THE COLLECTED WORKS OF
SAMUEL TAYLOR COLERIDGE · 14

TABLE TALK

General Editor: KATHLEEN COBURN
Associate Editor: BART WINER

THE COLLECTED WORKS

1. Coleridge's room at No 3 The Grove, Highgate,
from the watercolour by George Scharf engraved as the frontispiece
to Volume II of *Table Talk* (1835), with Coleridge later inserted
at the table for S. C. Hall *A Book of Memories* (1871).
Columbia University Libraries, reproduced
by kind permission

THE COLLECTED WORKS OF

Samuel Taylor Coleridge

Table Talk

RECORDED BY HENRY NELSON COLERIDGE
(AND JOHN TAYLOR COLERIDGE)

I

EDITED BY

Carl Woodring

ROUTLEDGE

✛ BOLLINGEN SERIES LXXV
PRINCETON UNIVERSITY PRESS

The Collected Works, sponsored by Bollingen Foundation,
is published in Great Britain
by Routledge
11 New Fetter Lane, London EC4P 4EE
ISBN 0–415–02614–8
and in the United States of America
by Princeton University Press, 41 William Street
Princeton, New Jersey
ISBN 0–691–09881–6
LCC 86–60477
The Collected Works constitutes
the seventy-fifth publication in Bollingen Series

The present work, number 14 of the Collected Works,
is in 2 volumes, this being 14: I

Printed in the United States of America
by Princeton University Press

THIS EDITION
OF THE WORKS OF
SAMUEL TAYLOR COLERIDGE
IS DEDICATED
IN GRATITUDE TO
THE FAMILY EDITORS
IN EACH GENERATION

CONTENTS

━━━━━━━━ I ━━━━━━━

━━━━━━━━ II ━━━━━━━

EDITOR'S APPENDIXES

LIST OF ILLUSTRATIONS

━━━━━ I ━━━━━

━━━━━ II ━━━━━

ACKNOWLEDGEMENTS

A FTER Henry Nelson Coleridge and Sara (Coleridge) Coleridge, these two volumes of Table Talk owe most to colleagues in the Bollingen edition, especially Kathleen Coburn, Bart Winer, David V. Erdman, J. R. de J. Jackson, H. J. Jackson, George Whalley, R. A. Foakes, J. C. C. Mays, John Colmer, Lewis Patton, J. B. Beer, and Thomas McFarland. Alwyne Coleridge gave permissions and advice at various times, as did E. L. Griggs, whose editing of Coleridge's letters has put this edition of table-talk much in debt. For generosity in answering queries and providing crucial information I am grateful to Lorna Arnold, Anne K. Mellor, Hermione de Almeida, G. Thomas Tanselle, Joel H. Wiener, John Clubbe, Gordon N. Ray, Virginia Murray, Eric W. Nye, Trevor H. Levere, Bishop C. Hunt Jr., Marshall Clagett, Coleman O. Parsons, Maurice Valency, Marsha Allentuck, Willard B. Pope, Benedict Read, Curtis Wilson, H. Dietrich Irmscher, Basil Savage, Richard Madden, James F. Mathias, Caleb Mason, Doris A. R. Clatanoff, Katharina Mommsen, Nilda Garcés, Charles C. Gillispie, Winifred Courtney, Fran Carlock Stephens, and Mary R. Wedd. For direct aid in search I am indebted to Janet Careswell, Mary Dering, Joseph Fichtelberg, Steven Jones, Valerie La Porte, Lisa Stahl, Victoria Yablonsky, and particularly Roland Maradino. Other students—Isabel Arenas, Francis Gretton, Alicia Martinez, and Stephen H. Sumida—helped in a graduate seminar so long ago they will have forgotten. Michael Neth has made the index.

Colleagues and administrators at Columbia University in the City of New York have provided endless support; specific details have come from Hubert F. Babinski, Martin Meisel, Karl Kroeber, John H. Middendorf, S. F. Johnson, Joseph A. Mazzeo, Ludwig W. Kahn, Arthur C. Danto, Steele Commager, Stephen Koss, Samuel Devons, Isaac Barzilay, and André Kaminski. These and other colleagues at Columbia, and colleagues from elsewhere attending conferences and annual meetings, have reduced the clouds by listening patiently.

Major friends and patrons of any editor are librarians. My list for heartfelt thanks is long: Eugene Sheehy, Kenneth Lohf, Rudolph Ellenbogen, and others in the Columbia University Libraries; F. W. Roberts, Cathy Henderson, Ellen S. Dunlap, June Moll, Sally Leach, and the staff of the Harry Ranson Humanities Research Center, University of Texas

at Austin; Lorna D. Fraser—and always Freda Gough—in the Victoria
College Library, University of Toronto; Dale M. Bentz and Frank Paluka
of the University of Iowa Libraries; Stephen Gill, Nesta Clutterbuck, and
the Trustees of Dove Cottage, Grasmere; Lola L. Szladits of the Henry
W. and Albert A. Berg Collection and the staffs of the research divisions
of the New York Public Library; Herbert Cahoon, Robert Priest, and the
staff of the Pierpont Morgan Library; O. B. Hardison Jr., Betsy Walsh,
and Mrs. Yeandle of the Folger Shakespeare Library; Connell Gallagher,
University Archivist and Curator of Manuscripts at the University of
Vermont; W. H. Bond and many others over many years in the Houghton
Library, Harvard University; James Thorpe, Alan Jutzi, and the staff of
the Henry E. Huntington Library; I. R. Willison among many who made
long searches pleasant in the British Museum Library; Frank Walker,
Fales Library, New York University; Mihai H. Handra (and Donald H.
Reiman and Doucet Fischer, informative editors), the Carl H. Pforzhei-
mer Library; Nona D. S. Martin, the Bodleian, Oxford; Malcolm Cor-
mack, Keeper of Paintings and Drawings, Fitzwilliam Museum, Cambridge; H. A. Harvey, College Archivist, King's College, University of
London; Stephen T. Riley, Massachusetts Historical Society; R. Burnett, National Library of Scotland; Ruth Salisbury, University of Pittsburgh Libraries; Patricia Mowbray, St Thomas Hospital, London; Patrick Strong, College Library and Collections, Eton College; the library
staff of the Royal Academy, Burlington House; George H. Healey and
the subsequent staff of the Cornell University Library; Richard Spoor
and Seth Kaston, the Burke Library of Union Theological Seminary.

The aid of Elizabeth Powers of the Princeton University Press continues as the galley proofs pass through various hands.

For permission to publish from manuscripts talk recorded by contemporaries not in Coleridge's family, I am grateful to the National Library
of Scotland (for Sterling), the University of Iowa Libraries (Sterling's
annotations on *Table Talk*), the University of Pittsburgh Libraries (Sterling on Allsop), Gordon N. Ray (Sterling Letters to Maccall), the Folger
Shakespeare Library (Collier), Duke University Library (transcription
from Allsop), University of Pennsylvania Library (a page from John
Taylor Coleridge), and the Library of the University of Vermont
(Wheeler). I am obligated to John G. Murray for permission to publish
records and correspondence of John Murray Publishers Ltd, and to Virginia Murray for gracious aid in uncovering the documents. Routledge
and Kegan Paul have permitted publication of details from their records.
I have drawn frequently on *The Diary of Joseph Farington* published by
the Yale University Press.

For permission to reproduce photographs I am obliged to the Columbia University Libraries for the Beerbohm and for the Scharf as modified for S. C. Hall; to the Victoria College Library for the pages and bits from H. N. Coleridge's papers; and to the Print Collection, New York Public Library, Astor, Lenox and Tilden Foundations, for the David Scott. The *Silenus* of Rubens is reproduced by courtesy of the Trustees, The National Gallery, London.

A grant from the Penrose Fund of the American Philosophical Society in 1972 helped push the work forward in that year.

I have designated no one above as "the late". The edition has been through long trials; George Whalley, Barbara Rooke, and E. E. Bostetter live in my work as in memory. My greatest debts are to Bart Winer, without whom there would have been no publication, and to Mary Frances Ellis, who has urged for years that the labour pass into other hands.

CARL WOODRING

Columbia University
14 May 1987

Bart Winer, the Associate Editor of *The Collected Works of Samuel Taylor Coleridge*, sought perfection and regarded elegance as a minimal achievement. In contact with the Bollingen Foundation from 1944, he was minister and physician to the Coleridge editon from its inception in 1960. Dividing each year between the resources of New York and of London, he pursued every detail from the choice of copy texts to the glossarial indexes, many of which he prepared. With typical dedication, he was intensely involved in every stage of the *Table Talk*, before and after I thought the mountain of typescript ready for final editing in 1982. Before his death in New York on 19 February 1989, he carefully laid out the procedures for Michael Neth, who has constructed the index and has caught a substantial number of the errors that Bart Winer would have caught.

C.W.

25 November 1989

EDITORIAL PRACTICE, SYMBOLS, MANUSCRIPTS, AND ABBREVIATIONS

THE text of Samuel Taylor Coleridge's talk in this volume follows the record by Henry Nelson Coleridge in manuscript diaries of 1822–7 and 1830–4. Appendix A lists abbreviations in the manuscripts that have been expanded for clarity. Initials have been expanded into proper names for persons and places identified within the entries in which they occur either in manuscript or in editions published by Henry Coleridge. The few names not so identified but reasonably certain have been supplied within square brackets. Ampersands have been expanded. Throughout the text and apparatus the infrequent square brackets enclose editorial interpolations. The divisional bars between entries are Henry Coleridge's except where indicated. The dates are his and are given in his varying form, but his division bars beneath dates have been omitted. Punctuation has been freely modified, usually towards the changes in *Table Talk* (1835), but dashes are retained where they may preserve the rhythm of Coleridge's speech. Henry's indentation of paragraphs has been ignored.

The textual apparatus, signalled by superscript letters in lower-case italics, records those words in the manuscripts, other than the abbreviations listed in Appendix A, that have been modified in the present edition. The apparatus indicates as cancelled those words crossed through by Henry Coleridge; words overwritten but legible are so indicated. Cancelled letters that leave the intended word uncertain are not recorded. Words inserted above the line are accepted into the text without notice.

Major changes of the text in the 1835 or 1836 editions are remarked in the editor's footnotes, which are numbered and printed in double columns. Minor variations between the manuscripts and the 1835 edition are not noted. The presence or absence of pairs of small triangles in ink at the top of the various pages in the manuscripts, which seem to have been used in checking the material, has not been recorded.

The text of the second edition (1836) is included in this edition as the first appendix in the second volume, Appendix H. There the dates, headings, and divisional bars between entries are retained as published, with bars supplied from the manuscripts or 1835 edition where an entry ended at the bottom of the page in 1836. The topical "Contents" and index of 1836 are omitted. The latter part of the Preface of 1835, which Henry Coleridge thought too ephemeral to reprint in 1836, is included within square brackets, as are other passages dropped between 1835 and 1836. Entries published in 1835 but dropped in 1836 are inserted where they originally appeared. Each entry is given a sequential number, in square brackets, preceded by 35 for those few entries published in 1835 but dropped thereafter; e.g. [35:426]. As dates and sequence vary between the manuscript and 1835 versions, those entry numbers, in square brackets, appear for cross-reference at the end and to the right of the corresponding entries in the manuscript version. Entries without such numbers have not been published in any previous edition of *Table Talk*.

All of John Taylor Coleridge's contributions to *Table Talk* have been gathered in an opening section. Coleridge's talk recorded by him in 1811 and sent by him for publication at the end of Henry Coleridge's volumes is here reprinted from the first edition. The account of Coleridge's talk of 9 Jan 1823, published under 1 May 1823 (36:47), is given from John Taylor Coleridge's diary, as published in Bernard Lord Coleridge *This for Remembrance* (1925) 324–61, and the anecdote by him published as a footnote to 30 Jul 1831 (36:311n) is given in this edition from his commonplace book, now in the Library of the University of Pennsylvania. Talk reported by others and included in the present edition is distributed among appendixes, the editor's introduction, and footnotes to particular topics. In quotations from these works single quotation marks have been changed to double and missing initial or end quotation marks have been silently supplied.

Editions referred to in the footnotes are, where practicable, those Coleridge used.

Coleridge manuscripts, where quoted, are printed literatim, including cancellations, except that "it's", "its' ", "your's", "yours' " have been standardised to "its" and "yours". The following symbols are also used in quoting from mss (with "wild" as an example):

[wild]	A reading supplied by the editor.
[?wild]	An uncertain reading.
[?wild / world]	Possible alternative readings.
[wild]	A tentative reading (owing to obliterations, torn paper, etc).
[. . .]	An illegible word or phrase.
⟨wild⟩	A later insertion by Coleridge.

Strokes, dashes, and other symbols are Coleridge's.

ABBREVIATIONS

(Place of publication is London, unless otherwise noted)

AA   *Annual Anthology* [ed Robert Southey] (1799–1800)

Allsop   [Thomas Allsop] *Letters, Conversations and Recollections of S. T. Coleridge* (2 vols 1836).

AM   S. T. Coleridge *The Rime of the Ancient Mariner*.

AP   *Anima Poetae: from the Unpublished Notebooks of S. T. Coleridge* ed E. H. Coleridge (1895).

A Reg   *The Annual Register* (1758–).

A Rev   *Annual Review and History of Literature* (1802–8).

AR (1825)	S. T. Coleridge *Aids to Reflection* (1825).
AR (1831)	S. T. Coleridge *Aids to Reflection* (2nd ed 1831).
AR (1843)	S. T. Coleridge *Aids to Reflection* ed Sara Coleridge (5th ed 1843).
AV	"Authorised" or "King James" Version of the Bible
BCP	*The Book of Common Prayer and Administration of the Sacraments and Other Rites and Ceremonies of the Church According to the Use of the Church of England.*
BE	*Biographia Epistolaris* ed A. Turnbull (2 vols 1911).
BL (1817)	S. T. Coleridge *Biographia Literaria: or Biographical Sketches of My Literary Life and Opinions* (2 vols 1817).
BL (1847)	S. T. Coleridge *Biographia Literaria* ed H. N. and Sara Coleridge (2 vols 1847).
BL (1907)	S. T. Coleridge *Biographia Literaria . . . with His Aesthetical Essays* ed John Shawcross (2 vols Oxford 1907).
BL (CC)	S. T. Coleridge *Biographia Literaria* ed James Engell and W. Jackson Bate (2 vols London & Princeton 1983) = *CC* vii.
Bl Mag	*Blackwood's Magazine* (Edinburgh and London 1817–).
BM	British Library, Reference Division, formerly "British Museum Library"
B Poets	*The Works of the British Poets* ed Robert Anderson (13 vols Edinburgh & London 1792–5; vol xiv 1807).
Bristol LB	George Whalley "The British Library Borrowings of Southey and Coleridge" *Library* iv (Sept 1949) 114–31.
C	Samuel Taylor Coleridge
C&S (1830 ed 1)	S. T. Coleridge *On the Constitution of the Church and State, According to the Idea of Each* (1830 but appeared Dec 1829).
C&S (1830 ed 2)	S. T. Coleridge *On the Constitution of the Church and State, According to the Idea of Each* (2nd ed 1830).
C&S (CC)	S. T. Coleridge *On the Constitution of the Church and State* ed John Colmer (London & Princeton 1976) = *CC* x.
Carlyon	Clement Carlyon *Early Years and Late Reflections* (4 vols 1836–58)
C at H	L. E. Watson *Coleridge at Highgate* (London & New York 1925).
C Bibl	J. H. Haney *A Bibliography of Samuel Taylor Coleridge* (1903).
CC	*The Collected Works of Samuel Taylor Coleridge* general ed Kathleen Coburn (London & Princeton 1969–)
C Fille	Earl Leslie Griggs *Coleridge Fille: A Biography of Sara Coleridge* (1940).
CH	*Coleridge: The Critical Heritage* ed J. R. de J. Jackson (1970).
CIS (1840)	S. T. Coleridge *Confessions of an Inquiring Spirit* ed H. N. Coleridge (1840).
CIS (1849)	S. T. Coleridge *Confessions of an Inquiring Spirit and Some Miscellaneous Pieces* ed H. N. [and Sara] Coleridge (1849).

CL	*Collected Letters of Samuel Taylor Coleridge* ed Earl Leslie Griggs (6 vols Oxford & New York 1956–71).
C Life (C)	E. K. Chambers *Samuel Taylor Coleridge* (Oxford 1938).
C Life (G)	James Gillman *The Life of Samuel Taylor Coleridge* (1838).
C Life (H)	Lawrence Hanson *The Life of Samuel Taylor Coleridge: the Early Years* (1938).
C Life (JDC)	James Dykes Campbell *Samuel Taylor Coleridge* (1894).
CM (CC)	S. T. Coleridge *Marginalia* ed George Whalley (London & Princeton 1979–) = *CC* xii.
CN	*The Notebooks of Samuel Taylor Coleridge* ed Kathleen Coburn (New York, Princeton & London 1957–).
Collier	*Seven Lectures on Shakespeare and Milton by the Late S. T. Coleridge* ed John Payne Collier (1856).
Collier (1971)	*Coleridge on Shakespeare: The Text of the Lectures of 1811–12* ed R. A. Foakes (1971).
Colmer	John Colmer *Coleridge: Critic of Society* (Oxford 1959).
Cottle E Rec	Joseph Cottle *Early Recollections Chiefly Relating to the Late Samuel Taylor Coleridge* (2 vols 1837–9).
Cottle *Rem*	Joseph Cottle *Reminiscences of Samuel Taylor Coleridge and Robert Southey* (1847).
CRB	*Henry Crabb Robinson on Books and Their Writers* ed Edith J. Morley (3 vols 1938).
CR (BCW)	*Blake, Coleridge, Wordsworth, Lamb, etc. Being Selections from the Remains of Henry Crabb Robinson* ed Edith J. Morley (Manchester 1922).
CRC	*The Correspondence of Henry Crabb Robinson with the Wordsworth Circle* ed Edith J. Morley (2 vols Oxford 1927).
CRD	*Diary, Reminiscences and Correspondence of Henry Crabb Robinson* ed Thomas Sadler (3rd ed 2 vols 1872).
C Talker	R. W. Armour and R. F. Howes *Coleridge the Talker* (2nd ed New York & London 1969).
C Rev	*The Critical Review; or, Annals of Literature* (1765–1817)
C 17th C	*Coleridge on the Seventeenth Century* ed R. F. Brinkley (Durham, N. C. 1955).
DC	Derwent Coleridge
DCL	Dove Cottage Library
De Q	Thomas De Quincey
De Q Works	*The Collected Writings of Thomas De Quincey* ed David Masson (14 vols Edinburgh 1889–90).
DNB	*Dictionary of National Biography* (1885–).
DW	Dorothy Wordsworth

DWJ	*Journals of Dorothy Wordsworth* ed E. de Selincourt (2 vols 1941).
DWJ (1958)	*Journals of Dorothy Wordsworth: The Alfoxden Journal 1798, The Grasmere Journals 1800–1803* ed Helen Darbishire (1958).
EC	Edward Coleridge
Ed Rev	*The Edinburgh Review* (Edinburgh & London 1802–1929).
EHC	Ernest Hartley Coleridge
Eichhorn *AT*	Johann Gottfried Eichhorn *Einleitung ins Alte Testament* (3 vols Leipzig 1787).
Eichhorn *NT*	Johann Gottfried Eichhorn *Einleitung in das Neue Testament* (3 vols Leipzig 1804, 1810–11).
EM	*Encyclopaedia Metropolitana* (29 vols 1817–45).
EOT	S. T. Coleridge *Essays on His Own Times, Forming a Second Series of "The Friend"* ed Sara Coleridge (3 vols 1850).
EOT (CC)	S. T. Coleridge *Essays on His Times in "The Morning Post" and "The Courier"* ed David V. Erdman (3 vols London & Princeton 1977) = *CC* III.
E Poets	*The Works of the English Poets from Chaucer to Cowper* ed Alexander Chalmers (21 vols 1810).
Farington *Diary*	*The Diary of Joseph Farington* ed Kenneth Garlick and Angus D. Macintyre (New Haven 1978–).
Friend (CC)	S. T. Coleridge *The Friend* ed Barbara E. Rooke (2 vols London & Princeton 1969) = *CC* IV.
Gillman SC	*Catalogue of a Valuable Collection of Books Including the Library of James Gillman, Esq* (Henry Southgate 1843). Marked Copies: BM SC Sg 64 (2) and SC Sg a 53.
G Mag	*The Gentleman's Magazine* (1731–1907).
Halévy	Elie Halévy *A History of the English People in the Nineteenth Century* tr E. I. Watkin (2nd ed 6 vols 1949–52).
Hansard	*The Parliamentary Debates from the Year 1803 to the Present Time* . . . (1812–35): 41 vols (1803–20) in 1812–20; 2nd series 25 vols (1820–30) in 1820–30; 3rd series 356 vols (1830–91).
HC	Hartley Coleridge
HCL	*Letters of Hartley Coleridge* ed Grace Evelyn and Earl Leslie Griggs (Oxford 1937).
HCR	Henry Crabb Robinson
HUL	Harvard University Library
HEHL	The Henry E. Huntington Library and Art Gallery, San Marino, California
HNC	Henry Nelson Coleridge
H Works	*The Complete Works of William Hazlitt* ed P. P. Howe (21 vols 1930–4).

IS	*Inquiring Spirit: a New Presentation of Coleridge from His Published and Unpublished Prose Writings* ed Kathleen Coburn (rev ed Toronto 1979).
JDC	James Dykes Campbell
Johnson's *Dictionary*	Samuel Johnson *A Dictionary of the English Language* (8th ed 2 vols 1799).
JS	John Sterling
JTC	John Taylor Coleridge
L & L	*Coleridge on Logic and Learning* ed Alice D. Snyder (1929).
LB (1800)	William Wordsworth [and S. T. Coleridge] *Lyrical Ballads, with Other Poems* (2 vols 1800).
LCL	Loeb Classical Library
Lects 1795 (CC)	S. T. Coleridge *Lectures 1795: On Politics and Religion* ed Lewis Patton and Peter Mann (London & Princeton 1971) = *CC* I.
Lects 1808– 19 (CC)	S. T. Coleridge *Lectures 1808–1819: On Literature* ed Reginald A. Foakes (2 vols London & Princeton 1987) = *CC* V.
LL	*The Letters of Charles Lamb to Which Are Added Those of His Sister Mary Lamb* ed E. V. Lucas (3 vols 1935).
LL (M)	*The Letters of Charles and Mary Anne Lamb* ed Edwin W. Marrs, Jr (Ithaca N. Y. 1975–).
L Life	E. V. Lucas *The Life of Charles Lamb* (1921).
L Works	*The Works of Charles and Mary Lamb* ed E. V. Lucas (7 vols 1903–5).
Logic (CC)	S. T. Coleridge *Logic* ed J. R. de J. Jackson (London & Princeton 1979) = *CC* XIII.
LR	*The Literary Remains of Samuel Taylor Coleridge* ed H. N. Coleridge (4 vols 1836–9).
LRR	S. T. Coleridge "Six Lectures on Revealed Religion, Its Corruption and Political Views" ms transcript by E. H. Coleridge (in *Lects 1795*).
LS (1817)	S. T. Coleridge *A Lay Sermon, Addressed to the Higher and Middle Classes, on the Existing Distresses and Discontents* (1817).
LS (CC)	S. T. Coleridge *Lay Sermons* [being *The Statesman's Manual* and *A Lay Sermon*] ed R. J. White (London & Princeton 1972) = *CC* V.
MC	*Coleridge's Miscellaneous Criticism* ed T. M. Raysor (Cambridge, Mass. 1936).
M Chron	*The Morning Chronicle* (1769–1862).
Method	S. T. Coleridge's *Treatise on Method as Published in the Encyclopaedia Metropolitana* ed Alice D. Synder (1934).
Migne *PG*	*Patriologiae cursus completus . . . series Graeca* ed J. P. Migne (162 vols Paris 1857–1912).
Migne *PL*	*Patriologiae cursus completus . . . series Latina* ed J. P. Migne (221 vols Paris 1844–64).

Minnow	*Minnow among Tritons: Mrs S. T. Coleridge's Letters to Thomas Poole 1799–1834* ed Stephen Potter (1934).
Moore *Journal*	Thomas Moore *Journal* ed Wilfred S. Dowden (Newark, N. J. 1983–).
M Post	*The Morning Post* (1772–1937).
M Rev	*The Monthly Review* (1749–1845).
Mrs C	Sara Coleridge née Fricker (wife of C)
MS A	Henry Nelson Coleridge's diary with C's table-talk through 2 Jun 1824 (University of Texas).
MS B	HNC's principal record of C's table-talk, 24 Feb 1827–23 Jun 1834 (Victoria College Library).
MS C	Workbook of HNC with table-talk for 28 Jun–5 Jul 1834 (University of Texas).
MS D	Fragment of a letter from C to Derwent Coleridge (Victoria College Library) similar to published table-talk of 10 Jul 1834.
MS E	MS dated 2 Jun 1827 of table-talk rearranged from MS A (University of Texas).
MS F	Fragments cut from a revised ms of table-talk (mostly in Victoria College Library).
N	Notebook of Samuel Taylor Coleridge (numbered or lettered) in ms. References are given by folio.
NED	S. T. Coleridge *Notes on English Divines* ed Derwent Coleridge (2 vols 1853).
N F°	Coleridge's folio notebook, now in the Henry E. Huntington Library.
NLS	S. T. Coleridge *Notes and Lectures upon Shakespeare and Some Other Old Poets and Dramatists with Other Literary Remains* ed Sara Coleridge (2 vols 1849).
NTP	S. T. Coleridge *Notes, Theological, Political and Miscellaneous* ed Derwent Coleridge (1853).
NYPL	New York Public Library
ODCC	*The Oxford Dictionary of the Christian Church* ed F. L. Cross (London 1971).
OED	*The Oxford English Dictionary, Being a Corrected Reissue . . . of "A New English Dictionary on Historical Principles"* (12 vols Oxford 1970).
Omniana	*Omniana, or Horae otiosiores* ed Robert Southey [with articles by C] (2 vols 1812).
Parl Deb	*Cobbett's Parliamentary Debates* (22 vols 1803–12).
Parl Hist	*The Parliamentary History of England* ed William Cobbett and John Wright (36 vols 1806–20)
Phil Trans (RS)	*Philosophical Transactions of the Royal Society* (1665–1886).

P Lects (1949)	*The Philosophical Lectures of Samuel Taylor Coleridge* ed Kathleen Coburn (London & New York 1949).
PML	The Pierpont Morgan Library
Poole	M. E. Sandford *Thomas Poole and His Friends* (2 vols 1888).
PW (1852)	*The Poems of Samuel Taylor Coleridge* ed Derwent and Sara Coleridge (1852).
PW (EHC)	*The Complete Poetical Works of Samuel Taylor Coleridge* ed E. H. Coleridge (2 vols Oxford 1912).
PW (JDC)	*The Poetical Works of Samuel Taylor Coleridge* ed James Dykes Campbell (1893).
QR	*The Quarterly Review* (London & Edinburgh 1809–).
Rees	Abraham Rees *Cyclopaedia* . . . (39 vols 1819).
RES	*Review of English Studies* (1925–).
RS	Robert Southey
RS CH	*Robert Southey: The Critical Heritage* ed Lionel Madden (1972).
RSL	Royal Society of Literature
RSV	The [American] Revised Standard Version of the Bible: NT 1946, OT 1952.
RX	John Livingston Lowes *The Road to Xanadu* (rev ed Boston 1930).
SC	Sara Coleridge (daughter of C and wife of HNC)
SC Memoir	*Memoir and Letters of Sara Coleridge* ed Edith Coleridge (2nd ed 2 vols 1873).
SH	Sara Hutchinson
SHL	*The Letters of Sara Hutchinson from 1800 to 1835* ed Kathleen Coburn (Toronto 1954).
Sh C (1960)	*Coleridge's Shakespearean Criticism* ed T. M. Raysor (2nd ed 2 vols 1960).
S Letters (Curry)	*New Letters of Robert Southey* ed Kenneth Curry (2 vols New York & London 1965).
S Life (CS)	*Life and Correspondence of Robert Southey* ed C. C. Southey (6 vols 1849–50).
S Life (Simmons)	Jack Simmons *Southey* (1945).
SM	S. T. Coleridge *The Statesman's Manual: or, The Bible, the Best Guide to Political Skill and Foresight. A Lay Sermon Addressed to the Higher Classes of Society* (1816).
SM (CC)	S. T. Coleridge *The Statesman's Manual* ed R. J. White (London & Princeton 1972). In S. T. Coleridge *Lay Sermons (CC* VI).
Studies	*Coleridge: Studies by Several Hands on the Hundredth Anniversary of His Death* ed E. Blunden and E. L. Griggs (1934).
Sultana	Donald Sultana *Samuel Taylor Coleridge in Malta and Italy* (Oxford 1969).

SW & F	*Shorter Works and Fragments* ed H. J. Jackson and J. R. de J. Jackson = *CC* 11
TL	S. T. Coleridge *Hints Towards the Formation of a More Comprehensive Theory of Life* ed Seth B. Watson (1848).
TLS	*The Times Literary Supplement* (London 1902–).
Towle	Eleanor A. Towle *A Poet's Children* (1912).
TT	Mss of *Table Talk* by HNC.
TT (1835)	*Specimens of the Table Talk of the Late Samuel Taylor Coleridge* ed H. N. Coleridge (2 vols 1835).
TT (1836)	*Specimens of the Table Talk of Samuel Taylor Coleridge* ed H. N. Coleridge (2nd ed 1836).
TT (1851)	*Specimens of the Table Talk of Samuel Taylor Coleridge* ed H. N. and Sara Coleridge (3rd ed 1851).
TT (1884)	*The Table Talk and Omniana of Samuel Taylor Coleridge* ed T. Ashe (1884).
TT (1917)	*The Table Talk and Omniana of Samuel Taylor Coleridge* with a Note on Coleridge by Coventry Patmore (1917).
UT	University of Texas (Harry Ransom Humanities Research Center)
UT Grantz	Carl L. Grantz "Letters of Sara Coleridge: A Calendar and Index" (PhD dissertation University of Texas 1968).
V & A	Victoria and Albert Museum
VCL	Victoria College Library, University of Toronto
W&C	*Wordsworth and Coleridge: Studies in Honor of George McLean Harper* ed E. L. Griggs (Princeton 1939).
Watkins	C. T. Watkins *A Portable Cyclopaedia* . . . (1810).
Watchman (CC)	S. T. Coleridge *The Watchman* ed Lewis Patton (London & Princeton 1970) = *CC* II.
WL (E rev)	*Letters of William and Dorothy Wordsworth: the Early Years* ed Ernest de Selincourt, rev Chester L. Shaver (Oxford 1967).
WL (L)	*Letters of William and Dorothy Wordsworth: the Later Years* ed Ernest de Selincourt (3 vols Oxford 1939).
WL (L rev)	*Letters of William and Dorothy Wordsworth: the Later Years* ed Ernest de Selincourt, rev Alan G. Hill (3 vols Oxford 1979–81).
WL (M rev)	*Letters of William and Dorothy Wordsworth: the Middle Years* ed Ernest de Selincourt, rev Mary Moorman (2 vols Oxford 1969–70).
W Life	Mary Moorman *William Wordsworth, A Biography* (2 vols Oxford 1957–65).
W Mem	Christopher Wordsworth *Memoirs of William Wordsworth* (2 vols 1851).
Woodring	Carl R. Woodring *Politics in the Poetry of Coleridge* (Madison, Wis 1961).

W Prose	*The Prose Works of William Wordsworth* ed W. J. B. Owen and J. W. Smyser (3 vols Oxford 1974).
W Prose (1876)	*The Prose Works of William Wordsworth* ed Alexander B. Grosart (3 vols 1876).
WPW	*The Poetical Works of William Wordsworth* ed Ernest de Selincourt and Helen Darbishire (5 vols Oxford 1940–9).
WW	William Wordsworth
WW LC	*Wordsworth's Library: A Catalogue* ed Chester L. and Alice C. Shaver (New York & London 1979).

CHRONOLOGICAL TABLE
1772–1834

1772	(21 Oct) C b at Ottery St Mary, Devonshire, to the Rev John and Ann (Bowdon) Coleridge, youngest of their 10 children	George III king (1760–1820) Wordsworth 2 years old Scott 1 year old *M Post* began
1774		Southey b
1775		American War of Independence Charles Lamb b
1776		Adam Smith *Wealth of Nations* Gibbon *Decline and Fall*
1778	C at Ottery Grammar School	Hazlitt b Rousseau and Voltaire d
1780		(Jun) Gordon Riots
1781	(4 Oct) C's father died	Kant *Kritik der reinen Vernunft* Schiller *Die Räuber*
1782	(Jul) Enrolled at Christ's Hospital, Hertford (Sept) Christ's Hospital, London, with C. Lamb, T. F. Middleton, Robert Allen, J. M. Gutch, Le Grice brothers; met Evans family and G. Dyer	Priestley *Corruptions of Christianity* Rousseau *Confessions*
1783		Pitt's first ministry (–1801)
1784		Samuel Johnson d
1785	Walked the wards of London Hospital with his brother Luke	De Quincey b Paley *Principles of Moral and Political Philosophy*
1787	First contribution to Boyer's *Liber Aureus*	
1788	(early summer) Elected Grecian; met Evans family	
1789		(14 Jul) French Revolution Blake *Songs of Innocence* Bowles *Sonnets*
1790		Burke *Reflections on the Revolution in France*
1791	(Sept) Jesus College, Cambridge, Exhibitioner, Sizar, Rustat Scholar; met S. Butler, Frend, Porson, C. Wordsworth, Wrangham	(Mar) John Wesley d Paine *Rights of Man* pt I (pt II 1792) Boswell *Life of Johnson* Anti-Jacobin riots at Birmingham
1792	Browne Prize for Greek ode on the slave-trade	Pitt's attack on the slave-trade Fox's Libel Bill

1793 One of four placed first for Craven Scholarship
(May) Attended Cambridge trial of Frend
(15 Jul) First poem in *Morning Chronicle*
(2 Dec) Enlisted in 15th Light Dragoons as Silas Tomkyn Comberbache

(21 Jan) Louis XVI executed
(1 Feb) France declared war on England and Holland
(Mar–Dec) Revolt of La Vendée
(16 Oct) Marie Antoinette executed
(16 Oct) John Hunter d
Godwin *Political Justice*
Wordsworth *An Evening Walk* and *Descriptive Sketches*

1794 (7–10 Apr) Returned to Cambridge
(Jun) Poems in *Cambridge Intelligencer;* set out with Joseph Hucks to Oxford; met Southey, planned pantisocracy; Welsh tour
(Aug) Joined Southey and Burnett in Bristol; met Thomas Poole; engaged to Sara Fricker
(Sept) Returned to Cambridge; with RS published *The Fall of Robespierre* (Cambridge); *Monody on Chatterton* published with *Rowley Poems* (Cambridge)
(Dec) Left Cambridge; sonnets in *M Chron;* "Noctes Atticae" with Lamb at Salutation and Cat
(24 Dec) Began *Religious Musings*

(23 May) Suspension of Habeas Corpus
(28 Jul) Robespierre executed; end of the Terror
(Oct–Dec) State Trials: Hardy, Tooke, and Thelwall acquitted of charge of treason
(–1795) Paine *Age of Reason*
Paley *Evidences of Christianity*

1795 (end Jan) RS brought C back from London to Bristol; lodgings with RS and Burnett; met Joseph Cottle
(Feb) Political lectures
(Feb/May) *Moral and Political Lecture* published
(May–Jun) Lectures on Revealed Religion
(16 Jun) Lecture on the Slave-Trade
Portrait by Peter Vandyke
(Aug–Sept) Quarrel with RS; pantisocracy abandoned; met WW in Bristol
(4 Oct) Married Sara Fricker
(26 Nov) Lecture on the Two Bills
(3 Dec) *Conciones ad populum* published
(Dec) *An Answer to "A Letter to Edward Long Fox"* and *Plot Discovered* published; *Watchman* planned

(Jun–Jul) Quiberon expedition
(26 Sept) WW and DW to Racedown
(Nov) Directory began
(3 Nov) Treason and Convention Bills introduced
(18 Dec) Two Acts put into effect
Lewis *Ambrosio, or the Monk*

1796 (9 Jan–13 Feb) Tour of Midlands to sell *The Watchman*; met Erasmus Darwin and Joseph Wright (painter)
(1 Mar–13 May) *The Watchman* in ten numbers
(16 Apr) *Poems on Various Subjects*
(19 Sept) Hartley C b; reconciliation with RS
(31 Dec) *Ode on Departing Year* in *Cambridge Intelligencer*; move to Nether Stowey

(Jul) Robert Burns d
(Sept) Mary Lamb's violent illness
(Nov) Catherine of Russia d
England treating for peace with France
Threats of invasion of England
Jenner performs first smallpox vaccination

1797 (Mar) WW at Stowey
(5 Jun) C at Racedown
(Jul) DW, WW, and Lamb at Stowey;
DW and WW in Alfoxden House
(16 Oct) *Osorio* finished; *Poems, to which are now added, Poems by Charles Lamb and Charles Lloyd*
(13–16 Nov) Walk with Wordsworths to Lynton and *Ancient Mariner* begun

(Feb) Bank of England suspended cash payments
(Apr–Jun) Mutinies in the British fleet
(9 Jul) Burke d
(17 Oct) France and Austria sign peace treaty
(Nov) Frederick William II of Prussia d
(Nov) *Anti-Jacobin* began

1798 (Jan) C's Unitarian sermons at Shrewsbury; Hazlitt heard C preach; Wedgwood annuity £150 accepted
(Mar) *Ancient Mariner* completed
(Apr) *Fears in Solitude*
(14 May) Berkeley C b
(18 Sept) *Lyrical Ballads* published; WW, DW, Chester, and C to Hamburg; met Klopstock
(Oct) C to Ratzeburg

(Feb–Oct) Irish rebellion
(Apr) Helvetic Republic
(12 Jun) Malta taken by French
(Jul) Bonaparte invaded Egypt
(9 Jul) *Anti-Jacobin* last number
(1–2 Aug) Nelson's victory in Battle of Nile
Lloyd *Edmund Oliver*
Bell introduced Madras system of education in England

1799 (10 Feb) Berkeley C died
(11 Feb) C at University of Göttingen; met Clement Carlyon, George Greenough
(c 6 Apr) C had news of Berkeley's death
(May) Ascent of the Brocken
(29 Jul) In Stowey again
(Sept–Oct) Devon walking tour with RS; met Humphry Davy in Bristol; experiments with nitrous oxide
(Oct–Nov) First Lakes tour, with WW
(26 Oct) Met Sara Hutchinson
(27 Nov) Arrived in London to accept *M Post* offer
(Dec) DW and WW at Town End (later Dove Cottage)

(Nov) Directory overthrown
(Dec) Constitution of Year VIII; Bonaparte First Consul
Schiller *Die Piccolomini* and *Wallensteins Tod* published
Royal Institution founded

1800 (Jan–16 Apr) *M Post* reporter and leaderwriter; translating *Wallenstein* at Lamb's
(Apr) To Grasmere and WW
(May–Jun) In Stowey and Bristol
(24 Jul) Moved to Greta Hall, Keswick
(Sept–Oct) Superintended printing of *Lyrical Ballads* (2nd ed)

(25 Apr) Cowper d
(14 Jun) Battle of Marengo
Burns *Works* ed Currie
(Aug) Union of Great Britain and Ireland
(5 Sept) Malta after long siege fell to England

1801 (Jan) *Lyrical Ballads* (1800) published; prolonged illnesses
(Jul–Aug) With SH at Stockton
(15 Nov) In London writing for *M Post*
Christmas at Stowey

(Mar) Pitt resigned over Emancipation
Addington ministry (–1804)
(Jul) Bonaparte signed Concordat with Pope
Davy lecturer at Royal Institution
RS *Thalaba*

1802 (Jan) In London; attended Davy's lectures at Royal Institution; writing for *M Post*
(Mar–Nov) In the Lakes, severe domestic discord

(25 Mar) Peace of Amiens
(18 Apr) Erasmus Darwin d
(8 May) Bonaparte Consul for life
(2 Oct) WW married Mary Hutchinson
(Oct) French army entered Switzerland

(4 Apr) *Dejection*
(Aug) Scafell climb; visit of the Lambs
(Sept–Nov) Writing for *M Post*
(Nov) Tour of S Wales with Tom and Sally Wedgwood
(23 Dec) Sara C b

Edinburgh Review founded
Cobbett's *Weekly Political Register* founded
Paley *Natural Theology*
Spinoza *Opera* ed Paulus (1802–3)

1803 (Jan–Feb) In Somerset with Wedgwoods and Poole; with Lamb in London; made his will
(Jun) *Poems* (1803) published
(summer) Hazlitt, Beaumonts, and S. Rogers in Lakes visited C; Hazlitt's portrait of C
(15–29 Aug) Tour of Scotland with WW and DW
(30 Aug–15 Sept) Continued tour alone
(20 Dec) To Grasmere on way to London

(Feb) Act of Mediation in Switzerland
(30 Apr) Louisiana bought by U.S. from France
(18 May) England declared war on France
(25 May) Emerson b
(Sept) Emmet's execution in Ireland
Cobbett *Parliamentary Debates* (later Hansard)
Hayley *Life and Posthumous Writings of Cowper*
Chatterton *Works* ed RS and Cottle
Malthus *Principles of Population* (2nd ed)

1804 (Jan) Ill at Grasmere, then to London; portrait by Northcote; Joseph Farington met C at Beaumont's
(27 Mar) To Portsmouth
(9 Apr–18 May) In convoy to Malta
(by Jul) Private secretary to Alexander Ball, High Commissioner at Malta
(Aug–Nov) Sicily, two ascents of Etna; stayed with G. F. Leckie

(12 Feb) Kant d
(Mar) Code Napoléon
(Apr) 2nd Pitt ministry (–1806)
(18 May) Napoleon made Emperor
(12 Dec) Spain declared war on Britain
Blake *Jerusalem* begun

1805 (Jan) Appointed Acting Public Secretary in Malta; news of loss of John Wordsworth in *Abergavenny*
(Sept–Dec) in Sicily
(Dec) To Naples and Rome

(Apr) Third Coalition against France
(9 May) Schiller d
(26 May) Napoleon King of Italy
(17 Oct) Napoleon's victory at Ulm
(21 Oct) Nelson's victory at Trafalgar
(2 Dec) Austerlitz
Hazlitt *Principles of Human Action*
Knight *Principles of Taste*
Scott *Lay of the Last Minstrel*
RS *Madoc*

1806 (Jan) In Rome, met Washington Allston, Washington Irving, the Humboldts, Tieck and Schlegel; to Florence and Pisa
(23 Jun) Sailed from Leghorn
(17 Aug) Landed in England; London, job-hunting and recovering his books and papers; at Parndon with the Clarksons and to Cambridge
(26 Oct) In Kendal with Wordsworths and SH
(Nov) Keswick, determined to separate from Mrs C
(21 Dec) Joined Wordsworth and SH at

(Jan) Pitt d; "Ministry of all the Talents" under Grenville, who resigned (Mar 1807) after rejection of Bill to open all commissions to RCs
(6 Aug) Holy Roman Empire ended
(26 Aug) Palm executed
(13 Sept) Fox d
British blockade
(Oct) Jena
(Nov) Berlin Decree and Continental System
Arndt *Geist der Zeit* (–1818)

Coleorton; crisis of jealous disillusionment with them

1807 Coleorton; heard WW read *Prelude* and wrote *Lines to William Wordsworth*
(4 Apr) Left for London with Wordsworths
(Jun) With his family at Stowey
(Aug) Met De Quincey; alone in Bristol and at Stowey with Poole
(Nov) In London

(Mar) Portland ministry (–1809)
(25 Mar) Abolition of slave-trade
(Jul) Peace of Tilsit
(2 Sept) Bombardment of Copenhagen by British fleet
(Dec) Peninsular War began
Davy and oxymuriatic acid
WW *Poems in Two Volumes*
RS *Letters from England by Don Espriella; Specimens of the Later English Poets*
C. and M. Lamb *Tales from Shakespeare*

1808 (15 Jan–Jun) In rooms at *Courier* office, Strand; lectures at Royal Institution on poetry and principles of taste; illnesses, Bury St Edmunds
(Feb–Mar) WW in London
(1 May) Wordsworths moved to Allan Bank
(Jun–Aug) Bristol, Leeds, Keswick
(Jul) Review of Clarkson's *History of the Abolition of the Slave-Trade*
(1 Sept) Arrived Allan Bank, Grasmere; instructed Mrs C to send all his books there
(Nov) First prospectus of *The Friend*; Kendal
(Dec) Took up residence at Allan Bank

Bell-Lancaster controversy
Sir Arthur Wellesley to Portugal
Crabb Robinson *Times* correspondent in Peninsula
(1 May) Hazlitt married Sarah Stoddart
(30 Aug) Convention of Cintra signed
(Dec) Napoleon invaded Spain; Dr. T. Beddoes d
Dalton *New System of Chemical Philosophy* and publication of atomic theory
Lamb *Specimens of English Dramatic Poets*
Scott *Marmion*
John and Leigh Hunt's *Examiner* began
Goethe *Faust* pt I

1809 (1 Jun–15 Mar 1810) *The Friend*, 27 numbers plus supernumerary
(7 Dec–Jan 1810) "Letters on the Spaniards" in *Courier*

(Feb) *Quarterly Review* founded
(9 Mar) Byron *English Bards and Scotch Reviewers*
(May) Napoleon captured Vienna
WW *Convention of Cintra* pamphlet
(21 Sept) Canning–Castlereagh duel
Perceval ministry (–1812)
Schlegel *Über dramatische Kunst und Litteratur*

1810 (Mar) SH left Grasmere for Wales; last number of *Friend*
Met Francis Jeffrey; met T. A. Methuen at Corsham House
(Oct) To London; Montagu precipitated quarrel with WW; with Morgans in Hammersmith
(Nov) Personal association with HCR began

(Mar) Battle over admission of press to House of Commons
(Apr) Burdett imprisoned
(Jul) Napoleon annexed Holland
George III recognised as insane
WW *Guide to the Lakes*
Mme de Staël *De l'Allemagne*
Scott *Lady of the Lake*
RS *Curse of Kehama*

1811 (Mar–Apr) Miniature painted by Matilda Betham; met Grattan
(20 Apr) First table-talk recorded by John

(5 Feb) Prince of Wales made Regent
RC claims in Ireland; scheme to set up representative assembly in Dublin

Taylor Coleridge
(Apr–Sept) Contributions to *Courier*;
J. Payne Collier met C
(18 Nov–27 Jan 1811) Lectures on
Shakespeare and Milton at Scot's Cor-
poration Hall, Collier, Byron, Rogers,
HCR attending; George Dawe bust of
C

(Nov to 1815) Luddite uprisings
Shelley *Necessity of Atheism*

1812   (Feb–Mar) Last journey to the Lakes to
collect copies of *Friend*
(Apr) With the Morgans, Berners Street,
Soho
(May–Aug) Lectures on drama in Wil-
lis's Rooms; portrait by Dawe
(May) Lamb and HCR patch up WW
quarrel
(Jun) Catherine Wordsworth d
(Jun) *The Friend* reissued
(3 Nov–26 Jan 1813) Shakespeare lec-
tures in Surrey Institution
(Nov) Half Wedgwood annuity with-
drawn; RS and C *Omniana*
(Dec) Thomas Wordsworth d

(11 May) Perceval shot; Liverpool PM,
resigned but resumed after Canning
(pro-Catholic) declined to serve with
Wellesley
(18 Jun) U.S. declared war on Great
Britain
(22 Jun) Napoleon opened war on Russia
(Oct–Dec) Retreat from Moscow
Combe *Tour of Dr Syntax in Search of
the Picturesque*
Byron *Childe Harold* vol I

1813   (23 Jan) *Remorse* opened at Drury Lane
Morgan's financial affairs deteriorating,
he escaped to Ireland in Sept
(2 Sept) Met Mme de Staël
(Oct–Nov) Moved to Bristol; lectures on
Shakespeare and education
(Dec) Established the Morgans at Ashley
Cottage near Bath, returned ill to Bris-
tol

(1 May) Wordsworths moved to Rydal
Mount
(May) Grattan's Bill for Relief of Ro-
man Catholics abandoned
(Jul–Aug) Peace Congress at Prague
failed
(10 Aug) Austria declared war on
Napoleon
(Sept) RS Poet Laureate
(autumn) Wellington successful in
Peninsula; Switzerland, Holland, It-
aly, Rhineland, Spain, Trieste, Dal-
matia freed of French rule
RS *Life of Nelson*
Northcote *Memoirs of Reynolds*
Leigh Hunt imprisoned for libel (1813–
15)

1814   (Apr) Lectures at Bristol on Milton, Cervantes, Taste; lecture on French Revolution and Napoleon; under medical
care of Dr. Daniel for addiction and su-
icidal depression
(3 May) Charles Danvers d
(1 Aug) *Remorse* performed in Bristol
(Aug–Sept) Allston portrait of C; Allston's exhibition of paintings; essays
"On the Principles of Genial Criticism" in *Felix Farley's Bristol Journal*
(10 Sept) Joined the Morgans at Ashley
Cottage

(1 Jan) Invasion of France by Allies
(1 Mar) Castlereagh's treaty with Austria, Prussia, and Russia against
Napoleon
(6 Apr) Napoleon abdicated
(May) First Treaty of Paris; Napoleon
exiled to Elba; Restoration of the
Bourbons
(8–9 Jun) Cochrane perjury trial
(Sept–Jun 1815) Congress of Vienna
(24 Dec) Peace of Ghent signed by Britain and U.S.
Inquisition re-established in Spain
WW *Excursion*

(20 Sept–10 Dec) "To Mr. Justice Fletcher" in *Courier*
(c 5 Dec) Moved with the Morgans to Calne, Wilts, to be treated by Dr Page

Scott *Waverley*
Cary's *Dante* completed

1815 (Jun) *Remorse* performed at Calne
(Jul–Sept) Dictating *Biographia Literaria*
(Aug–Scpt) *Sibylline Leaves* and *Biographia Literaria* sent for publication in Bristol

(Mar–Jun) The Hundred Days: Napoleon escaped from Elba to France
(6 Apr) Allies mobilise vs Napoleon
(18 Jun) Waterloo
Restoration of Louis XVIII
Napoleon from Plymouth to St Helena
(20 Nov) Second Treaty of Paris
WW *Poems* of 1815; *The White Doe of Rylstone*
Scott *Guy Mannering*

1816 (Feb) Grant from Literary Fund, and gift from Byron
(Mar) London: illness
(10 Apr) Sent *Zapolya* to Byron
(15 Apr) Accepted as patient and housemate by Dr Gillman, Moreton House, Highgate
(May–Jun) *Christabel* published (three editions); renewed acquaintance with Hookham Frere; offered Stuart tract or essays on Catholic Question
(Dec) *Statesman's Manual* published; Hazlitt's antagonistic reviews in *Examiner* (Jun, Sept, Dec) and *Edinburgh Review* (Dec)

(24 Apr) Byron left England
(21 Jun) Motion for relief of Roman Catholics rejected in the Lords
(7 Jul) Sheridan d
Parliamentary Committee on Education of the Poor
(Nov) *Cobbett's Political Register* reduced price to 2d
(2 Dec) Spa Fields Riot
Shelley *Alastor and Other Poems*
Peacock *Headlong Hall*
Maturin *Bertram*
J. H. Frere ms tr of Aristophanes

1817 (Apr) Second *Lay Sermon* published
(14 Apr) *Remorse* revived
(Jun) Conversations with Tieck
(Jul) *Biographia Literaria, Sibylline Leaves* published
(summer) Met Joseph Henry Green
(Sept) Met Henry Cary
(Nov) *Zapolya* published; C's tr of Hurwitz's *Hebrew Dirge* for Princess Charlotte; Tieck visited C

(13 Feb) RS *Wat Tyler*
(4 Mar) Habeas Corpus suspended
(27 Mar) Sidmouth Circular on libels
(Apr) *Blackwood's Magazine* founded as *Edinburgh Monthly Magazine*
(May) Motion for Relief of Roman Catholics rejected in the Lords
(6 Nov) Princess Charlotte d
Elgin Marbles purchased by government and placed in BM
Keats *Poems*
Hazlitt *The Characters of Shakespear's Plays*
Moore *Lalla Rookh*
Ricardo *Principles of Political Economy*
Cuvier *Le règne animal*

1818 (Jan) "Treatise on Method" in *Encyclopaedia Metropolitana* published
(Jan–Mar) Lectures on poetry and drama
(Jan) Met Thomas Allsop
Annotated 1817 Catholic Emancipation debate in copy of Hansard
(Apr) Two pamphlets supporting Peel's

(28 Jan) Habeas Corpus restored and never again suspended
(1 Jun) Parliamentary motion for universal suffrage and annual parliaments defeated
(Jun) Westmorland election
Keats *Endymion*

Bill against exploitation of child-labour

(summer) Portrait by Thomas Phillips

(Nov) *The Friend* (3-vol edition)

Portrait by C. R. Leslie

(Dec) Lectures on the History of Philosophy (–Mar 1819); literary lectures (–Mar 1819)

(Aug) *Blackwood's* and *Quarterly* attacks on Keats

Hallam *Middle Ages*

Hazlitt *Lectures on the English Poets*

Lamb *Collected Works* (Vol II dedicated to C)

Peacock *Nightmare Abbey*

1819 (Mar) Financial losses in bankruptcy of publisher Rest Fenner

(29 Mar) Lectures ended

(11 Apr) Met Keats in Millfield Lane; HC elected Fellow of Oriel; revived interest in chemistry; occasional contributions to *Blackwood's* (to 1822); B. W. Procter met C at Lamb's

(May) Grattan's Motion for Relief of Roman Catholics defeated

(Jun) Grey's Bill to abolish Declaration against Transubstantiation defeated

1820 (May) HC deprived of Oriel Fellowship

(Aug) Green began to act as weekly amanuensis to record C's work on Old and New Testament

(Oct) DC to St John's Cambridge

(Dec) High opinion of new friend, Hyman Hurwitz

(29 Jan) George III d; accession of George IV

Cato Street Conspiracy

(Feb) Parliament dissolved

(Jun) Grattan d; Plunkett became main Irish spokesman

Revolution in Spain and Portugal

(Aug–Nov) Trial of Queen Caroline

Crawfurd *History of the Indian Archipelago*

Godwin *Of Population*

Keats *Lamia and Other Poems*

Lamb *Essays of Elia*

Shelley *Prometheus Unbound*

RS *Life of Wesley*

WW *The River Duddon*

1821 (Apr–May) Projected 3 Letters to C. A. Tulk MP on Catholic Question

(Jul) Reunion with brother George

(autumn) Invitation to lecture in Dublin declined

HNC essay on C in *Etonian*

(Feb) Plunkett's Motion for Relief of Roman Catholics with two securities (ban on foreign correspondence and veto on appointments) passed by Commons, rejected in Lords after intervention of Grenville (Apr)

(Feb) Keats d

Napoleon d

Greek War of Liberation

De Quincey *Confessions of an English Opium Eater*

Hazlitt *Lectures on Elizabethan Drama*

Mill *Elements of Political Economy*

RS *Vision of Judgment*

1822 (spring) C's "Thursday-evening class" began; SC's tr of Martin Dobrizhoffer *An Account of the Abipones, an Equestrian People of Paraguay*

(Nov) Meeting with Liverpool and Canning at Ramsgate

(Nov–Feb 1823) Mrs C and SC visit C at Highgate

(30 Apr) Canning's Catholic Peers Bill carried in Commons, rejected in the Lords

(Jul) Shelley d

(Aug) Castlereagh d; Canning became Foreign Secretary

(Nov–Dec) Faction-fights between Orangemen and Catholics in Ireland

(17 Dec) Met Thomas Moore
(29 Dec) HNC began recording Table Talk
Edward Irving's first visit

Byron *Vision of Judgment*
Grattan *Speeches*
Shelley *Hellas*
Blanco White *Letters from Spain*
WW *Ecclesiastical Sketches*

1823 (Mar) HNC and SC secretly engaged
(Jun) W. E. Channing's visit
(Sept) Sought admission to BM through Sir Humphry Davy
(Nov, before 10th) Gillmans moved to 3 The Grove; C's attic study

(Apr) Plunkett's Motion for Relief of Roman Catholics abandoned for lack of support
(May) First meeting of Catholic Association in Dublin; in London (Jun)
War between France and Spain
Hazlitt *Liber Amoris*
RS *History of the Peninsular War*

1824 (Mar) Elected Royal Associate, RSL, with annuity of £100
DC took BA Cambridge
(Jun) Carlyle and Gabriel Rossetti called at Highgate
(Jun–Jul) DC seriously ill at Highgate
John Taylor Coleridge became editor of *Quarterly Review*
Met J. G. Lockhart

(Apr) Byron d
Foundation of London Mechanics' Institution
Cary tr *The Birds* of Aristophanes
Godwin *History of the Commonwealth of England*
RS *The Book of the Church*

1825 (Apr) Prati called on C and introduced him to Vico's work
(May) *Aids to Reflection* published
(18 May) "On the *Prometheus* of Aeschylus" delivered to RSL
(May) 6 essays promised to publisher, J. A. Hessey
(Jun) Partnership of C's publishers, Hessey & Taylor, dissolved
(Jul) Blanco White visited C
(Nov) Corrected proofs of Hurwitz's *Hebrew Tales*; proposed three lectures on projected London University
(Dec) Received Blanco White's *Letters from Spain* and *Poor Man's Preservative*

(Feb–May) Burdett's Motion for the Relief of Roman Catholics passed in Commons, defeated in the Lords
(May) Liverpool's speech on Coronation Oath; quoted with approval by Canning
(Aug) Frere arrived in England
Brougham *Practical Observations upon the Education of the People*
Butler *The Book of the Roman-Catholic Church*
Hazlitt *Spirit of the Age*
Mill *Essays on Government*
Blanco White *Poor Man's Preservative Against Popery* and *Practical and Internal Evidences Against Catholicism*

1826 (spring) Intensive work on Daniel and the Apocalypse
(summer) Frere spent long periods with C
(Sept) Frere obtained promise of sinecure of £200 from Liverpool for C
(Dec) C occupied his renovated bookroom

General Election with Corn Laws and Catholic Emancipation as main issues
England sent troops to Portugal
HNC *Six Months in the West Indies*
Turner *History of Henry VIII*
RS *Vindiciae Ecclesiae Anglicanae*
Blanco White *A Letter to Charles Butler*

1827 (Feb) Lord Dudley Ward intended to speak to Liverpool on C's behalf
(4 Feb) J. A. Heraud's first visit
(10 May) Thomas Chalmers called at Highgate; C's serious illness; visit

(Feb) Liverpool seized with paralysis
(Mar) Burdett's Bill rejected in Commons; Canning PM
(8 Aug) Canning d
(Aug) Goderich ministry

from Poole
(15 Jul) DC ordained
(Aug) John Sterling visited C
(30 Aug) HNC suspended record of Table Talk
(6 Dec) DC married Mary Pridham
Sir George Beaumont d, leaving £100 to Mrs C

University of London founded
Blake d
Hallam *Constitutional History*
Hare *Guesses at Truth*
Irving tr of *The Coming of Messiah*
Keble *Christian Year*
Tennyson *Poems by Two Brothers*

1828 (22 Apr) Fenimore Cooper met C with Scott at W. Sotheby's
(21 Jun–7 Aug) Netherlands and Rhine Tour with Dora and WW; J. C. Young, T. C. Grattan met C
(Aug) *Poetical Works* (3 vols)
Hyman Hurwitz appointed Professor of Hebrew, London University
(Aug) Onset of prolonged intermittent illness, with strong presentiment of death

(Jan) Wellington ministry
(Apr) Repeal of Test and Corporation Acts
(May) Burdett's Bill for Relief of Roman Catholics passed in Commons, rejected in Lords (Jun)
(Aug) Peel and Wellington in correspondence over the Catholic Question
(Dec) Lord Liverpool d
Russia goes to war with Turkey
Brougham *A Speech on the Present State of the Law of the Country*
Hazlitt *Life of Napoleon* vols I, II

1829 (Jan–Feb) Refused to sign Petition against Catholic Emancipation
(5 Mar) W. P. Wood visited C
(spring) Illness delayed writing of *Church and State*
(c May) *Poetical Works* (2nd ed)
Poetical Works of Coleridge, Shelley, and Keats (Galignani Paris)
(3 Sept) SC married her cousin HNC; Lady Beaumont left C £50; Poole visited Highgate
(17 Sept) C wrote his will
(Sept) Mrs C left Greta Hall for good
HNC and SC living in Gower Street
(Dec) *On the Constitution of the Church and State* published

Meetings held throughout the country to petition against Catholic Emancipation
(Jan) King agrees to discussion of Catholic Emancipation in Cabinet
(Feb–Mar) Bill passed to suppress the Catholic Association
(31 Apr) George IV gave reluctant assent to Catholic Emancipation
(May) Sir Humphry Davy d
Arnold *Sermons*
Hurwitz *The Elements of the Hebrew Language*
RS *Sir Thomas More*
[Isaac Taylor] *Natural History of Enthusiasm* (May)

1830 (c Apr) *On the Constitution of the Church and State* (2nd ed)
(13 Apr) HNC resumed record of Table Talk
(Jun) HNC and SC settled in Hampstead; Herbert Coleridge b
(2–17 Sept) C remade his will
(18 Sept) Hazlitt d
Republication of *The Devil's Walk* "by Professor Porson"

Reform agitation
(Jun) Death of George IV; accession of William IV
(Nov) Grey ministry
Greece independent
Comte *Cours de philosophie positive*
Lyell *Principles of Geology*
Tennyson *Poems Chiefly Lyrical*

1831 Last meetings with WW; *Aids to Reflection* (2nd ed)
(14 May) Emma Willard visited C
(May) Royal Society of Literature annuity withdrawn; refused personal grant from Grey; Frere made up the loss

(Mar) Lord John Russell introduced Reform Bill in Commons
(22 Apr) Dissolution of Parliament
(8 Oct) Lords rejected Second Reform Bill
(16 Nov) Wellington ministry resigned

(23 Sept) J. S. Mill, Henry Taylor, James Stephen visited C

(12 Dec) Final Reform Bill introduced
In U.S.A. issue of slavery intensified
Hegel d
J. S. Mill *The Spirit of the Age*
(Jul) Review of *C&S* in *Eclectic Review*
Walsh *Popular Opinions on Parliamentary Reform*

1832 Legacy of £300 from Steinmetz
(20 Mar) W. R. Hamilton's first visit
(27 Apr) H. B. McLellan's visit
(29 Sept) HCR brought W. S. Landor to C
(Sept) Portrait by Moses Haughton

Grey resigned; Wellington failed to form ministry; Grey recalled
(May) Reform Bill passed
Scott d
Green *Address Delivered in King's College*
Martineau *Illustrations of Political Economy*
Park *The Dogmas of the Constitution*

1833 HC's *Poems* dedicated to C
(24–9 Jun) To Cambridge for meetings of British Association;
R. A. Willmott recorded C's conversation
(Jul) Harriet Martineau visited C
(5 Aug) Emerson called at Highgate
HC's *Northern Worthies* published

(Feb–Apr) Debates over disturbances in Ireland
(Feb–Jun) Debates over tithes for Church of Ireland
(Jul) Temporary defeat of Miguel by Pedro in Portugal
Arnold *Principles of Church Reform*
Carlyle *Sartor Resartus*
Keble's sermon on "National Apostacy" began Oxford Movement
Lamb *Last Essays of Elia*
Mill "Corporation and Church Property"
Smith *Seven Letters on National Religion*
Tracts for the Times (Newman et al)

1834 (Mar–Jul) *Poetical Works* (3rd ed) 3 vols published separately; reviewed by HCR in *Quarterly* (Aug)
(30 Jun) Edwin Wyndham-Quin (later Earl of Dunraven) visited C
(5 Jul) C's last conversation with HNC
(25 Jul) C died at Highgate 6.20 A.M.
HNC set to work on *Table Talk*
(3 Sept) HNC formulated plans for *Literary Remains*

(Feb) New Poor Law introduced
(Apr) London Conference to oppose Miguel and his Spanish ally, Carlos
(Apr) Petition to admit Dissenters to Cambridge degrees
(Dec) Malthus d
(27 Dec) Lamb d
Bentham *Deontology*

EDITOR'S INTRODUCTION

H ENRY NELSON COLERIDGE'S *Specimens of the Table Talk of Samuel Taylor Coleridge* is an anthology, at once coruscating and convenient, of the poet's topics. More than an anthology, it is a chrestomathy designed to introduce and display Coleridge's vocabulary, the range and variety of his interests, and the keenness of his observations. *Table Talk* is the first in a line continued by the *Anima Poetae* edited by Ernest Hartley Coleridge in 1895 and *Inquiring Spirit* edited by Kathleen Coburn in 1951. E. H. Coleridge thought of *Anima Poetae* as supplementing the *Table Talk* by drawing on manuscript sources, but H. N. Coleridge had in fact found little reason to distinguish between topics on which the poet conversed and subjects explored in his notebooks and marginalia. Despite the encyclopaedic quality he gave to the *Table Talk* as chrestomathy, the manuscripts now available in the present edition do display, more clearly than the entries that H. N. Coleridge was able to publish in 1835, the informal and personal turn that private conversation often gave to general topics; the informality of everyday private talk was one element, though not the chief, that Henry as nephew and son-in-law hoped to catch in his record. He did not expect to capture the full effect epitomised in Washington Allston's memory of Coleridge in 1805, ". . . I am almost tempted to dream that I have once listened to Plato in the groves of the Academy",[1] but he did hope to popularise Coleridge as the Plato or, failing that, the Giordano Bruno of their fallen time.

Coleridge did not follow the progress of the nephew's record of his talk, and may never have known of its existence; but he would have had reasons for approving equally of the conception and of the title. He admired "inordinately" the *Colloquia Mensalia; or The Familiar Discourses of Dr. Martin Luther at His Table . . .* (1652).[2] He admired and annotated also the *Table Talk* of the pungent scholar John Selden (1689). The title has Shakespearian sanction. In *The Merchant of Venice* (III v 88), when Jessica offers Lorenzo praise before dinner, he answers, "No,

---

[1] Jared B. Flagg *The Life and Letters of Washington Allston* (New York 1892) 64.

[2] Luther was more than a model for C: "His Table-talk is next to the Scriptures my main book of meditation, deep, seminative, pauline, beyond all other works in my possession, it *potenziates* both my Thoughts and my Will." C to EC 8 Feb 1826: *CL* VI 561.

pray thee, let it serve for table-talk''. In *Coriolanus* table-talk might be said to rank with grace and benediction: Aufidius' lieutenant reports on Coriolanus' popularity (IV vii 4):

> Your soldiers use him as the grace fore meat,
> Their talk at table, and their thanks at end . . .

Henry Coleridge had something more elevated in mind than Sidney's definition of table-talk, in *An Apologie for Poetry*, as ''words as they chanceably fall from the mouth''. If Luther, Selden, and Shakespeare are the height of the scale, at the contemporary base the term had currency. William Hazlitt followed *The Round Table* of 1817 with *Table Talk; or, Original Essays* in 1821–2. More pertinently, Volume x of *Constable's Miscellany* (Edinburgh 1827) was entitled *Table-Talk; or, Selections from the Ana, Containing Extracts from the Different Collections of Ana, French, English, Italian, and German.*[3] The Preface to this miscellany spoke of the ''same blending of moral apothegms, of critical remarks, of serious and comic anecdotes, of scientific or literary information'' to be found, ''more or less modified by natural habits, and the state of human knowledge'', in the *ana* of French, Turk, Arab, or Greek, or the ''Bon Mots of Cicero''. The engraved title-page to this volume of 1827 depicted a dining table set for eight, with the doorway beyond, the guests yet to arrive. The setting was apt for Coleridge's entrance.

As an admirer of Luther and Selden, Coleridge would agree that such talk must not be completely personal, nor of a kind to be kept strictly private. Luther's was the talk ''held with diverse Learned Men'', as proclaimed on the title-page of one of the editions Coleridge annotated. Anthony Carlisle, Coleridge complained in 1812, unprofessionally detailed ''to a Woman, who made it the subject of common Table Talk'', everything ''I had confided to him as a Surgeon''.[4] The woman who repeated Carlisle's indiscretion debased the function of conversation at the table. Proper table-talk is informal discourse suited to all the circumstances, personal, intellectual, and civic, of the hearers. It is not ''common'', for not all are capable of such discourse.

Table-talk recorded to be published would also be suited to the circumstances and needs of the time. Henry Nelson Coleridge saw that the public situation, as discussed in the dining salons of 1823–35, called in two particular ways for his uncle's advent. In a proper symposium all prominent views need to be heard in order for truth to be recognised; Socrates' superiority becomes clear in the context of related but defective,

---

[3] More specialised, *Dramatic Table Talk or Scenes . . . Serious and Comic in Theatrical History and Biography* ed   Richard Ryan (3 vols 1825–30).
[4] *CL* III 408.

inferior opinions. After 1791 James Boswell's *Life of Samuel Johnson* had provided a dominant portrait not only of one whose talk met no counterbalancing voices but also of a talker distinctively wrong, in Henry Nelson Coleridge's opinion, for the times. In 1785 *Dr Johnson's Table Talk* had been arranged by Stephen Jones in alphabetical order, after the manner of Selden's; there was a new edition, amplified from Boswell's *Life*, in 1798 and again in two volumes in 1808. The younger James Boswell issued *The Table Talk of Samuel Johnson, LL.D.* in two volumes in 1818. Henry Nelson Coleridge's Introduction of 1835 clearly sets up Johnson as the talker to be surpassed and overcome.[5] Coleridge's works in prose, from *The Friend* on, had spoken to the needs of all who had survived the Age of Johnson, but readers had been few. The strength of his poems alone, deflected by C's uncertain aim in such books as the *Biographia Literaria*, could not convert or redeem an age given over to utilitarian self-interest, *laissez faire*, and the blinders of common sense. A record of the higher reaches of C's conversation could better meet the needs of the time by making his mind available to a wider audience than had yet heard it aright. Although sometimes as entertainment rather than philosophic message, reviewers also saw Coleridge as successor and rival to Johnson. Henry Nelson Coleridge had considerable additional success in provoking reviewers into comment on his antithesis of the expansive Coleridge and the constricted Sir James Mackintosh. All agreed that Coleridge was the more copious talker.[6]

"If our author's poetry is inferior to his conversation, his prose is utterly abortive", William Hazlitt wrote in 1825, giving the general reason that "the world is growing old" and the specific reason that Coleridge's faculties "have gossiped away their time, and gadded about from house to house, as if life's business were to melt the hours in listless talk".[7] The more sensitive to Hazlitt's charge that his talk had been a sign of inertia

[5] Making comparison easier, John Murray issued simultaneously James Boswell *The Life of Samuel Johnson, LL.D.* (8 vols 1835) and advertised it in *TT* (1835).

[6] De Q, as will be seen, set up Macaulay as the challenger for C's title, and others saw a resemblance: see App F 16, vol II, below.

[7] *The Spirit of the Age* (2nd ed 1825) 57, 70, 71. Basil Willey's explanation for the superiority of C's conversation to commissioned composition contrasts sharply with Hazlitt's: ". . . to be at his best his mind must be in action and growth, and his feelings ardent as he composes. Thus he shines most of all in conversation, where he can range freely and follow the scent wherever it leads; next best, in marginal annotations, in notebooks and in letters, where formal arrangement is not expected. Least of all in set composition, where the requirements of order and strict progression freeze the genial current, and often inhibit him altogether." *Samuel Taylor Coleridge* (1972) 179. Subsequent discussions of C's difficulties with "set composition" have begun with the question of his eclectic borrowing rather than with the strength of his spontaneity.

because he suspected Southey and Wordsworth of making similar assessments, Coleridge himself defended from time to time the energies he had expended in informal daily instruction. He justified his reluctance to lecture in Leeds in 1823 by assessing the cost to himself as greater than any instruction or pleasure he could currently give "either by a series of Lectures, or even by conversation, by which I have in the course of my Life atchieved ten fold more than by all my public Efforts, from the Press or the Lecture-Desk".[8] He had proclaimed the virtues of his conversation more directly in *Biographia Literaria*: "Would that the criterion of a scholar's utility were the number and moral value of the truths, which he has been the means of throwing into the general circulation; or the number and value of the minds, whom by his conversation or letters, he has excited into activity, and supplied with the germs of their after-growth!"[9] If Coleridge rather than his nephew is to be considered as the begetter of the *Table Talk*, his credo is announced; if a distinguished rank be denied him, the passage in *Biographia Literaria* continues, he could "dare look forward with confidence to an honorable acquittal".

If the *Table Talk* were arranged by topic, under headings and subheadings with such continuity as the nephew always felt free to provide any unpublished prose by Coleridge that seemed to need it, then the result would not only equal any of Coleridge's other works in range of favourite subjects, but would match most of them in clarity and portions of some of them in fulness of exposition of difficult but treasurable pronouncements. Such an arrangement by subject would lose the high degree of spontaneity retained in the nephew's manuscript version—reaching its height, perhaps, in 1830–32—and would cost us the sense of conversational flow from day to day in the last decade of Coleridge's life, with all the conversational repetitions and revisions in differing contexts. In the workbooks as the nephew and his heirs preserved them, we have both an anthology and a record of Coleridge in maturity.

COLERIDGE AS TALKER

It was universally acknowledged, although various and conflicting interpretations underlay the acknowledgement, that S. T. Coleridge was the greatest talker of his age. By 1790 his recitals of what he had read or heard overawed fellow Bluecoats at Christ's Hospital. Clement Carlyon and George Greenough, who studied and travelled with him in Germany in 1799, each felt the compulsion, like many after them, to record snip-

---

[8] To Dr Williamson [11] Nov 1823:   [9] *BL* ch 10 (*CC*) ɪ 220.
CL v 310.

pets from his astonishing conversation. Carlyon recalled years later Coleridge's vitality during their pedestrian tour through the Harz Mountains: "He never appeared to tire of mental exercise; talk seemed to him a perennial pastime; and his endeavours to inform and amuse us ended only with the cravings of hunger or the fatigue of a long march . . ."[10] Charles Lamb, among the first and the last to hear the golden flow with unillusioned love, epitomised his friend in the album of a London bookseller:

In him was disproved that old maxim, that we should allow every one his share to talk. He would talk from morn to dewy eve, nor cease till far midnight; yet who ever would interrupt him,—who would obstruct that continuous flow of converse, fetched from Helicon or Zion? He had the tact of making the unintelligible seem plain. Many who read the abstruser parts of his "Friend" would complain that his works did not answer to his spoken wisdom. They were identical. But he had a tone in oral delivery which seemed to convey sense to those who were otherwise imperfect recipients.[11]

Close friends like Lamb and Wordsworth could hear in "the unintelligible made plain" both angelic wisdom and airy nothings. Others would either experience irreproachable wisdom or be decidedly vexed by a seemingly vaporous unintelligibility.

So many hearers reported Wordsworth's appraisals to them of Coleridge's conversational power that they have made it seem one of Wordsworth's most interesting topics. Mrs John Davy, a neighbour in Ambleside, made notes on his remarks to her assembled guests in 1844: "He said that the liveliest and truest image he could give of Coleridge's talk was, 'that of a majestic river, the sound or sight of whose course you caught at intervals, which was sometimes concealed by forests, sometimes lost in sand, then came flashing out broad and distinct, then again took a turn which your eye could not follow, yet you knew and felt that it was the same river: so,' he said, 'there was always a train, a stream, in Coleridge's discourse, always a connection between its parts in his own mind, though not one always perceptible to the minds of others.' "[12] His remarks to Henry Nelson Coleridge on 15 Oct 1829 distinguish an early and a late Coleridge, but trace a unifying genius in both:

S. T. C. never did *converse* in the common sense of the word; he would lay hold of another person's suggestion, & then refine upon it, divide & subtilize it till he

---

[10] Carlyon I 130. Joseph Farington was fascinated with the report of Sir George Beaumont on 29 Nov 1803: ". . . *Coleridge*, a few years ago a violent Democrat but now quite opposite,— abt. 32 years old,—of great genius,— a Poet,—prodigious command of words,—has read everything." Farington (1978–) VI 2174.

[11] *L Life* 666; *L Works* I 351–2.

[12] Margaret Fletcher, Mrs Davy, in *W Mem* II 443; *W Prose* (1876) III 441–2.

had made it entirely his own. He borrowed largely, but he had a right to do so, for he gave away as largely. He is now too often dreamy; he rarely comes into contact with popular feelings & modes of thought.—You cannot incarnate him for a minute. The activity of his imagination, wͨh I must call morbid, disturbs his sense & recollection of facts. Many men have done wonderful things—Newton—Davy &c; but S. T. C. is the only wonderful man I ever knew.[13]

Wordsworth commented similarly to Samuel Rogers that the only intellect that ever astonished him became in later life "a little dreamy and hyper-metaphysical".[14] On 27 May 1830, after Wordsworth's remarks of October, Henry Nelson Coleridge brought Coleridge around to a comparison: "W's conversation runs round & round again in eddies—it never progresses—My fault is the ōr way—I skip from one thing to anͬ too fast & unconnectedly."[15]

As Coleridge was in a unique position to know how far he understood the meaning of his own words, and as moreover he was one of the most persistent and telling critics of his mental processes, conversational and otherwise, it is worth asking whether he perceived his leaps from one subject to the next as disruptions in his own thought or as sudden accelerations, simply too abrupt for his hearer, in the momentum of his progress from initiative through demonstration and illustration to full exploration.[16] Tentatively, supported by the dual assumption that he did not always converse the same way and that he was aware of conversing in more than one way, we can most usefully interpret his words on skipping "from one thing to another too fast and unconnectedly" as eliding two perceived faults: sometimes he leaped from one point to another that beckoned enticingly ahead, without making a secure logical connexion between them; at other times he saw the connexion—and on occasion even foresaw it as he began the periphrasis—but did not make the connexion clear to his audience. Because of Henry Nelson Coleridge's method of recording each subject in a separate entry, these faults do not lie on the surface of the *Table Talk*; neither disconnexion nor continuity can be found in his final record without attentive search.

Even the best known attempt to describe one of Coleridge's harangues as a series of leaps by Hartleian associations half buried in memory—the account by John Keats of an encounter on Hampstead Heath in April

---

[13] App D, below, from MS B ff 9–9ᵛ. For publication in his *QR* review of *PW* (1834) HNC added Sir Walter Scott among those thought by WW to have done wonderful things, and in print Newton became Georges Cuvier. *CH* 621.

[14] Alexander Dyce *Recollections of the Table-Talk of Samuel Rogers* ed Morchard Bishop (1952) 147n.

[15] MS B f 18ᵛ.

[16] The criteria come from C's "Essays on Method" in *Friend (CC)* I 448–524.

1819—can be shown to illustrate Wordsworth's analogy of a winding river.

I walked with him a[t] his alderman-after dinner pace for near two miles I suppose In those two Miles he broached a thousand things—let me see if I can give you a list—Nightingales, Poetry—on Poetical sensation—Metaphysics—Different genera and species of Dreams—Nightmare—a dream accompanied by a sense of touch—single and double touch—A dream related—First and second consciousness—the difference explained between will and Volition—so m[an]y metaphysicians from a want of smoking the second consciousness—Monsters— the Kraken—Mermaids—southey believes in them—southeys belief too much diluted—A Ghost story—Good morning—I heard his voice as he came towards me—I heard it as he moved away . . . Good Night!"[17]

The connectives from subject to subject, on the way from initiative to full demonstration for a novice, can be supplied from similar juxtapositions in the published works. The comprehensive index in each volume of *The Collected Works of S. T. Coleridge* makes the process available without detailed exposition here, but one can go representatively from Coleridge's description of his metaphysics as "the referring of the mind to its own consciousness for truths indispensable to its own happiness", on to "those rapid alternations of the sleeping with the half-waking state, which is *the true witching time* . . . the fruitful matrix of Ghosts" (in a passage on Luther's inkpot thrown at the devil), and on to a distinction between this state, when "a sort of under-consciousness blends with our dreams" and we "dream *about* things", and the fuller sleep of the nervous system when we "*dream the things*".[18] These passages equally illustrate the transitions from metaphysics to dreams to double touch to first and second consciousness to metaphysics again. A river of subliminal transitions can be similarly traced through many of the conversations recorded by Henry Nelson Coleridge.

In August 1814 Coleridge had analysed in a notebook the hazards of such an encounter with him as Keats had undergone:

There are two sorts of talkative fellows whom it would be injurious to confound/ & I, S. T. Coleridge, am the latter. The first sort is of those who use five hundred words more than needs to express an idea—that is not my case—few men, I will be bold to say, put more meaning into their words than I or choose them more deliberately & discriminatingly. The second sort is of those who use five hundred more ideas, images, reasons &c than there is any need of to arrive at their object/ till the only object arrived at is that the mind's eye of the bye-stander is dazzled with colors succeeding so rapidly as to leave one vague impression that there has been a great Blaze of colours all about something. Now this is my case—& a

---

[17] *The Letters of John Keats 1814–1821* ed Hyder Edward Rollins (2 vols Cambridge, Mass 1958) II 88–9.

[18] *Friend (CC)* I 108, 140; *SM (CC)* 80.

grievious fault it is/ my illustrations swallow up my thesis—I feel too intensely the omnipresence of all in each, platonically speaking—or psychologically my brain-fibres, or the spiritual Light which abides in the brain-marrow as visible Light appears to do in sundry rotten mackerel & other *smashy* matters, is of too general an affinity with all things/ and tho' it perceives the *difference* of things, yet is eternally pursuing the likenesses, or rather that which is common [between them]/ bring me two things that seem the very same, & then I am quick enough [not only] to shew the difference, even to hair-splitting—but to go on from circle to circle till I break against the shore of my Hearer's patience, or have my Concentricals dashed to nothing by a Snore—that is my ordinary mishap.[19]

This passage displays the same imagistic sense of "all in each" that Coleridge's talk must characteristically have contained.

The tape recorder has shown how fragmentary and uncompleted most casual discourse is. Newsmen learned that President Kennedy was no more given to complete sentences or explicit transitions than President Eisenhower had been. Before the tape recorder, it was impossible to cap-

[19] *CN* II 2372. C was more apologetic in late Nov 1828, when he learned, in his words, "that he is a most remorseless *Talker*—and that if his Ears were as long as his Tongue, his Consociates might well apprehend that their Patience would be *brayed*, tho' perhaps not *in a mortar*—and expect Rain in spite of Blue Skies and Sunshine". To Mrs Joshua Bates: *CL* VI 774.

He had been chastened by reading in *La Belle Assemblée* VIII (Dec 1828) 258–9 a tribute to Sir George Beaumont, signed "N. M.", published simultaneously in *The Anniversary* for 1829 ed Allan Cunningham pp 157–62: "We remember once of meeting at his table that wizard in conversation, Coleridge the poet. The discourse at first was discursive, and shifted with the shifting dishes; it glanced upon art, upon prose romances, and then shone full upon poetry. Coleridge burst out like a conflagration. We had met the inspired man before, and were aware of the untiring fascination of his eloquence, and how effectually he could keep a listener captive. It was at a midnight supper; he took up a prawn, and from that diminutive text preached upon the flux and reflux of the ocean, the wild theory of St. Pierre, the immensity of the leviathan, and the magnificence of the great deep. Had we supped with a whale entire, he could not have done more with his subject. At the baronet's table, however, he seemed less inclined to pursue his wild career, though verse presented an ample field, and Lady Beaumont found time to say, 'I wish, Mr. Coleridge, you would give us a volume of such poems as the Genevieve.' 'The Genevieve, my lady,' said the Bard, in a voice as musical as the inimitable poem itself, 'I shall give you a far worthier work than the Genevieve.' He then proceeded to draw the character of a work of a devout nature, in which his learning and his talent would be poured freely out; and if the excellence of the book equal the splendid summary of its contents, it will be a treasure to the church. From this a transition to the Revelations was easy and natural; but if it had been neither, the orator would have made it both, for he is unequalled in the art of transition, and never seems embarrassed for a moment. From the Revelations, the hand of his friend the Rev. Edward Irving was then seeking to lift the veil, and to this new and magnificent task the Poet turned with sparkling eyes and glowing brow—he had found a theme suitable to his own lofty imagination, and as mystical as his own mind. How he soared! He appeared to think that the Apocalypse was a divine poem rather than a Revelation." Can N. M. be the Nicholas Mitchell who turned on C, RS, and WW in *Poets of the Age* (1832)? *WL* (*L* rev) II 518n.

ture fully either nuance or detail in such conversation as Coleridge's. Within what was possible, Henry Nelson Coleridge's revisions in the manuscripts of Table Talk show that he often had to sacrifice the rhythm of spoken sentences in the more serviceable cause of retaining the key words that Coleridge had chosen "deliberately & discriminatingly". The redundancy of "ideas, images, reasons &c" that we can assume to have been normal in the actual conversation is absent from the earliest years of Henry Nelson Coleridge's record; even in the later years, if one can judge by comparison with the letters, notebooks, and fuller marginalia, the redundancy was usually lost in the interest of the intellectual kernel and highlighted phrase. Many who had listened to Coleridge at Highgate with enchantment or perplexity must have felt a sudden illumination as the subjects they had strained yearningly toward now flashed before them in the compact paragraphs of *Table Talk*.

When the great talkers are classified as to purpose or method—talking for victory, talking to entertain, talking to arouse—Coleridge usually emerges as the supreme monologuist who astounded, and astounded in part by seeming to need no external stimulus. It was Mme de Staël's definition of him, often quoted, that he was "a master of monologue, mais qu'il ne savait pas le dialogue".[20] Sensitive to the charge that he allowed the intrusion of no other voice, he protested once in 1819: "And even in conversation, I can affirm most sincerely that any interruption, or admonition that I have lost the bit and curb, and am reducing the conversation to a mono-drama, or dialogue (in which one of the two *dramatis personae* is forced to act the mute) of tongue *versus* ear, is received by me not only thankfully, but with unfeigned pleasure."[21] In the *Table Talk* itself, the entries for 29 June 1833 end with Coleridge beckoning to an unnamed entrant: "I am glad you came in to punctuate my discourse, which I fear has gone on for an hour without any stop at all."

---

[20] When HCR found Mme de Staël so quoted by HNC in *QR*—and in *TT* (1835) ii 217n—he somehow believed that he was the only person she had honoured with her *bon mot* and therefore that he must have been HNC's hidden source (*CRD* i 201), but she had said it also to JTC at Coppet in 1814 after she had met C in Sept 1813: Bernard, Lord Coleridge *The Story of a Devonshire House* (1905) 241.

Joseph Cottle says that during his residence in Bristol C gave little chance for "true, interchangeable conversation": "On almost every subject on which he essayed to speak, he made an impassioned harangue of a quarter, or half an hour; so that inveterate talkers, while Mr. Coleridge was on the wing, generally suspended their own flight, and felt it almost a profanation to interrupt so impressive and mellifluous a speaker. This singular, if not happy peculiarity, occasioned even Madame de Stael to remark of Mr. C. that 'He was rich in a Monologue, but poor in a Dialogue.' " Cottle *Rem* 77. One of De Q's accounts of C as conversationalist cites Staël. *De Q Works* x 281.

[21] To Joseph Hughes: *CL* vi 1049.

Henry Nelson Coleridge explains both the prolongation and the compulsiveness as "the habit of his intellect, which was under a law of discoursing upon all subjects with reference to ideas or ultimate ends".[22] Although Coleridge preened himself on ability to lower his subjects to suit all kinds and conditions of listeners, he suffered less from complaints that he talked over the heads of his auditors than from his own certainty of indiscretions in the presence of strangers. He made a memorandum in 1804:

> In company, indeed with all except a very chosen few, never dissent from any one as to the *merits* of another/ especially, in your own supposed department/ but content yourself with praising in your turn the really good. . . . Coleridge! Coleridge! will you never learn to appropriate your conversation to your company? Is it not desecration, indelicacy, a proof of great weakness & even vanity to talk to &c &c, as if you [talk]ed [with Words]worth & Sir G. Beau[mont?]²³

How far the discretion of H. N. C. saved us from the indiscretions of S. T. C. cannot be known, but the manuscripts now published reveal more than the family thought it discreet to publish in 1835, and some of the reviewers professed to be shocked by a variety of casual remarks. The personal, derogatory remarks now revealed will afford, at worst, titillation.

Not all hearers of Coleridge or readers of the *Table Talk* were pleased to sacrifice indiscretion for elevation. To a charge that Coleridge's talk is difficult to follow, however, the retort of Dr Johnson seems just: "Sir, I have found you an argument; but I am not obliged to find you an understanding."[24] In the perceptive footnote already cited, Henry Nelson Coleridge defended his uncle against Johnson's supposed superiority to "discursive and continuous" talkers like Burke and Coleridge, an assumption of superiority implicit in Mme de Staël's *bon mot*: "And if dialogue must be cut down in its meaning to small talk, I, for one, will admit that Coleridge, amongst his numberless qualifications, possessed it not. But I am sure that he could, when it suited him, converse as well as any one else, and with women he frequently did converse in a very winning and popular style, confining them, however, as well as he could, to the detail of facts or of their spontaneous emotions."[25] In 1827 Henry Nelson Coleridge had made a suggestion to Sara, his fiancée: "It would be well worth your while to be very attentive to your father's conversation, when you are with him, and endeavour afterwards to preserve some of

²² Entry 36:545n, 4 Jul 1833, *TT* (1835) II 217n.
²³ *CN* II 2193.
²⁴ Jun 1784 in *Boswell's Life of John-* son ed George Birkbeck Hill rev. L. F. Powell (6 vols Oxford 1934–50) IV 313.
²⁵ Entry 36:545n.

it, as I have done. Especially as he talks to you on plainer subjects."[26] It was not altogether or even largely a matter of stooping. The lode of simplicity in Coleridge's temperament and character, overlooked in most studies of his intellectual and literary borrowings, put him into direct communion with those he loved and with innocent, kindly souls in general.

He seems in fact to have charmed by innocence as well as by eloquence. Women of taste but without the intellectual aggressiveness of a Staël tended to proclaim him abundantly lovable. "Indeed", concluded the widow of the actor Charles Mathews, "I do not know whether he was not a more charming companion when he stooped his magnificent mind to the understanding of the less informed and little gifted, than when he conversed with higher intellects."[27] The generous innocence that Anne Mathews illustrates in Coleridge's love of flowers was praised also by Sarah Flower Adams, the daughter of Coleridge's first publisher, who reports, in "some such words" as Coleridge's, a flowery apostrophe to an engraving (over Lamb's mantel) of a girl half listening to an admonition against the roses of life.[28] Anne Gillman wrote after Coleridge's

---

[26] MS E, following E 57.

[27] *Memoirs of Charles Mathews* (4 vols 1838–9) III 190. Not every woman allowed herself to be taken in. Katharine Byerley Thomson (1797–1862), who had suffered the disillusionment of going to the Royal Institution when Coleridge announced that he had left his lecture at home, made a general assessment: ". . . he was *so* eloquent—there was such a combination of wit and poetry in his similes—such fancy, such a finish in his illustrations; yet . . . It was all fancy, flourish, sentiment." *Recollections of Literary Characters and Celebrated Places* (2 vols 1854) II 59–60. For Mrs Thomson's memory of C's tearful narration to her, when a child, of the woeful history of Mary of Buttermere see II 58. There was never a chance that the utilitarian Harriet Martineau would succumb either to C's sentiment or to his economics: *Autobiography* (3 vols 1877) I 396–9.

[28] "After some time he moved round the room, to read the different engravings that hung upon the walls. One, over the mantel piece, especially interested his fancy. There were only two figures in the picture, both women. One was of a lofty, commanding stature, with a high intellectual brow, and of an abbess-like deportment. She was standing in grave majesty, with the finger uplifted, in the act of monition to a young girl beside her. The face was in profile, and somewhat severe in its expression; but this was relieved by the richness and grace of the draperies in which she was profusely enveloped. The girl was in the earliest and freshest spring of youth, lovely and bright, with a somewhat careless and inconsiderate air, and she seemed but half inclined to heed the sage advice of her elder companion. She held in her hand a rose, with which she was toying, and had she been alive you would have expected momentarily to see it taken between the taper fingers, and scattered in wilful profusion. Coleridge uttered an expression of admiration, and then, as if talking to himself, apostrophized in some such words as these: 'There she stands, with the world all before her: to her it is as a fairy dream, a vision of unmingled joy. To her it is as is that lovely flower, which woos her by its bright hue and fragrant perfume. Poor child! must thou too be re-

death to his daughter: "We believe that he possessed a more heavenly nature than was ever before given to Man—yet not that he was perfect—But surely he was born with sweetness beyond compare—".[29]

Although the motivations of that letter might make its sentiment suspect, Thomas Allsop (whom Mrs Gillman and Sara Coleridge regarded as a radical boor) wrote publicly in an almost identical vein: "Of all the men, ordinary or extraordinary, I have ever known, Coleridge was the one in whom the *child-like*, the almost infantile, love and joyance, giving birth to or rather intermingled with perfect sympathy and identity of feeling, most predominated. His mind was at once the most masculine, feminine, and yet *child-like* (and, in that sense, the most innocent) which it is possible to image."[30] All those closest to Coleridge, if we exempt Mrs Coleridge and Sara Hutchinson on the ground of their own temperaments, have left witness of his sweetness and simplicity.

The innocence they agree on would have coursed through many of the conversations from which Henry Nelson Coleridge and others have dislodged selections, but innocence was harder to make interesting at second hand than learning, anecdote, brilliantly keen distinctions, and touches of malice. Few of the reports from men gathered by Richard W. Armour and Raymond F. Howes in *Coleridge the Talker: A Series of Contemporary Descriptions and Comments* include among the sayings that astounded them any specific instances of kind or innocent language. They were astounded by what other talkers could not attain, the breadth of his knowledge, the continuous flow, and the rhythm of surprises in his *Weltanschauung*.

The charges of unintelligibility measure his audience. One can retain full sympathy with his listeners while categorising those who dispraised

---

minded of the thorns that lurk beneath? Turn thee to thy monitress! she bids thee clasp not too closely pleasures that lure but to wound thee. Look into her eloquent eyes; listen to her pleading voice; her words are words of wisdom; garner them up in thy heart; and when the evil days come, the days in which thou shalt say "I find no pleasure in them," remember her as thus she stood, and, with uppointing finger, bade thee think of the delights of heaven—that heaven which is ever ready to receive the returning wanderer to its rest.' " *Monthly Repository* NS IX (1835) 167; Bertram Dobell *Sidelights on Charles Lamb* (1903) 307–9 (var).

[29] VCL S MS F 3.71. Cf the Gillmans' phrases on the tablet in St Michael's Church, Highgate: "Under the pressure of a long | And most painful disease | His disposition was unalterably sweet and angelic; | He was an ever-during, ever-loving friend, | The gentlest and kindest teacher, | The most engaging home companion." Mary Shelley's brief praise on 18 Jan 1824 was the highest she could give: "Seeing Coleridge last night reminded me forcibly of past times: his beautiful descriptions reminded me of Shelley's conversations." *Mary Shelley's Journal* ed Frederick L. Jones (Norman, Oklahoma 1947) 192.

[30] Allsop II 175–6.

on this score as (*a*) persons—the largest group—who were unfamiliar with much of his terminology and most of his topics, (*b*) persons of inferior intelligence or slow wit, whatever the degree of knowledge, (*c*) persons with an impatient disinclination to listen, (*d*) persons of opposed or differing opinion who were irritated into inattention by aspects of his thought or his expression, (*e*) persons envious or temperamentally unsympathetic, (*f*) persons who would have preferred to do the talking, and (*g*) persons who embodied a mixture of these characteristics. Is this categorisation intended to deny that Coleridge was ever unintelligible? Not at all. He was capable of speaking what was not fully intelligible to him, let alone his hearers; he was also capable—to go beyond Lamb's phrase—of making not only the unintelligible but also the intelligible less than plain. Nor does the categorisation mean that we have no surviving report of discontent from a hearer in better command of several of Coleridge's subjects than he was.

We may take as the norm comments by Samuel Rogers to Alexander Dyce:

Coleridge was a marvellous talker. One morning, when Hookham Frere also breakfasted with me, Coleridge talked for three hours without intermission about poetry, and so admirable, that I wish every word he uttered had been written down.

But sometimes his harangues were quite unintelligible, not only to myself, but to others.[31]

---

[31] Dyce *Recollections of Rogers* 146. Henry Hart Milman is similarly reported on 23 Jul 1854, like Rogers at second hand: "The Dean used often to see and hear S. T. Coleridge, but his wonderful talk was far too unvaried from day to day; also, there were some absolute deficiencies in it, such as the total absence of wit; still, it was very remarkable. 'But,' he added, 'I used to be wicked enough to divide it into three parts: one third was admirable, beautiful in language and exalted in thought; another third was sheer absolute nonsense; and of the remaining third, I knew not whether it were sense or nonsense.' " Caroline Fox *Memories of Old Friends . . .* ed Horace N. Pym (Philadelphia 1882) 320. This work (p 71) gives us a version of C's rapid departure from Rome to escape Napoleon's retaliation against C's articles in the *M Post* "very offensive to Napoleon's dignity".

The painter Joseph Farington reacted somewhat like Rogers and Milman when he first met C at Sir George Beaumont's 25 Mar 1804: "The evening was passed not in conversation but in listening to a succession of opinions, & explanations delivered by Coleridge, to which I attended from a desire to form a judgment of his ability. It was all metaphysical, frequently perplexed, and certainly at times without understanding His subject. Occasionally there was some brilliance, but I particularly noticed that His *illustrations* generally disappointed me & rather weakened than enforced what He had before said. . . . His Dialect particularly when reading is what I shd. call *broad Devonshire*, for a gentleman.— His manner was good natured & civil & He went on like one who was accustomed to take the lead in the Company He goes into." Farington (1978–) vi 2276.

Rogers's example of another who "could not make head or tail of Coleridge's oration" (on a different occasion) was Wordsworth.

Perhaps there was advantage in having an intensive exposure to Coleridge for a limited number of months, not (unless you were Lamb) for life—the optimum time was about two years for Gioacchino de' Prati (1790–1863), the Italian patriot brought to Coleridge by Sir James Stuart and his wife's sister, Mrs Henry Woodcock:

We did not leave the house without visiting the garden, which was a favourite place of our poet; here he took me under his arm, and we began to converse together in German. Coleridge spoke this language quite correctly, and with a soft Hanoverian accent. German literature stood highly in his favour; this sympathy for the German was only equalled by his aversion for the French. He seemed to take so much interest in me, that he made me promise to be with him the next day an hour or two before the company which was wont to visit him, did assemble. "We shall," said he "have a private talk here in the garden if the weather be fine, otherwise you will excuse my taking you in my room, which is my place of rest, my study, and my library."

On returning home, Mrs. W., the sister of the noble baronet, who introduced me to C., asked me how I was satisfied with my new acquaintance. "Satisfied," answered I, "I am delighted, enraptured; I find concentrated in him all the talents which I have left with regret on the continent. As a poet, he reminds me of Schiller, as a philosopher, he equals Schelling, and as a speaker, he excels Fichte. As far as I could judge of those different talents combined together, he stands between Göethe and Lessing. I shall see him to morrow, and I expect a great treat from a private conversation which he promised me."

Accordingly I went, and my visits were repeated at least once a week for two years running, when by a series of mishaps I was obliged to leave the metropolis. . . .

Men of real genius have something in them, which distinguishes them from men of mere talent. This something is like all internal powers of Nature—indescribable, and yet must be felt by every one who comes within their atmosphere. It is a latent light or life, which emanates from them, and is possessed of electrical generative power. If a man of talent speaks, we listen with satisfaction, we may learn that which we do not know; but, if a man of genius unfolds the depths of his thoughts, his thoughts become as it were seeds, which germinate within our mind, and make us think and feel that which we never would have thought or felt before, unless previously acted upon by the master mind. This is the cause of the charm and the power of the conversations of S. T. Coleridge. Whether he was speaking on metaphysics, theology, poetry, history, or the most trifling subjects of common occurrence, his genius threw a new light upon the object of his discourse, and compelled his company to think in their turn, and to examine the question in a point of view, which, without his aid, would for ever have escaped their minds. His friends assembled at Mr. Gillman's towards tea time, and remained there till late in the evening.

I often spent the morning and afternoon with him, and had the pleasure of conversing with him for whole hours, which I reckon among the most agreeable and instructive ones I ever spent in my life. For he was not only a deep philosopher and poet, but a man possessed of great knowledge in many sciences, and was moreover the most pleasant and humorous companion in the world. No day elapsed in which he did not amuse me with some pleasant anecdote, in which he or some of his friends cut the principal figure.[32]

Even John Taylor Coleridge, who had listened carefully as early as 1811, grew weary despite continuing wonder:

June 1825.—This week I have seen a good deal of my Uncle Sam. He sate with me one day in Chambers for a long time and he dined here on Friday. . . . He is certainly a most surprising man, but I cannot say that his conversation instructs or amuses me much. It is somewhat obscure, partly from real depth and height, partly also I suspect from the imperfectness of the expression. He astonishes you, he electrifies you almost as he goes on, but you cannot remember the train afterward, nor much of the separate members. But after all, the universality of his knowledge is the most wonderful part of him—he is a real improvisatore on *every* subject and a quack in none.[33]

Against this norm, Sir Henry Holland (1788–1873) is the almost perfect embodiment of all the designated traits of discontent:

I saw Coleridge . . . rarely, and never took a place among the worshippers at his shrine. I recollect him only as an eloquent but intolerable talker; impatient of the speech and opinions of others; very inconsecutive, and putting forth with a plethora of words misty dogmas in theology and metaphysics, partly of German origin, which he never seemed to me to clear up to his own understanding or to that of others. What has come out posthumously of his philosophy has not removed this imputation upon it. I suspect his "Table Talk," as we have it in the very agreeable volume bearing this title, to have been sifted as well as abridged by the excellent judgment of the Editor.[34]

Leigh Hunt was interested in few of Coleridge's subjects outside belles-lettres and the political opinions that Coleridge opposed to his own. Fortunately Hunt was also a conveyer of personal and domestic detail:

I heard him the other day, under the grove at Highgate, repeat one of his melodious lamentations, as he walked up and down, his voice undulating in a stream of music, and his regrets of youth sparkling with visions ever young. At the same time, he did me the honour to show me, that he did not think so ill of all modern liberalism as some might suppose, denouncing the pretensions of the money-getting in a style which I should hardly venture upon, and never could equal; and asking, with a triumphant eloquence, what chastity itself were worth, if it were a casket, not to keep love in, but hate, and strife, and worldliness? On the same occasion, he built up a metaphor out of a flower, in a style surpassing the famous

---

[32] *Penny Satirist* 6 Oct 1838 p 2, 13 Oct p 4; partly reprinted in *C Talker* xxi.
[33] "Diary of John Taylor Coleridge" in Bernard, Lord Coleridge *This for Re-membrance* (1925) 42.
[34] *Recollections of Past Life* (1872) 205–6.

passage in Milton; deducing it from its root in religious mystery, and carrying it up into the bright-consummate flower, "the bridal chamber of reproductiveness." Of all "the Muse's mysteries," he is as great a high-priest as Spenser; and Spenser himself might have gone to Highgate to hear him talk, and thank him for his "Ancient Mariner." His voice does not always sound very sincere; but perhaps the humble and deprecating tone of it, on those occasions, is out of consideration for his hearer's infirmities, rather than produced by his own. He recited his "Kubla Khan," one morning, to Lord Byron, in his Lordship's house in Piccadilly, when I happened to be in another room. I remember the other's coming away from him, highly struck with his poem, and saying how wonderfully he talked. This is the impression of every body who hears him.

It is no secret that Mr. Coleridge lives in the Grove at Highgate with a friendly family, who have sense and kindness enough to know that they do themselves an honour by looking after the comforts of such a man. His room looks upon a delicious prospect of wood and meadow, with coloured gardens under the window, like an embroidery to the mantle. I thought, when I first saw it, that he had taken up his dwelling-place like an abbot. Here he cultivates his flowers, and has a set of birds for his pensioners, who come to breakfast with him. He may be seen taking his daily stroll up and down, with his black coat and white locks, and a book in his hand; and is a great acquaintance of the little children. His main occupation, I believe, is reading. He loves to read old folios, and to make old voyages with Purchas and Marco Polo; the seas being in good visionary condition, and the vessel well-stocked with botargoes.[35]

In contrast with Hunt, Philarète Chasles was prepared upon arrival at Highgate (probably in 1820) to grasp Coleridge's philosophical and political thought:

In all his conversations which were not direct instruction, one could not but lament some obscurity and mistiness; but in listening and endeavouring to follow

---

[35] James Henry Leigh Hunt (1784–1859) *Lord Byron and Some of His Contemporaries; with Recollections of the Author's Life, and of His Visit to Italy* (2nd ed 2 vols 1828) ii 52–4.

Thomas Colley Grattan had heard C in Brussels in June 1828; he introduced specifically remembered comments with a general impression of drowsy flow: "In almost everything that fell from Coleridge that evening there was a dash of deep philosophy—even in the outpourings of his egotism—touches not to be given without the whole of what they illustrated. In a word, the impression made on me by his voluptuous and indolent strain of talk, flowing in a quiet tone of cadenced eloquence, was that he was by far the most pleasing talker, but by no means the most powerful, I had ever heard. He led you on beside him by the persuasive elegance of diction, but never drove you forward by the impetuous energy of argument. 'He had,' as Bishop Burnet said of William Penn, 'a tedious, luscious way that was not apt to overcome a man's reason though it might tire his patience.' But Coleridge's talk was not absolutely tiresome, only somewhat drowsy. I thought it would be pleasant to fall asleep to the gushing melody of his discourse, which was rich in information and suavity of thought. But there was something too dreamy, too vapoury to rouse one to the close examination of what he said. Logic there no doubt was, but it was enveloped in clouds. You were therefore delighted to take everything for granted, for everything seemed to convince—because it took a shape and colour so seductive." *Beaten Paths; and Those Who Trod Them* (2 vols 1862) ii 113–14.

him, I experienced nothing of that weariness and disgust that the systems of Bentham caused in me, neither that vacuum which the theatrical and pompous Foscolo induced. Vibrating to all emotions, capable of comprehending all systems, possessing rich treasures of memory and a truly independent spirit, with a taste for all philosophical reveries and caprices, and luxuriating in beauty, with the ability to reproduce his brilliant and deep thought with all the fascination of genius, Coleridge appeared to me a sort of mystical Diderot. Unhappily, the feebleness of his frame, much increased from his fatal indulgence in opium, did not permit him to draw up as a whole his magnificent system of aesthetic Christianity, of which he has only bequeathed some vestiges.

It would be impossible to enumerate the variety and depth of studies from which he reaped such fruits. He was familiar with the brilliant prose of Jeremy Taylor, the sonnets of Bowles, and the essays of Addison; also the works of Jean Jacques and Rabelais, Crebillon and Goldsmith, enchanted him. Romance, history, poetry, the dramatic art, the fine arts, he essayed them all, and enjoyed all. The erudite and occult sciences claimed his regard; the metaphysics of Fichte, Kant, Winckelmann, and Hegel counted him among their adepts. Coleridge has neared all shores.[36]

William Jerdan, who claimed possession of a device for stopping Coleridge's flow, reported also that Coleridge was often wrought to tears by thinking of a man who remembered something he said:

About this time [1824] I became acquainted with Mr. Coleridge, who was then residing with his stanch friend, Mr. Gillman, at Highgate; and on many occasions enjoyed the pleasure of his social conversation, I was going to say, but it must be called what it was, most eloquent outpourings, *de totidem rebus et quibusdem aliis.* I am not aware that I am yet overtaken by the foible of garrulous old age; but in my earlier years and prime I know I was accounted an excellent conversationalist, chiefly because I was an excellent listener, and also for a certain knack I had of drawing out the lions of the company. Thus by exposing, or rather immolating myself, by provoking Hook, I could always pitch him into the right key; and with Coleridge, by throwing in some extraneous vagary, I rarely failed to divert him into other topics from any dissertation which was becoming too far prolonged or too metaphysical. Coleridge gave lectures full of glowing ideas and glorious imagery; but they did not contribute much of the *aurum palpabile*; and yet he was wonderfully enthusiastic about them. A gentleman who had heard him ''discourse'' a number of years before, repeated a passage which had made a strong impression, and dwelt upon his memory; and Coleridge's delight was measureless. His countenance gleamed with ecstacy, and his large grey eye filled with tears of exultation. It was curious to witness the extraordinary effect of so trifling an incident; but I have heard him relate the anecdote and repeat the passage many times as the highest compliment ever paid to him.[37]

[36] Victor Euphémion Philarète Chasles (1798–1873) ''Improvisations of Coleridge'' *Notabilities in France and England* (New York 1853) 122. The chapter on C, from *Études sur les hommes et les moeurs aux XIXe siècle* (Paris 1850), is reprinted in *Mémoires* (2 vols Paris 1876–7) I 167–73. Chasles attempts to place C with regard to German philosophy.

[37] *The Autobiography of William Jerdan, with His Literary, Political, and Social Reminiscences and Correspondence During the Last Fifty Years* (4 vols 1852–3) III 34–5.

With the lapse of another fourteen years, Jerdan remembered more favourably "the Old Man Eloquent" and the method of diverting him:

He could rarely fatigue an attentive listener. It was only when his "philosophy" (with which he abounded on all occasions) betrayed him into abstruse paradoxes and metaphysical refinements that his rich colloquialism took the shape of dissertation, and was delivered with a fervent eloquence, most powerful in lecture, but subversive of conversation; and these bursts were so admirable that there was seldom any disposition to interrupt them. When it did occur that they went wandering into all cognate matters and consonant sentiments, it was the easiest thing possible, by throwing in some absurd remark or irrelevant question, to divert the current into quite another channel, and enjoy and re-enjoy the versatility and depths of an inexhaustible mind.[38]

Bryan Waller Procter (1787–1874), with a memory largely for anecdotes, was both amused and respectful:

Samuel Taylor Coleridge was like the Rhine,

That exulting and abounding river.

He was full of words, full of thought; yielding both in an unfailing flow, that delighted many, and perplexed a few of his hearers. He was a man of prodigious miscellaneous reading, always ready to communicate all he knew. From Alpha to Omega, all was familiar to him. He was deep in Jacob Behmen. He was intimate with Thomas Aquinas and Quevedo; with Bacon and Kant, with "Peter Simple" and "Tom Cringle's Log;" and with all the old divines of both England and France. The pages of all the infidels had passed under his eye and made their legitimate (and not more than their legitimate) impression. He went from flower to flower, throughout the whole garden of learning, like the butterfly or the bee,—most like the bee. He talked with everybody, about anything. He was so full of information that it was a relief to him to part with some portion of it to others. It was like laying down part of his burden. He knew little or nothing of the art of painting; yet I have heard him discuss the merits and defects of a picture of the poorest class, as though it had sprung from the inspiration of Raffaelle. He would advert to certain parts, and surmise that it had been touched upon here and there; would pronounce upon its character and school, its *chiaroscuro*, the gradations, the handling, etc., when in fact it had no mark or merit or character about it. It became transfigured, sublimated, by the speaker's imagination, which far excelled both the picture and its author. Coleridge had a weighty head, dreaming grey eyes, full, sensual lips, and a look and manner which were entirely wanting in firmness and decision. His motions also appeared weak and undecided, and his voice had nothing of the sharpness or ring of a resolute man. When he spoke his words were thick and slow, and when he read poetry his utterance was altogether a chant.

One day, when dining with some lawyers, he had been more than usually eloquent and full of talk. His perpetual interruptions were resented by one of the guests, who said to his neighbour, "I'll stop this fellow;" and thereupon addressed the master of the house with "G——, I've not forgotten my promise to

[38] *Men I Have Known* (1866) 120.

give you the extract from 'The Pandects.' It was the ninth chapter that you were alluding to. It begins: 'Ac veteres quidam philosophi.' " "Pardon me, sir," interposed Coleridge, "there I think you are in error. The ninth chapter begins in this way, 'Incident saepe causae,' etc." It was in vain to refer to anything on the supposition that the poet was ignorant, for he really had some acquaintance with every subject. I imagine that no man had ever read so many books and at the same time had digested so much.

Coleridge was prodigal of his words, which in fact he could with difficulty suppress; but he seldom talked of himself or of his affairs. He was very speculative, very theological, very metaphysical, and not unfrequently threw in some little pungent sentence, characteristic of the defects of some of his acquaintance. In illustration of his unfailing talk, I will give an account of one of his days, when I was present. He had come from Highgate to London, for the sole purpose of consulting a friend about his son Hartley ("our dear Hartley"), towards whom he expressed, and I have no doubt felt, much anxiety. He arrived about one or two o'clock, in the midst of a conversation, which immediately began to interest him. He struck into the middle of the talk very soon, and held the "ear of the house" until dinner made its appearance about four o'clock. He then talked all through the dinner, all the afternoon, all the evening, with scarcely a single interruption. He expatiated on this subject and on that; he drew fine distinctions; he made subtle criticisms. He descended to anecdotes, historical, logical, rhetorical; he dealt with law, medicine, and divinity, until, at last, five minutes before eight o'clock, the servant came in and announced that the Highgate stage was at the corner of the street, and was waiting to convey Mr. Coleridge home. Coleridge immediately started up oblivious of all time, and said, in a hurried voice, "My dear Z———, I will come to you some other day, and talk to you about our dear Hartley." He had quite forgotten his son and everybody else, in the delight of having such an enraptured audience.[39]

For the early years most reports of Coleridge's conversation derive from encounters with him on walking tours, in his lodgings, at dinner parties (or Rogers's breakfasts), or on visits to such convivial friends as Charles and Mary Lamb. Soon after he went to live with James and Anne Gillman at Moreton House, Highgate Hill, in 1816, friends began to bring visitors there, increasingly on Thursday evenings until those evenings became an open house to friends and institutionalised as a "class" in 1822, with few interruptions until 1829, when Coleridge wrote to Allsop of "our former Thursday Evening *Conver*- or to mint a more appropriate term, *One*versazioni".[40] The Thursdays were suspended in late 1830 through most of 1831. At 3, The Grove, Highgate, where the Gillmans moved in December 1823 (with a house-warming for 150 guests on 1 June 1824), there was a special upper room for Coleridge; in his

[39] *An Autobiographical Fragment* . . . ed Coventry Patmore (1877) 144–7. Procter dates this episode 1823. After severe trials to C in 1820–2, HC had gone to the Lakes, whence the reports to C were favourable. *CL* v 248, 255, 268n, 273, 286, 295, 335.

[40] *CL* vi 790.

room, rather than in the parlour or the garden, visitors gathered during the long periods of illness in his final five years.

Coleridge was seldom "visible" before noon; the dinner hour was four—later a more fashionable five or five-thirty, but on Thursdays the hour of dining remained four, in order that they might "see a few intelligent friends from Town—from 6 to 10 or 11".[41] Philarète Chasles, writing of an occasion in 1820, or perhaps more likely 1822 or 1823:

> We arrived at eight at the small but elegant residence of Coleridge; about thirty persons were already assembled in a small blue room, simply furnished. Coleridge was discoursing. Standing in front of the chimney upon which he leaned back, with head erect and arms crossed, his dreamy eyes lost in abstractions, transported by the inspirations of his own genius, he seemed to be addressing, not the auditors, but replying to his own thoughts. His voice was vibratory, rich and full, his features harmonious, his ample brow, shaded by dark brown curls, in which here and there some silver lines intruded, the beautiful contour of his mouth, sweet in expression, also the softness of his expressive eyes, won favour unheard.[42]

Chasles was a voluminous and rapid essayist, critic, and novelist; one wonders about the brown hair merely touched with silver and about the audience of thirty ("une trentaine de personnes"). In July 1825 Coleridge wrote to Daniel Stuart:

> There is one thing too, that I can not help considering as a recommendation to our Evenings, that in addition to a few Ladies & pretty Lasses we have seldom more than 5 or 6 in company, and these generally of as many different professions or pursuits—. A few weeks ago we had present, two Painters, two Poets, one Divine, an eminent Chemist & Naturalist, a Major, a Naval Captain & Voyager, a Physician, a colonial Chief Justice, a Barrister and a Baronet—& this was the most numerous Meeting, we ever had—[43]

A year later, mildly protesting the perception of Edward Coleridge that his uncle's mind was cloudy and eddying, Coleridge again emphasised the variety of persons "that had at different times been with me during the last 3 or four months—Merchant, Manufacturer, Physician, Member of Parliament & keen politician, chemist, Clergymen, *poetic* Ladies, Painters, Musical Men, Barristers & Political Economists—to each of whom, in turn, I had talked in his own way, & . . . they had all expressed their admiration of the *clear* point of view, in which I placed things".[44]

[41] *CL* IV 783, V 365, VI 532, 584, 732, 746; *C at H* 143.

[42] Chasles *Notabilities in France and England* 119.

[43] *CL* V 474.

[44] *CL* VI 592. Richard Monckton Milnes, 1st Baron Houghton (1809–85), recalled publicly, at the unveiling of the bust of C in Westminster Abbey (1885), that when he and Arthur Hallam visited C as mere students from Cambridge, he "received them as Goethe or as Socrates might have done". James Pope-Hennessy *Monckton Milnes* (2 vols New York 1951–5) II 254.

In a marginal note defending his schedule, "seldom up, till 12 at noon", he expatiated: "Too true; and add that he is as seldom in bed, till 3 in the morning; but likewise do not forget, that from 12 to 4, from 7 to 10, and from 11 to 3, he is at work, either collecting, or correcting, or composing."[45] The results of that working schedule were bestowed upon the friends and the variety of professional persons who assembled after 6 P.M. one evening a week.

We have at second hand the first impressions of Mary Pridham, who married Derwent Coleridge in December 1827: "I remember Mrs. Derwent Coleridge's telling me of her recollections of her father-in-law in her early married life. She listened with great wonder, she said, to the flow of his discourse; there was no hesitation or pause—on and on it went. The bedroom candles would be brought in and placed on a table near the door of the drawing-room. Coleridge would move slowly across the room, continuing his discourse the while, continuing it as he went through the hall to the staircase, continuing it as he slowly mounted the stairs, until his voice was lost in the distance."[46]

What had been marvellous in a boy of sixteen became at Highgate a marvel conditioned by one's expectations and by Coleridge's failing health. Charles Valentine Le Grice, a fellow student at Christ's Hospital and Cambridge, after almost forty years saw the ancient wonder again on 18 June 1833 at the Gillmans' and on 26 June at Trinity College:

I visited Coleridge at Highgate. A most melancholy sight—his hair white: his frame debilitated—an aged broken down man! His faculties still—shall I say perfect—this I fear I cannot say—but still predominant—his talk eloquent. He spoke of Wordsworth—Scott—Ossian—Brougham. I listened—and was full of sad thoughts. O Coleridge! and does the tale of thy life end in this? . . .

O how changed! All things are changed! I deeply see and feel that "All is vanity". I write this still with a heart grateful for many blessings.[47]

Emerson, an eager disciple, also arrived too late for the fulfilment of his best hopes, on 5 Aug 1833: "I was in his company for about an hour, but . . . his discourse . . . was often like so many printed paragraphs in his book—perhaps the same—so readily did he fall into certain commonplaces. As I might have foreseen, the visit was rather a spectacle than a conversation, of no use beyond the satisfaction of my curiosity. He was

---

[45] Annotation on *The Dramatic Works of Ben Jonson, and Beaumont and Fletcher* ed George Colman (4 vols 1811) III flyleaf: *CM (CC)* I 392.

[46] Ellis Yarnall *Wordsworth and the Coleridges* (1899) 133.

[47] Richard Madden "The Old Familiar Faces: An Essay in the light of some recently discovered documents of Charles Valentine Le Grice referring to Lamb, Coleridge and Wordsworth" *Charles Lamb Bulletin* NS No 6 (Apr 1974) 115.

old and pre-occupied, and could not bend to a new companion and think with him."[48] He had written of Coleridge in a commonplace book of 1824–36: "He is a god to me who shall rightly define & divide."[49] But in 1833 he had things of his own to say and much to ask; Coleridge, though frail, had attacked Unitarianism with vigour; and Emerson had read Carlyle.

Carlyle was both the most dyspeptic and the most eloquent of Coleridge's detractors. Perhaps he knew how much he owed to Coleridge, how effectively Coleridge had anticipated his exploitation of German thought, and how solidly—despite the opium, adenoids, and other infirmities—Coleridge had earned what all Carlyle's emotions told him was excessive attention from disciples who could just as well have been Carlyle's. His first surviving report went on 24 June 1824 to his brother John:

Besides Irving I have seen many other curiosities. Not the least of these I reckon Coleridge, the Kantean metaphysician and quondam Lake poet. I will tell you all about our interview *when we meet*. Figure a fat flabby incurvated personage, at once short, rotund and relaxed, with a watery mouth, a snuffy nose, a pair of strange brown timid yet earnest looking eyes, a high tapering brow, and a great bush of grey hair—you will have some faint idea of Coleridge. He is a kind, good soul, full of religion and affection, and poetry and animal magnetism. His cardinal sin is that he wants *will*; he has no resolution, he shrinks from pain or labour in any of its shapes. His very attitude bespeaks this: he never straightens his knee joints, he stoops with his fat ill shapen shoulders, and in walking he does not tread but shovel and slide—my father would call it *skluiffing*. He is also always busied to keep by strong and frequent inhalations the water of his mouth from overflowing; and his eyes have a look of anxious impotence; he *would* do with all his heart, but he knows he dare not. The conversation of the man is much as I anticipated. A forest of thoughts; some true, many false, most part dubious, all of them ingenious in some degree, often in a high degree. But there is no method in his talk; he wanders like a man sailing among many currents, whithersoever his lazy mind directs him—; and what is more unpleasant he preaches, or rather soliloquizes: he cannot speak; he can only "*tal-k*" (so he names it). Hence I found him unprofitable, even tedious: but we parted very good friends I promising to go back and see him some other evening—a promise I fully intend to keep. I sent him a copy of Meister about which we had some friendly talk. I reckon him a man of great and useless genius—a strange not at all a great man.[50]

He wrote more colourfully in August to Thomas Murray:

[48] Ralph Waldo Emerson (1803–82) *English Traits* (1856) 7.

[49] *The Journals and Miscellaneous Notebooks of Ralph Waldo Emerson* ed William H. Gilman et al (14 vols Cambridge, Mass 1960–78) VI (ed Ralph H. Orth) 209. Emerson copied passages from *TT* (1835) in *Journals* VI 174, 188, 193, 200, 209, 341.

[50] *The Collected Letters of Thomas and Jane Welsh Carlyle* (Durham, N. C. 1970–   ) III 90–1.

Charles Lamb is a ricketty creature in body and mind, sprawls about and walks as if his body consisted of four ill-conditioned flails, and talks as if he were quarter drunk with ale and half with laudanum. Coleridge is a steam-engine of a hundred horses power—with the boiler burst. His talk is resplendent with imagery and the shows of thought; you listen as to an oracle, and find yourself no jot the wiser. He is without beginning or middle or end. A round fat oily yet impatient little man, his mind seems totally beyond his own controul; he speaks incessantly, not thinking or imagining or remembering, but combining all these processes into one; as a rich and lazy housewife might mingle her soup and fish and beef and custard into one unspeakable mass and present it trueheartedly to her astonished guests.[51]

To Jane Welsh in November he used one of Coleridge's favourite similes: "Poor Coleridge is like the hulk of a huge ship; his mast and sails and rudder have rotted away."[52] John, the brother, educated to be a doctor, was readier to receive instruction. On 16 May 1830 he wrote to Thomas: "Coleridge has been unwell of late, but is now getting better. I saw him yesterday for the second time. I believe there is no man in the island puts more thought through himself."[53] But Thomas Carlyle, as Charles Richard Sanders has summarised the case, "might have been a happier man if there had never been a Coleridge".[54]

Thomas De Quincey (1785–1859), who shared Carlyle's envy of Coleridge, particularly of his subtler grasp of German thought, was able to respond with a nearer balance. In a first piece after Coleridge's death, which scandalised all Coleridge's friends, he insisted on the logical cohesion of the transitions in Coleridge's talk.[55] He returned for further appraisal in 1845:

There is another accomplishment of Coleridge's, less broadly open to the judgment of this generation, and not at all of the next—viz. his splendid art of conversation,—on which it will be interesting to say a word. Ten years ago, when the music of this rare performance had not yet ceased to vibrate in men's ears, what a sensation was gathering amongst the educated classes on this particular subject! What a tumult of anxiety prevailed to "hear Mr. Coleridge," or even to talk with a man who *had* heard him. Had he lived till this day, not Paganini would have been so much sought after. That sensation is now decaying, because a new generation has emerged during the ten years since his death. But many still remain whose sympathy (whether of curiosity in those who did *not* know him or of admiration in those who *did*) still reflects as in a mirror the great stir upon this

[51] Ibid III 139.
[52] Ibid III 199. For Carlyle's most famous account of C, in his *Life of Sterling*, see App N. vol II, below.
[53] National Library of Scotland MS 1775 A. 60, quoted in C. Richard Sanders "The Background of Carlyle's Portrait of Coleridge in *The Life of John Sterling*" *Bulletin of the John Rylands University Library of Manchester* LV (1973) 44–5.
[54] *Coleridge and the Broad Church Movement* (Durham, N. C. 1942) 151.
[55] In *Tait's Edinburgh Magazine* 1834: *De Q Works* II 152–3.

subject which then was moving in the world. To these, if they should inquire for the great distinguishing principle of Coleridge's conversation, we might say that it was the power of vast combination "in linked sweetness long drawn out". He gathered into focal concentration the largest body of objects, *apparently* disconnected, that any man ever yet, by any magic, could assemble, or, *having* assembled, could manage. His great fault was that, by not opening sufficient spaces for reply, or suggestion, or collateral notice, he not only narrowed his own field, but he grievously injured the final impression. For, when men's minds are purely passive, when they are not allowed to react, then it is that they collapse most, and that their sense of what is said must ever be feeblest. Doubtless there must have been great conversational masters elsewhere, and at many periods; but in this lay Coleridge's characteristic advantage, that he was a great natural power, and also a great artist. He was a power in the art; and he carried a new art into the power.[56]

[56] "Coleridge and Opium-Eating" *Bl Mag* LVII (1845) 129; *De Q Works* v 204–5 (var).

In an essay on "Conversation" in *Tait's Edinburgh Magazine* Oct 1847, De Q found C below the ideal talker: ". . . all reputation for brilliant talking is a visionary thing, and rests upon a sheer impossibility: viz. upon such a histrionic performance in a state of insulation from the rest of the company as could not be effected, even for a single time, without a rare and difficult collusion, and could not, even for that single time, be endurable to a man of delicate and honourable sensibilities.

"Yet surely Coleridge *had* such a reputation, and without needing any collusion at all; for Coleridge, unless he could have all the talk, would have none. But then this was not conversation. It was not *colloquium*, or talking *with* the company, but *alloquium*, or talking *to* the company. As Madame de Staël observed, Coleridge talked, and *could* talk, only by monologue. Such a mode of systematic trespass upon the conversational rights of a whole party gathered together under pretence of amusement is fatal to every purpose of social intercourse, whether that purpose be connected with direct use and the service of the intellect, or with the general graces and amenities of life. The result is the same under whatever impulse such an outrage is practised; but the impulse is not always the same; it varies, and so far the criminal intention varies. . . . Meantime, Coleridge's habit of soliloquizing through a whole evening of four or five hours had its origin neither in arrogance nor in absolute selfishness. The fact was that he *could* not talk unless he were uninterrupted, and unless he were able to count upon this concession from the company. It was a silent contract between him and his hearers that nobody should speak but himself. If any man objected to this arrangement, why did he come? For, the custom of the place, the *lex loci*, being notorious, by coming at all he was understood to profess his allegiance to the autocrat who presided. It was not, therefore, by an insolent usurpation that Coleridge persisted in monology through his whole life, but in virtue of a concession from the kindness and respect of his friends. You could not be angry with him for using his privilege, for it was a privilege conferred by others, and a privilege which he was ready to resign as soon as any man demurred to it. But, though reconciled to it by these considerations, and by the ability with which he used it, you could not but feel that it worked ill for all parties. Himself it tempted oftentimes into pure garrulity of egotism, and the listeners it reduced to a state of debilitated sympathy or of absolute torpor. Prevented by the custom from putting questions, from proposing doubts, from asking for explanations, reacting by no mode of mental activity, and condemned also to the mental distress of hearing opinions or doctrines stream past them by flights which they must not arrest for a moment so as even to take a note of them, and which yet

The ideal listeners were young men trained in the sciences but interested in a broad range of humanistic subjects and feeling no rivalry with the white-haired sage. One such was Sir William Rowan Hamilton (1805–65), precocious mathematician, later Astronomer Royal of Ireland; at Trinity College, Dublin, he was twice winner of the Vice-Chancellor's Prize for English verse and was appointed Andrews Professor of Astronomy in 1827. He was elected President of the Royal Irish Academy in 1837. Hamilton's notes and correspondence show that he followed Coleridge's classical, historical, and theological lucubrations with precision and simultaneously with awe. When he says that he understands Coleridge on every subject except science, he does not question the accuracy or fulness of Coleridge's knowledge (except in mathematics, where he finds Coleridge unaware of the value to his own anti-materialistic doctrines of Boscovich's theory of a point), but he regards Coleridge's metaphysically idealistic applications of biology and physics as scientifically useless: "As to Coleridge and his obscurity in conversation, I assure you that whenever I thought him obscure I laid all the blame on myself."[57] He tells of an archdeacon who piqued himself on the clarity of his ideas concerning the classics, but, finding that Coleridge put those ideas into embarrassing confusion, abruptly ran from the house. Hamilton, earnest and eager as he was, felt also the charm of Coleridge's self-deprecation:

This reminds me of something that Coleridge once said to me, at the rooms of Dr. Thirlwall, the present Bishop of St. David's. I met Mr. Coleridge in these rooms, in Cambridge, in 1833, having, however, already in 1832, visited him several times in the neighbourhood of London, and listened to him there. You

they could not often understand, or, seeming to understand, could not always approve, the audience sank at times into a listless condition of inanimate vacuity. To be acted upon for ever, but never to react, is fatal to the very powers by which sympathy must grow, or by which intelligent admiration can be evoked. For his own sake, it was Coleridge's interest to have forced his hearers into the active commerce of question and answer, of objection and demur. Not otherwise was it possible that even the attention could be kept from drooping, or the coherency and dependency of the arguments be forced into light.

"The French rarely make a mistake of this nature. . . . It is not strange, therefore, that Madame de Staël noticed little as extraordinary in Coleridge beyond this one capital monstrosity of unlimited soliloquy,—that being a peculiarity which she never could have witnessed in France; and, considering the burnish of her French tastes in all that concerned colloquial characteristics, it is creditable to her forbearance that she noticed even this rather as a memorable fact than as the inhuman fault which it was. On the other hand, Coleridge was not so forbearing as regarded the brilliant French lady. He spoke of her to ourselves as a very frivolous person, and in short summary terms that disdained to linger on a subject so inconsiderable." *De Q Works* x 281–3.

[57] *Life of Sir William Rowan Hamilton* ed R. P. Graves (3 vols 1882–9) I 601.

may have heard that nobody ever talked with Coleridge; for the full and rapid torrent of his own eloquence of discourse soon absorbed all minor rivulets, such as other men could supply. However, I must acknowledge that he took very graciously, and in good part, any few words I ventured to throw in; and allowed them to influence, and in some degree to guide his own great, and sweet, and wondrous stream of speech. Presuming that he had forgotten those former visits of mine, which, however, he afterwards assured me that he had not done, I said to Coleridge, on being placed beside him by Dr. Thirlwall, at Cambridge, that I had read most of his published works: but, by way of being very honest, I added, But, sir, I am not sure that I understand them all. "The question is, sir," said he, "whether I understand them all myself."[58]

Viscount Adare,[59] a pupil of Hamilton's, visited 3, The Grove about three weeks before Coleridge's death and reported at once to his teacher. Lord Adare, B.A. in 1833 and F.R.S. in 1834, was an archaeologist in correspondence about astronomy with John F. W. Herschel, but he was less attuned than Hamilton to Coleridge's religious thought and literary interests:

Burlington Hotel, London, June 30, 1834.
I am so exceedingly obliged to you for the letter you were so kind as to give me for Coleridge. I took it to-day, and on inquiring if Mr. Coleridge was at home, I was told he had been ill and could not see anyone; but I begged the servant to take up the letter to him, and to my great delight he sent down to say he would see me—this I consider as a compliment to you. Up I went, feeling a mixture of pleasure and awe, and was shown into a small room, half full of books in great confusion, and in one corner was a small bed, looking more like a couch, upon which lay certainly the most remarkable looking man I ever saw; he quite surpassed my expectations; he was pale and worn when I first entered, but very soon the colour came into his cheeks and his eye brightened, and such an eye as it is! such animation, and acuteness! so piercing! He began by asking how you were, and telling me how ill he had been for three months, but he is now getting a little better; he said he was sure it would give you pleasure to know (as far as I could understand) that religion had alleviated very much his hours of pain, and given him fortitude and resignation. He then talked about the Church, but really I found it so difficult to follow him that I cannot recollect what he said, but even less can I remember what I should say were the subjects of conversation: this I think arises from a great want of method; but I say this, feeling I do him injustice: still it strikes me he rambled on; but I remarked how, when once or twice he was interrupted by people coming into the room and speaking to them, he resumed at the very word he left off at—he said he was sure you would feel very sorry at the line of conduct Thirlwall had pursued about some petition about the Dissenters, and how it had pained him.[60] Now and then he said something very droll, which made

[58] Ibid II 623.
[59] Edwin Richard Wyndham Wyndham-Quin (1812–71), 3rd Earl of Dunraven and Mount-Earl in the peerage of Ireland (1850) and 1st Baron Kenry of the United Kingdom (1866). At the time of his B.A. from Trinity College, Dublin in 1833 he bore the courtesy title of Lord Adare.
[60] See TT 16 Apr 1834 (36:637), MS B f 117; 31 May 1834, MS B ff 118ᵛ–19 (previously unpublished).

us laugh; and he conversed with so much vigour and animation, though he had difficulty in *speaking* at all. I ventured, when a pause came, to put in a word. This happened twice: the second time I asked him when we might hope for another work from him. He said he had one very nearly ready, and it would have been out, were it not for his illness. He gave me the plan of the book, but really he got so deep, using words in a sense not familiar to me, that I could not follow him, and I gazed on his eloquent and venerable countenance, as he went on describing the results of his thoughts. All I can tell you is, that his book is on *logic* of some particular kind, and is a sort of introduction to his great work, as he calls the one which Aubrey[61] says exists only in his brain. He gave me a sketch of this also, very brief: the title I thought beautiful, and would have given anything to have written it down for you: indeed, much as I enjoyed the visit, I wished you could have been in my place, for I know you would have enjoyed it so exceedingly, and could have recollected all. He also spoke beautifully about Kant, who, as well as Bacon, was, he says, an Aristotelian; but I was unable to comprehend his explanation of the sense in which he said their methods were similar. He says he will get some one to look out for that work of Kant's for you, which he says is very valuable, and he told me how little Kant is known or read in proportion to what he ought to be. I was with him more than half an hour—nearer an hour, I believe—and could willingly, as you may suppose, have staid all day; but I, with some resolution at last, got up and said something about fearing I had interrupted him. I told him how you liked Kant, and how delighted you would be at hearing he [Coleridge] was about to publish another work. I must say, since I came to London I have not felt so happy as this day; and I consider the visit to Coleridge has been productive of complete pleasure, unmixed with disappointment of any kind; and I know not how to thank you for sending me the letter. I had half a mind, when in Dublin, to have asked you for one, but I feared it might look assuming, as of course in myself I have no right to intrude upon Coleridge, ill as he is. His head is finer than I had expected, and his eye different. I supposed it black and rather soft, instead of being grey and penetrating.[62]

Henry Nelson Coleridge himself would have only one more opportunity to watch those animated eyes and listen to distinctions and relationships that Lord Adare could not quite grasp.

A century later Donald A. Stauffer was able to survey the records of Coleridge's conversation from Christ's Hospital to those final days:

Coleridge began to talk at an early age and never left off until he died at sixty-two. . . . .

The talk went on through the years until he had become in his own person a kind of *causerie célèbre*, the Sage of Highgate to whom people made pilgrimages or for whom they gave dinners—Carlyle and Hood and Hunt and Keats and Lockhart and Scott and even the acidulous Francis Jeffrey, with Cooper and Emerson from America. Not all of them liked the torrent of talk, particularly those who preferred to talk themselves. But a man who could hold for decades the austere Wordsworth and the simple Southey and the quirky Lamb, who could more-

---

[61] Sir Aubrey de Vere (1788–1846), 2nd Bt (1818), poet, admirer of C, and friend of SC.

[62] *Life of Hamilton* II 94–5.

over transform his nephew Henry Nelson Coleridge into the Boswell who recorded *Table Talk*, is no mere whisperer.

What did he talk about? Everything. Yet essentially his one never-entirely-forgotten subject was relationship—relating parts, or fusing disparates, within a single reality.[63]

That summary would have satisfied surgeons like James Gillman and Joseph Henry Green, who exchanged views on medical questions with Coleridge over a period of years, but above all learned from him that their profession, their faith, and their lives formed a single reality. Henry Coleridge, as a young barrister, listened to the same message.

HENRY NELSON COLERIDGE

Henry Nelson Coleridge, the recorder and editor of the *Table Talk*, was the fifth of six sons of James Coleridge (1759–1836), "The Colonel", who was the fourth son in the family of which Samuel Taylor Coleridge was the youngest. Henry, named for the hero of the hour, Admiral Horatio Nelson, was born on 25 October 1798 at Heath's Court (The Chanter's House), Ottery St Mary, Devonshire, where James, upon marriage to Frances Duke Taylor (1759–1838), had retired from the Army on half pay, as Captain of the 6th Foot, and became Lieutenant Colonel of the local militia.[64] Henry attended the King's School in Ottery St Mary, where George Coleridge (1764–1828), brother of the poet, was schoolmaster until his retirement in 1808. In 1809 Henry entered Eton College assisted by funds from "Aunt Brown" of Combesatchfield.[65]

Except when an outbreak of scarlet fever at Eton in 1811 sent him into quarantine for a few months at Heath's Court, he flourished, with popular vivacity and conspicuous learning. In 1818 the Task Prize of two books joined his lengthening list of honours. He wrote sprightly letters to his brother Frank in English, French, and Latin. Edward Coleridge, after he had become assistant master at Eton (he married the daughter of the master, John Keate), remembered that "the growing success of my Brother Henry at Eton, in some sort screwed me up" to work.[66] Henry

---

[63] "Introduction" *Selected Poetry and Prose of Coleridge* ed Donald A. Stauffer (New York 1951) x.

[64] Details concerning HNC are taken from *DNB; G Mag* NS xx (1843) 97–8; Edith Coleridge *Some Recollections of Henry Nelson Coleridge and His Family* (Torquay 1910) 3–11; "The Biographia non Literaria of Edward Coleridge" transcription in BM Add MS 47555; correspondence and papers of HNC and SC, at VCL, UT, BM, and elsewhere as designated. JTC began a memoir of HNC. UT ms.

[65] Dorothy Ayre Taylor (1755–1831), widow of Henry Langford Brown and maternal aunt of the Heath's Court Coleridges. Bernard Coleridge *Devonshire House* (1905) 68, 173.

[66] BM Add MS 47555 f 11.

acted the part of Captain Worthington in a school production of *The Poor Gentleman* by George Colman the Younger.[67] He contributed poems and critical essays to the "College Magazine", which circulated in manuscript. Influences from Southey, Byron, and Coleridge are as evident as his informed admiration of Wordsworth. One poem in quatrains, *The Bride of the Cave: A Ballad*, based on an episode in William Mariner *An Account of the Natives of the Tonga Islands* (1817) and anticipating Byron's use of the episode, was also printed in *Poetry of the College Magazine* (Windsor 1819) and published in the last number of *The Etonian*, August 1821.

After winning an Eton scholarship to King's College, Cambridge, where he was admitted on 7 March 1818 and matriculated for the Easter Term, Henry was second, in his first year, for the Davies University Scholarship, ahead of Thomas Babington Macaulay; the winner was the orientalist Thomas Pell Platt, B.A. and Fellow of Trinity College in 1820. In his second year Henry gained the Browne Medals for Greek and Latin Odes, and "had the mottoes to my Epigrams published for being good ones; that is the Epigrams".[68] In September he won the Porson Prize for an epigram, and in 1821 he won again the Browne Medal for a Greek Ode, which Coleridge had won in 1792. The two volumes of *The Etonian* (October 1820–August 1821), edited by Walter Blunt and Winthrop Mackworth Praed, contain at least sixteen contributions from him, several of them signed "Gerald Montgomery". Besides *vers de société* and other verse, including a parodistic imitation of Wordsworth— "I was a boy"—he contributed essays on the poetry of Wordsworth, Coleridge, and Lamb, and a mock-review of Southey, after the manner of *Criticisms on the Rolliad*.[69] Walter Graham depended heavily on the critical essays to declare Henry Nelson Coleridge at twenty-three "one of the most important early interpreters of Romantic criticism".[70] The volumes went through four editions by 1824.

It had been almost a condition of his aunt's aid that Henry would win a fellowship to King's. In 1817 he had assured his elder brother John that the idleness at King's would not infect him: "I don't think I can be idle,

---

[67] Derwent Coleridge "Memoir" *Poems of John Moultrie* (2 vols 1876) I xvi.

[68] HNC to JTC, BM Add MS 47557 f 55.

[69] *Etonian* I 8, 57, 67–8, 99–104, 210, 217–25, 251–6, 273, 307–18, 336–9, II 49–58, 97–105, 144, 340–8, 349–52, 400.

[70] "Henry Nelson Coleridge, Explicator of Romantic Criticism" *Philological Quarterly* IV (1925) 231. Graham concluded that HNC became with the review of C's poetical works in 1834 "the chief expositor of romantic criticism" (p 238); cf Graham on HNC in "Contemporary Critics of Coleridge" *PMLA* XXXVIII (1923) 286–8.

for it never affords me any pleasure.''[71] His vivacity made him welcome to friends whenever he turned from study. He has been called ''the most brilliant and captivating of the band of brothers'', with ''irresistible wit, sparkling and pointed''.[72] Besides Praed and John Moultrie, friends continued from Eton, his intimates at Cambridge were the poet Chauncey Hare Townshend, Macaulay, the Benthamite statesman Charles Pelham Villiers (1802–98) and his brother Thomas Hyde Villiers (1801–32), and the jurist Charles Austin. He overlapped in residence with his cousin Derwent. Moultrie addressed to Derwent the section of his poem *The Dream of Life* that reminiscently assesses Henry at Cambridge and after:

> Turn we next
> To him—thy kinsman, once my schoolfellow,
> And more than most of my compeers at school,
> Or thy collateral kindred, to us both
> By close-knit bonds united;—in those days
> A comely youth, though prematurely grey,
> And long ere manhood's noon upon his brow
> To wear the stainless silver of old age.
> Graceful he was in person and in mind,
> Enrich'd with classical accomplishments,
> And stores of various study—apt to learn,
> And with intense susceptibility
> Of soul and sense endued. Some deem'd him proud,
> And in himself too confident.—In truth,
> 'Twas not his nature to dissemble powers
> With which he had been gifted, nor the lore
> To which he had attain'd, and envious men,
> Who hated him for both, were prompt to blame
> That which they could not imitate:—yet few
> Were cast by nature in a finer mould,
> Or arm'd with apprehensions more acute,
> And exquisite of beauty and of truth,
> Moral and intellectual. To create
> Was not his province; but his mind received,
> And treasured, and retain'd, with ready tact,
> The lessons by profounder minds instill'd,
> Which, with expressive utterance, to the taste
> And apprehensions of the world at large
> He skillfully adapted.—Hence his task
> Was rightly chosen, when, in after years,
> He to the teaching of that Master Mind
> Subjected his whole soul—content to share
> The glory which must rest, in time to come,
> On those outpourings of immortal thought

---

[71] BM Add MS 47557 f 19.

[72] Bernard Coleridge *Devonshire House* 138.

By his sole pen preserv'd, or by his toil
Collected and arranged. His was, in truth,
A proud and happy lot, to have imbibed
Those lessons, while he lived, and after death
To link his own remembrance with the name
Of Earth's profoundest Teacher:—happier still
In that his toils were sweeten'd and sustain'd
By such treasure of connubial wealth
As few have e'er possess'd.[73]

The poem first appeared in 1843, soon after Henry's death. To Sara, as bereaved widow, Derwent defended Moultrie's description of Henry as "not creative" relative to others in the circle:

If anything is wanting to the description of Henry's character, it is connected with his conversational ~~persons~~ powers. There was about him a certain festive brilliancy, as to the manner, and, as to the matter, so happy a mixture of the speculative and the practical, the remote and the present, the results of reasoning and the results of observation, as to make him intellectually the most agreeable companion I ever knew: and the same power, as far as could be expected, appeared in his writings.[74]

Derwent distinguishes Henry's writings from his conversation by the absence of three qualities also absent from the *Table Talk*: voice, look, and occasion. The first two, *parole* and expression of face and eye, are almost unavoidably absent; the third, by a choice "not creative", leaves the advantage with Boswell's life of Johnson, where the contextual occasion is usually clear and the drama of combat is frequent.

Concurrently with Henry's intellectual achievements at Cambridge and after, there were ominous physical symptoms. During 1821 he had swelling of the knee and inflammation of the eye. Trouble with his sight would recur every two or three years; he had an especially "alarming inflammation of the eyes" in the spring of 1828.[75] He became Fellow of King's in 1821, and to begin preparation as a barrister he was admitted at the Middle Temple on 16 June 1821. By 1823 (when he took the BA home for periods of weeks and later months, from a "rheumatic complaint" or "spinous condition". He began to publish essay-reviews on classical Greek and other literary subjects in the *British Critic, Knight's*

---

[73] John Moultrie *Poems* with a Memoir by Derwent Coleridge (2 vols 1876) I 424–5. The poem next turns to SC. "The Poet's Daughter" (II 392–3) describes her as a seeming emanation from the dream of "bard or prophet saint"— which, the poet concludes, she was. In the title of a sonnet by Moultrie, "To

—— by Anticipation", VCL S MS F 4.25 has the blank filled in, in pencil, as "S. C."

[74] Quoted, SC to JTC, BM Add MS 47558 ff 198–9.

[75] SC to Elizabeth Crump Wardell, from Greta Hall, 5 Jul 1828. DCL ms.

Quarterly Magazine (continued from 1825 without Knight's name), and *Quarterly Review* (of which John Taylor Coleridge was editor from December 1824 to November 1825, when he was succeeded by J. G. Lockhart). In an age of anonymous writing Henry began to be known among Conservative editors and suspected by editors and publishers of the Opposition.

Meanwhile two events occurred of first importance. In August 1822 he left for a tour of France. This was not one of the important events, but he was to transcribe as a present for Sara Coleridge the letters he wrote to his father, from 6 August at Calais to 25 September from Rouen, along with his early record of her father's talk. At the end of 1822 Sara and her mother came to London. Henry Nelson Coleridge had dinner with Coleridge at the John Taylor Coleridges' on 28 December, and first saw Sara at Highgate on 5 January. Getting to know his cousin and uncle was doubly momentous for him and doubled again for posterity. In a letter to his sister "Fran" on 7 January he tried to be frivolous; he and John had walked to Highgate wet, prepared for one or the other to fall in love with Sara, a "lovely creature" in whom he detected *design*: "John went home, and I stayed to dine. My uncle talked at an immense rate, now in glimmer and now in gloom! I walked home at nine."[76] To his brother James on 11 March he was more serious, but not completely open:

My dear ~~Fanny~~ Jem

You have seen Sara—she is a pretty little thing is she not? I think she possesses the most cultivated and beautiful mind I have ever met with. I am much pleased that my Aunt Brown saw her . . . to invite her to Combsatchfield. She deserves and stands in need of much pity and protection. Her mother is a detestable fidgett, if not a tyrant. But that's entirely ⟨between⟩ you and me, if you please. My authority however is strong—even from the victim herself.

In the next B.C. there are two articles of mine—Werner and Kruitzner—and Ugo Foscolo and Petrarch.[77]

Before Sara and her mother left for Ottery on 5 March, she and Henry had been secretly betrothed. They expected opposition from both fathers:

---

[76] UT ms. Frances Duke Coleridge (1796–1842), usually "Fanny", later the second wife of the judge Sir John Patteson (1790–1861), a close friend of JTC and legal colleague of both JTC and HNC.

[77] BM Add MS 47558 f 93. In the spring of 1823 he wrote to Frank (f 94): "I met Edith Southey at Fanny's yesterday. She is a very fine girl indeed; not so pretty in face as Sara, but taller and more finished in her figure." HNC reviewed Byron's *Werner; or, The Inheritance: A Tragedy* (1822) and the tale dramatised by Byron, Harriet Lee *Kruitzner, or the German's Tale* (5th ed 1823), in *British Critic* 2nd s XIX (Mar 1823) 242–53: Byron was "beginning to be ridiculous" (p 243). HNC's review of Ugo Foscolo *Essays on Petrarch* (1823) followed in Apr, pp 373–88.

they were first cousins, they were both given to debilitating illnesses, and neither had a favourable prospect financially. Henry had assessed his intellectual capacities for his brother James on 11 January:

Even thus early in life, I know my strength to be in *discourse*, and not in *intention*, of mind. Accordingly, I am fond of, and understand, History, Poetry and Criticism. I affect Oratory and Theology, because none of these demand much analytic reasoning to comprehend, but rather call for a general admiration of the beautiful, a sense of what is just and pure in taste and execution, expansion rather than attention of thought, width rather than depth.[78]

Sara had recently proved her mental stamina by translating *An Account of the Abipones, an Equestrian People of Paraguay*, from the Latin of the Jesuit Martin Dobrizhoffer (3 vols 1822).

One of the signs that Henry had been smitten also by Sara's father appears in "Scibile", which he contributed to the inaugural number of *Knight's Quarterly Magazine* I (1823) 180–92. There he paraphrases loosely an elderly man of unfashionable ideas who is clearly Coleridge: "the old gentleman", in remarks "originally addressed to a young man", is grateful for Luther, prefers Clarendon as historian to Hume, finds in society a principle of Permanency and a principle of Progression, and has taught the young man to question whether Rossini is a better composer than Corelli, Haydn, Mozart, or Handel.

In 1824 Henry expected to visit Sara in the Lakes, but instead he went to Ottery with a recurrence of pain, variously diagnosed, according to the first paragraph of his *Six Months in the West Indies*, as "rheumatism proper, rheumatism gout, gout proper, and an affection in the spinous process". Colonel James ordered the engagement broken off. Coleridge, apparently ignorant of the attachment until 1826, declined then to interfere: he could not condemn his daughter to unhappiness. Sara, who had accepted John Taylor Coleridge's aid in ending the persistent proposals of marriage from John May Jr, assured him on 17 August that she would not consider herself disengaged from Henry even if he could not give his hand with his heart.[79] May had been at Eton with Henry; excluded by Dr Keate from the college-bound, he spent 1818 at Heath's Court, with Henry's brother the Rev James Duke Coleridge as his tutor. John Taylor Coleridge wrote to May on 24 August that Henry's attack this year had been much worse than the one in July 1823: "I took the gig and drove my father down to Falmouth to see Henry—since that time I am told he

---

[78] BM Add MS 47558 f 90. This letter continues with admiration of C and SC: "Her mother I do not very much like."

[79] UT Grantz 695, 699.

is much improved . . . then he had only been drawn in a Bath chair to the Baths—now he can walk for an hour or more at a time.''[80]

The next event, though less momentous than getting to know Sara and Coleridge, proved indicative both of Henry's health and of his character. To provide an improved climate for his "rheumatic" back, and to divert him from his engagement to Sara, it was decided that Henry would go to the West Indies with his cousin William Hart Coleridge (1789–1849), recently appointed the first Bishop of Barbados and the Leeward Islands. They were to sail from Plymouth in late November, but bad weather held them into December. "Henry has managed to catch cold".[81] Between his arrival at Barbados on 29 January 1825 and his final departure on 8 August, he set foot on most of the islands from Trinidad northward to Anguilla.

Six Months in the West Indies, in 1825 appeared anonymously over John Murray's imprint the first week in February 1826. Henry assigned the copyright to Murray for £200 to be paid in two instalments.[82] His acceptance of slavery until education could prepare the slaves for self-government, coupled with a "gay, laughing Epicureanism" and "lively sallies", provoked answers. One from Birmingham, in two parts, was entitled *The Young Logicians; or School-boy Conceptions of Rights and Wrongs. With a Particular Reference to "Six Months in the West Indies"* (1828). First, however, Henry had to deal with the family; a flippant reference at the outset to the "two cousins" Margaret and Lucy who gave food and medicines to the poor, recognisable as the widowed sisters Jane and Sarah (Mrs George and Mrs Luke Coleridge) caused all recoverable copies to be bought in and a less offensive leaf substituted. Sara found the advance sheets sent to Southey "delightfully vivacious & amusing", and Southey concurred.[83] Coleridge made a note that the author of this book, whose epithet and name he put into Greek characters, "my harum scarum nephew, Henry", had taken a position on slavery that in error "implies the direct politocratic power of the Gospel".[84] The thin concealment of Henry's identity, presumably from curious women, indicates that Coleridge did not predict in 1826 that Henry would become the first major explorer of the notebooks.

A second edition of *Six Months in the West Indies*, also anonymous, with additions, appeared later in 1826; and a third, with the name

[80] Bodleian MS Eng Lett c 289.
[81] JTC to May, ibid.
[82] Records of John Murray Publishers Ltd. The contract of 11 Feb 1826 was between John Murray and Henry Coleridge "of the Middle Temple Student at Law". HNC acknowledged receipt of the £200 immediately.
[83] *CL* VI 560n.
[84] *CN* IV 5402.

"Henry Nelson Coleridge, M.A., Late Fellow of King's College, Cambridge" on the title-page. A one-page Preface, signed "H. N. C., *Lincoln's Inn, October, 1832*", proclaimed the need for a new edition "when the right hand of the colonial power of England is hacked at with a pertinacious hatred, of which there is no example in the history of domestic treason or foreign hostility". Henry was seldom irresolute.

When the book first appeared, he had taken up residence at Lincoln's Inn, to begin practice as equity draughtsman and conveyancer. He was called to the bar by the Honourable Society of the Middle Temple on 24 November 1826. At the end of July Sara had come to visit Lady Beaumont and remained in London a year. Her longest period with the Gillmans extended from 17 September to 8 October. When she visited the John Taylor Coleridges in January 1827 consent had been given to the marriage whenever circumstances seemed more propitious. Not many in the family expected the arrival of propitious circumstances. Sara's brother Hartley wrote to Derwent:

Entre nous—I wish the dear girl had form'd another attachment. Worldly considerations apart, I do not think the author of the *Six Months' Residence* the likeliest person in the world to accord with the exquisite tenderness and susceptibility of her moral and physical constitution . . . our Sariola will require delicacy in a husband. . . . The *Six Months*, is very clever, and tolerably sensible, but there is a flippancy, a vulgarity about it, which I cannot esteem. . . . Neither do I think he feels sufficiently the moral enormity of the slave system . . . At all events, he writes temperately, and practically—avoiding the coarse-heartedness of the West-indian party on one hand, and the bravado of Macaulay and such like spouting-club heroes, on the other.[85]

Sara Hutchinson informed Edward Quillinan: "I am sorry to tell you (but it is a secret) that she is engaged to one of her Cousins—he who has written the conceited work about West India and who is very delicate in constitution—having had an affection of the spine—without fortune but what he can make by his wits & the Law—".[86] The Southeys, envious for their Edith, were afraid, not that the cousins would marry, but that Lady Beaumont might promote Sara's beauty and intellect into a liaison above her station.[87] But Wordsworth, who had wished her affectionately a thousand good wishes on her departure in 1822, wrote now a brief note: "I wish you were back again in Cumberland—and take care that you

[85] *HCL* 93. In Aug 1829, as the marriage approached, HC again appraised HNC for DC: "I could have wish'd . . . that she had chosen a richer man, and that a richer man had chosen her" (108).

[86] *SHL* 323; cf 341, 349. In 1832 SH referred to HNC as "an efficient person"

with whom she would have been willing to serve as guardian to WW's children (*SHL* 388).

[87] VCL S MS F4.29. But Edith urged SC to return promptly to Keswick rather than to go to DC's at Helstone. Ibid.

keep your health, and the good looks of which I hear so much—farewell my very dear Friend—''.[88]

Henry looked for sources of income additional to his chancery practice, which was as yet slow. He issued anonymously, and Murray published, two pieces of conservative thought on current issues: *Remarks on the Present State of the Roman Catholic Question*, 1827, and *A Letter to the Right Honorable the Earl of Winchilsea and Nottingham*, 1829.[89] Lord Winchilsea had withdrawn his support of the new King's College of London. In the preparations of 1828 to counterbalance University College by including instruction at King's in "the doctrines and duties of Christianity", Henry had been appointed Secretary to the Provisional Committee of the college at a salary (decided upon in 1829) of £300 a year.[90] Assessing in letters to Frank his financial ability to marry, he listed his other income as legal fees, mostly conveyancing £100 (= £200?), a pupil £105, reviewing £50, estimated gift from his father £50, and Sara's three per cent stock at £200 (he would sell it), all of which totalled £955, against debts of £475 and the need to borrow two or three hundred more.[91]

Henry and Sara were married in the church at Crosthwaite, Keswick, the "Cathedral of the Lakes", on 3 September 1829. Wordsworth had intended to take temporary lodgings for them in Grasmere, but in the event they remained in Keswick for a few weeks before going to London, where they stayed first with John and Frances Patteson and then moved into lodgings in Bernard Street, off Russell Square, and next to modest quarters in Gower Street, while Sara's mother went on to the Derwent Coleridges in Helston. Coleridge, too ill with erysipelas and other ailments to attend the wedding, revised his will and came at once to greet them. He could have noticed that both of them had nervous ailments almost equal to his. In the summer of 1830, after a pause in Highgate, they moved to 1 Downshire Place, Downshire Hill, Hampstead. Sara then sent for her mother, who arrived in time for Sara's confinement with the first child, Herbert, and remained until her death in 1845.

[88] *WL* (*L* rev) I 699 (should be dated 1822), II 186 (VCL S MS F5.42, 5.53). On 26 Apr 1829 to HCR, WW described SC as "one of the loveliest and best of Creatures". *CRC* I 207; *WL* (*L* rev) II 69.

[89] "I have nearly finished a letter to Lord W; to be signed Civis. I will give you good reason for not putting my name or consulting the Abp." HNC to JTC, endorsed 23 Apr 1829, BM Add MS

47557 f 80ᵛ. In 1833 Murray reported a loss on "Civis" of £10-16-0. UT ms.

[90] HNC and SC to Elizabeth Wardell. DCL ms. Additional information from H. A. Harvey, College Archivist, King's College.

[91] 21 Nov 1828, 12 Jun 1829. BM Add MS 47588 ff 105–8ᵛ. He was still burdened with debts in 1833: Bernard Coleridge *Devonshire House* 311.

After the move to Hampstead, Henry came home from Lincoln's Inn for week-ends and holidays. He usually walked the seven miles or so, sometimes by way of Highgate to see Coleridge. He continued to take pupils along with his chancery practice. Upon passage of the Reform Bill he was named by the Whig ministry as a revising barrister, which took him on circuit between the Trinity and Michaelmas law sittings to different regions of Somerset, Wiltshire, and Devon, in order to revise or certify the lists of eligible voters. He became also lecturer to the Incorporated Law Society of the United Kingdom on the principles and practice of equity, his contract renewed annually at least through 1835–6. On 9 September 1831 he wrote to Southey that his lot had been drawn for the army: it "costs near five pounds to get a tall man to stand in my shoes".[92]

He wrote *A Short Account of the Life & Death of Swing, the Kent Rick-Burner*, dated 1830 but actually 1831, a sober rebuttal published by Effingham Wilson (for John Murray) to offset *The Life and History of Swing, the Kent Rig-Burner*, published by the radical Richard Carlile in 1830. The more vigorously sarcastic style that one comes to expect of Henry Coleridge appears in *The Genuine Life of Mr. Francis Swing* (W. Joy & H. Hughes 1831), but the family collection now at the University of Texas includes four copies of *A Short Account* and one of the answered *Life and History*, but none of the *Genuine Life*. *Notes on the Reform Bill*, "by a Barrister", 1831, is usually attributed to John Taylor Coleridge, but Sara, who reported to Elizabeth Crump Wardell on 4 July 1831 that 3300 copies had been sold, thought her husband the author.[93] Coleridge, who annotated the first edition, wrote to Henry about an "excellent paragraph" in the second edition.[94] John warned Henry in 1831 "against too much *pamphleteering*; it is a dangerous line for a lawyer".[95]

More overtly and more durably, and perhaps more lucratively, Murray published Henry's *Introductions to the Study of the Greek Classic Poets*, Part I, in 1830, "Designed Principally for the Use of Young Persons at School and College"; there was a revised edition in 1834 and another in 1846. After a "General Introduction", the work concerns Homer. Part II never appeared, although Henry's reviews in the *Quarterly* contained materials towards such a volume. In 1831 he was asked by Edward Hawtrey, then assistant master of Eton, to stand for the position of professor

[92] UT ms.
[93] DCL ms. The copy in the BM, bound with other "Ottery Pamphlets on the Reform Bill", has a marginal note by C, pp 39–41: *CM (CC)* II 90.

[94] *CL* VI 858–9. The "excellent paragraph" C mentioned is readily identified as one on p 11 of the 2nd ed; see *CM (CC)* II 90.
[95] *Devonshire House* 304.

of humanity at Glasgow, but he declined.[96] John James Park (1795–1833), appointed professor of English law at King's College, London, in 1831, asked Henry to give a course of lectures in May and June of 1833; later that year Henry agreed to provide the Law Society of the United Kingdom with "a modern universal history from Mahomet to French Revolution", written out on two sheets every fortnight, at about £500 a year for three years, in addition to his lectures on equity.[97] In 1834 he took on another pupil, "one Grove of Swansea", who came to Lincoln's Inn from 10 A.M. to 4 P.M.[98]

After Coleridge's death Henry Nelson Coleridge became to the public above all the editor and chief custodian of the works of his uncle and father-in-law; he performed those functions in fact from 1830 on. To the family and friends he was also the loving husband of the accomplished and beautiful Sara, who was equally loving but frequently ill, and from 1830 to 1834 hysterical during and after pregnancies. Henry came to better terms with Hartley, and it was his dying wish that his executors remit £100 of a £500 loan to Derwent.[99] Hartley wrote a verse tribute immediately after Henry's death, but he had written a more affective sonnet beginning

> Kinsman—yea, more than kinsman—brother, friend,—
> O more than kinsman! more than friend or brother!
> My sister's spouse, son to my widow'd mother!—
> How shall I praise thee right, and not offend?
> For thou wert sent a sore heart-ill to mend.
> Twin stars were ye, thou and thy wedded love . . .[100]

When spinal paralysis immobilised Henry in December 1842, Sara wrote to various relatives the details of his choking phlegm, his occasional relief from spasms, and the regimen ordered by Sir Benjamin Brodie. On 17 January she began a journal, which she continued until January 1844 as a record of her reactions to Henry's dying and to other deaths that followed. The end came ten minutes to one o'clock on the afternoon of Thursday, 26 January 1843, at 10 Chester Place, Regent's

[96] HNC to RS 1 Oct 1831. UT ms.
[97] BM Add MS 47557 ff 100ᵛ, 102, 103.
[98] Ibid f 103.
[99] SC to DC. UT Grantz 40, 43. In 1836, when CW's son Christopher was a candidate for headmaster of Harrow School, he asked HNC to write a letter of recommendation.
[100] *To H. N. Coleridge* in *Poems*, with a Memoir of His Life by His Brother (2 vols 1851) II 52. HC dated 28 Jan 1843 his poem *On the Death of Henry Nelson Coleridge Addressed to a Friend* (II 177–9); HNC's nephew Arthur Duke Coleridge (1830–1913)—son of Frank—wrote in a copy of *Poems* acquired 8 Mar 1856, at II 179, "Much of this Letter omitted".

Park (whither they had moved in 1837): "So ends the great charm of this world to me".[101]

Sara was glad that the children had not seen the end; nor could they remember "the blooming brilliant face I first saw at Mr Gillman's at Highgate".[102] Herbert, born in 1830, went on to a brilliant career; Edith, born in 1832, among other accomplishments was memoirist of her parents, notably of her mother. No likeness of Henry is known to exist (Edith said he could not afford to have his portrait painted), and this Introduction has given the longest available biographical account of him. His brother John drafted a memoir, but only fragments of it have survived among the family papers.

HNC AND STC

Henry, aged twelve, had accompanied his brother to Richmond in April 1811, when John, almost twenty-one, recorded their uncle Samuel's conversation more fully than Henry was able to do in 1823. When he saw and heard Coleridge a second time, at John's, on 28 December 1822, seeds of the *Table Talk* were planted.

Henry's opportunities to visit and record talk in 1823–4 did not depend solely on his love of the poet's daughter. In June 1823 Coleridge would be "always delighted to see" Henry.[103] A year later Coleridge wished "he would come oftener".[104] But it is clear that the opportunity afforded Henry to meet Charles Lamb, Edward Irving, and J. Blanco White at Highgate on 15 December 1825 resulted from Coleridge's enthusiasm for Henry's brother Edward, an enthusiasm heightened because Edward was trying to help Henry Gillman through difficulties at Eton.[105] Coleridge was no more pleased than the next with *Six Months in the West Indies*. He found the levities and olfactory images too reminiscent of Southey's similar offences, with the addition of impertinent coxcombry that might bring ruin to the family name.[106] Even before he learned how intense the attachment between Henry and Sara, he saw in the indiscreet words, "I love my cousin . . . almost my sister ere my wife", the possibility that knowledgeable readers would make an identification with Sara.[107] In short, the book was pleasant and informative but scandalous.

---

[101] UT ms.
[102] SC to JTC: UT Grantz 722.
[103] *CL* v 279.
[104] C to JTC 3 May [1824]: *CL* v 361.
[105] Ibid 521.
[106] C to EC [8 Feb 1826]: *CL* vi 560.

Dangerous signs; as illustrated in RS, "all men of cold constitutions are naturally immodest".
[107] C to EC 26 Jul 1826: *CL* vi 589. The reference is to *Six Months* 117.

Nor was Henry's conduct toward his uncle acceptable. William Hart Coleridge, before he went out as Bishop of Barbados, had visited Coleridge at Highgate several times; after his return he seemed studiously to avoid The Grove. Coleridge complained to Edward and Henry that his neighbours assigned denigrative reasons for the Bishop's absence; Edward expressed "manly indignation", but Henry, though signing himself "dutifully", defended the Bishop.[108] As if sensitive to the disapprobation, Henry preserved no record of his uncle's talk between his return from Barbados and his father's consent to the engagement with Sara in early 1827. A copy of Henry's *Remarks on the Catholic Question* was presented "with HNC's affectionate respects",[109] but Coleridge felt a sufficiently lingering chill to assure Derwent that he would have liked a sinecure through the Liverpool ministry on Hartley's account, and "now you & Mary; and Sara and—for her sake & *since so it is*—Henry".[110]

Surprisingly, after transcribing his entries for Sara in January 1827 (MS E), Henry continued to record talk through August and then ceased until April 1830. All indications point to frequent meetings and to mutual affection and respect during this period. On 20 February 1828 Coleridge subscribed himself "your affectionate Friend".[111] Paradoxically this letter contains a passage that Henry was to publish as Table Talk in 1835 under the date of 1 May 1833.[112] Once in 1829, in a paradox for the most unstoppable talker of his age, Coleridge "was engaged in a more than commonly interesting conversation with, or rather listening to, my nephew, Henry Nelson Coleridge, respecting his plans, which . . . include my daughter's change of *state* tho' not of name".[113] Mrs Gillman invited Sara and Henry to spend a week with them beginning 23 March 1830, after Hilary law term.[114] Henry was currently giving editorial aid toward the second edition of *On the Constitution of the Church and State*, and would soon perform the same function for *Aids to Reflection*. By a codicil to his will on 2 July 1830, naming J. H. Green as executor, Coleridge designated Green, Gillman, and Henry trustees for Hartley's portion of his bequest. When Henry remarked in a review-article on Hesiod (*Quarterly Review* March 1832) that "Milton seems to have taken a pregnant hint for a part of his grand description . . . in Paradise Regained", Coleridge protested in the margin: "Now on my Conscience,

[108] *CL* vi 560–1, 586.
[109] BM C 126 i 3 (5).
[110] Undated: *CL* vi 705.
[111] *CL* vi 730.
[112] Entry 36:495 in the numbers assigned in the present edition to *TT* (1835), *TT* (1836).
[113] C to Mrs George Frere [9 Feb 1829]: *CL* vi 785.
[114] VCL S MS F 3.62.

Henry! this is the only *flat* remark, I ever heard from YOU or knew of your making".[115]

The entries in Henry's workbooks from February through August 1827, like those of 1822–4, represented important intellectual events in a diary, with Coleridge reported in the third person. In April 1830 the record began with increased vigour, a greatly improved skill in conveying nuance, and a conviction that the task would in time have major public significance. On 8 June 1830 Henry wrote to his father that the fifty pages he had already accumulated would "make one of the most interesting *Table Talks* that ever was published".[116] John, particularly, watched with interest as the work grew.

The manuscript version of *Table Talk* published in *The Collected Works of S. T. Coleridge* greatly reduces the number of days to which talk is assigned. Aside from the clear evidence of the manuscripts, many of the previously published dates would be excludable on the basis of biographical data. On a few occasions Henry was present during Coleridge's rare excursions to London or his equally rare visits to Hampstead. Illness made such visits from Coleridge increasingly unlikely. Most of the recorded talk Henry heard at the Gillmans' during his week-ends of relief from Lincoln's Inn or during the vacations between law sittings— whenever he himself during such periods was not on circuit as revising barrister or visiting his parents or other relatives. In the gap between his entries of 11 September and 26 October 1831 he and Sara left the baby with Sara's mother and visited in Ottery.[117] Sara's confinements and other illnesses seem to have kept Henry with her no more often than they sent him to Highgate with news of her health. Saturdays predominate. For many of the months when Henry was seeing Coleridge, the earlier portion of Sundays was reserved for J. H. Green. Some of Coleridge's letters to Henry represent afterthoughts following their conversations; others remark on Henry's current illness or absence. From 1830 the dates in the manuscripts include most of the opportunities Henry can have had to accomplish his purpose.

Sara's opportunities would have been fewer still. Her nervous prostrations before and after her confinements were prolonged. When she was not restricted to Downshire Hill (and Coleridge simultaneously restricted to The Grove), she was often away seeking rest, at Ottery, Brighton, or

---

[115] *CM (CC)* II 88.

[116] UT ms, quoted at length TT 6 Jun 1830 n1, below. By the "50 quarto pages" he mentions in that letter he apparently refers to MS B and ignores the earlier entries of MS A.

[117] SC to Elizabeth Wardell 2 Nov 1831. DCL ms.

elsewhere. She spent five weeks in Brighton in the autumn of 1832. Mrs Coleridge's language of surprise at her husband's "power of continuous talking" after Edith's christening in August 1832 indicates that he had not been a frequent visitor to Hampstead.[118] Sara, confessing on 27 March 1833 to Elizabeth Wardell that she had not been well since the birth of Edith, from a complaint "entirely nervous", wrote that neither she nor her father had been really well since the christening.[119] Soon after that letter she went into "nervous misery" from her next pregnancy. Twins, Berkeley and Florence, were born 14 January 1834. Their death on the 19th elicited a sonnet from Hartley and a poem from Henry; Coleridge worried for Sara, but he was not up to verse. Sara, near exhaustion from worry about herself, her son, her daughter, and her father, felt relief that the house would not be further crowded by twins.[120] Although the first of five editions of her *Pretty Lessons in Verse for Good Children* appeared in the summer of 1834, she had written the verses for Herbert, she said, on her back.

Even when Sara apologised for not contributing more to the *Table Talk*, it is clear that she had especially in mind the brief opportunities before her marriage:

As to my contributions to "Table-Talk", I am ashamed to say that they really amount to a mere nothing. Two or three short memorables I remember recording; and I often wonder now how I could have been so negligent a listener. But there were several causes for this. In the first place, my father generally discoursed on such a very extensive scale, that it would have been an arduous task for *me* to attempt recording what I had heard. Henry could sometimes bring him down to narrower topics, but when alone with me he was almost always on the star-paved road, taking in the whole heavens in his circuit. Another impediment was this. When I was at Highgate (I think of it with grief and shame, for I ought perhaps to have had my mind in better order), my heart and thoughts were very much oppressed and usurped by a variety of agitating personal matters; I was anxious about my brothers, and their prospects—about Henry's health, and upon the subject of my engagement generally. . . . What I wish to convey to you is, that if I could have seen years ago how useless taking thought for all *those* things really was, and how permanently valuable every relic of my father's mind would be (which I did not then perceive *to the extent* that I do now, though well aware of his great powers), I should have tried to be an industrious gleaner, instead of loitering about the harvest-field as I did.[121]

---

[118] *Minnow* 165; cf Mrs C to Emily Trevenen, that C "talked incessantly with the greatest vigor and eloquence"—"on that day, if never in his life before, a most extraordinary person" (addition to a letter from SC, UT ms).

[119] DCL ms.
[120] SC to Elizabeth Wardell 19 Jan 1834. DCL ms.
[121] *SC Mem* I 123–4.

After her marriage Sara would have been seldom "alone with" her father when his conversation was on its "star-paved road".

In sum, most of the conversation recorded in *Table Talk* was heard by Henry, usually alone with Coleridge, at the Gillmans'. John Gibson Lockhart, who associated Coleridge with temperate hope and had found him more hopeful at Ramsgate in the summer of 1833 than he seemed in remarks on the Reform Bill in *Table Talk*, in his review of the work imagines Coleridge and Henry in nightly gloom. He may close in too narrowly the scene he asks his readers to picture with Henry as listener, but his description rests at least partly on knowledge and not on mere speculation. Instead of "the *stage directions*, so useful and entertaining in the case of Boswell", we may supply for the *Table Talk*, he says, "one melancholy formula—*place*, Mr. Coleridge's bed-room—*time*, night—*present*, the poet in his arm-chair, physically worn and exhausted by a day of pain, but refreshed and invigorated by the recent entrance of his dear young friend, to whom it is a sort of necessity of his nature that he should unburthen himself of some of the innumerable trains of thought and reflection that have been occupying him, as far as bodily sufferings might permit, since their last meeting".[122] But we must also, says Lockhart, see the nephew as "loving and respectfully attentive".

From the summer of 1832 Henry had been at work assembling texts for a new edition of Coleridge's *Poetical Works*. He hunted down juvenilia that Sara would later exclude on the grounds of Henry's "mixture of high taste and low taste, passion & unselectness, delicacy (or particularity) and exceeding freeness—dignity and familiarity".[123] "I have endeavoured to collect every thing", Henry wrote to John, "& the arrangement & corrections give me much trouble".[124] Like Ernest Hartley

---

[122] *QR* LIII (1835) 80. HNC wrote to John Murray on 18 Dec 1834 that after meeting that day with Lockhart concerning the Table Talk he could promise "to attend to his suggestions". UT ms.

[123] SC to DC 23 Jan 1852, UT Grantz 96: "My dear Henry found these poems in old MS. books &, in all the ardour of first love, would insert them in the new edition. . . . I think by this time he would have been ready to discard these *puerilia*. But the truth is, it is *our judgment versus H.N.C.* not our judgment against STC, either unbiassed, or swayed by friends, which constitutes our great exertion of editorial boldness. The

fact must have been, that my Father never troubled his head about the edition of 1834—left ⟨it⟩ entirely to Henry.— Had he given the matter a thought, he never COULD have sanctioned the publication of poems he scorned in 1796." She continues similarly in Grantz 133, 134, 136.

[124] 20 Mar 1834, BM Add MS 47557 f 103ᵛ. Discussions with Murray probably account for the sentences that follow: "this edition, which is stereotyped, will never be superseded. If S.T.C. should hereafter write a̶n̶y̶ much more poetry it would be added in anōr volume of the same size".

Coleridge later, he assigned titles that have been accepted as if they were the poet's. One assumes that he resurrected nothing without the poet's consent, but he included in the three volumes of 1834 his own poem *On Berkeley and Florence Coleridge*, as by "a friend".[125] Except that he lacked Ernest Hartley Coleridge's unguided freedom to publish as Coleridge's verses culled from the notebooks and could not feel free to make changes arbitrarily in the text of the poems, Henry seems to have had the same trust that Coleridge had expressed to him regarding the preface to the second edition of *Aids to Reflection* in 1830: ". . . I assure you, that I have quite confidence enough in your taste & judgement to give you a Chart Blanch for any amendments in the style".[126] The first volume was available by 20 March, the second in April; the third was listed among new books in the *Literary Gazette* for 19 July. To the third volume, containing the translation from Schiller's *Wallenstein*, Henry added on a final leaf one of Coleridge's dullest poems, as if in a last victory for "unselectness".[127]

To cap his stewardship during his uncle's lifetime, Henry also wrote and carefully revised the most important of all reviews of the *Poetical Works*, that for the *Quarterly*, reprinted in the *Museum of Foreign Literature, Science, and Art* of Philadelphia. His authorship of the review, undertaken at Lockhart's suggestion, had not been revealed to Coleridge. Knowing that the review would, as usual, be altered by the editor, Henry adjured Lockhart: "as S.T.C. & oͬs [others] can hardly fail to recognize the writer, you will not insert any expressions touching on my poor Uncle's personal or private life or adventures".[128] With this problem in mind, Henry modified before sending off the review such passages as one, already referred to, quoting Wordsworth:

We had the pleasure, one clear October day, of accompanying Mr Wordsworth from Rydal to the summit of Bow Fell. A thousand things make that excursion memorable to us; but we refer to it now only as being the occasion on wͨh Mr Wordsworth said, in concluding an elaborate description of the friend of his youth, "Many men have done wonderful *things*—as Newton, Davey, Scott &c; but Coleridge was the only wonderful *man* I ever knew".[129]

Intermediately in the manuscript this was reduced to begin, "We think we have somewhere heard repeated a remark by Mr Wordsworth that", with changes to indirect quotation and past tense. In the *Quarterly* it be-

<hr />

[125] *PW* (1834) II 149–50. The identity of the friend was clear enough from the poem.

[126] 1 Dec 1830: *CL* VI 849.

[127] *Love, Hope, and Patience in Edu-* cation, from *The Keepsake* for 1830: *PW* (1834) III 331.

[128] UT ms.

[129] UT ms. For HNC's original record, see App E.

gan, "Perhaps our readers may have heard repeated a saying of Mr. Wordsworth".[130] Henry decided to save for a work less anonymous the remark of Mme de Staël to "one of Mr Coleridge's nephews at Coppet, 'Your uncle ~~was~~ is excellent at monologue, but he does not understand *le dialogue*' ".[131]

Henry's review is almost an annex, or in the circumstances an antechamber, to the *Table Talk*. Much comes directly from his record of his uncle's conversation, even to the description of Mackintosh's manner of speaking that serves in the review as the antithesis of Coleridge's.[132] One of his many additions to the page proofs[133] elaborates on Coleridge's insistence that his poetry was more musical than pictorial.[134] The remark of Naldi, in illustration of Coleridge's taste in music, survives both in the review and in *Table Talk*.[135] The long account of Coleridge's Faust, Michael Scott (in *Table Talk* under the date 15 February 1833), appears in the review unchanged.[136] There are other parallels. And yet occasionally, perhaps from the vanity of authorship, Henry suppresses from *Table Talk* Coleridge's conversation as the source of critical interpretations and judgements in the review. In a startling example, Coleridge is quoted in the manuscript on 1 July 1833 concerning the seminal idea of *Christabel* as "witchery by daylight";[137] after Henry had appropriated that interpretation in the review, he removed it from the text of *Table Talk* and cited the *Quarterly* reviewer as the source.[138] The charitable view is that he not only expected knowledgeable readers to identify the author of the review-essay but also to recognise in his authorship the ultimate authority for both general and specific interpretations as Coleridge himself. In any view, Henry was trying to promulgate the best that had been thought and said in his time, to make it prevail, and to honour the thinker of it, Samuel Taylor Coleridge.

He could not have expected that the poet's death and the publication of *Table Talk* would follow so quickly that comparison of the two texts would show either that Coleridge was himself the chief source of the essay or that his purported conversation had been modified to fit the views of his nephew. To the extent that Henry did anticipate the poet's death, his fine description in the review-essay of Coleridge's conversation,

[130] *QR* LI I (1834), reprinted *CH* 621.

[131] So the version of his ms of the review, f 4.

[132] *CH* 623; cf *TT* 36:35.

[133] VCL S MS F 121, proof p 6; cf *CH* 627, 632–3.

[134] TT 31 Mar 1832, MS B f 57ᵛ.

[135] *CH* 627–8; *TT* 36:282, 5 Oct 1830; MS B f 33ᵛ.

[136] *CH* 640–1.

[137] MS B f 97ᵛ.

[138] *TT* (1835) II 22 (36:546). Another parallel between *TT* and the *QR* review, on language in Milton and Shakespeare, is acknowledged at 3 Jul 1833 (36:542n).

though it pressed him hard to improve upon it in the Preface to *Table Talk*, can be considered an advertisement for the collection he was preparing:

Those who remember him in his more vigorous days can bear witness to the peculiarity and transcendent power of his conversational eloquence. It was unlike anything that could be heard elsewhere; the kind was different, the degree was different, the manner was different. The boundless range of scientific knowledge, the brilliancy and exquisite nicety of illustration, the deep and ready reasoning, the strangeness and immensity of bookish lore—were not all; the dramatic story, the joke, the pun, the festivity, must be added—and with these the clerical-looking dress, the thick waving silver hair, the youthful-coloured cheek, the indefinable mouth and lips, the quick yet steady and penetrating greenish grey eye, the slow and continuous enunciation, and the everlasting music of his tones,—all went to make up the image and to constitute the living presence of the man. He is now no longer young, and bodily infirmities, we regret to know, have pressed heavily upon him. His natural force is indeed abated; but his eye is not dim, neither is his mind yet enfeebled. . . .

Mr. Coleridge's conversation, it is true, has not now all the brilliant versatility of his former years; yet we know not whether the contrast between his bodily weakness and his mental power does not leave a deeper and a more solemnly affecting impression, than his most triumphant displays in youth could ever have done. To see the pain-stricken countenance relax, and the contracted frame dilate under the kindling of intellectual fire alone—to watch the infirmities of the flesh shrinking out of sight, or glorified and transfigured in the brightness of the awakening spirit—is an awful object of contemplation; and in no other person did we ever witness such a distinction,—nay, alienation of mind from body,—such a mastery of the purely intellectual over the purely corporeal, as in the instance of this remarkable man. Even now his conversation is characterized by all the essentials of its former excellence; there is the same individuality, the same *unexpectedness*, the same universal grasp; nothing is too high, nothing too low for it; it glances from earth to heaven, from heaven to earth, with a speed and a splendour, an ease and a power, which almost seem inspired: yet its universality is not of the same kind with the superficial ranging of the clever talkers whose criticism and whose information are called forth by, and spent upon, the particular topics in hand. No; in this more, perhaps, than in anything else is Mr. Coleridge's discourse distinguished: that it springs from an inner centre, and illustrates by light from the soul. His thoughts are, if we may so say, as the radii of a circle, the centre of which may be in the petals of a rose, and the circumference as wide as the boundary of things visible and invisible.[139]

Henry recorded several topics of lively conversation on 5 July 1834. On the 23rd Sara wrote to Emily Trevenen, and Mrs Coleridge added a few words: "We send twice a day to Highgate; when H[enry] goes, poor father begs not to see him, nor anybody, but the Doctors and attend-

---

[139] *QR* LII 2–3; *CH* 621–2.

ants".[140] On the 26th Henry asked Lockhart to append to his review a notice of Coleridge's death on 25 July.[141] Reporting that action to John on 7 August, he disparaged his review: "I am afraid the whole is crude, & I takes no pleasure in the performance".[142] On 8 August he reported to James on their Aunt Sara's health:

> She is the widow of a great man—the greatest, in my judgment, since Milton. The impression he has made is profound, tho' at present in this country not very extensive. In America his influence is more general, &, if I mistake not, there will be a burst of power & glory around his memory very shortly in England.[143]

In October Sara mentioned the Table Talk to Mrs Wardell: "Henry has some notices of *his own* respecting my father which will appear by & by—But they have nothing to do with the MSS. in the hands of Mr Green". Her father admired and trusted Henry. "My husband too was greatly attached to him & deeply sensible of his good & great qualities; Mrs Gillman will testify that he was ever loving & respectfully attentive to my Father & it is not a little that would satisfy her on this score".[144]

Henry had begun work immediately on the *Table Talk*, with an eye also for the *Literary Remains* to follow. "I hope", he wrote to John Taylor Coleridge when he had reached the last sheets of the second volume, they "will add in a substantial way to the fame & utility of S. T. C.".

> Few, I believe, will give me credit for the labor of putting the text together; it reads nicely now, but the materials committed to me were fragmentary in the extreme. I think I understand the poetical & critical part of S. T. C.'s mind better than any other of the persons at all in the way of undertaking such a work; & if I have done him no harm, I believe you will think I have done him great good.[145]

He prepared a new edition of *The Friend*, with a synoptical plan of the contents and additional documents, for 1837; a fourth edition of *Aids to Reflection* and a third of *Church and State* in 1839. In 1840 he made public for the first time Coleridge's *Confessions of an Inquiring Spirit* and began work on a new edition of *Biographia Literaria*,[146] which Sara was to complete for publication in 1847. Wordsworth accepted twice over Sara's dedication to him of the *Biographia*, but urged her to tone down such references as that to the "latest writings of my dear Henry".[147]

[140] UT Grantz 1352. SC wrote similarly to HC the same day: Grantz 509.
[141] National Library of Scotland MS 924.10.
[142] BM Add MS 47557 f 106. Cf HNC to Poole 17 Sept 1834: "It is inadequate—but right, I believe as far as it goes . . .". BM Add MS 35344 f 112^v.

[143] BM Add MS 47558 f 119.
[144] Postmarked 13 Oct 1834. DCL ms.
[145] HNC to JTC 31 Jul 1836, BM Add MS 47557 f 123.
[146] HNC to Thomas Tracy 21 Apr 1840, HUL MS Am 661 (7).
[147] VCL F MS F5.61.

Those two volumes, completed by Sara with annexes more acute, learned, and original than her husband had provided in his eagerly devout series of volumes, were the first fruits of her succession to him in editing aright the works of their beloved mentor.

HENRY NELSON COLERIDGE'S *TABLE TALK*

Specimens of the Table Talk of the Late Samuel Taylor Coleridge, as it was entitled in 1835, is the labour of Henry Nelson Coleridge, amplified as noted in the edition by his brother John, "Mr Justice Coleridge", and, as not noted, compressed here and there into discretion by John and others. A correspondent in the *Times Literary Supplement* commented on marginalia displayed in the bicentennial exhibition at the British Museum: "Coleridge is as learned in his remarks on Gilbert White's *The Works in Natural History* as he is entertaining on Martin Luther's *Colloquia mensalia* (whose title he used for his *Table Talk*) . . .".[148] One can speak of the content of *Table Talk* as deriving directly from S. T. Coleridge, but the title and much more came from Henry. S. T. Coleridge used no title for his table-talk.

Most of the talk occurred tête-à-tête at Highgate. On 29 December 1822 Henry summarised in his diary what he had heard his uncle say the previous evening at the John Taylor Coleridges'. He was present when Coleridge came to dinner again on 9 January and 26 April 1824. On 24 July 1831 Henry and Sara encountered him unexpectedly at the British Gallery. The conversation of 9 August 1832 occurred at Hampstead, and possibly that of 8 September 1830 also. At the Gillman house-warming on 1 June 1824 others were present while Henry listened; on 4 April 1832 one or more Unitarians were present, and on 8 June 1833 someone more concerned than Henry for the rights of Negroes. When Henry visited on 13 May 1832 others were present, Coleridge was in poor spirits, and no record of talk resulted. Occasionally there is the hint of a dissenting voice in the room. The recorded talk may of course include still other days at Hampstead and further days when Henry was not alone with his uncle, but the bulk of the Table Talk resulted from Henry's congenial stimulus to the flow of talk. In 1823–4, 1827, and 1830–4 (the years of Henry's report from Highgate), even when Coleridge was not up to holding open Thursdays, visitors acquainted with the Thursdays were often present; it is noteworthy that the dates in the manuscript include only five Thurs-

[148] A Special Correspondent "Coleridge at the British Museum" *TLS* 21 Jul 1972 p 852.

days,[149] with no clear indication of an augmented audience on those five. The person who enters to "punctuate" the discourse on 29 June 1833 could be one of the Gillmans. For the most part *Table Talk* contains what Coleridge said to his nephew, not all of what he said and little of it designed exclusively for Henry, but said directly to him.

One of the strongest signs that what Henry recorded is conversation comes in instances of mishearing. On 27 December 1831 he thought he heard an Italian phrase attributed to "Franccsco Tcssela"; unable later to identify a Tessela, he modified the entry in 1835 to avoid specification. The name Coleridge pronounced was almost certainly Francesco (that is, Francis) "de 'Salez' ".[150] On 26 September 1830 Henry wrote "Fall of Fiers" for Fall of Foyers. On 21 May 1832 he wrote "Hollerus", which he later changed to Hugo de St Victor. On 4 May 1833 John Scotus Erigena first came to him as "J. Scotus—& Ramus"—the other John Scotus and Ramus. Possibly it was Coleridge who said "the Abbé Raynal" on 7 July 1832 when he meant Giovanni Ignazio Molina, but perhaps Henry's ear or memory supplied the more obvious authority on Chile.[151] Once or twice Henry seems to have scribbled notations for what he had not heard clearly, failed later to make an identification, and generalised the entry in print to evade the question.[152] Henry's brothers, his father, and of course Sara knew that he was recording conversation for eventual publication, but lapses in proper names and in titles of works by major authors support other evidence that Coleridge was not consulted concerning the work in progress. Nowhere in the manuscripts is there evidence that Henry returned at a later date to correct a name misheard.

With no clear exceptions, each day's entries represented a new beginning in the manuscript record. Entries for a given date more often than not begin by differing from the last entry of the preceding date in ink, in thickness of nib, and in size and slant of letters. Entries within a date vary, but less often, and perhaps never without special significance. When Henry's penmanship within a date varies, only the next date of record limits our guess as to the period of time that elapsed while he

[149] 30 Aug 1827, 27 May 1830, 23 Sept 1830, 9 Aug 1832, 28 Aug 1833.

[150] MS B f 54ᵛ (36:343).

[151] MS B f 32ᵛ (36:275), f 63 (36:385), f 87 (36:501), f 66 (36:392). On Molina see *CN* III 3789n.

[152] E.g. MS B f 90, 15 May 1833 (36:515), on one of Goethe's lyrics. Lockhart, in his review of *TT* (1835),

tells us that Henry "commonly set down, before going to bed, what fragments he had been able to carry away". *QR* LIII (1835) 79. Lockhart had been in effect the publisher's editor for the volumes; HNC would have met with him almost from the moment that Murray agreed to publish the TT.

made the record that survives. Determinations of a fresh beginning are made easier by his tendency to begin a long entry in a tightly controlled script but to allow the script to become larger and looser as he proceeds. A direct contrast frequently appears: a small, neat record on one date will be followed by a larger script with a thicker nib on the next date, or vice versa. Because of such characteristics, it has been possible in the annotations to refer to insertions of a word or a sentence or two "in a later script", meaning Henry's hand but distinguishable from the original script of the entry by a combination of pen, ink, and penmanship. Such changes also make it nearly certain that he recorded Coleridge's talk in his workbooks near to the time when he heard it. (The successive workbooks that make up the manuscript version are described at the end of this Introduction).

Henry's injunction to Sara in March 1827 was to listen closely to her father's talk "and endeavour afterwards to preserve some of it, as I have done". The "afterwards . . . as I have done" is one of our few external clues. The manuscript entries now published in *The Collected Works of S. T. Coleridge* were made soon after Henry heard the remarks. How soon? Do the surviving manuscripts represent transcriptions from an initial record not preserved? The balance of evidence, including especially revisions current with first recording in the workbooks, suggests that these entries were normally the initial record, made soon after each return from Coleridge to the location of the workbook. Henry is often more hesitant, with more changes in language, at the commencement of an entry, and then progressively fluid; one would expect the opposite if he were transcribing from an earlier draft. On 28 January 1832, for example, the running corrections indicate that exact wording was not established when he began to write.[153] At one point, where he first writes and then cancels "& accor" in a sentence that later includes "& accordingly", it might be thought that his eye has leaped ahead in copying from an earlier version, but all other corrections in the entry suggest rather that he began to conclude the sentence before perceiving that an intermediate clause would make the thought clearer.

At the very beginning, the next day after hearing Coleridge at dinner on the 28th, he recorded the event of the dinner in his diary and summarised briefly what he had heard Coleridge say. A similar pattern continued through 1827. At first Sara was as important to the diary as her father; next Coleridge's talk seemed to be what was most worth recording; soon the workbooks were used chiefly to record Coleridge's talk but

[153] MS B f 55ᵛ (36:348).

also occasionally to transcribe his words from manuscript sources and, rarely, to jot notes on Henry's own reading, both when that reading was directed by Coleridge's remarks and when (as far as we can tell) it was not. He recorded, not conversations or monologues, but Coleridge's topics, apparently at first without regard to the order of topics or to transitions between them. At first, in 1823 and 1824, he used a cautious past tense throughout, as if to certify only what Coleridge said on each particular occasion, not what his opinions could be said to be over a longer period. Later on he probably recorded the topics more nearly in the order they were spoken, but with few transitions, for by then he had erected the principle that his was a record of separable topics.

The workbooks would seem probably to have been in general the first written record. There are signs here and there, however, of transcription. On 13 April 1830, the first date of his new beginning, he wrote "but he never in any way led to bottom the Religion", a syntactic impossibility where the phrase "but he never" anticipates the first words of the next clause; he then crossed out the initial "but he never" and wrote "& so far as it" above the line.[154] This error might well result from the mind getting ahead of the hand in composition, but it could easily occur from letting the eye get ahead in transcription from an intermediate source. Dates out of order also could be explained if some of the entries at that point had been written first on a loose sheet or scrap of paper available after a short delay for transcription into the diary. Entries dated 31 March 1830 follow entries dated 20 April, and are themselves followed by Wordsworth's remarks of 15 October 1829.[155] One begins to believe that Henry used intermediate notations only or largely in early 1830, but there is a similar return to 9 August 1832 after entries dated 11 August.[156] Did the return of 23 September 1830 to note Coleridge's remarks on Huskisson on the 19th result from finding a temporarily misplaced notation or from a sudden memory on the 23rd of something said four days before?[157] What does it mean that the date 25 June 1831 occurs three times in succession for table-talk, each separated by notes from Henry's own reading of Machiavelli?[158]

Although an increase in skills brought fuller and fuller records, one does not imagine Henry carrying his red workbook to the Gillmans' and back, and still less imagines him sitting at the Gillmans' taking notes from *The Prince* between brief conversations with Coleridge. General

[154] MS B f 7 (36:127).
[155] MS B ff 8–10.
[156] MS B f 72.
[157] MS B f 32. A slip of the pen in writing "19" on a later date is a less likely possibility.
[158] MS B ff 37^{v}–9.

psychology requires the postulate that he kept the diary at Lincoln's Inn until his marriage in 1829, that he later kept at Hampstead each book currently used for recording table-talk, and that he sometimes made notes at Lincoln's Inn to preserve topics of Coleridge's conversation until it was convenient to transcribe them at Hampstead. Of her father's talk Sara made entries in the red book only two or three times, but she occasionally transcribed there passages from Coleridge's early letters to her mother or similar documents. This occasional presence of Sara's hand also suggests that the workbooks remained most of the time at Hampstead.

How far is the language Coleridge's? Comparison with other utterances by the Coleridge of 1822–34, whether on the particular topic at issue or on other subjects, reveals similarities, sometimes to the point of identity, in image, syntax, and range of vocabulary. Clearly Henry preferred to report Coleridge's own words, but it is equally clear that he did not feel bound either to the syntax or to the diction originally chosen for the record. The revision of one word, whether closer to the word Coleridge pronounced or farther away, often entailed further revision for stylistic harmony. Henry's continued changes to the text in 1835 and 1836, along with his free revisions in *Literary Remains* when dealing with unfinished or unpolished documents in Coleridge's hand, suggest very strongly that he was more interested in clarity of content, from his original record on, than in reportorial precision. Unfortunately for precisionists, he considered himself superior as a popular stylist to Coleridge—and he proved to be so.

From 1832 on, his workbooks include transcriptions from Coleridge's marginalia and similar documents. About 10 June 1832 he had copied into the red workbook, from a collection of tracts by John Asgill, Coleridge's note on the charm for cramp at Christ's Hospital; in 1835 he published it as table-talk of that date.[159] To plump up an entry concerning Richard Baxter on 12 July 1827 in the published versions, he included a remark he had transcribed on 6 August 1832 from marginalia in *Reliquiae Baxterianae*.[160] He appropriated, and assigned to various dates, *sententiae* copied by his brother Edward from Coleridge's notebooks and recopied by Henry on 1 September 1832.[161] One of these, on a woman's friendship, he published in a footnote with the explanation that he found it ''on a page dyed with an imprisoned rose-leaf''.[162] Two more were reversed, combined, and added to the text in 1836.[163] Most of these, as it happens, were from Jean Paul Richter's *Geist*—one more way of adding

[159] MS B f 64 (36:390).
[160] MS B f 70 (36:101). He followed this with another passage (36:102) taken from the Baxter.
[161] MS B f 73. EC's ms is VCL BT 25.
[162] 36:117, *TT* (1835) I 88 and n.
[163] 36:583, *TT* (1835) II 258–9.

by accident to Coleridge's reputation for plagiarism. The leaf was torn from the workbook, probably when Henry was preparing *Literary Remains* and the second edition of *Table Talk*.

Aware that he had come along when his uncle's earlier brilliance had been dulled somewhat by years and illnesses, Henry wished to capture as far as he could the range in tone as well as topic. A "retrospect" in the *Christian Observer*, attributable to the Reverend Thomas A. Methuen, drew upon *Table Talk* for its list of Coleridge's characteristics as a talker: conversational fluency; sprightly, occasionally severe, sayings; imagination; classical wealth; gigantic memory; theological views; and religious character.[164] Among the elements in the range caught by Henry but unspecified by Methuen are a wealth of knowledge, interest, and perception concerning English literature and English history, particularly of the seventeenth century; areas of European history and literature, especially but not solely theological or religious; Biblical as distinct from theological views; political theory and contemporary politics; the anecdotal, comic and good-humoured as well as "severe"; sociological observation; as much science as Henry could absorb; and *obiter dicta*, sometimes wry, sometimes buoyant, concerning current verse and fiction. To achieve this range Henry kept both ear and eye open. When the manuscript record of Coleridge's discussion of Whigs and Tories on 28 January 1832 could be amplified from a letter Henry received from Coleridge in May of that year, the published versions included the amplification.[165] Lacking the opportunity to hear Coleridge's last words, Henry borrowed appropriate words to end the table-talk from a letter of 1827 to Derwent.[166]

Going through Coleridge's notebooks in 1835–6 in search of materials for *Literary Remains*, Henry decided that some entries were more appropriate for the second edition of *Table Talk* than for "Omniana", possibly because he thought them especially characteristic.[167] It seems probable that the small "T.T." above some of these entries in Coleridge's notebooks was usually a notation of Henry's in 1835–6 of suitability for *Table Talk*, even though he included some of them instead among the "Omniana" of *Literary Remains*. Beginning in 1834 or 1835, he drew a

---

[164] Πίστις "Retrospect of Friendly Communication with the Poet Coleridge" *Christian Observer* XLIV (May 1845) 257–63. After quoting Staël, he modified her remark (259): "On the whole, perhaps, his vast conversational powers were too little exercised in *dialogue*".

[165] 36:348, *TT* (1835) II 22; MS B f 55ᵛ; *CL* VI 905.

[166] 36:664 from *CL* VI 705. The date is conjectural. The fragment is at VCL; when DC gave it to HNC is not known.

[167] E.g. *CN* III 3497, 3554, 3938, 4128, 4304; cf *TT* 36:116, 362, 509.

vertical line through each item in his own workbooks that he prepared for
publication in *Table Talk* or *Literary Remains*. Some of these are single
lines down the page when everything on the page appears in *Table Talk*
(1835). No line is present for items not prepared for publication by him.
Separate, differing lines are present for items he published after 1835.
From these three variations, it seems probable that he drew the vertical
lines at the time of transcribing from the workbooks in expectation of
publication. Such lines are present for all items that survive in MS F,
which is a collection of scraps cut from the revised manuscript at the instigation of various members of the family who objected to this entry or
that. MS F seems to tell us that Henry, not a clerk, transcribed for *Table
Talk*. Once he had obtained fuller access to the notebooks, he ceased to
rely on his miscellaneous transcriptions in the workbooks—from *Reliquiae Baxteriana*, for example—for the texts he published.[168]

Among other changes for the revised manuscript, Henry altered a substantial portion of the dates. He adjusted the dates for three discernible
reasons. Occasionally he chose to consolidate remarks on the same subject where his original record shows a return to the subject after a period
of days or years. As the earliest entries were individually lean and of little
bulk collectively, he moved parts of later entries to the earliest dates.
There are in fact few instances of this change, but from these few the purpose is evident. Most of all, he broke up the large blocks of talk from a
single day and created new dates, usually successive to the actual date of
record, for more even distribution over the calender. This change has the
effect, probably incidental, of making it seem that the sessions with
Coleridge came more frequently than they did. Distribution has also the
effect, probably not incidental, of lightening the printed page. His handling of 21 July 1832 seems a clear example of his freedom with dates
for the purpose of punctuation to the eye of the reader.[169] In revision (MS
F) he created the date 24 July for Coleridge's remarks of the 21st concerning his opposition to the slave trade in 1796. When disapproval by
his advisers caused the omission of this entry from the printed versions,
he retained the date 24 July for Coleridge's remarks on the futility of the
new infant schools.[170] By a piece of isolated mischief, he transferred to
Earl Grey under date of 20 March 1831 what had been recorded of
Jacques Necker on 14 August 1831.[171] Where dates survive on the scraps

---

[168] When he acknowledged notes from
JTC for *TT* he had laid out plans also for
LR: "What I shall do is, to set a fellow to
transcribe the parts roughly designated
by me first on even pieces of paper, &
then consider & class them afterwards."

HNC to JTC 13 Aug 1834, BM Add MS
47557 f 108.
[169] MS B ff 67–9.
[170] MS B f 68ᵛ (36:406).
[171] MS B f 49 (36:293).

of MS F, they are identical with the original dates in the workbooks, thereby suggesting that the distribution of dates occurred for the most part at a late point in the preparation of *Table Talk*.[172] If it occurred after John Murray or his representatives had seen the manuscript, punctuation to the eye might have been the principal consideration.

The creation of smaller units by distribution of a day's long talk over several dates proved so successful that references to the *Table Talk* have usually, for more than a century, been identified by the published dates of the entries concerned. Publication now of the original dates in the manuscript may in this sense seem inconvenient, but relatively few of Henry's changes of date involved changes in sequence of entries, although he did alter the order of entries within dates as a procedure separate from the change in date. Cross-references in the present edition between the manuscript and published versions should ease the burden of transition to new dates. (See also Appendix V, Table of Comparative Dates, vol II, below.) Luckily, few scholarly arguments have hinged on a specific date in Coleridge's utterances to his nephew. It has been wrong to assume on the basis of *Table Talk* that Coleridge expressed a given opinion on a given date, but scholars fortunately have realised that *Table Talk* as published rarely opens totally new vistas on Coleridge's thought. The dates have been a convenience without diverting intellectual history into gross error. Nevertheless, the present edition is a watershed for reference, even within *The Collected Works of S. T. Coleridge*.

Perhaps it is equally fortunate that close linguistic study of *Table Talk* has been minimal. Stylistic changes between the manuscripts and the printed versions scream out less than changes of date, but a student comparing the manuscript version with previously printed versions will notice immediately both verbal and substantive changes. Sometimes, as in the early entry on *Othello*, Henry enlivened the printed version by inserting connectives and pauses: "whereas", "in fact", "you see", "See how utterly".[173] From a sentence on the inheritance of Christianity through the mother, at the end of the first long paragraph in MS A, the words "and with the tone of her voice" were omitted in MS E but expanded in 1835 to read "and with the first-remembered tones of her blessed voice".[174] A clause on John Dryden (indebted to Pope) progresses in the manuscripts from "he *gets* warm" through "his chariot wheels *get* hot".[175] Such verbal changes occur in clusters throughout

---

[172] E.g. the entry on Harriet Macklin, not published, is dated 15 Aug 1832 in MS B 72ᵛ and in MS F. *TT* (1835) II 94–5 had reached 19 Aug in the redating of the 9–11 Aug sequence.

[173] MS A p 99, 6 Jan 1823 (36:1–2).
[174] MS A p 97; MS E 11 (36:28).
[175] MS B f 108, 23 Oct 1833 (36:601).

Henry Nelson Coleridge's work. Are they his improvements or attempts at restoration of what was originally heard? Sometimes one, no doubt, and sometimes the other. Probably some of them, though not restorations of what was originally heard, come from the rhythm of Coleridge's voice when he returned to the same subject at a later date. In any event, Henry's chief effort was not to recapture the exact words, but to convey Coleridge's thought with verbal approximations to his force of expression.

Most of the parlour Latin, absent from the manuscripts, enters in 1835. Hearers with Greek usually included more Greek phrases than Latin tags in their reports of what Coleridge said, in conformity with Henry's manuscript version rather than with the *Table Talk* of 1835 or 1836. Most of the specific examples of Latin—*siccissimis pedibus, ad hominem et pro tempore, Gradus ad Philosophiam*—were probably intruded by Henry at will, but their intrusion may restore something of the flavour that Coleridge's letters and notations, as well as his publications, suggest he gave normally to his talk. Educated hearers may have noticed the Greek, which was usually pertinent to the topic, whereas the Latin tags would have seemed an ordinary decoration in educated speech.

With the question of restoration or invention we reach an embarrassment. Some of the most famous sentences in the published *Table Talk* are not in the manuscripts: "To see him act, is like reading Shakespeare by flashes of lightning."[176] "I have a smack of Hamlet myself, if I may say so."[177] "Upon my word, I think the Œdipus Tyrannus, the Alchemist, and Tom Jones, the three most perfect plots ever planned."[178] The remark about "a smack of Hamlet" may not at first have seemed pertinent to the discussion of *Hamlet*, though memorable enough. Or Henry may have heard it on another occasion and remembered it when transcribing his original record. The image of Kean is supported by William Jerdan's testimony and has the true Esteesian ring. So also has the pronouncement on the three perfect plots, although it seems dragged from elsewhere into the contrast of Fielding and Richardson; Henry had no later opportunity of hearing the remark in a different conversation.

[176] 36:34, 27 Apr 1823; MS A p 102. George Rowell calls it "the century's most quoted piece of dramatic criticism". Introduction *Victorian Dramatic Criticism* (1971) xiii. William Jerdan, in *Literary Gazette* 23 May 1835 p 321, says of the passage as printed that it "was uttered in our company"; he offers a substitute for one phrase, but takes no exception to the sentence on flashes of lightning. We may take it that HNC (a) heard C say it on a later occasion, (b) was informed by another who heard C say it, or (c) heard it in 1823, but remembered it later than 1827.

[177] 36:80, 24 Jun 1827; MS B f 4.

[178] 36:661, 5 Jul 1834; MS C p 41. Another piece of wit not in the workbooks is dropped into a paragraph on Junius: "Horne Tooke and a long sentence seem the only two antagonists that were too much for him." 36:542, 1 Jul 1833; MS B f 96ᵛ.

Many of the modifications between the workbooks and the printed page remove or meliorate possible offences, especially where those prospectively offended would be otherwise more friendly than Whigs or Unitarians could be expected to be. Harsh language concerning the "ignorant zealotry & sordid vulgarity of the leaders of the day", the Whig ministers, could stand.[179] In correspondence concerning *Table Talk*, Henry seems totally unconscious of falsification in meliorating some statements but leaving occasional belligerences unchanged. In an antithetical sentence on the geologist Lyell, Coleridge may have said "most of what he denies is false", as the manuscript affirms, but the revision of 1835 removes an ambiguity and thus clarifies Coleridge's meaning: "He affirms a great deal that is true, and he denies a great deal which is equally true . . .".[180] Sometimes the suppression of a proper name accomplishes the dramatic sense of an opponent's presence along with anonymity, as when "you" replaces a newspaper in "What the Times says about the quarrel in the United States is sophistical".[181] If Henry's prudential revisions in MS F had in mind his own advisers and Murray's as much as the public beyond them, he was wrong only in not being prudent enough for the advisers.

After setting to work on the table-talk soon after Coleridge's funeral, Henry was able to thank John on 13 August 1834 for a first instalment of notes and to promise an important step in his procedure: "I shall submit the Table Talk, when drawn out, to you, Lockhart & Green—three very distinct represīves [respresentatives] of feelings & opinion. My own capital judgment will come last."[182] A month later he apparently sent John his workbooks along with (presumably) a first portion of his revision. John replied in alarm on the 18th:

My dear Henry,
  I have read some not all the books I return—I wish I had had more time—to read them all—You will not be surprised to hear me say, that I have been electrified by many of the paragraphs & delighted and instructed by more.
  But in my opinion you *must omit many of these*—as at present advised, I think many decidedly wrong and pernicious—that that is not all, thousands will read these *dicta*, who will never read their justification, or explanation, or modification—what will be the consequence—1st many pious Christians (infirmiores paullo if you please) will be offended—some will be perverted—some will pervert.
  In editing these dicta depend on it you have S T C's reputation and his means

---

[179] MS B f 77, 20 Jan 1833 (36:454).
[180] MS B f 94, 29 Jun 1833 (36:531). In revising, HNC would have seen that he had originally begun the sentence

with "A great deal" instead of with "Much".
[181] MS B f 84, 8 Apr 1833 (36:484).
[182] BM Add MS 47557 f 108.

at least of doing harm where he is wrong, sometimes even where he is right, more in your power than Mr Green will have.

Are some of the subjects here such as OUGHT to be printed upon from a note of half a conversation—do consider this? Inspiration for instance—take the note about the Gadarene Possession, & look at St Luke c. VIII, especially v. 28th—ask yourself did the possessed say, what is there recorded—if he did what becomes of the note—if he did not, what becomes of St Luke's VERACITY—I don't say ACCURACY—

I feel so much fellow interest in this with you, that I hope you will sell or print nothing, till I can talk over the whole matter with you.

My pencillings are mere hasty "jottings"—wrong or right—but do let me *talk* with you.

Yours ever
JTC.

Septr 18th 1834[183]

Henry must have received a second note immediately. On the 21st, in response to John's misgivings, he defended both Coleridge and himself:

I am much obliged by your note—you must read the whole collection, the latter part of w̄ch is more literary & less liable to exception. Some of your objections proceed from your not having graduated in Trismegisti philosophia—as where you object to the possibility of ~~con~~ propositions involving a contradiction in terms being each true—This very contradiction according to the syllogistic logic confined to the finite forms of the Understanding, & yet, by our inner certainty of the truth, evincing the necessity of referring them to a higher logic—that of Ideas & the Reason—is S. T. C.'s definition, or characteristic of an Idea—See Aids to Reflection p. 226 in the old edition & Church & State p. 12—He cites, *Before* Abraham *was*, I *am*, & &c. But as to all the notes on Inspiration & the genuineness of books of the Bible—I upon the whole agree with you upon their omission. It will make a hole in the materials, but that must not be regarded. All these things will appear ere long—but at least I shall not have the responsibility, & what is more, they will appear from his own pen. One or two short notes may still remain. You know his view of Possession is Lardner's & others—Lardner argues it in an aside & comes to a very ⟨clear⟩ conclusion for common readers— S. T. C.'s views are not peculiar in this—but in furnishing a view of what is called inspiration, w̄ch leaves the character & authority of the text in harmony with that conclusion. Not to lose time, I have sent back the books, wishing you to peruse them all accurately—& if you can send them to town by about the first week in October—that will do. I shall do nothing with them at present. I think your meñdum should be printed, however we will look at it. . . . I start for Bath tomorrow morning,—& begin at Bradford Tuesday.[184]

John devised a system of crosses to indicate on MS F three degrees of advisability against publishing. The surviving scraps show that one cross

---

[183] UT ms.

[184] BM Add MS 47557 f 114. On 2 Nov HNC assured RS: "I will take care to publish nothing w̄ch can hurt private feelings, or w̄ch indeed S. T. C. might not have said or written in his own person openly." UT ms.

was at least sometimes enough to secure omission from print. One of the later censors used a similar system of × 's, so that entries in MS F occasionally bear notations like × × × + + in the margin. But again, one × was sometimes enough to bury an entry concerning practices of the clergy, Biblical inspiration, or members of the Coleridge family. Edward and Derwent seem to have been the next censors after John; their verbal objections or queries, where recoverable, appear in the annotations to the present edition. As they were written in pencil on the verso of the leaf preceding the leaf commented on, and only the entries subsequently omitted have survived from MS F, few of these queries have been recovered.

Because of the censorship by Henry's brothers and others close to the project, the present edition includes as no earlier edition does personal remarks on Wordsworth, Southey, and Scott; anecdotes about Coleridge's father, mother, and brother George; comments on his own poems; axioms concerning sexual passion; and a wide range of Biblical criticism. Of the last, as Henry pointed out to John, we have had the essence from works published by Henry in 1838–40 and by others who came after him. In eliminating what seemed the most daring of Coleridge's comments on the Bible, the circle overruled one of his basic assumptions, forcefully expressed in a notebook entry of 1804:

So far from deeming it, in a religious point of view, criminal to spread doubt of God, immort. & virtue . . . in the *minds* of individuals, I seem to see in it a *duty*—lest men by taking the *words* for granted never attain the feeling or the true *faith* . . . whereas to *doubt* has more of faith, nay even to disbelieve—than that blank negation of all such thoughts & feelings which is the lot of the Herd of Church and Meeting Trotters.[185]

The scraps of MS F represent Henry's conciliatory approach to those in the circle who took another view. His original transcription of the passages represented what his brothers regarded as Coleridge's lack of caution and Henry's usual temerity.

On 25 September 1834, in Melksham, Wiltshire as revising barrister, Henry wrote to Murray:

I shall probably wish to publish soon a volume of selected specimens of S. T. Coleridge's Table Talk wc̄h have been preserved by me. I set a high value on them for their own merit, & also for their relative interest, in respect of Mr Coleridge's name & now rapidly increasing public. You have my offer of the MS, & I have no objection to its ⟨being⟩ submitted to Mr Lockhart; but the contents, consisting of short paragraphs, are so peculiarly liable to quotation &c, that I must

---

[185] *CN* II 2296.

be particular with you as to not letting the MS. ~~to~~ be exposed except to a confidential person.[186]

Whatever the intermediate exchanges, he wrote again on 1 December:

I send with this my MS. of "Specimens of the Table Talk of the late S. T. C." With the exception of some few additional notes, & a preface or introduction of a sheet & a half or two sheets, the copy is fit for the press as it is. The little poems at the end were omitted by accident in the late edition of S. T. C.'s poetical works, & the exclusive right to them is not mine—but their present publication is permitted.

Now my wish & intention are to sell this work, if I can get what I think it is, under the circumstances, fairly worth; & with that view I offer it to you in the first place. And I shall be obliged by your letting me ⟨have⟩ the MS. back again with your decision ⟨upon it⟩ with as little delay as may be convenient to yourself. I need not request you to keep the MS. safe & secret.

On the 13th Henry asked, on the advice of "some of my friends who have read the work", four hundred guineas in two instalments, the second to be paid six months from the day of publication. On the same day Murray answered, "I agree, according to your proposal"—to pay the amount asked in three instalments, the last to come twelve months from publication. He added a second paragraph: "I wish you would appoint some day about 4 o clock to meet Mr Lockhart at the Athenaeum, as he has read the MS & has one or two things to suggest."[187] On the 18th Henry gave assurances on this point: "I have talked with Mr Lockhart this morning touching the Table Talk, & will attend to his suggestions. I am ready for the printer when ever you choose to give directions." He had further news for Murray on the 13th: "I have added a small paper of further reminiscences from my brother, & I think it probable that before printing I shall be able to get some more." If the "further reminiscences" were John's notes from April 1811, any that arrived later (if used) were inserted as a footnote.[188]

Henry had been considering the addition of table-talk remembered by still other listeners. On 3 September he had written to Thomas Poole: "If you can give me any *dicta* of S. T. C. with dates as near as possible, I wish you would, as I think of making a miscellaneous chapter of Table Talk from other sources than my own." Readers of the present edition may smile at the request for "dates as near as possible", but Henry had

---

[186] One of some forty-five letters from HNC to John Murray, 1826–41, retained by John Murray Publishers Ltd with others from SC. This correspondence shows that Murray regularly sent to HNC copies of *QR*, which would then be available to C.

[187] UT ms.

[188] I.e. 36:666–7: *TT* (1835) II 343–57; and note to 36:310, *TT* (1835) I 243n–4.

in mind the ascertaining of the decade, or some such period of time, in which Coleridge had expressed a remembered opinion or observation. In the same letter he proposed that Poole write "a memoir—short & leading", but preferably with a chronological record of "whatever you remember remarkable in the sayings & doings of S. T. C.—recording the opinions & feelings of the time", to serve as a prefix to *Table Talk*.[189] On the 17th he was agreeing that such materials could be sent to Green.[190] A year later Poole sent a portion of what was desired.[191]

Henry's plans for his Preface were at least partly formed by 2 November, when he wrote to Southey of "a selection from a volume of recollections of S. T. C.'s conversations, with some notes & a preface, in wĉh I must needs say a word to that abandoned man, De Quincey". It was in this letter that he made the rash promise: "I will take care to publish nothing wĉh can hurt private feelings".[192]

In December Henry sent "a good deal" of copy to the printer and corresponded with Murray about the illustrations. At the beginning of 1835, printing was held up for a month or more, probably to wait on copy from Henry. On 3 January he wrote to Sara: "I am writing my preface, & get on very draggingly, & unsatisfactorily with it; but something of the sort must be done, & after I get back, the printing will, no doubt, proceed rapidly, as Murray will have it come out with the next Qu[arterly]."[193] The hope of having Poole's memoir may have been one cause of delay in Henry's Preface; by April, waiting on Poole as a cause for delay gave way to the need Henry felt to answer unfavourable proleptic treatment of *Table Talk* in the *Edinburgh Review* and *Westminster Review*. A later reviewer explained a final delay as arising "from a wish to make arrangements that would secure the advantage of copyright in America".[194] Henry's Preface was dated from Lincoln's Inn 11 May 1835, less than two weeks before publication.

Henry was not enthusiastic about the two illustrations chosen by Murray: (1) as frontispiece to Volume I, a lithograph by Louis Haghe (1806–85) from the portrait by Thomas Phillips (1770–1845) owned by Murray, engraved with Coleridge's complimentary-close-with-signature and mounted;[195] (2) as frontispiece to Volume II, the lithograph by George

---

[189] BM Add MS 35344 ff 110–11; the first sentence quoted is a postscript on the flap.
[190] Ibid ff 112–13.
[191] Ibid 118–24. Poole had corresponded with SC as well as HNC from the time of C's death: *Poole* II 294–300, 303–8; Poole to SC, totally co-operative,

13 Nov 1834: UT ms.
[192] UT ms.
[193] UT ms.
[194] *Dublin University Magazine* VI (Jul 1835) 1.
[195] On 17 Aug HNC wrote to JTC that he had seen Phillips's copy of the portrait, for which he asked "sixty guineas,

Scharf (1788–1860) from his own water-colour of Coleridge's room at The Grove, engraved from a copy owned by J. H. Green.[196] In presenting copies of the published volumes to Poole on 25 May 1835, Henry lamented, "The lithograph is vile; but I have not to answer for it."[197]

In April 1835 Murray paid A. Spottiswoode of New-Street-Square £159.11.9 for printing 2000 copies. Eleven copies were sent to Stationers' Hall for copyright, fifty copies were presented, and 1939 copies sold for £913.6.0, with a profit on 30 June 1838 of £92.8.8. Here was a work of commercial success such as Coleridge's prose had never enjoyed.

Enough copies were sold soon after publication to put a second edition immediately in view. In August Henry was "painfully doing a dull article on Hartley's Worthies for the Q.R.", specifically "for the money coming in aptly in the dead noon of vacation".[198] In September at Heath's Court, with *Literary Remains* as well as a new edition of *Table Talk* pressing upon him, he saw "but very little time for doing any thing to the Esteesian papers".[199] His clerk was busy transcribing materials for *Literary Remains*, but Henry must have found time for his own progress toward the end of the year, for he was able to write to Murray on 19 January 1836:

I send the first vol. of the Table Talk, corrected, & with several new passages inserted—enough to warrant you in calling this an edition with additions, if you like. I have cut out from the Preface all the matter of a temporary or controversial interest, &, now reduced to half its length, it contains that only wᶜh is proper & necessary for a permanent introduction to the work. I have done the same with the notes. The other volume you shall have similarly treated in a few days.

It would save time & trouble, if you will direct a correction of the proofs ac-

---

twenty less than the price for the original", but would probably ask more after C's death. BM Add MS 47557 f 109. HNC thought the best portrait that by Allston owned by Josiah Wade. Haghe was the first to practise lithography successfully in Britain. The portrait itself, painted in 1818, is reproduced as the frontispiece to *Friend (CC)* I. It is still in the possession of John Murray Publishers Ltd. SC wrote to DC 22 Jan 1852: "The frontispiece to the Table Talk is odious, and yet Phillips' picture—the original at Salston House—is very pleasing." UT ms.

[196] HNC to Murray 22, 26 Dec 1834. The water-colour, now in the Coleridge Cottage, Nether Stowey, is reproduced

in *CM (CC)* opposite I cxv; the lithograph is reproduced from a signed proof in *CL* opposite VI 659.

[197] BM Add MS 35344 ff 114–15.

[198] HNC to JTC 11 Aug 1835, BM Add MS 47557 f 117; cf f 118ᵛ. See *QR* LIV (Sept 1835) 330–55; HC to SC, *HCL* 177 ("It looks too like a family concern. I think the praise excessive, but let that pass."). The praise is not let pass by Elizabeth Story Donno "The Case of the Purloined Biography: Hartley Coleridge and Literary Protectivism" *Bulletin of Research in the Humanities* LXXXII (1979) 469–70.

[199] HNC to SC 12, 17 Sept 1835, UT ms.

cording to the accompanying copy—the same to be sent to me, with the name of the printer. After that there need be no delay.

He continued his excisions and additions through Volume II. On 10 March he told John that the second edition in one volume was "nearly finished in printing".[200]

Murray's account books show a payment to Spottiswoode in June for printing 2000 copies. Edward Finden re-engraved the frontispiece portrait. For advertising £50.4.1 was added to the £57.18.7 spent in advertising the first edition. But sales of the second edition dropped off rapidly. In June 1838 there were 1177 on hand; after Henry's death in 1843 there were 822 copies, but what had been loss in 1838 had become a profit of £26.8.10. These profits increased by £69.13.0 when 796 copies were remaindered to H. G. Bohn.

For the second edition, Henry removed from the Preface his responses to reviews and his denunciation of De Quincey's charges in *Tait's Edinburgh Magazine* that Coleridge was a frequent plagiarist. In the rebuttal of De Quincey, Henry had relied mostly on a defence by Julius Hare published in the January number of the *British Magazine*.[201] From the table-talk itself he dropped conjectures concerning Shakespeare's text that had been rejected in letters to him from Alexander Dyce; he eliminated an entry called by the *Westminster Review* a "coarse, indecent attack on Malthus" and a passage (with a note by himself) considered libellous by Sir Francis Head, whom it concerned.[202] He omitted an uncomplimentary reference to Sotheby's translation of Virgil's Georgics; George Burnett's name; claims of journalistic success denied by Daniel Stuart; and similar bits to which objection had been taken during 1835.[203] He meliorated other passages, and made verbal changes throughout. He added a large number of new entries, mostly brief and mostly from Coleridge's notebooks or marginalia. As he says in the letter of 19 January to Murray, he dropped several footnotes of temporary interest, some written in further rebuttal to reviews and journals. He rescued as new annotation some of the defences carried away in reducing the Preface; for example, the fuller explanation of Coleridge's remarks on Plato and Xenophon, which the *Edinburgh Review* had declared contradictory.[204] Instead of the miscellaneous poems at the close, he substituted the letter to Adam

[200] BM Add MS 47557 f 121ᵛ.
[201] *TT* (1835) I xxxix–lxix.
[202] *TT* (1835) I 128 (35:170), II 88 (35:426), 295–6 (35:625), 306–8 (35:635).
[203] *TT* (1835) I 74 (36:88), 157 (36:215), 173 (36:228).
[204] *TT* (1836) 9n, 26 (36:15, 50) from *TT* (1835) I lxvn–lxvi.

Steinmetz Kennard, which he had transcribed in MS C probably with *Table Talk* in mind.

The text of this second edition, except for the addition of two notes by Sara in the third edition of 1851 and gradual accumulation of small errors, is the text by which the *Table Talk* had been known to readers for more than a century and a half. After 1850 the demand for *Table Talk* rose again quickly and remained strong. There were editions or reprintings in 1851 (2000 copies), 1852 (1000 copies), 1858 (500 copies), 1865 (500 copies), 1870 (750 copies), 1874 (750 copies), and 1882 (1250 copies). In 1884, although John Murray Ltd sold the stereotype plates to Grant of Edinburgh and editions appeared simultaneously with the imprints of George Bell and Sons (Bohn's Standard Library) and George Routledge and Sons (Morley's Universal Library), Murray retained the steel plate for the frontispiece and printed 1000 copies in March. Walter Scott and Oxford University Press were among later publishers of the work. Although *Biographia Literaria* has been the critical favourite of the twentieth century, *Table Talk*, in the words of Lucy Watson, "has been perhaps the most popular of all books either relating to or written by S. T. Coleridge".[205]

The first edition of 1835 is much closer to Henry Nelson Coleridge's manuscripts than the second edition, and the chief difference between them is the addition in the second edition of materials from written sources, so that the intervening century and a half has been inadvertently mistaken in following the second edition (or third) rather than the first. *Table Talk* (1836) does, however, include Henry Nelson Coleridge's considered revisions, and its extremity of difference from the manuscripts makes it appropriate for reprinting as an appendix in *The Collected Works of S. T. Coleridge* along with the manuscript version. Above all, it is the text known to generations of readers. But no future generation can neglect the manuscript version now published. It is representative of the need for a scholarly edition that the reference to "Skelton's Richard Sparrow" has been neither corrected nor challenged in any edition, although Dyce called Henry Nelson Coleridge's attention to the error.[206] For another example, in entry 36:49 (1 May 1823) "John, xv.28" is incorrectly interpolated for John 14.28, and no subsequent editor has corrected it. More important than the correction of careless error, the manuscripts supply names where the sensibilities of 1835 and 1836

[205] *C at H* 94. *Aids to Reflection* and perhaps other works by C would have maintained an equal readership in the United States through most of the nineteenth century.

[206] *TT* (1835) I 60 (36:72); MS B f 1ᵛ (10 Mar 1827).

required blanks. Occasionally, also, names can be supplied even though Henry failed to make the proper identification. If the manuscript version is not ideal, it must be utilised in preparing any edition truthful to H. N. Coleridge's own intentions.

REVIEWS OF 1835

Because of the lapse of months between printing and publication, with the premature appearance of the official review by John Gibson Lockhart in the *Quarterly*, the daily newspapers noticed and quoted *Table Talk* before most of the monthlies and quarterlies had their chance. William Cobbett quoted Coleridge as sounding American.[207] Henry Taylor, who achieved sudden celebrity with *Philip van Artevelde* in June 1834 and was sensitive to competition, remembered that "the favourite theme of every magazine and journal" for the next year and more was Coleridge—less like the usual attention after a celebrated death, Taylor said, than "like the noisy inebriety of an Irish funeral".[208] *Table Talk* appeared during this inebriety.

Lockhart's official review has been cited earlier on the reasons for the lack of Boswellian drama in *Table Talk* and on Coleridge's relative cheerfulness concerning the condition of England after passage of the Reform Bill.

We ourselves happened to have several long conversations with him . . . not many months before his illness confined him to his chamber; and then, in the open air, walking by the sea-side, his tone of prediction was undoubtedly more hopeful than the reader of his sick-bed *talk* might be able to conjecture. We think it right to record that he more than once expressed his belief that, under the circumstances in which the Reform bill had placed the country, there was much more likelihood of good than of evil results from extending still further the electoral suffrage. The great mischief, he always said, had been placing too much power in one particular class of the population, the class above and below which attachment to our old institutions in church and state is most prevalent.[209]

Lockhart added Joseph Spence's *Observations, Anecdotes, and Characters of Books and Men* (1820) to the *ana* with which *Table Talk* could worthily compete. Like all the reviewers after him, and according to the general practice of the era, he quoted liberally from the volumes under

---

[207] In repudiating this view as not comprehensive, HNC rejected equally the opposite generalisation: "It suits the M. Chronicle in a paragraph I saw the other day, to say that S. T. C. vituperated Parliamentary Reform: no such thing, he only abused this Reform Bill— a very different thing, I conceive." HNC to Poole 15 Jun 1835. BM Add MS 35344 ff 116–16ᵛ.

[208] *Autobiography of Henry Taylor 1800-1875* (2 vols 1885) I 191.

[209] *QR* LIII (Feb 1835) 79–103; quotation p 103.

consideration. His own favourites he classified under the headings of Shakespeare; other writers; politics, including popular education; and "the actual business of life—men and manners in general".[210]

Most of the reviewers of *Table Talk* had heard Coleridge discourse. For fifteen years nearly every literate person had known somebody who could have secured a welcome at The Grove. Two who did not boast of personal knowledge, Thomas Perronet Thompson (1783–1869) in the *Westminster Review* and Herman Merivale (1806–1874) in the *Edinburgh Review*, abused the work in April, early enough for Henry Nelson Coleridge to answer in his Preface. Thompson had access only to Lockhart's review in the *Quarterly* and to the passages quoted there.[211] He condemned Coleridge as a turncoat who attacked economists and defended slavery: "the Tory sophist was a man of little soul", erected into a higher being to satisfy the needs of a party characterised by "the remoteness from useful truth and the clinging to all harmful darkness".[212]

Merivale, a barrister of the Inner Temple since 1832, probably kept in mind the nephew, his brother Mr Serjeant Coleridge (made Justice of the King's Bench in 1835), and their brother-in-law the justice Sir John Patteson as much as he regarded the sayings of the poet. His review in the *Edinburgh* is on the whole fair, though chilly in tone. Coleridge had achieved "that celebrity as a converser, or rather a discourser, which rendered him, during the latter years of his life, again an object of public curiosity and interest".

Conversation, in the ordinary sense of the word, was not to be met with in his company. His visitors came only for the purpose of hearing the dissertations of a lecturer. . . .

The theory of dreams and apparitions; the doctrines of phrenology, animal magnetism, and similar semi-medical questions; the singular forms in which enthusiasm or other disturbing causes have influenced the passive faculties of the mind;—all these topics . . . afforded a frequent exercise to his wandering fancy. On such subjects, and on the Platonic, or Kantian theory of mind, to which they invariably led him, he would hold forth to his audience, mazed and half-entranced. . . .

We do not deny, that the editor of these volumes has acquitted himself in a manner highly creditable. . . . He has endeavoured to reduce to the form of aphorisms the sayings of one of the most eloquent, but least concise and definite of reasoners; and has extracted in this manner, in unconnected fragments, much which was evidently wrapt up in the texture of some fine-spun but continuous theory.[213]

[210] Ibid 97.

[211] Jerdan said that the *Westminster* reviewer "reviewed the first reviewer out of the materials he himself had furnished". *Literary Gazette* 23 May 1835 p 321.

[212] *Westminster Review* XXII (Apr 1835) 531–7; quotation p 537. HNC responded in *TT* (1835) I xxxin.

[213] *Ed Rev* LXI (Apr 1835) 129-35; quotations 130, 131, 133.

Henry Nelson Coleridge found in the review much to resent. Without any intention of "correcting all the mistakes of the Edinburgh Reviewer", he cited the misconstruing of Coleridge on Xenophon and Plato and rejected the reviewer's declaration that Coleridge was "an unconscionable plagiary, like Byron".[214] The following October, reviewing *Memoirs of the Life of the Right Honourable Sir James Mackintosh*, Francis Jeffrey took the opportunity to turn the contrast between Coleridge and Mackintosh on its head. He attacked fiercely the work of "the admiring, or rather idolizing, nephew", and accused the uncle of general incompetence needlessly prolonged.[215]

On 25 April *The Printing Machine; or, Companion to the Library and Register of Progressive Knowledge* reviewed *Edinburgh Review* No 123, with a rebuttal on *Table Talk*:

We think it is, upon the whole, the ablest of the numerous accounts of this extraordinary man that have appeared since his death—with the exception of the admirable series of papers by M. de Quincy in "Tait's Magazine," which, notwithstanding some things that may, perhaps, be excepted to, are the only exposition of the genius, the philosophy, and the personal history and character of Coleridge yet attempted, that in spirit and power is worthy of the subject.

Along the way, the reviewer took on Lockhart's review in contrast with Merivale's, which he found to be,

throughout, tolerant and liberal, and perfectly free from the party animosity and spite in which the writer of the paper on the same work in the last number of the "Quarterly Review" chose so plentifully, and with such singular bad taste, to indulge.[216]

Table Talk afforded literary reviews and magazines a special opportunity to memorialise or epitomise Coleridge's career. William Jerdan (1782–1869), editor of the *Literary Gazette*, gave the work a lead review on 23 May and a second instalment the following week. The first began: "This publication has made some noise in the political, polemical, and party periodicals, before it reached our sphere."[217] He praised Henry Nelson Coleridge for making of crumbs from the table "a feast worthy

---

[214] *TT* (1835) I lxv–lxviii.

[215] *Ed Rev* LXII (Oct 1835) 242–8; quotation p 243.

[216] III 275. A writer in the same *Printing Machine* (III 23) had said in a delayed review of Lamb's *Works* on 10 Jan 1835: "Even his friend Coleridge, who thought so profoundly, and much of whose poetry has so exquisite a finish, has left things behind him which may, in comparison with his more elaborate or hap- pier efforts, be said to be hastily or carelessly constructed; and since his death it has been somewhere stated that a few of his poems were all of his published compositions which, if he could have had his wish, he would have preserved."

[217] *The London Literary Gazette; and Journal of Belles Lettres, Arts, Sciences, &c* No 957 (23 May 1835) 321–2; No 958 (30 May 1835) 340–2.

of his friend and the public''. Jerdan claimed a greater acquaintance than one would suspect from other sources:

Coleridge we knew well, and many a delighted hour we have spent in his society. His sagacity was profound, his eloquence, when dissertating (for he rarely conversed), overpowering, though sometimes, even in linked sweetness, too long drawn out; his manner of telling anecdotes wonderfully playful and amusing; his sketches of character epigrammatic, and often terribly keen; and his very mysticism replete with the deepest thought and most original combinations.[218]

The second notice, besides quoting "brief and pithy remarks", told of an episode with Theodore Hook and two anecdotes heard from Coleridge by Jerdan, who later retold them in his reminiscences with changes suggesting that neither version was precise.[219] In a story about Coleridge's father trying to teach a schoolboy an ironic "Ha! ha! ha!" in a performance of his own play (previously declined by Garrick), the adolescent victim was first one of Coleridge's brothers and then Coleridge himself. In a story of a man who could quote at Cambridge in 1833 from Coleridge's "first lecture" some thirty years earlier, the person with a pleasing memory was first a clergyman from Devon or Cornwall and later "a working man". There were verbal changes in quoting Coleridge's praise of Theodore Hook as conversational wit. Jerdan had not returned for authority or consistency to his review; the variants in his two anecdotes were of no significance to him, and would not have been to Coleridge the teller as distinct from Coleridge in the rôle of hearer or reader. The point of each anecdote remained the same; to Jerdan the importance of the episode in Cambridge was that Coleridge proudly told each visitor in succession of the flattering encounter.

Like the *Literary Gazette* its chief competitor, the *Athenaeum*, gave *Table Talk* a two-part review on 23 and 30 May.[220] Charles Wentworth Dilke, who had taken over the *Athenaeum* in 1830, was determined to fight puffery by preventing any influence upon his reviewers from publishers or authors. Disciples of Coleridge, however, the "Apostles" Frederick Denison Maurice, John Sterling, and Richard Chenevix Trench, had controlled the new weekly until Dilke lifted the editorial and financial burdens from Sterling, and they remained active contributors in 1835.[221] The *Athenaeum* reviewer believed Henry Nelson Coleridge's method to be as successful as any listener to Coleridge could expect:

[218] P 321. Jerdan was not pleased (322) by the reference to the *Literary Gazette* in *TT* (1835) I 173 (36:228); he rejected C's theory of a revolution "when the press fell off from literature": 36:366, *TT* (1835) II 42.
[219] *Men I Have Known* (1866) 120–2.
[220] Pp 387–8, 406–7.
[221] Leslie Alexis Marchand *The Athenaeum: A Mirror of Victorian Culture*

. . . His conversation, if it is to be so called, was a self-evolved speculation of the moment, a thinking aloud. It required almost as comprehensive a mind as his own to follow out his chain of reasoning—his linked subtleties; and no man that ever lived, not Coleridge himself, could have recorded it fully and faithfully two hours after.[222]

The reviewer was surprised, however, by the recorded remarks on current issues: "We were quite startled at the crude bald dogmatism, which we found upon occasions reverently set down here—so utterly opposed to Coleridge's conciliatory and gentle nature." Avoiding the religious interests of Maurice, Sterling, and Trench, the review quoted from entries on contemporary writers and more extensively on poets of the past, for "every word uttered by Coleridge on this subject deserves to be treasured up as fine gold".[223] With the intention of publishing a life of Coleridge, Dilke sent a messenger to Paris to talk to Underwood and Mackenzie, who had known Coleridge in Malta; if he had received by May their word that "there was more humbug in Coleridge than in any man that ever was heard of",[224] their attitude is not reflected in the *Athenaeum* review. Underwood, like Jerdan, was struck by Coleridge's tendency to repeat the same remarks, as if spontaneously, to each visitor in succession.

In June a disciple in the *Monthly Review* began the dozen pages allotted to *Table Talk* with a paean to the poet and sage.[225] Coleridge "stands in the foremost rank among men of genius", as "one of the most extraordinary and worthy, even of that small phalanx"; poetic and metaphysical, an exemplar of the best in Christianity and humanity, he was "still greater and lovelier" than those virtues imply. "Indeed there was nothing ordinary about him." As a talker he had an "almost matchless voice", with "a splendid fluency of diction", "very subtle perceptions", and "glorious illustrations". His system "combined physiology and metaphysics". Totally unlike the plagiarist described by De Quincey in *Tait's*, "if ever there was an independent and original thinker, that man was Coleridge". After quoting mostly literary entries from Henry Nelson Coleridge's record, with a sprinkling of the Biblical, but before quoting at length from John Taylor Coleridge's account of his uncle's talk in 1811, the reviewer summarised his attitude toward *Table Talk* with guarded vagueness:

(Chapel Hill, N.C. 1941) 6–22, 105. The editor's marked file for 1835 was not available (ibid p ix).

[222] *Athenaeum* 23 May 1835 p 387.

[223] Ibid 407.

[224] Sir Charles Wentworth Dilke (1810–69) *The Papers of a Critic* (2 vols 1875) I 32.

[225] *M Rev* 4th s II (Jun 1835) 250–61.

There are many opinions in these volumes, from which we must dissent. There is also querulousness, owing, no doubt, to the discourser's bodily infirmities and his frequent dejection of mind. But one cannot read and examine any considerable portion of his Talk, without admiring and loving the man—without desiring to read more, and without feeling enlightened either by some discovery or warmed by a kindred glow of zeal, imagination, or piety. [226]

The *Dublin University Magazine* divided a long review between the numbers for July and September. [227] Few other reviewers had praised so specifically the *Table Talk* itself—"one of the most interesting books which we have ever read" and "two of the most amusing volumes in the language". After initial praise, the review turned to Coleridge's poetry, his prose works, and his residence with the Gillmans. Once more Coleridge was defended against the charges of plagiarism from De Quincey and the *Edinburgh Review*. [228] Returning to a general appraisal at the beginning of the September instalment, the reviewer insisted that *Table Talk* "must be regarded as a genuine part of his works, and in all fairness considered as a record of about the same value as any other volumes of his prose". [229] The reviewer intended "The highest praise to this book which it is possible a work of the kind can receive".

An equally laudatory review by John Abraham Heraud (1799–1887) appeared in *Fraser's Magazine* for August, near to the date when Heraud delivered his *Oration on the Death of Coleridge* at the Russell Institution. [230] He endorsed Henry Nelson Coleridge's Preface still again in refuting De Quincey's charge of plagiarism. We have "our own memoranda of the conversation of Coleridge", he said, with better notes on the Trinity than those in *Table Talk*; but he had for Henry Nelson Coleridge "a very profound esteem" and "high laud". [231]

In July the "Ecclesiastical Record" of the *British Critic, Quarterly Theological Review, and Ecclesiastical Record* (xviii 255) concentrated into two sentences praise for Coleridge, the two volumes, and their editor: ". . . it would be a grievous wrong not to mention with passing, but cordial and almost reverential praise, the 'Table Talk' of the late Mr. Coleridge; a publication, which contains outpourings of an overflowing mind, and is singularly interesting, from the oracles which that extraordinary man took an especial pleasure in delivering on the subject of re-

---

[226] Ibid 259.

[227] *Dublin University Magazine* VI (1835) 1–16, 250–67.

[228] Ibid 7–13, 251.

[229] Ibid 250. T. M. Raysor wrote a century later: "The selections from *Table Talk* are indispensable to any collection of Coleridge's criticism." *MC* 401n.

[230] *Fraser's Magazine for Town and Country* xii (Aug 1835) 123–35. John Abraham Heraud is well represented in *C Talker* 257–62, 394, 409.

[231] *Fraser's* 123, 128, 131.

ligion and ecclesiastical polity. The Editor, too, has done his part well, because he has not done too much; but has kept himself subordinate to his distinguished kinsman.'' Henry preserved a copy of this and of similar praise from the *British Magazine and Monthly Register of Religious and Ecclesiastical Information*: ''The editor of that work deserves the most affectionate thanks of all good men for having preserved to us so many precious records of the wisdom & power of this great philosopher.''[232]

The Reverend Thomas Frognall Dibdin (1776–1847), the bibliographer, quarrelled respectfully with Coleridge (as reported in *Table Talk*) in several footnotes before he reviewed *Table Talk*, Coleridge, and the reviewers all together in a long footnote attached to a reference to ''poetic prose'' in his own remarks on Coleridge as talker:

I speak in reference to Mr. Coleridge's conversation. A pretty correct notion may be formed of this conversation from the ''*Specimens* of Mr. Coleridge's *Table Talk*,'' just published, in two very *taking* duo-decimo volumes, with a portrait of the ''Talker'' prefixed. I saw Mr. Phillips in the execution, or rather, perhaps, finishing, of that portrait—and I thought it, and yet think it, abundantly resembling—''VIR IPSISSIMUS.'' Could sound have come from the lips, or action been imparted to the eye or hands of that painted portrait, there was COLERIDGE HIMSELF. The lithographised copy prefixed to the ''Specimens'' is unworthy of all parties concerned. The ''Table Talk'' itself has been copiously and vigorously reviewed in the Quarterly and Edinburgh Critical Journals. I incline to give the latter Review the preference; simply because it is more close, pointed, and pertinent. The Quarterly Reviewer seems himself to be both a poet and a relation; and, in parts, has allowed his attachment to control the exercise of impartiality. This is natural and pardonable, *per se*. On the other hand, the Magazines of *Blackwood* and *Tait* have been yet more copious in their notices of the celebrated deceased. The *pro* and the *con* have been exhibited with more formidable powers of contrast in these respective Periodicals. . . . Yet each critical artist gives us an interesting picture; and it is still a resemblance of the intellectual powers of Coleridge. If I might offer a very humble opinion upon this ''Table Talk'' (to which the preceding pages have more than once or twice referred with satisfaction), I should bring forward the expression of regret that the subject of POLITICS (cameleon-like and fleeting!) had been introduced; or comparisons instituted of great departed philosophers. When Mr. Coledridge [sic] talks of its requiring ''two Bacons to make one John Milton,'' or ''two or three such men as Newton and Galileo to make one Kepler''—it surely does imply the possession of something like superhuman powers in the judge, to institute such a comparison! Was Coleridge deeply read in the *Calculus* of Newton? And upon *what* book, after the *Bible*, does INSPIRATION ITSELF seem to brood as upon the *Principles* of Newton?[233]

[232] UT ms.

[233] *Reminiscences of a Literary Life* (2 vols 1836) I 255n–6.

In the reviews the rivalry of Coleridge and Mackintosh is seen for what it is, a religious war between objectively oriented empiricists and an opponent struggling in all his works and words to depress empiricism to a lower rung and keep it there by a God-given idealism of spirit. The utilitarians wished to see Coleridge as a puppy raised by others, in their yearning for a moon, to the highest rung of illusion. For the opponents of utilitarian empiricism, Coleridge was a prophetic hero; spirit was in danger, the Church was in danger and therefore learning (Coleridge's clerisy) was in danger, God was in danger, the Bible needed rescue. For the *Edinburgh* old scores were still unsettled. Coleridge's revaluations in political, ecclesiastical, and literary history faded behind his confrontations with the present; no reviewer thought his views of Richard Baxter or of Beaumont and Fletcher of prime interest to the reader. Apparently his revaluations of and within the seventeenth century had been absorbed in the world of letters and were no longer news.

It is difficult to praise the *Table Talk* in the terms of the *Dublin* reviewer, as "of about the same value as any other volumes of his prose", without charging those volumes, as it is conventional to charge them, with a failure of ordonnance. The *Dublin* reviewer, seeking a record of vital ideas well expressed, however discretely packaged the ideas, nevertheless would seem to share the spirit of Coleridge's own praise of volumes gathering the table-talk of Luther and Selden. Like Coleridge, he followed with pleasure the quick dartings of ambitious exploration powered by moral fervour.

Probably few since the first reviewers and Emerson have read the *Table Talk* through as a single adventure. Yet Henry Coleridge has caught something of adventure, partly in his own reach for a fuller and fuller record of a mind but more in the scudding flights of a human spirit in its aspiration for a worthy death. In that record of adventure, he was right to call upon the letter to Derwent—"I am dying"—as the last entry.

PERSONAL RESPONSES TO *TABLE TALK*

Most of the responses from individuals were more specific than the questions raised by reviewers. General assessments by individuals are more interesting than informative. The painter C. R. Leslie (1794–1859), who knew Coleridge well, averred in his recollections: "It is not the lot of any one, twice in his life, to meet with so extraordinary a man. I now read over and over again what his nephew has recorded of his conversation, and I can vouch for the exactness with which his manner is preserved in those precious little volumes.''[234] J. C. Hare (1795–1855) came to a quite different conclusion. He felt that only his friend John Sterling could have captured the strengths of Coleridge's conversations, "their depth, their ever varying hues, their sparkling lights, their oceanic ebb and flow; of which his published Table-talk hardly gives the slightest conception''.[235] Robert Southey formed immediately an opinion similar to Hare's: "S. T. C.'s 'Table Talk' came to me yesterday. . . . There was no week in which Coleridge's talk would not have furnished as much matter worthy of preservation as these two volumes contain. Henry Coleridge has kept marvellously clear of indiscretion in his perilous talk.''[236] Aside from seeing the value of not reporting all Coleridge said, Southey assumed that he had been often the subject of remarks he had rather not see in print. And we can be sure that Coleridge "in his perilous talk" said things about Southey that Henry Nelson Coleridge suppressed even from his workbooks. To Henry himself Southey sent a "kind acknowledgment of the Table Talk" with several factual corrections and captious queries that appear in the present edition as annotations to the respective entries involved.[237] According to Sara, in expressing his pleasure in the volumes Southey said to Henry, " 'You have dealt well with Dequincey & the Benthamite Reviewer' i.e. him of the Westminster.''[238]

Carlyle and Emerson took the volumes as representative of Coleridge. Froude's version of Carlyle's immediate confidence to his journal has been corrected:

Coleridge's Table Talk: insignificant; yet expressive of Coleridge. A great Possibility—that has not realized itself. Never did I see such apparatus got ready for thinking, and so little thought. He mounts scaffolding, pullies and tackle, gathers all the tools in the neighbourhood, with labour, with noise, demonstration, precept, abuse,—and sets three bricks. I do *not* honour the man; I pity him (with the *opposite* of contempt); see in him one glorious up-struggling ray (as it were), which perished, all but ineffectual, in a lax, languid, impotent *character* (*gemuth*): this is my theory of Coleridge,—very different from that of his admirers here.[239]

[234] Charles Robert Leslie *Autobiographical Recollections* ed Tom Taylor (2 vols 1860) I 44.

[235] Julius Charles Hare ed *Essays and Tales by John Sterling, with a Memoir of His Life* (2 vols 1848) I xv–xvi. Samuel Carter Hall (1800–89), declaring that nobody could have caught the "superabundance" in the way it was remembered, called *TT* (1835) "only a collection of scraps, chance-gathered". *A Book of Memories* (2nd ed 1871) 43.

[236] RS in *Correspondence of Henry Taylor* ed Edward Dowden (1888) 64. RS must really have written "perilous task".

[237] UT ms. HNC replied to RS 27 Jun 1835.

[238] SC to Mrs H. M. Jones c Jul 1835. UT Grantz 1149.

[239] Journal entry of 26 May 1835, quoted in Sanders "The Background of Carlyle's Portrait of Coleridge in *The Life of John Sterling*" *Bulletin of the John Rylands University Library of Manchester* LV (1973) 45–6.

Emerson, despite his disappointment from inability in 1833 to rouse Coleridge to new questions, stated briefly to his brother William on 27 July 1835 an opinion that may be taken as diametrically opposed to Carlyle's: "Coleridge's Table Talk is, I think, as good as Spence's or Selden's or Luther's; better."[240]

Most of Coleridge's friends from earlier days were appalled by the remarks Henry Nelson Coleridge reported concerning the Reform Bill. The issue was real; even the Whig leaders were afraid that the country might be on the edge of revolution. Lockhart and other reviewers had been discreet on the point, and individual correspondents were only slightly less cautious, but those who had known both Coleridge and Henry Nelson Coleridge were not more shocked than suspicious. Thomas Allsop's *Letters, Conversations and Recollections of S. T. Coleridge* (1836) was not a work that those near Coleridge at the end could admire, but older friends were glad at least to see the political pall of *Table Talk* brightened by any source from which light might come. Hartley, as a letter to his mother on 16 May 1835 makes clear, had prepared himself for the worst Henry could do:

> The *Table Talk* has been reviewed both in the *Edinburgh* and *Quarterly*, but I have not read either review. I might have done so, but I wish to read the Book itself first. I hope *Henry has been very, very, careful as to what he has recorded*. Dear papa often said things which he *would not himself have published: and I have heard him utter opinions both in Religion and in Politics not very easy to reconcile with what he has published*.[241]

Henry saw this letter and perhaps others quoting Hartley, who wrote in January 1836 to reassure him:

> . . . What makes you think that I dislike your 'Table Talk'? I might have fears lest it should be Mali exempli—fears which Allsop has shewn not to be wholly groundless. I might tell Derwent, that the book gave me no feeling of my father's manner, which it does not pretend to do, but the execution of the work I greatly admire, and Derwent well observes that it were sad indeed if so much excellent criticism, so much moral, religious, and political wisdom were to perish with the lips that uttered it. I have not seen Allsop's book.[242]

On 18 January Hartley wrote again to his mother: "But on this head, permit me to say, that my Father's opinions on many points of public import were considerably different during the years wherein I last conversed with him, from those which Henry has recorded. He admitted the necessity of a reform in parliament, and though I could never have imagined

---

[240] *The Letters of Ralph Waldo Emerson* ed Ralph L. Rusk (6 vols New York 1939) I 448.

[241] *HCL* 174.
[242] Ibid 181.

that he could have much admired little Johnny Russell's unprecedented piece of stupidity and blundering, call'd 'the Reform Bill', I thought he would have been thankful, as I am, for any thing which got rid of the idolized abominations of the old system, not as better in itself, but as necessary, transitory, and, at least, making room for something better.''[243] Sara, who had heard similar political objections from other readers of *Table Talk*, would have none of it from Hartley, to whom she wrote on 21 January:

As to our differences in regard to politics they give me little concern except as to the different view it leads us to take of our dear Father's mind. That Henry has not only faithfully reported what he heard, but that he has reported *all* he heard, as far as he could remember it, on the subjects in question, ⟨without picking & culling⟩ I feel quite confident both from my knowledge of Henry's character & conduct on other occasions, & from what I myself recollect of my Father's Conversation. Besides I refer the objector to the Church & State & other works which my Father published in his latter years. Has my husband printed anything as coming from him which is not accordant with the tone and substance of those deliberate productions? Derwent says that my Father would naturally, from the courtesy of his temper, put forward the most Tory side of his opinions *to* a Tory. But the truth is, unless sincerity was to be sacrificed, my Father with all his ingenuity and subtlety, could not have seemed to agree with Henry on politics unless he had really done so in the main. The real truth is that I believe some of my husband's opinions on the Catholic Question, the Reform Bill, the Church, Political Economy &c to have been to a *certain degree* moulded by those of my Father— at any rate I think they took a more determinate shape from his . . .[244]

On 8 May Hartley assured Henry that ''nothing could be more remote from my intention than to accuse you of misrepresentation or suppression'', but he reiterated at still greater length what he understood Coleridge's view of reform to be.[245]

A letter from Coleridge's old friend Thomas Poole, when he first received *Table Talk* as a gift from Henry and glanced over a few entries, has been lost, but subsequent correspondence shows that its tenor was similar to Hartley's. Henry's immediate—and long—reply to ''one or two of the remarks'', although important as a description and defence of his procedure, can be represented here by quotations; it has been in print, with insignificant omissions, since 1888:

As to the mere fidelity of my reporting, I assure you that the only liberty taken by me, was to omit—perhaps, in a few instances, also to soften—language of the same sort as that to wͨh you object. When you wrote, you had not, I think, read the whole book; but I think, when you have done so, you will acquit me of making a Tory of S. T. C. altho' of course his reprobation of modern Whig politics

[243] Ibid 184.
[244] UT Grantz 512. SC refers first to "our Father" and thereafter to "my Father".
[245] *HCL* 189.

cannot be approved by you. I am sure I cannot myself go quite so far in some points as he expresses himself in the Table Talk—either as to the Church or as to personal loyalty to the King; but you see it had no weight with me in my report. . . . The dates of what he sa[id] are given throughout, & that it is a faithful rec-or[d,] taken generally, for ~~these~~ those latter years of his life, I doubt not.[246]

On 22 June Poole generously apologised and explained: ". . . my impression was, that had I been conversing with Coleridge, I should have induced him to have *much modified* his assertions. . . . *No*, I AM SURE that your report *is most correct*; and further, that you are quite entitled to the high credit you disclaim; viz. of representing the *Individuality* of his conversation. . . . *Your Notes* are always pertinent and often *very interesting . . .*".[247] A letter from Josiah Wade, another friend from Bristol days, among Henry Nelson Coleridge's papers at the University of Texas, is dated 26 September 1836 and must refer to *Literary Remains* rather than to *Table Talk*: "I sincerely thank you for the two Volumes you kindly ordered the publishers to send me. I have read them with delight—those for Mr. Gutch I have forwarded to him at Worcester . . .". Wade had given all pertinent papers in his possession, including some that proved explosively pertinent, to Joseph Cottle, who said he was authorised to write Coleridge's life; the Gillman–Coleridge circles, and even Poole, were in despair over Cottle's desire to counteract the picture of Coleridge in *Table Talk* by making clear the horrors of addiction to opium, a moral project in which Southey alone encouraged him. The issue was not whether Coleridge had taken laudanum, but how hard he had been able to fight against it and whether he had been able to overcome its debilitating effects.

Daniel Stuart, like Cottle, was eager to make public his own version of the past. Like Cottle, he manipulated his memory to the point of modifying documentary evidence. Unlike Cottle, he had a direct effect on the second edition of *Table Talk*. Southey had suggested to Henry Nelson Coleridge on 7 November 1834 that Stuart and Cottle would be willing and reliable informants.[248] The following September Stuart began with Henry in a very low key: "The Table Talk is so well written and so well gives Coleridge's opinions that it would be presumption in me to attempt

[246] HNC to Poole 15 June 1835: BM Add MS 35344 ff 116–17; cf *Poole* ii 303–4.

[247] Ibid f 118; *Poole* ii 305.

[248] VCL S MS F4.21. ". . . Stuart, who will be very willing to give you all the information he possesses,—& it is much. So will my old friend Cottle." James Gillman, after publishing a notice that nothing of C's was to be published without consent of the executors, wrote to HNC of Cottle on 11 Jul 1836: ". . . send Mr Poole the copy of my first letter to Mr Cottle, but his conduct has been so dishonest & he has proved himself so miserable a fanatic that I leave him to the care of the Law when required". VCL S MS F3.66.

to add to it. Some facts I will give, which you many use as you please."[249] Recital of his facts did not bring forth, as he expected, attention, apology, and retraction. Like Cottle and Southey, he regarded himself as a martyr to Coleridge's irresponsibilities. *Table Talk*, by what he considered an equivocal reference to him as "Mr. Stewart, of the Courier, a very knowing person", and by reporting Coleridge's claim to have raised the circulation of the *Morning Post* to 7000 copies a day (under the dates of 1 May 1832 and 7 June 1830), had added to the ingratitude and concomitant offences of *Biographia Literaria*. A month later he clarified the grounds of his plea:

When you was writing, or rather publishing the Table Talk, why did you not apply to me who was at hand ready & willing?—Why? but that, as it appears to me, you were impressed with unfavourable, disagreeable feelings respecting me, and did not wish me to come within your sight. You who were to write his life, did not know the character of the Man, after all your intimacy.

The sentence on Henry's ignorance of his uncle's character was an afterthought, squeezed in for added intimidation. Later the tone changed again:

. . . were it to be said hereafter, that Coleridge made the fortune of both the newspapers, and was neglected [and] deserted by me in the days of his poverty; that attack upon me could be well supported by reference to his Literary Biography & Table Talk, by his Will, by the want of notice at his funeral, and last but not least of all, by this, that Henry Coleridge his favourite . . . never applied for information to Mr. Stuart. . . . What but indignation and contempt could have prevented Henry from applying to Stuart, which he did not for a year, and only then when recommended to do so by Southey: and still more, not a word of kindness or kind allusion to Stuart, either in the Biography or Table Talk, but the contrary.[250]

His use of the third person suggests that he had already determined upon making the letters public. When sure that neither Henry Nelson Coleridge nor Gillman would incorporate his account of Coleridge within their own publications, Stuart published his version in the *Gentleman's Magazine*, in three instalments, quoting in the process letters from Coleridge and portions of this correspondence with Henry Nelson Coleridge.[251] Meanwhile, in the second edition of *Table Talk*, he had become "Mr. Stuart . . . who was very knowing in the politics of the day"; and the reference to the *Morning Post* under date of 7 June 1830 had disappeared completely. The latter change, a poor substitute for the desired

[249] Stuart to HNC 19 Sept 1835: VCL S MS F6 f 2ᵛ.
[250] 22 Oct 1835: ibid ff 1–1ᵛ.
[251] *G Mag* NS IX (May, Jun 1838) 485–92, 577–90, X (Jul 1838) 22–7.

retraction in Henry's Preface of Coleridge's remarks both here and in
Biographia Literaria, gave Stuart a springboard:

"Table Talk" is an imitation of Boswell's Life of Johnson, and some future Mr.
Croker, amplifying and enriching it by new, amusing, and interesting anecdotes,
may hold me up as an ungrateful person, who was rolling about in my carriage,
while Coleridge, who made my fortune, was starving in Mr. Gillman's garret.
To shield myself from such consequences therefore I reluctantly come forward
to tell a plain tale . . .[252]

Had Stuart rested on his known generosity and not introduced distortions
of his own, some future Mr Croker could have annotated with praise.

Henry Crabb Robinson, who can be counted among those displeased
by the tone of remarks on reform in *Table Talk*, had baited Coleridge as
one more favourable toward Stuart than he himself was but also as one
equally acquainted with Stuart's slippery methods of conducting the
Morning Post and *Courier*.[253] Robinson is the author of a leaf that has
survived among the Coleridge papers in the Victoria College Library:

As a Set off to Comments that I am afraid will not be acceptable, I will give a
Specimen that you would gladly have made use of.
    S. T. C. was praising one day his old friend D. S. who I understand was on
many occasions generous to him—I could not help putting some awkward questions—on which he said
    Why my dear Sir, if I am pressed, which I don't like to be about Dan's char-
acter I should say—Dan is a Scotchman who is content to get rid of the itch when
he can afford to wear clean linen—[254]

The same leaf contains a second piece of table-talk:

Another time he replied to some commonplace sentimental morality
    Oh Sir you mistake it altogether—That is not goodness, that is goody-ness—
The Goody is in your T: T:[255]

Robinson had *Table Talk* in mind when he complained to Mary Wordsworth on 27 October 1836:

[252] Ibid IX 485. To blunt Stuart's argument SC added a final section (XVI) to
her Introduction to *EOT* I xc–xciii. She
lacked the original correspondence and a
complete file of *M Post* and *Courier* necessary to make C's case even stronger.
    [253] *CRB* I 37; *EOT (CC)* I lxvii–lxxxv.
    [254] VCL S MS F11.3, No 475. In 1815
HCR recalled C's words differently but
to the same effect: "He is a Scotchman,
glad to get rid of the itch now he can afford to wear clean linen." *CRB* I 170.
    [255] In 1853, revising his report of a
meeting with Cottle 29 Aug 1836 at

which he recommended Cottle's omission of public statements against C's executors, he reworded notes apparently of
Mar–Apr 1836, before he was aware of
the availability of *TT* (1836). He began
with a remark of C's concerning societies for the propagation of the Bible:
" 'Ay, sir, there can be no doubt that
these are good men, very good men, who
are so zealous in widely spreading these
societies. It is a pity they want sagacity
enough to foresee that in sending the Bible thus everywhere among the instructed and the reprobate, they will be

It is quite provoking to see an attempt made to exhibit one of the profoundest thinkers and most splendid talkers of his age, as vulgarly orthodox—To think with the Wise and talk with the vulgar is an odious maxim of spurious prudence—C: cannot be said to talk *with* the vulgar, but he talked *to* them at least And he was gratified by feeling and exciting sympathy—[256]

Where the majority complained that the transcendental flow was missing from isolated entries, and the advisers had feared Henry Nelson Coleridge's lack of taste, Robinson remembered Coleridge as much earthier than the *Table Talk* or *Literary Remains* suggested.

When Mrs Henry M. Jones of Hampstead revealed her views of selections given in the reviews and of what the reviewers said about them, Henry and Sara sent her a copy of *Table Talk* with a defence from Sara:

The "Printing Machine" and other critical publications find fault with the Editor of "Table Talk" for not having done what they themselves admit no reporter upon earth could do—they all allow that it was impossible to represent on paper the ample sweeping current of my Father's discourse. They add however that the work has preserved much valuable matter, which would otherwise have perished, that it serves in some measure to confirm and elucidate my Father's written works, and ought always to be printed as a companion to the "Friend" &c. This was all that Henry expected to do—he dreamt not of placing Coleridge the Talker before his readers, but merely ⟨hoped⟩ to preserve some part of his talk.

~~Some~~ One of my Father's Whig friends insinuates that if he had told his own story he would have told it more Whiggishly.—the spirit of party is "father to this ~~thought~~—"—it is not true. Henry is a man of honour, though as some may

---

propagating, instead of the old *idolatry*, a new *bibliolatry*.'

"Will the forthcoming volume of the 'Table-talk' contain a wiser word than the above? Perhaps not an acuter than those in the following: 'That is not goodness', said Coleridge in my presence, to some one who was urging rather a commonplace and sentimental morality,—'that is not goodness, but should be called *goodyness*.' " *CRD* II 230. His reference to "goodyness" in *TT* is specifically to *TT* 36:568 (*TT* 17 Aug 1833 n 6, below).

[256] *CRC* I 320–1. HCR, after an evening with WW that included HNC on 16 Apr, began to read "a third of volume one" of *TT* (1835) in the Athenaeum Club 25 May 1835: "This book will be harshly and unjustly estimated I think. A more difficult book, not original, I cannot well imagine. Coleridge's sayings were curious as well as wise in their connection, but without their connection

they may to the ordinary reader seem merely odd. His puns and strong sayings are recollectable and repeatable; not so the wiser and deeper words that fell from him. I have seen nothing yet in this book at all equal to what I recollect. The preface contains a severe but well-merited rebuke of De Quincey for his shameful article in *Tait's Magazine*." *CRB* II 464. The next day, before finishing I he started on II, "very heavy indeed", more political especially in 1831, "chiefly on the Reform Bill, Malthus, and the Church—all the very topics on which he is most bigoted and least ingenious"; he continued on 1 Jun "with very mixed feelings—pleasure greater than approbation, and very little concurrence in feeling". *CRB* II 465. He called on HNC 26 Jun with tidings of SH's death. *CRB* II 465. For the exchange of letters that followed on 17–18 Nov, see App F 35, below.

think an illiberal Tory . . . If Henry had wished to please his own party through thick and thin he would not have printed many of the opinions recorded in Table Talk. . . . I wonder what Mr Herman Merivale thinks of his papa's last letter in Blackwood—It ~~was~~ is more Conservative than ever: much the same I suppose that my brother Hartley, dear fellow, will think of the Table Talk. I wish *he* had preserved specimens of my father's discourse. I am sure we would have given him free leave to print all the radicality he ~~had~~ ever heard my Father utter—it might have seemed inconsistent with some of the sayings and doings of the Tory party, but I am confident it would not have been so with his own "Idea of Church & State."[257]

Among other letters to which Henry had to draft answers, most were intended either as corrections on specific points or, like the letter from William Edmondstoune Aytoun (1813–65), as a strengthening of Henry's hand against De Quincey, particularly on the matter of Coleridge's source with regard to Pythagoras' abstention from beans.[258]

Across the Atlantic, where Harper and Brothers issued the *Table Talk* in 1835, printed in two volumes and bound as one, few reviewers had the opportunity to compare their own recollections with Henry Nelson Coleridge's. On 30 August 1836 Henry wrote to the Rev Thomas Tracy (1781–1872) of Newburyport, Massachusetts, a Germanist whose translations Henry tried to place with London publishers: "You gratify me very much by your kind recommendation of the Table Talk;—it will I think, be hereafter an interesting document."[259] A visitor from Germany, Friedrich Ludwig Georg von Raumer (also 1781–1872), who was to achieve popularity in North America before he wrote its history, read the two volumes of *Table Talk* at the Athenaeum in Pall Mall on a rainy 26 June 1835. Not only was *he* "delighted with the varied, interesting remarks of this extraordinary man"; he also found that the Athenaeum copy had already become marked "with great *nota benes* of English approbation".[260] Hartley called Raumer's praise of *Table Talk* and Coleridge to Henry's attention.[261]

The corrections communicated to Henry by Alexander Dyce (1798–1869), already mentioned, are specific enough to be quoted most appropriately in annotations. It is worth noting here, however, that Dyce's letter begins, as a correction to Henry's Preface, with his celebrated account, heard from Wordsworth in 1835, of the collaboration on *The*

[257] Jul 1835? UT Grantz 1149.

[258] UT ms.

[259] HUL MS Amer 661.

[260] Friedrich von Raumer *England in 1835* . . . tr Sarah Austin [and H. E. Lloyd] (1836) 285–6. Raumer noted with admiration the observation that every man is an Aristotelian or a Platonist and the disgruntled verses on Cologne.

[261] "He speaks highly of the Table talk and of my father, though some of the sentiments are at variance with his own." *HCL* 194.

Ancient Mariner, first published by Derwent and Sara as a note in their edition of Coleridge's poems.[262] Dyce's memories of Coleridge were heightened by recollections of the actor Charles Mathews lovingly caricaturing him:

Coleridge, *when thinking aloud*, would address any one he met: and I have heard the elder Charles Mathews act, with matchless humour, a scene (founded, he said, on fact), of which the following is a fragment,—mimicking to the life the solemn tones of Coleridge, and the surprise and squeaking voice of the urchin whom he addressed:—

"*Coleridge, walking near Highgate, meets an apothecary's boy.*

Coleridge. I have been considering, boy, that though I have known several persons good because they were religious, I have seldom known persons religious because they were good—

Boy. Sir?

. . . .

Coleridge. Boy, did you never reflect on the magnificence and beauty of the external universe?

Boy. No, sir, never," &c, &c.

Mathews was a very frequent visitor to Coleridge, who had a great regard for him.[263]

[262] *PW* (1852) 383–4.

[263] *The Reminiscences of Alexander Dyce* ed Richard J. Schrader (Columbus, Ohio 1972) 178–9.

William Maginn put into the mouth of Theodore Hook a parody of C in "The Fraserians" *Fraser's Magazine* XI (Jan 1835) 15–16: " 'Yes,' said Hook, 'he would not only have aided in the discussion of questions literary and political, but in the discussion of any thing else that is before us. I confess I could not help laughing at the fuss made about the sobriety, and temperance, and so forth, of Coleridge, in the newspapers, immediately after his death, when I knew so much of his habits.'

" 'Why,' said Jack Churchill, 'I have been informed by Barnett or Tarbor, I forget which, of the Spring Gardens' Coffee-house, that Coleridge's bill, when he stopped there, was something like that of Falstaff's,—a halfpenny worth of bread to a hogshead of sack. It was soda water and brandy, eighteen-pence—glass of brandy, sixpence—roll of bread, twopence—glass of sherry, ninepence—brandy and water, cold, a shilling—roll of bread, twopence—pint of sherry, three shillings—mutton chop, a shilling—bottle of port, six shillings—glass of brandy, sixpence—pint of porter, threepence—roll of bread, two-pence—paper, sixpence—brandy and water, seven shillings—anchovy toast, a shilling—glass of brandy, sixpence—small beer, twopence—and so forth, day after day. Coleridge was a wet customer.'

" 'I shall never forget,' remarked Hook, 'the first time he was introduced to me, or I to him, which you please. Mathews, who was always a great friend and admirer of his, promised to bring him down to dine with me, when I lived close by Putney Bridge; but he could not meet him in time. Old Cole, nevertheless, found out the way, but did not arrive until we had almost finished our wine.'

" 'By my soul, then,' interrupted Ainsworth, 'that must have been at rather a late hour, if I may judge by your present habits.'

" 'Never mind,' returned Theodore; 'I mean that he came about half-past nine o'clock, we having dined at six; so that we had nearly arrived at our brandy and water, which was what I meant when I said we had finished our wine; and into

A. G. L'Estrange's memories of Coleridge seem to have fused both with his memories of Mathews mimicking Coleridge and with the memories of others reported to him. After retelling from William Harness of an occasion when Coleridge raised his hands and head "in the manner which Charles Mathews so cleverly caricatured", he tells with omniscient au-

the room he walked, with a countenance as solemn as a mustard-pot. Mathews jumped up, and introduced him as rapidly as possible. "Mr. Coleridge, Mr. Hook—Mr. Hook, Mr. Coleridge." I bowed; he bowed. I offered him a chair; he accepted it. I asked him if he would take any claret; he inclined his head in assent. I filled his glass; I filled my own. I emptied mine; he emptied his. But not a word did he speak. I made some observation about the heat or the cold of the weather, but to no effect: he was silent. I filled him another glass. He opened his mouth, it is true; but it was only to swallow the claret. Can this, thought I, be the great speaker? Good God, the man's dumb! The thought had scarcely passed through my pericranium when our old friend, acting the part of Balaam's ass, opened his mouth and spake. You all remember the chant of his voice: I had never heard him speak before, and the first words that saluted my ears were, "When we reflect upon the state of Spain—" "Sir!" said I; but it was of no use, out flowed the gush of eloquence. "When we reflect upon the state of Spain, the mind naturally reverts—(your health, Mr. Hook!)—to the subjugation of the Peninsula in the days of the Visigoths, when the Mahometan hosts, introduced by the treachery of native grandees, having succeeded in defeating the legitimate prince, broke down the force of the Spanish nation for a moment, and made themselves masters of tower, and town, and tented plain—(thank you, Mr. Hook; the glass is full enough)—until the Goths were driven into the eternal fastnesses of the everlasting mountains, thence to rebound, under the conduct of the gallant Pelayo, destined to drive gradually, by successive shocks, into the sea, the infidel invaders; and planting at last the banners of Ferdinand and Isabella over the towers of Granada, deserted by Boabdil, to regain for Christendom the land of Spain. (Thank you; the claret is very good indeed.) So, when a more godless army than that introduced by the treachery of Count Julian crossed the Pyrenees under Napoleon Buonaparte—more godless, I say, because the infidelity of Jacobinism is worse and more unchristian in feeling and principle than that of the Moslem—they, too, won tower, and town, and tented plain; but the hills that lift up their heads into heaven, those they won not. And from them came rebounding the might of Spain, supported by the gallant army of the Duke of Wellington; and as the towers of Granada saw the last of the Islam, so did Vittoria chase from Iberian land the relics of the Frenchman. (Your health, Mr. Hook—thank you.) Now you may inquire why I have thought it necessary to institute this comparison between the Mahometan and Jacobinical invaders of Spain. ['I declare to Heaven,' here interjected Hook, 'I did not see the necessity; but as Coleridge did, he proceeded.'] It was occasioned thus: I arose this morning saddened and depressed by influences which I could not account for, and I went to dissipate my chagrin in one of those green lanes abounding about Highgate, and which are every where the characteristic and the main ornament of the scenery of England. And as I there roved along, on lowly fancies bent, I saw seated across a stile two of those gallant fellows whose dress denoted them to be of the Guards of Britain, and from whose bosoms depended the medal which proved that they had shared in the glorious day of Waterloo. And I thought upon that day, and then upon him who won it—and then upon his military career—and then upon his deeds in freeing the Peninsula from the insolent foe; and while thus musing, there came into my head the parallel

thority of how Coleridge among the children of Highgate "would lay his hand on the shoulder of one of them and walk along discoursing metaphysics to the trembling captive . . . 'I never,' he exclaimed one day to the baker's boy—'I never knew a man good because he was religious, but I have known one religious because he was good.' "[264] A moral can be extracted: initial reactions to *Table Talk* were based not only on fixed attitudes but also, like most of the materials in this Introduction, on extremely fallible memories of what Coleridge at some time or another said. Only the reviewers proclaimed what he should have said, and that very briefly in comparison with their quotations of what he was said to have said.

THE MANUSCRIPTS OF *TABLE TALK*

The earliest surviving materials from Henry Nelson Coleridge's record of his uncle's conversation, and probably the earliest made, appear in three workbooks with dated entries. The major part of the record sur-

which I have been in some measure endeavouring to make out for the information of the company. (Your health, Mr. Hook.) 'Such,' continued Theodore, 'were the first words I heard from Coleridge. I thought myself exceedingly lucky that he had seen only two Guardsmen lounging over a hedge; for if he had seen a troop, the oration would not have been over until the present moment. I can bear testimony, however, to the fact, that he never lost a glass of wine while he was pouring forth his sentences. If he was getting rid of words *ore rotundo*, he was beyond doubt swallowing claret *ore aperto* at the same moment.'

" 'Certainly,' said Barry Bryan Cornwall Procter, 'there were times when it was quite impossible to refrain from laughing at the ultra eloquence of my friend Coleridge. I was a regular member of his Thursday night's *conversazioni*, as were Mr. Irving, of whom we have been speaking, and Mr. Basil Montagu, with whom I generally went. And the drollest part of the thing was that it had infected, as if by contagion, all the establishment of Gillman, with whom he resided. I recollect calling one day with Basil Montagu to visit Coleridge, who happened at the time to be in London. The servant-

maid who opened the door replied to our question, that she did—not—know—but—that—if—we—were so—kind—as—to wait—for—the—shortest portion—of—time—she—would—inquire of—the—lady—of—the—house. Every other inquiry we made was answered in the same fashion; and at last, when out of the infinite verbiage we had discovered that he was staying at Blandford Place, Pall Mall, a little fellow about ten years of age was consulted as to the particular address, and he answered, as oracularly as Coleridge himself, "He — dwells — at — Blandford Place — close — by — the — street — called — Pall Mall — as — to the —precise — number — I cannot — inform— you — but — there — being — only — two — houses — in — the —place — if — you — do — not — find — that —he — lives — at — number — one—you—may—apply—with—the —certainty—of—discovering—him— at — number — two." And this was from a gaffer not higher than the table.' "

[264] A. G. L'Estrange *The Literary Life of the Rev. William Harness* (1871) 143–4.

vives in MS B, in the Victoria College Library, Toronto. The earliest entries appear in MS A, the latest in MS C. The mss designated D, E, and F are ancillary to the original record of MSS A, B, and C.

MS A

A red roan quarto workbook, originally 136 ruled leaves 22.3 cm × 18.5 cm, watermarks "JM 1816" and "JM & M 1816", gathered in eights. Paginated, possibly by HNC, to p 110. Three later leaves are loose but reinserted in sequence.

Location: Harry Ransom Humanities Research Center, the University of Texas at Austin.

Intended as a diary, "The Confessional" (know thyself), the book is headed on p 1:

> Henry Nelson Coleridge. Wednesday 7. February. 1821
> King's College. Cambridge.
> ————————————————
> The Confessional.
> Γνῶθι σεαυτόν.

At the end of 1822 HNC's encounter with his uncle Samuel and his cousin Sara focused the entries more narrowly. For nearly a year, ending 2 Jun 1824 (p 110), C's conversation took almost sole possession; his reported remarks continue from recto to verso of each leaf. Leaves after p 100 were used for notes on HNC's reading. On p 75 HNC copied five passages from C's marginalia in "Baxter Life"; it is not clear why the leaf had been left blank; the verso remains blank. Beginning on p 97 with the conversation of 28 Dec 1822, HNC made entries on the versos only for that day and then for 5 Jan 1823. Afterwards he turned back to p 96 and made a series of short undated entries on the blank versos; i.e. pp 96, 98, 100, 102. These entries must have been made before 13 Feb, because table-talk with that date takes up on p 102; thereafter HNC continued on both sides of each leaf. Earlier, besides his diary, he had transcribed notes on family genealogy (pp 26–9), epigrams from C (p 32), and brief passages from *Omniana* (p 34).

MS B

A red roan workbook (now disbound), originally 136 unruled leaves 22.3 cm × 18.3 cm, watermark "JM 1816"; 122 foliated leaves survive, including 12 loose leaves reinserted in sequence; gathered in eights.

Location: Victoria College Library, University of Toronto.

MS B is the basic record, containing entries from Coleridge's conversation dated 24 Feb 1827 through 23 Jun 1834. From time to time

HNC—occasionally SC—copied into this workbook passages from C's letters to Mrs C, C's marginalia, and, from transcriptions made by EC, C's notebooks. A few leaves contain notes from HNC's reading. A passage from Voltaire on Shakespeare was transcribed on ff 3ᵛ–4 as pertinent to C's remarks on *Hamlet*.

Lines inked vertically through separate entries or entire pages, in MSS A, B, and C, indicate passages published in *TT* (1835) or transcribed from these workbooks for publication in *LR*. It can be conjectured, then, that the leaves were torn out by HNC himself, after the transcriptions for *TT* (1835), so that a clerk could copy the passages for *LR*. Some of these leaves are inked "T. T." in the upper right-hand corner, but they had not been returned to MS B when the mss passed from the family to the Victoria College Library.

One unlocated leaf followed f 67; five leaves are missing from the first gathering; leaves once conjugate with f 115, f 116, and f 117 are missing; they almost certainly contained no table-talk. F 121ᵛ, f 122, and f 123 are blank; f 122ᵛ andᶠ 123ᵛ contain notes by HNC on Greek, Latin, and Joachim du Bellay. Transcriptions from MS B by Ernest Hartley Coleridge refer to an earlier foliation.

MS C

Dark red leather workbook with gold-stamped borders, six fleur-de-lys decorations, and lyres in each corner of front cover; leaves 22 cm × 18.5 cm, watermark "Smith & Allnutt 1827"; gathered in sixteens. Pages 1 through 39 have been numbered. Stubs indicate the removal of leaves from the beginning (before the numbering of pages) and following the entries of table-talk. Labelled on p 1: "Sara's Poetry".

Location: Harry Ransom Humanities Research Center, University of Texas, Austin.

Entries by HNC of C's conversation dated 28 Jun 1834 and 5 Jul 1834 on ff 20ᵛ–21ᵛ (pp 40–2), followed immediately on ff 21ᵛ–22ᵛ (pp 42–4) by HNC's transcription of C's letter to Adam Steinmetz Kennard, published by HNC, not for the first or last time, in *TT* (1836) 319–20.

Earlier than the table-talk, HNC had transcribed in this workbook verses exchanged between "Emma" (SC) and "Henry" dated 1823–8. After recording family dates provided by her aunts, SC next entered lists of her poems and then transcribed poems she had written during widowhood.

MS D

One leaf of a letter in C's hand to DC, made available by DC to HNC, perhaps specifically for its use in *TT* (1835) ɪɪ 341, under the date of 10

Jul 1834, as C's last words to his audience. In *CL VI* 705 the fragment is dated ''October 1827?''. The rest of C's letter has not been found.

Location: Victoria College Library, Toronto.

MS E

Workbook of grey paper over boards, half leather (red), leaves 22.2 cm × 18.4 cm. Headed ''Letters written during a tour in France from August 6th to September 29th 1822. Given to Sara Coleridge by her admiring and affectionate friend and cousin Henry Nelson Coleridge. *2. Jan. 1827.*'' Following the ten numbered letters on 51 leaves, HNC transcribed for SC, on the rectos of 17 leaves, the table-talk of 1822–4 from MS A, numbering the entries in the sequence of their physical appearance there, beginning with the first undated entry on MS A, p 96. Two numbers, 3 and 43, are repeated in error. Entry 34 (presumably the known entry 36:37, on the national debt) has been cut from MS E. No 57, on the marriage of first cousins, was cut from MS E but has been returned to it. The mutilated page ends with a note in SC's hand: ''H. N. Coleridge, from m.s. of Table Talk of STC. S.C. 1849''. While the mss were held by the family, a scrap from MS F p 73, with anecdotes of C's father and his brother George (24 Jul 1830), was pinned over the gap beneath No 56 in MS E, where it remains. The leaves of the workbook following these transcriptions have remained blank. The text of MS E is given in the present edition as Appendix B.

MS F

Single leaves and identifiable scraps cut from a revision of the table-talk submitted by HNC to other members of the family, probably in Oct or Nov 1834, certainly between Sept 1834 and the printing of *TT* (1835). The loose leaves and fragments bear watermarks dated 1833 and 1834, variously from ''C Wilmot'', ''J. Whatman'', and other papermakers. The family attempted to preserve all these fragments with MS B.

Location: Victoria College Library, Toronto.

The preserved fragments of MS F account almost completely for the total of those entries cancelled with a vertical line in MS B but not published in *TT* (1835). Surviving page numbers and other physical indicators suggest that MS F followed approximately the sequence of MS B. The entries bear pencilled crosses and x's, with a few pencilled notes (usually on the verso of a fragment of MS F that directly preceded the page referred to in the objecting note), all from censors within the family—unless there are unidentifiable marks of objection from John Gibson Lockhart, who read the work, and probably the version of it represented in MS F, for John Murray.

One scrap, for 24 Jul 1832, bears what appears to be an entry number, an inked 319, and may come from an earlier transcription than the other surviving fragments. One pencilled sequence of numbers was introduced after the entries were excised, or possibly at the time of their excision. As indicated in the description of MS E, one scrap of two anecdotes from MS F (24 Jul 1830) has been erroneously attached to MS E.

The identifiable text of MS F, with a fuller description, is given in the present edition as Appendix C.

TABLE TALK

TABLE TALK

Recorded by

JOHN TAYLOR COLERIDGE

a20th April, 1811, *at Richmond.*[1]

We got on politics, and he related some curious facts of the Prince and Perceval.[2] Then, adverting to the present state of affairs in Portugal,[3] he said that he rejoiced not so much in the mere favourable turn, as in the end that must now be put to the base reign of opinion respecting the superiority and invincible skill of the French generals. Brave as Sir John Moore was, he thought him deficient in that greater and more essential manliness of soul which should have made him not hold his enemy in such fearful respect, and which should have taught him to care less for the opinion of the world at home.[4]

We then got, I know not how, to German topics. He said that the language of their literature was entirely factitious, and had been formed by Luther from the two dialects, High and Low German; that he had made

a From *TT* (1835) II 343–57 (36:665, 666)

[1] In *TT* (1835) HNC appended "The following Recollections of Mr. Coleridge, written in May, 1811 . . . communicated to me by my brother, Mr. Justice Coleridge". John Taylor Coleridge (1790–1876), the son of C's oldest surviving brother, Col James Coleridge (1759–1836), was then twenty. HNC, aged twelve, had accompanied his brother on this visit to their family friend John May (1775–1856) in Richmond. May is prominent in the life and letters of RS. Bodleian MS Eng Lett c 289 consists of letters from JTC to May from 1 Mar 1811 to 17 Jan 1827.

[2] The Prince of Wales, Prince Regent from 5 Feb 1811, would become George IV in 1820. Spencer Perceval (1762–1812), Prime Minister from 1809 but insecure; the Prince sought unsuccessfully to displace him without inducting the Whigs. On the day before this conversation C published in the *Courier* 19 Apr 1811 "The Regent and Mr. Perceval (Respecting General Crawford's Rumoured Appointment)", and no doubt the "curious facts" had something to do with placemen: see *EOT* (*CC*) II 110–21.

[3] After a series of disasters to the British and Portuguese, André Masséna, Marshal of France, began a disastrous retreat towards the Mondego, following the battle of Barrosa on 5 Mar. Both Masséna and Marshal Ney were pressed by the pursuing British from 11 Mar until Wellington drove them into Spain on 5 Apr. Arthur Bryant *Years of Victory 1802–1812* (1944) 396–414.

[4] Sir John Moore (1761–1809), lieut-gen (1805), was appointed commander-in-chief of the forces in Spain in Oct 1808. He declined an appeal to march towards Madrid, besieged by Napoleon. Proceeding north to unify his armies, he learned that Napoleon was bringing greatly superior forces to the aid of Marshal Soult. He retreated across mountainous terrain to Corunna, where, mortally wounded, he began the embarkation of his troops and learned that the French had been defeated. Cf C's letter to Daniel Stuart 18 Apr 1809: "*Afraid* of every thing, and only still more afraid of being *thought* to be afraid". *CL* III 200. Naming Walter Scott and Hookham Frere, Bryant (p 273) denounced the "ignorant amateurs" who reviled Moore as a "timid procrastinator".

it, grammatically, most correct, more so, perhaps, than any other language:[5] it was equal to the Greek, except in harmony and sweetness.[6] And yet the Germans themselves thought it sweet;—Klopstock had repeated to him an ode of his own to prove it, and really had deceived himself, by the force of association, into a belief that the harsh sounds, conveying, indeed, or being significant of, sweet images or thoughts, were themselves sweet.[7] Mr. C. was asked what he thought of Klopstock. He answered, that his fame was rapidly declining in Germany; that an Englishman might form a correct notion of him by uniting the moral epigram of Young, the bombast of Hervey, and the minute description of Richardson.[8] As to sublimity, he had, with all Germans, one rule for producing it;—it was, to take something very great, and make it very small in comparison with that which you wish to elevate. Thus, for example, Klopstock says,—"As the gardener goes forth, and scatters from his basket seed into the garden; so does the Creator scatter worlds with his right hand."[9] Here *worlds*, a large object, are made small in the hands of the Creator; consequently, the Creator is very great. In short, the Germans were not a poetical nation in the very highest sense. Wieland was their best poet: his subject was bad, and his thoughts often impure; but his language was rich and harmonious, and his fancy luxuriant. Sotheby's translation had not at all caught the manner of the original.[10] But the

---

[5] Cf C's remarks on Luther and the German language in *BL* ch 10 (*CC*) I 210 and see 7 May 1830, below (after n 6).

[6] Cf Satyrane's Letters III *BL* (*CC*) II 197 and C's note; cf also *BL* ch 19 (*CC*) II 89n–90 (C's note).

[7] Friedrich Gottlieb Klopstock (1724–1803), author of *Der Messias* (1748–73), *Oden* (1771). On the visit of C and WW to Klopstock in 1798 see Satyrane's Letters III *BL* (*CC*) II 194–206 and nn; *CL* I 436–7, 441–5, VI 736, and 2 Sept 1833 n 30, below.

[8] Edward Young (1683–1765), author of *The Complaint; or, Night Thoughts on Life, Death, and Immortality* (1742). James Hervey (1714–58), devotional writer, author of *Meditations and Contemplations* (2 vols 1746–7), a popular prose work of pious gloom. Samuel Richardson (1689–1761), the novelist, author of *Clarissa* (1748). Cf HCR two months later, 28 Jul 1811: "Coleridge talked of German poetry, represented Klopstock as compounded of everything

bad in Young, Hervey, and Richardson." *CRB* I 42. *BL* ch 23 (*CC*) II 210–11 also compares German and Young, Hervey, and Richardson. On Richardson see also 5 Jul 1834 n 12, below.

[9] Not found as given. In *Die Gestirne*, dated 1764 in *Oden* (1771), God strews flowers around the graves of the dead as once the stars threw light around them. God as sower of stars appears in *Der Messias* I 221–6, X 980–3. Klopstock *Werke* (10 vols Leipzig 1799–1806) III 12, IV 178. The material sublime of immense space recurs throughout *Der Messias*, e.g. I 346–7, 593–600, II 259–68, VIII 144–53, 260–8, IX 430–46. C bought the *Oden* (2 vols) in Hamburg in 1798. *CN* I 340 and n.

[10] Christoph Martin Wieland (1733–1813) *Oberon: Ein Gedicht in vierzehn Gesängen* (Weimar 1780), Eng tr 1798 by William Sotheby (1757–1833). C "was severe on the want of purity in his *Oberon*"; he preferred *Liebe um Liebe*. HCR Diary 15 Nov 1810: *Misc C* 387. A

Germans were good metaphysicians and critics: they criticized on principles previously laid down; thus, though they might be wrong, they were in no danger of being self-contradictory, which was too often the case with English critics.

Young, he said, was not a poet to be read through at once. His love of point and wit had often put an end to his pathos and sublimity; but there were parts in him which must be immortal. He (Mr. C.) loved to read a page of Young, and walk out to think of him.

Returning to the Germans, he said that the state of their religion, when he was in Germany, was really shocking. He had never met one clergyman a Christian; and he found professors in the universities lecturing against the most material points in the Gospel. He instanced, I think, Paulus, whose lectures he had attended.[11] The object was to resolve the miracles into natural operations; and such a disposition evinced was the best road to preferment. He severely censured Mr. Taylor's book, in which the principles of Paulus were explained and insisted on with much gratuitous indelicacy.[12] He then entered into the question of Socinianism, and noticed, as I recollect, the passage in the Old Testament; "The people bowed their faces, and *worshipped* God and the king."[13] He said, that all worship implied the presence of the object worshipped: the people worshipped, bowing to the sensuous presence of the one, and the conceived omnipresence of the other. He talked of his having constantly to defend the Church against the Socinian Bishop of Llandaff, Watson.[14]

---

marginal note on W. M. L. De Wette *Theodor* (2 vols 1822) suggests that C counted Wieland with Goethe as an immoral influence. *CM (CC)* ii 190–1. Cf *BL* ch 15, Satyrane's Letters iii *(CC)* ii 22, 202–3.

[11] Heinrich Eberhard Gottlob Paulus (1761–1851), rationalist German theologian, known to C in 1811 as "Paulus of Jena", editor of Spinoza. C would later annotate extensively Paulus *Das Leben Jesu* (2 vols in 1 Heidelberg 1828), "this strange Book" by "Paulus of Heidelberg", who was also of "original incurable Coarseness and Vulgarity" of mind. *CM (CC)* iv. His denunciation of Paulus in a notebook entry of Jun 1810 *(CN* iii 3906) was probably provoked by accounts of his work by William Taylor in the *M Rev*. Merton A. Christensen "Taylor of Norwich and the Higher Criticism" *Journal of the History of Ideas*

xx (1959) 179–94. In 1820 C equated William Hart Coleridge's knowledge of Paulus with his own knowledge of Eichhorn, "the Founder and Head of this daring School", whose lectures he had attended in Göttingen. *CL* v 46; cf iv 811, 851. JTC may have confused C's allusions to Eichhorn with his remarks on Paulus.

[12] The book, by William Taylor (1765–1836) was (anon) *A Letter Concerning the Two First Chapters of Luke* (Norwich 1810).

[13] 1 Chron 29.20 (var). Socinianism will be a frequent subject in TT.

[14] Richard Watson (1737–1816), bp of Llandaff from 1782. C's earliest objections, like WW's, would have been political, after Watson's change from principles consonant with C's in 1795–6. *Lects 1795 (CC)* 66n, 89n–90; *CL* i 193, 196n, 197. As a neighbour in the Lakes,

The subject then varied to Roman Catholicism, and he gave us an account of a controversy he had had with a very sensible priest in Sicily on the worship of saints. He had driven the priest from one post to another, till the latter took up the ground, that, though the saints were not omnipresent, yet God, who was so, imparted to them the prayers offered up, and then they used their interference with Him to grant them. "That is, father, (said C. in reply),—excuse my seeming levity, for I mean no impiety—that is; I have a deaf and dumb wife, who yet understands me, and I her, by signs. You have a favour to ask of me, and want my wife's interference; so you communicate your request to me, who impart it to her, and she, by signs back again, begs me to grant it." The good priest laughed, and said, "*Populus vult decipi, et decipiatur!*"[15]

We then got upon the Oxford controversy, and he was decidedly of opinion that there could be no doubt of Copleston's complete victory.[16] He thought the Review had chosen its points of attack ill, as there must doubtless be in every institution so old much to reprehend and carp at. On the other hand, he thought that Copleston had not been so severe or hard upon them as he might have been; but he admired the critical part of his work, which he thought very highly valuable, independently of the controversy. He wished some portion of mathematics was more essential to a degree at Oxford, as he thought a gentleman's education incomplete without it, and had himself found the necessity of getting up a little, when he could ill spare the time. He every day more and more lamented his neglect of them when at Cambridge.[17]

Llandaff had become by 6 Jul 1801 "that beastly Bishop, that blustering Fool, Watson". *CL* II 740. On 4 Dec 1808, with a pontifical letter, he had subscribed to *The Friend*, warning that he could not take easily attacks on Locke; C's innocuous letter "To R. L." in that work may be addressed to him. *Friend* (*CC*) I 19n, II 440, 472–3. By 12 Jan 1810 C saw him as "an avowed Socinian", a phrase expanded in 1818 into "I have myself heard him boastfully profess opinions of the very lowest Socinianism". *CL* III 273–14, IV 857.

[15] "The people wish to be deceived, and let them be deceived". Attributed by Jacques Auguste de Thou *Historia sui temporis* to a legate of Pope Paul IV, c 1556, modifying a Latin proverb, "Qui vult decipi, decipiatur". Cf *Historia* (4 vols Frankfort 1625–8) I 348.

[16] Edward Copleston (1776–1849), Fellow of Oriel (1795–1814), professor of poetry (1802–12), was the leader of the Noetic, "pre-Tractarian" group at Oxford. Early in 1810, responding particularly to Sydney Smith's charge of useless rigour in Latin and Greek at Oxford, in a review of Richard Lovell Edgeworth's *Essays on Professional Education* in *Ed Rev* XV (Oct 1809) 40–53, Copleston published *A Reply to the Calumnies of the Edinburgh Review Against Oxford* (Oxford 1810). Smith, Richard Payne Knight, and John Playfair combined for a review of the pamphlet in *Ed Rev* XVI (Apr 1810) 158–97. Later in 1810 Copleston published *A Second Reply* and in 1811 *A Third Reply*.

[17] In an annotation on an endleaf of Gotthilf Heinrich von Schubert *Allgemeine Naturgeschichte* (Erlangen 1826)

Then glancing off to Aristotle, he gave a very high character of him. He said that Bacon objected to Aristotle the grossness of his examples, and Davy now did precisely the same to Bacon: both were wrong; for each of those philosophers wished to confine the attention of the mind in their works to the *form* of reasoning only by which other truths might be established or elicited, and therefore the most trite and common-place examples were in fact the best.[18] He said that during a long confinement to his room, he had taken up the Schoolmen, and was astonished at the immense and acute knowledge displayed by them; that there was scarcely any thing which modern philosophers had proudly brought forward as their own, which might not be found clearly and systematically laid down by them in some or other of their writings. Locke had sneered at the Schoolmen unfairly, and had raised a foolish laugh against them by citations from their *Quid libet* questions, which were discussed on the eves of holidays, and in which the greatest latitude was allowed, being considered mere exercises of ingenuity. We had ridiculed their *quiddities*, and why? Had we not borrowed their *quantity* and their *quality*, and why then reject their *quiddity*, when every schoolboy in logic must know, that of every thing may be asked, *Quantum est? Quale est?* and *Quid est?* the last bringing you to the most material of all points, its individual being.[19] He afterwards stated, that in a History of Speculative

---

C lamented his youthful neglect of mathematics as crippling to his later philosophical study, with a "remorse that turns it to a Sin". *CM* (*CC*) IV. Cf *CN* IV 4542, 4672. He had an opportunity for further remorse in 1833, when he received a work of higher algebra, W. R. Hamilton *On a General Method of Expressing the Paths of Light, and of the Planets, by the Coefficients of a Characteristic Function* (Dublin 1833). See also below, 1 Jul 1833 (at n 48).

[18] Copleston had proposed that the charges against Aristotle in *Ed Rev* were "of French growth". "Extracts from 'Replies to the Edinburgh Review' " William James Copleston *Memoir of Edward Copleston, D.D., Bishop of Llandaff* (1851) 300. He regretted also (p 303) Locke's "reflections on the folly and uselessness of logic". In *The Advancement of Learning* (*De augmentis scientiarum* bk III ch 4) Bacon repudiated Aristotle as the ravisher of innovative thought. In *Novum organum* I §§ 54, 63,

70, II § 35 he complained of abstractness among the ancients and Aristotle's corruption of "natural philosophy by his logic". *Opera omnia* (4 vols 1740) I 98, 280, 283, 286–7, 350. Humphry Davy's objection to Bacon has not been found. In "Historical View of the Progress of Chemistry" in *Elements of Chemical Philosophy* (1812) Davy cited Bacon's Preface to *Instauratio magna* in support of his own rejection of Aristotle's "erroneous practice" of advancing general principles for application to particular instances, "so fatal to truth in all sciences". *Collected Works* (9 vols 1839–40) IV 4 and n. In his works Davy typically praised Bacon for his knowledge and novelty; e.g. IV 15–16, VII 121–2.

[19] For the relation to Copleston see n 18, above. In *Some Thoughts Concerning Education* (1705) Locke, among many protests against excessive attention to logic, proposed (§ 94) a more practical education for a boy than that available in the schools, for "how much more use it

Philosophy which he was endeavouring to prepare for publication, he had proved, and to the satisfaction of Sir James Mackintosh, that there was nothing in Locke which his best admirers most admired, that might not be found more clearly and better laid down in Descartes or the old Schoolmen; not that he was himself an implicit disciple of Descartes, though he thought that Descartes had been much misinterpreted.[20]

When we got on the subject of poetry and Southey, he gave us a critique of the Curse of Kehama, the fault of which he thought consisted in the association of a plot and a machinery so very wild with feelings so sober and tender: but he gave the poem high commendation, admired the art displayed in the employment of the Hindu monstrosities, and begged us to observe the noble feeling excited of the superiority of virtue over vice; that Kehama went on, from the beginning to the end of the poem, increasing in power, whilst Kailyal gradually lost her hopes and her protectors; and yet by the time we got to the end, we had arrived at an utter contempt and even carelessness of the power of evil, as exemplified in the almighty Rajah, and felt a complete confidence in the safety of the unprotected virtue of the maiden. This he thought the very great merit of the poem.[21]

When we walked home with him to the inn, he got on the subject of the Latin Essay for the year at Oxford*, and thought some consideration of the corruption of language should be introduced into it. It originated,

* On Etymology.

---

is to judge right of men, and manage his affairs with them, than to speak Greek and Latin, or argue in mood and figure; or to have his head filled with the abstruse speculations of natural philosophy and metaphysics". *Works* (10 vols 1823) IX 84. In *An Essay Concerning Human Understanding* bk III ch 10 §§ 6–22 Locke made discreet attacks on abuse of language in "the schools"; in ch 6 § 9 and bk IV ch 12 § 12 he opposed all appeal to general principles, "essence being utterly unknown to us". *Essay* (23rd ed 2 vols 1817) I 479–80, II 25–37, 217–18. C defended Aristotle and the mediaeval Schoolmen against "the repeaters of Lord Bacon's assertions", and defended more generally "our great Schools", in *Logic* (*CC*) 210, 282, and throughout. Cf 31 Mar 1830 (at n 5), below.

[20] C had begun to argue in Feb 1801,

explicitly in opposition to Sir James Mackintosh, that Locke followed Descartes in teaching that human knowledge comes from "Ideas imprinted on the senses", perceived as inherent in operations of the mind and passions, or "formed by Help of Memory and Imagination". *CL* II 675, 681, 683, 685–6. Descartes' superiority to Hobbes and Locke, as well as his priority, is treated in *BL* chs 5, 8, 12 (*CC*) I 92–3, 129–30, 258. The "History of Speculative Philosophy" C was preparing may be either the "Compendium . . . from Pythagoras to the present Day" intended in 1815 for the Logosophia (*CL* IV 591) or the projected work on logic: see below, 29 Dec 1822 and nn 3, 4.

[21] *The Curse of Kehama* (1810) was reviewed in *Ed Rev* XVII (Feb 1811) 429–65. For RS see also 19 Sept 1830 and nn 23–5, below.

he thought, in a desire to abbreviate all expression as much as possible; and no doubt, if in one word, without violating idiom, I can express what others have done in more, and yet be as fully and easily understood, I have manifestly made an improvement; but if, on the other hand, it becomes harder, and takes more time to comprehend a thought or image put in one word by Apuleius than when expressed in a whole sentence by Cicero, the saving is merely of pen and ink, and the alteration is evidently a corruption.[22]   [36:665]

April 21.—Richmond.

Before breakfast we went into Mr. May's delightful book-room, where he was again silent in admiration of the prospect.[1] After breakfast, we walked to church. He seemed full of calm piety, and said he always felt the most delightful sensations in a Sunday church-yard,—that it struck him as if God had given to man fifty-two springs in every year. After the service, he was vehement against the sermon, as common-place, and invidious in its tone towards the poor. Then he gave many texts from the lessons and gospel of the day, as affording fit subjects for discourses.[2] He ridiculed the absurdity of refusing to believe every thing that you could not understand; and mentioned a rebuke of Dr. Parr's to a man of the name of Frith, and that of another clergyman to a young man, who said he would believe nothing which he could not understand:—"Then, young man, your creed will be the shortest of any man's I know."[3]

[22] Whatever C actually said—and it is curious that etymology was the subject for the essay in 1813, when JTC won the prize—C was perhaps not meaning to reject specifically the decadent style of Lucius Apuleius, Latin philosopher and rhetorician of the 2nd century A.D. In a note for Lect 3 of 1818 he praised Apuleius' "Tale of Cupid and Psyche" (*Metamorphoses* bks V–VI), the "most beautiful Allegory ever composed . . . tho' composed by an Heathen". *Lects 1808–19 (CC)* II 102; cf *Friend (CC)* I 485 and n. In the essays on method in *The Friend* he warned against using unusual words. *Friend (CC)* I 449.

[1] On John May see above, 20 Apr 1811 n 1.

[2] JTC reported similarly, but with fewer details of C's reaction, in a letter to his brother James. Bernard, Lord Coleridge *The Story of a Devonshire House* (1905) 191. Thomas Arnold wrote to JTC 12 Oct 1835: "I often think I could have understood your Uncle better if he had written in Platonic Greek.—His Table Talk marks him in my Judgment (as a far greater than either Southey or Wordsworth,) as a very great Man indeed,—whose equal I know not where to find in England.—It amused me to recognize in your Contributions to the Book divers Anecdotes which used to excite the open mouthed Admiration of the C.C.C. Senior Common Room in the Easter and Oct– [? = Trinity?] Terms of 1811, after your Easter Vacation spent with Th⁵ May at Richmond." Bodleian MS Eng Letts d 130.

[3] Samuel Parr (1747–1825), peda-

As we walked up Mr. Cambridge's meadows towards Twickenham,[4] he criticized Johnson and Gray as poets, and did not seem to allow them high merit.[5] The excellence of verse, he said, was to be untranslatable into any other words without detriment to the beauty of the passage;— the position of a single word could not be altered in Milton without injury.[6] Gray's personifications, he said, were mere printer's devils' personifications—persons with a capital letter, abstract qualities with a small one. He thought Collins had more genius than Gray, who was a singular instance of a man of taste, poetic feeling, and fancy, without imagination.[7] He contrasted Dryden's opening of the 10th satire of Juvenal with Johnson's:—

> Let observation, with extensive view,
> Survey mankind from Ganges to Peru.

which was as much as to say,—

> Let observation with extensive observation observe mankind.[8]

After dinner he told us a humorous story of his enthusiastic fondness for Quakerism, when he was at Cambridge, and his attending one of their meetings, which had entirely cured him.[9] When the little children came in, he was in raptures with them, and descanted upon the delightful mode

---

gogue, curate, Whig, and controversialist, prominent 1787–1809. C's interest in the man and in his ponderous style is reflected in *CL* I 101, 331, 585, v 340; *CN* I 101, 112, 278 and nn, III 3648; *Watchman (CC)* 15. This anecdote is cited, in Warren Derry *Dr. Parr: A Portrait of the Whig Dr. Johnson* (Oxford 1966) 274, as evidence of Parr's reluctance to reveal his own creed.

[4] The meadows, later Cambridge Park, belonged to the estate of the author Richard Owen Cambridge (1717–1802); there is an account of his life, works, and villa in *G Mag* LXXV (1805) 234–8.

[5] On Johnson as a talker and a prose writer see 1 Jul 1833 (at nn 25–8) and 23 Oct 1833 (at n 15), below. On Gray see *BL* chs 1 and 2 (*CC*) I 20, 40n–1; see also 23 Oct 1833 (at n 10), below.

[6] On *untranslatableness* as the infallible test of style in poetry see *BL* chs 1 and 22 (*CC*) I 23, II 142.

[7] In 1796, when the poetry of William Collins particularly excited him (*CL* I 279), C projected an "Edition of Collins & Gray with a preliminary Dissertation" (*CN* I 161). In *BL* ch 1 (*CC*) I 20 C remembered his collegiate "preference of Collins's odes to those of Gray".

[8] C made this point publicly in Lect 6 of the 1811–12 lectures (5 Dec 1811): *Lects 1808–19 (CC)* I 292, in which the misquotation of "Ganges" for "China" in line 2 of *The Vanity of Human Wishes* was not given. In *The Spirit of the Age* Hazlitt attributed to WW similar remarks concerning Johnson's tautology. *H Works* XI 93. Goldsmith's parody had preceded C and WW:

> Let observation with observant view
> Observe mankind from China to Peru.

Dryden's lines are

> Look round the Habitable World, how few
> Know their own Good; or knowing it, pursue.

[9] On C and the Quakers see 14 Aug 1833 (at n 3) and 3 Jan 1834 (at nn 12–15), below.

of treating them now, in comparison with what he had experienced in childhood. He lamented the haughtiness with which Englishmen treated all foreigners abroad, and the facility with which our government had always given up any people which had allied itself to us, at the end of a war; and he particularly remarked upon our abandonment of Minorca.[10] These two things, he said, made us universally disliked on the Continent; though, as a people, most highly respected. He thought a war with America inevitable;[11] and expressed his opinion, that the United States were unfortunate in the prematureness of their separation from this country, before they had in themselves the materials of moral society—before they had a gentry and a learned class,—the former looking backwards, and giving the sense of stability—the latter looking forwards, and regulating the feelings of the people.[12]

Afterwards, in the drawing-room, he sat down by Professor Rigaud,[13] with whom he entered into a discussion of Kant's System of Metaphysics. The little knots of the company were speedily silent: Mr. C.'s voice grew louder; and abstruse as the subject was, yet his language was so ready, so energetic, and so eloquent, and his illustrations so very neat and apposite, that the ladies even paid him the most solicitous and respectful attention. They were really entertained with Kant's Metaphysics![14] At last I took one of them, a very sweet singer, to the piano-forte; and, when there was a pause, she began an Italian air. She was anxious to please him, and he was enraptured. His frame quivered with emotion,

[10] Minorca, held by the British 1708–82 and 1798–1802, was restored to Spain in 1802. C had expressed concern in *The Friend* Nos 26, 27 (*CC*) II 356, 363, 367–8 (I 564, 571, 576, 578); *CN* II 2377; *EOT* (*CC*) III 186. He had traced in *The Friend* No 26 the process whereby the English "*gentlemanly* character" led to such errors abroad as "mistaking for vices, a mere difference of manners and customs". *Friend* (*CC*) II 350–1 (I 555–7).

[11] In the *Courier* of 7 May 1811 C regretted circumstances that "may force us against our wish into a war with the Republic". *EOT* (*CC*) II 128. On 13 May he expressed still less hope. *EOT* (*CC*) II 142.

[12] These needs of a "moral society" are fully explored in *C&S*.

[13] Stephen Peter Rigaud (1774–1839), astronomer and historian of mathemat-

ics, in 1810 had become Savilian professor of geometry and senior proctor of the University of Oxford. On 27 Sept 1815, trying to recollect what Rigaud had said of George Atwood's failure to derive the properties of the circle from the rectilinear, C reminded John May of "Mr Rigaud's genial kindness and instructive remarks" in conducting May, C, JTC, and HNC through the Royal Observatory at Kew—where Rigaud succeeded his father in 1814 as Observer to the King. *CL* IV 588 and n. C gave a fuller account of Atwood's failure in *The Friend* (*CC*) I 496–7.

[14] As here, reporters of C's conversation usually avoid detail concerning remarks on Kant's metaphysics, but see 7 Jan–13 Feb 1823 n 41, 9 May 1830 n 13, 14 Aug 1831 and n 23, and 22 Feb 1834 and nn 3–4.

and there was a titter of uncommon delight on his countenance. When it was over, he praised the singer warmly, and prayed she might finish those strains in heaven![15]

This is nearly all, except some anecdotes, which I recollect of our meeting with this most interesting, most wonderful man.[16] Some of his topics and arguments I have enumerated; but the connection and the words are lost. And nothing that I can say can give any notion of his eloquence and manner,—of the hold which he soon got on his audience— of the variety of his stores of information—or, finally, of the artlessness of his habits, or the modesty and temper with which he listened to, and answered arguments, contradictory to his own.—J.T.C.　　　[36: 666]

[*April* 1811]
*a*Curious instance of Roman Catholic blindness[1]

As M*r* Coleridge was descending from Mount Ætna with a very lively talkative Guide, they passed thro' a village called (I think) Nicolozzi,[2] where the host happened to be carrying thro' the streets; every one was prostrate, the guide became so, & not to be singular the traveller also. When they pursued their journey M*r* C perceived in his guide an unusual seriousness, & long silence, wc̄h after many hems & haws was interrupted with a low bow, & leave requested to ask a question, wc̄h of course was granted & the following dialogue followed. Signor are you then a Christian? I hope so. What are all Englishmen Christians? I hope & think they are. Why are you not Turks, are you not all to be damned eternally? I trust not through Christ. What you believe in Christ then? Certainly. This answer produced another long silence. At length he again spoke, still doubting the grand point of "the Christianity of his companion." I'm thinking, Signor, what is the difference between you & us,

---

a From JTC's commonplace book f 70 (36:311n)

[15] In JTC's version for James Coleridge, the "beautiful woman" sang "some Italian Arie" to C, who then, "sitting down by Mrs. May, recited some extempore verses on the singer". *Story of a Devonshire House* 191.

[16] HNC published one of the anecdotes under 25 Jul 1831 as a footnote. A version of it is given directly below.

[1] Given here from JTC's commonplace book (f 70) in the Library of the University of Pennsylvania, this anecdote was published by HNC in *TT* (1835)

as a footnote to 30 Jul 1831 (36:311n), with regularisation of quotation marks and other variations. Instead of the tendentious heading, HNC provided an explanatory introduction: "The following anecdote related by Mr. Coleridge, in April, 1811, was preserved and communicated to me by Mr. Justice Coleridge:—".

[2] Nicolosi. C ascended Mt Etna twice, on 20 and 26 Aug 1804: *CN* ii 2070–4 and nn.

that you are to be certainly damned? Nothing very material, nothing that can prevent our both going to heaven, I hope. We believe in God, Jesus Christ, & the Holy Ghost—"Oh those damned priests what lyars they are—but, (pausing) we cant do without them, we cant go to heaven without them." But tell me, Signor, what *are* the differences. "Why for instance we do not worship the Virgin." And why, Signor? "Because tho' holy & pure, We think her still a woman & therefore do not pay her the honor due to God." But do you not worship Jesus, who sits on the right hand of God? "We do." Then why not worship the virgin who sits on the left? "I did not know she did; if you can show it me in the Scriptures, I shall readily agree to worship her." O (said the man with uncommon triumph) securo[3] Signor, securo Signor.—[4]   [310n]

[9 *January* 1823][1]

[a]*January* 1823.—On Thursday my Uncle Sam and Sara dined with us,

[a] From JTC's diary as published in Bernard, Lord Coleridge *This for Remembrance* (1925) 34–61, which differs slightly from the version in *TT* under 1 May 1823

[3] "Surely . . . [I can show you it in the scriptures]". JTC and HNC understand the guide to declare with relief security in his own faith.

[4] Calling this "the usual travel-story . . . in illustration of local superstition", Sultana p 194 takes it as a later invention of C's, "because he represents himself in it as already a Trinitarian—several months before he actually became so". Joseph Cottle was sufficiently determined to make C no trinitarian until he found him so in 1807 that he dated as 1807 a letter of Oct 1806 that is itself no fruit of sudden conversion. Cottle *Rem* 337–40; *CL* II 1188–90.

[1] HNC's brother JTC had moved in 1818 with his bride, Mary Buchanan, to 7 Hadlow St, where they lived until 1824, when the street was absorbed by an expansion of the British Museum. As in Apr 1811, when JTC made his first record of C's talk, HNC was at this time also present. Two days later, 11 Jan, HNC wrote from 2 Pump Court, in the Temple, to his father, Col James, of the Chanter's House, Ottery St Mary: "My uncle talks like no other man in this world; upon all subjects whatever, and at all times, he pours forth more learning,

more just and original views, and more eloquence than I ever expect to witness again. He with his wife and daughter dined on Thursday at John's, and Rennell and Lyall came to meet him. My uncle held an almost continuous harangue from the time he entered the house till the moment he left it. Lyall, who had never seen him before, was much impressed with his astonishing powers. You should hear him upon Unitarianism! One expression was curious—'I am asked sometimes, how it is that I, who seem to understand the shallowness of Unitarianism so well, could ever have believed it—My answer is—I never did believe it—I only *disbelieved down* to Unitarianism. I only believed my own disbelief.' He has finished a work upon Logic, which he means to offer to Murray; and also the first half of his great work upon the Theology of St. John." BM Add MS 47558 f 91. On ff 90–1 he wrote: "John will tell you everything you may wish to know about Sara and her mother. I think her a most lovely girl, and one reason only prevents me from falling downright in love with her. She has scarcely any touch of ceruleanism about her, and talks with much anticipated pleasure of seeing

and Rennell and Lyall came to meet him.[2] I have heard him more brilliant, but he was very fine, and delighted both Rennell and Lyall very much. It is impossible to carry off or commit to paper his long trains of argument, indeed it is not always possible to understand them, he lays the foundation so deep and views every question in so original a manner. Nothing can be finer than the principles he lays down in morals and religion; the wonder, the painful wonder is that a man who can think and feel as he does—for I am convinced he feels as he speaks while he is speaking—should have acted and still act as he has done and does. His deep study of Scripture, too, is very astonishing; Rennell and Lyall were as children in his hands, not merely in the general views of theology, but in nice verbal criticism. He thinks it clear that St. Paul did not write the Epistle to the Hebrews, but that it must have been the work of some Alexandrine Greek, and, he thinks, Apollos.[3] It seemed to him a desirable thing for Christianity that it should have been written by some other person than St. Paul, for its inspiration being unquestioned it added another and independent teacher and expounder.

We fell upon ghosts, and he exposed many of the stories metaphysically and physically.[4] He seemed to think it impossible that you should really see with the bodily eye what was impalpable, unless it were a shadow; and what you fancied you saw with the bodily eye was in fact only an impression on the imagination; then you are seeing something "out of your senses," and your testimony is full of uncertainty. He observed how uniformly in all the best attested stories of spectres the appearance might be accounted for from the disturbed state of the mind or body, as in Dion [and] Brutus.[5] On Lyall saying he wished to believe

---

a play or an opera, or any such mundane divertisement, wͨͪ your Miss Barker kind of creatures think beneath their exalted ultra purified stupid insensibilities. She is really an acquisition to our family; it is a mechanical delight to feel that is 'all ain bluid' in yourself and in a being of so much loveliness, sweetness and intellect. Her mother I do not very much like.''

[2] Thomas Rennell (1754–1840), scholar and divine, was master of the Temple 1797–1827 and dean of Winchester 1805–40. William Rowe Lyall (1788–1857), editor and divine, was dean of Canterbury from 1845. In 1820 Lyall reorganised the *Encyclopaedia Metropolitana*, to which C had contrib-

uted in 1818. At the time of the visit in 1823 HNC reported that Lyall, married but childless, expected to go to Calcutta as bishop on the nomination of Charles Wynn, privy councillor and president of the Board of Control. BM Add MS 47558 ff 91, 91ᵛ.

[3] For C on Luther's attribution of Hebrews to Apollos, see below, HNC's TT, 7 Jan–13 Feb 1823 and n 35.

[4] On ghosts see also below, HNC's TT, 7 Jan–13 Feb 1823 and nn 5, 6.

[5] Dion (d 353 B.C.) of Syracuse, aware of a plot against his life, one night saw the apparition of a tragic Fury of great stature sweeping his house with a broom, a few days before his son's suicide and shortly before his own assassi-

them true, thinking they formed a useful subsidiary testimony of another state, he differed and thought it dangerous testimony, not wanted. It was Saul with the Scriptures and the Prophet, calling on the witch of Endor.[6] He explained very naturally, yet ingeniously, what has startled people often in ghost stories, such as Lord Lyttelton's, that when a real person has appeared, habited like the phantom, the ghost-seer has immediately seen two, the person and the phantom.[7] He said—and indeed it is obvious—that it must be so. The man under delusion sees with the eye of the body and the eye of the imagination; if no one were present, he would see the bed curtains with one and the spectre with the other. If therefore a real person comes, he would see him as he would have seen anyone else in the same place, and he sees the spectre, they do not interfere with each other. [36:46]

---

nation. Marcus Junius Brutus (c 78–42 B.C.), the conspirator against Julius Caesar, beheld and questioned a monstrous apparition that answered, "I am thy evil genius, Brutus, and thou shalt see me at Philippi." Plutarch *Lives*: "Dion" 55, "Brutus" 36, 48, tr Bernadotte Perrin (LCL). In defining the parallels between Dion and Brutus, Plutarch emphasises the apparitions. A work that C read attentively in 1795 on the subject of dreams, which he remembered in 1827 (see *CN* I 188n), Andrew Baxter (anon) *An Enquiry into the Nature of the Human Soul* (3rd ed 2 vols 1745), returned repeatedly to the apparitional dreams of Brutus and Dion, II 5, 85, 101–2, 134–40, 168. In his lecture of 8 Mar 1819 of the lectures on the history of philosophy, C referred to Dion and Brutus as having in common that "they were anxious, weary, in cold and bodily discomfort; the consequence of which is that the objects from without, weakened in their influence on the senses, and the sensations meantime, from within, being strongly excited, the thoughts convert themselves into images, the man believing himself to be awake precisely by the same law as our thoughts convert themselves into images the moment we fall asleep . . .". *P Lects* Lect 11 (1949) 319. On dreams see also below, 1 May 1823.

[6] 1 Sam 28.7–25. For details concerning the witch of Endor see 10 Mar 1827,

below, and nn 3, 4.

[7] Thomas Lyttelton, 2nd Baron Lyttelton (1744–79), "commonly called the wicked Lord Lyttelton" (*DNB*), was warned in a dream (24 Nov 1779) that he would die three days later. According to the version that his uncle, Lord Westcote, told Samuel Johnson and others, Lyttelton dreamed that a bird flew into his room, changed into a woman in white, and told him he would die in three days; whereupon he told his servants, friends, and acquaintances; spent three cheerful days; and died. When Boswell raised the subject on 12 Jun 1784 Johnson said, "I am willing to believe it". *Boswell's Life of Johnson* ed G. Birkbeck Hill rev L. F. Powell (6 vols 1934–50) IV 298–9. C told a similar story of his own father's death in a letter to Poole 16 Oct 1797: "He dreamt that Death had appeared to him, as he is commonly painted, & touched him with his Dart." He returned home, where his wife's cry awaked C, who, without knowing of his father's return, said, "Papa is dead." *CL* I 355. On reading Marcus Aurelius' account of remedies prescribed to him in a dream, C noted: "I am not convinced that this is mere Superstition. . . . My Father had a similar Dream 3 nights together before his Death, while he appeared to himself in full & perfect Health". *CM (CC)* I 163. For C on apparitions see also 1 May 1823 and n 5.

My uncle told us also at the same time the following striking story, which might well be dressed up and called "The Phantom Portrait."[8]

A stranger came, recommended to a merchant's house at Lubeck. He was hospitably received, but the house being full, was lodged at night in an apartment handsomely furnished but not often used. There was nothing that struck him particularly in the room when left alone, till he happened to cast his eyes on a picture, which immediately arrested his attention. It was a single head, but there was something so uncommon, unearthly, and frightful in it, though by no means ugly, that he found himself irresistibly attracted to look at it; and he could not remove from it, until his whole imagination was so filled by it that it broke his rest.

He dreamed and continually awoke with the picture staring at him. In the morning his host saw by his looks he had slept ill, and inquired the cause, which he frankly told him. The master of the house was much vexed and said the picture ought to have been removed, that it was an oversight, and it always was removed when the chamber was used. The picture was indeed, he said, terrible to everyone, but it was so fine and had come into the family in so curious a way that he could not make up his mind to part with it or destroy it. The story of it was this:—

"My father," said he, "was at Hamburg on business, and dining at a coffee-house, when he observed a young man of a remarkable appearance enter, and seat himself alone in a corner, and commence a solitary meal. His countenance bespoke the extreme of mental distress, and he observed him every now and then turn his head quickly round, as if he

---

[8] As HNC noted—*TT* (1835) I 42n—a version of this story is told by Washington Irving under the pseudonym of Geoffrey Crayon, Gent. in *Tales of a Traveller* (3 pts Philadelphia 1824) I 73–90. Irving, who was in London again in 1823, was writing "The Adventure of the Mysterious Picture" in Paris in Feb 1824. *Journal of Washington Irving* ed Stanley T. Williams (Cambridge, Mass 1931) 132. Irving's version adds one important character, Bianca. No German source for the tale has been discovered. An Introductory Note to *Tales of a Traveller* identifies the narrator of all the tales as "the same nervous gentleman" who told a tale in *Bracebridge Hall* (1822) claimed by the author of *Peveril of the Peak* (Walter Scott). Irving's observations in 1817, when he was introduced to C by Washington Allston, were recorded by a friend: "I was surprised by his volubility. He walked about, in his gray hair, with his right hand over his head, the thumb and finger of his right hand moving over his head, as if sprinkling snuff upon his crown." Stanley T. Williams *The Life of Washington Irving* (2 vols New York 1935) I 156. In Lect 4 of the 1818–19 series (14 Jan 1819), which alternated with the lectures on the history of philosophy, C probably related the story of the phantom portrait in connexion with the appearance in *Macbeth* of Banquo's ghost: he used for this lecture the annotations he had made in *The Dramatic Works of William Shakespeare* ed Samuel Ayscough (2 vols 1807), and on I 376 he wrote: "Tell the story of the *Portrait* that frightened every one—". *Lects 1808–19* (*CC*) II 310.

heard something, shudder, grow pale, and then go on after an effort as before. He saw this same man at the same place for two or three successive days, and at length became so much interested about him that he spoke to him. His address was not repulsed, and the stranger seemed to find some comfort in the tone of sympathy and kindness which my father used. My father found him an Italian, well-informed, poor, but not desperate, living economically on the profits of his art as a painter. Their intimacy increased, and at length the Italian, seeing my father's involuntary emotion at his convulsive turns and shudders, which continued as before, interrupting their conversation, told him his story.

"He was a native of Rome who had lived in some familiarity with, and been much patronised by, a young nobleman. But upon some slight occasion they had fallen out, and the nobleman, besides many reproachful expressions, had struck him. The painter brooded over the disgrace of the blow. He could not challenge the nobleman on account of his rank. He watched his opportunity and assassinated him. Of course, he fled his country, and finally had reached Hamburg. He had not passed, however, many weeks from the day of the murder before one day, in the crowded street, he distinctly heard his name called by a voice familiar to him. He turned short round and saw the face of his victim looking at him with a fixed eye. From that time he had no interval of peace. At all hours and in all places, and amidst all companies, however engaged, he heard this voice, and could never help looking round when he saw always this same face staring at him. At last, in a mood of desperation, he had deliberately drawn the phantom as it looked at him, and this was the picture. He said he had struggled long, but life was a burthen which he could no longer bear, and he was resolved, when he had made money enough, to return to Rome to surrender himself to justice and expiate his crime on the scaffold. He gave the picture to my father in return for the kindness he had shown him."[9]   [36:47]

[9] HNC wrote JTC on 13 Aug 1834: "I have received all your notes, for wᶜʰ I am much obliged." BM Add MS 47557 f 107. A reference to "your memorandum" in 1835 indicates that JTC's notes on 1811, placed at the end of *TT*, came much later than these notes on C's talk in 1823.

TABLE TALK

Recorded by

HENRY NELSON COLERIDGE

My uncle Samuel called upon John on the 28th. I had never seen him since I was a child at Richmond.[1] He seemed more like my uncle Edward than any one else.[2] He thought me like my father. He said he had finished a work upon Logic, but had still the preface to write;[3] he had also completed one half of his work upon St John. He expounded its aims and purpose. It is to demonstrate the a priori possibility and probability of a Revelation; the latter half will be on the historical evidence, for which he had many materials. St John had a twofold object in his Gospel and Epistles; to prove the divinity and the actual human nature and bodily suffering of Jesus Christ; that he was God and Man.[4] The notion that the effusion of blood and water from the Saviour's side was intended to prove the real death of the sufferer,[5] originated with some modern Germans, and is ridiculous; there is a very small quantity of water *occasionally* in the præcordia, but in the pleura, where wounds are not mortal, there is a great deal. St John meant to show he was a real man, and says, "I saw it with my own eyes! It was real blood, composed of lymph and crassimen-

a MS A p 97

[1] See JTC's record of TT, 20 Apr 1811, above, and n 1; also of 9 Jan 1823 n 1.

[2] C's second eldest brother was Edward (1760–1843), vicar of Buckerell. C had expressed imperfect sympathy in 1793: "I soon perceived, that Edward never thought—that all his finer feelings were the children of accident—and that even these capricious sensibilities were too often swallowed in the vanity of appearing great to little people." *CL* I 54.

[3] At least as early as 1803 C planned "The History of Logic with a Compendium of Aristotelian Logic prefixed". *CN* I 1646. Its history until he dictated the surviving portions to his pupils John Watson and Charles Stutfield Jr in 1822 and early 1823 is traced in *L&L* 66–103 and *Logic* (*CC*) xxxix–xlvii. On the importance of studying logic, and the need for "transcendental Logic", see *CN* I 1759, III 3670, 4228; *CL* v 340–1. Any

ms of the Logic extant in 1822–3 in C's hand has been lost, but there are sequential notes for the work in N 29: e.g. *CN* IV 4763-7, 4771, 4797–9.

[4] In 1814 in *Felix Farley's Bristol Journal* C wrote: ". . . I am about to put to the press a large volume on the LOGOS, or the communicative intelligence in nature and in man, together with, and as preliminary to, a Commentary on the Gospel of St. John . . . ". "On the Principles of Genial Criticism Concerning the Fine Arts" *BL* (1907) II 230. In his detailed description of the projected Logosophia in letters of 27 Sept and 7 Oct 1815 C listed the commentary on St John as the fourth of six treatises to be included. *CL* IV 589–92. On the Logosophia see also *BL* ch 12 (*CC*) I 263–4 and nn, 271n.

[5] John 19.34: "But one of the soldiers with a spear pierced his side, and forthwith came there out blood and water."

23

tum and not a mere celestial ichor.''[6] The verse of the three witnesses is spurious; it spoils the reasoning;[7] St John's logic is Oriental, consisting chiefly in *position*, whilst St Paul displays all the intricacies of the Greek system. Porson had shown that the balance of external authority is against the verse.[8] Christianity might be believed without the six first chapters of Daniel;[9] it was within us; it was associated with our mother's chair, and with the tones of her voice. [36:25–28]

Pindar was the sacerdotal poet; religion appeared in his writings mild and benignant; in Æschylus terrible, malignant, and persecuting; Sophocles was the mildest of the three tragedians, but the persecuting aspect was still maintained; Euripides was like a modern Frenchman, never so happy, as when giving a slap at the Gods altogether. It was a mistake to suppose Pindar a wild and extravagant poet. He was a tory. Ἀφίσταμαι,[10] something sacred about him.[11] [36:16]

[6] Taking heart from a medical account of survival despite loss of two quarts of "a serous fluid, slightly tinged with blood" from the thorax, C asked: "what will the Unitarians, who rest the proof of Christ's actual Death on the water from the side say of this and similar cases?" Annotation on John H. Fuge "Case of Gunshot Wound of the Heart" *Edinburgh Medical and Surgical Journal* XIV (1818): *CM* (*CC*) II 361–2. Of the many works underlying his discussion of the crucifixion, C resembles in the handling of the medical evidence a bishop towards whom he had been hostile, Samuel Horsley (1733–1806), Sermon 9 in *Sermons* (new ed 3 vols 1816) I 175–202, a similarity probably to be explained by the currency of the debate. Medical discussions of the subject referred to the coagulum, or blood clot, as *crassamentum*. From Karl Georg Schuster in J. G. Eichhorn *Allgemeine Bibliothek der biblischen Litteratur* (10 vols Leipzig 1789–1800) IV 1036–48 C learned that there was "not a word of coagulum" in such early commentators as Irenaeus and Tertullian; his point was first made by Origen against the Gnostics. *CN* IV 4626 and n. Cf the opening pages of the surgical lectures of Astley Cooper: "The blood is an uniform homogeneous fluid; in three or four minutes after it escapes it begins to coagulate, and a spontaneous separation takes place into serum and crassa-

mentum. The crassamentum is found again to be composed of red particles and coagulable lymph . . .". *A Series of Lectures on . . . Modern Surgery* "compiled from original manuscripts and documents" of Sir Astley Cooper by Charles Williams Jones (1819) 20.

[7] The verse of the three heavenly witnesses in 1 John 5.7 had been omitted by Erasmus in his Greek Testament of 1516 and 1519 but added in his edition of 1522. After two centuries of debate Gibbon in *The Decline and Fall of the Roman Empire* ch 27 called the verse spurious, which aroused George Travis (1741–97), archdeacon of Chester, to defence of the passage. C stands here with the best scholarship of his time.

[8] Richard Porson (1759–1808) *Letters to Mr. Archdeacon Travis, in Answer to His Defence of the Three Heavenly Witnesses, 1 John v. 7* (1790). The quarrel between Gibbon and Travis begun in *G Mag* continued there, and Gibbon was pleased to be supported by Porson in "the most acute and accurate piece of criticism which has appeared since the days of Bentley".

[9] For a fuller discussion of Daniel see 24 Feb 1827 and nn 5–8, below.

[10] Pindar *Olympian Odes* 1.52. Tr Sandys LCL (1915): "I stand aloof [Far be it from me to call one of the blessed gods a cannibal]."

[11] Is C saying that a political conser-

Kotzebue represents the petty kings of the islands in the Pacific exactly as Homer's Kings. All supposed descended from Gods. *b*Riches commanding influence.[12]   [36:17]

My uncle talked fluently; but his manner is not so good as I expected. Derwent has it precisely.[13]

January 6th—Sunday. 1823.

Went with John to Highgate to see Sara and her mother.[1] I dined and came away at nine. She is a lovely creature indeed, and perfectly unaffected. My uncle talked upon a thousand subjects. I remember the following remarks.

Othello was not a negro, but a high and chivalrous Moorish chief.[2]

b p 99

---

vative could not be extravagant in language, or has a transition been lost in the cryptic notation typical of HNC's earliest entries? In "Translations of Pindar" *QR* LI (Mar 1834) 18–54 HNC had expressed views near enough to C's to make C's possible priority a question not to be raised in 1835. He omitted the references to Pindar from 36:16 and a sentence in 6 Aug 1832. On Pindar's "sober majesty of lofty sense" see *BL* ch 18 (*CC*) II 86–7.

[12] Otto von Kotzebue (1787–1846), navigator and explorer, son of the German dramatist and Russian civil servant, August Friedrich Ferdinand von Kotzebue (1761–1819). He tells of conversations with the king Tamaahmaah of Owhyee in the Sandwich Islands and various chiefs in the Marshalls, Carolines, and islands in the Bering Sea, in *A Voyage of Discovery, into the South Sea and Beering's Straits, for the Purpose of Exploring a North-east Passage, Undertaken in the Years 1815–1818* tr H. E. Lloyd (3 vols 1821) I 209, 235, 246–7, 261, 292–356, II 6-7, 60–88, 97–118, 208–20. C's remark is made clearer by "Remarks and Opinions of the Naturalist of the Expedition" (Adelbert von Chamisso): "Though no particular marks of respect are shown to the chiefs, they, however, exercise an arbitrary right over

all property. . . . They appear to be subordinate to each other in several degrees, without our being able rightly to understand their respective relations. . . . The princes call their people together for war. The chief of each group joins the squadron with his boats." III 169–70. In the Carolines Chamisso detected a more regularised "feudal system": III 207–14. C made notes from these volumes in 1821 or 1822 (*CN* IV 4841, 4845) and read two later books by Kotzebue on voyages of discovery in 1828–31 (*CL* VI 1055–6). Cf "The Homeric Kings seem to have had little more or other power, than the Judges in Jewish History". Annotation on Heinrich Steffens *Die gegenwärtige Zeit und wie sie geworden mit besonderer Rücksicht auf Deutschland* (2 vols Berlin 1817) I 13: *CM* (*CC*) IV.

[13] DC (1800–83), C's youngest son, receives little attention in *TT*. He played a minor role in supplying documents and advice during HNC's preparation of *TT* (1835).

[1] At the invitation of Mrs Gillman, SC and Mrs C had arrived at Moreton House, South Grove, by 3 Jan. *CL* V 264 n 1. C had not seen SC since 1812, when she was ten; HNC met her for the first time. See JTC's record of TT 9 Jan 1823 and n 1, above.

[2] "Kean regarded it as a gross error to

Shakspeare learned the character from the Spanish poetry, which was prevalent in England in his time.[3] Jealousy is not the point in his passion; it was agony that the creature whom he had believed angelic, with whom he had "garnered up his heart", and whom he could not help still loving, should be proved impure and worthless. It was the struggle not to love her. It was a moral indignation and regret that virtue should so fall— "Pity on't, pity on't, Iago."[4] In addition, his honour was concerned; Iago would not have succeeded but by hinting that his honor was compromised. There was no ferocity; his mind was majestic and composed. He deliberately determined to die, and spoke his last speech with a view to show his attachment to the state, though it had superseded him. Schiller has the material sublime;[5] to produce an effect, he sets a whole town on fire, and throws infants with their mothers into the flames; or locks up a father in an old tower.[6] Shakspear drops a handkerchief, and

---

make Othello either a negro or a black, and accordingly altered the conventional black to the light brown which distinguishes the Moors. . . . Betterton, Quin, Mossop, Barry, Garrick, and John Kemble all played the part with black faces, and it was reserved for Kean to innovate, and Coleridge to justify . . . a light brown for the traditional black." F. W. Hawkins *The Life of Edmund Kean* (1869) I 221, quoted in the Variorum *Othello* (1886) 390, in which C's remarks are put in a larger context. On Othello as a Moor cf Lect 4 of 9 Nov 1813 at Bristol and Lect 5 of 21 Jan 1819 of the 1818–19 series: *Lects 1808–19* (*CC*) I 555, II 314. In a sour mood at Gibraltar in 1804 C noted: "on one side of me Spaniards, a degraded Race that dishonour Christianity; on the other Moors of many Nations, wretches that dishonor human Nature". *CN* II 2045 f 13ᵛ.

[3] August Wilhelm von Schlegel in Lect 12 of *Ueber dramatische Kunst und Litteratur: Vorlesungen* (2 vols in 3 pts Heidelberg 1809–12) II ii 3–4, with no mention of Spanish poetry, acknowledged English awareness of Spanish novels and romances but discovered no evidence that either country knew the poetic drama of the other. In a note on Beaumont and Fletcher *Dramatic Works* (1811) C declared it "an indispensable qualification" for an editor of those play-

wrights to have "an accurate and familiar acquaintance with all the productions of the Spanish Stage prior to 1620". *CM* (*CC*) I 389.

[4] *Othello* IV ii 57 (var) ("where I have garner'd up my heart"), IV i 195–6 (var), corrected in *TT* (1835).

[5] C's term for Schiller in 1794–6 was "Bard tremendous in sublimity" and for Schiller's *Die Räuber* (1781) "tremendous sublimity". *PW* (EHC) I 73; *Lects 1795* (*CC*) 70, 296. On Schiller's impact see *BL* ch 23 (*CC*) II 210; *CL* I 325, 491, and esp I 122 (3 Nov 1794 to RS): "Who is this Schiller? This Convulser of the Heart? Did he write his Tragedy amid the yelling of Fiends?" HNC's version in *QR* LII (Aug 1834) of C's remark is that a discussion of the respective sublimity of *Othello* and *The Robbers* led C to say, "Both are sublime; only Schiller's is the material sublime—that's all!" *CH* 648. That the phrase "material sublime" originated with C is easier to assume than to prove. Keats's use of the term, "From something of material sublime" (*To J. H. Reynolds, Esq.* line 69), was not published until 1848 but it attests the popularity of C's phrase by 1818.

[6] In *The Robbers* II iii (tr 1792) his followers tell how the hero Charles de Moor set fire to a town to rescue one of them but banished another for chucking an infant into the flames; in IV iv, after much

the same or greater effects follow.[7] Lear is the most tremendous effort of Shakspeare, as a Poet; Hamlet as a Philosopher or Meditater, and Othello is the union of the two. There is something gigantic and unformed in the former; but in the latter every thing assumes its due place and proportion, and the whole mature powers of his mind are displayed in admirable equilibrium.[8]   [36:1–2]

Privilege was a substitution for law, where from the nature of the circumstances a law could not act without clashing with greater and more general principles. The House of Commons *a*must of course have the power of taking cognizance of offences against its own rights. Sir Francis Burdett might have been sent to the Tower for the speech he made; but when afterwards he published it in a pamphlet, and they took cognizance of it, they forgot the right distinction of privilege and law.[9] As a speech they *alone could* notice it, consistently with their necessary prerogative of freedom of speech; but when it became a book, then the law was to look to it, and there being a law of libel, privilege, which acts only as a substitute of other laws, could have nothing to do with it. Wynn said, ''he would not shrink from affirming that if the House of Commons chose to burn one of their own members in Palace Yard, they had the inherent power to do it''.[10] This is for want of a due distinction between privilege and law.   [36:8]

a p 101

---

violence onstage, he rescues from the dungeon of a tower his aged father, who had been sealed there by the other son.

[7] *Othello* III iii to the end, v ii.

[8] *Lects 1808–19 (CC)* contains no exact parallel to this invaluable paragraph.

[9] In 1810 Sir Francis Burdett (1770–1844), then MP for Westminster, first in the House of Commons and then in Cobbett's *Political Register* denied that the Commons had a right to imprison a British citizen (Gale Jones) for breach of privilege in advertising disrespect for Parliament. Instead of the expected penalty of reprimand by the Speaker, the House voted by a majority of thirty-seven to have Burdett committed to the Tower. Repudiating the warrant, Burdett barricaded his house in Piccadilly for three days, with supporters rioting in the street. On 9 Apr he was taken to the Tower. He was released automatically on 21 Jun at the prorogation of Parliament. See M. W. Patterson *Sir Francis Burdett and His Times (1770–1844)* (2 vols 1931) I 242–93. In 1800 C had planned a public letter to Burdett on one of the baronet's many subjects of reform, solitary confinement. *CL* I 627; *CN* I 767. Although acknowledging that Burdett's ''private character is said to be very amiable'' and recommending that Daniel Stuart soften his attacks on Burdett in the *Courier*, C disliked Burdett's demagogic appeals to ''the People'', proclaimed his loathing for ''the Burdettites & Whitbreads'', and grew increasingly averse to Burdett personally. *CL* III 207–11, 410, IV 903; *CN* II 2955, III 3772, 4079. According to Allsop (II 73–4), C met Burdett at Horne Tooke's.

[10] Charles Watkin Williams Wynn (1775–1850), MP from 1797 and often in the cabinet, was a close friend of RS.

There are two principles in every European and Christian state; permanency and progression.[11] In the civil wars of England, which were as new and fresh now as they were 150 years ago, and will be so forever to us, these two principles came to a struggle. It was natural that the great and the good of the nation should be found in the ranks of either side. In Mahometan states there is no permanency,[b] and therefore they sink directly. They existed and *could* only exist in their efforts of progression; when they ceased to conquer, they fell to pieces. Turkey would long since have fallen, if it had not been supported by the rival interests of Europe.[12] They had no Church; religion and state were one; there was no counterpoise, no mutual support. This is the very essence of Unitarianism. They had no past; they were not an historical people; they existed only in the present. China was an instance of a permanency without any progression. The Persians were a superior people; they had a history and a literature; they had always been considered even by the Greeks, as quite distinct from the other barbarians. The Afghans were a brave republican people.[13] Europeans and Orientalists may be well represented

---

[b] ~~progression~~ permanency,

Wynn spoke in Parliament on the Burdett affair and voted on 6 Apr for the milder action of reprimand; the language substituted in *TT* (1835), "I have heard that one distinguished individual said", suggests that the remark was private. Of a similar occasion later RS wrote in Jan 1820 to John Rickman: "Wynn tells me he did all he could to persuade them to send Burdett to the tower for his speech at the meeting about Hobhouse." *S Letters* (Curry) II 210. RS was in London in Jun 1820, when Wynn's words would have been a live subject.

[11] As HNC noted in *TT* (1835), the principle is centrally affirmed in *C&S*, in which permanence is represented by "the land and landed property", the king, the national church, and the clerisy, and progression represented by "the four classes of the mercantile, the manufacturing, the distributive, and the professional". *C&S* (*CC*) 24–5. In 1820 C described the essential subject of Scott's novels as "the contest between the two great moving Principles of social Humanity—religious adherence to the Past and the Ancient, the Desire & the admiration of Permanence, on the one hand; and the Passion for increase of

Knowlege, for Truth as the offspring of Reason, in short, the mighty Instincts of *Progression* and *Free-agency*, on the other." *CL* v 35.

[12] The more obvious rivals were Russia, Austria, France, and Britain. C. W. Crawley described European books about Turkey before 1789 as depicting "a strange world, open perhaps to possible attack and liable to internal decay, but static, self-contained and not very sensitive to external influences"; those during and after the Napoleonic wars treated Turkey "as one more theatre of European war and diplomacy, as a world in which positive winds of change are blowing not only from outside but from within". *The New Cambridge Modern History* x (Cambridge 1965) 526.

[13] Afghanistan had achieved a large degree of autonomy from Persia in 1747 and subsequently virtual independence under Durani rulers. Internal affairs were near chaos from 1816 until 1826, when Dost Mohammad Khan of Kabul secured control. His consolidation of powers and diplomacy would provoke the British to war in 1838. C had earlier expressed a much less favourable view of the Persians, as having provided the Romans

by two figures standing back to back; the latter looking to the East, that is backwards; the European westward, and forwards.[14]   [36:9]

[7 January–13 February 1823]

[a]Negatively there might be more of the sayings of Socrates in the Memorabilia than in Plato; that is, there is less of what is *not* Socrates's[b] but the general spirit and impression left by Plato, is more Socratic.[1]

[36:15]

There was a want of harmony in Lord Byron.[2] It was unnatural to connect very great intellectual powers with utter depravity. Such combination did not exist *in rerum naturâ.*[3]   [36:4]

[a] p 96   [b] ~~Plato's~~ Socrates's

with a debased religion and "a perfect stream of astrologers and nativity-casters and magicians". *P Lects* Lect 7 (1949) 238.

[14] At this point HNC turned back in MS A to fill the blank versos opposite the table-talk he had already recorded. That he thought of all the remarks on pp 96–100 as C's is evident from their inclusion in MS E as well as in the later versions. In MS E his numbered entries begin with p 96, the first page of table-talk in the physical sequence from left to right. He must have made these undated entries between 7 Jan and 13 Feb 1823, for p 102 follows the end of these jottings with a continuation of his diary on 13 Feb.

[1] Xenophon (c 434–355 B.C.) left three works concerned with the life and teachings of Socrates: *Memorabilia, Symposium,* and *Apology.* An annotation on Xenophon *Memoirs of Socrates. With the Defence of Socrates, Before His Judges* tr Sarah Fielding (2nd ed 1767) was published by H. J. C. in *N&Q* 7th ser VII (1889) 90–1. C applauded a depreciation of Xenophon and added his own in 1818 or later: "I feel the want of a *commanding point*, of a *staple*, both as an Historian and as a Moralist. For in my strictest sense of the term, I should hesitate to admit Xenophon as a *Philosopher.*" Annotation on Hugh James Rose (1795–1838) *Prolusio in Curia Cantabrigiensi recitata, nonis jul.*

MDCCCXVIII (Cambridge 1818) 24: *CM (CC)* IV. When the contrast recurs on 1 May 1823 (36:50) (see below, at nn 14 and 15), C distinguishes between the moral aspects of Socrates, reported by both disciples, and the attribution of Pythagorean metaphysics to Socrates in Plato's accounts.

[2] In *TT* (1835), but not in MS E, the statement is made to concern "Lord Byron's verses". Julian Charles Young reported a conversation of C with August Wilhelm von Schlegel at Mrs Charles Aders's house at Godesberg in Jul 1828: "Schlegel praised Scott's poetry. Coleridge decried it, stating that no poet ever lived of equal eminence, whose writings furnished so few quotable passages. Schlegel then praised Byron. Coleridge immediately tried to depreciate him. 'Ah,' said he, 'Byron is a meteor. Wordsworth there' (pointing to him) 'is a fixed star. During the first *furore* of Byron's reputation, the sale of his works was unparalleled, while that of Wordsworth's was insignificant, and now each succeeding year, in proportion as the circulation of Byron's works has fallen off, the issue of Wordsworth's poems has steadily increased.'" Julian Charles Young *A Memoir of Charles Mayne Young* (1871) 112. On Byron see also 2 Jun 1824 at n 10 (36:61).

[3] "In the nature of things".

Old Mortality is the best of the Scotch Novels. Guy Mannering also.[4]

[36:3]

————

He ridiculed the ghost story in Wesley's life.[5]

Define a ghost—visibility without tangibility; that is also the definition of a shadow; therefore they must be the same; because no two different things can have the same definition.[6]   [36:13]

————

This is not a logical age.[7] A friend had lately given him some political pamphlets of the 17th century, in the time of Charles and the Cromwellate.[8] *There* the premises were frequently wrong, but the deductions were

[4] *Guy Mannering* (1815) and *Old Mortality* (1816), like all the novels of Sir Walter Scott before 1827, were anonymous. *Old Mortality*, which appeared with *The Black Dwarf* as the first of the "Tales of My Landlord", pleased C on a rereading in late 1823. *CN* IV 5038. C annotated fifteen of the novels in three sets of Scott's collected novels. Although declining to recommend them as a substitute for history, he averred in *C&S* that a statesman who had not learned from history how a great principle trampled on would avenge itself in the consequences "might in my opinion as profitably, and far more delightfully have devoted his hours of study to Sir Walter Scott's Novels". *C&S (CC)* 100. Of *Guy Mannering* C wrote that though "far from admiring [it] the most yet read with the greatest delight". Annotation on *Ivanhoe* in *Historical Romances* (1824) II 233–5: *CM (CC)* IV.

[5] RS *The Life of Wesley; and the Rise and Progress of Methodism* (2 vols 1820) I 21–2 tells of the occurrences in Wesley's father's house that witnesses believed to be supernatural. C wrote in the margin: "All these Stories, and I could produce 50 at least equally well authenticated and as for the veracity of the Narrators and the single fact of their having seen and heard such & such sights or sounds, above all rational scepticism, are as much like one another, as the symptoms of a same Disease in different patients. And this indeed I take to be the true and only solution/ a contagious nervous Disease, the acme or intensest

form of which is Catalepsy." *CM (CC)* IV. The reference to "Wesley's life" is omitted from *TT* (1835), perhaps to avoid offence to RS.

[6] C gave similar definitions in *Logic (CC)* 130 and in two marginal notes. "And as for Ghosts, it is enough for a man of common sense to observe that a Ghost and a Shadow are concluded in the same definition, viz. Visibility without Tangibility." Daniel Defoe *The Life and Adventures of Robinson Crusoe* (2 vols 1812): *CM (CC)* II 166. The other appears in James Gillman's copy of *SM*: "Reflections, Shadows, Ghosts, Apparitions, i.e. *disembodied* Souls that yet *appear*, are all creatures of the same kind, and comprized in the same general Definition, Visibility without Tangibility." *SM (CC)* 81n. Cf a note of 1806: "Strong proof of the imaginary nature of Ghosts/ i.e. the sensation in the *ex toto* of Nature producing the Ghost, not the Ghost the Terror . . .". *CN* II 2878. On ghosts see also below, at n 14 (36:13), and JTC's record of 9 Jan 1823, above.

[7] Complaining similarly of the decay of logic as early as 1803, C wondered if the "multitude of Maxims, Aphorisms, & Sentences & their popularity among the French, the beginners of this Style", might not be "proof & omen" of the decay. *CN* I 1759. In 1804 he blamed "utter want of Logic" for "careless observation followed by careless narration of Facts, recklessness with regard to Truth" among men educated in "the present system". *CN* II 2205.

[8] C's lifelong interest in the political

always legitimate; whereas in these days the premises are commonly sound, but the conclusions false. He had paid a merited tribute to Oxford in his work on Logic for preserving that study in the schools.[9] Geometry is not a substitute for logic.[10]   [36:14]

Christianity proves itself, as the Sun is seen by his own light. It is; its evidence is involved in its existence.[11]

Either we have an immortal soul or we have not; if we have not, we are beasts; the first and wisest beasts, but still beasts; we only differ in degree, and not in kind; but we are not beasts by the concession of materialists, and by our own consciousness; therefore it must be the possession of a soul within us, that makes the difference.[12]   [36:11]

Read the first chapter of Genesis without prejudice, and you will be convinced at once. After the creation of the animals, Moses pauses—Let

---

and religious disputations of the Cromwellian period is reflected in TT both in general discussions of Charles I and his advisers and in such specific comments as his praise of Richard Baxter. C annotated three bound volumes of political pamphlets, one called "Civil War Tracts" consisting of 39 pamphlets "relating to the Civil Wars", the other two called "Cromwellian Tracts" I and II consisting of 26 and 24 pamphlets respectively: *CM (CC)* II 42–3, 110–12. See also *Friend (CC)* I 410–11, concerning a "volume of old tracts" of Charles I's time.

[9] See above, 29 Dec 1822 and n 3. On the absence of Oxford from the "Logic" as we have it, see *Logic (CC)* lxi.

[10] In 1810 C had noted that "Mathematics cannot be a substitute for Logic". *CN* III 3670.

[11] This remark is omitted from *TT* (1835), and the next (36:11) is expanded in 1835 for clarification. C had written in 1816: "Reason and Religion are their own evidence. The natural Sun is in this respect a symbol of the spiritual. Ere he is fully arisen, and while his glories are still under veil, he calls up the breeze to chase away the usurping vapours of the night-season, and thus converts the air itself into the minister of its own purifica-

tion: not surely in proof or elucidation of the light from heaven, but to prevent its interception." *SM (CC)* 10. In *BL* ch 24, defending this passage against the charge that it encouraged disbelief in miracles, he declared Christianity self-evident in "the experience derived from a practical conformity to the conditions of the Gospel—it is the opening Eye; the dawning Light; the terrors and the promises of spiritual Growth; the blessedness of loving God as God, the nascent sense of Sin hated as Sin, and of the incapability of attaining to either without Christ". *BL (CC)* II 244.

[12] The transition from the sunlike self-evidence of Christianity to the distinguishing soul in man can be made by way of Plotinus, whom C adapts in *Friend (CC)* I 418 to say that "the intelligential soul" contemplates truth because "it is itself of the nature of truth": see *Enneads* 3.8.3–4. As HNC noted in *TT* (1835), C similarly distinguished man from beasts in *C&S* ch 5, in the footnote HNC quoted and a few pages earlier: ". . . individuals who have directed their meditations and their studies to the nobler characters of our nature . . . will be led by the *supernatural* in themselves to the contemplation of a power which is likewise super-*human* . . .". *C&S (CC)* 44.

us make man after *our own image*! and the passage—He breathed into him a *living soul.*[13]   [36:12]

If a[c] ghost is a soul, a soul is substance; and though we might not see it, yet we must feel it. e.g. the wind. A visible substance [d]without susceptibility of impact, is an absurdity. Ghosts are always said to perform trifling and foolish tricks; but the soul which is reason could not turn a spoon round &c.[14]   [36:13]

My uncle was reciting his tragedy at some house, and was in the midst of Alhadra's description of the death of her husband,[15] when a scrubby boy with a shining face set in dirt burst open the door with—"Please, ma'am, master says, will you ha' or will you not ha' the pin round?"[16]
[36:7]

The servant maid at M[r] Gillman's came once into the room, and said, there was someone below, who asked if there was any poet there, and she

[c] ~~the~~ a   [d] p 98

[13] In the King James Version "The First Book of Moses, Called Genesis" 1.26: "And God said, Let us make man in our image, after our likeness"; 2.7: "And the Lord God formed man of the dust of the ground, and breathed into his nostrils the breath of life; and man became a living soul." Attribution of the Pentateuch to Moses, which had entered Jewish tradition in the fourth century B.C., was accepted for practical purposes even by Eichhorn *AT* I 38, 112, II 211–392, but had been challenged by linguistic analysis. Expanding the entry to include the Bible language more exactly, *TT* (1835) added: "Materialism will never explain those last words." The sequence of thought included the discussion of logic, 36:14. Cf "And yet the present form of the whole Pentateuch I cannot help thinking later than Moses." Annotation on Eichhorn *AT: CM (CC)* II 390.

[14] The return to ghosts continues C's attack on the "Boa Constrictor of Materialism". *CL* VI 737. Fuller discussions centring on ghosts are reported by JTC and HNC for 9 Jan (see above) and 1 May (see below).

[15] *Remorse* IV iii 52–94, quoted in HNC's note in *TT* (1835) (with "further" for "farther" in line 89). Written

as *Osorio: a Tragedy* in 1797. *Remorse* was revised, performed at Drury Lane 23 Jan 1813, running for twenty nights, and published the same year. See *PW* (EHC) II 869–71.

We have from George Greenough C's account in 1799 of how *Osorio* failed to be performed in 1797–8: "Coleridge wrote his play . . . wholly at ye Instigation of Sheridan—gave up some emoluments wholly on that account—delivered it to Linley who gave it to Sheridan—Sheridan said it was impossible that anything could be better adapted for representation than ye two first acts and that the whole was excellent for ye Closet. He lent it to Grey, Grey to Whitbread, Whitbread to Sir Francis Burdett and so on till at last Col[eridge] heard Miss de Camp act one of ye Scenes in a public company. Meanwhile Sheridan will give no answer—will not even give audience to Coleridge." Greenough "Diary" 198: *London Mercury* Apr 1931 p 561; *W&C* 230.

[16] If "round" here is a noun, as indicated in the hyphenated "pin-round" of *TT* (1835), the term has escaped all the standard dictionaries. Whether "round" is noun or adverb, the question seems to mean "Would you like to have the pin passed around?" Various folk customs

knew, she said, that Mr C. was a Poet. Down goes my Uncle gravely to the door, and opens it; when a louting[e][17] boy screamed in his face, "Any pots[f] for the Angel?"[18]

John Kemble would correct any body.[19] He was discoursing in his measured manner after dinner, when the servant announced his carriage; but he took no notice of this, but went on; this was repeated twice more at intervals; at last the servant said upon entering the 4th time, "Mrs. Kemble says, Sir, she has the rheumatize, and cannot stay". "Add *ism*", said John, and proceeded in his discourse.[20]   [36:5, 6]

Mathews was performing before the King. The King was pleased with the imitation of Kemble, and told this anecdote—"I liked Kemble very much; he was one of my earliest friends; he was talking and was out of snuff; I offered him my box; he declined taking any; 'He a poor actor could not put his fingers into a royal box.' I said—'Take some, you will

---

[e] lout~~y~~ing   [f] pot~~ess~~

---

associate drinking with pins of various kinds.

[17] The word was perhaps written as "louty", to mean loutish, but rewritten as "louting"; as transcribed in MS E it is clearly "louting". Citing Spenser and Jonson, Johnson's *Dictionary* (8th ed 1799) says of the verb "to lout": "To bend; to bow; to stoop. Obsolete. It was used in a good sense."

[18] Reporting that he heard this anecdote from C at dinner with Thomas Monkhouse on 4 Apr 1823, when WW, Samuel Rogers, and Charles Lamb were also present, Thomas Moore remarked, "Improbable enough". Moore *Journal* II 623–4. Among "some tolerable things" C told a related anecdote: "One of a poor author, who, on receiving from his publisher an account of the proceeds (as he expected it to be) of a work he had published, saw among the items, 'Cellerage, 3*l*, 10*s*, 6*d*.,' and thought it was a charge for the trouble of *selling* the 700 copies, which he did not consider unreasonable; but on inquiry he found it was for the *cellar*-room occupied by his work, not a copy of which had stirred from thence." Ibid. Cf a fuller version of the anecdote in *BL* ch 10 (*CC*) I 178–9. In the transcription of TT for SC, HNC

wrote opposite this entry, "Credat Judaeus": let who will believe it. MS E 15. The entry was not printed, and no scrap survives in MS F to indicate that it was transcribed for use in 1835. Stirred to memory by the anecdotes in *TT* (1835), Daniel Stuart wrote to HNC on 19 Sept 1835: "Before Coleridge was known to me, he told me [he] had offerred some Poems to Debrett the Bookseller in Piccadilly for a small sum, and that Debrett recommended that he should write something 'warm'. Coleridge did not attend to this. Have we any 'warm' Poets?" VCL S MS F 6 f 4.

[19] John Philip Kemble (1757–1823), actor and theatre manager, died at Lausanne on 26 Feb. For C's rapid and lasting disenchantment with Kemble, see *CL* I 318, 357, 635, III 14.

[20] A version of this anecdote, given as witnessed by Charles Mathews at Lord North's and related by Mathews to George III, appears along with the King's capping anecdote (next paragraph) in Mrs Anne Jackson Mathews *Memoirs of Charles Mathews, Comedian* (4 vols 1838–9) III 296–7. HNC's changes in *TT* (1835) show that he either never understood or later forgot that C's source for the anecdote was Mathews.

obl*eege* me.' John said, 'It would become your royal jaws better to say "obl*ige*" me.' "[21]   [36:6]

St John used Λόγος[22] technically; Philo-Judæus had so used it before,[23] and it was commonly understood of the *Schechinah*.[24] Πρὸς τὸν Θεὸν

[21] In May 1814 C wrote from Bristol to the comic actor Charles Mathews (1776–1835) with praise and advice. *CL* III 500–1. In 1819, when Mathews moved to Ivy Cottage, Kentish Town, he and C became neighbours and warm friends. See *Memoirs* III 188–95; *CL* IV 940–1, V 10–11, 33, 39, 139, 235, VI 753 n 5. Tom Moore reported of a day with Mathews, 21 Sept 1825: "Mathews's imitation of Coleridge admirable; the 'single-*moindedness*,' &c. &c." Moore *Journal* II 833. Herman Merivale, reviewing *TT* in *Ed Rev* LXI (Apr 1835) 153, identified the anecdote, "if we mistake not", as one that Mathews "has long been in the habit of imparting to large assemblies of friends at the Adelphi", where Mathews gave a long series of popular performances under the generic title "At Home". Merivale's explanation was that C was too secluded to know "whether the anecdotes which he was fond of recounting were or were not public property". Nothing in the ms version of the two anecdotes suggests that C was claiming them as his personal experience. In 1835 HNC introduced such transitional phrases as "I remember a party" to heighten the drama; he thereby unintentionally created the suggestion that C told as his own what he had probably heard with others at one of the trial runs for "At Home" that Mathews gave at Ivy Cottage for friends. The apt pun of a "royal box" does not appear in Mrs Mathews's version. She wrote in the *Memoirs* of C's "beautiful simplicity of manner", his charming way of bending to lesser intellects, his tenderness with the sick, his many trips to her garden, his attempt once to walk through a mirror in leaving their house, a dinner on 5 May 1819 at the Gillmans' to meet Lamb. Although C had the two anecdotes concerning Kemble from Mathews, an account of Kemble's correction of the pronunci-

ation of the Prince Regent (not yet King) was published between C's retailing and *TT* (1835), as coming from a source other than Kemble, in James Boaden *Memoirs of the Life of John Philip Kemble, Including a History of the Stage from Garrick to the Present Period* (2 vols 1825) II 559. Boaden reports two episodes: on the first, Kemble modestly suggested that he did not himself pronounce "oblige" in the French manner; on a later occasion, the Prince took snuff from a box he had presented to Kemble as a gift and then pronounced "obliged" correctly.

[22] "Word": John 1.1. In attempting to adapt the theosophy of Jakob Böhme to contemporary science, C, in a marginal note, linked the Logos to Creation: "Hence in the Logos (distinctive Energy) is *Light*, and the Light became the *Life* of Man—Now [that] the Blood is the Life, is affirmed by Moses—and has been forcibly maintained by John Hunter." *The Works of Jacob Behmen* (4 vols 1764–81): *CM (CC)* I 624.

[23] C encountered in 1795 a discussion of Philo's trinitarian doctrine of the Logos in Ralph Cudworth *The True Intellectual System of the Universe* ed Thomas Birch bk 1 ch 4 ("2nd ed" 2 vols 1743) I 465–6, 550–3; see *Lects 1795 (CC)* 86–7. Cudworth and John Whitaker *The Origin of Arianism Disclosed* (1791), which C annotated, cited as source Eusebius Pamphili *Preparatio evangelica* bk 7 ch 13, bk 11 chs 24–5 (Migne *PG* XXI 545–7, 886, 912). Eusebius quoted works of Philo since lost. C referred appreciatively to Philo on the Logos in *CL* IV 632, 803, 850; *P Lects* Lects 7, 10 (1949) 239–40, 299; *SM (CC)* 95; *C&S (CC)* 84n; *CN* III 3824. He defended Philo against Eichhorn in annotations on *Apokryphischen Schriften* 172 and *NT* II 111. *CM (CC)* II 433, 458.

[24] Usually spelled Shekinah or Shek-

"with God" is an unfortunate translation, that would be σὺν τῷ Θεῷ.[25] Προς meant the utmost possible proximity without confusion;[g] likeness without sameness.[26] The Jewish church understood the Messiah to be a divine person.[27] Philo-Judæus expressly cautions against supposing it a mere personification, a mere symbol; it was a substantial [h]self-existent Being. Those, who were afterwards called Gnostics, were a kind of Arians, and thought the Λόγος was an after-birth.[28] They placed ἄβυσσος

hinah, meaning " 'dwelling', Divine Presence, the numinous immanence of God in the world"—*Encyclopaedia Judaica* (16 vols + New York 1971–). For identifications of the Shekinah with the Logos, see Whitaker pp 40, 70, 93–4. In 1819 C expounded the cabbalistic doctrine of the seventh Sephiroth as "the Messiah or the Shekinah", who "was to be the same as the second person of the triad, and to be in the Shekinah a concentration of all the seven spirits of the manifestation, a doctrine which must have been very early indeed in the Church, because we find a clear reference to it in the beginning of the Apocalypse". *P Lects* Lect 10 (1949) 299. The reference is to Rev 1.4: "Grace be unto you, and peace, from him which is, and which was, and which is to come; and from the seven Spirits which are before his throne."

[25] The two Greek phrases, "hard by God" (at least in the construction C places on πρὸς), "in company with God"—John 1.1: "and the Word was with God". In an informal but considered passage on the subject, probably in 1818, C wrote: "Therefore God alone is a self-comprehending Spirit; and in this incommunicable *Adequate* Idea of himself (Λόγος) his Personality is contained—πρὸς τὸν Θεόν (very ill translated by the preposition, with) καὶ Θεός. Philo has asserted the same, and anxiously guards against the misconception that the Logos is an Attribute or Personification or generic or abstract term.— *Est* enim, et est Deus alter et idem." *CL* IV 850. Concerning a similar assertion see *SM (CC)* 95 and n 3. C must find in "alter et idem" some such trinitarian phrase as "different and yet one with".

On C's fuller handling of the "Deus idem et alter" in the Opus Maximum see J. Robert Barth *Coleridge and Christian Doctrine* (Cambridge, Mass 1969) 89–93. One of C's fullest glosses on John 1.1 is an annotation on an endleaf of Heinrich Steffens *Ueber die Idee der Universitäten* (Berlin 1809): "I would have followed St John's example, and have called the Ens Supremum, or the absolutely Real, the co-eternal Offspring of the Absolute Cause of Reality, THE WORD relatively to the Eternal Mind, the Reason, the living self-subsistent Reason; relatively to the Absolute Will & as its only adequate Exponent—& then have shewn its incorporation in the Visible World—and lastly, its incarnation or personal Humanization in the Son of Man, *the* CHRIST." *CM (CC)* IV.

[26] On the Logos as person see e.g. *CL* IV 632, 850 and *CM (CC)* II 433.

[27] In a long marginal note in Lamb's copy of Jeremy Taylor ΣΥΜΒΟΛΟΝ ΘΕΟΛΟΓΙΚΟΝ: *or A Collection of Polemicall Discourses* (3rd ed 2 pts in 1 vol 1674) I 813–31 C discussed the opinions of the "Rabbis of best name" concerning the Messiah, the millennium, and a future state (Saeculum Futurum). He granted a distinction: "The Christian Doctrine of a Suffering Messiah, or of Christ as the High Priest & Intercessor has of course introduced a modification of the Jewish Scheme". *CM (CC)* V.

[28] When C gave an account, in LRR in 1795, of Gnostic beliefs he was dependent largely on Joseph Priestley "Of the Principles of the Christian Gnostics" *An History of Early Opinions Concerning Jesus Christ* (4 vols Birmingham 1786) I 139–49. *Lects 1795 (CC)* 195–202. Par-

and σιγη before him.[29] Therefore John said ἐν ἀϱχῇ ἦν ὁ Λόγος.[30] He was begotten in the first simultaneous burst of Godhead, if such expression can be used in speaking of Eternal Existence.   [36:31,32]

Snuff was the final cause of the human nose.[31]   [36:21]

Great writers wrote best when calm and exerting themselves upon subjects unconnected with party or passion. Burke never shows his powers, except he is in a passion.[32] The French Revolution was alone a subject fit

aphrasing Priestley on the gnostic Valentinus, C said in 1795 (p 199): "Their genealogy of Christ is amusing from its absurdity. . . . Logos and Zoe were the offspring of Nous and Αληθεια, that is, of pure Intelligence and Truth, and Nous and Aletheia were the offspring of Bythus and Sigè, or, Abyss and Silence." On the Gnostics see also 6 Jun 1830, below, and nn 9 and 10.

[29] The "Abyss" (or "Depth") and "Silence". Cf Gilles Quispel's summary of the gnostic Valentinus in Irenaeus *Adversus haereses* 1.1.1: "In invisible and ineffable heights the perfect Aeon, called Depth, was pre-existent. Incomprehensible and invisible, eternal and unbegotten, he was throughout endless ages in serenity and quiescence. And with him was Silence. And Depth conceived the idea to send forth from himself the origin of all and committed this emanation, as if it were a seed, to the womb of Silence." *Gnostic Studies* I (Istanbul 1974) 31.

[30] John 1.1: "In the beginning was the Word". Cf "St John clearly meant the words εν αϱχη as synonymous with *Eternally* or From all Eternity." Annotation on Böhme *Works: CM (CC)* I 681.

[31] HNC may have missed an attribution of the remark to RS, whose poem *Snuff* in *AA* (1800) II 115–16 had defended snuff as the reason for the human nose: "Why but for thee the uses of the Nose | Were half unknown . . . ". C noted in 1810: "Sarah Coleridge says, on telling me of the universal Sneeze produced in the Lasses while shaking my Carpet that she wishes, my Snuff would *grow*: as I sow it so plentifully." *CN* III 3826, copied (var) by HNC in MS B f 112.

[32] Edmund Burke (1729–97), Irish

Protestant statesman (MP from 1765), appears prominently in C's thought from schooldays to *C&S* (1830) and later. C here denies to him the highest rank, but he is "a great man" (below, 5 Apr 1833 at n 22), superior to Dr Johnson (below, 1 Jul 1833 at nn 25–7), indeed of "measureless superiority to those about him" (*Friend—CC—*I 189). "He referred habitually to *principles*. He was a *scientific* statesman; and therefore a *seer*." *BL* ch 10 (*CC*) I 191. Charles Valentine Le Grice recalled of C at Cambridge: "What little suppers, or *sizings*, as they were called, have I enjoyed; when Aeschylus, and Plato, and Thucydides were pushed aside, with a pile of lexicons, &c., to discuss the pamphlets of the day. Ever and anon, a pamphlet issued from the pen of Burke. There was no need of having the book before us. Coleridge had read it in the morning, and in the evening he would repeat whole pages verbatim." "College Reminiscences of Mr. Coleridge" *G Mag* 2nd ser II (1834) 606. Like Burke and most British writers then and since, C found the French Revolution characterised by "its sanguinary and sensual abominations". *Friend (CC)* I 410; cf 327. As the remark recorded by HNC indicates, C felt more certain about the causes of the Revolution than its consequences and implications. Although never underestimating the despotism of the French monarchy, he found even more culpable the corruption of moral and political philosophy that preceded the Revolution, which thus became the "closing *monsoon*" of the self-proclaimed Enlightenment. *Friend (CC)* I 482; cf 85, 180–1; *SM (CC)* 14–17, 33–4, 61–2.

for him. We are not yet aware of the important consequences of that event. We are too near it. [36:19]

Goldsmith did every thing happily.[33] [36:20]

Δακρύοεν γελάσασα[34] looked like an expression of Moschus or Bion.[35] Pindar called it[36] [36:18]

A rogue is a roundabout fool; a Knave[i] in *circumbendibus*.[37] [36:22]

He did not believe St Paul to be the author of the Epistle to the Hebrews; he thought Luther's conjecture very probable, that it was Apollos, an Alexandrian Jew.[38] The plan was too studiously regular for St Paul. It was

[i] Knave ⟨fool⟩

[33] C's infrequent references to Oliver Goldsmith (1728–74), whether to *The Deserted Village, Retaliation, The Traveller, The Vicar of Wakefield*, or *The Citizen of the World* or other essays, express a measured contentment, usually with such phrases as "delightful Poems with good sense" (but "without the passion . . . of the poetic character"), "an overpowering Delight to a Lad of Feeling", "in so happy a manner", "with so much humour". *CN* I 829, II 2516; *Friend (CC)* I 189; *SM (CC)* 24n.

[34] *Iliad* 6.484; tr Richmond Lattimore: "smiling in her tears"—Andromache taking her son Astyanax again as Hector returns to battle.

[35] *TT* (1835) is more explicit: "It sounds to me much more like a prettiness of Bion or Moschus." Reviewing *TT* in *Ed Rev* LXI (Apr 1835) 151, Merivale objected to C's reservation: "But the phrase, 'smiling in tears', only represents a natural appearance, which may be observed on the face of any woman or any child: no fanciful antithesis, but a real picture. We see no reason why Homer . . . may not have remarked and portrayed it, long before more artificial poets tortured it into point and epigram." Bion of Smyrna and Moschus of Syracuse were second-century B.C. pastoral followers of Theocritus. RS and Robert Lovell employed the pseudonyms "Bion" and "Moschus" in *Poems* (1794).

[36] Uncompleted in MS A and MS E 22 and omitted from *TT* (1835).

[37] A jocular macaronic: *circum* + *bend* as a Latin ablative plural. Johnson gave as the first definition of a rogue, "A wandering beggar; a vagrant; a vagabond." Later than the original entry "Knave" was cancelled and "fool"— the reading of MS E 23 and *TT* (1835)— written above it.

[38] The Biblical account of Apollos begins at Acts 18.24: "And a certain Jew named Apollos, born at Alexandria, an eloquent man, and mighty in the scriptures, came to Ephesus." For his doctrines as a source of contention see 1 Cor 1.12, 3.4–6. Luther's Preface to his translation of the Epistle to the Hebrews suggests Apollos as author. Eichhorn *NT* III 477, noting Luther's suggestion, accepted equally the possibility of some other unknown apostolic author. C wrote in Anne Gillman's Bible: "It was evidently written by some converted Jew of Alexandria: by a singularly happy conjecture, Luther assigned it to Apollos. Whoever was the Author (for Luther's is but a conjecture) it is the Work of an Apostolic Man & worthy of its place in the Christian Canon." *CM (CC)* I 467. Writing to J. H. Green in 1829 C dated the work as apostolic rather than, like Matthew and the Apocalypse, "the earliest post-apostolic". *CL* VI 784. See also above, 9 Jan 1823 (at n 3).

evidently written during the yet existing glories of the temple. For 300 years the Church had not affixed St Paul's name to it; but its inspiration, independently of its genuineness as to St Paul, was never doubted.[39] The three first gospels showed the history, that is, the fulfillment of the prophecies in the facts; St John declared explicitly the doctrine, *oracularly* and without argument; because being pure reason, it could only be proved by itself; St Paul wrote for the understanding, and proved the doctrine by human logic.[40]   [36:29, 30]

The Persians came from Elam, who was a son of Japheth; hence their European superiority.[41] Kant had declared the existence of three races of mankind.[42] If two races*j* cross, a third is different from either; a white and

j ~~ef a~~ race⟨s⟩

[39] So Eichhorn *NT* III 477; see also 506–26. Among others, Origen, c A.D. 250, listed Hebrews among the acknowledged books.

[40] A notebook entry of 1815 clarifies C's view of the three synoptic gospels: "I think it highly probable and even supported by both internal Evidence, and the practice of the early Fathers and Apologists, that the Gospels, the first three at least & more especially, were written not as Evidence for Unbelievers and *Convertendis* but for those who had received the Faith, had been satisfied as far as external Evidence can satisfy in a religious Code . . .". *CN* III 4255. He accepted without alarm Eichhorn's conclusion (*NT* I 511–12) that Matthew could not have been written before A.D. 70. See *CM (CC)* II 450. On the attribution of the book to Matthew see C's note on Eichhorn *AT: CM (CC)* II 400. In a marginal note on Eichhorn *NT* C was more more specific than in this TT entry concerning John: his purpose was "to represent the Messias as the Regenerator and Redeemer of Man", his object "to emancipate the idea of personëity from the phænomenal notion of Outline, and (generally) from the sensuous Definite in space and time". *CM (CC)* II 456; cf II 462.

[41] HNC, appealing to Gen 10.22, noted in MS E 27: " + This is a mistake. Elam was the son of Shem." Elam, an ancient country between Media and the Persian Gulf, annexed by Persia c 600

B.C., was occupied by a non-Semitic people of uncertain origin. Gen 14.1 names "Chedorlaomer king of Elam"; the Elamites are referred to in Ezra 4.9, Dan 8.2, Acts 2.9. Presumably C made Elam a son of Japheth by a slip of the tongue—not so puzzling as Elam and the other "sons" of Shem have been to Biblical scholars. The first assumption implicit here is that extant humanity descends from the three sons of Noah: Shem, Ham, and Japheth. The racial link of the Persians and Europeans is explained by C's notes of Jan 1818 for his lecture on the emergence of a new literature shortly before Petrarch. *CN* III 4384 ff 158ᵛ–157ᵛ. "Madai, the Son of Japhet, and probably with others of the elder Brothers of Javan, became the Ancestors of the Medes and of the Persians, who are to this day happily characterized as the Europeans of Asia . . .". Ibid f 157. C read widely concerning the migration of races, and returned to the subject on 24 Feb 1827, below (at nn 12–14).

The sentence concerning Elam is omitted from *TT* (1835). What C calls the "European superiority" of the Persians was a special emphasis of Sir William Jones, who assigned Persian, and in a later migration of Sanskrit, to the tribe of Ham. Discourse of 23 Feb 1792 "On the Origin and Families of Nations" *Works* (13 vols 1807) III 185–95.

[42] Although deriving racial differences from Gen 9.19, "These are the

a negro produce a mulatto; but different species produce by chance; sometimes the offspring are like one species, sometimes another. English and Spaniard.[43]   [36:10, 65]

———

[k]The *understanding* suggests the materials of reasoning; *Reason* decides upon them. The first can only say—this *is* or *ought* to be so; the last says—it *must* be so.[44]   [36:33]

———

27. April. 1823.

[a]My uncle Samuel dined at John's.[1] He talked very fluently and intelligibly. I never heard him to more advantage.

[k] p 102
[l] HNC's diary continues (pp 102–3) with notes on his own life and reading
[a] MS A p 103

———

three sons of Noah: and of them was the whole earth overspread", Kant declared the existence of four races, as determined largely by colour of skin: white, copper, black, and olive: "Von den verschiedenen Racen der Menschen" (1775) and "Bestimmung des Begriffs einer Menschenrace" (1785) in *Vermischte Schriften* (Halle 1799) II 607–60. Among C's several attempts to reconcile "the Mosaic Triad" with the accounts of Kant and Blumenbach concerning the geographical dispersal of races, see especially *CN* IV 4548, C's annotations on Johann Friedrich Blumenbach *Über die natürlichen Verschiedenheiten im Menschengeschlechte* (Leipzig 1798)—*CM (CC)* I 535–41—and below, 24 Feb 1827 and nn 12–14.

[43] After noting in MS E 27 that C should have said, not "different species", but "rather 'varieties of the same species' ", HNC expanded in *TT* (1835) for clarification. Charles Darwin (1809–82) was not able to carry questions of heredity beyond C's assumptions; the science of genetics awaited developments about 1900 from the principles of Gregor Johann Mendel (1822–84).

[44] The distinctions between reason and understanding that are fundamental to C's philosophical writings take their chief impulse from Kant's *Kritik der*

reinen Vernunft (1781). The moral aspect of the distinction emphasised in this entry in TT derives from the *Kritik der praktischen Vernunft* (1788). Kant's thought "took possession" of C "as with a giant's hand" in 1801—*BL* ch 9 (*CC*) I 153—but he rejected Kant's limitation on the capacity of reason to know ultimate truth. For C the ideas of reason are constitutive, not merely regulative: "Thus, God, the Soul, eternal Truth, &c. are the objects of Reason; but they are themselves *reason*." *Friend (CC)* I 156. The understanding operates only on the experience of the senses; the moral necessities of reason are supersensuous. C began to define the differences as early as Oct 1806: *CL* II 1198. See esp *SM* App C: *SM (CC)* 59–93. He explained the distinction "more popularly" in *Friend (CC)* I 154–61. Detailed discussions occur in "The Reason and the Understanding", two pages of notes at HEHL, and in HEHL MS HM 17299 (N F°) p 118 (of 1827), and in *AR* (1825) 196–7, 207–28. See also below, 9 May 1830 (at n 13).

[1] At the end of Jan 1823 SC and Mrs C left Highgate to stay with JTC in London until their departure for Devon, where they arrived at Fair Mile on 20 Mar. Although HNC and SC became engaged during this period, C saw neither of them. *CL* V 271; *The Story of a Devon-*

Kean was original, but copied from himself.[2] His rapid descents from the hyper-tragical to the infra-colloquial, *b*though sometimes productive of great effect, were often unreasonable.[3] He was not a thorough gentleman enough to play Othello. [36:34]

Sir James Mackintosh was the King of the Men of Talent.[4] He was an elegant converser. He once gave breakfast to my uncle and Sir H. Davy,

b w̶c̶h̶ though

---

shire House p 282. In the available days of March, C was too ill to see them, but in the interval before HNC next saw him, on 26 Apr, he was notably present for dinner parties given on 4 Apr by Thomas Monkhouse and on 5 Apr by Mr and Mrs Charles Aders; see *CRB* I 292–3; *CRC* I 125; Moore *Memoirs* IV 49–50; [HCR] "Charles Lamb and Thomas Moore" *Athenaeum* 25 Jun 1853 pp 771–2. On 26 Apr, a Saturday, with SC and her mother remaining in Devon, C was scheduled to dine, and did dine, with his brother, Col James Coleridge, and wife, visiting at the Hadlow St residence of their son, JTC. *CL* v 273.

[2] Edmund Kean (1787–1833), from his triumphant return to Drury Lane in 1814 onwards, was famous as a tragedian who burst into momentary "hits" of furious theatricality. On 28 Feb 1823 C wrote to Godwin: "As to Kean, it would be superfluous to say a word—a man, whose genial originality, whose unique and multiform energy in the evolution of Thought, Passion, and Character, in one word whose intense Genius in re-creating the creations of the World's first Genius, are granted—I had almost said—*conclaimed*—even by those whose Preconceptions of Tragedy are at variance with his—." *CL* v 269. Godwin had apparently suggested that C submit his translation of Schiller's *Wallenstein* to Kean for production; C promised to do so "with very little expectation of the result". Perhaps C's expectation had sagged even lower by April, but HNC may have recorded only qualifications to what he considered conventional or universal praise, and C's hopes of production by Kean were alive later in the year.

S Life (CS) v 142. Hazlitt, who is representative of the major writers in preferring Kean's bursts of passion to Kemble's classical control, concluded after two seasons that Kean's acting "is always energetic or nothing". *H Works* v 223. When Joseph Hughes referred in a sermon to "the Siddons, the sublime, tremendous, super-tragical Kean", C objected only to the one word "the": see John Leifchild *Memoir of the Late Rev. Joseph Hughes, A.M.* (1835) 274; *CL* VI 1051; Joseph Hughes *Attachment to Life* (1822) 5–6.

[3] In a review of *TT* (1835) William Jerdan said of this passage that it "was uttered in our company, and the phrase then was, 'super-tragic to the sub-colloquial;' but both are good, and very pithy". *Literary Gazette* 23 May 1835 p 321. Jerdan did not remark specifically on the famous sentence introduced at this point in *TT* (1835): "To see him act, is like reading Shakespeare by flashes of lightning." Henry Blake McLellan heard C say of the historian Pufendorf on 27 Apr 1832: "His mind is like some mighty volcano, red with flame, and dark with tossing clouds of smoke, through which the lightnings play and glare most awfully." *Nation* 14 Jul 1910 p 32.

[4] Sir James Mackintosh (1765–1832), Scottish philosopher and historian, was the lifelong exemplar for C of talent without genius. He had defended the French Revolution in *Vindiciae Gallicae* (1791) but soon recanted. Daniel Stuart's brother-in-law and related by a second marriage to Josiah and Thomas Wedgwood, a legal officer and then judge in Bombay (1804–11), lecturer, and MP,

then an unknown young man.[5] There was much conversation about Locke &c.[6] Afterwards Mackintosh said to my uncle "That's a very extraordinary young man; but he is gone wrong upon some points." There

Mackintosh recommended offices for C's talents (rather than for his genius) on various occasions. Francis Jeffrey, in reviewing *Memoirs of the Life of the Right Honourable Sir James Mackintosh*, spent seven pages counterattacking this passage and the denigration of Mackintosh in HNC's Preface. *Ed Rev* LXII (1835) 242–8. Jeffrey presented a case of Mackintosh's orderliness against C's multifarious incompetence. Jerdan's review of *TT* (1835) also noted the passage: "Of Mackintosh we have heard Coleridge speak more bitterly; more bitterly than we will repeat of the dead, and especially as we remember one of the fiercest cuts of all was in the shape of an epitaph." *Literary Gazette* 23 May 1835 p 321. In 1800 C assured Godwin that Davy "defends you with a friend's zeal against the Animalcula, who live on the dung of the great Dung-fly Mackintosh". *CL* I 588. This is the tone also of C's lampoon, which he discussed on 31 Mar 1833, below (at n 6). Attending a series of lectures by Mackintosh in 1800, C found certain points "vague & unmeaning", others "ludicrous or *approaching* to the Ludicrous", for Mackintosh asserted "the old Tale of no abstract Ideas" and made "Idea (of course) mean Image". *CN* I 634. A notebook entry of 1805 seems to confirm the suspicion of scholars that Mackintosh is referred to in the motto affixed to *LB* (1800) and after, "Quam nihil ad genium, Papiniane, tuum!", which Thomas Hutchinson translated "How absolutely *not* after your liking, O learned jurist!" See *CN* II 2468n. See also JTC's report of 20 Apr 1811, above (at n 18). For further details of the relationship between C and Mackintosh see Woodring 151–3, 252 nn 22–3.

[5] Sir Humphry Davy (1778–1829), chemist, president of the Royal Society in 1820, was C's friend from 1799. About 1814 C wrote that they had been "for many years at a great distance from each other—but that may happen with no real breach of Friendship . . . we are now separated". *CN* III 4221. Perhaps there is a double meaning in his public reference after Davy's death to "my illustrious (alas! I must add, I fear, my *late*) friend". *C&S (CC)* 91. Cottle testified to their friendship in 1807: "Having introduced Mr. Davy to Mr. C. some years before, I inquired for him with some anxiety, and expressed a hope that he was not tinctured with the prevailing scepticism since his removal from Bristol to London. Mr. C. assured me that he was not: that *his* heart and understanding were not the *soil* for infidelity. I then remarked, 'During your stay in London, you doubtless saw a great many of what are called "the cleverest men," how do you estimate Davy, in comparison with these?' Mr. Coleridge's reply was strong, but expressive. 'Why, Davy could eat them all! There is an energy, an elasticity in his mind, which enables him to seize on, and analyze, all questions, pushing them to their legitimate consequences. Every subject in Davy's mind has the principle of vitality. Living thoughts spring up like the turf under his feet.' With equal justice, Mr. Davy entertained the same exalted opinion of Mr. Coleridge." Cottle *Rem* 328–9. On Davy see also JTC's report of 20 Apr 1811, above (at n 18).

[6] In Feb 1801 C wrote a series of letters to Josiah Wedgwood (with copies to Poole) to prove that Locke, particularly in *An Essay Concerning Human Understanding* (1690), gained a high reputation "to which he had no honest claim" and "to which T. Wedgwood & *after* him Mackintosh have laboured to raise him". *CL* II 677–703. For "Locke &c" *TT* (1835) reads "Locke and Newton, and so forth". On Locke see also JTC's report of 20 Apr 1811, above (at nn 17 and 18), and below, 14 Aug 1831 (at n 27).

was a freshness about the mind of Davy which was strongly contrasted with that of Mackintosh. Davy's thoughts were like the flower plucked wet with the dew; nay more, you could see them growing in the rich garden of his mind. The mind of Mackintosh was a hortus siccus;[7] full of specimens of every kind of plant, but dwarfed, ready cut and dried. He was like a liquor shop, where if you ask for gin, out they pour it from this phial; if for brandy, from that; so whatever was the subject, Mackintosh had a pre-arranged discourse upon it. In short he was, as the chief of men of talent, of course very powerful; but he possessed not a ray of Genius. After leaving Davy you would remember many sayings and things which would stick by you for days and set you thinking for yourself; but, although you would admire Mackintosh and be much taken with his fluency and brilliancy, you would carry off nothing. Coleridge proposed to write on his forehead, "Warehouse to let."[c8] He dealt too much in generalities for a [d]lawyer. He was deficient in power in applying his principles to the particulars in question. Robert Smith had more logical ability; but he always aimed at conquest by any means.[9] Mackintosh was candid.   [36:35]

[c] lett.'   [d] p 104

[7] "Dry garden"; a collection of dried plants. C noted in Dec 1799: "Mackintosh intrudes, not introduces his beauties. Nothing grows out of his main argument but much is shoved between—each digression occasions a move backward to find the road again—like a sick man he recoils after every affection", whereas the writer of genius "varies his course yet still glides onwards—all lines of motion are his—all beautiful, & all propulsive". *CN* I 609. Davy's imagery from nature for C in 1803 is quite unlike C's flower "wet with dew": "Brilliant images of greatness float upon his mind, like images of the morning clouds on the waters. Their forms are changed by the motions of the waves, they are agitated by every breeze, and modified by every sunbeam." *BE* I 251.

[8] Hazlitt had publicly quoted C as calling Mackintosh in 1798 "a clever scholastic man—a master of the topics,—or as the ready warehouseman of letters, who knew exactly where to lay his hand on what he wanted, though the goods were not his own". "My First Acquaintance with Poets" *Liberal* II (1823) 30. In

TT (1835), in which the passage about the "liquor shop" was omitted, "Warehouse to let" struck Jeffrey as the meanest insinuation in an "unjust" and "arrogant" attack: "It can scarcely mean (though that is the most obvious sense) that the head was empty. . . . If it was intended to insinuate that it was ready for the indiscriminate reception of any thing which one might choose to put into it, there could not have been a more gross misconception . . .". "Memoirs of Sir James Mackintosh" *Ed Rev* LXII (1835) 205–55. For James Fenimore Cooper's comparison of C and Mackintosh (C lectured, whereas Mackintosh conversed), Samuel Rogers on C vs Mackintosh, and the Rev Robert Hall's estimate of Mackintosh, part of which SC quoted in *TT* (1851) 15n, see App F 1, below.

[9] Robert Percy ("Bobus") Smith (1770–1845), politician, advocate-general of Bengal 1803–10, only a little less renowned for wit than his elder brother Sydney. C named him in 1792 as "a man of immense Genius" who was competing with C for prizes at Cambridge. *CL* I 34. In 1808 he included both Smiths with

Canning was very irritable, surprisingly so for a wit who was always giving hard knocks.[10] He should have put on an ass's skin before he went into Parliament. The Cabinet could hardly stand; it was composed of such jarring materials. Canning and Plunket must both feel mortified and wounded.[11] Lord Liverpool was the stay of the Ministry, but he was not a man of a directing mind. He could not ride on the whirlwind. He served

Mackintosh among those whose presence made him feel "like a Child—nay, rather like an Inhabitant of another Planet—their very faces all act upon me, sometimes as if they were Ghosts, but more often as if I were a Ghost, among them—at all times, as if we were not *consubstantial*''; therefore, he concluded, "I must have some *analogon* of Genius''. *CN* III 3324. Mme de Staël reportedly enjoyed Robert's victories over her in conversation, and "Mr. Canning used to say, 'Bobus's language is the essence of English.' " *A Memoir of the Reverend Sydney Smith by His Daughter, Lady Holland, with a Selection from His Letters* ed Mrs Austin (3rd ed 1855) I 99.

[10] George Canning (1770–1827), statesman, had resigned as governor-general of India, returned to Parliament, and in Sept 1822 became for the second time Foreign Secretary. First shifting from the Whigs as a student at Oxford, Canning had become a protégé of Pitt in opposition to the French Revolution; in 1797–8, with George Ellis, he edited the *Anti-Jacobin, or Weekly Examiner*, in which he pilloried C and his friends. Until Canning refused office in 1812, C disliked and distrusted his "insolent & womanish mind''. *CL* III 168, 195, 260; *EOT (CC)* II 13n. From 1804 Canning's restlessness with his ministerial colleagues was publicly known; in 1809 he appalled C by fighting a duel with Castlereagh. *CL* III 227, 241. But he subscribed to *The Friend* through William Sturges–Bourne, and in later years was sent copies of C's works as they appeared. After Frere introduced Canning to C in 1816 C thought him "highly gifted'', "judicious'', and "nobly principled'' (*CL* IV 654, 671), but wrong on Catholic emancipation, the "one issue

on which Canning was not equivocal''. Peter Dixon *George Canning: Politician and Statesman* (New York 1976) 204. Concerning the attacks of the *Anti-Jacobin* on the Pantisocrats, Gillman wrote: "Canning had the faculty of satire to an extraordinary degree, and also that common sense tact, which made his services at times so very useful to his country. . . . He never attempted a display of depth, but his dry sarcasm left a sting which those he intended to wound carried off *in pain and mortification.*'' *C Life* (G) 70–1. John Hookham Frere, replying to Mrs Gillman from Malta that he had rather not be mentioned in a book that so misrepresented Canning's motives, explained that "this very common tact, teaches him to avoid any *display of depth* as invidious and open to ridicule and subsequent misrepresentation''. UT ms. C reacted strongly pro or con to each of Canning's public acts in 1822–6. *CN* IV 4920, 4938, 5234, 5330.

[11] *TT* (1835) omitted C's judgement that the cabinet "could hardly stand''. William Conyngham Plunket (1764–1854), Irish barrister and politician, created 1st Baron Plunket in 1827, had introduced two bills for Catholic emancipation in 1821, but they were rejected by both the House of Lords and the Irish clergy. When Plunket declined to reintroduce the bills in 1822, Canning came forward with a more modest compromise, which passed in the Commons but lost decisively in the Lords. When Daniel O'Connell's Catholic Association began its growth and agitation in 1823, Canning, in a quandary, recommended to Plunket that Catholics enter a period of quiescence. Plunket, as attorney-general of Ireland, was to create more trouble for Canning and the ministry in Dec 1824 by attempting to prosecute O'Connell.

as the isthmus to connect one part of the ministry with the other. He always gave the common sense of the matter.[12]					[36:36]

The national debt had made more men rich than had a right to be so. It was like an ordinary, where three hundred tickets have been distributed, but where there is only room for one hundred. So long as you can amuse the company with any thing else, or make them come successively, all is well, and the whole 300 fancy themselves sure of a dinner; but if suspicion of a hoax should arise, and they were all to rush into the room at once, there would be 200 without a potatoe for their money, and the table would be occupied by the landholders who lived on the spot.[13]	[36:37]

The poor laws were the necessary accompaniments of increasing commerce and manufacturing systems. In Scotland they did without them, till Glasgow and Paisley became great manufacturing places, and then people said, "We must subscribe for the poor, or we shall have poor laws".[14] So they made themselves poor laws in order to avoid having

[12] Robert Banks Jenkinson, 2nd Earl of Liverpool (1770–1828), Prime Minister 1812–27, was harsh against the Irish rebels but favoured concessions to the Catholics unsatisfactory to Plunket on one hand and to Sir Robert Peel's anti-emancipation views on the other. HNC is reporting C's views in a relatively early stage of the whirlwind. Personal memories were fresh: Frere had arranged for C to dine with Liverpool and Canning on 17 Jun 1820; encountering C at Ramsgate in Nov 1822, Canning recognised him before Liverpool did, but the Prime Minister treated him better. *CL* v 55, 257.

[13] C is here less favourable towards the national debt than in fuller discussions of 31 Mar 1833, below (at n 2), and *The Friend* for 9 Nov 1809 (virtually unchanged in 1818): *Friend (CC)* I 228–44, II 159–69. In 1809, likening the debt to a husband and wife playing cards against each other, so that what one loses the other gains, he explained in passing why landholders would not gain from national bankruptcy. "Suspicion of a hoax" had in fact arisen: Pitt's precipitous increase in the national debt had led to a run on the Bank of England in Feb 1797 of such intensity that cash payments were sus-

pended until 1819. By 1815 the accumulated debt was £834,000,000; by 1818 interest and charges on the debt had reached almost two-thirds of the total annual governmental expenditure. C. P. Hill *British Economic and Social History 1700–1914* (1957) 117, 236; Elie Halévy *A History of the English People in the Nineteenth Century* (rev ed) vol II: *The Liberal Awakening 1815–1830* tr E. I. Watkin (1949) 37–40.

[14] Economic historians are barely willing to concede that Glasgow and Paisley subscribed for the poor. Assessments for relief of the sick and disabled were made legal in Scotland by an Act of 1574, but the Scots resisted relief to the able-bodied and rejected the Speenhamland policy of supplementing labourers' wages, not only in C's time but even in the Scottish Poor Law Act of 1845. New textile machinery advanced rapidly in Glasgow and Paisley in the third quarter of the eighteenth century. Mule-jenny operatives held meetings in Glasgow in 1787 in an attempt to establish minimum wages. In 1812 the weavers of Lanarkshire were encouraged by magistrates and the Court of Session in the establishment of a fixed scale of wages, but refusal of employers to accept the scale,

poor laws. It was absurd to*ᵉ* talk of Queen Elizabeth's Acts creating the Poor Laws.[15] The inequality and mischief consisted in the agricultural interest having to pay them all; for though perhaps in the end the land became more valuable, yet at the first the farmers bore all the brunt. The poor's rates were the consideration given for having labour at demand. It was the price. There ought to be a fixed revolving period for the equalization of rates.[16]   [36:38]

ᵉ ~~of~~ to

along with the absence of public relief, led first to a strike and then to imprisonment of the leaders. Meanwhile the industrial centres had moved slowly towards voluntary assessments and relief. Glasgow, which had built a Town's Hospital in 1733, began to provide the outdoor relief of one meal in 1774 and later converted the allowance to cash. David Bremner *The Industries of Scotland: Their Rise, Progress, and Present Condition* (Edinburgh 1869) 273–84; I. F. Grant *The Economic History of Scotland* (1934) 198–9, 272–3; P. H. Campbell *Scotland Since 1707: The Rise of an Industrial Society* (Oxford 1965) 204–8. When in 1819 an excess of Paisley shawls brought collapse to the industry, and unemployment, the General Assembly of the Kirk refused assistance on the Scottish principle of relief only for sickness or calamity. Sir John Clapham *An Economic History of Modern Britain* (3 vols Cambridge 1963–4) I 585.

[15] The Act 14 Eliz 1572 c 5 had directed the levy of a compulsory poor rate; 18 Eliz 1575/6 c 3 required the unemployed to be set to work. A. E. Bland, P. A. Brown, and R. H. Tawney eds *English Economic History: Select Documents* (1914) 372–3. By the Act 43 Eliz 1601 c 2 the poor without maintenance were consigned to work on materials to be provided by the parish; the Act provided for the apprenticeship of poor children and for relief of those incapable of work, but made no provision for idle agricultural workers. C. R. Fay *Life and Labour in the Nineteenth Century . . .* (Cambridge 1945) 91–2; cf *LS (CC)* 122n.

[16] The Speenhamland settlement of 1795, embodied in 36 Geo III c 83, authorised home relief by tying poor rates to the price of bread and the number of children in a family, with the effect of subsidising wages out of the rates and thus securing to farmers a cheap labour reserve. Fay 98–108; E. P. Thompson *The Making of the English Working Class* (1963) 221–8. To Allsop C complained that the poor laws, taking from the poor the independent feelings of an Englishman, made them more improvident. Allsop I 27. "I hold it impossible", he said in *LS* of the Speenhamland settlements, "to exaggerate their pernicious tendency and consequences". *LS (CC)* 221. C's complaint of the burden to landholders has been accepted by historians as valid. The costs of poor-law administration, which had risen from £619,000 in 1750 to almost £8,000,000 in 1818, "fell only on real property or tithes; they were distributed unequally over this limited field of wealth, since assessment to the poor rate was strictly parochial. The law of settlement, which had been grafted into the Elizabethan system towards the end of the seventeenth century, enabled manufacturers in towns to escape the burden of maintaining unemployed workmen in times of depression; they could take men from their villages in good times, and send them back again when there was no work for them." E. L. Woodward *The Age of Reform 1815–1870* (Oxford 1949) 431. In a note on Patrick Colquhoun's definition of poverty in *A Treatise on Indigence* (1806) as "the state of every one who must labour for subsistence", C protested that poverty inhered only in "such unceasing bodily Labor" that all

The conduct of the Whigs was inconsistent. It originated from the fatal error which Fox committed in persisting, after the three first years of the French Revolution, when every shadow of freedom was vanished, in eulogizing the men and measures of France.[17] So he went on gradually departing from all the principles of English *f*policy and wisdom, till at length he became the panegyrist through thick and thin of a mad military frenzy under the influence of which even the very name of liberty was detested. Thus his party became the absolute abettors of the invasion of Spain, and did all in their power to thwart the efforts of this country to resist it;[18] at present, when the invasion is by a Bourbon, and the cause

f p 105

improvement of mind was precluded. *CM (CC)* II 98.

[17] Charles James Fox (1749–1806) led the "New Whigs" in a policy of reconciliation with France from Dec 1792 until his death, except for five years of semi-retirement from Parliament and brief spasms of disquiet over Napoleonic threats to England's survival. C supported Fox's motions to employ every species of negotiation in pursuit of peace up to 1 Mar 1796—*Watchman (CC)* 16–20—but first began to waver with Bonaparte's victories in the Italian peninsula from the end of March; he became increasingly troubled when the Directory rejected British overtures for peace, Spain declared war against Britain in October, and the French attempted to land in Ireland in December; and he broke permanently with Fox and the Revolution when the French found pretexts for invading Switzerland in Mar 1798; he then continued to show as much hostility as Pitt towards a treaty of peace. C's language, as usual, is milder than RS's: "The Foxites, from the beginning of the war, through all its changes had uniformly taken part against their country; consistent in this and in nothing else, they had always sided with the enemy, pleading his cause, palliating his crimes, extolling his wisdom, magnifying his power, vilifying and accusing their own government, depreciating its resources, impeding its measures, insulting its allies, calling for disclosures which no government ought to make, and forcing them sometimes from the weakness and the mistaken liberality of their opponents." *History of the Peninsula War* (2nd ed 6 vols 1828–37) I 67. Cf *Friend (CC)* I 220, 267; *EOT (CC)* I 425–34.

[18] When Napoleon sent troops into Spain in Feb 1808 he had designs not only on Spain but also, as C and others were fully aware by 1823, on Gibraltar and Morocco. With little opportunity to prevent actions, the Opposition party found much to complain of after actions had been taken. On 30 Jun 1808 the cabinet decided to send troops under Sir Arthur Wellesley into Portugal, in order to divert French pressure from the Spanish army and the (more effective) guerrillas. The Convention of Cintra that concluded this action was almost universally condemned for permitting the French troops a free departure. A British expedition under Sir John Moore into northern Spain in October ended in encirclement, retreat, and defeat at Corunna on 16 Jan 1809 (see JTC's report of 20 Apr 1811, at n 4). A British force under Wellesley entered Spain in July and withdrew in August. *A Reg* (1809) 27–40; RS *Peninsular War* I 445–9, III 328–86, IV 235–63, 326–56. At the time, in the *Courier* for 9 Dec 1809, C made clear that the press troubled him more than the Opposition in Parliament; when the Duke of Alva led the armies of Philip II in 1567, C wrote, "Then, as now, infamous sophists were found, who, both in conversation and from the press, declaimed on the advantages of submission, and the

of the Spaniards neither united nor sound in many respects, they would precipitate this country into a crusade.[19] Coleridge in 1808–9 met Lord Darnley accidentally,[20] when Lord D. said to him: "Are you mad, Mr. C." "Why, my Lord? What have I done that argues derangement of mind?" "Why, I mean those essays of yours on the 'Hopes and Fears of a people invaded by foreign armies';[21] the Spaniards are absolutely conquered; it is absurd talking about their chance of resisting." "Very well, my Lord! We shall see! But will your Lordship permit me in a year or

vanity of resistance." *EOT (CC)* II 54. Henry Brougham, anonymously, in *Ed Rev* XIII (Oct 1808) 215–34, XIV (Apr, Jul 1809) 244–64, 442–82, XV (Oct 1809) 197–236, had summarised the reasons for despair. Daniel Stuart, editor of the *Courier*, had tried to answer such doubts in a series of articles 8 Nov–22 Dec 1808, and C had followed with a more vigorous series, admitting less gloom, in Dec 1809 and Jan 1810 (see n 21, below). And cf *W Prose* I 227.

[19] In 1820 scattered rebellions had broken out in Spain against the tyrannical powers of Ferdinand VII (1784–1833), king in 1808, 1814–20, and 1823–33. When meetings supplementary to the Congress of Verona took up the question of Ferdinand's forced subordination to the Constitutionalists, Wellington refused to join in alliance for military intervention. The Bourbon King Louis XVIII of France, after threatening in Jan 1823 that French troops were ready to restore Ferdinand's royal prerogatives, sent an invading force on 7 Apr. Upon the reassembling of Parliament after Easter, when the government released documents revealing that Canning had assured the French of Britain's opposition to war and strict neutrality should war ensue, Sir Francis Burdett spoke for retaliation against the Bourbon invader, and John Cam Hobhouse and Sir Robert Wilson deplored Canning's unheroic encouragement of French action against the liberal cause in Spain (9–17 Apr). But Halévy concluded that Brougham was in collusion with Canning and that the apparent bellicosity of Hobhouse, Wilson, and others (excepting Burdett) was tempered by the realisation that support from leaders of industry and commerce depended upon reduction of public expenditure and avoidance of war. *The Liberal Awakening* 168–79. Ambivalence pervaded Parliament and the cabinet; Canning himself saw the trap his policy had baited; C, on 27 Apr close to the unfolding events, backed off only to observe the paradox of Whig behaviour over a period of three decades.

[20] John Bligh, 4th Earl of Darnley (1767–1831), was a prominent Whig; several of his speeches on Ireland and the Irish poor were published 1824–31. In Sept 1814 C had reported the first encounter with Darnley, but not the second, to Stuart: "Earl Darnley on the appearance of my Letters in the Courier concerning the Spaniards bluntly asked me, whether I had lost my senses—& quoted Lord Grenville at me—". *CL* III 531. In 1812 C had expected Darnley to serve as an announced patron of his lectures on the drama at Willis's Rooms: *CL* III 389.

[21] "Letters on the Spaniards" *Courier* 7 Dec 1809–20 Jan 1810: *EOT (CC)* II 37–100. HNC praised the series in a letter to Thomas Tracy of Newburyport, Mass on 29 Mar 1837: "He wrote nine or ten long letters in the Courier newspaper in 1809 on the subject of the then doubtful Spanish cause, which are amongst the most prophetic effusions I know. It is to them that he refers in the early part of the Table Talk." HUL MS Am 661(4). The eighth letter promised a ninth, which did not appear. For a high assessment of the treatment of nationalism in the eight letters, see Colmer 123–5.

two's time to retort your question upon you, if I should have grounds for so doing?'' ''Certainly that's fair''.

Two years afterwards, when affairs were altered in Spain, Coleridge met Lord Darnley again about the same place, and after some little conversation, he said ''Does your Lordship remember giving me leave to retort a certain question upon you about the Spaniards? Who is mad now?'' ''Very true! it is very extraordinary! It was an ingenious conjecture!'' ''I think that is hardly a fair term. Has any thing happened which I had not foretold, or from other causes, or under other conditions?''[22]	[36:39]

Many votes were given for Reform in the House of Commons which were not sincere. While it was well known that the measure never could be carried in Parliament, it was as well to purchase some popularity by voting for it.[23] When Hunt and his associates, before the Six Acts, created a panic, the Ministers lay on their oars for three or four months, until the general cry from even the Opposition was, ''Why do not the Ministers come forward with some measure?''[24]	[36:40]

---

[22] Apparently the subject of Darnley's blunt question arose because of a sentence in *The Times* on 4 Mar 1823 concerning ''Astonishing Events'' and a remark of Canning's that any man who had dared predict the outcome of the Peninsular War ''would have been called a Madman'', leading C to record that ''Lord Darnley told me I must be out of my senses—This was on occasion of my 8 Essays in the Courier on the grounds of Hope in a Nation['s] struggle against disciplined Armies''. BM MS Egerton 2800 f 129: *EOT (CC)* III 264.

[23] Few sessions of Parliament since the 1780s had been without a motion for Reform, and C's observation on safely wasted votes in favour of Reform could apply to any of them. The sentence that follows suggests a reference to the period of agitation and renewed ''panic of property'' after 1815.

[24] Henry Hunt (1773–1835), the ''Orator'', had been imprisoned for acts of personal violence in 1800 and 1810. After raising the Cap of Liberty above his colours on the hustings in the Westminster election of 1818 (and securing 84 of 15,669 votes counted), he began to step up his activity as a radical. He took

the chair at the Smithfield meeting of 21 Jul 1819 to petition for reform of suffrage and for repeal of the Corn Laws and at St Peter's Fields in Manchester on 16 Aug, when a charge of cavalry called forth the sobriquet of ''Peterloo Massacre''. In September Hunt presided over a meeting at the Crown and Anchor where the music included *Ça ira, Scots Wha Ha'*, and *See the Conquering Hero Comes*. Of ten charged with violating the sedition act of 1817 at Manchester on 16 Aug, five were sentenced in May 1820, among them Hunt. Details of these events are heightened in *Memoirs of Henry Hunt, Esq. Written by Himself* . . . (3 vols 1820–2) and in Robert Huish *The History of the Private and Political Life of the Late Henry Hunt* . . . (2 vols 1836). Lord Eldon, one of those who thought that ''the Ministers lay on their oars'', wrote to Sir William Scott at the end of Sept 1819 that Parliament must try a harsh remedy; ''if Ministers will not try it, they ought to make way for other Ministers, who either will try it, or some other measure which may occur to them''. On 17 Oct Henry Addington, 1st Viscount Sidmouth, the Home Secretary, admitted to Eldon that meetings and

The present Ministry existed on the weakness of the Opposition. The latter had pledged themselves to such desperate measures, that they never would have the support of the country.[25]   [36:40]

The present adherents of the Romish Church were not Catholics; we are the Catholics. We can prove that we hold the doctrines of the primitive Church for the first 300 years. The council of Trent made the Papists what they are.[26] A foreign Romish Bishop *had declared that that the Protestants were more like the Catholics before the Council of Trent, than their present descendants.[27] The course of Christianity and the Christian Church may be likened to a great river which covered a large channel and bore along with its waters mud and gravel and weeds, till it met a great rock in the middle of the stream; by some means or other the water flows purely and separated from the filth in a deeper and narrower course on one side of the rock, and the refuse of the dirt and troubled waters went off on the other, and then cries out, "We are the River!"[28]

* p 106

---

violence continued: "Would that I could persuade myself of the sufficiency of our means, either in law or in force, to curb that spirit, or to control and crush its impending, and all too probable results." Horace Twiss *The Public and Private Life of Lord Chancellor Eldon* (3 vols 1844) II 346–7. Called into emergency session, Parliament between 23 Nov and 29 Dec passed the Six Acts, which prevented the postponement of trial, prohibited assembly for military drill, restricted the number and identity of persons at public meetings of grievance, restricted freedom of the press, and permitted search of private houses and seizure of arms. Hunt, released from Ilchester on 30 Oct 1822, had attracted adverse attention in Parliament on 21 Feb and 1 Mar 1823.

[25] The Liverpool ministry, in office since 1812, included in 1823, besides Liverpool and Canning, Sir Robert Peel (1788–1850), Home Secretary; Frederick John Robinson (1782–1859), later Viscount Goderich (1827) and Earl of Ripon (1833), Exchequer; William Huskisson (1770–1830), Navy and Board of Trade. The Opposition was pledged to Catholic emancipation, and in 1822 Lord John Russell (1792–1878) had intro-

duced a bold plan of parliamentary reform.

[26] The purpose of the Council of Trent (1545–63) was to maintain or restore the unity of Christendom by the reform of discipline and a firmer definition of Church doctrine. In formulating a clear doctrinal system, the Council confuted Lutheran errors, declared the Vulgate authentic, and in 1563 declared anathema errors in the Thirty-nine Articles of the Anglican bishops. Decrees of the Council came into force in 1564. C was to remind readers in 1830 that "the *Roman* Catholic Church dates its true origin from the Council of Trent". *C&S (CC)* 140n. HNC (anon) *Remarks on the Present State of the Roman Catholic Question* (1827) 41 echoed C: ". . . the frantic Council of Trent . . . transmuted the old Catholics into Papists".

[27] "Mr. Coleridge named him, but the name was strange to me, and I have been unable to recover it." *TT* (1835) I 31n.

[28] The same argument is expressed in the same simile but with homelier diction—"with a great deal of Filth & Folly floating on it"—in a notebook entry of 1810 headed "Answer to Papists". *CN* III 3872.

A person said, "But you will call them civilly Catholics?" "No, I will not! I will not tell a lie upon so solemn an occasion!*ʰ* They are not Catholics! If they were, then we are heretics, and *Roman* Catholics makes no difference. Catholicism is not capable of degrees. Properly speaking there can only be one body of Catholics ex vi termini;²⁹ if Roman Catholics be allowed, then there may be English, Irish &c; which with respect to a difference in religious tenets is absurd."³⁰   [36:41, 42]

The Romish religion is so flattering to the passions of men, that it is impossible to say how far it would spread amongst the higher orders, if the disabilities attending its profession were removed.³¹   [36:43]

———

Milton's Latin style is perhaps better than his English. His style is as characteristic of him as a stern Republican, as Cowley's is of him as a Gentleman.³²   [36:54]

———

Literal interpretation of the Bible was the best after all. The Zendavesta must have been copied from the writings of Moses; for in the description

ʰ MS E 39 closes the quotation after "occasion" rather than after "absurd", below. The change, confirmed in the revision of 1835, makes the rest of the paragraph not part of the answer to an unnamed person, but a fuller explanation given to HNC on 27 Apr 1823

²⁹ "From the meaning of the expression".

³⁰ Of the name *Roman Catholic* as a "downright contradiction in terms" because of the "parasitical and suffocating *Epithet*", in notes on two copies of *The Friend*, C punned on "bull" as an Irish blunder in distinguishing *Catholic* from "the papal *Bull* of *Roman* Catholic". *Friend (CC)* I 135n. The notebook entry of 1810 gives the positive side of the argument: "What is the *visible* Catholic Church?—The aggregate of all Christian Churches throughout the World—Why do we attribute unity to it? First and chiefly, because they are all members of one Head, Jesus Christ—and secondly, because they are all united in the bond of brotherly Love, by the command of their Head & King." *CN* III 3872.

³¹ HNC in *TT* (1835) called the readers' attention to C's poem of 1826, *Sancti Dominici Pallium*, which declares Charles Butler's "half-truths" in *Vindication of "The Book of the Roman Catholic Church"* (1826) as dangerous as "the full lie" of an anonymous pamphlet by John Milner answering (less courteously than Butler) *The Book of the Church* (1824) by RS: *PW* (EHC) I 448; on the date see *CM (CC)* I 856. The poem and the conversation of 27 Apr are closely related.

³² According to C's Lect 14 of 13 Mar 1818, Cowley's prose had "variety of excellence"; "probably the best model of style for modern imitation in general", it rivalled Addison's prose for "mere ease and grace", with superiority in thought and fancy. *Lects 1808–19 (CC)* II 241, 236. The designation of "a Gentleman", however, is probably pejorative. In *BL* ch 24 *(CC)* II 235n–6, C protested against Johnson's preference for Cowley's Latin poems over Milton's. In a marginal note on Lamb's copy of John Donne *Poems* (1669) C called Cowley a legitimate child of Donne whose soul-mother was perhaps an intellectually discursive "sickly Court-royalty". *CM (CC)* II 219. See also C's annotations on Cowley *Works* (1681): *CM (CC)* II 102–6.

of the Creation, the first chapter of Genesis is taken literally except that the sun is created *before* the light, and the herbs and plants after the sun; which are the two points they did not understand, and therefore altered as errors.[33] There are only two acts of creation properly so called—the earth and man, the intermediate acts seem more as the results of secondary causes, or at any rate a modification of materials.[34]　　　[36:44]

[33] Of the *Avesta* (*Zend* means "commentary") C could have misinformation from many sources. The edition in French in 1771 by Abraham Hyacinthe Anquetil-Duperron, *Zend-Avesta, Ouvrage de Zoroastre*, was called by the young William Jones (mistakenly so) a collection of worthless fabrications. For fifty years the authenticity of the work was debated, until about 1825, when scholars began to study the original texts. The works making up the *Avesta* were attributed to a Zoroaster (a Greek form of the Persian Zarathustra) of about the sixth century B.C., said by some to be an imposter who eventually eclipsed the Zoroaster of pre-history. Humphrey Prideaux, drawing upon Thomas Hyde *Historia religionis veterum Persarum* (Oxford 1700) and abu-al-Faraj al-Isfahani *Specimen historiae Arabum, sive . . . de origine et moribus Arabum succincta narratio . . .* (1650), counted the history of creation and the deluge among the "great many things taken out of . . . the Old Testament" and slightly altered; for example, the six days of creation in Genesis are converted into six periods of several days each. Prideaux *The Old and New Testament Connected in the History of the Jews and Neighbouring Nations, from the Declension of the Kingdoms of Israel and Judah to the Time of Christ* (1716) 224–5. With help from classical sources, Hyde had extrapolated the Zoroastrian cosmology and history of creation from the psalms and songs (Gāthās), hymns (Yashts), and liturgical portion (Yasna) of the *Avesta*. There is an apparent paradox in C's speculation that the authors of a cosmology based on the primal opposition of light and darkness could not comprehend a creation of light prior to the sun, but C is speaking of difficulties in Genesis, not of limitations in the *Avesta*. In 1818 he copied some of the "Oracles of Zoroaster" from his chief source, *The History of the Chaldaick Philosophy* (1701) pt XIX, which belongs to, but has a separate title-page and pagination from, Thomas Stanley *The History of Philosophy* (3rd ed 1701); C's annotated copy is in the Berg Collection, NYPL. The first five oracles, he noted, "contain the whole *Principles* of Schelling". *CN* III 4424. The excursus on the *Zendavesta* in TT is motivated by the opening sentence on literal interpretation of the Bible, omitted from *TT* (1835). Although HNC may have missed or suppressed evidence of C's doubts, the moral drawn from the *Avesta* in 1823 was that one should attempt no correction of supposed errors in the Biblical account. At probably about this time C discussed claims for the *Zendavesta* as less disruptive of his convictions than claims for the Egyptians. See *CN* IV 4794 and cf 4558, 4562, 4639, 4640, 4794, 5162, 5434 and nn.

[34] Eichhorn *AT* explained some problems of sequence in the Biblical account of creation as resulting from a conflation of separate "Jehovah" and "Elohim" versions, but C proposed to accept the result by taking the details of Gen 1.1–25 as incidental to the creation of an earth awaiting the human; the sequence is to be taken as one of explanation rather than of chronology. When Eichhorn declared the version in Genesis superior to all other theogonies and cosmogonies, C objected, in a marginal note, to the Biblical "separation of the Vegetable from the Animal Creation by an intermediate Creation of the present Solar System"; i.e. the herb and the tree (Gen 1.11) before the sun (vv 13–18). *CM (CC)* II 393–4. In a long note of 1818 on this subject, C found eminently satisfactory,

Pantheism and Idolatry naturally ended in each other; for all extremes meet.[35] The Judaic religion was the exact medium, the true compromise.[36]   [36:45]

[a]1st. May—

My uncle in great force at John's.[1]

He treated the subject of ghosts and dreams at great length, and said there was a difference in the credibility to be attached to them.[2] Dreams

---

[a] MS A p 107

---

scientifically as well as mythopoetically, everything in the account not involving "the firmament", which left him with no "tolerable solution" to Gen 1.6–8. *CN* III 4418. For C. A. Tulk on 12 Jan 1818 he had explained Gen 1 in terms of his theory of polarity. *CL* IV 804–9. Two years or so later he re-examined the chapter in the light of available scholarship. *CN* IV 4562, 4794.

[35] Pantheism produces polytheism, C would explain on 15 Aug 1832, below (at n 3), because "worship of abstract Nature could never exist in a people at large". That "extremes meet" was his favourite axiom; see e.g. *Friend (CC)* I 110 and n 5; *EOT (CC)* I 138, II 336; in a notebook entry he cited the "1000th" instance of that adage: *CN* IV 5402.

[36] The discussion centres still in the Biblical account of creation. In the notebook meditation of 1818 C observed that Gen 1.1 "precludes the systems of Cosmotheism, Pantheism, and a primal Element—in short, every possible form of the eternity (i.e. unbeginningness) of the World or any part of the World"; in the editor's words, "an infinite Creator but a transcendent event set forth in finite terms" is for C "the exact medium". *CN* III 4418 f 11[v] and n. That the medium is between pantheism and "Idolatry" implies also approval of the forms of worship prescribed in the later books of the Old Testament, the law and the prophets.

[1] HNC wrote to his brother Francis, at Ottery St Mary, from "2 Pump Court, May day": "Uncle Sam dined in Had-low Street last Saturday, and dines there again to day at his own instance, which we were pleased at. He laughed at my father's stories about country rates, and 'nacking off half' &c. He was looking remarkably well and rosy; and talked like a dragon." UT ms. Those known to be present are C, JTC and wife, Col James Coleridge and wife, and HNC.

[2] C felt that he had never said enough about dreams and apparitions. In 1809, in *The Friend*, amplifying his discussion of Luther's throwing an inkpot at the Devil, he promised further essays on "Dreams, Visions, Ghosts, Witchcraft, &c.", to be based on his knowledge from books and testimony—and personal experience. *Friend (CC)* II 117. He expressed similar hopes in *CL* II 707 (to Poole in 1801) and in *BL* ch 13 *(CC)* I 306. Clement Carlyon heard C and Humphry Davy discuss dreams and ghosts in 1803. Carlyon I 198–241. In some "Desultory Remarks" on drama, probably used for one of the lectures at the Royal Institution in 1808, C distinguished between "*ordinary* Dreams" and "the Night-mair . . . when the waking State of the Brain is re-commencing" and the mind converts physical causes of discomfort into "a present Image". BM Add MS 34225 ff 54–6: *Lects 1808–19 (CC)* I 135–6. In Lect 11 of 3 Mar 1818 he described the mind as acting similarly in dreaming and in such Oriental works as the Arabian Nights— "an exertion of the fancy in the combination and recombination of familiar objects so as to produce novel and wonder-

had nothing in them which was absurd and nonsensical, and though most of the coincidences may be readily explained by the diseased system of the dreamer and the great and surprising power of association, yet it was impossible to say whether or not an inner sense did not exist in the mind, which was but seldom developed, and which might have a power of presentiment.[3] All the external senses have their correspondents in the mind; the eye can foresee before an object is distinctly apprehended, why should not a corresponding power of the soul? The power of prophecy might have been merely a spiritual excitation of this dormant quality; hence the seers often required music &c.[4] Every thing in nature had a tendency to move in cycles, and it would be a miracle if out of such myriads of cycles moving concurrently, some coincidences did not take place. No doubt many such happen in the day time, but then our senses drive out the remembrance of them, and render the impression hardly felt; but when we sleep the mind acts without interruption. Terror produces them and the imagination; which creates such a picture out of a small particle.[5] In St Paul "speaking with tongues" means the speaking

---

ful imagery", and in Lect 12 of 6 Mar 1818, drawing equally on books, reported instances, and personal experience, he discussed dreams and apparitions and the supposed instances of witchcraft, confuting "the reality of apparitions". *Lects 1808–19 (CC)* II 191, 199–210. He had been willing, as in the *Ancient Mariner*, to suspend disbelief in Cudworth's principle that invisible spirits are "real and substantial inhabitants of the world". *True Intellectual System* I 715. For the next twenty years he emphasised something nearer to the explanation in John Ferriar *An Essay Towards a Theory of Apparitions* (1813) that irregularities of the nervous system and lingering images in the ordinary process of vision accounted for most spectral effects. On the inadequacies of metaphysics alone and empirical psychology alone see C's annotation on Richard Baxter *Reliquiae Baxterianae* (1696): *CM (CC)* I 281. It is against the unquestioning acceptance of a "mechanical Psychology" that he returns to the subject of apparitions in 1823. On dreams and ghosts see also JTC's report of 9 Jan 1823, above (at nn 4–7), and on ghosts see 7 Jan–13 Feb 1823, above (at n 6).

[3] In *TT* (1835) I 36n HNC cited and quoted *SM* App C, where C distinguishes from the almost-waking dreams in which we dream *about* things those deep dreams "so exact, minute, and vivid" that the dreamer, as one "of tender feelings and reflecting habits", can be said to "*dream the things themselves*"; we should not be surprised, he says, "if such dreams should sometimes be confirmed by the event, as though they had actually possessed a character of divination". *SM (CC)* 80–1.

[4] In *TT* (1835) the "seers" became "Hebrew seers"; in *TT* (1836) the instance of Elisha before Jehoram is added (2 Kings 3.15), with a reference also to the conjunction of musical instruments and prophecy in 1 Sam 10.5.

[5] In 1808 C related "a fact of Vision" to prophetic hallucination (*CN* III 3280), but without reference to the terror assumed here, explicit in many notebook entries concerning his dreams, and basic to a poem like *The Pains of Sleep: PW* (EHC) I 389. A classic example for C of induced excitation is Luther and the ink-pot, in one of "those rapid alternations of the sleeping with the half waking state, which is *the true witching time*".

with the tongue without consciousness. 1. Cor.[6]

Ghosts are absurd. When a real ghost, that is, some man dressed up has appeared, the effects have always been, when believed, most terrible, convulsion, idiocy, madness, death. But after all these stories of ghosts, the next day the seer is quite well, a slight headache or so, and that's all.[7] Allston[b] told of a youth in the University of Cambridge near Boston, that he determined to fright a Tom Painish companion.[8] He ap-

[b] Alston

Friend (CC) II 117. A prior cause of terror, C said in a note for Lect 12 of 1818, produces the bodily sensation that in turn causes the apparition. *CN* III 4396: *Lects 1808–19 (CC)* II 207. For C on the imagistic and symbolic language of dreams, see *CN* III 4409; on the psychological and moral elements in dreams, "Fear, Hope, Rage, Shame, and (strongest of all) Remorse", see *CN* III 4046.

[6] In 1 Cor 12.10, 13.1, 14.2, to speak with divers or alien tongues is a spiritual gift akin to prophecy, as also in Acts 2.4, 10.46, 19.6. SC provided a note on C's views of this subject in *CIS* (1849) 221–30. See also 24 Feb 1827, below (at nn 2–4).

[7] *TT* (1835) contrasts here (36:46) descriptions of prophecy in the OT. Joseph Farington (1747–1821) told how C disposed of a much-bruited ghost as early as 25 Mar 1804: "At Lady Beaumont's desire I related the story of the *Apparition* of his Brother [John] appearing to Captn. Wynyard. It was told at the private instigation of Lady Beaumont who was desirous to hear Coleridge's opinion upon it.—He gave a decided opinion upon it that it [was] an 'Ocular Spectrum', a deception created by the disordered imagination of Captn. Wynyard when in a nervous, languid state, & that Coll. Sherbroke who also professed to have seen the apparition had the notion of it excited by the sudden assertion of the other." Farington *Diary* VI 2276.

[8] Washington Allston (1779–1843), A.R.A. 1818, a painter who published poems and a novel, was born in South Carolina, entered Harvard in 1796, met C in Rome in 1806, and returned to the U.S. from England in 1818. His first portrait of C was left unfinished upon C's departure from Rome in 1806. After being tended by C during an illness in 1813 at Salt Hill, Allston completed in 1814 for Josiah Wade what HNC recommended to Murray, for *TT* (1835), as the "best portrait of my late Uncle". It was purchased by the National Portrait Gallery in 1864. C's essays of 1814 "On the Principles of Genial Criticism Concerning the Fine Arts" were designed in part to call public attention to an exhibition of Allston's paintings in Bristol. *BL* (1907) II 219–46.

Ralph Waldo Emerson reported of his visit to C in 1833: "He asked me whether I knew Allston, and spoke warmly of his merits and doings when he knew him in Rome; what a master of the Titianesque he was, &c., &c. . . . Going out, he showed me in the next apartment a picture of Allston's, and told me 'that Montague, a picture-dealer, once came to see him, and glancing towards this, said, "Well, you have got a picture!" thinking it the work of an old master; afterwards Montague, still talking with his back to the canvas, put up his hand and touched it, and exclaimed, "By Heaven! this picture is not ten years old!" '—so delicate and skilful was that man's touch." Emerson *English Traits* (1856) 5, 7; cf Fenimore Cooper's similar account in 1828, John Wheeler's in 1829, and Henry Blake McLellan's in 1832: C thought Allston "in imagination and color almost unrivalled". *Gleanings in Europe: England* 260, Wheeler's ms diary, and *Journal of a Residence in Scotland* (Boston 1834) 232. The picture

peared in costume. "This is a good joke—come I shall be offended. I will give you five minutes"—he fired his pistol—and fell dead.[9]

[36:46]

The eye by a slight convulsion often saw a portion of the body, which it of course projected forward, which explained many stories of persons seeing themselves lying dead.

*c*If a ghost be a spirit, it must be a substance like the wind, and therefore capable of impact—but it is not. If it be a shadow it must have a substance of which it is the shadow. Unless there is an external substance, the bodily eye *cannot* see it; therefore *that* which is supposed to be seen, is in fact not seen, but produced from the mind. External objects naturally produce sensation; but here sensation, as it were, produces the object.

[36:13]

He had no doubt the Jews believed in a future state. The story of the witch of Endor proved it.[10]

[36:48]

The pet texts of a Socinian were enough to confute him.[11] If Christ were a mere man, it would have been ridiculous to call himself the Son of

c p 108

Emerson mentioned is Allston's adaptation of Titian's *Adoration of the Magi*. William H. Gerdts and Theodore E. Stebbins Jr *"A Man of Genius" : The Art of Washington Allston (1779–1843)* (Boston, Mass 1979) 101.

[9] The erratic question marks of MS A have been corrected from the clearer version in MS E 43. The ending was further elaborated in *TT* (1835). Cottle *Rem* 274–5, which also tells the story, is probably a crib from this account as published in *TT* (1835).

[10] C is here refuting Unitarians but particularly William Warburton (1698–1779) *The Divine Legation of Moses* (2 pts 1737–41). Warburton argued that the law of Moses was of divine origin but lacked the socially necessary doctrine of future rewards and punishments. In 1 Sam 28 the Witch of Endor, who had a "familiar spirit", called up the dead Samuel before Saul. In marginal notes C called attention to evidence in the OT of belief in immortality: Mal 3.14–18 and Job, esp 32.8; see annotations on the Bible and Böhme *Works: CM (CC)* I 445–

6, 675. *TT* (1835) enlarged the remark about the Witch of Endor from the talk of 10 Mar 1827, below, and also borrowed from C's marginalia. It also recommended the reading of John Webster *The Displaying of Supposed Witchcraft* (1677) and—anachronistically for talk of 1823—George Francis Lyon *The Private Journal of Captain G. F. Lyon, of H.M.S. Hecla, During the Recent Voyage of Discovery under Captain Parry* (1824).

[11] Socinians derive from the two Sozzini, Lelio (1525–62) and his nephew Fausto (1539–1604), both anti-trinitarian. Fausto (in Latin, Faustus Socinus) established the sect in Poland in 1587. Here, in keeping with his normal usage, C refers to the Unitarians of his own day. Although the Socinians believed the birth of Christ miraculous, and in general held a higher view of the Son than did the Unitarians, their rejection of Christ's power of mediation to atone for human sin, substituting instead a doctrine of divine example, enabled C to call down upon the Unitarians, merely by using the

Man; but being God and Man, it then became a peculiar and mysterious title. If he were a mere man, Christ's saying, "my father is greater than I," would have been as unmeaning.[12] It would be laughable enough to hear Coleridge say, "my Remorse succeeded indeed, but Shakspeare is a greater dramatist than I";[13] but how immeasurably more foolish would it be for a man however good and wise to say—"but Jehovah is greater than I". [36:49]

Plato's works are logical exercises for the mind; nothing positive is advanced. Socrates may be fairly represented in the moral parts, but in the metaphysical disquisitions it is Pythagoras.[14] Xenophon is quite different.[15] [36:50]

May. 8.—1824.

My Uncle at Highgate was in good spirits and health.[1] He approved of Milton's definition of poetry, that it was simple, sensuous, impassioned;

earlier name, all the vituperation exercised upon the Sabellians and Socinians by his favourite seventeenth-century divines. That the conversation moved to Socinians from Jewish belief in immortality is perhaps explained by C's defence of his friend Hyman Hurwitz in a letter of 1820—"how far nearer is an orthodox Jew to an orthodox Protestant Christian, than the Socinian is". *CL* v 132. In 1822 (as in 1819) he had objected to those crying "Fire" at Calvinistic Methodism "while the Dry Rot of virtual Socinianism is snugly at work in the Beams and Joists of the venerable Edifice". *CL* v 199; cf iv 966. For C on Socinianism as "a dance, in which self-complacent blank-headedness and blank-heartedness are the two blind fiddlers", and other remarks on the Unitarians, see App F 2, below.

[12] John 14.28.

[13] For *Remorse*, which opened at Drury Lane on 23 Jan 1813 and ran for twenty nights, a record for the era, see 7 Jan–13 Feb 1823, above, and n 14.

[14] Lives of the Greek philosopher Pythagoras (of the 6th century B.C.) by Porphyry and Iamblichus attribute to him a

theory of numerical correspondences, the teaching that earthly life is for the purification of the soul, and other elements of religious mysticism evident in some of the later works of Plato. For C on Pythagorean elements not expressed in Plato's writings, see *P Lects* Lects 4–6 (1949) 158–9, 164–5, 175–6, 187–220.

[15] For Xenophon vs Plato on Socrates see also 7 Jan–13 Feb 1823 and n 1, above. Stanley *History of Philosophy* 120 finds an enmity between Xenophon and Plato confirmed "by the Epistle of *Xenophon* to *Aeschines*, wherein he condemns *Plato*, that not being satisfied with the Doctrine of *Socrates*, he went to the *Pythagoreans* in *Italy*". C read Stanley at Christ's Hospital. *CL* vi 843.

[1] We have no TT from HNC between May 1823 and May 1824. HNC's diary has only two entries for this period: "Kept Easter Term, and Trinity Term. 1823." "Wrote Scibile for Knight's Quarterly Magazine. No. 1." "Scibile" *Knight's* i (1823) 180–92 is attributed in the table of contents to Joseph Haller. Between May and Jul 1823 HNC suffered an onset of the serious illness that was to take him to the West Indies in Aug

easy to be apprehended, abounding in sensible images, and informing them with the spirit of the mind.[2]   [36:53]

Wordsworth never had any of those losses of personality, which Hartley had so much.[3] In composing the wanderings of Cain, Wordsworth would not put down any *a*thing he thought good, lest it should be thrown away.[4] The latter poetry of Wordsworth, though it had its merit, was different and inferior to his former.[5] The three books of the Eneid were bad.[6] Landor's orthography seemed absurd.[7] There was nothing to be ex-

a p 109

1824 and lead eventually to his death. See JTC to John May 29 Jul 1823, Bodleian MS Eng Lett c 289.

On 10 Jun 1823 C wrote to JTC: "My love to Henry—tell him, I shall be always delighted to see him when he can make a day's countrification". *CL* v 279. The weekly visits of Edward Irving and Basil Montagu on Thursdays had ended when Irving moved to Essex, and C felt the gap. To JTC on 3 May 1824 he mentioned "some words that fell from Henry when he was here last (I wish, he would come oftener)". *CL* v 361. This wish brought a visit from HNC Thursday, 8 May, to No 3 The Grove, where in Nov 1823 the Gillmans had moved from Moreton House.

[2] In *Of Education* (1644) Milton wrote that logic came first among "organic Arts": "To which Poetry would be made subsequent, or indeed rather precedent, as being less suttle and fine, but more simple, sensuous, and passionate." *A Complete Collection of the Historical, Political, and Miscellaneous Works of Milton* ed Thomas Birch (2 vols 1738) I 139. In 1811 C explained "sensuous" as "appealing to the senses, by imagery, sweetness of sound, &c.". *CL* vi 1025; cf *BL* ch 10 *(CC)* I 172. See also C's notes for "a future Lecture on the moderns" of 1808: *CN* iii 3287.

[3] HNC recorded casual, entirely personal remarks such as this on WW and HC only in the early years, when he did not equate the recordable with the publishable.

[4] In a Prefatory Note in 1828 to the fragment *The Wanderings of Cain*, which originally was to be written in

concert with WW, C assigned "a taste so austerely pure and simple" as WW's as the reason for WW's "look of humourous despondency fixed on his almost blank sheet of paper" when he had failed to match a Canto I to C's Canto II. *PW* (EHC) I 287. For notes by C on the composition in 1797, see *RX* 538 and *AR* (1825) 383n.

[5] The context suggests a reference to poems by WW after about 1815. The sentences in this entry are obviously summaries of expatiation on the various subjects.

[6] WW's translation of *Aeneid* bks 1–3 (lacking 3.588–706) is reprinted from the *Philological Museum* of 1832 in *WPW* iv 286–357. In letters of Jan–Feb 1824 to Lord Lonsdale, WW explained the principles on which he had diverged from the translation by Dryden. *WL* (*L* rev) I 246–7, 250–2. A few weeks before this conversation with HNC, C had written to WW himself that a literal translation of Virgil was impossible; and to have WW produce "page after page without a single *brilliant* note, depresses me, and I grow peevish with you for having wasted your time on a work *so* much below you, that you cannot *stoop* and *take*". *CL* v 353.

[7] Walter Savage Landor (1775–1864) first advanced his ideas on English orthography, citing Milton as his authority, in a footnote to *Gebir* I 100 (2nd ed 1803 pp 345–6). He recommended and practised *therefor, wherefor, precede, excede, hight* for *height*, final *t* in participles like *whipt* and *blest*, and *red* as the preterite of *read*. His fullest discussion had just appeared, in Mar 1824, in

pected from Egypt. Every thing really fine in that country was Grecian.[8] [36:52]

Remarkable contrast between the religion of the tragic poets and the popular ones of Greece. The former are always opposed to the Gods.[9] The ancients had no idea of a *fall* of man, though they had of a gradual degeneracy. Prometheus was Jesus Christ and the Devil together.[10] There were the popular, the sacerdotal, and the mysterious religions.[11] If you take from Virgil his language and metre, what do you leave him?[12]

[36:51, 55]

"Samuel Johnson and John Horne (Tooke)", a dialogue in *Imaginary Conversations with Literary Men and Statesmen* destined to grow longer with each subsequent edition. HNC did not print this comment.

[8] A year later, when he planned to denigrate Egyptian antiquities in his "Papers" for the RSL, C gave a simple explanation to JTC: "My Belief . . . is: that all Inscriptions, Hieroglyphics, &c earlier than Moses are ancient Forgeries—that the wisest Ancients were well acquainted with these pretended Kings &c & regarded them as mere Egyptian Lies—". *CL* v 442; cf 423 and "On the Prometheus of Aeschylus" *LR* ii 323–8. In Lects 1–2 of Dec 1818 on the history of philosophy he had reduced the Egyptian contribution to fancy, sensuality, and "some geological facts of the past ages". *P Lects* (1949) 85, 91, 95, 109–11. In Lects 6–7 he blamed Egypt for Roman importation of false gods and magic. Ibid 221, 232, 238. What he called the "idolatrous *Polytheism*" of the Egyptians (*CL* vi 561) was so described by Cudworth *True Intellectual System* ch 4 § 18 i 309—"the Greeks and Europeans generally received their polytheism and idolatry from the Egyptians"—but Cudworth was one of several authors familiar to C who paid tribute to Egypt's gift to Greece of literature, learning, and culture (ibid i 311). C had explained to himself Herodotus' emphasis on influences from Egypt as an excessive reliance on the priests of Dodona. *CN* iv 4794. C had an ally in William Mitford, who acknowledged in *The*

History of Greece (5 vols 1784–1818) the arguments of Warburton and James Burnett, Lord Monboddo that "we owe alphabetical writing to the genius of Egypt", but inveighed against "the arrogant and exploded absurdity of Egyptian vanity" (i 84–6). C could imagine (as in *CN* iv 4618) that the Greeks might borrow emblems from Egypt, but not as easily as he could imagine inscriptions lying if reported by Bonaparte's savants; of Jean François Champollion's work he said "they are Stones, of which I cannot make Bread". *CN* iv 4794, 5219.

[9] *TT* (1835), in mitigation, has the tragic poets "opposed in heart to the popular divinities". In "On the Prometheus of Aeschylus" C connected the tragic poets with the philosophic content of myth and "the Homeric and cyclical poets with the popular religion". *LR* ii 330.

[10] Prometheus served as transgressor and redeemer in giving "reason theoretical and practical", which should have been "the sole property and birth-right" of divinity, to "a favored animal", man, who was thereby ennobled. *LR* ii 353.

[11] *TT* (1835) added: "represented roughly by Homer, Pindar, and Æschylus".

[12] This expresses C's usual view of Virgil. When the Marquis d'Argens *Kabbalistische Briefe* extolled the beauty of the lines on Marcellus (*Aeneid* 6.863–4) as more beautiful each time he read them over, C retorted in the margin that "the metre and composition" comprise "*sobs* of Harmony", but "what one deep feeling that goes to the human

June 2.ᵈ 1824.[1]

C. thought Granville Penn's book against Buckland a miserable performance.[2] Science would be put an end to, if every phenomenon was to be referred to an actual miracle. It was absurd to refer every thing to the deluge. The deluge, which left an olive branch standing and bore up the ark peaceably on its bosom, could not have caused the tremendous rents and fissures observable on the earth. The tropical animals discovered in England and Russia could not have been transported in the perfectly natural

---

heart? I see not one''. *CM (CC)* I 110. In Sept 1834 SC wrote to HNC: "In regard to poor Virgil—whom Dryden rather unfairly . . . contrasts with Homer . . . I believe my Father thought his genius by no means of a high order. Still there *was* genius . . .''. UT Grantz 591. But perhaps C would stand by his clarification to Godwin in 1801: "I have received, & I hope, still shall, great delight from Virgil, whose versification I admire beyond measure, & very frequently his Language.'' *CL* II 743; cf II 672. C told Gillman that Thomas Fanshaw Middleton (1769–1822) had discovered him reading Virgil "for pleasure" at Christ's Hospital and in consequence called him for the first time to Boyer's attention. *C Life* (G) 19. C's father had written: "That Sounds add a Grandeur to Sense, we may see amply proved by *Longinus*; and to produce this Effect, *Virgil*, with the best Poets, varied Numbers by every Contrivance, and, that the Harmony might be compleat, introduced into *Italy* all the Freedom of *Grecian* Poetry.'' John Coleridge "On Liberty in Poetry" *A Critical Latin Grammar . . .* (1772) 157.

[1] On Sunday, 1 Jun, the Gillmans and C had a housewarming at The Grove, to which 150 guests had accepted invitations. *CL* v 365. C was having a rare bout of good health; on the 3rd he attended a ball at the Aders's in Euston Square. On 2 Jun HNC recorded in his diary what he had heard or overheard C say, probably 1 Jun.

[2] In 1822 Granville Penn (1761–1844) published *A Comparative Estimate of the Mineral and Mosaical Geologies* to defend the Bible with his own peculiar theories in opposition to French geologists. William Buckland (1784–1856), professor of mineralogy and reader in geology at Oxford, president of the Geological Society (1824) and soon to be Canon of Christ Church, Oxford (1825), published in 1823 *Reliquiae Diluvianae; or, Observations on the Organic Remains Contained in Caves . . . Attesting the Action of an Universal Deluge*. In *A Supplement to A Comparative Estimate . . .* (1825) Penn rejected the "hyaena-den hypothesis" of Buckland and the theories of Georges Cuvier, but frequently quoted *Reliquiae Diluvianae* without challenge. C's objection to Penn's illogic is explained by a letter of about the same date to the sister of John Frederic Daniell, author of *Meteorological Essays* (1823): C predicted that Daniell's "Coalescence with the Granville Penn Party and the Pressing of Moses & the Bible into the Service of Geological Theory" would end like other such attempts in "the triumph of Infidels", for the "Bible must be interpreted by it's known *objects* and *Ends*; & these were the moral and spiritual Education of the Human Race.—These ends secured, the truths of Science follow of their own accord—.'' *CL* v 372. On 3 Jun HCR heard C, Davy, and J. H. Green "patronising" Penn's "absurd attack on geology". *CRB* I 307. During C's time in Malta, Penn was an intermediary between Lord Camden and Alexander Ball. On 18 Sept 1805 Ball wrote to Penn from Malta introducing C as one who had been satisfactory as a secretary. Transcription in DCL.

state by such a flood; they must evidently have been the natives of the places in which they are found.[3] The climates must have been altered; and supposing an inconceivably sudden evaporation to have produced an intense cold, the solar heat would not be sufficient afterwards to overcome it. The polar cold was not to be accounted for merely by the comparative distance of the Sun. No rain is mentioned *previously to the deluge. The rainbow did not exist before.[4]   [36:56, 57]

The Earth was Memory—The Air and Heaven Futurity.[5]   [36:58]

The fondness for dancing was the reaction of the reserved manners of English women; it was the only way in which they could throw themselves forth in natural liberty.[6]   [36:59]

We had no idea of the perfection of the ancient tragic dance; the pleasure received had for its basis Difference, and the more unfit the vehicle was, the more lively was the curiosity and intense the delight at seeing the incongruity overcome.[7]   [36:59]

The ancients understood some principles in acoustics, which we have lost. They conveyed the voice distinctly in their theatres by means of a pipe, and created no echo or confusion.[8] Our theatres were fit for noth-

a p 110

[3] The reviewer of Penn in *B Critic* NS XXI (Apr 1824) 387–402 found the objection made here by C applicable also to Buckland's hypothesis. C's next sentences rebut Penn's argument that the contents of the "hyaena's den" and similar caves could have been contemporaneous with the rocks where they are embedded, if gases created by putrifaction of the animals, while the strata were still soft, formed the caves where the fossils were discovered. C was rejecting also such theories of catastrophic change as Buckland's—that the cold waters of the deluge, upon hitting the central fires of the earth and thus setting off volcanic explosions, might have created mountain ranges and burned away extinct species. See also 29 Jun 1833 n 16, below.

[4] God set his "bow in the cloud" as "a token of a covenant between me and the earth" in Gen 9.13. *TT* (1835) expanded the last two sentences into a separate entry (36:57), adding: "However, I only suggest this."

[5] *TT* (1835) clarified the first clause: "The Earth with its scarred face is the symbol of the Past". C thus makes the vista confronting Noah at the moment of the covenant emblematic for all subsequent generations.

[6] When De Wette argued in *Theodor* (1822) that dances are an allegory of sexual love, C protested: "In England at least, our young Ladies think as little of the Dances representing the moods and manœvres of Sexual Passion as of the Man-in-the-Moon's whiskers: & woe be to the Girl, who should so dance as to provoke such an interpretation." *CM (CC)* II 190.

[7] Of choral dancing in Greek tragedies, as C says, almost nothing was known. Into the vacuum C inserts the doctrine of representational sameness with aesthetic difference, or "incongruity overcome": cf 1 Jul 1833, below (at n 34), on imitation as "the mesothesis of Likeness and Difference".

[8] Cf Schlegel *Ueber dramatische Kunst und Litteratur* I 81–2: "Ueberhaupt darf man annehmen, dass die Theater der Alten nach vortrefflichen akoustischen Grundsätzen gebaut waren." Tr John Black: "We may without hesitation venture to assume, that the

ing; they were too large, and too small.[9]   [36:60]

Nothing of Lord Byron's would live, nor much of the poetry of the day. The *art* was so neglected; the verses would not scan.[10]   [36:61]

Up to 21, a father has power; after that age, authority or influence only. Show me one couple unhappy on account of limited circumstances only, and I will show you ten wretched from other causes. S.T.C. would of himself disapprove marriage between first cousins; but the Church had decided otherwise on the authority of Augustine, and that was enough.[11] A slight contrast of character was very material to happiness in marriage.[12]   [36:62, 63, 64]

---

theatres of the ancients were constructed on excellent acoustical principles.'' In the same paragraph Schlegel mentioned contrivances for reinforcing the voice (''darin angebrachten Verstärkungsmitteln der Stimme'') and commented on the smallness of modern theatres (in Germany). Vitruvius Pollio (1st century B.C.) *De architectura* (Rome 1486), the chief source for later confusion between Periclean lumber and Hellenistic marble in the theatres, in bk v ch 5 described bronze sounding vessels arranged in the theatre according to the harmonics of the octave, but Schlegel had amplifiers in mind, and C either amplifiers or conduits for sound.

[9] Covent Garden had been rebuilt in 1809 to seat nearly 3000, with a stage 68' × 82'; Drury Lane, rebuilt in 1812 and later remodelled, seated about 2500. Both were too small, said *TT* (1835), ''for a bull-fight''.

[10] C spoke often of the metrical deficiencies of Lord Byron and of recent verse generally. Charles Robert Leslie (1794–1859) reported remarks, probably of 1813: ''He thought Lord Byron's misanthropy was affected, or partly so, and that it would wear off as he grew older. He said that Byron's perpetual quarrel with the world was as absurd as if the spoke of a wheel should quarrel with the movement of which it must of necessity partake.'' *Autobiographical Recollections* ed Tom Taylor (2 vols 1860) I 49. For C's sympathy with Byron in 1816 see *EOT (CC)* II 427–9 and nn. HNC, who had reviewed *Werner, a Tragedy* adversely, indeed vituperatively, in *B*

Critic for Mar 1823, took an opportunity to attack Byron, in a defence of C against plagiarism, in the Preface to *TT* (1835) I lxv–lxviii, dropped from *TT* (1836). But the present entry continued in *TT* (1835) with C's praise of *Don Juan* III, particularly III 32, on Lambro's return home, and with HNC's defence, against C's objection, of Byron's rhyming ''again'' with ''then''. The stanza put C in mind of the ''festal abandonment'' in paintings by Nicolas Poussin (1594–1665).

[11] To HNC this discussion concerned his engagement to SC, but C, although disturbed by HNC's indiscretion in *Six Months in the West Indies in 1825* (1826)—''I love a cousin . . . almost my sister ere my wife''—protested his innocence of the affair until Mrs Gillman told him the meaning of HNC's reference. *CL* VI 589–91. In a long memorandum on the subject, probably written in the summer of 1826, C pointed out that St Augustine's reversal of Theodosius and St Ambrose had not led to a removal of ''the prejudice against and the aversion to the marrying the Child of a Father's or Mother's Brother or Sister''. BM MS Egerton 2800 f 151; *CL* VI 590n–1. Some of the language of the memorandum is repeated in a marginal note on Luther *Colloquia Mensalia* (1652) 451, dated 19 Aug 1826: *CM (CC)* III.

[12] For C's avuncular letters of advice on marriage see *CL* V 152–8, 181–4, VI 793–6. For his conversation on 10 Jun 1824, the date used by HNC for this entry in *TT* (1835), see *CRB* I 307–8. Among those present were the painter William Collins, Edward Irving, Henry

*a*Highgate. 24. Feb. 1827.[1]

*b*S.T.C.—There is no miracle of a gift of tongues in the second chapter of Acts.[2] The only language used in divine service was Hebrew, and the text says that after the descent of the Holy Ghost the Christians came out and spoke ἑτέραις γλώσσαις i.e. with *other* tongues or in reality profane or secular tongues,[3] and this it was, that they should speak of the things of God in any other language but Hebrew, which filled the assembled multitude, who were Jews, with wonder. As if a Romish priest had spoken his vernacular tongue in the service instead of Latin.*c*[4]

---

a MS B f 1   *b-c* For the variant in MS F see App C, below

Taylor, and E. Chance, a glass-manufacturer.

HNC's first cycle of recorded TT and his diary end here together on 2 Jun 1824. Subsequent pages of MS A contain notes on his own reading.

[1] HNC later in 1824, mostly for reasons of health, accompanied his cousin, William Hart Coleridge, bp of Barbados, to the West Indies. After his return in mid-1825 (and writing *Six Months in the West Indies*), he saw C on occasion (*CL* v 508, 521, vi 571) but made no surviving record of TT. SC came to London in the summer of 1826 for a year. In Jan and Feb 1827 she was staying with the JTC family, who had moved to a spacious house at 65 Torrington Square. On 2 Jan 1827 HNC presented to SC, still no closer kin than cousin and fiancée, both MS A and his rearranged transcription, MS E. At the end of MS E he wrote: "These are all the Memorabilia, my love, I have. It would be well worth your while to be very attentive to your father's conversation, when you are with him, and endeavour afterwards to preserve some of it, as I have done. Especially as he talks to you on plainer subjects. Thine devotedly *HNC. 2. Jan. 1827.*" On Saturday, 24 Feb, HNC began again to record C's conversation at the Gillmans'; one may surmise that SC was also present. Beginning a new notebook specifically for C's TT (in this edition called MS B), HNC continued straight through on both sides of each leaf.

[2] The subject of miraculous tongues possibly arose because C had talked with Edward Irving on 4 Feb. *C Talker* 259. On the authority particularly of Acts 2, Irving was encouraging members of his congregation to "speak with tongues". See also above, 1 May 1823 (at n 6).

[3] "With other tongues": Acts 2.4. Not discussed by Eichhorn *NT. Aliis* (other) is glossed as *novis* (new) in Matthew Poole *Synopsis criticorum aliorumque S. Scripturae interpretum* (4 vols, with vol iv in 2 pts, 1669–76) iv i 1403. C's set of Poole, left with WW, went later to Irving. *WW LC* 348. For C on Acts 2 see *CL* vi 784.

[4] C had no reason to predict that Mass would be said in vernacular languages. The entry on tongues was omitted from *TT* (1835). Cf C's explanation in an annotation on *Omniana* of the gift of tongues: "On the inrush of the Spirit the new Converts ⟨to Jesus⟩ from all parts of the Roman Empire, then met at Jerusalem/ rushed out of the House, and addressed the crowd, each his own countrymen, and to the scandal of some & surprize of all, in the vernacular ⟨dialects⟩ instead of the sacred (Syro-chaldaic) Language—just as if a man should pray aloud in a Catholic Church in any other than Latin Prayers." He concluded that "the *miracle*, they had witnessed, was a fulfilment of Joel's Prophecy— viz. that Laymen should preach in the Spirit in the Common Tongue". *Omniana* ed RS with contributions by C (2 vols 1812) i 226–7: *CM (CC)* iii.

First six chapters of Daniel were the most corrupt of the books of the Old Testament. They were evidently spurious. The genuine book began at the seventh chapter. Doubts as to Daniel.[5] Certainly written before our Savior.[6] Christ said to the Jews, when you shall see the abomination of desolation &c. i.e. not a passing storm by the frantic reformer Antiochus Epiphanes, but by the wise and tolerant Romans—*then* you may know that indeed your destruction is come.[7] ⟨S.T.C. now thinks *all Daniel* a forgery.⟩[8]   [36:66]

Ecclesiastes was the next corrupt. Evidently not by Solomon, but attributed by the Jews in their passion to ascribe every thing to him.[9]

[36:66]

[5] C wrote in 1825: "Six first chapters of Daniel—I value not at a farthing the *faith* of the Man who can believe them—in fact, such belief arises from the want of facts." *CN* IV 5260, at greater length in 5287. In an annotation on Irving *Sermons* (3 vols 1818), on a leaf tipped in between I 74 and 75, he called Daniel 7–12 "the Dream-book compiled under the name of Daniel", and in *CIS* he specified Dan 1–6 among those passages of the Bible most likely to be questioned by a sceptical reader because the language is irreconcilable with the assumed date. *CM (CC)* III and *CIS* (1840) 25, 82. E. S. Shaffer has observed that C was readier than Eichhorn to find in books of the OT a series of interpolators. *"Kubla Khan" and "The Fall of Jerusalem": The Mythological School in Biblical Criticism and Secular Literature 1770–1880* (Cambridge 1975) 78. But C was cautious about imposing such views on others, a reluctance apparent in letters of 1826–7 to Basil Montagu, EC, and H. F. Cary. *CL* VI 550, 561, 568–71, 683. To Richard Chenevix Trench and to John Sterling in 1832 C did not argue the contemporaneous writing of Daniel and Maccabees "until pressed". R. C. Trench *Letters and Memorials* ed M. Trench (2 vols 1888) I 124. The impetus behind these remarks is C's contention that "it is the spirit of the Bible, and not the detached words and sentences, that is infallible and absolute". *CIS* 73. Further, as he said in the first reference to Daniel in TT, 29 Dec 1822 (at n 9), Christianity is within.

[6] Jesus cites Dan 9.23, 27 in Matt 24.15.

[7] Antiochus IV Epiphanes (c 215–163 B.C.), King of Syria from 175 B.C., stormed Jerusalem in 170 B.C. and desecrated the Temple in pursuit of his intention to destroy the Jewish religion. C is arguing that the book of Daniel was composed shortly after this "abomination" and that both Jesus and his hearers recognised the allusions to a specific event. For a clarification c 1828 see N 36 f 67 (*CN* V).

[8] In Letter 4 of *CIS* (1840) 54, C referred to "the Grecisms and heavier difficulties in the biographical chapters of Daniel" as an unanswerable objection that could be made by an infidel to the authenticity of the book. Cf Eichhorn *AT* III 340–90. HNC's insertion of the last sentence in this entry is the only instance in TT of a later insertion that declares a change in C's opinions. C's considered opinion that Daniel is a compilation of smaller works originally discrete is now common among Biblical scholars.

[9] In a marginal note on Eccles 1.12 in Anne Gillman's Bible, C assigned the work on linguistic grounds to the same age as Esther and Dan 1–6. *CM (CC)* I 433. In *TT* (1835) Solomon became "their *grand monarque*", a phrase perhaps readier to HNC's pen than to C's tongue.

Esther not genuine.[10]
Hebrew in its heighth in Isaiah.[11]   [36:66]

Blumenbach said there were five races—Kant three.[12] One great Iapetic original of language, under which Greek, Latin and species, perhaps

[10] In Letter 6 of *CIS* (1840) 82 C said that a "spiritual physician" may grant to the infidel that Esther, like Dan 1–6, possesses "a traditional and legendary character unlike that of the other historical books" of the OT. Although Deborah in Judges 4–5 is his usual example of the morally repulsive, he renounced the vindictiveness of Esther, Ps 109.6–20 and 137.9, along with Dan 1–6, in *CIS* 25; cf p 54. The discussion of Daniel, reduced and mitigated in MS F, was clipped from that ms before it was further reduced in *TT* (1835), and the remark about Esther in MS B was omitted from *TT* (1835).

[11] In *TT* (1835) the discussion of the OT on 24 Feb concerns not so much the authorship of different books as the rise and fall of Hebrew in "force and purity" as a language. Modifying an earlier note on Eichhorn *AT* of 5 Jun 1827, C declared it not "mere guess" but fact that the compilers of "Isaiah" lost track of the various authors to whom they had given that name. *CM (CC)* II 405–6, 408.

[12] For Kant's identification of four races on the basis of skin-colour see 7 Jan–13 Feb 1823 and n 42, above. Blumenbach (1752–1840) in *De generis humana nativa varietate* (1775) distinguished four races; in the 2nd ed 1781, five: Caucasian, Asiatic or Mongolian, American, Ethiopian, and Malay. After visiting England in 1791–2, apparently influenced by Sir Joseph Banks, he introduced into the 3rd ed of 1795, as *Über die natürlichen Verschiedenheiten im Menschengeschlechte*, the question of possible degeneration into races and varieties as a result of environmental factors. He was the first to replace differentiation by skin-colour with distinctions of skeletal structure and posture. He had a collection of skulls, still extant, which C would have seen. Carlyon I 190–1. In 1795 and later he emphasised the distinctness and unity of the human species; in all editions he argued that the process of degeneration was reversible and concluded therefrom that slavery was pernicious. In *Beyträge zur Naturgeschichte* (2 vols Göttingen 1806–11) he paid tribute to the Negro as lacking only opportunity to equal the European in accomplishment. C had attended Blumenbach's lectures on physiology and natural history at Göttingen in 1798–9. As the only English student animated and bold enough to question him, C became a favourite. *CL* I 472, 494, 497, 590–1; *CN* I 1657, 1738; *BL* ch 10 *(CC)* I 207; Carlyon I 161–91. Blumenbach's son, who accompanied the English visitors on a walking tour to the Brocken, remembered C "often and affectionately". George Bellas Greenough to C, *W&C* 234. In 1803 C took notes from Blumenbach *Handbuch der Naturgeschichte* (Göttingen 1799), which he proposed to translate. *CN* I 1738–53. He remained an admirer of Blumenbach and defended him against what he regarded as misrepresentation and mistranslation by others. *Friend (CC)* I 59, 154–6. He worked out three of his varying schemes to modify Blumenbach on race in N 26 ff 99ᵛ–100 *(CN* v), N 27 ff 80–78 *(CN* IV 4548), and BM Add MS 34225 ff 135–6ᵛ. All his speculations on race begin in the conviction that the greatest threat to any human soul is to assume that it was formed by the environment. The salience of the question is clear in *CN* IV 4548, 4668, 4697, 4839, 4984, *CL* VI 723, and in marginal notes on Antoine Desmoulins *Histoire naturelle des races humaines* (Paris 1826) and Steffens *Caricaturen des Heiligsten* (2 vols Leipzig 1819): *CM (CC)* II 176–8, IV.

Sanskrit, Ιαόνες,[13] one branch with a tendency to migrate southwest, the other—Goths, Germans, Swedes—northwest. Shemitic—Hebrew.[14]   [36:65]

---

[a]10 March. 1827. Highgate—

S.T.C. In all other nations but the Jews, the people look backwards and also exist for the present; but with the Jewish scheme every thing is prospective, preparatory; nothing is done for itself alone, but all is typical of something to come.[1]   [36:67]

No doubt there was a popular belief in a future state, wholly independent of their Mosaic law.[2]   [36:48]

[a] MS B f 1[v]

[13] Ιωαονες in *CN* III 4384 f 158[v], *CN* IV 4507, and *CM* (*CC*) II 578. Edward Hawkins annotated *Samson Agonistes* 715–16, "bound for th'isles of Javan"—"that is, Greece, for *Javan* or *Ion* the fourth son of Japheth is said to have peopled Greece and Ionia". *The Poetical Works of John Milton* (4 vols Oxford 1824) III 275n. About 1828, in a long note at the end of J. G. Gruber's edition of Blumenbach *Über die natürlichen Verschiedenheiten im Menschengeschlechte* (Leipzig 1798), C proposed to reconcile Blumenbach (and Kant) with the account in Genesis by distinguishing the "Generous" or historic race, comprising Semitic (religious), Iapetic (sciential, philosophic), and Hammonic (symbolic, literary) tribes, from the pure "Degenerous" or unhistoric (African), and the mixed (Mongolian, American, Malay). *CM* (*CC*) I 539–41. By this theory, the Celtic tribes (C specifies Welsh, Irish, and French), and perhaps the Slavic, would descend from the Semitic-Iapetic by intermarriage with the Hammonic. *TT* (1835) reproduced at this point (36:65) the diagram of racial degeneration that HNC had recorded on 15 Aug 1832 (below). Aside from anthropological and Biblical questions, the origin of races was of special interest in C's day for aesthetic and political reasons—

e.g. the superiority of the Goths, formerly declared barbarous—and because of the recent discovery of the Indo-European family of languages.

[14] *TT* (1835) interpreted safely: "The Hebrew is Semitic." The ms spelling, "Shemitic", preserves the origin in Noah's son Shem.

[1] Presenting a more static view of the OT in his lectures on religion in 1795, C said in Lect 2: "To preserve one nation free from Idolatry in order that it might be a safe receptacle for the precursive Evidences of Christianity, was the principal design of the Mosaic Dispensation." *Lects 1795* (*CC*) 137; cf 116. C was probably thinking of the messianic sense of greater influence to come for God's dispersed people that pervades the OT (e.g. Gen 9, Isa 9.2–7, 11.1–12, Jer 23.5–8, Ezek 34.11–31) and continued in Jewish aspirations for a return of Israel to Zion. Byron had written in *Hebrew Melodies* (1815) that "The Harp the Monarch Minstrel swept" still sounds "In dreams that day's broad light can not remove".

[2] Continuing the train of thought evoked by Warburton's *Divine Legation*, C returned to his argument of 1 May 1823; the two discussions are combined in *TT* (1835) (36:48).

In the original it is a "*bladder*" and not *witch* as we translate it.[3] Saul is not said to have *seen* Samuel; and the prophecy is nothing but what had been well known for three years before.[4]					[36:48]

In the Roman Catholic Question, the existence of the Irish Protestant Church is the real question.[5] He would vote for the claims with this distinct declaration that at no time and under no circumstances could a branch of the Romish Hierarchy as at present constituted become an estate of the Realm.[6]					[36:70]

---

[3] In so interpreting 1 Sam 28.11, C drew especially on John Webster (1610–82) *The Displaying of Supposed Witchcraft* (1677) 30: "And the Woman at *Endor* (falsely called a Witch, or a Woman that had a familiar Spirit, when in the Hebrew she is only called the Mistress of the Bottle, as we shall manifest hereafter) must needs be a Deceiver and Imposter . . ."; cf 128–9, on the Pythoness as "the Mistress of the Bottle, or of the oracle . . . at Endor there is a Woman that was Mistress of the *Ob*, the Bottle or Oracle". C annotated this work, and referred to it in a note on Exod 22.18 in Anne Gillman's Bible: "Webster has shown clearly, that Witch (mulier inflata, bladder-woman) was a fortune-telling Ventriloquist—always in the service of the false Gods—Pythoness. So the Witch of Endor." *CM (CC)* I 420. On 10 Mar 1820 C had written jocularly to Hyman Hurwitz of his conscience as "the most fearful of the *Ōboth*, the pre-eminent *Kosem Kesamim*", making clear his meaning of ventriloquist and necromancer. *CL* v 20. He played with the association of witch and bladder in Letter 4 of *CIS* (1840) 45–6. For similar remarks see C's annotations on J. A. Hillhouse *Hadad* (New York 1825): *CM (CC)* II 1108–9. See also 36:48 n 3, below.

[4] C argued this case at length in N 18 (*CN* III 3753) and in a marginal note on Argens *Kabbalistische Briefe* (*CM—CC*—I 110). In notes on Luther *Colloquia Mensalia* (1652) 370, 388, 391, he called on the authority of Webster to divorce the "Imbecilities" of belief in witchcraft from "the *Ob*, and *Obim*" of the Bible. *CM (CC)* III.

[5] As expanded in *TT* (1835) (36:70), C charged the "leading Irish Romanists" with seeking to destroy the Protestant Church in Ireland in order to re-establish their own. In 1817 he had argued that the admission of any Catholic into Parliament would "establish an irresistible *Right* to be the Established Church in Ireland for the Catholic Hierarchy". Annotation on Hansard XXVI (1817) 400: *Parliamentary Debates: CM (CC)* IV. On C's fears that the removal of disabilities would lead to repeal of the Union, see *EOT (CC)* II 243; *C&S (CC)* xlv. The present entry is the kind that made C's more liberal friends suspect HNC of tampering with the record, for HNC wrote in 1827 in *Remarks on the Present State of the Roman Catholic Question* 17: "There are many, no doubt, amongst them whose secret aspirations of ambition, envenomed by religious hatred, stop at nothing short of levelling the Protestant Church, and setting up their own in its place. These are a small but influential section of the grand army." And on p 33: ". . . the essence of the Opposition is,—Security to a Protestant Establishment in Church and State."

[6] C stated this condition in *C&S* as "at no time and under no circumstances has it ever been, nor can it ever be, compatible with the spirit or consistent with the safety of the British Constitution, to recognize in the Roman Catholic Priesthood, as now constituted, a component Estate of the realm, or persons capable, individually or collectively, of becoming the Trustees and usufructuary Proprietors of that elective and circulative property, originally reserved for the perma-

Understanding stands under the phænomenon, and gives it objectivity.
We know *what* a thing is by it—[7]   [36:75]

James Gurney's character in King John.[8]   [36:72]

Skelton's Richard Sparrow.[9]   [36:72]

Difference of French Church now and before the Revolution.[10]

Proverbs old and Solomonian, if not of Solomon, as the Davidical
psalms.[11]   [36:68]

---

nent maintenance of the National Church", and the exclusion to be maintained "wholly irrelative to any doctrines received and taught by the Romish Church as Articles of Faith". *C&S (CC)* 156–7.

[7] *TT* (1835) adroitly combined with this entry that on the Hebrew *Bineh* from 23 Sept 1830, below, as examples of the power of a pun to facilitate understanding. As the entries of 10 Mar 1827 are unusually telegraphic, the original context may have been a discussion of puns. In an annotation on Böhme *Works* C wrote: "All men who possess at once active fancy, imagination, and a philosophical Spirit are prone to *Punning*; but with a presentiment, that the Pun itself is the buffoon Brutus concealing Brutus, the Consul." *CM (CC)* I 610. On "understanding" see also *Logic (CC)* 239.

[8] *TT* (1835) presented this as an instance of Shakespeare's power in the smallest matters, or with the least material (*"in minimis"*). Gurney, a servant to Lady Faulconbridge, speaks four words. When asked by the Bastard, "wilt thou give us leave a while?" Gurney answers: "Good leave, good Philip." *King John* I i 231.

[9] *TT* (1835) reads: "And pray look at Skelton's Richard Sparrow also", which shows that HNC forgot in 1835 the point of C's remark and that he probably missed the connexion in 1827 with *King John*. The Bastard answers Gurney, "*Philip*, sparrow, *Iames*", usually rendered by editors as "Philip? sparrow!

James". Alexander Pope's edition of 1725 provided an annotation: "Philip is a common name for a tame sparrow." Zachary Grey (1688–1766) had made the literary connexion explicit in *Critical, Historical, and Explanatory Notes on Shakespeare, with Emendations of the Text and Metre* (2 vols 1754) I 277: "But I imagine that Shakespeare had an eye to *Skelton's* poem, entitled *Philip* Sparow." C may have said more than Pope and Grey; he certainly would have said no less. When *TT* (1836) was announced, Alexander Dyce called HNC's attention to the error of Richard for Philip (UT ms), but neither HNC nor any subsequent editor corrected it.

[10] Apparently not remembering C's point, HNC omitted this entry from *TT* (1835). After the Concordat of 1801 between Pius VII and Napoleon, which was in effect with slight modifications until 1905, C declared in 1802 that "the Church of France at present ought to be called—*a standing* church—in the same sense as we say a *standing* army". *CL* II 803; cf 806. C's comments on the Concordat in the *M Post* 12 Oct 1802—*EOT (CC)* I 366—lack the clear distinction of his letters between an established and a standing Church.

[11] I.e., as made clear in *TT* (1835), the Proverbs are only Solomonian as the Psalms are only Davidical. Eichhorn, after stressing the widespread and ageless sources and analogues of particular proverbs, proposed that some were by Solomon, some were of his time and *Sa-*

Internal energy and external modifiability are in inverse proportions. In man the former is greater than in any animal and hence being less changed by [b]climate. Highest and lowest man are not half so much altered as different kinds of dogs.[12]   [36:71]

P. Sarpi's style more like Guicciardini—Very interesting.[13]   [36:73]

Bartram's voyage to Florida.[14]   [36:74]

[b] f 2

---

lomonisch, and some, earlier or later in origin, were assimilated as Solomonlike. *AT* III 44. On clear textual evidence, Eichhorn separated the Psalms into those by David, by the bard Assaph (Asaph), by the Korahites (musicians in the Temple), and by accretion in later prophetic times. *AT* III 416–17. C, proposing in a marginal note on Eichhorn *AT* that Ezra began the work of collecting all available moral and religious books in Hebrew and that Nehemiah carried on this collecting for the Temple, continued more specifically: "The Psalms, I doubt not, like the Greek Anthologies, appeared in two or three successive Collections—first, those extant before the Captivity & then, those that were composed during the Captivity, and on the Return, or during the Building & on the opening of the Temple—third, the two were united, and others of all the 3 Periods that had escaped the former Compilers, added." *CM (CC)* II 377. With reference to Ps 27.4 (and 68.29), C wrote in Anne Gillman's Bible that "a Ps. of D. must often mean no more than a Davidic Psalm: as we say, a Pindaric Ode." *CM (CC)* I 428.

[12] Here "external modifiability" refers, not to the adaptability of an individual to environment, but to the acquisition of physically apparent characteristics, which C presumes to be inheritable. Cf "the living power will be most intense in that individual which, as a whole, has the greatest number of integral parts presupposed in it; when, moreover", in addition to interdependence each integral part has most the character of a whole. *TL* (1848) 44–5. C would have heard Blumenbach, in the lectures of 1799, contrast the unity of the human species with the variety of canine breeds, but the observation does not require a learned source.

[13] Paolo Sarpi (1552–1623), Venetian prelate, historian, and scientist, counselled the republic of Venice in its conflict with Pope Paul V. His *Istoria del concilio Tridentino* (1619) was published in London under the pseudonymous anagram Pietro Soave Polan, in a translation by Nathanael Brent, as *The History of the Council of Trent* (1620). Sarpi's account, which begins with Luther and Huldreich Zwingli in 1500, overlaps slightly with the *Storia d'Italia* (Florence 1561–4) of Francesco Guicciardini (1483–1540). C may have said that Sarpi's style is more like Guicciardini's than like Machiavelli's, but HNC settled in *TT* (1835) for "very interesting" and "deserves your study". Eugenio Donadoni described Sarpi as equally noble with the historians of Guicciardini's generation, serious, rapid, and "more spirited and immediate". *A History of Italian Literature* tr Richard Monges (2 vols New York 1969) I 286–8. Apparently C first learned of Sarpi from Gilbert Burnet *Life of William Bedell* (1685) 253–9: see *EOT (CC)* II 406n.

[14] William Bartram *Travels Through North & South Carolina, Georgia, East & West Florida, the Cherokee Country, the Extensive Territories of the Muscogulges, or Creek Confederacy, and the Country of the Chactaws . . .* (Philadelphia 1791). A copy of this work acquired from James Webbe Tobin was presented by C to SH with a pedagogical comment: "This is not a Book of Travels, properly

18. March—Highgate.[1]

S. T. C. There are seven parts of speech, and they agree with the five grand and universal divisions into which all things fall;—two of them being modifications only. 1. Prothesis. 2. Thesis. 3. Antithesis. 4. Synthesis. 5. The Indifference of the Thesis and Antithesis.[2]

I.[a] The first and previous form is that of the Noun-Verb, or Verb Substantive, I am = Prothesis or Identity with Being.

II. The Noun = Thesis.

III. The Verb = Antithesis.

} Each of these may be converted i.e. they are only opposed to each other.

[a] The "I" was a later insertion, the first part of the table having been part of the first paragraph

speaking; but a series of poems, chiefly descriptive, *occasioned* by the Objects, which the Traveller observed.—It is a *delicious* Book . . .''. He asked her to remember an evening when he read to her from Bartram's Introduction. *CM (CC)* I 227. In Apr 1818 C wrote his name in a copy of the 2nd ed of 1794, now in VCL. For speculations concerning Bartram's influence on C in 1794–8, see *RX* esp 8–11, 46–59, 186–92, 364–72, 455, 513–15. In various notes to *CN* I, *RX* is extended or modified. In *BL* ch 22 *(CC)* II 155 C quoted Bartram's description of deep soil and stately trees as an analogy for WW's genius. This brief entry is expanded to two sentences in *TT* (1835).

[1] It is accident only that on this same day SH wrote from Keswick to her cousin John Monkhouse: "Sara C. (celestial *blue* as Q[uillinan] calls her) is at Highgate with her Father." *SHL* 341.

[2] For *TT* (1835) HNC arranged the pentad into a table conforming with *AR* (1831) 170, whereby "4. Synthesis" became "Mesothesis. 4" and "Indifference"—in *AR* (1825) 172n the "Punctum Indifferens sive *Amphotericum*"—became "Synthesis. 5". (In TT he began the first entry for 18 Mar as a running paragraph, at first omitting the roman numeral I. His failure to anticipate the tabular form is significant as an indication that he was not copying from a document.) Of the many places where C tabulated the progression from prothesis to synthesis as a pentad, tetrad, or heptad, one of the most informative is that in a letter to James Gillman Jr, written in a copy of *C&S* (1830) 150–61 and printed in *C&S (CC)* 233–4. In a letter to Hurwitz of 16 Sept 1829 *(CL* VI 816–18) C applied the pentad to grammatical forms, as in this entry, and to colours, as in 24 Apr 1832, below (36:371). For some other occurrences see marginalia on Baxter *Reliquiae Baxterianae* and Hegel *Wissenschaft der Logik* (2 vols 1812–16): *CM (CC)* I 347, II 991. The astronomer William Rowan Hamilton (1805–65) told how, by a long algebraic struggle, he arrived at approximately the point where C, virtually innocent of mathematics, achieved his "terrific note about the *Pentad*". Hamilton to Aubrey de Vere 13 May 1835, in Robert Perceval Graves *Life of Sir William Rowan Hamilton* (3 vols 1882–9) II 142. William Page Wood, Lord Hatherley (1801–81), less sympathetic, not only experienced from C an outpouring of "all the riches of his prodigious memory, and all the poetry of his brilliant imagination", but "heard the whole of the poet-philosopher's favourite system of Polarities—the Prothesis, the Thesis, the Mesothesis, and Antithesis—showered down on a young lady of seventeen, with as much unction as he afterwards expounded it to Edward Irving". *A Memoir of . . . Baron Hatherley* ed W. R. W. Stephens (2 vols 1883) I 51–2.

IV. Thesis or Noun modified by = Adnoun or Adjective.
Antithesis or Verb i.e. a quality

V. Antithesis or Verb modified
by Thesis or Noun = Adverb.

VI. Participle i.e. partaking of
the Noun and Verb i.e. of Thesis = Synthesis.
and Antithesis

VII. Indifference of the Noun
and Verb = Infinitive Mood.[3]

[36:76]

---

[b]Interjections are parts of Sound, not of Speech. Conjunctions are the same as prepositions, only prefixed to a sentence or member of a sentence, instead of a word. The inflections of Nouns are modifications as to Place—Conjugations of Verbs as to Time.

Genitive case, dependence.

Dative, transmission.[4]

[b] MS B f 2[v]

[3] C's lifelong interest in grammar made inevitable his applying to the parts of speech the "*Logical Pentad*, or Heptad, of *forms*", as here, in *CN* IV 4644, and in the letter to Hurwitz of 16 Sept 1829 (*CL* VI 816–18). For Hurwitz he pointed out that there can be but one perfect prothesis, "The Eternal I AM", possessing "the identity or co-inherence of Act and Being". As *TT* (1835) and the other grammatical pentads make clear, the infinitive, as the indifference between thesis and antithesis, is the mesothesis. Notes on grammar and logic with reference to Greek appear in N 29 ff 25–31: *CN* IV 4644, 4697–8, and elsewhere. *TT* (1835) promised, in a footnote, that the Greek grammar compiled by C for his children would appear in *LR*, but it did not, and the note was dropped from *TT* (1836). C prepared a dialogue on Italian grammar for SC's study at Keswick (VCL F MS 2.21) and a Latin grammar, in 1825, for Henry Gillman's use at Eton (VCL S MS F 2.19). According to Grattan's account of a conversation in Belgium in 1828, C had compiled a succinct German grammar of ten pages: "This led to his favourite topic, grammar. Every conversation on that subject was a general treatise on its philosophy, its construction, and its value." Thomas Colley Grattan *Beaten Paths; and Those Who Trod Them* (2 vols 1862) II 118. C's father published *A Critical Latin Grammar* in 1772.

[4] Johnson's dictionary had defined the genitive as "a case, which, among other relations, signifies one begotten . . . or one begetting"; the dative as "the case that signifies the person to whom any thing is given"; and the ablative as the sixth case in Latin "which, among other significations, includes the person from whom something is taken away". C treated the Latin ablative as a subdivision of the dative, or, in 1825, as "the *border*-land between the Greek Genitive and Dative". *CL* V 490. The speculation in 1825 led to affectionate memory of a passage in his father's Latin grammar: "The *Quale-quare-quidditive* Case is so called, because it denotes the Manner of doing; *how*, the Cause *why*, or the Instrument *with which*, the Prior Case effects it's End . . .". *Critical Latin Grammar* ii. C's general rule is that "Cases are *Pre*positions affixed and agglutinated to the nouns or adnouns, they govern"; his chief philosophic motive for attending to

Absurd to talk of Verbs governing. In Thucydides every case has been found absolute.—[5]

Middle Voice absurd. τύπτομαι and τύπτομαι must be the same.[6]

Declensions[c] of the tenses formed out of adjuncts of the verb substantive—τυπτω[7] = τυπτ' ειμι—ετυπτ–ημην[d]—ετυφθ- ην.[8] ε̲ is the prefix significant of a past time.[9]   [36:76]

Magnetism = Length. Electricity = Breadth or Surface. Galvanism = Depth.[10]   [36:77]

---

[c] ~~Conjugations~~ Declensions   [d] ημ of ημην apparently cancelled

---

cases is the conviction that words do not refer to things, but rather to our thoughts of things, or our thoughts of the "modes of appearance" that things achieve by "moving, acting, or being acted on". *CL* VI 817.

[5] In *TT* (1835) HNC provided examples of nominative and dative absolutes from Thucydides and an accusative absolute from Sophocles, problematic because it may be a nominative.

[6] "I strike myself", or "I strike for myself" (middle); "I am struck" (passive). As middle and passive forms of a verb are identical in the present (as in C's example) and in all tenses except the future and the aorist, C presumably means that it is unnecessary to specify a middle voice, as distinct from the passive, wherever the same form renders both passive and reflexive shades of meaning. The middle voice was becoming obsolete when written Greek became the dominant literature.

[7] "I strike".

[8] C derives the indicative from the root plus ειμι, *sum*, "I am". He then derives the first and second aorist, with passive signification, from ε, prefix for the past; the root; and ην, "was". "Declensions" replaced the cancelled "Conjugations" in MS B; *TT* (1835) reads "inflections".

[9] Called by grammarians "the temporal augment".

[10] *TT* (1835) had C apologising: "Perhaps the attribution or analogy may seem fanciful at first sight, but I am in the habit of realizing to myself . . ." etc. Yet not only C but the foremost chemists, phys-

iologists, and other scientific students puzzled endlessly over the meaning and interrelations of electricity, magnetism, and galvanism. The spatial equivalents set forth in this entry derive from the *Naturphilosophen*, especially Schelling and Steffens. C modified progressively both the Germans' changing schemes and his own. In 1809 he had compared electricity with free will, "infinite in its affinities, infinite in its modes of action". *EOT (CC)* II 52. In Nov 1818 he wrote to Tulk: "Schelling . . . is beyond doubt a Man of Genius, and by the revival and more extensive application of the Law of Polarity (i.e. that every Power manifests itself by opposite Forces) and by the reduction of all Phænomena to the three forms of Magnetism, Electricity, and constructive Galvanism, or the Powers of Length, Breadth, and Depth, his System is extremely plausible and alluring at a first acquaintance. . . . But as a *System* . . . like Behmen's it is reduced at last to a mere Pantheism . . ." *CL* IV 883. Johann Wilhelm Ritter (1776–1810) experimentally found electricity and magnetism to be identical, but the discovery by Oersted in 1819 that a conductor carrying electrical current induced magnetism in other objects was accepted by Davy as the basis of experiments in 1820–1: Davy *Electro-Magnetic Researches . . .* (1821) 1–2. So intense was the experimentation and theorising that John Murray of Birmingham declared in Nov 1822 that the relations of galvanism to heat and magnetism were perplexed, obscure, and "utterly unknown". *Philosophical*

Three colors only—Red = Prothesis or Color κατ᾽ ἐξόχην.[11] Yellow = Thesis. Blue = Antithesis. These are indecomponible.[12] [36:371]

Pantheism of Spinoza.

W. − G. = 0. i.e. The World without God is an impossible Idea.

G. − W. = 0. i.e. God without the World is ditto.[13]

Christian Scheme.

W. − G. = 0. i.e. as in Pantheism.

G. − W. = G. i.e. But God without the World is God self-sufficing.[14] [36:69]

---

*a*24th June 1827.[1] S. T. C.

Spenser's Epithalamium sublime, and the swan-like movement of the

a f 3

Magazine and Journal LX 358. C followed the experiments, but found greater satisfaction in the theorising of the major *Naturphilosophen.* L. Pearce Williams attributed to C, Davy, and Schelling the "sense of interconnectedness of phenomena" through an organic doctrine of polarity that enabled Faraday to lay the foundation of the field theory by discovering electromagnetic induction. *Michael Faraday* (1965) 63–6. For Philarète Chasles' report of C's remarks on electricity, magnetism, and galvanism see App F 3, below. See also below, 6 Aug 1831 (at n 3) (36:319).

[11] "Par excellence", or "in itself".

[12] The three primary colours. C preferred to think of colours as pigments adding up to black rather than as components in the spectrum of light. For a fuller treatment see *CN* IV 5290 and n. HNC omitted this entry from *TT* (1835), presumably because it was superseded by the entry of 24 Apr 1832, below (at n 3) (36:371).

[13] The entry on Spinoza is crowded into the ms and undatable. HNC probably took it from an annotation on James Abraham Hillhouse *Hadad* (1825): *CM (CC)* II 1106–7. For C's definitions of Spinozism in 1799 and his remarks on

Spinoza and Spinozism some twenty-odd years later ("Spinoza . . . withdraws God from the universe") and in 1830 ("to talk of God becoming flesh appears to me very much like talking of a square circle") see App F 4, below.

[14] In a marginal note on Böhme's *Aurora* C wrote in 1818 that he had read Giordano Bruno (1548–1600) "at a time, when I . . . was myself intoxicated with the vernal fragrance & effluvia from the flowers and first-fruits of Pantheism, unaware of its bitter root, pacifying my religious feelings meantime by the dim distinction, that tho' God was = the World, the World was not = God—as if God were a Whole composed of Parts, of which the World was one!" *CM (CC)* I 602–3. HNC's note to *LR* I 329 could be taken as suggesting that C wrote out tables of this sort on paper for listeners to his conversation.

[1] There is no HNC-recorded TT from 18 Mar to this date. On 8 May C wrote to HNC that they could meet on the 9th at C. A. Tulk's or, if he remained in London a second night, he would come after breakfast on the 10th to HNC's rooms at 1 New Square, Lincoln's Inn. *CL* VI 682. Later that Thursday, the 10th, C was in Highgate, for Basil and Mrs Montagu

Prothalamium.[2] Spenser's attention to the metre and rhythm sometimes so minute as to be painful. [36:78]

Volpone the greatest of Ben Jonson's plays; full of poetry in the smaller poems.[3] [36:86]

Measure for Measure a hateful play though Shakspearian in every part.[4] Our feelings of justice are wounded in Angelo's escape.[5] Isabella unamiable, and Claudio detestable. [36:85]

---

carried there Edward Irving and Thomas Chalmers (1780–1847), who found C's "mighty unremitting stream" of conversation astonishing but unintelligible, although he perceived a communion between C and Irving "on the ground of a certain German mysticism and transcendental lake-poetry which I am not yet up to". William Hanna *Memoirs of the Life and Writings of Thomas Chalmers* (3 vols New York 1851) III 167–8.

At about this point in MS B, HNC began to give the entries the date of the talk recorded rather than a diary-date of his recording. Of Sunday, 24 Jun 1827, his memory was lyrical; see his footnote to 36:78.

[2] Edmund Spenser's "Epithalamion" was published as a conclusion to the *Amoretti* in 1595; *Prothalamion, or, A Spousall Verse . . . in Honour of the Double mariage of . . . the Ladie Elizabeth and the Ladie Katherine Somerset* in 1596. The *Prothalamion* likens the brides to two swans "softly swimming downe" to Essex House. Contemplating an epithalamium for the marriage of Frances Duke Coleridge in 1824, C reread aloud to himself Spenser's "delightful Ode, which needs only the omission of something less than a third to be the most perfect Lyric Poem in our language". *CL* v 357. Earlier he had specified the substitution needed to raise the poem above "the very best 3 or 4 Odes in our Language" as a few stanzas of "moral Tenderness" instead of two or three of those least beautiful on "things & feelings purely bodily". *CM (CC)* I 80. On Spenser see also 31 Mar 1832 and n 2, below.

[3] *TT* (1835) referred to *Volpone* (1605) by its subtitle and translation, *The Fox*. In the entry of 16 Feb 1833, below (at n 33) (36:459), *The Alchemist* is

called perfect in plot; elsewhere C qualifies this praise. Cf "the more I study his writings, the more I admire them—and the more the study resembles that of an ancient Classic, in the minutiæ of his rhythm, metre, choice of words, forms of connection, &c, the more numerous have the points of Admiration become". Note on an endleaf of Jonson *Dramatic Works* (1811): *CM (CC)* III. C judged the dramas "of worth far inferior to his Poems". Annotation on *B Poets: CM (CC)* I 62. Yet it is Jonson's dramas, not his poems, that C studied and cited throughout his maturity.

[4] The connexion, that in *Volpone* and in *Measure for Measure* alone among Shakespeare's plays "there is no goodness of heart in any of the prominent characters", was made in a note by C on Jonson *Dramatic Works* I 235; on an endleaf he also wrote: ". . . the Measure for Measure is the only play of Shakespear's in which there are not some one or more characters, generally many, whom you follow with affectionate feeling. For I confess, that Isabella, of all Shakespear's female Characters interests me the least: and the M. for Meas. is the only one of his genuine Works, which is painful to me". *CM (CC)* III. C's remarks to HNC echo his marginal note on the play in John Morgan's copy of Shakespeare *Works* ed Lewis Theobald (8 vols 1773) I [305]: "This Play, which is Shakespeare's throughout, is to me the most painful, say rather, the only painful, part of his genuine Works." *CM (CC)* IV.

[5] Escape from punishment for cruelty and lust: "the pardon and marriage of Angelo not merely baffles the strong indignant claim of Justice . . . but it is likewise degrading to the character of Woman". Ibid.

Monsieur Thomas and the little French lawyer of Beaumont and Fletcher admirable.[6] Much wit in Beaumont and Fletcher. One of the most deeply tragic scenes existing is in Rollo, where [Edith][b] prays for her father.[7]   [36:87]

No jealousy, properly speaking in Othello.[8] There is no predisposition to suspicion, which is an essential term in the definition of the word. Iago's suggestions are quite new to him; they do not correspond with any thing of a like nature in his mind before. If Desdemona had been guilty, we should not have thought of calling Othello's conduct jealous. He could not act otherwise than he did with the lights he had; jealousy can never be strictly right. Othello very different from Leontes[c] or even Leonatus.[9] The jealousy of the first is made to proceed from an evident trifle, and hate is almost mingled with it; and Leonatus accepting the wager and exposing his wife to the trial is a sign of a jealous temper previously.[10]   [36:79]

Love is the admiration and cherishing of the amiable qualities of the loved object upon the condition of yourself being the object of their action.[11] The qualities correspond. The courage of the man is loved by the

b Blank in ms   *c* Leontius

[6] Beaumont and Fletcher *Monsieur Thomas* (pub 1639, based on a novel of 1610); *The Little French Lawyer* (pub 1647).

[7] *The Bloody Brother* (pub 1639) III i, entitled in C's edition of Beaumont and Fletcher *Dramatic Works* (1811) *The Tragedy of Rollo*. *TT* (1835) continued the entry: "and then, when she cannot prevail, rises up and imprecates vengeance on his murderer", and quoted Edith's imprecation in a footnote. The play was printed as *The Tragoedy of Rollo, Duke of Normandy* "Written by John Fletcher Gent" (Oxford 1640) and in 1718 as *The Bloody Brother, or Rollo* "Written by Mr Francis Beaumont, and Mr John Fletcher". Fletcher may have had a collaborator for the play other than Beaumont. In a note on the tragedy C called it "perhaps, the most energetic of Fletcher's Tragedies", but compared it unfavourably with Shakespeare's *Richard III*; praising act III sc i in greater detail than in HNC's record, he declared the next scene "not only unnatural, but disgusting". *CM (CC)* I 397–8. He objected also to act II sc i in Lamb's copy of

Beaumont and Fletcher *Fifty Comedies and Tragedies* (2 pts 1679): *CM (CC)* I 368.

[8] "I have often told you", the entry began in *TT* (1835), which interpolated, with reference to *Othello* III iv 30–1, v ii 345, and perhaps III iii 183: "Desdemona very truly told Emilia that he was not jealous, that is, of a jealous habit, and he says so as truly of himself."

[9] C contrasted the jealous Leontes of *The Winter's Tale* with Othello in Lect 6 of 5 Jun 1812, in Lect 4 of 9 Nov 1813 at Bristol, and in marginalia: *Lects 1808–19 (CC)* I 471, 555. The "morbid suspiciousness of Leonatus" in *Cymbeline* is included in the record in *LR* II 266–7.

[10] Within two weeks of this conversation with HNC, C proposed to talk with Alaric A. Watts about an edition of Shakespeare with "critical notes, prefaces, and analyses, comprizing the results of five and twenty Years' Study". *CL* VI 695.

[11] *TT* (1835) quoted from the Friend's speech on love in "New Thoughts on Old Subjects; or Conversational Dialogues on Interests and Events of Com-

woman, whose fortitude is coveted as it were by the man—his vigorous intellect is answered by her infallible tact. *ᵈ*The whole frame of a woman mysterious—the indrawing and retiring of the pudenda denoting modesty—the prominence of the bosom showing the large action of tenderness and maternal care.*ᵉ¹²*   [36:84]

Our version of the Bible most valuable in having preserved a purity of meaning to many of the plain terms of natural things; without this our vitiated imaginations would refine away the language to mere abstractions.¹³   [36:88]

French have thus lost a poetical language.¹⁴   [36:88]

Sotheby's translation of totam Venerem, "Love" in the Georgics absurd.¹⁵   [35:88]

S. T. C. had the perception of individual images very strong, but a dim one of the relation of place; i.e. he substituted another relation for the real one.¹⁶   [36:89]

Craniology very imperfect at present—though some things could not be by accident.¹⁷ There will be endless confusion until some names or

ᵈ f 3ᵛ
ᵈ⁻ᵉ For the variant in MS F see App C, below

mon Life", published in the *Amulet* for 1828 and in *PW* (1834) II 120–1; cf *PW* (EHC) I 464–5. *TT* (1836) added a final sentence from Notebook L: *CN* III 3531 (var). HNC may have remembered some of the phrasing from conversation. C had made the point emphatically in Satyrane's Letters II *The Friend* No 16 of 7 Dec 1809: "there is a sex in our SOULS". *Friend (CC)* II 209.

¹² In MS F, with the intention of publishing it, HNC bowdlerised this anatomical observation, but three triangles marked it for excision.

¹³ One of C's purposes in *SM* was to distinguish between the simple language of the senses in the King James Version of the Bible and the common illusion that its meaning is plain and simple. The vitiation of the imagination by abstractions is a theme less persistent in C's work than in WW's, but there is sufficient consonance for C to denounce William Pitt in 1800 for "Abstractions defined by abstractions"—*EOT (CC)* I 223—and to deplore in *SM* the "unenlivened generalizing Understanding" responsible for spreading "the general contagion" of

the "mechanic philosophy". *SM (CC)* 28.

¹⁴ To the plight of the French in replacing poetic concreteness with abstractions, *TT* (1835) added that "Blanco White says the same thing has happened to the Spanish".

¹⁵ The phrase *totam Venerem* does not appear in Virgil's *Georgics*; the Latin reference is to the act of mating. C's remark, expanded in 1835 with *Georgics* 3.64 and 3.97 as examples, was dropped in 1836. See 36:88. On the polyglot *Georgics* given to C by Sotheby at this time, see 11 Aug 1832 n 2, below.

¹⁶ *TT* (1835), converting this entry to the first person, included a more concrete sentence: "I remember the man or the tree, but where I saw them I mostly forget." HNC's long footnote to the entry explained that C, like his father, "could not find his way". The conversation has moved from concreteness vs abstraction in language to C's own characteristics and practices with regard to idealisation and particulars.

¹⁷ HNC's footnote in *TT* (1835) explains the connexion between this and

proper terms are discovered for the organs, which are not taken from their application. The fore part of the head is generally given up to the higher and intellectual powers—the hinder part to the sensual.[18]

[36:90]

S. T. C. was at a dinner—one man was silent during the first part and S. T. C. thought there was something in him—till some apple-dumplings came in—when he cried out—"them's the jockies for me!"[19]   [36:91]

---

f S. T. C.[20]

Hamlet is the prevalence of the abstracting and generalizing habit over the practical. He does not want courage, skill, will or opportunity; but every incident sets him thinking; and it is curious and yet quite consonant with philosophy[21] that Hamlet who all the play seems to be reason itself, at last is impelled by mere accident to effect his object.[22]   [36:80]

f MS B f 4; ff 3ᵛ–4 contained HNC's note on "Voltaire on Hamlet"; see n 20, below

---

the previous entry: Johann Friedrich Kaspar Spurzheim (1776–1832), originator with Franz Gall of phrenology, had, in a gathering at Sotheby's that knew better, declared C to have a large bump of direction-finding "Locality" and no bump of "Ideality", the organ of poetry. Sotheby, who provides another link in the conversation, coincidentally took Fenimore Cooper to Highgate in 1828: "The conversation had wandered to phrenology, and Mr. Coleridge gave an account of the wonders that a professor had found in his own head, with a minuteness that caused his friend [Sotheby] to fidget." *Gleanings in Europe: England* 261. If fidgeting resulted from embroidery by C, Sotheby did not point out the discrepancies to Cooper.

[18] C's mixed responses to phrenology are even clearer in the entry of 24 Jul 1830, below (at n 14) (36:255).

[19] As a diminutive of John, *jockey* came early to mean a horserider; although *jock* was low slang for private parts as early as 1790, the Coleridges were unaware of any such connotation or the word *jockies* would have been censored. The germinal episode was recorded by C in 1803: "Ay! them's the

Chaps for I!—a young Rider, long silent, making a dart at the Jellies on their first appearance." *CN* i 1528. The young rider who said "Chaps" was by definition a jockey. *TT* (1835) begins this entry: "Silence does not always mark wisdom", and closes: "I wish Spurzheim could have examined the fellow's head." The thrust of the story includes both the illusion of intelligence in silence and the inadequacy of craniology and physiognomy: appearances deceive.

[20] In MS B ff 3ᵛ–4, preceding this entry, HNC transcribed for contrast Voltaire's account of *Hamlet* as "une pièce grossière et barbare", in which the hero goes mad in the second act and his mistress in the third; in sum "le fruit de l'imagination d'un sauvage ivre"—from "Dissertation sur la tragédie ancienne et moderne" prefixed to *Semiramis, Tragédie* (1748).

[21] "Hypothesis or system upon which natural effects are explained"—Johnson's third definition of "philosophy". *TT* (1835) reads: "and, at the same time, strictly natural" for the phrase.

[22] At least as early as 1810, and perhaps earlier, C began to describe Hamlet as suffering from excessive reflective-

S. T. C. 8th July 1827.[1]

Bull and Waterland are the classical writers on the Trinity.[2]   [36:93]
In the Trinity there is the 1. Ipseity. 2. Alterity. 3. Community; or God
i.e. the Absolute Will = Identity or Prothesis; The Father = Thesis; The
Son = Antithesis; The Spirit = Synthesis.[3]   [36:93]

---

ness. HCR learned 23 Dec 1810 why "real objects" were faint to Hamlet. *CRD* I 162; *CR (BCW)* 35. Of the surviving fragments, the closest to the epitome is Lect 12 of 2 Jan 1812: *Lects 1808–19 (CC)* I 386. C's analysis of Hamlet's character is a celebrated and influential contribution to Shakespearian criticism. *TT* (1835) concludes with the famous sentence: "I have a smack of Hamlet myself, if I may say so." George Daniel (1789–1864) remembered C as contending c 1817 "that Shakespeare might possibly have sat to himself for the portrait, and from his own idiosyncrasy borrowed some of its spiritual lights and shades . . .". *Recollections of Charles Lamb* (1927) 17.

In print the talk of 24 Jun ends with an anecdote (36:92), to follow and cap that on silence broken by "the jockies", on a stranger's use of the term "majestic" to describe the Falls of the Clyde.

[1] Like the last date, this was also a Sunday. J. H. Green's weekly sessions with C, which had taken place on Sundays, had been changed to Tuesdays. *CL* VI 697.

[2] George Bull, bp of St David's (1634–1710) *Defensio Fidei Nicaenae* (Oxford 1685); Daniel Waterland (1683–1740), master of Magdalene College, Cambridge *The Importance of the Doctrine of the Holy Trinity Asserted . . .* (2nd ed 1734). C annotated the Waterland and a later edition of the Bull (Ticino 1784–6); he also annotated Waterland *A Vindication of Christ's Divinity* (2nd ed 1719). The *Defensio* is still a classic. On C's copy, mentioned in HNC's footnote to this entry in *TT* (1835) but now lost, see *CM (CC)* I 800. In designating Bull as the capstone of a course in Platonic philosophy for clergymen in 1812, C proclaimed "the gigantic merits of that Glory of the English

Church, yea, of Protestantism". *CN* III 3934. He continued to think of Bull and Waterland as the chief stays against Arianism, to be read by all clergy—e.g. in *CL* IV 850 and *AR* (1825) 308n—but he expressed strong reservations concerning their philosophic, as distinct from their sacerdotal, depths: neither Bull nor Waterland had discovered the "I AM" in the Father and therefore neither realised that belief in the Trinity is reason itself: marginalia on *Vindication* 42, 228–35, and endleaves. *CM (CC)* V. In later years he may have treasured them more for his own notes than for Waterland's text. *CL* VI 962–3; *C Talker* 208. In 1827 publication of Waterland's *Works* was almost completed (11 vols Oxford 1823–8). In Nov 1825 C went through two of the six volumes of the Irish divine Philip Skelton (1707–87): "On the subject of the Trinity he is a *Master*—and worthy to be named with Bull and Waterland." *CL* V 510.

[3] In HEHL MS HM 17299 (N F°) p 162 C diagrammed the Trinity as: 1. Self-ness; the "I AM"; Father. 2. Otherness; "reflex act of self-consciousness"; Thou; Son. 3. Synthesis of I-AM and Thou; "Life, Love, the Holy Spirit". Restated in *AR* as a tetrad: "1. Prothesis, or the Identity of T[hesis] and A[ntithesis], which is neither, because in it, as the transcendent of both, both are contained and exist as one. Taken *absolutely*, this finds its application in the Supreme Being alone, the Pythagorean TETRACTYS; the INEFFABLE NAME, to which no Image dare be attached; the [Pythagorean] Point, which has no (real) Opposite or Counter-point". *AR* (1825) 173n. Two versions of the tetrad in the F° Notebook distinguish between the Identity as "The Absolute Will, the Good" or "The Absolute Subjectivity = the Absolute *Will*, the only Absolute *Good*"

Athanasian Creed is first persecuting, then tautological and lastly heretical. Unknown author.[4]   [36:94]

[a]Exalted human nature without common sense in Don Quixote; nothing but the common sense in Sancho. Sancho reverences Don Quixote even when he is cheating him.[5]   [36:425]

In the scene with Ophelia, Hamlet probably beginning with great tenderness, but perceiving her reserve and coyness, fancies there are some listeners, and then to sustain his part, breaks out into all that coarseness.[6]   [36:83]

Mrs Jordan's angelic voice, and her playing in Viola.[7]

[a] f 4[v]

and the Ipseity as "the Supreme Will" or "The *relatively* Subjective". HEHL MS HM 17299 pp 162–3, dated 6 Mar 1832. In a still fuller version of the tetrad possessed by DC and preserved by HNC (on four cards that determine the date as 1833 or later), C equated the Identity with θεος (no article) in John 1.18 ("No man hath seen God at any time") and the Ipseity with the θεος of John 5.18(?), said by Jesus to be his Father. VCL S MS 6. In a marginal note on Claude Fleury *Ecclesiastical History* C called his tetradal distinctions "the scheme of S[t] John". *CM (CC)* II 726. The advantage of the tetrad form is that the Prothesis assures the unity of Father, Son, Spirit.

[4] The creed beginning "Quicunque vult salvus esse", attributed until the seventeenth century to St Athanasius (c 293–373) of Alexandria, remains in translation in the liturgy of the Church of England. Surviving records express C's dislike of "the (Pseudo-) Athanasian Creed". *CL* IV 686, v 87–8, VI 684. He objected chiefly that the creed "does not confess the subordination of the Persons" to the Godhead, more loosely stated as failure to subordinate the Son to the Father. He objected also, as TT shows, to the damnatory clauses (based on Mark 16.16). For *TT* (1835) HNC absorbed a similar statement from 25–6 Aug 1827, below (at n 12), and borrowed from 8 Oct 1830, below (at n 11); also, "persecuting" became "if not persecuting, which I will not discuss, certainly containing harsh and ill-conceived language". Carlyon I 281–314 discussed

C's statements with partial approval. In Sept 1825 C declared his outward, as distinguished from his inward, creed to be the "Apostles' as expanded in the Nicene"; i.e. the Son not merely "born of the Virgin Mary" but "was incarnate by the Holy Ghost of the Virgin Mary, and was made man". *CN* IV 5243 and n.

[5] This comment on *Don Quixote*, omitted at this point in *TT* (1835), is utilised (in 36:425) with the comments of 11 Aug 1832, below.

[6] *Hamlet* III i. C speculates similarly in an annotation on Shakespeare *Works* ed Theobald (on VIII 166–7) and in another on Shakespeare *Dramatic Works* ed Samuel Ayscough (2 vols 1807) (on II 1017). *CM (CC)* IV. In print the entry is moved back to 24 Jun in order to consolidate the comments on *Hamlet*.

[7] Dorothea Jordan (1762–1816), née Bland, first acted the rôle of Viola in *Twelfth Night* in Nov 1785, as her second rôle at Drury Lane. She acted the part frequently until her retirement (from Covent Garden) in 1814. C reported in 1800 that she intended to sing stanzas of WW's *The Mad Mother* in Sheridan's *Pizarro* "if she acted Cora again". *CL* VI 1013. John Genest, who included the words *vocis suavitate* ("in sweetness of voice") on her tombstone, wrote later: "Mrs. Jordan's voice was not only sweet, but distinct, she articulated particularly well—tho' she was not a professed singer, yet the little songs, which she frequently introduced, were much admired—she was sometimes called on to sing a song the 3d time—". *Some Ac-*

The Pope should never have affected temporal sway, but rested on the superstitious awe of him and lived in his impregnable castle.[8]   [36:97]

Epistle of Barnabas genuine; 1st of Clement also.[9] Γνῶσις[10] very apparent in the Epistle to the Hebrews.[11]   [36:225]

Origen, Jerome and Augustine the great fathers.[12]

Basil, Gregory Nazianzen and Chrysostom great rhetoricians.[13]

[36:107]

---

count of the English Stage, from the Restoration in 1660 to 1830 (10 vols Bath 1832) VIII 429–31. For Sarah Flower Adams's report of C's conversation c 1825 on "the effect of different sounds upon his sensations" and "the exquisite witchery" of Mrs Jordan's voice, see App F 5. HNC's brief notation in TT died in MS B.

[8] Annibale Francesco della Genga (1760–1829), who was elected Pope in Sept 1823, becoming Leo XII, directed his political activities particularly against the press, the Carbonari, Freemasons, Jews, and Bible societies. The consolidation of this entry in TT (1835) with that on "a history of the Popedom" (at n 27, below) suggests that HNC took the reference as generically concerned with changes in the rôle of Popes over time. Clement VII (Pope 1523–34) took refuge in Castel Sant' Angelo against Charles V, but was captured there in 1527. Paul V (Pope 1605–21) quarrelled with Venice and began the Villa Borghese. Both the papal apartments in Sant' Angelo and the tunnel that connects the castle with the Vatican were extant in C's day and survive to be seen by visitors.

[9] C had read both these epistles in Wake's translation in William Hone's The Apocryphal New Testament (1820) and discussed their authorship at length in Apr 1826. CN IV 5351–5; CM (CC) I 488–92. Both were read in some early churches but were not eventually accepted into the canon. The "Epistle of Barnabas", so described in the mss, was as early as Clement of Alexandria (c 150–c 215) attributed to Barnabas, the companion of Paul (e.g. Acts 4.36–7, Gal 2.11–13). It is now thought that this attribution is improbable and that the work was written early in the second cen-

tury. It is, however, generally accepted that there is no good reason to doubt the tradition, again vouched for by Clement of Alexandria, that Clement I, bp of Rome (c 30–c100), was the author of the epistle known as 1 Clement, sent from the church at Rome to the church at Corinth. Eichhorn NT I 114–22 accepted both epistles as giving evidence of the state of the NT text at the end of the first century by their quotations from it.

[10] Gnosis knowledge; immediate knowledge of spiritual truth attainable only through faith; intuitive knowledge.

[11] On gnosis in Barnabas and Hebrews see 6 Jun 1830, below (at nn 12–13); 31 Mar 1832, below (at nn 28–30); 3 Jan 1834, below (at n 24).

[12] TT (1835) added "in respect of theology" (versus rhetoric). Origen, surnamed Adamantius (c 185–c 253), Greek Father, head of a celebrated catechetical school in Alexandria; after degradation by a synod founded a school in Caesarea. St Jerome (Eusebius Hieronymus, c 340–420), hermit (374–9), with a knowledge of Greek and Hebrew Augustine lacked, was responsible for the Vulgate; with Ambrose, Augustine, and Gregory the Great, one of the original four Doctors of the Church. St Augustine (Aurelius Augustinus, 354–430), bp of Hippo; C quoted him usually at second hand. Jerome, we learn later (3 Jan 1834, at n 27, below), was "very inferior" to Origen.

[13] St Basil, called Basil the Great (c 329–79), metropolitan of Cappadocia; vigorous against Arianism. St Gregory Nazianzen (c 325–c 390), surnamed Theologus, bp of Constantinople, defended the Nicene Creed. St John Chrysostom (c 345–407), patriarch of Constantinople; his works occupy 13 vols in Migne. All three were Fathers of the

Rhenferd[b] possessed the immense learning and robust sense of Selden with the acuteness and wit of Jortin.[14]   [36:108]

Mr Frere[15] said that a spirit could do many things, but could not carry parcels;—in reference to the Monastery or Abbot.[c16]

b Renfurt   *c* Abbott

Eastern Church. Pope Benedict XIV (d 1758) added Chrysostom and Gregory Nazianzen, along with Anselm, Isidore, and Peter Chrysologus, to the list of Doctors. Alerted by a reference to the funeral orations of Gregory Nazianzen, C wrote: "These funeral Orations are valuable, and it would be worth while to make a collection of those, that are extant, of different Fathers chronologically arranged. They supply important Data for a History of the Progress of Superstition in the Christian Church." Annotation on Fleury *Ecclesiastical History: CM (CC)* II 749.

[14] Jacob Rhenferd (1654–1712), German orientalist; John Jortin (1698–1770), ecclesiastical historian and critic with a lively style; son of Renatus Jordain, a Huguenot refugee. John Selden (1584–1654), jurist, orientalist, antiquarian, member of the Long Parliament. C praises and sometimes makes further comparison of Rhenferd, Selden, and Jortin in annotations on John Oxlee *The Christian Doctrines of the Trinity and Incarnation Considered and Maintained on the Principles of Judaism* (2 vols 1815) I 4–5, in which he observes that Rhenferd has "in Jortin's best manner displayed the gross ignorance of the Gentile Fathers in all matters relating to Hebrew Learning", and in Rhenferd *Opera philologica* (Utrecht 1772), which he was reading at this time (Jul 1827), writing on a flyleaf on 6 Jul: "This truly excellent and enlightened Theologian constantly reminds me of Erasmus—or rather our Jortin. Jortin & Rhenferd were the spiritual Heirs of Erasmus . . . Rhenferd has the wit and humor & classical taste of [Jortin], with the vast Learning and robust Intellect of [Selden]—& the *good sense* common to both." *CM (CC)* III, IV. For similar praise see *SM (CC)* 111, *P Lects* (1949) 98. C cited the *Table Talk* of "the great SELDEN" in *AR*

(1825) 360n; in the work itself he wrote: "There is more weighty bullion good sense in this book, than I ever found in the same number of pages of any uninspired writer." *CM (CC)* IV. The only surviving marginalia on Selden *Table Talk* (1689) were rescued by H. F. Cary, who copied them from the Westminster Library copy in which C had written them. These include the exclamation: "O to have been with Selden over his glass of wine, making every accident an outlet and a vehicle of wisdom!" "Renfurt" is corrected to Rhenferd in an erratum notice for *TT* (1835) I 96 (at I [lxxii]), but the occurrence at I 85 was overlooked; both were corrected in *TT* (1836).

[15] John Hookham Frere (1769–1846), a friend and colleague of Canning in the *Microcosm* at Eton and in the *Anti-Jacobin* of 1797–8, and often in diplomatic offices from 1796 until his retirement in 1818. He was "dear friend and patron", as C's will calls him, if not from their acquaintance and rivalry at Cambridge (*CN* I 1656), then at least from 1816 (*CL* IV 637).

[16] *The Monastery: A Romance* by the Author of *Waverley* (3 vols Edinburgh 1820) ch 8. When Halbert Glendinning and the orphan Mary Avenel went up to the White Lady of Avenel, "behold she was passed away", but "on the very ground where the white woman was sitting, they found the Lady of Avenel's book, and brought it with them to the tower". The book is Lady Alice's Bible, "a thick black volume with silver clasps" (chs 4, 5). On 8 Apr 1820 C had read notices of *The Monastery* but not the novel itself. *CL* V 35. A note on the novel in his set of *Historical Romances of the Author of Waverley* (6 vols in 3 Edinburgh 1824), probably written after 1827, objected to the supernatural, specifically in ch 12, as having "abun-

Correctness of language in Greek writers down to Theocritus;[17] in Latin to the Augustan age; in Italian to Tasso's artificial style;[18] in England in the Elizabethan age and before the Restoration.[19]   [36:99]

He deprecated much the cant of the evangelicals of the day; wished

---

dance'' of fancy with the "blankest absence" of imagination (III 18–19), a view C had held of Scott's poems and continued to hold of most of the novels. In a note on ch 3 of the sequel to *The Monastery, The Abbot* (also 1820), in the same set (IV 42–3), C generalised from Halbert's "supposed experiences" with the White Maiden of Avenel: "Sir W. S. should never have meddled with the Supernatural, for he can not blend it with the Natural." *CM (CC)* IV. A scrap inserted at MS B f 49, probably but not certainly cut from MS F, indicates that HNC failed to remember the association of this entry with Scott, or wished to preserve the joke without it, and tried unsuccessfully to establish a different context. See App C, MS F, below.

[17] In *TT* (1835) this became "Observe the superior truth of language", "truth" being closer than "correctness" to C's views on the nature of language and the function of style. Theocritus fl c 270 B.C. C had noted in 1809: "All the Greek Writers after Demosthenes & his Contemporaries what are they but the Leavings of Tyranny . . . Theocritus appears the only man of true poetic Genius under a Tyranny." *CN* III 3497. A clergyman who met C in 1815 reported: "Of the *classical wealth* of Mr. Coleridge, I need not speak at any length. He was once described in my hearing, and by a man sufficiently qualified to estimate his merits, as 'a ripe and pregnant scholar.' Such unquestionably he was. Without attempting to call to mind any instance of his scholarship, both Greek and Latin, I may say, without fear of contradiction, that, like a subtile spirit, it pervaded all his discourse as well as his compositions, and gave to them that peculiar character which could not but gratify the taste of every classical hearer. With the Grecian dramas, poems, orations, and history, he was confessedly familiar.

This added much to the weight and interest of his conversation. It was evidently that of a man who had devoted days and nights to the enthusiastic study of the classics; who had deeply imbibed their spirit, and who had happily imitated their models. To say thus much (and far more might justly be recorded to the same effect) is but to transcribe, however imperfectly, the opinions generally entertained of him in the literary world." [Thomas A. Methuen] "Retrospect of Friendly Communication with the Poet Coleridge" *Christian Observer* NS LXXXIX (1845) 260.

[18] In *BL* ch 1 C wrote that his master at Christ's Hospital had moulded his taste to prefer Demosthenes to Cicero, Homer and Theocritus to Virgil, and Virgil to Ovid, and after comparing Lucretius, Terence, and Catullus with the Roman poets of the silver and bronze ages, and with those of the Augustan era, "on grounds of plain sense and universal logic to see and assert the superiority of the former, in the truth and nativeness, both of their thoughts and diction". *BL (CC)* I 8–9. C began to earn the right to appraise Italian styles in 1804; see "Coleridge's Knowledge of Italian" *CN* II App A pp 397–404. C had earlier owned WW's copy of Torquato Tasso (1544–95) *La Gerusalemme liberata* (4th ed 2 vols Paris 1783): *WW LC* 305, 355.

[19] In a note stimulated by poetic tributes in Latin to Donne, C seemed to draw the line after the Restoration: Virgil and Horace, "or the best of their Successors" compared with "Lucretius, Catullus, Plautus, & even Terence—the difference is—as between Row, D[r] Johnson &c, & the writers of Eliz. & James". Annotation on Donne *Poems* (1669): *CM (CC)* II 240. In Lect 14 of 13 Mar 1818, on the development of English style, C blamed the decline on the commercial

parts of Luther were translated;[20] to a man *d*who said such and such feelings were the "marrow" of religion, he answered by recommending him to try to walk to London on his marrow only.[21] Nothing in nature is sinful in itself. There is in the whole chain of being, even in the lowest, though scarcely apparent, an effort at individualization, but it is almost lost in the mere nature; in the next stage, it becomes apparent and separate, but still subordinate; then it is on a par with the nature, which is the lowest state of man.[22] Certain of our natural desires are those which only remain in our most perfect state on earth as the means of the higher power's *acting.*   [36:95, 96]

Difference of Reason and the Understanding[23]

d f 5

---

spirit that spread through literature after the Revolution; the worst is visible from 1700: "From the common opinion that the English style attained its greatest perfection in and about Queen Anne's reign I altogether dissent . . . The classical structure of Hooker—the impetuous, thought-agglomerating, flood of Taylor—to these there is no pretence of a parallel; and for mere ease and grace, is Cowley inferior to Addison, being as he is so much more thoughtful and full of fancy?" *Lects 1808–19 (CC)* II 235–6.

[20] Martin Luther (1483–1546), in C's words "the great Father and Founder of the Evangelical Church, that dear large hearted Man of God, the heroic Luther— he whose Faith removed Mountains", the antithesis of "Pseudo-evangelicals" who fancy "impurity & evil in the most innocent things". To William Worship 29 Dec 1826: *CL* VI 656. In *TT* (1835) emphasis falls upon language, with "improve" and "prayerful" joining "marrow" as cant-words, and the discussion of individuation, detached as a separate topic, assigned to the following day. The ms version recommends Luther as a restraint against excessive attention to feelings and to sin. C granted to Bunyan, as explained better by Luther (and by St Paul in Rom 7.7–13), that "the discovery of Sin by the Law tends to strengthen the Sin". Annotation on John Bunyan *The Pilgrim's Progress* (1820): *CM (CC)* I 819.

[21] *TT* (1835) changed the gender of this misguided evangelical to a "young lady".

[22] HNC's note to this passage in *TT* (1835) quotes at length from a parallel, inspirational passage in *AR* (1831) 105– 6; cf *AR* (1825) 111–12. Progressive individuation throughout the scale of life is set forth in *TL* (1848) 46–50 and BM Add MS 34225 f 148. C's scheme of gradations, agreeing with the vitalistic theory of the surgeon John Abernethy (1764–1831) that function precedes structure, involves temporal evolution only to the extent that it allows for a progressive unfolding in the days of creation in Gen 1–2. Whether introduced casually by C on 8 Jul or intruded by HNC, the "chain of being" is the traditional term, traced by Arthur O. Lovejoy in *The Great Chain of Being: A Study of the History of an Idea* (Cambridge, Mass 1936) from Plato to its "temporalizing" by the Romantics. For C, however, it is "one proof of the essential vitality of nature, that she does not ascend as links in a suspended chain, but as the steps in a ladder; or rather she at one and the same time *ascends* as by a climax, and expands . . . [by] concentric circles". *TL* (1848) 41. On "ascent" as increase in power, see *CN* IV 4517, 4583, 4862, 5150, 5182. In this entry C opposes his theory of life to the dualism of the Wesleyan conviction that nature is evil. *TT* (1835) omitted "Nothing in nature is sinful in itself".

[23] Omitted at this point in *TT* (1835) as subsumed under 36:33 (from 7 Jan–13 Feb 1823, above, at n 41) and 36:172 (from 9 May 1830, below, at n 13).

A Maxim is the conclusion upon observation of matters of fact. An Idea or Principle is prospective and carries knowledge within itself. Maxims all retrospective.[24] [36:81]

Polonius a man of maxims; whilst descanting on matters of past experience, admirable; advising or projecting, a mere dotard. Hamlet as the man of ideas despises him.[25] [36:81]

A man of maxims like Cyclops with one eye, but that eye placed in the back of his head.[26] [36:82]

History of the Popedom a great subject.[27] [36:97]

Scanderbeg a fine subject for Walter Scott.[28] [36:98]

Becket*[e]* also but too much for Walter Scott; the conflict between arms or force and the men of letters.[29] [36:98]

[e] Beckett

[24] C, following Kant, as in *The Critique of Practical Reason* I i 1–3, defined maxims as "GENERALIZED past *experiences*" and identified principles with ideas, "in the light of which alone the Past can be safely applied to the Future", in a marginal note on Samuel Johnson (the Whig) *Works* (1710) 306: *CM (CC)* III. In print the three remarks on maxims appear together as part of the discussion of *Hamlet*, dated 24 Jun 1827. Maxims vs principles, with understanding vs reason, return on 14 Aug 1831, below (at n 20) (36:327).

[25] C's discussions of *Hamlet* usually emphasise the degree to which we see Polonius through Hamlet's eyes—as in Lect 1 of 28 Oct 1813 at Bristol, Lect 3 of 7 Jan 1819 of the 1818–19 series, and Lect 1 of 11 Feb 1819—although he once cites Polonius as an example of Shakespeare's "unceasing war against Pedantry"—in Lect 4 of 6 Feb 1818. *Lects 1808–19 (CC)* I 520, II 116, 300, 352. That Polonius attempting to apply principles or ideas is "a mere dotard" is compatible with C's most famous description of him as "the personified *Memory* of wisdom no longer actually possessed". Lect 5 of 10 Feb 1818: *Lects 1808–19 (CC)* II 129.

[26] A second twist to an early notebook entry: "Learning without philosophy a *Cyclops*." *CN* I 662. Cf *SM (CC)* 43 and n 1, in which experience is a Cyclops.

[27] On the history of the Popedom see 24 Jul 1830, below (at nn 1–5), 4 May

1833 (at nn 3–4), and 31 May 1834 (at nn 9–11).

[28] Scanderbeg (Iskender Bey), by birth George Castriota (1403–68), Albanian national hero. Brought up as a hostage, Moslem, and Turkish soldier, he became a Christian champion against the Ottomans. An isolated reference like this one to Scanderbeg calls attention to the breadth of C's attentive reading more directly than keenly discriminative remarks upon some topic he often returned to. He left with WW his copy of Jacques de La Vardin, Lord of Plessis Bourrot *The Historie of George Castriot, Surnamed Scanderbeg, King of Albanie* tr Zachary Jones (1596): *WW LC* 339.

[29] Thomas à Becket (c 1118–70), saint, martyred in Canterbury Cathedral. About 1810 C named as the most glorious subject left by Shakespeare to later poets the "Struggle between the men of arms & of Letters, Becket". *CN* III 3654 f 9. Objecting in 1820 to the unmeaningful strife between Saxons and Normans in *Ivanhoe*, he wished that Scott had chosen instead "the struggle between the Men of Arts & the Men of arms in the time of Becket". *CL* v 35. His variant use "Letters" and "Arts" points to Becket as representative of the clerisy, the custodians of the spiritual wealth of the nation. For Scott's report of an evening with C, who harangued on "the Samo-thracian Misteries" and on Homer, on 22 Apr 1828, see App F 6, below.

S. T. C. *a*25ᵗʰ–26ᵗʰ Aug. 1827.[1]

The doctrine of the polarization of Light is superseding the Newtonian theory.[2]

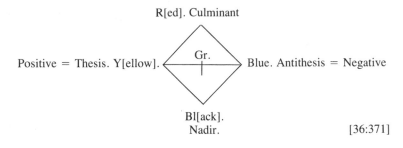

R[ed]. Culminant

Positive = Thesis. Y[ellow].   Gr.   Blue. Antithesis = Negative

Bl[ack].
Nadir.   [36:371]

*b*It is the green ray which is the most magnetic, and not the blue.*c*[3] People may not be able to distinguish colors from a general weakness, which, in

a–c For the variant in MS F see App C, below   *b* MS B f 5ᵛ

[1] HNC's notes on talk of the summer of 1827 are brief prods to the memory on the wide range of topics noted. C described at this period his own "languor of volition": "I have for the last three or four months been under a depression of spirits, which I cannot easily characterize". *CL* VI 697. Yet the few extant letters show him mobile and able to "converse at times with a literary friend with unabated vigour; but all must be *continuous*". Ibid. MS B makes record of one weekend in August, distributed in *TT* (1835) over four days in July. MS F gives the entry on colours the actual date, 25 Aug, but the date disappeared when the entry was cancelled to avoid duplicating the entry of 24 Apr 1832, below (36:371). A change of script for the last four entries—in larger letters, different slant—possibly demarks subjects of the 26th rather than the 25th. But the dateline "25ᵗʰ–26ᵗʰ" must have preceded all the entries; it was executed in the same script as the entries up to the distinction between prose and poetry.

[2] Sir Isaac Newton (1642–1727) had advanced the corpuscular theory of light in his *Opticks* (1704). In 1802–3 Thomas Young (1773–1829) presented three papers in *Phil Trans* (RS) proposing "the undulatory system of light" in opposition to the corpuscular theory. Augustin Jean Fresnel (1788–1827) is credited with establishing the wave theory of light in 1815–16. Meanwhile, C could have followed a series of experiments in the polarisation of light by Sir David Brewster (1781–1868) published in *Phil Trans* (RS) 1813–16. Polarisation contradicted the corpuscular theory and could be explained by the wave theory. C's reference to a crystal giving shape to light in Essay III "On the Principles of Genial Criticism"—*BL* (1907) II 232—may draw a little upon Brewster's experiments, but this entry derives less from experimental developments—although C usually noted them—than from the theorising of Goethe *Zur Farbenlehre* (1810) and the *Naturphilosophen* who followed him, as can be seen more clearly in the fuller diagram and comments of 24 Apr 1832, below (at n 3) (36:371). C left with WW his copy of Newton *Opticks* (3rd ed 1721): *WW LC* 345.

[3] *TT* (1835) transformed this sentence into a prediction that red, yellow, and orange rays would be proved capable of communicating magnetic action. Most experiments in polarisation were con-

the same manner as dusk or twilight renders all colors one, may render imperceptible the differences. The defect is most usual in the Blue ray or negative pole.[4]   [36:110, 111]

William III. a greater man than any of his ministers.[5]   [36:114]

Burke's Essay on Taste a poor thing.[6]   [36:104]

---

ducted on gems and crystals; Davy and others consolidated polarisation with magnetic experiments. In 1796–7 C had borrowed from Erasmus Darwin (who had acknowledged his own second-hand source) a note concluding from variations in flashes of light from flowers of different colour that "there is something of electricity in this phenomenon". *PW* (EHC) I 99n–100; *RX* 464–5. C was dissatisfied with Lorenz Oken's treatment of colours in *Erste Ideen zur Theorie des Lichts, der Finsterniss, der Farben und der Wärme.* IV (Jena 1808) 40: *CM (CC)* III.

[4] George Palmer *Theory of Colors and Vision* (1777), politely refuting Newton, had isolated colour-blindness from degrees of visual acuity. The chemist John Dalton, first in 1794 and then in the *Memoirs* of the Philosophical Society of Manchester, had ascribed his own colour-blindness to a defect in "a *coloured medium*" that constituted "one of the humours" of the eye. William Charles Henry *Memoirs of the Life and Scientific Researches of John Dalton* (1854) 24–7, 240–3; Sir Henry E. Roscoe *John Dalton and the Rise of Modern Chemistry* (New York 1895) 70–89. C had met Dalton and had observed similar cases. *CN* II 1059 and n. In *Logic (CC)* 118, 142 he refers twice to an eye insensible to blue and one that sees everything as yellow. This may possibly derive indirectly from David Hume's admission of one exception to the derivation of all simple ideas from simple physical impressions: a person who had seen all colours "excepting one particular shade of blue" would, if all shades of blue except that one were set in gradations before him, "perceive a blank, where that shade is wanting". *A Treatise of Human Nature* bk I pt i § 1 (1739–40).

[5] William III (1650–1702), as husband of James II's Protestant daughter Mary, was invited from the Netherlands to be King of England, Scotland, and Ireland from 1689. He was cold to the claims of party, but his chief ministers besides Robert Spencer (1640–1702), 2nd Earl of Sunderland, a crafty politician whom William was afraid to alienate, were the Whig junto including John, Baron Somers (1651–1716), who framed the Declaration of Right; Thomas Wharton, 1st Marquis of Wharton (1648–1715), controller of the king's household; Edward Russell (1653–1727), Earl of Orford, admiral and lord justice; and Charles Montagu (1661–1715), 1st Earl of Halifax, charged in 1701–3 with malfeasance in office. HNC was to hear the comparison of William and his ministers refined on 13 May 1833 (after n 19). C counted among "that great & good man's excellencies" William's recognition that Great Britain's commercial and colonial superiority could not be maintained in separation from "the great European Commonwealth of Nations", with the misfortune that "he was not endowed with the power of communicating his superior wisdom to others persuasively". Annotation on Henry Brooke *The Fool of Quality* (1776): *CM (CC)* I 732–3. See the addition in 36:114.

[6] Burke's "Introductory Discourse Concerning Taste", added to *A Philosophical Enquiry into the Origin of Our Ideas of the Sublime and Beautiful* (1756) from the 2nd ed (1759) onward. The "Discourse" declared tastes, from "principles entirely uniform", different only in degree; imagination, which includes "wit, fancy, invention, and the like", derived solely from the senses; opium was a "nauseous morsel", and the seacoast of Bohemia an offence to

Bolingbroke's style not comparable to that of Cowley or Dryden.[7]

_____

[36:103]

Ariosto a greater poet than Tasso.[8]   [36:105]

_____

Berkeley can only be confuted or answered by one sentence.[9] So with

those of good taste (1801 pp 12–21). *TT* (1835) expanded the entry to condemn the whole *Enquiry*. If Carlyon's record is accurate, C had moved from Burke to Kant on the sublime (*Critique of Judgement* pt 1 § 25) by 1799: "When we were ascending the Brocken, and ever and anon stopping to take breath, as well as to survey the magnificent scene, a long discussion took place upon the sublime and beautiful. We had much of Burke, but more of Coleridge. Of beauty much, but more of sublimity, which was in accordance with the grandeur of surrounding objects. Many were the fruitless attempts to define sublimity satisfactorily, when Coleridge, at length, pronounced it to consist in a suspension of the power of comparison." Carlyon I 51.

[7] In *TT* (1835), "not in any respect equal". Henry Saint-John (1678–1751), 1st Viscount Bolingbroke, statesman and orator; friend of Swift and Pope; author of works mostly political collected in 5 vols 1754, 11 vols 1786, 8 vols 1809. In preparing a contribution for the *Courier* in 1811 C seems to have read three tracts by Bolingbroke edited by David Mallet in 1753: *EOT (CC)* III 236n. Although *A Dissertation upon Parties* and *Letter on the Idea of a Patriot King* had not gone without occasional praise, few would have ranked Bolingbroke's prose stylistically with Cowley's or Dryden's. The eighteenth century is being put down as usual. On Cowley's style see also 27 Apr 1823, above (at n 32).

[8] Lodovico Ariosto (1474–1553), Italian poet best known for the chivalric epic *Orlando furioso* (1516–32); Torquato Tasso (1544–95), known to C for the heroic epic *Gerusalemme liberata* (1575). C owned and annotated a copy of *Orlando furioso* (Venice 1713): *CM (CC)* I 116–17. For remarks on Ariosto see *Friend (CC)* II 219; *CN* II 2598, 2670, III

3284, 3557, 4115. J. P. Collier noted on 20 Oct 1811 that C "seemed to have little admiration for Ariosto, and perhaps less for Tasso, but I think he did not know much of them", although Collier reveals C's familiarity with the Edward Fairfax translation, as *Godfrey of Bulloigne* (1600), of the opening cantos of *Gerusalemme liberata*; see App K, below. By Feb 1812 C was preparing the course of lectures that was to include treatments of both Ariosto and Tasso, particularly in relation to Spenser. *CL* III 364. In 1818 he lectured on Tasso and Ariosto and on Ariosto in 1819: *Lects 1808–19 (CC)* II 90–5 passim, 399–400. He knew Sir John Harington's translation of the *Orlando*, and read other works in Ariosto *Opere in versi e in prosa* (Venice 1741). *CN* II 2670n, 2770n, III 3305n, 4115n. *Gillman SC* includes three sets of *Orlando* (4 vols Birmingham 1773, 4 vols Milan 1821, and 6 vols Pisa 1815). On Tasso see also 8 Jul 1827, above (at n 18).

[9] If the Anglo-Irish philosopher and clergyman George Berkeley (1685–1753) is summarised as asserting that what others have regarded as an external world of things is indeed a coherence of idea in the mind of God that arouses in us the perception of a coherent natural order, then Berkeley could be refuted either by the counter-assertion of materialists that a physical world of things does exist apart from our perception of qualities or, in Hume's way, by calling into question our certainty of either substances or our perceptual ideas of substance. As C rejects both Hume's scepticism and all materialism, his own quarrel is with Berkeley's inconsistency in building a pure idealism upon Locke's empirical premise: "This great man" thereby assured only "partial emancipation from the fetters of the mechanic phi-

Spinoza—his premiss granted, the logic is irresistible.[10] [36:115]

The Reformation narrowed reformation.[11] As soon as men called themselves names, then all hope of farther amendment was lost. [36:113]

Athanasian Creed blasphemous, tautological, deficient and nonsensical.[12] [36:94]

---

[d]St John's Gospel genuine authority. St Luke's fair ground for belief in facts. St Matthew's one of the many gospels to the Hebrews.[e][13]

[d-e] For the variant in MS F see App C, below

---

losophy". Note on Berkeley *Siris: CM (CC)* I 410. Like the materialists, Berkeley, according to C, failed to distinguish between perception and sensation. *CN* IV 4540; cf *Logic (CC)* 127–8. In 1818 C described Berkeley's system as the entirely subjective and Spinoza's as the entirely objective. *CL* IV 863. C sought a reconciliation of the subjective and objective that would be free of pantheism. That he named his second son Berkeley in 1798 is emblematic of the comfort he took, then and after, from Berkeley's faith and clarity. Carlyon I 90 said that C in Germany in 1799 "took opportunities of analysing and illustrating the philosophical tenets" of Berkeley and David Hartley. Kant deflected but did not end C's admiration for Berkeley, whose *Treatise Concerning the Principles of Human Knowledge* he studied in 1820–5—rejecting its subjective idealism. *CN* IV 4540, 5276–7.

[10] Baruch or Benedict de Spinoza (1632–77), Jewish philosopher born in Amsterdam, is to C and to history the pre-eminent expounder of pantheism: the universe, including thought and divinity, is one substance. HCR recorded on 3 Nov 1812 C's one-sentence rejection of Spinoza: "Did philosophy begin in an IT IS instead of an I AM, Spinoza would be altogether true". *CRB* I 112. He borrowed from HCR that day Spinoza *Opera quae supersunt omnia* ed H. E. G. Paulus (2 vols Jena 1802–3), which he annotated during the next year, favourably except for noting (I 453–7) that "Spinoza begins with the Phantom of a Thing

in itself, i.e. an Object". *CM (CC)* IV. C was thinking of consistency and inconsistency in Spinoza and Berkeley in 1810 when his thirst for antithesis set Spinoza's absolute, ontosophical system against the only other self-consistent system, Kant's relative, anthropological philosophy (*CN* III 3756)—an opposition repeated in the lectures on the history of philosophy: *P Lects* Lect 2 (1949) 107. *TT* (1835) borrowed for this entry the metaphor of the adamantine chain from 28 Jan 1832, below (at n 4). C had noted in 1820 the "odious consequences" of the Spinozistic chain. *CN* IV 4737.

[11] In Feb 1826 C had given EC a more specific period: ". . . the Reformation in my opinion fell back after Luther, instead of advancing". *CL* VI 562. This entry suggests a reason for the retrogression. *OED* dates the term "Reformation" in English from 1563. C refers not to political organisation, under which by 1530 rebels called themselves Protestant, but to the potential for ecclesiastical and religious self-reform.

[12] HNC combined this entry with that of 8 Jul 1827, above (at n 4).

[13] These three sentences represent telegraphically C's own reflection on the internal evidence and import of the gospels. That there were "many" gospels is declared in Luke 1.1. C believed that the authors of the Bible were divinely inspired to say all that is necessary for salvation, but not often either taking down God's exact words or divinely informed. *CIS* (1840) 13. For C on Matthew see *CN* III 3879, 4402, and *CM (CC)* I 446–7.

Algernon Sydney's style reminds neither of books or blackguards.[14]

[36:103]

Luther in parts the most biblical writer known.[15]   [36:100]

A nobleman—a common Mæcenas—would be the best President of the Royal Society.[16]

J. Behmen remarked that it was not wonderful that there were separate languages for France, Germany &c; but rather that there was not a dif-

[14] Algernon Sidney (1622–83), republican and martyred hero to the Whigs, was beheaded as a traitor for advocating resistance to designated acts by a monarch, in a manuscript that he denied any intention of publishing, issued in 1698 as *Discourses Concerning Government*. Named several times as a hero of liberty in C's Bristol lectures on politics in 1795, twice in *The Watchman*, in *M Post* of 11 Mar 1800 and *Courier* of 9 Dec 1809, repeatedly in *The Friend*, in *SM* App E, and as late as *C&S* (1830), the nephew of Sir Philip remained for C as for WW a faultless patriot. By consolidation with an earlier entry, *TT* (1835) sets Algernon Sidney's style in contrast with Bolingbroke's. In the process, the grammatical problem of "neither . . . or" dissolves into "as little . . . as". Of the *Discourses* (1772), which C annotated—*CM (CC)* IV—he said in Lect 14 of 13 Mar 1818 that many parts of the treatises were "excellent exemplars of a good modern practical style". *Lects 1808–19 (CC)* II 236. Cf "the *Blackguard Slang*, which passed for *easy* writing from the Restoration of Charles to the accession of Queen Anne". Annotation on *The Picture of Cebes: CM (CC)* I 182.

[15] C wrote similarly in Anne Gillman's Bible: "Of all our Divines, Luther most fully mastered the sense & spirit of St Paul." *CM (CC)* I 460. He referred her specifically to *Colloquia Mensalia* ed Henry Bell (1652), which he called in 1826 "my *Bosom* book" and "next to the Scriptures my main book of meditation, deep, seminative, pauline". *CL* VI 561, 656. C heavily annotated the volume—*CM (CC)* III—and quoted passages from it in his notebooks—*CN* IV 4594, 4599, 4600, 4664, 4665. In a defence of RS's *Wat Tyler* in 1817 C referred to the "heroic Luther", "a Poet". *EOT (CC)* II 471. Luther is one of the heroes of TT. In *TT* (1835) Luther became "the most evangelical writer I know, after the apostles and apostolic men", which is certainly what C meant, whatever his exact words in Aug 1827.

[16] *The Times* reported on 10 Apr that Sir Humphry Davy, who was seriously ill in Italy, was resigning as president of the Royal Society. As the Society was financially dependent upon the annual subscription of members, its size had been allowed to grow until active scientists formed a small minority increasingly at odds with aristocratic members. The secretary, Gilbert Davies, to whom Davy had written officially on 1 Jul, was elected interim president, which he remained until 1830, when Charles Babbage, in *Reflections on the Decline of the Sciences in England, and on Some of Its Causes*, so attacked the Society and "the feeble occupant of its desolated kingdom" (p 54) that something like C's suggestion was realised in the choice of a royal patron, Augustus Frederick, Duke of Sussex, as president (1830–9). The controversies during Davy's presidency had increased to an uproar over the awarding of Royal Medals in their first year (1826) without regard to the purpose of reviving scientific activity in Britain by honouring research "completed and made known . . . in the year preceding". Babbage 117–19. This entry was unpublished.

ferent language for every geographical degree of latitude.[17] See the infinite variety of languages amongst the barbarous tribes of South America.[18]   [36:109]

---

*f*Baxter's Life by himself a most inestimable book.[19]   [36:101]

The elements had been well shaken during the interregnum and civil wars *g*in the time of Charles I.*h*[20] and nothing but the cowardliness and

f MS B f 6   *g–h* temp. Car I;

[17] Jakob Böhme, anglicised Behmen (1575–1624), explained how "the Spirit of God formed, through the Nature of the Properties, the *Language* and Speech in every *Country*; first the seventy-two Head Languages out of Nature, and afterwards the *collateral Affinities*, proceeding from the Senses of every Head Language; as we plainly see, that a Man does scarce find, in any Place of the World, among all the Head Languages, one and the *same* Sense in any Head Language, within the Compass of fifteen or eighteen Miles . . .". *Mysterium Magnum* pt 2 ch 35: *Works* (4 vols 1764–81) III i 198. Böhme was much more important to C than TT suggests, as his annotations on these volumes, ch 9 of *BL (CC)* I 146–7, and Lect 11 in *P Lects* (1949) 327–31 testify and John Beer *Coleridge the Visionary* (1959) demonstrates. C "conjured over" Böhme's *Aurora* at Christ's Hospital (*CL* IV 750–1). He annotated the *Works* from 1808 until at least as late as Mar 1826 (*CM—CC*—I 555), and defended the "Theosopher" e.g. in a note on Baxter *Reliquiae* (*CM—CC*—I 296). C seems to approve of Böhme on the diversity of languages; he rejected as the "one *absurd*" thing in the *Works* Böhme's assumption that the sounds of his own language, German, are the "very language of the total universal nature". *CM (CC)* I 607. He offered to show that Böhme was inspired in the sense that orthodox divines called the Bible inspired. *CN* IV 4793.

[18] Among many possible sources for an impression of variety among languages of the South American Indians, RS *History of Brazil* (3 vols 1810-19) I 224–5 and n sufficiently justifies C's re-

mark: "[Lorenzo Hervas y Panduro] enumerates sixteen Brazilian tribes or nations speaking dialects of this [Tupi and Guarani] tongue, and fifty-one whose languages are different. . . . He supposes, however, that there may be, as some writers have stated, a hundred and fifty barbarous languages spoken in Brazil." C read about the Chilean languages in 1810; see *CN* III 3789, and 7 Jul 1832 n 7, below.

[19] C annotated two copies of Richard Baxter (1615–91) *Reliquiae Baxterianae* ed Matthew Sylvester (1696): *CM (CC)* I 240–361. HNC's note in *TT* (1835) described it as "a very thick folio of the old sort" in which C found lessons for "the modern political Dissenters". Baxter, a Presbyterian scholar and divine, was a chaplain in Cromwell's army (1645–7); he was offered a bishopric at the Restoration and was later imprisoned by Judge Jeffreys (1685–6). C praised the "perspicuity and perspicacity" of Baxter's understanding and "the candour and charity of his spirit". *CM (CC)* I 273. A note in praise of Baxter's veracity (*CM—CC*—I 306), which HNC transcribed in MS B f 70, is moved to this entry in *TT* (1835); a comparison of C's own lot with Baxter's (*CM—CC*—I 299) is incorporated in HNC's note to this entry.

[20] From his ascension in 1625, Charles I (1600–49) was in difficulties with Parliament over the Calvinistic majority as well as finances. He declared war in 1642, surrendered to the Scots in 1646, and was executed 30 Jan 1649. *TT* (1835) specified the period of the Long Parliament, which defied Charles when called in 1640 and was dissolved in 1652 by Cromwell, and the Protectorate,

impolicy of the Dissenters at the time of the Restoration could have prevented their obtaining, what was so necessary, a real reformation on a wider basis. But by going over to Breda with their stiff flatteries they put Sheldon and the Bishops on the side of the Constitution.[21]   [36:112]

---

[i]Prose = words in the best order.
Poetry = the best words in the best order.[22]   [36:106]

---

[i] A change of script in this and the next three entries—HNC's hand, but a blunter nib, larger letters, different slant—possibly demarks subjects of the 26th rather than the 25th

---

which began under Cromwell's assumption of the title Protector in 1653. The Rump of the Long Parliament, which met intermittently until it dissolved itself in 1660, was predominantly Presbyterian and intolerant of all other sects. It ended, as the interregnum ended, with the restoration in 1660 of Charles II and the episcopacy. C's analysis is not greatly unlike that reflected in the works of Baxter, except for the charge of cowardliness.

[21] "Constitution" here refers primarily to the Church establishment and the forms of religious service based upon it. In Apr 1660, when Gen Monck was arranging the recall of Charles II from the United Provinces, Charles moved back and forth between Breda and Brussels; in some pertinent accounts Dissenters seeking pardon for friends carried presents to Brussels, but Charles's Declaration "dated as from Breda" renewed Breda's symbolic importance in history. What C calls "stiff flatteries", touched on in Gilbert Burnet *History of His Own Time* bk I (2 vols 1724–34) I i 88, briefly in *Reliquiae Baxterianae* ii ch 2 ("some went voluntarily"), and in other works read by C, are apparent (allowing for Clarendon's bias) in Edward Hyde, Earl of Clarendon (1609–74) *The History of the Rebellion and Civil Wars in England* bk xvi (3 vols 1707) III 598: "Several Persons now came to *Breda*, not, as heretofore to *Cologne*, and to *Brussels*, under disguises, and in fear to be discover'd, but with bare faces, and the pride and vanity to be taken notice of, to present their duty to the King; some being imployed to procure Pardons for those who thought themselves in danger . . . others

brought good Presents in *English* Gold to the King . . .". C read Clarendon and made notes in N 18 in 1810: *CN* III 3740–2. Gilbert Sheldon (1598–1677), bp of London 1660–2, abp of Canterbury 1663–77, had the King's ear in 1660, but C refers specifically to the Savoy Conference of 1661 held in Sheldon's quarters adjacent to the Savoy Chapel in the Strand, where established bishops meeting dissenting ministers fended off any change in the Prayer Book or other ecclesiastical arrangements. On Burnet and his *History of His Own Time* see also 15 Jun 1830, below (at n 7), and on Sheldon and the Savoy Conference see 7 Jun 1830, below (at nn 5 and 10).

[22] C is extending the definition of Jonathan Swift, who had said in "A Letter to a Young Gentleman Lately Entered into Holy Orders" (1720): "Proper Words in proper Places, make the true Definition of a Style." For C "the best order" for prose will not be up to the best for poetry. In *BL* ch 18 *(CC)* II 60–88 he argued (against WW's virtual identification of the language of poetry with the language of prose) that metre, order of words, and choice of words bring each other into harmony (in ch 13, into fusion) in the process of poetic creation. In notes for a lecture of 1808 he observed that the name poetry is reserved for "measured *words*"; more fully in 1809 he noted that poetry demands "severer keeping" in language because it "presupposes a more continuous state of Passion". *CN* III 3286 f 7[v], 3611. *TT* (1835) made this entry a cautionary axiom for "clever young poets", with the implication of *BL* ch 4 that forced diction is endemic among beginners in poetry. *BL (CC)* I

Always a natural oppugnancy to C. Wordsworth.[23]

Genius may co-exist with wildness, idleness, folly—even crime—but not long with selfishness and an envious disposition indulged in.[24]

[36:116]

The Man's desire is for the Woman. The Woman's desire is for the desire of the Man.[25]

[36:117]

S. T. C. 29th–30th Aug. 1827.[1]

Jeremy Taylor a good book for a young man to study for the purpose of imbibing noble principles, and at the same time of exercizing the caution

79. This entry is one of twelve from *TT* in *The Oxford Dictionary of Quotations* (2nd ed 1955).

[23] Christopher Wordsworth (1774–1846), brother of the poet, was a strong disciplinarian as master of Trinity College (1820–41) and vice-chancellor of Cambridge University (1820–1, 1826–7). C had generally admired his published work. *CL* II 820, III 274, 282–3, V 477. But presumably the reference is largely personal. On 12 Jan 1810, to Poole, in contrasting the sacrifices of WW with the worldly success of his brothers, C had asked specifically of Christopher's wife (née Priscilla Lloyd), "Are such People *conscious* of their Hypocrisy?" *CL* III 274. Mary Moorman summarised WW's relations with his youngest brother: "Christopher was reserved and somewhat remote", and "in spite of mutual admiration and loyalty, they were never intimate". *W Life* (M) II 424. C sounded both personal and antiprelatic in 1830 when he observed that for those like the master of Trinity who identify the character of the Church of England with "that of those Diseases of the Age, Charles I., Laud, & Sheldon, I must submit to be scowled at, as an Alien and an Adversary". Annotation on John Miller *Sermons* (Oxford 1830): *CM (CC)* III. If the entry had been publishable, it would have followed 36:112, with a transition through Christopher Wordsworth's "*Who Wrote ΕΙΚΩΝ ΒΑΣΙ-*

ΛΙΚΗ" Considered and Answered (2 pts 1824–5), which C had annotated (as well as the *Six Letters to Granville Sharp . . . on the Uses of the Definitive Article in the Greek Text of the New Testament—* 1802).

[24] The positive expression of this point appears best in Lect 5 of the lectures on the history of philosophy of 18 Jan 1819: genius knows self only as reflected in the features of nature and other persons. "A man of genius finds a reflex to himself, were it only in the mystery of being." *P Lects* (1949) 179; cf 168, 291. The model is Shakespeare, who "darts himself forth, and passes into all the forms of human character and passion"; he "becomes all things, yet for ever remaining himself". *BL* ch 15 *(CC)* II 27–8. C explored this aspect of genius further in an annotation on Bunyan *Pilgrim's Progress*: "Enthusiasm . . . is almost a Synonime of Genius—the moral *Life* in the intellectual *Light*, the Will in the Reason". *CM (CC)* I 818. *TT* (1835) extended the paragraph with a remark on "envy" from C's notebooks as transcribed by EC.

[25] *TT* (1835) prudently inserted in the second sentence the words "rarely other than" and added a note, as from "a page dyed red with an imprisoned rose-leaf", a passage HNC had copied from EC's transcription from C's notebooks.

[1] Like the previous date, the script in these entries continues in the same hand

and thought of the reader in detecting its*a* numerous errors.[2]   [36:118]
Hooker perhaps has been over-credited for his judgment.[3]   [36:119]
As an instance of an Idea[4] = The Continuity and yet the Distinctness,
of Nature.[5] Also = Vegetable Life is always striving to be something

a ~~his~~ its

---

up to the last entry, on painting, which in *TT* (1835) is the sole item assigned to 30 Aug.

[2] Jeremy Taylor (1613–67), Anglican prelate, chaplain to Laud and Charles I; bp of Down and Connor and administrator of Dromore (1661–7). C may refer to the popular combination of *Holy Living* (1650) and *Holy Dying* (1651)—he annotated a combined edition of 1710—but he probably refers here to the more notorious ΘΕΟΛΟΓΙΑ ΈΚΛΕΚΤΙΚΗ. *A Discourse of the Liberty of Prophesying* (1647), which he annotated in ΣΥΜΒΟΛΟΝ ΘΕΟΛΟΓΙΚΟΝ: *or A Collection of Polemicall Discourses* (3rd ed 2 pts in 1 vol 1674). The annotations, both in general judgements and in specific comments, sustain the ambivalence of this entry. In a note on one of the discourses, *A Dissuasive from Popery*, C wrote: "I love thee, Jeremy! but an errant theological *Barrister*—that thou wert . . . .". *Polemicall Discourses* i 419: *CM (CC)* v. On Taylor and *The Liberty of Prophesying* see also 4 Jun 1830, below, and n 1. For a general survey see R. F. Brinkley "Coleridge's Criticism of Jeremy Taylor" *Huntington Library Quarterly* XIII (1950) 313–23.

[3] Richard Hooker (c 1554–1600), Anglican theologian, called from an epithet on his monument "the Judicious". In c 1824–6 C had annotated *The Works* (1682): *CM (CC)* II 1131–67. He had commended certain passages to correspondents, particularly "A Learned and Comfortable Sermon of the Certainty and Perpetuity of Faith in the Elect". *CL* VI 607, 617; cf annotations on the Bible and on Bunyan *Pilgrim's Progress* (1820): *CM (CC)* I 453, 826–7. C's reference in the traditional way to this "judicious author" in *BL* ch 4 *(CC)* I 88 may be a concealed irony, as suggested in the running theme of the marginalia that

Hooker was capable of conceptions but "to the tranquil Empyrean of *Ideas* he had not ascended": "Hooker was truly *judicious*—the consummate Synthesis of Understanding and Sense." *CM (CC)* II 1146. In 1826 C read *Ecclesiastical Polity* with dedication (*CN* IV 5437, 5443, 5450). The language for this entry in *TT* (1835) is tentative and deferential. C's pupil Basil Montagu edited *Selections from the Works of Taylor, Hooker, Hall, and Lord Bacon* (1805). On Hooker see also 30 May 1830, below (at n 8).

[4] C cited Hooker as an example of a writer who confused an idea with a conception: "Every Conception has its sole reality in its being referable to a Thing or Class of Things, of which or of the common characters of which it is a *reflection*. An Idea is a POWER . . . that constitutes its own Reality . . .". Annotation on Hooker *Works: CM (CC)* II 1134. HNC's note in *TT* (1835) quoted C's definition of an idea in *C&S* (1830) and examples of misuse of the word after the disastrous rise of "the Mechanic Philosophy". *C&S (CC)* 13, 64. According to Bacon, C wrote, what in *natura naturata* is called a law, in *natura naturans* is called an idea. HNC also referred to the last paragraph of *SM* App E, in which an idea is described as "an educt of the Imagination actuated by pure Reason, to which there neither is or can be an adequate correspondent in the world of the senses". *SM (CC)* 113–14.

[5] This idea is fully developed in *TL*: ". . . the most comprehensive formula to which life is reducible, would be that of the internal copula of bodies, or (if we may venture to borrow a phrase from the Platonic school) the *power* which discloses itself from within as a principle of *unity* in the *many*. . . . I define life as *the principle of individuation*, or the power which unites a given *all* into a *whole* that

that it is not; Animal Life to be itself.[6] Hence in a plant the parts—root—stem, branches, leaf &c remain after they have each produced another status of the whole; in the animal nothing remains distinct of the previous state, but is incorporated into and constitutes the Self.[7]   [36:120]

[b]Jeremy Taylor most probably slandered himself even in his base assertion in a sermon after the Restoration that he had written the "Liberty of Prophesying" as a ruse de guerre, because the Church at that time needed toleration.[8]

[b] f 6[v]

---

is presupposed by all its parts." *TL* (1848) 41–2. Comparative physiologists had raised specific issues. Albrecht von Haller (1708–77) had objected that the *vis essentialis* of Kaspar Friedrich Wolff (1733–94) did not explain why in any given species the *vis* or force maintains the type and yet simultaneously creates a variety of types; to answer the problem of continuity and novelty (epigenesis), C's mentor Blumenbach had proposed a *nisus formativus* that is not a causal force but an effect, like gravitation and attraction, ever recurring in the same way to conserve the form by nutriment and restore it after mutilation. See Hans Driesch *The History & Theory of Vitalism* tr C. K. Ogden (1914) 53–64.

[6] "Also" became in *TT* (1835) less ambiguously "or this", a second instance of an idea. Among the examples in *TL* of the striving of a plant to become something else is the apparent dawn of voluntary motion in the vegetable world, in the stamens and anthers, at the time of impregnation. The point in TT may be no more than what is apparent in the illustrations: a root remains when the leaves unfold but the egg becomes the fowl and the tadpole becomes the frog.

[7] "Self" here seems to mean not the intrinsic that survives, but an Aristotelian formal cause realised in individuation. Even so, can the second "idea" not be reduced to verbal paradox by describing the indicated difference between plant and animal as the plant's retention of all its essential stages and the animal's abandonment of successive selves? In a marginal note on J. C. Heinroth *Lehr-*

buch der Anthropologie (1822) C found no more than "a progressive metamorphosis by successive evolution of the three forms or forces of the Vital Principle" in admitting "that the human Fœtus exists as a Plant, an Insect, and an Animal; but each state specifically in reference to *the Man*". *CM (CC)* II 1026.

[8] The sermon has not been traced; C's marginalia, quotations, and references show that he was familiar with several miscellaneous volumes of Taylor's sermons. His language is similar to that in this entry, but harsher, in an annotation on *The Liberty of Prophesying: Polemicall Discourses* i 919: *CM (CC)* v. Anthony à Wood (1632–95), insisting that Taylor should not be condemned in such a good cause, described the work as lying "in ambuscado", a "stratagem . . . to break the presbyterian power, and so countenance divisions between the factions, which were too much united against the loyal clergy". *Athenae Oxonienses* ed Philip Bliss (4 vols 1813–20) III 786. Michael Lort (1725–90), the antiquary, reported that Taylor desired all copies of *The Liberty of Prophesying* gathered and burned in the marketplace of Dromore. C. J. Stranks *The Life and Writings of Jeremy Taylor* (1952) 259 and n. Robert Aris Willmott, who had listened to C in 1833, said that C read *The Liberty of Prophesying* "with the highest admiration and the liveliest apprehension". *Bishop Jeremy Taylor, His Predecessors Contemporaries and Successors* (2nd ed 1848) 123. C has baffled scholars from his day to this by remarking in *Omniana* I 237 that "there is ex-

Painting is the intermediate something between a Thought and a Thing.[9]   [36:122]

---

[a]31. March. 1830.[1]

The result of my system will be to show that so far from the World being

[a] f 8; the entries for 13, 18, and 20 Apr followed in MS B

---

tant in manuscript a folio volume of unprinted sermons by Jeremy Taylor". *LR* I 303; *TT* (1884) 365. C objected to two adjacent passages on toleration in a volume of Taylor's sermons he had read and annotated, the "Epistle Dedicatory to A Sermon Preached at the Opening of the Parliament of Ireland" on 8 May 1661 and the sermon itself. 'ΕΝΙΑΥΤΟΣ, *a Course of Sermons for All the Sundays in the Year* (5th ed 1678) supplement 60, 61: *CM (CC)* v. This entry on Taylor's self-slander reached MS F, but was then excised, possibly because HNC found no evidence for it, but probably because Taylor returns at greater length on 4 Jun 1830 (36:223).

[9] C distinguished thoughts from things in *BL* ch 2: ". . . where the ideas are vivid, and there exists an endless power of combining and modifying them, the feelings and affections blend more easily and intimately with these ideal creations, than with the objects of the senses; the mind is affected by thoughts, rather than by things; and only then feels the requisite interest even for the most important events, and accidents, when by means of meditation they have passed into *thoughts*." *BL (CC)* I 31; cf ch 5 I 90. The ideal against which C measured the other forms of art is poetry, which is thought and not thing, though he granted that Raphael does not require the indignity of translation for those whose native tongue is not Italian. "On the Principles of Genial Criticism" I: *BL* (1907) II 221. In *TT* (1835) the word "something" was improved to "somewhat".

The reviewer of *TT* (1835) in the *Literary Gazette* 23 May 1835 p 322 commented in quoting this entry: "We may observe here that Coleridge had an ex-

quisite taste and judgment in the fine arts, particularly painting: we have heard the most sententious and able criticism fall from his lips, both on ancient and modern productions." Typically in 1811 C stressed the need for formal harmony from belief in the ideal: "C. spoke of painting as one of the lost arts. Some time after, C., speaking of a great picture by West, said, 'In this picture are a number of figures, each of which is painted as it might have been if it had been a single figure, no one figure having any relation to or influencing any other figure, & tho' they ought to be under each a light of its own, yet each figure looks as if it were in the open-air.' He explained the *ideal* beauty to be that wh. is common to all of a class, taking from each individual that wh. is accidental to him." *CR (BCW)* 41. When in 1799 Greenough observed that the grandeur of nature could hardly have been formed simply for the relish of man, C "directed me to observe still farther that men were less durable than their works, which, as far as we see, are formed for their pleasure only . . . from hence he wished to draw a new argument for the immortality of the soul: for if this be admitted, the means will be only adequate to the end". "Diary" 56: *London Mercury* Apr 1931 p 560; *W&C* 229.

[1] SC remained in the London area another two months, but the record of talk pauses. Two leaves torn from a different workbook contain in HNC's autograph four entries dated 19 Nov and 11, 16, 23 Dec 1827 as he waited to hear from SC on her way to Liverpool and then to Keswick: "My soul is quite sick for your blessed companionship, and yet that alone gives me any spiritual life at all. Yet are we not entirely ill-starred; for

a Goddess in petticoats, it is rather the Devil in a straight waistcoast.[2]

[36:134]

The controversy of the Nominalists and Realists was the greatest and most important of any that have ever occupied the human mind. They were both right and both wrong. They maintained the poles of the same Truth, which Truth neither saw, for want of a still higher premiss.[3] Duns Scotus was the head of the Realists; Occam, his pupil, of the Nominalists.[4] Occam, though prolix, was a most extraordinary writer. Two

---

never do I think a more tender and more disinterested passion burned in two hearts than in ours now. In this we are happy; a thousand sweet delights of mind and sense we lose indeed, by not being married, but we must not complain." VCL S MS 30.

C and HNC continued to correspond, visit, and grow closer in 1828 and into 1829. *CL* VI 719, 728, 749, 785, 787. In Aug 1828 HNC went to Keswick to visit SC and again a year later to marry—on 3 Sept 1829 in the parish church of Crosthwaite. On returning to London he and SC lived for a few months in lodgings. On 15 Mar 1830 Mrs Gillman invited them to The Grove "on the 23d for a week". VCL S MS F 3.62. From the time of this visit, or immediately after it, the record of talk takes up where it had left off in 1827. (In MS B, 31 Mar follows entries dated 13, 18, and 20 Apr. Perhaps HNC was transcribing from a loose sheet that had been mislaid, which would account for the chronological disorder of the ms.)

For HNC's record of WW's conversation dated 15 and 16 Oct 1829 (MS B ff 8ᵛ–10), see App E, below.

[2] The strait waistcoat, which came into use in the eighteenth century for the restraint of violent lunatics and less frequently as prisoners, appears as "Straight Waistcoat Madhouse &c—a stratagem" in one of C's earliest notes (*CN* I 47, which *RX* 457–8 n 56 relates to the Cambridge *University Magazine*, an advertisement for which had it disappearing in a strait waistcoat on its way to the press). In C's journalism strait waistcoat became more often a metaphor for tyranny, particularly for military despotism. *EOT (CC)* I 105–6, 282 and nn, II

78. In Satyrane's Letters C had noted the contrasting "prodigal plumpness of petticoat behind"—*Friend (CC)* II 211—begging for metaphorical application. Although this TT entry may be indirectly a pronouncement concerning the perpetually sinful condition of humanity, it can be taken as a philosophical rejection of the optimism of the empiricists and corpuscular scientists concerning the content and progressive acceptance of their own views. Others heard "Nature" where HNC heard "World": "No! Nature is not God; she is the devil in a strait waistcoat." Julius Charles Hare *The Mission of the Comforter* (2nd ed Cambridge 1850) 410, quoted in *SM (CC)* 71n; see also App I, vol II, below.

[3] The higher premise, to be found in "my system" of the previous entry, is that Realism (taking universals as necessary, knowable, and real) and Nominalism (holding that universals are merely convenient for generalising from particulars) are two views of the same power, a power that is both behind and in particulars.

[4] Long interested in the philosophic issues, C lectured on the Realist-Nominalist controversy in Lect 9 of the lectures on the history of philosophy of 1819, distinguishing three periods in the controversy. *P Lects* (1949) 265–88. Lect 11 of the same series, *SM* App D and E, and *CN* III 3628–9 illustrate C's superimposition of the conflict in his own time between materialist "realists" and Platonistically oriented idealists. In 1801 he had gone to Durham Cathedral with the intention of reading Joannes Duns Scotus (c 1265–c 1308) "in order to wake him out of his present Lethargy", but found only one work there, *De sententiis. CL* II

*b*thirds of the schoolmen of eminence were British. The schoolmen made the languages of Europe what they are. We laugh at the quiddities of the Schoolmen now; these quiddities are the parts of their language which we have rejected; but we never think of the mass which we have adopted and have in daily use.[5]   [36:135, 136]

My mind is in a state of philosophical doubt as to animal magnetism.[6]

b f 8ᵛ

746; annotation on Baxter *Reliquiae: CM (CC)* I 255. From the paucity of available books, he later felt "too little conversant" with Duns Scotus to be sure that he was the only Englishman with metaphysical genius. Annotation on Hooker *Works: CM (CC)* II 1136. The "Scotus" that C planned in 1803 to include in a work on "Revolutionary Minds" (*CN* I 1646) would logically be Duns Scotus and not Scotus Erigena. C wrote long notes on Duns Scotus on the front flyleaves of vol VIII pt ii of Wilhelm Gottlieb Tennemann (1761–1819) *Geschichte der Philosophie* (10 vols in 11 Leipzig 1798–1817). A few leaves further on, C called William of Ockham or Occam (c 1300–c 1349) "a truly great man and worthy of his title, Venerabilis Inceptor". *CM (CC)* v. C honoured Ockham first because his attacks on Realism led to a closer examination and clearer comprehension of idealism and secondly because Occam's razor, the principle that entities must not be unnecessarily multiplied, led to the Baconian advance beyond Aristotle and Aquinas. BM MS Egerton 2801 ff 100–1, quoted in *P Lects* (1949) 439 n 39; cf *CL* v 326 n 2. As late as 1823–4 C's knowledge and views of Scotus and Occam depended in part on Tennemann VIII 759–69, 863, 880. *CN* IV 5087–8 and nn.

[5] C defended the scholastic churchmen in his lectures on the history of philosophy of 1819 and in various contexts, as here for introducing the abstract portion of modern European vocabularies, and in *TL* (1848) 28 for reviving, after barbarism, "the science of *Metaphysics* and *Ontology*". He listed as one of his specialties, when made an Associate of the Royal Society of Literature in 1824, "The influences of the Institutions and Theology of the Latin Church on Philosophy, Language, Science and the Liberal Arts from the VIIth to the XIVth Century". *CL* v 344. On the quiddities of the Schoolmen see also JTC's record of 20 Apr 1811 (at n 17).

[6] C's disinterestedness with regard to animal magnetism is almost as impressive as his suspension of disbelief in phrenology. Franz (or Friedrich) Anton Mesmer (1734–1815), Austrian physician, after concluding experimentally that a *fluidum* pervading the universe can flow curatively through a magnet inside a *baquet* with protruding rods for twenty or more patients to grasp, practised cures in Paris by which the *gravitas*, or animal magnetism, from the magnetic attraction of the spheres, flowed through his hands into the patient. In 1795 C had defended Edward Long Fox's belief in the curative powers of such magnetism. *Lects 1795 (CC)* 327–8. He ridiculed curative magnetists in 1809, but recanted in 1818: *Friend (CC)* I 59 and n, II 51. Among books on the subject C read and annotated Carl Alexander Ferdinand Kluge (1782–1844) *Versuch einer Darstellung des animalischen Magnetismus* (Berlin 1815), Mesmer *Mesmerismus* ed Karl Christian Wolfart (Berlin 1814), and Wolfart *Erläuterungen zum Mesmerismus* (1815): *CM (CC)* III, IV, V. As the quotation in HNC's long note to this entry in *TT* (1835) said and C's letters of 1817–24 amply confirm, C sought the latest opinions from such visitors as the informed Ludwig Tieck (1773–1853) and the naturalist Gottfried Reinhold Treviranus (1776–1837). *CL* IV 730–1,

Chenevix did some odd feats at St Thomas's Hospital.[7] Von Spix, the eminent naturalist, makes no doubt of the matter, and talks coolly of giving doses of it &c.[8] The Torpedo affects a third or external object by an exertion of its own will; that power is not properly electrical.[9] [36:140]

739, 745, 749, 883, 886–7, v 349–51. He recommended the subject for an article in *EM*, and in Jul 1817 drafted such himself. *CL* IV 886; BM Add MS 36532 ff 7–13; *IS* 45–50; *CN* IV 4512. On mesmerism as a partial explanation of ancient priests and oracles, see *P Lects* Lects 2, 10 (1949) 104–5, 304–5, and C's note on Webster *The Displaying of Supposed Witchcraft* 70: "... it enables us to explain the Oracles & a score other superstitions". *CM (CC)* V.

His interest was stimulated again in 1822 by Johann Carl Passavant *Untersuchungen über den Lebensmagnetismus und das Hellsehen* (Frankfurt 1821) and M. Loewe *A Treatise on the Phenomena of Animal Magnetism* (1822). *CN* IV 4908 and n. In 1824 he was tempted to try animal magnetism on the child of a neighbour. *CL* V 350. Later his scepticism of such therapy again increased: annotation on Gotthilf Heinrich von Schubert (1780–1860) *Allgemeine Naturgeschichte oder Andeutungen zur Geschichte und Physiognomik der Natur* (Erlangen 1826) 755–9, 997. *CM (CC)* IV. On 24 Jun 1824 Carlyle wrote that C was full of magnetism (apparently in two senses, both favourable): "He is a kind, good soul, full of religion and affection, and poetry and animal magnetism." *The Collected Letters of Thomas and Jane Welsh Carlyle* ed C. R. Sanders et al (Durham, N.C. 1970–) II 109.

[7] Richard Chenevix (1774–1830), chemist and mineralogist, was given the opportunity by John Elliotson (1791–1868)—translator of Blumenbach *The Institutions of Physiology* (2nd ed 1817) and founder of the Phrenological Society—to perform experiments at St Thomas's, which Chenevix reported in the *London Medical and Physiological Journal* LXI (Mar–Jun 1829) 219–30, 491–501, LXII (Jul–Oct 1829) 113–25, 210–20, 315–24. Chenevix reported success with 164 patients suffering from fe-

ver, rheumatism, epilepsy, diseased liver or lungs, gout, or scrofula, but acknowledged that some diseases resisted the cure. Whether because the Chenevix experiments were controversial or because they seemed of little permanent interest, the sentence concerning him was not printed in *TT* (1835).

[8] Johann Baptist von Spix (1781–1826), Bavarian naturalist and disciple of Schelling. With Dr Carl F. P. von Martius he reported on Brazilian hospitals and such diseases as dysentery and malaria, but not mesmeric cures, in *Reise in Brasilien . . . in den Jahren 1817 bis 1820* (2 vols Munich 1823–31).

[9] Most physiological debates about animal magnetism concerned the nervous system: was it cutaneous, fluidic, productive of a magnetic field, or in some other way a version of electromagnetic force? The torpedo (electric ray or cramp-fish, *torpedinidae*), besides the need felt by all students of electrical phenomena to explain its power to numb other creatures, raised the possibility that a Mesmer could physically shock his patients without touching them. Scientific reports on the torpedo were unceasing. Erasmus Darwin recounted his own experiments with the gymnotus electricus in a footnote to *The Economy of Vegetation* I line 202; cf *The Temple of Nature* (1803) III 111–12. Debates concerning electrical and chemical explanations for the "torpedo electricus" had appeared in *Phil Trans* (RS) XC (1800) 403–32, CVI (1816) 120, CVII (1817) 32–5, and (by Davy) CXIX (1829) 15–18. C referred to the benumbing "torpedo touch" metaphorically at least three times in 1795–6: *CL* I 155, *PW* (EHC) I 163n, *Lects 1795 (CC)* 45. *TT* (1835) added a sentence about a steady gaze causing a blush, with a second sentence, "Account for that", implying that the blush could not occur if the stare were only supposed.

Spinoza, at the end of his life, in his last letter, seems to have gained a glimpse of the truth. He began to suspect his *premiss*.[10] His Unica Substantia is^c in fact a mere Notion, a *subject* of the Mind and no *object* at all.[11]   [36:138]

Plato's works are preparatory exercises of the mind. He leads the mind to see that contradictory propositions are each true—which therefore *must* belong to a higher Logic—that of Ideas. They are contradictory only in the Aristotelian Logic.[12] I have read several of the works of Plato

^{c} ~~was~~ is

[10] C wrote a similar note in Spinoza *Opera* (2 vols Jena 1802–3), which he had borrowed from HCR—that the greatest of all pantheists, who had begun by considering God as an object, was at the end about to reach the true conclusion that God is the identity of subject and object, the ground of all existents (I 584): "I think his Epist. 72. authorizes us to believe and of so pure a Soul, so righteous a Spirit, as Spinoza, I dare not doubt, that this *Potential* Fact is received by the Eternal as Actual". *CM (CC)* IV. For an acknowledgement of strength in the argument that unlearned men managed to convert nearly the whole world see Letter 72, of 15 Jul 1676, in Spinoza *Opera* I 680–1. John Abraham Heraud (1799–1887) reported the same points as HNC in *An Oration on the Death of Samuel Taylor Coleridge* (1834): " 'If only half the truth be taken, the conclusion must be erroneous. This was the case with Spinoza. While Spinoza supposed that phenomena were Objects only, and not Subjects also, not all the powers of heaven and earth,' said the eloquent and venerable man, 'could invalidate his argument. But some time before his death, Spinoza began to suspect that they were Subjects as well, which half of the truth added to the other half, will lead to a correct result. The things of experience and sense are Subject-Objects.' " *C Talker* 259. HCR doubted C's sincerity in 1812 in kissing the *Opera* engraving of Spinoza while declaring his philosophy false (*CRB* I 112), but C's painful sincerity in facing the dilemma of Spinozistic pantheism is eloquently argued by McFarland *Coleridge and the Pantheist Tradition* 53–190, esp 107. C declared a near reverence for Spinoza in 1830 and 1832: *CL* VI 850, 893. On the first flyleaf of Schelling *Philosophische Schriften* (Landshut 1809) C counted "*Spinoza's Ethice*, with his Letters &c as far as they are Comments on his Ethics", along with Bacon's *Novum Organum* and Kant's *Critique of Pure Reason* (each with their supporting works), as "the three greatest Works since the introduction of Christianity". *CM (CC)* IV.

[11] According to C, to say with Spinoza that no *substantia* besides God can be granted or conceived (*Ethics* prop 14: *Opera* II 46) is to speak of a substance that is God *or* nature, and therefore to have a mere notion of a combinative *unica substantia*. In *AR* (1825) 161–2 he wrote that one loses all prayer, all "Faith, Love, Fear and Adoration", and therefore loses the Idea of God, in "the indivisible one and only substance (*substantia una et unica*) of Spinoza, of which all Phaenomena, all particular and individual Things, Lives, Minds, Thoughts, and Actions are but modifications".

[12] In an annotation on Tennemann *Geschichte der Philosophie* VIII i endleaf (referring to VIII i 130 on Anselm) C gave as one reason for the superiority of Platonists their ability to understand the Aristotelians, without the reverse being true. *CM (CC)* V. About 1802 he had made a great leap from his condition in 1796, when he could declare to John Thelwall, with regard to definitions of life, "Plato says, it is *Harmony*—he might as well have said, a fiddle stick's end—but I love Plato—his dear *gorgeous* Nonsense!" *CL* I 295.

several times with profound attention, but not all his writings. I soon found that I had read Plato by anticipation. He was a consummate Genius. [36:139]

---

*a*13. April 1830. S. T. C.

If the prophecies of the Old Testament are not rightly interpreted of Jesus Christ, there is no prediction whatever contained in it of that stupendous event, the rise and establishment of Christianity, in comparison with which all the preceding Jewish history is as nothing.[1] With the exception of the book of Daniel, which the Jews themselves never classed amongst the prophecies,[2] and an obscure text of Jeremiah,[3] there is not a passage in all the Old Testament which favors the notion of a temporal Messiah. What could such a Messiah have been but a virtuous Buonaparte? What moral object could there be, for which he should come?[4] [36:123]

a f 6ᵛ, following the entries for 29–30 Aug

[1] Of Ps 72, a prediction for "the king's son" usually described as David's prayer for Solomon, C wrote in the Book of Common Prayer: "The 72ⁿᵈ Psalm ad mits of no other interpretation except of Christ as the Jehovah incarnate." *CM (CC)* I 706. He endorsed Baxter's "sound & irrefragable argument" that passages in the OT are not to be taken as spoken only of such private persons as David, "but as Types of Christ". Annotation on *Reliquiae Baxterianae: CM (CC)* I 316. He endorsed even more strongly Baxter's suggestion that prophecies are to be interpreted of general movements, never of individuals; the prophecies of Antichrist may be fulfilled in paganism or popery but must not be applied to any one Pope: annotation on Webster *The Displaying of Supposed Witchcraft* 138: *CM (CC)* v. Cf C's letter to Hurwitz of 4 Jan 1820 on the OT prophecies as demonstrating "the identity of the doctrines of the Old Testament and of our Gospel". *CL* v 2–3.

[2] Cf C's annotation on John Davison (1777–1834) *Discourses on Prophecy* (1825): ". . . the Jewish Church ranked the book of Daniel in the third class only, among the Hagiographic . . .". *CM*

(CC) II 156. In a note on one of his sources for this information, Eichhorn *AT* I 109, C admitted the "infatuation" of Josephus in favour of Daniel. *CM (CC)* II 375. In a later margin of the same work C wrote: ". . . the Selecters and Compilers of the Hebrew Canon . . . degrad[ed] Daniel to the Hagiographi, to the Authors of which they conceded only the lowest grade or sort of inspiration— scarcely more than we attribute to favorite devotional Books". *CM (CC)* II 409. On Daniel see also above, 29 Dec 1822 (at n 9) and 24 Feb 1827 (at nn 5–8).

[3] Jer 23.5, echoed in 33.15, promises "a righteous Branch" of David who shall reign as king and prosper.

[4] Of Jer 32.26–44 C had written in Mrs Gillman's Bible: "That the *Spirit* of these Promises will be fulfilled whenever the Jews present the moral conditions . . . I see no reason to doubt", although he could not reconcile fulfilment with Christian sacrifice. *CM (CC)* I 438. More generally he had declared in 1824: "The Bible must be interpreted by it's known *objects* and *Ends*; and these were the moral and spiritual Education of the Human Race." *CL* v 372; cf *CIS* (1840) 55–6, 71–2. In an annotation on A. C. A.

Hyman Hurwitz said he owned he did not expect a Messiah; but he thought it might possibly be God's will and meaning that the Jews should remain a quiet light among the nations for the purpose of pointing at the doctrine of the Unity of God.[5]

But this truth of the essential Unity of God has been preserved and gloriously preached by Christianity alone. The Romans never shut up their temples, nor ceased to worship a hundred Gods at the bidding of Jews; the Persians, the Hindus and Chinese learned nothing from the Jews of this great Truth. From the Christians they did learn it in various degrees—and are still learning it. Indeed the light of the Jews is as the light of a glowworm, which gives no heat and illumines nothing but itself.[6]

[36:124]

Hurwitz objected that the vulgar notions of the Trinity were at variance with this doctrine. Few thought of the Trinity as S. T. C. did.[7]

My own superior light—if superior—consists in this, that I more clearly see that the doctrine of the Trinity is an Absolute Truth transcending my human means of understanding it or demonstrating it.[8] I may be

---

Eschenmayer *Psychologie in drei Theilen als empirische, reine und ungewandte* (Stuttgart & Tübingen 1817) he declared that "the Prophecies of the Bible are all *conditional* in proportion as they are particular". *CM (CC)* II 544. *TT* (1835) added to Bonaparte an alternative, Sesostris.

[5] The name of C's friend Hyman Hurwitz (1770–1844), professor of Hebrew at London University from 1829, is suppressed from *TT* (1835). C's attempt to praise Hurwitz's forthcoming *Hebrew Tales* in the "Advertisement" to *AR* in 1825 had been thwarted for similarly innocent but prudential reasons. *CL* v 458, 460. Their names were linked publicly in *Israel's Lament* (1817), which C translated from the Hebrew of Hurwitz; in *Hebrew Tales* (1826), which included three translations by C; and in *AR* (1825) 205n, in which Hurwitz, "my friend", is called "that pious, learned, strongminded, and single-hearted Jew, an Israelite indeed and without guile". *TT* (1835) substituted for his name "some excellent men—Israelites without guile". C applied the phrase from John 1.47 to his father (*CL* I 355) and to the wife of Washington Allston (*C Talker*

285). HCR had noted wryly in 1811: "Coleridge's antipathy to the Irish I cannot share in. But then, he has no aversion to Turks or Jews, so I am the best Christian after all." *CRB* I 29; cf *CR (BCW)* 40.

[6] The post-Exilic monotheism of the Jews (C answers Hurwitz) has had a world-wide effect only through Christianity; the Jewish religion as such, though of moral and spiritual value to the Jews, carries no evangel to the world of 1830. Cf C's use of the metaphor of the glowworm in an annotation on Marcus Aurelius: *CM (CC)* I 169–70 and in *CL* VI 595–6.

[7] This paragraph, which reports Hurwitz's continuation of the debate with C, dropped out of *TT* (1835). The following paragraph includes C's rebuttal: although Hurwitz is correct in arguing that the vulgar do not perceive the triune godhead in C's way, yet the instinctive belief of the vulgar in one God sustains C's claim that Christians teach others to believe in the unity of God.

[8] For elucidation of C's views on the Trinity, expressed throughout TT and elsewhere, see James D. Boulger *Coleridge as a Religious Thinker* (New Ha-

able to express my belief in more *b*logical terms than many others, but go and ask any Christian—a professed believer in the Trinity—whether he believes in a plurality of Gods: he will start with horror at the imputation; he may not be able to explain his exact creed, but he will tell you that he *does* believe in one God and in one God only—reason as you may upon it. [36:125]

What all the Christian Churches of the East and West—what Roman Catholic and Protestant believe in common—I call Christianity. The Unitarians and Socinians are not Christians in any proper sense of the word. Almost all the theological disputes have been about additions and appendices to Christianity as *commonly* believed.[9] [36:126]

There is no hope of converting the Jews in the way and with the spirit unhappily adopted by our Church and indeed all other modern Churches.[10] In the beginning of Christianity, the Jewish Christians undoubtedly considered themselves, as of the blood of Abraham with whom the promise had been made, a superior order—Witness St Peter's conduct in the Acts.[11] St Paul protested against this, so far as it went to make Jewish observances compulsory on Christians who were not of Jewish blood, *c*and so far as it*d* in any way led to bottom the Religion on the Mosaic Covenant of Works:[12]—but he never denied the birth-right of the chosen seed; he himself evidently believed that the Jews would ultimately be restored, and he says that if the Gentiles have been so blessed by the rejection of the Jews—how much rather shall they be blessed by

---

b f 7   *c–d* ~~but he never~~ & so far as it

---

ven 1961) esp 133–8; McFarland *Coleridge and the Pantheist Tradition* esp 227–43; Barth *Coleridge and Christian Doctrine* esp 9 11, 85–108.

[9] The last sentence, omitted from *TT* (1835), broadens the argument from C's (customary) rejection of Unitarians from the ecumenic body of Christians into an affirmation of central Christian doctrine by finding the general cause of theological differences in accretions to the central doctrine. One element in the conversational transition from Jews to Unitarians is C's belief that contemporary Unitarians "virtually" rejected the Old Testament. *CL* v 4.

[10] In the letter to Hurwitz of 4 Jan 1820 (n 1, above) on conversion of the Jews, C repudiated procedures parallel to those of Anglican missions abroad and proposed instead (*a*) retention by Jews of the noble heritage of God's commands and promises to them as a people and (*b*) a demonstration that Jesus was a tree whose fruits could be available to them by the termination of all persecution based on their reluctance to reject their antique heritage and gather under the Christian shade. *CL* v 1–9.

[11] Acts 2.14–36 (Peter's sermon on Jesus as the expected Messiah); 11.8 (Peter's declaration that he obeyed the dietary laws); 15.7 (his rôle as apostle of circumcision).

[12] Paul debates with Peter in Acts 15; in Gal 2 he tells how he rebuked Peter for attempting to force Judaic practices on the Gentiles.

the conversion and restoration of Israel![13] Why do we expect the Jews to abandon their national customs? The Abyssinian Church said that they claimed a descent from Abraham, and in virtue of such ancestry they observed circumcision, but they rejected the Covenant of Works, and rested on the promise fulfilled in Jesus Christ. The Abyssinians were permitted to retain their customs.[14] If Rhenferd's[e] Essays were translated—if the Jews were made acquainted with the argument—if they were addressed kindly—if they were not required to abandon their distinctive customs as a nation, but were invited to become Christians of the seed of Abraham—there would be a Christian Synagogue in a year's time.[15] As it is, the Jews are the lowest of mankind; they of the lower orders have not a principle of honesty in them; to grasp and be getting moneys for ever is their one occupation.[16]

[e] ~~the~~ Renfurt's

[13] Rom 11.16–27 says as much metaphorically: "if the root be holy, so are the branches"; cf Gal 3.21–9.

[14] In the fifth century the church in Abyssinia followed the Coptic Church of Alexandria into Monophysite heresies; in the sixth century Jewish influence penetrated (although the Abyssinian rite of circumcision may have been for sanitary reasons). When Socinios (Negus Susenyos) attempted to impose Catholicism under the influence of Portuguese Jesuits, the nobility and clergy forced his abdication in 1632; his son restored the Abyssinian Church. C's interest in the Abyssinian Creed as early as 1795— *Lects 1795 (CC)* 308—suggests that one source of his information was James Bruce (1730–94) *Travels to Discover the Source of the Nile* (5 vols Edinburgh 1790; 6 vols Dublin 1790–1), which C read in 1794. *RX* 133–4. Religious developments are included in Bruce's "Annals of Abyssinia, translated from the Original" bks II–IV in vols II–III; bk v ch 12 describes Abyssinian religious practices in 1769. Bruce stresses ties to Alexandria rather than descent from Abraham.

[15] This seems to propose that Rhenferd's *Opera philologica*, by showing the interrelationships of Christian and non-Christian sects of the first century A.D., in a translation from the Latin,

could persuade modern Jews to achieve Pauline elevation morally and spiritually while retaining the Mosaic law. On the last point, C's letter to Hurwitz was emphatic: ". . . it is my confirmed Opinion, that were 'an Israelite, of the seed of Abraham,' to become a Christian, he would not the less remain bound by virtue of his Lineage to perform every *jot* of your Law, as far as it is declared or evidently implied, in the Books of Moses". *CL* v 3. C found confirmation of his view that "whatever was ordained for them, as Abrahamidae is not repealed by Christianity" in John Hacket *A Century of Sermons* (1675): *CM (CC)* II 916. On Rhenferd see also 8 Jul 1827, above, and n 14.

[16] *TT* (1835) included confirmation concerning the poor in Holywell St and Duke's Place from a "learned Jew" who sounds like the C that HCR heard on an undeclared date: ". . . I *once* heard Coler. say 'When I have been asked to subscribe to a society for converting Jews to Xtnty. I have been accustomed to say, "I have no money for any Charity, but if I had, I wd. subscribe to make them first *good* Jews & then it wd. be time to make good Christians of them." ' " *CR (BCW)* 40. Since the 1770s synagogue authorities had worked with civil authorities to reduce crime among impoverished Jews. Elkan Na-

In Poland the Jews are great landholders, and are the worst of tyrants.[17] They have no sort of sympathy with their ⸿laborers and dependants—they never meet them in common worship. Sir Robert Inglis's opposition to the Bill is weak.[18] Land in the hand of Jews from being the organ of Permanence would become the order of Rigidity in a Nation; by their intermarriages within their own pale it would be perpetually entailed. Then again if a popular tumult were to take place in Poland—who can doubt that the Jews would be the first object of Murder and Spoliation?[19]   [36:127]

f f 7ᵛ

than Adler *London* (Philadelphia 1930) 150–60. *TT* (1835) carried a footnote on C's friendships with Hurwitz and other cultivated Jews, and continued with a passage dropped in 1836: "Mr. C. once told me that he had for a long time been amusing himself with a clandestine attempt upon the faith of three or four persons, whom he was in the habit of seeing occasionally. I think he was undermining, at the time he mentioned this to me, a Jew, a Swedenborgian, a Roman Catholic, and a New Jerusalemite, or by whatsoever other name the members of that somewhat small, but very respectable, church planted in the neighbourhood of Lincoln's Inn Fields, delight to be known. He said he had made most way with the disciple of Swedenborg, who might be considered as a convert, that he had perplexed the Jew, and had put the Roman Catholic into a bad humour; but that upon the New Jerusalemite he had made no more impression than if he had been arguing with the man in the moon." The Swedenborgian Charles Augustus Tulk (1786–1849), M.P. for Poole 1835–7, would have been among those discomfited by this note. On the "New Jerusalemites" see the correction in n 6 to 2 May 1830, below.

[17] Jews were allowed to practise farming in Poland as early as the twelfth century, and a few Ashkenazi Jews in and near Lithuania had been encouraged in the 1820s to extend their monopolistic leases on agricultural produce into direct production—*Encyclopaedia Judaica* XIII (1971) 726–35—but it is not clear in what sense their power to mistreat the

Polish peasantry included ownership of land. Ch 10 of Robert Johnston *Travels Through Part of the Russian Empire and the Country of Poland . . .* (1815) gave a strongly anti-Semitic account of Jewish tyranny over Lithuanian servants. C noted in 1799 the contrasting oppression of Jews in Germany. *CL* I 473.

[18] Sir Robert Harry Inglis, Bt (1786–1855), Tory M.P. representing Oxford University, spoke against the motion introduced by Robert Grant (1779–1838, knighted 1834) on 5 Apr "to repeal civil disabilities for British-born subjects professing the Jewish religion". Inglis opposed even the introduction of the bill, on the grounds that the constant practice of Parliament had been to protect Christianity. He asserted that Jews had already "a right to purchase land, and to dispose of it by sale or testament", but he believed that any bill not explicitly Christian should pay no regard at all to the religion of an individual, Jew, Turk, or Mohammedan. Hansard NS XXIII 1287–324; *A Reg* for 1830, Hist 109–15. The bill, supported by Macaulay's maiden speech on 5 Apr, received a second reading on 17 May, when it was set aside for a later session; it was to be passed in 1833. Although the reference to Inglis is omitted from *TT* (1835), Grant's bill clearly occasioned the discussion.

[19] The argument against rigidity is consonant with *C&S*, written in 1829, rev Jan 1830. Is the implication of the final sentence that the Jews in England should be protected from the full rights of citizenship for their own safety?

In the Miracles of Moses there is a remarkable intermingling of actions which we should now a days call Providential with such as *we* should still call Miraculous. The passing of the Jordan is perhaps an instance of the purest and sheerest miracle recorded in the Bible; it was done apparently for the Miracle's sake, and to show to the Jews the descendants of those who had come out of Egypt that the *same* God, who had appeared to their fathers and who had by miracles in many respects providential only pre-served them in the Wilderness, was *their* God also.[20] The Manna and Quails are provisions of Providence in great part.[21] The passing of the Red Sea is caused by a strong Wind which we are told drove back the Waters.[22] Then the death of the First Born was purely miraculous.[23] Hence both Jews and Egyptians might learn that it was one and the same God who interfered specially and who governed all the world generally. The [g]second to thirteenth chapters[h] of Exodus were inserted by another Writer.[24]   [36:128]

---

[i]Doubts have been entertained of the genuineness of the book of Joshua—but I think the internal testimony irresistible.[25]

Observe the different coloring given by the poetic spirit of David to the battles &c recorded in prose in the Chronicles.[j][26]

Take away the first verse of Genesis—and what remains or immediately follows is an exact history of Pantheism.[27] Pantheism was taught in the

[g–h] 2[d] to 13th capitā
[i–j] For the variant in MS F—especially the insertion, "It sometimes . . . hand"—see App C, below

[20] Josh 3.14–17; cf 2 Kings 2.8, 13.
[21] Exod 16.12–35.
[22] Exod 14.16–29.
[23] Exod 11.5, 12.29. For C's dispar-agement of miracles as the "extra-essen-tial", derived from and not preceding faith, see *CL* II 1189–90; *CN* II 2640; "Definition of a Miracle" in *LR* I 370–2; *SM (CC)* 10 and n.
[24] Exod 2–13 recounts the life of Moses from birth to the eve of the pass-ing of the Red Sea. The sentence was omitted from *TT* (1835). In a note on Eichhorn *AT* C wrote that "Eichhorn has purposely *slurred over* the first 14 Chap-ters of Exodus". *CM (CC)* II 396.
[25] Some of the inconsistencies and ev-ident interpolations in Joshua, with the names of some questioning scholars, are given in Eichhorn *AT* §§ 445–54 II 392–

416. For C's comment see *CM (CC)* II 399. This entry was rewritten in MS F but not published.
[26] E.g. Ps 60 and 1 Chron 18–20.
[27] That the opening of Genesis is pol-ytheistic was said in a number of works read by C. In a marginal note on Sir Thomas Browne *Religio Medici* C de-clared Gen 1 literal and Gen 2.4ff, of greater antiquity, symbolical. *CM (CC)* I 783. At another time he saw in Gen 1–2.4 "the physical theory of the Earth" and 2.4ff and ch 3 "the moral and spir-itual theory or philosopheme of Man", co-ordinated as one assurance. Annota-tion on Eichhorn *AT: CM (CC)* II 389. In C's view Eichhorn on the polytheism and on the multiple authorship of Gen 1 was anticipated in Böhme *Aurora* ch 22. An-notation on Böhme *Works: CM (CC)* I

Mysteries of Greece, of which the Cabeiric were the purest and most ancient.[28] [36:129]

---

18. April 1830.

In the present age it is next to impossible to predict from specimens, however favorable, that a young man will turn *ᵃout a great Poet*—or rather *a* Poet at all. Poetic Taste, dexterity in composition and ingenious Imitation, very often produce poems that are very promising apparently. But Genius, or the Power of doing something new, is another thing. Tennyson's sonnets partake of the excellencies of those of Wordsworth and Southey.[1] [36:130]

I never had and never *could* feel any horror at Death, simply as Death.[2] [36:132]

ᵃ f 8

---

616. The same annotation shows that C knew also, if only through Eichhorn, of the rôle of Jean Astruc (1684–1766) in establishing philologically the Elohim-Jahveh sources of Genesis, in *Conjectures sur les mémoires originaux dont il paroît que Moyse s'est servi pour composer le livre de la Genèse* (Brussels 1753).

[28] On the Mysteries and Cabiri see Lect 11 of 3 Mar 1818: *LR* I 184–8; *CN* III 4385; C's RSL essay "On the *Prometheus* of Aeschylus" *LR* I 323–59; and annotations on Böhme *Works* (*CM—CC*—I 616, 659, 665, 678), on George Stanley Faber *A Dissertation on the Mysteries of the Cabiri* (2 vols Oxford 1803; *CM—CC*—II 573–85). C's principal source was Schelling *Ueber die Gottheiten von Samothrace* (Stuttgart & Tübingen 1815). For Walter Scott's memory of C on the Cabiri as germinal to all fairy tales see App F 6, below.

[1] Specifically of Sonnet 11 ("It is a Summer's gloaming") in *Sonnets and Fugitive Pieces* (Cambridge 1830) 14, by Charles Tennyson, later Turner (1808–79), Alfred's brother, C wrote: "This (and indeed a large proportion of these Sonnets) stands between Wordsworth's & Southey's and partakes of the excellencies of both." C granted "poetic taste with both the feeling & plastic power of a poet" but predicted greatness only if "he will be a philosopher and pure from the World"—not C's usual way of distinguishing genius from taste. *CM (CC)* V. The original volume, on which C made his annotations, has since disappeared; C may have extended it towards HNC as he spoke. In 1823 he had complained of the poor "metrical arrangement" of "modern Poems", in a note on *The Battle of the Bridge*, sent to him by the author, one S. Maxwell, and in Feb 1830 had been the reluctant reader of a poem in ms by the "very poor Poet" Charles Whitehead (1804–62). *CM (CC)* III; *CL* VI 826–7. HC wrote to HNC in May 1836 that he was happy to see in *TT* evidence that C was reconciled to "those excellent men" RS and WW, though he himself could not admire RS's "laureate poetry". *HCL* 190.

[2] Although HNC read Montaigne, C's aversion to the French may have kept from him the classic demonstrations, in *Essais* bk I 20, bk II 6, bk III 13, that death is not to be feared. He was sensitive to the higher ground taken by Spinoza *Ethics* pt v scholium to prop 38: ". . . mors eo minus est noxia, quo

It is a small thing that the patient knows of his own state, yet some things he *does* know better than his physicians.[3]   [36:131]

———

20. April. 1830.

At the accession of George IV. there was no blackguard in St Giles's, who did not hug himself and think that he was an honester man than the King.[1]

It makes me proud of my country to think how great the influence of private morals is! The old King, in spite of his homeliness, his obstinacy and his craziness, with all the national misfortunes around him, was almost universally beloved and popular; George IV. has counted his months with victories and yet not one ray of the public glory fell on him![2]

———

Good and bad men are each less so than they seem.[3]   [36:133]

———

*a*S. T. C. 25. April 1830[1]

A *Fall* of some sort or other—the creation, as it were, of the Non-Absolute—is the fundamental *Postulate* of the Moral History of Man. With-

---

a f 10; for ff 8ᵛ–10, conversation by WW 15–16 Oct 1829, see App E, below

---

Mentis clara et distincta cognitio major est et consequenter, quo Mens magis Deum amat''—*Opera* ed Paulus ɪɪ 295— tr Elwes: ''. . . death becomes less hurtful, in proportion as the mind's clear and distinct knowledge is greater, and, consequently, in proportion as the mind loves God more''.

[3] C is at once speaking of his own ill health and generalising from it.

[1] The squalid rookery of St Giles's, notorious for poverty and crime, lasted until it was cut through by New Oxford St in 1847. As St Giles was the patron saint of cripples, ''St Giles's parish'' was originally outside the walls of the city, where lame beggars were banished; the name served C's purposes both actually and symbolically. Before and during the Regency (1811–20), the heir of George ɪɪɪ was ridiculed by the public

caricatures and the radical press for loose and extravagant conduct.

[2] George ɪᴠ, who had secluded himself at Windsor, was reported in Apr to be near the death that would come on 26 Jun. C was pronouncing a valediction.

[3] HNC seems to be searching along here for ways to get C into the anthologies of common wisdom. This is one of three aphorisms combined in *TT* (1835) under the date 19 Apr 1830.

[1] In MS B, these entries were preceded by those dated, out of sequence, 31 Mar: see n 1 to that date. The conversations of 13 Apr and 20 Apr, which preceded that of 31 Mar in the ms, had fallen on Tuesdays during the vacation between Hilary and Easter law terms, when HNC could have remained away from Lincoln's Inn. 25 Apr was a Sunday.

out this hypothesis Man is unintelligible; with it, every phenomenon is explicable. The Mystery itself is too profound for human insight.[2]

[36:141]

_b_Madness is not simply a bodily disease. It is the sleep of the Spirit with certain conditions of wakefulness; _c_that is,_d_ lucid intervals. During this sleep or recession of the Spirit, the lower or bestial states of Life rise up into action and prominence. It is an awful thing to be eternally tempted by the perverted senses; the Reason _may_ resist—it _does_ resist, for a long time—but too often, at length, it yields for a moment and then the man is mad for ever. An act of the will is in many instances precedent to complete insanity.[3] Bishop Butler said he was all his life struggling against

_b_ f 10^v   _c-d_ =

[2] In *SM* App C, after attributing the "original temptation, through which man fell" to the "rational instinct", C cited Rom 8.19 23 and 2 Cor 3.18 on the image of the Lord in glory, lost after the Creation by the vanity of the self, so that fallen man has only religion to express, though finitely, "the *unity* of the infinite Spirit by being a total act of the soul". *SM (CC)* 61, 90. That man is a fallen creature "diseased in his *Will*", as C declared in *The Friend* on 11 Jan 1810 (*CC* II 279), self-analysis had long since convinced him. He defended the agreement of Calvin, Luther, and Zwingli on original sin against the Arminianism or (in his view) "Grotianism" of later centuries. *AR* (1825) 156–8. The fall into sin—the problem of evil—is not to C a *mere* mystery; in *SM* he cited Eph 1.17–18 and 3.9 to steer a course between mystery and knowledge of God. *SM (CC)* 46. The "fearful Mystery" remains, he declared in his creed of 3 Nov 1810; "Guilt is justly imputable to me prior to any given act, or assignable moment of time, in my Consciousness". *CN* III 4005 ff 4–4^v.

[3] Some of C's earliest theories concerning madness came from David Hartley (1705–57) *Observations on Man* (2 vols 1749), which he read and annotated in the 1791 ed with notes by H. A. Pistorius. He cited Hartley on irrational attention to one idea (from a disturbance in the medullary substance) in *Watchman*

No 1 *(CC)* 32. Hartley, who first introduced madness in connexion with physically induced sleep, later ascribed instances not to bodily causes alone but also to such mental excesses as "ambitious, or covetous desires". *Observations* (1791) I 55, 165, 400–3. In Lect 7 of 25 Mar 1819, on *Don Quixote*, madness was to be considered "without pretension to medical science". *CN* III 4503: *Lects 1808–19 (CC)* II 415. Yet his fourfold classification there, of a man being out of his senses or his wits, or suffering loss of reason or derangement of sensations (*Lects 1808–19—CC*—II 418; cf Lect 8 of 20 Feb 1818: ibid II 165), corresponds, despite different terminology, with the classification in Thomas Arnold (1742–1816) *Observations on the Nature, Kinds, Causes, and Prevention of Insanity* (2 vols 1806), which was available to C at Highgate (*Gillman SC*). A similar classification appears under "The Soul and Its Organs of Sense" in *Omniana* II 14–16. For a well-supported suggestion that C took a deep personal interest in William Battie *A Treatise on Madness* (1758) see *CN* III 3431n. Pts ii and iii of C's *The Three Graves* trace the progression of madness in the heroine— *PW* (EHC) I 267–84—and a similar interest appears in his use of "The Story of Maria Eleonora Schöning" in *Friend (CC)* I 342–55. Responding to Darwin's explanation that madness derives from the devilish suggestions of his senses, which would have maddened him, if he had relaxed the stern wakefulness of his Reason for a moment.[4]

[36:142]

[e]Mead is[f] right in denying the demoniac possessions of the New Testament but wrong in saying they were only bodily diseases.[5] The Spirit becomes devilish in madness—but the belief that little individual devils got inside the man is absurd. St John expressly says—they were otherwise called Lunatics or Moon-blasted.[6]

[e-k] For important variants in this passage in MS F see App C, below　　　[f] ~~was~~ is

---

"excess of action of the sensorial power of volition", Thomas Beddoes nevertheless similarly described delirium and madness as states of "abstraction and agitation" in which "the mind acts with unusual energy". *Hygëia* (11 pts in 3 vols Bristol 1802–3) iii ii 45–60. Unlike Hartley and C, both Darwin and Beddoes avoided moral explanations, as did the three writers on madness reviewed in *Lancet* xii (14 Apr 1827) 51–6, J. G. Spurzheim, Paul Slade Knight, and Alexander Morison.

[4] *TT* (1835) reads: "I think it was Bishop Butler", meaning that HNC had not found the remark in the works or biographical sketches of Joseph Butler (1692–1752), bp of Durham, author of *The Analogy of Religion Natural and Revealed to the Constitution and the Course of Nature* (1736). C's "appears to be an apocryphal anecdote", according to Ernest Campbell Mossner "Coleridge and Bishop Butler" *Philosophical Review* xlv (1936) 207. C's version is repeated in Thomas Bartlett *Memoirs of the Life, Character and Writings of Joseph Butler, Late Lord Bishop of Durham* (1839) 221. On pp 225–6 Bartlett reports a similar remark by Butler on another occasion, as from *Anecdotes Illustrative of the Assembly's Shorter Catechism* (Edinburgh 1825), a work probably compiled by John Whitecross. If the authenticity of C's anecdote is questioned, a second candidate arises: John Butler (1717–1802), bp of Hereford, a chaplain to George iii. C's friend Samuel Butler (1774–1839) did not become bp of Lichfield and Coventry until 1836.

[5] Richard Mead (1673–1754), English physician educated at Utrecht, Leyden, and Padua, ch 9 "De daemoniacis" in *Medica sacra* (Amsterdam 1749) 47–58; in English as "Of Demoniacks" in *The Medical Works of Richard Mead, M.D.* (1762) 617–25: "That the Demoniacks . . . mentioned in the gospels, laboured under a disease really natural, though of an obstinate and difficult kind, appears to me very probable . . ." (p 617); and ". . . with regard to this power of the devils over human bodies, believed equally by the Jews and other nations . . . the divinity ought not to be made a party concerned in imposing diseases, which may possibly have natural causes; unless it be expressly declared that they were inflicted immediately by the hand of God" (p 623). After "Mead" MS F inserts "& Lardner", with reference to Nathaniel Lardner (1684–1768) *The Case of the Demoniacs Mentioned in the New Testament* (1758): most of the cases are "distempers" (pp 24, 39, 66); Matt 17.15 concerns epilepsy (p 25). C is rejecting materialistic and rationalistic explanations that minimise the significance of spiritual disturbance. C read Lardner (*Works*, 11 vols 1788) with admiration for his "truly Christian Spirit", though he came to think him a "dull man" inclined toward Socinianism. *CL* ii 821–4; vi 894; *Friend (CC)* i 30n; *CN* iii 3907 f 56.

[6] Perhaps this is a reference to John 10.20, "He hath a devil, and is mad" (Δαιμόνιον ἔχει καὶ μαίνεται). Poole *Synopsis criticorum* iv i 1275 and Arthur Young *A Dissertation on the Gospel-*

St Luke wrote his history from the accounts and documents of other persons, some eyewitnesses and others not. He tells what was told him with the strictest veracity, and draws no conclusions from the narrative.[7] During or just after Christ's miraculous cure of a madman a herd of swine are frightened and run into the sea. Those are the facts. Like most madmen, the man in this instance assumed the name of some other *g*person or thing. "I am Legion"; says he;—the Roman name running in his fevered imagination—he then acts as a madman, to rush into the swine, that hated and galling mark and sign of the Jewish subjugation to the Roman dominion. The swine are frightened and the Jewish mob, who firmly believed these possessions, cried out "the Devils have entered the swine".[8] To this day we say the Devil is in him.—

g f 11

Daemoniacks (1760) both accepted the view of "the great Mr. Mede" on this passage that "the Daemoniacks were no other than what we call Madmen and Lunaticks" (Young p 30). Matt 4.24 names "those which were lunatick" σεληνιαζομένους, moon-stricken) among the diseased and tormented brought to Jesus. RSV follows Mead, Lardner, and Young (and James Moffatt) in translating Matthew's list as "demoniacs, epileptics, and paralytics". Referring to the madmen of Matt 17.15, 18, C wrote: "St. John names them not at all, but seems to include them under the description of diseased or deranged persons". *LR* I 212.

[7] About to speak specifically of Luke 8.26–39 on Jesus' driving of a legion of devils into the Gadarene swine, C refers first to 1.1–3.

[8] C gave a similar interpretative paraphrase of Luke 8 in a note on Webster *The Displaying of Supposed Witchcraft* 78. *CM (CC)* V. Lardner, Young, and Eichhorn all appeal to Josephus and Justin Martyr on the common Jewish belief in demonic possession. Distinguishing between such common superstition and the purposes of Jesus, as C distinguished in Luke's account between the recorded facts and the interpretation then common, Young (p 40) agreed with Lardner: the Saviour's task was "to cure the Distemper, not the mistake of the People".

Writing to a Unitarian in 1802, C was reluctant to let anybody off so easily: Jesus' mission was to subvert false doctrine and respect the swine as private property. *CL* II 823–4. The interpretation in TT is consonant with C's argument that "belief in Angels and that sort of poultry is nowhere countenanced" in the Bible, unless in Job, as John Frere learned in Dec 1830 when he cited the words of Jesus on the casting out of devils (Mark 9.29 or Matt 17.21) as an exception to C's thesis: "*C.* There is nothing I say in the New Testament to countenance the belief in Angels. For what are the three first Gospels? Every one must see that they are mere plain narrations, not of things as they are but of things as they appeared to the ignorant disciples—but when we come to John, Mr. F., there we find the difference. He told things as they were, and therefore you must not believe everything that you read implicitly; and with respect to Devils entering into a man, why it is quite absurd. What do we mean when we say a thing is in another? Why 'in' is merely a relative term. [The argument, though I was compelled to assent to it, I am sorry to say was far above my comprehension, and therefore I could not catch it, still less bag it and carry it away,—however it proved that there could be no Devils and still less could there be Devils in a man.] Spirit therefore was not more in a

Compare the awfully solemn manner in which in the Old Testament the prophets relate the communications of God to them—Deuteronomy—Isaiah &c—with the preface of St Luke.[9] If you suppose what is commonly called inspiration of Scripture to be dictation, see what horrid blasphemies—what disgusting absurdities you run into! Try the Psalms by this test! The Spirit of God doubting what he knew infallibly!—fearing what he could not fear!—hating what he could not strictly hate![10] The spirit of Grace is evident in the Scriptures, and it is enough for us.

Conceive St Luke's case thus: The Duke of Wellington made me his secretary, and said, "You shall write a history of the War, and I will give you from my own mouth a detailed account of all that took place. I will dictate the language or the matter to you." Then, having received a perfect account of the whole War from the Duke's own mouth, I begin my book thus—"Whereas several corporals, some in[h] service, and some out, and a serjeant's wife have written accounts and pamphlets concerning the war—I also have[i] availed myself of their assistance and have attempted to set out the following history"—without hinting a word about the Duke's authority.[11]

[j]The Apostles were teaching and preaching Christianity; they had something else to do besides simply recording anecdotes of our Saviour's life and actions. St John in his Gospel mentions nothing but what was the occasion and foundation of a doctrine. St Luke clubs eight chapters together of our Lord's parables, without reference to time or place.[k12]

---

[h] ~~weh~~ in   [i] ~~will~~ ⟨have⟩ avail⟨ed⟩   [j] f 11[v]   [k] [See [e-k], above]

---

man than it was out of him, the mistake arising from a misconception of the word *in*. As for all notions of men with wings, of course they are absurd in the extreme." E. M. Green "A Talk with Coleridge" *Cornhill Magazine* NS XLII (1917) 408–9.

[9] Luke 1.1–4, contrasted with, say, Isa 8.1: "Moreover the Lord said unto me, Take thee a great roll, and write in it with a man's pen . . .".

[10] C's point is clear enough; e.g. fear in Ps 52.6, 72.5, hatred in 26.5, 139.21–2, and perhaps the doubt in 74.1, "O God, why hast thou cast us off for ever?" and 74.22, "Arise, O God, plead thine own cause". For the argument see *CIS* (1840) 34–7, 44–58. Nothing in this long entry survived the family censorship of MS F.

[11] C paraphrases Luke 1.1–3 to show that an author whose account has been dictated by the highest authority could only with absurdity acknowledge as his sources other redactors of accounts from witnesses. Moffatt's translation follows C's line exactly: "Inasmuch as a number of writers have essayed to draw up a narrative of the established facts in our religion, exactly as these have been handed down to us by the original eye-witnesses who were in the service of the Gospel Message, and inasmuch as I have gone carefully over them all myself from the beginning, I have decided . . . to write them out . . .".

[12] C's statement is true in essence, if not in detail; time and place are referred to even in Luke 15–16, but do not determine the order of presentation in Luke 8–21, which includes parables assigned more clearly to occasions in Mark or Matthew or both.

Nature is—the sum total of the laws and powers of the material world, which for the sake of perspicuity we reduce to Unity, and for the convenience of Language we personify.[13]

---

29. April 1830.

Plants exist *in* themselves; Insects *by* themselves; Men *for* themselves.[1]
Growth only in Plants; Irritability or better Instinctivity in Insects.[2]

[36:145]

[13] This carefully neutral definition is consonant even with C's acceptance in 1795 of arguments for divine creation from universal design—LRR Lect 1 in *Lects 1795 (CC)* esp 89–94—but a note to C's "Essays on the Principles of Method" had distinguished energetic nature, *forma formans* (in Schelling's terms), from material nature, *forma formata*, "the sum total of all things, as far as they are objects of our senses, and consequently of possible experience—the aggregate of phaenomena, whether existing for our outward senses, or for our inner sense". *Friend (CC)* I 467n. In *BL* ch 12 he confined the word "nature" to objective phenomena, but continued in later works to toy with a nature he had called in *The Friend* "a vision of the Most High" and "the aggregated *material* of duty". *BL (CC)* I 254–5; *Friend (CC)* I 112; cf *SM (CC)* 71–2, *C&S (CC)* 175–6, 185.

The entry in MS B has no vertical line to indicate use by HNC.

[1] C said he had seen "in earliest manhood" that the relation of vegetable and animal "was not a harmony of resemblance, but of contrast". *Friend (CC)* I 470. In a marginal note on Hugh J. Rose's copy of *The Friend* C corrected his discussion of the scale of life to stress individuation rising to the wakefulness of the philosopher: "Plants are Life dormant; Animals = Somnambulists". *Friend (CC)* II 75n. The scale from the productivity of plants to self-consciousness in humanity is a central subject in Schelling, Steffens, Schubert, and other *Naturphilosophen*, and also for Blumenbach and other physiologists of whom C

was a frequent reader. On the plant as love and the insect as lust see *IS* 224–5.

[2] Albrecht von Haller had set forth in 1752 the distinctions between productivity or growth in plants, irritability or contractility in all muscular tissues and therefore in all animals, and sensibility in all tissue supplied with nerve. These distinctions were basic to all subsequent natural history and physiology. C defined instinct, in "On Instinct in Connexion with the Understanding"—*AR* (1825) 238–42—as "a power of selecting and adapting means to proximate ends *according to circumstances*" (p 239), a definition that distinguishes insects from vegetables rather than from higher animals, and shows why C preferred instinctivity to irritability as the distinguishing leap in classification. The general lawgiver on instinct was Hermann Samuel Reimarus (1694–1768) *Allgemeine Betrachtungen über die Triebe der Tiere hauptsächlich über ihre Kunsttriebe* (Hamburg 1762), but C and J. H. Green were stimulated to definition by Jean Pierre Huber *The Natural History of Ants* (in French 1810, tr 1820) and the confirmation of Huber in William Kirby and William Spence *An Introduction to Entomology* (4 vols 1815–26)—see *AR* (1825) 210, *AR* (1843) I 183–90, II 328–34. C's chief purpose in all these explorations was to preserve reason as a higher power than instinctive intelligence. The brief entries at this point in TT belong to a wide area of interest and information. The context in C's own *Weltanschauung* for the theory of life set forth in *TL* can be seen in his letter to EC of Jul 1826 (*CL* VI 593–601) or the an-

Insect because the life is in sections; diffused equally over all parts.[3]

[36:146]

Brown's theory will not account for Sleep; and Darwin's will not account for Death.[4]

[36:143]

---

notated version of it in *C&S (CC)* 173–85. Green consolidated his and C's definitions of instinct in App F of *Vital Dynamics* (1840), reprinted in *AR* (1843) II 328–34. *OED* cites the *TT* (1835) passage as the earliest appearance of the word "instinctivity"; C had used it as early as 1824. *CN* IV 5168.

[3] Kirby and Spence *Introduction to Entomology* III (1826) 4–5 traced to Aristotle the name and the defining segmental description of insects (*entoma*); C emphasised the diffusion of life through all the parts. There are notes of c 1822–4 on insects in N 28: *CN* IV 4879–96, 5175–83 passim. C left with WW his Friedrich Christian Lesser *Théologie des insectes* tr Pierre Lyonnet (2 vols The Hague 1742) and François Huber *New Observations on the Natural History of Bees* (Edinburgh 1806). WW LC 336, 340.

[4] John Brown (1735–88), a testy Scottish reformer of medicine, argued in *Elementa medicinae* (Edinburgh 1780) that life depends upon an even supply of stimulation or excitability; all illness can be classified as *asthenic*, from debility, or *sthenic*, from an excess excitement, leading in turn to debility. Death results (in Beddoes's translation) from "a perfect extinction of the excitement, either from a complete exhaustion or extreme abundance of excitability". Brown *The Elements of Medicine* pt ii ch 7 tr Brown, rev Beddoes (2 vols 1795) I 266. For C's intense early interest in the Beddoes edition see *CN* I 388 and n. In *Zoonomia; or, The Laws of Organic Life* (1794–6) Erasmus Darwin (1731–1802) advanced the materialistic hypothesis that all the phenomena of life derive from excitement of fibrous motions (irritative, sensitive, voluntary, or associate) by a single subtle fluid, the "sensorial power"; external stimulants working through this

"spirit of animation" caused a contraction of fibres in the organism thus animated. To Heinroth's proposal, in *Lehrbuch der Anthropologie* (1822), that life is sustained by magnetic power, C objected in a note dated Aug 1826: "the *function* is put for the *Principle*. And this may constitute the difference between Sleep and Death—that in Sleep the restoration of the exhausted irritability and sensibility is found in the functions of Vegetive Life—in Death by a deeper retraction into the common Principle of all 3 Powers." *CM (CC)* II 1008.

If John Brown is the counter-theorist to Darwin referred to, HNC could assume that educated readers would know what sort of theories were at issue. Darwin had a more explicit antagonist on the subject of sleep in Thomas Brown (1778–1820) *Observations on the Zoonomia of Erasmus Darwin, M.D.* (Edinburgh 1798) and more general works of 1820 and 1822 on the human mind, all of which rebutted Darwin's materialistic associationism. Darwin said that in sleep the power of volition is totally suspended, with muscular motions and the nerves of sensation continuing unchanged; T. Brown answered that it is the body rather than volition that changes in sleep: Darwin explained only the phenomena of sleep, not sleep. *Observations* 345–70. C himself rejected anecdotally the idealist's view of sleep: *BL* ch 18 *(CC)* II 63–4.

C remembered "frequent amicable disputes" in the period of Darwin's ascendancy over others—*BL* ch 1 *(CC)* I 19—and he debated religion with Darwin himself at Derby in 1796 (*CL* I 177). He is reported by others in 1799 and 1804: "Coleridge always spoke with disrespect of the celebrated Dr. Darwin. His excessive vanity, he said, betrayed itself on all occasions; and he expressed

It is said that every excitation is followed by a commensurate exhaustion; the excitation of Nitrous Oxide is an exception; it leaves no exhaustion on the bursting of the bubble.[5] It prevents the decarbonating of the blood, and would produce apoplexy. The blood becomes black as ink. The voluptuous sensation is produced by the compression and resistance.   [36:144]

If an inscription be put on my tomb, it may be that I was an enthusiastic Lover of the Church, and as enthusiastic a Hater of the Individuals who now govern it, and have betrayed it.[6]   [36:150]

---

doubts of the truth of many of the facts brought forward by him in support of his opinions. His infidel philosophy he looked upon as most contemptible.'' Carlyon I 88. And ''Coleridge sd. Dr. Darwin was 'a great *plagiarist*. He was like a pigeon picking up peas, and afterwards voiding them with excrementitious additions'.'' Farington *Diary* VI 2276. C's point, that Darwin plagiarised from nature, is carefully explained by David W. Ulrich in the *Wordsworth Circle* XV (1984) 78–9. Cf C's remarks on RS, 19 Sept 1830 (at n 23), below.

[5] Humphry Davy conducted experiments with nitrous oxide (''laughing gas'') at Thomas Beddoes's Pneumatic Institution, Clifton, in 1799–1800. Beddoes mentions C's first experience with the exhilarant in a postscript to *Notice of Some Observations Made at the Medical Pneumatic Institution* (Bristol 1799). C's report concerning this and three other dosages, of Oct 1799 and perhaps May or Jun 1800, appears in Davy *Researches, Chemical and Physical; Chiefly Concerning Nitrous Oxide . . .* (1800) 516–18: ''The first time I inspired the nitrous oxide, I felt a highly pleasurable sensation of warmth over my whole frame, resembling that which I remember once to have experienced after returning from a walk in the snow into a warm room. The only motion which I felt inclined to make, was that of laughing at those who were looking at me. My eyes felt distended, and towards the last, my heart beat as if it were leaping up and down. On removing the mouth-piece, the whole sensation went off almost instantly.'' The second time: ''My heart beat more violently than the first time. This was after a hearty dinner.'' The doses were five to seven quarts; C's third experience was still more violent: ''Towards the last, I could not avoid, nor indeed felt any wish to avoid, beating the ground with my feet; and after the mouth-piece was removed, I remained for a few seconds motionless, in great extacy.'' He concluded: ''The fourth time was immediately after breakfast. The first few impressions affected me so little that I thought Mr. Davy had given me atmospheric air: but soon felt the warmth beginning about my chest, and spreading upward and downward, so that I could feel its progress over my whole frame. My heart did not beat so violently; my sensations were highly pleasurable, not so intense or apparently local, but of more unmingled pleasure than I had ever before experienced.'' C's accounts appear in full, with a few changes in punctuation, in Davy *Collected Works* III 306–7 and in an informative study by Suzanne R. Hoover ''Coleridge, Humphry Davy, and Some Early Experiments with a Consciousness-altering Drug'' *Bulletin of Research in the Humanities* LXXXI (1978) 17–18. In Lect 12 of 6 Mar 1818 C gave an example of wilful mishearing five minutes after he had inhaled nitrous oxide at the Royal Institution: *Lects 1808–19 (CC)* II 210.

[6] *TT* (1835) mitigated this fierce passage by omitting ''the Individuals who now govern it'', adding ''be they who they may'' to the final clause, and supplying an emollient footnote. C objected particularly to the arguments from expediency by the current leaders of the

The black Colonel in the Beggar Girl is a very good character.[7]

[36:149]

*a*The Dog alone of all brute animals has a στόργη[8] or affection *upwards* to Man.[9]   [36:147]

The Ant *b*and Bee are*c* much nearer Man in the Understanding or Faculty of adaptive means to ends than the Elephant &c.—[10]   [36:148]

a f 12   *b-c* is & Bee are

Church; e.g. HNC's friend Charles James Blomfield (1786–1857), bp of London from 1828: *CL* vi 846–7. On C's changed opinion of William Howley (1766–1848), abp of Canterbury from 1828, see esp *CL* v 440, 475, vi 586. In 1832, after Howley introduced three bills in the Lords to mollify opponents of the Church, C contrasted Asgill with "our Clergy, at least all such as the B. of L., Arch B. of Cant.—of Dublin &c, the Paleyians and Mageeites". Letter to HNC [7 May 1832]: *CL* vi 902.

[7] Agnes Maria Bennett (c 1750–1808) *The Beggar Girl and Her Benefactors* (7 vols 1797). Col Buchanan, who had turned "a sort of black" from a bilious disease in India, hid his kindness in adopting the beggar girl, Rosa, by saying, "You see that creeping bundle of filth sweeping the path with rags after me" (i 8, 56). The first of her benefactors, he sent presents from India and left a deposit for Rosa, but "the blackamoor Colonel left no will" (ii 120). On 8 Apr 1820 to Allsop, C included "Betty (in Mrs Bennett's Beggar-girl)" as better than the best of Scott's "*female* characters" (*CL* v 34), and on a leaf listing four novels by Mrs Bennett that he would like to read (said to have been removed from a copy of *Conciones*), C called *The Beggar Girl* "the best novel . . . since Fielding". Ms in Fales Library, New York University. According to HNC's note to this entry in *TT* (1835), C's usual praise of *The Beggar Girl* ended in commendation of Jane Austen. SC observed to HCR in 1847 that WW'S lack of appreciation of humour explained "his disregard for Jane Austen's novels, which my Father & Uncle so admired". *CRC* ii 643.

[8] "Love", especially of parents for offspring. In the contrast of plant and insect in BM MS Egerton 2800 f 155, C concluded that both join "in the submissive love of the female—and with the victory of the former in the στοργή" and thus combine in the bird, for "the hatching and brooding are vegetable processes". *IS* 225. For uses of the word *storgè* in authors read by C see *CN* iii 3765n.

[9] C wrote similarly of the dog and "of the storgè or maternal instinct of beasts" in *Friend (CC)* i 155. Distinguishing canine breeds, in a note on Steffens *Caricaturen des Heiligsten* (1819) ii 74, C declared "the *man-minded* Pudel, the Philanthropist κατ' εξοχην of a philanthropic Genus". HNC's note to this entry in *TT* (1835) repeated C's opinions on the affections of dogs and the intelligence of ants. The conversation would have had heightened interest in the presence of advocates for the cat and the horse. C. R. Leslie reported: "I once found Coleridge driving the balls on a bagatelle board for a kitten to run after them. He noticed that, as soon as the little thing turned its back to the balls it seemed to forget all about them, and played with its tail. 'I am amused,' he said, 'with their little short memories.' " *Autobiographical Recollections* i 50.

[10] In a letter of 12 Feb 1821 to Tulk on reason and understanding, with citations of "Huber's Treatise on Ants", C distinguished vital power, "by which *means are adapted* to proximate ends"; instinct, "*which adapts* means to proximate ends"; and understanding, which so adapts "according *to varying circumstances*". *CL* v 137; cf *AR* (1825) 239, as cited in n 2 to 29 Apr 1830, above. In TT the ant and bee are given a medial position higher than all other animals ex-

2. May. 1830.

Holland and the Netherlands ought to be seen once, because no other country is like them. Every thing is artificial. You must admire the combinations of vivid green and water and building; but every thing is so distinct and rememberable that you would not improve your conception by visiting the country a hundred times over. It is interesting to see a country and a nature made, as it were, by Man, and to compare it with God's nature.[1]

Remark the identity (it is more than proximity) of dirt and filth in Holland; in all that concerns the dignity of and reverence for the human person, the most disgusting dirtiness; in all that concerns property, a painted cleanliness that is quite persecuting. You must not walk in their gardens; hardly look into them.[2]   [36:151]

They seem very happy and comfortable, but it is the happiness of an-

---

cept man. Thomas Andrew Knight *Phil Trans* (RS) xcvii (1807) 239 is quoted by Kirby and Spence *Introduction to Entomology* ii (1817) 201: "Brutes . . . have language to express sentiments of love, of fear, of anger; but they seem unable to transmit any impression they have received from external objects. But the language of bees is more extensive; if not a language of ideas, it is something very similar." The passage in *Friend (CC)* i 155 on "animal *reason*" cites the "halfreas'ning elephant" from Pope *Essay on Man* 1.7.16. It is not clear why MS B recorded the entries on C's tomb and *The Beggar Girl* as an interruption to the entries on forms of life.

Talk dated 29 Apr, Thursday, may have occurred a day or so earlier or later; under the date 29 Apr 1830 SC wrote to HNC that she hopes to go to Mrs Gillman's but still expects him to return from Lincoln's Inn at five o'clock the next day. UT ms.

[1] When C accompanied WW and his daughter Dora on a tour of Belgium and the Rhineland in Jul–Aug 1828 they returned by way of Nijmegen, Utrecht, Amsterdam, Leiden, and Rotterdam to Antwerp. *CL* vi 749. Dora kept a journal of the tour (now at DCL). The *polderland*, below sea level, had been made habitable by dikes and drainage ditches. Netherlands, besides a minimum of natural land frontiers, has a sufficient lack of picturesque undulation to encourage artificial planting and other decoration by human hand. C's "Holland" refers to that nation; "the Netherlands" apparently to Belgium and Luxembourg, Low Countries under the control of the Hapsburgs until 1794 and known then as the Austrian and Spanish Netherlands.

[2] *TT* (1835) included in this entry, from MS B f 104ᵛ, C's two verse epigrams on the stenches of Cologne: *PW* (EHC) i 477. *TT* (1836) kept the note on "filthy habits of the people" but omitted the verses, which had been printed in *PW* (1834) ii 144. It is the "painted cleanliness", with the famed Calvinistic Protestantism, that made Holland more apt for C's paradox than the Rhineland. A reputedly sour visitor had noted of Amsterdam in 1815 its "universal propriety & cleanliness—ever chearful, ever busy—whiteness of the linen, & the red & white complexions of the women & children", and near Amsterdam "every house like the cottages of the *rich* in England—Walked in three Gardens". *The Italian Journal of Samuel Rogers* ed J. R. Hale (1956) 292–5. Rogers read these notes to WW in 1823, before WW left on a tour of Holland from which he returned "well pleased". *CRB* i 292, 296. WW reported near the end of the journey in 1828 that "Mʳ Coleridge is not in the best plight". *WL* (*L* rev) i 621.

imals; in vain do you look for the sweet breath of Hope and Advancement among them.[3]

As to their villas and gardens, they are not to be compared to an ordinary London merchant's box. [36:152]

I should like to see Strasbourg.[4]

Religion is the most gentlemanly thing in the world.[5] [36:153]

The Walkerite[a] creed is a sort of Calvinism and Quakerism mixed together.[6] [36:156]

I never could get any information from the Biblical Commentators. Cocceius is the best; but they have an art in skipping all difficulties.[7]

[36:155]

[a] Walkerites

[3] *TT* (1835) quoted, in a footnote, WW's couplet on the necessity of hope for true nobility (reading "For" for "That") from a sonnet of 1803, "These times strike monied worldlings with dismay", which declares, like C's *Fears in Solitude*, that riches bring worldliness, timidity, and contraction of spirit. On the importance of "hope" to C, see *CN* II 3067n.

[4] In notes for Lect 2 of 13 Jan 1818 of the literary series and in Lect 8 of the lectures on the history of philosophy of 1819, influenced by Friedrich Schlegel, C had cited the cathedral of Strasbourg (in German, Strassburg), with those of York and Milan, as the quintessence of Gothic symbolism and the victory of Christian aspiration over pagan order. *CN* III 4384 f 153ᵛ: *Lects 1808–19 (CC)* II 74; *P Lects* (1949) 256–7. Entry previously unpublished.

[5] *TT* (1835) expanded this sentence to specify superiority to the army, reputed "embellisher of manners". C's point becomes clearer in later references to St Paul, especially 5 Jul 1834 (sentence after n 13).

[6] John Walker (1768–1833) abandoned the established Church of Ireland and founded his own intensely Calvinistic sect in Dublin in 1804 as The Church

of God. He removed to London in 1819. The Walkerites, often called the "Separatists", are the "New Jerusalemites" of n 16 to 13 Apr, above. HNC's interest derived partly from the proximity of Walker's church to HNC's office in Lincoln's Inn Fields, and presumably also from the details that RS officiously assumed HNC not to know. RS corrected simultaneously HNC's note to this entry in *TT* (1835) and the one of 13 Apr: "Vol. 1. 97, 116. The Swedenborgians are the New Jerusalemites. Sara can tell you who the Walkerites are:—a mere handfull. Some of them were here once, the homo (whose name I forget) (I think it was Chase) was connected with Hurst the booksellers firm, & Sara & her mother had fallen in with some of his connections in London. I noticed them in a sentence in the Q.R.—but cannot call to mind the place, nor the particulars of the sect." UT ms. One obituary jocosely explained Walker's departure from Dublin as his taking 1 Cor 16.20 literally and having each congregationist kiss the person in the next seat. *G Mag* CLXIII (1833) ii 540–1. *TT* (1835) I 116n disappeared after RS's challenge, along with the note of 13 Apr it (and RS) referred to.

[7] Johannes Cocceius, or Johann Koch (1603–69), professor of theology at Lei-

*a*3. May. 1830.

Women have their heads in their hearts. Man seems to have been destined for a superior being; as things are, I think women generally better creatures than men.[1] They have weaker appetites and weaker intellects, but much stronger affections. A man with a bad heart has been sometimes saved by a strong head; but a corrupt woman is lost for ever. Boys are usually prettier infants than girls.   [36:154]

---

7. May 1830.

Horne Tooke was pre-eminently a ready-witted man.[1] He had that clearness which is founded on shallowness; he doubted nothing, and therefore gave you all he himself meant with great completeness. His voice was

a f 12ᵛ

den. Often in 1820–6 C recommended Cocceius with such phrases as "the best & most spiritual" and "learned & generally judicious". *CL* v 480, vi 550, 557–8, 562. He borrowed a copy of Cocceius *Opera omnia* (10 vols Amsterdam 1701) from a Mr Tudor in 1825 and used it for the next two years before returning it (with his annotations written in vol v). *CM (CC)* ii 46. In a note on RS *Life of Wesley* i 297 he wished RS had read Cocceius on Gen 1, but in a note on Anne Gillman's Bible, probably in 1826, he found that on Matt 17.25–6 (as elsewhere) Cocceius, "the only Commentator in my possession", is "prolix where there is no difficulty and regularly fails me wherever I need help". *CM (CC)* iv, i 451. As early as 1819, and with renewed vigour after Eichhorn's death in 1827, C regarded him as "the best of the *historical* Critics", with Richard Field *Of the Church* above Cocceius for divinity—but Eichhorn a blind man confronting colours. *CL* iv 929; note on Eichhorn *NT: CM (CC)* ii 491. He queried on a flyleaf Eichhorn's failure to mention Cocceius, "the first rational Commentator on the Apocalypse", in *Commentarius in Apocalypsin Joannis: CM (CC)* ii 504. Among other Biblical commentaries C consulted were those in Gillman's library: the composite commentaries of Simon Patrick, William Lowth, Richard Arnald, and Daniel Whitby (7 vols 1748–65). *Gillman SC*.

[1] C wrote to W. R. Hamilton in Apr 1832: "Man's heart must be in his *head*. Woman's head must be in her heart." *CL* vi 893–4. When Mrs Gillman first approved and then disapproved a sentence of C's on Scotsmen, C reportedly answered: "A woman judges by her instinct, and not by reason. I'll strike it out, but I've more respect for your first impression than I should probably have for your argument." Anecdote from Richard H. Dana Jr in Flagg *Life and Letters of Allston* 358. In Aug 1833 C supported the belief of Walter Scott's niece Anne that women were too veracious to value a good joke. *CL* vi 958–9.

[1] John Horne, later Tooke (1736–1812), radical politician and philologist. C had praised him in verses of 1796, when both the politics and the philology seemed admirable, but described him to Thomas Wedgwood in 1800, in terms he never after abandoned, as "a clear-headed old man" with "a sort of charletannery". *CL* i 224–5, 559; *PW* (EHC) i 150–1. For a succinct account see James C. McKusick "Coleridge and Horne Tooke" *Studies in Romanticism* xxiv (1985) 85–111.

very fine and his tones exquisitely discriminating. His mind had no progression. All that is worth any thing (and that is little) in the Diversions of Purley is contained in a short pamphlet-letter to Mr Dunning; then it was enlarged to an octavo, but not a foot of progression beyond the pamphlet; at last two quarto volumes, and yet, excepting Morning Chronicle lampoons and political insinuations, nothing added to the pamphlet.[2] It argues a base and unpoetical mind to convert so beautiful a subject as that of Language into a political squib.[3] All that is true in his book is taken from Lennep, who gave it for so much as it was worth, and pretended not to make a system of it;[4] Horne Tooke affects to explain the whole origin and philosophy[a] of Language by what is in fact only a mere accident of its history. The abuse of Harris is most shallow and unfair; Harris was dealing (not very profoundly, it is true) with the philosophy of Language; and the moral and metaphysical causes &c;[5] Horne Tooke in writing

[a] ~~history~~ philosophy

[2] Ἔπεα πτερόεντα, *or, The Diversions of Purley* pt 1 (1786) was expanded into two large quartos in the 2nd ed, I (1798), II (1805) and further augmented in an edition ed Richard Taylor (1829). Horne Tooke himself said in 1786 p 102 that the three chapters following were slightly changed from *A Letter to John Dunning, Esq.* (1778). Hazlitt, who thought *Diversions of Purley* "one of the few philosophical works on Grammar that were ever written" but agreed with C that the essence "(and indeed, almost all that is really valuable in it) is contained in his *Letter to Dunning*", summarised the argument: "The whole of his reasoning turns upon showing that the Conjunction *That* is the pronoun *That*, which is itself the participle of a verb, and in like manner that all the other mystical and hitherto unintelligible parts of speech are derived from the only two intelligible ones, the Verb and the Noun." *Spirit of the Age* (2nd ed 1825) 113–14. C would have liked parts of John Fearn (1768–1837) *Anti-Tooke; or an Analysis of the Principles and Structure of Language, Exemplified in the English Tongue* (2 vols 1824–7), which refuted in Coleridgian metaphor the grammarians' error that word represents idea represents object: instead, words are militiamen, for "*all that happens* DURING THE FRAY, HAPPENS TO THE SUBSTITUTE: and the Constituent, who is not present, has nothing at all to do with it" (II 337). Horne Tooke's general linguistic principle is that "Words are the *signs* of things" (1786 p 25). Otto Funke *Englische Sprachphilosophie im späteren 18. Jahrhundert* (Bern 1934) 88 quotes C on Horne Tooke with disapproval, but grants that the *Grundanschauungen of Purley* appears in the pamphlet of 1778. C is scolded also by Hans Aarsleff *The Study of Language in England 1780– 1860* (Princeton, N.J. 1967) 61n.

[3] *Diversions of Purley* included throughout such political examples as the rise and fall of kingdoms (1786 pp 123– 4). In pt 2, which is dedicated to the jurors who acquitted Horne Tooke in 1794, ch 1, entitled "The Rights of Man", is a dialogue with Francis Burdett; II 141–3 concerns Gilbert Wakefield, with blanks (until 1829) of political censorship; and there are other such passages.

[4] Johan Daniel van Lennep (1724– 71), Dutch philologist. His *Praelectiones academicae, de analogia linguae graecae* ed Everardus Scheidius (Utrecht 1790) derives other parts of speech from forms of the noun and verb. Scheidius was here editing Lennep's *In analogiam linguae Graecae* (Utrecht 1779); see also *CM* II 380n.

[5] *Letter to Dunning* 16–24, 66–7 belittled James Harris (1709–80) *Hermes or*

about the formation[b] of words only thought he was explaining the philosophy of Language, which is a very different thing. Horne Tooke was very shallow in the Northern dialects. What stuff is all that about the genders of the Sun and Moon in German![6] Originally, before Luther, [c]in the Plat-Deutsch of the north of Germany, there were only two articles—Die (masculine and feminine) and Das (neuter). Then it was Die Sonna in a masculine sense, as we say *The* Sun. Luther, in constructing the Hoch-Deutsch, took the article Der (m.) from the Ober-Deutsch, and constituted the three articles of the present High German—Der, Die, Das.[7] Naturally therefore it would then have been Der Sonna; but here Luther was led by the analogy of the Latin Grammar, and as Sonna had the ar-

---

[b] ~~verbal~~ formation   [c] f 13

A Philosophical Inquiry Concerning Universal Grammar (1751; 3rd ed 1771). *Diversions of Purley* quoted Robert Lowth's praise of *Hermes* in order to refute it. In general a follower of Aristotle, Harris speculated on the causes of grammatical gender not unlike C on *Die* and *Das*, but to Horne Tooke's complete scorn (1786 pp 73–80). In *BL* ch 16 C praised Harris "on the means of acquiring a just taste". *BL (CC)* II 36n.

[6] Although he essayed Anglo-Saxon (Old English), Horne Tooke referred to Gothic in 1778–86 only for examples. His ms notes in Edward Lye *Dictionarium Saxonico et Gothico-Latinum* ed Owen Manning (2 vols 1772) show close attention (now in BM). C is pointing to Horne Tooke's knowledge of classical rather than of Germanic languages, without intended reference to romance languages. Harris expounded an Aristotelian distinction that the sun was masculine "from communicating Light, which was native and original, as well as from the vigorous warmth and efficacy of his Rays", and the moon feminine, "from being the Receptacle only of another's Light, and from shining with rays more delicate and soft" (1771 p 45). With examples and authorities, Horne Tooke responded that the genders were reversed in Asiatic and in Anglo-Saxon and other northern languages; English poets from Shakespeare on had simply followed "their Greek and Latin masters" (1786 pp 75–7 and nn; in 1798 he added an example of his point from John

Gower). C concluded his discussion by noting that Harris's distinction, which he would like to accept, is valid only if primitive speakers knew that the moon's light was reflected. *TT* (1835) expanded the sentence with a Latin tag, *decantata fabula*, "oft-sung tale": see 36:157 n 1. C seems not to have known that John Bruckner, roused by Priestley's acceptance of Horne Tooke on the moon and finding an earlier application of Horne Tooke's principle by Albert Schultens, had pointed out that *Maan* in Low Dutch, and possibly the moon in languages he and Horne Tooke were both weak in, was feminine. "I. Cassander" *Criticisms on The Diversions of Purley* (1790) 22–3, 79.

[7] C gave related accounts in *BL* ch 10 *(CC)* I 210 and in a stray leaf watermarked 1816, in HNC's hand and probably torn from MS B (VCL S MS 20 Clutch 4; cf VCL LT 17). C's explanation of Luther's sources for *Neuhochdeutsch* is as near to the explanations of later authorities as they are to each other; e.g. Paul Pietsch *Martin Luther und die hochdeutsche Schriftsprache* (Breslau 1883) 36, 92, 101; Friedrich Kluge *Von Luther bis Lessing: Sprachgeschichtliche Aufsätze* (2nd ed Strassburg 1888) 132. Luther's translation of the NT in 1522 established the form of modern written German. And see n 10, below. Luther's German is described as partly new, partly regional by R. E. Keller *The German Language* (1978) 380–4.

bitrary feminine termination of the Latin, he left it with its old article Die, which originally meaning masculine and feminine now meant feminine only. The Minnesingers and all the old poets always use the Sun as masculine, and since Luther's time, the poets feel the awkwardness of the classical gender affixed to it so much, that they scarcely ever allude to it, but say Phœbus instead.[8] There never was a nation that did not consider the Sun as the masculine power. The Moon does not so clearly demand a feminine as the Sun a masculine sex; it may be considered negatively; yet if the reception of its light from the Sun were known, *that* would be a good reason, as being the recipient, for making her feminine.   [36:157]

English article *The* is from the *Die* of the Plat-Deutsch—and no doubt originally *That* was used for *Das*, as a neuter article.[9]   [36:158]

The Plat-Deutsch was a compact language like the English, not admitting much agglutination; the Ober-Deutsch was fuller, richer, and fonder of agglutinating words together.[10]   [36:159]

Horne Tooke said his friends might, if they pleased, go as far as Slough; he should go no farther than Hounslow; but that was no reason why he should not keep them company as far as their road was the same.[11] The

---

[8] C discussed this development more fully, again with a rejection of Horne Tooke, in a letter of 1825 to EC. *CL* v 490–1.

[9] The discovery in the 1780s by Sir William Jones and others of the place of Sanskrit in the Indo-European family of languages and the formulation of Grimm's Law on consonant-shifts by Jakob Grimm (1785–1863) in 1822, from an enunciation by Rasmus Christian Rask (1787–1832) in 1818, had collectively made it possible to express such relations between Platt-Deutsch and English as cognate rather than as direct English indebtedness to the German dialects. Considered vis-à-vis the etymologies of the Cambridge scholar Jacob Bryant (1715–1804) in *A New System, or, an Analysis of Ancient Mythology* (3 vols 1774–6; 3rd ed 6 vols 1807), C is a model of precaution.

[10] In *BL* ch 10 *(CC)* I 207–9 C attributed his knowledge of Teutonic lan-

guages and early Germanic literature to study at Göttingen under Thomas Christian Tyschen (1758–1834), professor of Oriental languages, and there is confirmation in a letter of 6 May 1799 to Poole. *CL* I 494.

[11] John "Major" Cartwright (1740–1824) testified at Horne Tooke's trial for treason in 1794 that in 1792 the accused had shown "that his objects did not go to the same lengths as those of Mr. Paine and others" by appeal to travel in a public coach: "And, still pursuing his simile of the stage-coach, he said—When I find myself at Hounslow I get out, those that want to go further may go to Windsor, or where they like; but when I get to Hounslow (applying it to the House of Commons), there I get out, no further will I go, by God." *The Trial of John Horne Tooke, for High Treason . . .* taken in shorthand by Joseph Gurney (2 vols 1795) I 458. Windsor and Hounslow recur in the same metaphor at II 11, 21, 51,

answer is; suppose you know a man is about to commit a robbery at Slough *d*though you do not mean to be his accomplice, have you a right to walk arm in arm with him to Hounslow, and by giving him your countenance, prevent his being taken up? The History of all the World tells us that immoral means will ever intercept good ends.[12]   [36:160]

Enlist the interests*e* of stern morality and religious enthusiasm in the cause of political liberty, as in the time of the old Puritans, and it will be irresistible; but the Jacobins played the whole game of Religion and Morals and Domestic Happiness into the hands of the Aristocrats. Thank God! that they did so! England was saved from civil war by their enormous, their *providential*, blundering.[13]   [36:161]

Can a politician, a statesman, slight the feelings and convictions of the whole Matronage of his country? They are as influential as the Men.[14]

[36:162]

Horne Tooke always made a butt of Godwin.[15] He was a keen, iron man.   [36:163]

d f 13*v*   *e* ~~cause~~ interests

214, 215, 240, 275, 276, 393. The remark is quoted in *Memoirs of Henry Hunt, Esq., Written by Himself* I 502–3 and by Hazlitt *Spirit of the Age* (2nd ed 1825) 110. All give Windsor, not Slough, as the further stage.

[12] Hazlitt objected to Horne Tooke's stopping, C to his going on that road at all; both condemned the concealment of prudential motive. C saw at the base of the prudential always a sacrifice of ends. By "intercept" C adds experiential and metaphysical dimensions to his rejection on moral grounds of Matthew Prior's prudential words, "The end must justify the means" (often traced back to Publilius Syrus Sententia 244: "Honesta turpitudo est pro causa bona"). C had published lines in an *Epigram* of 1802 (*PW*—EHC—I 381):

Greatness and goodness are not *means*,
    but *ends*!
Hath he not always treasures, always
    friends,
The good great man?

[13] Cf "to think filial affection folly, gratitude a crime, marriage injustice, and the promiscuous intercourse of the sexes right and wise . . . cannot increase

the probability that you are a PATRIOT". *Watchman (CC)* 99. By "Jacobin", he declared in *M Post* 21 Oct 1802, he meant one who believed that the happiness of the individual can and must be secured by a government based on universal suffrage and an equal right to property, and moreover—creating a tighter link to the previous entry—endorsed any means necessary to these ends. "Once a Jacobin Always a Jacobin" *EOT (CC)* I 368–70.

[14] Whatever the degree of feminism in this remark, C is making a near equation of the convictions of respectable married women with his own. In an essay of 1820 on Queen Caroline he referred to "that class which is least exposed to the influences of party spirit, the Matronage of the Realm". *EOT (CC)* III 258.

[15] Of William Godwin (1756–1836) Hazlitt had written, "In company, Horne Tooke used to make a mere child of him—or of any man!" *Spirit of the Age* 51. One biographer, noting that Horne Tooke "soon conceived and maintained a poor opinion of Godwin", drew first on this entry in *TT*. Godwin's diary, which recorded a moment of relief on 21 May 1795 from Horne Tooke's

Shiraz wine is bad raisin wine.[16] I never could see any merit in the translations of Persian poetry which I have read. I never saw a ray of Imagination, and only a glimmering of Fancy.[17] The Sacontala is pleasing.[18]

Poetry is something more than Good Sense; but it must be Sense at all events; as a Palace is more than a house, but it must be a House.[19]

---

customary rallying upon "the visionary nature of my politics", repeatedly recorded such remarks as Horne Tooke's declaring *Political Justice* "a very bad book" that "would do a great deal of harm". Ford K. Brown *The Life of William Godwin* (1926) 36, 60, 96–7, 307. *TT* (1835) added that Godwin "had that in him which Tooke could never have understood", and "I saw a good deal of Tooke at one time". Godwin's qualities included the creative energy of a novelist and the Platonic idealism emphasised in F. E. L. Priestley's Introduction to *Enquiry Concerning Political Justice and Its Influence on Morals and Happiness* (3 vols Toronto 1946) III 8–20, 80, 163–4. In Sept 1800 C wished Godwin to "*philosophize* Horn Tooke's System" in the endeavour to eliminate the antithesis of words and things, "elevating, as it were, words into Things, & living Things too". *CL* I 625–6. For HCR on C concerning Godwin and Godwin's detractors, see App F 7, below.

[16] Shiraz or Syrah, dark wine of Persia or its namesake of Hermitage on the Rhône. "It has considerable character, a slightly raisin-like taste with a suggestion of bitterness", said Hugh Johnson on the variety popular in South Africa. *Wine* (1966) 235. George Saintsbury, who gave Hermitage a special place in ch 1 of *Notes on a Cellar-Book* (1920), confessed it was "not a delicate wine", but declared it "the *manliest* French wine I ever drank" and praised the vine, "whose ancestors are said to have been of Shiraz stock imported by the Crusaders". Cf an anecdote of Sir Walter Scott's concerning "a butt of *sheeraz*" an Oriental friend had sent him. J. G. Lockhart *Memoirs of Sir Walter Scott* (5 vols 1900) III 195. HNC probably knew the wine as an after-dinner alternative to port. The transition to the next entry shows that C was aware of the connexion

with Shiraz, the ancient Persian city of wines and poets. His remark, omitted from *TT* (1835), adds emphasis to his opinion of Persian poetry.

[17] When HCR took W. S. Landor to Highgate on 29 Sept 1832 C's opinion was unchanged. "The stay was too short to allow of our entering upon literary matters. He spoke only of Oriental poetry with contempt . . .". *CRB* I 413–14. Besides translations and adaptations by Sir William Jones into English, Latin, and French, most of them included in his collected works of 1799 (reprinted 1807), there had been a number of editions and translations, mostly from Calcutta under stimulus from Jones, of such classical poets as Firdausi (c 941–c 1019), Nizami (c 1140–c 1203), and Hafiz (1320–89). Jones, linguist and jurist, was not dependent upon his services to Persian poetry for C's inclusion of him with two other Orientalists as "scholars of highest rank in the world of letters". *Friend (CC)* I 479n. In addition to the intense activity of English Orientalists, C was aware of German translation, adaptation, quotation, and citation by F. and A. W. Schlegel and of the reflection of this activity in such works as Goethe's *Westöstlicher Divan* (1819). C himself observed that there were no European translations from Persian until the eighteenth century. *CN* III 4500 and n. On C's distinction of imagination vs fancy, see *BL* chs 12–13 *(CC)* I 293–305 and 304 n 4.

[18] *Sakuntalā* or *Shakuntalā*, a drama in seven acts by the fifth-century Hindu dramatist and poet Kālidasā, was translated by Sir William Jones as *Sacontala; or the Fatal Ring: An Indian Drama* (Calcutta 1789), with a 5th ed by 1796. Its influence is felt in the Prologue of Goethe's *Faust* and in Schiller's *Maria Stuart* III i.

[19] As the paragraphing in *TT* (1835)

Arabian poetry is another thing. The Arabian Nights Tales are probably Greek in origin. We have a great loss in the Milesian Tales.[20] Job is pure Arab poetry.[21]   [36:164]

Sir Thomas Munro[f] and Sir Stamford Raffles both great men; but more genius in the latter.[22]   [36:166]

[f] Monro

suggests, this remark implies that Persian poetry, in the translations C had seen, lacked sense. That poetry, according to a sentence inserted in *TT* (1835), is also "deficient in truth".

[20] *TT* (1835) began this entry: "Arabian poetry is a different thing", but the transition led only to the *Arabian Nights' Entertainments*. In 1836, "Arabian poetry" was dropped and the Tales were declared "delightful". C's informal remarks of a lifetime, as well as his poetic practice, confirm the epithet: e.g. *CN* I 58, III 4315, 4317; *Friend (CC)* I 148; Lect 11 of 3 Mar 1818: *Lects 1808–19 (CC)* II 191; *CL* I 347, v 36, 496; *RX* 16, 459–61. What editions C knew is not on record. C, WW, and Lamb consistently defended the *Arabian Nights* and fairy legends as better for children than cautionary tales and other utilitarian fare specifically designed for the very young.

In *TT* (1835) HNC annotated the reference to the Milesian Tales. Some scholars have identified HNC's Aristides of Miletus as compiler of tales from Antonius Diogenes. In 1818 and 1819 in notes for the lectures of 3 Mar 1818 and 11 Mar 1819 C took from Friedrich Schlegel *Geschichte der alten und neuen Litteratur* I 277—as amplified in Terrick Hamilton's "Introduction" to *Antar, a Bedoueen Romance* (1819)—the deduction, sustained with a few qualifications by later scholarship, that the *Arabian Nights* was Persian in origin. *Lects 1808–19 (CC)* II 192, 403 (*CN* III 4500). Here, as in Lect 11, C attempted through the Milesian Tales to establish a Greek source for the Persian originals of the *Arabian Nights*.

[21] *TT* (1835) added: "of the highest and most antique cast"—C's view of truth required an obligation of the Greeks to the Hebrew Bible similar to that of the Persians to the Greeks. Eichhorn *AT* § 641 declared Job so Arabian in structure, tone, idiom, traditional sayings, poetic fantasy, customs, and landscape that the Hebraic author not only must have been born and raised there but must have come from stock able to instil bedouin idioms and customs in him from earliest childhood. *AT* III 500, 507–9. Robert Lowth noted that Idumea in Arabia Petrea had been recognised as the scene of Job as early as the Septuagint. *Lectures on the Sacred Poetry of the Hebrews* tr George Gregory (2 vols 1787) II 347–52 and n. C's works often apply quotations from Job to modern situations. The structural superiority of *Paradise Regained* to *Paradise Lost* C attributed to Milton's taking Job as its model. Annotation on William Hayley *The Life of Milton* (1796): *CM (CC)* II 968–9; conversation with HCR Dec 1810: *MC* 388–9. Joseph Dacre Carlyle (1759–1804) translated *Specimens of Arabian Poetry* (1796) and more specimens in *Poems* (1805), but no poetry from Arabic known to be available to C would suggest a resemblance to Job. On Job see also 27 May 1830 (at n 11) (36:208).

[22] Sir Thomas Munro (1761–1827), 1st Bt; Sir Thomas Stamford Raffles (1781–1826), knighted 1817. In 1819 Raffles occupied Singapore and persuaded the East India Company to acquire it; after he was recalled in 1824 for disobeying orders he founded the Zoological Society. Sophia, Lady Raffles *Memoir of the Life and Public Services of Sir Thomas Stamford Raffles, F.R.S.* (3 vols 1830) was reviewed in *QR* XLII (Mar 1830) 405–50. Munro, governor of Madras 1820–7, had been an able administrator, admired by the Indians as well as by the British. George Robert Gleig *The Life of Major-General Sir Thomas*

Think of the sublimity or rather profundity of that passage in Ezekiel—"Son of Man! shall these dead bones ᵍlive?" "Lord God! Thou knowest!"²³ [36:165]

I never found an idea in any speech or writing of Brougham's.²⁴ Those enormously long speeches are a proof of intellectual weakness. Canning had a sense of the beautiful and the good;²⁵ Brougham never speaks but to abuse, detract, degrade. No man can rightly see an abuse, till he has first mastered the idea of the use of a thing. How beautiful is the idea of the unpaid magistracy of England! Brougham never seems to think of it but as connected with brewers, and barristers, and tyrannical Squire Westerns!²⁶ [36:167]

ᵍ f 14

Munro, Bart and K.C.B. (2 vols 1830) was reviewed in *QR* XLIII (May 1830) 81–111. Murray, who published the book on Raffles, often provided HNC with early copies of *QR*. Reviews there may account for the juxtaposition of Munro and Raffles in TT and for the addition, "the world says otherwise", in *TT* (1835). *QR* gave to both very high praise. The reviewer of the life of Munro quoted Canning's superlatives (p 81) and defended "such good and great men" (p 111). The volumes on Munro appeared separately before and after the Raffles; *Ed Rev* did not review the life of Raffles until July. In 1832 C remembered favourably Raffles' often successful attempts to save British possessions despite the policies of Castlereagh. HEHL MS HM 17229 (N Fᵒ) p 152. Munro and Raffles as "great men" served the empire; Raffles contributed to scientific advance as well.

²³ Ezek 37.3 (var), "corrected" in TT (1835). By "or rather profundity" C reserves the word "sublimity" for more precise applications. In 1805 he had asked in personal despair a question from Ezek 33.11 (or 18.31), "Why will ye die?", meaning, Why do you go on sinning? *CN* II 2454. In letters of 8–15 May 1830 he was expressing repeatedly "a heavy presentiment respecting my own sojourn here". *CL* VI 832–7.

²⁴ Henry Peter Brougham (1778–1868), one of the editors of the Whig *Ed Rev*, reformer, especially of legal procedures; late in 1830 to be made Lord

Chancellor and Baron Brougham and Vaux. In a speech of six columns on law reform, "He felt that he was taking up too much of the house (hear, hear) . . .". *The Times* 30 Apr 1830. His name is suppressed in *TT* (1835), but the reference to "the unhired magistracy" would have made identification easy. About this time C received newspapers, including *The Times*, from E. Chance of Hurst, Chance & Co one day after publication. *CL* VI 840–1, 845. On Brougham see also 21 Nov 1830, below (at n 1).

²⁵ Since C's remarks of 27 Apr 1823, first Canning's public and private actions and then his death in 1827 had mellowed C enough to make Canning the heroic opposite to Brougham's rôle as Thersites the impudent disparager.

²⁶ Brougham had spoken against the unpaid magistracy on 29 Apr. Among the "inferior judges", he said, were "tradesmen, who know nothing of law", although it was better to have such judges in Courts of Request "than to have none". Hansard NS XXIV 258. In Hansard the speech takes thirty-two columns; the apologies for trespassing on the indulgence of the House come at 258, 268–9. The blank for Brougham's name in C's last sentence, *TT* (1835), gave way in *TT* (1836) to a more cautious "some men never seem". Seeking a favour for his friend Hurwitz in 1827, C complimented Brougham on his defence of Queen Caroline in 1820, one of the few occasions when C's position on a

I thought Horner a much superior man.[27]   [36:167]

Canning flashed such a light around the Constitution that it was difficult to see the ruins of the building through it.[28]   [36:168]

9[a] May. 1830.

Shakspeare is the Spinozistic Deity, an omnipresent creativeness.[1] Milton is Prescience; he stands ab extra, and drives a fiery coach and four, making the horses feel the iron curb which holds them.[2] Shakspeare's poetry is characterless; [b]that is,[c] it does not reflect the individual Shakspeare; but John Milton himself is in every line of the Paradise Lost. Shakspeare's rhymed verses are excessively condensed; epigrams with the point every where; but in his blank verse, he is diffused with a linked sweetness long drawn out.[3] In Cymbeline the line—

[a] ~~10~~ 9   [b-c] (i-e)

---

public issue coincided with Brougham's. *CL* VI 668. Squire Western is the irascible father of the heroine in Fielding's *Tom Jones*.

[27] As a Whig politician from Edinburgh and a contributor to the *Ed Rev*, Francis Horner (1778–1817) was aligned with Brougham. C may have been intimate with Horner in London in 1804; to his brother Leonard (1785–1864) C wrote in 1827 of "my knowlege of your Brother and (I need not say) the reverence in which I hold him". *CL* VI 709, 1017. In 1815 C had praised Horner as the only opponent of the Corn Bill who had held firm. *CL* IV 553.

[28] This sentence parodies Canning's own language, as on 17 May 1810, when he declared that "the fabric of monarchy could never be supported except the throne was surrounded, not merely by a decent, but a gorgeous splendour", and 21 May, when he defined the issue of Reform as a question whether the House should declare itself inadequate to perform its duties: "Let the venerable fabric, which has sheltered us for so many ages, and stood unshaken through so many storms, still remain unimpaired and holy; sacred from the rash frenzy of that ignorant innovator who would tear it down, careless and incapable of any sub-

stitution". *Parl Deb* XVI 1092, XVII 161. Speaking against the West Indies planters on 16 Mar 1824, he described the power of Parliament with reference to colonial possessions: "The transcendental power is the *arcanum* of empire, which ought to be kept back within the *penetralia* of the constitution. It exists, but it should be veiled." Hansard NS X 1106.

[1] This is C's finest surviving tribute to Shakespeare as pantheistically, dynamically living throughout the body of his works. The editor of *CN* points to the appositeness of this conversation to an entry of 1810: "The Poet & his Subject, are they not as the Δημιουργος [demiurge, creative spirit] and ὑλή [hyle, matter] of Plato". *CN* III 3952 f 72.

[2] Prescience, though a divine attribute, here distinguishes Milton's foreknowledge of each of his works, through rigid planning of every detail, from the vitality, plenitude, and openness to every emerging potentiality in Shakespeare's evolving creativeness. C later, in *TT* (1835) (36:404), related to Milton a similar characteristic in WW (though the comparison does not appear in the TT passage on which the entry is based, 21 Jul, 1832, below).

[3] Milton *L'Allegro* line 140.

The twin stones on the numbered marge[4]—ought to be
The grimed stones on the umbered marge.
No man can understand Shakspeare's superiority fully, until *d*he has ascertained by comparison all that which he possessed in common with several other great dramatists of his age, and then calculated the surplus which is entirely Shakspeare's own.[5]   [36:169; 35:170]

A worn out metaphor is no longer a metaphor; it suggests no visual image.

Take up arms &c—[6]

"Take up arms" means only *oppose, resist*; besides, it must be remembered, that many figures and breaks which Shakspeare would not have used in an Ode or a Sonnet, he might properly employ in Dramatic dialogue. A speaker in the heat of passion may begin a sentence with one figure, break off, as it were, and join on again with another visually*e* incongruous with the former. For there is a Logic of Passion consistent with itself, though not so in actual nature.[7]

d f 14ᵛ   *e* ~~grammatically~~ visually

---

[4] *Cymbeline* I vi 35–6 (var). C's emendation was printed in *TT* (1835), but Alexander Dyce pointed out in a letter to HNC that "umber'd" had been proposed by Richard Farmer (in *An Essay on the Learning of Shakespeare* 1767), but that "the text is certainly right as it stands". UT ms. Herman Merivale, reviewing *TT* in *Ed Rev* LXI (1835) 150–1, found in the emendation evidence that C "had very little acuteness in verbal criticism, or accurate taste in style". He explained: "Few men of genius have been good verbal critics." HNC withdrew the entry in 1836.

[5] Of C in 1799 Carlyon I 92 reported: ". . . Coleridge dwelt a good deal on the circumstances which, in his opinion, must have largely contributed to the developement of Shakespeare's dramatic powers, which, great as they were by nature, owed their vast expansion, he maintained, to the cheering breath of popular applause, or the enthusiastic gale, rather, of admiration, to which there was no check in the habits or literature of society in that period. There were no writhings, moreover, he added, in those days from the stings of a trafficking criticism, against which he has elsewhere feelingly inveighed . . .". By 1818, even allowing for the rhetoric of a public lecture, Shakespeare was a pineapple growing beside a melon and a gourd: the warmth and soil shared with others did not account for "the golden hue, the ambrosial flavor, the perfect shape of the Pine Apple, or the tufted Crown on its head". Lect 7 of 17 Feb 1818: *Lects 1808–19 (CC)* II 147.

[6] *Hamlet* III i 58 ("to take arms"); *1 Henry VI* III ii 70 ("take up arms"). Not in *TT* (1835), not cancelled in MS B; not in surviving MS F.

[7] C affirms "a Logic of Passion" for aesthetic uses, not for "general nature". In *The Friend* of 8 Jun 1809 he praised Burke for applying "even the recondite laws of human passions" to political affairs; in the revised *Friend* he acknowledged Cicero's ability to persuade through "fractional truths integrated by fancy, passion, accident" and selective memory; with Lear and Hamlet as examples, he generalised that "in many instances, the predominance of some mighty Passion takes the place of the guiding Thought, and the result presents the method of Nature, rather than the habit of the Individual". *Friend (CC)* II 21–2, I 428–9, 456. Supported by Schelling's view that art is the mediative bond between the soul and nature, C argued in *BL* ch 18 that metre provides a

Shakspeare's rhythm is so perfect that you may be sure you don't understand the real force of the line, if it does not run well as you read it. The necessary mental pause after every hemistich or imperfect line is always equal to the time that would have been taken up in reading the complete verse.[8]   [36:169]

> The mounting Sire up on a mountain standing

ought to be,

> The *monarch* Sire—Edward III.[9]   [35:170]

The Trinity is the Will—the Reason or Word—the Love or Life; as we distinguish these three, so we must unite them in one God. The Union must be as transcendant as the Distinction.[10]

Irving's notion is Tritheism—nay rather Tri-Dæmonism. His opinion about the sinfulness of the Humanity of Jesus is absurd—and frenzied.[11]

---

logical restraint to passion in poetry, and in Lect 13 of 10 Mar 1818 that in art "by excitement of the Associative Power Passion itself imitates Order". *BL (CC)* II 64–6; *CN* III 4397 f 48: *Lects 1808–19 (CC)* II 218. Yet Shakespeare is "the only one who has made passion the vehicle of general Truth". Lect 4 of 6 Feb 1818: *Lects 1808–19 (CC)* II 122. None of this entry appeared in *TT* (1835).

[8] In offering the impetuous flow of Shakespeare's versification as the surest distinguishing characteristic of legitimate passages in his work, C said in Lect 1 of 28 Oct 1813 at Bristol that "perfection in the flowing continuity of interchangeable metrical pauses is constantly perceptible". *Lects 1808–19 (CC)* I 521. Shakespeare attains "sweet and appropriate melody" because "his thoughts were harmony itself, and they naturally created a language suitable to themselves". *CN* III 3290, notes for Lect 4 of 1 Apr 1808: *Lects 1808–19 (CC)* I 80; *Sh C* (1960) I 123n.

[9] *Henry V* II iv 57. Dyce, rejecting both C's "monarch" and Lewis Theobald's "mounting", told HNC that "the common text is right,—'*mountain* sire, on *mountain* standing'; & more in Shakespeare's style than the conjectures". The passage was dropped from *TT* (1836), along with that on *Cymbeline* (n 4, above).

[10] Amplified in a marginal note on De

Wette *Theodor*: "The sense & import of the Trinity is to me abundantly clear . . . Now all real distinctions are resolved into three genera generalissima, or absolute Ideas—1. Absolute Will. 2. Realized Will, or real, i.e. Spiritual Being, Idea, pure Intelligence—these being but different terms for the same Conception. 3. Communicate Unitive Life: Feeling and Act, Spirit, Love.—And the Deity exists entire and absolute at once in each of these." *CM (CC)* II 198. He wrote similarly in 1805 of the "distinguishable Triplicity in the indivisible Unity". *CN* II 2444. In a marginal note on Isa 42.1 in Mrs Gillman's Bible, C observed the difficulty of "two Natures . . . united in one Person" (Jesus). *CM (CC)* I 435. He found it easier to define the Trinity philosophically than to locate it scripturally. R. P. Graves tried to set down C's view of triunal acts as given to William Rowan Hamilton: "The unity of God, being adopted as a paramount truth, the supposition was made that the *action* of God might be regarded as either mediate or immediate; that the Second Person in the Holy Trinity, the Son, the Logos, was God *expressing himself by external means*, that the Third Person, the Holy Spirit, was God acting *immediately* upon every being susceptible of spiritual (or vital) influence . . . ". *Life of Hamilton* I 548.

[11] In Jul 1822 Edward Irving (1792–

ᶠBody is not Carcase. How can there be a sinful Carcase? Irving caught many things from me, but would never attend to any thing which he thought he could not use in the pulpit. I told him the consequence would be that he would fall into grievous errors. Sometimes he has five pages together of the purest eloquence, and then an outbreak of almost madman's babble.[12]　　　　　　　　　　　　　　　　　　　　[36:174]

ᶠ f 15

1834) came from Glasgow to the Caledonian Church in Hatton Garden, London. C's first reaction, in Jul 1823, was to "the super-Ciceronian . . . Pulpiteer" (*CL* v 280), but close acquaintance led to Irving's dedication to C of *For Missionaries After the Apostolic School* (1825); to C's qualified but spirited tribute to him in *AR* (1825) 372n–3 as closer to Luther in "*Gospel* Morality" than any other "Wrestler" alive; and to C's note in *Reliquiae Baxterianae* to the effect that Irving had found the proper mean between the Church and the individual congregation. *CM (CC)* I 307–8. The popular Irving opened his larger Regent Square Church in 1827, but first began to accumulate troubles with his translation of *The Coming of Messiah in Glory and Majesty* (2 vols 1827), a millenarian work by Manuel Lacunza ("Juan Josafat Ben-Ezra"). C was so impressed by the improvements in Irving's style in this work that he "dare not speak of it in the unmeasured terms of rejection and regret, which the greater number even of his friends and admirers use". HEHL MS HM 17299 (N Fᵒ) pp 112–13. J. A. Heraud reported later that C "mentioned with particular commendation to us Irving's preface to Ben Ezra, as being written in pure English, undefiled, though with too much *vehemence* of style". *Fraser's Magazine* XII (1835) 131. In *C&S*, as referred to in HNC's note in *TT* (1835), C wrote again of "the genial power" his friend Irving shared with Luther, although he had "no faith in his prophesyings; small sympathy with his fulminations"; and substantial theological differences with him. *C&S (CC)* 142n–3. On 31 Oct 1831 HNC wrote to RS that C "seldom corresponds with Ir-

ving any more", but that acquaintances "2 months ago witnessed a show when they got together". UT ms. Mar 1830 had marked the beginning in Irving's church of uttering "unknown tongues". For *The Orthodox and Catholic Doctrine of Our Lord's Human Nature* (1830) Irving was charged with heresy but acquitted; he was barred from his church in 1832 and condemned in 1833 by the Presbytery of Annan, his birthplace (see 14 Aug 1833 and n 27, below).

C blamed Irving's tritheism on his "too exclusive attention to the Distinctities under the unhappy translation of hypostasis by Person, and of thus introducing diversity of Attributes where only the eternal Proprieties of Form, Subsistency, and essential Relations dare be affirmed". Annotation on a front flyleaf of vol I of Irving *Sermons* (3 vols 1828); in other notes he complained of his "glaring Tritheism" and "palpable Tri-angelism". *CM (CC)* III. For Irving on the sinfulness of Christ see n 12, below; also 14 Aug 1833, below (at n 27) (36:561).

[12] With frequent reference to "sin in the flesh", Irving wrote in *Our Lord's Human Nature* that Christ "met all sin, and all weakness, and all mortality, and all corruption, and all devils, and all creature-oppression, and all creature-rebellion in his flesh; in his body, he strangled them there, he resisted, he overcame, he captured them" (p 8). Cf an annotation on Irving *Sermons* I (140) xxxiv–lviii: "With the dissolution of the Unity . . . it is not a Body but a Carcase. And in strict propriety of language we cannot even say—the Body is now a Carcase, but must say—There is a Carcase instead of a Body", though chemical energies such as carbon, hydrogen, ni-

Until you have mastered the essential difference in kind of the Reason and the Understanding, you cannot escape a thousand difficulties in philosophy.[13]   [36:172]

Homer is a concrete name for the Rhapsodies of the Iliad. Of course there was a Homer, and twenty besides.[14] I will engage to compile twelve

---

trogen remain in the carcass. *CM (CC)* III. Several weeks later (31 May 1830) Thomas Chalmers heard C speak of Irving and body vs carcass; see App F 8, below.

[13] For C on reason vs understanding see 7 Jan–13 Feb 1823, above (at n 41). *TT* (1835) declared this "fundamental difference" between the terms the *Gradus ad Philosophiam*, with Coleridgian play on *Gradus ad Parnassum*, a systematic aid towards the writing of Latin verse.

[14] In *The Friend* (1818) C referred to the Greek "Orpheus, Linus, Musaeus, and the other mythological bards, or perhaps the brotherhoods impersonated under those names". *Friend (CC)* I 503. In Lect 2 of 30 Jan 1818 he acknowledged the existence of sceptical opinion with regard to single authorship of the *Iliad* or the *Odyssey*: "In Homer you have a poem perfect in its form, whether originally so, or from the labour of after critics, I know not . . . ". *Lects 1808–19 (CC)* II 79–80. By 28 Dec 1818 he was approaching the position of the two entries on Homer in *TT*: "Though I profess myself perfectly sceptical . . . whether the *Iliad* of Homer was a poem written by one man or whether it is a choice of an immense number of poems, written upon the same subject, strung together by Pisistratus or some other . . . I can see no probability of Homer being a particular person. Rather (what is already hazarded respecting Orpheus and Musaeus and so forth) I should say it implied a fraternity of men who had wandered through the countries, and . . . gradually introduced those traditions or this, properly-speaking, poetic and sensuous mode of propagating truths which Herodotus attributes to Homer." *P Lects* Lect 2 (1949) 89. Cf *CM (CC)* II 397, 1126. HCR reported on

16 Jun 1825: "Coleridge referred to an Italian Vico who is said to have anticipated Wolf's theory concerning Homer (which Coleridge says was his at college)." *CRB* I 320–1. C had recently read Giovanni Battista Vico (1668–1744) *Principii d'una scienza nuova* (1725, rev 1730, 1744) in the Milan 1816 edition with equal enthusiasm for Vico's view of history as in the account of organic human societies and (bk III) his view of the Homeric epics as early poems from northeastern Greece and slightly later poems from the west arranged by Pisistratidae into *Iliad* and *Odyssey*. *CN* IV 5071, 5204, 5231–2. According to HNC in a note to this entry in *TT* (1835), C became a "decided Wolfian" by reading Vico. Whether C saw that Vico's argument against single authorship might be intended to apply also to the Bible, he drew the parallel in his first note: *CN* IV 5071, and cf the Eichhorn passage in *CM (CC)* II 397. For Fenimore Cooper's report of C's conversation on Homer on 22 Apr 1828, and for the views of HC and WW, see App F 9, below.

Not long before the conversation of 9 May HNC had written an account of the origin and preservation of the *Iliad* for his *Introductions to the Study of the Greek Classic Poets* (1830, rev 1834, 1846). In 1830 he reported the arguments of Friedrich August Wolf (1759–1824) *Prolegomena ad Homerum* (1795) and Christian Gottlob Heyne (1729–1812) that the Homeric epics were compilations of minstrelsies repeatedly rearranged and edited. After the conversations of 1830 and 1832 (23 Apr, below, on Vico), HNC added a translation from Vico bk III to his 2nd ed of *Introductions* (1834) 73–98.

books with characters just as distinct and consistent from the Metrical Ballads of England about Arthur and the Round Table Knights.[15] The different qualities were traditional. Guyon is always courteous &c.[16] So of the Romances of Spain.[17] The Iliad has no subjectivity whatever; it is a clear stream which reflects on its bosom the heaven and the trees and flowers and men on its banks—every thing but itself.[18] In the Lyric Poets, Individuality begins to appear; but we have so little that we cannot fully judge. In the Dramatists, the Individual and the Subjective are intense.

There is a Subjectivity of the Poet—as of Milton, who is himself before himself in every thing he writes.[19]

And a Subjectivity of the Persona or Character as in[g] Shakspeare's characters—Hamlet &c.[20]   [36:171]

The Odyssey was written by one single Poet, no doubt.[21]

———

[h]The general harmony between the operations of the mind and heart and the words which express them in almost all languages is wonderful; whilst the endless discrepancies between the names of things is very well

[g] ~~of~~ in   [h] f 15ᵛ

[15] To sustain his claim, C could have found Arthurian ballads in the various editions of *Reliques of Ancient English Poetry* ed Thomas Percy; *A Select Collection of English Songs* ed Joseph Ritson (3 vols 1783); and in scattered sources. Metrical romances were more plentifully available in *Scotish Poems* ed John Pinkerton (1792); *Ancient Engleish Metrical Romanceës* ed Joseph Ritson (3 vols 1802); *Specimens of Early English Metrical Romances* ed George Ellis (3 vols 1805, 2nd ed 1811); *Sir Tristrem* ed Walter Scott (1804); *Select Remains of the Ancient Popular and Romance Poetry of Scotland* (1822) and *Early Scottish Metrical Tales* (1826), both edited by David Laing; *Ancient Metrical Tales* ed Charles Henry Hartshorne (1829). *TT* (1835) inserted "and other chronicles", which would include further compilations by Thomas Warton, Ritson, and other works of the Arthurian revival, including the edition of Sir Thomas Malory with an Introduction by RS: *The Byrth, Lyf, and Actes of Kyng Arthur* (2 vols 1817).

[16] C probably named Gawain, called "the Courteous" in the Arthurian ro-

mances, not Guyon, who is the knight of Temperance in Spenser's *Faerie Queene*. *TT* (1835) substituted: "Tristram is always courteous, Lancelot invincible, and so on."

[17] *TT* (1835) specified "of the Cid". The popular ballads of the fifteenth century are called in Spanish *romances*. J. G. Lockhart's *Ancient Spanish Ballads, Historical and Romantic* (1823) collected his translations from *Bl Mag* and *Edinburgh Annual Register*. In *BL* ch 3 C praised RS's *Cid* (1808) as "unique". *BL (CC)* I 59, 59n–60.

[18] In *TT* (1835) the *Iliad* became "the Homeric poetry". The two sentences on the lyric poets and dramatists of Greece dropped out, perhaps to make the entry more compact.

[19] See above, "Milton himself is in every line of the Paradise Lost".

[20] *TT* (1835) added "Lear".

[21] Omitted from *TT* (1835). HNC's *Introductions* (1834) draws upon Wolf to weight the case for rearrangement from rhapsodies, but retains the possibility that the "primitive order" originated by a single poet (p 69) was editorially restored.

deserving notice. There are nearly a hundred names in the different German dialects for the Alder-tree. You may take a useful distinction between words and mere names of things.[22]   [36:173]

How wonderfully beautiful is[i] the delineation of the characters of the three Patriarchs in Genesis.[23] To be sure, if ever man could without impropriety be called or supposed the Friend of God, Abraham was that man. We are not surprized that Abimelech reverenced him.[24] He was peaceful because of his conscious relation to God; in other respects, he takes fire, like an Arab Sheik, at the injuries suffered by Lot, and goes to war with the kinglings immediately.[25]   [36:175]

Isaac is, as it were, a faint shadow of Abraham, born in possession of the power which his father had acquired, he is always peaceful and meditative; and it is curious to observe his timid and almost childish imitation of his father's stratagem about his wife. Isaac does it beforehand and without any necessity.[26]   [36:176]

Jacob is a regular Jew, and practises all sorts of tricks and wiles, which according to our notions of *honor* now a days we cannot approve. But you will observe that all these tricks are confined to matters of prudential arrangement—to worldly success and prosperity; and I think we must not exact from men of an imperfectly civilized age the same conduct as to mere temporal and bodily abstinence, which we have a right to look for from Christians. Jacob is always careful not to commit any violence; he shudders at blood-shed.[27] He is the exact compound of the timidity and

ⁱ ~~are~~ is

²² This entry provides one of C's more telling thrusts against empiricism. The Indo-European languages, he argues, reveal a much greater agreement on ideas and feelings than on objective phenomena. Ideas, he contended in *SM* App E, at the beginning of *C&S*, and elsewhere, are anterior to things. *SM (CC)* 100–3; *C&S (CC)* 12–13 and nn. Conceptions, like names, follow consciously the perception of things; words of mind and heart, as ideas, can be conscious or unconscious. To German dialects *TT* (1835) added Arabic for "many more remarkable instances". This entry continues C's logical demonstration of Shakespeare's superiority to Milton and even more to the objective *Iliad*. It also continues the refutation of Horne Tooke on language: see 7 May nn 1, 2, and 15, above.

²³ Abraham, Isaac, and Jacob in Gen 12–35 and Jacob in 42–50 on Joseph.

²⁴ Abimelech, the king of Gerar who made a covenant with Abraham (Gen 21.27–32), had given him silver, sheep, oxen, servants, and land (20.14–16) because God warned him in a dream to give back Abraham's wife. To clarify C's interpretation, *TT* (1835) added Ephron, a Hittite who indulged Abraham's wish to pay for land in which to bury Sarah (23.10–16).

²⁵ Gen 14.12–16.

²⁶ To explain the doublet in Gen 20 and 26, in the absence of any other acceptable reason why Isaac should call his wife his sister, many scholars assume a common legend prior to both accounts.

²⁷ *TT* (1835) cited Gen 34, wherein Jacob "held his peace" after Shechem defiled Dinah, Jacob's daughter.

gentleness of Isaac, and of the underhand craftiness of his mother Rebecca.[28] No man could be a *bad* man who could love as he loved Rachel. I dare say Laban thought no worse of Jacob for his plan of making the ewes bring forth ring-streaked lambs.[29]　　　　　　　　　[36:177]

---

10. May. 1830.

If a man's conduct cannot be ascribed to the Angelic nor to the Bestial within him—what is *a*left for us to refer it to, but the Fiendish? Passion without any Appetite is Fiendish.[1]　　　　　　　　　[36:178]

Lord Eldon's doctrine that Grammar Schools must mean Latin and Greek Schools is founded on gross historical ignorance.[2]　　　　　　　　　[36:181]

a f 16

[28] After Rebekah disguised Jacob with a goatskin to deceive the blind Isaac into a blessing intended for Esau, she sent Jacob to her brother Laban to save both sons from each other (Gen 27). Laban, as implied in C's sentence about him, is equally crafty, and so is Rachel. Gen 31.32–5.

[29] Gen 30.28–43. C's drift is clear and his view tenable, although Jacob saw that Laban's countenance "was not toward him as before" (31.2).

[1] C had written in *The Friend* of 15 Feb 1810: "A being absolutely without morality is either a beast or a fiend, according as we conceive this want of conscience to be natural or self-produced . . .". *Friend (CC)* II 321. Appetite (in the terms of TT) would be the natural cause. In 1811 and 1814, in the *Courier*, he variously described "the wary fiend" as displacing within the immoral individual the angelic spirit of law. *EOT (CC)* II 268–9, 392–3. C rejected on both Christian and rational grounds the concept of possession by devils.

[2] The immediate subject of conversation was the Free Grammar School founded at Highgate by Sir Roger Cholmley (or Cholmeley) c 1562–5. In 1818 and 1820 Brougham introduced bills in Parliament to empower grammar schools to teach not only statutory Greek and Latin but also reading, writing, and arithmetic. In 1822 a suit and counter-suit, along with a new bill, centred on the desire of the Highgate governors to enlarge the chapel adjoining the school with funds of the Highgate Charity left by Cholmley. On 30 Apr 1827 John Scott (1751–1838), 1st Earl of Eldon, Lord Chancellor 1801–27, decreed that the Charity was "for teaching the learned languages", including Hebrew. By further decrees in 1829 and act of Parliament in 1830, the governors were freed to erect a new chapel but the school was raised to the rank of a public school instead of the "effective School for the poor" that C desired. John H. Lloyd *The History, Topography and Antiquities of Highgate* (1888) 135–53; *CL* v 171–5, 190, 235–8, vi 833–5. On 10 May the bill had its second reading in the Commons; it was to be amended and passed on 24 May. Alderman Wood's son, later Baron Hatherley, was invited to The Grove the second week of May to clarify the issues for his father. For C's laudatory description of Cholmley's School as an example of the appreciation of "our great ancestors" for "learning, *in conjunction with common Arithmetic*, the A B C and the rudiments of Grammar" see *L&L* 105–6; *Logic (CC)* 20. Lloyd (pp 318–44) gives an account of C at The Grove, but does not connect him with the long struggle over the Grammar School.

It is intolerable when those men, who have no other knowledge, have not even a competent knowledge of that world in which they are always living and to which they refer every thing.[3]   [36:182]

The best way to bring a clever young man, who has become sceptical and unsettled, to reason, is—to make him *feel* something in any way. Love, if sincere, will in nine cases out of ten bring him to a sense and assurance of something real and actual, and that will make him *think* to a sound purpose, instead of dreaming that he is thinking.[4]   [36:179]

---

12. May 1830.

A Democracy according to the prescript of Pure Reason would be a Church. There would be focal points, but no superior.[1]   [36:184]

Though contemporary events obscure past events in a living man's life; yet as soon as he is dead, and his whole life is a matter of history, one action stands as conspicuous as another.[2]   [36:183]

The almost universal feeling of the People for the late Queen proved a good deal of virtue left amongst them. It compensated in some degree for the baseness of the Lords.[3] Brougham lost that cause. If Brougham be-

---

TT (1835) appropriately transferred to this entry C's remark on Jonson's *Grammar* (see 13 May 1830, below, at n 16), and Eldon's "gross . . . ignorance" prudentially became "insufficient knowledge".

[3] In sequence, this remark seems to apply to Eldon, but in a fuller context it probably applies more to Brougham, who shared C's view of the original intention and current need in grammar schools but not C's sympathy with the Highgate governors.

[4] C's insistence from his earliest days that the "*Heart* should have *fed* upon the *truth*" (*CL* I 115) leads through his letters and published works towards the conviction expressed here. The primacy of love in preventing or curing scepticism and despair, a lesson that the Wanderer teaches the Solitary in *The Excursion*, was known to both C and WW by

1797.

[1] This maxim is explained more fully on 19 Sept 1830, below (36:259, 260).

[2] George IV would not die until 26 Jun, but reports that he was near death could have prompted this reflection and the remarks that follow.

[3] When the ministers brought in a Bill of Pains and Penalties to deprive Caroline of her title and all royal privileges and immunities, trial by her proximate peers began in the House of Lords 17 Aug 1820; it ended in withdrawal of the bill on 10 Nov. Residences of the officers of the House of Lords were occupied by paid witnesses, were barricaded against the mob, and were heavily guarded. For a brief, lively, documented account of the noisy support afforded Caroline by the populace, see Arthur Bryant *The Age of Elegance* (New York 1950) 391–8.

lieves the Queen really guilty, I think him the wickedest man in England, after his declaration at Edinburgh.[4]

The People were too manly to consider whether the Queen was guilty. "What right had the King to complain!" was their just argument.[5]

---

*a*13. May. 1830.

No doubt, Chrysostom and the other rhetorical Fathers contributed a good deal by their rash use of figurative language to advance the superstitious notion of the Eucharist; but the beginning had been much earlier.[1] In Clement, indeed, the mystery is treated as it was treated by John

a f 16ᵛ

[4] Brougham, as attorney-general to the Princess of Wales, along with her more sedate solicitor-general, Thomas Denman, defended the Princess before the bar of the Lords. On 10 Nov the bill passed its third reading in the Lords by nine votes, but the Earl of Liverpool, as Prime Minister, announced that the bill would not be introduced in the Commons. C, believing that Caroline's guilt remained unproved, could judge that Brougham "lost that cause" by persuading few in the Lords or elsewhere of her innocence. In Oct 1820, planning to publish his own defence of Caroline, C found himself in agreement with William Cobbett that Brougham deserved condemnation for "his hollow complimentary phrases to the Ministry & the House of Lords". *CL* v 115–19. (For the draft of C's defence see *EOT—CC*—III 257–60.) In parliamentary debates of Feb 1821 Brougham declared his perfect faith that Caroline was not guilty: "For the truth of this assertion, I desire to tender every pledge that may be most valued and most sacred. I wish to make it in every form which may be most solemn and most binding; and if I believe it not, as I now advance it, I here imprecate on myself every curse which is most horrid and most penal." Hansard NS IV 503. Could he have made a stronger declaration in Edinburgh? Alderman Wood, Caroline's chief supporter, had been at odds with Brougham and contributed to her distrust of Brougham in 1820; a visit from Wood's son (*CL* VI 835) may have stimulated C's suspicion on 12 May of Brougham's hypocrisy. It is even possible that William Page Wood was either present to hear C's remarks or had just left.

[5] As early as Jul 1796, in verses *On a Late Connubial Rupture in High Life*, C had taken the side of Caroline—"Thou'rt a wretch *at home*!"—against her royal husband. *CL* I 223–4; *PW* (EHC) I 152. A vertical line through this entry in MS B indicates that it was transcribed, but it was not published and does not survive in MS F. A later champion, a judge and sergeant-at-arms, used language less measured than C's: "The King had been hated for his evil deeds when he was Prince, and when he was Regent, and that this unfaithful and cruel husband should be allowed by Parliament to torture a wife, who had never done him an injury, was driving the people of the country to a pitch of madness." Sir Edward Abbott Parry *Queen Caroline* (1930) 288.

[1] St John Chrysostom said innocently enough in Homily 82.4 on "my body" in Matt 26.26–8 that Christ has given only to the mind and nothing to the senses; but in Homily 8.5 on Rom 4.1–2 Christ on the communion table is the Victim whereof all partake, and in Homily 24.3–4 on 1 Cor 10.13 the bread at communion is the body of Christ and all who partake thereof become that one body. Migne *PG* LX 465–8, LXI 201–3.

and Paul, but in Hermas[b] we see the seeds of the error, and far more in Irenæus, and so it went on till the Idea was changed into an Idol.[2]

[36:185]

The errors of the Sacramentaries on the one hand and of the Romanists on the other are equally great; the former have volatilized the[c] Eucharist into a Metaphor; the latter have condensed it into an Idol.[3]   [36:186]

Jeremy Taylor contends in his zeal against Transubstantiation that the sixth chapter of John has no reference to the Eucharist; if so, St John wholly passes over this sacred Mystery.[4] It *is* a mystery; it is the only

[b] Hermes   [c] the ~~sacred~~

Jeremy Taylor *The Real Presence and Spiritual of Christ in the Blessed Sacrament Proved Against the Doctrine of Transubstantiation* § 12 pars 11, 12, 17 complained of Chrysostom's rhetoric, as in "the Table or Altar is as the manger in which Christ was laid", but found his doctrine on the Eucharist sound and Anglican. *Polemicall Discourses* i 252–3, 260–1. The "superstitious notion" is the Roman Catholic doctrine of transubstantiation, or conversion of the whole substance of the bread and wine into Christ's body and blood, with only the sensory accidents of appearance remaining unchanged. HNC's note in *TT* (1835) tells us that the conversation began with his quoting John Selden on the subject.

[2] Clement of Alexandria contributed to discussion of the Eucharist in *Paedagogus* 2.2 and *Stromateis* 3.2, but C may have referred to Clement of Rome (see 8 Jul 1827 n 9, above). Hermas *The Shepherd*, an apocalyptic work probably composed in Rome A.D. c 160 (complete in Latin and Ethiopic, fragmentary in Greek), does not deal directly with the Eucharist. Could "Hermas" be a slip of the ear or tongue for Ignatius or Barnabas? The *Epistle of Barnabas* does not refer specifically to the Eucharist, but Anglican apologists often cited its repudiation of carnal sacrifices and its discussion in §§ 5–6 of the rôle of the Lord's blood and flesh in salvation. Hermas and Barnabas usually appeared in the same collections, and C's comments on one tend to evoke the other. St Irenaeus (c 125–c 202), a Father of the Greek Church, bp of Lyons, made much-debated references to the Lord's body and blood in *Adversus haereses* 1.13.2, 5.2.2–3, 5.7.2–3.

[3] In this context "the Sacramentaries" are those who deny the real presence of Christ in the Lord's Supper. In a note dated 14 Dec 1827 in the Book of Common Prayer C recommended perusal of the Communion Service as "the surest Preventive and Antidote to . . . the lethargizing Hemlock . . . of the Sacramentaries, according to whom the Eucharist is a mere *practical Metaphor*, in which Things are employed instead of articulated sounds". *CM (CC)* i 713 (cf 862). *CN* ii 2103n observes that C used the word *Idolatry* with increasing frequency during and after the residence in Malta that increased his anti-clericalism.

[4] After feeding the five thousand, Jesus said, "He that eateth my flesh, and drinketh my blood, dwelleth in me, and I in him." John 6.56. Taylor, in the *Real Presence* iii "Of the sixth Chapter of St Johns Gospel" § 1 wrote: "In this Chapter it is earnestly pretended that our blessed Savior taught the mystery of *Transubstantiation* . . .", to which C replied in the margin: "I cannot but think that the same mysterious truth, whatever it be, is referred to in the Eucharist & in John VI". *Polemicall Discourses* i 188: *CM (CC)* v. Elsewhere, to Böhme's observation on John 6.53, 60, C answered that these are hard sayings "for the disciples of the crude or dead *Letter*, and for the Doctors of abstraction & mere moral meanings". Annotation on *Mysterium Magnum: Works: CM (CC)* i 673.

mystery in our Religious Worship. When many left Jesus and complained that his sayings were hard—he does not attempt to detain them by any explanation, but only tells them that his words are Spirit.[5] If he had really meant that the Eucharist should only be a*d* memorial or a celebration of his death, would it have been even honest to let these disciples go away from him upon such a gross misunderstanding? Would he not have said "You need not make a difficulty; I only mean so and so after all?"   [36:186]

Arnauld and the other learned Catholics are irresistible against the Sacramentary doctrine.[6]   [36:187]

The Sacrament of Baptism applies itself and has reference to the Faith or Conviction and is therefore only to be performed once; it is the *Light* of Man.[7] The Sacrament of the Eucharist is a Symbol of all our *Religion*; it is the *Life* of Man. We want it always; it is commensurate with our Will.[8]

[36:188]

d a̶n̶ an

[5] John 6.63. In *SM* App C, C recommended study of the Bible with "spiritual partaking of the Redeemer's Blood, of which, mysterious as the symbol may be, the sacramental Wine is no mere or arbitrary memento". *SM (CC)* 88. Annotating Johnson the Whig *A Second Five Years' Struggle Against Popery and Tyranny: Works* (1710) 199, C said that he holds "Transsubstantiation in a certain sense" because he takes the "body" of Mark 14.22 ("Hoc est corpus meum") to be other than the carnal material nailed to the cross. Similarly, on Sherlock *A Vindication of the Doctrine of the . . . Trinity and the Incarnation* (1690) 4, C answered that he would prefer transubstantiation, with the body "having an esse not in the percipi", to "impanation", or consubstantiation. *CM (CC)* III, IV. When *AR* (1825) went into print, C announced a disquisition on the Eucharist as ready for publication (p 376); cf *CL* v 434, 444.

[6] Antoine Arnauld (1612–94), Jansenist theologian. His *La Perpetuité de la foi de l'Eglise Catholique touchant l'Eucha- riste, défendue contra le livre du Sieur Claude, Ministre de Clarenton* (Paris 1669–79), reissued with additional doc-

uments (5 vols Paris 1704–13), gave a formidable list of believers, Latin and Greek, in "la présence réelle", and related the doctrines of Zwingli, Calvin, and the Swiss Sacramentaries to eleventh-century heresies. C referred to Arnauld's "Great Work" in a note of Sept 1824 on the Eucharist. *CN* IV 5161. SC, defending C's departures from commonly held Anglican doctrines, was more vehement than he in declaring consubstantiation "as empty a doctrine as the dogma insisted on by the Council of Trent". *CIS* (1849) 261.

[7] C's fullest discussion of baptism, in *AR* (1825) 354–76, gives something like a history of his opinions on the topic. In the aphorism on baptism with which the discussion begins, Robert Leighton (1611–84) calls baptism "the Word unfolding the Sacrament . . . the Word as a Light", and says, in C's *rifaciménto*, "This (*sacrament*) of Baptism, the Ancients do particularly express by *Light*."

[8] *AR* (1825) 131 begins C's "Elements of Religious Philosophy" by declaring: "*If* there be a Will, there must be a Spirituality in Man", and vice versa. Further on, p 195, he says that "Christianity is not a Theory, or a Speculation;

Ἐξ ἄνωθεν—from above—When our Saviour says that Pilate could do nothing against him unless it had been given him from above—he means from the Sanhedrin.[9] It would have been a poor truism to say he could do nothing against the will of God. The Assumption of Messiahship was no crime in the eyes of the Jews; they hated Christ, because he would not be *their* Messiah; on the other hand the Romans cared not for Christ's assuming to be Son of ᵉGod. The crime in *their* eyes *was* the assuming, or the charge of assuming, a kingly character.[10]   [36:189]

See how Caiaphas the high priest understands the words of our Lord as to his being Son of God![11] Not in the sense of being full of his spirit, or doing his commands, or walking in his ways, in which sense Moses, the Prophets, nay, all good men are sons of God—no! he tears his robes in sunder, and cries out—Blasphemy! What need have we of further evidence? It was no crime to assume to be the Messiah; but to assume to be the Son of God was indeed blasphemy unless true.[12]   [36:190]

One striking proof for the genuineness of the Mosaic books is this. They contain precise prohibitions (by way of predicting the consequence) of

ᵉ f 17

---

but a *Life*. Not a *Philosophy* of Life, but a Life and a living Process.'' The Eucharist is the ever-renewable symbol of that life. In a marginal note on Leighton *The Genuine Works* ed Philip Doddridge (4 vols 1819) I 157, C qualified the distinctions: ''The Life is the Soul of the *Body*. But the Soul is the life of *the Man*, and Christ is the Life of the Soul.'' *CM (CC)* III.

[9] C so glossed John 19.11 in Anne Gillman's Bible: ''from above means from the Sanhedrin, or Jewish Senate who to gratify their malice basely betrayed & gave up their one remaining privilege—that of judging offences against their Laws . . .''. *CM (CC)* I 458. The common interpretation was that ''from above'' ascribed the power as from God, but C is dealing with the rest of Jesus' words to Pilate, ''therefore he that delivered me unto thee hath the greater sin'', as made clearer in the much fuller version of this entry in *TT* (1835). For C on this issue in Eichhorn *NT* II 261–4, see *CM (CC)* II 465, 485. As ex-

panded in *TT* (1835) C calls ''dry-footed'' the explanatory versions of Erasmus and of Samuel Clarke (1675–1729) *A Paraphrase on the Four Evangelists* (2nd ed 2 vols 1714) II 211, in which Jesus asks, ''was it not my Father's Will, that for great and wise Reasons I should at this Time submit to be delivered to you by the Envy and Malice of the *Jews*''. C declared Clarke overrated in his own time as Johnson in his and Byron in C's: note on endleaf of Waterland *Vindication of Christ's Divinity: CM (CC)* V. Erasmus' paraphrase of John, to the same effect as Clarke's on John 19.11, was first published at Basel in 1523. Erasmus returns, still without flattery, on 15 Jun 1833, below (at n 7) (36:525).

[10] For the Greek phrases in the expansion of this entry in *TT* (1835) see 36:189.

[11] Matt 27.63–5, Mark 14.61–4.

[12] This entry is expanded in *TT* (1835) for clarity and conversational flavour.

all those things which David and Solomon did and gloried to do.—e.g. raising cavalry—alliance with Egypt, laying up treasure and polygamy.[13] Would *such* prohibitions have been fabricated then or even afterwards? Impossible! [36:191]

———

The manner of the predictions of Moses is very remarkable. He is like a man standing upon an eminence and addressing[f] people below him, and pointing to things which he can and they cannot see. He does not say You will act in such and such a manner and the consequences will be so and so; but—so and so will take place, because you will act in such a way.[14] [36:192]

———

Talent, lying in the Understanding, is often inherited; Genuis rarely or never.[15] [36:193]

[f] ~~look~~ addressing

[13] Deut 17.15–20 promises that God will choose a king for Israel, but this king, to prolong his days in his kingdom, "shall not multiply horses to himself, nor cause the people to return to Egypt . . . Neither shall he multiply wives to himself . . .". Yet Solomon had a great cavalry (1 Kings 4.26, 10.26); David had more than one wife (1 Sam 18.27, 25.42–3); Solomon had 700 wives and 300 concubines (1 Kings 11.3), including a wife gained, along with trade in horses and linen, from a treaty with her father the Pharoah of Egypt. C's argument, that such awkwardness would not have been deliberately created in the age of Solomon or later, is strengthened by the justification for God's mitigation of the prophesied consequences in 1 Kings 11.1–13. In LRR Lect 3 C had grappled with current arguments, summarised in Paine *The Age of Reason* pt 1 (1794), that those Biblical prophesies not conveniently vague were forgeries after the purported fulfilment. *Lects 1795 (CC)* 149–56.

[14] In Deut 4.25–8 Moses comes nearest to prophesying action and consequence without moral contingency. C's metaphor of the "eminence" is biblically present in Moses' ascents of Mt Sinai to receive the law and in such supporting symbols as concealment by clouds and Moses' shining face at descent. Exod 34.29–35. In an undated note, C concludes that the mission of Moses was "not the lasting existence or Unity and Well-being of the Jewish *State*; but the gradual Diffusion of the Doctrine of One God". VCL S MS F 2.11.

[15] In a notebook entry of 1800 C did not require the inheritance of genius to be apparent before the age of fifteen. *CN* I 669. In 1822 he claimed to avoid despair over WW's "Head & Heart" by the knowledge that genius, like reason, is "a Presence vouchsafed, like a guardian Spirit" rather than, like talent or understanding, "a personal property". *CL* v 234. His fullest contrast of genius, talent, sense, and cleverness appears in *Friend (CC)* I 110, 419–23. Genius includes originality and imagination; its distinctive mark, as Aristotle noted, is metaphor; talent requires only the ability to acquire, arrange, and apply. Ibid 419; *CL* IV 667; *BL* chs 2, 4 *(CC)* I 31, 81; *EOT (CC)* I 220, II 101. Frequently C applied the distinction to critical moments of national and intellectual history, particularly when nature and historic event concur with "the great revolutionary moments of individual genius". *Friend (CC)* I 480n; cf *EOT (CC)* I 208, 316, II 67, 81–2; *SM (CC)* 14.

Ben Jonson used Grammar expressly as distinct from Greek and Latin.[16]   [36:181]

---

[a]18. May. 1830.

Motives imply weakness and the existence of evil and temptation. The Angelic Nature would act from Impulse alone. A due medium of Motives and Impulse is the only practicable object of our moral Philosophy here.[17]   [36:194]

---

19. May. 1830.

It is a great error in Physiology not to distinguish between what may be called the General or Fundamental Life—the Principium Vitæ—and the Functional Life—the Life in the Functions.[1] Organization must presuppose Life as anterior to it; without Life there could not be or remain any Organization; but there is also *a* Life in the Organs or Functions, distinct from the other. Thus a[a] Flute presupposes—demands the existence of a

[a] f 17[v]   [a] ~~are~~ a

[16] *The English Grammar. Made by Ben. Iohnson. For the Benefit of All Strangers, Out of His Observation of the English Language Now Spoken, and in Use* (1640) 35: "*Grammar* is the art of true, and well speaking a Language: the writing is but an accident." The mottoes are in Latin, but English writers are cited for all examples in bk II "Of Syntaxe". This entry continues the discussion of Lord Eldon's doctrine concerning grammar schools: see 10 May, above (at n 2).

[17] The "here", meaning in this fallen, unangelic world, is omitted from *TT* (1835). In the Prospectus of *The Friend* (1809) C proposed as a subject for the work "The Origin and Growth of moral Impulses, as distinguished from external and immediate Motives". He disallowed Francis Jeffrey's objection to the phrase "moral Impulses". *CL* III 140.

[1] The error was promulgated by William Lawrence (1783–1867), surgeon at St Bartholomew's Hospital 1824–65, in lectures to the Royal College of Surgeons, 1815, published as *An Introduc-* tion to *Comparative Anatomy and Physiology* (1816) and consolidated in *Lectures on Physiology* (1822). In rebuttal to his teacher, John Abernethy, surgeon at St Bartholomew's 1815–27, who argued in lectures at the College of Surgeons, 1814, in *An Enquiry into the Probability and Rationality of Mr. Hunter's Theory of Life* (1814 = 1815), and in *Physiological Lectures* (1817) that the *principium vitae* of the great John Hunter (1728–93) was an informing spirit anterior to organisation, Lawrence answered that, spirit aside, as irrelevant, life is an assemblage of all the functions and is dependent on organisation—and Hunter knew it and said so. For C's intimate involvement in this debate, see *L&L* 17–23; *CL* v 49n–50; *CN* IV 4518. For other speculations by C on the rôle of organisation in life see Lect 12 in *P Lects* (1949) 358; *CN* III 4461. In 1848 Seth B. Watson regarded as unique in England C's theory that "rocks and mountains . . . share with mankind the gift of Life". *TL* (1848) 9.

Musician as anterior to it—without whom no flute could ever have existed:—yet again without the instrument, there could be no Music.[2]

[36:195]

It often happens that on the one hand the Principium Vitæ, or Constitutional Life, may be affected without any, or with the least imaginable, affection of the Functions; as in inoculation where one pustule only has appeared and no other perceptible symptom, and yet this has so affected the constitution, as to indispose[b] it to infection under the most accumulated and intense contagion: on the other hand Hysteria, Hydrophobia and Gout will *disorder* the functions to the most dreadful degree and yet often leave the Life untouched.[3] In Hydrophobia the Mind is quite sound, and the patient feels his muscular and cutaneous life removed forcibly from under the control of his Will.[4]

[36:196]

[b] ~~fortif~~ indispose

[2] This analysis derives ultimately from Aristotle's formal, material, efficient, and purposive causes in *Physics* 2.3 and his unmoved mover (C's musician) in *Metaphysics* 12.7.

[3] "Inoculation", botanical grafting, became the general term for "transplanting a distemper from one subject to another". Edward Jenner (1749–1823), a pupil of Hunter's who first vaccinated with cow-pox in 1796, published *Inquiry into Cause and Effects of the Variolae Vaccinae* (1798). C made a notebook entry in 1803 concerning the social success of inoculation. *CN* I 1521. Until about 1808 vaccination was a joke for caricaturists, and C found ultimate absurdity in the line "Inoculation, heavenly maid! descend!". *BL* ch 18 *(CC)* II 85. But in 1811 he wrote a deferential letter to Jenner asking for materials to write both an account in the *Courier* and a poem on the origin and progress of Jenner's discovery. *CL* VI 1025–7. Jenner had become emblematic of "systematic war against the existing evils of nature". *Friend (CC)* I 101–2. Like Abernethy, C saw the importance of diagnosing disease, equally with health, as a condition in which the whole person is involved, with the fear that empirical and analytic materialism would focus on local disease and individual symptoms as if they were detachable from the organism; unlike Abernethy, C was willing to view functions as consequent upon structure. On the general issue of organisation, somewhat as he had written in *TL*, C wrote to J. H. Green in May 1820; in May 1828 he wrote to Green of evidence he had found in the *London Medical Gazette* of 26 Apr that an agent "intelligible but not sensible" determined the growth of muscles in the beetle *Scarabaeus nasicornis*. *CL* V 47–50, VI 737. Some of the physicians and surgeons C knew are named in *L&L* 24–5, and some of the many pertinent works he read are listed in John Harris "Coleridge's Readings in Medicine" *Wordsworth Circle* III (1972) 85–95.

[4] In 1824, urging James Gillman to publish a revision of his monograph of 1812, *A Dissertation on the Bite of a Rabid Animal*, C had proposed that the nerves, in hydophobia, are alive to external excitants but "lifeless and alien to the Life a centro"; i.e. that the nerves act on the brain without the brain acting on the nerves. *CL* V 378; cf 387. Reviewing in 1813 a piece in *The Watchman* from Thomas Beddoes, concerning a presumed case of hydrophobia twelve years after the dog's bite, C deduced from this instance and his long-held belief that "no Disease was ever yet cured, but merely suspended" that inoculation prevented the permanent absorption of poison from smallpox and measles. *Watchman (CC)* 275n. In N 29 C wrote on hydrophobia: *CN* IV 4514.

Hysteria might be called Mimosa, from its counterfeiting so many diseases and even death itself.[5]   [36:197]

Hydrocarbonic Gas should be inhaled by way of experiment in case of Hydrophobia.[6]   [36:198]

Hydrocarbonic Gas produces the most death-like exhaustion without any previous excitement.   [36:198]

There is a great difference between Bitters and Tonics.[7] Where weakness proceeds from excess of irritability, then Bitters ᶜact beneficially;

ᶜ f 18

[5] Hysteria, convulsive agitations in women, supposed to proceed from disorders in the womb; the symptoms were reported to be a lump rising in the throat, a gurgling of the bowels, alternative laughing and crying, irritability of mind, and sometimes the appearance of coma. It was supposed that bodily disturbances in hysteria caused psychological difficulties, and not the reverse. *Mimosa pudica*, the sensitive plant, regular-flowered but an anomaly because the folding of its leaves from cold, darkness, or touch gave it (beyond the productivity of plants) the irritability of animals—distinctions supposedly absolute in the scale of organic nature, as explained in *C&S (CC)* 179–80. Known to students of belles-lettres from Darwin *Loves of the Plants* I 299–312 and n and Shelley's poem *The Sensitive Plant*, the mimosa turned up frequently in scientific discussions of the seventeenth to nineteenth centuries. Science and poetry are brought together in Robert M. Maniquis "The Puzzling *Mimosa*: Sensitivity and Plant Symbols in Romanticism" *Studies in Romanticism* VIII (1969) 129–55.

[6] Allowing for increased refinements and continuing confusions in the laboratory, hydrocarbonic gas would seem to be the "inflammable air" of William Nicholson *The First Principles of Chemistry* (1790) 177–9; the "carbonated hydrogen gas" of Lavoisier *Elements of Chemistry in a New Systematic Order* tr Robert Kerr (Edinburgh 1790) 111; the "carburetted hydrogen" of William Thomas Brande *A Manual of Chemistry* (1819) 152, 155 and of Dalton *A New System of Chemical Philosophy* (2 vols 1808); and the hydrocarbonate or

"heavy inflammable air" of Brande (3rd ed 1836) 483–4. Cottle described Davy's "numbness and loss of feeling in the chest" from inhaling "carburetted hydrogen gas". *Rem* 268–9. Beddoes reported of one typical dosage of "hydrocarbonate air" that the patient became "vertiginous and nearly insensible, his pulse at one period being nearly imperceptible". *Considerations on the Medicinal Use, and on the Production of Factitious Airs* (3rd ed Bristol 1796) 39. Letters from other physicians reported occasional success with its use in prescribing for *phthisis pulmonalis*, causing a few deaths and always some vertigo. Ibid 32–9, 85–93, 105–9. Hydrophobia, from the bite of a dog affected with rabies, was one of Gillman's specialties (see n 4, above). In the desperate search for successful treatment, Abernethy had reported in a lecture at St Bartholomew's on his failure to stop the spread of rabies by cutting out the area where he had supposed the poison would lodge for a while. *Lancet* VI (1825) 394–5. The subject arose twice in *The Watchman: (CC)* 256, 273–4.

[7] "Bitters" was the name given first in the eighteenth century to bitter medicines such as quinine and alcohol tinctured with the extract of gentian-root, quassia-root, or the like; "tonics", such as arsenic and digitalis, were prescribed to restore tone or firmness to muscles. For apoplexy, asthma, hysteria, and other diseases, the standard *Materia Medica* of William Cullen (1710–90), and others indebted to it, recommended "Tonic bitters, such as colombo, gentian, quassia"; hence C's corrective remarks.

because all Bitters are poisons and operate by stilling and depressing and lethargizing the irritability. But where weakness proceeds from the opposite cause of Relaxation, then Tonics are good; because they *brace* up and tighten the loosened string. *Bracing* is a correct metaphor. Bark goes near to a combination of a Bitter and a Tonic; but no perfect medical combination of the two properties is yet known.[8]   [36:199]

The study of Specific Medicines is too much disregarded now. No doubt the hunting after specifics is a mark of ignorance and weakness in Medicine; yet the neglect of them is a proof also of Immaturity; for in fact all Medicines would be found specific in the perfection of the Science.[9]

[36:200]

The Epistle to the Ephesians is improperly so called; it is evidently a Catholic Epistle, addressed to the whole of what may be called St Paul's diocese.[10] It is the divinest composition of man. It embraces every doc-

---

[8] Peruvian bark, *cinchona*, is recommended by Cullen and others for fevers, chronic rheumatism, erysipelas, menorrhagia, hysteria, and other complaints. And see n 9, below. Elm, willow (the venerable predecessors of aspirin in supplying acetyl), and other prescribed barks were usually specified by the full name; "bark" normally meant Peruvian bark. See also 7 Apr 1832, below (at n 2), and 2 Sept 1833 (at n 5).

[9] It has been said, but is untrue, that C had little serious interest in scientific detail. Although higher reason led him to medical consideration and treatment of the human organism as a whole, understanding could encourage the experimental advance in specific details of medicine and, as here, the advocacy of specific medicines. The highly influential Cullen had speculated that some medicines act on solids of the body and some on the fluids; John Brown had discarded this distinction and had substituted the generalised treatment of either deficient or excessive excitability. C. F. S. Hahnemann, the founder of homeopathy, who enters TT in May 1832, was a vehement advocate of the return to specific medicines, which could be prescribed under his system in much smaller doses than under earlier regimens.

Hahnemann said in *Organon der Rationellen Heilkunde* (1810) that his theory came to him when translating Cullen on the effects of Peruvian bark.

[10] The implications of this remark become clearer as a marginal note of Sept 1830 on Blomfield *A Charge Delivered to the Clergy of His Diocese*: Eph 4.16 on "the whole body fitly joined together" shows, said C, that Paul addressed "the whole body of *Eccalumeni*—the nearest Copy of which is, perhaps, a Quaker Community . . . The Gospel *has* no PRIESTS, *can* have no Priests . . .". *CM (CC)* I 529. Eichhorn *NT* III 249, 285, described the Epistle to the Ephesians as *Circularschreiben*, C's "catholic circular charge" of 15 Jun 1833, below (at n 5), addressed to parties unknown to us rather than specifically to a congregation in Ephesus. In Anne Gillman's Bible C called it "the elaborate & highly finished Circular Charge, misnamed Ep. to the Ephesians". *CM (CC)* I 465; cf 459. HNC wrote to SC on 22 Sept 1832: "S.T.C. says it is a catholic charge by Paul to all his Asiatic converts". UT ms. Paul's authorship has been questioned because the style is impersonal and the theme of the unified church is unique to this epistle.

trine of Christianity; first those doctrines peculiar to Christianity and then those precepts common to it with natural religion.

The Epistle to the Colossians is the overflowing, as it were, of St Paul's mind upon the same subject.[11]   [36:201]

The present system of taking oaths is horrible. It is awfully absurd to make a man invoke God's wrath upon himself if he speaks false; it is a sin to do so.[12] The Jews' oath is an *adjuration* by the Judge to the wit ness—"In the name of God I ask you &c."[13]

The more oath-taking, the more lying.[14]   [36:202]

---

27. May. 1830.[1]

I had *one* just flogging. At thirteen, I went to a shoemaker and begged him to take me as his apprentice. He, being an honest man, immediately took me to Bowyer; Bowyer got into a great rage, knocked me down and even pushed Crispin rudely out of the room.[2] Bowyer asked me why *a*I

a f 18ᵛ

[11] The close relation of the Epistle to the Colossians and that to the Ephesians has been universally noted, but explanations differ. In a period of eclectic worship the Colossians apparently needed a stronger reminder of the supremacy of Christ.

[12] C has several notes, especially in the margins of *Reliquiae Baxterianae*, on "the folly, mischief, and immorality of all Oaths but judicial ones", for oaths "are 999 times out of 1000 abominations", and the legal ones are cruelly administered. *CM (CC)* I 271–2, 274–5, 342–3. Hobbes *Leviathan* pt 1 ch 14 (1651) 71 had noted the extreme force of the judicial oaths: "unlesse he performe, he renounceth the mercy of his God, or calleth to him for vengeance on himselfe". William Paley, though he would have the law "spare the solemnity of an oath", declined to make the distinction essential to C between calling upon God to witness and invoking His vengeance. *The Principles of Moral and Political Philosophy* bk III pt 1 ch 16 (7th ed 2 vols 1790) I 192–3.

[13] Matt 26.63: "I adjure thee by the living God", as specified in the fuller version of C's remarks in *TT* (1835). In 1810, reading Sir William Blackstone's *Commentaries on the Laws of England*, C defended against Quaker objections, despite Matt 5.33–7, the calling of God to witness. *CN* III 3830.

[14] *TT* (1835) added: "generally among the people". On reading the entry, HC "rejoiced with the angels in Heaven to find that my revered parent thoroughly sympathized with my abhorrence of the present system of administering oaths". 8 May 1836: *HCL* 192.

[1] During law terms HNC normally saw C only when he returned from London to Hampstead for the weekend. During May, however, he was seeing him frequently, often during the week: 2, 9 and 30 May were Sundays, and 7 May a Friday, but weekday meetings were Monday (3, 10 May), Tuesday (18 May), Wednesday (12, 19 May), and Thursday (13, 27 May). For the changes in dating in *TT* (1835) see the Table of Comparative Dates, App V, below.

[2] The Rev James Boyer (1736–1814), master of the upper grammar school at

had made myself such a fool; to which I answered that I had a great desire to be a shoemaker and that I hated the thought of being a clergyman. "Why so?" said he:—"Because, to tell you the truth, Sir, I am an Infidel." For this Bowyer flogged me well, and, I think, wisely. Any Evangelical whining or remonstrances would have gratified my vanity and confirmed me in my absurdity; as it was I got laughed at and ashamed.[3]

[36:203]

The Anti-American articles of the Quarterly Review have been most pernicious.[4] The Americans regard what is said of them in England a thousand times more than they do any thing in any other country. They are excessively pleased with any kind of favorable expressions, and never forgive any slight or abuse.   [36:205]

Christ's Hospital 1776–99, appears in *BL* ch 1 and in C's letters as a grotesquely but salubriously severe taskmaster. See *BL (CC)* I 8–11 and e.g. *CL* VI 843. Leigh Hunt, who said Boyer once called C "that sensible fool, Collĕrĭdge", doubted that he deserved C's praise in *BL*, on the grounds that his "objection to a commonplace must have been itself commonplace". *Autobiography* ch 3 ed J. E. Morpurgo (1948) 74. For versions of C's prayer that Boyer be wafted to heaven by cherubs with no bottoms see ibid and n 43 p 472. Even before C's remarks of 1830 and 1832 in TT, Hunt's comments were available in his "Recollections", *Lord Byron and Some of His Contemporaries* (1828), but C praised Boyer solemnly in one of his last letters, 27 May 1834: *CL* VI 983. Crispin, martyred c 286 on 25 Oct (*Henry V* IV iii 40), according to legend made shoes and is the patron saint of shoemakers; the name suffered further reduction when assigned in French comedy to the conventional impudent valet.

[3] The epithet "Evangelical" does not appear in *TT* (1835). Cf "the cant of the evangelicals" in 8 Jul 1827, above (at n 20). Examples were plentiful in the Cheap Repository Tracts, instituted by Hannah More, and in the *Children's Friend* and similar periodicals conducted by members of the Bible Society. In "The History of Joseph Green. Part II" *Child's Companion; or, Sunday Schol-*

ar's *Reward* I (1824) 45–50, Joe said that he had missed Sunday School because of a headache, but he had gone nutting. "His teacher was very sorry to find that Joe had been so wicked; he spoke to him of the sin of breaking the Sabbath, and of the lies he had told; he said that these two sins led to many more, and that the little boys who thus began, would go on from sin to sin, if they were not checked. . . . Joe cried very much when he was put on the form . . . before the whole school."

[4] Articles written during 1829 by John Barrow (1764–1848), most pertinently a review of two books of travel in the United States in *QR* XLI (Nov 1829) 417–46. One of the books was Capt Basil Hall *Travels in North America in the Years 1827 and 1828* (3 vols Edinburgh 1829), which returns to TT in entries for 20 Aug 1830 (at n 6) and 8 Apr 1833 (at n 8). Both books enabled the reviewer to notice "noisy patriots", "well-sounding principles", "trickery and deceit", "the absence of an effective executive head", "the pains taken to nourish hatred towards England", "the excessive use of ardent spirits", and nothing "to excite envy or jealousy". *TT* (1835) generalised the opening sentence to conceal the reference to *QR*. There was no specific need to protect RS, who had reviewed favourably George Head's book on the wilds of Canada in *QR* XLII (Jan 1830) 80–105.

The last war to us was only something to talk or read about; but to the Americans it was the cause of misery in their own homes.[5]   [36:206]

The misanthropy of the concluding part of Hall's North America is most horrible.[6]   [36:257]

A few civil verses I wrote in Miss Barbour's Album were published in America, and have called forth raptures of gratitude and sympathy.[7]

I do not call the sod under my feet my country; but language—religion—government—blood—Identity in these makes men of one country.[8]

[36:207]

[5] Among many possible sources, visitors to Highgate from the United States since the war of 1812–15 (e.g. Wheeler and Barbour in n 7, below) could have reported humiliations beyond the burning of public buildings in Washington. And C could remember that fears of invasion in England, without actual landings, had sharpened both imagination and emotions. See e.g. *Fears in Solitude: PW* (EHC) I 256–63. R. M. Milnes, who went to Highgate in 1830 with Arthur Hallam, was advised by C: "Go to America if you have the opportunity; I am known there. I am a poor poet in England, but I am a great philosopher in America." T. Wemyss Reid *The Life, Letters, and Friendships of Richard Monckton Milnes* (2 vols 1890) II 424.

[6] On Basil Hall see n 4, above, and 20 Aug 1830 (at n 6) and 8 Apr 1833 (at n 8), below.

[7] *Lines Written in Commonplace Book of Miss Barbour, Daughter of the Minister of the U.S.A. to England* of Aug 1829—*PW* (EHC) I 483—had been sent to the New York *Mirror* of 19 Dec 1829, in which the thirteen lines appeared under the heading "The Mother and Daughter Land" with answering verses by the sender, Daniel Bryan:

In countless bosoms here thy generous tone
Shall find high thoughts congenial to thy own;
No loftier name commands our deep regards,

Than his whose spirit in thy numbers breathes . . .

"Enlightened thousands here", the lines continue, have been spellbound by C's Mariner. James Barbour (1775–1842), the U.S. Minister to Great Britain 1828–9, received a DCL from Oxford. John Wheeler, who succeeded the Coleridgian James Marsh as President of the University of Vermont in 1833, visited C with Miss Barbour and others on 28 Jul and 1 Aug 1829. App R, vol II, below. The entry has a vertical cancellation indicating transcription, but it was not printed and does not survive in MS F.

[8] Cf the poem for Miss Barbour (n 7, above) lines 3–6:

'Tis not the clod beneath our feet we name
Our country. Each heaven-sanctioned tie the same,
Laws, manners, language, faith, ancestral blood,
Domestic honour, awe of womanhood . . .

C warmly commended local attachments, but he contrasted rich national spirit with mere fondness for soil in "Letters on the Spaniards" II in the *Courier* 8 Dec 1809—*EOT (CC)* II 46—and elsewhere, and began his second Lay Sermon by exhorting the middle stations of society: "To what purpose, by what *moral* right, if you continue to gaze only on the sod beneath your feet?" *LS (CC)* 124.

Wordsworth's[b] conversation runs round and round again in eddies—it never progresses—My fault is the other way—I skip from one thing to another too fast and unconnectedly.[9]

The Books of Moses were the Homer of the Jewish Poets and Prophets.[10]

---

[c]The Book of Job is an Arab Poem antecedent to the Mosaic dispensation.[11] It represents the mind of a good man not enlightened by an actual revelation, but seeking about for one. In no other book is the desire and necessity for a Mediator so intensely expressed. The Personality of[d] God; the *I Am* of the Hebrews is most vividly impressed on the book, in opposition to Pantheism.[12]　　　　　　　　　　　　　　　　[36:208]

It should be observed that all the imagery in the speeches of the men is taken from the East, and is no more than consonant to actual existence—a mere representation of the forms of Nature. But when God speaks, the tone is exalted and almost all the images are taken from

---

[b] W.'s　　　[c] f 19　　　[d] of ~~the~~

---

[9] This entry was abandoned in MS B, presumably as too personal for publication. Some of C's other remarks on his own conversation are included in the Editor's Introduction.

[10] Not transcribed for publication, perhaps as insignificant, perhaps as signifying too much in the suggestion of human authorship rather than divine inspiration as formative influence on the later books of the OT. In a strikingly similar statement, evoked by the Warburton controversy that underlies this remark of C's and those that follow, Robert Lowth included style as well as content in refuting Warburton's parallel of Job and Ennius: "Job is rather the Homer of the Hebrew Classics; who, with the venerable air of antiquity, and the force and spirit of original genius, has, at the same time, that elegance of language and beauty of composition, which the more polished and refined ages never surpassed." *A Letter to the Right Reverend Author of "The Divine Legation of Moses Demonstrated"* (2nd ed 1766) 80. A few pages later (p 92), setting aside Job as of doubtful date, Lowth acknowledged: "Moses stands at the head of the Hebrew Writers;

not only in point of time, but in regard also of literary Merit, as an Historian, as an Orator, and as a Poet."

[11] To the entry for 7 May 1830, above (at n 21), this opening sentence adds the suggestion that Job is the earliest book of the Bible in its surviving form. In *BL* ch 10 C called Job "the sublimest, and probably the oldest, book on earth". *BL (CC)* I 202. Cf C's remarks to John Frere of Dec 1830 (in App F 10, below). When Eichhorn remarked that Job has often been called a drama, C answered that "Milton far more judiciously considers [it] as a didactic Epic Poem". Annotation on *AT: CM (CC)* II 413. For a compromise see the end of n 14, below. Lowth had accepted the dramatic quality of the poem but denied its resemblance to Greek tragedy. *Lectures on the Sacred Poetry of the Hebrews* tr Gregory II 363n–4. In Anne Gillman's Bible, after Job 21, C noted: "I seem, thro' great part of this most precious as most ancient Poem, to feel that the *Clew* of the argument is yet to be given." *CM (CC)* I 426.

[12] On pantheism vs "I Am" see *CM (CC)* II 392 and the last entry for 13 Apr 1830, above (at n 27) (36:129).

Egypt—crocodile—war horse &c. Egypt was then the first monarchy that had a splendid court.[13]   [36:210]

Satan in the Prologue does not mean the Devil—Diabolus—There is no calumny in his words; he is the circuitor—the accusing spirit—the Attorney General.[14] But after the Prologue which was*e* necessary to bring the imagination into a proper state for the dialogue, we hear no more of this Satan.   [36:211]

Warburton was quite wrong in setting this book down as low as Ezra.[15] His only reason is this appearance of Satan.[16]   [36:212]

I think the passage about the Redeemer may fairly be taken as a burst of determination, a quasi prophecy—"I know not *how* this can be; but in spite of all my difficulties, I *do* know that I shall be recompensed."[17]

[36:209]

e was ~~nothing~~

[13] Michaelis, remarking in his commentary on Lowth that some of the imagery in Job was borrowed from Egypt, appealed to his own Dissertation recited before the Royal Society of Göttingen. His full Latin commentary was reprinted at Oxford in 1763. Lowth, in turn, noting that Isaac Newton's *Chronology* also put Job before Moses, wrote in *A Letter to the . . . Author of "The Divine Legation"* 75: "The Country of Job was upon the borders of Egypt; and the Age of Job was when the Empire of Egypt was arrived at a high degree of improvement in all the arts of civil Society."

[14] C seems to combine Job 2.2, "circuivi terram et perambulabam" (AV "going to and fro in the earth, and . . . walking up and down") with 1 Pet 5.8, "adversator vester diabolus . . . circuit" ("your adversary the devil . . . walketh about") to make Satan = Circuitor = Adversary, as in his note on the Gospel of Nicodemus: ". . . the same Satan, in its etymon, Circuitor, who walks over earth seeking whom to devour, as well as its derivative sense, Adversarius". *CN* IV 5351. For C's remarks to John Frere on Job in Dec 1830 see App F 10, below. In a marginal note on Webster *Displaying of Supposed Witchcraft* 18, C makes similar remarks on the Circuitor, with the additional explanations that the derivative senses of inspector to informer to false accuser to common enemy of mankind are all later than Job and that the prologue of "this incomparable drama, or epico-dramatic Poem" need not be thought a later accretion. *CM (CC)* v.

[15] That Job was written in the time of Ezra, who went from Babylon to Jerusalem in 458 B.C., the seventh year of the reign of Artaxerxes I (Ezra 1.7), is argued throughout vol I of William Warburton (1698–1779) *The Divine Legation of Moses Demonstrated* (3 vols 1738–41). Warburton declared later—(4th ed 5 vols 1765) v 109—that the author was Ezra himself.

[16] Warburton bk VI § 2 (1738–41) II 530: "The finding *Satan* in the Scene is a certain Proof that the work was composed in the Age we assign to it." The survey of the refutations of Warburton available to C in Isaac d'Israeli *Quarrels of Authors, or Some Memoirs of Our Literary History* (3 vols 1814) I 3–134 is greatly extended in A. W. Evans *Warburton and the Warburtonians: A Study in Some Eighteenth-Century Controversies* (Oxford 1932). C offered an extended rebuttal to Warburton, on the grounds that the object of Mosaic legislation was to create a nation, in N 29: *CN* IV 4708.

[17] Job 19.25–6. *TT* (1835), to ameliorate C's rejection of prophetic inspiration, began the entry: "I now think, after many doubts".

*f*The first six chapters of Daniel cannot have been written by the same person who wrote the rest.[18] They are full of Greek words—there could have been *no* Greek words in any thing written by Daniel—and there *are* no Greek words in the rest of the book.

The *fourth* monarchy is clearly the Greek.[19] There is no sort of intimation of the Romans. The monarchies are designated by their known heraldic signs.*g*[20]

The Psalms ought to be translated afresh; or rather the present version should be revised. Scores of passages are utterly unmeaning as they now stand.[21] If the primary visual images had been preserved, the harmony would have been perceived.[22]   [36:213]

f f 19ᵛ
f–g For the variant in MS F see App C, below

[18] Of other remarks on Daniel in TT see esp 24 Feb 1827, above (at nn 5–8).

[19] Dan 2.40–4, on "the fourth kingdom". Cf C's annotation in Anne Gillman's Bible, in which he enumerates the four kingdoms: ". . . 4. Greek. And to the Grecian Empire after the Death of Alexander I apply v. 41–43". *CM (CC)* I 440. And cf the note on John Davison *Discourses on Prophecy: CM (CC)* II 155–6. The apocalyptic vision of the fourth beast (Dan 7.7), or king, with iron teeth and ten horns, is presumed to be Alexander the Great of Macedon, who became master of Asia 333–331 B.C. There are Greek names for musical instruments in Dan 3.5. Eichhorn called attention to the Greek words: *AT* § 614 III 348.

[20] Before the emblem of Alexander, Dan 7.4–6 describes a lion with eagle's wings (Babylonian), a bear with three ribs (Medo-Persian), and a leopard with four wings and four heads (Cyrus of Persia). Eichhorn noted the "Babylonischen, Medischen, Persischen und Griechischen" emblems. *AT* § 614 III 350.

[21] In the margins of the Book of Common Prayer C commented on the meaning, intelligibility, or imagery in Psalms 8, 68, 72, 74, 82, 87, 104 ("which in some parts is scarcely intelligible" in the Psalter version), 110, and 126. *CM (CC)*

I 705–10. He carried the Psalms in his head enough to misremember in 1824 the imagery of Ps 91.5–6. *CL* v 327. He had made a metrical paraphrase of Ps 46 in 1799. *CL* I 532; *PW* (EHC) I 326. On the place of the Psalms in C's daily meditation see letters of 1827–34, esp *CL* VI 681–2, 725, and HNC's long note to this entry in *TT* (1835), which includes a transcription, with HNC's usual small improvements, of *CN* III 3890 on Matt 27.46 as a recitation of Psalm 22. C repeated this happily encountered "hypothesis" in notes on Anne Gillman's Bible and twice where he was grieved to observe that Irving had not taken up his repeated suggestion. *CM (CC)* I 427–8; annotations on Irving *Sermons* (1828) I 75, 200–4: *CM (CC)* III. HNC's note acknowledged that C allowed less prophetic or typological character to Psalms than did *A Commentary on the Book of Psalms* by George Horne, which went through twelve editions between 1776 and 1825. C's remarks ignore the emphasis of Orientalists on the difficult and probably corrupt state of the Hebrew text.

[22] *TT* (1835) said more precisely "oftener preserved". C's "harmony" refers to the parallelism of content in the repetitive patterns of Hebrew poetry noted by Lowth and subsequent commentators.

30. May. 1830.

The fault of the Ancient Mariner consists in making the moral sentiment too apparent and bringing it in too much as a principle or cause in a work of such pure Imagination.[1]   [36:214]

I took the thought of "grinning for joy" in that poem from a friend's remark to me, when we had climbed to the top of Plinlimmon and were nearly dead with thirst. We could not speak from the constriction, till we found a little puddle under a stone. He said to me—"You grinned like an idiot." He had done the same.[2]   [36:215]

Undine is a most exquisite work.[3] It shows the want of any sense of the fine and the exquisite in the public taste that this beautiful work never

[1] *TT* (1835) transferred for consolidation with this entry the exchange with Mrs Barbauld of 31 Mar 1832, below. C holds to the same view of the "moral sentiment" with and without Mrs Barbauld.

[2] "They for joy did grin"—*AM* line 164: *PW* (EHC) I 193. *TT* (1835) incorrectly identified the friend as "poor Burnett", meaning George Burnett (c 1776–1811). "Plinlimmon" is an error of misspeaking or mishearing. From C's letter of 22 Jul 1794 to Henry Martin (*CL* I 94) and from Joseph Hucks *A Pedestrian Tour Through North Wales in a Series of Letters* (1795) 62, we know that the mountain climbed in Jul 1794 was Penmaenmawr and that the companions were Berdmore and Brookes. *TT* (1836) replaced Burnett with a nameless "companion". SC did not tamper with the text of the 3rd ed and consequently made no change in *TT* (1851) 87, but in *BL* (1847) II 338n she had quoted this entry with the companion identified as Berdmore and the peak as "Penmaenmaur". *BE* I 35n and *C Life* (H) 46, 432 n 68 both followed SC, but *RX* 210 cautiously declined to choose between Berdmore and Brookes as the companion. Thomas Berdmore of Jesus College, Cambridge, B.A. 1795, had matriculated in 1792. RS's list of errors for HNC in 1835 had included: "*Beardmore* not Burnett was

the name you heard. He & Brookes joined S.T.C. & Hucks on their Welsh tour." UT ms. Berdmore could be counted among the "chance-started friendships" of *To the Rev. George Coleridge* line 20, a line to which Hucks took exception in his *Poems* (Cambridge 1798) 148, as noted in *PW* (JDC) 588. C said in 1794 that the climb was "most dreadful". If he had also climbed Plynlimmon, he or Hucks would have let us know. For other uses of "grin" and "grinning" see *CN* II 1496 f 71ᵛ, III 4397 f 52ᵛ; *BL* ch 8 *(CC)* I 139; *CL* I 557; WW *Peter Bell* line 825. Literary ramifications of the tour are studied in Herbert Wright "The Tour of Coleridge and His Friend Hucks in Wales in 1794" *Nineteenth Century* XCIX (1926) 732–44.

[3] Baron Friedrich Heinrich Karl de La Motte-Fouqué (1777–1843), German romanticist of Huguenot descent, author of *Undine, eine Erzählung* (1811, in his quarterly *Die Jahreszeiten*, tr George Soane 1818). Apparently the copy C lent to HC about 1820 belonged to Mrs Gillman. *CL* v 42. C associated Undine "before she had a Soul" with HC's lack of a self-conscious "I". *CL* v 110–11. C thought *Undine* "founded on a tradition recorded in Luther's Table Talk"—see *CN* IV 4594—which is not inconsonant with the presumed source in Paracelsus.

made any impression. Her character before she receives a soul is most
marvellously beautiful.   [36:216]

*a*How much more really imaginative is Undine than any of Scott's
novels!⁴

Is it not most extraordinary that the Church of England should so utterly
disregard congregational singing!—that in that particular part of the public worship in which, more than in all the rest, the common people might
and ought to join—which by its association with music is meant to give
a fitting vent and expression to the Emotions—that in this part, I say—
we should all sing as Jews!⁵ In Germany, the hymns are known by heart
by every peasant; they advise*b*, they argue from the hymns, and every
soul in the church praises God like a Christian with words which are natural and yet sacred to his mind!⁶

No doubt this proceeded at the Reformation from the fear of introducing any thing but what they supposed was the word of God in their theory
of the inspiration of the New Testament.⁷   [36:220]

Hooker said that by looking for that in the Bible which it is impossible
that any Book can have—we lose the benefits which we might reap from
it as being the best of Books.⁸   [36:221]

---

a MS B f 20   *b* advise ~~in~~

⁴ *TT* (1835) omitted the direct comparison with Scott, but HNC's note there explained, with examples, that C thought
"Scott's best characters and conceptions
were *composed*". The note in 1835, but
not in 1836, specified *Undine* (Philadelphia 1824), a pirated reprint of the Soane
translation. A note by EHC in the BM
copy says that George Ticknor gave it to
SC.

⁵ The "should" here suggests a meaning such as "We ought to sing congre-
gationally as the Jews do in the syn-
agogues". That suggestion is apparently
incorrect. In the greatly extended version
in *TT* (1835) "should" is omitted; after
"Jews" is added "or, at best, as mere
men, in the abstract, without a Saviour";
and other changes make clear a meaning
that in the Anglican churches of 1830 the
people sing together only as provided by
the Psalter, which had none of the explicit Christian content that hymns would
afford. One addition acknowledged the

importance of the hymns given to Methodists by the brothers Wesley—John
(1703–91), founder of Methodism;
Charles (1707–88), author of 6500
hymns—and George Whitefield (1714–
70), their more Calvinistic co-worker.

⁶ *TT* (1835) prefaced this part of the
entry: "Luther did as much for the Reformation by his hymns as by his translation of the Bible." Even before he went
to Germany, C was struck by the report
of Pliny (called to C's attention by Paley's *View of the Evidences of Christianity*) that early Christians sang together
hymns "to Christ as to a deified man".
Lects 1795 (CC) 173.

⁷ In the revision of this sentence in *TT*
(1835), the English Reformers dreaded
"being charged" with the introduction
into worship of anything except Scripture.

⁸ Hooker *Of the Laws of Ecclesiastical
Polity* bk II § 8: "And as incredible
praises given unto men, do often abate

In dreams even, there is nothing fancied without an antecedent quasi cause. It could not be otherwise.[9]   [36:222]

The Pilgrim's Progress is one of those few books which may be read repeatedly over at different times, *c*and each time with a different pleasure. I read it once as a theologian—once as a devotional book—another time as a poet &c. I could not have believed beforehand that Calvinism could be painted*d* in such exquisitely delightful colors.[10]

There is great theological acumen in the book.   [36:218]

c f 20ᵛ   *d* ~~dressed~~ painted

and impair the credit of their deserved commendation: so we must likewise take great heed, lest in attributing unto Scripture more than it can have, the incredibility of that, do cause even those things which indeed it hath most abundantly, to be less reverently esteemed." *Works* (1682) 124.

[9] Andrew Baxter, who attributed all dreams to "the agency of living invisible beings", agreed with most writers available to C that dreams are of two kinds, reasoned and confused; C here assimilates the two kinds to each other. C always assumed an influence from external causes on the content of dreams. In notes on the half-faith of illusion, probably written for the 1808 lectures, he wrote: ". . . the mind . . . which at all times, with and without our distinct consciousness, seeks for and assumes some outward Cause for every Impression from without, and ⟨which⟩ in Sleep by aid of the Imaginative Faculty converts its Judgements respecting the Cause into a present Image, as being the Cause,—the mind, I say, in this case deceived by past experience attributes the painful sensation received to a correspondent Agent— An assassin, for instance, stabbing at the Side, or a Goblin sitting on the Breast, &c . . .". BM Add MS 34225 f 56ᵛ: *Lects 1808–19 (CC)* I 136. It has been argued that C is chiefly indebted in this passage and elsewhere on dreams to *The Loves of the Plants* and *Zoonomia* of Erasmus Darwin. Elisabeth Schneider *Coleridge, Opium and Kubla Khan* (Chicago 1953) 91–105. But one could hardly overestimate the number of med-ical and other sources encountered by C after reading Baxter in 1795 having, at the least, brief references citing dreams or revealing theoretical bases of opinion on dream. By 1830 he probably knew the amalgam of Darwin, Thomas Brown, Blumenbach, Elliotson, Dugald Stewart, George Combe, Spurzheim, and Rees's *Cyclopaedia* in Andrew Carmichael "An Essay on Dreaming, Including Conjectures on the Proximate Cause of Sleep" *Philosophical Magazine and Journal* LIV (1819) 252–64, 324–5. Perhaps his remark on 30 May was stimulated by the recent appearance of the associationist John Abercrombie (1780– 1844) *Inquiries Concerning the Intellectual Powers and the Investigation of Truth* (Edinburgh 1830, issued in London by John Murray), with its long section in pt 3 on dreaming, somnambulism, insanity, and spectral illusions. When Eichhorn argued that Ezekiel and other prophets must have worked their visions out in advance, C answered that he "should infer the contrary", for he had himself experienced "the wonderful intricacy, complexity, and yet clarity of the visual Objects". Annotation on *AT: CM (CC)* II 403. He made a systematic analysis of the "Language of Dreams" in 1818. *CN* III 4409. He thus far confirms Beddoes *Hygëia* III i 64: "*Reasoning dreams* are regular through wrought-up scenes . . .".

[10] C's almost altogether laudatory remarks on John Bunyan (1628–88), including marginalia in the edition of *Pilgrim's Progress* published by R. Edwards (1820) and in that with a life

Martin is a poor creature.[11] It seems as if he looked at Nature through bits of stained glass, and was never satisfied with any appearance that was not prodigious.[12] He never schooled his imagination to the apprehension of the true Idea of the Beautiful.   [36:217]

The wood-cut of *Slay good* is admirable; but this is too fine a book for it. It should be on sixpenny brown paper and larger.[13]   [36:218]

There are three sorts of Prayer—Public—Domestic—Solitary. Each has its peculiar uses and character. The Church ought to publish and authorize a directory of forms for the two latter.[14]

---

of Bunyan by RS (1830, HNC's copy)—*CM (CC)* I 802–27—are largely collected in *C 17th C* 474–86. C usually granted that Bunyan was a Calvinist, but commented on the epithet in RS's "Life of Bunyan": "*I* have met with nothing in his Writings (with the exception of his Anti-paedobaptism, to which too he assigns no *saving* importance) that is not much more characteristically *Lutheran*". *CM (CC)* I 810. Scott, in *The Heart of Midlothian* ch 31, calling Bunyan "a rigid Calvinist", received a similar riposte from C: "Calvinism never put on a less rigid form, never smoothed its brow & softened its voice more winningly than in the Pilgrim's Progress." Annotation on *Novels and Tales of the Author of Waverley* (12 vols Edinburgh 1823) x 65: *CM (CC)* IV. In *TT* (1835) HNC gave in a note C's praise of Bunyan's "whole saving Truth", dated 14 Jun 1830, without giving the dispraise of RS's cold view that immediately follows in HNC's copy. C found Hermas "poor, and unevangelic" compared with Bunyan. *CM (CC)* I 802–3, 817.

[11] This and the previous remark on Bunyan were stimulated by the presence before C of the copy given to HNC by John Murray of *The Pilgrim's Progress. With a Life of John Bunyan by Robert Southey* (1830), with two illustrations from the painter John Martin (1789–1854) engraved by W. R. Smith as the frontispieces to pts i and ii, *The Valley of the Shadow of Death* and *The Celestial City*, pp 1, 216. C would have seen large paintings by Martin and probably his illustrations to *Paradise Lost* (1825–7). Martin's habitual placing of small figures in vast architectural and mountainous or cavernous vistas, with bold contrasts of light and colour, can be seen in reproduction in Christopher Johnstone *John Martin* (1974); William Feaver *The Art of John Martin* (1976); Thomas Balston *John Martin 1789–1854: His Life and Work* (1947). Balston (p 100) juxtaposes C's remarks with the less metaphysical scolding of Martin by Macaulay in *Ed Rev* LIV (1831) 450–61.

[12] C had experimented with coloured glasses to accentuate tonal values as early as 1803. *CN* I 1412, III 4227 and nn.

[13] In the List of Embellishments "Great-heart daring Giant Slay-good to combat", with separate captions on p 350 for "Mr. Great-heart armed" and "Feeble-mind in grip of Slay-good". The design by William Harvey (1796–1866) was cut by Thomas Mosses (fl 1829–61). Although based upon a doctrine of decorum, C's judgement also recognises the aesthetic values of the rough medium, associated by 1830 with such low works as broadsides and children's books, and distinguishable from the refinements of wood-engraving on the end-grain of hard wood introduced by Thomas Bewick. C apparently felt that the quality of the paper and print in this book called for engraving or etching of a metal plate.

[14] In a marginal note on Donne *LXXX*

The decay of the Devotional Spirit in the English Clergy is amazing. Witness the contemptible compositions which proceed from time to time from[e] Lambeth[15] and the Bishops generally, whenever a[f] new Prayer is to be offered. Instead of New Forms of Prayer—they[g] were happily blundered by the hawker into New Former Prayers.   [36:219]

I think the Church giving God the option of killing poor old George III. or hanging up the madness over his head exceeded any thing I ever read for base and soulless meanness of Devotional Imagination.[16]

---

[e] from ~~the~~   [f] ~~they~~ a   [g] there

Sermons (1640) C insisted similarly that "solitary, family, and templar" devotions are "distinctions in *sort*", not merely of degree. *CM (CC)* II 283. He distinguished private from public worship more fully in *CN* III 4021. In *AR* (1825) 376 he announced as forthcoming his own exposition of "the philosophy of Prayer". His most poignant declarations, in the depths of addiction to opium in 1813–15, maintained a distance from the "*delirious* Superstition" that the supplicant can influence God's will; rather, as he said in *AR* (1825) 81, one reaches out to "a divine Comforter" when the "*whole* man" prays in "absolute Necessity" for "penitent Resolution". *CL* III 478–9; *CN* III 4183; marginal note on No 19 "Homily on Prayer" on the back flyleaves of *Sermons or Homilies of the United Church of England & Ireland* (1815): *CM (CC)* IV. T. A. Methuen heard C say in 1815: "Sir, it is my fixed persuasion that no man ever yet prayed in earnest, who never felt the misery of being unable to pray. For when the soul feels that she is sinking, as it were, from Him who is the author of all happiness, she beseeches Him to stretch out his hand and suffer her to sink no further." *Christian Observer* XLIV (1845) 262. In a copy of the Book of Common Prayer he wrote: "Prayer *is Faith* passing into act—a union of the will and the Intellect realizing in an *intellectual act*." *CM (CC)* I 702. To EC in 1826, after a recent illness, C confessed that his prayers had had "too much of thought and feeling, and too little of Will and Striving". *CL* VI 554–5. HNC's note in *TT* (1835) quoted De Q's memory of

C's vigorous remarks on prayer when they first met and his own memory of C's tearful comments of 1832. C made notes for an essay on prayer in 1796 (*CN* I 257–60, 263) and again in 1826 (*CN* IV 5383, 5411, 5420; *CL* VI 545).

[15] Lambeth Palace, the official residence of the abp of Canterbury, not specified in *TT* (1835). The spirit of C's remarks in this entry and the next is ironically present in a radical parody that includes "Psalms from the New Version": William Hone *The Form of Prayer, with Thanksgiving to Almighty God, To Be Used Daily by All Devout People Throughout the Realm, for the Happy Deliverance of Her Majesty Queen Caroline from the Late Most Traitorous Conspiracy* (1820).

[16] In Dec 1810 "The Prayer for the Restoration of His Majesty's Health" asked God to teach both the royal family and the people "patiently to adore thy inscrutable Providence"—"whether it shall seem fit to thine unerring wisdom, presently to remove from us this great calamity, or for a time to suspend it over us". *A Reg* (1810) Chronicle 420. If this is the prayer C had in mind, perhaps he thought that removal of the calamity of madness other than by death would be no manifestation of "inscrutable Providence". Models of tact were available in the prayers for the King's recovery issued in 1789. Robert Huish *Memoirs of George the Third* (1821) 521, 529. The vertical cancellation of the previous entry carries through this one, but the "option" was not published and does not survive in MS F.

*h*Works of Imagination should be composed in very plain language—The more purely Imaginative they are, the more necessary it is to be plain.[17]

The Pilgrim's Progress is the lowest style of English without being slang or ungrammatical; if you were to polish it, you would at once destroy the reality of the Vision.   [36:218]

---

4. June. 1830.

Taylor's was a great and lovely mind; yet how much and perniciously was it perverted by his being a protégé of Laud's and entertaining such intensely Popish feelings of Church authority. His Liberty of Prophesying is an admirable work, and written, no doubt, to save the Church of England from persecution;[1] but if we believe Taylor's argument, what do

h f 21

[17] A remarkable statement that has not been considered outside the context of the published paragraph on *Pilgrim's Progress*. More than an assertion about style, it carries the force of Lamb's argument in "Detached Thoughts on Books and Reading" that "the better a book is, the less it demands from binding". *L Works* II 173.

[1] C compared and contrasted Taylor with Milton in the "Apologetic Preface" (c 1815) to *Fire, Famine, and Slaughter: PW* (EHC) II 1103–4. He had counted Taylor as one of "*my men*" in 1796. *CL* I 245. Of 1799 there is strong indirect evidence: "Jeremy Taylor was an author from whose works Coleridge always professed to have derived the greatest possible delight; and he more particularly referred us to his 'Ductor Dubitantium,' and his 'Holy Living and Dying.' He illustrated what he said of him, by quotations given with so much emphasis and kindred feeling, as bespoke a perfect brotherhood between them." Carlyon I 95 (the discussion of Taylor continues to p 97). Though Thomas A. Methuen lost a ms that C gave him in 1815: "One point, however, I distinctly recollect: namely, that though Jeremy Taylor, among the moderns, was 'the os et lyra Ecclesiae,' he was in others doctrinally unsound; especially as to the depravity of human nature, and the value of a death-

bed repentance." *Christian Observer* XLIV (1845) 261. On the despair paradoxically resulting from Taylor's cheerful Arminianism, see *CL* v 404–5 and an annotation on *Reliquiae Baxterianae: CM (CC)* I 269.

In *A Discourse of the Liberty of Prophesying*, which C annotated in *Polemicall Discourses* (1674) i 939–1079 (see above, n 2 to 29–30 Aug 1827), Taylor argued in § xx, "How far the Religion of the Church of Rome Is Tolerable", that a prince who tolerates Jews must surely tolerate all sects of Christians: "Let the Prince and the Secular Power have a care the Commonwealth be safe. For whether such or such a Sect of Christians be permitted is a Question rather politicall then religious . . ." (i 1075). In *The Friend* C quoted "the eloquent Bishop" on the limitations of tolerance, but noted the Romanist and Socinian dangers of Taylor's thought. *Friend (CC)* I 282–3, 433. (The announcement of a forthcoming edition of *The Friend*, in *TT* 1835 I 166n, was withdrawn from *TT* 1836. It was published by William Pickering in 1837.) C reached beyond Taylor to Laud himself on 7 Jun 1830 (at n 6) (36:232). HCR heard C on 23 Dec 1810: "Taylor's *Holy Living & Holy Dying* he declared to be a perfect poem in its details. Its rhythm may be compared with the *Night Thoughts*." *CR*

we come to? Why, nothing more or less than this—that so much can be said for every opinion and sect—so impossible is it to settle *any* thing by reasoning or authority of Scripture that positive authority alone can be appealed to. The whole book is the precise argument used by the Papists to induce men to admit the necessity of a supreme and infallible head of the Church. As Charles II.[2] well said of such works and of the Church of England generally—"When you contend with the Papists, you use the arguments of the Puritans; when you contend with the Puritans, you immediately adopt all the weapons of the Roman Catholics." Taylor never speaks with the slightest symptom of affection or respect of Luther, Calvin or of any of the Reformers; at least not in any of his learned works; but he *saints* every trumpery monk or friar down to the very latest canonization by the modern Popes.[3] I think Taylor was in heart very near to Socinianism. The cross of Christ is scarcely ever seen or alluded to; compare him with Donne, and you will feel the difference in this respect.[4] In Edward VI. time, the Reformers feared to admit almost anything of human authority; *they* had seen and felt the abuses—the atrocious consequences [a]of the Popish theory of Christianity—and I doubt not they in-

[a] f 21[v]

(BCW) 36. C was rough on Taylor in a marginal note on John Howie *Biographia Scoticana: CM (CC)* II 1176–9.

[2] *TT* (1835) inserted "or James II., I forget which"; i.e. HNC was the first editor who failed to find the source.

[3] C wrote similarly in a marginal note on *The Liberty of Prophesying* § xiii par 8: "It is characteristic of the Man, and the Age, Taylor's high-strained reverential epithets to the names of the Fathers—and his rare and naked mention of Luther, Melancthon, Calvin—the least of whom was at least equal to S[t] Augustin, & worth a brigade of the Cyprians, Firmilians &c. And observe! always SAINT Cyprian". *Polemicall Discourses* i 1028: *CM (CC)* v. "So confident", goes a typical phrase of Taylor's, "as *Luther* sometimes was". *Of the Sacred Order and Offices of Episcopy: Polemicall Discourses* i 47.

[4] *TT* (1835) added as from C: "Why is not Donne's volume of sermons reprinted at Oxford?" and a stronger note, beginning "Why not, indeed!", from HNC. C wrote extensive and favourable comments on two copies of the folio *LXXX Sermons* (1640): *CM (CC)* II 245–338. For Methuen's report on C's quoting Donne and on William Page Wood's on C's enthusiasm for Donne's poetry, see App F 11, below. But of both Donne and Taylor C had a reservation: "Even in Donne . . . there is a strong *patristic* leaven—. In Jeremy Taylor, this Taste for the Fathers, and of all Saints and Schoolmen before the Reformation amounted to a dislike of the Divines of the Continental protestant Churches, Lutheran or Calvinist". *CM (CC)* II 260. (See also n 3, above.) In marginalia on Taylor, in *Friend (CC)* I 433n, and elsewhere, he calls Taylor Latitudinarian, Sabellian, or Socinian. He believed that such a charge by Baxter in *Reliquiae* I 370 referred to Taylor: *CM (CC)* I 334. C's conclusion that the argument of *The Liberty of Prophesying* leads either to Catholicism or to agnosticism is accepted by C. J. Stranks *The Life and Writings of Jeremy Taylor* (1952) 259 and n.

tended to reconstruct the religion upon the plan of the primitive ages.[5] But the Puritans pushed this to an absolute Bibliolatry[6]—they would not put on a corn-plaster without scraping a text on it. The learned however soon felt that this was wrong; that a knowledge of the Fathers and of early tradition was absolutely necessary, and unhappily the excess of the Puritans drove them into an extreme of denying the Scriptures to be capable of affording a rule of faith without the positive dogmas of the Church.[7]

[36:223, 224]

---

6. June. 1830.[1]

*a*Such is the temper of the Bishops and the high Churchmen now a days that I am sure that if I or any other writer were to maintain and satisfactorily prove the truth of all the great articles of Faith holden by the Church of England and to demonstrate their harmony with the laws of Morals and Mind; if I were to silence the opposition or even convince the incredulity of the Sceptic by taking away his most ready weapon of attack—yet if I were to doubt the authenticity of the book of Daniel or suggest that Inspiration did not mean verbal Dictation—I should be universally condemned, and sneered at as being unorthodox and an enemy to

a-c For the variant in MS F see App C, below

[5] Reformers like Hugh Latimer (c 1485–1555) and Nicholas Ridley (c 1500–55), among those appointed court preachers during the brief reign of Edward vi (1547–53), because they feared to admit any religious practices on human authority alone lest popish practices return—so goes C's argument—appealed to the authority of Scripture without intending to declare the Bible the sole source of divine revelation, a view left to the Puritans. C had projected a history of the conflict between Puritan and hierarchy from the time of Edward i. *CL* v 299.

[6] *Bibliolatrie* is Lessing's word, discussed by him in "Bibliolatrie" *Sämmtliche Schriften* xvii 61–74, as noted in *CIS* (1849) xxxiii. C could have seen the word in English, however; citations in *OED* begin with John Byrom 1763, "If to adore an image be idolatry, To deify a book is bibliolatry." In a note on Wil-

liam Chillingworth *Works* (1742) C accused the Protestants of playing into the hands of the Romanists "by needless & impossible deifications of a *Book*". CM *(CC)* ii 39.

[7] An additional sentence in *TT* (1835) makes it clearer that the discussion still concerns Taylor, who chose to deny the usefulness of Scripture in adjudicating differences of faith and thereby put excessive stress first on the tolerance of individual differences and then on the authority of the Church as a solution to the problems of tolerance.

[1] The censorship of the first two paragraphs by the Coleridge family (they had been transcribed by HNC with slight change in MS F, but were vetoed with the mark + +, probably by JTC) demonstrates C's point that he would be condemned as unorthodox for saying what he here says.

the Church!² Yet what is the fact? Is not this supposed inspiration of the Bible the handle which every infidel and railer at Religion invariably takes up? Well! may they do so—yet how unjustly if understood in the only way compatible with fact or common sense! What a mass of gratuitous difficulties—shall I not say, horrible blasphemies—does the Church create and as it were appropriate ᵇby this strange doctrine!³

I well remember, when only nine years old, listening with intense eagerness to the story of Jael murdering Sisera as read in Church,⁴ and to the war song of Deborah—the most sublime composition in the world⁵—and when the words "Blessed shall Jael be &c" were read, putting down my head between my hands and knees, and murmuring from my soul as even now I do—"Cursed shall Jael be above women &c"—

She murdered the innocent sleep.⁶

Deborah's song—when we think for a moment what light she had—her situation—her nation and all the circumstances—is, as I have said, in my judgment the sublimest of human compositions⁷—But the Holy Ghost to have *inspired* that Song!! It is awful to utter the supposition.ᶜ

ᵇ MS B f 22   ᶜ See ᵃ⁻ᶜ, above

² The general argument is that of *CIS* (1840). In the Introduction to *CIS* (1849) J. H. Green attempted to report the degree of C's indebtedness to Lessing's distinction between the essential religion in the Bible and those elements in the Bible superadded to the religion. Doubts about the book of Daniel appear several times in TT. In a note on Chillingworth *Works* C asked if he should be damned for rejecting the first six chapters of Daniel as scholars rejected passages attributed to Cicero, as belonging in style to a later age. *CM (CC)* II 36–7. His most detailed rejection of Dan 1–6 occurs in a marginal note on Francis Wrangham *The Life of Dr. Richard Bentley* (1816) 5: *CM (CC)* V; he wrote on the subject to Wrangham (*CL* IV 802). C was on a frontier; Priestley repeatedly expressed astonishment that Thomas Belsham doubted the authenticity of Daniel. Joseph Towill Rutt *Life and Correspondence of Dr Priestley* (2 vols 1832) II 335–74.

³ How the doctrine of direct dictation of Scripture by God creates blasphemies is illustrated in the discussion of Jael and Deborah that follows.

⁴ Judges 4.17–22, which returns on 31 Mar 1832, below (at n 21). This paragraph earned one + of rejection in MS F.

⁵ Judges 5. "Blessed above women shall Jael . . . be" (5.24) is preceded by "Curse ye Meroz . . . curse ye bitterly the inhabitants thereof; because they came not to the help of the Lord . . ." (5.23). "The Song of Deborah, translated in the parallelisms of the Original", a version of Judges 5.1–11 in C's hand, survives with a journal of 16–17 Sept 1798 in the Berg Collection, NYPL.

⁶ *Macbeth* II ii 33.

⁷ In a note for Lect 5 of 2 Dec 1811 C wrote of the "passionate repetition of a sublime Tautology (as in the Song of Debora)" and in *BL* ch 17 declared such repetitions "to be a beauty of the highest kind; as illustrated by Mr. Wordsworth himself from the song of Deborah" (i.e. in a note to *The Thorn: WPW* II 513). *CN* III 4113 ff 17ᵛ–18: *Lects 1808–19 (CC)* I 267; *BL (CC)* II 57.

It is delightful to think that the beloved Apostle was born a Plato.[8] To him was left the almost oracular utterance of the Mysteries of the Christian Religion; whilst to St Paul was committed the task of explanation, defence and assertion of all the doctrines and especially of those metaphysical ones[d] touching the Will and Grace, for which his active mind, his learned education, his Greek Logic made him preeminently fit.[9]

[36:227]

In the first century Catholicity was the test of a Book or Epistle—whether it were Evangelicon or Apostolicon—being canonical.[10] This Catholic spirit was opposed to the Gnostic or peculiar spirit—the humor of fantastical interpretation of the Old Scriptures into[e] Christian meanings.[11] This Gnosis it is which St Paul says puffeth up—not *knowledge* as we translate it.[12] The Epistle of Barnabas, of the genuineness [f]of which I

---

[d] ones ~~of~~   [e] ~~by~~ into   [f] f 22ᵛ

[8] In John 21.24 (cf 13.23, 19.26, 21.7, 20) the author identifies himself as the disciple whom Jesus loved; the other gospels confirm that John's intimacy with Jesus is equal to that of Peter and James. The Gospel and Epistle of John could be Platonic to C because their philosophy, founded in the Logos, is profoundly Greek, rational, and ideal. HNC's note in *TT* (1835) quoted *SM* on all Scripture as "the form of reason itself". *SM (CC)* 18.

[9] Whether Paul speaks "of himself, of the Apostles, of the Prophets, or of the Churches, all is calm, and sober, tho' earnest, *prose*—strong sound Sense, with complete Self-possession!" C's note on Eichhorn *NT: CM (CC)* II 499.

[10] Although he gained his assurance from Eichhorn and other Biblical scholars, who would have reinforced his awareness of such passages on the Apostolic as 1 Cor 12.28 (in distinction from the original witnesses of Jesus' acts), C was sufficiently familiar with such pre-Nicene champions of catholicity as Irenaeus, Clement of Alexandria, and Ignatius of Antioch to know how works of "peculiar spirit" were refuted and rejected.

[11] Both this definition and C's choice of examples, the epistles of Barnabas and Hebrews, put the Gnostics in a favourable light. After reading Rhenferd on illusory views of early sects, C wrote concerning an account of the gnostic Basilides: "It is much to be regretted, that none of the Writings of the Gnostic Christians have been suffered to survive/ & that we can only refer to such convicted Bigots & Blunderers as Epiphanius & Irenæus!—". Annotation on Fleury *Ecclesiastical History: CM (CC)* II 713. Gnosis was "the supposedly revealed knowledge of God and of the origin and destiny of mankind, by means of which the spiritual element in man could receive redemption"; specifically, this was the esoteric knowledge that the "supreme remote and unknowable Divine Being" was separated by the mischance of emanations or "aeons" from the Demiurge, or Creator, who "was the immediate source of creation and ruled the world, which was therefore imperfect and antagonistic to what was truly spiritual". "Gnosticism" *ODCC*. On C's knowledge of the Gnostics, see 7 Jan–13 Feb 1823, above (at n 25).

[12] 1 Cor 8.1: γνῶσις φυσιοῖ, "Knowledge puffeth up". C wrote similarly, in a note on Donne *LXXX Sermons*, of "the Gnosis, i.e. the science of detecting the mysteries of faith in the simplest texts of Old Testament History, to the contempt or neglect of the literal & contextual

have no sort of doubt, is an example of this Gnostic spirit.[13] The Epistle
to the Hebrews is the only instance of Gnosis in the canon; it was written
evidently by some Apostolical man before the destruction of the Temple,
and probably at Alexandria.[14] For three hundred years it was not admitted on account of this difference in it from the other Scriptures; but its
merit was as great, and the Gnosis in it so kept within due bounds that its
admirers at last succeeded, especially by affixing St Paul's name to it, to
have it included in the Canon. Fortunately for us they did so.   [36:225]

Tertullian, a great liar, says something about an autograph of St
Paul's. Origen expressly says the reverse.[15]   [36:226]

Men generally, especially Churchmen, hate a slightly differing Friend
more than an opposing Enemy. You see now, how it is—the High

---

sense . . . It was *Gnosis*, and not Knowlege, as our English Testaments absurdly
render the words, that Paul warns
against, & most wisely, as *puffing* up—
inflating the heart with self-conceit, and
the head with idle fancies." *CM (CC)* II
285. Cf also Eichhorn *NT: CM (CC)* II
482–3. That "knowledge which puffeth
not up" is a prayerful need in *SM* App C:
SM (CC) 71.

[13] On the Epistle of Barnabas see 8 Jul
1827 and n 9, above. The translation of it
in *The Genuine Epistles of the Apostolic
Fathers* by William Wake (1657–1737),
abp of Canterbury, was included with
Wake's Hermas in the collection read by
C in Apr 1826: William Hone *The Apocryphal New Testament* (1820)—*CN* IV
5351–4; *CM (CC)* I 488–92. Barnabas 6–
16 is filled with typological interpretations of Christ as the figure of OT prophecies; the extreme example is § 9: Abraham circumcised 318, meaning 10 + 8
= IH = Jesus, + 300 = T = the
Cross. C rejected "the *lunacy* of the Understanding" in "the Epistle attributed
(and I think justly) to S[t] Barnabas", in a
note repeating that Paul meant Gnosis,
not knowledge. Eichhorn *NT: CM (CC)*
II 482.

[14] As suggested by Luther; see 7 Jan–
13 Feb 1823, above (at nn 35–6). C lamented in a marginal note that the Epistle
to the Hebrews, intended to elevate the
Jewish religion, had been "the chief oc-

casion and mean of literalizing and debasing" Christian doctrine. Eichhorn
NT: CM (CC) II 499.

[15] Quintus Septimus Florens Tertulli-
anus (c 160–c 230) *De praescriptione
haereticorum* ch 36: "ipsae authenticae
litterae" (the very apostolic writings); cf
De monogamia ch 11: "in Graeco au-
thentico" (in the genuine Greek). Migne
PL II 58, 996. Eichhorn had given assurances that no one had seen the original
Hebrew of the Gospel of Matthew. *NT* I
467. *TT* (1835) softened "great liar" to
"amongst his many *bravuras*", but C
seldom let up on Tertullian's "strange
impudence of fanaticism". *CN* III 3891.
Despite efforts of a favourite author to
rescue Tertullian from misrepresentations, C protested that "a Believer in all
the assertions & narrations of Tertullian,
and Irenæus would be a more wonder-
working Jonas, or John-ass! For he must
have swallowed Whales." Annotation
on a back flyleaf of Waterland *Importance of the Doctrine of the Holy Trinity
Asserted* (1734): *CM (CC)* V. More leni-
ently, C counted Tertullian among the
early bishops, "fervent, pious, and holy
Men but neither Critics nor Philosophers", who put doctrine above fact.
Annotation on F. E. D. Schleiermacher
A Critical Essay on the Gospel of St Luke
tr Connop Thirlwall (1825) Introduction:
CM (CC) IV.

Church hate the Evangelicals and Calvinists ten thousand times more than they do Unitarians—much less open Infidels, whom they seem to pet and favor.[16]   [36:229]

---

[g]Wordsworth,[h] like many other great and thinking men, was kept a long time from admitting the truths of Revelation, solely and exclusively because of the verbal Inspiration doctrine, which he had been taught to be a part of the Religion.[i][17]

I am persuaded that a Review would amply succeed even now, which should be started upon a published code of Principles—Critical—Moral—Political and Religious—which should announce what sort of books it would review—namely works of *literature* [j]as contra distinguished from all that offspring of the Press which in the present age supplies what was formerly done by conversation and speech—and should really give a fair account of what the Author *intended* to do in his own words, if possible, and also one or two fair specimens of the execution—which should never descend for one moment to personality—and should be provided before commencement with some dozen powerful articles upon fundamental topics to appear successively.[18] By such a plan I raised the Morning Post in a year from 900 to 7000 a day.[19] You see the great

---

[g–i] For the variant in MS F see App C, below   [h] W—th   [j] MS B f 23

---

[16] Totally restated in *TT* (1835) to declare the personal application: C will be "holden in worse repute . . . than the Unitarians and open infidels". The restatement avoids the questionable use of "much less", called in H. W. Fowler *A Dictionary of Modern English Usage* "a matter of difficulty even for those who are willing to be at the pains of avoiding illogicality"—as C was.

[17] Revised in MS F, but not published.

[18] C had promised Joseph Hardman in Mar 1828 to draw up a scheme of contents for "our Quarterly *Excursive* Magazine". *CL* VI 730. He consistently opposed the "arbitrary dictation and petulant sneers" of the reviews in being. *BL* ch 3 *(CC)* I 62 (the discussion in *BL* chs 2–3 is resumed in chs 21–2: I 40–63, II 107–16, 156–8). On 25 Oct 1812 Lady Beaumont reported C's opinion on "*Reviews* & the multiplication of newspapers as tending to amuse the mind superfi-

cially, and that at former periods when Lord Bacon and other great Philosophers and deep thinkers lived there being no such light matter in circulation the minds of men were employed in a more solid manner". Farington *Diary* XII 4228–9. C was of the same mind in 1827. *CL* VI 696–7. He was troubled when JTC became editor of *QR* and delighted when he ceased to be editor. *CL* V 361, 422, 525. He declared in 1826: "I cannot, at least will not, write in reviews". *CL* VI 608. He wrote acidly in a marginal note probably of 1833 on HC *The Worthies of Yorkshire and Lancashire*: "I would put H. on a year's *Fast* from all Review and Magazine Reading—as one means of getting rid of the constant itch to be witty . . .". *CM (CC)* II 64.

[19] *TT* (1835) changed "900" to "an inconsiderable number", but even a change of the 7000 would have failed to appease Daniel Stuart (1766–1846), who

Reviews are almost ashamed of reviewing in the old style, and have taken up Essay writing; hence such works as the Literary Gazette are set up for the purpose of advertizing new books of all sorts for Circulating Libraries.[20] The Median is still left to be taken.   [36:228]

Blanco White's Review was commenced without a single principle to direct it, and with the absurd disclaimer of certain public topics.[21] I pro-

---

had owned and edited the *M Post*. In a long letter to HNC on 19 Sept 1835 he protested: "Could Coleridge have written the Leading paragraph dailey, his services would have been invaluable; but an occasional Essay or two, now and then when Coleridge wanted money, could produce little effect. . . . It was the earliest and fullest accounts of [news events . . .] that raised the Morning Post, from 350 when I took it in August 1795 to 4500 when I sold it in August 1803. It never sold 7000 dailey ~~as~~ which Coleridge is said to have declared he raised it to, in one year; nor had any dailey Paper then ever sold 7000 dailey." VCL S MS F 6 f 1ᵛ. On 7 Oct he supplied the further details that the circulation of Aug 1795 was raised to 1000 in 1797, when "Mʳ Pitts additional tax . . . reduced it to 700 dailey." HNC dropped the offending sentence in 1836, but Gillman's attempt in *C Life* (G) 152–4 to placate Stuart was without avail. In *G Mag* for May and Jul 1838 (NS IX 485, X 22–4) Stuart published his version of his correspondence with everybody concerned. SC dealt mildly with the problem in *BL* (1847) II 391–408. Drafts of her first remarks and part of her fuller treatment in *EOT* (1850) I xc–xciii—in which she suggested that 7000 was the circulation of the *Courier* after writings by C that "made a sensation" according to Stuart himself—survive in VCL MS F 10.3. She might have suggested alternatively that C was doing the customary journalistic multiplication from subscribers to readers, as he did in writing to Josiah Wedgwood in 1800. *CL* I 569. Perspective on Stuart's deviousness and C's acknowledged service to him is provided by the editor of *EOT (CC)* esp I lix–lxxxiii. C wrote to Poole in Mar 1800 that he had declined Stuart's offer of half

shares in the *M Post* and *Courier*, and George Greenough heard him repeat in Jan 1801 that he had achieved for the *M Post* "so extensive a sale that the proprietor of it in gratitude offered to take him into partnership which he refused". *CL* I 582; *W&C* 234. Stuart acknowledged directly to C in Sept 1802 that his contributions had lifted the circulation of the *M Post* above the seasonal norm. *EOT (CC)* III 169. On 7 Dec 1809 C was allowed to boast in the *Courier* itself that his writings had achieved a "great increase of circulation". *EOT (CC)* II 37.

[20] The *Literary Gazette and Journal of Belles Lettres, Arts, Sciences*, a weekly source of information about new books, was founded in 1817, with William Jerdan (1782–1869) as editor. It had a rival from Jan 1828 in the *Athenaeum*. Jerdan, one of the founders of the RSL, had proposed C as Associate in 1824. *CL* v 329. His *Autobiography* (4 vols 1852–3) and *Men I Have Known* (1866) include memories of C's conversation, partly reproduced in *C Talker* 273–6. Circulating libraries, for lending new books by subscription, had been growing in number since the 1720s; their reputation as "the *slop-shops* in literature" is surveyed in ch 1 of J. M. S. Tompkins *The Popular Novel in England 1770–1800* (1932) and in Q. D. Leavis *Fiction and the Reading Public* (1932). In the *SM* C attacked circulating libraries and "the periodical press" as "the two public *ordinaries* of Literature". *SM (CC)* 36 and n.

[21] The *London Review*, "Published Quarterly" in Feb 1829 and for one more number. C initially thought it suitable for an article on Virgil's *Georgics* as a variety of didactic poetry, with judgements on the fitness for translating the work of the various European languages repre-

foundly reverence Blanco White; the Doblado's letters are exquisite.[22]

---

7. June. 1830.[1]

Southey's life of Bunyan is beautiful. I wish he had illustrated that mood of mind which exaggerates the inward depravation, as in Bunyan &c, by

---

sented in Sotheby's polyglot edition; but by 23 Mar he feared that his friend's review had "the want of *prominence*". *CL* VI 771, 787. Article I, headed "*The Times, the Morning Chronicle, &c. &c. The Edinburgh Review, The Quarterly Review, &c. &c.*", with the running-headline "Journals and Reviews", served as a statement of policy, mostly negative, remarking "that our object will be to stimulate instead of palling curiosity,—instead of manufacturing thoughts for the reader, to induce him to think for himself", and renouncing strong political feelings of a kind to distort the sentence of a judge: "Nor, in fact, do we choose to acknowledge any [opinion] more specific than a sincere attachment to Christianity, and a sincere desire for social improvement, with the least possible disturbance of established order." I 6, 8. The attempt, said White, was "still-born"; it "totally failed of success". *The Life of the Rev. Joseph Blanco White, Written by Himself . . .* ed John Hamilton Thom (3 vols 1845) III 130, 132. Some of C's writing plans died with the review. *CN* IV 5240, 5250.

[22] Joseph Blanco White, earlier José María Blanco y Crespo (1775–1841), was ordained a Roman Catholic priest in Spain in 1800, then an Anglican priest in 1814. He and C sought and found each other in 1825 (*CL* V 476, 481) and remained friends until Blanco White moved to Dublin in 1832. His sonnet *Night and Death*, addressed to C in 1825 and sent by Gillman to the *Bijou* (1828), was declared by C "the finest and most grandly conceived Sonnet in our Language". *CL* VI 713, 716. Among works by Blanco White, C annotated *Letters from Spain* by "Don Leucadio Doblado" (2nd ed 1825); *The Poor Man's*

Preservative Against Popery (1825); *Practical and Internal Evidence Against Catholicism* (1825), and *A Letter to Charles Butler, Esq.* (1826). *CM (CC)* I 500–25. C praised the *Preservative* to EC and to its author for "the charm of novelty". *CL* V 520, 522. He composed verses upon a second answer to Butler by Blanco White in 1826: *PW* (EHC) I 448–50; *CL* VI 980 and n; *CM (CC)* I 856–60. Cf "O that Blanco White would write, in Spanish, the Progress of a Pilgrim from the Pope's Cave to the Evangelist's Wicket Gate and the Interpreter's House!—". Annotation on Bunyan *Pilgrim's Progress: CM (CC)* I 814. But Blanco White's pilgrimage took him into Unitarianism and beyond after C's death, so that SC had to rescue C from a charge of association with Blanco White's late infidelity. *CIS* (1849) 237–41. In *TT* (1835) the passage at the end of the entry read: "I profoundly revere Blanco White; his Doblado's Letters are exquisite; but his Review was commenced without a single apparent principle to direct it, and with the absurd disclaimer of certain public topics of discussion." Blanco White and his review were both excised in *TT* (1836).

[1] HNC wrote to his father from Highgate on 8 Jun: "My uncle is at present quite come round, I think, & is very lively & entertaining in his conversation. His influence is undoubtedly very extensive, & his popularity slowly but constantly increasing. No public critic *now* denies his genius & the pre-eminence of his works—at least his poems. In this last point Tory & Radical seemed to agree. For a long time past I have been in the habit of noting down the remarkable things he says in conversation; I have 50 quarto pages of such memorabilia, &

extracts from Baxter's Life of himself.[2] It is, however, very extraordinary that Southey, admitting, as he does, that the Church and all parties generally were under a common delusion of believing an intolerance of *some* doctrines necessary, should still at this time of day pour out all his anger on the Puritans only. Besides what a *a*mistake it is to call these Puritans Dissenters;[3] before St Bartholomew's day, they were essentially a part of the Church and had as determined opinions in favour of a Church Establishment as the Bishops themselves.[4]   [36:231]

Southey talks of Baxter and the other erring and good men—but not one word of the Lauds and Sheldons who drove all these men astray.[5]

a f 23[v]

---

they would even now make one of the most interesting *Table Talks* that ever was published. I hope my collection may be doubled & more. You would be excessively struck with the vigor & originality & wisdom displayed upon ten thousand different subjects. The Johnsoniana seem to me poor stuff in comparison." UT ms. His count of fifty quarto pages ignores the earlier sixteen pages in MS A.

[2] In RS's "Life" of Bunyan prefixed to *The Pilgrim's Progress* (1830) he developed at length (pp viii–xliii) the argument that Bunyan's self-accusations of sinfulness (i.e in *Grace Abounding to the Chief of Sinners*) had been mistaken for evidence of depravity in his early life. In an annotation on p xlii C praised the "good sense and kind feeling—the wisdom of Love" in this approach. *CM (CC)* I 805. In a note on the life prefixed to *Pilgrim's Progress* (1820), in which the biographer referred to Bunyan's "open course of wickedness", C praised "our excellent Laureate" for reducing this charge "to its proper value". *CM (CC)* I 817. At 11 PM on 8 Jun 1830 C wrote in N 45 ff 21–21[v] what the editor of *CM (CC)* calls "quasi-marginalia" to the same effect as the conversation of 7 Jun. *CN* V. As C acknowledges later in the present entry, RS mentioned Baxter, and quoted *Reliquiae Baxterianae* on p xiv of his "Life", but not on the point C asks for, which could be richly supplied from Baxter's first two chapters in *Reliquiae*.

[3] If RS called the Puritans Dissenters it was unobtrusive, but he did make clear his disapproval of their "nonconformity", a term that allows for a willed failure to conform to the doctrines and usages of the Church without requiring the open separation of dissent. If neither C nor HNC's record blurred the distinction, perhaps HNC or somebody else present had called the Puritans Dissenters just before we are admitted to the scene. *TT* (1835) further clouded the reference by inscrting a sentence in praise of Bunyan's *Grace Abounding*.

[4] The massacre of the Huguenots began in Paris on 23–4 Aug 1572. In the 1560s Puritan liberty in ceremonial had turned to defiance of the rules of minimum observance; in 1566–7 nearly forty Puritan clergy in London suffered deprivation. "This precarious state of religion was the more terrible, because of the Parisian massacre." Daniel Neal (1678–1743) *History of the Puritans* . . . abridged by Edward Parsons, with the life of the author by Joshua Toulmin pt 4 ch 4 (2nd ed 2 vols 1811) I 169. In 1570 Pope Pius V published a bull excommunicating Queen Elizabeth. Attempts to replace episcopacy with presbyterian forms of Church government began in 1582. Henry Offley Wakeman *An Introduction to the History of the Church of England* rev S. L. Ollard (1923) 325–40.

[5] When RS wrote (p xv): ". . . while the bestial herd who broke in rejoiced in the havoc, Baxter and other such erring though good men stood marvelling at the

Laud was not exactly a Papist, to be sure; but he was on the road with the Church with him to a point, where Popery would have been inevitable. A wise and vigorous Popish King would very soon, and very justifiably too in that case, have effected a reconciliation between Rome and the Church of England when the line of demarcation was so obliterated.[6]　　　　　　　　　　　　　　　　　　　　[36:232]

Southey talks also of the bestial herd &c. Well! Whatever may have been the faults of the Puritans under Cromwell—to call them immoral as compared with the Cavaliers after the Restoration is really too much.[7]

[36:233]

The Presbyterians hated the Independents more than the Bishops, which induced them to effect the Restoration.[8]　　　　　　[36:234]

---

mischief which never could have been effected, if they had not mainly assisted in it'', C asked in the margin: ''But would these erring good men have been either willing or able to assist in this work, if the more erring Lauds and Sheldons of very equivocal goodness had not run riot in the opposite direction?'' *CM (CC)* I 803. He renewed this quarrel at pp lxi–lxv: *CM (CC)* I 805–6. SC, in *BL* (1847) II 422–5, defended C's persistent distaste for William Laud (1573–1645). Laud, as abp of Canterbury (1633–40) after holding a succession of episcopal and political offices under Charles I, compelled the uniformity of churchmen with such vigour that he was vengefully impeached, committed to the Tower, tried, and beheaded under the Commonwealth. Gilbert Sheldon, abp of Canterbury (1663–77), who played a rôle under Charles II similar to Laud's under Charles I, appears prominently in C's readings in Baxter, Clarendon, and Gilbert Burnet. HC explained what sorts of things C said before HNC knew him: ''He was, as far as his nature allowed him to hate any thing, a king-hater, and a prelate-hater, and spoke of Charles 1st and of Laud with a bitterness in which I never did and never can sympathize.'' *HCL* 189.

[6] C hypothesises a king wiser than he took any of the Stuarts to have been; even so, his ''very justifiably too in that case'' seems an exercise of historical imagination and detachment.

[7] To the words of RS quoted in n 5,

above, C's note on p xv continues: ''And the bestial Herd!—Merciful Heaven! Compare the whole body of Parliamentarians . . . with the morals and manners of the Royal & Prelatical Party in the reign of Charles II. *These* were indeed 'a bestial Herd' ''. He noted accurately that Baxter and Burnet both testified to ''the moral discipline'' under Cromwell. *TT* (1835) preserved C's view of the Cavaliers without reference to RS.

The moral certitude that C and RS shared with regard to public policy in 1794 took different routes. C referred to RS in the 1820s as ''Hugh Hussee'', meaning ''Heu! et Eheu'', ''Alas! Alas!'' *CN* IV 4985 and n.

[8] This motivation was so generally reported that it may need a query as to its significance in characterising C for readers of TT. An unlikely explanation of the need for C's comment had been provided: ''The presbyterians . . . seeing no likelihood of restoring the covenant . . . entered into a kind of confederacy with the royalists, to restore the King and the old Constitution. The particulars of this union are not known, because the historians who write of it being all royalists, have not thought fit to do so much honour to the presbyterians.'' Neal *History of the Puritans* pt 2 ch 4 II 450; cf 465. Baxter *Reliquiae Baxterianae* pt 1 ch 8 named Edmund Calamy (1600–66) and Edward Montagu (1602–71), 2nd Earl of Manchester, as the Presbyterians who chiefly ''encouraged and persuaded'' Gen Monck to restore Charles II. In a

The conduct of the Bishops to the King at Breda was wise and constitutional.[9] They knew, however, when the forms of the constitution were restored, all their power would revive again of course.   [36:235]

[b]In the accounts we have of the Savoy Conference, it is clear that the Churchmen never intended to yield one single letter, good, bad or indifferent.[c][10]

Intense study of the Bible will keep any writer from being *vulgar* in style.[11]   [36:236]

What frightful, what genuine Superstition is exemplified in that bandying of texts and halftexts, just [d]as memory suggested or chance brought them before Bunyan's eyes![12]   [36:231]

---

15. June. 1830.

Rabelais is a wonderful writer.[1] Panurge is a pollarded man; the man

[b-c] For the variant in MS F see App C, below   [d] f 24

---

note on Baxter C said that reading the Presbyterians reduced his "anti-prelatism". *CM (CC)* I 319. Presbyterians wished uniform Church government by elders, without a superior hierarchy; Independents, who believed that each body of men agreeing to do so could organise its own church, favoured a political republic. Oliver Cromwell, an Independent, had acted to exclude the Presbyterians from power.

[9] The bishops generally maintained a position of simultaneous readiness and official neutrality. They were in correspondence privately with Edward Hyde, Charles's Lord Chancellor and chief adviser, largely through John Barwick (1612–64), whom they sent among themselves to gather episcopal opinions on the succession and then in 1659 to Breda to report on the state of church affairs and to stand prepared for any instructions from Charles to the bishops. Neal pt 2 ch 4 II 470–1; Barwick in *DNB*. Letters from Barwick to Charles, earlier than this mission, had been published in *A Collection of Original Letters and Papers, Concerning the Affairs of England, from the Year 1641 to 1660. Found Among the Duke of Ormonde's Papers* ed Thomas Carte (2 vols 1739) II 201–4,

256–7; for C's knowledge of Carte see 11 Apr 1833, below (at n 5).

[10] In 1661 twelve Presbyterian and twelve Episcopalian leaders, with nine assistants to each side, met 15 Apr–24 Jul at the Savoy Palace, residence of Gilbert Sheldon, then bp of London, in an unsuccessful attempt to compromise on a form of service. Among the accounts available to C were *Reliquiae Baxterianae* pt 2 ch 4; Burnet *History of His Own Time* pt 1 bk II (2 vols 1724–34) I 179–82; Neal pt 2 ch 6 II 498–506. Baxter, who was charged to prepare a reformed liturgy for consideration by the conference, published *An Accompt of All the Proceedings of the Commissioners of Both Persuasions, Appointed by His Sacred Majesty, According to Letters Patent, for the Review of the Book of Common-Prayer, &c.* (1661). Revised in ms, the entry was not published.

[11] C is saying once again that Bunyan's style is not either "slang or ungrammatical".

[12] I.e. constant quotation and paraphrase in *The Pilgrim's Progress*, not always fitted to the narrative, reveals a form of idolatry, superstitious bibliolatry.

[1] C annotated *The Works of Francis*

with every quality except the Reason. Gargantua is the Reason; Panurge the Understanding. I know no example more illustrative of the distinction between the two.[2] Rabelais had no other mode of speaking the truth in those days but in such a form as this; as it was he was indebted to the king's protection for his life.[3] It is in vain to hunt about for a hidden meaning in all that he has written; you will observe that after any particularly deep blow, as the Papimania,[a] Rabelais, as if to break the blow and to appear unconscious of what he had done, writes a chapter or two of pure buffoonery.[4] His morals are high—as to his manners, to be sure, I

---

[a] Pappomania,

Rabelais tr. M. Le Du Chat and others (4 vols 1784), which disappeared after two of the notes were published in *LR* I but recently reappeared in a private collection. In a note dated 15 Sept 1829 C wrote on II 254–5: "It is impossible to read Rabelais without an admiration mixed with wonder at the depth & extent of his Learning, and his multifarious Knowlege—and original Observation, beyond what Books could in that age have supplied him with!" *CM (CC)* IV. HNC had transcribed the more general of the notes in MS B f 72ᵛ, on or shortly after 15 Aug 1832, when he himself was reading the histories of Gargantua and Pantagruel and had C's notes at hand, HNC to JTC: BM Add MS 47557 f 92. In MS B f 72ᵛ HNC included from these, as C's highest praise, "I class R. with the creative minds of the world—Shakspeare—Dante—Cervantes &c". In 1815 C drafted verses on "wisest Rabelais! wise, humane & good", and in Lect 9 of 24 Feb 1818 on the "Nature . . . of Humour" conjectured that the ribaldry of Rabelais was a disguise to attack the priesthood and the court of France. *CN* III 4264; *Lects 1808–19 (CC)* II 179. Later, his suggestion that "Pepys could have been the *Panurge* of the incomparable Rabelais" led C to wonder how Rabelais could have been French except on the (Coleridgian) hypothesis of a "continued dilution of the Gothic blood" from the reign of Henry IV. Annotation on *Memoirs of Samuel Pepys, Esq. F.R.S.* ed Richard, Lord Braybrooke (2 vols 1825) II i 254–5: *CM (CC)* IV.

[2] *TT* (1835) altered "Gargantua" to "Pantagruel". Cf "In Ch. 9 [of bk III] Pantagruel stands for the *Reason* as contra-distinguished from the understanding & choice—i.e. Panurge—and the humour consists in the latter asking advice of the former on a subject, in which the Reason can only give the necessary Conclusion, the Syllogistic Ergo, from the Premise provided by the Understanding itself . . .". Annotation on Rabelais *Works* II 258–61. On reason vs understanding see 7 Jan–13 Feb 1823, above, and n 44.

[3] Before *Pantagruel* was condemned by the Sorbonne in Oct 1533, Rabelais had come under the protection of Jean du Bellay (c 1492–1560), then bp of Paris; when bk III was published in 1546, he was a Cardinal and still Rabelais' protector. By 1537 Rabelais enjoyed the patronage of Francis I, but was soon abroad with Guillaume du Bellay. As Henry II had resolved his differences with the Pope when the first version of bk IV was published in 1548, it, like bks I–III, was condemned. "The Life of Dr. Francis Rabelais" *Works* (4 vols 1807) I 10–11 tells of a hoax such that Rabelais, "come to Paris, was immediately brought before the king, who knowing him asked him . . . where he had left the Cardinal du Bellay". As a presumed poison was found to be only ashes, Rabelais was ordered released. But the retailer of this anecdote says immediately, "I would not . . . be answerable for its truth." More soberly, the "Life" says that "King Francis had found the reports of his enemies to be unjust" (I 19).

[4] In bk IV chs 48–9 the Papimanians

can't say much.[5]   [36:237]

Swift's saying of King William's motto "Recepit, non rapuit"—"that the Receiver was as bad as the Thief"—was[b] very happy.[6]   [36:237]

The effect of the Tory[c] wits attacking Bentley with such acrimony has been to make them appear shallow, incompetent scholars.[7] Neither Bent-

[h] ~~is~~ was   [c] Tor~~iesy~~

---

consider the Pope to be God on earth; in chs 50–1 Rabelaisian humour is more obvious than satire in the treatment of the Pope's decretals.

[5] Cf "I could write a treatise in praise of the morality and moral Elevation of Rabelais' Works, which would make the Church stare, and the Conventicle groan—and yet should be the truth, & nothing but the truth." Annotation on a front flyleaf of vol I of Rabelais *Works*. Havelock Ellis tells how he acquired a copy of Rabelais' masterwork in response to a description of Rabelais in Macaulay's *Essays* as an indecorous buffoon and about 1875, in Sydney, planned an essay to announce that Rabelais was in reality a profound thinker and daring pioneer: "A few months later I discovered that . . . the task was unnecessary. I had procured Coleridge's *Table Talk* from England, and in that book I found a passage about Rabelais, of but a few lines only, but embodying an estimate indeed unlike that of the Philistinish Macaulay, an unqualified and enthusiastic recognition of Rabelais's immense genius. Here was a fellow-adventurer who had discovered the same spiritual continent that I had discovered! No critical judgment has ever caused me such a leap of joy. I still treasure my copy of this precious little book." *My Life: Autobiography of Havelock Ellis* (Boston, Mass 1939) 134–5. On Rabelais see also 11 Aug 1832, below (at n 7).

[6] "When Dean Swift was informed by a friend that William the Third had, upon his arrival, taken the following motto—*I have not stolen, but received*: 'Aye,' said the splenetic Dean, 'I always thought the *receiver* as bad as the *thief*.' " *National*

Anecdotes; Interspersed with Historical Facts; English Proverbial Sayings and Maxims . . . (3 pts 1812) i 33–4. C's precise source is untraced. In his Bristol lecture against the slave-trade C had asked: ". . . is it not an allowed axiom in Morality . . . that the Guilt of all attaches to each one who is knowingly an accomplice?" *Lects 1795 (CC)* 247. *TT* (1835) provided a transition to this entry by inserting a sentence on Swift as "the soul of Rabelais dwelling in a dry place", for which see 11 Aug 1832, below, and n 9. Vol v including *Gulliver's Travels* (now at UT), out of Swift *Works* (13 vols Edinburgh 1768) from WW's library, contains a note by C on the back endleaves distinguishing his position from that of most critics who "complain of the Houyhnhnms" and ranking pt 4 as "the highest effort of Swift's genius", with *A Tale of a Tub* ahead of Lilliput and Brobdingnag, and Laputa to be expunged. *CM (CC)* IV. C took Swift's other writings seriously enough to copy extracts (VCL S MS F 2.11) and to practise Swift's ironic methods in pieces for the *Courier* 26 Sept 1811, 1 Apr 1812, and 31 Mar 1818: *EOT (CC)* II 311n, 341–7, 484–9. In Oct 1820 C had commented on "the bad effect of Wit" in a sermon of Swift's. *CN* IV 4727. He noted a passage from *A Tale of a Tub* in N 30: *CN* IV 5041. On Swift vs Defoe and Asgill see below, 23 Apr 1832 (at n 4).

[7] Richard Bentley (1662–1742), Cantabrigian scholar and critic. For proving in an essay of 1697 and in its expansion, *Dissertation upon the Epistles of Phalaris* (1699), that the "letters of Phalaris" were a forgery, and thus supporting the Moderns against the Ancients, he

ley nor Burnet*d* suffered in the least from their hostility. Burnet's*e* book is a truly valuable book; his credulity is great, but his simplicity is equal, and he never deceives you for a moment.[8] [36:238]

---

25. June 1830

The Fresco paintings by Giotto and others in the Cemetery at Pisa are most noble.[1] Giotto was a contemporary*a* of Dante, and it is a curious

d Burnett   *e* Burnett's   *a* f 24*v*, the leaf beginning with the last syllables, "porary"

---

was attacked by Charles Boyle, later Earl of Orrery, by Alexander Pope, Samuel Garth, and Conyers Middleton, and most notably by Swift in *A Full and True Account of the Battel Fought Last Friday, Between the Antient and the Modern Books in St. James's Library* (1704). Swift was supporting his patron Sir William Temple, whose praise of Phalaris had set off the controversy. C recognised Bentley's great accomplishments as a classical scholar. In Dec 1797 he took notes from Bentley's *Remarks upon a Late Discourse of Free-thinking in a Letter to F. H. DD*. (1743, a new ed 1792). *CN* I 311–14. Bentley was a notorious tyrant as master of Trinity College, but C was content to repeat an innocuous Cambridge anecdote about him in *M Post* 11 Dec 1801: *EOT (CC)* I 294. Bentley's tampering with the text of *Paradise Lost* seems to be accepted without demur in a (deliberately) obscure note of 1804, and C praised his "sound Restoration" of Greek texts. *CN* II 2120; annotation on Beaumont and Fletcher *Dramatic Works: CM (CC)* I 376.

[8] Gilbert Burnet (1643–1715), bp of Salisbury *Bishop Burnet's History of His Own Time* (2 vols Dublin 1724–34), which C annotated. He also annotated RS's copy of Burnet *The Life of William Bedell, D.D.* (1685) and—of "so sensible and powerful a reasoner"—*The History of the Reformation of the Church of England* (2 vols Dublin 1730, London 1683). *CM (CC)* I 830–49. On an endleaf of *Bedell* C noted that "Burnet was notoriously rash & credulous" but grossly calumnious only of Sir Henry Wotton. *CM (CC)* I 843. C had an axe to grind against the Scots, in the *Courier* 16 Sept 1811, when he quoted the *History of His Own Time* on the grounds of the "known veracity, and now universally admitted impartiality" of "that excellent and primitive Bishop". *EOT (CC)* II 291–2. The collocation of Burnet and Swift is explicable either by direct reference or in response to a mention by someone else present of Swift's acerbic marginal notes on Burnet's *History of His Own Time*, which had been variously published from transcriptions and from Swift's own copy in John Barrett *An Essay on the Early Part of the Life of Swift* (1808) 186–228 and in the edition of Burnet revised by Martin Joseph Routh (6 vols Oxford 1823). Representative of what are announced on the title-page of the Burnet as "the cursory remarks of Swift" are "Nonsense", "Poor malice", "Puppy", "Sad trash", "A damnable lie!", and, of a reference to Baxter's many books (I 327), "Very sad ones".

[1] C visited Pisa in May and June 1806, in June with Thomas Russell of Exeter, who was studying art in Rome. *CN* II 2848, 2856–2858, *CL* II 1173, 1202; Farington *Diary* 2 Nov 1810: x 3782–3. The frescoes in the Campo Santo had in the past been ascribed primarily to Giotto di Bondone (c 1276–c 1337). C was impressed most of all by *The Triumph of Death*, on the south wall, ascribed by Vasari and generally in C's day to the Florentine artist Andrea Orcagna (c 1308–68). C's Lect 4 of the lectures on

question whether the painters borrowed from the poet, or vice versâ.[2] Certainly Michael Angelo and Raphael fed their imaginations highly with these grand drawings; especially Michael Angelo, who took from them his bold yet graceful lines.[3]   [36:239]

the history of philosophy contains his fullest surviving description of it: ". . . the effect of the appearance of Death on all men—different groups of men—men of business—men of pleasure—huntsmen—all flying in different directions while the dreadful Goddess descending with a kind of air-chilling white with her wings expanded and the extremities of the wings compressed into talons and the only group in which there appeared anything like welcoming her was a group of beggars. The impression was greater, I may say, than that which any poem had ever made upon me. There, from all the laws of drawing, all the absence of color (for you saw no color—if there were any you could not see it, it was gone) it was one mighty idea that spoke to you everywhere the same." *P Lects* (1949) 167–8; cf Lect 1 of 27 Jan 1818: *Lects 1808–19 (CC)* II 62–3. C's inclusion of the beggars indicates that he perceived the "mighty idea" as including triumph *over* death. Hazlitt, writing in "My First Acquaintance with Poets" that neither he nor C had any "idea of pictures" in 1798, intimated that C continued in ignorance: "He sometimes gives a striking account at present of the Cartoons at Pisa, by Buffamalco and others; of one in particular, where Death is seen in the air brandishing his scythe, and the great and mighty of the earth shudder at his approach, while the beggars and the wretched kneel to him as their deliverer. He would of course understand so broad and fine a moral as this at any time." *Liberal* II (1823) 44n–5. Hazlitt gave a more favourable report on C's enthusiasm for painting, including again *The Triumph of Death*, in *The Spirit of the Age*. *H Works* XI 33–4. His casual errors are correctible either from C or from Giovanni Rosini *Descrizione delle pitture del Campo Santo di Pisa coll'indicazione dei monumenti* (Pisa 1829)—a handbook that does not men-

tion the Algarotti (at n 6, below). At Benjamin Robert Haydon's on 27 Dec 1818, after C's first reference to the *Triumph* in his lecture of 27 Jan, Keats saw an engraving of it in *Pitture al Fresco del Campo Santo di Pisa intagliate da Carlo Lasinio* (Florence 1812) and interpreted the fresco quite differently from C's description. Robert Gittings *Keats* (Boston & Toronto 1968) 279–81 and Pl 39. After C saw the cemetery, its walls were further damaged by fire in 1823 and by heavy gunfire in 1944.

[2] In Lect 1 of 27 Jan 1818 of the literary lectures and in Lects 4, 5, and 14 of the lectures on the history of philosophy of 1819, as he had in a letter sent with a copy of *BL* in 1817 in an effort to educate Lord Liverpool, C proclaimed "the coincidence of the revival of Platonism by Dante and Petrarch with the appearance of Giotto, and the six other strong masters, preserved in part in the Cemeterio at Pisa, and the culmination of the 'divine Philosophy,' with Michael Angelo, Rafael, Titian, and Correggio". *CL* IV 759; cf *Lects 1808–19 (CC)* II 60; *P Lects* (1949) 167, 193–4, 393, 398. HNC, in a footnote in *TT* (1835), dealt with the friendship of Giotto and Dante.

[3] Greeting Samuel Rogers on his return from Italy in 1815, C trusted that he had seen Michelangelo's *Moses* and Sistine Chapel and "that rude but marvellous pre-existence of his genius in the Triumph of Death and its brother frescoes in the Cemetery at Pisa". The *Moses* and the cemetery each had "a life of its own in the spirit of that revolution of which Christianity was effect, means, and symbol". *CL* IV 569. In Lects 4 and 5 of the lectures on the history of philosophy C acknowledged in the frescoes at Pisa the same stiffness of outline as in earlier, Aristotelian painters of the Middle Ages, but found also a dawning of Platonism with "bewitching grace" as in

People may say what they please about the gradual improvement of the Arts. It is not true of the substance.[4] The Arts and the Muses both spring forth in the youth of nations like Minerva from the front of Jupiter—all-armed; manual dexterity may be improved indeed by practice.

[36:240]

Painting went on in Power till in Raphael it attained the apex, and in him too I think it began to turn down the other side. The Painter began to think of overcoming difficulties.[5]

After this the descent was rapid, till sculptors began to work inveterate likenesses of perriwigs in marble—as see Algarotti's tomb in the cemetery at Pisa[6]—and painters did nothing but *copy*, as well as they could,

Raphael, but "without that which can equally explain". *P Lects* (1949) 167, 193. Leigh Hunt, in an epistolary essay of 1822, was in agreement with C about the influence of the frescoes: ". . . it is an injustice to the superabundance and truth of conception in all this multitude of imagery, not to recognise the real inspirers as well as harbingers of Raphael and Michael Angelo, instead of confining the honour to the Massacios and Peruginos". "Letters from Abroad. Letter I.—Pisa" *Liberal* I 1822) 114.

[4] Hazlitt had put his own mark clearly on this sentiment. Between 1814 and 1819 he had published or had said in lectures at least six times, with minor variations: "Nothing can be more contrary to the fact, than the supposition that in what we understand by the *fine arts*, as painting, and poetry, relative perfection is only the result of repeated efforts in successive periods, and that what has been once well done, constantly leads to something better. What is mechanical, reducible to rule, or capable of demonstration, is progressive, and admits of gradual improvement: what is not mechanical, or definite, but depends on feeling, taste, and genius, very soon becomes stationary, or retrograde, and loses more than it gains by transfusion. The contrary opinion is a vulgar error . . .". Lect 3 of *Lectures on the English Poets: H Works* v 44; earlier appearances of the statement are listed IV 390n. In "Why the Arts Are Not Progressive?— A Fragment", the last piece in *The Round Table* (2 vols 1817), and again in

Lect 3 (on Shakespeare and Milton) Hazlitt listed poets and painters who demonstrate that "giant sons of genius" attain "the utmost limit of perfection" near the beginning of their respective arts. *H Works* IV 161, v 45. Titian and Correggio join Raphael and Michelangelo in making the demonstration.

[5] That painting reached its peak in Italy about 1520 had been accepted without much cavil since that date. To the artists after Raphael who tried sophisticated experiments with unexpected problems the descriptive name of Mannerism was assigned long after C's day, although Vasari used the word *maniera* for those like himself who made difficulties to be overcome. Absence of the Venetian colourist Titian from C's remarks is probably not accidental. His focus is on Tuscany and Rome. The aesthetic principle involved is expressed in a couplet of Charles Alphonse du Fresnoy's poem on the art of painting, as translated by William Mason (lines 615–16) and attached in 1797 and later editions of Reynolds *Discourses*:

Then as the work proceeds, that work submit
To sight instructive, not to doubting wit.

[6] Count Francesco Algarotti (1712–64), Italian critic, philosopher, and connoisseur, friend of Voltaire and Frederick the Great. His sepulchre has survived. Hunt (n 3, above) had written: "Here is a handsome monument, with a profile, to Algarotti, erected by Freder-

the external face of Nature.[7]

Now in this age, we have a sort of reviviscence not, I fear, of the Power—but of a Taste for the Power of the early times.[8]   [36:241]

You may get a motto for every sect or line of thought or religion from Seneca—yet nothing is ever thought out in him.[9]   [36:242]

Basil Montagu[b] is a fine house made up of passages leading to nothing at all.[10]

[b] B. M.

---

ick of Prussia. . . . In truth, these modern gettings up of renown, in the shape of busts and monuments to middling men of talent, appear misplaced when you come to notice them.'' Nevertheless, Hunt continued, the old frescoes bring into harmony even the Algarotti and a more recent monument to Lorenzo Pignotti (I 109–10).

[7] On C's distinction of copy vs imitation see 1 Jul 1833 (at n 35), below.

[8] C's terms were provided by Sir Joshua Reynolds: ''It must be remembered, that this great style itself is artificial in the highest degree: it presupposes in the spectator, a cultivated and prepared artificial state of mind. It is an absurdity therefore, to suppose that we are born with this taste, though we are with the seeds of it, which, by the heat and kindly influence of this genius, may be ripened in us. . . . When the Student has been habituated to this grand conception of the Art, when the relish for this style is established, makes a part of himself, and is woven into his mind, he will, by this time, have got a power of selecting from whatever occurs in nature that is grand, and corresponds with that taste which he has now acquired, and will pass over whatever is common-place and insipid. . . . That the Art has been in a gradual state of decline, from the age of Michel Angelo to the present, must be acknowledged; and we may reasonably impute this declension to . . . indolence,—not taking the same pains as our great predecessors took . . .''. *Discourses* xv (the last, 1791).

[9] C occasionally recorded aphorisms

from the tragedies, epistles, and essays of Seneca (c 4 B.C.–A.D. 65). *Lects 1795 (CC)* 209; *EOT (CC)* III 59; cf *CN* I 884, 1507, II 2615, 3086, III 3523, IV 4853, 5089. Although on 1 Jul 1833 (below) C names Seneca as exemplifying a lack of fusion in style, and in a letter of 27 Oct 1826 named him with other authors as having ''a sort of *memorandum* character'' essentially Roman, he had written to Poole in 1809 that his own complicated style resembled Bacon's, based in turn on Seneca's, in contrast with illogical books of the day that imitated the French with the consequent effect of ''a mere bag of marbles, i.e. aphorisms and epigrams on one subject''. *CL* III 234, VI 639. C's signature and WW's appear on a Seneca now at Cornell University: *L. Annaei Senecae philosophi, et M. Senecae rhetoris quae extant opera* ([Antwerp] 1609).

[10] Most probably the remark refers to Basil Montagu (1770–1851), legal and miscellaneous writer who specialised in bankruptcy, editor of Bacon (16 vols 1825–36) and friend of WW. HCR, who first met him in 1815, had been told by WW that Montagu was ''a *philanthropised courtier*''; at his death HCR summarised: ''He was a man of generous impulses, but wanting consistency and full of ostentation and pretence.'' *CRB* I 170, II 716. After a chequered friendship that began in 1797 or earlier, C left one of three gold mourning rings to Montagu in his will of 17 Sept 1829. *CL* VI 1000. The initials ''B. M.'' for Montagu occur in a letter of 11 Sept 1830 to HNC, in which C jests that certain key ideas pour

He is insane with the privilege of acting upon common occasions as if he were really sane.[11]

---

*a*2. July. 1830.[1]

Every man is born an Aristotelian or a Platonist.[2] I don't think it possible that any one born an Aristotelian *can* become a Platonist, and I am sure

a f 25

---

out of C "as inevitably as the great *Bacon* from B.M.—nolens volens." *CL* VI 847. A vertical line carries through this entry and the next to the bottom of f 24ᵛ, but they were not published and have not been found among the scraps of MS F.

[11] HNC's creation of a separate entry makes it uncertain that this remark concerns "B. M.". More than two years after Montagu's indiscretion of Oct 1810 led to the notebook entry, "W. authorised M. to tell me, he had no Hope of me!", C described to Poole his difference with WW as "occasioned *in great part* by the wicked folly of the Archfool Montague", an "acknowledged Wretch". *CN* III 3991 f 36; *CL* III 437–8. But C had begun to forgive when Montagu took in HC in the crisis of 1820. *CL* v 93. Of the son Basil Caroline Montagu (Dec 1792–Jun 1830) it would have been difficult to say that he acted as if sane "upon common occasions"; it would have been equally difficult to regard him as the "fine house" of the previous entry.

[1] On 24 Jun HNC and SC had taken occupancy of a furnished house, 1 Downshire Place, Downshire Hill, Hampstead, near enough for C to visit during periods of good health. In the letter of 8 Jun to his father (see 7 Jun 1830 n 1, above) HNC explained that he would be able to walk from Lincoln's Inn in an hour for supper at home. Until he could "get things quite right" for SC, who was expecting a child in Sept, she visited with the EC family at Eton. The talk of 2 Jul (Fri), and also the notation of 15 Jul, below, occurred before her return. Letters of 29 Jun–15 Jul 1830. UT mss.

[2] C's distinction between the Platonist, for whom ideas are constitutive, and the Aristotelian, for whom ideas are regulative only, occurs most lucidly in a letter of 14 Jan 1820 to James Gooden. *CL* v 13–15. C's choice for the contrast was sharpened by Goethe's discussion in *Zur Farbenlehre* (1810) II 140–1 of discipleship in Western thought to the Platonic or Aristotelian systems and perhaps by F. Schlegel *Vorlesungen über Litteratur* I 136–45, II 77. After C had read these works he commented on the distinction in marginalia on Tennemann *Geschichte der Philosophie* I 107 ("the two genera generalissimi of Philosophizing") and at greater length VIII i 130. *CM (CC)* v. In Jan 1819, before he began to thread the distinction through his own lectures on philosophy, he asked J. H. Green to make *Zur Farbenlehre* available to him again specifically for the passage in which Goethe "compares Plato with Aristotle". *CL* IV 911. In his readiness for the suggestion from Goethe he had previously (1810) described the two possible systems of philosophy as that of Spinoza, the absolute or ontosophical, and that of Kant, the relative or anthropological. *CN* III 3756. The matter is finely discussed in *P Lects* (1949) 52–5, with nn on 413–15. C emphasises even more strongly that one is born either Platonist or Aristotelian in a marginal note on Hooker: *CM (CC)* II 1147. HNC's note to this entry in *TT* (1835) called attention to the final words of *SM* App E, in which C came down in 1816 on the side of Plato

no born Platonist *can* ever change into an Aristotelian. They are the two classes of men beside which it is next to impossible to conceive a third. The one consider Reason a Quality or Attribute; the other consider it a Power. I believe Aristotle never could get to understand what Plato meant by an Idea; there is a passage indeed in the Eudemus which looks like an exception, but I doubt not of its being spurious, as[b] that whole work is supposed to be.[3] With Plato Ideas are *constitutive* in themselves.

Aristotle was and is still the sovereign lord of the Understanding—the Faculty judging by the Senses. He was a Conceptualist, but never could raise himself into that higher state, which was *natural* to Plato and is so to others, in which the Understanding is distinctly *contemplated* and looked down upon from the Throne of Actual Ideas or Living, Inborn, Essential Truths.[4]

Yet what a mind was Aristotle's! Only not the greatest that ever animated the human form! The parent of *Science*, properly so called; the founder or editor of *Logic*.[5] But he confounded Science with Philoso-

[b] as ~~indeed~~

and Plotinus, for ideas as constitutive, against the regulative of Aristotle and Kant. *SM (CC)* 114. HNC took the "Whether" and "problem" there to express indecision, but a just paraphrase would be, "Whether to go to heaven or to hell is the highest problem of life."

[3] Eudemus of Rhodes, Greek mathematician and astronomer of the fourth century B.C., is the supposed editor of the summary of Aristotle's lectures on ethics known as the *Eudemian Ethics*. HNC's questioning note in *TT* (1835) seems to require of the Aristotelian source a clearer definition of Platonic ideas than C's remark demands. C's position is carefully measured, but possibly confuses the *Eudemian Ethics* with Aristotle's lost early work, *Eudemus*, a dialogue on the soul as "idea," occasioned by the death of Eudemus of Cyprus. C's source is untraced, but see W. K. C. Guthrie *History of Greek Philosophy* (Cambridge 1962–81) VI 66–73. In 1818–19, finding it alleged that Aristotle's point of view was so contradictory that he could not have comprehended the spirit of Plato's speculations well enough to grasp the meaning of ideas properly, C had answered: "That Aristotle did not,

and as a mere tho' most eminent Philologist, ⟨could not⟩ *behold* the *Ideas* of the divine Philosopher, is most true; but that he should so grossly misunderstand his *words*, as to have persisted in taking as constitutive what Plato had taught as only regulative—this is little less than impossible." Annotation on Tennemann *Geschichte der Philosophie* III 26–7: *CM (CC)* V.

[4] Although Kant had made it possible for C to join Plotinus among the "others" who looked down upon the understanding, C expressed the enthronement in a way to exclude Kant.

[5] In Feb 1824, insisting to George Skinner of Cambridge on the importance of logic equally with mathematics, C lamented that a "recent perusal of Aristotle's Analytics & Topics with a superficial looking thro' his Metaphysics convinces me . . . that we have not even a philosophic statement . . . of what parts possessed only a temporary and accidental Value and what possess a permanent worth". *CL* V 341. In the essays on method C offered among his defences of Aristotle against detraction by Bacon that the most eminent of recent zoologists and mineralogists admired Aristotle

phy—which is an error. Philosophy is the middle state between Science or Knowledge and Wisdom or Sophia.[6]   [36:243]

The Duke of Wellington has failed in a foolish attempt to govern a great Nation by word of command ᶜin the same way as he commanded a highly disciplined army.[7] He is unaccustomed to, and despises the inconsistencies, the weaknesses, the bursts of heroism followed by prostration and cowardice which invariably characterize all popular efforts; he forgets that after all it is from such efforts that all the great and noble institutions of the world have come, and that on the other hand the discipline and organization of armies has been only like a cannon ball, the object of which has been Destruction.[8] The Duke does not stand in the light of an

ᶜ f 25ᵛ

---

as "the first clearer and breaker-up of the ground in natural history". *Friend (CC)* I 483. C had written in a footnote to *The Friend* of 14 Sept 1809 that Aristotle by constructing a table of the mental faculties proved "his Penetration and philosophical Genius" as "the first systematic Anatomist of the Mind". *Friend (CC)* II 77n.

[6] In a letter of 27 Feb 1819, with a nod towards Steffens, C defined philosophy as "the Love of Wisdom and the Wisdom of Love". *CL* IV 922n. In *BL* ch 9 it is "an affectionate seeking after the truth". *BL (CC)* I 142. In the second essay on method he had written of philosophy as intermediary: "Religion . . . is the ultimate aim of philosophy, in consequence of which philosophy itself becomes the supplement of the sciences . . . as the convergence of all to the common end, namely, wisdom". *Friend (CC)* I 463. C could believe his distinctions worth making; both philosophy and science are defined in Johnson's *Dictionary* as knowledge (the first is also argumentation, the other an art attained by precepts), and wisdom itself is (1) "the knowledge of divine and human things" or (2) prudence.

[7] Arthur Wellesley (1769–1852), commander in the Netherlands (1794–5), India (1797–1805), Copenhagen (1807), the Peninsula (1808–13), France (1813–14, 1815); created 1st Duke of

Wellington (1814); Prime Minister from Jan 1828. When the first leader of the Commons under Wellington, William Huskisson, was forced to resign in 1828 over the issue of rotten boroughs, former members of the Canning cabinet resigned with him. In 1829 Sir Charles Wetherell was forced from the office of attorney-general because he refused to draw up a bill for Catholic emancipation. Wellington himself wrote to Harriet Arbuthnot in Dec 1829: "I feel myself to be situated as I was in the Command of the Army; without resource excepting in my own Mind and knowing that where I was not myself to give directions matters would go wrong." Elizabeth Longford *Wellington, Pillar of State* (1972) 204. Mrs Arbuthnot admitted that he had a "dictatorial & arbitrary spirit". Ibid 339. C's strong language is subdued in the published version.

[8] HNC's note in *TT* (1835) cited *Wallenstein* pt 1, *The Piccolomini* I iv 68–71 on the destructiveness of the cannonball. *PW* (EHC) II 613. These lines are Octavio's answer to his son Max's proposal that it be allowed the privilege of the chieftain (lines 56–60):

to move and act
In all the correspondencies of greatness.
The oracle within him, that which lives,
He must invoke and question—not dead books,

ordinary prime minister, but is a substitute for the King; but yet his jealousy will not permit him to allow any one else to hold that office. He has only succeeded in getting even such a monarchist[d] as Peel to act for him in the Commons by accepting a man who had ruined himself for ever by his glaring inconsistency.[9] [36:244]

How base and baseless (to pun a little!) has been the foreign policy of this country! The stock-jobbing and moneyed interest prevails over national honor, and national justice. The country gentlemen join in this. Canning felt this keenly, but said it was difficult to contend with the moneyed men.[10] As if this mighty and imperial Island must go to war, in order to

---

[d] monarchis

Not ordinances, not mould-rotted papers.

Perhaps C reminded HNC on 2 Jul of this debate between the Piccolomini; it applies aptly to his view of Wellington.

[9] Sir Robert Peel, leader of the Commons, had been Home Secretary in Wellington's administration from its inception in Jan 1828. He had succeeded his father as 2nd Bt on 3 May 1830. After active opposition to Catholic emancipation until the party and cause of Daniel O'Connell gained strength in Parliament as well as in the country at large throughout 1828, Peel had convinced Wellington that they must bring in a bill favouring emancipation. He tried to explain his reversal in a speech of 5 Feb 1829. Wetherell's vehement address of 18 Mar, directed ostensibly against Brougham, applied equally to Peel: "He had no speech to eat up. He had no apostacy to explain . . . He had not to say that a thing was black one day and white another. He would rather remain as he was, the humble member for Plympton, than be guilty of such apostacy—such contradiction—such unexplainable conversion—such miserable, such contemptible apostacy." Hansard NS XX 1263–4, where "He had" = "I have." Peel, immediately voted out of his Oxford seat for what TT calls his "glaring inconsistency", was returned in 1830 as MP for Tamworth. Wellington had considered

since May resigning the government into Peel's hands. Longford 207. On 2 Jul, William IV's tenure of only six days as King added to the Duke's enduring strength as the hero of Waterloo to account for the hyperbole of C's "substitute for the King". Objections such as C's were to bring the fall of Wellington and Peel from office on 16 Nov. Brougham was to write that Peel by the Catholic bill "conferred a great benefit on the country at the cost of large sacrifices to himself", including the sacrifice, "his adversaries remarked", of "all claims to political consistency, and of all authority and weight in the country". *Ed Rev* LIII (Jun 1831) 481. The last two sentences of this entry were omitted from the published version.

[10] Although Miguel is not mentioned at this point in *TT* (1835), policy with regard to Portugal is the central thrust of the entry. Canning had been troubled over Portugal from 1822 until his death. His famous speech of 12 Dec 1826—"I called the New World into existence to redress the balance of the Old"—was a defence of his counter-intervention in Portugal to repulse incursions that were supported by Spain and allowed by France for the purpose of restoring arbitrary rule. In similar crises of Jun 1824 and early 1826 Canning had successfully manoeuvred to avoid sending British troops. Dixon *George Canning* 245–51. As leader of the Commons in the Liver-

bring that mean monster Miguel to reason![11] If, as is reported, England, Russia and Austria have negotiated with Pedro for the ͤunion of his daughter with that wretch and stipulated for an entire renunciation of the Charter—I do hope for the sake of our dear Country, that there is still public spirit enough left to overwhelm the infamous ministers who are concerned in the transaction![12]   [36:245]

I once sat in a coach opposite a Jew—a symbol of Clothes Bags—an Isaiah of Hollywell Street[13]—he would close the window—I opened it—he

ͤ f 26

pool administration, Canning had also felt the pressures and hostility of the country gentlemen and what *TT* (1835) called "the city train-bands" (for the ms "moneyed men"), in 1825–6, when a speculative boom had been followed by a crash, a panic run on small banks, release of corn by the government, and a new Corn Bill (crippled by Wellington).

[11] King John (João) VI of Portugal had left his son Dom Pedro (1798–1834) to succeed as Emperor of Brazil in 1823 when he himself returned to a constitutional regime in Lisbon. When John summoned the Portuguese Cortès in 1824, his second son Dom Miguel (1802–66) attempted a coup but failed. Ambassadors of Spain, Russia, Prussia, and Austria all protested against assembly of the Cortès and John's installation of a pro-British ministry. When John died in 1826, Pedro renounced the throne of Portugal in favour of his daughter the Infanta Maria (1819–53), with his sister Isabella as Regent and with the betrothal of Maria to Miguel. In Feb 1828, with support from all the absolutist powers, Miguel entered Portugal; in July he had himself crowned King. Throughout 1829, and despite provocation from Miguel in 1830, Wellington insisted on non-intervention until after the date of C's expostulation. Although Wellington had opposed Canning's intervention, he had referred privately as early as 24 Mar 1828 to Miguel's "acts of folly amounting to madness". Longford 156. In 1830 Miguel blockaded Terceira, in the Azores, where the government of Maria

II had been established. On 2 Jul C knew that the blockade had led to Miguel's seizure of British merchantmen as prizes. *The Times* 1 Jun 1830; *A Reg* for 1830 History 298. "Extracts from Table Talk &c" preserved from HNC by SC includes an earlier reaction by C: "Too hopeless for indignation I turn sick at heart from the perusal of the State Papers respecting the relations & conduct of our Government toward . . . Don Pedro . . . to the present 21 June *1829*." VCL S MS 20.

[12] Although diplomatic efforts to prevent the impending civil war in Portugal had included an attempt to bring about the marriage of Miguel and Maria originally sanctioned by Pedro, Miguel at this date had been married several months. Antonio G. Mattoso *História de Portugal* (2 vols Lisbon 1939) 268–71. As C's remark illustrates, news of Portuguese affairs reached the London press by very indirect and unofficial means.

[13] *TT* (1835) had added to the record of MS B (13 Apr 1830, above, at n 16) a reference to Duke's Place (off Houndsditch) and Holywell St, Shoreditch (built on the site of rubbish accumulated after the Great Fire of 1666) as places where Jews were concentrated. In the eighteenth century the itinerant "old Clo'-man", who wore a long gaberdine, was by far the most visible of Jews in London; in C's lifetime their numbers and visibility steadily decreased. Sir Walter Besant *London in the Eighteenth Century* (1903) 85–6, 178, 262. In Duke's Place, inhabited by Jews from 1650, the Great

closed it again—Upon which I looked gravely at him and said—"Son of Abraham! thou smellest! Son of Isaac! thou art offensive! Son of Jacob! thou stinkest damnably! See the man in the Moon! He is holding his nose at thee at that distance: Dost thou think that I sitting here can endure it any longer?" The Jew was astounded—opened the window himself, and said "he was sorry he did not know before I was so great a shentleman!!"[14] [36:248]

Bourrienne's Memoirs are most admirable.[15] He has one remark, when comparing Buonaparte with Charlemagne, which I had attempted to express in the Friend, but which Bourrienne has condensed into a sentence worthy of Tacitus, or Machiavel or Bacon, i.e. that Charlemagne was above his Age, Buonaparte was only above his competitors, but under his *Age*.[16] Buonaparte was never great except as an Actor; when not acting a part, he was contemptible. [36:246]

Synagogue was opened 1722, rebuilt 1790. Most of the Jews clustered in Aldgate and Whitechapel were Ashkenazim, in London commonly known as "Dutch Jews". Adler *London* 119, 150–3. C condemned Jewish neglect of "their Poor", as a contrast with Quakers, in a marginal note on "Ueber das Lustspiel die Juden" in Lessing *Sämmtliche Schriften* xxiii 125–6. *CM (CC)* iii.

[14] C's anecdotes sometimes report aggressive behaviour towards others (see e.g. Methuen's two examples, below, App F 12), but his practice in letters confirms rather the many reports of his hearers that he normally spoke sharply only of persons not present. More frequently he offended by absent-mindedly or half-consciously denouncing a group or a doctrine, e.g. Unitarianism, in the presence of an adherent. Perhaps C could have laughed with a hearer of this anecdote who pointed out that its teller had invited the episode by not looking like a gentleman. *TT* (1835) inserted ahead of this anecdote another (36:247), in which C accepts the justice of a Jewish ragpicker's retort, and it bridged the anecdotes with a generalisation that he had never borrowed money from Jews. In these entries C's friendship with Hurwitz makes no imprint; HNC's advisers, so alert on other subjects to the difference between

private utterance and public influence, seem to have taken for granted the social assumptions here exposed. In print "shentleman" became "gentleman".

[15] Louis Antoine Fauvelet de Bourrienne (1769–1834), French diplomat *Mémoires de M. de Bourrienne, Ministre d'État, sur Napoléon, Le Directoire, Le Consulat, L'Empire, et la Restauration* (10 vols Brussels 1829), tr as *Private Memoirs of Napoleon Bonaparte* (4 vols 1830), which C annotated. Private secretary to Napoleon (1797–1802), Bourrienne had offered his services to Louis xviii, who named him Minister of State. More recently he had been the chief spokesman for Charles x in the Chamber of Deputies. Between the utterance and publication of C's remarks, Barry E. O'Meara, who had been Napoleon's surgeon at St Helena, rebutted Bourrienne in *Observations upon the Authenticity of Bourrienne's Memoirs of Napoleon* (1831). When SC finished reading the *Mémoires*, she praised the character-portraits but noted that Scott's life of Napoleon was more romantic. SC to HNC 12 Sept, 6 Oct 1833. UT Grantz 578. Historians use Bourrienne with caution.

[16] "In my opinion an immense difference exists between them. Charlemagne was really superior to his age, which he endeavoured to associate with his glory

*ᵃ*15. July. 1830.

Bourrienne is the French Pepys; with right feelings, yet always wishing to participate in what was going on, be it what it might be.¹ He is the only writer that has shown Buonaparte to the world as he really was.

[36:246]

---

24. July 1830.

During the middle ages the Papacy was in fact nothing but a confederation of the learned men against the barbarism and ignorance of the times.¹ The Pope was chief of this confederacy, and so long as he re-

---

ᵃ f 26ᵛ

---

by advancing it in knowledge, whereas Bonaparte was superior, not to his age, the glory of which he wished to engross, but merely to the men of his age, which is a very different thing." Bourrienne *Private Memoirs of Napoleon* III 38. Cf C's annotation: *CM (CC)* I 715. In 1809 C had developed in two numbers of *The Friend* his reference to Napoleon on 7 Sept as "the mimic and Caricaturist of Charlemagne"; he argued, mostly by implied contrast and comparison, that Charlemagne was "an Hero" with a government "splendid abroad and fearfully oppressive at home". *Friend (CC)* II 62–6, revised I 82, 84–90. His material on Charlemagne was avowedly adapted from Michael Ignaz Schmidt *Geschichte der Deutschen* (Ulm 1785). Napoleon had evoked the comparison with Charlemagne, notably at his coronation in 1804 and upon taking Vienna in 1805. That C would think of Niccolò Machiavelli (1469–1527) with Tacitus and Bacon as a writer of laconic aphorisms follows from his uses of *Il Principe* and *Discorsi* in *Friend (CC)* I 123, 274, 324; *EOT (CC)* I 421.

¹ C's marginalia on Samuel Pepys (1633–1703) praised his diary for its "minuteness & truth of portraiture", but disparaged the author as prudential and calculating, filled with "Self-love and Self-interest", with "the queerest & most omnivorous Taste" enabling him to declare Shakespeare's plays silly trash. Annotations on *Memoirs* ed Braybrooke (1825) II i 348, 125, 151: *CM (CC)* III. To say that X was the French, or Swedish, or local Y was a common nineteenth-century formula, almost a disease, later parodied as in "Coleridge was the Wordsworth of poetry".

¹ *TT* (1836) corrected the opening phrase to "the early part of the middle ages"; *TT* (1835), in the final sentence of the entry, corrected "the beginning" to "the middle" of the sixteenth century. How far the supremacy of early "successors to St Peter" had been acknowledged in their own time was a boiling issue between Roman Catholic and Protestant theologians and historians that had certainly not cooled in C's time. Here C accepts that supremacy as both acknowledged and just from the fourth through the twelfth century, as he does in a marginal note explaining that "as long as the Christian Churches were disjoined specks amid Paganism in the first Half— & till Gotho-Celtic Christendom was organized in the second—the Papacy was a Good". H. E. G. Paulus *Das Leben Jesu* (2 vols Heidelberg 1828) I vi–vii: *CM (CC)* IV. The Scottish Calvinist William Mackray dated the "spiritual supremacy of the Roman pontiffs" from the seventh century, their consolidation of temporal power from the eighth. *An Essay on the Effect of the Reformation on Civil Soci-*

tained that character exclusively, his power was just and irresistible. It preserved for us and all posterity all that we have now of the illumination of past ages. But as soon as the Pope made a separation between his character as first Clerk in Christendom and as a secular Prince; as soon as he began to squabble for towns and castles, then he at once broke the charm and gave birth to a revolution.[2] From that moment those who still remained true to the cause of truth and knowledge became opponents of the Roman See. Wicliffe rose—Huss—Jerome—the Albigenses; in short every where, but especially throughout the North of Europe the breach of feeling and sympathy went on widening—so that all Germany, England, Scotland &c started like a Giant out of sleep at the first blast of Luther's trumpet.[3] Nay, in France one half of the people, and that the most

---

ety in Europe (1829) 14n. C, as reported, omits to mention as a cause of the Reformation the greatly increased papal claims to spiritual supremacy, as in the naming of bishops and the administration of ecclesiastical courts.

[2] Lands were given to the Popes from the fourth century onwards. The donation of the exarchate of Ravenna in 754–6 by the father of Charlemagne, Pepin the Short, marks the beginning of the Papal States. Boniface VIII, Pope 1294–1303, was the first to proclaim a temporal as well as spiritual ascendancy, although territorial conflicts between the Popes and secular rulers had been frequent since the eighth century. Julius II (1443–1513), Pope 1503–13, as one Italian sovereign competing for territory and temporal power with other Italian sovereigns, best fits C's description of a squabbler for towns. C, in terms of *C&S*, here traces a change from the responsible ascendancy of a clerisy to the rise of "*Anti-Christ, i.e.* a usurped power *in* the church itself". *C&S (CC)* 139. He was mindful of the gradual replacement of Alexandria by papal libraries as the chief preserver of cultural records, notable as early as the destruction of Alexandrian rolls by Theodosius I in A.D. 391.

[3] Cf Ps 78.65 (66) in BCP: "So the Lord awaked as one out of sleep: and like a giant refreshed with wine." Kant, awakened by Hume from his dogmatic slumbers, "took possession" of C "as with a giant's hand". *BL* ch 9 *(CC)* I 153. The trumpet-blast derives from Josh 6.5, Rev 1.10, 4.10, as in John Knox *The First Blast of the Trumpet Against the Monstruous Regiment of Women* (1558) and in "the blast of a trumpet from the clouds" in *EOT (CC)* II 432. John Wycliffe (c 1320–84), Oxford theologian who expounded in the 1370s the doctrine that authority, because it derives from the grace of God, can be forfeited by worldly misdeeds; John Huss (1373–1415), of Prague, excommunicated in 1410 for preaching the doctrines of Wycliffe, tried and excommunicated at the Council of Constance, burned at the stake; Jerome (c 1360–1416) of Prague, like Huss a Bohemian reformer influenced by Wycliffe, condemned and burned by the Council of Constance. Jerome studied at Oxford. Wycliffe's name is spelled variously; "Witcliffe" may preserve C's pronunciation (as his habit of writing "Edingborough" does). The Albigenses, of Albi and other centres in southern France, are usually counted as contributors to the anti-hierarchal unrest of the Reformation, but they had survived through the centuries as Manichaean Cathari in descent from Marcion and other Gnostics; they actively resisted treatment as heretics from 1205 until they were eliminated by the Inquisition in the fourteenth century. Luther nailed his ninety-five theses to the church door at Wittenberg 31 Oct 1517. *TT* (1835) inserted the Coleridgian sentiment that the "great British schoolmen led the way", words justified by 4 May 1833, below (at n 5).

enlightened and richest embraced the Reformation. The seeds were deeply and widely spread in Spain and Italy—and as to the latter, if James I. had been an Elizabeth, I have no doubt at all that Venice would have publicly declared itself against Rome.[4] It is a profound question to answer why it is that since the beginning of the sixteenth century,[a] the Reformation has not advanced one step in Europe.   [36:249]

In the time of Pope Leo X. Atheism or Infidelity [b]was almost universal in Italy amongst the high dignitaries of the Roman Church.[5]   [36:250]

Citizen John Thelwall had something good about him. We were once sitting in Somersetshire in a beautiful recess.[6] I said to him—"Citizen

[a] Divisional bar mistakenly placed after this line   [b] f 27

[4] During the reign of James I (1603–25), with Sir Henry Wotton as his ambassador to Venice in 1604–12, 1616–19, and 1621–4—the interruptions resulted from indiscretions and diplomatic failures by Wotton and in London—tensions between Venice and Spain offered the best opportunity for testing the renewed ties between Venice and Rome. In 1508–10 Pope Julius II had formed the League of Cambrai specifically for the humiliation of Venice. W. Carew Hazlitt gives a full account in *The Venetian Republic: Its Rise, Its Growth, and Its Fall A.D. 409–1797* (2 vols 1915) II 154–200, 513–22.

[5] Leo X, Giovanni de' Medici (1475–1521), Pope 1513–21, had hastened the Reformation by the open sale of indulgences; his bull of 1520 excommunicated Luther. Qualified versions of C's generalisation could be sustained even from Guicciardini's contemporary *Storia d'Italia* (1561–4), in 1830 available as *Istoria d'Italia* ed Giovanni Rosini (9 vols Pisa 1820). In the Italian states in 1830, said C, Philosopher "is the name of Courtesy for an Infidel". *C&S (CC)* 138. William Roscoe *The Life and Pontificate of Leo the Tenth* ch 15 (4 vols Liverpool 1805) III 137–79, esp 142–8, justified charges of paganism and Platonism against the clergy under Leo.

[6] John Thelwall (1764–1834), reformer and poet in the earliest years of his friendship with C, WW, and RS; "Citizen" in his enthusiasm for the French Revolution; in later years a lecturer in elocution. On his eventful visit to C and WW at Nether Stowey and Alfoxden in 1797, see *CL* I 339–44; *Poole* I 232–44; *C Life* (H) 204–11; Bertram R. Davis "Wordsworth, Coleridge, Southey and the Spy" *TLS* 7 Nov 1968 p 1261. *TT* (1835) identified the recess as in the Quantock Hills. On 18 Jul 1797 Thelwall wrote to his wife from C's "enchanting retreat": "We have been having a delightful ramble to-day among the plantations, and along a wild, romantic dell in these grounds, through which a foaming, rushing, murmuring torrent of water winds its long artless course. There have we . . . passed sentence on the productions and characters of the age . . .". *Poole* I 232–3. In the winter of 1842–3 WW recited to Isabella Fenwick a version blander than C's: "I remember once, when Coleridge, he, and I were seated together upon the turf on the brink of a stream in the most beautiful part of the most beautiful glen of Alfoxden, Coleridge exclaimed, 'This is a place to reconcile one to all the jarrings and conflicts of the wide world.'—'Nay,' said Thelwall, 'to make one forget them altogether.' " *WPW* I 363. The version that Cornelia A. H. Crosse repeated from John Kenyon is almost identical to that in TT; C says "the very place", and the answer ends: "it is the place to make one forget the necessity of treason". Crosse *Red-letter Days of My Life* (2 vols 1892) I 102.

John! this is a fine place to talk treason in!" "Nay! Citizen Samuel!"
replied he, "it is a place to make a man forget that there is any necessity
for treason."   [36:251]

Thelwall thought it very unfair to prejudice a child's mind by inculcating
any opinions before it should have come to years of discretion and be
able to choose for itself. I showed him my garden and told him it was my
botanical garden. "How so?" said he—"it is covered with nothing but
weeds." "O" I replied—"that is only because it has not yet come to its
age of discretion and choice. The weeds, you see, have taken the liberty
to grow, and I thought it unfair in me to prejudice the soil towards roses
or strawberries."[7]   [36:252]

Swift chose the name of Stella (properly a man's name with a feminine
termination) to denote the mysterious epicœne relation in which poor
Miss [Johnson][c] stood to him.[8]   [36:253]

That Legislation is iniquitous which sets Law against the common and
unsophisticated feelings of Nature.[9] If I were a Clergyman in a smug-

[c] Blank in ms; *TT* (1835) reads "Johnston"

[7] Dating this episode earlier on 18 Jul 1797 than the exchange in the "beautiful recess", in a fuller account for Hugh J. Rose in 1818, C attributed to Rousseau the philosophy of education he was parodying; he probably also wished to imply that his "Botanic Garden" differed from that of such radical *coxcombs* as Erasmus Darwin. *CL* IV 879–80. He compensates for poorer gardening with superior political perceptions. C had told different versions of the anecdote in two of his lectures on education, that of 3 May 1808 at the Royal Institution and Lect 7 of 18 Nov 1813 at Bristol: *Lects 1808–19 (CC)* I 106, 586. See also John Sterling's note on the anecdote, in App I, vol II, below.

[8] Letters from Swift to Hester (or Esther) Johnson (1681–1728) were first published in vol XII of *The Works of Dr. Jonathan Swift* (13 vols Edinburgh 1768)—a volume of which C annotated (see 15 Jun 1830 n 6, above)—and they were first entitled *The Journal to Stella* in the *Works* ed Thomas Sheridan (17 vols 1784). *On Stella's Birth-day* had appeared in *Poems* (1735). Sidney's *Astrophel* had been unusual in England, until

after C's day, in applying the name Stella to a woman. Most biographies had told how Swift, sixteen years older, had helped educate her, saw her daily but always in the company of Rebecca Dingley or another, addressed endearments and baby-talk to her (and Dingley); biographers also mentioned the mystery of her parentage and the possibility that she and Swift were secretly married. *Epicene* refers grammatically to nouns in Greek and Latin with one form for either sex; Ben Jonson and others had used the word in the sense C gives it here.

[9] The precept conforms to C's discussion in *The Friend* of "contra-natural laws". *Friend (CC)* I 443, 499. References to law and nature throughout that work imply that legislation can either be natural or be iniquitous because contra-natural. Herman Merivale commented on this passage in his review of *TT*: "It would be a singular rule of morality which should make right or wrong depend on the correctness in political economy of the violated law. All taxation, all Government 'set law in conflict with the

gling town, I would not preach against smuggling. I would not be made
a sort of clerical revenue officer. Let the Government which by absurd
duties fosters smuggling prevent it itself, if it can. How could I show my
hearers the immorality of[d] going twenty miles in a boat and honestly buy-
ing with their money a keg of brandy, except by a long deduction which
they could not understand? But were I in a place where wrecking went
on—see if *I* would preach on *any* thing *else*![10]   [36:254]

---

[e]My father, after explaining and insisting on a text, used always to say in
his sermons—"But that I may give you this injunction in the most solemn manner, hear the very words uttered by the Spirit of God—" and
then he thundered out the Hebrew original. It did more good than all the
rest of his sermon. The clowns in the gallery put their necks out and
opened their mouths and were evidently impressed with something of a
sense of the grand and holy.[11]

[d] of ~~boys~~   [e] f 27[v]   [e-g] For the variant in MS F see App C, below

---

unsophisticated feelings of our nature.' " *Ed Rev* LXI (1835) 142.

[10] Ottery St Mary, as HNC did not
need to be reminded, lay near enough to
the coast to make smuggling an ancient
subject there. From 1816, when the various "temporary" war duties of 1803
had been made "perpetual", smuggling
had increased along the southern coast
from Seaford to Plymouth, according to
a tour by the Board of Customs in 1822;
tariff adjustments had been made in
1825, and continued dissatisfaction
would bring more in 1833, but the use of
foreign ships for many products besides
brandy continued to be controlled. Henry
Atton and Henry Hurst Holland *The
King's Customs* (2 vols 1910) II 64, 109–
40, 329–31. C had witnessed a wreck
and wrecking—"a *diffusion* of Property"—at Ramsgate in 1824. *CL* v 397–
402.

[11] Of the learning of John Coleridge
(1719–81) we know something from his
collateral positions as master of the
King's New Grammar School, chaplain
priest of the Collegiate Church, and vicar
of the Parish of Ottery St Mary; his two
Latin grammars, with a list in his *Miscellaneous Dissertations on the xvii. and*

xviii. Chapters of Judges (1768) of the
Greek and Latin studies required of his
pupils; and anecdotes relating him by his
simplicity and absence of mind to Fielding's Parson Adams. *C Life* (C) 3–6, *C
Life* (G) 1–9. C wrote of him in the second of his autobiographical letters to
Poole in 1797 as "a profound Mathematician, and well-versed in the Latin,
Greek, & Oriental Languages". *CL* I
310. HNC gave an account of him,
mostly from C, in *BL* (1847) II 311–15,
325. The fuller account in Bernard,
Baron Coleridge *The Story of a Devonshire House* (1905) 11–20 may depend
upon the present entry for one paragraph:
"From the oaken pulpit in the church at
Ottery St. Mary would flow quotations
from the Bible in Hebrew, which the
gaping congregation, on the assurance of
the preacher, believed to be the very
words of the Holy Ghost" (p 19). The
version in *De Q Works* II 164–5 must
have come from C—though De Q owned
the two Latin grammars. For an anecdote
concerning C's father and a student acting in a play see App F 13, below. This
TT entry and the next were not published. (The entries, cut from MS F, are
now at UT, attached to MS E 56.)

My poor brother George preached morning and evening at Ottery on Scandal—and on Smuggling.[12] In the afternoon people congratulated my mother. She looked[f] rather blank upon the occasion, and said—"George was, no doubt, very clever and fine—but for her part, she must say—she did not like any *new doctrines.*"[g]

And, to be sure, she did love gossip, and as to smuggling—decent brandy could not be obtained without it.[13]

Spurzheim is a good man, and I like him; but he is dense and the most ignorant German I ever knew.[14] If he had been content with stating certain remarkable coincidences between the moral qualities and the configuration of the skull, it would have been well; but when he began to map out the cranium, he fell into infinite absurdities. You know, every act, however you may distinguish it by name, is truly the act of the entire man; the notion of distinct organs therefore in the brain itself is absurd. It is just quackery committed by Spurzheim, to say that he has actually

[f] ~~smiled~~ looked   [g] See [e-g], above

[12] George Coleridge (1764–1828), after four daughters by John's first wife the sixth son by his second—from 1792 the third of five surviving sons—succeeded their father as master of the King's School and chaplain priest. Of "reflective mind & elegant Genius", in learning next after C, gravely moral (*CL* I 311), George served in lieu of father to C, with disapproval of C's conduct increasingly evident to C himself. C's epithet "poor" simply acknowledges George's death thirty months earlier.

[13] Ann Bowdon Coleridge (1727–1809) comes alive in this anecdote as in no other record. C was revealingly brief to Poole: "My Mother was an admirable Economist, and managed exclusively." *CL* I 310. Among C's memories reported by Gillman, she disliked "your harpsichord ladies". *C Life* (G) 6. C was close enough to his mother's sentiments in 1806 to recognise in a sea captain "a prejudice against Smuggling almost peculiar to Americans". *CL* II 1186.

[14] Spurzheim was "beyond all comparison", said C in 1817, "the greatest Physiognomist that has ever appeared". *CN* III 4355. He was ignorant by comparison with other *Germans* C knew. C had found it very difficult to be serious when he read in Nov 1815 *The Physiognomical System of Drs. Gall and Spurzheim* (2nd ed 1815). *CN* III 4269; *CL* IV 613. But in 1817, after Spurzheim had visited C, he became "a true man"; attacks by the *Ed Rev* and by John Gordon *Observations on the Structure of the Brain, Comprising an Estimate of the Claims of Drs. Gall and Spurzheim to Discovery in the Anatomy of That Organ* (Edinburgh 1817) became evidence of "the malignity and malignant ignorance of Scotchmen". *CN* III 4355. When John Abernethy addressed the Royal College of Surgeons and presented to C his *Reflections on Gall and Spurzheim's Physiognomy and Phrenology* (1821), anticipating "nothing but mischief" from their "Cranioscopy" (p 7), and Spurzheim called at Highgate to take a life-mask of C's face, C was ready for the genial mockery of a letter to Montagu in May 1825 (*CL* v 460) and a note of c 1825 to Green (BM MS Egerton 2800 f 188). See also HNC's note to *TT* (1835) 36:90 and 24 Jun 1827 n 17, above. Lectures by Spurzheim on phrenology were printed in *Lancet* VII 16 Apr–17 Sept 1825.

discovered a *different material* in the different parts or organs of the brain, so that he can tell a piece of Benevolence from a bit of Destructiveness &c. Besides it is constantly found that so far from there being a concavity[h] in the interior surface of the cranium answering to the convexity apparent [i]on the exterior—the interior is convex too. Dr Baillie thought there was something in the system, because the notion of the brain being an extendible net served to explain those cases where the intellect remained after the solid substance of the brain was dissolved in water.[15] That a greater or less development of the forepart or hind part of the head shows that a person has more or less of the reasoning being in him, is certain.

The line across the forehead denoting music is a very general mark.[16]

[36:255]

---

20. Aug. 1830.

This French Revolution is a[a] preventive process, and the nation must have improved immensely under the influence of a free and regular government (for such it in general has been since the restoration) to have

---

[h] con~~vex~~ity   [i] f 28   [a] a ~~ease~~

---

[15] Matthew Baillie (1761–1823), physician extraordinary to George III, had argued in the earliest editions of *The Morbid Anatomy of Some of the Most Important Parts of the Human Body* (1793, 1795) that different emotions of the mind, conveyed along nerves to different muscles, thereby changed countenance and attitude to express emotion in a universal language. On hydrocephalus, he declared it unclear whether the water of the brain is "altered in its properties" or only in amount (1793 pp 304–5). In 1815 C found that Baillie accepted in "the last edition" of *Morbid Anatomy* Spurzheim's argument that in hydrocephalus the brain is not disorganised but only expanded. *CL* IV 613–14. In the 3rd ed (1807) Baillie wrote (440n): "A distinguished author has, in a late publication, insisted very strongly upon the existence of an immediate communication between the two lateral ventricles of the brain, and has expressed great surprise that it has been denied by several teachers of anatomy in London." Denying that the connexion was direct, Baillie retained the same note, and the same text on hydrocephalus, in the 4th and 5th eds (1812, 1818). C had direct access to the 3rd ed of 1807. *Gillman SC*. *TT* (1835) quoted in a footnote C's ironic reference to the bump of benevolence on the head of the murderer John Thurtell (1794–1824): *AR* (1825) 147n–8; (1831) 143n.

[16] C's acceptance of physiognomical evidence for musical power may come as a surprise, but the entire Boston Medical Association attended Spurzheim's funeral. *The Picturesque Pocket Companion and Visitor's Guide Through Mount Auburn* (Boston, Mass 1839) 99. Prominent physiognomists before Gall and Spurzheim included Giambattista della Porta (c 1538–1615), James Parsons (1705–70), Johann Kaspar Lavater (1741–1801), and Shakespeare.

conducted themselves with such moderation in success. There is something very fine and dignified in conducting Charles X. all through France, and receiving him every where with tricolored[b] flags and silence.[1] [36:256]

If he is to live here—there should be a perfect understanding that it is not to put this country in any uneasy situation with respect to any foreign powers.[2]

As to Spain, if in case of Revolution, no fit member of the royal family can be found—I think a republic the only resource—the least evil; and the clergy ought to be largely interested in it.[3]

A State regards Interests—a Church Persons.[4] [36:260]

[b] triclored

[1] The *Moniteur* announced on 26 Jul ordinances signed by Charles x as a *coup d'état* to dissolve the Chamber of Deputies, restrict the press, and establish a new method of election. By 28–9 Jul Paris was in insurrection. Ministers resigned, Charles x abdicated, and on 9 Aug Louis Philippe, until then Duke of Orléans, accepted the crown from the two Chambers. From mixed sources *The Times* and *M Chron* passed on "confused and often contradictory" reports on Charles's slow movement, under safe conduct provided by Commissioners and Garde de Corps of the Provisional Government, from Rambouillet to Maintenon to Cherbourg. A "profound silence" either prevailed throughout the journey or was maintained with difficulty by the escorts, depending on whether you read *The Times* of 18 or 19 Aug; the tricolour was hoisted at Valogne on the 12th. Historical summary supports C: "Every village and town flew the tricolor from its highest tower or steeple; sullen crowds lined streets to watch the sad procession pass." David H. Pinkney *The French Revolution of 1830* (Princeton, N.J. 1972) 177. *TT* (1835) omitted the sentence on the reception of Charles, the opening clause on "a preventive process", and the last two paragraphs of the entry.

[2] Charles and his entourage had embarked for England on 16 Aug. On the 20th they remained on the two United States ships that had brought them to Cowes. Charles would reside for a time at Lulworth Castle, Dorsetshire, before removing to Holyrood Castle, Edinburgh. It was clear that troubles brewing in Holland, Belgium, and Spain would be intensified by the events in France; revolts were to follow also in Greece and Poland. A *Times* editorial of 20 Aug on "the self-invited guest" speculated on how Austria, Prussia, and the Netherlands would react.

[3] The notoriously tyrannical Ferdinand VII, who had been re-established on the Spanish throne by Napoleon in 1814 and by French troops under sanction of the Holy Alliance in 1823, had recently abolished the Salic law of succession to exclude his brothers Don Carlos and Don Francisco, who were now leading a faction against him. When *TT* (1835) was in preparation, the long Carlist revolt against Ferdinand's daughter Isabella II had begun. If HC, HCR, Allsop, and others less conservative than HNC had known of the suppression of this sentence, their opposition to the political sentiments expressed in *TT* would have had the kind of ammunition they sought.

[4] The germ of this idea is developed on 19 Sept 1830, below (36:260).

The United States do not constitute a State; they are in a transitional state now.[5]

*c*Basil Hall's book on North America is disgusting, especially after he had been stifled with hospitalities.[6] *I* see nothing, even in his accounts, but foibles which make me like the Americans better. How much more amiable is the American fidgettiness and anxiety about the opinion of other nations and especially of the English, than the John Bullism, which affects to despise the sentiments of the rest of the world.[7]

As to Hall's stuff about the Loyalty to the person*d* of the English—I feel none of it.[8] I respect the man, while the King is translucent through

c f 28ᵛ   *d* [i.e. of the King]

[5] It has been noted that the term "United States" was at first descriptive, usually in the phrase "these United States", and that the change from a plural to a singular verb, after survival of the Civil War had made one nation, has not converted those members of Parliament who say "a church of the Church of England" but "one of the United States". Allen Walker Read "Is the Name *United States* Singular or Plural?" *Names* XXII (1974) 129–36. C's observation was not published by HNC.

[6] Basil Hall (1788–1844), captain in the Navy, *Travels in North America in the Years 1827 and 1828* (3 vols Edinburgh 1829): see 27 May 1830 n 4, above. Hall had achieved prominence with books on travel in Korea, Chile, Peru, and Mexico, and by interviewing Napoleon. C's epithet "disgusting" was too much for *TT* (1835), and the opening sentence was dropped. The hospitalities were reported by Hall himself.

[7] As early as Mar 1801 C expressed to Poole his "indignation to hear the *croaking* accounts, which the English Emigrants send home of America. The society is so bad—the manners so vulgar—the servants so insolent. . . . It is arrant ingratitude . . .". *CL* II 709. SC, in "Mr. Coleridge's sentiments concerning British America", reported similarly on C's private remarks. *EOT* I lxxiv. HNC's note to this entry in *TT* (1835) quoted from C's "Sketches of the Life of Sir Alexander Ball" his praise of the

"*gentlemanly* character" of the English, with its one disadvantage of "contemptuous and insolent demeanor" towards "the inhabitants of countries conquered or appropriated". *Friend (CC)* I 555–7. The "fidgettiness" had been denied: "Do we worry and fret ourselves about what is said of us in America? Certainly not." An American *Captain Hall in America* (Philadelphia 1830) 5.

[8] The clearer if less colloquial wording of *TT* (1835) is "the English loyalty to the person of the King". In ch 17, the last, Hall reported a conversation in which he contrasted "the absence of loyalty in America" with the more than loyalty in Britain (III 393–6): "I mean, that we have universally, throughout the nation, a feeling of personal attachment to the King on the throne—a pride and pleasure in his happiness and success, and a resolute determination to support him, as a matter of habit, duty, and sentiment. . . . It pervades all ranks and classes. . . . It is the grand symbol, if I may so call it,—the masonic secret,—by which the distinction of ranks is preserved." From this exposition, which C rejects, Hall went on to speak of the Church as the rudder of the nation. C here expounds the doctrine of the two bodies of the King. He had defended the Presbyterians for distinguishing the mortal incumbent Charles II from the King as an appeal to "the most venerable maxims of English Law;—(the King never dies—the King can do no wrong, &c)"

him—I reverence the glass case for the saint's sake within—otherwise it is to me mere glazier's work—putty and glass.   [36:257]

Charles Lamb^e said—that Chapman's Ode to Pan was the grandest thing he had ever read—it was like Milton in rhyme.[9]

The version of the Odyssey is not so quaint as that of the Iliad, and excellent it is.[10]

---

8. Sept. 1830.[1]

The fatal error into which the character of the English Reformation threw the Church has borne bitter fruit ever since—I mean that of the Church's

^{e} C. Lambe

---

in *Friend (CC)* I 177n. He had also, however, acknowledged Hall's side of the question by quoting favourably (or filtering, as he admitted to Emerson) William Sedgwick *Justice upon the Armie Remonstrance* (1648) 30–1 on "the oppressed suffering king" Charles I, whose "being is not solitary, but as he is in union with his people, who are his strength in which he lives". *Friend (CC)* I 413. He noted in *M Post* 6 Aug 1800 that the Monarch had long since become "more an office, and less a person". *EOT (CC)* I 242. The distinction of the two bodies was essential to John and Leigh Hunt's defence in 1812 for calling the Prince Regent a fat Adonis of fifty, and it is implicit in Byron *The Vision of Judgment*.

[9] We have a version of Lamb's words in a letter of 17 Aug 1824 to Sir Charles Abraham Elton: "Reverend Chapman! you have read his hymn to Pan (the Homeric)—why, it is Milton's blank verse clothed with rhyme." *LL* II 304 (the date corrected by George L. Barnett). When Lamb wrote to C on 23 Oct 1802 that Chapman's Homer "has *most* the continuous power of interesting you all along, like a rapid original, of any", he followed two quotations from Chapman's *Iliad* with a promise, "I will tell you more about Chapman & his peculiarities in my next", but we have no next letter with references to Chapman. *LL* (M) II

82–3. George Chapman (c 1559–1634) tr Homer's *Iliad* (1598, 1611), *Odyssey* (1614), *The Crowne of All Homers Works*, *Batrachomyomachia Or the Battaile of Frogs and Mise. His Hymn's and Epigrams* (1624). The *Hymn to Pan* was included in later editions of *The Whole Works of Homer* than the 1616 cited in n 10, below.

[10] When C sent to SH in 1808 his annotated copy of *The Whole Works of Homer: Prince of Poetts in His Iliads and Odysseys* tr Chapman (1616), he enclosed a letter beginning: "Chapman I have sent in order that you might read the Odyssey/ the Iliad is fine but less equal in the Translation as well as less interesting in itself. . . . Excepting his quaint epithets which he affects to render literally from the Greek . . . it has no look, no air, of a translation". *CM (CC)* II 1119–20. Lamb thought that Chapman "improved upon Homer, in the Odyssey in particular". *LL* II 304. The vertical line on f 28^v of MS B carries through the two entries on Chapman, but they were not published and have not been found among the scraps of MS F.

[1] HNC spent late August with his parents and other relatives in Devon. On 27 Aug SC addressed a letter to him at Combesachfield, where he was visiting "Aunt Brown". Just before his departure, Mrs C arrived in Hampstead for SC's confinement and for residence

ever clinging to Court and State instead of cultivating the People.² The Church ought to be a Mediator between the People and the Government—between the rich and the Poor. As it is, the Church has let the hearts of the People be stolen from them. See how ᵃdifferently the Church of Rome always acted. They were wiser in that, as in many other things.³

For a long time the Church of England has been positively cursed and rotted and blighted with—Prudence. Would to God there were a little ᵇimprudent Zeal!ᶜ —ᵈzealous imprudence!ᵉ⁴   [36:258]

thereafter with the HNCs. On 12 Sept Mrs C reported to Poole HNC's return home "with bright eyes indeed, but with considerable pain in the back and loins . . . We have, at present, a great deal of Mʳ Henry's company, and hope to have him at [home] for upwards of a month longer . . .". *Minnow* 159–62. 8 Sept was a Wednesday.

² Henry viii's claim to be obeyed as the supreme head of the Church in England was endorsed by Parliament in several statutes between 1531 and 1534. The case made by Gilbert Burnet *The History of the Reformation of the Church of England* (3 vols 1679–1715) is summarised in Wakeman and Ollard *An Introduction to the History of the Church of England* 196: "The English Reformation began as a matter of policy, an affair of kings and ministers and parliaments." The clergy accepted the King as supreme head of the Church Established by Law in convocations of Canterbury and York "as far as the law of Christ permits". Bishops had served in the highest legislative body of England since Saxon times, but after the separation from the papacy Henry, Mary, and Elizabeth all suspended the licences of recalcitrant bishops. It was attention to King and Parliament, not to the people, that could keep one in office as vicar of Bray. C's language here is greatly toned down from *Conciones* and LRR Lects 5 and 6 in 1795, when the Church of England was "the Religion of Mitres and Myster-

ies, and the Religion of Pluralities and Persecution", like the Church of Rome in "intimate alliance with the powers of this World", so that the "very officers of Religion are converted into machines of Despotism". *Lects 1795 (CC)* 66–7, 210, 221. He had continued in *The Friend* to argue specifically that juries "are not the representatives of religion, but the guardians of external tranquility", from the general principle that "Law and Religion should be kept distinct". *Friend (CC)* ɪ 91, 94.

³ The revision of *TT* (1835) omitted the "many other things".

⁴ The conversation is related to, and probably provoked by, Charles James Blomfield *A Charge Delivered to the Clergy of His Diocese* (1830). On the flyleaves of the copy presented by Blomfield to HNC, C wrote on 11 Sept that this bp of London might well find in jeopardy a Church "by the partiality of the two houses of Parliament allowed and authorized to exact such and such Sums from the Land-owners, Farmers &c, no consent asked on their part, independent of their attendance on its Ministry and without any recognizable proportion to the claimants' Services". *CM (CC)* ɪ 527. Prudence, which can never rise to wisdom or reason, is commended by C throughout *The Friend* and elsewhere as necessary to government, but it is inadequate for morality, poetry, or religion. In the Preface to *TT* (1835) ɪ xxix—*TT* (1836) xvi, and see *C&S (CC)*

19. Sept. 1830.[1]

It has never yet been clearly seen and announced that Democracy, as such, is no proper element in the constitution of a State.[2] The Idea of a State is undoubtedly a government ἐκ τῶν ἀρίστων[3]—an aristocracy. Democracy is the healthful blood which circulates through the veins and arteries, which supports the system, but which ought never to appear externally and as the mere blood itself. [36:259]

A State in Idea is the opposite of a Church. A State regards Classes and not Individuals, and it estimates Classes not by internal merit, but external accidents, as property, birth &c.[4] But a Church does the reverse of this, and disregards all external accidents, and looks at men as individual persons—allowing no gradation of ranks, but such as greater or less holiness and wisdom necessarily confer.

A Church is therefore in Idea the only pure Democracy—

The Church so considered and the State, exclusive of the Church, constitute *together* the Idea of a State in its largest sense.[5] [36:260]

195n for re-use in 1839—HNC quoted as additional conversation a plea from C that revenues taken from the Church by Henry VIII and later be restored for "the education of the people".

[1] On 12 Sept the Gillmans visited Mrs C and SC at Hampstead and took HNC in their carriage back to Highgate to see C, who was "very poorly". *Minnow* 160. MS B contains no record of the visit. Either C or HNC could have paid the visit of Sun, 19 Sept, but Thurs, the 23rd (the date of the subsequent entries) was C's day "at home". Greater privacy on the 19th is implied in C's telling remarks on Hazlitt and on RS and Lamb, which became in print (under 22 Sept) blandly general and anonymous in application. HNC's care in assigning the appraisal of Huskisson to the 19th displays a concern with accuracy of dating in 1830 that disappeared during the preparation of TT for publication.

[2] C had written to T. G. Street in Mar 1817: "Alas! dear Sir! what is Mankind but *the Few* in all ages? . . . But either by an Aristocracy, or a Fool-and-Knave-ocracy man must be governed." *CL* IV 714. At no time had he felt strong sympathy for democracy or for the demagogues nourished by it. A week after congratulating RS in 1794 for making the "adamantine Gate of Democracy" turn on its "golden Hinges", he confessed to the same fellow-revolutionist a fear that he had "caught the Itch from a Welch Democrat". *CL* I 83, 89. In the *M Post* 26 Dec 1799 he praised the English for a national character made up of "the influence of a Court, the popular spirit, and the predominance of property". *EOT (CC)* I 48. The "popular spirit" would achieve fruition through government by the select few. An aristocracy was sharply superior to an absolute monarchy or a democratic republic because in those extreme forms "the Nation, or People, delegates its whole power". *C&S (CC)* 96.

[3] "From the best [men]".

[4] This agrees with Johann Gottlieb Fichte (1762–1814) *Die Staatslehre, oder über das Verhältniss des Urstaates zum Vernunftreiche* (Berlin 1820), but without Fichte's emphasis on "der rechtmässige Oberherr", supreme ruler, made legitimate by his teaching of truth to the public. *Sämmtliche Werke* ed I. H. Fichte (8 vols Berlin 1845–6) IV 447.

[5] In a copy of *C&S* C defined the state "in the largest sense" as the nation, and set forth in a marginal note for the Rev

All temporal Government must rest on a compromise of Interests and Abstract Rights.[6] Who would listen to the county of Bedford, if it were to declare itself disannexed from the British State, and to set up for itself.   [36:261]

The Brussels[b] riot (I give it no higher name!) is a wretched parody on the second French Revolution.[7]   [36:285]

The government of the King of Belgium is a mild government, and the Brabanters are not agreed upon a separation, and they are even now beginning to be sick and ashamed of the false position in which they have placed themselves.[8] The effect of a separation would of course be an im-

---

a f 29[v]   *b* Brussells

James Gillman a pentad with the explanation: "The State (i.e. the *Nation*— n.b. NOT the People) is the Prothesis; *including* both the *State* in its *thetic* sense, *and* the Church, the antithesis . . .". *C&S (CC)* 117, 233. There he subtilised *C&S*; here he clarifies the subtilisation. In May 1826 C had developed the argument that Protestantism promotes nationalism. *CN* IV 5373. In N 44 ff 75–6, to the same effect and of about the same date as this conversation, C suggested that it is natural in "progressive Civilization" for the state to "display a transition into the character of a Church"— quoted in *C&S (CC)* lx. In the Preface to *C&S* (1839) HNC attempted to show how C took up a position with regard to Church and State intermediate between the known positions of Richard Hooker and William Warburton. *C&S (CC)* 196–9.

[6] The opposition of interests and rights to be compromised is less common in C's writings than the need to compromise the personal interests and the general welfare of the citizen—e.g. *EOT (CC)* I 75, II 53, III 119—although he does acknowledge, as a refuge against insults and compulsion from Napoleon in 1809, "the common rights of human nature" (II 53). Of his many declarations from 1796 on that "abstract rights" exist only as a phrase, the clearest and most famous occurs in *SM (CC)* 64. The present sentence, despite its language of antithesis between interests and rights, should be glossed as recommending a compromise between local and national interests or sentiment. Good sense, C said in *The Friend*, brings to a country or an age "a feeling of the necessity and utility of *compromise*". *Friend (CC)* I 420.

[7] The Congress of Vienna had joined Belgium with Holland in 1815 as the Kingdom of the Netherlands under King William I (1772–1843). C's view of the Belgian uprising is no more contemptuous than that of *A Reg* for 1830 History 247: "On the afternoon of the 25th of August, a mob of the lowest classes in Brussels commenced a riot, directed principally against a local tax, affecting the price of bread . . . and, during the night, the city was in the possession of this half-drunken and half-armed rabble, composed of the dregs of society, and unemployed workmen, bent on pillage and mischief." Less scornful accounts, still with an air of parody, located the commencement of the revolt at the Brussels Opera House, stimulated by the representation of a revolutionary rising in Naples in *La Muette de Portici* by Daniel Auber. "Respectable citizens" set forth their demands on the 27th; 6000 troops arrived by the 28th; King William entered Brussels on 1 Sept, received the committee of grievance, and issued a proclamation of gratitude for the restoration of order. C's sentence is delayed in *TT* (1835) to combine it with his remarks of 5 Oct, below (at n 5) (36:285).

[8] *TT* (1835) omitted this paragraph, perhaps for its ephemerality, perhaps for its misjudgement.

position of customs on the borders, and how would they like that with their nearest neighbour? As to their uniting with France—that is another matter, which would affect England and Europe.[9]

The most likely and the most desirable thing that can happen to France with her immense army of Gens d'armes, is that by not being called into action, it may at first become very irksome to the men on service themselves, and ultimately fall into general ridicule like our Train Bands.[10] The evil in France and throughout Europe seems now especially to be the subordination of the legislative power to the direct physical powers of the nation. The legislature was weak enough before; now since this new Revolution of 1830 it is absolutely powerless, and does manifestly depend even for its existence on the will of a popular commander of an irresistible army. There is now in France a daily tendency to reduce *c*the Legislative Body*d* to a mere Deputation from the Provinces and Towns.[11]   [36:262]

I don't know whether I deceive myself, but it seems to me that the young men, who were my contemporaries, fixed certain principles in their minds and followed the legitimate consequences, in a way which I rarely see now. No one seems to have any distinct convictions—right or wrong; the mind is completely at sea—rolling*e* and pitching on the waves of Facts and personal Experiences.[12] H. V. is, I suppose, one of the rising young men of the day[13]—yet, the other evening he went on talking *f*and

---

c–d ⟨the⟩ Legislat~~ure~~ive ⟨Body⟩   *e* ~~wandering~~ rolling   *f* f 30

---

[9] The London Conference of major powers, meeting over the status of Greece, now turned its attention to Belgium. In November, to little immediate effect, it would recommend Belgian independence from King William and Holland.

[10] *TT* (1835) reads "trained bands" (I 202), but had introduced "train-bands" at I 185, changed to "trained-bands" in *TT* (1836) 97 (36:245). *OED*: "Train-band . . . A trained company of citizen soldiery, organized in London and other parts in the 16th, 17th, and 18th centuries." The fading of this corps was apparently making the previously common name unfamiliar to compositors in 1834–6. The *gens d'armes*, from an elite cavalry created by Charles VII in 1445, had been greatly increased under Louis XIV and XV; from re-establishment in 1815

they became the national force to maintain order. In the next sentence "powers of the nation" is clarified in print as "force of the people".

[11] The distinction between a representative and a deputy or a delegate is as basic to C as later to John Stuart Mill. In a personal elucidation of *C&S* for Jonathan Green, C wrote that a proper legislature, such as the King, Lords, and Commons provided, "is an Organ for the Representation of the Interests of the Nation, not a Means for the transmission and collection of the Opinions or Wishes of the People". *C&S (CC)* 31n. On representation see also *EOT (CC)* I 327–8.

[12] To his observation of 7 Jan–13 Feb 1823, above (at n 7), C now adds an older man's complaint that a lack of principles led the young into illogic.

[13] The initials H. V. are written decid-

making remarks with great earnestness, some of which were palpably irreconcilable with each other. You say Facts give birth to, and are the ground of, Principles. But, unless you had a Principle of selection, why did you take notice of those particular Facts. You must have a Lantern in your hand to give light; otherwise all the materials in the world are useless, for you can neither find them, and if you could, you could not arrange them.

But *that* Principle came from Facts!—To be sure: but there must have been antecedent Light again to see those antecedent Facts. The Relapse may in imagination be carried back for ever—but you can never imagine a man without a previous Aim or Principle.[14]

Then what do you say to Bacon's Induction? This—that it is *not* what is now a days so called, but which is in fact *De*duction only.[15]   [36:263]

edly enough. A later hand has made the surname "Vinars" or "Vinar". A likely identification is the Benthamite politician Thomas Hyde Villiers (1801–32), a friend of HNC's at Cambridge; M.P. for Hedon (1826–30), Wootton Bassett (1830), and Bletchingly (1831). Speaking in the Commons on commercial relations with Portugal, 15 Jun 1830, he had given the history of treaties with Portugal, read extracts from reports, and given statistics concerning the wine trade. Hansard NS XXV 370–84. Hyde Villiers, with Mill, Carlyle, and John Romilly, accompanied Henry Taylor to see C at an unknown date. Una Taylor *Guests and Memories: Annals of a Seaside Villa* (1924) 58.

[14] C had begun *The Friend* in 1809 by decrying the "perpetual flux" of facts, qualified in 1812 to admit facts "acquired by reflection". *Friend (CC)* II 6–7 and nn. All true method requires an initiating idea. Throughout C's later works, facts are confined to the level of the understanding. W. P. Wood visited C with Irving and the Montagus on 11 Dec 1828: "We found a large party at Highgate, and Coleridge was very entertaining. He read to us a fine passage from a manuscript on the foolish objection to theory and demand for facts. 'Such men,' he observed, are 'preparing their souls for the office of turnspit at the next

metempsychosis.' " *Memoir of Hatherley* I 157.

[15] C sustained through most of his life the heroic task of freeing Bacon from his traditional rôle as the first of the inductive Baconians to replace Aristotelian logic with reliance on sensory experience. C granted the existence of purely inductive Baconians, but excluded Bacon from their number. HNC's note to this entry in *TT* (1835) directed the reader to passages in C's "Essays on Method" that declare Plato's procedure inductive and Bacon's principles in the *Novum organum* based, not on sensation or experience, but on experiment directed by *"Lux Intellectûs, lumen siccum*, the pure and impersonal reason". *Friend (CC)* I 486–93; cf 467n–8. C had assured Godwin on 4 Jun 1803 that the Verulamian logic is "bonâ fide the same" as the Platonic. *CL* II 947. For C's steady attention to Bacon in the 1820s see *CL* V 15, 332n, 493, 496, VI 676. In *CIS* (1840) 56 he defended the "spirit of wisdom" of the philosopher identified simply in *C&S (CC)* 13 as "Lord Bacon, the British Plato", who "describes the Laws of the material universe as the Ideas in nature". Aubrey de Vere confessed that he could square Lord Adare's report of C's calling both Kant and Bacon Aristotelians only if C thought Plato and Aristotle shared the

If I compare Robert Southey with an Ideal, then I know nothing in which he excells; but if with the authors of the day, I think he well deserves the rank and reputation which he has;—which is only inferior to Walter Scott's.[16]

His History is neither the Epic of Herodotus, nor the Pragmatic Narrative of Thucydides.[17] It is a mere tale of all the striking things to be found in his documents without a single principle or[g] leading intention. For example: He told me, he should leave out the Indian Episode in his History of Portugal—as if it were possible to write the history of[h] *Portugal* without that part of *its* history included![18]

The object of Thucydides was to show the ills resulting to Greece from the separation and conflict of the two spirits or elements of Democracy and Oligarchy.[19]   [36:264]

[g] of or   [h] of the

---

same method—a polite way of saying that Adare must have misheard. *Life of Sir William Rowan Hamilton* II 137. The set of Bacon's *Works* at Rydal Mount, with a life by David Mallet (4 vols 1740), was marked as belonging to C. *WW LC* 315.

[16] This comparative estimate of Scott and C's brother-in-law, Robert Southey (1774–1843), who had accepted in 1813 the office of poet laureate after Scott declined it, includes, as few later estimates were likely to do, the full range of their work as men of letters, and thus not excluding the verse and editorial endeavours of the two, Scott's life of Napoleon, or RS's biographies, histories, and colloquies. In John O. Hayden *Scott: The Critical Heritage* (1970) 552–3, RS is omitted from the list of writers with whom reviewers compared Scott. In 1816 Josiah Conder had compared RS and WW as "our two greatest living poets", with RS found superior in various characteristics. *Eclectic Review* 2nd s VI 4. RS was admired as a poet by Shelley, but not by C or WW. Hazlitt had praised RS's prose extravagantly in *The Spirit of the Age* (2nd ed 1825) 181.

[17] RS *History of Brazil* (3 vols 1810–19), part of his projected history of Portugal, was published as a subject of popular interest, but it no longer looms as

large as his *History of the Peninsular War* (3 vols quarto 1823, 1827, 1832), which had begun to appear also in octavo (6 vols 1828–37). RS is here being judged by C against the two polar kinds of great histories. The classical historians will be treated more fully on 14 Aug 1833, below (at nn 11ff) (36:557).

[18] In 1800 RS determined "to undertake one great historical work, the History of Portugal", and had not abandoned the possibility in 1830. Unpublished portions of the work have been lost, but he told John May in 1806 that the portions then completed included the history of the Portuguese in India to 1539, with three volumes on that subject a part of the plan. *S Life* (Simmons) 84, 119. Vasco da Gama found a sea route to India in 1498; Portugal conquered Goa in 1510 and shattered the power of the Moslem rulers around the Indian Ocean; the Portuguese flourished in India until driven out by the British in the eighteenth century. India had a significant place when RS wrote of his work to John Rickman in 1803, although he did not specifically mention India in reporting his progress to C on 19 Feb 1804. *S Life* (CS) II 235, 264.

[19] In Lect 10 of 1818, on Dante, as edited by HNC, C had given in illustration of the advance in history from chronicle

*i*The object of Tacitus was to demonstrate the desperate consequences of the loss of liberty on the Minds and Hearts of Men.*j*20 [36:264]

The best piece of history ever written by Southey was the first part of the Peninsular War, as it was in the Edinburgh Annual Register.[21]

His opinions now are mine occasionally of ten years ago. I can put my finger upon *mine own* in all his books.[22]

Southey picked Nature's pockets, as a poet, instead of borrowing from her. He went out and took some particular image, for example a water-insect—and then exactly copied its make, colors and motions. This he put in a poem. The true way for a poet is to examine Nature, but write from your recollection, and trust more to your imagination than your memory.[23] [36:265]

i f 30ᵛ   *j* & the

to a moral theme "Thucydides, whose object was to describe the evils of democratic and aristocratic partizanships". *Misc C* 146.

[20] Cornelius Tacitus (c 55–c 120) *Histories* and *Annals*, both of which depict imperial oppression. After Thucydides and Polybius, C's third example of a writer with a moral stance was Tacitus, "whose secret aim was to exhibit the pressure and corruptions of despotism". *Misc C* 146. In Lect 14 of 13 Mar 1818 he condemned "the *falsetto*" of Tacitus in contrast with Cicero, but earlier (c 1809), in a note on Barclay's *Argenis*, had indirectly praised Tacitus' style for "energy and genuine conciseness". *Lects 1808–19 (CC)* ii 237, *CM (CC)* i 221. C's books and journalism frequently quote or cite Tacitus. Counting Thucydides and Tacitus with Machiavelli, Bacon, and Harrington as "red-letter names" for worldly wisdom, clear reasoning, and plain facts, he found them nevertheless anticipated in every single truth by the Bible. *SM (CC)* 17.

[21] "History of Europe", which RS wrote for the *Edinburgh Annual Register* 1808–11, was much concerned with Peninsular events. His pages for 1808 ended with the "termination of our First Campaign in Spain". For 1809, when most of the thirty-three chapters concerned Portugal or Spain, an "Advertisement" by the "Writer of the Historical Part" explained that the plethora of events and availability of a mass of documents accounted for both the great length and the delay in publication. These materials were reworked for his *Peninsular War*.

[22] There never was a serious chance that these remarks on RS would be published by HNC. C told Cottle in 1814 that *The Origin . . . of the New System of Education* by RS was "a dilution" of C's lecture on education at the Royal Institution in 1808. *CL* iii 474.

[23] To pick nature's pockets, in the manner of RS or Erasmus Darwin, is to work by fancy with "fixities and definites" instead of dissolving and recreating with the imagination. *BL* ch 13 *(CC)* i 304–5. *Thalaba the Destroyer* (2 vols 1801) iii 442ff describes an Egyptian locust (bk iii st 33):

> The admiring girl survey'd
> His out-spread sails of green;
> His gauzy underwings,
> One closely to the grass-green body furl'd,
> One ruffled in the fall, and half unclosed.
> She view'd his jet-orb'd eyes,
> His glossy gorget bright,
> Green glittering in the sun;
> His plumy pliant horns,
> That, nearer as she gazed,
> Bent tremblingly before her breath.
> She mark'd his yellow-circled front
> With lines mysterious vein'd . . .

Kehama[k] &c.[24] are pieces of Mosaic—Chinese paintings. A[l] bit of red follows a[m] bit of blue[n] all in equal prominence. They were taken from books, and clapped bodily into the frame; hence there is no perspective, no lights and shadows;—all is Glare.[25]

Some of his humorous things are excellent.[26]

The Life of Wesley is a most delightful book for a lounge.[27] It is curious to see how Southey becomes the man whose life he writes; he shows Wesley to have been, as he was, a jesuit and yet eulogizes him with enthusiasm, and condemns poor Whitfield in toto—who was a much honester man.[28] I have noted as many as ten different opinions of

[k] Kehana   [l] ~~One~~ A   [m] ~~another~~   [n] ~~red~~ blue

RS quoted in a note his source for this description: Frederick Lewis Norden *Travels in Egypt and Nubia* tr Peter Templeman (2 vols 1757) I 51. The next paragraph of C's remark in TT implies that RS usually "picked Nature's pockets" by way of books. Fireflies are described briefly in *Roderick, the Last of the Goths* (1814) x 39–40. On 13 Mar 1811 C "said S. was not competent to appreciate Spanish poetry; he wanted modifying power. He was a jewel setter; whatever he found to his taste he formed it into, or made it the ornament of a story." *CR (BCW)* 38.

[24] The "&c" refers presumably to the long narrative poems besides *The Curse of Kehama* (1810): *Thalaba, Madoc* (1805), and *Roderick.* C's private remarks contrast with his public praise of these poems in *BL* ch 3 *(CC)* I 59–60, 64. On *Kehama* as mythological scraps "tacked and fitted", see J. P. Collier's report, App K, below.

[25] Reynolds, although he granted in Discourse II that aging and varnish obscured the colours of the masters, recommended something like du Fresnoy *The Art of Painting* lines 489–90 tr Mason:

Forbid two hostile colours close to meet,
And win with middle tints their union sweet . . .

The sculptor John Flaxman, in unpublished verses favourable to Chinese art (as sparsely known in Europe), typically noted the bold lines and colours in "long blue petticoats" and "Gold and green spitting dragons"—quoted in David Irwin *English Neoclassical Art* (1966) 142.

[26] C recommended RS's best known humourous poem, *The March to Moscow* (1814), and defended his publication of "playful poems" against abuse by the critics, in *BL* ch 3 *(CC)* I 60, 64n. C's notes calling attention to particular works by RS were dropped by SC from *BL* (1847) I 60–1, thus obscuring her reaction to his inexact citation of "the incomparable 'Return to Moscow' and the 'Old Woman of Berkeley' ". Macaulay's anonymous attack on RS in *Ed Rev* L (Jan 1830) 528–65 had denied the existence of humour in RS: "A more insufferable jester never existed." *RS CH* 345.

[27] Current meanings for "a lounge" were (a) a spell of reclining or strolling lazily and (b) a place, as in a hotel, for passing the time in indolence. *OED.* Johnson's *Dictionary* gives only the verb, from the Dutch, "To idle; to live lazily". Cf "*Lounge-*book" in C's letter to Davy 9 Oct 1800: *CL* I 631.

[28] In *The Life of Wesley; and the Rise and Progress of Methodism* (2 vols 1820) ch 4 RS introduced George Whitefield as less logical and less formed for command than John Wesley, but more ardent; later Whitefield is said to have none of Wesley's ambition, but "a great longing to be persecuted" (I 232). RS did not condemn him "in toto", but thought it "might be suspected that Whitefield had grown deranged by the

Southey in this book—all asserted dogmatically and even vehemently—and all irreconcilable one with another.

The solemn morality poured forth on the subject of Nelson's connection with Lady Hamilton seems to me disproportioned to the merits of the case.[29] Nelson had very many grounds of *°palliation*—and it would have been fair to have compared him with his fellow admirals—in which comparison I believe he would have appeared an angel.

The Metre of Thalaba bears the same relation to Metre truly understood that Dumb Bells do to Music; both are, I presume, for exercise; pretty severe too, I think.[30]	[36:266]

° f 31

perpetual reading of Fox's Martyrs'' and found it no wonder that ''the suspicion of hypocrisy'' hung over one given both to exaggerated humility and to ''ebullitions of spiritual pride'' (I 234–5, 368). C came to a different view: ''Whitefield's Ultra-Calvinism is Gospel gentleness and Pauline sobriety compared with Wesley's Arminianism in the outset of his career.'' Annotation on *The Genuine Works of Archbishop Leighton* (4 vols 1819) III 204: *CM (CC)* III. With the *Life of Wesley* annotated by C at hand in time for the note to *TT* 36:140 on animal magnetism, HNC wrote to RS on 1–6 Feb 1835 that he had traced in ink and transcribed C's notes in vol I and SC had transcribed all and traced in ink most of those in vol II; he was therefore returning the work to RS. UT ms. C had written (I 356): ''R. Southey is an Historian worth his weight in diamonds, & were he (which Heaven forfend!) as fat as myself, and the Diamonds all as big as Birds' eggs, I should still repeat the appraisal.'' *CM (CC)* IV.

[29] In *The Life of Nelson* (2 vols 1813) ch 3 RS referred frequently to the ''most unfortunate attachment'' of Admiral Nelson to Lady Hamilton, née Emma Lyon (c 1761–1815), which, if it was not criminal, carried ''criminality enough'' in weaning Nelson's affection from his wife. RS blamed ''that acquaintance with the Neapolitan Court'' (ch 3) for ''disgraceful'' treachery by Nelson (ch 6) in turning over to the Sicilian court rebels who had surrendered under a

treaty thus abrogated by Nelson. The reviewer in *B Critic* XLII (1813) 360–6 had sided with RS: ''The great error of all, the unfortunate and unjustifiable infatuation in favour of Lady Hamilton, to the prejudice of the natural and legitimate claim on his affection and his honour, is introduced with much feeling and delicacy. That other momentous deviation also from the path of rectitude which took place in the Bay of Naples, equally discreditable to Nelson's prudence, honour, and humanity, is introduced with some, though not quite its due share of animadversion.'' *RS CH* 173.

[30] In the Preface to *Thalaba* RS wrote with pride of the variability allowed by the irregular blank metres he had first encountered in Frank Sayers (1763–1817) *Dramatic Sketches of Northern Mythology* (1790). George Saintsbury preferred *Thalaba* (sampled in n 23, above) to most other long attempts at ''rhymeless Pindarics'' or ''staves varied in line-length but destitute of rhyme''. *A History of English Prosody* (3 vols 1910) III 38–9, 51–3. The apparatus for exercise at New College, Oxford, named ''dumbbells'' because its design copied the apparatus for ringing church-bells, had been superseded no later than 1785 by the short bar with rounded knobs on each end that affords equally unmusical exercise. Avoiding the question of prosody, C had written in *BL* ch 3 of ''the pastoral charms and wild streaming lights of the 'Thalaba,' in which sentiment and imagery have given permanence even to the

I certainly always did say there was something original and powerful about Hazlitt at a time that Poole and Wordsworth were quite incredulous about it.[31] I still think there was by Nature, but the Devil that was in him—the brutal savagery of mind—prevented any development. When he was asked how he could think of calling Christabel an obscene poem—having often declared it to be one of the most beautiful in the language—he said "Because I thought it was the only thing that would sting him"—meaning me. "But why do you wish to sting him?" "Because I hate him"—"Why do you hate him?" "Because he has served me, damn him!"[32] I did serve him to be sure with a father's care at Stowey—

excitement of curiosity". *BL (CC)* I 64. In *TT* (1835) *Thalaba* became anonymously "some of the modern poems I have read". For C on the "depravity of the spirit of the times" as a mark of "the absence of poetry" see App F 14, below.

[31] William Hazlitt (1778–1830) had died the previous day, 18 Sept. His meetings with C in Shrewsbury and Nether Stowey in Jan–Jun 1798 are best known from his essay "My First Acquaintance with Poets" *Liberal* II (1823): *H Works* XVII 106–22. In his lecture of 1818 "On the Living Poets" Hazlitt said of C: "He was the first poet I ever knew. His genius at that time had angelic wings, and fed on manna." *H Works* V 167. On 8 Mar 1798 C wished to be remembered to "young Mr Haseloed" with "respect due to his talents" and a renewed invitation to visit Nether Stowey. *CL* I 394. Besides C's testimony that WW and Thomas Poole (1765–1837) saw in Hazlitt no great promise we have the negative evidence that no notice of Hazlitt by WW or Poole in 1798 survives and that Hazlitt repeatedly referred only to C as making him aware in 1798 of his own powers, in contrast with WW's remark even later that in *An Essay on the Principles of Human Action* (1805) Hazlitt had said "what every shoemaker must have thought of". *H Works* IX 3–4. There is a cloudy hint of Hazlitt's low assessment of WW (c 1800) in *CN* I 624.

[32] Hazlitt had written of *Christabel* anonymously: "There is something disgusting at the bottom of his subject, which is but ill glossed over by a veil of Della Cruscan sentiment and fine writ-

ing—like moon-beams playing on a charnel-house, or flowers strewed on a dead body." *Examiner* 2 Jun 1816 p 349. In the previous paragraph he had quoted the line "Hideous, deformed, and pale of hue" from the ms possessed by his wife, Sarah Stoddart. C had written in *BL* ch 24 that the poem was reviewed in *Ed Rev* with "malignity" and "personal hatred"—"and this review was generally attributed (whether rightly or no I know not) to a man, who both in my presence and in my absence, has repeatedly pronounced it the finest poem of its kind in the language". *BL (CC)* II 239. Jeffrey, taking this passage as referring to him, denied that he either reviewed *Christabel* or ever called it "a fine poem at all". *Ed Rev* XXVIII (1817) 508n, 510n. The similar language in TT strengthens the implication that C was pointing in *BL* to Hazlitt, but Jeffrey's extension of remarks concerning him in *BL* to include the review of *Christabel* suggests that he had at least heavily reworked the version submitted to him, in accordance with his frequent practice. C's letter of 27 Feb 1817 to Murray, often cited as evidence that C thought Hazlitt the reviewer in *Ed Rev*, probably refers to Hazlitt's review of *SM*. *CL* IV 706 and n. An entry in N 42 ff 10–11 indicates that C had come by 1829 to think Thomas Moore the reviewer in *Ed Rev*. Kathleen Coburn "Who Killed Christabel?" *TLS* 20 May 1965 p 397. The entry in TT throws no direct light on the vexed questions of who reviewed *Christabel* in *Ed Rev* and who C thought reviewed it there. Whatever C thought in 1817, that

I got him through Sir George Beaumont into a money-making way in painting old ladies,[33] and when he was in danger of his life or limbs at least for his horrid brutality to a girl at Keswick I gave him all the money I had and clothes and helped him to escape. Southey got him over the mountains to Grasmere where I was then.[34]

---

*P*It has been very injurious to Charles Lamb's mind and reputation that he has lent himself to such men as Hazlitt &c.[35] Lamb thinks any thing odd

P f 31ᵛ

---

he identified Hazlitt as the reviewer in the *Examiner* is sufficient impetus for the remarks in TT. In a letter of 5 Dec 1816 to R. H. Brabant, after declaring that "at my own risk I saved perhaps his Life from the Gallows, most certainly his character from blasting Infamy" (see n 34, below), C used almost exactly the language reported by HNC. "His reason I give in his own words—'Damn him! *I hate him*: FOR I am under obligations to him.'" And C had continued aptly enough: "You would scarcely think it possible, that a monster could exist who boasted of guilt and avowed his predilection for it." *CL* IV 693.

[33] Although the wording might suggest that C provided at Nether Stowey in 1798 not only "a father's care" but also, through Beaumont, income for Hazlitt, the latter action is to be assigned to Keswick in 1803. Hazlitt became an art student in London in the autumn of 1798, but he did not begin to paint portraits commercially until his return from Paris in Feb 1803. And there is no evidence that C was acquainted before 1803 with Sir George Howland Beaumont (1753–1827), landscape painter, friend and patron of C, WW, and the National Gallery. We learn initially from RS in Dec 1803 that Beaumont commissioned a portrait of C by Hazlitt (on C's reaction to the portrait see his letter to WW [23 Jul 1803]: *CL* II 958). *S Life* (CS) II 238. To HCR in 1811 Hazlitt complained that Beaumont's promise of patronage ceased when Hazlitt, led on by C, defended Junius against C in Beaumont's presence. *CRB* I 24. On a quarrel over religion see *CN* I 1616–18.

[34] This episode, which occurred on Hazlitt's return to Keswick in Oct 1803, was not mentioned immediately, in surviving reports of his visit, by any of the concerned parties. That he hurriedly left his effects behind is clear from *CL* II 1024–5 and *WL* (*E* rev) 446–7. The versions of later years vary in details: from C angry about the reviews in 1816 (*CL* IV 670, 693, 735); by way of HCR's understanding from a similarly angry WW on 15 Jun 1815 that Hazlitt had escaped from the incensed populace to WW, "who took him into his house at midnight, gave him clothes and money (from three to five pounds)" (*CRB* I 169); from WW's conversation of 29 Mar 1824 in *The Diary of Benjamin Robert Haydon* ed W. B. Pope (5 vols Cambridge, Mass 1960–3) II 470. C had warned Thomas Wedgwood on 16 Sept 1803, before the episode of Hazlitt's second visit, that he was "addicted to women, as objects of sexual Indulgence". *CL* II 990. Hence the later references to more than one reprehensible act, but we can assume only one hurried escape, when RS sent Hazlitt to Grasmere, where C was with WW and either one or both provided clothes and money. As to priority in making the story known, RS wrote to John Rickman on 11 Jan 1814 as if the details were either familiar or available upon request. *S Letters* (Curry) II 92–3.

[35] Charles Lamb (1775–1834), C's friend from the years when they were both at Christ's Hospital (1782–9), had met Hazlitt in C's company at Godwin's 22 Mar 1803. Herschel Baker *William Hazlitt* (Cambridge, Mass 1962) 153n.

or ugly powerful.[36]
Hood learnt his punning from Lamb.[37]

The "&c" cannot be identified with precision, but Lamb's "Letter of Elia to Robert Southey, Esquire" in *London Mag* VIII (Oct 1823) 400ff takes pains to defend his friendships with Thomas Holcroft (1745–1809), dramatist, radical, and freethinker, heartily disliked by C; Hazlitt; and James Henry Leigh Hunt (1784–1859), the essayist, editor of the *Examiner* and other periodicals, imprisoned in 1813 for libelling the Prince Regent. Before listing some fifteen identifiable persons presumed to be less offensive to RS than Hazlitt, Hunt, and Holcroft, the "Letter" to RS declares: "In more than one place, if I mistake not, you have been pleased to compliment me at the expence of my companions. I cannot accept your compliment at such a price. . . . You have put me upon counting my riches." *L Works* I 229. It is possibly pertinent to the drift of C's personal remarks on 19 Sept that Hunt's expansion of a passage on the hauteur of RS in *The Feast of the Poets* (1815) 12 included a memorable nod at C:

For Coleridge had vexed him long
    since, I suppose,
By his idling, and gabbling, and
    muddling in prose.

Hunt clarified the reference in notes by explaining that C had "done his best" in pamphlets and newspapers to deserve such offices in government as his friends RS and WW held; that C's friends lamented his waste of "great natural talents"; that his "strange periodical publication, called the Friend", had defended Nelson's attack upon Copenhagen, whatever C now claimed his meaning to be; and that C ought to know better than to think that Hunt would try to get *Remorse* condemned (pp 78–87). John Beer relates this passage to Lamb's and C's interest in the friendship of Sidney and Fulke Greville: "Coleridge and Lamb: the Central Themes" *Charles Lamb Bulletin* NS No 14 (1976) 115–18.

[36] In the essay "Charles Lamb" in

Appreciations Walter Pater observed the prevalence of humour over wit; "and such union of grave, of terrible even, with gay, we may note in the circumstances of his life, as reflected hence into his work". C may have had in mind such interests as those revealed in Lamb's essays ("Witches, and Other Night-Fears", "Hogarth", "Old China"), or, continuing with personal acquaintances, Lamb's unremitting praise for such as the digressive coxcomb and erotic draughtsman, Thomas Griffiths Wainewright (1794–1847), whose best known pseudonym was "Janus Weathercock". Neither Lamb nor C knew of his prowess as forger and poisoner. And see n 39, below.

In 1811, although HCR's record does not mention Lamb until 29 Mar, Charles and his sister Mary would probably have come up a few days earlier: "*March* 24. A call on Coler. He expatiated largely on the powerful effect of brotherly & sisterly love in the formn. of char[acte]r. Certain peculiarities in his wife, Mrs. Southey, Mrs. Lovell he ascribed to their having no brother. I recollect too, but it was on some other occasion, his saying that he envied Wordsworth his having had a sister & that his own character had suffered from the want of a sister. Today he also spoke of *incest*. The universal horror he ascribed not to *instinct* (if I mistake not *Southey*, he said, believed in the *instinct*). He was of opinion that fatal consequences had been found to follow from the intercourse. And therefore a religious horror had been industriously excited by priests—he spoke of novelty as exciting, & of habitual presence as repressing desire. *March* 29. With Coler. at Hazlitt's. Before Lamb came, Coler. praised his *serious* conversation & Hazlitt ascribed his puns to *humility*." *CR (BCW)* 38.

[37] Thomas Hood (1799–1845), poet and editor, had emerged as a prince of punsters in *Odes and Addresses to Great People* (1825, with John Hamilton Reyn-

Poor dear Charles! What society has he kept and what habits have been his! Yet *nothing* ever left a stain on his mind—which looked upon the degraded men and things around him as Moonshine on a Dunghill[38]— which shines and takes no pollution. All things are shadows to Lamb except those which move his Affections.[39]   [36:267]

---

[a]19. Sept. 1830.

What a melancholy thing is poor Huskisson's death![40] So far as we know, he is the last of our Statesmen.

---

[a] f 32; in the ms this entry follows the entry on Hurwitz, below, before the repeat of the date 23 Sept 1830

---

olds) and *Whims and Oddities* (1826–7). In *The Plea of the Midsummer Fairies, Hero and Leander, Lycus the Centaur, and Other Poems* (1827) the most obvious influence is from Keats, but the first poem was dedicated to Lamb (by a commendatory letter) and the second to C. When C came upon a copy of the anonymous *Odes and Addresses*, he wrote at once to praise Lamb as author: "The puns are nine in ten good—many excellent—the *Newgatory* transcendent." *CL* v 473. Lamb identified the authors by return mail, but declared the puns an excess: "A Pun is a thing of too much consequence to be thrown in as a makeweight." Lamb reminded C that he had met this punster at Islington, where Hood and Lamb were neighbours; entering the room as Lamb wrote, Hood was pleased by C's error. *LL* III 8. Hood reported two meetings with "the 'Old Man eloquent' " in Islington, the first when C and Mrs Gillman came to dine with the Lambs, the second with "one of his sons", presumably DC. "Literary Reminiscences IV" *Hood's Own: or, Laughter from Year to Year* (1846) 550–62; reprinted from the 1839 ed in *Thomas Hood & Charles Lamb: The Story of a Friendship* ed Walter Jerrold (1930) 122–4.

[38] See 36:23.

[39] This last paragraph was published in *TT* (1835) as of an unnamed "gentle creature's mind". Lamb had protested the inappropriateness of "gentle-hearted Charles" in C's *This Lime-tree Bower My Prison. LL (M)* I 217–18, 224. On C's and WW's continuation of the epithet "gentle" see Edmund Blunden *Charles Lamb and His Contemporaries* (Cambridge 1933) 126–32. Godwin— whose atheism was a staining influence resisted by Lamb throughout a friendship of thirty-odd years—urged in 1808, as Lamb's publisher, that some of the descriptions of violence in *The Adventures of Ulysses* would result in "excluding the female sex" from among parental readers, but Lamb typically stood firm: "If you want a book that is not occasionally to *shock*, you should not have thought of a Tale which was so full of Anthropophagi & monsters. I cannot alter those things without enervating the Book . . . ". *LL* (M) II 278–9. In 1804 C made a note of one whose "pure mind met Vice and vicious Thoughts by accident only", as a poet seeking a rhyme might encounter an impure word. *CN* II 2275.

[40] This entry and the date followed the entries of 23 Sept in MS B. William Huskisson (1770–1830), secretary of the Treasury 1804–5, 1807–9, president of the Board of Trade 1823–7, Colonial Secretary 1827–9, was killed in an accident near Manchester on 15 Sept. Did HNC suddenly remember that C had made this remark when news of the loss was fresher than on the 23rd? In 1811 in

^a23. Sept. 1830.

I never read such wretched stuff as those two books of Whately's^b on Logic and Rhetoric.[1] There are two kinds of Logic. 1. Syllogistic 2. Criterional. How any one can by any spinning make more than ten or a dozen pages about the first is inconceivable to me; all those absurd forms of syllogisms are one half pure sophisms and the other half mere forms of Rhetoric. All Logic[2] is 1. *Seclusion* 2. *Inclusion*. 3. *Conclusion* = the Understanding—the Experience—Reason = This *ought*—this *is*—this *must* be so. The Criterional Logic or Logic of Premises is of course much the most important and it has never been treated on.[3]   [36:268]

---

^a f 31^v   ^b Whateley's

---

the *Courier* C had set against Huskisson's defence of the bullionists the principle that money is "*whatever* has a value among men according to what it *represents*, rather than to what it *is*". *EOT (CC)* II 132, 239. Nor would C have been automatically drawn to such Huskissonian policies as opposition to the claims of agriculturists, Ricardian reduction of tariffs in support of commerce, or co-operation with Joseph Hume in the reduction of restraints against combinations of labour. A close associate of Canning for twenty years, clearly superior to other financiers in government in his time, Huskisson was generally credited with enabling the Canning government to survive the economic crisis of 1825. Canning's death probably accounts above all other reasons for C's melancholy generalisation. The entry died in MS B, perhaps because of the judgement it passed on Wellington, Peel, and other political eminences who remained.

[1] Richard Whately (1787–1863) *Elements of Logic, Comprising the Substance of the Article in the Encyclopaedia Metropolitana, with Additions* (1826) and *Elements of Rhetoric* (1828). As C seems to have had in hand a draft of his long-planned Kantian, criterional logic by Jun 1823—*Logic (CC)* xxix, xlvii—it is not surprising that he looked with disdain on Whately's syllogistic *Logic* and associationist *Rhetoric*, both of which had proved by further editions before 1830 to be the popular handbooks they remained throughout the century.

That the *EM* was widely acknowledged as an idea initiated by C was no salve for the choice of the narrowly deductive Whately as author of the articles there on logic and rhetoric. *L&L* 38–9. As dean of Oriel College in 1820, Whately had informed the provost of HC's intemperance, which resulted in his being deprived of his fellowship; Whately advised HC not to "cherish any hopes" of reclaiming it but to endeavour "to derive moral profit *from* what has befallen you". *CL* v 59, 64.

[2] Meaning "All syllogistic logic", as clarified in *TT* (1835). When mental operations other than logic are excluded, "a thousand syllogisms would amount to nine hundred and ninety-nine superfluous illustrations of the syllogism itself, that is, of what a syllogism is". *Logic (CC)* 51. In 1814 C had represented more favourably the first step, to "Seclude— or Decide—To cut off from—to set apart = judgement—an act of inclosure of the common use of our Reason". *CN* III 4228.

[3] HNC's guardedly optimistic note, *TT* (1835) I 207n, was dropped in 1836: "Mr. Coleridge's own treatise on Logic is unhappily left imperfect. But the fragment, such as it is, will be presented to the world in the best possible form which the circumstances admit, by Mr. Joseph Henry Green, who, beyond any of Mr. C.'s friends, is intimately acquainted with his principles and ultimate aspirations in philosophy generally, and in psychology in particular." Green's table of contents

The object of Rhetoric is = Persuasion.
Logic = Conviction.
Grammar = Significancy.
There wants a fourth between them all = the Rhematic or Logic of Sentences.[4]   [36:269]

---

[c]Hurwitz tells me that the Hebrew word for Understanding signifies—Between—which is a curious confirmation of my argument.[5]   [36:75]

---

[d]23. Sept. 1830.[6]

What a loss we have had in Varro's mythological and critical works![7]

It is said that the works of Epicurus are probably amongst the Herculanean MSS.[8] I do not feel much interest about them, because by the consent of all antiquity Lucretius has preserved a complete view of his system.[9]

[c] f 32   [d] The separate date 19 Sept 1830 with the entry on Huskisson intervened

---

entitled pt 2 of C's *Logic* "The Criterion or Dialectic"; the wise querist first asks, said C, "What is the universal and sure criterion of any and every knowledge?" *Logic (CC)* vii, 107.

[4] *Logic (CC)* 22: ". . . the doctrine of arranging words and sentences perspicuously; an art which has hitherto had no appropriate title . . . and which I therefore propose to distinguish by the term 'rhematic' . . . Thence rhetoric, or the art of declaiming persuasively; and lastly logic, as the art and science of discoursing conclusively." A table that follows in the *Logic*, with a counterpart in N 29 (*CN* IV 4771), lists the four sciences of words, Grammar, Rhematic, Rhetoric, and Logic, for the fitting together of letters, words, persuasions, and reasonings.

[5] Giving the word as "*Bineh* . . . from a root meaning *between* or *distinguishing*", HNC published this entry under the date 13 Mar 1827, combining it with the definition of "understanding" in 10 Mar 1827 (at n 7), without mention of C's friend Hurwitz.

[6] In MS B the entry of 19 Sept on Huskisson's death intervened. The date is repeated in the ms at this point.

[7] Marcus Terentius Varro (116–c 27 B.C.), grammarian, poet, satirist, antiquarian, geographer, jurist, author of over fifty works, said by Quintilian to be the most learned of the Romans. Cf "Varro's Opus Grande Rerum Divinarum et Humanarum—Ah! that is a Loss!" —inspired by Vico. *CN* IV 5232 f 39. This lost work, *Antiquitatum rerum humanarum et divinarum*, was divided into two parts, the first twenty-five books on *res humanae*, the remaining sixteen books on *res divinae*. In the margins of Faber *Mysteries of the Cabiri*, observing that the "ancient Mystae" showed themselves pantheists by making "the lowest first, the highest posterior", C cited Varro, "himself the reformer of the Samothracian Rites". *CM (CC)* II 575; cf 583 and *CN* IV 4091.

[8] C had brought home from Malta a list of papyri excavated and unrolled at Herculaneum (now VCL S MS F 14.15), *CN* II Notes App B p. 410; *C&S (CC)* 82n. From the papyri at Herculaneum Johann Conrad Orelli had published fragments of Epicurus *De natura*, Περὶ φύσεως, from bks II and XI, at Leipzig in 1818.

[9] Titus Lucretius Carus (c 99–c 55 B.C.) *De rerum natura* gives the fullest

I regret the loss of the works of the old Stoics—Zeno &c.[10] [36:270]
Socrates was only a poetical character to Plato, who built up a system
of his own. The several disciples of Socrates caught some particular
points from him, and made systems of philosophy upon them. Socrates
had no system.[11] [36:271]
I hold all claims set up for Egypt as having been the origin of Greek
Philosophy as groundless.[12] It sprang up in Greece itself, and began with
physics only—then it took in the Idea of a living Cause—and made
Pantheism out of the two.[13] Socrates introduced ethics and taught duties,
and Plato conceived the Idea of a God the Maker of the World.[14]

The measure of Human Philosophy was full, when Christianity came
to add what before was wanting—Assurance.[15]

After that the Neo-Platonics[e] joined Theurgy with Philosophy, and ultimately degenerated into Magic and mere Mysticism.[16] [36:272]

[e] Platonic(s)~~icians~~

---

extant exposition of the atomistic Epicu-
rean system, with its emphasis upon serenity as the chief end of life. In Lect 6 of
the lectures on the history of philosophy,
after giving a biography and analysis of
Epicurus based on Tennemann, C said:
"The physiology of Epicurus so fully detailed in [Lucretius] I have no concern
with". *P Lects* (1949) 216. By "all antiquity" C apparently refers to works
less obvious than Diogenes Laertius
*Lives and Opinions of Eminent Philoso-
phers*. None of Cicero's attacks on the
Epicureans mentions Lucretius.

[10] The writings of Zeno the Stoic
(336–264 B.C.) and his followers in the
"old Stoa" are known through quotation
and biographical treatment in Diogenes
Laertius, Stobaeus, Cicero, Plutarch,
and other sources, and as modified in the
works of the later Roman Stoics by way
of the otherwise lost Middle Stoa. In an
annotation on Tennemann I 197–201 C
criticises Zeno's conceptions of space
and time. *CM (CC)* V.

[11] Cf C's earlier references to Xenophon, 7 Jan–13 Feb 1823 (at n 1) and 1
May 1823 (at n 15), above. For his fullest discussions of Socrates see *P Lects*
Lects 3 and 4 (1949) 136–42, 153–6, in
which he says almost the opposite of the
present remark; i.e. that Plato's dialogues contain "the true opinions of Soc-

rates" but "by no means convey the
opinions of Plato" (156; cf 163–5).

[12] Cf 8 May 1824 (at n 8), above
(36:52), concerning what he had called
this "mere fancy, the mere jargon of the
later Platonists". *P Lects* Lect 2 (1949)
95. Napoleon had made Egyptian antiquities a French preserve; on controversies consequent in the 1820s see *CN*
III 4317n.

[13] Of the Stoics C charged in 1819 that
"throughout they confounded God and
Nature". *P Lects* Lect 6 (1949) 219.

[14] After describing Socrates as moral
and religious, Tennemann defined Plato's God as "einer ausserweltlichen In-
telligenz", an extra-mundane intelligence. *Geschichte der Philosophie* II
375–7. On God as maker of the world
see e.g. *Timaeus* 29D–34B, 38C; *Republic* X 597D; *Sophist* 265B–E.

[15] Even in Plato, C had said in Lect 6
of the lectures on the history of philosophy, "nowhere do we find a living God
to whom we may be privileged to say,
'Our Father' "; Christianity brought
with such a God the conviction of the im-
perishableness of "personal identity". *P
Lects* (1949) 223–4.

[16] Proclus and other Neoplatonists
"connected philosophy with magic, with
the power of names and numbers, and
the whole secret trade which we know

Plotinus was a man of wonderful ability, no doubt *and some of the sublimest passages I ever read are in his works.[17]   [36:273]

I was amused the other day with reading in Tertullian that Spirits or Dæmons dilate and contract themselves and wriggle about like worms— lumbricis similes.[18]   [36:274]

---

26. Sept. 1830.

The five finest things in Scotland are 1. Edinburgh. 2. The Antechamber of the Fall of Foyers.[a] 3. The view of Loch Lomond from Inch M——[1] the highest island. 4. The Trossachs. 5. The view of the Hebrides from some point, I forget where.[2]

f f 32ᵛ   *a* Fiers.

---

little of, but which they professed under the name of theurgy'', and, ''worst of all, the moral into physical God-likeness''. *P Lects* Lect 8 (1949) 250 and n; cf 243, 296. In a marginal note on Plotinus *Operum philosophicorum* ed Marsilio Ficino (Basel 1580) C ascribed such theosophy, like the witchcraft of other ages, to ''Despotism with civil Wars''. *CM (CC)* IV.

[17] ''Beautiful passages there are in Plotinus—exquisite morality—fine observations so that you would believe him to be a Christian'', but unlike Plato and Aristotle, who struggle to move thought upward, ''in the works of Plotinus it is all beginning, no middle, no progress''. *P Lects* Lect 7 (1949) 241–2. Lamb, apostrophising C in ''Christ's Hospital Five and Thirty Years Ago'', told how strangers had stood entranced ''to hear thee unfold, in thy deep and sweet intonations, the mysteries of Jamblichus, or Plotinus (for even in those years thou waxedst not pale at such philosophic draughts)''. *Elia* (1823) 48. *CN* shows C reading and drawing upon Plotinus at all stages. His surviving notes to the *Enneads*, some of them dictated or transcribed, praise Plotinus on love; explicate *sensus, ratio*, and *mens*; and speculate on Plotinus as a ''Whitewitch'' (cf n 16, above). Quotations in C's works come from the heart of Plo-

tinus' thought on the intelligential soul and on the universe as symbolic representation. *Friend (CC)* I 418, 524; *BL* ch 12 *(CC)* I 240–1. On Plotinus see also 7 Jan–13 Feb 1823 n 12, above.

[18] C was reading, in Webster *Displaying of Supposed Witchcraft* ch 10 (1677) 213, ''what seems to have been the opinion of *Tertullian*'', as recorded in N 29 (*CN* IV 4621): ''Daemones sua haec corpora contrahunt, et dilatant, ut volunt: sicut etiam lumbrici, et alia quaedam insecta'' (''Spirits dilate and contract these bodies of theirs at their pleasures, as do worms and some other insects''). Cf Tertullian *Apologeticus adversus gentes* § 22: ''Omnis spiritus ales: hoc et angeli et daemones, igitur momento ubique sunt'' and ''suppetit illis ad utramque substantiam hominis adveniendam mira subtilitas et tenuitas sua'' (''Every spirit is winged: in this both the angels and daemons agree: therefore in a moment they are everywhere'' and ''their own wondrous subtle and slight nature furnisheth to them means of approaching either part of man'': tr C. Dodgson 1842).

[1] Inch Tavannach: *TT* (1835); *DWJ* I 251–3; *CN* I 1462.

[2] C had written to RS 13 Sept 1803: ''There are about four Things worth going into Scotland for, to one who has been in Cumberland & Westmoreland/— the view of all the Islands at the Foot of

But the intervals between the fine things in Scotland are very dreary; whereas in Cumberland and Westmorland it is a cabinet of beauties; each thing beautiful in itself and the passage to another lake or mountain is itself a beautiful thing again. The Scotch lakes are so like one another from their great size that you are obliged in a picture to read the names; but the English Lakes, especially Derwent water—or rather the whole vale of Keswick, is so rememberable that after having been once seen, no one ever requires to be told what it is.[3] This Vale is about as large a basin as that of Loch Lomond; the latter is covered with water; in the former case, we have two Lakes with a charming river to connect them, and lovely villages at the foot of the mountains and other habitations, which give an air of life and cheerfulness to the whole place.   [36:275]

The Land Imagery of the North of Devon is most delightful.[4]

[36:276]

I wrote Kubla Khan in Brimstone Farm between Porlock and Ilfracombe—near Culbone. And at Porlock I wrote Christabel, [b]and the Ancient Mariner.[5]

[b] f 33

Loch Lomond from the Top of the highest Island, called Inch devannoc [Inchtavannach]: 2. the Trossachs at the foot of Loch Ketterin 3. The Chamber & antichamber of the Falls of Foyers . . . 4th & lastly, the City of Edinburgh.—Perhaps, I might add Glen Coe . . .". *CL* II 989. C had visited the Cavern and Falls of Foyer, after parting from WW and DW on 29 Aug 1803. *CN* II 1481, 1492–5. On the Trossachs see *CN* II 1470, *CL* II 978; Edinburgh as vista, *CN* II 1513, *CL* II 988–9.

As succinct as this entry is, it contrasts vividly with the complaints of RS; e.g.: "It rained during our halt, and continued to rain heavily when the carriage stopt above the Fall of Foyers. The ladies stept from the coach upon the wall, to look down the glen, and I went with Mr Telford some way down. It is not creditable to the owner of this property, that there should be no means of getting at the bottom of the Fall, and no safe means of obtaining a full view from any point, except from the high road, where it is so foreshortened as to be seen to great disadvantage." RS *Journal of a Tour in Scotland in 1819* ed C. H. Herford (1929) 177–8.

[3] *TT* (1835) added: "when drawn".

[4] I.e. the hills along the Bristol Channel, from Leeford to Ilfracombe; but C probably would think simultaneously of Culbone and Porlock, eastward in Somersetshire. The word "Imagery", in Johnson's meaning of "sensible representations", is applied to objects of nature by C in *The Destiny of Nations* line 182, "And clouds slow-varying their huge imagery", and often by WW, as in *To H. C. Six Years Old* lines 9–10, "Suspended in a stream as clear as sky, | Where earth and heaven do make one imagery". *PW* (EHC) I 138; *WPW* I 247. C included this meaning in the final essay on method when he delineated one kind of mental antecedent as "an image or conception received through the senses, and originating from without, the inspiriting passion or desire being alone the immediate and proper offspring of the mind". *Friend (CC)* I 513. C told how he made sketches in and near the Quantocks for his poem-to-be *The Brook*. *BL* ch 10 *(CC)* I 195–7.

[5] A notebook entry of Nov 1810 lamenting that the Wordsworths did not take his side against Charles Lloyd in 1798—"it prevented my finishing the Christabel—& at the retirement between

Wordsworth[6] said he could make nothing of Love except that it was Friendship accidentally combined[c] with Desire. Whence I conclude that Wordsworth was never in love. For what shall we say of the feeling which a man of sensibility has towards his wife with her baby at her breast? How pure from sensual Desire—yet how different from Friendship![7] [36:277]

[c] ~~united~~ combined

Linton and Porlock was the first occasion of my having recourse to Opium" (*CN* III 4006 f 23)—would seem to date as after May 1798 rather than "the summer" of 1797 the writing of *Kubla Khan* in retirement at "a lonely farm-house between Porlock and Linton, on the Exmoor confines of Somerset and Devonshire". *PW* (EHC) I 295–6. In the Crewe MS of *Kubla Khan* C said that he wrote the poem "at a Farm House between Porlock & Linton, a quarter of a mile from Culbone Church, in the fall" of 1797. *TLS* 2 Aug 1934 p 541; *CL* I 349. He had taken laudanum to relieve mental distress as early as 1795. *CL* I 188; cf 250. HNC left this entry in MS B, whence it was published by Morchard Bishop "The Farmhouse of Kubla Khan" *TLS* 10 May 1957 p 293. Bishop took "Brimstone" as the extant Broomstreet Farm, locally pronounced "Brimson". *CN* III 4006n. The *Ancient Mariner*, conceived by C and WW between Alfoxden and Watchet on 13 Nov 1797, was read to the Wordsworths on 23 Mar 1798. *WL* (*E* rev) 194; *DWJ* (1958) 15. In Nov 1797 C mentioned casually to Joseph Cottle that he had "written a ballad of about 300 lines". *CL* I 357. Bits of *Christabel* pt 1 seem to peep through C's letters and notebooks in 1797 and early 1798; in the Preface of 1816–34 he said it was written at Stowey in 1797, but it has been assigned more easily to the spring of 1798. *Christabel* ed EHC (1907) 2–5. The designation of Porlock in conversation with HNC in 1830 has at least a symbolic importance; like the specification of the farmhouse for *Kubla Khan*, the place carries more freight in his memory than the numerals of 1797 or 1798. To readers it may have been enough that he wrote the two poems when he lived—the high point of his life—at Stowey; to himself apparently there was a breakthrough, twice, at Porlock, away from the "inmates of my cottage" and the "lime-tree bower my prison". *PW* (EHC) I 178, 240.

[6] Blank in *TT* (1835), "A person" in *TT* (1836). Isolating this entry under a separate date, HNC was willing to risk having WW recognise himself as C saw him, whatever WW had actually said. *TT* (1836) softened the judgement to "I concluded"—as if it seemed so to C only at that moment. The conversation with WW may have occurred as early as 1808 (*CN* III 3284n); C was explicit with HCR on 12 Mar 1811: ". . . Wordsworth is by nature incapable of being in Love, tho' no man more tenderly attached—hence he ridicules the existence of any other passion, than a compound of Lust with Esteem & Friendship, confined to one Object, first by accidents of Association, and permanently, by the force of Habit & a sense of Duty". *CL* III 305. In 1808, when C distinguished between the friendship WW might feel for him, promoting the welfare of each equally, and his own love for WW and SH, preferring their welfare to his and receiving happiness from the sacrifice, he attributed WW's satisfying prudence to a happy marriage, in contrast with his own unrestful love. *CN* III 3284, 3304.

[7] In a marginal note on De Wette *Theodor* C similarly rejected "the common opinion" that love "is no more than Friendship + Lust", for "all, who are capable of Love, know that it must be exclusive" because "Friendship is Sympathy, but Love Correspondence . . . the Union of opposite Poles". *CM (CC)* II

Sympathy constitutes Friendship—but in Love there is a sort of Antipathy or opposing Passion. Each strives to be the other, and both together make up a one whole. [36:277]

Luther has sketched the most beautiful picture of the nature and ends and duties of the Wedded Life, I ever read.[8] [36:278]

St Paul says it is a great Symbol—not Mystery as we term it.[9] [36:278]

———

Why need we talk of a fiery Hell? If the Will—the law of our nature—were withdrawn from our Memory, our Fancy, our Understanding, our Reason—no other Hell could equal for a spiritual being what it^d would^e then feel.[10] [36:280]

———

^{d} ~~we~~ it ^{e} ~~sh~~ would

———

197. Perhaps the most pertinent of C's many discussions of love and wedded union is the note on Sir Thomas Browne *Religio Medici: CM (CC)* I 751–2. Only in *TT* (1835) is the discussion of conjugal love broken by a divisional bar between this paragraph and the next.

[8] Luther *Colloquia Mensalia* ch 50 "Of Matrimonie" (1652) 445–54. At p 447 C improved the text to say that desire "should be occasioned by our Love" rather than having "imagined Love" originate in desire. *CM (CC)* III. C may have had in mind Luther's sermon preached on the marriage of Sigismund von Lindenau in Merseburg 4 Aug 1545, with Heb 13.4 as text.

[9] Eph 5.32, μυστήριον. HNC's note in *TT* (1835) gives the passage. In annotating Rev 17.5 C gives five possible meanings of the word. *CM (CC)* I 471–2. In Poole *Synopsis criticorum* IV ii 817 *mysterium* is glossed as the symbol relating Christ's marriage to the church with the marriage of Adam and Eve. In 1826 C described sacraments, including marriage, as symbol or mystery with a sensible sign and a spiritual substantive act. *CN* IV 5348. RSV retains "mystery", but James Moffatt reads with C, "This is a profound symbol, as I take it, of Christ and the church", and the New English Bible gives it as "a truth" concerning Christ and the Church.

[10] *TT* (1835) expanded to explain the result as "mental anarchy", "conscious madness—a horrid thought". In *The Friend* (1818) C attacked Paley's doctrine of general consequences because it "draws away the attention from the *will*, that is, from the inward motives and impulses which constitute the essence of *morality*, to the outward act". *Friend (CC)* I 314; cf I 444–5, II 279–80. C. R. Leslie reported on a visit of 1817 or 1818: "When Allston was suffering extreme depression of spirits, immediately after the loss of his wife, he was haunted, during sleepless nights, by horrid thoughts; and he told me that diabolical imprecations forced themselves into his mind. The distress of this to a man so sincerely religious as Allston, may be imagined. He wished to consult Coleridge, but could not summon resolution. He desired, therefore, that I would do it; and I went to Highgate, where Coleridge was at that time living with Mr. Gillman. I found him walking in the garden, his hat in his hand (as it generally was in the open air), for he told me that, having been one of the Blue-coat boys, among whom it is the fashion to go bare-headed, he had acquired a dislike to any covering of the head. I explained the cause of my visit, and he said, 'Allston should say to himself, *"Nothing is me but my will."* These thoughts, therefore, that force themselves on my mind are no part of *me*, and there can be no guilt in them.'"

"Most women have no character at all" said Pope, and meant it for satire.[11] Shakspeare, who knew man and woman better, saw that in fact it was the perfection of woman to be *characterless*. Every man wishes for Desdemonas, Ophelias and creatures who, though they may not always *understand* you, do always *feel* you and *feel*[f] with you.[12]　　　　[36:279]

---

^a5. Oct. 1830.[1]

In Politics, what begins in Fear usually ends in Folly.[2]　　　　[36:281]

^f fel+l　　　^a f 33^v; a cancelled date, 3 or 8, preceded the final "5"

If he will make a strong effort to become indifferent to their recurrence they will either cease, or cease to trouble him.' " *Autobiographical Recollections* I 51–2. Emerson heard C say on 4 Aug 1833 that "the will was that by which a person is a person; because if one should push me in the street, and so I should force the man next me into the kennel, I should at once exclaim, 'I did not do it, sir,' meaning it was not my will". *English Traits* (1856) 6. If WW's presence continues in C's remarks to HNC, the link occurs in a letter of 8 Aug 1820 to Allsop, in which C denounced WW's "Confusion of God with the World" and rewrote *The Brothers* lines 182–3 as

The thought of Death sits easy on the Man,
Whose earnest *Will* hath lived among the Deathless.

CL v 95. He explained to HCR 20 Dec 1810 "that religious belief is an act not of the understanding but of the will. To become a believer, one must love the doctrine & must resolve with passion to believe, Not sit down coolly to enquire whether he shd. believe or no." *CR (BCW)* 33–4.

[11] Alexander Pope *Moral Essays* Epistle 2, *To a Lady* (1735) 2: " 'Most women have no Characters at all' ", as a quotation from Martha Blount (the lady addressed) describing women as many-faceted. Johnson's *Dictionary* cites Pope's line to illustrate the meaning "Personal qualities; particular constitu-

tion of the mind"; i.e. most women have no ruling passion.

[12] In Lect 1 of 17 Dec 1818, on *The Tempest* (in the lectures on Shakespeare that alternated with those on philosophy), C said: "Shakespeare saw that the want of prominence, which Pope notices for sarcasm, was the blessed beauty of the woman's character, and knew that it arose not from any deficiency, but from the more exquisite harmony of all the parts of the moral being constituting one living total of head and heart." *Lects 1808–19 (CC)* II 270. Did C more than most wish for a Desdemona as wife? EHC transcribed a note for Lect 6 of 16 Nov 1813 at Bristol, including "9—lastly the female no character—". *Lects 1808–19 (CC)* I 573.

[1] 5 Oct, the date HNC settled on, was Tuesday. The final paragraph was crowded into the ms at a later time. SC's son Herbert was born 7 Oct, 11 AM.

[2] C's repeated attacks from 1795 to 1802 on the "panic of property"—e.g. *Lects 1795 (CC)* 30–1; *EOT (CC)* I 68–9, 381—illustrate the consistent connexion throughout his political writings of fear with folly. In the *Courier* 6 May 1811, on the bullion controversy, he found in commercial history "that in every instance where either a real danger or a groundless panic has produced a general alarm, in both cases the *alarm* has been the true source of nine-tenths of the whole calamity". *EOT (CC)* II 127; cf 462. On 26 Sept 1811 he objected to Hobbes's recommendation that mon-

An Ear for Music is a very different thing from a Taste for Music.

I have no Ear whatever. I could not for my life sing an air. But I have the intensest delight in Music, and can detect bad from good.[3] Naldi said to me once that I did not seem to be much interested with a piece of Rossini's music which had been just performed. I said it sounded to me like nonsense verses. But I could scarcely contain myself when a thing of Beethoven's followed.[4]   [36:282]

I think the Belgians a set of ungrateful miscreants, and were I King of the Netherlands I would banish *them* as Diogenes did the Corinthians. It is a wicked rebellion without one just cause.[5]   [36:285]

---

archs, like God, instil fear. Ibid II 312. In Malta he had noted a diplomat whose sentences repeated "For fear—for fear, for fear—now of Russia—now of this". *CN* II 2295.

[3] Gillman heard C similarly on this occasion or another: "I believe I have no ear for music, but I have a taste for it." *C Life* (G) 357. C left a fuller record of his own: "I have no technical knowledge of Music. . . . It converses with the *life* of my mind. . . . Yet I wish I did know something more of the wondrous mystery of this mighty *Art Magic*, were it but to understand why . . . I should feel so utter, so extreme a difference between the Musical Compositions of Beethoven, Mozart, and our own Purcell for instance, and those of the equally celebrated Rossini and others which are just like nonsense verses to me, which I know to be meant for a Poem because I distinguish the rhymes." N 52: *IS* 214. J. H. Green is apparently the transcriber of a more philosophic analysis of meaning in music, in a ms now VCL LT 21.

[4] Giuseppe Naldi (c 1770–1820), Italian baritone, left London for Paris in 1819. On 2 Mar 1813, when "Purcell was his hero", C talked to Charles Aders and HCR about music, seemingly "with more feeling than knowledge". *CRB* I 122. Plato set him to speculating about music in 1817. *CN* III 4337. We know that he attended musical evenings given by Mr and Mrs Aders in Euston Square on 21 Dec 1822, 5 Apr 1823 (when WW

slept and Flaxman was bored, but C's "enjoyment was very great indeed"), and other occasions—all too late for Naldi. *CRB* I 288, 293; *C at H* 95. Leigh Hunt heard Naldi several times in Mozart operas at Covent Garden in 1817–18. *Examiner* (1818) 57–8, 492. HNC had already utilised this entry in *QR* Aug 1834. *CH* 627–8.

[5] To the Brussels riots of 25–6 Aug and 19–20 Sept, C's reactions of 19 Sept (see above, at n 7) continue. Prince Frederick William Charles's attack on the barricades of Brussels on 23 Sept put the Belgians at civil war; on 4 Oct the provisional government declared Belgium independent; King William entrusted the southern provinces to his son, the Prince of Orange. *A Reg* for 1830 History 257–60. Diogenes Laertius *Lives* 6.2.6 tells of Diogenes the Cynic (c 412–323 B.C.), who was sold as a slave in Corinth: "When some one said to him, 'The people of Sinope condemned you to banishment,' he replied, 'And I condemned them to remain where they were.' " LCL, tr C. D. Yonge. *TT* (1835) substituted: "Were I King William, I would banish the Belgians as Coriolanus banishes the Romans in Shakspeare", citing *Coriolanus* III iii 120–4. Corinth was notorious for its courtesans; "Corinthian" in 1830 meant "licentious libertine", as in Pierce Egan *Life in London, or the Day and Night Scenes of Jerry Hawthorn, Esq. and Corinthian Tom* (1821–3).

I never felt the heavenly superiority of the prayers of the English Liturgy, till I had attended some Kirks in the country parts of Scotland.[6]

[36:283]

----

*b*I call these strings of school-boys or girls which we meet near London— "Walking Advertisements."[7]   [36:284]

----

8. Oct. 1830.

Galileo was a great genius and so was Newton; but it would take two or three Galileos and Newtons to make one Kepler.[1] It is in the order of

b Entry crowded into ms at later time

[6] One of C's several defences of "our excellent Liturgy", in the margins of *Reliquiae Baxterianae*, gives a context for the bald Scottish kirks of this entry: "But for our blessed and truly apostolic & scriptural Liturgy, our Churches ⟨Pews⟩ would long ago have been filled by Arians and Socinians, as too many of their Desks and Pulpits already are". *CM (CC)* I 343; cf 261–2, 320. In a note of 1810 he similarly contrasted "our noble Liturgy" with "the meanness of the Conventicles". *CN* III 4020. Neither C nor DW mentioned attendance in kirks during the tour of Aug–Sept 1803.

[7] Writing to C. A. Tulk in Feb 1818 of Blake's poem *The Little Vagabond*, C imagined the response of "a Saint of the new stamp, one of the Fixt Stars of our eleemosynary Advertisements . . . with the whites of his Eyes upraised at the *audacity* of this poem". *CL* IV 837. In the copy of *TT* (1835) presented to him by HNC, now in the Cornell University Library, WW wrote beside this entry: "I have heard them called The March of Intellect."

[1] Johannes Kepler (1571–1630), German astronomer, was ranked by C almost with Giordano Bruno. In 1799 C translated or adapted an epigram on Kepler, "No mortal Genius yet had clomb so high". *CN* I 432 f 49ᵛ; *Friend (CC)* I 252n, II 201n. On certain points of character, C said, one turns from Bacon to Kepler "as from gloom to sunshine";

Kepler "seemed born to prove that true genius can overpower all obstacles". *Friend (CC)* I 485. Kepler rises from data to theory to idea. *L&L* 136. He was "the beginning of truly scientific astronomy". *P Lects* Lect 11 (1949) 331. Galileo Galilei (1564–1642), Italian astronomer and physicist who stressed observation and sound evidence; condemned by the Inquisition to silence, he was visualised by C as "blind in a dungeon". *Friend (CC)* I 57, 58. Possibly as an alter ego, C was drawn to the configuration of character overcoming obstacles—Kepler, Böhme, Bunyan, George Fox. Carlyle questioned C's elevation of Kepler above Newton; see App M (Allsop), vol II, below. T. F. Dibdin protested in behalf of the incomparable Newton in *Reminiscences of a Literary Life* (2 vols 1836) I 159n, 256n. Robert Small, in *An Account of the Astronomical Discoveries of Kepler* (1804), after tracing Kepler's steps to the laws of planetary motion, proposed in conclusion that "no person, in any age, ever soared higher than Kepler, above the common elevation of his contemporaries" (p 305; the laws on 290, 299). Among the books in WW's library marked as belonging to C was *Mathematical Collections and Translations* tr Thomas Salusbury, containing works of Galileo, Kepler, Benedetto Castelli, Didacus à Stunica, Descartes, and others (5 vols 1661–5). *WW LC* 330. The brief passage in Latin from

Providence that the inventive, generative, constitutive mind—the Kepler—should come first; and then the patient and collective mind—the Newton—should follow and elaborate the pregnant Queries and illumining Guesses of the former. The Laws of the Planetary System are due to Kepler. Gravitation he had fully conceived, but because it seemed inconsistent[a] with some received observations on Light &c. he gave it up in allegiance, as he says, to Nature. Yet he says it vexed and haunted him—Vexat me et lacessit.[2]

We praise Newton's clearness and steadiness; he was clear and steady when working out by the help of an admirable geometry, no doubt, the Idea brought forth by another; but he never attempted to sound the Law of the Distances of the Planets—upon which it was that Kepler racked his brain. [b]And surely the fact of an increasing series from Mercury to Mars—then a decreasing one from Jupiter is marvellous.[c3] But Newton had his ether, and could not rest in—he could not and did not conceive—the idea of a Law; he thought it a physical thing after all.[4]

[a] f 34; the leaf beginning in mid-word, "sistent"

[b-c] Cancelled with vertical lines; "marvellous" cancelled with horizontal line

---

Galileo's *Dialogus de systemata* that C copied about 1801 may have come from an intermediate source. *CN* I 937D.

[2] "It vexes and irritates me." Kepler came very near to a general theory of gravitation; see a letter to David Fabricius 11 Oct 1605. *Gesammelte Werke* (19 vols Munich 1937–75) xv 240–80, quoted in Max Caspar *Kepler* tr. C. Doris Hellman (1959) 138.

[3] A restatement of Kepler's third law of planetary motion, announced in *Pro suo opere harmonices mundi apologia* (1619), that the squares of the time of orbit of the five primary planets, and of the earth, about the sun, are proportional to the cubes of their mean distances from the sun; as C put it in *SM*, "all their orbits in the divine order of their ranks and distances". *SM (CC)* 51. Among several changes and rearrangements in this entry, *TT* (1835) gave Kepler's laws of motion in orthodox form. In *CN* IV 4652 C discusses Kepler's three laws: see 4652n and 4775 and n.

[4] For the full range of C's judgements on Sir Isaac Newton (1642–1727), from delight with "the beauty & neatness of his experiments" (*CL* II 709) to the

"monstrous FICTIONS" of his metaphysical assumptions (*CL* IV 750), see *C 17th C* 393–408. For his early reading of Newton see *CN* I esp 82–3, 88. C wrote to Poole in 1801: "I believe the Souls of 500 Sir Isaac Newtons would go to the making up of a Shakspere or a Milton. . . . Newton was a mere materialist—*Mind* in his system is always passive—a lazy Looker-on on an external World." *CL* II 709. As he will say on 27 Dec 1831, below, "Facts are not Truths". C shared with Pope the usual objection to Newton's ether, as showing him "ashamed to assert a mere Mechanic Cause, and yet unwilling to forsake it intirely". *The Dunciad* IV 473n. But C rejected the "subtle fluid" on more strictly logical grounds on 29 Jun 1833, below (at n 7) (36:530). Bryan Robinson had attempted a Christian justification in *Sir Isaac Newton's Account of the Aether* (Dublin 1745) 50–1. Roger Cotes, in his preface to the 2nd ed of Newton's *Principia Mathematica* (1709), had declared ether unnecessary if gravitation be considered as an essential property of matter.

Think of Newton's ravings about Daniel and the Revelation, and the miserable feebleness with which he worked himself into a sort of Unitarianism! And as for his Chronology, I believe those who are most competent to judge, rely on it less and less every day.[5] [36:286]

Personal Experiment is wanted to correct Observation of those experiments which Nature makes for us—i.e. the phenomena of the Universe; but Observation is more wanted to direct and substantiate the course of Experiment. Experiments of themselves cannot advance Knowledge; they amuse for a time and then pass off the scene and leave no trace behind them.[6] [36:287]

Bacon, when like himself, (for no man was ever more inconsistent) says Prudens Quæstio &c.[7] [36:288]

---

[5] Newton's *Observations upon the Prophecies of Holy Writ, Particularly the Prophecies of Daniel and the Apocalypse of St. John* came to C's attention, in Newton *Opera quae exstant omnia* ed Samuel Horsley (5 vols 1779–85), as early as 1796. *CN* I 83 and n. *The Chronology of Antient Kingdoms Amended* (1728) appears in *Opera*, also in vol V. Vol IV includes *Four Letters to Dr. Bentley Containing Some Arguments in Proof of a Deity* (1756), which C could take as "a sort of Unitarianism". In 1816 C described Newton as curing himself of belief in astrology. *SM (CC)* 85, in which page the editor notes C's overestimation of Newton's rationality. The overestimation does not infect C's view of Newton as interpreter of the Bible. "Revelation" becomes "Revelations" in *TT* (1835).

[6] William Page Wood had apparently heard C on this subject on 11 Dec 1828: "But I cannot go along with him in rejecting Bacon's theory of induction as the groundwork of an insight into general laws. Coleridge has indicated this in the 'Friend', and quoted a ludicrous passage from Hooke, who requires ten times more from the philosopher than Cicero did from the orator." (See *Friend—CC—*I 483–4.) And again on 29 Jan 1829: "Coleridge launched forth at some length upon Bacon's inductive method, at the request of Montagu. I think he clearly failed in his attempt to depreciate

experiment. The instances he selected—namely, the continued observation of the heavenly bodies, which led to nothing more than the Ptolemaic system, till Kepler's time, and his still more favourite one of the isolated nature of the facts attending magnetism and electricity till the present day—may tend to show that the *experientia literata* is nothing without a master-mind, which Bacon himself asserts; but if Coleridge means anything, he must mean that Kepler could have equally demonstrated his laws by one single observation, as from the result of the observations of ages; a proposition which cannot be maintained. . . . To use Coleridge's favourite simile, the human mind may be the kaleidoscope, but it is a dull instrument if there be no extrinsic object to work upon. He was happy in one image, not so much as an illustration, but as a pleasing touch of fancy. He said that Nature had for ages appeared to wish to communicate her stores of higher knowledge by the phenomenon of the compass, but that she was too distant from us, and we could only watch the trembling of her lips without catching the sound." *Memoir of Hatherley* I 157, 175–7.

[7] "Prudens quaestio—dimidium scientiae est." Bacon *De augmentis scientiarum* bk V ch 3: *Works* I 148–9. "The forethoughtful query", as C translates it in *The Friend*, is "half of the knowledge sought". *Friend (CC)* I 489. Quoted in

At the Reformation the first Reformers were beset with an almost morbid anxiety not to be considered heretical in point of doctrine. They knew that the Romanists were on the watch to fasten ^d^the brand of heresy upon them whenever a fair pretence could be found; and I have no doubt that it was the excess of this fear which at once led to the burning of Servetus and also to the thanks offered by all the Protestant Churches to Calvin and the Church of Geneva for burning him.⁸ ^e^Hence, amongst other things, the Athanasian Creed was preserved; a composition, the original of which was in Latin and cannot be traced within fifty years of the man whose name it bears—which emanated from no General Council—which in the beginning and end is intolerant and persecuting and in the middle is heretical in a high degree.⁹ I mean in particular the flagrant omission or rather denial of the essential article of the Filial subordination in the Godhead, which Bull and Waterland have so labored to enforce in their writings which make the Church of England the classical authority on the subject of the Trinity even in the eyes of the Church of Rome itself—and by not holding to which Sherlock staggered to and fro between Tritheism and Sabellianism.¹⁰   [36:289, 94]

---

^d^ f 34^v^   ^e–m^ For the variant in MS F see App C, below

Logic (CC) 107 and often. C seems to have first found the quotation c 1797 in Sir James Steuart *An Inquiry into the Principles of Political Oeconomy* (2 vols 1767) I vi; see *CN* I 307 and n; *Friend (CC)* I 110, 489, and nn. The discussions of 8 Oct of experimental method and of the responsibilities of clergymen may have been directed at James Gillman Jr, who would be ordained and become Fellow of St John's College, Oxford, in 1831. To help in his preparation for the Oxford examinations, C had borrowed for him in August a translation of the *Novum organum* but warned him against Bacon's "unfair & often untrue" attacks on the Platonic and Aristotelian schools. *CL* VI 843–4. Against received opinion, C argued that Bacon was a Platonist. *Friend (CC)* I 483–93; *P Lects* Lects 9 (1949) 331–4. In earlier notes he had quoted Bacon against "modern Psilosophers" who "Talk big words of Lord Bacon", like the Pharisees who appealed to Moses with the intention of murdering Christ. *CN* III 3244. In a margin of Proclus *On the First Book of Euclid's Elements* tr

Thomas Taylor (2 vols 1792) I 76 he wrote of the offence against Bacon (whom every Platonist "must revere") by all modern chemists except Davy. *CM (CC)* III. He defended the conduct of "our illustrious Verulam" as far as he honestly could against Lucy Aikin *Memoirs of the Court of King James the First* (2 vols 1822) I 109, 190–6, II 30–74, 194–223. See *CN* IV 4932, 5046, 5051, 5055.

⁸ C defended Calvin's condemnation of Servetus at greater length on 3 Jan 1834, below (at n 3) (36:613). For heretical views of the Trinity, Servetus was tried, condemned, and imprisoned by the Inquisition in 1553; he escaped, but was arrested in Geneva on Calvin's order and burned 27 Oct 1553.

⁹ On the Athanasian Creed see 8 Jul 1827 and n 4, above. HNC moved part of this entry to that date. Carlyon I 283–314 took issue with C as reported in *TT*; not so HC, writing to HNC in 1836: "I am glad my father continued to disapprove of the Athanasian creed." *HCL* 193.

¹⁰ Aided by Bull and Waterland, C wrote extensive, mostly hostile notes on

In considering the question—how far a man is bound in point of conscience and honor to assent to every thing contained in the Prayer Book,
before he takes Orders—I recommend you to put a Clergyman in these
four points of view. 1. In the Desk.[11] 2. In the Pulpit. 3. As a Pastor. 4.
As a Man of Letters.

Now, if the points upon which you have a difficulty, are such that they
are quite collateral to the Liturgy, and such that it would be most impertinent to introduce any discussion of them in the pulpit and worse than
impertinent to broach them in*f* your pastoral communications with your
flock—and which therefore have no proper place but in your book-room
and with learned friends—I cannot understand how any doubts or difficulties of such a kind should deter*g* you from taking orders. I put all subscriptions for the present out of the Question; for, undoubtedly, if you
cannot do the duty of *h*a Clergyman of the Church of England without
violating your conscience,*i* you must not take Orders, if the Articles were
abolished tomorrow. What the use of these Articles is, I never could find
out—but that is not to the point.

You will remember that the Church of England binds you by one of
her own Articles to believe that she is *fallible*—and that all Churches
have erred—and that the Scriptures are *alone* infallible.[12] You have the
strictest obligation, therefore, to carry in mind that the doctrines of the
Church of England *may* be erroneous,*j* so far as you are unable to reconcile them with the Word of God. Accordingly it is beyond a doubt that
you may conscientiously reject in your mind the Athanasian creed as

---

f ~~as a Past~~ in   *g* ~~render it~~ deter   *h* f 35   *i* conscience, ~~or~~   *j* erroneous, ~~& in~~

William Sherlock (c 1641–1707) *A Vindication of the Doctrine of the Holy and
Ever Blessed Trinity, and the Incarnation of the Son of God* (1690). *CM (CC)*
IV. In those notes C protests repeatedly
that Sherlock is ambiguously either
tritheist or Sabellian. This common
seventeenth-century language for the
heresies of three equal gods or one-dom-
inant-over-two can be seen typically in
Waterland's objection that Samuel
Clark, in admitting to his adversaries
"no *Medium* between *Tritheism* and *Sabellianism*", left none for himself. *A
Vindication of Christ's Divinity* (2nd ed
1719) 329–30.
    [11] Desk, litany-desk: "In a church or
chapel: A sloping board on which books
used in the service are laid." *OED*. C is

distinguishing degrees of orthodoxy incumbent upon a clergyman. These remarks, transcribed in MS F but not published, are explicable as addressed to
James Gillman Jr in HNC's presence. In
Jan 1830, when HNC offered to steer
young Gillman towards the profession of
law, C announced himself as "on the
whole" an advocate "for his entering
under the mild yoke of the Clerical
Profession". *CL* VI 826.
    [12] Article 19 declares that the Churches
of Jerusalem, Alexandria, Antioch, and
Rome have erred; the "visible Church
of Christ" is one where "the pure Word
of God is preached". Article 6 declares
the sufficiency of Holy Scripture for salvation.

manifestly heretical and uncharitable, and still remain a faithful Church Minister. Besides in the Desk, you are not using your own words or staking your own authority or warranting any thing;—it is well understood that you are only a Voice, an Officer of the Church. If you are amongst peaceful people, don't read the Athanasian Creed; if there are informers, read it, because the Rubric, which is by Act of Parliament, orders it.[13]

In the Pulpit you appear for yourself—and I would *there* explain the true doctrine of the Trinity and either leave the contrast to be made by the audience, or I would point out with decency the imperfections of the Athanasian creed which I had been obliged to read in the morning. You are no more[k] obliged to leave the Church or not enter it because of the Athanasian Creed, than a Judge is obliged to leave the bench because he disapproves the actual Law. The fact is, nine-tenths of the enlightened clergy of the Church of England condemn this[l] Creed.[m][14]

---

[n]As Pastor, I am sure your doubts need not trouble you; they do not enter into the performance of any pastoral duty.

I am supposing, of course, that you are not a Socinian or Unitarian:— that you believe in the Redemption of Man by the blood of Jesus and that your salvation is by Grace alone. Unless you believe this—you cannot, indeed, without the grossest want of faith and honesty enter the Church; for these are points on which you must insist in the pulpit and in the cottage.[15]

As to Articles of Discipline—the only way to assent to them is to obey them. Beyond obedience there can be no obligation.[16]

---

[k] more ~~concerned in conscience as a Clergyman in reading the~~   [l] this ~~vile~~
[m] See [e-m], above   [n] f 35[v]

---

[13] For objections entered on MS F see App C, below.

[14] A pencilled "Qu" in MS F queries these last sentences. Questioning of the Athanasian Creed was widespread, and condemnation of it not unique to C.

[15] These two beliefs are fully supported by Articles 11–18 of the Church of England.

[16] C seems to refer to the "common order and discipline" set forth in the Book of Common Prayer; on the when, how, and what services are to be performed, C's clergyman is required to conform, not to believe. What he says elsewhere about the Eucharist and baptism would make this a less than Cole-

ridgian solution; here he is trying to ease a young man over a point of conscience, with the result of frightening the clerical members of his family. Technically England was under the Canon Law confirmed by Act of 25 Henry VIII c 19; all subsequent efforts to establish a common book of ecclesiastical discipline had failed, and continued after C's time to fail. In a substantial note on Philip Skelton Discourse 73 "The Pastoral Duty" *Complete Works* (6 vols 1824) III 394–9, C argued that "Christian *Discipline*, enforced only by spiritual motives . . . and submitted to for Conscience' sake", is to be distinguished from discipline enforced by ecclesiastical authority, as in

21. Nov. 1830.

Brougham never makes a figure in quietude.[1] He astounds fools by a certain enormity of exertion; he takes an acre of canvass on*a* which he scrawls every thing. He thinks aloud; every thing, good, bad and indifferent in his mind,—out it comes; he is like the Newgate gutter flowing with guts, garbage, dead dogs and mud.[2] He is preeminently a man of many thoughts with no ideas. Hence he is always so lengthy; because he must go through every thing to see any thing.   [36:290]

It is a melancholy thing to live when there is no vision in the land. Good God! where are the Statesmen to meet this awful crisis?[3] Not one of our reformers asks himself the question—"*What* is it that I propose to myself?"[4]

   Is the House of Commons to be constructed on the principle of a rep-

a ion

---

excommunication, which "is incompatible with a Church established by Law". *CM (CC)* IV. Cf *C&S (CC)* 45.

[1] Brougham had just received the great seal as Lord Chancellor of England, with elevation to the peerage as Baron Brougham and Vaux, following the resignation of the Wellington government on 16 Nov. The victorious Whigs had taken these steps to get Brougham safely out of the Commons. He had spoken often in recent weeks, on the Reform Bill, disturbances in the streets, slavery, and the shakiness of the Tory ministry. He had been one of the founders of the *Ed Rev* in 1802, and C's hostility is clear in notes (perhaps of 1804) to *An Inquiry into the Colonial Policy of the European Powers* (2 vols Edinburgh 1803): "the disease of Brougham's mind is mistaking the *contingent* for the *necessary*"; Brougham is "the Lord of the Marvellous". BM MS Egerton 2800 ff 107–7ᵛ. In the *Courier* 21 Oct 1814 C identified Brougham in all but name as a "brazening" barrister who vended his impudence, and similarly again in 1817. *EOT (CC)* II 390; *LS (CC)* 144–5. Writing in behalf of Hurwitz, C flattered Brougham on 9 Feb 1827 for the one act C approved of, service to the nation by defending Queen Caroline. *CL* VI 668. See also 12

May 1830 and n 4, above, and, for C against Caroline's prosecutors, *CN* IV 4803, 4826–7. For further on Brougham see App M (Allsop), vol II, below, and C's annotations on Brougham *A Speech on the Present State of the Law of the Country* (1828): *CM (CC)* I 738–40. For JTC's appraisal of Brougham as "always cunning and ready" see Bernard Coleridge *This for Remembrance* 31.

[2] Opposite this entry in MS F, in pencil probably by EC: "I should omit the *guts*". The significant omissions in *TT* (1835) are "Brougham" (replaced by a dash) and "guts".

[3] The crisis, from the threat of a Reform Bill, included the defeat of the Wellington ministry over the Civil List, 15 Nov. *TT* (1835) reduced "crisis" to "emergency", but Sir Archibald Alison wrote after longer reflection: "Thus fell the Wellington Administration, the most important event in the domestic history of England since the Revolution, in the general annals of Europe since the battle of Waterloo." *History of Europe from the Fall of Napoleon in MDCCCXV to the Accession of Louis Napoleon in MDCCCLII* (8 vols 1854–71) IV 1.

[4] Dropping the quotation marks, *TT* (1835) added the wooden words, "to effect in the result".

resentation of interests, or of a delegation of Men?[5] If on the former, we may perhaps see our way; if on *b*the latter—then I say you can never stop short of universal suffrage—and women in that case have as good a right to vote as the men.[6]   [36:291]

---

*a*20. March. 1831[1]

S. T. C. It is false that Government is founded on Property taken as Property in the abstract; it is founded on *unequal* Property; and the *inequality* is a necessary term in the position.[2] The terms Higher, Middle and Lower

b f 36   *a* WW's conversation of 11 Mar 1831, recorded on f 36, precedes this date

[5] C is thinking of the aptness for the day of his arguments in *C&S*: in a "democratic Republic" as under absolute monarchy, "the Nation, or People, delegates its whole power". *C&S* (CC) 96. On 29 Nov, writing to H. F. Cary that he had been very ill, C reported that Green "yesterday" declared the second *Lay Sermon* also current in its message. *CL* VI 847–8.

[6] HNC's note to this entry in *TT* (1835) quoted, as equally "in the nature of a *reductio ad absurdum*", C's essay in *The Friend* refuting Rousseau's *Contrat social*. *Friend (CC)* I 195–6. C was not advocating the universal suffrage that would include women as voters; but in 1796 he had stood with Mary Wollstonecraft against Gibbon, on the question of Germanic women earning intellectual respect without losing, as Gibbon claimed, "attractive softness". *Watchman (CC)* 90–1 (a sketch in which RS may have had a hand). Even in reminding Mrs C that theirs was a "marriage of unequal & unlike Understandings & Dispositions", C wished her to see that such a marriage was not the only kind. *CL* II 887.

[1] Sun, 20 Mar 1831 marks the only date of recorded talk—except from WW—between Sun, 21 Nov 1830 and Sat, 25 Jun 1831. (For WW's talk of 11 Mar 1831 see App E, below.) HNC visited C, but there were many distractions. Herbert, born to SC and HNC on 7 Oct, was christened 10 Dec. At Christmas DC came from Cornwall to Highgate for a

fortnight and remained in the area until after 20 Jan. WW, in the London area from December to April, paid visits to Highgate. C talked at length one evening in December with John Frere, but the open Thursdays were suspended. *C Talker* 221. C's surviving letters from this period—half of which are addressed to HNC—remark on worsening health. *CL* VI 846–69. On 7 Feb HNC wrote to RS that C was very low—"He says, 'my spirit is like Ariel pent up in a tree's trunk!' "—on 21 Mar that C had been set up by sulphur baths. UT ms. In December and January HNC was working on the 2nd ed of *AR*; in May and June he was occupied in attempts to secure a restoration of C's grant from the RSL. On the morning of 14 May C was cordial to the American feminist, Emma Hart Willard (1787–1870). *C Talker* 360–1.

[2] In "Once a Jacobin Always a Jacobin", *M Post* 21 Oct 1802, recollecting his definition in the *M Post* of 7 Dec 1799 but ignoring the "aspheterism" of Pantisocracy, C said he had always believed that "that government was best, in which the power was the most exactly proportioned to the property". *EOT (CC)* I 32, 373. In 1809 he expanded the phrase to "power or political influence". *Friend (CC)* I 223, II 146. He had dropped the emphasis of 1799 on "good" government requiring circulation of property (but see below, 25 Jun 1831 n 1). On 19 Apr 1811 he found "a tolerably fair proportion" of influence

Classes are delusions; no such divisions exist in society as Classes; there is an inextricable blending and interfusion of persons from top to bottom, and no man can trace a line of separation between them,[3] except such a confessedly unmeaning and unjustifiable line of political empiricism as £10 householders.[4] I declare[b] this measure of the Government has made me ashamed of the Country. Not a ray of Principle in their whole plan; not a hint of the effect of the change upon the Balance of the Estates; not a remark upon the *nature* of the[c] Constitution of England, and the character of the property of so many millions of its inhabitants. Half the wealth of this country is purely artificial—existing *only* in and on the credit given to it by the integrity and honesty of the Nation.[5] This property *appears* a heavy burthen to the numerical majority of the people, and they believe that it causes all their distress. And they are now to have the maintenance of this faith committed to their keeping![6] The lamb to the wolves! Fools—fools—fools—Motley fools!   [36:292]

Lord Grey, like Necker, has asked the people to come and help him against the Aristocracy.[7] The people came fast enough at Necker's bid-

---

[b] f 36[v], the leaf beginning mid-word, "clare"   [c] the ~~English~~

"or the power of acquiring it" in Britain. *EOT (CC)* II 117. In the essay on Rousseau he had explained the necessity for inequality—"the nature of the earth and the nature of the mind unite to make the contrary impossible". *Friend (CC)* I 200; cf II 132. In Switzerland (and Buttermere) power could be nearly equal because ownership of land and cattle was nearly equal, but civilisation rises above this agrarian level. *EOT (CC)* I 327, 370, 406.

[3] In the *Courier* 19 Apr and 13 Sept 1811 and 2 Nov 1814 C had declared the interdependence and "chain of Connexion" among the higher, middle, and lower ranks of England. *EOT (CC)* II 117, 281, 394.

[4] The bill placed before Parliament by Lord John Russell on 1 Mar extended the franchise to householders who had occupied for six months prior to annual revision of the register a house with a rental value of £10 or more. Although restrictions and qualifications varied thereafter, the £10 minimum endured. At the second reading on 20 Mar the bill had a majority of one vote.

[5] This is consonant with C's defence of the National Debt both earlier and later in TT and in *Friend (CC)* I 223–5.

[6] The revision in *TT* (1835) to "maintenance of this property committed to their good faith" is not in itself any clearer, but both versions refer to the difference between the credit of the coherently governed nation and the loss of that credit by transferring it to individuals who believed it a mere burden. The printed version softened the previous sentence to "in many instances, a heavy burthen" and omitted the reiteration of "Fools". Awareness of such softening made SC and HNC defend fiercely the reporting in *TT* as an understatement of C's conservatism.

[7] Charles Grey (1764–1845), 2nd Earl Grey (1807), a Foxite Whig from 1786, had constructed a new ministry committed to the Reform of Parliament. Jacques Necker (1732–1804), as director general of finance and chief adviser to Louis XVI, both recommended and issued the King's convocation of the States-General, which convened 4 May 1789. Escalating demands and turmoil followed at once.

ding—but some how or other, they would not go away again.⁸ Can Lord Grey be sincere in this measure?⁹   [36:293]

ᵃS. T. C. 25. June 1831.

The three great ends which a Statesman ought to propose to himself in the government of a Nation, are 1. Security to Possessors. 2. Facility to Acquirers and 3. Hope to All.¹   [36:294]

A Nation is the unity of a People. Parliament and King are the Unity made visible. The Lords and the King are as integral portions of this manifested Unity as the Commons.²   [36:295]

I can forgive the Ministers every thing except their evident neglect of, if not hostility to, that last remaining fragment of our Nationalty*ᵇ*—the Church. Is it not extraordinary that Brougham seems never to be able to

---

ᵃ f 37ᵛ; ff 36ᵛ–7 contain adages from Machiavelli *Il Principe* copied by HNC   ᵇ Nationality

---

Necker's consequent (second) dismissal led immediately to the storming of the Bastille on 14 Jul and therefore to the Revolution and Terror that C calls before his hearers. In 1788–9 Necker repeatedly brushed aside protests from the nobility that he was extending too much power to the Third Estate.

⁸ Taking a hint from this sentence, *TT* (1835) transferred to Grey as conjuror the parable applied to Leopold on 14 Aug 1831, below (at n 10). HNC thus created an anachronism, for Grey did not request the dissolution of Parliament until 21 Apr.

⁹ Earlier on this day (20 Mar) C and WW would have exchanged rhetorical questions and condolences over the crisis. On 27 Apr Mrs C wrote to Emily Trevenen that earlier than the 20th "we had gone in a fly to Highgate" and found C "a little better from the use of the sulphur bath", but "Henry was there last Sunday and found him very infirm"; HNC had hoped to see the Wordsworths, but missed them. UT ms, quoted by Molly Lefebure "*Toujours gai . . .*" *Charles Lamb Bulletin* NS No 30 (Apr 1980) 112. Henry Taylor wrote in May that he had seen much (in Apr) of WW, who "spends his time wholly in

society". Taylor *Correspondence* ed E. Dowden (1888) 38–9. HNC recorded and translated on ff 36ᵛ–7 adages from Machiavelli *Il Principe* chs 2, 3, 7, 10; reference to the political crisis and C's remarks does not seem to be intended.

¹ On 21 Aug C would write to Charles Stutfield that a legislature is but a means to right government, "the best definition of which would be—that which under the circumstances most effectually provides Security for the Possessors, Facility for the Acquirers and Hope for all". *CL* VI 870. See also the "positive ends" of government in *The Friend (CC)* I 252. "Facility to Acquirers" in this entry restores the emphasis of 1799 on the circulation of property. In a note of 1808 on Barclay *Argenis* (1629) C had distinguished the "Republican", who hoped for amelioration by attributing vices to circumstances, from the "Philo-despotist", who believed vices common and irremoveable. *CM (CC)* I 224. On 24 Jun 1831 (the day before the conversation) Lord John Russell laid a modified Reform Bill before the Commons for debate.

² For lines from George Wither that C found apt, see HNC's note to this entry.

raise his mind for one moment to the consideration of the Established Church as any thing else than a club of beneficed parsons? He never seems to have a clear conception of the *good* of any institution.[3]

In that imperfect state of society in which our system of representation began, the interests of the country were nearly commensurate with its municipal divisions; the county, the towns, and the seaports almost exactly represented the only interests then existing—the landed, the manufacturing or shop-keeping, and the mercantile. But for a century past this division has become notoriously imperfect; some of the most vital interests of the nation[4] are now totally unconnected with any English locality; and yet now when the evil and the want are known, cwe are to abandon the accommodations which the necessity of the case had worked out for itself, and begin again with a rigidly territorial plan of representation![5] The miserable tendency of all is to destroy our Nationalty,*d* which consisted in our Representative Government, and to convert it into a degrading Delegation of the Populace.[6] There is no Unity for a People

c f 38   d Nationality

[3] This paragraph was omitted from *TT* (1835). Ten years earlier, the *Speech of Mr. Brougham, Delivered on the Trial of the Cause, The King Versus J. A. Williams, for a Libel on the Clergy, at the Durham Summer Assizes, Aug. 6th, 1822* (Durham 1822) had set Brougham's tone of scornful irony. In Scotland, he said, there was no bishop, no minor canon, no curate, "nay, the poor benighted creatures are ignorant even of tithes" (p 5); whereas in Durham the prodigiously large establishment was laying "the inhabitants under a load of obligation overwhelming in its weight", for "the Clergy swarmed in every corner" and the people, like sheep, were "fleeced, and hunted, and barked at, and snapped at, and from time to time worried" (p 6); in short, as Milton and Gilbert Burnet noted before him, there was "corruption" in the priesthood (p 15). Brougham's speeches on Reform maintain a similar view of the clergy.

[4] "Nation" became "empire" in *TT* (1835).

[5] C is defending indirect and virtual representation, rotten boroughs, and other departures from quantitative representation with the argument that the drift away from the "territorial", which could no longer be also the representation of occupational interests, had been compensated for by the growth of government *for* the people—a position he had passionately rejected in *The Plot Discovered* and other early lectures and pamphlets. *Lects 1795 (CC)* 131, 306–13. His subsequent journalism indicates that events in France rather than events or words in England began to change his mind. John Colmer *Coleridge Critic of Society* (Oxford 1959) 22–4 relates the change to C's shift in ethical theory from necessity to free will. The system of parliamentary elections came gradually into being in the thirteenth century; C's point is that barons from seaports and from areas of more and less density of population represented the occupations predominant in each of those areas.

[6] In *TT* (1835) "consisted" became "consists, in a principal degree", which narrowed the implications of the original past tense. On C's distinction of people from populace see *LS (CC)* 164n and n 3, and cf "Wordsworth . . . did me the honor of once observing to me, the *Peo-*

but in Representation of National Interests; a Delegation of the Passions or Wishes of the People is a rope of Sand.*ᵉ⁷*   [36:296]

---

*ᶠ*S. T. C. 25. June 1831.⁸

Undoubtedly it is a great evil that there should be such an evident discrepancy between the Law and the Practice of the Constitution in the matter of the Representation. Such a direct, yet clandestine contravention of solemn Resolutions and established laws is immoral and greatly injurious to the cause of legal loyalty and general subordination in the minds of the People. But then a Statesman should consider that these very contraventions of Law in Practice point out to him the places in the Body Politic which need a remodelling of the Law. You acknowledge a certain necessity of indirect Representation in the present day, and that *ᵍ*it has been instinctively obtained by means contrary to Law—Why then do you not wisely approximate a useless Law to the useful Practice—instead of abandoning both Law and Practice for a completely new system of your own?⁹   [36:296]

ᵉ The paragraph above, which makes up the first half of 36:296 as published, seems to have been written later (i.e. in a different script of HNC's) than the paragraphs above it. See also n 8, below
ᶠ Preceded by passage copied from Machiavelli and remarks on it
ᵍ f 38ᵛ

---

ple and the *Public* are two distinct Classes". Annotation on Barclay *Argenis* (1659): *CM (CC)* I 220.

⁷ In political writings from 1795 to 1830 C had described the Crown as "representing the unity of the people". *C&S (CC)* 20 and n. In a letter to Sotheby 3 Jun 1831 the King was "the consecrated Symbol of the Unity and Majesty of the *Nation*". *CL* VI 863. In a draft of *C&S* he had rejected the idea of individuals being "component parts of an Organic Unit", as ignoring the integrity of each "imperishable Person"; here in TT, as in *C&S (CC)* 219, he locates the only true unity of a people in religion. On 19 Jun HNC sent a copy of the 3rd ed of his own tract on Reform to RS. UT ms. After this entry HNC copied a passage from Machiavelli ch 15 and noted the excellence of chs 18 and 23.

⁸ The three headings dated 25 Jun 1831 (Sat), separated by notations from HNC's reading in Machiavelli, may indicate either immediate records of separate conversations on a day spent with C or subsequent transcriptions from disjunct records of the day's talk. On both f 38 and f 38ᵛ, when the date 25 Jun recurs, the entries begin in a small controlled hand that grows progressively larger and more hurried.

⁹ In short, laws should be adjusted to the current facts of representation instead of distorting the Constitution, under the name of Reform, to fit earlier facts no longer appropriate or relevant. C had written of Reform and reformers in *The Friend* of 30 Nov 1809: ". . . the wisdom of Legislation consists in the adaptation of Laws to Circumstances. . . . In other words, the spirit of the Statute interpreted by the intention of the Legislator would annul the Letter of it." *Friend (CC)* II 198, I 246. For once, WW was more colloquially metaphorical than C:

The malignant duplicity, and unprincipled tergiversations of the Times are to me detestable; but I like the Morning Chronicle—because it is open in its endeavors to destroy the Church and to introduce a Republic.[10] There is an honesty in that paper which I approve, though I would with joy lay down my life to save my country from the consummation which that paper desires.[h][11]   [36:297]

S. T. C. 25.[i] June. 1831.

I have been exceedingly impressed with the pernicious precedent of Napier's history of the Peninsular War.[12] This is a specimen of the true

[h] A remark about Machiavelli follows
[i] The entries on Napier and RS appear in *TT* (1835) under 26 Jun; "25" may have been a slip

---

"Our Constitution . . . grew . . . as a skin grows to, with, and for the human body. Our Ministers would flay this body, and present us, instead of its natural Skin, with a garment made to order, which . . . [may] prove such a Shirt as, in the Fable, drove Hercules to madness and self-destruction". *WL (L* rev) II 500–1. If the repetition of "you" in this entry indicates direct address to someone with the opinions ascribed, that someone was not HNC.

[10] In *TT* (1835) *The Times* became "the specific Whig newspapers" and the *M Chron* was similarly generalised. By chance, *The Times* 24 Jun carried an editorial on Lord Plunket's charge of libel against the newspapers for reporting that Sir Robert Bateson accused the Lord Chancellor of Ireland (Plunket) of intimidation in the election. C refers to larger tergiversations. Amid its "duplicity" over Reform and the emancipation of non-Anglicans, *The Times* had reported on 3 Jun that Lord Grey, finding that C had lost his "pittance", had agreed to grant temporarily an annuity from the Treasury; on 4 Jun it published a letter from Gillman explaining that C had felt it his duty to decline the grant of £200 made on representation through Brougham to Grey. The annuity paid to C since 1824 as a Royal Associate of the RSL had been withdrawn in May, because William IV declined to continue

the pensions of the Royal Associates.

[11] Both the originality and the vigour of this comment deserve notice. The now-famous remark attributed to Voltaire, that he disapproved of what you say, but would defend to the death your right to say it, was not known in C's day and appears first as a distant paraphrase in S. G. Tallentyre (E. Beatrice Hall) *The Friends of Voltaire* (1917) 199. C's remark inverts *Hamlet* III i 62–3: " 'Tis a consummation | Devoutly to be wish'd. To die—to sleep." HNC follows this entry of f 38[v] with the notation, "Machiavel. Prince Cap. XVI. admirable."

[12] Sir William Francis Patrick Napier (1785–1860) *History of the War in the Peninsula and in the South of France* (5 vols 1828–40); vol III appeared in 1831. C proposed a review of vol I for *QR* in 1828, to show it both erroneous and "in the highest degree unhealthy". *CL* VI 734–5. G. P. Gooch, calling Napier's "the finest military history in English", admitted its pronounced bias. *History and Historians in the Nineteenth Century* (Boston, Mass 1959) 286. A similar survey calls Napier's work vivid and fair, "but it scandalized the Tories by its admiration of Napoleon". James Westfall Thompson and Bernard J. Holm *A History of Historical Writing* (2 vols New York 1942) II 293. Possibly C knew that Napier was the reviewer of the Swiss-Russian Baron Henri Jomini's *Principes*

French Military school; not a thought for the justice of the war—not a consideration of the damning and damnable iniquity of the French invasion. But all is looked at as a mere game of exquisite skill, and praise is regularly awarded to the most successful players. How perfectly ridiculous is the prostration of Napier's mind before the name of Buonaparte! I declare I know no book more likely to undermine the national sense of Right and Wrong in matters of Public import,[13] than this[j] work of Napier's.   [36:298]

Southey's history is on the right side and starts from the right point; but Southey was very partial to the [k]Spaniards personally, and in noticing in the prominent manner it deserved the nationality of the Spaniards, he never saw that their nationality was not one founded on any just ground[l] of good government, or wise laws;[m] but in a more personal feeling—an antipathy to strangers.[14] Every thing in this sense is national in Spain— Even the Catholic Religion is in a genuine Spaniard's mind exclusively national; he does not regard the professions of the Italian or Frenchman at all in the same light with his own.[15]   [36:299]

Napier is a man who would like to play just such a war game as that of Buonaparte.[n]

If A. has a hundred means of doing a certain thing, and B. has only one means[o] of doing it, is it very wonderful or does it argue very transcendant superiority, if A. surpasses B.? Buonaparte was the child of circumstances, which he neither originated, nor controlled. He had no chance of preserving his power but by continual warfare; not a thought of wise tranquillization of the shaken elements of France seems to have passed through his mind—and I believe that at no part of his reign, could he have survived one year's continued peace. He never had but one obstacle to contend with—Physical Force—very commonly the least difficult enemy a General subject to Court Martial and a Court of Conscience has to overcome.[16]   [36:298]

---

j ~~such~~ this   *k* f 39   *l* ~~view~~ ground   *m* laws; ~~or paternal~~   *n* ~~Buonaparte~~   *o* mean

---

de la guerre in *Ed Rev* XXXV (1821) 377–409.

[13] In *TT* (1835) "Public import" became "foreign interference".

[14] RS *History of the Peninsular War* (3 vols 1823, 1827, 1832). At the outset (I 1–12), RS praised the Spanish for "those holy feelings" of "national independence, national spirit", of "unexampled patriotism and endurance", despite "the imbecility, misrule, and dotage" of their despots; in the Preface (I v) he claimed to have been fully persuaded from 1808 on that England need only "perform its duty as well as the Spaniards and Portugueze" to ensure a glorious issue.

[15] C's "Letters on the Spaniards" No 2 (*Courier* 8 Dec 1809) had protested against religious journals that "dwelt on Spanish intolerance in religion". *EOT* (*CC*) II 47 and n.

[16] Denunciation of Napoleon Bonaparte runs through C's journalism and letters from 1796 to 1817. C's most con-

*a*S. T. C. 7. July. 1831.[1]

The darkest despotisms on the continent have done more for the cultivation and elevation of the Fine Arts, than the English Government. A great musical composer in Germany and in Italy is a great man in society; a dignity and rank is universally conceded to him. Without that sort of encouragement and patronage such arts as music and painting never will come to great eminence.[2] In this country there is no reverence for the Fine Arts, and the base spirit of a money-amassing philosophy would meet any proposition for the fostering of Art by the commercial maxim of Laissez faire—Paganini indeed will make a fortune, because he can actually sell his notes;[3] but Mozart himself might have languished in a

a f 39ᵛ

centrated portraits, comparing him with the Emperor Julian and Charlemagne, but never completing the comparison with Pitt, appear in *EOT (CC)* ɪ 207–16, 226 and n, ɪɪ 349–55; *Friend (CC)* ɪ 83–90. *TT* (1835), omitting the sentence on Napier's desire to play war, placed this paragraph before that on RS; *TT* (1836), by removing the divisional bar, made it part of the entry on Napier's "prostration".

[1] DC and his wife Mary were in lodgings across from the HNCs from June to November. SC to Elizabeth Crump Wardell 4 Jul, 2 Nov 1831. DCL mss. During the summer Mrs C paid her last visit to Keswick.

[2] Among the possible instigations to this generalisation are the struggle by C's friends over the discontinuance of the annuity paid to the Royal Associates—succinctly described in *C Life* (EKC) 322–3—and the summer exhibition of the British Institution for Promoting the Fine Arts, which C had identified in 1819 with the adage that those who "know nothing about art" are in a position to determine its successes. *P Lects* Lect 2 (1949) 95 and n. (And see n 3, below.) Other Londoners, like C, noted the triumphs of Gioacchino Rossini, other Italian composers, and Carl Maria von Weber, director of opera in Dresden, who died executing *Oberon* and other commissions in London. Beethoven, who worked mostly in Vienna, received gratefully a few days before his death a loan of £100 from the London Philharmonic Society. Specifying German and Italian royal patrons, C typically passes over the most notable institution for "cultivation and elevation", the Institut de France, reorganised several times under Napoleon and again in 1816. HNC does not quote C on the significant social changes; Alfred Einstein, tracing from Handel the movement from church patronage to popularity and from Beethoven the growth of artistic independence, describes the situation as hindsight enables historians to see it: "More and more the creative musician freed himself from society; he placed himself more and more in opposition to it, and he became increasingly isolated when he did not succeed in conquering it." *Music in the Romantic Era* (New York 1947) 16. C could not have had in mind any English composer of 1800–30 of more than mediocre talent.

[3] Nicolò Paganini (1782–1840), Italian violinist and composer, epitomised the passionate virtuoso of the era just begun. Performance of a new work in Paris brought the London *Athenaeum* to salute his virtuosity on 13 and 20 Feb 1830, pp 91–3, 105–6. Performance, not published scores, is meant by "his notes", changed in *TT* (1835) to "actually sell the tones of his fiddle at so much a scrape". A notice in the *M Chron* 18 May 1831 that the prices at the King's

garret[b] for any thing that would have been done for him here.[4] [36:300]

The allowing the muskets to be removed from the Tower for the convenience of the Birmingham manufacturers is a very disgraceful transaction.[5] The Duke of Wellington behaved in a very spirited and becoming way upon an application of the same sort last year. If the British Government had said ''We will cheerfully accommodate the Belgian or any other Government with a supply of arms, nation with nation'', there might be no harm in it; but for the Government to enter into a speculation with[c] the manufacturers of the country itself for the sake of getting improved Markets—is bad in my opinion.

There are three classes into which all the women past 70 that ever I knew were to be divided. 1. That dear old soul. 2. That old woman. 3. That old witch.[6]   [36:301]

[b] garrett   [c] twds [towards?]

Theatre would range from half a guinea in the gallery to ten guineas for a box in the grand tier, double the normal, led to general uproar, cancellation of the performances, and Paganini's departure for Calais. Announcing that he had misunderstood the English reluctance to meet his usual doubling of prices, Paganini returned and began on 3 Jun a triumphant series that included two ''last'' concerts, one ''by particular desire'', a fourth from ''solicitation of the musical world'', and more. *M Chron* reported on 4 Jul: ''His gains are said already to have got beyond 5,000 *l.*, and this earned in one brief month!!!'' The ''gains'' on tour and in London, including the ''Farewell Concert'' on 20 Aug, can be traced in *The Times* and other newspapers. Tom Moore thought that Paganini ''abuses his powers'' as a player by ''tricks and surprises''. Moore *Memoirs* VI 210. A pseudonymous letter in the *M Chron* 24 May 1831 said all that would be needed for C's general remarks: ''Abroad most of the great Theatres are supported in great part by the Governments, and not by the prices of admission. They are in fact . . . donations to the public of theatrical entertainments, and the prices are consequently far below what I may call the natural prices. Here things are upon a wholly different footing. All our theatres are private speculations, and all our prices are consequently wound up to their full pitch. To double prices here, is, therefore, a very different thing from doubling them at the continental theatres.'' On C's general interest in patronage see *CN* II 2746n.

[4] Wolfgang Amadeus Mozart (1756–91), after several years of near-poverty and heavy debts, declined in illness a decent offer to work in London; he died in Vienna and was buried there in a pauper's grave. Had C known the details of Mozart's life, he would have been fascinated by Mozart's belief that the stranger who commissioned the *Requiem* in Sept 1791 was an apparition of death.

[5] Incident untraced. *The Times* 23 Apr 1831 had reported from *Galignani's Messenger* word of a contract for Birmingham gunmakers to supply muskets to France.

[6] This entry, with the characteristics of a set piece and in isolation from its context, points up both the austerity of HNC's selections and the topicality of the remarks that interested him on 7 Jul.

S. T. C. 24. July 1831.[1]

Observe the remarkable difference between Claude and Teniers in their powers of painting vacant space.[2] Claude makes his whole landscape a plenum; the air is quite as substantial[a] as any other part of the scene. Hence there are no true distances, and every thing presses at once and equally upon the eye. There is something close and almost suffocating in the atmosphere of some of Claude's sunsets. But never did any one paint air, the thin air, the absolute[b3] apparent vacancy between object and object, so admirably as Teniers. That picture of the Archers exemplifies

---

[a] f 40, the leaf beginning "stantial"   [b] absolute~~ly~~

---

[1] In the afternoon of 24 Jul (Tues) C attended the annual loan exhibition of old-master paintings held by the British Institution for Promoting the Fine Arts, at the British Gallery in Pall Mall. HNC and SC did not accompany him, but encountered him there. See HNC's footnote to 36:302. The entries of 24 Jul continue on other subjects, and the ms also contains among them topics transcribed, in the hands of both HNC and SC, from C's letters of 1802–4 to Mrs C. It therefore seems probable that C returned with them to Hampstead. The published remarks, interspersed as they are with transcriptions from the letters, may have been digressions from a conversation about the crucial stages of C's separation from SC's mother, who seems to have been absent.

For his annotations identifying the paintings C referred to, HNC had before him the catalogue, *British Institution for Promoting the Fine Arts in the United Kingdom. Founded, June 4, 1805, Opened, January 18, 1806* (1831). From a distinguished German visitor we learn that "Every year the wealthy possessors of pictures lend some out of their collections, to form an exhibition, which is open to the public by day, and to a numerous but select company in the evening, when the room is brilliantly lighted with gas. Tickets for the day are sold; those for the evening given." Friedrich Ludwig von Raumer *England in 1835* tr Sarah Austin and H. E. Lloyd (Philadelphia 1836) 246. From the time of its founding, C had encountered high praise

for the British Institution and the generous motives of its proprietors; e.g. John Britton *An Historical Account of Corsham House, in Wiltshire* (1806) 1–8, 25, which C studied in 1814 (*CN* III 4227n), and *The Director: A Weekly Literary Journal* (2 vols 1807) I 139, 204, 365–6. C's lectures on the fine arts at the Royal Institution were announced in I 27 of this work, which he owned. *WW LC* 325.

[2] In the exhibition, works ascribed to the French landscape painter Claude Gellée, called Claude Lorrain (1600–82), included *Sea Port, Evening; View of Tivoli with Rome in the Distance; Landscape with the Flight into Egypt; A Sunset View in the Mediterranean; Landscape, Cattle and Figures.* Besides the work specified by C, three paintings were ascribed to David Teniers the Younger (1610–90): *Sea Shore with Fishermen; A Man Shooting Wild Fowl; An Interior with Figures Gambling.* Earlier accustomed to engravings, C was exhilarated in 1804 to see Sir George Beaumont's "famous Rubens, two Claudes, a Gaspar Poussin!!" *CL* II 1110. In Sept 1826 he identified with some confidence a Teniers amid questionable works. *CL* VI 614.

[3] First written and later published as "absolutely", but the "ly" is clearly cancelled by three lines characteristic of HNC. Did C say and mean "absolute (apparent) vacancy"? At the end of the entry HNC began to write "the infinity of apparent space" but corrected it to "the apparent infinity of space".

this excellence.[4] See the distances between those ugly louts! How perfectly true to the fact![5]

But Oh! what a wonderful picture is that of Rubens'—"The Triumph of Silenus"![6] It is the very revelry of Hell; every evil passion is there that could in any way be forced into juxta position with joyance[c]—Lust and hard by it see the Hate; every part is pregnant with libidinous Nature without one spark of the Grace of Heaven. The Animal is triumphing—not over—but in the absence, in the non-existence of, the Spiritual part of Man. I could fancy that—

> all the souls that damned be,
> Leaped up at once in anarchy,
> Clapped their hands and danced for glee.[7]

[c] ~~Lust hard by Hate, Violence~~

[4] Newly acquired by Francis Bernard, Earl of Bandon, and exhibited as *Figures Shooting at a Target*: "The Archers. A Landscape, with some cottages on the left; and a party of eight peasants distributed along the fore-ground, amusing themselves with archery. . . . The spire of a church rises above the cottages, and a shepherd, keeping sheep, is seen in the distance. Dated 1645. . . . This little picture has ever held a high reputation for its peculiar smartness and freedom of penciling, its silvery tone of colour, and tasteful composition." No 528 in John Smith *A Catalogue Raisonné of the Works of the Most Eminent Dutch, Flemish, and French Painters* . . . (9 pts 1829–42) III 400–1. Of a similar painting by Teniers in the Hermitage, Leningrad, there is a copy in the Belvedere Palace, Vienna.

[5] With the implication, as everywhere in C and reinforced here by the "But" that follows, that fact is not enough, even for the representation of "thin air".

[6] Lent by Sir Robert Peel in 1831, now in the National Gallery, the painting was described about 1835 by G. F. Waagen: "A Bacchanalian scene of eight figures, among whom a drunken Silenus is the principal; 4 ft. 7 in. high, 6 ft. 6 in. wide; on canvas. In the expression of drunken glee, in body and depth and clearness of colouring, it is inferior to none of the pictures by Rubens of this kind, but far ex-

cels all that I have seen in taste and in decorum, and especially in the beauty of a nymph, painted with the most fascinating freshness and fulness of his bright golden tone. At the same time, this picture, surrounded as it is here [at Peel's] with elegant subject pictures, seems to me to have too massive an effect." *Treasures of Art in Great Britain* (4 vols 1854–7) I 399. Once owned by Cardinal Richelieu, the *Silenus* had undergone a change protested in the *M Chron* 4 Jul 1831: "We are great friends of decorum, but we marvel that Sir Robert, or any one who could appreciate such a picture, should have suffered a coarse drapery to be thrown over Silenus by a modern hand. In such a subject, classical in all its parts, what harm in a naked figure?" The work of Peel's breeches-maker was removed in the late 1940s. The whole was subsequently attributed to "the studio of Rubens"; before C's time it was thought to be by Sir Anthony Van Dyck. SC wrote to Emily Trevenen on 26 Jul 1831 that C was "particularly struck" by Rubens's "Silenus & Satyr's Scream"; "Mr. Wordsworth too always had a great deal to say about Rubens." UT Grantz 1338. SC's way of referring to the *Silenus* suggests that C may have commented on the (screaming) open mouth of the satyr to the right of Silenus.

[7] *Fire, Famine, and Slaughter* lines 8–10: *PW* (EHC) I 237.

That Landscape next on the left hand is only less magnificent than dear Sir George Beaumont's, now in the National Gallery.[8] It has the same charm. Rubens does not take for his subject grand or novel conformations of objects;[d] he has, you see, no precipices, no forests, no frowning castles &c—nothing that a poet would take at all times, and a painter take in these times! No! he takes little ponds, old tumble-down cottages—that ruinous chateau—two or three peasants—a hay rick and such humble images, which looked at *in* themselves and *by* themselves convey no pleasure and excite no surprise; but he—and he Peter Paul Rubens alone— handles these every day ingredients of all common landscapes, as they are handled in nature—he [e]throws them into a vast and magnificent whole consisting of Heaven and Earth and of all things therein.[9] He extracts the latent poetry out of these common objects—that poetry and harmony which every man of genius perceives in the face of Nature, and which many men of no genius are taught to perceive and feel after examining such a picture as this. In other landscape painters the scene is confined and as it were imprisoned; in Rubens the landscape dies a natural death; it fades away in [f]the apparent infinity of[g] space. [36:302]

[h]The more I see of pictures the more I am convinced that the ancient art of painting is gone and something substituted for it very pleasing, but different and that in kind not in degree only.[i] Portraits by the old masters, take for instance the pock-fritten lady by Cuyp,[10] are pictures of men and

---

[d] objets   [e] f 40ᵛ   [f-g] the ⟨apparent⟩ infinity of ~~appar~~

[h-j] In SC's hand. She also wrote a shorter version of the following paragraph and then transcribed on f 41 the passage described in n [k], below. At the bottom of f 40ᵛ and continuing beneath SC's transcription on f 41, HNC expanded the passage on the godlike and the beastly in Rubens that SC had cancelled: "Rubens's men & women are beasts as his animals are endued with ~~the~~ energy & animation almost spiritual."

[i] ~~alone~~ only.

---

[8] The work exhibited is identified by HNC as Rubens *Landscape with Setting Sun*, lent by Charles Long, 1st Baron Farnborough, from his energetic collecting at Bromley Hill Place; by his gift in 1838, it is National Gallery NG 157: oil on wood, 19 inches high, 33 inches wide, now called *A Landscape with a Shepherd and His Flock*. "The great charm of this picture is the glowing evening light, with the rays of the sun—an effect as bold as it is poetical." Waagen I 351. The more impressive Rubens donated by Beaumont to the National Gallery in 1826 is *Autumn, Château de Steen* (NG 66). Sir Charles Holmes *The National Gallery* (3 vols 1935) II 60 noted the influence of this painting on Turner, Constable, and Crome. Waagen I 351 on this painting approaches C on the smaller landscape: "All that art could effect by means of single trees and by shadows of clouds, to produce variety in an extensive level surface, is done here, while the execution is so minute that singing birds are seen upon the trees: the landscape is also enlivened by numerous figures of men and animals."

[9] Like the other details C specifies, even "that ruinous chateau" is neither obviously present nor obviously absent in *Landscape with Setting Sun*; with this painting as example, C praises Rubens's consistent ability to fuse observation with an ideal vision not available to Teniers.

[10] Albert Cuyp (c 1620–91) *Lady with a Fan* (No 9 in the 1831 catalogue), lent

women—they fill not merely occupy a space—they represent individu-als:[11]—modern portraits, a few by Jackson and Owen perhaps excepted, give you not the man—not the inward humanity, but merely the external mask, that in which Tom is different from Bill.[12] There is something affected and meretricious, even in the Snake in the Grass and such pictures by Sir Joshua Reynolds.[13] [36:306]

The Italian masters differ from the Dutch in this that ages in their pictures are perfectly ideal: the infant that a Madonna holds in her arms cannot be guessed of any particular age—it is humanity in infancy. The babe in the manger in a Dutch painting is a fac simile of some real new born bantling—it is just like one of the little rabbits.[j][14] [36:303]

j See *h–j*, above

by the Rev Heneage Finch. Smith v 353 describes it, 32 by 26 inches oval: "A Portrait of a young Lady, with an oval-shaped countenance, slightly marked with the small-pox: her hair is turned back, and a black velvet cap covers her head. Her dress consists of black speckled silk, and a plain muslin kerchief with a b[l]ack rosette on the bosom. The right hand only is seen, holding a fan. Such is the richness of the colouring, the breadth of the effect, and the extraordinary look of nature in this picture, that it may be said to vie with the best productions of Rembrandt." Lent again by Finch, it was exhibited at the British Institution in 1852 as *A Dutch Lady*. Algernon Graves *A Century of Loan Exhibitions 1813–1912* (3 vols 1913–15) I 244.

[11] *TT* (1835) clarified: "individuals, but individuals as types of a species".

[12] John Jackson (1778–1831), R.A., was included in *Library of Fine Arts* I (1831) 445 as one of the leading portrait painters of the day; he was praised for "great delicacy and truth" by Waagen II 335; cf 152. Sir George Beaumont was a major patron of both Jackson and William Owen (1769–1825), R.A. A "beautifully modelled and expressive" portrait of Beaumont's mother by Owen, now in the National Gallery of Victoria in Melbourne, is reproduced in T. S. R. Boase *English Art 1800–1870* (Oxford 1959) Plate 8 p 14. Portraits of Sir John Soane by both Jackson and Owen, and of Chantrey and Northcote by Jackson, hang in the Soane Museum. Jackson had

died 1 Jun, in St John's Wood; on 14 Jun WW asked Samuel Rogers who could best paint WW for St John's, Cambridge: "Had Jackson been living, without troubling you I should have inquired of himself whether he would undertake the task; but he is just gone . . .". *WL* (*L* rev) II 402.

[13] The reviewer in the *M Chron* 4 Jul 1831 of the exhibition said of No 6, Reynolds *Snake in the Grass*, lent by Sir Robert Peel: "A picture too well known to be described, and too much admired to need praise to recommend it." The full title of the painting (finished about 1788, purchased for the nation in 1871, and now in the Tate Gallery) is *A Nymph and Cupid: "The Snake in the Grass"*. There is a second version in the Soane Museum and a third in the Hermitage, Leningrad, with the descriptive title *Love Unbinding the Zone of Beauty*. At the Uffizi in Florence in 1806 C had been reminded by a Parmigianino of works by Reynolds with a similar simper. *CN* II 2853. Facing a Correggio painting in Parma, Tom Moore, Jackson, and Chantrey in 1819 had been reminded of a similar "grotesque sweetness" in Reynolds. Moore *Journal* I 262.

[14] The expansion in *TT* (1835) obscures the point that the rabbits are in the Dutch painting, not merely in the mind of such fathers as HNC. Yet C was on poetic record as being "only sad" when he first saw HC's "face of feeble infancy". *PW* (EHC) I 154; *CL* I 236.

So long as Rubens confines himself to space and outward figure—to the mere animal man with animal passions, he is, I may say, a God amongst painters. His Satyrs, *k*Silenuses, Lions, Tigers &c are almost godlike; but the moment he attempts any thing involving or presuming the spiritual, his gods and goddesses, his nymphs and heroes,*l* become beasts, absolute, unmitigated beasts.[15]　　　　　　　　　[36:302]

Carlo Dolce's representations of our Saviour are pretty, to be sure; but they are too smooth to please me.[16] His Christs are always in sugar candy.　　　　　　　　　[36:304]

That is a very odd and funny picture of the Connoisseurs at Rome by Reynolds.[17]　　　　　　　　　[36:305]

k f 41. The top of f 41 contains a transcript in SC's hand of C's letter to Mrs C [2 Sept] 1803; see n 15, below

l heros

[15] At Brussels in Jun 1828 C was heard to say "of Rubens's picture of The Boar Hunt, in the Prince of Orange's Collection, 'It is a perfect dithyrambic—every piece of it forms a separate epithet of beauty.' " Grattan II 112.

At the top of f 41 SC transcribed several sentences on the Trossachs and Glen Coe from C's letter of [2 Sept] 1803 to Mrs C: *CL* I 978–9.

[16] One painting by the Florentine Carlo Dolci (or Carlino Dolce, 1616–86) was exhibited, No 171, *St John*, lent by Thomas Hamlet. Thomas Methuen reported differently the C of 1814: "Again, when admiring Carlo Dolce's inimitable picture of Christ consecrating the elements, he thus addressed me, 'Other painters have represented the humility of our blessed Saviour; but it was not (as in the masterpiece before us) the humility of one who could have called on the Father, and he would presently have sent him more than twelve legions of angels.' " *Christian Observer* XLIV (1845) 260. This painting would be the version of Dolci's *Christ Blessing the Bread and Wine* at Corsham House, owned by Paul Cobb Methuen (1752–1816), Thomas's father, when C stayed there for a few days in late Sept or early Oct 1814. *CL* III 535–6; *CN* III 4227 and n. The epithet

"inimitable" is Methuen's, but C was always likely to flatter the valued possessions of a host. Holmes I 132 sides with the later C: "it is hard to be patient with . . . Dolci, although there is often a certain corrupt attractiveness in his colouring". C's praise in 1814 had been anticipated by John Britton *Historical Account of Corsham House* 75: "This truly great man was one of those prodigies who give early indications of future eminence. . . . His works are distinguished by peculiar delicacy of composition, by a pleasing tone of colour, by the graceful air of his heads, and by a placid repose diffused throughout the whole." Besides *Our Saviour Breaking the Bread* (No 134 p 50), Britton lauded *Our Saviour at the Pharisee's House* (No 53 p 38) and two other works by the "truly great" Dolci (pp 31, 51, 75).

[17] No 133, *Portraits of Distinguished Connoisseurs, Painted at Rome*, 70 by 45 inches, lent by Lord George Cavendish. Reynolds painted several such caricatures of identifiable English visitors to Rome in 1751, one as a parody of Raphael's *School of Athens*. Ellis K. Waterhouse *Reynolds* (1941) 38. Reynolds often spoke and wrote with contempt of "half-learned connoisseurs, who have quitted nature and have not acquired

*m*It is now twenty years since I read Chillingworth's Book;[18] but certainly it seemed to me that his main position that the Bible—the mere Book itself—is the sole exclusively conclusive ground and standard of Christian Religion is perfectly untenable against the Roman Catholics.[19] It entirely destroys the conditions of a Church, of an authority residing in a religious community—and all that holy sense of brotherhood which is so sublime and consolatory to a meditative Christian. Had I been a Papist, I should not have wished for an easier or more vanquishable opponent in controversy. I certainly believe Chillingworth to have been a Socinian in some sense.[20] Lord Falkland, his friend, said so in substance.[21] I do not deny his skill in dialectics. He was more than a match for Knott to be sure.   [36:307]

m f 41ᵛ

art''. *The Literary Works of Sir Joshua Reynolds* ed Henry William Beechey (2 vols 1835) II 353; cf 124.

[18] William Chillingworth (1602–43), Oxford theologian. His "Book", as HNC noted in *TT* (1835), is *The Religion of Protestants a Safe Way to Salvation; or, An Answer to a Booke Entitled Mercy and Truth* (Oxford 1638). It was included in Chillingworth *Works* (10th ed 2 pts in 1 vol 1742), two copies of which C annotated. *CM (CC)* II 24–41. *Mercy and Truth* (1634), by Matthew Wilson, S.J. (1582–1634) under the pseudonym Edward Knott, was reprinted and answered chapter by chapter in Chillingworth's *Religion of Protestants*.

[19] C wrote in Chillingworth *Works* that the "true and effectual way to confute the Romanists" is first to abandon "needless & impossible deifications of a *Book*" and next to expose the indeterminacy revealed by "their own ridiculous disagreements as to what and to whom the term Church and the attribute infallibility are to be determined", with the result that "A or B or C are infallible, but which neither they nor we know". *CM (CC)* II 39. Chillingworth argued that a Protestant need seek religious authority only in the Bible, as C noted in Mar 1810. In answer to "the Chillingworthian Divines", also in 1810, he praised the Anglican Church for its reliance on "the Tradition of the first 3 or 4 Centuries" as an aid in interpreting

Scripture; in 1812 he recommended more specifically reliance on "the Councils regularly called & confirmed". *CN* III 3743 f 21, 3812, 4143.

[20] C identified as one example of Socinian tendency Chillingworth's advice to comprehend what in Scripture is clear, but to leave the rest obscure until the Holy Ghost pleases to clarify. *CM (CC)* II 39.

[21] Lucius Cary, 2nd Viscount Falkland (c 1610–43) entered Chillingworth's controversies posthumously with *Of the Infallibility of the Church of Rome* (1646), which was republished in 1660 as *A Discourse of Infallibility* with an answer by Thomas White and a reply, along with two discourses of episcopacy, one by Falkland, the other by Chillingworth. Henry Spencer, 1st Earl of Sunderland, shortly before he was killed with Falkland at Newbury in 1643, wrote in a letter to his lady of Chillingworth's "*dispute last night* with Lord Falkland, in *favour* of SOCINIANISM, *wherein* he was by his Lordship *so often* confounded". John Whitaker *The Origin of Arianism Disclosed* (1791) 484–5. C annotated Whitaker. Falkland's *Of the Infallibility of the Church of Rome* and his reply to the Catholic answerer White do not refer directly to Chillingworth, but he rebutted the charge that Protestants could fall readily into Arianism and had trouble with the Catholic demand for a guide to support the reader of Scripture;

I must be bold enough to say that I do not think that even Hooker puts the idea^n of a Church on the true foundation.^{o22} [36:308]

---

^{p}S. T. C. 24. July. 1831.

The superstition of the peasantry and lower orders generally in Malta, Sicily and Italy exceeds common belief. It is unlike the superstition of Spain, which is a jealous fanaticism, having reference to^q Catholic Christianity, and always glancing on Heresy.^{23} The popular superstition of Italy is the offspring of the climate, the old associations, the manners—the very names of the places. It is pure paganism, undisturbed by any anxiety about orthodoxy, or animosity against heretics. Hence it is much more pleasing and good natured to a traveller's feelings, and certainly not a whit less like the true religion of our dear Lord than the gloomy idolatry of the Spaniards.^{r24} [36:309]

^{n} ~~foundation~~ idea
^{o} Following this HNC transcribed a sentence from a letter of C's; see n 22, below. About six lines have been cut from the letter just above the passage transcribed; see *CL* II 1038
^{p} f 42 ^{q} to ~~the~~
^{r} After this SC copied a paragraph from C's letter to Mrs C 19 Feb 1802; see n 24, below

---

his reply improves upon Chillingworth: "Christ is our unquestionable, and infallible Governour, and his Will the Principle by which we are guided, and the Scripture the place where this Will is contained, which if we endeavour to find there, we shall be excused, though we chance to misse, and therefore want not your guide . . .". *Discourse* (1660) 199; on Arianism see pp 240–6. Falkland is named first of Chillingworth's "intimate friends" in the "Life" introducing Chillingworth *Works* (3 vols 1820) I 2.

^{22} By "bold enough" C does not merely rephrase the reservation about Hooker that he had expressed earlier (29–30 Apr 1827, at n 2), but allows a degree of humility in suggesting that the true foundation was achieved in *C&S*.

Following this entry, on f 41^v, under the date "1804. Jan 29", HNC transcribed hastily a sentence on C's love of his children, from the end of C's letter to Mrs C dated by *CL* II 1038 "Jan. 24 [25], 1804".

^{23} Like WW, C thought it better to be "suckled in a creed outworn" than to be a mechanist without faith; and, like

WW, he depicted superstition sometimes with condescending affection and sometimes as a powerful vehicle of passion. But within the context of embattled trinitarianism he made a note in 1819: "Superstition the Giant Shadow of Humanity with its back to the setting Sun of true Religion". *CN* III 4491. In Lect 10 of the lectures on the history of philosophy he noted the universal adaptability of "superstitious stories", especially those suggestive of magic. *P Lects* (1949) 296–7. Several notebook entries of 1804 remark on the adverse effects of Catholicism in Sicily; e.g. as religion it is comparable to poison sold as patent medicine. *CN* II 2324; cf 2206, 2216. A note in *C&S* suggests that he took his information on current Catholicism in Spain from Blanco White. *C&S (CC)* 122. The "gloomy idolatry" (end of paragraph) of Spain in previous centuries was a commonplace that C did not need to stress in publications or marginalia; his early interest in books on the era of Philip II (1527–98) was renewed by the Peninsular War.

^{24} There is no divisional bar to sepa-

S. T. C. 24 July . 1831.

42

The superstition of the peasantry & lower orders generally in Malta - Sicily & Italy exceeds common belief. It is unlike the superstition of Spain, which is a jealous fanaticism, having reference to Catholic Christianity, & always glancing on Heresy. The popular superstition of Italy is the offspring of the climate, the old associations, the manners - the very names of the places. It is pure paganism, undisturbed by any anxiety that orthodoxy, or anxiously against heretics. Hence it is much more pleasing & good natured to a traveller's feelings, & certainly not a whit less like the true religion of our dear Lord than the gloomy idolatry of the Spaniards.

Feb. 19. 1802.

// little Subligni [alias Underwood] fell in love lately with a fair Jewess & went to Mr D'Israeli requesting his interference & offering immediately to become a convert & be circumcised. This is nakedly the fact without a word of Decoration — — I like Subligni hugely. //

I well remember, when in Valette, asking a boy who waited on me what a certain procession then passing, was, & his answering with great quickness & seriousness, that it was I. C, who lives here / rta di casa qui /, & when he comes out, it is in the shape of a wafer. Rut Eccelenza, said he smiling & crossing himself - non è Chiesa. I beg pardon, I had forgotten.

S. T. C. 30. July 1831.

Argill was an extraordinary man & his pamphlet is invaluable. He undertook to prove that man was literally

2. A page from H. N. Coleridge's workbooks, MS B f 42,
for 24 July 1831, with a passage transcribed by Sara Coleridge from
her father's letters to her mother. Victoria College Library,
reproduced by kind permission

I well remember, when in Valletta,[s] asking a boy who waited on me
what a certain procession, then passing, was, and his answering with
great quickness and seriousness,—that it was Jesus Christ *who lives here*
(sta di casa qui),[25] and when he comes out, it is in the shape of a wafer.
"But Eccelenza," said he smiling and correcting himself, "Non è Cris-
tiano! I beg pardon, I had forgotten."[26]   [36:310]

S. T. C. 30. July 1831.

Asgill was an extraordinary man, and his pamphlet is invaluable.[1] He undertook to prove that man was literally [a]immortal, and was expelled from
two Houses of Commons for blasphemy or atheism.[2] I expected to find
the ravings of an enthusiast[b] or the sullen snarlings of the infidel; whereas
I found the very soul of Swift—an intense, half self deceived humorist.
I scarcely remember elsewhere such uncommon skill in logic—such law-
yer-like acuteness and yet such grasp of common sense. Each of his ax-

[s] Valette,   [a] f 42[v]   [b] enthusiastie

rate the two paragraphs relating to Malta,
but SC here transcribed the paragraph on
"Subligno" (T. R. Underwood) from
C's letter of 19 Feb 1802 to Mrs C: *CL* II
786.
[25] "Is at home here". C was in Valletta, the capital of Malta, May–Aug
1804 and from Nov to Aug 1805. C himself gives the name variously as Valette,
Vilette, La Vallette, Valletta.
[26] Implying that the boy had been
taught to distinguish Protestants from
Christians, as C distinguished Unitarians
from Protestants. For the longer colloquy
given as a footnote to this entry in *TT*
(1835) see above, JTC's record of Apr
1811.
[1] John Asgill (1659–1738), "eccen-
tric writer" (*DNB*), to C "a prime Dar-
ling of mine—the most honest of all
Whigs". *CL* VI 901. C annotated in
1827–8, with an afterthought in 1832, *A
Collection of Tracts Written by John Asgill, Esq* (8 pts in 1 vol 1715). The
"pamphlet" referred to is the first of the
tracts, as noted by HNC in *TT* (1835): *An*
*Argument Proving, That According to
the Covenant of Eternal Life Reveal'd in
the Scriptures, Man May be Translated
from Hence into That Eternal Life, Without Passing Through Death* (1700); C's
notes are given in *CM (CC)* I 121–9. Although uncertain whether Asgill was "in
jest or in earnest", producing "sound
Logic" or "original Humor", C planned
in 1832 a facsimile edition. *CL* VI 901–2,
906–7. HNC described the project to RS
on 27 Jun 1835 as "amongst S.T.C.'s
agenda non acta; he wrote many notes
upon such as he had", pointing out that
Asgill's publisher listed at the end of the
collection many other tracts. UT ms.
Preparing his own account of Asgill for
The Doctor vol IV, RS had declared on 6
Jun: "Coleridge knew only part of his
history." *Correspondence of Henry Taylor* ed Edward Dowden (1888) 64.
[2] The addition in *TT* (1835), "I really
suspect because he was a staunch Hanoverian", derives from f 61, 21 Apr
1832, below. (Altered in 1836 to
"Really I suspect".)

ioms or paragraphs is in itself a whole, and yet a link between the preceding and following; so that the whole series forms one argument.[3]

[36:311]

The French are like grains of gunpowder; each by itself contemptible, but^c in^d aggregation most terrible![4]

[36:312]

Was there ever such a miserable scene as that of the exhibition of the Austrian Standards in the French House of Peers the other day! Every other nation but the French would see that it was an exhibition of their own falsehood and cowardice! A man swears that the property entrusted to him is burnt, and then, when he is no longer afraid, produces it, and boasts of the atmosphere of "honor" forsooth! through which the lie did not transpire![5]

[36:312]

If sixty or seventy new peers are created, and sixty or seventy of the old peers do not for that very reason vote against Ministers, whatever they might have done otherwise, the House of Lords, as an Estate of the Realm, will be annihilated, and the Revolution is begun.[6] The form of

^{c} but ~~terrible~~ ^{d} in ⟨the⟩

[3] Among small changes in the entry— e.g. "humorism" for "humorist"—*TT* (1835) added a final clause, "and yet each is a diamond in itself".

[4] *TT* (1835) retained the divisional bar omitted in 1836, but like the later edition added "smutty" to the epithets and made the generalisation follow the comments on the Austrian standards. The order in MS B suggests, perhaps less accurately than the revision, that the generalisation led to an illustration chosen from the current news. Julian Charles Young reported C's conversation in Jul 1828 at Godesberg: " 'I hate,' he would say, 'the hollowness of French principles: I hate the republicanism of French politics: I hate the hostility of the French people to revealed religion: I hate the artificiality of French cooking: I hate the acidity of French wines: I hate the flimsiness of the French language:—my very organs of speech are so anti-Gallican that they refuse to pronounce intelligibly their insipid tongue.' " *A Memoir of Charles Mayne Young* (1871) 115.

[5] The speech, or as C would have it, the admission of Charles Louis Huguet, Marquis de Semonville (1759-1839), in the Chamber of Peers on 26 Jul 1831 was reported in *The Times* 29 Jul and quoted in HNC's explanatory footnote in *TT* (1835).

[6] An obvious transition in the conversation was neglected in HNC's record. The *M Chron* and *The Times* had both been reporting in July on the progress of threats to the French peers that if Casimir Perier's bill to modify the mode of creating peers was not passed, then Charles x would create enough new peers to pass the bill. Thirty-six new peers were created, and the bill was passed. Unknown to C, Charles x was in the process of abdicating; the hereditary peerage would be abolished 19 Nov. *A Reg* for 1831 History 361–6. C was reacting to rumours, later to be confirmed, that Grey's government was similarly threatening the creation of new peers to assure passage of the Reform Bill. The account in *A Reg* 252–4 of threats against the Lords if they failed to pass the bill does not mention

Government will be ipso facto changed; the Crown, or rather the Ministers which have assumed absolute power in partnership*e* with the Commons.[7]

---

*'*I earnestly hope that the Times and Morning Chronicle may succeed in their attempts to procure deputations from Manchester, Birmingham &c to the House of Commons to remonstrate with the members on account of delay.[8] I know nothing so likely to open the eyes of the nation to the mad career which these wretched Ministers are running—and cause it to see the fearful precipice on which we now stand.

As there is much Beast and some Devil in Man—so is there some Angel and some God in him. The Beast and the Devil may be conquered, but in this life never destroyed.[9] [36:313]

I will defy anyone to answer the arguments of a St Simonist except on the ground of Christianity and its precepts and assurances.*g*[10] [36:314]

e ~~conformity~~ partnership   *f* f 43

g Following this and on f 43ᵛ SC copied passages from C's letters to Mrs C; see n 10, below

---

new peerages, nor does Brougham in "The Dissolution and General Election, with Suggestions to the Peers", a review of *Friendly Advice, Most Respectfully Submitted to the Lords, on the Reform Bill* in *Ed Rev* LIII (Jun 1831) 478–501. For Grey's meetings and correspondence with William IV on the subject in Apr–May 1832, see Halévy III 54 and 26 Oct 1831 n 9, below.

[7] I.e. the power of the Lords will be eliminated; the Ministers, in lieu of the Crown, will share power with the Commons. This entry and the next are cancelled with a vertical line in the ms, but were not published.

[8] Leading articles on Reform in *The Times* throughout July stressed the claims of Manchester, Birmingham, and Leeds for greater representation. The *M Chron* gave prominent place to the speeches at public rallies of such radical supporters of the bill as William Cobbett, whose trial during July for inciting labourers to violence gave further prominence to his calls for assemblies and deputations. Both newspapers regularly reported petitions for Reform from commercial and industrial cities.

[9] By assigning this entry and the next to a separate date, HNC eliminated the transition in thought: reform of government could never bring either perfection or the great improvements promised by the reformers.

[10] Claude Henri de Rouvroy, Comte de Saint–Simon (1760–1825) propounded in several works, culminating in *Le nouveau Christianisme* (1825), a doctrine of social reorganisation under the leadership of scientists and industrialists to bring about social harmony. The Saint-Simonists reached their crest under Barthélemy Prosper Enfantin (1796–1864) and Amand Bazard (1791–1832) in *L'Exposition de la doctrine de Saint–Simon* (1828–30) and Enfantin *La Religion Saint–Simonienne* (1831). Their tenets included public control of production, redistribution of property, abolition of private inheritance, and gradual improvement in the lot of women. Reviewing *L'Exposition, première année* (1828–9) at about this time in *QR* XLV

*a*S. T. C. 6. Aug. 1831.

There is the love of the Good for the Good's sake, and the love of the Truth for the Truth's sake. I have known many—especially women— love the Good for the Good's sake; I have known but very few indeed love the Truth for the Truth's sake. Yet without the latter, the former may be, as it has a thousand times been, the source of persecution of the Truth—the pretext and the motive*b* of Inquisitorial cruelty and of Party zealotry. To see clearly that the love of the Good and the True are ultimately identical, is given only to those who love both sincerely and*c* without other ends.[1]   [36:315]

---

*d*Iron is the most ductile of all hard metals, and the hardest of all ductile metals. With the exception of Nickel, in which it is dimly seen, Iron is the only metal in which the Magnetic Power is visible. Indeed it is almost impossible to purify Nickel of Iron.[2]   [36:318]

a f 43ᵛ   *b* ~~cause~~ motive   *c* ~~for~~ &   *d* f 44

(Jul 1831) 407–50, RS dealt severely with their "new Christianity (?)", but came a small way toward C by concluding that "no system which has yet been advanced under cover of pious fraud has ever been presented to the world so temperately, so reasonably, nor with so much ability as theirs" (p 447). He had written similarly in a letter of 14 Mar 1830. *S Life* (CS) vi 92. C's Christian "assurances" are of life hereafter; the "precepts" include conviction of human fallibility, with "much Beast and some Devil" in each "never destroyed". RS had More say, "The root of all your evils is in the sinfulness of the nation." *Sir Thomas More: or, Colloquies on the Progress and Prospects of Society* (2 vols 1829; 2nd ed 2 vols 1831) ii 324. Spinoza provides the chief example of C's propensity to say of a logical argument unacceptable to him that it was irrefutable if you accepted its premise.

Following this entry and on f 43ᵛ SC copied passages from C's letters to Mrs C of 19 Feb, 1 Apr 1804 and 29 Sept 1806. *CL* ii 1069, 1115, 1184.

[1] In the first of the essays "On the Communication of Truth" in both 1809 and 1818 *Friend*, though in changed language, C argued that "Truth, Virtue, and Happiness, may be distinguished from each other, but cannot be divided", that well-being "can be built on Virtue alone, and must of necessity have Truth for its foundation". *Friend (CC)* ii 40, i 39. In Lect 4 of the lectures on the history of philosophy he noted in the Socratic principle that knowledge is "the source of all virtue and therein of all happiness" a validity only when knowledge was given to a mind predisposed to virtue. *P Lects* (1949) 150–1. Along with such changes as providing the noun "love" with the verb "is" instead of "are", *TT* (1835) added as rhetorical balance, after "few, indeed" in the second sentence, "and scarcely one woman". Coventry Patmore, asserting that C was clearest and best in *TT*, remarked that elsewhere "in his love of pure truth", C "fell often into hopeless obscurity from forgetfulness of the fact that truth is only intelligible in its application to the realities of life", but everywhere for C "truth was the pure white ray which his intellect followed whithersoever it went". "Great Talkers—Coleridge" *St James's Gazette* 13 Mar 1886, reprinted *TT* (1917) xi.

[2] Of standard works, C is closer to Brande's revision of 1836 than to his *Manual of Chemistry* (1819) 288: "Nickel is a white metal, which acts

Galvanism is the union of electricity and magnetism, and by being continuous exhibits an image of Life—I say an image only—it is Life in Death.[3]   [36:319]

_____

Heat is the mesothesis of Light and Matter.[4]   [36:320]

_____

There is but one exception that I know of to the rule that Aeriforms must pass through Fluids in their way to Solids—and that is the [   ]^e which united in certain proportions project a white powder.[5]

^{e} Blanks left in ms for names of gases

_____

upon the magnetic needle, and is itself capable of becoming a magnet. It is difficultly fusible . . . It is malleable, and its specific gravity is about 8,5.'' The advance in C's lifetime can be seen from William Nicholson *The First Principles of Chemistry*, which repeated in 1795 the language of the 1st ed of 1790, which C acquired and left with WW (*WW LC* 345): nickel is ''of great hardness'', ''always magnetical, whence it has been supposed to contain iron in its purest state'', malleable, and ''scarcely more fusible than pure iron'' (1795 p 345); it is ''not yet applied to any use'', some suppose it an alloy of copper with ''substances'' (p 347).

[3] Speculation of this sort occurs throughout German *Naturphilosophie*, but not in articles on galvanism and electricity in popular encyclopaedias in England. Galvanism was named for Luigi Galvani (1737–98), physician and physicist of Bologna, who announced in 1794 his discovery that electrical current caused a twitching in the muscles of frogs. Watkins *Portable Cyclopaedia* (1810) defined galvanism as ''the influence of metals by mere external contact with the animal body''. What this entry adds to that on 18 Mar 1827 (at n 10, above) (36:77), is the graphic image. Life-in-Death diced with Death for the Ancient Mariner, and won (*AM* 193–6); according to the trope of 1831, the Mariner was as dead as one of Galvani's frogs. Attacking atomistic chemistry and related mechanistic doctrines from France, C described practitioners of Linnaean classification as delighting to

''peep into Death to look for Life''. *SM (CC)* 77.

[4] C here converts chemical experimentation into his pentad of polarity, with light as thesis and matter as antithesis. This entry and the next are best considered against opinions HNC's readers might hold. In Watkins, e.g., heat not from the sun is caloric, ''a fluid extremely elastic and subtle'' that ''produces heat''. Under *Fluidity* Watkins explained that ''whenever a solid is converted into a fluid it combines with a certain dose of caloric''. Humphry Davy had quoted Lavoisier on light and ''calorique'' as one a modification of the other, before declaring that ''light and heat are totally distinct''. ''An Essay on Heat, Light, and the Combinations of Light'' in *Contributions to Physical and Medical Knowledge, Principally from the West of England* ed Thomas Beddoes (Bristol 1799) 67. Davy was modified somewhat in a work that C owned (*WW LC* 362), Thomas Young *A Syllabus of a Course of Lectures on Natural and Experimental Philosophy* (1802) 147: ''Hence, it becomes highly probable, that heat differs from light, in the same respects as the rays of light differ from each other; and that the scale is continued into the invisible rays which Ritter and Dr. Wollaston have observed to produce chemical effects. And it may be concluded, that the states of luminous and heated bodies are similarly related.''

[5] Attending Davy's lectures in Jan 1802, C noted: ''Muriatic Acid . . . combines with all the alkalis/ ex. gr. the muriatic acid Gas with the Volatile Al-

Look through the whole history of Roman Catholic countries, and you
will uniformly find the leaven of this besetting and accursed principle of
action—that the *End* will sanction any Means.[6]   [36:316]
The conduct of this country to King William of Holland has been base
and unprincipled beyond anything I remember in our history since *f*the
time of Charles II.[g] Certainly Holland is one of the most important allies
which England has. And under this precious ministry we have as it were
in a moment thrown it and Portugal into the hands of France![7] Will not
this awake the people from their slumber. The nation is now like a man
palsied in every part of his body, but one, on which part he is so *h*mor-
bidly sensitive that he can't bear to be breathed upon.*i*[8]   [36:317]

f-g temp Car. II.   *h* f 44*v*
i After this SC copied passages from C's letters to Mrs C, to f 47*v*; see n 8, below

---

kali—the 2 aeriform substances become
a white solid''; the gas was hydrogen
chloride, the alkali ammonia. *CN* I 1098
ff 20–1 and n. William Nicholson,
whom C knew at least as editor of *A
Journal of Natural Philosophy, Chemistry, and the Arts*, described a more complicated experiment whereby ''alkaline
and marine acid air'' over mercury
formed a white cloud that itself precipitated a ''solid white salt''. *A Dictionary
of Chemistry* (2 vols 1795) I 73. In 1818
C had recorded speculations concerning
the function of mercury in the solidifying
of gases. *CN* III 4410. C accused the *Naturphilosophen* of failure to distinguish
between fluidity and aerity. Annotations
on Hans Christian Oersted *Ansicht der
chemischer Naturgesetze* . . . (Berlin
1812) 28 and Steffens *Grundzüge
der philosophischen Naturwissenschaft*
(Berlin 1806) 87: *CM (CC)* III, IV. C's
remark was not published, presumably
because HNC failed to identify the
gases.
    [6] ''Look'' and ''observe'' as impera-
tives are more common in *TT* than in C's
prose generally; they appear more frequently in the writings of RS. The priority of ends over means had been a staple
of quotable authors in England throughout the eighteenth century.
    [7] Conferences on Belgium at London,
under the guidance of Viscount Palmerston, the Foreign Secretary, sustained his

policy of weakening both William and
the French in Belgium and Luxemburg.
In early January Palmerston had favoured the Prince of Orange, but in June
Prince Leopold of Saxe-Coburg was
elected King by the Belgian Assembly in
accordance with agreements achieved by
Palmerston to exclude Louis Philippe if
Leopold agreed to marry Louis Philippe's daughter. When Leopold claimed
Luxemburg, with connivance or tempo-
risation in London, troops of the Prince
of Orange crossed into Belgium on 5
Aug. Palmerston had promised on 16 Jun
to lend naval support to the French in an
effort, ultimately successful, to drive
William out of Belgium. The language
of this entry is modified in *TT* (1835).
SC, whether to note C's prescience or his
Francophobia—or by coincidence—
copied into MS B after this day's talk C's
similar language to Mrs C from Malta,
12 Dec 1804, to the effect that Ministers
by favouring Naples would ''throw Sicily into the hands of France''. *CL* II
1157.
    [8] *TT* (1835) clarified by adding
''whilst you may pinch him with a hot
forceps elsewhere without his taking any
notice of it''. The one sensitive spot is
Reform; foreign affairs illustrate the
palsy.
    Beginning here—there is no divisional
bar in MS B—on f 44*v* and continuing to
f 47*v* SC copied passages from C's letters

*a*S. T. C. 14. Aug. 1831.[1]

The character of all nations in their colonial dependencies is in an inverse ratio of excellence to their character at home.[2] The best people in the mother country will be the worst in the colonies; the worst in the mother country will be the best abroad. The reason is obvious—In countries, well governed and happily conditioned, none or very few but those who are desperate by vice or folly*b* will be willing to leave their homes and settle in another hemisphere; and of those who do go, the best are always striving to acquire the means of leaving the colony and returning back to their native land. In ill-governed and ill-conditioned countries, on the contrary, the most respectable of the people are willing and anxious to emigrate for the chance of greater security and enlarged freedom; and if they succeed in obtaining these blessings in almost any degree, they have little inducement, on the average, to wish to abandon their second and better country. Hence in the former case, the Colonists consider themselves as mere strangers, sojourners—birds of passage—and shift to live from hand to mouth without regard to lasting improvement to their place of temporary commerce; whilst in the latter case, men feel attached to a community to which they are individually indebted for otherwise unattainable benefits, and for the most part learn to regard it as their abode and to make themselves as happy and comfortable in it as possible.

Analogous to this—though not founded on precisely the same principle—is the fact that the severe *c*naval discipline*d* is always found in the ships of the freest nations, and the most lax discipline in the ships of the most oppressed*e*.[3]—Hence the naval discipline of the Americans is the

---

a f 48   *b* folly—~~or~~   *c–d* discipline ~~on board ship~~   *e* oppressed &

---

to Mrs C of 21 Aug 1805, 16 Nov 1802, 12 Dec 1804, and 5 Jun 1804 (on Valletta): *CL* II 1171, 882–3, 1157, 1158, 1137–9. She wrote only two lines on f 47ᵛ; HNC left the rest of the page blank (there is no similar blank elsewhere in MS B).

[1] C was ill both before and after 14 Aug (Sun), with "the retrocession of the morbid action to the intestinal Canal in a type resembling Cholera". Letter of 10 Nov 1831: *CL* VI 874. On 21 Aug, in the only surviving letter between 14 Jun and 13 Sept, C spoke of a "sad relapse, last night, from which I obtained a reprieve only this Evening". *CL* VI 869.

[2] In a notebook of 1810, analysing the inverse ratio of "Freedom & Virtue" at home and abroad, C found six causes. *CN* III 4018. In 1804 he had begun a note, "Of the French & Spanish Colonists why so much better than the English & Dutch . . .", but the continuation makes clear that he is recording an observation with which he disagrees. *CN* II 2270. In 1799 he had soberly described to Josiah Wedgwood differences in vassalage in different countries. For a reservation concerning such characterisations see *CL* I 464–70.

[3] For some of C's opportunities to observe crewmen and naval officers see *CN* II 1993, 2044, 2051, 2060, 2228, 2308, 2451; *CL* II 1150–6, V 396–8, 401.

sharpest—then that of the English[4]—then that of the French—(I speak as it used to be), and on board a Spanish ship, there is no discipline at all.

——————— *f*   [36:321]

[g]I cannot contain my indignation at the conduct of the Ministers towards Holland. They have undoubtedly forgotten the true policy of the country in regard to Portugal in permitting the war faction in France to take possession of the Tagus and bully the Portuguese upon so flimsy—indeed false—a pretext.[5] Yet in this instance, something may be said for them. Miguel is such a wretch that I acknowledge a sort of morality in leaving him to be cuffed and insulted; though, of course, this is a poor answer to a statesman who alleges the interest and policy of the country.[6] But as to the Dutch and King William—the first, as a nation, the most ancient ally, the alter idem of England, the best deserving of the cause of Freedom, and Religion and Morality of any people in Europe; and the second, the very best sovereign now in Europe, with perhaps the exception of the excellent King of Sweden,[7]—was ever any thing so infamously mean and cowardly as the behavior of England? The Five Powers have[h] throughout this wretched Conference been actuated exclusively by a selfish desire to preserve peace—I should rather say—to smother war at the expence of the ruin of a most valuable, but inferior Power. They have over and over again acknowledged the justice of the Dutch claims, and the absurdity[i] of the Belgian pretences; but as the Belgians were also as impudent as they were iniquitous—as they could not yield *their* point—why then— that peace may be preserved—the Dutch must yield theirs! A foreign Prince comes into Belgium, pending these negotiations, and takes an unqualified oath to maintain the Belgian demands: What could King Wil-

f Divisional bar supplied; not in ms   *g* f 48ᵛ   *h* have ~~been~~   *i* ~~impudence~~ absurdity

[4] In a long note at this point explaining that C did not mean to rate English liberty lower than U.S. liberty, HNC in *TT* (1835) quoted *C&S* (1830 ed 2) 120–1, concluding that "where every man may take liberties, there is little Liberty for any man". *C&S (CC)* 95–6, 96n. HNC called attention also to *The Friend* (1818) I 129: see *Friend (CC)* I 70–6.

[5] French ships carrying troops reached the mouth of the Tagus 8 Jul 1831. In 1830 Britain had sent warships to the Tagus with an ultimatum against illegal seizure and forcible entry charged by British subjects against Miguel.

[6] Miguel's appeal for British help against the French in support of a faithful ally had been rejected by Palmerston.

[7] Jean Baptiste Jules Bernadotte (1763–1844), who served as general, ambassador, and minister of war under Napoleon, was elected crown prince of Sweden in 1810 and ascended the throne in 1818 as Charles XIV of Sweden and Norway. Allied with Britain, he contributed to the defeat of Napoleon at Leipzig (1813). As monarch he was celebrated for peace and for such domestic improvements as the Göta Canal and educational reform. C admired both present and past Swedish kings and people. *CN* III 4147 f 6, 4482.

liam do, or the Dutch do, if they meant ever hereafter to call themselves[j] independent, but [k]resist and resent to the uttermost[l] this outrage?[8] It was a crisis, in which every consideration of state is inferior to the strong sense and duty of national Honor. When the French appear in Belgium— King William retires;—"I now see", he may say, "that the Powers of Europe are determined to abet the Belgians. The justice of such proceeding I leave to their conscience. It is no longer a question whether I am tamely to [m]submit to rebels and an usurper—it is no longer a quarrel between Holland and Belgium—it is an alliance of all Europe against Holland; in which case I yield. I have no desire to sacrifice my people."[9]

[36:322]

Will the French retreat? I don't believe it. I doubt the obedience of the Army. King Leopold is like the Conjurer who had called up the Devils with infinite zeal and pains; when they come thronging about him, grinning and howling and dancing and whisking their tails in diabolic glee— the poor wretch is frightened out of his wits—and when they ask what he wants of them—all he can stammer out—is—"I pray you begone down again."

> Yes! Yes! we'll go down, we'll go down!
> But we'll take you with us to swim or to drown![10]

[36:293]

---

[j] themselves ~~an~~   [k–l] resist ∧ to the utter²most ⟨& re¹sent⟩   [m] f 49

[8] The London Conference of the Five Powers, Britain, Austria, Prussia, Russia, and France, took up the Belgian question intermittently from January to November. C's "foreign Prince" is Leopold. Charles William Stewart, 3rd Marquis of Londonderry, reminded the Lords on 28 Jul that he had earlier asked "whether our old and most faithful ally had not been sacrificed by Ministers in the recent proceedings relative to Belgium? His own opinion was, that it would appear that the King of Holland had been sacrificed—had been basely and treacherously treated by his Majesty's present Ministers." George Hamilton Gordon, 4th Earl of Aberdeen, observed similarly that the King of Holland, though he had acted "with the utmost degree of fairness, candour, and good faith", had been "most harshly and cruelly treated". Hansard 3rd s v 462, 1020.

[9] *The Times* 12 Aug 1831: "The Dutch Government, as might have been expected, has yielded to the remonstrances of its friends in the London Conference, and has consented to withdraw its troops within its own frontier. This was announced in Parliament last night, and must appear to all the friends of European tranquillity and national independence a . . . valuable triumph . . .". *The Times* acknowledged that William "has been hardly treated in being required to subscribe to one set of conditions, while he had given his consent to another on the engagement that the arrangement was to be final". *The Times, M Chron,* and *Ed Rev* continued to support the Belgians against the Dutch. An English fleet had sailed towards the Scheldt on 12 Aug. C's words of defence for William simultaneously castigate Grey's government.

[10] In shifting this analogy to Necker and Grey in *TT* (1835) (36:293) HNC, in a footnote, took the couplet as a para-

When Leopold said he was called to *"reign over* 4,000,000 noble Belgians"[11]—I thought it would have been nearer the truth if he had said that he was called to *"rein in* 4,000,000 restive asses."   [36:323]

I was uncommonly amused at the grave pleasantry of Sir George Murray in asking Ministers if they had contemplated a successor to Leopold—who has been King some fortnight.[12]

O. P. Q. in the Morning Chronicle is a clever fellow.[13] He is for the greatest possible happiness for the greatest possible number of men for the greatest possible time! So am I—so are you, and every one round the tea table. First, however, what does O. P. Q. mean by the word "Happiness": and secondly, How does he propose to make other persons agree in *his* definition of the term? Don't you see the ridiculous absurdity of setting up that as a principle or motive of action which is in fact a necessary and essential instinct of our very nature—an inborn and inextinguishable desire? How can creatures susceptible of Pleasure and Pain do otherwise than desire happiness? But what Happiness? The Indian *n*Savage in scalping his fallen enemy pursues *his* happiness naturally and adequately. An Indian Bentham or O. P. Q. would necessarily hope for the greatest possible indulgence in scalping for the greatest possible number of Indians.[14] There is no escaping this absurdity, unless you

n f 49ᵛ

---

phrase of RS *A Ballad of a Young Man That Would Read Unlawful Books, and How He Was Punished: The Minor Poems of Robert Southey* (3 vols 1815) III 92–5. A somewhat nearer parallel is Goethe *Der Zauberlehrling: Musenalmanach* for 1798 (the year of RS's ballad). Goethe is thought to have taken the story from a translation of Lucian by Christoph Wieland in 1788, but the spectacular failure of a novice in magic is a common theme in German and other folklore. C himself in the *M Post* 15 Jan 1800 had referred to "the fable of the Magician, who having ordered his ministering imps to destroy the infernal abodes, was himself torn in pieces by them, and carried off in a whirlwind". *EOT (CC)* I 107. Then the magicians were Pitt and his cabinet.

[11] C's source untraced.

[12] Sir George Murray (1772–1846), general and statesman, M.P. for Perth from 1823, Colonial Secretary 1828–30,

asked questions about foreign policy on 12 Aug: "There was one other point on which the British public would naturally look for information, namely, whether any, and what kind of provision had been made to secure a successor to the present king of Belgium. During the present contest he was daily exposing himself to peril, and it would be exceedingly satisfactory to know if in the event of his death, who was to become his successor." *M Chron* 13 Aug 1831. Continuing "the grave pleasantry", he asked if it were the son of the French king, then in the French army of 50,000 in Belgium.

[13] John Wilks (d 1846), swindler (*DNB*), contributed regularly to the *M Chron* at this time over the initials O.P.Q. In beginning a new series on 26 Jul 1831 he announced: "I belong to the party which desires the 'greatest possible happiness of the greatest number for the greatest period of time'."

[14] O.P.Q. came down repeatedly for

come back to a standard of Reason and Duty, as imperative upon our mere pleasurable sensations. O! but I am for the happiness of others! Of others! are you indeed? I happen to be one of those others—and so far as I can judge from what you show me of your habits and views, I would rather be excused from your banquet of happiness. *Your* mode of happiness would make me miserable. To go about doing as much *good* as possible to as many men as possible—is indeed an excellent thing for a man to propose to himself; but in order that you may not sacrifice the real good and happiness of others to your particular views, which may be quite different from your neighbour's—you must do *that* good to others, which the Reason, common to all men, pronounces to be good to all.[15] In this sense your maxim is so true as to be a*º* truism. But it is objected that in fact I do these good actions for the pleasure of a good conscience![16] Heaven help us and our logic! Don't you see that if Conscience, which is in its nature a consequence, were thus anticipated and made an antecedent—a party instead of a judge—it would*ᵖ* dishonor your draft upon it—it would not pay the demand? Don't you see that in truth the very fact of acting with this motive properly and logically destroys all claim upon conscience to give you any pleasure at all?   [36:324, 325]

There are, no doubt, many good men in the House of Commons. Sir Robert Inglis and Peel and others.[17] But they never have the courage to take their stand upon Duty, and appeal to all men *as men*—to the Good and the True which exists for *all*, and of which *all* have an apprehension.

º ~~the~~ a   *ᵖ* would ~~not~~

---

the "greatest happiness principle" of Jeremy Bentham (1748–1832) as the way to a future free of the "despotic authority which has hitherto disposed of nations". Perhaps only to identify the Indians as of North America, *TT* (1835) specified "a Chickasaw, or Pawnee Bentham". It is C, however, who assumed that an Indian might find his greatest happiness in scalping. C's copy of Pierre Étienne Dumont's translation from Bentham, *Traités de législation civile et pénale* (3 vols Paris 1802), was left with WW. *WW LC* 317. Presumably C had not acquired the work when he noted its existence in 1804. *CN* II 1967.

[15] O.P.Q had written from Paris on 18 Feb that the "whole state of your social and political society is disorganized—is perishing—and must be changed". *M Chron* 21 Feb 1831. He denounced the "London Protocolists" for not considering the wishes and happiness of the Belgians in their deliberations to secure peace. Perhaps C's appeal to the common reason, able to declare what is good for all, is to be taken as less Rousseauistic and Godwinian than it sounds, with an emphasis on the limited "good to all" that remains when individual preferences have been subtracted.

[16] *TT* (1835), making the rest of the paragraph a separate entry, attributed the objection to "old Hobbes".

[17] This is the Peel who on 2 Jul 1830 (above, at n 9) "had ruined himself for ever by his glaring inconsistency"—an observation prudently omitted from *TT* (1835). Inglis (see 13 Apr 1830, above, and n 18) had become Tory M.P. for Oxford by defeating Peel there on the issue of Catholic emancipation in 1829.

They always set to work by appealing to individual interests; the measure will be advantageous to linen drapers, or bricklayers or brewers et id genus omne.[18] Whereas their adversaries, the Demagogues, always work on the opposite*q* principle; they always appeal to Man as Man; and, as you know, the most terrible convulsions in society have been wrought by such phrases—as Rights of Man—Sovereignty of the People &c; which no one understands—which apply to no one in particular, but to all in general. The Devil works in the same way—he is a very clever fellow—I have no acquaintance with him, but I respect his talents.*r*[19] Consistent Truth and Goodness will in the end overcome every thing; but inconsistent Good can never contend with consistent Evil. I look in vain for some man to sound the word Duty in the ears of this Generation.[20]	[36:326]

The English Public are not yet ripe to comprehend the essential difference between the Reason and the Understanding,—between a Principle and a Maxim—an eternal Truth and a mere conclusion from a generalization of a great number of Facts.[21] A man having seen a million moss

q f 50, the leaf beginning mid-word, "site"
r talents; he always seduces ((I mean in the large way)) by appealing to men

[18] "All persons of that sort". Usually such Latin tags first emerge in *TT* (1835); this one becomes "and so forth" in *TT* (1835), in which the words "this clause will bear hard on bobbin-net or poplins" may be anachronistic. *OED* records no use of "bobbin-net" before Charles Babbage mentioned the new machine (for the imitation of bobbin-lace) in 1832.

[19] That the Devil appeals with generalisations adds a twist to Antonio's observation that the "devil can cite Scripture". *The Merchant of Venice* I iii 99.

[20] C had sounded the word "Duty" in his first address of 1795—*Lects 1795 (CC)* 43—and in *The Watchman* of 17 Mar 1796 *(CC)* 122n; he had sounded it with increasing emphasis ever since. He called for a union of truth and goodness. William Page Wood recorded on 5 Mar 1829: "Went to Coleridge's in the evening with Montagu and young Edgeworth, a brother of Miss Edgeworth . . . Coleridge wandered into metaphysical depths and mazes, talking of the characteristic of reason or the pure idea being

the impossibility of defining it; its definition involving contradictions, &c. &c. If he means simply to say that that which understands cannot itself as a whole be understood, I can agree with him; otherwise I should feel some difficulty, when no proposition is offered, to assent. His illustrations were occasionally very beautiful. I like also his idea of truth, of its being an eternity, as it were, in itself, which we cannot feel ere we arrive at perfect conviction." *Memoir of Hatherley* I 189–90. Godwin in 1793 had been well before C in denying "the right in certain cases to do as we list"; for Godwin all rights were passive, none active, and all subservient to the duty each individual must pay to reason, justice, utility, and the passive rights of others. *Enquiry Concerning Political Justice* bk II chs 5–6, bk VIII ch 1 (3rd ed 2 vols 1798) I 158–82, II 422–3.

[21] In early lectures and journalism upon current events C had understandably proclaimed the superiority of facts over the opinions of his aversaries. He gradually began to assign the accumula-

roses all red concludes from his own experience and that of others that all moss roses are red. That is a maxim with him—the greatest amount of his knowledge on the subject. But it is only true until some gardener has produced a white moss rose; after which the maxim is good for nothing. Again suppose Adam watching the Sun sinking under the horizon for the first time; he is seized with gloom and terror, relieved with scarce a ray of hope of ever seeing the glorious light again. The next evening when it declines, his hopes are stronger, but mixed with fear; and even at the end of 1000 years, all that a man can*s* feel, is hope*t* and an expectation so strong as to preclude anxiety.[22] Compare this in its highest degree with the assurance which you have that the two sides of any triangle are greater than the third. This demonstrated of one triangle is seen to be eternally true of all imaginable triangles. This is the truth perceived at once by the Reason, wholly independently of experience. It is and must ever be so, multiply and vary the shapes and sizes of triangles as you may.[23]   [36:327]

---

s ~~could~~ can   *t* ~~an assurance~~ hope

---

tion of facts not only to the mere understanding but more specifically to utilitarians, as in his attacks in the *Courier* on the educational system of Joseph Lancaster. *EOT (CC)* II 327–33, 393–7. For attacks on deductions from fact see *CN* III 3737, 4268, 4358 and nn.

[22] In initiating "Skeptical Doubts Concerning the Operations of the Understanding" Hume had written: "*That the sun will not rise tomorrow*, is no less intelligible a proposition, and implies no more contradiction, than the affirmation, *that it will rise.*" *An Inquiry Concerning Human Understanding* § 4 pt 1. Four paragraphs later, he pointed out that Adam's rational faculties could not have enabled him to infer "from the fluidity and transparency of water, that it would suffocate him; or from the light and warmth of fire, that it would consume him". *Essays and Treatises on Several Subjects* (4 vols Edinburgh 1825) II 24, 25–6. Hume did not attribute "gloom and terror" to Adam or to others limited by induction. The accepted doctrine, summarised in the Transcendental Analytic bk II ch 2 of the *Critique of Pure Reason*, assumed that repeated observation and comparison of observations led first to the dis-

covery of an invariable rule and then to a general conception of cause. Kant (with Hume before him) found in such an accumulation of observations only a supposititious universality and therefore only a supposition of necessary cause.

[23] Richard Price (1723–91), a nonconformist friend of revolutions, had written in a work first published in 1758: ". . . from any *particular* idea of a triangle, it is said we can frame the *general* one; but does not the very reflexion said to be necessary to this, on a greater or lesser triangle, imply, that the general idea is already in the mind? How else should it know how to go to work, or what to reflect on?—That the universality consists in the *idea*; and not merely in the *name* as used to signify a number of particulars, *resembling* that which is the immediate object of reflexion, is plain . . .". *A Review of the Principal Questions and Difficulties in Morals* (2nd ed 1769) 37–8. C had used the triangle as his example in explaining to Thomas Clarkson in Oct 1806 the characteristics of universality and necessity that distinguish reason from understanding. *CL* II 1198. Hume, in the paragraph before the sentence on the sun quoted in n 22, above, had de-

"We have behaved very unfairly to Ireland; we have not civilized the natives, and yet we have interfered so far as to prevent them from cutting each other's throats to any useful extent.[24] We were bound to let the Irish run an equal race with other savages—either civilize them forcibly—or else leave them to keep down their verminous population in the way common to all other savage tribes—by mutual homicide. Five and twenty years ago and more I said in "sport" that the time might come, when the English themselves would cry out against the Union; that time is now come, and the cry will ere long become a loud one.[25] The true English character has since the peace very materially suffered from the deluge of Paddyism in England, which the Union originated and will, if preserved, augment. The connection of Ireland with England has been from first to last a source of unqualified evil and weakness to England; the soldiers and sailors obtained from Ireland might have been obtained, and better, in England and Scotland, and their whole number has been required to keep Ireland itself in that sort of murderous armistice in which, for the most part, it has ever been.[v]

It used to be said that 4 and 5 make 9. Locke says that 4 and 5 *are* 9. Now I say that 4 and 5 *are not* 9, but that they will *make* 9. When I see 4 objects which will form a square and 5 which will form a pentagon—I see

[u] f 50[v]   [u-v] For the variant in MS F see App C, below   [v] See [u-v], above

clared: "Though there never were a circle or triangle in nature, the truths demonstrated by Euclid would forever retain their certainty and evidence."

[24] These harsh remarks on the Irish population, though toned down in MS F, were cut from that ms and left unpublished. Similar language in the *M Post* 15 Jan 1800 was explained on 22 Jan as describing a condition for which England was to blame, and not "the poor sufferers in Ireland". *EOT (CC)* i 106, 117–21. Taking a similar line herself, SC explained in 1850: "My Father never ceased to be heartily sorry for these our misdoings, and he ever held the burden of them only to be lightened by confession and amendment, not by indiscriminate accusation of the Irish and their *Celtic blood*. Not but that he strongly felt the defects of their present national character, and the trouble to England connected with the guardianship of so unruly

a ward. I have heard him laughingly suggest, that it would be a blessing to Albion if Erin and all her emerald plains could be snatched up by some Titan Angel to whom belongs the ordering of the terraqueous globe, like a green nest in the talons of an enormous Roc, and dropped in the middle of Polynesia to tempest the Pacific. But such as these are dangerous thoughts to indulge, and lead to harsh dealings." *EOT* i xxxix. SC cited evidence that Englishmen talked similarly in Spenser's day.

[25] The United Kingdom of Great Britain and Ireland came into being on 1 Jan 1801. In 1803 C remembered his pain when Pitt, whom he thought contemptible, brought about "the Irish Union, deemed by me a great & wise measure". *CN* i 1606. By "five and twenty years ago" C does not mean to date his change of opinion precisely in 1806. See also 17 Dec 1831 (at n 3), below.

that they are two different things—when combined, they will form a third different figure which we call 9. When separate they *are not* it, but can *make* it.[26]   [36:328]

S. T. C. 11. Sept. 1831.[1]

Drayton is a sweet poet, and Selden's notes to the Poly-Olbion well worth reading.[2] Daniel[a] is a superior man; his diction is preeminently

[a] Daniell

[26] This entry reverts to the discussion of reason and understanding, which it follows in *TT* (1835). Kant had added to *Critik der reinen Vernunft* Einleitung 5.1 (2nd ed Riga 1787) 13, tr John Watson (1888): "At first sight it may seem that the proposition 7 + 5 = 12 is purely analytic, and follows, by the principle of contradiction, from the conception of a sum of 7 and 5. But when we look more closely we see that the conception of the sum of 7 and 5 is merely the idea of the union of the two numbers, and in no way enables us to tell what may be the single number that forms their sum. . . . To get beyond the separate ideas of 7 and 5, I must call in the aid of perception, referring to my five fingers, or to five points . . . The propositions of arithmetic are therefore all synthetic." C uses Kant's numbers to illustrate the point in *Logic (CC)* 201. Confirmation of C's appeal to usage in the propositions of arithmetic appears in Hazlitt's surprising acceptance of Horne Tooke's explanation that "and" = "add": "Thus the word, *And*, he explained clearly enough to be the verb *add*, or a corruption of the old Saxon, *anandad*. 'Two *and* two make four,' that is, 'two *add* two make four.' " *The Spirit of the Age* (2nd ed 1825) 116. C's most extended denigration of the empirical philosopher John Locke (1632–1704) occurs early, in letters to Josiah Wedgwood in Feb 1801 and in continuation to Poole in Mar. *CL* II 677–803, 708–9. See also JTC'S report of 20 Apr 1811 (at nn 19, 20) and HNC's of 27 Apr 1823 (at n 6), above. HCR heard C

speak "with great contempt" of Locke on 23 Dec 1810: see App F 15, below.
[1] On 4 Sept, anticipating a visit to Ottery St Mary the following week, HNC wrote to the family: "My Uncle is much as usual—very grand & eloquent, & my memorabilia augment rapidly." BM Add MS 47557 f 86. Knowing that he and SC would depart on the 12th, he visited C on Sunday the 11th.
[2] Most of C's references to the poetry of Michael Drayton (1563–1631) are ambiguously for and against. In Jul 1802 he quoted to William Sotheby six lines from *Poly-Olbion* as displaying a "vile commonplace trashy style" rare in Drayton. *CL* II 811–12. In 1805 he found the fable of the maddening rain, which he himself had essayed in Lect 6 on religion in 1795 and would elaborate in *The Friend* No 1, in Drayton's *The Moon-Calf*, "most miserably marred in the telling". *Lects 1795 (CC)* 215, *Friend (CC)* I 8–9, *CN* II 2626. His citations from Drayton can be found in *B Poets* III, including the Latin line quoted by John Selden in the "Address to the Reader" prefixed to *Poly-Olbion* and supplied as a motto to *LB* (1800). *CL* I 617; *CN* II 2468. C referred Byron in 1816 to the werewolf in Drayton *The Man in the Moone* lines 12–13, and in *BL* ch 20 called WW's *To Joanna* a "noble imitation of Drayton". *CL* IV 628; *BL (CC)* II 104. From Drayton's weightedly historical works (and historical matter is his chief link with Daniel) C selected the mythic, particularly moon-myths. For C on Drayton's *Nimphidia* and *Ideas* see *CM (CC)* I 57. *TT* (1835) specified Sel-

pure—of that sort which I believe has always existed somewhere in society—just such without any alteration as Wordsworth or Sir George Beaumont might have spoken or written in the present day.[3]   [36:329]

My system is the only attempt that I know of ever made to reduce all knowledges into harmony; it opposes no other system, but shows what was true in each, and how that which was true[b] in the particular in each of them became error because it was only half the truth. I have endeavored to unite the insulated fragments of truth and frame a perfect mirror.[4]

[b] truthe

den's notes to "the early part" of *Poly-Olbion* and inserted in the entry a paragraph on "instances of sublimity" in Drayton, with a sample taken near the end of *Poly-Olbion* VII. In his note in *TT* (1835) HNC quoted praise of Drayton in RS *The Doctor* ch 36 pt 1 (2 vols 1834) II 33–6.

[3] WW's "austere purity of language both grammatically and logically" is likened to that of Samuel Daniel (1562–1619), "whose diction bears no mark of time", and their sentiments are equally characterised as simple and timeless, in *BL* ch 22 *(CC)* II 142, 146–7. In 1805 C found Sir John Davies (c 1585–1618) an even better exemplar than Daniel of the standard of purity established in Elizabethan English. *CN* II 2645. Daniel is prominent in C's life. On 8 Mar 1804, two months after he had found in Daniel passages for his own projected "Comforts and Consolations", he sent "Daniel's Poems with the eminent Passages of the Hymen's Triumph (for which alone I have sent them) *marked*" to Sir George Beaumont, named in the present entry for correctness and ease of speech. *CN* II 1793–5, 1835 f 66; *CL* II 1079. In 1808 C annotated the *Civil Wars* in Lamb's copy of Daniel *Poetical Works* (2 vols 1798) and wrote two letters on the blank leaves asking Lamb to think more highly of the poem. *CM (CC)* II 116–30. He also copied two stanzas from the poem into N 18, used in the *Courier* 7 Dec 1809. *CN* III 3655; *EOT (CC)* II 42. In the *Courier* of 20 Sept 1814 he quoted lines as from the *Civil Wars*, but they

have not been found in that poem. See *EOT (CC)* II 378 and n 12. Of Beaumont HCR noted in 1823: "Sir George is himself a very elegant man and talks well on matters of art." *CRB* I 291. Farington's diary records with respect Beaumont's opinions on a wide range of subjects.

[4] René Wellek, troubled for more than fifty years by C's eclecticism and his attempts to reconcile empirical and idealistic approaches that all systematic philosophers have declared incompatible, assessed such claims as this of 1831: "Coleridge differs from almost all preceding English writers by his claim to an epistemology and metaphysics from which he derives his aesthetics and finally his literary theory and critical principles. He aimed at a complete systematic unity and continuity even though in practice he left wide gaps. But he made an attempt and he insisted rightly on the significance of the attempt." *A History of Modern Criticism, 1750–1950: The Romantic Age* (New Haven 1955) 158. C is certainly not saying that he hopes to arrive "finally" at literary theory; nineteenth-century readers of this entry would have sympathised with his desire to bring all knowledge in aid of their reflections on divinity and faith. C recognised his own revulsions against system even in the act of reconciling "insulated fragments of truth". *TT* (1835) began the entry: "My system, if I may venture to give it so fine a name". In N 29 C wrote: "One main Object of my Work is to establish the difference of the Spiritual alike from 1. the Notional; 2. the Phae-

I show to each system that I fully understand and ᶜrightfully appreciate what that system means; but then I lift up that system to a higher point of view, from which I enableᵈ it to see its former position where it was indeed, but under another light and with different relations; so that the fragment of truthᵉ is not only acknowledged, but explained. So the old astronomers discovered and maintained much that was true, but because they were placed on a false ground, and looked from the wrong point of view, they never did—they never could—discover *the* truth—that is the whole truth.[5] As soon as they left the earth—their false centre—and took their stand in the Sun—immediately they saw the whole system in the true light—and their former station remaining—but remaining a part of the prospect. I wish in short,ᶠ to connect by a moral copula Natural History with Political History—or in other words, to make History scientific, and Science historical—to take from History its accidentality—and from Science its fatalism.[6]   [36:330]

I never from a boy could under any circumstances feel the slightest dread of death; in all my illnesses I have ever had the most intense desire to be released from this life[7]—unchecked by any but one wish—viz. to be able to finish my work on Philosophy. Not that I have any author's vanity on

---

nomenal; and 3. the Carnal—and that it alone is the Truth that verily and indeed is." *CN* IV 4924.

[5] I.e. the Copernican revolution, regarding the solar system no longer as geocentric but as heliocentric, made possible "the famous Kepler . . . whom we all know as the beginning of truly scientific astronomy". *P Lects* Lect 11 (1949) 331.

[6] In *LS* (1817) in quoting Berkeley *Siris* C substituted for Berkeley's rejection of fatalism and Sadducism "the doctrines of Necessity and Materialism, with the consequent denial of men's responsibility, of his corrupt and fallen nature, and of the whole scheme of Redemption by the incarnate Word". *LS (CC)* 192 and n 4. It is for these losses through the corpuscular experimental sciences that C attempts to compensate while bringing greater exactness to such study of prophetic history as to "create the noblest kind of Imaginative Power in your Soul, that of living in past ages"; give power to "anticipate the Future"; and "live a truly human life, a life of reason, in the Present". Annotation on *Reliquiae Baxterianae: CM (CC)* I 280.

[7] Henry Taylor, who took John Stuart Mill, James Stephen, and "Mr Elliot" (M.P., according to *CL* VI 872) to Highgate on 22 Sept, wrote of C: "Poor man, he has been for two months past under the influence of cholera and other extra disorders, by which he seems sadly enfeebled and even crippled"; there was consequently "not such continuous and unintermitted eloquence as I have sometimes heard from him, but the 'flash and outbreak of a fiery mind' from time to time". *Correspondence* ed Dowden 39. C wrote of a "sad relapse" as early as 21 Aug, and similarly to J. H. Green in the only known letters from September (there are none from October). To Poole on 7 Oct HNC wrote that C "has had two very severe attacks of the prevailing cholera, & suffered dreadfully under them". *CL* VI 874n.

the subject; God knows, I should be absolutely *glad*, if I could hear that the *thing had* already been done before me.[8] [36:331]

Illness never in the smallest degree affects my intellectual powers—I can *think* with all the vigor I can ever possess in the midst of pain—but I am beset wth the most wretched—unmanly[g]—reluctance shrinking from action.[9] I could not take the pen in hand to write down what I was thinking—for all the world. [36:332]

---

^a26. Oct. 1831. S. C.[1]

Few men of Genius are keen; but almost every man of Genius is subtle.[2] If you ask the difference between keenness and subtlety—I answer that

[g] unmanningly   [a] f 51ᵛ; for HNC's note in the space above the date see n 1, below

[8] The *"thing"* is the subject of the previous paragraph (36:330), the reconciliation of empirical demonstrations with certainty that the human mind can know ultimate reality. His "work on Philosophy" was probably the Opus Maximum.

[9] C had written to Richard Sharp on 15 Jan 1804 of a severe illness at Grasmere, "not that my inner Being was disturbed—on the contrary, it seemed more than usually serene and self-sufficing—but the exceeding Pain . . . had taken away from me the connecting Link of voluntary power . . . between the Vital and the Organic—or . . . Mind and it's sensuous Language". *CL* ii 1032. McLellan reported of his visit of 27 Apr 1832: "I inquired whether his mental powers were affected by such intense suffering; 'Not at all,' said he, 'my body and head appear to hold no connexion; the pain of my body, blessed be God, never reaches my mind.' " *Journal* 231. In MS A p 75 HNC copied variatim a marginal note, which he dated 7 Feb 1821, from *Reliquiae Baxterianae*, in which C compared his lot with Baxter's, but noted "how much less have my bodily Evils been, & yet how very much greater an impediment have I suffered them to be! . . ." *CM (CC)* i 299.

[1] Although C was very ill during much of this period, the gap from 11 Sept to 26 Oct (Wed) is accounted for by HNC's absence in Devon. To Mrs C, who remained in Hampstead with Herbert, HC wrote with ironic reference to the fears in Devon of disturbances over Reform: "If I understand aright, Sara and her spouse are gone to Ottery without the Bab." *HCL* 134, HNC and SC returned together on 23 Oct. SC to Elizabeth Crump Waddell 2 Nov 1831: DCL ms; SC letters at UT. The entries for 26 Oct are in HNC's hand, but the "*S.C.*" beside the date may mean that it was Sara who reported (and perhaps first recorded elsewhere) the talk. HNC wrote to RS on 31 Oct that C had been desperately ill but was now getting about again. UT ms.

In the space above the date, f 51ᵛ, HNC wrote a note about an "admirable sermon" of Robert South in *Sermons Preached upon Several Occasions* (3 vols Oxford 1679). As space remains unused at the bottom of f 51, the note may occupy space originally left vacant for TT (to be filled in by SC?).

[2] C frequently defined genius by noting its opposites, as in TT distinguishing genius from talent and excluding from genius both selfishness and envy. The keenness he allows here is usually confined to the clever. In 1825 Gioacchino de' Prati listened to C at Highgate: "To show how hard it is for one who translates to give the true meaning of his au-

it is the difference between a point and an edge. To split a hair is no proof of subtlety[b] for subtlety[b] acts in distinguishing differences—in showing that two things apparently one[c] are in fact two; whereas to split a hair is to cause Division and not to perceive Difference.[3]   [36:333]

There is undoubtedly a limit to the exertions of an Advocate for his Client. He has a right—it is duty—to do every thing which his Client might honestly do—and to do it with all the effect which any exercise of skill, talent or knowledge of his own may produce. But he has no right—nor is it his duty—to do that for his Client which his Client in foro conscientiae[4] has no right to do for himself—as for example to put in evidence a forged deed or will, knowing it to be so forged. As to mere confounding of witnesses by skilful cross-examination, I own I am not disposed to be very strict. The whole thing is perfectly well understood on all hands, and it is little more in general than a sort of cudgel playing between the Counsel and the Witness.[d] It is of the utmost importance[e] in [f]the administration of justice, that knowledge and intellects should be as

---

[b] subtilty   [c] t̶h̶e̶ one   [d] P̶r̶i̶s̶o̶n̶e̶r̶ Witness.   [e] importance. t̶h̶e̶   [f] f 52

---

thor—take, for instance, our word clever and the German gemüthlich. Neither can the German convey, but by periphrasis, ideas which the single word 'clever' signifies, nor [the English] that which the Germans understand under 'gemüthlich.'

"A clever man is not merely a man of talent—indeed, he may possess but moderate talents, little knowledge, and be clever.

"The clever man is a product [produce: 1838] of a certain tact acquired by great practice. Yes, talent is a natural gift, cleverness an artificial one. The clever man does not what is the best, but that which is most to the purpose; his actions are not the offspring of principle, but of circumstances, to which he knows how to accommodate himself. If he is an artist, he produces that which fetches the greatest money; if a politician, he advises that which is most feasible for certain purposes; in morality, in religion, in every thing he is a latitudinarian. In fact, clever men are those which Tacitus calls *callidi temporum et sapientes*. Now, what language can convey the ideas which we associate with the one word

'clever'? and who can translate your 'gemüthlich'? The very nature of the English, that which we call sterling English, is an antithesis to that which you call gemüthlich. In fact, our peculiarity is to be stern or humorous. In the whole gallery of Shakspeare's characters, there is not one trace of 'gemüth' or 'gemüthlich.' " *Penny Satirist* II (1838) 4, quoted in M. H. Fisch "The Coleridges, Dr. Prati, and Vico" *Modern Philology* XLI (1943) 122; cf *C Talker* xxiii–xxiv.

[3] C distinguished "distinction" from "division", because "Distinct *notions* do not suppose different *things*", in *Friend (CC)* I 177n (II 104n). In another typical example, a note on *Reliquiae Baxterianae*, he amplified a contrast by John Kenyon to protest the tendency of RS to see "all Difference as Diversity". *CM (CC)* I 331.

[4] "In the law-court of the conscience". HNC would have special interest in questions of law. If he is supposed to be absent during these remarks, however, C's advice to other lawyers—e.g. young men brought by JTC—could have been heard by SC.

far as possible equalized: hence the necessity for an order of Advocates—men whose duty[g] it should be to know what the Law allows—but whose interests should be wholly indifferent as to the persons or characters of their Clients. Necessary means to a legitimate end are themselves legitimate; and if a certain latitude in examining witnesses is, as experience seems to have shown, a necessary mean towards the evisceration of truth—I have no doubt in saying that such latitude is morally justifiable.[5] We must be content with a certain quantum in this life; the necessities of society demand it; we must not be righteous overmuch—nor wise overmuch—and, as an old father says—in what vein may there not be a plethora, when the Scripture tells us that there may be too much of virtue and of wisdom.[6]

Still I think that upon the whole the Advocate is placed in an unfavourable position for his moral being—and indeed also for his intellect in its higher sphere. Therefore I would recommend an Advocate to devote a part of his leisure time to some study of the metaphysics of the Mind or metaphysics of Theology—something, I mean, which shall call forth all his powers and center his wishes in the investigation of Truth alone, without reference to a side to be supported. No studies give such a power of distinguishing as metaphysical, and in their natural tendency they are ennobling and exalting. Some such studies are wanted to counteract the operation of legal studies and practice—which sharpen indeed, but like[h] a grinding stone—narrow[i] as they sharpen.   [36:334]

[j]I cannot say what the French Peers *will* do; but I can tell you what they *ought* to do.[7] "So far", they might say, "as our feelings and interests as individuals are concerned in this matter—if it really be the prevailing wish of our fellow-countrymen to destroy the hereditary Peerage—we shall without regret retire into the ranks of the private citizens. But we

---

[g] duties̶y̶   [h] s̶h̶a̶r̶p̶e̶n̶ like   [i] b̶y̶ narrow̶i̶n̶g̶ ̶a̶t̶ ̶t̶h̶e̶ ̶s̶a̶m̶e̶ ̶t̶i̶m̶e̶ ̶(̶i̶n̶ ̶t̶h̶e̶   [j] f 52ᵛ

[5] The opening clause, "Necessary means to a legitimate end are themselves legitimate", is omitted from *TT* (1835). The point is not that ends justify convenient or prudential means; rather, a legitimate end justifies a means to that end when no alternative means are discernible. *TT* (1835) introduced a dozen verbal changes, mostly qualifications by expansion.

[6] Prov 23.4, "cease from thine own wisdom", and Eccles 1.18, "in much wisdom is much grief", strike notes repeated throughout the Bible. In Luke 10.41 Martha is reproved for being "careful and troubled" in serving Jesus:

"God reckons righteousness apart from works" (Rom 4.6 RSV)—all confirming Eccles 7.16: "Be not righteous over much; neither make thyself over wise . . .". C's "old father" untraced.

[7] On threats to the French peerage see 30 Jul 1831 and n 6 above. Reports from Paris in *The Times* had continued to link the precarious state of the French peerage to rejection of the Reform Bill by the British House of Lords (20 Sept, 15 Oct, 22 Oct, 31 Oct). C invented language for beleaguered groups at least as early as his words for the oppressed people of Denmark in *The Plot Discovered: Lects 1795 (CC)* 315–18.

are bound by the provisions of the existing constitution to consider ourselves collectively as essential to the well-being of France; we have been
placed here on purpose to defend what France a short time ago, at least,
thought a vital part of its Government; and what answer could we make
hereafter to France itself, if she*k* should come to see what we still think
to be an error in the light in which we view it? We should be justly
branded as traitors and cowards, who had deserted the post which we
were specially appointed to maintain. As a House of Peers, therefore—
as*l* one branch*m* of the Legislature*n*—we can never in honor or conscience
consent to a measure, of the impolicy and dangerous consequences of
which we are convinced. If therefore, this measure is demanded by the
country—let the King and the Deputies form themselves into a Constituent Assembly, and then assuming to act in the name of the total nation,
let them decree the abolition. In that case we yield to a just, perhaps, but
a revolutionary act—in which we do not participate, and against which
we are upon the supposition quite powerless. If the Deputies, however,
consider themselves so completely in the light of Delegates as to be at
present absolutely pledged to vote without freedom of deliberation—let
a concise, but perspicuous summary of the ablest arguments that can be
adduced on either side be drawn up and printed and circulated throughout
the country—and then after two months, let the Deputies demand fresh
instructions on this point. One thing as men of honor we declare beforehand *o*that—come what will—none of us who are now Peers will ever
accept a Peerage created de novo[8] for life.''[9]   [36:335]

---

20. Nov. 1831.

These wretched Ministers have been guilty of two preeminently wicked
things in their conduct upon this Reform Bill.[1] They have endeavored to

k ~~the~~ she   *l* ~~the~~ as   *m* ~~constitue~~ branch   *n* Legislati~~ve~~ure   *o* f 53

[8] ''Anew''.

[9] In 1831 discussions like C's of the
threatened conversion of hereditary peerages into seats for life in the upper house
of the legislature were pointed more towards Reform in Britain than towards the
crisis in France. At Lord Grey's urging
William iv had signed patents for the creation of new peers in June and September. With the Reform Bill yet to be
passed, a petition was introduced in the
Commons on 20 Oct, the day of prorogation, to vote an address to the King

asking for the creation of ''such a number of Peers as might be thought requisite
for the success of a new Reform Bill''.
Hansard 3rd s viii 929. The younger Pitt
and his successors had more than doubled the number of peers to serve political ends, but after September William iv
refused further creations for Grey's purpose of swamping conservative lords.

[1] After Parliament was dissolved on
22 Apr and Grey's party greatly strengthened by the election in June, the Reform
Bill was reintroduced on 24 Jun with

carry a fundamental change in the material^a and mode of action of the Government of the country by so exciting the passions and playing upon the necessary ignorance of the numerical majority of the nation—that all freedom and utility of discussion by competent heads in the proper place should be precluded. In doing this they have used, or sanctioned, arguments which may be applied with equal or even greater force to the carrying of any measure whatever—however atrocious in its character and destructive in its consequences. They have appealed directly to the argument of the greater number of voices—no matter whether those voices were drunk or sober, competent or not competent; and they have done the utmost in their power to rase out the sacred principle of a Representation of Interests; and to introduce the mad and barbarizing scheme of a Delegation of Individuals.[2] And they have done all this without one word of thankfulness to God for the manifold blessings of which the constitution as settled at the Revolution—imperfect as it may be—has been the source or vehicle to this great Nation,—without one honest statement of the manner in which the anomalies in the practice grew up,^{b} or any manly

---

^{a} ~~form~~ material ^{b} up, ~~& the~~

---

changes including a clause that denied the franchise to those who made payments on their £10 rent more frequently than half-yearly; after the Commons passed the revised Bill on 22 Sept it was rejected by 41 votes in the Lords on 8 Oct. Parliament, prorogued on 20 Oct for further adjustments to the bill, was set to convene again on 22 Nov. HNC's anonymous *Notes on the Reform Bill, by a Barrister* had a 2nd ed with a Preface dated April, 1831, and a 3rd dated in the same form, "Lincoln's Inn, June, 1831". A copy of the 3rd among the family papers at UT bears on the title-page, not in his hand, "H. N. Coleridge/ Hampstead".

[2] C's first general defences of representation as against delegation from "universal suffrage" arose in analysis of the new constitutions of 1799 and 1802 in France, but the clear antithesis even then was between the methods of election to Congress in the United States and "government by popular representation", a genial principle that ancient Greece and Rome had left it to the English to discover. *M Post* 7, 26–31 Dec 1799, 25 Sept 1802: *EOT (CC)* I 31–6,

46–57, 327–8. From Locke's *Two Treatises of Government* (1690) had stemmed the widely accepted premise that each man was the best judge of his own self-interest and the increasingly common deduction that each should have an equal vote in the determination of national policies that concerned the self-interest of each. The first strong challenge to these doctrines came from Rousseau *Du contrat social* bk II ch 3, although C attributed to Rousseau the spread among the "vain, ignorant, and intoxicated populace" the doctrine of the inalienable sovereignty of the people. C treated Rousseau's distinction between the *volonté de tous* and the *volonté générale* as a rhetorical and unconsidered admission of "the nothingness of the whole system", and defined the general will as "a casual over-balance of wills". *Friend (CC)* I 193–4 (II 127–8). That the later political positions of C, WW, and RS on the issues of this entry derived chiefly from Burke is the influential argument of Alfred Cobban *Edmund Burke and the Revolt Against the Eighteenth Century* (1929).

declaration of the inevitable necessities of government which those anomalies have answered,—with no humility, nor fear, nor reverence like Ham the accursed they have beckoned with grinning faces to a vulgar mob to insult over the nakedness of a parent:[3]—when ^cit had become them—if one spark of filial patriotism had been within their breasts—to have marched with silent steps and reverted faces to lay their robes upon his destitution. 2. They have made the King the prime mover in all this political wickedness;—they have made the King tell his[d] people that they were deprived of their Rights, and by direct and necessary implication that they and their ancestors for a century past had been slaves; they have made the King vilify the memories of his own brother and father.[4] Rights! There are no Rights whatever without correspondent Duties. How can a Christian, who owes even his Righteousness to God, claim a Right as of his own—when without Righteousness there can be no Right?[5] Look at the history of our Constitution, and you will see that our ancestors never upon any occasion stated as a ground for claiming any of their privileges an inherent right in themselves—you will no where in our

^c f 53ᵛ   ^d ~~the~~ his

[3] Gen 9.22–4. But it was Canaan, the son of Ham, who was cursed. Gen 9.25.

[4] On Grey's explanation that this would be the final reform, William IV gave unconditional assent to the Reform Bill in March. The King's speech opening Parliament on 21 Jun asked for action: "I have now to recommend that important question to your earliest and most attentive consideration"; his speech on the prorogation of Parliament on 20 Oct, which is probably most sharply in C's mind, went further: "The anxiety which has been so generally manifested by my people for the accomplishment of a Constitutional Reform . . . will I trust, be regulated by a due sense of the necessity of order and moderation in their proceedings. To the consideration of this important question the attention of Parliament must necessarily again be called at the opening of the ensuing Session; and you may be sure of my unaltered desire to promote its settlement, by such improvements in the Representation as may be found necessary for securing to my people the full enjoyment of their rights, which, in combination with those of other orders of the State, are essential to the support of our free Constitution." Hansard 3rd s IV 84, VIII 928. "Thus William IV, in reality a convinced Tory, encouraged the popular belief, a belief very useful to the Cabinet, that for the first time for a century the sovereign belonged to the popular party." Halévy *History* III 27.

[5] Representative assertions by C that rights obtain only with correspondent duties appear in *EOT (CC)* II 145, 380 n 2, 387, 393n–4. C's views on the Christian context of rights, claims, and duties are presented in Colmer *Coleridge: Critic of Society* 12, 157. Although C's attacks on abstract rights owed much to Burke, Godwin's stress upon duties of the individual to the general utility of society (14 Aug 1831 n 20, above) was probably C's earliest prod to derive right from obligation to God. C here uses "Righteousness" in the Pauline sense of faith, achievable through the Atonement, in the absolute sinlessness of God. Rom 1.17, 3.21–6. In *LS* (1817) C rejected the Evangelical reduction of righteousness to an aim of good works while taking for granted spiritual truths. *LS (CC)* 194.

Parliamentary records find the miserable sophism of the Rights of Man—No! they were too wise for that! they took good care to refer the claim to Custom and Prescription, and boldly—sometimes very impudently—asserted*e* it upon traditionary and constitutional grounds.[6] The Bill is bad enough, God knows—cumbrous—-impracticable—revolutionary,—but the arguments of its advocates, and the manner of their advocacy are a thousand times worse than the Bill itself.[7]   [36:336]

———

3. Dec. 1831.[1]

A Religion—that is, a true Religion—must consist of Ideas and of Facts both; not of Ideas alone without Facts,—for then it would be mere Philosophy; nor of Facts alone without Ideas of which those Facts *a*should be the symbols, or out of which they should arise, or upon which they should be grounded—for then it would be mere History.[2]   [36:337]

e asserted a   *a* f 54

[6] In making prescription and custom sacred by repeated homage to them, Burke had almost made the words as well as the arguments sacred to his own rhetoric. On 16 Jun 1784 he had declared the Commons "a legislative body corporate by prescription, not made upon any given theory, but existing prescriptively—just like the rest". *The Speeches . . . of Edmund Burke* (4 vols 1816) III 47. In defining prescription as "Rules produced and authorized by long custom; custom continued till it has the force of law", Johnson's *Dictionary* quoted Shakespeare, Bacon, South, Dryden, and Addison.

[7] *TT* (1835) added: "and you will live to think so". *TT* (1836) also added a paragraph from N L (*CN* III 3554), amplifying only the first clause, "I will not run into a vulgar abuse of the vulgar". The notebook entry is marked "T. T.", perhaps at the time of transcription for this entry. On 25 Nov HNC wrote to RS that Robert Lovell Jr had dined with "us" a week before. UT ms. Lovell might have brought news of the Reform Bill from Rickman—see Orlo Williams *Life and Letters of John Rickman* (1912) 204–5,

268–92—but is probably not otherwise to be associated with the present entry.

[1] As the only surviving letter from C for Dec 1831 is a note to J. H. Green on the 15th to communicate "a gleam of Convalescence" (*CL* VI 877), we are lucky to have TT for 3 (Sat), 17 (Sat), and 27 (Tues) Dec.

[2] C's earlier discussions of true philosophy as preparation for religion and conversely of "idea-less philosophy" as productive of comfortless religion—*P Lects* Lect 7 (1949) 246; *SM (CC)* 30; cf *AR* (1825) 228–30—and of religion as "the Poetry and Philosophy of all mankind"—*LS (CC)* 197—had flowered belatedly into a definition of religion as "philosophy evolved from idea into act and fact by the superinduction of the extrinsic conditions of reality". *SM (CC)* 64n, in which the passage, first published in *SM* (1839), is taken as referring to *Friend (CC)* I 520. On 21 Jun 1829, in a copy of *The Friend* (1818), C described religion as the union of reason and imagination. *Friend (CC)* I 203n. The present entry, which points towards symbolic truth available to philosophic comprehension in the Biblical record and the

17. Dec. 1831.

I am quite sure that no dangers are to be feared by England from the dis-annexing and independence of Ireland at all comparable with the evils which have been, and will yet be, caused to England by the Union.[1] We have never received one particle of advantage from our association with Ireland—whilst we have in many most vital particulars violated the principles of the British Constitution solely for the purpose of conciliating the Irish Agitators, and endeavoring—a vain endeavor! to find room for them under the same Government.[2] Mr Pitt has received great credit for effecting the Union; but I believe it will sooner or later be discovered that the manner in which, and the terms upon which, he effected it, made it the most fatal blow that ever was levelled against the peace and prosperity of England.[3] From it came the Catholic Bill![4] From that has come this Reform Bill! And what next?   [36:338]

history of Christianity, specifies scriptural revelation in contrast to C's more usual insistence that all history be read as prophetic. The clarity of the present entry is no more than approached by *CIS* (1840) 6–7, in which Christianity is declared "spiritual, yet so as to be historical; and between these two poles there must likewise be a midpoint, in which the historical and spiritual meet".

[1] Irish agrarian riots and refusals to pay the tithe in January had led directly to parliamentary debates in Feb 1831 on repeal of the Union. Hansard 3rd s II 349–55, 604–6. For the rest of the year Ireland was thought to be at its most lawless since 1822. On Ireland see also 14 Aug 1831 (penultimate entry), above.

[2] Since 1804, and loudly since 1811, the chief Irish agitator for repeal of the Union had been Daniel O'Connell (1775–1847). Elected to Parliament but refusing to take the oath of supremacy in order to take his seat, he was arrested early in 1831 on the charge of evading the various proclamations against his Catholic Association of 1823 and the subsequent forms in which he had resurrected it; he had been almost immediately released into further agitation. C would probably be aware also of the quieter but increasingly effective agitation by Thomas Wyse (1791–1862),

M.P. for Tipperary from 1830.

[3] Of C's contempt in 1799–1800 for "the bribery and corruption attendant on the bringing in of Irish Union", remarked by the editor of *EOT (CC)*, this entry is clearer evidence than *CN* I, cited in 14 Aug 1831 n 25, above. C's attack on Pitt's character and methods in "Pitt and Bonaparte: Pitt" appeared in the *M Post* 19 Mar 1800 during Pitt's application of "secret influence" to bring about the Act of Union. *EOT (CC)* I xciv, 219–26.

[4] The Catholic Emancipation Act (10 Geo IV c 7) became law 13 Apr 1829, accompanied by an act raising the property qualification for the franchise in Irish counties. In the *Courier* of 3 Sept 1811 C had ascribed to a meeting of Irish Catholics in Dublin a programme to maim the Anglican Church: "Let us first secure the means of a Catholic Parliament, with Catholic officers of state, then dissolve the union with Great Britain, and then—*Caetera quis nescit?*" (Who does not know the rest?) *EOT (CC)* II 273. Of such a programme to make Roman Catholicism the one religion of the realm he now, in this entry, traces the progress and predicts the fulfilment. The logic of events, which all sides could see, was that admission of the Catholics into Parliament was a step in the separation of

The case of the Irish Church is certainly anomalous, and is full of practical difficulties. On the one hand it is the only Church which the Constitution can admit—on the other, such are[a] the circumstances[b]—it is a Church that can not act as a Church towards five-sixths of the persons nominally and legally within its care.[5]   [36:339]

The difference between an inorganic and an organic body lies in this:— in the first—a sheaf of corn[6]—the *Whole* is nothing more than a[c] collection of the individual phænomena;[d] [e]in the second—a man—the whole is the[f] effect of, or result from, the parts—is in fact every thing and the parts nothing.[7] A State is an Idea intermediate between the two—the Whole

[a] ~~is~~ are   [b] ~~nature~~ circumstances ~~that~~   [c] ~~the~~ a   [d] phænomena ~~of the individual unities~~
                       [e] f 54ᵛ   [f] ~~any~~ the

Church and State. In Oct 1827 C had attempted the formulation of a scheme to alleviate the evils suffered by the population of Ireland as the one plan under which the extension to Irish Catholics of franchise, ability to sit in Parliament, and legal qualification to hold public office "could be either desirable for Ireland, or palatable to the Country at large". *CL* vi 702. After passage of the Catholic bills of 1829, O'Connell had added to his platform a stress upon general reform of Parliament second only to his insistence upon repeal of the Act of Union. On 5 Feb 1829 William Page Wood had found himself in general agreement with C: "We discussed the King's speech, which was delivered today at the opening of the Parliament, and agreed as to the gross absurdity of the insertion of the bishops and clergy as detached from the Church, in the recommendation for Catholic emancipation. The event, however, forms an epoch in our history." *Memoir of Hatherley* i 181.

[5] The Union of Great Britain and Ireland in 1801 had affirmed the official title of the United Church of England and Ireland. Fears of the political power of the See of Rome made the United Church "the only Church which the Constitution can admit" in Ireland, as distinguished from the constitutional Presbyterian Church of Scotland. Conflicts between desire for reform and fear of subordination to a foreign power are summarised in Halévy *History* i 390–4, 475–85, ii 262–81, iii 136–44. Halévy surveyed also (i 468–9) the range of estimates in C's day of the Irish Catholics as four-fifths to six-sevenths of the population in Ireland. The tithe and the church cess (local tax rates) remained as a double charge upon Irish adherents to a church whose lands had been confiscated for the benefit of the church maintained by their forced tithe and cess. The sense of crisis over the anomaly C describes would remain until 1835, when the Church of England won victories in Parliament, at the hustings, and in popular opinion.

[6] In the marginal note on Steffens quoted in n 8, below, C contrasted an organism with "a heap of Corn", a phrase used also in *CN* iv 5086. Did HNC not mishear "sheaf" for "heap"? The long letter to EC of Jul 1826 described "the scale of Organic Nature from the Plant to the highest order of Animals". *CL* vi 597. The version of that letter offered as *C&S* App (1830) retained the same language and included a reminder that "whatever *is, lives*". *C&S (CC)* 183.

[7] With man as distinguished here, cf *BL* ch 13 on imagination, which "dissolves, diffuses, dissipates, in order to recreate . . . It is essentially vital, even

being a result from and^g not a mere total of, the parts—and yet not so merging the constituent parts in the result, but that the individual exists perfectly within it.[8] Extremes meet.[9] At Athens, each individual Athenian was of no value, but taken together—as Demus[10]—they were every thing in such a sense that no individual citizen was any thing: In Turkey there is the sign of unity put for unity—but in fact there is no State at all—and the whole consists of nothing but a vast collection of neighbourhoods.[11]   [36:340]

^{g} ~~the~~ &

---

as all objects (*as* objects) are essentially fixed and dead". *BL (CC)* I 304. Elsewhere this transforming power is named reason: "Every man is born with the faculty of Reason: and whatever is without it, be the shape what it may, is not a man or PERSON, but a THING." *Friend (CC)* I 189. Or again, it is "the idea of moral freedom" that modifies the "whole practical being" in all that a person says, feels, does, or suffers, "even as the spirit of life, which is contained in no vessel, because it permeates all". *C&S (CC)* 17–18. *TT* (1835) converted the noun "result" into the verb "results", probably by typographical error in 1835 but with no serious harm. Other applications by C of the organic relation of parts to whole are discussed in *CN* III 4111n.

[8] When a dialogue of Lessing's asked whether men are made for the state or the state for men, C answered in the margin that both may be true: "Not only is the Whole greater than a Part; but when it is a Whole, and not a mere All or Aggregate, it makes each part that which it is." *Ernst und Falk:* Lessing *Sämmtliche Schriften* (30 vols Berlin 1784–96) VII 245–6: *CM (CC)* III. C recommended the dialogues in *C&S (CC)* 114n–15; cf 65 n 5. In a note on Steffens C suggested that the immanence of *idea* could make the state an organism: "A State is not an aggregate [of] Units, like a Heap of Corn or of Sand-grains; b[ut] an Organismus, the Laws of the parts of which [are?] Reflexes of the Law of the Whole. But the Law *real* (not merely phænomenal). Whole is *an Idea.*" Annotation on *Caricaturen des Heiligsten* (2 vols Leipzig

1819) II 437. He had defended his own definitions of government and state against Steffens' in notes on II 356–8, 362–6: *CM (CC)* IV.

[9] Into this favourite adage *TT* (1835) inserted "especially in politics", but C applied it to all subjects. In the first of three applications in *The Friend* he said that "to collect and explain all the instances and exemplifications" of this proverb "would constitute and exhaust all philosophy". *Friend (CC)* I 110. On 11 Dec 1803 he noted eleven instances of extremes meeting. *CN* I 1725. "Extremes meet" is Axiom 1 of *AR* (1825) 1.

[10] Δῆμος, the citizens collectively. In the letter of Jul 1826 to EC, Demos, or "Demosius, of Toutoskosmos" is an owlet representative of "*this* world", as the antithesis of a mystic. *CL* VI 594; *C&S (CC)* 165, 174. For C in 1831 as well as for the Athenians, the citizen is nothing except as an organ of the whole.

[11] For C's distinction of government vs neighbourhood see *Friend (CC)* I 199–200, quoted in *C&S (CC)* 83. William Eton *A Survey of the Turkish Empire* (1798) 23–38, 284–333 stressed the divisions of authority within the Turkish state and the declining power of the Porte over the pashaliks and provinces. Later, more thorough studies, such as Ami Boué *La Turquie d'Europe* (4 vols Paris 1840) III 181–255 emphasised the strength of municipal structures of governance. Although C concentrates, as if abstractly, on the Turkish reversal of the relation of individual to state in ancient Athens, Turkey was a current topic. As

If men could learn from history—what lessons it might teach us! But Passion and Party blind our eyes, and the light which Experience gives is a lantern on the stern which shines only on the waves behind us![12]

[36:342]

When the Government and the Aristocracy of this country had subordinated Persons to things, and treated the one like the other: the Poor with some reason and almost in self defence, learnt to set up Rights above Duties.[13] The code of a Christian Society is—Debeo et tu Debes—;[14] of Heathens or Barbarians, Teneo—Teneto—si potes.[15]   [36:341]

C spoke, the Sultan's forces were falling back under attacks from Egypt begun in November, only the latest in a series of progressive signs of weakness, with losses to Russia in 1828–9, the surrender in 1830 of Algiers to France and of Greece under pressure from Britain and Austria. In the *Courier* 30 Aug 1811, as a warning to Napoleon against aggression, C found the Turkish people united. *EOT (CC)* II 258–62.

[12] In the *M Post* 2 Jan 1800 it was "ambition and vanity" that made experience, "like the lights placed in the stern of the vessel", illumine only the track "already passed over"; the simile was repeated in that language in the *M Post* on 25 Sept 1802, and in *The Friend* of 28 Sept 1809 it became: ". . . human experience, like the Stern lights of a Ship at Sea, illumines only the path which we have passed over". *EOT (CC)* I 67, 324; *Friend (CC)* II 106 (I 179–80); cf *SM (CC)* 12. In the *Courier* 10 Dec 1814 he complained that Justice William Fletcher had, except for sudden turns of his "dark lanthorn", put out the light previously waved to beckon readers to follow him in his printed Charge to the Grand Jury of Wexford. *EOT (CC)* II 416. Earlier, in the *Courier* 22 Dec 1809, C had lamented that those who opposed the Spanish cause would respect his "analogous facts of experience derived from history" more than his arguments "de-

duced from the general nature of things". *EOT (CC)* II 83. C wrote similarly of the power of history to free from "party Zeal" in *Memoirs of the Life of Colonel Hutchinson* (1806): *CM (CC)* II 1197.

[13] *TT* (1835) quoted in a note to this entry *C&S* (1830 ed 2) 10–*CC* 15–16—on the equivalence of erroneous subordination of ends to means and erroneous treatment of persons as things. C had asserted this Kantian principle in the essay on Rousseau's theory of government. *Friend (CC)* I 189–90 (II 125). The statement of 1831, with the corrective "almost" and "some reason", is a reminiscence of 1795, when C could say, "Poverty is the Death of public Freedom", and 1796, when he published "Extract from Dr. Beddoes' Postscript to His Defence of the Bill of Rights Against Gagging Bills". *Lects 1795 (CC)* 126; *Watchman (CC)* 344–6.

[14] "I ought, and you ought". Cf Luke 6.38, Acts 20.35.

[15] "I keep [mine]—keep [yours] if you can". There is an unascribed Latin proverb, "Capiat qui capere possit" (Let him take who can take). Cf WW *Rob Roy's Grave* (c 1805) lines 37–40:

the good old rule
Sufficeth them, the simple plan,
That they should take, who have the
    power,
And they should keep, who can.

27. Dec. 1831.[1]

Francesco *Tessala*'s[2] definition of Beauty was—*il più nell' uno*[a]—Multitude in unity—and there is no doubt that such is the Principle of [b]Beauty;[3] and it is one of the most characteristic and most infallible criteria of the different ranks of men's intellects[c]—the instinctive habit which all superior minds have of endeavoring to bring, and of never rest-

[a] *il piu nel' uno* =   [b] f 55   [c] intellects =

[1] HNC wrote to his father from Hampstead on this date of the Gillmans' kind attention to "my poor Uncle" in his illness; of a reference in an earlier letter he explained that C's "great friend & disciple is Mr Greene the eminent surgeon", i.e, Joseph Henry Green (1791–1863), who had been in attendance as regularly as ever.

[2] Almost certainly C said "Francesco de Salez", meaning St François de Sales (1567–1622), Savoyard nobleman and Doctor of the Church, a leader of the Counter-Reformation in France. C wrote to William Sotheby in Jul 1829: "Più NEL UNO is Francesco de Salez' brief and happy definition of the Beautiful . . .". *CL* VI 799n; cf *PW* (EHC) I 481n. In a letter to HC, probably of 1820, C first seems to attribute "*Uno nel Più*" to "the Italian Philosophers", but then explicitly to "the philosophic Saint & Bishop of Geneva (Francesco Sales)". *CL* V 99–100. The repeated "Francesco" can be accounted for by C's ownership of an Italian translation of St Francis's *Traité de l'amour de Dieu*: Francesco di Sales *Il Teotima o sia il trattato dell'amor di Dio* (2 vols Padua 1790)—listed in *WW LC* 329, now in VCL, with one note by C. *CM (CC)* II 792–3. At the end of bk I ch 1 of this *Treatise* St Francis said that God reduces the multitude and distinctions of what is to a perfect unity, but C's favourite phrase does not appear in the Italian translation. When Blanco White called St Francis the "least morose of all Roman Catholic saints", in *Practical and Internal Evidence Against Catholicism* (1825), C sympathised in a marginal note with St Francis's recommendation of ritualistic, physical discipline. *CM*

(CC) I 516. For other references to St Francis see *CN* III 3560, 3907, 3922, and IV 4909. As no actual "Tessela" was discovered by HNC, *TT* (1835) began the entry: "The old definition of beauty in the Roman school of painting". On a linkage of God and the poet in creating unity from diversity see John Black *Life of Torquato Tasso* (2 vols Edinburgh 1810) II 132–4.

[3] In notes for Lect 13 of 10 Mar 1818 (*CN* III 4397 f 50v), published by HNC in a different form as "On Poesy or Art", C wrote: "the notion of Beauty, namely, the many seen as one". Cf *LR* I 221. With apologies for restoring a mediaeval word, he wrote in 1814 of beauty as "multëity in unity", and several years later of life as "the principle of unity in multëity". "On the Principles of Genial Criticism" III: *BL* (1907) II 230; *TL* (1848) 42. A spiderweb is offered as a paradigm of unity, without specification of the manifold, in *CN* III 4229—beauty requires multëity within the unity. For applications of the idea to God, love, and poetry, see *CN* II 3201, III 4111 f 12v; *BL* ch 13 (*CC*) I 304, ch 14 (*CC*) II 13. Emerson copied the Italian phrase from *TT* (1835) into his notebooks, used it instantly in the lecture "Michael Angelo Buonarroti" and a second time in "Nature"; he accepted from HNC the attribution to "Italian artists". *The Journals and Miscellaneous Notebooks of Ralph Waldo Emerson* ed William H. Gilman et al (6 vols Cambridge, Mass 1960–6) V 116, VI 200, 225; *The Early Lectures of Ralph Waldo Emerson* ed Stephen E. Whicher et al (Cambridge, Mass 1961) I 101, II 264.

ing till they have brought into Unity the scattered Facts which occur in conversation or in the statements of men of business. To attempt to argue any great question upon Facts only is absurd; you cannot state any Fact before a mixed audience which an opponent as clever as yourself cannot with great ease twist towards another bearing, or at least meet by a contrary Fact, as it is called. Facts are not Truths—they are not Conclusions; they are not even Premisses, but in the nature[d] and parts of Premisses— the Truth depends on, and is only arrived at by, a legitimate deduction from *all* the Facts which are truly material.[4] [e]You see how M[acaulay][f5]—that frothy school-boy—was mauled on the score of his Facts by Croker—a very clever and witty fellow.[6] By the by, Croker's was an excellent speech indeed.[g7]   [36:343]

---

[d] nature ef,   [e-g] For the variant in MS F see App C, below   [f] M.

[4] In *The Friend* 25 Jan 1810 C had insisted that the accumulation of facts from experience could rise at best from "*contingent* circumstances" and could lead at best to greater rather than less probability. *Friend (CC)* I 158 (II 295).

[5] Thomas Babington Macaulay (1800–59), 1st Baron Macaulay (1857), historian, a "mainstay" (*DNB*) of the *Ed Rev*. The name is spelled out in MS F, in which HNC was prepared to identify his (and DC's) friend from Cambridge days but not to retain C's epithet "frothy schoolboy". Macaulay was already notorious for the phrase "as every schoolboy knows". *TT* (1835) eliminated the individual: "I wonder why facts were ever called stubborn things: I am sure they have been found pliable enough lately in the House of Commons and elsewhere." C as early as 1824 deplored DC's proximity to the "brutish Anti-Faith" of Macaulay (*CL* V 330, VI 336, 726, 797), and HC in 1826 congratulated DC, prematurely, on getting free of "*that* set" (*HCL* 93–4). On 1 Mar 1832 C admitted the strengths of one of Macaulay's "best & least flashy speeches". *CL* VI 889. For C vs Macaulay see also App F 16, below.

[6] John Wilson Croker (1780–1857), Tory politician credited with introducing the name "Conservatives", contributor to *QR*. His edition of Boswell's *Life of Johnson* had been slashed by Macaulay in *Ed Rev* LIV (Sept = Aug 1831) 1–38.

In earlier years C had regarded Croker as the epitome of ministerial intimidation of the press (*CL* IV 639); for his objections to Croker's indifference towards the Church see *CL* VI 903; *C&S (CC)* 161 and n. In 1818 Croker had warned William Blackwood against attacks on C and WW, "who are certainly respectable writers, to say the least of them, and, I understand, worthy men. I never saw either of them but once at dinner, and therefore I am impartial." Myron F. Brightfield *John Wilson Croker* (1940) 229; cf 230. HCR had noted on 13 Oct: "Read Macaulay's *Edinburgh* review of Croker's edition of Boswell's *Life of Johnson*.The exposure of Croker's blunders in facts is complete." *CRB* I 392. In *Bl Mag* XXX (Nov 1831) 829–39 John Wilson enumerated Macaulay's false charges of inaccuracy in Croker's Boswell.

[7] Macaulay's observation that episodes in the French Revolution offered parallels with resistance to the Reform Bill led immediately to the most eloquent of Croker's attacks upon him (20 Sept 1831): "Good God! Sir, where has the learned Gentleman lived,—what works must he have read,—with what authorities must he have communed, when he attributes the downfall of the French nobility to an injudicious and obstinate resistance to popular opinion? The direct reverse is the notorious fact, so notorious, that it is one of the common-places

How inimitably graceful children are before they learn to dance! I think there is a clear sympathy between dogs and little children.[8]

[36:346, 347]

I prefer the principles upon which the Government has been upon the average carried on from the Revolution to the accession of William IV.,[9] but if the old system must be abandoned—rather than submit to the abominable operation of this infamous Bill—I would a thousand times over prefer a universal suffrage by all householders.[10]

Even to a Church—the only pure Democracy—because in it Persons are alone considered and one Person is equal to another a priori—even to[h] a Church, Discipline is an essential condition. But a State regards Classes—and Classes as they represent classified Property—and to introduce a system of [i]Representation which must inevitably render all discipline impossible—what is it but Madness—the madness of Ignorant Vanity and reckless Obstinacy?[j][11]

[36:344]

---

[h] ~~in~~ to   [i] f 55[v]   [j] ~~Passion?~~ Obstinacy?

---

of modern history." Hansard 3rd s VII 314 (Croker's long speech was published by Murray). In a politer response of 16 Dec Croker cited Hume's *History of England* against Macaulay and reminded the House of his "not very successful allusions to the history of France" on 20 Sept. Ibid IX 401–2.

[8] *TT* (1835) added in explanation that a little child is rarely attacked by a large dog. C promised in the first, introductory essay of *The Friend* to base his arguments not only on books but also on self-reflection and 'Observation of the Ways of those about me, especially of little Children". *Friend (CC)* II 8. HNC may have lost a transition between the gracefulness of children and their sympathy with dogs.

[9] I.e. 1688–1830. In 1688, when a group of prominent Englishmen invited William of Orange to take over the administration of government, the "Glorious Revolution" established the principle of limited monarchy by which the crown was held, not from divine right, but by the choice and consent of Parliament. The Declaration of Rights of 1689 secured freedom of all subjects from

such misdeeds of a sovereign as James II was charged with in the Declaration. Particularly to C's taste, the Revolution Settlement had provided that none of Roman Catholic faith could wear the crown. More to the point of his protest against "this infamous Bill", the hereditary House of Lords and the weighted suffrage of the landed gentry provided a stability and a restraint on the mercantile classes that C regarded as essential. As he was to say a month later (28 Jan 1832, below) (36:348), his ideal Whig and ideal Tory agreed 'in the necessity and benefit of an exact Balance of the three Estates". Supporters of the Bill were claiming that the £10 suffrage, however they adjusted it, should be accepted and simultaneously that no further reform of Parliament would be needed in the future.

[10] This entry was not published, and has not been found among the fragments of MS F. Perhaps HNC thought it redundant in the light of the entry on disfranchisement of 3 Mar 1832, below (36:351).

[11] *The Friend* of 28 Sept 1809 told how C learned from Sir Alexander Ball

I have known and know many Dissenters who profess to have a zeal for Christianity—and I dare say they have: but I have known very few indeed who did not hate the Church of England a thousand times more than ever they loved Christianity.[12] There never was an age since the Apostles, in which the catholic[k] spirit of Religion was so dead, and put aside for love of sects and parties.[13]   [36:345]

---

28. Jan. 1832.

The ideal Tory and the ideal Whig (and some such there have really been) agreed[a] in the necessity and benefit of [b]an exact[c] Balance of the three Estates;[1] but the Tory was more *jealous* of the Balance being deranged by the People—the Whig,[d] of its being deranged by the Crown.[2] But[e] this

---

[k] Catholic   [a] agreed ~~exactly~~   [b-c] a⟨n exact⟩   [d] Whig ~~was~~   [e] ~~Hen~~ But

---

the danger of severe discipline and the value of moderate discipline. *Friend (CC)* II 99–100 (I 169–70). *BL* and other works argued that genius should be disciplined as James Boyer disciplined C. The essay on the Sophists in *The Friend* (1818) traced the obvious relation between moral and political discipline. *Friend (CC)* I 438–9. The discipline of the Church refers technically to divine laws of faith and morals that had been administered, before Henry VIII, under Canon Law; the Commination Service on Ash Wednesday laments the decay of "the said discipline" among the members of the Church.

[12] *TT* (1835) inserted a sentence excepting certain Wesleyans, just as in an earlier entry, 30 May 1830 (after n 5), a sentence concerning Methodists, not in the ms, was inserted. *CN* III 3901 of 1810 typically condemned Methodist and similar sects that emphasise the vileness of the individual "me" in contrast with St Paul's concern for "us".

[13] C's suspicion of sectarian division grew as his respect for the Church of England increased. A phrase in *LS* (1817) justifying British pride in "the number and respectability of our sects" was omitted from *LS* (1839). *LS (CC)* 127 and n. In the addendum "On the

Third Possible Church" in *C&S* C condemned with humour the "extreme sects of Protestantism, whether of the Frigid or of the Torrid Zone, Socinian or fanatic". *C&S (CC)* 135.

[1] Although application of the word "estate" to more than one class dates from the Normans in England, Johnson's *Dictionary* did not acknowledge that sense; debates over the French Revolution transferred to England references to the three estates of nobility, clergy, and commons. C seldom used the term or the conception until he found it useful in *C&S (CC)* 42 and passim; cf *LS (CC)* 169n.

[2] The original Tories, in the political sense, were opposed in 1679–80 to the exclusion of the Roman Catholic James from succession to the throne. In 1688–9 the allegiance of most of their leaders shifted to a king, William III, whose power was limited by "the People". C's observation that they "remained Tories" possibly notices the taint of Jacobinism that clung to some leading Tory families in 1715–45, but probably refers to his definition of a Tory as one who feared a reduction in the balancing power of the Crown. In a note of 1809 he contemplated with sympathy and subtlety the conversion of the Jacobites to the Han-

was a habit—a jealousy only; they*ƒ* both agreed in the ultimate preservation of the Balance, and accordingly they might each, under certain
circumstances, without the slightest inconsistency pass from one into the
other, as the ultimate object required it. This the Tories did at the Revolution; but remained Tories as before.[3]   [36:348]

If you admit Spinoza's premiss, it is in vain to attack his conclusions. His
logic is an adamantinc chain![4]   [36:115]

---

*ᵃ*22. Feb. 1832.[1]

The Church is the last relique of our nationalty.*ᵇ*[2] Would to God that the
Bishops and the Clergy in general could once fully understand that the
Christian Church and the National Church ought as little to be con-
founded as divided![3] I think the fate of the Reform Bill of comparatively

ƒ ~~& accor~~ they   *ᵃ* f 56   *ᵇ* nationality

---

overian side for the reason that "feelings
remain when Principles are forgotten".
CN III 3528. Of Samuel Johnson "the
Whig" C had declared: "S. Johnson was
not a Whig: for a Whig implies a compromise between two opposite *Principles*: & S. J. was a Man of *Principle*."
Johnson *Works* (1710) 305: *CM (CC)* III.

[3] *TT* (1835) continued with remarks
similar in language to C's letter of early
May 1832 to HNC concerning an essay
on Whiggism to accompany C's projected edition of tracts by John Asgill.
CL VI 905.

[4] The irony beneath this remark, lost
when it was combined with a similar observation concerning Berkeley under the
date 23 Jul 1827 in *TT* (1835) (see 25–6
Aug 1827 and n 10, above), is clear from
11 Apr 1833, below (36:489): "Hence
you may set out like Spinoza with all but
the Truth, and end with a conclusion
which is altogether monstrous, and yet
the mere deduction be irrefragable".

[1] Before and after 28 Jan (Sat) C suffered from "nervous Rheumatism" in
limbs and viscera. One of the secret orders to Thomas H. Dunn for opium is
dated 6 Jan 1832. Yet C's few letters for
January and February range from a dis-

interested analysis of betrothal, addressed to James Gillman Jr and Susan
Steel, through the high spirits of his
"Elegiac Farewell to my black Tin Shav-
ing-pot", to a fanciful proposal to have
the Reform Bill caricatured in a public
print as a locomotive dragging caravans
over "the Church, chancery, the Colonial Interests, &c". *CL* VI 883. Among
the subjects discussed with HNC were
the speech imagined for Lord Wicklow
and the possibility of republication of
C's essays of 1817–18 on taxation and
"the National Church, and it's Revenue", as we know from C's letter
"Thursday Night" to HNC. *CL* VI 884–
5. According to C's medical account to
Green, his active hours on Wednesday
were short: he went to bed after taking
"at half-past 5 a few spoonfuls of Bread
Pudding". *CL* VI 887. The next day he
was much better. SC's son Herbert was
brought to him from Hampstead on Sat,
25 Feb. UT ms.

[2] Such is the central thesis of *C&S*
concerning the "National Church."

[3] *C&S* distinguishes from each other
the state, concerned with the property of
individuals collectively; the established
Church of England; the National Church

minor importance; the fate of the national church occupies my mind with greater intensity. [36:349]

I could not help smiling in reading Lord Grey's speech in the House of Lords the other night—when he asked Lord Wicklow whether he (Lord W.) seriously believed that he (Lord G.) or any of the Ministers intended to subvert the institutions of the Country.[4] Had I been in Lord Wicklow's place, I would have answered—"Waiving[c] the charge of personal consciousness against the noble Earl and all but one or two of his colleagues, upon my honor and in the presence of Almighty God, I answer Yes! You have destroyed the freedom of Parliament; you have shut the door of the House of Commons to the property, the birth, the rank, the wisdom of the people, and have flung it open to their passions and their follies. You have disfranchised the gentry and the real patriotism of the nation—you[d] have agitated and exasperated the mob, and thrown all political power into the hands of that class—the shop keepers, which[e] in all countries and in all ages has been,[f] is now, and ever will be the least patriotic, and the least conservative,[g] of[h] any.[5] You are now preparing to destroy for ever

---

[c] "Waving   [d] & you   [e] wch ~~of all ōrs~~   [f] been, &   [g] conservative, ~~the least~~   [h] of ~~all~~

---

of the clerisy, engaged in "producing and re-producing, in preserving, continuing and perfecting, the necessary sources and conditions of national civilization"; and the universal Christian Church as "the *sustaining, correcting, befriending* Opposite of the world". *C&S (CC)* 53, 114. In the "Thursday Night" letter to HNC, probably of 23 Feb, C put his stress on equitable taxation for the benefit of the established Church. *CL* VI 884–5.

[4] William Forward Howard, 4th Earl of Wicklow and Viscount Wicklow of Ireland (1788–1869), speaking 17 Feb on the subject of tithes in Ireland, carefully ascribed to the ministers "sincere and zealous dispositions" to discharge their duties "for the good of the country", but he spoke of others as no friends to the Church. Rising to reply, Grey asked: "Could that Noble Earl believe that they were persons likely to shake the foundations of the laws, and to subvert the institutions of the Country? The Noble Lord reproached them with proposing the extinction of tithes, and accused them of a design to overthrow the laws,

and with having denounced the law as a grievance." *M Chron* 18 Feb 1832.

[5] C seems barely to distinguish here between the patriotic and the conservative. His distinction in *C&S* between forces of conservation and forces for change, and his preference for conservation, are adumbrated in *SM* App E and in his contrast, in *The Friend*, of trade and literature. *SM (CC)* 108–9; *Friend (CC)* I 507–9. In *The Watchman* he had exploited the bad repute of the word "patriot" after Bolingbroke's attempt to appropriate it in *Letters on the Spirit of Patriotism* (1749), but by 1809 he could define patriotism as "a necessary link in the golden chain of our affections and virtues." *Friend (CC)* II 323. C found shopkeepers in short supply of affection for everything inherited that needed to be conserved. Contemplating the subjects of this conversation as they appear in *C&S*, HCR noted on 4 Jan 1832: "He exposes himself to the charge of being desirous to appear more of a Tory than he really is, leaving an opening to back out when assailed by his Liberal friends". *CRB* I 400.

the constitutional independence of the House of Lords; you are for ever displacing it from its supremacy as *ᶦa coordinate estate of the Realm; and whether you succeed in passing your Bill by actually swamping our votes by a *batch* of Peers, or by frightening a sufficient number of us out of our opinions by the threat of one—equally you will have broken down the triple assent which the Constitution requires to a valid Law, and have left the King *alone* with the Delegates of the Populace!''[6]   [36:350]

---

3. March 1832.

I am afraid the Conservative party see but one half of the truth.—The mere extension of franchise is not the evil; it is that the franchise is nominally extended to *such* classes and in *such a manner* that a disfranchisement of all above and a discontenting of all below the favored class areᵃ the unavoidable results.[1]   [36:351]

---

17. March. 1832.[1]

Wordsworth'sᵃ face is almost the only exception I know to the observation that something feminine is discoverable in the countenances of all

ᶦ f 56ᵛ   ᵃ ɪs are   ᵃ W.W.'s

[6] The operative word in C's rejection is ''Delegates'', as distinguished from representatives. The properly constitutional ''triple assent'' is not of the three estates, but of king, lords, and commons.

[1] In Dec 1803 C had noted that ''it is politic to allow every man *a vote*—not that he is always entitled to it''. *CN* ɪ 1760. On 1 Mar 1832 he had complained, in what remains of a letter to HNC, of the Marquis of Chandos's failure to oppose effectively the conversion of the metropolitan district into boroughs. *CL* vɪ 888–9. After *TT* appeared, HNC wrote on 15 Jun 1835 to Poole to say that the *M Chron* was wrong to say that C vituperated Reform, for ''no such thing; he only abused this Reform Bill— a very different thing''. BM Add MS 35344 f 116ᵛ. The entry of 3 Mar can be contrasted with WW to Haydon 8 Jul 1831, quoting his own words to Lord John Russell: ''. . . the Mass must either

be your zealous supporters, said I, or they will do all in their power to pull you down—that power, all at once, are you now giving them through your ten pound renters who to effect their purpose will soon call in the aid of others below them till you have the blessing of universal suffrage . . .''. *WL (L* rev) ɪɪ 408. The single brief entry of 3 Mar may not reveal C's poor health so much as the intensity with which all conversations were concentrated on the Reform Bill. Yet C was unquestionably very low. In diary entries of this period, he noted a ''reprieve'' in ''comparatively a night of ease and refreshment'' on 6 Mar, and similarly on 7 Mar, but ''*spotty*''; on the 8th he turned to prayer, and on the 9th to autobiography. HEHL MS HM 17299 (N Fᵒ) pp 155–78.

[1] After seeing C on Sat, 3 Mar, HNC wrote to JTC: ''Poor S.T.C.'s maladies increase upon him, & the loss of his £100 annuity distresses him. Some crisis will,

men of Genius.² Look at that face of old Dampier, a rough sailor but a man of exquisite mind—how soft is the air and delicate the shape of his temples!³   [36:352]

I think it very absurd and misplaced to call Raleigh and Drake and others of our old naval heroes of Elizabeth's age*ᵇ*—Pirates.⁴ No man is a pirate unless his contemporaries agree to call him so. Drake said—the subjects of the King of Spain have ruined me—ergo I will try to ruin the King of Spain's subjects.⁵ Would it not be silly to call the Argonauts pirates in our sense of the word?⁶   [36:353]

ᵇ ages

I think, take place in his health soon. . . .'' BM Add MS 47557 f 87. C's letters continue to refer to "the languor of Illness", but Sat, 17 Mar finds him wide-ranging and vigorous. On 20 Mar, in fact, from 4 to 5.30 PM, he had one of the most entranced and competent listeners of his life, young William Rowan Hamilton, who returned on the 23rd for two hours more. Graves *Life of Hamilton* I 552, II 538–9.

² Although WW's name was suppressed in *TT* (1835), early readers could identify the one genius without qualities of androgyny by comparing this entry with the statement that "Wordsworth has the least femineity in his mind" in Allsop II 228, reprinted by Ashe in *TT* (1884) 339; cf App M, vol II, below. For C's ruminations in 1808 on the need for English pronouns to acknowledge the sharing of characteristics by male and female, see *CN* III 3238, 3308, 3399.

³ I.e. an engraved portrait of William Dampier (1652–1715), captain in the Royal Navy, pirate, and hydrographer, possibly the frontispiece in *A Collection of Voyages* (3 vols—4 with William Funnell *A Voyage Round the World*—1729), which C was reading in 1807–11. *CN* II 3224–6, 3240n. Dampier was a favourite. *Friend (CC)* I 541 (II 289); *CL* VI 979; *RX* 49, 478–9; annotation on Defoe *Robinson Crusoe: CM (CC)* II 165.

⁴ Sir Walter Raleigh or Ralegh (c 1552–1618), the Elizabethan courtier, historian, and poet, who joined his brother-in-law Sir Humphrey Gilbert in an expedition against the Spanish in 1578. Sir Francis Drake (c 1540–96),

circumnavigator and admiral, commissioned by Elizabeth as a privateer to plunder Spanish ships and towns, 1570–2.

⁵ Probably C's authority is "The Life of Sir Francis Drake" by Thomas Fuller, who said that because Drake's goods were taken with Capt John Hawkins' "by the Spaniards at S. John de Ulva" in 1567, "Drake was perswaded by the Minister of his ship that he might lawfully recover in value of the King of Spain, and repair his losses upon him any where else"; though knighted, "it grieved him not a little, that some prime Courtiers refused the gold he offer'd them, as gotten by Piracy". *The Holy State* bk II ch 22 (1663) 124, 128 (C's annotated edition). As a sequel to the events at San Juan de Ulua (Vera Cruz), Drake took diamonds and other plunder from the Spanish at Nombre de Dios (at the isthmus of Panama) in 1573. Perhaps the person C is answering is RS, who was to say publicly in 1834 in *Lives of the British Admirals, with an Introductory View of the Naval History of England* (5 vols 1833–40) that apparently those who went with Drake "on this piratical voyage thought they were engaged in an honest cause", but that the Spaniards "naturally and properly" considered it "an act of piracy" (III 116–17). Hume had given scolding accounts of acts of "violence and piracy" by both Drake and Raleigh. *The History of England from the Invasion of Julius Caesar to the Revolution in 1688* (8 vols 1802) V 234–5, 377, VI 93–8.

⁶ Jason and his crew of heroes sailed

^cIt is curious to mark how certainly—I may say instinctively—the reason has always pointed out to men the ultimate end of the various sciences, and how immediately afterwards they have set to work like children to realize that end.[7] Now they applied to their appetites—now to their passions—now to their fancy and latterly to the understanding—lastly to the intuitive reason again. There is no doubt but that Astrology would be the last achievement of Astronomy—there must be chemical relations between the planets—the difference of magnitudes as compared with that of distances is not explicable otherwise—but this, though as it were blindly and unconsciously seen, led immediately to fortune-telling and other nonsense.[8] So Alchemy is the theoretic end of Chemistry—there must be a common law, upon which all can become each and each all— but then it was turned to coining gold, &c.[9]   [36:354]

^c f 57

---

in the ship *Argo* to Colchis and recovered the golden fleece of the ram that had saved his cousins from their wicked stepmother. In most versions stealth, violence, abduction, and murder are involved, all normal occurrences in legends of a heroic age. Pindar's is the earliest version of the story. For Valerius Flaccus *Argonautica* see 2 Sept 1833 and n 15, below. By the implied transition to the next subject, piracy is an early form of naval heroism as astrology and alchemy are early forms of science.

[7] For clarity, *TT* (1835) added "by inadequate means". The entry traces the history of sciences from the inadequate to the adequate, from alchemy to chemistry, from astrology to astronomy, all proceeding from an idea serving as the initiative towards progression.

[8] I.e. intuitive reason led mediaeval searchers in a direction they would have taken had they consciously posited, as C does, chemical relations among the planets to explain the discrepant tables of magnitude and distance. C had treated variously the interrelations of curiosity, theurgy, and superstition, at the time of the great alchemists, in Lect 12 of 6 Mar 1818 of the literary series and in Lect 11 of 1819 of the lectures on the history of philosophy. *Lects 1808–19 (CC)* II 210–11; *P Lects* (1949) 319–21 and nn. In *Friend (CC)* I 57 (II 50) he had cited purchase from the astrologer of "foresight

without knowledge or reflection", along with the promise of riches from an alchemist, as evidence that professions in the fifteenth century were "licensed modes of witchcraft". In 1816 he praised astrology as at least better than French infidelity, and repeated his appeal of 1795 to Newton's interest in astrology. *SM (CC)* 84–6, 85 n 4.

[9] In the lectures on the history of philosophy of 1819 C had lamented that the alchemists "abandoned all ideas", but proclaimed a debt to them "for chemistry as it now exists"; he had praised the alchemist Cornelius Heinrich Agrippa for foreshadowing the experiments of C's time in electricity and magnetism. *P Lects* Lects 9, 10 (1949) 300–5. In Lect 12 of the literary series of 1818 he had described the theory of the alchemists as "the same with that of the Heraclitic physics, or the modern German *Naturphilosophie*, which deduces all things from light and gravitation, each being bipolar". *Lects 1808–19 (CC)* II 211. See also *CN* III 4414. In every instance, he found in the alchemists positive lessons for his own day. In a letter of 11 Nov 1823 he referred to his "Pride of being a fellow-lecturer with the Father and Founder of philosophic Alchemy", Humphry Davy, in 1808. *CL* V 309. His remarks to HNC show why he was drawn to the search by the *Naturphilosophen* for a "common law", though repelled

I solemnly declare that I have heard but two arguments of any weight adduced for the passing of this Reform Bill—and they are in substance these—1. We will blow your brains out if you don't pass it. 2. We will drag you through a horsepond if you don't pass it; and there is some cogency in both.[10]   [36:355]

The Bill is a tapeworm lie with some 80 or 90 Knots or nodes[d] in it.

Talk to me of your pretended crisis! Stuff[e]—A vigorous government in one month would change all the data for your reasoning. Would you have me believe that the events of this world are fastened to a revolving cycle with God at one end and the Devil at the other—and that the Devil is now uppermost? I tell you as a Christian Statesman and a lover of the welfare of my country that your Bill is a wicked bill and as absurd and dangerous as[f] wicked.[11] Are you a Christian and talk about a crisis in that fatalistic sense?   [36:356]

---

^a31. March 1832.

There are two classes into which all Poets may be divided; one the Picturesque, who by an inborn felicity view and present every thing in the completeness of actual objectivity; of these Pindar and Dante are the

---

^d [rings? word not clear]   ^e & Stuff   ^f & as   ^a f 57^v

---

by their rigid fantasies. Attitudes towards the alchemists similar to C's are implied in the opening speeches of Goethe's Faust and expressed in Mary Wollstonecraft Godwin Shelley *Frankenstein, or the Modern Prometheus* (3 vols 1818) ch 2.

[10] In *TT* (1835) "some cogency" became "a great deal of force", a pun and more colloquial, to go with the repeated "don't" in suggesting the language of the populace. In a marginal note on Johnson the Whig *Works* (1710) 304, C condemned in similar language the requirement of an oath of allegiance after conquest: "Give me your money, or I'll blow out your Brains!—Swear that you will give me your money, or I'll blow out your Brains!—I confess, I see small difference between the two . . .". *CM (CC)* III. C had called Green's attention to an editorial in *The Times* (12 Sept 1831) urging the troops, in C's words, to

"mutiny and refuse to obey command". *CL* VI 871–2. After reading the passages on Reform in *TT* (1835) HC wrote to Mrs C that C's views had been different in their last conversations: "He admitted the necessity of a reform in parliament, and though I could never have imagined that he could have much admired little Johnny Russell's unprecedented piece of stupidity and blundering, call'd 'the Reform Bill', I thought he would have been thankful, as I am, for any thing which got rid of the idolized abominations of the old system . . .". *HCL* 184.

[11] This sentence and that on the "tapeworm lie" were omitted in *TT* (1835), probably as excessive. The phrase "as a Christian Statesman" suggests that C is imagining, as on 22 Feb and often, a fitting speech for a member of the conservative opposition to toss at Lord Grey.

chief,[1] and they have a subordinate class, derived from and congenial with them, who although they rarely present pictures, are full of picturable matter; Southey is a remarkable instance of this latter kind of power—Spenser is another.[2] This[b] first class corresponds with Painting or the Painter; the other or second class corresponds with Music and the Musician—has few or no proper pictures, but a magnificent mirage[3] of words instead—and gives you the subjective associations of the Poet instead of the external object. I remember but two pictures in all Milton—

---

b ~~The other~~ This

---

[1] Although MS B stressed later as well as here this distinction between picturesque and musical poets, *TT* (1835) omitted it. HNC omitted from *TT* (1835) all C's references to Pindar (c 522–443 B.C.), whether by chance or in his own capacity as expert on the supreme Greek master of choral lyrics. It has been suggested that C's distinction between musical and picturesque was influenced by Schiller's description of Klopstock as a musical, not a picturesque poet. *Sh C* (1960) I xxiv n 3.

[2] C took a great variety of positions with regard to the relation of picture to music in Spenser. In a note for Lect 4 of 1 Apr 1808 at the Royal Institution, attributing to Shakespeare an "exquisite sense of Beauty, both as exhibited to the eye in combinations of form, & to the ear in sweet and appropriate melody", C made Spenser an equal in sweetness of melody, whether he intended to include also equality in beauty "to the eye". *CN* III 3290: *Lects 1808–19 (CC)* I 80. In Lect 6 of 5 Dec 1811 he compared Spenser's ability to give a sense of concreteness of space, with no sense of particular place, with Shakespeare's ability to remove his characters from any particular period of time. *Lects 1808–19 (CC)* I 289. In notes for Lect 6 of 18 Mar 1819 he observed the "marvellous independence or true imaginative absence of all particular place & time" in *The Faerie Queene* and praised the "indescribable sweetness of his verse", while pointing out the "scientific construction of his metre". *CN* III 4501: *Lects 1808–19 (CC)* II 409. At dinner with Thomas

Monkhouse on 4 Apr 1823, according to Thomas Moore, "Coleridge said that Spenser is the poet most remarkable for contrivances of versification: his spelling words differently, to suit the music of the line, putting sometimes 'spake,' sometimes 'spoke,' as it fell best on the ear, etc. etc. To show the difference in the facility of reciting verse, according as they were skilfully or unskilfully constructed, he said he had made the experiment upon Beppo and Whistlecraft (Frere's poem), and found that he could read three stanzas of the latter in the same time as two of the former. This is absurd." Moore *Journal* II 624.

In the present entry C distinguishes RS and Spenser, not for picture-making, but for the capacity of inspiring illustration or mental images. The supplanting in C's day of the assumption that poetry is like painting, *ut pictura poesis*, by an analogy with music as more "expressive of spirit and emotion" is traced by M. H. Abrams *The Mirror and the Lamp: Romantic Theory and the Critical Tradition* (New York 1953) 50–3, 88–94.

[3] Written "mirāge" in MS B. HNC's bar usually indicates an abbreviation, but here he may have intended to recall C's pronunciation or to indicate the French source of a word new to English (the first citation in *OED* is 1803, the earliest figurative use 1812). By "magnificent mirage" a work gives an impression of pictorial objectivity but simultaneously added sense of mental associations that coalesce in internal vision. Mirage, like music, turns from a linkage of objective word and thing to subjective suggestion.

Adam bending over the sleeping Eve—and Dalilah approaching Samson.[4]   [36:418]

If I belong to any class of poets, it is most preeminently to the latter. If I have ever drawn any pictures, they are in Christabel.[5]

Mrs Barbauld told me that the only faults she found with the Ancient Mariner were—that it was improbable, and had no moral.[6] As for the probability—to be sure that might admit some question—but I told her that in my judgment the chief fault of the poem was that it had too much

[4] C makes the same point again on 6 Aug, below (at n 10), and HNC's pastiche of Lect 10 of 1818 has a similar remark: *LR* I 177–8. Milton's two passages are quoted in footnotes in *TT* (1835). In Lect 9 of 16 Dec 1811 C declared that "the Picturesque power of Shakespeare . . . of all the poets that ever lived was only equalled by Milton & Dante". *Lects 1808–19 (CC)* I 361. Even if it does not extend the contrast between Milton (with C) as musical and Pindar, Dante, Spenser, and RS as picture-making, C's contrast of Shakespeare and Milton in Lect 4 of 28 Nov 1811 applies at least obliquely to the denial of objective pictures in Milton, who "attracted all forms & all things to himself into the unity of his own grand ideal", whereas Shakespeare "became all things well into which he infused himself". *Lects 1808–19 (CC)* I 253; cf *BL* ch 15 *(CC)* II 27–8. Keats's graphic representation of this distinction has replaced for most students C's expression of it. In *BL* ch 22 *(CC)* II 127–8 C quoted *Paradise Lost* IX 1101–10, on the "pillar'd shade" of fig-trees in Malabar as "poetic painting" addressed to the imagination, "*creation* rather than *painting*". To paint is to represent the visible by appeal to the senses.

[5] This remark has significance particularly for the "conversation poems" in blank verse and other pieces that have been praised for faithful pictorial detail. In *BL* ch 15 C saved his highest praise for "richness and sweetness of sound", because "the sense of musical delight, with the power of producing it, is a gift of imagination; and this . . . may be cultivated and improved, but can never be learnt". *BL (CC)* II 20. To be a musical rather than a pictorial poet was to emu-

late the greatest with some degree of success. For HNC's remarks on C's attention to versification see App F 17, below.

[6] As C had made a similar remark without reference to Mrs Barbauld on 30 May 1830, above, HNC consolidated the two entries under 36:214 (as of 31 May). Anna Letitia Barbauld (1743–1825), miscellaneous writer, née Aikin, had been a favourite of C's until about 1804. He praised her style in 1796; he asked that copies of *Poems* (1796), *LB* (1800), and other works be sent to her; in 1797 he walked twenty miles to Bristol and back to see her; in Mar 1798 she was "that great and excellent woman"; after seeing her several times in 1800 he continued to praise her "very great" acuteness and "wonderful *Propriety* of Mind". After RS attributed to her, in error, a harsh review of Lamb's *John Woodvil* in the *A Rev*, for which C would "cut her to the Heart", and probably for other reviews, she became "Mrs Bare-Bald". *CL* I 197, 201, 341, 393, 420, 577–8, II 1039, 1191, VI 1013. For other remarks on the Aikin family see *CL* I 392; *CN* II 2303, IV 4707. John Frere heard C say in 1830 that an abusive review by Mrs Barbauld had ruined the sale of *Wallenstein*. *Cornhill* NS XLII (1917) 407. C's *Poems* (1803) was roughly handled in *A Rev* II (1804) 556, as C was not likely to forget, but the review of *Wallenstein* in John Aikin's *M Rev* 2nd s XXXIII (1800) 128–31 was by John Ferriar. Although branding the plot as "insufferably tedious", the reviewer declared C "the most rational partizan of the German theatre" among an admittedly dubious lot. For anecdotes concerning C and the Aiken family see App F 18, below.

3. ''He blesses the Creatures of the Calm'',
from David Scott *Scenes from Coleridge's Rime of the Ancient Mariner*
(Edinburgh 1837). Print Collection, New York Public Library,
reproduced by kind permission

moral, and that too openly obtruded on the reader.[7] It ought to have had
no more moral than the story of the merchant sitting down to eat dates by
the side of a well and throwing the shells aside, and the Genii starting up
and saying he must kill the merchant, because a date shell had put out the
eye of the Genii's son.[8]   [36:214]
   It is an enormous blunder in these engravings of David Scott,[9] brought
here by Mr Aitken,[10] to represent the Ancient Mariner as an old man on
board ship. He was in my mind the everlasting wandering ᶜJew—had

ᶜ f 58

[7] In *QR* LII (Aug 1834) 28 (*CH* 644
var) HNC as reviewer of *PW* (1834) had
seemed to say that he, not C, thought the
Arabian tale apt: "'Mrs. Barbauld, meaning to be complimentary, told our poet,
that she thought the 'Ancient Mariner'
very beautiful, but that it had the fault of
containing no moral. 'Nay, madam,' replied the poet,'if I may be permitted to
say so, the only fault in the poem is that
there is *too much!* In a work of such pure
imagination I ought not to have stopped
to give reasons for things, or inculcate
humanity to beasts. "The Arabian
Nights" might have taught me better.'
They might—the tale of the merchant's
son who puts out the eyes of a genii by
flinging his date-shells down a well, and
is therefore ordered to prepare for
death—might have taught this law of
imagination; but the fault is small indeed
. . .'". HNC went on to make it clear that
for him C's distinction is between unen-
cumbered imagination and inculcated
moral. He would not have had the pilot
and hermit witnesses to the sinking of the
ship or other "out-of-the-world wonders". Lowes based his interpretation of
AM as a work of "pure imagination"
upon the *TT* entry (*RX* 300–3); T. M.
Raysor, with no knowledge of the mss of
TT, speculated that the *QR* version "expresses a sounder critical judgment than
the version in *Table Talk*, and is therefore more credible". "Coleridge's Comment on the Moral of 'The Ancient Mariner' " *Philological Quarterly* XXXI
(1952) 90. For some of the other interpretations of the "moral" of *AM*, see
Martin Gardner *The Annotated Ancient
Mariner* (New York 1965) 186–90.
   [8] HNC's long quotation from "The

First Night. The Merchant and the Ge-
nie", as a note to *TT* (1835) (36:214),
seems to come with small variants from
The Arabian Nights Entertainments
(14th ed 4 vols 1778) I 24. C referred to
the same tale in 1816. *CN* III 4315, 4317
and nn.
   [9] David Scott (1806–49), Scottish
painter, brother of William Bell Scott.
Associate of the Scottish Academy from
1830, and Academician upon his return
from Italy in the autumn of 1832, Scott
began in 1831 the series of twenty-four
outline drawings for publication a-
chieved after C's death: "*The Rime of
the Ancient Mariner*. Illustrated by
Twenty-Five Poetic and Dramatic
Scenes, Designed and Etched by David
Scott, Member of the Scottish Academy
of Painting. Edinburgh: Alexander Hill,
50 Princes Street; Ackermann & Co.
London M.DCCC.XXXVII." The engraved title-page, "Scenes from Coleridge's Rime of the Ancient Mariner by
David Scott, S.A.", also dated 1837, is
counted, for its vignette, among the
twenty-five illustrations. A "Life of
David Scott" by A. L. Simpson is prefixed to the popular edition of 1885.
   [10] Probably John Aitken (1793–1833),
until lately the editor of *Constable's Miscellany*, which he had taken over with
Hurst, Chance, & Co, and *The Cabinet,
or The Selected Beauties of Literature*, in
which he published pieces by Lamb in
1824, 1825, and 1831. An introduction
of Aitken to C could have come through
Thomas Hurst, a neighbour and C's publisher in 1830–1. Lamb asked Edward
Moxon for "Mr. Aitken's Town address" in Oct 1831. *LL* III 325.

told this story ten thousand times since the voyage which was in early youth and fifty years before.[11]

I certainly understand the γυναι, τι εμοι και σοι[12] in John to have aliquid increpationis[13]—a mild reproof from Jesus to Mary for interfering in his ministerial acts by requests on her own account.[14] I do not think that γυναι was ever used by child to parent as a common mode of address; between husband and wife it was; but I cannot think that μητερ[15] and γυναι were the same things in the mouth of a son speaking to his mother. No part of the Christopædia is found in John or Paul; and after the baptism there is no recognition of any maternal authority in Mary.[16] See the two passages, where she endeavors to get access to him when he

---

[11] MS B here gives us more directly than previously available C's own observations. Scott's Mariner, bearded from the start, seems to grow older on the voyage. C's objection to this "enormous blunder" suggests a close identification with the Mariner as a young man as well as with the later sufferer. His words date the wedding feast fifty years after the voyage, with narrations to the Hermit and the Guest separated by 10,000 others and yet by implication both early among the many retellings between the voyage and the reader's encounter with the Wandering Mariner. HNC wrote in the *QR* review of 1834: "It was a sad mistake in the able artist—Mr. Scott, we believe—who in his engravings has made the ancient mariner an old decrepit man. That is not the true image; no! he should have been a growthless, decayless being, impassive to time or season, a silent cloud—the wandering Jew. The curse of the dead men's eyes should not have passed away. But this was, perhaps, too much for any pencil, even if the artist had entered fully into the poet's idea. Indeed, it is no subject for painting." *CH* 645. HNC thus makes the "grey-beard loon" as young in appearance as the mariner who set off merrily. Did C examine Scott's last drawing, "All Absolved"?—the mariner kneels with mediaeval knights and ladies in a church where divine or priestly hands reach out from above the altar to absolve him. That HNC does not report the whole conversation is indicated by the absence of comment on the wedding feast, a clear transition to the next entry on the marriage feast at Cana.

[12] John 2.4 (var): "Woman, what have I to do with thee?" (AV); "O woman, what have you to do with me?" (RSV).

[13] "Something of a rebuke".

[14] At Cana the mother of Jesus observed, "They have no wine". Commentators before and after C debate whether γύναι, "woman", would be used in civil address to a person of dignity.

[15] "Mother".

[16] From the absence in the Gospel of John of all details concerning the childhood of Jesus, C deduced that the accounts in Matthew and Luke of his heredity and his early years were late additions, perhaps "a poetic Romance,/ allegorico-cabalistic, a Christopædia" of A.D. 80 or 90. *CN* IV 5075. Cf marginal notes on Blanco White *Letters from Spain*, Chillingworth *Works*, Donne *LXXX Sermons*, and Richard Field *Of the Church: CM (CC)* I 506, II 35, 266, 661. A comparison of C's position with Herder's theory that oral and legendary material helped shape both the primary documents and the final form of the Gospels is made by E. S. Shaffer *"Kubla Khan" and the Fall of Jerusalem* (Cambridge 1975) 79, 321–2.

is preaching—"Whosoever doeth the will of my &c."[17] and also the recommendation of her to the care of John.[18]   [36:357]

---

[d]My deep conviction is that the true course is, to recognize Christianity in the Scriptures, not to piece it up by a selection of texts.[19] So long as I thought it absolutely necessary to make[e] every part and parcel of the writings contained in the collection called the Bible agree with and tend to the proof of Christianity, I read in terror, and according as the mood was, I either outraged my common sense and reason, or else violated the plainest dictates of the moral[f] conscience. But all would not do! Thank God! the verbal inspiration doctrine did *not* make an infidel of me—as it has done with many—I rejected it altogether;—I saw the absurdity—the wickedness—the horrible blasphemy attending it.[20] I became sensible that such a mode of interpreting the Scriptures has no more warrant in the example and practice of the ancient Church and the greatest lights amongst the fathers than it can have in reason. That[g] which is most beautiful—most natural—most justifiable when regarded under all the actual [h]conditions of time, place, action &c—becomes a mill-stone around the neck of a sincere believer—a stumbling block in the path of every [devout reasoner].[i]

What! because Deborah—a mother in Israel—flushed with conquest—in the expression of her triumph—in the last working up of her

---

[d-j] For the variant in MS F see App C, below   [e] make ~~my~~   [f] ⟨the⟩ moral ~~it~~
[g] That ~~is~~   [h] f 58[v]   [i] Blank left in ms; see MS F: devout reasoner . . . strange doctrine.

---

[17] Matt 12.50: "For whosoever shall do the will of my Father which is in heaven, the same is my brother, and sister, and mother." *TT* (1835) cited Mark 3.35, a slightly differing version. In the preceding verses Jesus responds to a desire of his mother and brothers to speak to him by asking, "Who is my mother, or my brethren?" Mark 3.33. Luke 8.19–21 gives a briefer version.

[18] John 19.25–7. *TT* (1835) added correctly, "at the crucifixion". After a session with C in Oct 1832, R. C. Trench reported: "He has finished his great work on St. John—the labour of his life, and which will probably be the greatest acquisition which Christian literature has received for the last century and a half." *Letters and Memorials* I 124. C rejected Eichhorn's belief that the Apocalypse was written by the same author as the fourth gospel in favour of Eusebius' hypothesis that the Apocalypse was written by a different John, an elder at Ephesus under John the Evangelist. Annotation on Eichhorn *NT: CM (CC)* II 490. He welcomed Eichhorn's defence of the fourth gospel as authentic.

[19] This paragraph and the following one, on Deborah's praise of Jael, are omitted from *TT* (1835). In MS F they are marked in pencil, probably by EC, with the words "Move this".

[20] Among examples that drove others to infidelity C cited, in the narration of Jesus' trials before Pilate, Luke's variants from John, "who was an ear and eye witness"—a discrepancy irreconcilable with the doctrine of inspiration as "*infusion* or some mode or other of divine *information, virtually* a dictation to the inspired Amanuenses". HEHL MS HM 17299 (N F°) p 114.

war ode—called Jael blessed for ridding Israel of her great enemy[21]—am I, a disciple of Christ Jesus in England, to *think* that Jael was really blessed, was really not cursed, for the most cruel—most brutal—most dastardly act of assassination that ever yet combined murder with treachery and violation of the sacred rights of hospitality!*j*[22]

There may be Dictation without Inspiration and Inspiration without Dictation; they have been grievously confounded.[23] Balaam and his Ass were the passive organs of Dictation; but no one, I believe, will venture to call either of those worthies inspired.[24] It is my profound conviction that St Paul and St John were divinely inspired, but I totally disbelieve the dictation of any one word, sentence or argument throughout their writings. Observe, there was Revelation—all Religion is revealed; revealed religion is in my judgment, a mere pleonasm; revelations of facts were undoubtedly made to the Prophets—revelations of doctrines were as undoubtedly made to John and Paul; but is it not a mere matter of the senses that John and Paul each dealt with those revelations—expounded them—insisted on them just exactly according to his own natural strength of intellect—habits of reasoning—moral and even physical temperament? Understand the matter so—and all difficulty vanishes; you read without fear lest your faith meet with some shock from a passage here and there which you cannot reconcile with immediate dictation by the Holy Spirit of God without an absurd violence offered to the *k*text.

j See *d-j*, above   *k* f 59

[21] Judges 5.24–7. See 6 Jun 1830 n 5, above.

[22] Cf the gloss to *AM* lines 79–82, "The ancient Mariner inhospitably killeth the pious bird of good omen."

[23] The fullest exposition of C's distinction between dictation and inspiration is in *CIS*, which HNC prepared for publication in 1840. J. Robert Barth ascribes to C a belief in inerrant revelation, in which God's infallible intelligence is at issue, but including inspiration that allows for learning by natural means. *Coleridge and Christian Doctrine* (Cambridge, Mass 1969) 53–8. James D. Boulger notes rather C's emphasis in *CIS* and elsewhere on the receptivity of the reader of Scripture. *Coleridge as Religious Thinker* (New Haven 1961) 113–17. John Sterling wrote to Trench 28 Jan 1833 that he had seen C frequently: "I have been allowed to copy his notes on Pearson on the Creed [copy now lost].

. . . Much of his comment hinges on his view of the inspiration of Scripture, from which I think you would entirely dissent. He has given me, in the course of one of his conversations, an illustration of the pentad relating to this subject, which I will add here:—1. Prothesis—Christ the Lord. 2. Mesothesis—the Spirit. 3. Thesis—the Church. 4. Antithesis—the Scriptures. 5. Synthesis—the Preacher." Trench *Letters and Memorials* I 132. *CN* IV 4909 is a note of Jul 1822 against the assumption of dictation.

[24] In Num 22.28–30 the Lord "opened the mouth" of the ass to speak to Balaam. As in *CIS* C chooses examples to make absurd the doctrine that every word spoken by a character in the Bible was dictated by God. The ass asks, "Was I ever wont to do so unto thee?", which might mean, Did I ever ride you?, or Did I ever take up a sword to kill you? Balaam answers, "Nay."

You read the Bible as the best of all books—but still as a book, and make use of all the means and appliances which learning and skill under the blessing of God can afford towards rightly apprehending the genuine[25] sense of*l* it, not solicitous to find out doctrine in mere epistolary familiarity or facts in an*m* allusion to national traditions.[26]   [36:358]

Tertullian amongst his many lies—he was an enormous liar—says he had seen the autograph copies of the Apostles' writings;[27] the truth is, the ancient Church were not guided by the genuineness alone of a writing to pronounce it canonical—its Catholicity was the test applied to it.[28] I have not the smallest doubt that Barnabas's epistle is genuine—but it is not catholic—it is full of the γνῶσις[29] though*n* of the most simple and pleasing sort—so of Hermas—the Church would never admit either into the Canon—though the Alexandrians always read Barnabas for 300 years in their churches.[30] It was 300 years before the epistle to the Hebrews was admitted—on account of his γνῶσις; at length by help of the venerable prefix of Paul's name, its admirers fortunately succeeded.[31]   [36:359]

So little did the early Bishops and preachers think their Christianity wrapped up in and solely to be learnt from the New Testament.—in fact there was no such collection for 300 years*o*—that I remember a letter from [Melito]*p* to a friend of his a Bishop in the East—in which he most evidently speaks of the Christian Scripture very much as of works of which the Bishop knew little or nothing.[32]   [36:360]

---

l of ~~the writing~~   *m* ~~the~~ an   *n* tho' ~~in~~   *o* yrs   *p*Dash in ms

[25] *TT* (1835) changed "genuine" to "general", a persuasive correction.

[26] *TT* (1835) inserted a Latin tag confining the allusion "to the particular person and for the time".

[27] See 6 Jun 1830 at n 15, above.

[28] Cf 6 Jan 1830 (paragraph following n 8), above (36:225). Eichhorn is the chief stimulus to many of the remarks in this paragraph. For representative observations on the NT canon see *CL* VI 784; *CN* III 4415 (for Eusebius "the Balance after centuries of doubt turns in favor of the Authenticity''); and C's marginal notes on Lessing *Sogenannte Briefe an verschiedene Gottesgelehrnte* in *Sämmtliche Schriften* XVII 95, 112–25, 130: *CM (CC)* III.

[29] "Knowledge''; see above, 7 Jan–13 Feb 1823 nn 25–6; 6 Jul 1827 n 10; 6 Jun 1830 nn 10–11. On 5 Feb 1829 W. P. Wood heard C on the "quickening

spirit'' of 1 Cor 15.45: "In the evening went to Coleridge's. He discoursed somewhat mystically on some points of Christian philosophy. Speaking of the πνεῦμα ζωοποιοῦν, for instance, of St. Paul, he conceives it to be something not requiring the understanding as a condition of life, but as being in itself a source of life; but how shall we comprehend that which he admits we cannot in the very terms of his proposition?'' *Memoir of Hatherley* I 180.

[30] See above, 8 Jul 1827 n 9; 13 May 1830 n 2; 6 Jun 1830 n 12.

[31] See above, 7 Jan–13 Feb 1823 nn 38–9; 6 Jun 1830 n 13; Eichhorn *NT* III 51–2, 442, 453, 464, 477; marginal notes on *Eternal Punishment Proved to Be Not Suffering, But Privation* and Fleury *Ecclesiastical History: CM (CC)* II 563–4, 706.

[32] Eusebius   *Historia   ecclesiastica*

4. April 1832.[1]

I make the greatest difference between *ans* and *isms*. I should deal insincerely with you,[2] if I said that I thought Unitarianism was Christianity;—no—it has nothing to do with the religion of Christ Jesus: but God forbid that I should doubt that you and many other Unitarians, as you call yourselves, are very good Christians. We do not win Heaven by Logic.[3]

4.26 quoted a letter from Melito "the eminent Bishop of Sardis" (115–85) in answer to a request from Onesimus, a bishop previously pastor at Ephesus, for "extracts from the Law and Prophets regarding the Saviour and the whole of our Faith"; Melito went to the trouble of ascertaining the canonical books of the OT, which he listed for Onesimus' edification. Eusebius 3.36, 4.13, 25–6; tr G. A. Williamson (1965). The letter does not mention books of the NT. In a marginal note on Rhenferd *Opera philologica* 123, probably of 1827, C refers to Melito's letter with "sundry other passages in the Fathers of the 3 first Centuries" as demonstrating a sufficient ignorance of the OT to account for their "strange interpretations of the N.T.—of the Apocalypse, especially". *CM (CC)* IV. Melito's letter is translated in Eichhorn *AT* I 120–.

[1] The only prolonged period after 1801 when we can believe C to have gone without opiates lasted from 23 Mar to 13 May 1832. *CL* VI 892–908. The long conversation of Sat, 31 Mar on Scripture and its commentators was one fruit of C's good spirits. On Wed, 4 Apr HNC left SC ill at Hampstead and found C unrecovered from cholera but reluctant to consult Gillman, who was himself ill along with the rest of the household. C had been concerned for several weeks over the lingering disease of Unitarianism in the Lawrence family. C had known Miss S. Lawrence as governess in the home of Peter Crompton and his "angel wife," near Liverpool, in 1808 and 1812. On 18 Mar 1832 he had promised her he would receive her friend William Rowan Hamilton, mathematician and astronomer, who was visiting from Dublin (see 17 Mar 1832 n 1, above). After two

visits, of 20 and 23 Mar, in a letter dated by Hamilton's biographer "April, 1832", C deplored the Unitarianism of the Lawrence family in language similar to that of the TT entry of 4 Apr. *CL* VI 893–4, redated Mar, on the dubious theory that C can have provided Hamilton with an autograph on only one occasion. It may be that HNC, visiting alone, heard C recite what he intended to say, or read what he had said, in the letter to Hamilton.

[2] If a member or members of the Lawrence family are the Unitarians addressed, Hamilton was probably also at Highgate. C wrote to Hamilton, under the same date of 4 Apr, of his inability to find a promised volume of Kant. *CL* VI 896.

[3] Details of these paragraphs appear in a different order in the letter to Hamilton: "I was affected . . . to find her and her family still on that noiseless sand-shoal and wrecking shallow of Infra-Socinianism, yclept most calumniously and insolently, Unitarianism: as if a Tri-unitarian were not as necessarily Unitarian as an apple-pie must be a pie. . . . [From reading *Aids to Reflection* you will] be aware that though I deem Unitaria*nism* the very *Nadir* of Christianity, and far, very far worse in relation either to the *Affections*, the *Imagination*, the Reason, the Conscience, nay even to the UNDERSTANDING, than several of the forms of *Atheism*—*ex. gr.* than the Atheism of Spinoza . . . yet I make an impassable chasm between *an* and *ism*, and while I almost yield to the temptation of despising Priestleyianism as the only *sect* that feels and expresses contempt or slander of all that differ from them; the poison of hemlock for the old theological whiskey and its pugnacious effects; yet I am per-

What do you mean by exclusively assuming the title of Unitarians?—as if Triunitarians were not necessarily Unitarians—as much as an *ᵃapple-pie must of course be a pie.[4]

If I could contemn any men for their religious tenets, it would be the Unitarians; for they themselves universally call all believers in the orthodox doctrine either fools or knaves; to be sure they were forced to make an exception of me—and it annoyed them that were so forced; but they had flattered me so much as the champion of their cause that they could not pretend that I was not master of all they could say for themselves—and they could not for the life of them make out that I had any sinister or interested motive; so they set me down for a visionary, and fond of a paradox as a theme for display in conversation.[5]

ᵃ f 59ᵛ

---

suaded that *the Word* works *in* thousands, to whose ears the *words* never reached, and remained in the portal at the unopened door. . . . the *Socini* were Christians—though grievously inconsistent in their logic. But it is not in the ways of logic that we can be raised to heaven." *CL* vi 893–4. The difference between *ans* and *isms* begins in a distinction like William Blake's between the individual and the condition or "state": one must forgive the individual but can hate the individual's condition. That C had both talked and written to Hamilton about the Unitarianism of the Lawrence family is clear from Graves *Life of Hamilton* i 536, 538–42.

[4] *TT* (1835) added: "The schoolmen would, perhaps, have called you Unicists; but your proper name is Psilanthropists—believers in the mere human nature of Christ." C had distinguished between the "Psilanthropist, (or Socinian)" and the Christian "Theanthropist" in Nov 1810. *CN* iii 4006. In *LS* (1817) he denied that Socinians could rightfully call themselves Unitarians, "for Unity or Unition, and indistinguishable *Unicity* or Oneness, are incompatible terms", and continued in words similar to those of *TT* (1835): "Their true designation, which simply expresses a fact admitted on all sides, would be that of *Psilanthropists*, or assertors of the *mere* humanity of Christ." *LS (CC)* 176–7. Near the end of

BL C denied any attempt to make a final judgement concerning the individual Unitarian's love of God. *BL* ch 24 *(CC)* ii 246. By 1807 C was using the word "psilosophy" to mean pseudo-philosophy *(CN* ii 3121, 3158); the same suggestion of barrenness attaches to the word "psilanthropist". Before this entry C had recorded similar views, in Jul 1825, in a copy of Blanco White *Practical and Internal Evidence Against Catholicism: CM (CC)* i 512–13. Cf *CN* iv 4797, 4857. He defined current Socinianism in 1825 in *CN* iv 5213.

[5] C's open conflict with former Unitarian friends dates from his Bristol lectures of 1814. Although he had begun by 1796 to speak of Joseph Priestley as an atheist *(CL* i 192), his debates with J. P. Estlin were conciliatory as late as 1808, when he had begun to deplore, particularly, Socinian influence on the Anglican clergy *(CL* iii 146). He wrote in *SM:* "It is not the *sect* of Unitarian Dissenters, but the *spirit* of Unitarianism in the members of the Established Church that alarms *me." LS (CC)* 100. But Estlin and his friends had had enough in 1814 when C "stated a mere matter of fact" that Milton "represented Satan as a sceptical Socinian" *(CL* iii 477). This paragraph of personal reminiscence was transcribed in MS F but did not appear in the published *TT.*

I think many forms of Atheism more agreeable to the mind than Unitarianism; in particular I prefer the Spinozistic scheme infinitely.[6] The Socinians were to be sure most unaccountable logicians—but swallow their bad reasonings and you come to a doctrine on which the heart may rest for some support. They adore Jesus Christ.[7] But Unitarianism is the worst of Atheism joined to the worst of Calvinism, like two asses tied tail to tail. They have no covenant with God, nor are bound to Him in any respect; they acknowledge that they look upon Prayer as a sort of self-magnetizing[8]—a getting the body and temper into a certain status desirable per se, but without any reference to the Being to whom the prayer is addressed.[9]   [36:361]

It is curious to trace the truth of the law of Polarity in the history of Politics, Religion &c.[10] When the maximum of one tendency has been at-

---

[6] C had written to Thomas Clarkson 13 Oct 1806: "Unitarianism in it's immediate intelligential . . . consequences, is Atheism or Spinosism—God becomes a mere power in darkness, even as Gravitation, and instead of a moral Religion of practical Influence we shall have only a physical Theory to gratify ideal curiosity—no Sun, no Light with vivifying Warmth, but a cold and dull moonshine, or rather star-light, which shews itself but shews nothing else—". *CL* II 1196. He described briefly to J. H. Green in Oct 1833 his note on the endleaves of Waterland *Vindication of Christ's Divinity* as that "on Pantheism as the only possible *speculative* Atheism: & that it *is* Atheism; & that Socinianism stops short of it, only because it is lazy, and lily-livered . . .". *CL* VI 962; the note in *CM (CC)* V. By speaking similarly to Emerson on 5 Aug 1833 C gave great displeasure. *English Traits* 16–18. Cottle reported an occasion apparently of 1807 when "a zealous Unitarian minister" met with C: "It was natural to conclude, that such uncongenial, and, at the same time, such inflammable materials would soon ignite. The subject of Unitarianism having been introduced soon after dinner, the minister avowed his sentiments, in language that was construed into a challenge, when Mr. Coleridge advanced at once to the charge, by saying,

'Sir, you give up so much, that the little you retain of christianity is not worth keeping.' We looked in vain for a reply. After a manifest internal conflict, the Unitarian minister very prudently allowed the gauntlet to remain undisturbed. Wine he thought more pleasant than controversy." *Rem* 326–7. C noted in 1809: "Socinianism is not a *Religion* but a Theory". *CN* III 3581. With Allston as intermediary, C enjoyed a visit from William Ellery Channing (1780–1842)—"He has the love of wisdom and the wisdom of love", C wrote to Allston 13 Jun 1823—but even one sermon of Channing's "Unitarian Christianity" was too much. William Henry Channing *Memoir of William Ellery Channing* (3 vols 1848) II 218–19; *CN* IV 5292 and n.

[7] The words "they adore J.C." is a later insertion in MS B, perhaps as late as the time of publication. *TT* (1835) inserted sentences on Faustus and Laelius Socinus similar to those under 23 Jun 1834, below (36:652).

[8] Mesmerising, self-charging. On animal magnetism see 31 Mar 1830 n 6, above.

[9] After this entry *TT* (1836) inserted a version of *CN* III 3938 (36:362).

[10] Derived from C's polar logic, this law of historical polarity, similar to Hegel's dialectic, is defined in *Friend (CC)* I 94n: "EVERY POWER IN NATURE AND

tained there is no gradual decrease—but a direct transition to the minimum,[b] till again the opposite tendency has attained its maximum and
then you see another corresponding revulsion. With the Restoration
came in the Mechanico-corpuscular philosophy which with the increase
of manufactures, trade and arts made[c] every thing in philosophy—religion—poetry objective;[11] till at length[d] attachment to mere external
worldliness and[e] to forms got to its maximum, when the French Revolution broke out, and with it immediately every thing became subjective
without any [f]object at all—The Will of the People, the Rights of Man
were subject and object both.[12] We are now, I think, on the turning
point—this Reform is the ne plus ultra of that tendency of the public
mind which substitutes its[g] own undefined notions or passions for real
objects and historical actualities. There is not one of the Ministers, except the one or two revolutionists among them, who have ever given us
a hint throughout this long struggle as to *what* they really do believe will
be the product of this Bill—what sort of House of Commons it will make
for the purpose of governing this empire soberly and safely.[13] No! they

---

[b] minimum, ~~of the opposite tendency~~   [c] ~~began converted~~ made   [d] length ~~the maximum of~~
[e] & ~~attachment~~   [f] f 60   [g] itself

IN SPIRIT *must evolve an opposite, as the sole means and condition of its manifes-*tation: AND ALL OPPOSITION IS A TEND-ENCY TO RE-UNION."
[11] In LRR 1 in 1795 C had adapted the arguments of Ralph Cudworth, particu-larly, against the corpuscular materialists who descended from Descartes and Hobbes. *Lects 1795 (CC)* 96–103. His most vivid rejection appeared in the con-clusion of *AR* (1825) 386–99. For bring-ing a "debasing Slavery to the outward Senses" into religion, he blamed Priest-ley next after Paley. As representative mechanico-corpuscular atheists *AR* names the chemists Jöns Jakob Berzelius and Charles Hatchett.
[12] *TT* (1835) changed "Will" to "Sovereignty". When an opponent of the Reform Bill objected to the phrase "the Sovereignty of the People" be-cause "such a Sovereignty never has ex-isted", C gave a better reason: "because 'the Sov. of the people' is *nonsense* and involves a contradiction". Annotation on Sir John Walsh *Popular Opinions on Parliamentary Reform, Considered* (4th

ed 1831) 8: *CM (CC)* V. In this and four other anti-Reform tracts C found the chief defect to be "the absence of *all* concessions". Note on *A Dialogue on Parliamentary Reform* (1831): *CM (CC)* II 210.
[13] HCR reported on 12 Apr: "I had an interesting morning with Mrs. Aders, having driven with her to Mr. Gillman's. We saw Coleridge in bed—he looked beautifully; his eye remarkably brilliant and he talked as eloquently as ever. His declamation was against the Bill: he took strong ground, resting himself on the de-plorable state to which a country is re-duced when a measure of vital impor-tance is acceded to merely from the danger of resistance to the popular opin-ion. A yielding to a government by the people for fear of the mob is a desperate remedy." *CRB* I 405. McLellan, visiting from the United States, had a slightly dif-ferent perspective on 27 Apr: "Speaking of the state of the different classes of England, he remarked 'we are in a dread-ful state; care like a foul hag sits on us all; one class presses with iron foot upon the

have actualized for a moment a wish—or a fear—a passion—but not an Idea. [36:363]

---

7. April 1832.

There are two grand divisions under which all contagious diseases may be classed: 1. Those which spring from organized living beings, and from the life in them and which, as it were, enter into the life of those in whom they reproduce themselves—such as small-pox and measles; these become so domesticated with the habit and system that they are rarely received twice. 2. Those which spring from dead organized or inorganized matter, and which may be comprehended under the wide term Malaria.[1]

You may have passed a stagnant pond a hundred times without injury; you happen to pass it again in low spirits and chilled precisely at the mo-

---

wounded heads beneath, and all struggle for a worthless supremacy, and all to rise to it move shackled by their expenses; happy, happy are you to hold your birthright in a country where things are different; you, at least at present, are in a transition state; God grant it may ever be so! Sir, things have come to a dreadful pass with us, we need most deeply a reform, but I fear not the horrid reform which we shall have; things must alter, the upper classes of England have made the lower persons, *things*; the people in breaking from this unnatural state will break from their duties also.' " *Journal* 231–2.

[1] A severe epidemic of Asiatic cholera had swept through Europe in 1831, reaching England by November and London (including C) in Feb 1832. C designates his second class of diseases as malarial with reference to the unwholesome atmosphere exhaled by marshes and without benefit of the later discovery of a specific parasite conveyed by the bite of a mosquito. He had encountered classifications of diseases all his life, e.g. in Daniel Sennertus *Opera omnia* (Lyons 1666) and Erasmus Darwin *Zoonomia*. *CN* I 1000C, III 4461n, *BL (CC)* II 31–2 and n, *WW LC* 353. Although the sequence from the Reform Bill to cholera in TT is perhaps acciden-

tal, C related the two epidemics, as in a letter of 26 Jul 1832 including his verses on "Cholera cured beforehand". *CL* VI 916–18. In 1821 he applied theories of contagion to the spread of religions and revolutions. *CN* IV 4836. The reviewer of *TT* in the *Literary Gazette* 30 May 1835 p 341 lamented that C's "ideas about epidemic disease seem to us to lack his usual sense and intelligence". The preparation of "Observations on Egypt" for Sir Alexander Ball in 1804 had involved C in reporting on the plague and other communicable fevers. *EOT (CC)* III 194, 202. C read the major English medical journals, in 1819 the *Jahrbücher der Medicin als Wissenschaft* ed A. F. Marcus and F. W. J. Schelling, and the transactions of societies and academies that included medical reports. *CN* IV 4641, 4868, 4894, 5189. He expands the basic distinction accepted by Erasmus Darwin between "epidemic complaints, which are generally termed influenza" and "arise from vapours thrown out from earthquakes", and "diseases properly termed contagious" that "originate from the putrid effluvia of decomposing animal or vegetable matter". *The Temple of Nature* (1803) IV 119n; cf *The Botanic Garden* IV 82 and n.

ment of the explosion of the gas; the malaria strikes on the cutaneous or veno-glandular system and drives the blood from the surface; the shivering fit comes on, till the musculo-arterial irritability reacts and then the hot fit succeeds; and unless bark or arsenic—particularly bark, because it is bitter as well as tonic—be applied to strengthen the veno-glandular and to moderate the musculo-arterial system, a man may have the ague for thirty years together.[2]

But if instead of being exposed to the solitary *ᵃ*malaria of a pond, a man travelling through the Pontine Marshes permits his animal energies to flag and surrenders himself to the drowsiness which generally attacks him, then blast upon blast strikes on the cutaneous system and passes through it to the musculo-arterial and so completely overpowers the latter that it cannot react and the man dies at once, instead of only catching an ague.[3]

———

There are three factors of an epidemic or atmospheric disease: 1. and the principal is the predisposing state of the body. 2. the specific virus in the atmosphere. 3. the accidental circumstances of weather, locality, food, occupation &c.[4] Against the second we are powerless—its nature,

ᵃ f 60ᵛ

[2] C's classification of bodily systems, by no means standard, is approximated by Blumenbach and more closely by Steffens, not at all in the current English proposals concerning causes and treatment of cholera. Peruvian bark, cinchona, was widely prescribed for intermittent fevers; there is a long account in *The Edinburgh New Dispensatory* (Edinburgh 1797) 139–43. C had been familiar with it from 1796 or earlier. *CN* I 235, III 4224. C's "Zöo-dynamic Triad" is set forth in an endleaf note on Steffens *Beyträge zur innern Naturgeschichte der Erde* (Freiburg 1801) 74 (*CM—CC*—IV), partly quoted in *CN* III 4225n.
[3] C made the same distinction between the small effect in an ordinary ague of a virus in explosive water-blasts "from a stagnant or emptying Pond" and the overwhelming of the cutaneous and veno-glandular systems by "a continued Volley of these Water-blasts, as in the Pontine Marshes", in a letter to J. H. Green on 24 Feb 1832. *CL* VI 888. C had read works by Richard Mead, among many others, on pestilential contagion

and plague. He left in Grasmere Diego Saverio Piccolo *Descrizione della peste di Messina nel 1743* (Messina 1745)— *WW LC* 347—but acquired other tracts on epidemic diseases and had Gillman's library—and Green's—on call. He annotated in 1821 Sir John Pringle *Observations on the Diseases of the Army* (5th ed 1765), with a proposal to divide fevers into three kinds, hydroseptic, as in the Pontine marshes; aeroseptic, "or chemico-atmospheric, Typhus and Plague"; and zooseptic, as in smallpox; with perhaps a fourth, from excessive exercise of muscles and the respiratory organs, thus unduly exciting "the Arteriality or the Irritable system". *CM (CC)* IV. In 1806 C would have passed through or near the Pontine marshes, which remained notoriously malarial from antiquity until the 1920s.
[4] C's letter of 24 Feb to Green, finding it little likely that such diseases as cholera came from a specific virus, gave attention rather to the three apparently influential factors of "the Predisposition of the Patient, the unknown Virus, and the

causes, sympathies are too subtle for our senses to find data to go upon; against the first[b] medicine may act profitably; against the third a wise and sagacious medical police[5] ought to be adopted; but above all let every man act like a Christian in all charity and love and brotherly-kindness, and sincere reliance on God's providence.[6]

Quarantine cannot keep out an atmospheric disease—but it can and does always increase the predisposing causes of its reception.[7]   [36:364]

All harmony is founded on a relation to rest—on relative rest. Take a metallic plate, and strew sand on it; sound[c] an harmonic chord over the sand, and all the grains will whirl about in circles or other geometrical figures, but always round or as it were depending on some point of sand relatively at rest; sound a discord, and every grain will whisk about without any order at all, in no figures and with no points of rest.[8]

---

b 1st ~~wise & temperance~~   *c* ~~draw~~ sound

---

predisposing Circumstances, in which word I include . . . state of atmosphere, soil, air, temperature & condition of the Habitat, &c". *CL* vi 887. C had found confirmation of his theory in a communication from John Lizars, professor of surgery in Edinburgh, reprinted in the *M Chron* 22 Feb 1832. In an earlier marginal note C had suggested "contagious" as the name for diseases ordinarily requiring immediate contact and "infectious" for those "supposed to stain, corrupt, or *infect* the air", with "epidemic" for diseases produced in different places at the same time, "whether from the atmosphere or gasses from the soil". *Edinburgh Medical and Surgical Journal* xiv (1818): *CM (CC)* ii 362–3.

[5] I.e. a system of regulations for preserving order.

[6] C had noted on 1 Mar 1832 that every epidemic disease "should awaken us to the deep interest which every man of every country has in the well-being of all men, and in the consequent progressive *humanization* of the Surface & with it the Atmosphere of the Planet itself". HEHL MS HM 17299 (N F°) p 152. C wrote to Green on the day of this conversation (7 Apr) of "Mr Gillman's odd aversion to allow any sick person in his own house". *CL* vi 898. DW had written

to HCR 1 Dec 1831: "One visible Blessing seems already to be coming upon us through the alarm of the Cholera. Every rich man is now obliged to look into the miserable bye-lanes & corners inhabited by the Poor; & many crying abuses are . . . about to be remedied—". *CRC* i 225.

[7] C had denounced the quarantine laws in a note of 1810 (*CN* iii 3730); he was vehement in the note of 1 Mar 1832: "The Quarantine is a cruel Superstition of Fear. Where the Disease is simply contagious, as the Small Pox, Measles, &c. there is no need of it. Common Caution & Medical skill suffice. When this very disease becomes *epidemic*, thro' uncomprehended influences, the Quarantine is mockery." HEHL MS HM 17299 (N F°) p 152. In Jun 1831 the Board of Health had recommended a strict quarantine against Asiatic cholera. Rejecting the proposal as unpopular, the Government created in Nov 1831 a new Central Board of Health, which shortened the period of quarantine and "declared against all coercive attempts to isolate the disease". William Munk *The Life of Sir Henry Halford, Bart* (1895) 86.

[8] Approximately the results described by C were first announced by Ernst Florenz Friedrich Chladni (1756–1827) in

The Clerisy of a Nation—its learned^d—its poets—its writers^9 are these points of relative rest. There would be no harmony without them.
[36:365]

---

^{a}21. April. 1832.

There have been three silent revolutions in England: 1. When the Professions fell off from the Church. 2. When Literature fell off from the Professions. 3. When the Press fell off from Literature.^{1} [36:366]

Common phrases are, as it were, so stereotyped now by conventional use that it is really much easier to write on the ordinary politics of the day in the newspaper slang than it is to make a good pair of shoes. An apprentice has as much to learn now to be a shoemaker as ever he had; but an ignorant coxcomb with a competent want of honesty may very effectively wield a pen in a newspaper office with infinitely less pains and preparation than were necessary formerly.^{2} [36:367]

^{d} learned ~~men~~ ^{a} f 61

Entdeckungen über die Theorie des Klanges (Leipzig 1787). After initially using circular and rectangular plates of glass and copper, he reported in *Die Akustik* (Leipzig 1802) on variations in the geometrical figures produced by variations in the shapes of the vibrating plates. It is the harmonic response of the metallic plate that creates patterns in the sand. C might have learned of the "Chladni figures" at Göttingen, where further experiments were carried out by Georg Christoph Lichtenberg (1742–99), or from Thomas Young, who had studied acoustical phenomena in 1801–3 at the Royal Institution (where he worked with Davy and Sir Joseph Banks) after becoming interested, about 1800, in Chladni's experiments.

^{9} C had defined the clerisy "of the nation, or national church" as "the sages and professors of law and jurisprudence; of medicine and physiology; of music; of military and civil architecture; of the physical sciences . . . in short, all the so called liberal arts and sciences . . . as well as the Theological". *C&S (CC)* 46. The word here printed as "writers" is

overwritten and almost illegible in MS B; *TT* (1835) substituted "or philosophers, or scholars".

^{1} Rejecting the conventional theory of progressive revolutions, C in *C&S* gave a general historical context for intellectual degeneracy. *C&S (CC)* 61–8. In 1812 Lady Beaumont told Joseph Farington "that Coleridge considers *Reviews* & the multiplication of newspapers as tending to amuse the mind superficially, and that at former periods when Lord Bacon and other great Philosophers and deep thinkers lived there being no such light matter in circulation the minds of men were employed in a more solid manner." Farington *Diary* XII 4228–9. The "same gradual retrograde movement" is traced in *BL* ch 3 *(CC)* I 56–9. Against this passage in *TT* the *Literary Gazette* 30 May 1835 p 341 protested that "the mere periodical press of our time might measure strength with the best writers of any previous epoch".

^{2} C would seem to be tracing a rapid decline from his own years as journalist, which had gone a little past 4 Sept 1811 when he wrote in the *Courier* that

Asgill was a staunch friend of the Hanover succession; and it was on that account—and not for his book—that the Tories persecuted him and got him expelled from the House of Commons.[3]   [36:311]

---

23. April 1832.[1]

The Genius of the Spanish is exquisitely subtle without being at all acute; hence there is so much humor and so little wit in their literature.[2] The Genius of the Italians, on the contrary, is[a] acute,[b] profound and sensual, but not subtile;—hence what they think to be humourous is merely witty.[3]   [36:368]

I think Defoe's and Asgill's irony often[c] times superior to Swift's.[4]

                                                                              [36:376]

---

[a] is ~~profoundly~~   [b] acute, ~~as well as~~   [c] ~~many~~ often

---

"Newspapers and Reviews . . . form nine tenths of the erudition of nine tenths of the readers throughout England"; yet even then (21 Sept) he characterised the commonly accepted style as "cementless aggregates". *EOT (CC)* II 276, 306. The style of other journalists and all addicts of the "unconnected periods of the fashionable Anglo-gallican taste" he had found "asthmatic". *CL* II 1179; *Friend (CC)* I 20; *CN* I 1758.

[3] Asgill's *Argument* was condemned to be burnt by the public hangman. C now adds to his remarks of 30 Jul 1831, above, on Asgill's expulsion the motivation that Asgill was a Hanoverian. HNC transferred the sentence to 36:311, with the qualification "I really suspect" (1835), changed in 1836 to "really I suspect". Asgill arises here as a prominent example of the better days of journalism, coming the more readily because C was at work on his projected collection of Asgill's tracts. *CL* VI 901–6.

[1] 21 Apr was Holy Saturday. During this Easter vacation, between law terms, HNC returned to Highgate on Monday, Tuesday, and the following Saturday.

[2] To his distinctions of genius, talent, sense, and cleverness among the English, French, and Germans, in *Friend (CC)* I 418–23 and in a letter to Thomas Boosey 4 Sept 1816 (*CL* IV 666–7), C here provides a postscript on the Spanish and Italians. In two copies of *The Friend* he distinguished between the sense in which Cervantes and Calderón are "in some sort characteristic of the *Nation* that produced them" and the sense of his general remarks on national characteristics. *Friend (CC)* I 420n–1.

[3] For similar classifications of peoples, besides *The Friend* as cited in n 2, above, cf *CL* IV 666–7; *CN* I 1762; *P Lects* Lects 5, 13 (1949) 190, 382, 416 n 25, 463 n 22.

[4] Of C's reserved opinion of Swift, it is noteworthy that HNC first wrote "many times superior"; transferred in print to 30 Apr, the phrase became "often finer". In a marginal note on *The Life and Surprising Adventures of Robinson Crusoe* (2 vols 1812), comparing the "contemptuous Swift" and the "contemned De Foe", C found Defoe more estimable because he drew sympathy from "the *whole* of my Being" in contrast with an author appealing "to but a *part* of my Being—my sense of the Ludicrous, for instance". *CM (CC)* II 158–

To estimate a man like Vico[5]—or any great man who has made discoveries and committed errors—you ought to say to yourself: "He did so and so in the year 1690[6]—a Roman Catholic at Naples; now what would he not have done if he had lived now and could have availed himself of all our vast acquisitions in physical science!"   [36:369]

After the Scienza Nuova, read Spinoza De præscripto &c.[7] They differed, Vico in thinking that Society tended to Monarchy, Spinoza in thinking it tended to Democracy.[8] Now Spinoza's Ideal Democracy has been realized, and by a contemporary—not in a Nation (for that is impossible) but in a sect—Fox and the Quakers.[9]   [36:370]

---

9. On 11 Aug, below (at n 11) (35:426) Asgill and Swift are named together as appropriate answerers of Malthus.

[5] Vico published *Principii d'una scienza nuova* at Naples in 1725. This *New Science*, defending history against Descartes as a human product, advanced a theory of the past as modified cycles best discovered through the study of language, myth, and customs. To Gioacchino de' Prati, from whom C had borrowed a copy of the work (3 vols 1816), he wrote on 14 May 1825: "I am more and more delighted with G. B. Vico". *CL* v 454. A few days earlier he had sent to the publisher a motto for *AR* from Vico *De antiquissima Italorum sapientia*, but it has been shown that C found the motto, with a passage rephrased in *Friend (CC)* I 476 and a quotation in *TL* (1848) 36, in J. H. Jacobi *Von den göttlichen Dingen und ihrer Offenbarung* (1811) in *Werke* (6 vols Leipzig 1812–16) III 351–3, which C acquired c 1816–17. M. H. Fisch "The Coleridges, Dr. Prati, and Vico" *Modern Philology* XLI (1943) 119–20. C still had Prati's copy in Oct 1833, when HNC took the volumes to Devonshire just in time to avoid their return to the revisiting Prati. *CL* VI 965. As in his respect for Paracelsus and Bruno, C would respond sympathetically to Vico's distinction between *certum*, the certainty of grammar and legal fact, and *verum*, the truth of rational justice and historical philology. For HCR's report of C's conversation on Vico see App F 19, below. See also 9 May 1830 n 14, above.

[6] *TT* (1835) retained "1690"; *TT* (1836) changed the date to 1720. In 1699, at thirty-one, Vico became professor of rhetoric at the University of Naples. A note in *TT* (1836) recommended to the reader the adaptation of Vico's theory of history by Jules Michelet (1827).

[7] *TT* (1835) cited in a note *Tractatus politicus* ch 6, "De Monarchia ex rationis praescripto". C cited the same chapter, to the effect that pure monarchy is a rational entity unknown in actuality, in *C&S (CC)* 23. In Spinoza *Opera* ed Paulus (2 vols Jena 1802–3), which C borrowed from HCR and annotated Nov 1812–Nov 1813, the passage occurs at II 332–4. C had the work sharply in mind when he referred to "an Aristocracy after the valuable Model of Spinoza" in a note assigned the date Apr 1812. *CN* III 4147 (par 6).

[8] Vico declared repeatedly in *Scienza nuova* that the natural succession of political forms (after the original families with their plebs) is aristocracy, democracy, and civil monarchy, with variations but in that order. Spinoza *Tractatus politicus* ch 8 § 12 asserted that democracies change into aristocracies and these at length into monarchies. In chs 6–7 Spinoza described the healthy tendency of political development to limit the monarch by council, judiciary, magistracy, and the like to serve the interests of all citizens in the commonwealth; he described limited monarchy rather than democracy. HNC included in "Omniana" C's somewhat similar contrast of Spinoza and Hobbes—*CN* III 3548—on the natural state of man as a state of war. *LR* I 362.

[9] The point is restated on 8 Apr 1833,

*a*24 April 1832.

Colors must be expressed by a Heptad, the largest possible form for things Finite, as the Pentad is the smallest possible form; indeed the Heptad of things Finite is in all cases reducible to the Pentad.[1] The adorable

a f 61ᵛ

---

below (at n 12) (36:485). C professed the religion specifically of George Fox (1624–91) on 7 Dec 1802. *CL* II 893. Writing on 31 Dec 1808 to Thomas Wilkinson, he again declared that "in the essentials of their faith I believe as the Quakers do", and praised William Penn's "Preface to G. Fox's Journal". *CL* III 155–7. Often he made a near equation of Fox, Bruno, and Böhme, partly on the basis of their unacceptability to empirical philosophers. *CN* I 1646 f 84; *CL* III 279, IV 590, 592; *BL* ch 9 *(CC)* I 149–50; *P Lects* Lect 11 (1949) 329. The notebooks repeatedly project a never-published eulogium of Fox. At the Lambs' 20 Dec 1810 C agreed with HCR that "everyone who utters a truth may be said to be inspired . . . & afterwards named *Fox* & other of the Quakers, Mad. *Guyon*, St. *Theresa* &c. as being *also* inspired"—the "*also*" meaning in addition to Jesus. *CR (BCW)* 33.

[1] See 25–6 Aug 1827 nn 2–4, above, and the pentad of grammar of 18 Mar 1827, above (36:76). This approach to colour derives from Goethe *Zur Farbenlehre* (Tübingen 1810), which C requested of HCR 7 Dec 1812 (*CL* IV 422); from Steffens "Ueber die Bedeutung der Farben in der Natur" *Schriften Alt und Neu* (2 vols Breslau 1821) II 5–35, with Steffens's modifications of Schelling's doctrine of polarity in *Schriften* I 3–66; in its less speculative aspects from William T. Brande *Manual of Chemistry* (1819)—*CN* IV 4570, 4855, 5290 and nn—and less directly from Lorenz Oken *Erste Ideen zur Theorie des Lichts, Finsterniss, der Farben und der Wärme* pt IV: *Über Licht und Wärme als das nicht irdische, aber kosmische materiale Element* (Jena 1808). Despite C's need for a unified philosophy of nature that the English empiricists did not satisfy, he rebuked the lesser *Naturphilosophen* in

notes on *Erste Ideen* and on Oken's *Lehrbuch der Naturgeschichte* (6 vols Leipzig and Jena 1813–26)—*CN* IV 4813–14—both for being too abstract and for substituting borrowed fact for the needed idea. He made similar protests in marginalia on Johann Christian Heinroth (1773–1843) *Lehrbuch der Anthropologie* (Leipzig 1822) and Johann Friedrich Meckel (1781–1833) *System der vergleichenden Anatomie* (6 vols in 7 Halle 1821–33). *CM (CC)* II 998–1031; III. On 14 Jul 1816 C returned to HCR works by Kant he had borrowed: "Coleridge talked about Goethe's work on the theory of colours: said he had some years back discovered the same theory, and would certainly have reduced it to form and published it had not Southey diverted his attention from such studies to poetry. On my mentioning that I had heard that an English work had been published lately developing the same system, Coleridge answered with great naïveté that he was very free in communicating his thoughts on the subject wherever he went and among literary people." *CRB* I 185. C had congenial support for his opposition to Newtonian optics in a book he had first laughed at as "a biggish one, to overthrow Sir Iky's System of Gravitation, Color, & the whole 39 Articles of the Hydrostatic, chemic, & Physiologic Churches" (*CL* III 414) but soon came to admire: Richard Saumarez *The Principles of Physiological and Physical Science* chs 7, 16 (1812) 146–55, 323–80. On C and Saumarez see *CL* III 418–20, v 309. There is a pentad of colours in VCL MS LT 1 and an octad of c 1827 in BM MS Egerton 2800 f 178ᵛ: *SW&F (CC)*. For Grattan's report of C's remarks on colours in 1828 see App F 20, below. And see the discussion in Trevor H. Levere *Poetry Realized in Nature* (Cambridge 1981) 149–58.

Tetractys or Tetrad is the form of God, which again is reducible into, and the same in reality with the Trinity.[2]

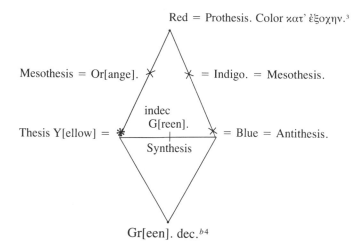

Red = Prothesis. Color κατ' ἐξοχην.[3]

Mesothesis = Or[ange]. ✳ ✳ = Indigo. = Mesothesis.

indec
G[reen].
Thesis Y[ellow] = ✳ ✳ = Blue = Antithesis.
Synthesis

Gr[een]. dec.[b][4]

The natural Green is indeconponible; = but you may make a Green of Yellow and Blue. [36:371]

The Destruction of Jerusalem is the only subject now remaining for an Epic Poem—a subject which should interest all Christendom as the Fall of Man, or as the War of Troy did all Greece.[5] There would be difficul-

[b] ~~indec.~~

2 Cf 8 Jul 1827 n 3, above.
3 "Pre-eminently".
4 "Gr. dec.", as explained in the sentence below the heptad, is decomponible green, a distinction derived from Goethe and Oken. Variants of the diagram appear on a covering sheet addressed to C and postmarked 23–5 Feb 1828 (VCL S MS F 2.13) and in a letter to Hyman Hurwitz 16 Sept 1829 (CL vi 818). A note in TT (1835) was omitted from TT (1836): "I trust this touch of the *polar* logic will not frighten the general reader. The students of Mr. Coleridge's later works are familiar enough with it; and the scheme is as simple as it is beautiful and comprehensive.—ED." A note on George Herbert *The Temple* (10th ed 1674) suggests that C saw an analogy between his pentad and the cross of Jesus. *CN* IV 5399; cf *CM (CC)* II 1036–7.

5 Acting for his father the Roman Emperor Vespasian, Titus levelled Jerusalem and destroyed the Temple in A.D. 70. The event would be most fully known to C from the works of the Jewish historian Josephus. C used William Whiston's translation from the Greek, *The Works of Flavius Josephus* (1737), often reissued. *CN* IV 5329, 5331n; *CL* VI 569. Stimulated by Eichhorn *Commentarius in Apocalypsin Joannis* (Göttingen 1791)—of which he annotated two copies—C interpreted the Apocalypse as narrating the final triumph of Christianity over paganism and Judaism, "typified in the Fall of Rome, the destruction of the Old and the (symbolical) descent of the New Jerusalem". *LS (CC)* 147n. In his *QR* review of Aug 1834 HNC quoted the remarks of 24 Apr with exactly the same additions and omissions

ties—as there are in all subjects—and they must be mitigated, palliated and thrown into the shade, as Milton has done with the numerous ones in the Paradise Lost;[6] but there would be a greater assemblage of grandeur and splendor than can now be found in any other theme. As for the old Mythology—incredulus odi:[7] and yet there must be a mythology for an Epic Poem; here there would be the completion of prophecies—the termination of the first revealed national religion under the violence of Paganism as the immediate forerunner and condition of the spread of a revealed mundane religion; the character of the Roman and the Jew, the awfulness, the completeness, the justice.[8] No materials would be wanted beyond the Bible, Josephus, Philo-Judæus and the Zelotæ.[9] I schemed it

as in *TT* (1835). He alluded in the review, but not in the published *TT*, to the "splendid drama" by "a younger poet" (*CH* 635), meaning Henry Hart Milman (1791–1868) *The Fall of Jerusalem, a Dramatic Poem* (1820).

[6] The preceding sentence, as expanded in *TT* (1835), referred to "Milton's Fall of Man" and "the Homeric War of Troy". In notes for Lect 5 of 11 Mar 1819 on Dante and his age, C said that the "comb[ination] of Poetry with Doctrines" is "one of the charac[teristics] of Xtn Poetry—but in this Dante has failed, far more than Milton". *CN* III 4498 f 138ᵛ: *Lects 1808–19 (CC)* II 400.

[7] Horace *Ars poetica* 188. Tr H. Rushton Fairclough (LCL 1916): "I discredit and abhor".

[8] This account subsumes C's view of prophecy as reported on 13 Apr 1830, above (36:123), and 21 Dec 1833, below (36:607–8). In a marginal note C interpreted the fall of Jerusalem, with reference to the words of Jesus in Mark 13.28–37, as closing one great epoch and more especially "the Type of the final close of the whole World of Time, i.e. of all *temporal* things". Philip Skelton *Complete Works* ed Robert Lynam (6 vols 1824) I 276–7: *CM (CC)* IV. Eichhorn, describing Revelation as a dramatic poem in three acts, interpreted Act I as an allegory of the fall of Jerusalem; C annotated the pages on Act I, the destruction of Jerusalem as the conquest

of Judaism by Christianity. C probably knew of David Pareus *A Commentary upon the Divine Revelation of the Apostle and Evangelist John* (Amsterdam 1644—the first tr into English), which described the work as "a Prophetical Drama" and was praised by Milton in several places, including the essay on tragedy affixed to *Samson Agonistes*. The subject of C's projected epic has been imaginatively deduced as "the confluence of cultures accomplished in Christ", for the "Jew and Babylonian, Greek, Roman, and Egyptian, Christian and Mohammedan yet to be born, were conquered by and absorbed into Christianity, in the great symbolic metropolis of the East . . .". E. S. Shaffer *"Kubla Khan" and the Fall of Jerusalem* 37; cf 17–18, 38–9, 53–5.

[9] Philo *On the Embassy to Gaius* (LCL Philo X 2–187). Flavius Josephus, earlier Joseph ben Matthias (37–c 100), governor and general in Galilee, surrendered to Vespasian and permanently joined the Romans; the pertinent works are his *History of the Jewish War* (7 bks) and his autobiography. Perhaps it was puzzlement over mention of the Zelotes, or Zealots, that led HNC to drop the sentence on sources from *TT* (1835). According to Josephus, opposition under their leader Judas to the census of Quirinius in Galilee A.D. 6, and their continued resistance to Roman taxation, precipitated the rebellion of A.D. 66–70 and thus led to the fall of Jerusalem. Cf Hastings

at twenty-five[10]—but alas! it was a scheme only for me! Venturum expectat.[11]   [36:372]

I never said that the Vox Populi was of course Vox Dei; it may be—but it may,[c] and with equal probability à priori, be [d]Vox Diaboli.[12] That the voice of 100[13] million of men calling for the same thing is a Spirit, I believe; but whether that be a spirit of Heaven or Hell, I can only know by trying the thing called for by the prescript of Reason and God's Will.

[36:373]

[c] may be—   [d] f 62

Dictionary of the Bible XII 849–55; *Encyclopaedia Judaica* XVI (1971) 947–50. One of the disciples of Jesus is designated as Simon Zelotes (Luke 5.15, Acts 1.13), but no substantial work by any member of the sect remains. Maybe C said something like "Philo-Judaeus on the Zelotes". Tacitus *Historiae* 5.1–13 gives a Roman view of Titus' destruction of the Temple. With aims somewhat like C's, Tasso had disastrously revised his masterwork into *Gerusalemme conquistata* (1593).

Josephus, Tacitus, the Zealots, and the later Dio Cassius and Eusebius are among the sources cited by Jacques Basnage *The History of the Jews from Jesus Christ to the Present Time* tr Thomas Taylor (1708) 53–61, which C read in 1820. *CN* IV 4709 and n.

[10] C wrote to Thomas Wedgwood on 20 Oct 1802: "I have since my twentieth year meditated an heroic poem on the Siege of Jerusalem by Titus—this is the Pride, & the Stronghold of my Hope." *CL* II 877. A year later he included the poem among projects that would require "enough of manly Strength & Perseverance to do one thing at a time". *CN* I 1646. On 20 Mar 1820 he wrote to Allsop: "Alas! for the proud times when I planned . . . the Scheme of the Hymns . . . and the Epic Poem on what still appears to me the one only fit subject remaining for an Epic Poem, Jerusalem besieged & destroyed by Titus". *CL* V 28; cf IV 687.

[11] "It awaits one who is to come".

[12] Alcuin Epistle 127 to Charlemagne c 800: "Vox populi vox dei", "the voice of the people is the voice of God". From 1809 C attributed to Sir Philip Sidney the thought that the voice might be from the devil; see 13 May 1833 and n 21, below. In a letter to his brother George 6 Nov 1794 C denied that he was a democrat, and in *BL* ch 10 and elsewhere denied that he had ever been one. *CL* I 126; *BL (CC)* I 179–87, 190, 194. In *The Plot Discovered*, inspired by Joseph Gerrald and the Earl of Abingdon, C had declared that a free press in a time of corruption would "swell into a deep and awful thunder, the VOICE OF GOD". *Lects 1795 (CC)* 312 and n. Charles Caleb Colton had written in *Lacon or Many Things in Few Words* (2 vols 1820–2) II 166: "The voice of the People is the voice of God; this axiom has manifold exceptions, and '*Populus vult decipi*,' is sometimes nearer the truth . . .". C declared the axiom "true or false according as it is understood". *Friend (CC)* I 50n.

[13] "Ten millions" in *TT* (1835). A census report by Lamb's (and C's) friend John Rickman had appeared in Jan 1832, *A Comparative Account of the Population of Great Britain in 1831* (2 vols). As corrected by later statisticians, the figures are 13 million for England and Wales, 24 million for the United Kingdom. Phyllis Deane and W. A. Cole *British Economic Growth 1688–1959* (Cambridge 1967) 6–8.

28. April 1832.[1]

Black is the negation of color in its greatest energy. Without lustre, it indicates or represents vacuity; add lustre to it, and it represents the highest degree of solidity. As for instance in the first case the dark mouth of a cavern; in the second a polished ebony box.[2]　　　　　[36:374]

In finite forms there is no real and absolute Identity. God alone is Identity. In the former Prothesis is a bastard Prothesis, a quasi Identity only.[3]　　　　　[36:375]

I know no genuine Saxon English superior to Asgill's.[4]　　　　　[36:376]

M——[5] is one of those men who go far to shake my faith in a future state of existence. I mean on account of the difficulty of knowing where to place him. I could not bear to roast him—he is not so bad as all that comes to; but then on the other hand, to have to sit down with such a

---

[1] On 27 Apr a young man from New England, Henry B. McLellan, visited C and recorded in his journal remarks on the condition of England that complement those reported by HNC. McLellan's record also indicates a responsiveness to his personal interests not always evident in reports by C's visitors. For the report, and a letter written a bit later, see App F 21, below.

[2] See 24 Apr 1832 and n 1, above. Between the years 1819 and 1825, reading Brande and thinking about Steffens, C had speculated about dark vs black, shade, cavern, and "a mass of ebony". *CN* IV 4855, 5290.

[3] The Trinity, with God as Identity, had come up on 24 Apr with reference to colours. Indeed, the first three topics recorded for 28 Apr seem to follow those of 23–4 Apr as if HNC or another opened the conversation with questions about C's recent remarks.

[4] *TT* (1835) combined the two sentences on Asgill of 23 and 28 Apr (36:376).

[5] Speculation on the identity of "M" is necessarily invidious. *TT* (1835) headed the entry "Adiaphori", indifferent, neither good nor bad. In a marginal note on William Ellery Channing *A Dis-course Delivered at the Installation of the Rev. Mellish Irving Motte* (1828) the word designated Unitarians: "Adiaphorites, or Uni-personalists, or better still Psilanthropists, are the proper names of the modern Socinians." *CM (CC)* II 22. That C next speaks of a parliamentary orator at once clear and shallow suggests either Macaulay, a current *bête noir*, or Mackintosh, a standing aversion (Mackintosh was to die a month later). The adjacent reference to C's Asgill project could have brought up John Murray's rôle as a possible publisher, but if "M" is Murray, this is one of C's milder comments about him. A week later, protesting to HNC Henry Hart Milman's presumption in "improving" C's poems, C referred to Murray first as "an Anthropoïd" and then as "the Anthropoïd". *CL* VI 902, 906. The apparent transition to Horner, identifiable as a star in the Scottish constellation, strengthens the candidacy of Mackintosh as the undesirable companion for C's heaven.

C applied a similar formula to Jane Harding, Mrs Gillman's sister, "whom no one could think of putting into Hell, & yet who would make a Hell of every other decent person's Heaven". *CN* IV 5053.

---

fellow in the very lowest pot-house in Heaven is[a] utterly inconsistent with the belief of that place being a place of reward to me.   [36:380]

I cannot say that I thought Horner a man of genius;[6] he seemed to me to be one of those men who have not very extended minds, but who know what they know well—shallow[b] streams, and clear because they are shallow. Still, I must say he struck me much more than Brougham.[7] There was a great goodness about him.[8]   [36:379]

---

[c]Horne Tooke's advice to the Friends of the People was profound—If you wish to be powerful, pretend to be powerful.[9]   [36:377]

Fox and Pitt constantly played into each other's hands. [d]Daniel Stuart of the Courier,[e] a knowing Scotchman, soon found out the gross lies and impostures of that Club as to their numbers and told Fox so;[10] and yet,

---

[a] is ~~beyond quite~~   [b] ~~clear~~ shallow   [c] f 62[v]   [d-e] D. Stewart of the C.

---

[6] Francis Horner as M.P. opposed the slave-trade and the Corn Bill of 1815, with C's blessing. *CL* IV 553. See 7 May 1830 and n 27, above.

[7] Besides their resemblance to Mackintosh as men of talent, not genius, Horner and Brougham were both Scottish Whigs involved in the *Ed Rev* from its inception.

[8] C may have visited Horner just before embarking for Malta in 1804. Writing to his brother Leonard Horner in behalf of Hurwitz in 1827, C assured him that he held Francis in reverence. *CL* VI 709, 1017.

[9] C's source uncertain. Describing the policy of "the associated Jacobins" as pretending to be "numerous and formidable", in Letter I to Fox, *M Post* 4 Nov 1802, C had pointed to Horne Tooke: "I believe, that this advice was early given them by a man, whose talents and attainments ought to have inspired a nobler ambition, than that of becoming the leader and tool-master of a London Corresponding Society." *EOT (CC)* I 380–1. C's antipathy to Horne Tooke can be documented even from TT, but G. B. Greenough had a different view from John Chester as late as 9 Jan 1801. Reporting on C's activities with *Wallen-*

stein and the *M Post* after they had parted in Germany, Greenough's journal continues: "He was introduced to Godwin, to Horne Tooke whom he likes very much, to Sheridan whom he detests and several others of the great men of the Age." *W&C* 234; *London Mercury* XXIII (1931) 564. C's *Verses Addressed to J. Horne Tooke*—*PW* (EHC) I 150–1—had praised even *The Diversions of Purley* when published in the London *Telegraph* 9 Jul 1796. *An Expository and Panegyrical Ode to Addington*, in *M Post* 27 May 1801, takes Horne Tooke's side by default against the Committee of Secrecy. *EOT (CC)* I 264 and n.

[10] *TT* (1835) changed the first part of the sentence to "Mr. Stewart . . . a very knowing person", without comfort to Stuart, who included this reason for protest among others in his letter of 7 Oct 1835 to HNC: "I must be permitted to add that after a perusal of his Letters, and a review of my conduct towards him, instead of feelng myself 'a knowing Person', I think I should be regarded as a very great simpleton. He never had a prime & manhood of Intellect in the sense he speaks of in the Literary Biography. He had indeed the great mind, the great powers, but he could not use them

instead of disclaiming them, as he ought to have done, he absolutely exaggerated their numbers and sinister intentions—and Pitt, who also knew the lie, took him at his word, and argued against him triumphantly on his own premiss.[11]

Fox's Anti-Anglicism or Gallicism, too, was a treasury of weapons to Pitt. He could never conceive the French right without making the English wrong.[12]   [36:378]

for the Press with regularity & vigour. He was always ill. Admitting all he says of his services to the Morning Post, yet after I left that Paper he did nothing to serve me, and yet he had at least 700£ of me, besides many acts of kindness." VCL S MS F 6 f 8. In 1838 Stuart protested that he had spoken to Fox only once and never on the subject of associations. "Anecdotes of the Poet Coleridge" *G Mag* NS IX 579, x 24. Although C was as careless with the facts in 1832 as in 1802, his point is that Fox by taking seriously associations favourable to France led to Pitt's success in putting before Parliament the papers of the Committee of Secrecy with an assurance on 15 May 1794 that the Society for Constitutional Information had "a deliberate and deep concerted plan for actually assembling a convention of all England" to wrest from Parliament the power given to it by the people and the constitution. *Parl Hist* XXXI 502.

HCR sent to HNC in 1835 "a *Specimen* that you would gladly have made use of": "Mr. C: was praising one day his old friend D. S. who I understand was on many occasions generous to him—I could not help putting some awkward questions—on which he said 'Why my dear Sir, if I am pressed, which I dont like to be about Dan's character I should say—Dan is a Scotchman who is content to get rid of the itch when he can afford to wear clean linen—' " VCL S MS F 11.3 No 475. Cf *CRB* I 37, 170.

[11] The Society of the Friends of the People was founded 11 Apr 1792 by Charles Grey and other parliamentary Whigs to maintain the freedom won in 1688–9 without the excesses of such associations as the Society for Constitutional Information. On the moderation of

their program see Carl B. Cone *The English Jacobins* (New York 1968) 126–32, 143. Horne Tooke was active in the more advanced Society for Constitutional Information, founded in 1780 in succession to the Constitutional Society that he had formed in 1771. He lent aid to the more radical (Painite) London Corresponding Society, founded by Thomas Hardy in 1792 to demand universal suffrage and annual Parliaments. Albert Goodwin *The Friends of Liberty: The English Democratic Movement in the Age of the French Revolution* (Cambridge, Mass 1979) 114, 120–3, 203–7, 218–21, 236–58.

[12] Granting at all times the error of Fox's coalition with Lord North in 1783, C in retrospect probably dates the errors he describes here from the sedition trials of 1794 or from Pitt's successful passage of the Treasonable Practices and Seditious Meetings Acts in 1795, over the protests of Fox, C, the Whig Club of Bristol, the London Corresponding Society, and the few similar associations that had survived the intimidations of 1794. In 1800 C still heard Pitt's eloquence without finding reason in it, whereas Fox spoke from "clear head, clean heart, and impetuous feelings". *CL* I 568. In the *M Post* 3 Dec 1801 C saw the Foxites as hoping like enthusiasts and the Pittites as fearing like fanatics but admitting that Jacobinism had never had the strength to justify real alarm. *EOT (CC)* I 278. By 1806 neither Pitt nor Fox was a wise statesman, but Pitt had the better measures. *CL* II 1179. *TT* (1835) had C remembering his own lines on "Goose and Goody at the Helm" in *A Character* (?1825) 62–8, with line 62 converted from third to first person. *PW* (EHC) I 453.

It was the error of Milton, Sydney and others of that age to think it possible to construct a purely aristocratical Government—defecated of all passion and ignorance and sordid motive. The truth is, such a government would be weak from its utter want of sympathy with the people to be governed by it.[13]   [36:383]

In two points of view*f* I reverence man—1. as a citizen, a part of, and in order to, a Nation[14]—2. as a Christian. If men are neither one or the other—but an aggregation of individuals who acknowledge no national unity, nor believe with me in Christ—I have no*g* sympathy with them nor*h* should I feel more remorse at their destruction to preserve the Nation, than if I held out a sword against yon thunder-cloud, and God's lightning.[15]   [36:381]

f view ~~of~~   *g* no ~~more~~   *h* nor ~~scruple~~

[13] Although the error C attributes to Milton and Algernon Sidney might be thought to stem from the lack of comprehension of common people, and even of prospective readers, often declared to be the chief failing in C's own political writings, he objects here to the philosopher-parliament being recommended, not the philosopher recommending it. C here gives the other side to his warnings against rule by the unenlightened masses; his select clerisy was not to govern but to civilise. In *The Ready and Easy Way to Establish a Free Commonwealth* (1660) Milton had recommended the subordination of an annually rotated senate to a sovereign council of "good Education and acquisite Wisdom": "For the ground and basis of every just and free Government . . . is a general Council of ablest men, chosen by the People to consult of public Affairs from time to time for the common good. . . . The grand or general Council, being well chosen, should be perpetual. . . . By this continuance they will become every way skilfullest, best provided of Intelligence from abroad, and best acquainted with the People at home, and the People with them." Milton *A Complete Collection of the Historical, Political, and Miscellaneous Works* ed Thomas Birch (2 vols 1738) I 594, 592–3. Sidney, throughout *Discourses Concerning Government*

(1698), argued that governors should be chosen on the basis of virtue, for only virtue carries the true marks of sovereignty; in ch 2 § 16 he declared that government best which mixes monarchy, aristocracy, and democracy. What C doubts is the prevalence of virtue. For other comments on aristocratic government see *CN* II 2223, IV 5376; *Friend* *(CC)* I 199 (II 131).

[14] *TT* (1835) read "or in order to", but C means man as such a part as to serve the state as an end. To illustrate this meaning of "order", Johnson's *Dictionary* cites Jeremy Taylor: "the virginity of the body is only excellent in *order* to the purity of the soul".

[15] *TT* (1835) simplified and mollified the language to "no more personal sympathy . . . than with the dust beneath my feet". The specific thrust of C's remark is that he can bear utilitarians only if they are Christian and Unitarians only if they believe in the organic nation. The utilitarian Unitarian Harriet Martineau, not yet totally anti-theological, visited Highgate at about this time: "He told me that he (the last person whom I should have suspected) read my tales as they came out on the first of the month; and, after paying some compliments, he avowed that there were points on which we differed: (I was full of wonder that there were any on which we agreed:) 'for in-

21. May. 1832.[1]

Professor Park talks about its being *doubtful* whether the Constitution described by Blackstone ever in fact existed;[2] in the same manner it is

stance,' said he, 'you appear to consider that society is an aggregate of individuals!' I replied that I certainly did: whereupon he went off on one of the several metaphysical interpretations which may be put upon the many-sided fact of an organised human society, subject to natural laws in virtue of its aggregate character and organisation together. After a long flight in survey of society from his own balloon in his own current, he came down again to some considerations of individuals, and at length to some special biographical topics, ending with criticisms on old biographers, whose venerable works he brought down from the shelf. No one else spoke, of course, except when I once or twice put a question; and when his monologue came to what seemed a natural stop, I rose to go. I am glad to have seen his weird face, and heard his dreamy voice; and my notion of possession, prophecy,—of involuntary speech from involuntary brain action, has been clearer since." *Autobiography*, with Memorials by Maria Weston Chapman (3rd ed 3 vols 1877) I 397–8.

[1] Surviving letters suggest that HNC visited Highgate each Sunday during May. He was there on 13 May, but there were other guests and C was feeling low. C's face was bloated from medication. *CL* VI 902–7. The talk recorded here may be for Sun, 20 May rather than Mon, 21 May.

[2] John James Park (1795–1833) *The Dogmas of the Constitution* Lect 1 (1832) 6–7: "The propositive or theoretic constitution of Great Britain (if it ever existed in a pure state, which is very doubtful,) has ceased to have any existence for upwards of a century and a half—has, for upwards of a century and a half, been superseded by a totally different machinery; but the fact has never been PUBLICLY recognized or recorded,—the substituted constitution has never been formally reduced to proposi-

tion; no De Lolme, or Blackstone, has descanted upon *its* virtues, or pointed out *its* defects; and a sufficient number of the forms of the old constitution have been tenaciously observed, to satisfy all persons who think merely by rote, that a government by separate and independent estates of King, Lords, and Commons, was, with certain irregularities or corruptions, still the government of the country." C annotated the work, warning HNC in his first note to beware of confounding the terms "theory" and "principle", and in answer to the above, wrote: "Very *doubtful*? Yes, as it is very doubtful that the moon is made of green cheese, and that the spirits of virtuous Welchmen made perfect are transplanted thither in the shape of mites! Blackstone's was the age of shallow law. Monarchy, aristocracy and democracy, as *such*, exclude each the other: but if the elements are to interpenetrate, how absurd to call a lump of sugar hydrogen, oxygen, and carbon!—nay, to take three lumps, and call the first hydrogen, the second oxygen, and the third carbon!" *CM (CC)* IV. *TT* (1835) follows the annotation almost word for word, including the sentence about Blackstone, which does not appear in the TT passage. Between the penning of this entry and the addition of HNC's explanatory and evaluative note in *TT* (1835), HNC had substituted as lecturer during the final illness of Park, who was professor of English law and jurisprudence at the newly established King's College, London. Park's announced purpose in *Dogmas* was to show that he saw through the delusion of Reform (Preface p vii). In it he quoted "part of a sentence" from the *C&S* of C, who was ready to improve him further by "a morning's Conversation" (*CL* VI 909). Later in the year C read Park's privately printed *Conservative Reform: A Letter Addressed to Sir William Betham* (1832), but his one annotation laments

doubtful whether the moon is made of green cheese, or whether the souls of Welshmen [a]do in fact go to heaven on the backs of mites.

To suppose the Crown, Lords and Commons to be three bodies representing Monarchy, Aristocracy and Democracy, and constituting[b] a Government—is like taking three bits of sugar and calling them Oxygen, Hydrogen and Carbon.[3]

Democracy as such is no legitimate ingredient of any Government whatever. The one and only principle of Government ought to be ἡ ἐκ τῶν ἀρίστων κρατεια.[4]

The Democracy of England—before the Reform Bill—was where it ought to be, in the Corporations, Vestries, Companies &c. The power in a democracy is in focal points without a Centre; and in proportion as such democratical power exists, the strength of the central Government ought to be intense; else the Nation falls to pieces.[5]   [36:382]

Mercury strongly illustrates the theory de vi minimorum.[6]—Divide five grains into fifty doses, and it may poison you irretrievably. I don't believe in all Hahnemann[c] says[7]—but he is a fine fellow and like most Ger-

[a] f 63   [b] coereationnstituting   [c] Hannemann

his own mortality, frailty, and "Impatient Cowardice of Pain". *CM (CC)* IV. HNC had known Park at Lincoln's Inn, and wrote to RS on 19 Jun 1831 that his own pamphlet on Reform involved Park's views. UT ms.

[3] The clarification of this analogy in *TT* (1835) concluded: "Don't you see that each is in all, and all in each?"

[4] "The power of the best men". This sentence was dropped from *TT* (1835), presumably as duplicating 19 Sept 1830 (at n 3) (36:259), possibly because of the strangeness of the Greek.

[5] *TT* (1835), among other clarifications, changed "power exists" to "power is strong". It also added a one-sentence paragraph on the increase in 1832 of "democratical action".

[6] "Of the power of the smallest". Doses of mercury reduced "to the millionth degree" are given as the chief example of the "strange doctrine of infinitesimal doses" in "New System of Cure—Hahnemann's Homöopathie" *Ed Rev* L (1830) 517. C had been so heavily dosed with mercury for cholera that he

claimed to see in his mirror "a Hottentot Venus", "*sub* Medicis et Mercurio". *CL* VI 909, 913. In 1833 he would be given mercury for gout and for influenza. *CL* VI 932, 936. HNC wrote of his eye trouble to his brother James 8 Aug 1834: "My numerous inflammations were always in the iris, & mercury was the specific". BM Add MS 47558 f 118. In a note on Hermann Boerhaave *A New Method of Chemistry* C quarrelled with Schelling about mercury as a fluid. *CM (CC)* I 548–9. C may have contrasted a need for the weakest and least in medicine with the need for the strongest and best in government (n 4, above).

[7] Christian Friedrich Samuel Hahnemann (1755–1843), German physician, argued in his first *Organon* of 1810 that "every disease is curable by such medicines as would produce in a healthy person symptoms similar to those which characterise the given disease". *Ed Rev* L (1830) 507. He was known in England primarily by translations and adaptations of his *Reine Arzneimittellehre* (6 vols Dresden 1822–7) and *Organon der*

mans is not altogether wrong, and like them also is *never^d* altogether right.   [36:384]

Six volumes of translated selections from Luther's works, two being from his Letters, would be a delightful work.[8] The translator should be a man deeply imbued with his Bible, the English writers from Henry VII to Edward VI, Latimer and the Scotch Divines, and with the old racy German.[9]   [36:385]

Hollerus—Luther's favorite divine—was a wonderful man, who in the twelfth^e century—the jubilant age of the Papal dominion—nursed the lamp^f of Platonic mysticism in the spirit of the most refined Christianity.[10]   [36:385]

^d ~~not~~ *never*   ^e 12 & 13   ^f lap

Heilkunst (Dresden and Leipzig 1829). Homeopathic principles seem to be what C was recommending to Green in a letter of 10 Apr 1824, yet in asking Green in Feb 1830 if he had ever looked into "Hahnemann's Organ der Heilung" (earlier than the *Ed Rev* article), C seemed to have no faith in the "Similia similibus minimissimum dose man". *CL* v 350, vi 828. Hahnemann founded a school of practice, but he did not invent homeopathy: Milton's essay prefixed to *Samson Agonistes* paraphrased Antonio Minturno and Robert Burton on the similarity of tragic purgation and homeopathic medicine—"salt to remove salt humours". Milton *Poetical Works* ed Edward Hawkins (4 vols Oxford 1824) iii 231. On the possibility that C was trying homeopathy to reduce his intake of laudanum as early as 1814, see *CN* iii 4236 and n.

[8] From 1809 to at least 1818 C regarded a life of Luther "proportioned to the grandeur and interest of the subject", with a volume of selections from his letters, a vital desideratum. *Friend (CC)* i 134, 139n (ii 114, 116n); *CL* iv 845–6. For sustained appraisal by C see *Friend (CC)* i 136–43 and Lect 10 of the lectures on the history of philosophy: *P Lects* (1949) 308–11. In a marginal note on Sir Thomas Browne *Works* C distinguished on 16 Mar 1824 between a little mind

that would ask what "a Luther" would be like in the nineteenth century and a great mind that would ask what the actual Luther did, taught, and sanctioned. *CM (CC)* i 795. Luther, most of all, made C prize "the intellectual growth of Protestant Germany" to Lessing and beyond. *CL* v 287.

[9] *Friend (CC)* i 139n (quoted in HNC's note to this entry in *TT* 1835) specified a knowledge of English writers from Edward vi to Charles i. *TT* (1835), omitting the Lutheran Hugh Latimer, narrowed the "Scotch Divines" to those of the sixteenth century. In quoting Edward Irving's honour roll of Reformers in 1830, C substituted the German Martin Bucer for the Scottish John Knox—*C&S (CC)* 142n—but here he proposes for the translator attention to style and manner rather than content.

[10] Instead of "Hollerus", whether or not he mentioned also a twelfth-century divine unremembered by HNC, could C have said "Taulerus", meaning Johannes Tauler (c 1300–61), "the Illuminated Doctor"? Of Tauler, a mystic mentioned several times in Luther's works, C inquired in a letter of 20 Jun 1817 to HCR, and he mentioned in a letter of Jan 1822 to John Murray his acquisition of Tauler's works. *CL* iv 742, v 205. In *TT* (1835) HNC substituted "Hugo de Saint Victor", not visibly a favourite of Lu-

9. June 1832.

If you take Sophocles, Catullus, Lucretius, the better parts of Cicero and so on, you may, with just two or three exceptions arising out of the different idioms as to cases, translate page after page into good mother English word by word without altering *a*the order.[1] But you cannot do so with Virgil or Tibullus; if you attempt it, you make nonsense.[2]   [36:386]

There is a remarkable power of the picturesque, a vivid manner, in the very old Roman writers—Ennius, Actius &c.—which was lost in the Augustan age.[3]   [36:387]

Much as the Romans owed to Greece in the beginning, whilst the mind was as it were tuning itself to an after effort of its own music, it suffered more by the influence of Greek literature afterwards when the Roman mind was formed and ought to have worked for itself. It then became a superfœtation upon, and not an ingredient in, the national character. With the exception of the stern pragmatic historian and the moral Satirist, it left nothing original to the Latin Muse.[4]

a f 63ᵛ

ther's. The works of Hugh (or Hugo) of St Victor (c 1096–1141) occupy Migne *PL* CLXXV–CLXXVII. In 1829 Irving gave C a copy of Hugh's "rare and intrinsically valuable Volume", *De sacramentis* (Strassburg 1485), but C's one annotation in it has nothing to do with Hugh or his work. *CM (CC)* II 1182–3. On various leaves of Tennemann *Geschichte der Philosophie* VIII C equated "St. Victore's Contemplation" (along with Jean Charlier de Gerson's) with his own "Positive Reason". *CM (CC)* V. In Jan 1834 C asked HNC to recommend to William Pickering that the new series of *G Mag* include biographies of "Hugo de St Victore, Ambrosius, Petrarch &c &c &c". *CL* VI 976.

[1] The point of the entry is enforced by the heading in *TT* (1835), "Sympathy of Old Greek and Latin with English". C expressed to James Gillman Jr, in a letter of 24 Oct 1826, his persuasion that Marcus Tullius Cicero (106–43 B.C.) could be rendered "word by word in English, in the exact order in which they stand in the Latin", with perhaps twenty exceptions per page, if one's models in English were Hooker, Milton, and Jeremy Taylor. *CL* VI 639–40. (To J. W. Mackail

Cicero created a language scarcely altered for nineteen centuries. *Latin Literature*—1895—62.) C is making less obviously his point that "to write Ciceronianly we must think in the age of Cicero". *CN* III 3365.

[2] Greater detail on these and other classical authors is reported on 2 Sept 1833, below (36:585–6). For Virgil see below at n 12 and above, 8 May 1824 and n 12; for Tibullus 2 Sept 1833 and n 13. On the styles of Tibullus, Ovid, and Catullus see *CN* II 2826.

[3] Ennius recurs on 2 Sept 1833 (see below and n 11), but not Lucius Accius (Actius or Attius, 170–c 86 B.C.), mentioned with Ennius by C to Collier.

[4] *TT* (1835) indirectly reported a protest by HNC that letter-writing, as by Cicero and Pliny, was also original to the Romans, but C countered by accepting as genuine the epistles attributed to Plato. Tennemann accepted them as genuine (as George Grote would later), but scholarship had challenged certain and sometimes all of the letters; debates are summarised in Reginald Hackforth *The Authorship of the Platonic Epistles* (Manchester 1913). The first moral satirist, by Roman tradition, was Gaius Lu-

A Nation to be great ought to be compressed in its increment by nations more civilized than itself—as Greece by Persia, Rome by Etruria and the Italian States and Carthage.[5] I remember an American[6] saying to me at Malta that he deplored the occupation of Louisiana by the United States and wished that country[7] had been possessed by England. He thought that if the United States got hold of Canada by conquest or cession, the last chance of his country becoming a great compact nation would be lost.   [36:388]

cilius (180–102 B.C.). In a note on Flögel *Geschichte der komischen Litteratur* II 16–17 C protested that the Greeks "had satirical Poems". *CM (CC)* II 757–8. Tacitus better than Livy meets his requirement of a historian drier than Greek predecessors.

HNC wrote in the peroration of his General Introduction to *Introductions to the Study of the Greek Classic Poets* (1830) 34–5: "And Latin—the voice of empire and of war, of law and of the state; inferior to its half-parent and rival in the embodying of passion and in the distinguishing of thought, but equal to it in sustaining the measured march of history, and superior to it in the indignant declamation of moral satire; stamped with the mark of an imperial and despotizing republic . . . one and uniform in its air and spirit, whether touched by the stern and haughty Sallust, by the open and discursive Livy, by the reserved and thoughtful Tacitus".

[5] Beginning with variations of style in certain Greek and Latin authors, C has moved through contemplation of influences on a national literature to influences in the formation of a nation emerging into strength. Besides such ancient historians as Herodotus, Dionysius of Halicarnassus, Polybius, and Livy, C had available to draw upon the *Universal History*, Rees, and such recent works as Mitford (see 11 Aug 1832 n 4, below), Hooke (see 4 May 1833 n 8, below) and Barthold Georg Niebuhr's history of Rome (3 vols 1811–32), of which the translation by Connop Thirlwall and Julius Hare had begun to appear in 1828. The comparative method in his comment, implicit in Plutarch, would have

been stimulated by C's reading of Vico. The impact of the Etruscans on Roman culture from the eighth century B.C. to the fourth (Etruria is roughly the territory of Tuscany and Umbria), and of Carthage until the demolition by Rome in 146 B.C., is apparent from all remains; the mixed peoples of Italia north and south of Rome gave to Latin literature such writers as Virgil, Catullus, Horace, Ovid, and Livy as well as more amorphous cultural strains.

[6] "Commodore Decatur" in *TT* (1835). Stephen Decatur (1779–1820) had been elevated to captain in the U.S. Navy after destroying the frigate *Philadelphia* on 16 Feb 1804 upon its capture by the Tripolitans. In an episode possibly more intriguing to C, Decatur had acted as second in 1802 in a duel that resulted in the death of the secretary to the governor of Malta. C, serving as secretary to the governor Sir Alexander Ball, saw a good deal of Decatur in Syracuse and probably in Malta. The language of the present entry echoes that of a passage in *The Friend* paraphrasing an "American commander, who has deserved and received the highest honours which his grateful country, through her assembled Representatives, could bestow". *Friend (CC)* I 297 (II 326). Although the identification of Decatur is probably correct, not only is HNC the source both in *TT* and in *Friend* (1837) II 141n, but HNC also identified as Decatur "an American officer of high rank" who was actually William Eaton (1764–1811). *Friend* (1837) II 74n; *Friend (CC)* I 254n. C referred specifically to Decatur in *CN* II 2228 and *CL* II 1150–2.

[7] *TT* (1835): "province".

I think metre precedes rhythm in order of nature.[8]

War in republican Rome was the offspring of its intense aristocracy of spirit, and stood to the State in lieu of Trade. As long as there was any thing ab extra to conquer, the[b] State advanced; when nothing remained but[c] what was Roman, then as a matter of course civil war began.[d9]

[36:389]

---

[a]7. July 1832.

It is hardly possible to conceive language more perfect than Greek.[1] If you compare it with the modern European tongues in the points of the

---

[b] ~~they~~ the   [c] b~~y~~ut

[d] Following this entry, on ff 64–5 HNC copied annotations from C's copy of Asgill *Collection of Tracts*; see n 10, below

[a] f 65

---

[8] Here, as in *CL* II 812 (to William Sotheby 13 Jul 1802) and *BL* ch 18 *(CC)* II 64–7, C is arguing for the primacy in human nature of passion over intellection. On similar assumptions concerning the "order of nature" were based such arguments as those of Vico, Lord Monboddo, Herder, and the Schlegels that the metre of poetry preceded the rhythm of prose temporally in the progress of civilisation. Wellek *History of Modern Criticism 1750–1950* (4 vols New Haven 1955–65) vols I, II. No one doubted that the earliest known compositions were in verse. This entry was omitted from *TT* (1835) and has not survived in MS F.

[9] C had written in *C&S*: "To early Rome, war and conquest were the substitutes for trade and commerce. War was their trade." *C&S (CC)* 25. In his extended comparison of France with Rome in the *M Post* 21 Sept–2 Oct 1802, he had predicted that "political amalgamation", as by ancient Rome, would be to "exchange national wars for civil wars". *EOT (CC)* I 325. His association of aristocracy with war is an appeal to British and European as well as Roman history, but the point was implicit when he distinguished the Romans from their Greek predecessors by Roman devotion "to war, empire, law". *Friend (CC)* I

505.

After recording C's remarks of 9 Jun HNC copied variatim into MS B (ff 64–5) C's marginalia from Asgill *A Collection of Tracts* (1715), headed "From his Asgill". The first annotation (the last in the volume) HNC published in *TT* (1835) under the date 10 Jun as "Charm for Cramp" (36:390); the other annotations he published in *LR* II 390–7. See *CM (CC)* I 121–9. The two leaves (ff 64–5) were torn from MS B for (we can assume) preparation of *LR*, but have now been reinserted in the ms. Unaware of the detached leaf that contained the "charm", EHC asked JDC in a letter of 16 May 1890 whether HNC had cheated or C falsely pretended spontaneity when HNC was visiting. UT ms.

[1] In N 20 C sighed because Greek, "that flexible Tongue", was not the universal language. *CN* III 3365 (1808). DC quoted from the "patient, laborious pains-taking" Greek grammar prepared for HC by C in 1806, in the "Memoir" prefixed to *Poems of Hartley Coleridge* (2 vols 1851) I xxix–xxxi and n, clxxxviii–cxcvii. C gave a briefer version to "My dearest Darl, Derwent", with doggerel verses. VCL S MS F 2.6. VCL LT 8 is a transcription of the HC version by HNC and his clerk. A com-

position and relative bearing of the vowels and consonants on each other and of the variety of terminations, [b]it is incomparably before all in the former particulars and only equalled in the last by German.[2] But that is the only point in which the German surpasses the other modern languages as to sound; for as to position,[c] nature seems to have dropped an acid into the language when a-forming, which curdled the vowels and made the consonants all flow together. The Spanish is very excellent for variety of termination. The Italian the worst.[3]   [36:391]

[b] f 66   [c] position of the

parison of Greek with English for brevity appears in *LR* I 337. There are speculations on Greek grammar in N 28 ff 40[v]–42[v]. Even more forcefully than C, James Burnett, Lord Monboddo (1714–99) wrote of "Greek, the language the most perfect that I know, or, I believe, that is known"—in sound, word-length, variety of termination, and articulation. *Of the Origin and Progress of Language* (2nd ed 6 vols Edinburgh 1774–92) IV 25; cf II 512–54; for comparisons of Greek and English, II and III passim. In 1825 C annotated for EC A. H. Matthiae *Copious Greek Grammar* tr E. V. Blomfield (2 vols 1824). *CM (CC)* IV.

C had gained his mastery of Greek slowly. Of his Greek ode on the slave-trade, in 1792, wherein Richard Porson offered to show 134 errors, C told Greenough in 1799 that "he first conceived the idea and afterwards hunted thro' the several poets for words in which to cloth[e] those ideas. It would be the same with Chatterton, supposing his book to be a forgery—and in this case Chatterton would no more fully comprehend his own writing than Coleridge does ye Greek". Greenough "Diary" 27 Jun 1799: *London Mercury* XXIII (Apr 1931) 562; *W&C* 231.

[2] C gave reasons in 1809 (*CN* III 3557) for "the superiority of the German language to all others". C had written to Poole from Hamburg 26 Oct 1798: "The German is a noble Language—a very noble Language". *CL* I 435. Two notes in *BL* laud German for its similarity to Greek in freedom to form compounds, but contrast "the woeful harshness of its

sounds". *BL* ch 19, Satyrane's Letters III *(CC)* II 89n–90, 197n–8. On agglutinations see also *CN* II 3160. A German grammar begun in N 3½ (*CN* III 4336) appears in *SW&F (CC)*. Grattan (II 118–19) tells of it in 1828: ". . . he strongly urged me to study German, of which I had only the slightest smattering. He told me he had compiled a grammar, never published, containing, he said, in ten pages, all that was of the least use to a learner of intelligence. This led to his favourite topic, grammar. Every conversation on that subject was a general treatise on its philosophy, its construction, and its value. I often afterwards longed for the little treatise he alluded to, which would have been of great value when I set really to work to follow Coleridge's advice, on the banks of the Neckar, and under the woods of Slierbach, with a still more gentle and accomplished guide, into the difficulties of that terrible German language".

[3] This sentence, which otherwise might be taken as a complaint against the limited range of sound in Italian poetry, became in *TT* (1835) "Italian prose is excessively monotonous". In the most detailed of C's many comparisons of languages, in Feb 1805, he found each superior in one characteristic or another—"the Italian is the sweetest, the Spanish the most majestic in its sounds"—and raised English above even ancient Greek in expressing "more meaning, image, and passion *tri-unely* in a given number of syllables". *CN* II 2431. But he rejected the suggestion that French, German, or any language is "unfit for poetry".

It is extraordinary that the Germans should not have retained or assumed the two beautiful sounds of the ^{d}soft and hard^e Theta. Thy, thick &c.[4]   [36:393]

Never take^f an iambus as a Christian name. A trochee,^{g} tribrachys or amphibrachys^h will do very well.[5] Edith and Rotha are my favorite names for women.[6]   [36:395]

It is very natural to have a Dual—Duality being a conception quite distinct from Plurality. Most very primitive languages have a dual—Greek—Welsh—the native Chilese as given in the Abbé Raynal.^{i7}

The neuter plural governing a verb singular is one of many instances in Greek of the inward and metaphysic grammar resisting the tyranny of

---

$^{d-e}$ ha$\overset{2}{\text{r}}$d & s$\overset{1}{\text{o}}$ft ^{f} ~~fix~~ take ^{g} ~~Trochees~~ ^{h} amphibrachy ^{i} Raynall

[4] *TT* (1835) substituted more pointed examples, e.g. "*thy thoughts*", and added a sentence contrasting the "grand word—Death" with *Tod*, suggesting to an English ear "a loathsome toad".

TT (1835) introduced under "July 8. 1832" (36:394), along with a footnote on Irving (reduced in 1836), an expansion of C's annotation on Park *Dogmas of the Constitution* xi: "This vile, barbarous, vocable 'talented'! Why not shillinged, farthinged, tenpenced, &c.? The formation of a participle passive from a noun, is a license that requires some peculiar felicity to excuse it." *CM (CC)* iv. See 36:394 nn 1, 2.

[5] *TT* (1835) omitted the amphibrach, of which Algretha and Lovenna (n 6, below) are examples, as Elaine and Annette are of iambs. The tribrach would seem a better candidate for omission.

[6] The daughter born to SC and HNC on 29 Jun would be christened Edith, after SC's aunt Edith Fricker Southey, on 9 Aug. Rotha, after the river Rothay, was a name given by C to DW, was what he called his goddaughter Dora Wordsworth at least once (*CL* vi 747), and the name of Dora's daughter, Rotha Quillinan, born in 1821. RS's daughter Edith May, born in 1804, was a favourite of C's and SH's. C had written to Mrs C on 5 Dec 1802, before the birth of SC: "If a Girl, let it be Gretha . . . unless you prefer Rotha—or Laura . . . You may take your choice of Sara, Gretha, or rather Algretha, Rotha, Laura, Emily, or Lovenna". He rejected Bridget as failing "to end with a vowel". *CL* ii 892. HNC's note in *TT* (1835) was omitted from *TT* (1836): "Rotha is a beautiful name indeed, and now finding its way southward from the lovely stream from which it was taken.—ED".

[7] C's knowledge of the dual in Chinese came from "An Essay on the Chinese Language" in a work anonymously edited by RS: Abbé Don Juan Ignatius Molina (1740–1829) *The Geographical, Natural, and Civil History of Chili* (2 vols 1809) ii esp 336–47. C probably used, in 1810, RS's own copy; see *CN* iii 3789 and n. Molina's Italian, translated for an edition in the U.S. by Richard Alsop and William Shaler, 1808, was used for the RS edition. C misspoke, HNC misheard, or HNC changed what he heard to the notorious freethinking Guillaume Thomas François Raynal (1713–96) *A Philosophical and Political History of the Settlements and Trade of the Europeans in the East and West Indies* tr J. Justamond (2nd ed rev 5 vols 1776). C borrowed Raynal's work from the Bristol Library 16–20 Apr 1795, but it gives no details of the Chilese language. Perhaps C mentioned Raynal peripherally on 7 Jul.

formal grammar. In truth there may be Multeity in Things, but there can only be Plurality in Persons.[8]

Observe also that in fact a neuter noun in Greek has no real nominative case, though it has a formal one, that is, the same word with the accusative; the reason is a Thing has no subjectivity, or nominative case, but exists only as an *object* in the accusative or other oblique case.[9]

[36:392]

Valckenaer's[j] treatise on the interpolation of the Classics by the later Jews and early Christians is well worth your attention.[10]   [36:396]

---

[k]I have read all the famous histories—and I believe some history of every country and nation that is or ever existed—but I never did so for the story itself as a story. The only thing interesting to me was the principles to be evolved from and illustrated by the Facts; after I had gotten my Principle, I pretty generally left the Facts to take care of themselves.[11] I never could remember any passages in books or the particulars of events, except in the gross. I can refer to them. To be sure, I must be a different man from Herder, who once was seriously annoyed with himself, because in recounting the whole regal table of the German Empire, I think, he missed some one of those worthies, and could not recall the name.[12]   [36:397]

[j] Valcknär's   [k] f 66[v]

[8] On "Multeity" see *BL* ch 12 *(CC)* I 287 and n 3; on "Plurality" see *Logic (CC)* 46. In *Logic (CC)* 228, 262, and 269 C identifies multeity with plurality.

[9] Neuter nouns in Greek have the same form for accusative, nominative, and vocative, arguably for the reason C gives.

[10] Lodewijk Kaspar Valckenaer (1715–85) *Diatribe de Aristobulo Judaeo* ed Johannes Luzac (Leyden 1806). C wrote on the half-title: "This Book is well worth reading: but of all books worth reading the most prolix, *lengthy*, & *fall-abroad!*" *CM (CC)* v. HNC in a note in *TT* (1835) confessed to uncertainty as to "which of the numerous works of this splendid scholar" was meant, but a letter of 21 Jul 1835 from Charles James Blomfield, bp of London, and another from Alexander Dyce gave him the title for the note in *TT* (1836). UT mss.

[11] HNC's note in *TT* (1835) quoted in full the related passage in *SM*; cf *SM (CC)* 11–12.

[12] Not Herder but Johannes von Müller (1752–1809), Swiss historian and editor of Herder's works. The anecdote is translated from Mme de Staël in the Preface to Müller *An Universal History, in Twenty-four Books* (3 vols 1818) I iv: "On one occasion he was requested, in order to decide a wager, to repeat the pedigree of the sovereign counts of Bugey: he performed the task immediately, but was not quite certain whether one individual of the series had been a regent or a sovereign in his own right; and he seriously reproached himself for this defect of memory". JS in his copy of *TT* (1835) makes the correction from Herder to Müller. In a note to 36:556 of 14 Aug 1833 HNC declared C "remarkably deficient in the technical memory of words". In C's own words of 22 Oct 1826: "In the gifts of passive or spontaneous Memory I am singularly deficient. Even of my own Poems I should be at a loss to repeat fifty lines." *CL* VI 631. Technology steadily reduces the standards for human memory. Müller edited

Schmidt was a Roman Catholic, but I have generally found him candid—as indeed almost all the Austrians are.[13] They are good Catholics,
but like our Charles II.[l] never let their religious[m] bigotry interfere with
their political well doing.[14] Kaiser is a most pious son of the Church—
yet he always keeps his Papa in order.[15]   [36:398]

I have the firmest conviction that Homer is a mere synonyme with the
Iliad.[16] You can't conceive for a moment anything about the *Poet*, as you
call him, apart from that Poem. Difference[n] of men there was in Degree,
not in Kind—one man was a better poet than another, but he was a poet
upon the same ground and with the same feelings.

The want of adverbs and conjunctions in the Iliad is[o] very characteristic. With more adverbs there would have been some subjectivity—or
the latter would have made them.

The Nation was then on the verge of the bursting forth of Individuality.[p][17]   [36:396]

> [l] ~~Stuarts~~ Ch. II.   [m] religio~~no~~us   [n] ~~The~~ difference   [o] are
> [p] For the stub of the leaf torn out following f 66ᵛ, see n 17, below

---

Johann Gottfried von Herder (1744–
1803) *Sämmtliche Werke* (14 vols Tübingen 1805–15), in which his name is
given as Johann Georg Müller.

[13] Michael Ignaz Schmidt (1736–94)
Geschichte der Deutschen (continued by
Joseph Milbiller 22 vols Ulm 1785–
1808). For C's use of this "voluminous
German work" see *Friend (CC)* I 84–8
(II 62–6); *CN* III 3553 and n.

[14] To the suggestion that Charles II
was "naturally humane", C answered
that the King enjoyed watching religious
factions destroy each other as if they
were toad and spider; such was "the
playful and humane disposition of this
engaging Tiberius". Note on Samuel
O'Sullivan *The Agency of Divine Providence Manifested . . .* (Dublin 1816)
157: *CM (CC)* III.

[15] C probably refers to Francis (i.e.
Franz) I (1768–1835), reduced from
Holy Roman Emperor (as Francis II) to
Kaiser of Austria in 1804, but possibly to
Gottlieb Philipp Christian Kaiser (1781–
1847) *Die biblische Theologie; oder Ju-
daismus und Christianismus nach der
grammatisch-historischen Interpretations-
methode* (2 vols Erlangen 1813–21).

[16] These remarks emphasise the objectivity of the *Iliad* rather than the multiple
authorship stressed on 9 May 1830,
above (at n 18) (36:171).

[17] Whatever the "then" of the composition or compilation of the *Iliad*, C's
point depends for validity upon the increased individuality of Greek literature
and art later than the Homeric poems—
unless he is to be taken as sensing a
"verge" of individuality in the *Odyssey*.
Only a stub remains of the leaf following f 66ᵛ in MS B. As the two brief, personal entries dated 20 Jul (Fri) in *TT*
(1835) repeat marginalia of a much earlier time, it can be conjectured that the
missing leaf contained these and other
transcriptions from C's marginal notes.
If so, it would have been torn out, as
other leaves were, for the preparation of
LR. If absence of the leaf is not to be explained in this way, we may have lost
more than a page of the originally recorded talk. The two notes in *TT* (1835)
came from C's annotations on Baxter *Reliquiae Baxterianae* (1696)—and were
omitted from the other Baxter notes published in *LR*. Perhaps the missing leaf
also included 36:394, on barbarous

*a*21. July 1832.

The characteristic merit of my verses is their musicalness.[1] There is nothing of it in Wordsworth; though there is a rhythm—a motion of a man walking in a dream. Wordsworth was always a spectator ab extra[2] of nature and society; he felt for, but never sympathized with, any man or event. Hence that exaggerated sentimentality occasionally seen in his poems. "Under the broad and open eye of the solitary sky"[3] applied to three or four jolly damsels on a plank is ridiculous—it would have been sublime if spoken of Jesus Christ, alone on the Mount after having retired from Jerusalem, when the Jews were factious for a Messiah King.[4]

[36:404]

The two first books of the Excursion should have been published alone under the name of the "Deserted Cottage", and they would have formed, what indeed they are, one of the most beautiful poems of the language.[5] The Pedlar was proper so far—it was felt that his character was wholly imaginative; but when he is afterwards brought on as a talker in the dialogue, all the propriety ceases—the pedlarship is absurd, and you

a f 67

slang, assigned in publication to 8 Jul 1832.

[1] As on 31 Mar 1832, above (at n 5), C's characterisation of his poetry as musical was not used in *TT* (1835). The remarks on WW, which follow, could not be published unaltered, but HNC's stress on the music and melody of C's poetry in the *QR* review of Aug 1834 may have hampered him from retaining this first sentence here or elsewhere in *TT*.

[2] "Observer from the outside". The phrase has been often noted from its appearance here and its repetition on 16 Feb 1833, published as 36:457, where it links WW with Goethe. C, like Keats, similarly linked WW with the Milton who "stands *ab extra*" in 36:169 (9 May 1830, above). The phrase had once served a different purpose: of the poem we know as *The Prelude*, addressed to C, he wrote to WW 12 Oct 1799 that it would "indeed be a self-elevation produced *ab extra*" to have this great work so addressed. *CL* I 538.

[3] *Stray Pleasures* line 16 (var): *WPW* II 160.

[4] Matt 24, Mark 13. C had a special

interest in Christ's prophecy, on the Mount of Olives, of the fall of Jerusalem and the coming of false Messiahs in the last days before his own return (see 24 Apr 1832, above, at n 5, and 2 Sept 1833, below, at n 23) (36:372, 588). WW's poem blunts C's objection by the argument that "a rich loving-kindness" scatters pleasures through the earth in "stray gifts to be claimed by whoever shall find"—the argument of Luke 12.6: God's eye is on such sparrows as these "damsels on a plank".

[5] The first complete version of *The Ruined Cottage* (1798) is given in *WPW* v 379–409. The history of this poem, with the incorporation of *The Pedlar* to form bk I of *The Excursion*, is given in Jonathan Wordsworth *The Music of Humanity* (1969) and in *"The Ruined Cottage" and "The Pedlar"* ed James Butler (Ithaca, New York 1979), a volume in the Cornell Wordsworth. This poem, which C had followed from Jun 1797 (*CL* I 327–8), he declared on 3 Mar 1815 "the finest Poem in our Language, comparing it with any of the same or similar Length". *CL* IV 564.

have a methodist parson instead.[6]   [36:401]

Can dialogues in verse be defended? Wordsworth undertaking a grand philosophical poem ought always to have taught the reader himself as from himself; a poem does not admit argumentation—though it does admit development of thinking. In prose there may be a difference; though I must confess that even in Plato and Cicero, I am always vexed that the authors did not say what they had to say at once in their own persons.[7] The introductions and little *b*urbanities are to be sure delightful—I would not lose them—but I have no admiration for the practice of ventriloquizing through another*c* man's mouth.[8]   [36:402]

Wordsworth should have first published his thirteen books on the growth of an individual mind,[9] far superior to any part of the Excursion: then the plan suggested and laid out by me was—that he should assume the station of a man in repose, whose mind was made up, and so prepared to deliver upon authority a system of philosophy.[10] He was to treat man as man—a subject of eye, ear, touch, taste, in contact with external nature—informing the senses from the mind and not compounding a mind out of the senses—then the pastoral and other states—assuming a satiric or Juvenalian spirit as he approached the high civilization of cities and

b f 67ᵛ   *c* another⸜s⸝

[6] Cf *BL* ch 22 *(CC)* II 134–5. The underlying issue is the "species of ventriloquism, where two are represented as talking, while in truth one man only speaks". Francis Jeffrey, whom experience had prepared even less than it had C for a moralising pedlar, asked: "What but the most wretched and provoking perversity of taste and judgment, could induce any one to place his chosen advocate of wisdom and virtue in so absurd and fantastic a condition? Did Mr Wordsworth really imagine, that his favourite doctrines were likely to gain any thing in point of effect or authority by being put into the mouth of a person accustomed to higgle about tape, or brass sleeve-buttons?" *Ed Rev* XXIX (1814) 30.

[7] The dialogue, Plato's normal form, is employed by Cicero in several works, e.g. *De oratore* and *De republica*. C's depreciation of Plato on this score takes some of the sting out of his objection to WW's use of dialogue.

[8] See n 6, above. All the remarks of this paragraph concern *The Excursion*, and all are based on a criterion important to WW himself, sincerity of emotion.

[9] The title-page of MS B of *The Prelude*, in 13 bks, as completed in 1805 and read to C after his return from Malta, reads "Poem, Title not yet fixed upon, by William Wordsworth, Addressed to S. T. Coleridge". Throughout 1832 WW corrected MS D *(WPW)*, which divides bk X (of 1805) to produce the 14 bks of the poem as published in 1850. The WW family and circle usually referred to the work as WW's poem on "the Growth of his own Mind". The title of C's lines in tribute, after several small changes, would become in 1834 *To William Wordsworth, Composed on the Night After His Recitation of a Poem on the Growth of an Individual Mind. PW* (1834) I 206; *PW* (EHC) I 403.

[10] In a letter of 30 May 1815 C reminded WW in similar terms of the plan he had laid out long before. *CL* IV 572–6.

towns,[11] and then opening a melancholy picture of the present state of degeneracy and vice—thence revealing the necessity for and proof of the whole state of man and society being subject to and illustrative of a redemptive process in operation—showing how this Idea reconciled all the anomalies, and how it promised future glory and restoration. Something of this sort I suggested—and it was agreed on. It is what in substance I have been all my life doing in my system of philosophy.[12]   [36:403]

Wordsworth spoilt many of his best poems by abandoning the [d]contemplative position, which is alone fitted for him, and introducing the object in a dramatic way. This is seen in the Leech gatherer,[13] and

[d] f 68

[11] Notably in bk III "Residence in Cambridge" and bk VII "Residence in London". A Juvenalian tone contrasting with "the pastoral and other states" occurs in other passages, also, as in the description of the child prodigy shaped by utilitarians—v (1805) 292–389, (1850) 293–363—and the derision of such faith in the understanding as the protagonist attempted after his return from France—(1805) x 806–901, (1850) xi 223–305.

[12] The final books of *The Prelude* attempt the redemptive process that C ascribed to his own philosophic system. *The Excursion* ends on a note of doubtful hope that renovation has supplanted the despondency of the Solitary. Julian Charles Young wrote of his hours with C and WW in 1828: "I must say I never saw any manifestation of small jealousy between Coleridge and Wordsworth; which, considering the vanity possessed by each, I thought uncommonly to the credit of both. I am sure they entertained a thorough respect for each other's intellectual endowments. . . . It must not be assumed that the reciprocal admiration entertained by the two poets for each other's gifts made them blind to each other's infirmities. . . . Coleridge . . . forward as he was in defending Wordsworth from literary assailants, had evident pleasure in exposing his parsimony, aye—even in the same breath in which he vaunted the purity and piety of his disposition." *A Memoir of Charles Mayne Young* (2nd ed 1871) 118, 122. HCR enjoyed greater intimacy on 21 Dec 1822: "The afternoon I spent at Aders's; a large party; splendid dinner prepared by a French cook and music in the evening. Coleridge was the *star* of the evening. He talked in his usual way, but as well and with more liberality and in seemingly better health than when I saw him last, some years ago. But he was somewhat less animated and brilliant and paradoxical. He had not seen Wordsworth's last works, and spoke less highly of his immediately preceding writings than he used and still does of his earlier works. He reproaches him with a vulgar attachment to orthodoxy in its literal sense. The latter end of *The Excursion*, he says, is distinguishable from the former, and *he* can ascertain from internal evidence the recent from the early compositions among his works. He reproaches Wordsworth with a disregard to the mechanism of his verse, and in general insinuates a decline of his faculties. Of Southey's politics he spoke also depreciatingly—he is intellectually a very dependent, but morally an independent man. In the judgment of Southey I concur altogether. Of Wordsworth I believe Coleridge judges under personal feelings of unkindness. The music was enjoyed by Coleridge, but I could have dispensed with it on account of Coleridge himself." To explain his preference for C, HCR quoted *Paradise Lost* II 556: "For Eloquence the Soul, Song charms the Sense". *CRB* I 288.

[13] *The Leech Gatherer* is the informal title by which family and friends continued to call *Resolution and Independence*: *WPW* II 235–40. As only nine of the 140

Ruth.[14] Wordsworth had more materials for the great philosophic Poet than any man I ever knew, or, as I think, has existed in this country for a long time[15]—but he was uttterly unfitted for the Epic or narrative style. His mental-internal action is always so excessively disproportionate to the actual business that the latter either goes to sleep, or becomes ridiculous. In his reasoning you will find no progression—it eddies—it comes round and round again, perhaps with a wider circle, but it is repetition still.[16]   [36:404]

No man was more enthusiastic than I was for France and the Revolution: it had all my wishes—but none of my expectations. Before 1793 I fully saw and often enough stated in public the horrid delusion, the vile mockery of the whole affair.[17] It was well said by *my brother James*[18] once,

ᵉ⁻ᶠ J. C.

lines are in dialogue, C's objection would seem to be to the structure of dramatic encounter. He wrote in *BL* ch 22: "Indeed this fine poem is *especially* characteristic of the author." *BL (CC)* II 126.

[14] *WPW* II 227–35. *BL* ch 17 counted *Ruth* among "the most interesting" of the "more or less dramatic" poems. *BL (CC)* II 43. C had been unreservedly fond of *Ruth* in 1800 (*CL* I 623, 632, II 713), but objected to the changes of 1803 (*CL* II 830), most of which were eliminated in 1805. The narrating "I" is much present in this poem, e.g. in apostrophes to Ruth similar to those that C's poetic voice addresses to Christabel.

[15] "Since Milton"—*TT* (1835). *BL* ch 22 concluded that WW "is capable of producing . . . the FIRST GENUINE PHILOSOPHIC POEM". *BL (CC)* II 156. Cf *CL* II 1034 (15 Jan 1804), IV 574 (to WW 30 May 1815). John Cam Hobhouse recorded in his diary 6 Jun 1816 an anecdote from Henry Hallam, who "told us that a plain man who was dining with Sotheby when Coleridge was present and had been declaiming long, at last put down his knife and fork and said: 'Somehow or the other, sir, it is odd one hears of no poets in these times.' Coleridge said, 'Pardon me, sir; I take it we have more poetry than has been known since the days of Milton. My friend Mr.

Wordsworth, for example.' He then repeated some rhapsody of Wordsworth." Lord Broughton *Recollections of a Long Life* (6 vols 1909) I 343. (The ms, in BM, differs only in punctuation.)

[16] Neither the version of the entry in *TT* (1835) nor C's explanations to WW of his disappointment in 1815 (*CL* IV 572–6) included the depreciations of the last half of this paragraph.

[17] HNC in a note to this entry in *TT* (1835) quoted *France: an Ode* (1798) lines 64–98; lines 22–63, not quoted, would further qualify C's claim to have seen through the Revolution before 1793. Cf *PW* (EHC) I 245–7.

[18] James Coleridge (1759–1836), "The Colonel", described in HNC's note to this entry in *TT* (1835) as a "soldier of the old cavalier stamp". To anyone of C's circle outside the family from Ottery, the "J. C." of MS B would be taken as Joseph Cottle, but HNC remembered the initials two years later as standing for his father. To be a Jacobin, in this entry, required the kind of dry ratiocination C associated with French thinkers. The Moravian Church of the Brethren, founded by the followers of John Huss in 1457, was revived at Herrnhut, Saxony, in 1722 under Nikolaus Ludwig, Graf von Zinzendorf (1700–60), with emphasis on conduct above doctrine. In 1809, not for the only time, C counted Zinzen-

when some one said I was a Jacobin—"No! Samuel*g* is no Jacobin—he is a hot-headed Moravian!" In truth I was in the extreme opposite Pole.

[36:405]

*h*The struggle about the Slave Trade and the Middle Passage excited my most fervent emotions.[19] Yet I then stated in the Watchman—and I lost some friends by it—that no good will be done by applying to Parliament—that it was unjust—and that in twenty years after a Parliamentary Abolition—the horrors of the Trade would be increased twenty-fold.[20] Now all acknowledge that to be true. *More* Africans are now transported to America for Slavery—the Middle *i*Passage is more horrible—and the Slavery itself worse.*j*[21]

g S.T.C.   *h–j* For the variant in MS F, dated 24 Jul 1832, see App C, below

i f 68ᵛ   *j* See *h–j*, above

---

dorf among his heroes of true faith vs "rational Religionists". *CN* III 3560 and n. From reading works on the Moravians by Heinrich Rimius and George Lavington, he came to conclusions, as on most subjects, partly favourable, partly not. *CN* III 4169, 4409 and nn.

[19] C won the Browne Gold Medal at Cambridge in 1792 for a Greek Sapphic ode on the slave-trade, printed in *PW* (JDC) 476–7, details 653–4 (n 248). C read the ode publicly in the Senate 3 Jul 1792. (For the ode see also 7 Jul 1832 n 1, above.) C lectured against the slave-trade at the Assembly Coffee House, Bristol, on 16 Jun 1795. *Lects 1795 (CC)* 235–51. For a survey of C's efforts for abolition of the trade, drawn partly from C's own survey for Thomas Clarkson, 3 Mar 1808 (*CL* III 78), see *Lects 1795 (CC)* 232–3. C modified the lecture for his essay "On the Slave Trade" *Watchman* 25 Mar 1796 *(CC)* 130–40. Opposition to slavery and the trade continued with less zeal throughout C's writing for the *M Post* and *Courier*; e.g. *EOT (CC)* I 126, III 202. C's remarks of 21 Jul were transcribed (var) in MS F, but were not published. (Possibly this scrap of MS F came from an earlier transcription than the other surviving fragments; it bears the number 319 in ink, apparently an entry number, not in a position to indicate the page. There is no equivalent among the other scraps.)

[20] No prediction by C that the horrors of the slave-trade would increase after abolition can be sustained from *The Watchman*. Perhaps it was an unsuccessful search through *The Watchman* that led HNC to drop the entry in 1835. The editor of *EOT (CC)* assigns to C a sentence in the *Courier* 26 Mar 1804 on "the far-celebrated farce of the Abolition of the Slave Trade". *EOT (CC)* III 83.

[21] Middle Passage, "the middle portion (i.e. the part consisting of sea travel) of the journey of a slave carried from Africa to America". *OED*. "In actual fact the volume of the trans-Atlantic slave trade grew substantially in the years immediately after 1807 . . .". J. D. Fage in *The New Cambridge Modern History* IX ed C. W. Crawley (Cambridge 1965) 579. Some estimated the numbers between 1825 and 1837, including Portuguese trade into Brazil, at 200,000 annually. W. E. Burghardt DuBois *The Suppression of the African Slave-Trade to the United States of America 1638–1870* (New York 1896) 143. Britain after 1807, notably under the leadership of Canning, had consistently pressed for treaties against the trade in slaves and for the right of search at sea. The treaty with France was signed 30 Nov 1831. British efforts of 1808–32 are tabulated in James Badinel *Some Account of the Trade in Slaves from Africa* (1842). Slavery and

I have no faith in Act of Parliament Reform. All the great, the permanently great, things that have been achieved in the world, have been so achieved by Individuals, working from the instinct of Genius or Goodness.[22] The rage nowadays is all the other way: the Individual is supposed capable of nothing—there must be organization—classification—machinery; as if the capital of National Morality were to be increased by making a Joint Stock of it. Hence you see these Infant Schools so patronized by Bishops and others, who think them a grand invention.[23] Is it found that an Infant School Child—who has been bawling all day a line of the Multiplication Table, or a verse of the Bible—grows up a more dutiful son or daughter to its[k] parents? In a great town, in our present state of society, perhaps it may be a justifiable expedient, but per se, the conception of public Infant Schools seems to me most miserably mistaken.[24]   [36:406]

[k] ~~the~~ its

the trade had been debated in the Commons 24 May 1832. Hansard 3rd s XIII 34–98. C was to write in 1833 in the margin of William Fitzwilliam Owen *Narrative of Voyages to Explore the Shores of Africa, Arabia, and Madagascar* (2 vols 1833) II 218: "After reading such accounts, as these, of the state of the Negroes in their own country, surely it is pardonable to think, that if the power and wisdom of Law, enforced by powerful and wise governments, had regulated the Middle Passage, and secured the right treatment, gradual Christianizing, and final emancipation of the Slave after his arrival in the Colonies, the transportation would have been a blessed Providence for the poor Africans!" *CM (CC)* III.

[22] In 1796 C regarded "the virtue and rationality of the People at large" as essential to effective change in "the *forms* of Government"; in 1818 he declared the "concurrence of nature and historic event with the great revolutionary movements of individual genius". Prospectus *Watchman (CC)* 4–5; *Friend (CC)* I 480n.

[23] The first infant school, for children under seven, was introduced by Robert Owen at New Lanark in 1816. Brougham praised more than once in the Commons Owen's experiments in "the formation of character"; with James Mill he opened a school on Owen's model at Westminster in 1818. In 1824 the London Infant School Society was founded, and in 1836 the Home and Colonial Infant School Society. By 1835, there were about 150 schools in England and Wales teaching cleanliness and order by example and practice, "training infant children", in Brougham's words, "before they were susceptible of what was generally called education". Hansard XLI (16 Dec 1819) 1197. Details are available in John William Adamson *English Education 1789–1902* (Cambridge 1930). Besides London University, Brougham had supported various "steam-intellect" societies, such as the institutes for workingmen called for in his *Practical Observations upon the Education of the People, Addressed to the Working Classes and Their Employers* (1825).

[24] *TT* (1835) introduced qualifying clauses that describe "the bishops and others" who supported an idea promoted by Brougham as "well-intentioned people" making "miserable mistakes". Anglicans and nonconformists had brought Owen's emphasis on environment towards the rote memory of the Madras system of Andrew Bell and his National

The pith of my^l system is to make the Senses out of the Mind—not the Mind from the Senses, as Locke etc.[25]   [36:407]

Could you ever discover any thing sublime in our sense of the term in Greek Literature? I never could.[26]   [36:408]

^{m}I should think the Proverbs and Ecclesiastes written about the time of Nehemiah.[27] The language is Hebrew with Chaldaic endings—totally unlike the language of Moses on the one hand, or of Isaiah on the other.[28]

[36:409]

Solomon introduced the commercial spirit in his Kingdom, and I can not think his idolatry could have been more than a state protection or toleration of the foreign worship.[29]   [36:410]

---

^{l} ~~the~~ my ^{m} f 69

Society for Promoting the Education of the Poor According to the Principles of the Established Church (1811) and the nonconformist British and Foreign School Society (1814) of the Quaker Joseph Lancaster.

[25] The "etc", replaced by "did" in *TT* (1835), indicates such empiricist disciples of Locke as David Hartley. This entry and the next were written hurriedly and loosely in the lower quarter of f 68^v; the "etc" may be HNC's hurried notation for obvious names—Hartley, Priestley—spoken by C. There is a pungent note on Pepys' diary for 3 Aug 1667: "Mercy on the Age, & the People, for whom Locke is profound, and Hume subtle." *Memoirs* (2 vols 1825) II i 100: *CM (CC)* IV.

[26] *TT* (1835) added a sentence of clarification: "Sublimity is Hebrew by birth", a proposition of Robert Lowth—*Lectures on the Sacred Poetry of the Hebrews* tr Gregory I 307—popularised by A. W. Schlegel and De Q. C wrote of Psalm 50 in Anne Gillman's Bible: "What can Greece or Rome present, worthy to be compared with the 50th Psalm, either in sublimity of the Imagery or in moral elevation?" *CM (CC)* I 420. He had asked Thelwall rhetorically in Dec 1796: "Is not Milton a *sublimer* poet than Homer or Virgil? Are not his Per-

sonages more sublimely cloathed? And do you not know, that there is not perhaps *one* page in Milton's Paradise Lost, in which he has not borrowed his imagery from the *Scriptures*?" *CL* I 281. For C on the sublime see e.g. *CL* I 349–50, 461–2, 466, 625; *CN* I 1517, III 4073; C's notes on George Dyer *Poems* (1801) and Herder *Kalligone* (1800): *CM (CC)* II 355, 1067, 1069–70. Longinus, Anne Dacier, Addison, and Pope had found the language of Homer comparable in sublimity with that of the Bible.

[27] *TT* (1835) inserted "or, perhaps, rather collected". Nehemiah was dated by Eichhorn (*AT* II 565, 571) to the Persian rule of Artaxerxes I (d 424 B.C.) or Artaxerxes II (d 359 B.C.). Proverbs and Ecclesiastes are later by internal evidence than Solomon, to whom they were ascribed.

[28] Less specifically in Eichhorn *AT* § 658 III 562–6.

[29] 1 Ki 5 tells how Hiram of Tyre (Huram in 2 Chron 2) contracted to supply Solomon with cedar and fir in return for wheat and oil; 1 Ki 10 and 2 Chron 9 tell how the Queen of Sheba and other rulers brought rich gifts to Solomon; 1 Ki 11.1–11 tells how Solomon loved many "strange women" ("outlandish women" in Neh 13.26) and built shrines to their gods.

28. July 1832.[1]

When a man mistakes his Thoughts for Persons and Things, he is mad. A madman is properly so defined.[2]   [36:411]

The sublime and abstruse doctrines of Christian Belief[a] belong to the Church—but the Faith of the Individual, centered in his heart, is or may be collateral to them.[3] Faith is subjective—"I throw myself in adoration before God, acknowledge myself his creature—sinful, weak, lost—and pray for help and pardon"—but when I rise from my knees, I discuss the doctrine of the Trinity as I would a problem in Geometry—in the same temper of mind I mean, not by the same process of reasoning, of course.[4]   [36:414]

---

[a] ~~Faith~~ Belief

[1] Writing to Emily Trevenen on 24 Jul of his own good health—"have walked to & from London this month past & more"—HNC reported also on his uncle: "S.T.C. is upon the whole not much below par—another man's zero." UT ms. He returned to Highgate on the next two Saturdays.

[2] Defining insanity as "a defective state, or disorder of the *intellectual powers*", Henry Clutterbuck, M.D. (1767–1856) in his Lect 17 on "mental derangement" had classified the possible errors: "The *perception* of objects may be false, or the *recollection* of them imperfect; or the *judgment* formed with respect to them, erroneous, and so on . . .". *Lancet* XII (21 Jul 1827) 485. John Abercrombie, in his strongly associationist *Inquiries Concerning the Intellectual Powers and the Investigation of Truth*, distinguished from the madman the poet or novelist who feels embodied in a character created by his imagination but then returns to "the ordinary relations of life,—were he then to act in a single instance in the character of the being of his imagination,—this would constitute insanity". *Inquiries* (3rd ed Edinburgh and London 1832) 235. Emerson copied the first sentence of this entry. *Journals* VI 193.

[3] In a note on Asgill's tracts C illustrated this distinction between collective belief and individual faith: "The *Faith* may be and must be the same in all who are thereby saved; but every man, more or less, construes it into an intelligible *Belief* thro' the shaping and colouring Optical Glass of his individual Understanding." *CM (CC)* I 123–4. He scolded Donne for confounding these. Notes on *LXXX Sermons: CM (CC)* II 300, 331–3. C publicly utilised the distinction in *Friend (CC)* I 432–3 and *BL* ch 10 *(CC)* I 203. HNC cited the distinction made in this entry to explain why C "exercised a liberty of criticism" with respect to incidents in the Scriptures that "will probably seem objectionable to many of his readers". *LR* III xi.

[4] This paragraph makes no distinction between doctrines and belief, but is representative of C in allowing the reason exercised on doctrines to include faith without being restricted by faith. C employed faith also in prayers for others, as in his "humble Intercession" for SC and Mrs Gillman in Nov 1833: "I thank God who has thus far given ear to my Prayers, and trust in his Mercy". *CL* VI 974. He wrote a long note, beginning: "Observe: we must not worship God, as if *his* Ways were as *our* ways", and ending, "Lo, I pray! O that I had the power of supplication! I believe! O Lord—help my unbelief", on the endleaves of *Sermons or Homilies of the United Church of Eng-*

4. Aug. 1832.

*^a*Charles Lamb*^b* translated my motto Sermoni propriora[1] by—Properer for a sermon.[2]   [36:412]
I hardly know any thing more amusing than the honest German Jesuitry of old Dobrizhoffer.*^c*[3] His chapter on the dialects is most valuable. He is surprized that there is no infinitive, but that they say, I wish, and I go—forgetting his own German and the English, which are the same.*^d*[4]
[36:415]

^{a–b} C. Lambe   *^c* Dobrizoffer

^d On ff 69*^v*–70 HNC transcribed marginalia from Baxter; see n 4, below

---

land & Ireland . . . in the Time of Queen Elizabeth (1813–15), specifically to No 19 "Homily on Prayer". *CM (CC)* IV.

[1] "More suitable to prose". Horace *Satires* 1.4.42 has "sermoni propiora" (nearer to prose). John Foster *An Essay on the Different Nature of Accent and Quantity with Their Use and Applications in the English, Latin, and Greek Languages* (1762) 201n defined *sermoni propiora* as "metrical lines composed on unpoetical subjects, in very unpoetic expression, with loose metre". This work was mentioned by C in *C Rev* Feb 1797—republished by George Whalley as C's in *RES* NS II (1951) 238–47—and has been nominated as the source of C's usage by Richard T. Martin "Coleridge's Use of *sermoni propriora*" *Wordsworth Circle* III (1972) 71–5.

[2] On 10 Sept 1802 C wrote to William Sotheby of his "moods of mind": "They are 'Sermoni propiora' which I once translated—'*Properer for a Sermon*'." *CL* II 864. C referred to the Horatian phrase in a note on Lamb's copy of Dyer *Poems: CM (CC)* II 353. He shared with others Lamb's "exquisite" sayings; e.g. in *CL* v 202–3, 222, 277, 328, 367, 411, 424, 455, 463, 590, VI 776. *TT* (1836) inserted at this point, under the date 25 Jul 1832, entry 36:413, on a saying by Mario Sforza, from MS B f 112, a transcription by HNC from C's N 18. See 36:413 and n.

[3] Martin Dobrizhoffer (1717–91) *An Account of the Abipones, an Equestrian People of Paraguay* (3 vols 1822). When

RS decided that the work deserved translation, he tried HC and probably DC for it, then passed the Latin to SC, who translated 5 vols and abridged to 3. Towle 90–2; *C Fille* 55; *LL* II 370; *The Letters of Robert Southey to John May 1797–1838* ed Charles Ramos (Austin, Texas 1976) 171. C had first seen an account of Dobrizhoffer in *Allgemeine Encyclopädie der Wissenschaften und Künste* ed Johann Samuel Ersch and Johann Gottfried Gruber vol I (Leipzig 1818) 126–32. Allsop I 109–10; *CL* v 96. In a footnote to this entry in *TT* (1835) HNC quoted RS *A Tale of Paraguay* (1825) canto III lines 136–80 (sts 16–20).

[4] Dobrizhoffer tr SC pt ii ch 16 II 157–82, esp 176: "The Abipones seem to want the infinitive, the place of which they supply in other ways . . .". *TT* (1835) added a sentence on the "pure mother English" of SC's translation. *TT* (1836) inserted a comment on Dobrizhoffer pt ii ch 8 from MS B f 73, HNC's copying from EC's transcriptions from C's notebooks; see 36:415 and n.

MS B f 69*^v* and the top of f 70 contain three passages transcribed under the heading "*B. Life*" from C's marginalia in George Frere's copy of Baxter *Reliquiae Baxterianae—CM (CC)* I 303–6. These include a sentence on Baxter's veracity, on f 70, incorporated in *TT* 36:101 (12 Jul 1827), cancelled with a vertical line to indicate that it had been transcribed for publication. See 25–6 Aug 1827 at n 19, above.

^a6. Aug. 1832.

I have generally found the Scotch to be either superficial Germans, or dull Frenchmen.[1] The Scotch will attribute merit to people of any nation rather than the English; the English have a morbid habit of petting and praising foreigners to the unjust disparagement of their own worthies.[2]

[36:416]

You will find this a good gage or criterion of Genius—whether it progresses and evolves, or only spins upon itself.[3] Take Dryden's Achitophel—every line adds to or modifies the character;[4] in Pope's Timon &c.

^a f 70

---

[1] C had also generally said as much, e.g. in a letter of 4 Sept 1816 to Thomas Boosey (*CL* IV 667) and in *Friend (CC)* I 423, in which the remark is attributed to a "whimsical friend of mine"; both quips, 1816 and 1818, occur in contexts distinguishing genius from talent and cleverness. The attribution to a whimsical friend may be explained by an anecdote recorded from Allston by Richard H. Dana Jr: "Allston was sitting with Mrs. Gillman and Coleridge in the garden at Highgate, when Coleridge read to them something which he had written, in which was the following passage: 'A Scotchman is a superficial German and a dull Frenchman.' " When Mrs Gillman remonstrated and said she would give a reason for omitting it, C answered: " 'No, madam; don't, for God's sake . . . for if you do you will spoil the whole. A woman judges by her instinct, and not by reason. I'll strike it out, but I've more respect for your first impression than I should probably have for your argument.' " Flagg *Life and Letters of Allston* 358. C's distaste for "Scotch feelosophers", like Cobbett's and Lamb's, is ultimately indistinguishable from their common English prejudice against Scots, as illustrated in the *Courier* of 4, 16, and 27 Sept 1811: *EOT (CC)* II 275–6, 289–92, 316–17. The Scots had fallen wrong on both sides, among stony places as Catholics and tares as Presbyterians. To the Germanophile Eliza Aders C wrote on 6 Feb 1826 in praise of his disciple John Watson: "He *loves* Germany & Germans—*dislikes* the Italians, and ABHORS the French—all as a good man ought to do—just as I would have had it! . . . I rank him now among the *judicious* Lovers & Haters". *CL* VI 553. For HCR's report of C's remarks on the "Scotch" see App F 22, below.

[2] As C puts it, this is a further example of English prejudice against Scots, but it anticipates Bernard Shaw's complaint in the Preface to *Major Barbara* (1905) that his debts to Samuel Butler brought only "vague cacklings about Ibsen and Nietzsche . . . Really, the English do not deserve to have great men."

[3] Genius is once more distinguished from talent, with Dryden here illustrating genius, and Pope mere talent. Genius, C observed in a note on Bunyan *Pilgrim's Progress*, requires enthusiasm but excludes fanaticism. *CM (CC)* I 818. The presence of progression thus implies the presence of enthusiasm. If HNC is reporting the topics in the order of their occurrence, the reference to national traits led in transition to French cleverness and talent vs German and English genius.

[4] John Dryden (1631–1700) *Absalom and Achitophel* (first published 1681) I 150–229. *TT* (1835) expanded to "Achitophel and Zimri,—Shaftesbury and Buckingham". In 1801 C wrote to Godwin: "Of Dryden I am & always have been a passionate admirer. I have always placed him among our greatest men.—You must have misunderstood me—& considered me as detracting when I considered myself only as dis-

the two or three first lines contain all the pith of the character—and the forty that follow are so much evidence or proof as it were [of]*ᵇ* the overt acts of jealousy or pride &c.⁵ Compare Charles Lamb's exquisite criticisms on Shakspeare, and Hazlitt's imitation of them. Hazlitt fed on the fragments or the crumbs which fell from Lamb's mouth when his wit was flickering in*ᶜ* the last stage of dying*ᵈ* consciousness.⁶   [36:417]

Pindar and Dante are certainly the two great picturesque poets.⁷

*ᵉ*It is remarkable that in no part of his writings does Milton notice the great painters of Italy, nor painting as an art—whilst every other page breathes his love and taste for Music.⁸ Yet it is curious that in one passage in the Paradise Lost Milton has certainly copied the fresco of the Creation in the Sistine*ᶠ* Chapel at Rome—I mean the lion breaking

---

ᵇ Word supplied by the editor   *ᶜ* ~~under~~ in   *ᵈ* lging [?]   *ᵉ* f 70ᵛ   *ᶠ* Blank in ms

---

criminating." *CL* ii 743. "Dryden *could* not have been a Platonist" (14 Jan 1820, *CL* v 15), but if "Pope was a *Poet*, as Lord Byron swears—then Dryden, I admit, was a very *great* Poet". Note on Pepys *Memoirs* ii i 110: *CM (CC)* iv. In defence of *The Hind and the Panther* against HC *The Worthies of Yorkshire and Lancashire* C noted "pleasing marks of the tranquil feeling in which this ingenious poem was written". *CM (CC)* ii 78.

⁵ Pope *Moral Essays* Epistle 4 (first published 1731) lines 98–176. No more than Pope's other detractors born in the late eighteenth century did C ignore him; in several marginal notes he rescues Pope's meaning from misinterpretation in Lessing "Pope ein Metaphysiker" *Sämmtliche Schriften* vii 163–80: *CM (CC)* iii.

⁶ The tribute to Lamb as a critic more original than Hazlitt remained in *TT* (1835), but the final sentence was dropped. The implication is that Hazlitt stole the least discriminating witticisms that Lamb was too drunk to remember. William Maginn was to say in 1833 in *Fraser's* viii (Jul 1833) 64: "Many a critic deemed original has lived exclusively by sucking Coleridge's brains. The late William Hazlitt was one of the most conspicuous thieves. There was not an observation—not a line—in all Haz-

litt's critical works, which was worth reading, or remembering, that did not emanate directly from our old friend the Platonist; other spoliators, more or less known, were as barefaced. It was always worse done than if Coleridge had done it, and sometimes vilely perverted in spirit; but still the seed was good, and he has thus strongly acted upon the public mind of his day." Maginn had probably heard the charge from C himself.

⁷ C is returning to the distinctions between the picturesque and musical poets of 31 Mar, above. The comments on Milton of that date are consolidated in 36:418, but the sentence on Pindar and Dante, though repeated in MS B from 31 Mar, was not published.

⁸ "It is also said that he had some skill in painting as well as in music, and that somewhere or other there is a head of Milton, drawn by himself; but he was blessed with so many real excellencies, that there is no want of fictitious ones to raise and adorn his character." Thomas Newton "Life of Milton" *The Poetical Works of John Milton* ed Edward Hawkins (4 vols Oxford 1824) i xciv. In marginal notes on Milton *Poems upon Several Occasions* ed Thomas Warton (1791) C found two subjects for paintings in *Ode on the Morning of Christ's Nativity* sts 15 and 23. *CM (CC)* iv.

through the soil[9]—an image which the necessities of the Painter justified, but which was wholly unworthy of the enlarged powers of the Poet. Adam bending over Eve, and Dalilah approaching Samson, are the only two pictures I remember in Milton.[10]   [36:418]

---

9 Aug. 1832.[1]

I think the Baptismal Service quite perfect[2] with the exception of the con-

[9] *TT* (1835) cited and had C quote *Paradise Lost* VII 463–6. Thomas Newton's note to this passage (1749, included in Hawkins, II 43n) explained: "He supposes the beasts to rise out of the earth . . . as Raphael had painted this subject before in the Vatican". Merritt Y. Hughes, rejecting what "Coleridge thought", claimed an adequate source in Lucretius *De rerum natura* 2.991–8. Milton *Complete Poems and Major Prose* (New York 1957) 357n. Trouble with what "Coleridge thought" arises in the mistaken specificity of the Sistine Chapel, for which HNC rather than C may be responsible. C is referring to the fresco of the fifth and sixth day of creation in the vault of the first bay of the inner loggia of the Vatican, designed by Raphael and executed by his pupil Giulio Romano. F. A. Gruyer *Essai sur les fresques de Raphaël* (2 vols Paris 1859) II 49–51. C referred to the loggia in Satyrane's Letters II, along with "Michael Angelo's Sestine Chapel", as "the Scripture Gallery of Raphael". *Friend (CC)* II 218; *BL (CC)* II 187. In the fresco, the lion to the left of God, clearly the king of all creatures until the arrival of man, is pulling his hindquarters out of the earth. To the right, only the large head of a horse has emerged.

[10] In a footnote in *TT* (1835) HNC quoted *Paradise Lost* V 8–18; *Samson Agonistes* lines 710–21. C's remark is repeated from 31 Mar 1832 (at n 4), above. During illness in 1830, C implied an identification of Milton with blind Samson and both with himself. HEHL MS HM 17299 (N F°) p 145.

[1] On Thurs, 9 Aug C was driven to Hampstead for the christening of Edith, the second child of SC and HNC. Mrs C thought him "on that day, if never in his life before, a most extraordinary person"; she reported to Poole that "he talked incessantly for full 5 hours to the great entertainment of Mrs May and a few other friends who were present". *Minnow* 165. SC wrote to Emily Trevenen on the 12th that from 3 PM to 10 PM C "talked incessantly with the greatest vigor and eloquence". UT Grantz 1341.

[2] Cf *AR* (1825) 367–8: "And then make present to your imagination . . . the softening, elevating exercise of Faith and the Conquest over the senses, while in the form of a helpless crying Babe the Presence, and the unutterable Worth and Value, of an Immortal Being made capable of everlasting bliss are solemnly proclaimed and carried home to the mind and heart of the Hearers and Beholders!" For C's varying beliefs and doubts concerning infant baptism see *CL* I 624–5, 632, VI 572; *CN* III 4462, IV 4750; *CM (CC)* I 262–6, 276–7; *AR* (1825) 354–76.

Edith was christened by James Gillman Jr. HNC wrote to JTC, one of the godparents: "Sara & I, Aunt S and S.T.C. stood & answered for my mother & you, Miss Trevenen & Frank." BM Add MS 47557 f 92. Edith's birthday is frequently given as 2 Jul, but SC wrote in the family Bible that Edith was born "June the 29th 1832, at half past nine o'clock A.M.". *CM (CC)* I 413. SC's dissatisfaction with J. H. Green's version of C's view of the sacraments, extracted in *AR* (1848) II 249–322, led her to adjoin to a letter to DC 1 Nov 1849 "three sheets to thee on Baptism". UT

ceit of the Deluge*a* out of the First*b* Epistle of Peter.[3] None of the services of the Church affect me so much as this. I never could attend a christening without tears bursting forth at the sight of the helpless innocent in a pious clergyman's arms.   [36:419]

The First Epistle of Peter is no doubt genuine—that is, I suppose it was in substance supplied by Peter. Of course the Apostle could not have written the Greek text, which in all probability was composed by Mark, a disciple of Paul's. In truth you see the Pauline phrases stuck in every where. But it is a most valuable work.[4]

*c*The Second Epistle cannot possibly be genuine. The mention of St Paul's Epistles is conclusive.[5] The Epistolion[6] was not collected for a long time after this age—and the title γράφαι Scriptures was never applied in the early Apostolic age to any thing but the Old Testament.*d7*

I have no doubt this Second Epistle and*e* those to Titus and Timothy were composed long after the Apostles' time.[8] It is evident that church government had assumed a certain degree of complexity at the date of those two works.

Suppose these three epistles removed, would the evidence for*f* a single fundamental article of our Faith be weakened? Can you not find in other parts of the *g*New Testament Canon all that you*h* could wish to find in these Epistles and better*i* expressed?

The Jews recognized three degrees of sanctity in their Scriptures—1. the writings of Moses who had the αυτοψια;[9] 2. the Prophets—3. the

---

a ~~Red Sea~~ Deluge   *b* ~~2nd~~ 1st   *c–d* For the variant in MS F see App C, below
e like   *f* ~~of~~ for   *g* f 71   *h* you ~~find~~   *i* MS F: much better

---

Grantz 65. She had treated baptism in her essay "On Rationalism", which had joined C's work in *AR* (1843) II 335–556.

[3] In the Anglican service Public Baptism of Infants, the priest paraphrases 1 Pet 3.20–1: "Almighty and everlasting God, who of thy great mercy didst save Noah and his family in the ark from perishing by water; and also didst safely lead the children of Israel thy people through the Red Sea, figuring thereby thy holy Baptism . . .". C's remark, like the paragraphs that follow, was omitted from *TT* (1835).

[4] Although C's chief authority here was probably Eichhorn, he had gone beyond Eichhorn in a marginal note: "With all due respect for Papius, Polycarp, Irenæus, Origen, Eusebius, and the Tradition of the Church, I must confess, that

my Judgement inclines to the opinion, that even the *first* Epistle of Peter was composed after Peter's Death, by some one of his Scholars; and that it is in all points analogous to the ⟨I⟩ Epistle to Timothy." Eichhorn *NT: CM (CC)* II 502. HNC transcribed this and the next three paragraphs in MS F, but they were not published.

[5] 2 Pet 3.16 mentions Paul's epistles. Eichhorn *NT* III 632, 637 argued that Paul's letters could not have been collected during the lifetime of Simon Peter.

[6] The epistles of the NT collectively, as distinct from the gospels, Acts, and Apocalypse.

[7] γραφαί, scriptures.

[8] See 15 Jun 1833, below (at n 6) (36:524).

[9] "Seeing with one's own eyes".

Good books.[10] Philo amusingly enough places his works somewhere between the second and third degrees.[11]   [36:420]
The claims of the Sanskrit for priority to the Hebrew as a language are ridiculous.[12]   [36:421]

---

[j]9. Aug. 1832[13]

The belief that Malta is the island on which St Paul was wrecked is so rooted in the common Maltese, and is[k] cherished with such a superstitious[l] nationality,[m] that the Government would run the chance of exciting a tumult, if it unwarily ridiculed it.[14] The supposition itself is quite absurd. Not to argue the matter at length, consider these few conclusive facts: The narrative speaks of the "barbarous inhabitants"[15]—Malta at

[j] f 72; the entries for 11 Aug intervened in the ms   [k] is ~~so superstitious~~   [l] superstitious~~ly &~~
[m] national~~ly~~ity

[10] Josephus, and especially Origen, reflect a division into Mosaic works of highest prophecy, other prophets, and moral works. For three classes extracted from Philo see Eichhorn *AT* §§ 27–33 I 86–94; on the traditional classification of Law, Prophets, and Hagiography see § 8 I 39–40. Finding Josephus cited as authority for the reading of Daniel in Jewish worship, C noted that "the Jewish Church ranked the book of Daniel in the third class only, among the Hagiographic". Annotation on Davison *Discourses on Prophecy: CM (CC)* II 156.

[11] Untraced. Philo says in *De migratione Abrahami* 7.31–5 that his writing sometimes rises by divine inspiration. LCL IV 150–2.

[12] The oldest surviving state of Sanskrit is in the Veda, possibly of 1500 B.C., probably contemporaneous with the earliest Hebrew writing, c 1000 B.C. Thomas Burrow *The Sanskrit Language* (3rd ed 1973) 3, 35. C rests ultimately upon the divine word of the Bible, as did Sir William Jones in his 3rd, 6th, and 9th discourses to the Asiatick Society at Calcutta in 1786–92 and his paper "On the Chronology of the Hindus" (1788) *Works* (13 vols 1807) III 27–8, 34, 107–8, 185–95, IV 1–2. Prepared to have his mind changed, Jones called the Mosaic books "the oldest composition perhaps in the world" (III 191). C had read some (later) Sanscrit literature in translation, and had commented on a review in *Ed Rev* XXXIII (1820) 431–42 of Franz Bopp *Über das Conjugationssystem der Sanskritssprache* . . . (Frankfurt 1816) and of Bopp's translation of part of the *Bhagavadgita*. *CN* IV 4697. See also *CN* IV 4832 and n.

[13] The next entries in MS B are from Sat, 11 Aug, followed by a return to the date of the christening, 9 Aug, whether from the recovery of notes is not clear. And see n 1, above, C talking "incessantly for full 5 hours".

[14] C here opposes the general opinion in his own time and later. Eichhorn concluded that shipwreck brought Paul to Malta in the winter of A.D. 62. *NT* II 70, III 50. Frank Sayers, admired by RS, cited Strabo in evidence that the Adriatic mentioned by Paul could have included the Ionian Sea: "Remarks Tending to prove that the Melita on which St. Paul was shipwrecked, is the Melita of the Mediterranean". *Disquisitions* (Norwich 2nd ed 1808) 117–20; *Collective Works* (2 vols Norwich 1823) II 107–20. The "Melita" of Acts 28.1 is "Malta" in RSV, James Moffatt, and the New World Translation of the Watch Tower Bible and Tract Society.

[15] βάρβαροι: Acts 28.2, 4.

the time was fully peopled and highly civilized, as[n] we learn from Cicero.[16] A viper comes out from the sticks upon the fire being lighted—the men are not surprised at the appearance of a snake, but[o] imagined him first a murderer and then a divine personage from the harmless attack.[17] In Malta there are no snakes at all. Now Melita[p] in the Adriatic was a perfectly barbarous island, and was and is now infested with serpents. Besides the context shews that the scene is in the Adriatic.[18]   [36:431]

The Maltese seem to have preserved a fondness and taste for architecture from the time of the Knights—naturally enough occasioned by the incomparable materials at hand.[19]   [36:432]

It may be doubted whether a composite language like the English is not a happier instrument of expression than a homogeneous one like the German. We possess such wonderful richness and variety of modified meanings in[q] our Saxon and Latin quasi-synonyms, which the Germans have

[n] ~~my~~ as   [o] but ~~at St~~ P   [p] ~~in~~ Mellta   [q] ~~by~~ in

[16] *Second Action Against Verres* 2.4.46. RS wrote to HNC: "Wynn in expressing the pleasure he derived from the Table Talk to me, remarks upon this that βάρβαρος was never used by the Greeks as meaning uncivilized" but simply the inability to speak Greek or to pronounce it properly. UT ms. HNC's reply to RS, of 27 Jun 1835, shows that he took a proprietary interest in C's position: "Mr Wynn's remark on βαρβαρος is of course just, taken generally; still I incline to think that the context of the passage in the Acts shows that rudeness & barbarism were principally intended. First the writer clearly understood what they said, & his remarking that the crew met with no common kindness from the islanders would be without point, unless you take his barbarians in a sense referring to their apparent want of civilization. Even Herodotus & the historians more commonly—unless by antithesis to the Greeks—call the Persians &c. by their proper names; & I no where remember any Greek writer under the empire calling the Romans βαρβαροι. What I think the most conclusive thing *for* our Malta, is, that St Paul reembarks on board an Alexandrian ship, wch is stated to have wintered in the island, apparently by

choice & in its course. Now in due course from Egypt, the Adriatic Melita would not have been visited; whereas Malta would. On the ōr hand, the wandering up & down Adria before the wreck is strong. But enough of this." UT ms. HNC's long note in *TT* (1835) argues the case from further evidence. *TT* (1836) introduced a separate note to dissociate HNC tactfully from C's interpretation of "barbarians".

[17] Acts 28.3–6.

[18] C's Melita in the Adriatic Sea is Mljet, an island now in the federative unit of Croatia, west of Dubrovnik, Yugoslavia. The context is provided by Acts 27, esp 27.27, "as we were driven up and down in Adria".

[19] In 1805–6 C had observed a Maltese sense for stone but not for woodwork: "Splendid doorways and Stone Balconies, with wretched Door and window shutters". *CN* II 2289. The underlying rock of Malta is chiefly porous limestone. *TT* (1835) in a footnote cited the evidence of Diodorus Siculus 2.12 that the Maltese taste for architectural refinement preceded the Knights—the military and religious Order of the Hospital of St John of Jerusalem, awarded sovereignty of Malta in 1530.

not. For "the pomp and prodigality of Heaven"[20] ʳthe Germans must
have said the "spendthriftness".[21] Shakspeare is particularly happy in
his use of the Latin synonyms, and in distinguishing between them and
the Saxon.[22]   [36:433]

_____

That is the most excellent state of society in which the patriotism of the
Citizen ennobles, but does not merge the individual energyˢ of the
Man.[23]   [36:434]

_____

ᵃ11. Aug. 1832.[1]

I like reading Hesiod—meaning the Works and Days.[2] If every verse is
not poetry, it is at least good sense, which is a good deal to say.

[36:422]

There is nothing real in the Georgics, except to be sure the verse.[3]
Mere didactics, unless seasoned with the personal interests of the time or
author, are inexpressibly dull to me.

ʳ f 72ᵛ   ˢ ~~charm~~ energy
ᵃ f 71; these entries preceded those for the second group under the date 9 Aug

[20] Thomas Gray *Stanzas to Mr. Bentley* line 20; subtitled "a Fragment" in
Gray *Works* (2 vols 1825) I 174–5.
Thomas Ashe—*TT* (1884) 182n—called
attention to the fuller version of these
comments in Lect 6 of 5 Dec 1811: *Lects
1808–19 (CC)* I 291–2.
  [21] *Verschwendung*, according to the
"guess" in the footnote to this entry in
TT (1835). C's attempts to name the
"best" language vary with the characteristics under consideration; he had a
deeper interest in the comparison of linguistic structures than in the rankings.
  [22] Probably the best known example
of C's point is *Macbeth* II ii 59–60:

The multitudinous seas incarnadine,
Making the green one red.

  [23] This aphorism is an augmentive ap-
pendage to C's published discussions of
social union, as in *Friend (CC)* I 251–3
(II 200–2), analysed in Colmer 107–11.
In a note of c 1809–10 on nationality, patriotism, and the individual, C had concluded: "Nationality in each Individual
quoad his Country is = the sense of his

Individuality quoad himself—i.e. sub-
sensuous, central, inexclusive, &c." *CN*
III 3654.
  [1] These entries preceded those with
the repeated date 9 Aug; see 9 Aug n 13,
above.
  [2] Hesiod, Greek poet of about the
eighth century B.C., author of *Works and
Days*, probably of *Theogony*, and perhaps of other extant poems attributed to
him in antiquity. HNC had published a
review-article on Hesiod in *QR* XLVII
(Mar 1832) 1–39. The remarks of 11
Aug arose because of what C in a letter of
7 Aug to HNC called the article's "second or plagiary Rain-bow" by John Eagles in *Bl Mag* XXXII (Aug 1832) 165–
76. *CL* VI 919. C's marginalia on HNC's
article—*CM (CC)* II 86–9—include two
remarks on the authorship of *Theogony*.
C had quoted "the wise Hesiodic Line",
Works and Days 40, in a letter to William
Sotheby of 1828. *CL* VI 736.
  [3] To HNC's declaration in the article
on Hesiod that "Hesiod and Virgil were
both poets in the truest sense of the
word", C responded: "Mentiris, Caris-

Such didactic poetry as that of the Works and Days followed naturally upon Legislation and the first ordered municipality.[4]   [36:423]

All Genius is metaphysical. The ultimate end is ideal, however [b]it may be actualized[c] by incidental and accidental circumstances.[5]   [36:424]

Don Quixote is not a man out of his senses, but a man in whom the Imagination and the pure Reason are so powerful as to make him disregard the evidence of sense when it opposed their[d] conclusions.[e][6] Sancho

---

[b-c] ~~the actualization takes place~~   [d] the⟨ir⟩   [e] conclusions ~~of his~~

sime! V. in *no* sense but that of having a good ear. But I forgot—you are an *Etonian*, & swear per Maronem''. *CM (CC)* II 88. HNC answered in a footnote in *TT* (1835). When Sotheby issued a magnificent folio *Georgica Publii Virgilii Maronis hexaglotta* in 1827, C wrote that he would pass the copy presented to him on to SC, because of the "Talent and Industry, that have made her Mistress of the Six Languages" and "the fine Taste and genial sentiment" that would enable her to admire Sotheby's English and Johann Heinrich Voss's German translations. *CL* VI 691. On the Voss see *CN* III 3557 and n (C's comments on the Voss refer to the Sotheby edition left to SC in C's will). On 9 Nov 1828 C wrote to Sotheby of a plan to write an article for Blanco White on didactic poetry, to include "the merits and defects of the Georgics". *CL* VI 771.

[4] The chief authority of the time, William Mitford *The History of Greece* (5 vols 1784–1818) I 15–17, 65, 83, discussed the beginnings of municipal government and noted Hesiod's hostility to the earlier type of "bribe-devouring" king. C referred to Mitford's work in *P Lects* Lect 8 (1949) 253 and used it in N 27 (*CN* IV 4507).

[5] The need for C to speak can be seen in Sir Joshua Reynolds's Sixth Discourse of 1774: "Genius is supposed to be a power of producing excellencies, which are out of the reach of the rules of art . . . But the truth is, that the *degree* of excellence which proclaims *genius* is different in different times and different places. . . . Invention is one of the great marks of genius; but if we consult experience, we shall find, that it is by being conver-

sant with the inventions of others, that we learn to invent . . .''. *Discourses Delivered at the Royal Academy* (2 vols 1825) I 88, 90–1.

[6] After planning to include *Don Quixote* as a subject for lectures in 1812, C in Lect 6 of 21 Apr 1814 at the White Lion in Bristol lectured on Miguel de Cervantes Saavedra (1547–1616), "by particular desire" giving a "Philosophic Analysis" of *Don Quixote*. He compared Quixote and Sancho in Lect 8 of 20 Feb 1818 and again in Lect 7 of 25 Mar 1819, for which there are notes in *CN* III. *Lects 1808–19 (CC)* II 5 and 14, 162, 419–20. In the latter lecture his notes came from *The Life and Exploits of Don Quixote de la Mancha* tr Charles Jarvis (4 vols 1809). See *CN* III 4503n. In Satyrane's Letters II he cited *Don Quixote* in arguing against dependence upon plot for interest. *Friend (CC)* II 218–19; *BL (CC)* II 187–8. From 1812 on, the subject always led him to contrast Quixote's intense motivation with other kinds of madness. Whether he lectured on Cervantes at Clifton as he hoped to do, he gave a sketch of the subject to Charles Leslie there in 1813: "He said, 'there are two kinds of madness; in the one, the object pursued is a sane one, the madness discovering itself only in the means by which it is to be gained. In the other, an insane intention is aimed at or compassed by means that the soundest mind would employ, as in cases of murder, suicide, &c. The madness of Don Quixote is of the first class, his intention being always to do good, and his delusion only as to the mode of accomplishing his object.' '' Leslie *Autobiographical Recollections* I 34–5.

is the common sense of the social man animal, unenlightened and unsanctified by the Reason. You see how he reverences his master.[7]

[36:425]

Rabelais is a wonderful author—the morality is uncommonly pure and high.[8] People talk about its all being^f political and historical—there are politics in the work of course, but the real scope is still higher and more philosophical. He as it were flashes you a glimpse of ^{g}a real^h face from a magic lantern, every^i now and then—and then buries the whole in mist.[9]

[36:237]

Swift was Anima^j Rabelaisii habitans in sicco—^{k}the soul of Rabelais dwelling in a dry Land.^{l10}

[36:237]

Is it not lamentable—is it not even more wonderful ^{m}that the monstrous sophism of Malthus should now have gotten possession of the leading men of the Kingdom![11] Such a lie in morals—and such a lie in fact as it

^{f} being ~~his~~ $^{g-h}$ ~~the true~~ a real ^{i} ~~all~~ every
^{j} ~~spiritus~~ Anima $^{k-l}$ ~~in the desert~~ the soul . . . Land. ^{m} f 71^v

[7] *TT* (1835) completed the sentence, "at the very time he is cheating him", from the record of 8 Jul 1827, above (at n 5). In a letter of 20 Oct 1829 to William Blackwood C offered to send two articles ready at hand, "a critique expository and vindicatory of Francis Rabelais' great work" and "2. Ditto on the Don Quixote". *CL* VI 821.

[8] This entry was consolidated with the comments on Rabelais of 12 Jun 1830, above, to form 36:237. *TT* (1835) added a sentence distinguishing the questionable manners of the work from the praiseworthy morality. Somewhat similarly C praised Boccaccio in 1818 for "a depth and fineness in the workings of the Passions" but censored a licentiousness "which has once or twice seduced even our pure-minded Spenser to a grossity" alien to "the delicacy of his morals". *CN* III 4388. HNC may have had in hand Gillman's copy of Rabelais with C's marginal notes, for on f 72^v, after the first entry for 15 Aug, HNC transcribed three of those notes.

[9] The magic lantern, utilising lenses to throw onto a screen a magnified image from a transparent slide or an opaque object such as paper, was increasingly used, as transparencies were, to super-impose images or to have one image fade into another. Defending RS in the *Courier* 18 Mar 1817, C represented Dante as realising the phantoms and torments of the Inferno on the slides of "their own magic lanthern". *EOT (CC)* II 459. The master of such effects on the stage as C describes was Philippe Jacques de Loutherbourg (1740–1812), whose Eidophusikon had opened in 1781. The term "magic lantern" was also applied to the *camera lucida*.

[10] In *TT* (1835) the sentence was moved to 15 Jun 1830, with "place" for "Land", joining the other remarks on Rabelais and Swift.

[11] Thomas Robert Malthus (1766–1834) argued in *An Essay on the Principle of Population* (1798, rev 1803) that only checks to population such as war and disease could reduce the misery of the poor, because population increases geometrically and food only arithmetically. The entry was published with minor changes, under the heading "*August* 12. 1832. MALTHUSIANISM", in *TT* (1835) but omitted from *TT* (1836). Thomas Perronet Thompson's review of *TT* (1835) voiced special outrage at the "coarse, indecent attack on Malthus"; C, he said, "abandons Ennius whom he

is too! I declare solemnly that I do not believe all the heresies and sects and factions which the ignorance and the weakness and the wickedness of man have ever given birth to, were altogether so disgraceful to man as a Christian, a philosopher, a statesman, or citizen as this abominable tenet. It should be exposed by reasoning in the form of Ridicule. Asgill or Swift would have done much—but like the Popish doctrines, it is so vicious a tenet, so flattering to the cruelty, and avarice, and sordid selfishness of most men, that I hardly know what to think of the result.[12]

[35:426]

———

Poor Steinmetz is gone![13] His state of sure blessedness accelerated—or may be he is buried in Christ, and there in that mysterious depth grows on to the spirit of a just man made perfect. Could I for a moment doubt this, the grass would become black beneath my feet, and this earthly frame a charnel house. I never knew any man so illustrate the difference between feminine and effeminate.[n]

[36:427]

[n] ~~I said Death is in~~

———

understands, to run a tilt at Malthus whom he does not". *Westminster Review* XXII (1835) 532. C annotated a copy of the *Essay* (1803), which he sent to RS, who also wrote notes in it while preparing the review he wrote for *A Rev* for 1803. For one of C's annotations see 8 Apr 1833 n 13, below.

[12] Adverse reactions to Malthus by WW, Hazlitt, Byron, Shelley, Carlyle, and Dickens as well as C are sampled and applauded in Harold A. Boner *Hungry Generations* (New York 1955). Defending Malthus, De Q wrote: "Amongst others, Mr. Coleridge, who probably contented himself *more suo* with reading the first and last pages of the work, has asserted that Mr. Malthus had written a 4to volume (in which shape the second edition appeared) to prove that man could not live without eating". *London Magazine* (Oct 1823): *De Q Works* IX 17.

Where Allsop (I 61–2) said that C quarrelled with Unitarians for adopting the "hateful opinions and views of Malthus", John Sterling wrote in the margins of his own copy (see App M, vol II, below): "I never could understand Coleridge's ignorance or on the other alter-native my own about this matter. The *rationale* of Malthusianism seems to be that unless [the poor] restrain themselves from begetting children whom they cannot support the population will perpetually be brought down to the only possible level by misery and disease and the mass of the survivors will be debased and stinted. Now surely this is at least not absurd or immoral. On this point it has long seemed to me that perhaps from some soreness at the prevalent views of an age so cruel to him, S.T.C. was unlike himself, was an enemy to calm and comprehensive enquiry into one whole set of phenomena. J.S."

[13] If Adam Steinmetz, C's young friend and disciple, died on 12 Aug, as the evidence indicates, then HNC omitted a date from MS B; for once, then, the published date, 14 Aug, is more probable than the date in the ms. The subsequent return of MS B to the date 9 Aug suggests confusion in HNC's record for a period of several days. C used language similar to that of this entry, without the final sentence distinguishing feminine from effeminate, in a letter to John Peirse Kennard dated and postmarked 13 Aug. *CL* VI 921. Kennard, who wrote to

A[o] loose, not well dressed youth,[14] met Mr Green[p] and me in Mansfield Lane—Green[p] knew him and spoke.[15] It was Keats—he was introduced to me, and stayed[q] a minute or so—after he had gone a little, he came back, and said, "Let me carry away the memory,[r] Coleridge, of having pressed your hand".[16] There is death in *his*[s] hand said I to Green[t] when he was gone.[17] Yet this was before the consumption showed itself. [36:428]

[o] A~~n~~ [p] G. [q] staid [r] ~~thought~~ memory [s] ~~that~~ *his* [t] G.

C of the death, was to name after Steinmetz the son to whom C addressed the letter that closes the mss of TT and *TT* (1836).

[14] The poet John Keats (1795–1821). HNC omits the transition from Steinmetz to Keats: upon receiving the letter from Kennard (n 13, above) C wrote at once to Mrs Gillman: "I have ever anticipated this event, and you well know have often, after his taking leave of me, said, 'Alas! there is death in that hand!' " He wrote to Kennard that more than once or twice he had said to Mrs Gillman, "Alas! there is Death in that dear Hand!" *CL* vi 920, 922. See also 15 Aug 1832 n 1, below. HNC wrote "I said Death is in" at the end of the entry on Steinmetz but crossed out the words. *TT* (1835) added "slack" to the description of Keats; Leigh Hunt denied "that appearance of 'laxity,' which has been strangely attributed to him in a late publication". *Book of Gems* ed Samuel Carter Hall iii (1838) 120; quoted in Edmund Blunden *Leigh Hunt: A Biography* (1930) 270.

[15] Green, surgeon at St Thomas's Hospital, professor of anatomy at the College of Surgeons and the Royal Academy, C's literary executor, had been one of Keats's demonstrators at Guy's Hospital. All editions of *TT* before *CC* have left the name blank. Richard Monckton Milnes *Life, Letters, and Literary Remains of John Keats* (2 vols 1848) ii 107n explained that the meeting occurred in 1817 and that the third person was Leigh Hunt (see n 16, below). SC wrote to Isabella Fenwick that Milnes had made a "double mistake": "It was not Leigh Hunt, but Mr Green, to whom my father addressed his remark about Keats' deathly hand, & this was, Mr Green says, some years after the period when Keats first knew Hunt, & was, apparently, in perfect health. It was certainly as late as 1819." UT Grantz 1100 (var). In *TT* (1851) 195n–6, SC dealt with the question at some length; for her note see 36:428, below.

[16] In a letter of 15 Apr 1819 to his brother George (and wife Georgiana) Keats reported that on 11 Apr "I took a Walk towards highgate and in the lane that winds by the side of Lord Mansfield's park I met M[r] Green our Demonstrator at Guy's in conversation with Coleridge"; they walked together "for near two miles I suppose". *The Letters of John Keats* ed Rollins ii 88. Milnes had received the information he published from John Hamilton Reynolds on 7 Jul 1848: "At the time this interview took place, Keats was in perfect health & strength for it was when he was first known to Leigh Hunt & myself." MS Trinity College, Cambridge. Donald Lange, in publishing the Reynolds letter, suggested that the agreement of C and Keats concerning the occasion of 1819 may not exclude an earlier meeting: "A New Reynolds–Milnes Letter: Were There Two Meetings Between Keats and Coleridge?" *Modern Language Review* lxxii (1977) 769–72.

[17] The fullest account based on C's memory comes from John Frere, who talked with C about Keats and other contemporaries in Dec 1830:

"*F*. You have not read much of Keats, Sir, I think.

"*C*. No, I have not. I have seen two Sonnets which I think showed marks of a

*"*The discipline at Christ's Hospital in my time was ultra-Spartan—all domestic ties were to be put aside. "Boy"—I remember Boyer*ᵛ* saying to me once when I was crying the first day of my return from holidays— "Boy! the School is your father! Boy! the School is your mother! Boy! the School is your brother—the School is your sister—the School is your first cousin and your second coz—and all your relations! Let's have no crying!"[18]   [36:429]

ᵘ f 72   *ᵛ* Bowyer

---

great genius had he lived. I have also read a poem with a classical name—I forget what. Poor Keats, I saw him once. Mr. Green, whom you have heard me mention, and I were walking out in these parts, and we were overtaken by a young man of a very striking countenance whom Mr. Green recognised and shook hands with, mentioning my name; I wish Mr. Green had introduced me, for I did not know who it was. He passed on, but in a few moments sprung back and said, 'Mr. Coleridge, allow me the honour of shaking your hand.'

"I was struck by the energy of his manner, and gave him my hand.

"He passed on and we stood still looking after him, when Mr. Green said, " 'Do you know who that is? That is Keats, the poet.'

" 'Heavens!' said I, 'when I shook him by the hand there was death!' That was about two years before he died.

"*F.* But what was it?

"*C.* I cannot describe it. There was a heat and a dampness in the hand. To say that his death was caused by the Review is absurd, but at the same time it is impossible adequately to conceive the effect which it must have had on his mind.

"It is very well for those who have a place in the world and are independent to talk of these things, they can bear such a blow, so can those who have a strong religious principle; but all men are not born Philosophers, and all men have not those advantages of birth and education.

"Poor Keats had not, and it is impossible I say to conceive the effect which such a Review must have had upon him, knowing as he did that he had his way to make in the world by his own exertions,

and conscious of the genius within him." *Cornhill* NS XLII (1917) 405–6.

[18] In marginalia C gave variously Boyer's disciplinary "Peripatetic" adage; e.g. "You must lay it in at the Tail before you can get it into the Head"; "You must make a lad *feel* before he will *understand*". *CM (CC)* I 354 and n. The methods of "old Orbilius Plagosus Boyer" (*CL* VI 843) had come up on 27 May 1830, above (at n 1) (36:203). Leapidge Smith, who was C's attendant or "boy" at Christ's Hospital, remembered an occasion when C, irritated by Boyer's challenge to his definition of a Greek word, made Smith light a rush candle, take it to Boyer, and say C lighted it (presumably to hold a candle before the devil as if he were a saint); Boyer said, "Tell Colly (he always called him so when pleased) that he is a good fellow". "Reminiscences of an Octogenarian" *Leisure Hour* IX (1860) 634. Smith is identified in the reprinting by John Beer *Coleridge's Variety* (1975) 61–3. Lamb, contrasting the "heavy hand" of Boyer with the easy touch of his own master, the Rev Matthew Field, in "Christ's Hospital Five and Thirty Years Ago", ended with "the pious ejaculation of C.—when he heard that his old master was on his death-bed—'Poor J.B.!—may all his faults be forgiven; and may he be wafted to bliss by little cherub boys, all head and wings, with no *bottoms* to reproach the sublunary infirmities." *Elia* (1823) 46. De Q, in *Bl Mag* Jan 1845, challenged C's view of him "as a profound critic" with an insistence that he aroused "hearty detestation" in all other pupils; he concluded from C's own testimony reported in *C*

No tongue can express Mrs Boyer. Val LeGrice[19] and I were once going to be flogged for some domestic misdeed, and Boyer was thundering away at us by way of prologue, when Mrs Boyer looked in,[w] and said, "Flog them soundly, dear,[x20] I beg!" This saved us! Boyer was so nettled at the interruption, that he growled out, "Away, woman—away!" We were let off. [36:430]

[a]15. Aug. 1832.

I was complaining yesterday that a paper of mine was lost;—"No, Sir!" said the cook[1]—"nothing[b] is lost in your[c] room, but every thing mis-

---

[w] i‑tn,   [x] D[r],   [a] f 72[v]; the entries for 9 Aug preceded these
[a-d] For the variant in MS F see App C, below   [b] ‑it nothing   [c] this your

---

Life (G) 24–5 on Boyer's threat to flog a woman that he was the greatest villain of the eighteenth century. *De Q Works* v 197.

[19] Charles Valentine Le Grice (1773–1858), "conversationalist and author" (*Concise DNB*), who signed as "Cergiel" his "College Reminiscences of Mr. Coleridge" *G Mag* NS II (1834) 606–7. Lamb described the "wit-combats" between C and Le Grice. *Elia* 48. WW begged Francis Wrangham on 12 Jul 1807 not to put his poems into Le Grice's hands for *C Rev* because he hated C and would persecute any friend of C's. *WL* (*M* rev) I 155. From Penzance on 19 Feb 1842 Le Grice wrote to HNC that DC had not liked his piece on C. VCL ms. For a sonnet and remarks by Le Grice on C, see Edmund Blunden "Elia and Christ's Hospital" *Essays and Studies* XXII (1936) 53–7; for other memories by Le Grice see Richard Madden "The Old Familiar Faces" *Charles Lamb Bulletin* NS No 6 (Apr 1974) 113–21.

[20] Could Mrs Boyer have called him "Doctor"? MS B reads "D[r]", *TT* (1835) "sir".

[1] Harriet Macklin, "my favourite Hand-maid". *CL* VI 939. C's last written communication, addressed to Green and Mrs Gillman, asked that HNC impress upon all Coleridges that he would hope from them contributions towards a leg-acy for "that most faithful, affectionate, and disinterested servant, Harriet Macklin". *CL* VI 990. HNC, quoting to his father C's whole letter, explained: "Harriet is Mrs Gillman's servant, & has been so for eight or nine years. She has always particularly attended on my uncle", recently as his nurse. UT ms. After acknowledging on 14 Aug receipt of JTC's notes for TT, HNC continued: "As to the present to Harriet at Highgate, I quite agree with you. Patteson must have nothing to do with it. . . . She is, I suppose, something about 35 or not quite so much." BM Add MS 47557 f 107[v]. On 28 Nov he reported to SC from Devon: "Every thing will go very well, I think, about the present to Harriette. Derwent offers any thing. I think we should at all events give £5 each, even if £50 is made up without it. Fanny insists on contributing." UT ms. As HNC "knew the poor creature" Macklin—the "Harriet" of MS F carries more conviction than "the cook" of MS B—either the anecdote was addressed to another hearer present or possibly the clause concerning the "poor creature" is HNC's. The entry was marked with a vertical line in MS B and transcribed in MS F but not published. In the letter to Kennard on 13 Aug, C reported: "When I announced the sad tidings [of the death of Steinmetz] to Harriet, an almost *unalphabeted*

laid!'' If you knew the poor creature who said this, you would think it inspiration.*d2*

Pantheism naturally produces Polytheism as its only popular exponent. A*e* worship of abstract Nature could never exist in a people at large.[3]

Blumenbach's five races are thus:[4]

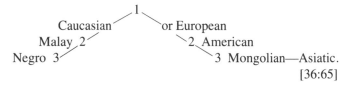

[36:65]

*a*1. Sept. 1832. S. T. C.[1]

In Chemistry and in Nosology by extending the Degree to a certain point, the constituent proportion may be destroyed, and a new kind produced.*b2*   [36:435]

---

d HNC copied several annotations from C's Rabelais after this entry; see n 2, below   *e* A̶n̶   *a* f 73
b HNC followed this entry with transcriptions, ff 73–75, from C's notebooks, from EC's ms; see n 2, below

---

but very sensible Woman, the Tears swelled in her eyes, and she exclaimed— 'Ah, Sir! how many a Thursday Night, after Mr Steinmetz was gone & I had opened the Door for him, I have said to them below—That dear young Man is too amiable to live: God will soon have him back.' '' *CL* vi 922.

[2] At this point in MS B HNC copied three paragraphs "From Rabelais" (Gillman's copy), published in *LR* i 138–9 and drawn upon for entry 36:237.

[3] A return to the subject of 27 Apr 1823 (at n 35) and 13 Apr 1830 (at n 27) (36:45, 129).

[4] Published in *TT* (1835) (36:65). The diagram on MS B f 72ᵛ has no vertical line to indicate publication from this source. For the relation of the diagram to Blumenbach's teachings, see 24 Feb 1827 n 12, above. For C's positions on the subject see J. H. Haeger "Coleridge's Speculations on Race" *Studies in Romanticism* xiii (1974) 333–57.

[1] After 15 Aug (Wed), HNC apparently visited C again on 1 Sept (Sat). C's letter of 28 Aug to HNC, enclosing the doggerel *Cholera Cured Beforehand*, indicates that they had not seen each other for some days. *CL* vi 922–5. On 30 Aug HNC wrote from Hampstead to JTC: "I . . . have had one or two days of continual quiet at home". BM Add MS 47557 f 93. He spent the free time, he said, reading Pindar, Horace, and Jonson; no immediate discussion of these authors with C is reflected in TT.

[2] By specifying nosology, the classification of diseases, rather than medicine or pharmacology, C may lodge the comparison with chemistry in analogy rather than in adjacency. Thomas Manning, a mathematician who had studied medicine, at Lamb's on 30 Dec 1817 "sometimes smiled as if he thought Coleridge had no right to metaphysicise on chem-

*a*S. T. C. 2. Jan. 1833.[1]

I certainly think that juries would be more conscientious if they were allowed a larger discretion.[2]   [36:438]

I cannot bring myself to think much of Mason's poetry. I may be wrong, but all those passages in the Caractacus, which we learn to admire at school, now seem to me one continued falsetto.[3]   [36:444]

a f 75ᵛ

---

istry without any knowledge of the subject". *CRB* ɪ 215. C listed four primers of chemistry in N 23 (*CN* ɪᴠ 4929) before adding Andrew Ure and Michael Faraday in N F° (*CN* ɪᴠ 5357), on 22 Apr 1826.

Except for the single sentence on chemistry and nosology, there is no further TT for 1832. The next heading in MS B, on this same page, f 73, is "S.T.C. copied from E's book MS." This was a ms booklet of brief passages copied by EC from C's notebooks. VCL BT 25. HNC copied thirty brief entries on three leaves of MS B, which have been torn out, probably by him. Two of the seven were published as TT of 1 Sept 1832 (36:436, 437); the others appear under 4 Aug 1832 (36:415), 23 Jul 1827 (36:116 and as a note to 36:117), and 30 Aug 1833 (36:583).

[1] Soon after the visit of 1 Sept 1832 HNC went on circuit to revise the lists of voters in Dorset and Devon. Correspondence between SC and HNC (at UT) shows that SC, as frequently before and after childbirth, was ill with nervous tension. HNC returned to Hampstead about 3 Oct; on that day he took SC to Brighton (*Minnow* 170), where she remained for a month. On 19 Oct HNC reached Bath for a continuation of the circuit; and both he and SC were at 1 Downshire Place again by 18 Nov. But the only reports of C during this period come from other sources. For Walter Savage Landor's visit with HCR to Highgate on 29 Sept and R. C. Trench's in early October see App F 23, below. HNC, who was in Ottery during Christmas week, next reported C's talk on Wed, 2 Jan.

[2] Bentham, the most influential legal reformer of the era, had increasingly opposed the jury system on the grounds that jurymen were intellectually inferior and inevitably corrupted. Mary P. Mack *Jeremy Bentham: An Odyssey of Ideas* (1963) 420–9. C, in turn, had most of his life, like many English authors before him, disparaged lawyers: they did not need genius, for talent could make an excellent lawyer, as common sense could make an adequate legislator. *CN* ɪ 669; *Friend (CC)* ɪɪ 139 (ɪ 213). But C was speaking to a lawyer, and the sentence was joined by two more in TT (1835).

[3] William Mason (1724–97), poet, a graduate of WW's college, St John's, Cambridge. His drama *Caractacus* was published 1759 and was performed in Dublin 1764 and at Covent Garden 1776. R. A. Willmott quoted WW: "The objection I have ventured to hint against Gray, is more unmitigated towards his friend Mason, of whose *Caractacus* I remember to have heard Mr. Coleridge say it was one continued *falsetto.*" *Conversations at Cambridge* (1836) 244. When Carlyon quoted the first five lines of Mason's *Elfrida* to C in 1799, "he asked me whose lines they were; and, singularly enough, confessed that he was unacquainted with Mason's beautiful imitations of the ancient drama". Carlyon ɪ 89–90. HC had called Mason "the most considerable" Yorkshire poet after Marvell, and "for many years of his life" England's "*greatest* living poet". "The Reverend William Mason" *Worthies of Yorkshire and Lancashire* (1832–3) 397–462.

I think there are only two things wanting to justify a surgeon in performing the Cæsarean operation—1. that he should possess[b] infallible knowledge. 2. that he should be infallibly certain that he is infallible.[4]

[36:441]

There undoubtedly ought[c] to be a declaratory act withdrawing expressly from the St John Longs and other quacks the protection which the Law is inclined to throw around the mistakes or miscarriages of the regularly educated practitioner.[5]   [36:440]

I should be sorry to see the honorary character of the fees of Barristers and Physicians done away with. Though it seems a shadowy distinction, I believe it beneficial. It contributes to preserve the idea of a Profession—of a class belonging to the Public—in the employment and remuneration of which no law interferes, but the citizen acts as he pleases in foro conscientiæ.[6]   [36:439]

[b] ~~be~~ possess   [c] ~~might~~ ought

[4] C could not grant infallibility even to the Scriptures, except in "the spirit of the whole". *CIS* (1840) 31–2, 53 ("the doctrine of infallible dictation . . . paralleled only by the Romish tenet of Infallibility"), 73. Of thirty-eight Caesarean sections performed in Great Britain between 1739 and 1845, four patients recovered; of eighty from 1846 to 1879, eighteen recovered. Robert F. Harris "The Caesarean Operation" *British Medical Journal* 3 Apr 1880 i 508. In 1816 John Abernethy had communicated an account by Kinder Wood of an unsuccessful Caesarean, "an operation, which, in this kingdom, has hitherto invariably proved fatal"; in 1819 J. J. Locker reported the first success in saving the lives of both mother and child. *Medico-Chirurgical Transactions* VII (1816) 264; IX (1819) 11–25. C treated the chief obstetricians of the day with grim humour in a letter to J. H. Green 5 May 1828. *CL* VI 739–40.

SC's continuing illness included a dread of childbirth. As the remaining subjects on this day concern medical practice, Gillman may have been present and perhaps other surgical or medical visitors to Gillman—who had had a tumour removed from his neck in September or October. *Minnow* 173. C, granting in 1800 that surgeons might become hard-hearted from habituation, nevertheless declared them "of all useful men, the most unequivocally useful". *EOT (CC)* I 250. In 1819 he commented that the medical profession generally was the only learned class in Britain to improve its professors within his lifetime. Annotation on "Medical Treatises" (transcript by SC): *CM (CC)* III.

[5] John St John Long (1798–1834), empiric, was tried in 1830 and 1831 for manslaughter for rubbing onto the bodies of female patients "certain noxious, unwholesome vapours, and a certain inflammatory, corrosive and dangerous liquid". *The Times* 1 Nov 1830, 21 Feb 1831. Conviction in a third case in Nov 1833 would not end the saga. *The Times* 2 Nov, 9, 10, 13 Dec 1833. He had counterattacked in *A Critical Exposure of the Ignorance and Malpractice of Certain Medical Practitioners in Their Theory and Treatment of Disease* (1831).

[6] "In the forum of the conscience". *TT* (1835) made this the second entry of the day, to follow that on juries and to account more naturally for the priority of barristers in the context of medical practice.

Can anything be more dreadful than the thought that an ^dinnocent child has inherited from you a disease or a weakness—the penalty in yourself of sin or want of caution?[7]   [36:442]

In the treatment of nervous cases, he is the best physician who is the most ingenious inspirer of Hope.[8]   [36:443]

4. Jan. 1833.

Naturally one would have thought that there would have been^a greater sympathy between the northern and north-western States of the Union and England than between England and the Southern States. There is ten times as much English blood and spirit in^b New England as in the Carolinas &c.[1] Nevertheless such has been the force of the interests of commerce^c that now and for some years past the people of the North hate England with increasing bitterness, whilst amongst those of the South who are jacobins^{d2} the British connection has become popular. Can there ever be any fusion of the Northern and Southern states? I think not. In fact the Union never could have lasted so long, if any serious question between the different States had arisen.[3]   [36:445]

^d f 76   ^a been a   ^b in the   ^c commerce &   ^d jacobinicals

[7] As a general topic the first focus would be on venereal disease, but HC's disaster in 1820 had brought at once to C's mind his own addiction: he had "long ago" written to warn HC against drunkenness, "conjuring him to reflect with what a poisoned dagger it would arm his Father's enemies—yea, and the Phantoms that half-counterfeiting, half-expounding the Conscience, would persecute his Father's Sleep". *CL* v 79.

[8] SC was seeking just such a physician. According to her mother, she had "great faith" in her physician at Brighton, "but no sleep". In May 1833 she would go under the care of Sir Henry Halford, president of the Royal College of Physicians. *Minnow* 171, 175.

[1] *TT* (1835) included Virginia with the Carolinas, but the inclusion of "spirit" makes the statement too subjective for assessment. South Carolina was currently prominent over the doctrine of nullification by states of acts by the na-

tional government. As C indicates, the chief issues were commercial: raw cotton was exported from the Southern states; textiles and other manufactured goods returned from Lancashire had encountered increasingly high tariffs for the protection of Northern factories.

[2] Jacobinism everywhere, C explained in *SM (CC)* 64, draws upon the passions and physical force of the multitude in order to base government and society on "the universals of abstract reason" in such doctrines as natural right instead of social privileges positively evolved through specific experience. In *TT* (1835) the phrase "who are Jacobins" is set off by commas, but the insertion of the word "amongst" above the line in MS B helps to indicate that HNC originally understood C to designate a certain number in the South, not all Southerners.

[3] The extensive addition in *TT* (1835) made C predict conditionally for the fu-

There is a great and important difference, both in politics and metaphysics, between *All* and the Whole. The first can never be ascertained as a standing quantity; the second, if ascertained by insight into its parts, remains for ever known.[4] Huskisson, I thought, satisfactorily refuted the Ship-owners[5]—and yet the Shipping Interest, who must know where the shoe pinches, complain to this day.[6]   [36:446]

---

7. Jan. 1833.

"Very far gone" is quam longissime[1] in the Latin of the article[2]—as far gone as possible, that is, as was possible for[a] Man; as far as was compatible with his having any redeemable qualities.[b] To talk of Man's being utterly lost to good is absurd, for then he would be a devil.   [36:447]

---

[c]No article of Faith can be truly and duly preached without necessarily

---

[a] for a   [b] qualityies.   [c] f 76[v]

---

ture a division of the Union into "two or three great governments". He projected a quite different vision on 8 Apr 1833, below (at n 6) (36:482). C's prophecy of 4 Jan was confirmed by events and historians; e.g. Edward Channing *A History of the United States* (6 vols New York 1905–25) VI 3: "Two such divergent forms of society could not continue indefinitely to live side by side within the walls of one government . . .", yet Channing was not able to cite firm prophecies of secession earlier than 1844.

[4] In *SM* App C, explaining the distinction of All and the Whole, C concluded that in Reason they are one; Reason is "the science of All as the Whole". *SM (CC)* 59–60, 63–4.

[5] Huskisson held office almost continuously from 1795. The speech C referred to was published with a statistical Appendix to show that the shipping trade had not been in decay since 1792 but had risen: *Shipping Interest. Speech of the Right Hon. W. Huskisson in the House of Commons, Monday, the 7th of May, 1827, on General Gascoyne's Motion, "That a Select Committee be appointed, to inquire into the present Distressed State of the British Commercial Shipping*

Interest" (1827). On Huskisson see also above, 27 Apr 1823 n 25, 2 Jul 1830 n 7, and 19 Sept 1830 n 39.

[6] A meeting of ship-owners to form an association was reported in *The Times* 10 Jun 1831. In early 1833 their interests were represented in the Commons by Joseph Hume, as they had been, he said, since 1821. *M Chron* 22 Feb 1833. Huskisson had permanently refuted the whole, but had not satisfied or silenced all.

After they talked on the 4th, C wrote to HNC at Lincoln's Inn—postmarked 5 Jan 1833, a Saturday—afterthoughts about sharing a small legacy with Mrs C, a subject not reflected in TT. *CL* VI 930–1.

[1] "As far as possible".

[2] No 9 of the 39 Articles, on Original Sin, "whereby man is very far gone from original righteousness". On "ut ab originali justitia quam longissime distet", Gilbert Burnet had noted in 1699 that the original ms of the Convocation read "whereby man is very far from his original righteousness". *An Exposition of the XXXIX Articles of the Church of England* (Oxford 1814) xxiii, 16.

and simultaneously infusing a deep sense of the indispensableness of a holy life.[3]   [36:449]

___

How pregnant with instruction, with Knowledge of all sorts, are our old divines! In this respect, as in so many others, how different from the majority of modern clergymen![4]   [36:450]

___

One mistake perpetually made—and with a pernicious tendency to Antinomianism—is to confound Sin with Sins.[5] To tell a modest girl, the watchful nurse of an aged parent, that she is full of sins against God is monstrous and as shocking to reason as unwarrantable by scripture—[but to tell her][d] that she and all men and women are of a sinful nature, and that without Christ's redeeming love and God's grace, she cannot[e] be emancipated from its dominion, is true and proper.[6]   [36:448]

___

Every attempt in a sermon to cause[f] emotion, except as the consequence

___

[d] Words supplied by the editor from *TT* (1835)   [e] cannot ~~tho' irreproachable by the law~~
[f] ~~move~~ cause

[3] A Pauline, Lutheran, and Anglican position: not justification by works, but a holy life as evidence of faith. Perhaps HNC found it the more memorable because of C's habitual emphasis upon faith.

[4] *TT* (1835) meliorated by contrasting "the sermons" of old vs "the major part of modern discourses".

[5] Where Jeremy Taylor wrote that God "appointed the evil which is the consequent of sin", C protested, "as if Sin were any thing but a *man* sinning or a man who *has* sinned! . . . Sin! the word, *Sin!* for abstracted from the Sinner it is no more". Annotation on *Polemicall Discourses* i 889: *CM (CC)* v. Rejecting Taylor's reasoning on the subject earlier in the volume, C had declared original sin "*an unaccountable Fact*". Ibid i 713: *CM (CC)* v. Cf *AR* (1825) 250–85. He sided with the "ignorant Rout" that raged against Richard Baxter for declaring unregenerate infants "loathsome in the Eyes of God". Annotation on *Reliquiae Baxterianae: CM (CC)* i 289. To the instruction in *A Companion to the Altar* that confession must be "of all our most heinous Sins", C wrote in a copy belonging to the Gillman family that he

agreed rather with the differing judgement of Luther, to whom he attributed an argument from St Francis of Sales against "recapitulation and renewing of sins". *CM (CC)* i 714 and n. C knew that Luther rejected the distinction between original and actual sins as a creation of Augustine's: "Of Sins" *Colloquia Mensalia* ch 9 (1652) 152. The published version of C's remark specified as perpetually in error "one of our unhappy parties in religion", which could point with more accuracy to Calvinist Presbyterians in Scotland, less accurately to the Evangelicals, among whom Charles Simeon, the Evangelical of greatest influence at Cambridge, said in C's way that Christ died "for the sins of men". *Christ Crucified* (3rd ed 1816) 96, 108.

[6] For C's scriptural authority see particularly Ps 51.5, Rom 3.9, 1 John 1.7. Among other annotations on Taylor *Polemicall Discourses*, C wrote on i 713: "Observe once for all: that I do not pretend to account for original Sin. I declare it to be an *unaccountable Fact*. How can we explain a Species, when we are wholly in the Dark as to the Genus?" *CM (CC)* v.

of an impression made on the Reason or the Understanding or the Will,[g] I hold to be fanatical and sectarian.[7]　　　　　　　　　　[36:451]

No doubt preaching in the proper sense of the word is more effective than reading, and therefore I would not prohibit it, but leave a liberty to the clergyman who feels himself able to accomplish it. But, as things now are, I am quite sure I should prefer going to Church to a pastor who read his discourse; for I never yet heard more than one preacher without notes,[8] who did not forget his argument in three minutes' time, and fall into vague, unprofitable declamation, and generally very coarse declamation too. These preachers never progress—they eddy round and round. Sterility [h]follows their ministry.[9]　　　　　　　　[36:452]

---

20. Jan. 1833.[1]

When the Church at the Reformation ceased to be extra-national, it unhappily became Royal; its proper bearing is intermediate between the Crown and the People with an inclination to the latter.[2]　　　[36:453]

The present prospects of the Church weigh heavily on my soul. Oh! that the words of a statesmanlike philosophy could win their way through the ignorant zealotry and sordid vulgarity of the leaders of the day![3]
　　　　　　　　　　　　　　　　　　　　　　　　　　　　[36:454]

The Quarterly Review's gravely setting to work to prove Seaward's Narrative not authentic is rather amusing.[4]

[g] Will　all playing upon the feelings by holding up images　　[h] f 77

---

[7] Although a long way from C's practice in 1795, the statement differs from conventional rationalism by allowing an appeal to the will.

[8] "Without book": *TT* (1835).

[9] *TT* (1835) cautiously specified "Sterility of mind". C was no longer accustomed to hearing sermons of any kind.

[1] After the visits of the 4th (Fri) and 7th (Mon) the Hilary sittings commenced and HNC returned regularly to his chambers at Lincoln's Inn. Except for the note to HNC in early January, we have no letter from C until 18 Mar, when he wrote to John Sterling, "I have been & now am, worse, far worse than when you left

me". *CL* vi 932. HNC returned to Highgate on 20 Jan (Sun). By 8 Feb WW heard that C was "more than usually unwell". *WL* (*L* rev) ii 590.

[2] See 8 Sept 1830 n 2, above. C developed both propositions of this sentence on endleaves of George Frere's copy of *Reliquiae Baxterianae*. *CM (CC)* i 355–8.

[3] In a rigmarole of 28 Aug 1832 to HNC, accompanying *Cholera Cured Beforehand*, C specified "the Lords Gray, Durham and the Reform Bill" as earning a place in hell for "emptying and stripping the Church". *CL* vi 923.

[4] A review of the latest novel by Jane

5. Feb. 1833.

If any modification of the Union takes place, I trust it will be a total divorce a vinculo matrimonii.[1] I am sure we have lived a cat and dog life of it. Let us have no silly saving of one Crown and two Legislatures; that would be preserving all the mischiefs without any of the good[a] of the Union.

I am deliberately of opinion that England in all its institutions has received unmingled injury from its union with Ireland. My difficulty is as to the Protestants, to whom we owe protection. But they themselves have greatly aided in accelerating the present horrible state of things, by using that as a remedy and a reward which should have been to them an opportunity.[2] [36:455]

I sometimes think it possible that the Dissenters may once more be animated by a wiser and nobler spirit, and see their interest in the Church of England as the bulwark and glory of Protestantism as at the Revolution. But I doubt their being able to resist the low factious malignity to the Church, which has characterized them as [b]a body[c] [d]for so many years.[3] [36:456]

If the Protestant Church in Ireland is removed, of course the Roman Catholic Church must be established in its place. There can be no resisting it in common reason.[4]

^a ~~goods~~ good   ^{b-c} body   ^d f 77ᵛ

Porter (1776–1850) *Sir Edward Seaward's Narrative of His Shipwreck, and Consequent Discovery of Certain Islands in the Caribbean Sea . . .* "Edited by Miss Jane Porter" (2nd ed 3 vols 1832)—1st ed 1831—*QR* xlviii (Dec 1832) 480–507. The reviewer (John Barrow), after summarising the narrative, found it contradicted by the known historical facts of the Navy, and therefore "a fabrication of a very modern date" (506) and indeed "an amusing romance in the school of Defoe" and "well worth a score" of such novels as those by Jane Porter (507). C and HNC may have had before them the review, where the running headline is "Interesting Events in the Life of Sir E. Seaward". HNC did not publish this entry.

[1] "From the bond of matrimony". The legislative Union of Ireland with Great Britain was consummated in 1801. The hearer might have found C and Mrs C in the metaphor of "a cat and dog

life". On the dissolution of the Union see also above, 17 Dec 1831 and nn 1–4.

[2] In a footnote in *TT* (1835) HNC quoted from *C&S* pt 2 (2nd ed 1830): *CC* 153–4.

[3] *TT* (1835) separated this attack on the Dissenters from the discussion of Ireland.

[4] Therefore, according to C's logic, although against his feelings of justice, the Protestant Church should remain established. Parliament would debate disestablishment in late February and again in April.

TT (1835) isolated this paragraph with a divisional bar at the end; the 3rd ed (1851) lost the division in consequence of being set from *TT* (1836), in which this paragraph ends the text of p 193. Subsequent Murray and Bohn editions are without the divisional bar. Not until the Oxford University Press edition, *TT* (1917) 206, was this entry again isolated by a bar as it had been in 1835.

How miserably imbecile and objectless has the[e] English government of Ireland been for forty years past![5] O! for a great man—but one really great man—who could feel the weight and the power of a Principle, and unflichingly put it into act![6] But truly there *is* no Vision in the land, and the people accordingly perisheth.[7] See how triumphant in debate and in action O'Connell is—because he asserts a broad principle and acts up to it—rests all his body on it, and has faith in it.[8] Our ministers have faith in nothing but expedients de die in diem;[9] *they* can have no principles of government, who in the space of a month recanted a life of political opinions, and threaten this and that innovation at the huzza of a mob or in pique at defeat. [36:455]

---

16. Feb. 1833.

Before the Faust was published,[1] I had conceived and drawn up the plan of a work, a drama, which was to be to[a] my mind what the Faust was to

[e] the ~~policy~~   [a] ~~the~~ to

[5] HNC had said in *Remarks on the Present State of the Roman Catholic Question* (1827): "an imbecile system of compromise" has now worked (p 56); "There has been for a long time a complete deliquium of the usual powers and duties of Government" on the Irish question (p 31); "There is *no* Government. . . . the Legislature is paralysed" (p 53).

[6] "O merciful Heaven! if it were thy good Will to raise us up among us *one* great good man, only *one* man of commanding mind, enthusiastic in the *depth* of his Soul, calm on the *surface* . . .". C to Poole 18 Apr 1801: *CL* II 721.

[7] Cf Prov 29.18. In an ambiguous marginal note of 8 May 1833 on Johnson the Whig C seems to say that the Irish will massacre as many Protestants as they can. *Works* (1710) 33: *CM (CC)* III.

[8] O'Connell, the "Liberator" of Ireland, was increasingly successful in belligerency since 1823. The awkwardness of his election in 1828 to a Parliament in which he could not be seated hurried the Catholic Emancipation Act of 1829. See above, 17 Dec 1831 and n 2.

[9] "From day to day", probably with the weight of vexation and weariness from 2 Pet 2.8.

[1] Goethe *Faust, ein Tragödie* (Berlin 1808), i.e. Part I. HNC, taking fright, quoted in a note in *TT* (1835) a passage from Abraham Hayward on Goethe's *Faust, ein Fragment* of 1790. HNC's changes in the text make C suspiciously defensive: "Before I had ever seen any part of Goethe's Faust, though, of course, when I was familiar enough with Marlowe's . . .". It is the published version, not the ms, that resembles Byron's several denials that *Manfred* was obliged to Marlowe or Goethe. Byron *Works: Poetry* ed EHC IV 80–2. HNC incorporated this entire entry in his *QR* review of C in 1834, with only an occasional verbal change after the opening variation: ". . . the curious fact that long before Goethe's *Faust* had appeared in a complete state, which we think was in 1807—indeed before Mr. Coleridge had ever seen any part of it—he had planned a work upon the same, or what he takes to be the same idea. This plan, like many of its fellows, is now in Ariosto's moon; yet its general shape deserves to be recorded, as a remarkable instance of unconscious coincidence between two great individual minds, having many properties in common." *CH* 639–40.

Goethe's.[b] *My* Faust was Michael Scott.[2] He appeared in the midst of his college of devoted disciples, enthusiastic, ebullient, shedding around him bright surmises of discoveries fully perfected in after times, and inculcating the study of Nature and its secrets as the pathway to the acquisition of Power. He did not love knowledge for itself, for its own exceeding great reward, but in order to be powerful. This poison-speck infected his mind from the beginning. The Priests suspect him—circumvent him—accuse him; he is condemned and thrown into solitary imprisonment. This was the Prologus or beginning of the Drama. A pause of [c]four or five years takes place, at the end of which Michael escapes from confinement, a soured, gloomy, miserable man. He cannot, will not study;—of what avail had all his study been to him? his knowledge, great as it was, had failed to preserve him from the cruel fangs of the persecutors; he could not command the winds, or the lightning to wreak their furies upon the heads of those whom he hated and contemned and yet feared. Away with learning—to the winds with all pretences to knowledge. We *know* nothing; we are wretches, fools, mere beasts. Anon I began to tempt him. I made him dream, and[d] gave him wine and passed women before him, whom he could not obtain. Is there no knowledge by which these pleasures may be commanded? *That way* lay witchcraft— and to witchcraft Michael turns with all his soul.[3] He has many failures and some successes—he learns the chemistry of exciting drugs and exploding powders, and some of the properties of transmitted and reflected light; his appetites and curiosity are both stimulated, and his old craving for power and mental domination over[e] others revives. Michael at last tries to raise the Devil, and the Devil comes at his call. My Devil was to be, like Goethe's, the Universal Humorist, who should make all things vain and nothing worth by a perpetual collation of the great with the little[f]

[b] In ms Goethe is spelled "Goëthe" four times in the entry
[c] f 78   [d] ~~I subjected~~ &   [e] ~~of~~ over   [f] ~~small~~ little

[2] Michael Scott or Scot (c 1175–c 1234), metaphysician, scholar, alchemist, born in Scotland, educated at Oxford and Paris, went to Bologna, then to Palermo, learned Arabic at Toledo; translator and astrologer to the emperor Frederick II; in legend a magician who possessed a demon horse and foretold his own death; in Dante *Inferno* xx 115–17, one familiar with fraud. C adumbrated the plan for "Michael Scott, the Person: Homo Agonistes, the Ens personans" in 1819. *CN* IV 4642; cf 4690.
[3] From his sympathetic study of such dubious martyrs to the cause of intellectual curiosity as Roger Bacon, Henry Cornelius Agrippa, Giordano Bruno, and Paracelsus, C constructed a generic explanation for their overreaching. William Godwin, after covering similar ground, would soon say in *Lives of the Necromancers* (1834) xii that he told their stories "to display the immense wealth of the faculty of imagination, and to shew the extravagance of which the man may be guilty who surrenders himself to its guidance".

in the presence of the infinite.[4] I had many a trick for him to play—some better, I think, than any in the Faust. Michael, meantime, is miserable, he has power but no peace—and he every day[5] feels the tyranny of Hell surrounding him. In vain he seems to himself to assert the most absolute empire over the Devil by imposing the most extravagant tasks—one thing is as easy as another to the Devil. "What next, Michael?" is repeated with[g] more imperious servility every day. Michael groans in spirit—his power is a curse—he commands women and wine—but the women seem fictitious and devilish to him, and wine does not make him drunk. He begins to hate the Devil and tries to cheat him. He studies again, and explores the deepest recesses of sorcery for a receipt to cozen Hell; but all in vain. Sometimes the Devil's finger turns over the page for him and points out an experiment, and Michael hears him [h]whisper— "*Try that* Michael!" The horror increases, and Michael feels that he is a slave and a condemned criminal. Lost to every hope, he throws himself into every sensual excess—in the mid career of which he sees Agatha, my Margaret,[6] and immediately tries to seduce her. Agatha loves him and the Devil facilitates their meetings; but she resists Michael's[i] attempts to ruin her and implores him not to act in a way to forfeit her esteem. Long struggles ensue—the result of which was to be that Michael's affections are called forth against his appetites, and the idea of the redemption of his lost Will dawns upon his mind. This is known to the Devil; and for the first time, the Humorist becomes severe and intimidating. A fearful succession of conflicts between Michael and the Devil takes place, in which Agatha helps and suffers. In the end, after subjecting Michael to every horror and agony, I make him triumphant, and pour Peace into his mind in the conviction of Redemption of Sinners through God's grace.[7]

In the Faust there is no causation—no progression.[8] The theme intended is, Misology caused by intense thirst of knowledge baffled. But a love of knowledge for itself would never produce such a misology—but

[g] with ~~the~~   [h] f 78ᵛ   [i] ~~his~~ Mich's

[4] Cf C's autobiographical letter to Poole Oct 1797: "from my early reading of Faery Tales . . . my mind had been habituated *to the Vast*", whereas those who appeal only to the senses "contemplate nothing but *parts* . . . and the Universe to them is but a mass of *little things*". *CL* I 354.

[5] *TT* (1835) read "every day more keenly". Here as usual HNC followed MS B more closely in the review of Aug 1834 than in the reuse for *TT*.

[6] Goethe's Margarete (Gretchen).

[7] *Faust* Part I ends with angels answering Margarete's call to God and the angelic hosts to save her; Mephistopheles stands by to take Faust on further adventures under their contract.

[8] This paragraph had to be displaced in the review (*CH* 639) and the sentences are reordered in *TT* (1835).

a love of it for power or base ends. Faust is a ready made sorcerer from the beginning—the *incredulus odi*[9] is felt from the first line. The sorcery and the sensuality are totally unconnected with each other and with the thirst for knowledge. I think Faust himself dull and meaningless. Mephistopheles and Margaret are excellent throughout. The scene in the Ale house is one of the best, perhaps the very best.[10] That on the Brocken is also very fine,[11] and all the songs are beautiful. The German is very pure. But there is no whole in Faust—the scenes are mere magic-lantern pictures[12]—and a large part of the work I think very flat and dull.

The young men in Germany and England who admire Lord Byron[j] prefer Goethe to Schiller; but you may depend upon it, Goethe does not, nor ever will, command the mind of the people of Germany as Schiller does.[13] Schiller had two legitimate phases.[14] The first as author of the

[j] Ld B.

[9] Horace *Ars poetica* 188. Tr H. Rushton Fairclough (LCL 1916): "I discredit and abhor". The Latin tag also appears above, 24 Apr 1832 (at n 7).

[10] "Auerbachs Keller in Leipzig" *Faust* 2073–2336.

[11] "Walpurgisnacht" *Faust* 3835–4222. Shelley's translation, with omissions "not out of an idle squeamishness", had been published as "May-Day Night" *Liberal* I (1822) 121–37.

[12] Here meaning isolated images without continuity.

[13] HCR recorded on 13 Jun 1824 that C "set Goethe far below Schiller, allowing no other merit than that of exquisite taste, repeating his favourite reproach that Goethe wrote from an idea that a certain thing was to be done in a certain style, not from the fullness of sentiment on a certain subject. He treats Goethe with more plausibility as utterly unprincipled." *CRB* I 308. HCR was pleased that Tennyson in 1845 "acknowledged the inferiority of Schiller", although with the "common opinion" (shared by C) that Goethe "wanted heart". *CRB* II 651. It has been generally granted to C's position that German feeling for Schiller is more intensely national than is German respect for Goethe. Heinrich Döring *Friedrich von Schillers Leben* (Heidelberg 1817) 176 tells of the adulation of Schiller at the first performance of *Die*

Jungfrau von Orleans in Leipzig (1801). The reviewer of *TT* in *Dublin University Magazine* VI (Sept 1835) 256 suggested that C might have preferred Schiller because he associated him with his own happy time of accomplishment and associated Goethe with such unfinished projects as that on Michael Scott. For C the chief issue is sexual morality. For HCR's reports of C's remarks, in 1812–13, on *Faust* see App F 24, below.

[14] Schiller considered as dramatist. In the Preface to *The Death of Wallenstein* (1800) C wrote: "The admirers of Schiller, who have abstracted their conception of that author from the *Robbers*, and the *Cabal and Love*, plays in which the main interest is produced by the excitement of curiosity, and in which the curiosity is excited by terrible and extraordinary incident, will not have perused without some portion of disappointment the Dramas, which it has been my employment to translate. . . . We scarcely expect rapidity in an Historical Drama; and many prolix speeches are pardoned from characters, whose names and actions have formed the most amusing tales of our early life. On the other hand, there exist in these plays more individual beauties, more passages the excellence of which will bear reflection, than in the former productions of Schiller." *PW* (EHC) II 724–5. He had

Robbers, which must not be considered with reference to Shakespeare, but as a work of the material sublime—and in that line it is undoubtedly very powerful indeed.[15] It is quite genuine and deeply imbued with Schiller's own soul. After this, Schiller outgrew the composition of such plays as the Robbers and at once *k*took his true and only rightful stand in the grand historical drama the Wallenstein.[16] Not the intense drama—he was not master of that—but of the diffused drama of history, in which alone he had ample score for his varied powers.*l* This is the greatest of his works*m*—not unlike Shakespeare's historical plays—a species by it-

k f 79   *l* powers. ~~He had fancy & imagination enough to make it poetical &~~

       m works—~~but it is not a whole~~

written to Sheridan in 1797: ". . . the impression from Schiller's 'Fiesco' is weak compared to that produced by his 'Robbers.' There are however great advantages in the other scale." *CL* i 304.

[15] On Schiller and the material sublime see 6 Jan 1823 (at n 5), above. One contrast is with a drier form that C, drawing on Kant, calls "an arithmetical sublime like Klopstock's". HNC's report of C's Lect 10 of 1818. *LR* i 176. Cf *Lects 1808–19 (CC)* ii 427.

[16] During the tedium of translating *Die Piccolomini* and *Wallensteins Tod* (omitting the prelude, *Wallensteins Lager*) from Schiller's ms, C had grumbled about the "dull heavy play"; "Prolix & crowded & dragging as it is, yet . . . quite a model for it's judicious management of the *Sequence* of Scenes"; "that accursed Wallenstein". *CL* i 610, 621, 643; cf 574, 577, 579, 583, 587; *PW* (EHC) ii 598n–9. He reportedly mixed praise with blame in Jun 1828: "Talking of the German language, on which subject he was quite at home, he bore testimony to its copiousness and power, by remarking that 'in reading the German translation of the Georgics if he did not pronounce the words he could believe that he was reading the original.' Of Schiller he said that 'he had reached the acme of his genius in the "Wallenstein". His previous works were too wild, his latter too formal. He was a man of deep feeling for moral beauty, and should have written half-a-dozen grand historical plays.' He observed that Fred-erick Schlegel, (whom by the way he pronounced to be a consummate coxcomb) had told him that his translation of 'Wallenstein' was better than the original. 'If so,' said Coleridge, 'it is because I struck out a word from almost every line. Wherever I could retrench a syllable I did so, and I cleared away the greatest possible quantity of stuffing.' " *Grattan Beaten Paths* ii 112–13. C may be responsible, or John Chester or George Greenough may be, for inaccuracies in Greenough's journal for 9 Jan 1801: "Called on Chester. . . . With regard to Col[e]ridge I learned that on his arrival in England he repaired forthwith to Stowey, only stopping at Bath long enough to change horses, and having seen his family and friends there and corresponded for some time with Wordsworth who had taken his sister down to the North of England to settle there, he returned to London last April, stayed there 6 weeks and then wrote to his wife to pack up all his goods and chattels and follow him as soon as possible since he had determined to leave Stowey and go to live in Cumberland. During these 6 weeks he got introduced to a number of booksellers of whom Longman in Paternoster row proposed to him the translation of Schiller's *Piccolomini* which he at first declined. The offer however having been very handsome and liberal, he afterwards accepted it and having written to Schiller an account of his intention, received from him the MS. copy." *London Mercury* xxiii (1931) 564; *W&C* 234.

self:—you may take up any scene, and it will please you by itself, just as you may in Don Quixote—which you read *through* once or twice only, but read *in* repeatedly. After this it was, that Goethe and other writers injured by their theories the steadiness and originality of Schiller's mind; and in every one of his works after the Wallenstein, you may perceive the fluctuations of his taste and principles of composition.[n][17] He got a notion of re-introducing the characterlessness of the Greek tragedy with a chorus, as in the Bride of Messina—and then that the tragedy ought to have a greater infusion of lyric verse.[18] Schiller affected to despise the Robbers and the other works of his first youth, whereas he ought to have spoken of them as of works not in a right line, but full of excellence in their way.[19] In his ballads and lighter lyrics Goethe is most excellent—it is impossible to praise him too highly in this respect. I like Wilhelm Meister the best of his prose works.[20] But neither Schiller's nor Goethe's prose style approaches to Lessing's, whose writings for manner are perfect.[21]

,

[n] composition. ~~One time & pl~~

[17] *Maria Stuart* (1800), *Die Jungfrau von Orleans* (1801), *Die Braut von Messina* (1803), *Wilhelm Tell* (1804).

[18] *TT* (1835) read, probably by misinterpretation, "and he was for infusing more lyric verse into it". May he not mean, though not well stated even in MS B, that Schiller swung from the classicism of the *Braut* to the more lyrical *Tell*? Schiller had given the *Braut* a subtitle, *Ein Trauerspiel mit Chören*, and introduced it with a defence of the chorus in ideal tragedy. *Sämmtliche Werke* (12 vols Stuttgart and Tübingen 1812–14) x 431–48. On 29 Jan 1811 "Coleridge seemed willing to censure Schiller's and Schlegel's ideas concerning the German idea of the Greek chorus", but HCR could not comprehend his reproach. *CRB* I 21; cf *BL* ch 23 *(CC)* II 210, quoted in n 19, below.

[19] *The Robbers*, C wrote in *BL* ch 23, was "the first fruits of his youth . . . and as such, the pledge, and promise of no ordinary genius. Only as *such*, did the maturer judgement of the author tolerate the Play. During his whole life he expressed himself concerning this production with more than needful asperity, as a monster not less offensive to good

taste, than to sound morals; and in his latter years his indignation at the unwonted popularity of the *Robbers* seduced him into the *contrary* extremes, viz. a studied feebleness of interest . . . a diction elaborately metrical; the affectation of rhymes; and the pedantry of the chorus." *BL (CC)* II 210.

[20] *Wilhelm Meisters Lehrjahre* (4 vols Berlin 1795–6), translated anonymously by Thomas Carlyle as *Wilhelm Meister's Apprenticeship* (3 vols Edinburgh 1824); *Wilhelm Meisters Wanderjahre* (Stuttgart and Tübingen 1821, rev 1829; the 1821 ed tr Carlyle in *German Romance* vol IV 1827).

[21] C was aware by 1796 of the dramatist and "the most formidable infidel", Gotthold Ephraim Lessing (1729–81); in 1798 he began to collect books and data with the intention of writing a life of Lessing. *CL* I 197, 455; *CN* I 377 and n. His extensive annotations on Lessing's *Sämmtliche Schriften* seem to date from 1813–16: *CM (CC)* III. He drew upon Lessing's "exquisite Dialogues on Freemasonry", *Ernst und Falk*, in the *Courier* 29 Sept 1814, and recommended in 1830 that a translation of them be published. *EOT (CC)* II 382 and n; *C&S*

Although Wordsworth and Goethe are not much alike to be sure upon the whole, yet they both have this quality of non-sympathy with the subjects of their poetry. They are always both ab extra—feeling *for* but never *with* their characters.[22] Schiller is a thousand times more hearty than Goethe.[23]   [36:457]

I was once pressed—many years ago—to translate Faust, and I so far entertained the proposal as to read the work through with great attention, and to revive in my mind my own former plan of Michael Scott.[24] But

---

(CC) 114n–15. For C's enduring interest in Lessing's *Anti-Goeze* see *Friend (CC)* I 34n.

[22] See 21 Jul 1832 n 2, above. With these remarks WW would have been able to contrast HCR's diplomatic letter of 13 Jul 1832 on "the great poet lately dead in Germany"; as a great admirer, HCR wished that Goethe "had as uniformly directed those powers in behalf of the best interests of mankind as you have done". *CRC* I 229. WW's judgement coincided with C's: "Goethe's writings cannot live", WW said to Felicia Hemans, "because *they are not holy.*" *Memorials of Mrs. Hemans* ed Henry F. Chorley (2nd ed 2 vols 1837) II 129; cf *W Prose* (1876) 435–6.

[23] In *Memorial Verses, April, 1850* Matthew Arnold, more representative of the English than C in his admiration for Goethe's "sage mind", yet contrasted WW's "healing power" with Goethe's power of diagnosis without cure. C assigned to Schiller a rôle more like that given in Arnold's poem to Byron: we "*felt* him like the thunder's roll". C wrote to Daniel Stuart in 1800: "To be known to Schiller was a thought, that passed across my brain & vanished—I would not stir 20 yards out of my way to *know* him." *CL* I 628.

[24] In Aug 1814 John Murray offered C £100 to translate *Faust* Part I. Asking 100 guineas and a set of Goethe's complete works in advance, C expressed qualms; the proposal faded away. *CL* III 521–5, 528, 536, IV 562, 648, 665 and n. In 1820 Thomas Boosey & Sons proposed that C supply copy for an edition of Moritz Retzsch's illustrations to *Faust*

Part I; C declined to connect himself with a work of bad repute, although he saw the possibility of omitting "the passages morally or prudentially untranslatable". *CL* V 43 and n. Upon seeing HNC's reference to the earlier proposal in his *QR* review of C's works (*CH* 639), HCR, who had been Murray's intermediary, first paraphrased C as answering that "he could not execute his purpose; it was burthensome", and then quoted him directly: "I felt I could make a better!"; upon which HCR granted that C on Michael Scott "certainly would have been more moral and more religious". *CRB* I 448. C spoke to Prati with more reserve than usual, c 1825–7: "Once when walking with him in the garden, we were speaking about the difficulty of translating. 'Truly,' said he, 'no one knows how difficult it is to translate well, but he who has attempted to translate a masterwork. I have done all the justice I could to "Wallenstein," but I could not venture upon translating the "Camp," which is perhaps the most original part of the work. I would have attempted to translate your favourite "Faustus," but I must give it up in despair. To translate it so as to make the English readers acquainted with the plot, is a foolish task. The beauty of this work consists in the fine colour of the style, and in the tints, which are lost to one who is not thoroughly *au fait* with German life, German philosophy, and the whole literature of that country. The antithesis between the slang of Mephistopheles, the over-refined language of Faustus, and the pastoral simplicity of the child of Nature, Margaret, requires a man's whole life to

then I considered with myself whether the time taken up in executing the translation might not more worthily be devoted to the composition of a work which, even if parallel in some points to Faust, should be truly original in motive and execution and therefore more interesting and valuable than any version which I could make—and secondly *o*I debated with myself whether it became my moral character to render into English—and so far certainly lend my countenance to language—much of which I thought vulgar, licentious and most blasphemous. I need not tell you, that I never put pen to paper as translator of Faust.[25]   [36:457]

In the romantic drama Beaumont and Fletcher are almost supreme.[26] Their plays are for the most part most truly delightful. I could read the Beggar's Bush from morning to night. How sylvan and sunshiny it is! The Little French Lawyer is excellent. La Writ is conceived and executed from first to last in genuine comic humor. Monsieur Thomas is also capital.[27] I have no doubt whatever that the first act and first scene of the

o f 79*v*

---

be made self-evident in our language. And therein lies Goethe's peculiarity. I would have wished also to translate some of Goethe's minor poems, which I esteem not only as the best productions of Goethe, but among the best of the modern lyrics. I found equal difficulty.' '' From the autobiography of Gioacchino de' Prati (1790–1863) *Penny Satirist* 13 Oct 1838 p 4; *Modern Philology* XLI (1943) 121–2. According to Prati, he had met EC and then JTC before Sir James Stuart took him to Highgate (about 1825). For John Frere's conversation with C in 1830 on *Wallenstein* and *Faust* see App F 25, below.

[25] The paragraph added to *TT* (1835) on the translation of *Faust* by Abraham Hayward (1801–84) may be taken as the gist of something said later by C and remembered as HNC prepared *TT*. On 11 Apr 1833 C offered to return John Sterling's copy because he had now been sent one by Hayward himself. Ashe—*TT* (1884) 193n—observed that Hayward's preface was dated 25 Feb 1833, but suggested that C might have seen a copy in private circulation—an example of problems raised by HNC's lack of care about

dates.

[26] Among the editions C annotated was the Stockdale, in which he wrote his name 29 Mar 1815 at Calne: *The Dramatic Works of Ben Jonson, and Beaumont and Fletcher*: the First Printed from the Text, and with the Notes of Peter Whalley; the Latter, from the Text, and with the Notes of the Late George Colman, Esq. (4 vols 1811). For C's notes on this edition and on Lamb's copy of *Fifty Comedies and Tragedies* (1679) see *CM (CC)* I 362–408; for other comments on Beaumont and Fletcher, *C 17th C* 649–52, 666–73.

[27] The specification of La-Writ (the little French lawyer) is an insignificant addition to the similar judgements on 24 Jun 1827, above (at nn 6 and 7) (36:87). In the Stockdale, C indicated that Seward's classification was wrong not to include in the first class *Monsieur Thomas, The Chances, The Beggar's Bush*, and *The Pilgrim*. *CM (CC)* I 376. In 1815 C thought of adapting for Drury Lane *The Beggar's Bush* and *The Pilgrim*. *CL* VI 1038; *CN* III 4245n; *CM (CC)* I 373, 376 n 9.

second act *p*of the Two Noble Kinsmen*q* are Shakspeare's.[28] Their plots are to be sure wholly inartificial; they only care to pitch a character into a position to make him or her talk. You must swallow all their gross improbabilities, and taking it all for granted, attend only to the dialogue.[29] How lamentable it is that no gentleman and scholar can be found to edit these beautiful plays![30] Did the name of criticism ever descend so low as in the hands of the two fools and knaves Seward and Simpson?[31] There are whole scenes that I could with certainty put back into their original verse—and more that could be replaced in the native prose.[32] Was there

p-q of the 2ᵈ of the (Love's) Pilgrimage 2. N. Kinsmen

[28] Cf Collier's fuller report of a conversation in 1811, App K, vol II, below. SC, in her review of Dyce's edition of Beaumont and Fletcher—*QR* LXXXIII (1848) 377–418—disagreed with C's suggestion on this point but otherwise cited him frequently with approval and supported aganst Dyce C's high opinion of *The Beggar's Bush*. For her authorship of the review, see SC to JTC (UT Grantz 831) and SC to Lockhart, cited in *The Wellesley Index to Victorian Periodicals 1824–1900* I (1966) 731 Item 932. SC had written to HNC of *The Maid's Tragedy* from Brighton on 14 Oct 1832: ". . . it appears to me that B. & F. eddy more about one feeling, one passion than Jonson or Shakespeare—there is little intricacy or underplot in their plays". UT Grantz 563.

[29] C has been paraphrased as saying that Beaumont and Fletcher, like Massinger, fail "to make parts conform to an idea of the whole"; their characters "have no inner consistency and no lived relationship to other characters in the same play, but are merely functionaries of the moment". Joseph W. Donohue Jr *Dramatic Character in the English Romantic Age* (Princeton, New Jersey 1970) 292. HNC recorded from the 17 Feb conversation nothing on social content, such as C's notes in the Stockdale that Beaumont and Fletcher were "passive-obedience Tories", influenced by Calderón and other Spanish dramatists into "romantic Loyalty to the greatest Monsters". *CM (CC)* I 380, 389, 398.

[30] In a note to this entry in *TT* (1835)

HNC proposed that Alexander Dyce (1798–1869) could meet the requirements. Later editions reprint the note, Ashe with a reference to "Mr. Dyce's admirable edition of . . . 1843" (11 vols 1843–6) and the observation that SC had not changed HNC's note in 1851. *TT* (1884) 194 n 1. In sending corrections for the announced 2nd ed, Dyce thanked HNC for the notice; he was busy, but "I could do a good deal for the text, which is detestable". UT ms. Dyce had published Fletcher's *The Humourous Lieutenant* as *Demetrius and Enanthe* in 1830. C had specified in marginalia to the Stockdale that an "authentic Edition" would require an editor who had "studied the philosophy of metre" and "all the productions of the Spanish Stage prior to 1620". *CM (CC)* I 376–7, 389.

[31] The Preface of 1750 by Thomas Seward (1708–90) and notes by Seward, Lewis Theobald (1688–1744), and J. Sympson are included in the Stockdale edition, as taken from *The Works of Mr Francis Beaumont and Mr John Fletcher*. Collated with all the former editions and corrected. With notes. By the late Mr Theobald, Mr Seward and Mr Sympson (10 vols 1750). C left his opinion insistently in the Stockdale; e.g. "Mᵣ Seward! Mᵣ Seward! You may be & I trust you *are*, an Angel; but you *were* an Ass." *CM (CC)* I 375; cf 374, 386, 391, 399.

[32] Noting several such transpositions in the Stockdale, C marked *The Scornful Lady* II i 98–111 into pentameter lines and complained: "Strange that neither

ever such an absolute disregard of literary fame as that displayed by Shakspeare and Beaumont and Fletcher![33]   [36:458]

In Ben Jonson you have an[r] intense[s] and burning art. Some of his plots—that of the Alchemist—are perfect. Ben Jonson and Beaumont and Fletcher would have made a great dramatist indeed, and yet not have come near Shakspeare. Yet, no doubt, Ben Jonson was the greatest man after Shakspeare in that age of dramatic genius.[34]   [36:459]

The styles of Samson[t] Agonistes and Massinger are the two extremes of the arc within which the diction of dramatic poetry may oscillate.[35] Shakspeare in his great plays is the midpoint. In the Samson[t] Agonistes colloquial[u] language is left at the greatest distance, yet something of it is preserved, to render the dialogue probable;[36] in Massinger the style is

[r] ~~the~~ an   [s] intense~~st~~   [t] Sampson   [u] ~~the rule is~~ colloquial

M[r] Th. nor M[r] S. should have seen that this mock-heroic Speech is in full-mouthed Blank Verse!" *CM (CC)* ι 382. After commenting throughout on Seward's (and Colman's) lack of ear, he noted of *The Woman-Hater* ι ii 1–27: "Prose printed as Blank Verse—as elsewhere in this edition blank verse is printed as prose." *CM (CC)* ι 408.

[33] I.e. disregard for current fame in allowing their dramatic works to appear in piracies with such wretched texts as to require in later ages editors of far greater powers than Seward or Colman. This remark is transitional to Jonson, who included his plays in *The Workes of Benjamin Jonson* (1616). *TT* (1835) in a footnote quoted *BL* ch 2 to the effect that Shakespeare, like other writers "of the greatest genius" (C included Chaucer, omitted in *TT*), had "the inward assurance of permanent fame". *BL (CC)* ι 33–5.

[34] Shakespeare, in political opinion "as in all other things, himself and alone, gives the permanent Politics of Human Nature". Annotation on Beaumont and Fletcher *Dramatic Works: CM (CC)* ι 389; cf 401. About 1807, with the Anderson edition of *The Works of the British Poets* before him, and acknowledging heresy, C held Jonson's "Dramas of worth far inferior to his Poems, and his Plays themselves chiefly valuable for the many & various passages which

are not dramatic", but in every characteristic except harmony he was superior to Juvenal. *CM (CC)* ι 62. Jonson, C once noted, "scarcely can be said to have any *Humor* at all". Annotation on Carl Friedrich Flögel *Geschichte der komischen Litteratur: CM (CC)* ιι 778. Despite the perfect plot of *The Alchemist, Volpone* (at least on 27 Jun 1827, above, at n 3; 36:87) was a greater play. A. W. Schlegel had praised equally the plots of *Volpone, The Alchemist,* and *Epicoene, or the Silent Woman. Ueber dramatische Kunst und Litteratur* Lect 13 (Heidelberg 1809–11) ιι ii 285. SC, who had been reading William Gifford's edition of Jonson (9 vols 1816), in a letter to HNC 6 Sept 1832 differed with some of his judgements; she would write more firmly on 16 Nov 1836: "What I remarked upon the 'Fox' I should say applied equally to the 'Alchemist': how could you introduce any sweetness or goodness into that piece without destroying the whole character of the composition? An acid ceases to be an acid, and becomes a syrup, if you fill it up with sugar." UT Grantz 557, 644.

[35] Philip Massinger (1583–1640) collaborated with Fletcher, among others. HNC caught more detail on 5 Apr 1833, below (from nn 2ff) (36:471).

[36] Milton's *Samson Agonistes, A Dramatic Poem* (1671) was also the mesothesis between real and ideal. *NTP* 404.

only differenced,^{v} but differenced in the smallest degree possible, from animated conversation by the vein of poetry.   [36:460]^{37}

---

^{w}I was just now reading Sir John Cam Hobhouse's answer to Hume or some other of that set upon the point of transferring the patronage from the Crown to the House of Commons.^{38} I think, if I had been in the House,^{x} I should have said—that ten or fifteen years ago, I should have considered^y J. C. H.'s speech quite unanswerable—it being clear constitutional law that the House of Commons has not, nor ^{z}ought to have^a, any share directly or indirectly in the appointment of the officers^b of the army or navy. But now that the King had been reduced by the means and procurement of the Baronet and his friends to a puppet, who so far from having any independent will of his own,^{39} could not resist a measure which he hated and condemned, it became a matter of grave consideration whether it was not necessary to vest the appointment of such officers in a body like the House of Commons rather than in a junta of Ministers, who^c are obliged to make common cause^d with the mob and democratic press for the sake of keeping their places.   [36:461]

---

^{v} differenced ~~from~~ ^{w} f 80 ^{x} H., ~~if~~ ^{y} considered ~~the~~ $^{z-a}$ ought have
^{b} ~~public~~ officers ^{c} who ~~at any time~~ ^{d} game [?]

For *Samson* as an imitation of Greek drama see Collier's report, App K, vol II, below. C drew on the work for metrical experiments, especially lines 80–150, 1072, and the "noble metre" of 1670, "Drunk with Idolatry, drunk with Wine". *CN* II 2224 ff 17, 23^v, 80, 3180. Any lectures in which C treated *Samson* are lost, and the only annotation presently located is *B Poets: CM (CC)* I 71–2.

^{37} *TT* (1835) inserted here a paragraph beginning with an appeal to *Hamlet* IV v 124, "There's such divinity doth hedge a king", to explain the result of C's attempt to imitate Shakespeare's manner in *Remorse*; namely, he "had been tracking Beaumont and Fletcher, and Massinger instead".

^{38} John Cam Hobhouse (1786–1869), statesman, friend and executor of Byron, succeeded his father as baronet in 1831; he was created Baron Broughton de Gyfford in 1851. On 14 Feb 1833 he answered Joseph Hume, concerning military sinecures and pensions, that half-pay and other grants should continue to emanate from the King; if Parliament conferred the original grants, "it would be impossible to calculate the extent of the invidious cavillings and canvassings which would accompany each detail of every case". Hansard 3rd s xv 698–703; *M Chron* 15 Feb. C's protest here against the Reform Bill resembles that made by WW to HCR on 5 Feb: "The extinction of the nomination-boroughs has nearly destroyed the internal check" to democracy from the Commons; the Bill has so trampled the Peers that they "will prove useless as an external check—while the regal power & influence has become, or soon will, mere shadows". *CRC* I 233–4; *WL* (*L* rev) II 588.

^{39} Without the irony of this mock-address as M.P., C had annotated Charles Dallison *The Royalist's Defence* (1648): "Our King represents the whole power of the nation and its Laws, but does not possess it." *CM (CC)* II 115.

9. March. 1833.[1]

The Penal Code in Ireland in the beginning of the last century was justifiable, as a temporary means of enabling Government to take breath and look about them; and if right measures had been systematically pursued in a right spirit, there can be no doubt that all or the greater part of Ireland would have become Protestant.[2] But unfortunately the drenching horn was itself substituted for the medicine.[3]   [36:462]

Lord Grey has in Parliament said two things—1. that the Coronation oaths only bind the King in his executive capacity. 2. that members of the House of Commons are bound to represent the wishes and opinions of their constituents and not their own—Put these two together, and tell me what part of the constitutional monarchy of England remains.[4] It is

---

[1] Two days later, on Mon, 11 Mar, HNC wrote to RS that he was reading his *Lives of the British Admirals* (vol I 1833), but HNC reported no conversation with C on this subject at this period.

[2] Royal assent was given in Mar 1704 to an "act to prevent the further growth of popery" by breaking up the estates of Roman Catholics in Ireland unless the eldest son became a Protestant and by forbidding education abroad; the code was incrementally made harsher as successive additions failed to achieve the desired result. J. C. Beckett *The Making of Modern Ireland 1603–1923* (1966) 168. According to an explanatory insertion into this paragraph in *TT* (1835), C's subject was the educational aspect of the penal laws, and the solution should have been Charter Schools.

[3] Johnson's *Dictionary*, quoting *1 Henry IV* II iv 107, defines "Drench" as "Physick for a brute". *OED* cites George Dampier in *Phil Trans (RS)* xx (1698) 50: "If it be for any Cattel, it must be . . . given with a Drenching Horn."

[4] C brings together Grey's position of 1829 that the Coronation Oath did not prevent the removal of the civil and political disabilities of the Catholics and his position in 1830–2 that the will of the people required the elected members of Parliament to pass the Reform Bill. Citing the position taken by Liverpool in 1825 and supported by Canning in May 1825 and Mar 1827, Grey had said in the Lords on 4 Apr 1829 that it would be dangerous if "the Coronation Oath should be viewed as binding the King in his legislative capacity". Hansard 3rd s XIII (1825) 750, 893, XVI (1827) 1003, XXI (1829) 326; for Grey cf XX (1829) 1076–8. After the Scots had imposed on William III in 1689 an oath "to root out all heretics and enemies of the true worship of God", the Coronation Oath to maintain "the Protestant reformed religion established by law" was enacted in 1 William and Mary c 6, which survived into the twentieth century. At about the time of his conversation C wrote that "the King is bound by the most solemn Oaths before God & to the Nation, to make abortive every projected Law, destructive of Freedom". Annotation on Johnson the Whig *Works* (1710) 310: *CM (CC)* III. (C dated a note on the Whigs, p 321, 15 May 1833.) In 1826, after Liverpool and Canning had taken the opposite position, C argued "that the King has and cannot but have, a great influence on the votes of both Houses: and that the Oath binds him in conscience not to use this influence to the endangerment of the Protestant Church". Annotation on Charles Butler *Vindication of "The Book of the Roman Catholic Church"* (1826): *CM (CC)* I 864. On the same subject, he noted it as strange that Rich-

clear the coronation oaths would be no better than Highgate oaths;[5] for in his executive capacity the King *cannot* do any thing against the doing of which the oaths bind him; it is *only* in his[a] legislative character, that he possesses a free agency capable of being bound. The Nation meant to bind *that*.[6]   [36:464]

---

[b]Divinity is essentially[c] the first of the Professions, because it is necessary for all at all times;[7] Law and Physic are only necessary for some at some times. I speak of course of them, not in their abstract existence, but in their applicability to man.   [36:465]

Every true Science bears necessarily within it the germ of a cognate Profession, and the more you can elevate Trades into Professions the better.[8]   [36:466]

What solemn humbug this modern Political Economy is![9] Can you tell

a ~~this~~ his   *b* f 80ᵛ   *c* ~~necessarily~~ essentially

---

ard Baxter "never appropriated the distinction between the King = the Executive Power, and the Individual Functionary". Note on *Reliquiae Baxterianae: CM (CC)* I 294. For a fuller exposition of C's position see *C&S (CC)* xxxvi–xxxix, 104–7 and nn, 196 (HNC's summary, 1839).

[5] In a note on Johnson the Whig C had written: "Much as I dislike Lord Grey & his Gang for their transferring the deliberative & determining functions from the Parliament to the Mob before the Hustings, & thus degrading Representatives of the Realm into Delegates of the Rabble, yet I dislike far more, yea, detest them for nullifying the kingly office, by reducing the Coronation Oaths to Highgate Oaths." *Works* (1710) 309–10: *CM (CC)* III. Public houses in Highgate had long administered a ludicrous oath on stag (or other) horns. William Hone *The Every-day Book* (2 vols 1826–7) II 79–87, 378.

[6] To the most embarrassing point made by Charles Butler (n 4, above), that Henry VIII, Edward VI, and Elizabeth swore to support the Catholic religion but did not, C answered that those oaths were "framed and imposed by the Romish Hierarchy", whereas the later Coro-

nation Oath was "actually the sense and positive Will of the Nation". *CM (CC)* I 866.

[7] I.e. all periods everywhere and every moment in a life. On 2 Feb 1826 C wrote to DC: "What is Christianity at any one period?—The Ideal of the Human Soul at that period." *CL* VI 552.

[8] Science, meaning exact knowledge tried in competition with error, applied in a self-aware calling, a designated field of knowledge *professed*—including and on the model of, but not confined to, the three fields designated in Johnson's *Dictionary*, "law, physick, and divinity". The "habitual consciousness of the ultimate principles to which your opinions are traceable", a *desideratum* in all who fill "the higher and middle stations of society", is a *duty* for the professional. *LS (CC)* 121; *Logic (CC)* 144–5. There seems to be a suggestion here also of the elevation of the individual, the "Hope to all" of 25 Jun 1831 (at n 1), above (36:294), the rationale of C's praise of the "oldest schools" for "raising a certain number of the more promising scholars into a higher rank, and qualifying them for the learned professions". *Logic (CC)* 19–20.

[9] C wrote to JTC on 8 May 1825: "In

me any truth in it which is not very plainly a simple deduction from the
Moral and Religious*d* credenda and agenda[10] of any good man, and with
which we were all previously acquainted, and upon which every man of
common sense instinctively acted? I know none.[11]   [36:467]

All is an endless, fleeting abstraction; *the Whole* is a reality.[12]   [36:468]

You talk about making this article cheaper by reducing its price in the
market from eightpence to sixpence. But suppose in so doing, you have
rendered your country weaker against a foreign foe—suppose you have
demoralized thousands of your fellow-countrymen—suppose you have
sown discontent between one class of society and another—your article
is tolerably dear I take it after all. Is not its real price enhanced to every
Christian and patriot a hundred fold?[13]   [36:467]

There is at present a curse upon the English Church and upon all the Governors of Institutions connected with the orderly advancement of national
piety and knowledge—it is the curse of *Prudence*, as they call it—in fact
Fear.[14]

d Religious ~~truths~~

---

my Conviction the whole pretended Science is but a Humbug. I have attentively
read not only Sir James Stewart [Steuart]
& Adam Smith; but Malthus, and Ricardo—and found (i.e. believe myself to
have found) a multitude of Sophisms but
not a single just and important Result
which might [not] far more conveniently
be deduced from the simplest principles
of Morality and Common Sense." *CL* v
442. On 27 Jul 1826 he wrote to EC that
"the Science professes to give light on
Rents, Taxes, Income, Capital, the Principles of Trade, Commerce, Agriculture—on *Wealth* and the ways of acquiring and increasing it", and yet not only
was it beyond the comprehesion of well-
informed merchants and manufacturers,
but no two professors of it understood
each other. *CL* vi 596, published by C in
C&S—(CC) 177. In Feb 1826 he made a
note against such economists as Ricardo.
CN iv 5330. C associated political economy with the *Ed Rev* and urged Blackwood in 1829 not to continue the recent
increase in space allotted to it in *Blackwood's. CL* vi 820.
  [10] "Things to be believed and acted

upon". HNC first wrote "Moral and Religious truths".
  [11] *TT* (1835) continued the subject
with an argument that political economy,
though striving to be a science, can only
produce works like *Utopia* (1516) by Sir
Thomas More or *The Commonwealth of
Oceana* (1656) by James Harrington.
  [12] The context here, as on 4 Jan 1833,
above (at n 4) (36:446), emphasises the
political or sociological relevance.
  [13] The collocation in MS B suggests
that the distinction of all and whole came
up in the discussion of political economy. The "you" addressed in this entry
and generally throughout 9 Mar implies
the presence of a hearer standing in
greater need than HNC of conversion.
  [14] In an annotation on Baxter *Catho-
lick Theology* C recommended that the
clergy give instruction to their congre-
gations instead of "the chopped straw of
their prudential discourses on given
Texts". *CM (CC)* i 234. On 29 Mar 1817
he had written to Daniel Stuart: "What
are the Clergy doing? Sleeping with their
eyes half-open! under attacks and en-
croachments such as that their Predeces-

Clergymen are now almost afraid in their pulpits to explain the grounds of their being Protestants. They are *c*completely cowed by the vulgar harassings of Lord King and Hume and such ignorant bravos.[15] There should be no *party* politics in the pulpit, to be sure—but every church in England ought to resound with national politics—I mean the sacred character of a National Church, and an exposure of the base robbery from the Nation*f* itself—for so it is—about to be committed by these Ministers, in order to have a sop to throw to the Irish ruffians.[16]

[36:463]

---

31. March 1833.[1]

What evil results to this country from the National Debt? I never could get a plain and practical answer to that question. As to taxation to pay the interest, how can the country suffer by a process, under which the money is never one minute out of the pockets of the people? You may as well

c f 81   *f* ~~poor~~ Nation

---

sors a century ago, even if asleep, would have *snored* more indignantly and more to the purpose than they either write or talk". *CL* IV 711; for the date see *EOT (CC)* II 473n. Of their fear of quite different challenges he complained similarly: he found typical the "poltroonery" of an Oxford-educated clergyman who advised silence concerning the theories of Eichhorn. BM MS Egerton 2801 f 234. *IS* 387.

[15] Peter King, 7th Baron King (1776–1833) had said in the House of Lords on 7 Feb 1833 that "seeing several Right Rev. Prelates in their places, he would take the opportunity of moving for some papers in relation to the revenues of the Church. . . . It could not be expected that any useful reform of abuses in the Church should come from the members of the Church themselves." The clergy had used all their influence and power "to protect the many abuses of the Church". *M Chron* 8 Feb 1833. On 26 Feb he was led to distinguish between human nature and "clerical nature" in presenting a petition from a parish that had driven away their rector for claiming the right "to extract tithe of herrings

taken on the high seas"; on the 27th a prominent bishop expressed regret that "the Noble Lord was upon all occasions so ready to malign the Clergy". Hansard 3rd s xv (1833) 1134; *M Chron* 27 Feb, 28 Feb. Joseph Hume (1777–1855) had added to his string of attacks on the revenues and property of the Church on 7 and 13 Feb. Hansard 3rd s xv (1833) 312, 619.

[16] *TT* (1835), with modifications towards the end of this entry, quoted from the 2nd ed of *C&S* ch 8 *(CC)* 75–6; cf *BL* ch 11 *(CC)* I 226–8.

[1] In the third week of March, when HNC was at Eton to conduct examinations, SC reported word from Mrs Gillman that C was in bed, a "sad sufferer". UT ms. HNC's next record comes on 31 Mar, the Sunday before Easter. During the holidays HNC returned on 5 Apr (Fri), 8 Apr (Mon), and 11 Apr (Thurs). To JTC he wrote on 2 Apr: "Poor S.T.C. is in a wretched state—& has a good deal lost his articulation;—*He* thinks from paralysis in the jaw—Green says it is from his teeth being loose." BM Add MS 47557 f 100.

say that a man is weakened by the circulation of the blood. There may, certainly, be particular local evils and grievances resulting from the mode of taxation or collection; but how can that debt be in any proper sense a burthen to the Nation, which the Nation owes to itself and to no one but itself?[2] It is a juggle to talk of the Nation owing the capital or the interest to the stock holders; it owes to itself only. It is really and truly nothing more than so much money or money's worth raised annually by the State for the purposes of quickening industry.[3]   [36:469]

I should like to see a well graduated property tax accompanied by a large loan.   [36:469]

One common objection to a property tax is, that it would tend to diminish the accumulation of capital. In my judgment, one of the chief sources of the bad economy of the country now is the enormous aggregation of capitals.[4]

[2] This is one of the paragraphs that particularly irritated T. P. Thompson: "Here is manifestly a man who does not know the difference between the mischief of throwing away the substance of the debt, and the inutility of attempting to remedy the mischief afterwards by refusing to pay the interest." *Westminster Review* XXII (1835) 534. C was in surprising company. Thomas Paine, against whom C had directed the essay on taxation cited in n 3, below, had written in *Common Sense, Addressed to the Inhabitants of America* (Philadelphia and London 1776) 31–2: "The debt we may contract doth not deserve our regard if the work be but accomplished. No nation ought to be without a debt. A national debt is a national bond: and when it bears no interest, is in no case a grievance." Patrick Colquhoun, the metropolitan commissioner of police, compared the national debt to amounts due from one to another member of the same family; "whatever is owing by the community at large to a part of the same community cannot in any degree increase or diminish the national capital". *A Treatise on the Wealth, Power, and Resources, of the British Empire* (2nd ed 1815) 281. Henry Taylor wrote to RS that when he, J. S. Mill, and others visited C on 22

Sept 1831, James Stephen remarked "that it was a pity he should talk at all upon such subjects as the National Debt, on which he was obviously so much less ripe than on subjects of criticism". *Correspondence* ed Edward Dowden (1888) 39–40.

[3] Every loan by British subjects to their government, said Colquhoun (p 283), "has been productive of national improvement: and hence it may be concluded, that the present *Domestic Debt* . . . yields an increase of wealth to the country in proportion to its magnitude". C is here more sanguine than he had been in 1823 (see 27 Apr 1823, at n 13, above; 36:37), though near his position of late 1825 (*CN* IV 5265, 5330). For a summary of his fluctuating views see Colmer p 147. In a note on Donne *LXXX Sermons* C connected the national debt unfavourably to the growth of usury. *CM (CC)* II 310–11. In a footnote to this entry in *TT* (1835) HNC quoted from the 1818 edition C's essay on taxation in *The Friend (CC)* I 229–30 (II 159–60).

[4] Pitt's "Property Tax" had been abolished in 1816, but Jan–Apr 1833 was a period of agitation against high taxation, with proposals of every sort for balancing the budget. Halévy *History of the English People* II 40, III 88–96. In

*a*When shall we return to a sound conception of the right to property—namely as being official, implying and demanding the performance of commensurate duties?*b5* Nothing but the most horrible perversion of humanity and moral justice, under the specious name of Political Economy, could have blinded men to this truth as to the possession of Land; the law of God having connected indissolubly the cultivation of every rood of earth with the maintenance and watchful labor*c* of man;*6* but money, stock, riches by credit, transferable and convertible at will, are*d* under no such obligations—and unhappily it is from the selfish autocratic possession of *such* property, that our land holders have learnt their present theory of *trading* with that which was never meant to be an object of commerce.   [36:469]

*e*I certainly did mean Mackintosh*f* in the "Two round spaces"—but as to meaning to lampoon him, as Fraser's Magazine says, from resentment, I never had other than kind feelings towards Mackintosh all my life.*7* He

> *a* f 81ᵛ   *b* dut~~y~~ies?   *c* ~~vigil~~ labor   *d* ~~is~~ are
> *e–i* For the variant in MS F see App C, below   *f* Mack.

journalism during the war with France C had considered capital primarily as involved in the purchase of commodities; as his interest increased in the conditions of employment in the factories, 1816–18, he began to see the private and joint-stock accumulation of capital as subverting the traditionally stable society in the ways denounced in *C&S. EOT (CC)* I 248, II 303, III 195, 203, 488.

5 To make the same point C had defaced a title-page on 1 Mar 1832: "But the maxims of Trade . . . universalized, and acting on the selfish superstition of absolute Property, 'an unqualified right to do what I like with my own'—have been the disease, & probably will be the ruin, of Great Britain." Annotation on Sir John Walsh *On the Present Balance of Parties in the State* (2nd ed 1832): *CM (CC)* v. The Benthamite position C is opposing is clear from Thompson's response in the *Westminster* (p 535; see n 2, above) to the sentence in *TT*: "What is visible upon the face of this, is that there is a mis-statement of the foundation of the right to property. It might as well have been said that the right to property was *religious*, and therefore was only inherent in bodies ecclesiastical. The right of property rests simply on the fact, that it promotes production; and the time is not far off, when the invasions of the right of property created and maintained by the unjust distribution of the legislative influence in the community, will be more than any form of unsound words will be able to protect."

6 Gen 3.19. In a marginal note of 18 Feb 1828 to one of Brougham's speeches, C had stated forcefully his rejection of any claim to absolute property "in any portion of the Land". *CM (CC)* I 739–40. In N 28 of about 1820 he had indicated the other pole of his position: "The overbalance of the Landed Interest in the H. of C. is the true Evil of the Borough System." *CN* IV 4684.

7 *Fraser's Magazine* VII (Feb 1833) 175–7 had reprinted "The Two Round Spaces on the Tombstone; being an Epitaph on the Late Sir James Mackintosh. By S. Taylor Coleridge, Esq. With an Epitaph on Himself, by the Same." C's purpose in writing the squib was given as resentment at attacks on C in the *Ed Rev*. For the verses and their history see *PW* (EHC) I 353–5 and nn. In May J. S.

was taken slightly ill in passing through Grasmere—snow was deep, and I remember being tickled, as I looked on the humble churchyard, with the thought that if he, a great Scotch Lawyer, should die there, and have a great tombstone in the middle of the ground, how odd and funny it would be. When I repeated the verses to Wordsworth[g] he smiled in his grave way—Southey[h] roared at them, and wrote them down and gave copies.[i][8]

---

5. April 1833.

To please me, [a]a Poem[b] must be either music or sense—if it is neither, I confess I cannot interest myself in it.[1]   [36:470]

The first act of the Virgin Martyr is as fine an act as I remember in any play.[2] The Very Woman is, I think, one of the most perfect plays we

[g] W.   [h] S.   [i] See [e-i], above   [a-b] (a) Poetrym

(John Sterling?) would provide *Fraser's* VII 620–1 with an "Authentic Version". Daniel Stuart, married to Mackintosh's sister, published the verses in the *M Post* 4 Dec 1800 without lines 15–16, which identified Mackintosh by "a black tooth in front". For a summary of C's attitudes towards "the great Dung-fly Mackintosh" (*CL* I 588) see Woodring 152–3, nn 22–3, Mackintosh as indexed in *EOT (CC)*, Carlyon I 68–70, IV 126–30, and, above, 27 Apr 1823 and n 4, 28 Apr 1832 and n 5.

[8] C sent the verses as a "Skeltoniad" to Davy 9 Oct 1800. *CL* I 632–3. A token of the spread of copies survives in one sent by Richard Heber to John Mitford, BM Add MS 28322. William Jerdan understood C to say once in the 1820s that RS had a hand "especially in an 'Inscription on a Gravestone', of remorseless animosity, which I cannot here repeat". *Autobiography* (3 vols 1852–3) III 312–13. HNC revised this entry, either to protect RS and WW or because one of them denied a favourable reaction; then the entry was cut from MS F and was not published.

[1] A casual remark, perhaps arising from a poem that did not please him; he is not attempting definition, which could be expected to put a premium on reconciliation into unity, as in *BL* ch 14 *(CC)* II 11–13. In his sense of poetry as music, C had support from Thomas Fuller, whose "generall Artist" in *The Holy State* bk II ch 7 (1642) 74 is not "a stranger to Poetry, which is musick in words; nor to Musick, which is poetry in sound".

[2] Massinger and Thomas Dekker (c 1572–1632) *The Virgin Martyr*, licenced 1620, quarto 1622. Lamb published about fifty lines from II ii in *Specimens of English Dramatic Poets* (1808). *L Works* IV 357–8. Lamb recommended Massinger to C in 1796. *LL* (M) I 30–1, 35, 63. A year later C borrowed the edition by J. Monck Mason (4 vols 1779) from the Bristol Library. *Bristol LB* 95. In early 1804 he was planning an essay on Shakespeare's relation to his age as represented in Sidney, Jonson, Beaumont and Fletcher, and Massinger (*CL* II 1054), which may have borne fruit in the lectures of 1808 at the Royal Institution. See e.g. Lect 15: *Lects 1808–19 (CC)* I 116–17. When he had DC reading Massinger—"three Plays & half of a fourth" in three afternoons of 1810 (*CL* III

have. There is some fun in that first scene between ᶜDon John and his master, Cuculo³—and can anything exceed the skill and sweetness of the scene between him and his mistress, in which he relates his story?⁴ The Bondman is also a delightful play.⁵ Massinger is always entertaining; his plays have the interest of Novels.

But like most of his contemporaries—except Shakspere—Massinger often deals inᵈ exaggerated passion.⁶ Malefort, however heᵉ may have had the moral will to be so wicked, could never have actually done all that he is represented guilty of, without losing his senses.⁷ He would have been mad. Regan and Goneril are the only pictures of the unnatural

ᶜ f 82   ᵈ in ~~the~~   ᵉ ~~a man~~ he

---

290)—he may have had at hand the edition by William Gifford (4 vols 1805) that he used for Lect 7 of 17 Feb 1818. *Lects 1808–19 (CC)* II 142, 152. In 1820 Massinger, Jonson, and Beaumont and Fletcher still provided the chief dramatic context of Shakespeare for C as for others. *CL* v 25–6. On Massinger see also *CN* II 3187, III 3445, 3656, 3801 and nn.

³ Massinger *A Very Woman, or the Prince of Tarent: a Tragi-Comedy* (licenced 1634, published 1655) III ii. Cuculo, steward to the viceroy of Sicily, instructs Don John Antonio, Prince of Tarent, whom he has bought as a slave. Lamb recommended the play to C in 1796, quoting IV iii 185–99, 208–14, 225–8, which he published in *Specimens. L Works* IV 350–2 (see n 2, above). Six of the lines, sent again to C on 14 Nov 1796, served as motto to Lamb's pieces in C's *Poems* (1797) 215.

⁴ *A Very Woman* IV iii. *TT* (1835) in a footnote gave the text with minor variants from *The Plays of Philip Massinger* ed William Gifford (4 vols 1813) IV 332–4.

⁵ *The Bond-Man; An Antient Storie* (performed 1623, published 1624). Gifford, who found in *The Virgin Martyr* "base and filthy" scenes but "beauties of no ordinary kind", declared *The Bondman* "at once steady and playful; impressive and tender". *Plays* (1813) I 119, II 118.

⁶ C practised consistently what he

called one of the "flat truisms" that Shakespeare was better than "even his own immediate Successors, Fletcher, Massinger &c". Annotation on Shakespeare *Works* ed Theobald (8 vols 1773) VII [87]. In Lect 6 of 5 Dec 1811 he proclaimed it "shame and sorrow" if one could answer the charge of indecency by comparison with Massinger and the others: "there is nothing common to Shakespeare & to other writers". *Lects 1808–19 (CC)* I 295; cf *C 17th C* 648, 657, 668–9, 678.

John Murray had published an edition of Massinger for family reading (3 vols 1830–1) with "omission of objectionable passages". Schlegel was on record in *Ueber dramatische Kunst und Litteratur* Lect 12 (1809–11) II ii 67: Shakespeare "hat in der That niemals die wilden blutdürstigen Leidenschaften mit einem gefälligen Aeussern überfirnisst, niemals die Bosheit mit einem falschen Schimmer von Seelengrösse bekleidet, und dafür ist er in alle Wege zu loben". (He "has never, in fact, varnished over wild and blood-thirsty passions with a pleasing exterior, never clothed crime and want of principle with a false show of greatness of soul, and in that respect he is every way deserving of praise". Tr John Black 1815.)

⁷ *The Unnatural Combat: A Tragedy* (acted c 1616, quarto 1631). In *Specimens* Lamb included lines from II i, the parley before Malefort senior kills his son in combat. *L Works* IV 355–7.

in Shakspere, the pure unnatural; and you observe that Shakspere has left their hideousness unsoftened or diversified by a single line of goodness or common human frailty. Whereas in Edmund, for whom passion, the sense of shame as a bastard, *f*and ambition,*g* offer some plausible excuses, Shakspere has placed many redeeming traits.[8] Edmund is what under certain circumstances any man of powerful intellect might be, if some other qualities and feelings were cut off. Hamlet is inclusively an Edmund, but different from him as a whole on account of the controlling agency of other principles which Edmund had not.

Remark the use which Shakspere always makes of his bold villains as vehicles of expressing opinions and conjectures of a nature too hazardous for a wise man to put forth directly as his own, or as from any reclaimable character.[9]   [36:471]

The parts pointed out in Hieronymo as Ben Jonson's bear no traces of his style; but they are very like Shakspeare; and it is remarkable that every one of them reappears in full form and development and tempered with mature judgment, in some of Shakspeare's great pieces.[10]   [36:472]

f-g —ambition,

[8] In the Stockdale Shakespeare ed S. Ayscough (2 vols 1807), in which C wrote notes for lectures delivered in 1818–19, he traced the effect in *Lear* on "united strength and beauty" of Edmund's pride in its encounters with "pangs of shame, personally undeserved". *The Dramatic Works of William Shakespeare* ed Ayscough II 928–32. In contrasting Beaumont and Fletcher's characters, on the endleaves of vol III of the Stockdale Jonson and Beaumont and Fletcher, C noted that even the "utter Monsters", such as Goneril and Regan, are kept out of sight. *CM (CC)* I 393–4.

[9] *TT* (1835) read "sustained character"; *TT* (1836) also changed "Remark the use" to "It is worth while to remark the use".

[10] Thomas Kyd (1558–94) *The Spanish Tragedie, or Hieronimo Is Mad Again*, published anonymously in 1594, frequently performed in 1592; identified as Kyd's by Thomas Heywood's chance reference in *Apology for Actors* (1612). References in the early records to "*Jeronimo*" led to confusions of this play with *The First Part of Jeronimo*, published 1605. C ended a note on *Titus Andronicus* in Shakespeare *Works* ed Theobald (1773) VI 208: "Yet I incline to think that both in this and in Jeronymo Shakespear wrote some passages, and that they are the earliest of his Compositions—". *CM (CC)* IV. For C's confidence that Shakespeare contributed see *CN* III 4486; *Friend (CC)* II 495 and n. Lamb included two scenes from the play in *Specimens: L Works* IV 10–11. Gifford felt that Edmund Malone had been too mildly doubtful of Jonson's rôle in "new additions to Jeronymo" if that meant *The Spanish Tragedy*. Gifford "Memoirs of Ben Jonson" in Jonson *Works* (9 vols 1816) I xvii. C's knowledge, like that of most of his contemporaries, was too slight to suppose that dramatic influences could account for characteristics found in Shakespeare. In a footnote to this entry *TT* (1835) proposed as Shakespeare's, in the act-division of Thomas Hawkins followed by Robert Dodsley, three passages (as two), III xi 24–51 and IV iii 201–15, 227–41.

I think I could point out to a half line what is really Shakspeare's in Love's Labour's Lost and some other of the non-genuine plays.[11] What he wrote in that play, is of his earliest manner—the all pervading sweetness which *ʰ*he never indeed lost[12]—and that extreme condensation which makes the couplets fall into epigrams, as in the Rape of Lucrece and Venus and Adonis. In the Drama alone, as Shakspeare soon found out, could the sublime poet and profound philosopher find the conditions of a compromise. In Love's Labour's Lost there are many faint sketches of some of his vigorous portraits in after life—especially Benedict and Beatrice.[13]   [36:473]

Gifford has done a great deal for the text of Massinger, but not as much as might easily be done. His comparison of Shakspeare with his contemporary dramatists is obtuse indeed.[14] It*ⁱ* proves that Gifford had not a sense of*ʲ* that which makes Shakspeare.[15]   [36:474]

In Shakspeare one sentence begets the next naturally; the meaning is all inwoven. He goes on kindling like a meteor through the dark atmos-

ʰ f 82ᵛ   *ⁱ* S. ~~had~~ It   *ʲ* ~~wҽh a true critic must have~~ of

[11] *TT* (1836), probably under the influence of Dyce, changed "non-genuine" to the more precise "not entirely genuine". In Lect 1 of 28 Oct 1813 at Bristol, but not as reported otherwise, C gave *Love's Labour's Lost* as an example to "distinguish what is *legitimate* in Shakespeare from what does not belong to him". *Lects 1808–19 (CC)* I 521. Generally he took it as an early play exhibiting experience of art rather than of nature.

[12] A word inserted above the line is represented here as "indeed"; HNC omitted it in 1835, perhaps as illegible, which it almost is. In a footnote in *TT* (1835) he also quoted C on the tension of creative power and intellectual energy in Shakespeare's narrative poems. *BL* ch 15 *(CC)* II 26. C goes on there to discuss the greater maturity of *The Rape of Lucrece*. Of *Venus and Adonis* the "first and most obvious excellence is the perfect sweetness of the versification". *BL (CC)* II 19–20. For another strong statement of Shakespeare's early vigour see Lect 3 of 25 Nov 1811: *Lects 1808–19 (CC)* I 230.

[13] C had made this point more expansively both in notes and in lectures. See

e.g. Lects 5 and 6 of 2 and 5 Dec 1811, Lect 4 of 29 May 1812, and an annotation on Shakespeare *Dramatic Works* ed Ayscough (1807) I facing 147. See *Lects 1808–19 (CC)* I 276 and n 32.

[14] William Gifford (1756–1826) ed *The Plays of Philip Massinger* (4 vols 1805, 2nd ed 1813). *TT* (1835) in a footnote added HNC's objections to C's. Two final sentences of the note were dropped in 1836: "The whole of the passage to which I allude seems to me to be the grossest miscarriage to be found in the writings of this distinguished critic. It is as bad as any thing in Seward, Simpson, & Co." In the note HNC quoted part of the offending sentence: "The claims of this great poet on the admiration of mankind are innumerable, but rythmical modulation is not one of them: nor do I think it either wise or just to hold him forth as supereminent in every quality which constitutes genius: Beaumont is as sublime, Fletcher as pathetic, and Jonson as nervous . . .". *Plays* (1813) I lxxix; (1805) I l–li.

[15] This sentence, which gave HNC trouble in MS B, was dropped from *TT* (1835).

phere—yet when the creation in its outlines is once perfect, then he seems to rest from his Labor and to smile upon his work and tell himself it is very good.[16] You see many scenes and parts of scenes, which are simply Shakspeare's disporting himself in joyous triumph and vigorous fun after a great achievement of his highest genius.   [36:475]

The old dramatists took great liberties in respect of bringing parties in scene together and representing one as not recognizing the other under some faint disguise. Some of their finest scenes are constructed on this ground. Shakspeare only avails himself of it twice, I think, in Twelfth Night, where the two are with great art kept apart till the end of the play and in the Comedy of Errors, which is a *proper farce*, and should be so considered. The definition of a Farce is—an improbability or even impossibility granted in the outset, see what odd and laughable events will fairly follow from it.[17]   [36:476]

I wrote the first twenty pages or so of Wordsworth's Cintra pamphlet.[18] But I own my sympathy was Wordsworth himself—not much about the Convention, though it was a disgraceful proceeding. Wordsworth was always subject to violent *ᵏ*political humors, or accesses of feeling—I

ᵏ f 83

[16] Cf Gen 1.31. The paragraph illustrates what it celebrates—genius as a jovial god.

[17] HNC published a similar note of C's on *The Comedy of Errors* as farce. *LR* II 114–15.

[18] This sentence was omitted from *TT* (1835). At Cintra 23–30 Aug 1808 the British generals agreed to facilitate the evacuation of the French forces from Portugal. In October WW, RS, and C projected a public meeting of protest. In Nov 1808 WW began to write for initial publication in the *Courier* the essays published as *Concerning the Relations of Great Britain, Spain, and Portugal . . . as Affected by the Convention of Cintra* (1809). For a fuller account see *W Prose* I 193–217. On 9 Jan 1809 C wrote to Stuart: "You will long ere this . . . have received Wordsworth's second Essay rewritten by me, and in some parts re-composed"; in a passage crossed out of the ALS but printed in *CL* III 164 he specified a passage both written and revised by him. He repeated this claim in a letter to Poole 3 Feb 1809. *CL* III 174. It is possible that the opening pages of WW's *Cintra* drew upon a speech by C for the proposed meeting, but more likely that in Apr 1833 he remembered the details inaccurately or—a little less likely—that HNC heard "first" when C said something else. To Poole on 4 Dec 1808, complaining as he frequently did that some of his best eggs had "crawled forth into Light to furnish Feathers for the Caps of others", C mentioned that "Wordsworth has nearly finished a most eloquent & well-reasoned Pamphlet". *CL* III 131; cf 134, 137. On 22 Jun 1809 he wrote to Thomas Woodruffe Smith, a subscriber to *The Friend*, that the tract, of which the opening "might with great advantage have been written in a more calm & argumentative *manner*", incorporated "sentiments & principles matured in our understanding by common energies & twelve years' intercommunion" (*CL* III 216–17)—a fourth possible explanation for the sentence in TT. See also *EOT (CC)* I cxxxv, III 98–103.

never was.[19] When very young I wrote and spoke very enthusiastically, but it was always on subjects connected with some grand general principle, the violation of which I thought I could point out. As to mere details of administration I really and honestly thought that ministers and men in office must of course know much better than any private person could possibly do—and it was not till I went to Malta and had to correspond with official characters myself that I fully understood the extreme shallowness and ignorance with which men of some note too were able to carry on the government of important departments of the Empire.[20] I then quite assented to Oxenstiern's saying—Nescis mi fili &c[21] [36:477]

Burke was indeed a great man. No man ever read history so philosophically as he seems to have done. Yet until he could associate his general principles with some sordid interest, panic of property, jacobinism &c he was a mere dinner-bell.[22] Hence so many half-truths in his speeches and writings. Nevertheless,[1] let us acknowledge his transcendant greatness— he would have been more influential if he had less surpassed his contem-

[1] ~~Yet~~ Nevertheless,

[19] C's first letter to Poole on WW's tract announced that the first essay in *The Friend* would be on principles: "What a beggarly thing your calculating Prudence is without high general Principles, as we have lately seen in that confluent Smallpox of Infamy, the Cintra Convention". *CL* III 131. Whatever the degree of accuracy in assessing his temperament and WW's (HNC prudently omitted the contrast from *TT* 1835), C insists that the passions aroused in him by political events were directed at the principles violated.

[20] From C's letters in 1806 the nearest candidate would seem to be Hugh Elliot (1752–1830), British minister at Naples. *CL* II 1182, 1202. Sultana 282 notes with reference to C's remarks that Sir John Jeffreys Pratt (1759–1840), 2nd Earl (1794) and 1st Marquis (1812) of Camden, secretary of war 1804–5, president of the council 1805–6 (and again 1807–12), was the official with whom C chiefly conducted official correspondence for Sir Alexander Ball.

[21] "An nescis, mi fili, quantula prudentia regitur orbis?"—another version is given in *TT* (1835)—"Do you not know, my son, with how little wisdom the world is governed?" The saying is attributed to Axel Oxenstiern, Count Axel Gustafsson (1583–1654), Swedish statesman, although given in variant forms, in most dictionaries of quotations. One of C's favourite books, John Selden's *Table Talk* (1786 and 1789 p 107) attributes to a "wise pope" the words "thou little thinkest what a little foolery governs the whole world".

[22] Burke was called the Dinner Bell because his protracted speeches made the other M.P.s go to dinner. Perhaps the nickname came the more readily from his "habitual undulating motion of the head". James Prior *Memoir of the Life and Character of the Right Hon. Edmund Burke* (1824) 527. On Burke cf 7 Jan–13 Feb 1823 (at n 29) (36:19). In 1795–1802 C often accused Pitt and his fellow ministers of creating a panic of property; he revived the term and the interest of others in it in 1811. *Lects 1795 (CC)* 30–1; *EOT (CC)* I 69, 225, 274, 381, II 309; *Friend (CC)* II 143 and nn. He recalled in 1802 the exaggeration of "Burke's 80000 Jacobins in England". *CN* I 1262.

poraries, as ^mFox or Pitt, men of much inferior mindsⁿ in all respects.[23]

[36:478]

---

8. April 1833.

I have a deep conviction that most of the European nations are more or less on their way, unconsciously indeed, to pure monarchy; that is, to a government in which under circumstances of complicated and subtle control the Reason of the People shall become efficient in the apparent Will of the King.[1] As it seems to me, the wise and good in every country will^a in all likelihood become every day more disgusted with the representative form of ^bgovernment, brutalized^c as it is and will be by the predominance of democracy in England, France and Belgium. The statesmen, we know, of^d antiquity doubted the possibility of the effective and permanent combination of the three elementary forms of government; and perhaps they had more reason than we have been accustomed to think.[2]   [36:480]

^eYou see how this House of Commons has begun to verify all the ill prophecies that were made of it—low, vulgar, meddling with every thing, assuming universal competency, and flattering every base passion—and sneering at every thing noble, refined and truly national. The direct tyranny will come on by and by, after it shall have gratified the multitude with the spoil and ruin of the old institutions of the Land.[3] As

^{m-n} Fox ⟨or Pitt⟩—a maen of a much inferior mind⟨s⟩   ^a must will
^{b-d} government, in the democracy in England—France & Belgium has got full eo posson of the
^c brutalized and   ^d See ^{b-d}, above   ^e f 83^v

---

[23] Hazlitt remembered the C of Jun 1798: "He thought little of Junius as a writer; he had a dislike of Dr. Johnson; and a much higher opinion of Burke as an orator and politician, than of Fox or Pitt. He however thought him very inferior in riches of style and imagery to some of our elder prose-writers, particularly Jeremy Taylor." "My First Acquaintance with Poets" *Liberal* II (1823) 44.

TT (1836) inserted after this entry 36:479, with the simile of the telegraph.

[1] *TT* (1835) made the conviction "deep, though parodoxical", and HNC added a footnote betting on democracy and referring to the comments on Vico and Spinoza of entry 36:370 (23 Apr 1832, at nn 7–9, above).

[2] On approval of mixed government by Plato, Aristotle, Polybius, and Cicero, see George H. Sabine *A History of Political Theory* (New York 1954) esp 77–80, 112–15, 154–5.

[3] C wrote in HC *The Worthies of Yorkshire and Lancashire*: "Our *pledged* House of Commons is *truly* & efficiently a *Democracy*—& therefore a Contradiction, and annulment of Aristocracy & Monarchy—both which change their natures, & become the Vassals, the κρατού-μενοι." *CM (CC)* II 68–9.

for the House of Lords there seems no hope whatever of them; they have been once humbled—beaten—and they cannot now recover it.[4] Besides, what is the use of ever so much fiery spirit, if there be no principle to guide and sanctify it? [36:481]

Can any humiliation be more complete—more pointed and unequivocal—than the House of Lords passing without a division the amendments of the Commons in this[f] Irish Coercion [g]Bill?[5] It is really extraordinary.[h]

The possible destiny of the United States of America—as a nation of 100-million of freemen, stretching from the Atlantic to the Pacific, living under the laws of Alfred, and speaking the language of Shakspeare and Milton—is an august conception.[6] Why should we not wish to see it realized?[i] America would then be England viewed through a solar microscope[7]—Great Britain in a state of glorious magnification. How deeply to be lamented is the spirit of hostility and sneering which the Quarterly Review and some of the popular books of travels have shown in treating of the Americans![8] They hate us, no doubt, just as brothers

[f] theis   [g–h] MS F: Bill! It is really quite extraordinary.   [i] ~~accomplished~~ realized?

[4] *TT* (1835) omitted the prediction but preserved the protest of the next sentence.

[5] By amendment to the bill for the suppression of disturbances in Ireland, the Commons had exempted from prosecution acts committed before the Act, "any offence created by this Act", acts considered as libel, and combination without violence. On 1 Apr the Lords divided over an amendment introduced in their own house, but the report of their deliberations has otherwise a refrain to catch a duller eye than C's: "The Clause as amended by the Commons agreed to." Hansard 3rd s xvii (1833) 1294–331.

[6] C's dream of Pantisocracy on the Susquehannah in 1794 never completely faded. Even with the War of 1812 threatening and the United States seeming as tyrannical as other nations that had replaced monarchy with commerce, C in a piece newly unearthed from the *Courier* of 19 Jul 1811 declared Britons and Americans countrymen "if the same language, the same books, the same laws, the same ancestry, and (with exception

of one single generation) the same history" mean more than "the clod under our feet". *EOT (CC)* ii 235. In Nov 1814 he felt that he could describe the virtues and vices of post-colonial America better than the *QR* and the *Ed Rev* had done it; on 25 Oct 1815 to Allston he was eloquent on the possibilities of reconciling parent and child. *CL* iii 543, iv 608–9.

[7] The solar microscope was a kind of camera obscura, with two lenses, that threw an enlarged image onto a wall or screen. See *CM (CC)* i 519 and n.

[8] William Jacob in *QR* xlviii (Dec 1832) 507–23 had shared the antipathies of William Gore Ouseley (1797–1866) *Remarks on the Statistics and Political Institutions of the United States* (1832) and *The Refugee in America: A Novel* (3 vols 1832) by Frances Trollope (1780–1863), who gained more lasting notoriety for *Domestic Manners of the Americans* (2 vols—4 eds—1832). Jacob chided the Americans for believing that they and not the French secured their freedom from Britain; described the infection of "political restlessness,—the miasma of democracy"; and ascribed to

hate—they respect the opinion of an Englishman upon themselves ten times as much as they do that of any other nation on earth. A very little humoring of their prejudices and some courtesy of language and demeanor on the part of England would work wonders, even as it is, with the public mind of the Americans. [36:482]

Captain Basil Hall's book is certainly a very entertaining and instructive work; but in my judgment his sentiments upon many points, and more especially his mode of expression are unwise, uncharitable—I might say, ungentlemanly.[9] Captain Hall was [j]treated in America with boundless attention—every house and almost the secrets of every house were thrown open to him—and the shock felt in that country on the perusal of his Travels was deep and lasting.[10] After all, are not most of the things shown up with so much bitterness by Hall mere national foibles—parallels to which every people has and must of necessity have? [36:483]

There are two possible modes of Unity in a State: One by absolute coordination of each to all and all to each; the other by subordination of classes and offices.[11] Now I maintain that[k] there never was an instance of the first, nor can there be, unless Slavery be established as its condition

[j] f 84   [k] that ~~with the trifling exception~~

"meanness" their tendency to complain of such remarks as his. In the *QR* just out an article on steam-navigation to India ridiculed American "pretensions even to the *invention* of the steam-boat" when in fact "infinitely inferior" machinery and "imperfect workmanship" led to loss of life on the rivers of the United States. *QR* XLIX (Apr 1833) 212–13. C was taking a side unusual for him in *Ed Rev* vs *QR*. "The Americans and Their Detractors" *Ed Rev* LV (Jul 1832) had questioned most Mrs Trollope and Capt Hall; William Empson, the reviewer, had named but largely ignored Godfrey Thomas Vigne (1801–63) *Six Months in America* (2 vols 1832). John Ramsay McCulluch in *Ed Rev* LVI (Jan 1833) 460–81 praised James Stuart (1755–1849) *Three Years in North America* (2 vols Edinburgh 1833) as "disinterested", in contrast with Hall, Mrs Trollope, and even the earlier (1821) Frances Wright (1795–1852).

[9] See 27 May 1830 nn 3, 5 and 20 Aug 1830 n 6, above. Hall had more recently published *Fragments of Voyages and Travels* (3 vols 1831–3), but C referred still to the *Travels* of 1829. JTC recorded a conversation of Feb 1832 with Hall about Scott's novels. Bernard, Lord Coleridge *This for Remembrance* (1925) 48–9.

[10] Sentence omitted from *TT* (1835). C had probably talked about Hall's book with McLellan and others, and it may have been referred to when C's verses for Miss Barbour "called forth raptures of gratitude" (27 May 1830, at n 6, above).

[11] Slavery in the United States would seem to be the point of departure for this paragraph. The sentence, sounding formidably polar, without examples to expand it would say merely that there must be either equality or inequality, but the biassed modifier, "absolute", means "unlikely".

and accompaniment, as in Athens, Sparta &c. The poor Swiss cantons are no *^l*exception.[12]   [36:485]

The mistake lies in confounding a State which must be founded on Classes and Interests and Unequal Property with a Church which is founded on the Person and has no*^m* merit but personal merit. Such a community may exist, as the Quakers—but in order to exist, it must be compressed and hedged in by another society—mundus mundulus in mundo immundo.[13]   [36:485]

I have no objection to your aspiring to the political*ⁿ* principles of our old Cavaliers—but embrace them all, fully, and not merely this and that feeling, whilst in*^o* other points you speak the canting foppery of the Benthamite or Malthusian Schools.[14]   [36:488]

The free class in a slave state is always the*^p* most*^q* patriotic class of people in an empire. For their patriotism*^r* is not simply the patriotism*^r* of other people—but an aggregate*^s* of lust of power and distinction and supremacy.[15]   [36:486]

What the Times says about the quarrel in the United States is sophistical and brutal as usual.[16] No doubt taxation may, and *^t*perhaps in some cases,

---

^l exception &c.—*unperfecit*   *^m* ~~not~~   *ⁿ* political *&*   *^o* you ~~in~~
^p ~~a~~ the   *^q* most ~~independent & quasi rebellious~~   *^r* ~~freedom~~ patriotism
^s aggregate ~~power~~   *^t* f 84ᵛ

---

[12] In the drafting of MS B, the Swiss cantons were apparently to be a "trifling exception". HNC appended "&c.—*unperfecit*" to the entry, perhaps as a reminder for later revision, not carried out.

[13] "A clean little world in an unclean big one". For the apparent debt to St Augustine see *C&S (CC)* 175 and nn 5, 6, a piece of cosmic buffoonery for which the earlier source is *CL* vi 595. C had discussed church and state in Dec 1831, above, as well as in *C&S*.

[14] The "you" of this entry suggests the presence of someone whose inconsistencies irritated C. Entry 35:426 on Malthusianism (11 Aug 1832) disappeared in *TT* (1836), but the harsh language here remained. On Malthus *An Essay on the Principle of Population* (1803) vii C wrote: "Merciful God! . . . The whole

Question is this: Are Lust & Hunger both alike Passions of physical Necessity, and the one equally with the other independent of the Reason, & the Will?—Shame upon our Race, that there lives the Individual who dares even ask the Question!" *CM (CC)* iii.

[15] A further generalisation from contemplating Southern states. HNC's first drafting did not mention patriotism.

[16] The prudential change of "the Times" to "you" in *TT* (1835) increased the air of hostile confrontation. *The Times* had reported on the debates of early 1833 over protective tariffs under President Andrew Jackson and the doctrine of nullification advanced by John C. Calhoun of South Carolina: 14, 17, 24, 31 Jan, 13 Feb, 4 Mar, 7 Apr; esp 4 Mar, in which congressional procedure

must press unequally, or apparently so, on different classes of people in a State; in such case there is a hardship—but in the long run the matter is fully compensated to the over-taxed class. For example, take the house-holders in London who complain so bitterly of the House and Window Taxes; is it not pretty clear that whether such householder be a tradesman who*u* indemnifies*v* himself in the price of his goods, a letter of lodgings who does so in his rent, a*w* stockholder who receives it back again in his dividends, or*x* a country gentleman who is saved so much fresh lcvy on his land or his other property—that one way or other, the thing comes at last pretty nearly to the same thing?—though the pressure for the time may be unjust and vexatious, and fit to be removed.[17] But when New England, a state of itself, taxes the admission of foreign manufactures in order to cherish manufacturers of its own and thereby forces the Carolin-ians, another state of itself, with which there is no intercommunion, which has no such desire or interest to serve, to buy worse articles at a higher price, it is altogether a different question—and is in fact down-right tyranny of the worst because the most sordid kind. What would you think of a Law which should tax every person in Devonshire for the pe-cuniary benefit of every person in Yorkshire? And yet that is a feeble comparison to the actual usurpation of the New England deputies over the property of the Southern States.[18]   [36:484]

Land was the only species of property which in the old time carried any respectability with it. Money alone, apart from some tenure of land, not

---

was called "this very absurd mode of transacting business"; condolences were extended to those subjected to nuisance by "the iron lungs of their orators".

De Q, in *Bl Mag* Jan 1845, gave as an example of C's "ineptitude" for politi-cal economy his belief that "if the taxes are exhaled from the country as vapours, back they come in drenching showers". *De Q Works* v 188–9.

[17] Since February petitions in support of the motion to repeal the house and window taxes had been presented in Par-liament; e.g. Lord Kenyon had presented one from Mary-le-bone; others were pre-sented to Hobhouse and Burdett at a meeting in Willis's Rooms. *M Chron* 28 Feb, 1 and 6 Mar. The level of agitation

was rising as C spoke, but the graduated tax on the number of windows in a house was to endure until 1851.

[18] The tariffs of 1816–33, including that of 1828 known in the South as the "Tariff of Abominations", protected ag-ricultural products of the West as well as manufactures in the Northeast. Although South Carolina had threatened to put into effect in Feb 1833 its doctrine of nullifi-cation of legislation in Washington that it regarded as unconstitutional, support from other states had not materialised. Although C and *The Times* may be re-garded as prophetic, the chief issue of 1832–3 as seen across the Atlantic was the charter of the Bank of the United States, renewed by Congress but vetoed

only did not make the^y possessor great and respectable—it^z only made him the object of plunder and hatred. Witness the history of the Jews in this country in the early reigns after the Conquest.[19]   [36:487]

---

11. April 1833.

There are three ways of treating any subject. 1. Analytically. 2. Historically. 3. Constructively or Synthetically. Of these the only one complete and unerring is the last.[1]

^{a}In the first you begin with a Definition, and that Definition is necessarily assumed as the Truth. As the argument proceeds, the conclusion from the first proposition becomes the base of the second and so on. Now it is quite impossible that you can be sure that you have included all the necessary and none but the necessary terms in your Definition; as, therefore, you proceed, the original speck of error is multiplied at every remove—the same infirmity of knowledge besetting each successive definition. Hence you may set out like Spinoza with all but the Truth, and end with a conclusion which is altogether monstrous, and yet the mere deduction be irrefragable: Warburton's Divine Legation is also a splendid instance of this mode of Discussion and of its inability to lead to the Truth.[2] In truth it is attempting to adopt the mathematical series of

^{y} ~~a man~~ the ^{z} ~~that~~ it ^{a} f 85

---

by Jackson. Henry Bamford Parkes *The United States of America: A History* (New York 1955) 217, 244–9. By the word "deputies" C meant to insult the system of direct representation in Congress.

[19] Jews, who came in the wake of the Norman Conquest of 1066, lent money to the barons and the warrior class at a high rate of interest and lived in stone houses until they were expelled from England by Edward I in 1290; but they depended entirely on the whim of each king for protection and suffered frequent abuse and pogroms, especially after the Third Crusade of 1190–3. Robert Henry *The History of Great Britain, from the First Invasion of It by Julius Caesar* (4th ed 12 vols 1805–6) VI 168–9, 278–81, VIII 336.

[1] Drawing directly upon Kant *Critik der reinen Vernunft* (2nd ed Riga 1787),

C began his discussion of synthetic judgements in *Logic* chs 6–8 *(CC)* 174–210 by defining synthesis as "the adding of one knowledge to another"; by the analytic process "we know what we know *better*; by the synthetic we know more".

[2] The larger argument of Warburton *The Divine Legation of Moses* is summarised in a book more to C's taste: "The history of nations has . . . demonstrated, that without some measure of religious faith, political security is a dream, and that impressions of futurity, in proportion to their truth, constitute the spring and safeguard both of public and of private welfare." Robert Vaughan *The Life and Opinions of John de Wycliffe, D.D.* (2 vols 1828) I 92. C annotated the volumes. (See also 13 May 1833 at n 23, below.) C was more concerned with Warburton's "mathematical" argument that the law of Moses had

proof—but in forgetfulness that the Mathematician is sure of the truth of his definition at each remove, because he *creates* it as he can do in pure figure and number. But you cannot *make* any thing true which results from or is connected with real externals; you can only *find* it out. The chief use of this first mode of discussion is to sharpen the wit, for which it is the best exercitation.

2. The historical mode is a very common one, in which the Author professes to find out the truth by collecting the facts of the case and tracing them downwards. But this mode is worse than the other. Suppose the question is as to the true essence and character of the English Constitution.[3] First, where will you begin your collection of facts? where will you end it? What facts will you notice, and how do you know that the class of facts which you select are necessary terms in the premisses—and that other classes of facts which you neglect are not necessary? And how do you distinguish phenomena which proceed from disease or accident from those which are the genuine fruits of the essence of the tree? What can be more striking in illustration of the utter unfitness of this line of investigation for arriving at the real truth than the political treatises and constitutional histories which we have in every library?[4] A Whig proves his

---

no doctrine of future rewards and punishments but must have been supported by an "extraordinary providence". On "mathematical or intuitive" synthesis see *Logic (CC)* 198–210. On Spinoza's "chain of adamant" see 25–6 Aug 1827 (at n 10) and 28 Jan 1832 (at n 4), above. C seems to have said something of the same sort when he kissed the engraved portrait of Spinoza in 1812. *CRB* I 112. Spinoza entered the talk of C heard by HCR with Charles and Mary Lamb on 20 Dec 1810: "Coleridge warmly praised Spinoza, Jacobi on Spinoza, and Schiller 'Ueber die Sendung Moses,' &c. And he concurred with me in thinking the main fault of Spinoza to be his attempting to reduce to demonstration that which must be an object of faith. He did not agree with Charles Lamb in his admiration of those playful and delightful plays of Shakespeare, 'Love's Labor's Lost' and the 'Midsummer Night's Dream'; but both affirmed that not a line of 'Titus Andronicus' could have been from Shakespeare's pen." *CRD* I 198.

[3] The Constitution provides an illustration of the thought underlying C's essays in *The Friend* and the opening chapters of *C&S* on the communication of truth and on the principles of human knowledge.

[4] The standard works on the Constitution in nearly every library were Sir William Blackstone (1723–80) *Commentaries on the Laws of England* (4 vols Oxford 1765–8), kept in print until 1876, and Jean Louis Delolme (c 1740–c 1806) *The Constitution of England* (1775, 4th ed 1784, "corrected" 1789, with apparatus 1807). C's emphasis here seems to be not on the standard works but on the miscellaneous accumulation of warring pamphlets and treatises that provide contradiction on the subject within any library. C found unfit a survey like Hume's of "continual fluctuation" in the history of the Constitution to Henry VII and later: "In each of these successive alterations, the only rule of government which is intelligible or carries any authority with it, is the established practice of the age, and the maxims of administration which are at that time prevalent and universally assented to." *History of England* (8 vols 1802) III 305, V 452n.

case [b]convincingly to the reader who knows nothing beyond his author; then comes an old Tory—Carte[5]—and ferrets up a hamper full of conflicting documents and notices, which prove his case per contra. A.[c] takes this class of facts; B. takes that class: each proves something true, neither of course proves *the* truth or any thing like *the* Truth.

You must commence with the philosophic Idea of the Thing, the true nature of which you wish to find out and manifest. You must carry your rule ready made if you[d] mean to measure aright. If you ask me how I can know that this Idea—my own invention—is the Truth, by which the phenomena of History are to be explained, I answer, in the same way exactly that you[e] know that your eyes are made to see with—and that is—because you *do* see with them.[6] If I propose to you an Idea or Self-Realizing Theory of the Constitution, which will manifest itself as in existence from the earliest times to the present, which comprehends within it *all* the facts which History has preserved and gives them a meaning as interchangeably causals or effects—if I show you that such an event or reign was an obliquity to the right hand, and how produced, and such another event a deviation to the left—that the growth was stopped here, accelerated there—that such a tendency is and has always been corroborative, and another tendency destructive of the main progress of the Idea towards realization—if this Idea not only like a kaleidoscope reduces all the miscellaneous fragments into order, but[f] also ministers[g] strength and knowledge and light to the true patriot and statesman for working out the bright Thought, and bringing the glorious Embryo to a perfect Birth—then I think I have a right to say that the Idea which led to this is not only true—but the Truth—the only Truth.[7] To set up for a statesman upon historical knowledge only is about as wise as to set up for a Musician by the

[b] f 85[v]   [c] On A.   [d] your   [e] you I you   [f] & but   [g] ministers to

[5] Thomas Carte (1686–1754) *A Collection of Original Letters and Papers, Concerning the Affairs of England, from the Year 1641 to 1660* (2 vols 1739), "published for the use of the world, and, without any reflections or observations of my own, submitted to the reader's judgment". Carte's Jacobite stance was clear from the documents selected and from his development of the case in *A General History of England* (4 vols 1747–55).

[6] In the Appendix to *C&S* (CC) 176 C argued that since shapes, colours, sounds, and odours answer to eyes, ears, touch, and smell, then the ideas of the good, immortality, freedom, and the beautiful must also imply "a world correspondent to them". In *The Friend* of 1818 he had modified slightly from Jacobi the definition of reason "as an organ bearing the same relation to spiritual objects . . . as the eye bears to material and contingent phaenomena". *Friend (CC)* I 155–6.

[7] In short, C's idea of the Constitution is reason itself, recognised when seen. For C's metaphorical use of the kaleidoscope, invented by David Brewster in 1816 and introduced to the general public in 1818, see e.g. *CN* III 4411, *AR* (1825) 258n; *Logic (CC)* 134, 163 and n.

purchase of some*ʰ* score of flutes, fiddles, horns &c. In order to make music, you must know how to play; in order to make your facts speak*ⁱ* Truth, you must know *what* the Truth is *ʲ*which ought to be proved—the Ideal Truth—the Truth which was consciously or unconsciously, strongly or weakly, wisely or blindly, intended at all times.[8]   [36:489]

Except in Shakspeare, you can find no such thing as a pure conception of wedded love in the old dramatists. In Massinger, Beaumont and Fletcher &c. it really is on both sides absolute lust. There is scarcely a suitor in all their plays, whose *abilities* are not discussed by the lady or her waiting women. In this, as in all things, how transcendant over his age and his rivals was our sweet Shakspeare![9]   [36:492]

I have not read through all young Tennyson's poems, which have been sent to me; but I think there are some things of a good deal of beauty in what I have seen.[10] The mischief is that he has begun to write verses without understanding what Metre is. Even if you write in a known and

ʰ ~~the~~ some   *ⁱ* speak ~~the~~   *ʲ* f 86

[8] For this philosophic passage HNC provided an apologetic and explanatory note in *TT* (1835).

[9] Citing *The Maid in the Mill* particularly, C noted that Beaumont and Fletcher's virtuous women were "Strumpets in their imaginations and Wishes". *CM (CC)* I 393; cf 397. Abilities were often represented by reference to "parts". Camiola, the titular heroine of *The Maid of Honour* by Massinger, responds chillingly to foolish Sylli's description of his own "good parts", but soon after declares directly to Bertoldo that he is "absolute and circular" in "all those wished-for rarities" that may take a virgin captive. I ii 17–25, 109–74. C's endeavour is to make Juliet's Nurse and Emilia's words to Desdemona chaste by comparison.

[10] Alfred Tennyson (1809–92), 1st Baron Tennyson (1884) *Poems* (dated 1833, issued Dec 1832). The new volume had been reviewed with savage irony by John Wilson Croker in *QR* XLIX (Apr 1833) 81–96. HNC, waiting until 24 Apr to thank John Murray for that number, said that he "liked all but the supposed demolition of Master Tenny-son, wch, as you will see, will be a feather in his cap". John Murray MSS. James F. A. Pyre traced Tennyson's versification from the "disorder of wild and irregular metres" in *Poems Chiefly Lyrical* (1830), through *Poems* (1833), in which the poet "is still inclined to invent his stanzaic system for each new poem rather than to accept any settled and well-known form", on to regularisation in "some standard and well-known metre" in both the revisions and the new pieces of *Poems* (2 vols 1842). *The Formation of Tennyson's Style* (Madison, Wisconsin 1921) 25–7 (for the phrases quoted). Pyre (pp 23–5) and Edgar Finley Shannon Jr—*Tennyson and the Reviewers* (Cambridge, Mass 1952) 42—concluded that C's remarks were definitely justified for 1830 and basically so in 1833. In Nov 1830, after the *Spectator* of 21 Aug in a generally favourable review had complained of "a vicious and irregular system in the arrangement" of Tennyson's rhymes, WW wrote to William Rowan Hamilton that the Cambridge poets of *Poems by Two Brothers* (1827) were "not a little promising". *WL* (*L* rev) II 354.

approved Metre, the odds are, if you are not a Metrist yourself, that you will not write harmonious verses—but to deal in new metres without knowing what Metre means is preposterous. What I would prescribe to Tennyson[k]—indeed without it he never can succeed—is[l] to write for the next two or three years in none but one or two well known and strictly defined metres, such as the heroic couplet, the octave stanza, or the octosyllabic measure of Allegro and Penseroso. He would probably thus get imbued with a sensation if not a sense of Metre without knowing it, just as Eton boys get to write such good Latin verses by conning Ovid.[11] As it is Tennyson's verses are neither fish nor[m] flesh in respect of construction.[12] I can't scan them.   [36:493]

In my judgment Protestants lose a great deal of time in a false attack when they labor to convict the Roman Catholics of false doctrines. Destroy the *Papacy* and help the Priests to wives, and I am much mistaken if the doctrinal errors—such as there really are—would not very soon pass away. They might remain in terminis,[13] but they would lose their sting and body, and lapse back into figures of rhetoric and warm devotion from which they most of them—such as Transubstantiation and Prayer for the Dead and to Saints—originally sprang.[14] But so long as the Bishop[n] of Rome remains Pope, and he [o]has an army of Mamelukes all over the world—we can do little by fulminating against doctrinal tenets.[15] In the Milanese and elsewhere in the north of Italy I am told there is a powerful feeling abroad against the Papacy; they seem to be something in the state of England in Henry VIII's reign.[16] How deep[p] a wound to morals and social purity has that accursed article of the celibacy of the Clergy been! Even the best men in Roman Catholic countries attach a no-

---

[k] T. ~~is~~   [l] ~~is~~ is   [m] or   [n] ~~Pope~~ Bishop   [o] f 86[v]   [p] deep ~~must be~~

[11] C may mean to indicate public schools generally, but Eton was highly regarded for its training in Latin verse; *TT* (1835), from an Etonian's knowledge of the regimen, added Tibullus.

[12] Sentence omitted from *TT* (1835). The word "construction" includes versification and possibly stanzaic form; HNC got as far as "ver" in MS B before substituting "construction".

[13] "In terminology".

[14] In a note on Baxter *Reliquiae*, C lamented that Protestant polemicists attempted to attack Romanism on too many points, and proposed instead that the system be undermined by a strong thrust at the doctrine of an infallible Church, on which he found the strength of all its other doctrines dependent. *CM (CC)* I 314.

[15] From the Reformation, hostile observers had called the "fighting slaves" of the Pope Mamelukes. Of the actual warrior caste of Mamelukes, powerful in Egypt until 1811, Napoleon had made C and all Europe especially aware. *EOT (CC)* I 183, 332, II 31, 32n, 203 (figurative as in 1833), III 205. Mamelukes had ruled Egypt and most of the Arabic world 1250–1517.

[16] C's source untraced.

tion of impurity to the marriage of a Clergyman—and can such a feeling be altogether without its effect on the estimation of the wedded life in general? Impossible, and the morals*q* of both sexes in Spain, Italy and France prove it abundantly.[17]   [36:490]

The Papal Church has been anti-Cæsarean, extra-national, and anti-Christian.[18]   [36:490]

The Romans would never have subdued the Italian tribes, if they had not boldly left Italy and conquered foreign nations, and so at last crushed their next door neighbours by external pressure.*r*[19]   [36:491]

---

*a*4. May 1833.[1]

Colonization is not only a manifest expedient—but an imperative duty on Great Britain. God seems to hold out his finger to us over the sea. But it must be a national colonization, such as was that of the Scotch to Amer-

---

q moral~~ity~~s
r On ff 86ᵛ–87 HNC transcribed two of C's marginal notes, one from Baxter, the other from Rabelais; see n 19, below
a f 87

[17] C's authority undetermined; all English Protestants knew the case proved.
[18] *TT* (1835) provided a clarifying phrase, "had three phases". There is a fuller record on 4 May, below (36:501).
[19] See 4 May 1833 n 7, below.
At this point in MS B, f 86ᵛ–7, under the heading "In B.'s life. 1 Sept. 1825", HNC transcribed two passages, the first from C's marginalia on Baxter *Reliquiae* i 365–6—*CM (CC)* I 330—the second from C's note on Rabelais *Works* (4 vols 1784) on a front flyleaf of vol II, on the birth-dates of Rabelais and Luther, Cervantes and Shakespeare. The second, succinct passage gave him the inspiration for the entry published in *TT* (1835) under the date 1 May 1833, 36:494. The date used for the entry is not in the Baxter marginalia but could have been recorded on f 88 from current conversation. The second entry under 1 May, 36:495, does not appear in MS B, but has its counterpart in a letter of 20 Feb 1828 from C to

HNC: *CL* VI 729.
[1] Near the end of the first week of April an epidemic of influenza struck down the Gillman household and a number of C's friends. On the 11th C warned John Sterling to remain at home, but he expected to see Sterling on the 25th. On the 14th C wrote to Green: "I am myself in the average of my endurable state. . . . I have not gone backward—I make no progress.—May God grant me removal, or the power of using the time assigned to me—". *CL* VI 935–7. On 4 May (Sat) HNC recorded enough conversation to cover three additional days in the published versions. C was well enough to leave the house on the 5th and 6th. *CL* VI 939.
The part of f 88 that might have borne a date has been cut away, but both the stub and internal references to days of the week make it likely that the last entry under 4 May (36:503), which is dated 10 May in *TT* (1835), actually continued the

ica; a colonization of Hope, and not such as we have alone encouraged and effected for the last fifty years, a colonization of Despair.[2] [36:496]

The wonderful powers of machinery can, by multiplied production, render the *Arte-facta* of life cheaper; but it cannot cheapen except in a very slight degree the immediate growths of Nature or the immediate necessaries of man. A shoe and a coat are as dear now as ever they were— perhaps dearer and no discoveries in machinery can materially alter the relative price of beef and mutton.[3] Now the *arte facta* are sought by the higher classes of society in a proportion incalculably beyond that in which they are sought by the lower classes—and therefore it is that the vast increase of mechanical powers has not cheapened life and pleasure to the poor as it has to the rich. In some respects no doubt it has done so, as in giving cotton dresses to maidservants and penny gin to all. A pretty benefit truly! [36:497]

The beneficial influence of the Papacy has been much overrated by some writers; and certainly no country in Europe received less benefit and more harm from it than England. In fact the lawful Kings and Parliaments of England were always essentially Protestant in feeling for a National Church, though Catholic in their Doctrine, and it was only the

---

talk of the former date. In a letter from SC to HNC at Lincoln's Inn, postmarked 10 May 1833, she wrote that she had been two days in completing her letter to him. UT ms.

[2] In memoranda ultimately for Ball on Brougham *An Inquiry into the Colonial Policy of the European Powers* (2 vols Edinburgh 1803) C proposed that a colony capable of maintaining itself should be afforded "all the privileges, it could enjoy as an independent state". BM MS Egerton 2800, quoted in Colmer p 168. In 1810 he made one note to the effect that compelling savages into civilisation would be justified if the means were appropriate both morally and prudentially and a balancing note on "the inverse ratio of the good behaviour of Colonists to the Freedom & Virtue of the Mother Country". *CN* III 3921, 4018. Earlier in the year he had asked publicly whether "Inhabitants of Countries conquered or appropriated by Great Britain" might not think the advantages little worth their

wounds from the "contemptuous and insolent demeanour" of individual Englishmen. *Friend* No 26 *(CC)* II 351. On 8 Oct 1827 he wrote to Stuart that he had sketched a memorial, with Canning in mind, of emigration and colonisation as a possible solution to population and crime in Ireland. *CL* VI 702. For C's conversation in Dec 1830 with John Frere on colonies see App F 26, below.

[3] *TT* (1835) qualified this statement to allow for inflation of currency and changes in what are regarded as "immediate necessaries". The changes were not enough for T. P. Thompson: "Machinery, it seems, cannot make *all things* cheaper. Has it been tried? Is not the making an honest use of the produce of machinery, prohibited by law? Do we not live in a country where commerce is illegal, and trade put down by Act of Parliament; and was not the propping of this state of things, one of the immediate objects of the writer?" *Westminster Review* XXII (1835) 533–4.

Usurpers, John, Henry IV, &c. that went against this policy.[4] All the great English Schoolmen—J. Scotus—and Ramus[5]—those morning stars of the Reformation,[6] were heart and soul opposed to Rome, and maintained the Papacy to be Antichrist. The Popes always persecuted *b*with rancorous hatred the national clerisies—the married clergy—and disliked the Universities which grew out of the old monasteries. *c*The Papacy*d* was, and is, essentially extra national and was always so considered in this country, although not believed to be anti-Christian.

[36:501]

The Romans had no national clerisy; their priesthood was entirely a matter of State, and as far back as we can trace it, an evident strong hold of the Patricians against the increasing powers of the Plebeians.[7] All we

b f 87*v*   *c–d* It

[4] Robert Henry, generally anti-clerical, in his *History of Great Britain* (12 vols 1805–6) notes with disapproval the compromises and capitulations of Kings John and Henry IV (VI 432–3, 442–4, VIII 2–15, 24–35, 40–7, 55–6, X 1–2, 25–6); on the papacy vs the married clergy see V 275–6, 296, 306–7, 316–18. Strained relations of the English kings with the Popes were continuous.

[5] *TT* (1835) read "Scotus Erigena, Duns Scotus, Ockham and others", with a footnote sharing HNC's new knowledge of Joannes Scotus Erigena (c 815–c 877). HNC's original inclusion of the French logician Petrus Ramus (Pierre La Ramée, 1515–72) may have resulted from C's quirky pronunciation of Erigena. Clearly HNC did not at first record all the names C mentioned. The "and Ramus" could be taken as an aside, meaning "like Ramus". Ramus, who became a Protestant, was killed in the Massacre of St Bartholomew. C mentioned Ramus in 1803 in his plans for a history of logic. *CL* II 947. Robert Henry summarised Ockham's opposition to the papacy, bk IV ch 4, VIII 228–31, and opposition from Rome to Wycliffe's learning and to the growth of his doctrines at Oxford, bk IV ch 4, bk V ch 2, VIII 231–5, X 12–13. Paul de Rapin de Thoyras *The History of England, as Well Ecclesiastical as Civil* tr (and continued by)

Nicholas Tindal (28 vols 1726–41) included besides Wycliffe only one episode of conflict between Oxford and the Pope's legate, in 1238 (III 341–2). Erigena's name means something like John the Scot of Ireland, of whom, said C, "we know nothing but that he was an Englishman". *P Lects* Lect 9 (1949) 270. Pope Nicholas I demanded that certain of his works be examined for heresy. Henry Bett *Johannes Scotus Erigena: A Study in Medieval Philosophy* (Cambridge 1925) 11. Reading with "great delight & instruction" in 1803 Erigena's *De divisione naturae* (Oxford 1681), which he also annotated, C interpreted as Unitarian his "curious & highly philosophical account of the Trinity". *CL* II 954; *CN* I 1369 and n; *CM* (*CC*) III. C proved no better pleased than Nicholas I with Erigena's translation from "the pretended Dionysius the Areopagite", which he found pantheistic—note of 1827 on an endleaf of John Oxlee *The Christian Doctrines of the Trinity and Incarnation Considered and Maintained* (vol I 1815): *CM* (*CC*) III. In 1817, however, he had attributed to Erigena an influence on his own doctrine of polarity. *CL* IV 775. In 1819 he called Erigena the "most extraordinary man, perhaps, of his age". *P Lects* Lect 9 (1949) 270.

[6] See 13 May n 24, below.

[7] In *C&S* ch 2, cited with relation to

know of the Romans is, that after an indefinite lapse of years, they had conquered some fifty or sixty miles round their city; then it is that they go to war with Carthage the great maritime power, and the result of that war was the occupation of Sicily. Thence they in succession conquered Spain and Macedonia and Asia Minor &c., and so at last contrived to subjugate Italy partly by a tremendous back blow, and partly by bribing the Italian States with a communication of those privileges, which the now enormously enriched conquerors possessed over so large a part of the world.[8] They were ordained by Providence to conquer and amalgamate the materials of Christendom; they were not a national people; they were truly Romanos rerum dominos[9]—and that is all.   [36:499]

Under Constantine the Spiritual Power became a complete Reflex of the Temporal: four Patriarchs, four Prefects &c. The Clergy and the Lawyers, the Church and the State, were opposed.[10]   [36:500]

I think this country is now suffering grievously under an excessive accumulation of Capital, which having no field for profitable operation, is in a state of fierce civil war with itself.[11]   [36:498]

---

this topic in 9 Jun 1832 n 10, above, C went on to say that the slave of Jamaica stood in better relation to his master than that "in which the plebeian formerly stood to his patrician patron". *C&S (CC)* 25. Although C would not have acknowledged the *Decline and Fall* as a source, Gibbon (chs 2, 15, 20) stressed the senatorial station and secular attachments of the Roman pontiffs, for his own purpose of praising the absence of distinction between spiritual and temporal powers (e.g. ch 2): "They knew and valued the advantages of religion, as it is connected with civil government."

[8] C is noticing as an oddity the way conflict with Carthage (270–146 B.C.) led the Romans to far-flung conquests before they spread over Italy. Roman actions as C sets them forth can be traced in Nathaniel Hooke *The Roman History: from the Building of Rome to the Ruin of the Commonwealth* (latest ed 6 vols 1830).

[9] Virgil *Aeneid* 1.282. "Romans, lords of the world".

[10] Constantine the Great, Flavius Valerius Aurelius Constantinus (c 280– 337), retained the four prefectures established by Diocletian, but added one for Rome and one for Constantinople, as Gibbon ch 17 explains. The authority of the three bishops of Alexandria, Rome, and Antioch over their respective provinces was acknowledged throughout Constantine's reign and recognised by the Nicene Council (325); a fourth, the bishop of Constantinople, attained that recognition in 381; the title of patriarch came later.

[11] Against reliance on protective markets, C insisted that the power of "the great *Machine*" of capital accumulated by the citizens of a commercial town be acknowledged. Annotation on Fichte *Der geschlossne Handelsstaat: CM (CC)* II 619. Colquhoun, writing at a time of high taxation for war, had proposed that parsimony and full employment, producing capital wealth not in "excess of property in the few, but the extension of it among the mass of the community" would bring economic health as mere revenue never could. *Treatise on Wealth* (1815) 6, 81–2, 118–21. C's remark, although not concerned explicitly with em-

I know no portion of history which a man might write with so much pleasure as that of the great struggle in the time of Charles I., because he may feel the profoundest respect for both parties.[12] The side taken by *any particular person was determined by the point of view which he happened to command of the prospect at the commencement of the collision which was inevitable—one line seeming longer to this man, another line to another. No man of that age saw the Truth, the whole Truth: there was not enough light for that; the consequence of course was a violent exaggeration of each party for the time. Charles became a Martyr, and the Parliamentarians Traitors or vice versa. The Grand Reform brought into act by and under William III. combined the principles truly contended for by*f* Charles I. and his Parliament respectively: the Great Revolution of 1831 has certainly to an almost ruinous degree dislocated the harmony of these principles of government again.*g* As to Hampden's speech, no doubt it means a declaration of passive obedience to the Sovereign, as the*h* creed of an English Protestant individual—every man, Cromwell and all, would have said as much—it was the antipapistical tenet, and almost vauntingly as[serted*i* on all occasions by Protestants up to that time. But it implies nothing of Hampden's creed as to the duty of Parliament.[13]   [36:502]

---

e f 88   *f* by the   *g* against   *h* ~~an~~ the
i-j A passage of about 17 lines, excised when a passage was cut from the verso, f 88ᵛ (leaving 3 lines at the foot of the leaf), is here supplied from *TT* (1835)

---

ployment, recommends an adjustment of capital to market.

[12] Most of C's remarks on Charles I and his ministers indicate that he felt equal respect for both sides only at lower levels of responsibility. In a note on Baxter *Reliquiae* he called this reign "at once the glory and the shame of the English Diocesan Church"; glory for the learning and "stupendous talents" of the prelates and clergy, shame for their cruelties and superstition. *CM (CC)* I 250.

[13] A current flurry over the speech of John Hampden (1594–1643) on 4 Jan 1641/2 after his impeachment by the King may have occasioned C's remarks on the period of Charles I. The flurry began with George Nugent Grenville, Baron Nugent (1788–1850) *Some Memorials of John Hampden, His Party, and His Times* (2 vols 1832). RS, reviewing the work in *QR* XLVII (Jul 1832)

457–519, pointed out (p 510) that Lord Nugent had "suppressed" Hampden's third duty of a subject: "Not to resist the lawful and royal power of the King . . . is the only sign of an obedient and loyal subject." Murray then published as a pamphlet *A Letter to John Murray, Esq. from Lord Nugent* dated "Sept. 18, 1832". Nugent (p 9) accused RS of suppressing Hampden's emphasis on "Lawful subjection to a King" and "Lawful obedience to laws". On 4 Nov 1832 RS promised to review the rejoinder in *QR* "for the unprovoked & brutal insolence in which his Lordship has indulged" in "that most insolent & mendacious performance". *The Letters of Robert Southey to John May* ed Ramos 252–3. *TT* (1835) added in a footnote HNC's remarks, with quotations apparently from the original publication of *A Discreet and Learned Speech* (1641/2).

[14][Well, I think no honest man will deny that the prophetic denunciations of those who seriously and solemnly opposed the Reform Bill are in a fair way of exact fulfilment! For myself, I own I did not expect such rapidity of movement. I supposed that the first parliament would contain a large number of low factious men, who would vulgarize and degrade the debates of the House of Commons, and considerably impede public business, and that the majority would be gentlemen more fond of their property than their politics. But really the truth is something more than this. Think of upwards of 160 members voting away two millions and a half of tax on Friday, at the bidding of whom, shall I say? and then no less than 70 of those very members rescinding their votes][j] on Tuesday following, nothing whatever having intervened to justify it, except that they found out that at least [k]seven or eight[l] millions more must go also upon the same principle, and that the revenue was [m]cut in two! Of course I approve the vote of recission, however dangerous a precedent: but what a picture of the composition of the House of Commons![15]   [36:503]

---

13. May. 1833.[1]

1. That which is digested wholly, and part of which is assimilated and part rejected is[a]—Food.[2]

[j] See [i-j], above   [k-l] 7 & 8 8 7 or 8   [m] f 88[v]

[14] Headed in *TT* (1835): "*May* 10.1833. REFORMED HOUSE OF COMMONS" but probably in MS B a continuation of 4 May, as indicated by the stub and by the correct references to Friday and Tuesday as the days of voting. Most of this entry, excised when a passage was cut from f 88[v], is supplied from *TT* (1835); see n [i–j].

[15] In a footnote *TT* (1835) gave accurate details. The vote on 26 Apr was 162 Aye, 152 No. On 30 Apr, when Althorp's motion to repeal the window tax lost, Ingilby first asked and lost an amendment to remove the reference to malt duty from that motion; when he brought in a bill pursuant to the action on Friday, the vote was 238 No (for the ministers), 76 Aye.

[1] 13 May (Mon) may possibly have been followed, on the half-page cut from MS B, by 14 May, but the considerable rearrangement of the entries of MS B in

TT (1835) there dated 13, 14, 15, 17, and 18 May, make it likely, given HNC's general practice of equable distribution, that HNC next visited C on 15 May (Wed), as indicated in the ms.

[2] In a note on Mesmer as quack, C wrote in 1830 or later: "All remedies without exception are in their effects Diseases. Were they not, they would be *Diet* not Medicines. A medicine is the medium aliquid between Food & Poison—each taken in its notional absoluteness. What is either assimilated or naturally expelled, is food; what the vital energy cannot act on but which acts on the vital energy is poison. What is digested, but not assimilated, is capable of being a medicine." RS *Life of Wesley* I 239: *CM (CC)* IV. Earlier he wrote more amusingly: "Poison to one animal, food for a second, medicine for a third. . . . 1. Digestible without assimilation = Poison. 2. Assimilable with reaction =

2. That which is digested wholly—and the whole of which is partly assimilable and partly not is[a]—Medicine.[3]

3. That which is digested—but not assimilated is[a]—Poison.[4]

4. That which is neither digested, nor assimilated is[a]—mere obstruction.

As to the stories of slow Poisons, I cannot say whether there was any, or[b] what, truth in them; but I believe a man may be poisoned by arsenic a year after he has taken it. In fact, I think that is known to have happened.[5]   [36:504]

---

[c][6][How can I wish that Wilson should cease to write what so often soothes and suspends my bodily miseries, and my mental conflicts![7] Yet

---

[a] =   [b] & or   [c-d] Half leaf of f 88[v] cut from ms; see [i-j], above, I 373, and n 6, below

---

Doctor's Stuff. Assimilable = Food. P.S. Almost all Food contains an unfoodful portion . . .''. Annotation on Ferdinand Friedrich Runge (1795–1872) *Neueste phytochemische Entdeckungen zur Begründung einer wissenschaftlichen Phytochemie* (2 pts Berlin 1820–1) i 35–6—*CM (CC)* IV—in which Runge's classification of plants led to C's remarks.

[3] C asked in a note on *The Book of Common Prayer*: "Is not the Sacrament Medicine as well *as food*?" *CM (CC)* I 714.

[4] In a note on Steffens *Beyträge zur innern Naturgeschichte* 74, C declared his persuasion that all poisons act on the irritable system, with vegetable poisons acting on its irritability and animal poisons acting on its sensibility. *CM (CC)* IV.

[5] Richard Mead *A Mechanical Account of Poisons, in Several Essays* mentions only that one dog died the day after poisoning (3rd ed 1745 p 219), and most volumes of materia medica cautioned concerning the speed with which arsenic worked. Anecdotes of delayed death from arsenic would therefore have a special interest, even in an era before the detective story. The principal authority, Matthieu Orfila (1787–1853) *A General System of Toxology* tr John Augustine Waller (2 vols 1815–17), has a section on arsenical poisons and a chapter "Of

Slow Poisoning", but no light on C's comments.

[6] The half-page (9.6 cm) cut from MS B at this point probably contained a version of entry 36:506, the remarks on John Wilson here given from *TT* (1835). The stub leaves no hint on the verso concerning what was cut or why. In print the entry follows that on Wilson's characterisation of Lamb, which survives at the bottom of MS B f 88[v].

[7] John Wilson (1785–1854), the "Christopher North" of "Noctes Ambrosianae" (1822–35) in *Blackwood's*, professor of moral philosophy at Edinburgh University (1820–51), and athlete, was one of the main supports of *Blackwood's* from its founding in 1817. With Alexander Blair, Wilson wrote the letter signed "Mathetes" in *The Friend* 14 Dec 1809, answered by WW. *Friend (CC)* II 222–32, 260–9 (I 377–405). Anonymously, he ridiculed *BL* in *Bl Mag* II (Oct 1817) 3–18. In "Noctes Ambrosianae" he praised C as a talker who "pours out wisdom like a sea"—though C "writes but indifferent books"—in Sept 1825, Apr 1827, Sept 1831. *Bl Mag* XVIII 384, XXI 479, 488, XXX 478–9; cf *C Talker* 365–7. C listed his own contributions to *Bl Mag* in *CN* IV 4930. C's relations with Wilson and *Bl Mag* are surveyed in David V. Erdman "Coleridge and the 'Review Business' '' *Wordsworth Circle* VI (1975) 29–41; Alan Lang

what a waste, what a reckless spending, of talent, aye, and of genius, too, in his I know not how many years' management of Blackwood! If Wilson cares for fame, for an enduring place and prominence in literature, he should now, I think, hold his hand, and say, as he well may,—

> "*Militavi* non sine gloria:
> Nunc arma defunctumque *bello*
> Barbiton hic paries habebit".[8]

Two or three volumes collected out of the magazine by himself would be very delightful. But he must not leave it for others to do; for some re-casting and much condensation would be required; and literary executors make sad work in general with their testators' brains.[9]]*d*   [36:506]

Wilson's character of Charles Lamb in the last Blackwood—Twaddle on Tweed—is very sweet indeed and gratified me much. It does Wilson honor, to head and heart.[10]   [36:505]

---

*e*I believe it possible that a man may, under certain states of the moral feeling, entertain something that deserves the name of Love towards a male object—an affection beyond Friendship and wholly aloof from Appetite.[11] In Elizabeth's and James's time it seems to have been almost fashionable—and perhaps we may account in some measure for it by

d See *c–d*, above   *e* f 89

Strout in *PMLA* XLVIII (1933) 100–28; Strout "Knights of the Burning Pestle" *Studia Neophilogica* XXVI (1953) 78–80; Heather J. Jackson "Coleridge's 'Maxilian' " *Comparative Literature* XXXIII (1981) 39–49. C had been receiving *Bl Mag* as a gift from William Blackwood. *CL* VI 884, 912.

[8] Horace *Odes* 3.26.2–4. Tr C. E. Bennett (LCL 1914): "I have served not without renown. Now this wall shall have my weapons and the lyre that has done with wars".

[9] Wilson published *The Recreations of Christopher North* (3 vols Edinburgh 1842), but his *Works* (12 vols Edinburgh 1855–8) awaited editing by his son-in-law, James Frederick Ferrier. In *TT* (1835) HNC risked a note, "True; and better fortune attend Mr. Coleridge's own!", which disappeared in 1836.

[10] In "Twaddle on Tweedside" *Bl Mag* XXXIII (May 1833) 856–7. In a foot-note in *TT* (1835) HNC quoted the "character", with changes of punctuation and mechanics; e.g. Wilson called the house where he had visited the Lambs in 1832 "their Bower of Rest". The same note takes from the *New Monthly Magazine* NS XLIII (Feb 1835) 198 the motto of *Poems* (1797). See note to 36:505.

[11] A few months later Tennyson was to write the lines on his "widow'd race" after the death of Arthur Hallam,

> Dear as the mother to the son,
> More than my brothers are to me,

later to become *In Memoriam* IX 18–20, and

> that dear hand that I should press,
> Those honoured brows that I would kiss,

bowdlerised when published by Hallam Tennyson in 1897.

considering how very inferior the women of that age were, taken generally, in education and accomplishment of mind to the men. Of course there were brilliant exceptions enough; but the plays of Beaumont and Fletcher—the most popular dramatists that ever wrote for the English stage—will show us what sort of women it was generally pleasing to represent.[12] Certainly the language of the two friends in the Arcadia is such as we could not now use except to women, and in Cervantes the same tone is sometimes adopted, as in the Novel of the Curious Impertinent.[13] And I think there is a passage in the Atlantis of Lord Bacon, in which he speaks of the possibility of such a feeling—but hints the extreme danger of entertaining it, or allowing it any place in a moral theory.[14] I mention this with reference to Shakspeare's sonnets—which it is supposed were addressed to the third*f* Earl of Pembroke, Herbert, whom Clarendon calls the most beloved man of his age, though his licentiousness was equal to his virtues.[15] I doubt this—I do not think Shakspeare, merely because he was an actor, would have thought it necessary to veil his emotions towards Herbert under a disguise, though he might if the real object had been a Laura or a Leonora.[16] It seems to me that the sonnets could only

f 2*d*

[12] Cf 11 Apr 1833 n 9, above.

[13] At the beginning of the *Arcadia* by Sir Philip Sidney (1554–86) Pyrocles was "full of admirable beauty", which "when *Musidorus* saw, though he were almost as much ravished with joy, as they with astonishment, he leaped to the mariner . . . saying, Dost thou live, and art well? who answered, Thou canst tell best, since most of my well being stands in thee . . ." and at the end "*Procles* . . . leap'd suddenly from their hands that held him, and passing with a strength strengthen'd with a true affection, through them that encompassed *Musidorus*, he embraced him as fast as he could in his arms. And kissing his cheeks, O my *Palladius*, said he, let not our virtue now abandon us . . .". *The Works of the Honourable S*ʳ *Philip Sidney, Kt. in Prose and Verse* (14th ed 3 vols 1725) I 7, II 782. In "The Curious Impertinent" *Don Quixote* I iv 6–8 Anselmo and Lothario "lov'd one another above all other Considerations; and mutually quitted their own Pleasure for their Friend's" (tr Charles Jarvis 1742)—but the event is unhappy; to test his wife's

virtue the foolish Anselmo drives Lothario to betray the honour of all three.

[14] In Bacon *The New Atlantis* (pub 1627) Joabin describes the customs in Bensalem—*Works* (10 vols 1803) II 108—as quoted in HNC's note in *TT* (1835).

[15] The first to identify the "W. H." of the dedication of Shakespeare's *Sonnets* (1609) as William Herbert, 3rd Earl of Pembroke (1580–1630) was James Boaden in 1832; B. H. Bright said he had told Joseph Hunter about Pembroke in 1819; Boaden answered that he had made the identification in 1812. *G Mag* CII (1832) ii 217–21, 296, 308–14. *TT* (1835) quoted from the pertinent passage in Clarendon *History of the Rebellion*, which continues: "To women . . . he was immoderately given up". Rev from Clarendon's ms (2 vols Oxford 1826) I 100–2.

[16] Laura, the inspirer of Francesco Petrarca (1304–74) *Canzoniere: Rime in vita e morte di Madonna Laura*. C owned and annotated *Le Rime* (2 vols London 1775) before 1812. *NLS* II 23–4. His copy, in the BM, bears HNC's

have come from a man deeply in love, and in love with a woman—and there is one Sonnet, which from its incongruity of tone I take to be a purposed blind.[17] These extraordinary sonnets form in fact a Poem of so many stanzas of fourteen lines each; and like the Passion which inspired them, the sonnets are always the same with a variety of expression—continuous if you regard the Lover's soul, distinct if you listen to him as he heaves them sigh after sigh.

These Sonnets, like the Venus and Adonis and Rape of Lucrece, are characterized by boundless fertility, and labored condensation of thought, with perfection of sweetness in rhythm and metre.[18] These are the essentials in the budding of a great Poet. Afterwards, habit and conscious power teaching to be more easy—precipitandus liber spiritus.[19]

[36:507]

[g]Samuel Johnson, whom to distinguish him from the Doctor, we may call the Whig, was a very remarkable writer. He may be compared to his contemporary De Foe, whom he resembled in many points.[20] He is an-

[g] f 89[v]

name, with the date 1829. In 1819 C noted in *Il Petrarca di nuovo ristampata* (Venice 1651) that it was a gift to him from H. F. Cary. *Studies in Philology* LII (1955) 497–8. C. made frequent notes from Petrarch's Latin works. The tradition that Tasso was locked in an asylum because of his love for Leonora d'Este (1537–81) is central to Goethe's *Torquato Tasso* (prose 1781, verse tragedy 1790) and accepted by Byron *The Lament of Tasso* (1817).

[17] HNC's note in *TT* (1835) suggested, surely correctly, Sonnet 20, "A woman's face, with Nature's own hand painted". On 2 Nov 1803 C addressed to HC a note in *B Poets* explaining that the "pure Love" in Sonnet 20 could best be understood by reading John Potter *Archaeologia Graeca; or the Antiquities of Greece* ch 9 (2 vols Oxford 1697–9) II 262–6. *CM (CC)* I 42–3 and nn.

[18] For C on the sonnets see *BL* chs 2, 15 *(CC)* I 33–6, II 23–5; *CN* II 2428, III 3289; for commentary on C's views, the New Variorum Shakespeare *The Sonnets* ed Hyder Edward Rollins (2 vols Philadelphia 1944) I 55, 96, 206, II 232, 345–9; *CM (CC)* I 81n.

[19] Gaius Petronius surnamed Arbiter (d A.D. 65) *Satyricon* 118. Tr "the free

spirit must speed onward". *TT* (1835) changed the cases to fit C's sentence. C used the phrase, italicising *liber*—"says Petronius Arbiter most happily"—in *BL* ch 14 *(CC)* II 14; in *CL* V 402, VI 732; and in *CN* IV 4721 to suggest improvement in Mrs Gillman's singing.

[20] C was reading and annotating at this time the Rev Samuel Johnson *Works* (1710): "Think only what a grand highminded Fellow Samuel Johnson (M[r]) verily was (*his* treatment and Defoe's make one feel the heterogenëity of William's own Character & that of his scoundrelly compromising Whig Ministers!)." Annotation on an endleaf: *CM (CC)* III. C's "thin folio" (see below, sentence after n 21) has 28 + 488 pages + endleaves for notes by C. Johnson, domestic chaplain to Lord William Russell, who was executed in 1683, resembled Defoe in writing works for which he was degraded, fined, imprisoned, pilloried, and whipped. When the case for his second imprisonment in 1686 was reversed in 1689, King William "gave him Three Hundred Pounds a year out of the *Post-Office* for his and his Son's Life, besides a Thousand Pounds in Mony; and likewise bestow'd a Place of about a Hundred Pounds a year on his Son".

other instance of King William's discrimination, which was so much superior to that of any of his Ministers. Johnson was the most formidable advocate of the Exclusion Bill, and he suffered by whipping and imprisonment under James accordingly. Like Asgill, he argues with that apparent candor and clearness till he has his opponent within reach, and then comes a blow of a sledgehammer.[21] I do not know where I could put my hand upon a book containing so much sense and sound constitutional doctrine as this thin folio of Johnson's works. And what party in this country would read so severe a lecture in it as our Whigs?   [36:511]

When Sir Philip Sidney saw the enthusiasm which agitated every man, woman and child in the Low Countries against Philip and D'Alva, he told Queen Elizabeth that it was the Spirit of God, and that it was invincible.[22] What is the spirit which seems to move and unsettle every other man in England and in the Continent at this time? Upon my conscience,

Works xvii. *TT* (1835) gave an informative (and misinformative) note on Johnson. C wrote on p 315 of the *Works* that this Johnson and Samuel Barrow gave him "palliative consolation" for being named Samuel. In the one surviving note of C's on Walter Wilson (1781–1847) *Memoirs of the Life and Times of Daniel De Foe* (3 vols 1830) C defended Defoe against his biographer and compared him with Addison as "little inferior in wit and humour, and greatly superior in vigor of style and thought". *N&Q* III (1851) 136. *CM (CC)* v.
   [21] On *Works* 302 C noted: "N.B.—Asgill evidently formed his style on S. Johnson's Pamphlets.—" The page contains an example of Johnson's clarity ending in a heavy blow: "It is vain to talk of Laws which secure to us our Lives, Libertys and Estates, when Passive Obedience comes into play . . . For if a Thing be not mine to keep, it is none of mine; but it is uncontroulably his, who can take it away without Controul." Another example is in *Julian the Apostate*, for which Johnson was imprisoned in 1683; he ends his questioning of passive obedience by asking "where is it said in the Word of the Lord . . . that the World was made only for *Banditti*, or that we are to yield up our selves to Cut-Throats and Assassinates, which the *Papists* have

ever been to poor *Protestants?*'' *Works* 33. C's note to this passage is dated 8 May 1833, five days previous to this conversation: *CM (CC)* III.
   [22] C's authority is Thomas Zouch *Memoirs of the Life and Writings of Sir Philip Sidney* (York 1808) 238–9 or (2nd ed York 1809) 239–40, 247. Zouch so interprets a letter he quoted from a ms life of Sidney by Thomas Comber. C first cited and quoted the passage in *The Friend* No 7 28 Sept 1809 *(CC)* II 107–8 (I 182). He said there that Sidney was convinced that "when the People speak loudly it is from their being strongly possessed either by the Godhead or the Daemon"—which is to translate what Sidney meant (according to Zouch) into words to be found in WW's *Cintra* separately from WW's own quotation from Zouch's Sidney. *W Prose* I 290, 339, 392–3. In *C&S* C translated Zouch's Sidney into "*Vox populi, vox Dei*". *C&S (CC)* 40–1. In *SM (CC)* 16 it is Sidney's "proof of the divine agency". On the question that has vexed editors, then, C probably meant in *The Friend* No 7 to quote WW openly (he goes on to commend *Cintra*) and probably had called WW's attention to Zouch's Sidney in connexion with a point WW also thereafter associated with Sidney.

and judging by St John's rule,[23] I think it is a special spirit of the Devil—
and a very vulgar Devil too!   [36:512]

Wicliffe's genius was perhaps not equal to Luther's, but really the more
I know of him from Vaughan and Le Bas, both whose books I like,[24] I
think him as extraordinary a man as Luther. He was much sounder and
more truly Catholic in his view of the Eucharist than Luther. And I find,
not without some pleasure, that my own view of it, which I was afraid
was original, is the one maintained by Ælfric[h] in the tenth century;[25] that
is to say, that the body broken has[i] no reference to the human body of
Christ, but to the symbolic body, the Rock that followed the
Israelites.[26]   [36:509]

James I. thought that, because all power in the State seemed to proceed
from the Crown, therefore[j] all Power remained *in* the Crown—as if, because the Tree sprang from the Seed, the stem, branches, leaves and fruit
were all contained in the Seed. The Constitutional doctrine as to the relation [k]which the King bears to the other components of the State is in
two words this—He is the Representative of the Whole of that, of which
he is himself a Part.[27]   [36:511]

---

[h] Alfic   [i] ~~had~~ has   [j] it therefore   [k] f 90

---

[23] Probably 1 John 4.2 on "the spirit of antichrist, whereof ye have heard that it should come".

[24] Robert Vaughan (1795–1868) *The Life and Opinions of John de Wycliffe, D.D.* (2 vols 1828), which C annotated, and Charles Webb Le Bas (1779–1861) *The Life of Wiclif* (1832). John Wycliffe or Wiclif (c 1320–84), "Morning Star of the Reformation", religious reformer, was educated at Oxford and resident there.

[25] Aelfric (c 955–c 1020), English abbot, *A Testimonie of Antiquitie* (1567), cited in Vaughan along with a letter from Aelfric to Wulfstan (II 76): The "housel is Christ's body, not bodily but spiritually. Not the body which he suffered in, but the body of which he spake when he blessed bread and wine, a night before his sufferings. The apostle . . . has said of the Hebrews, that they all did eat the same ghostly meat, and they all did drink the same ghostly drink . . . not bodily but ghostly, Christ being not yet born,

nor his blood shed when that the people of Israel ate that meat, and drank of that stone." C annotated this passage: "Now Berengarius . . . Bucer, and the Church Catechism distinctly assert the *real* presence, with and in the spirit of the Gospel (John vi), and contradistinguish *real* from *phenomenal*, substantive from accidental. The Romish doctors sensualize the doctrine into an idol; while the sacramentaries volatilize it into a metaphor; and alas! too large a number of our clergy are sacramentaries! Often I have had occasion to mourn the dissonance between the sermon and the service." *CM (CC)* v. C declared the elements of the Eucharist "not the phænomena, Flesh and Blood", but "it may be the Noumenon", in a marginal note on Jeremy Taylor *The Worthy Communicant* (1674) endleaves: *CM (CC)* v.

[26] *TT* (1836) here appended a paragraph from *CN* III 4128.

[27] One of C's more persistent political convictions was that the King of England

Every one who has been in love, knows that the Passion is strongest in absence, and the Appetite weakest, and that the reverse is the case in the presence of the beloved object.   [36:508]

There are many phases of Love—but the tenderest of all is the Love after Enjoyment.[28]

---

15. May. 1833.

Asgill formed his style evidently upon Samuel Johnson's, but he only imitates one part of it. Asgill never rises to Johnson's eloquence. Johnson is a sort of Cobbett-Burke.[1]   [36:511]

What is good in Faust, is very good, as the Boors and Margaret. But really I think as a whole the work is excessively overrated. I understand the continuation is poor, and almost doting.[2] Goethe's small lyrics are delightful; a piece called, I think—*a*Jon and Saly*b*—is very sweet.[3] Goethe showed good taste in not attempting to imitate Shakspeare's Witches, which are threefold,—Fates, Furies, and earthly Hags o' the cauldron.[4]   [36:515]

a–b Reading uncertain

"is the lawful representative and person-ification" of the "power and dignity resident in the majority of the common-weal". *M Post* 28 Jan 1800: *EOT (CC)* I 136; cf *The Plot Discovered* in *Lects 1795 (CC)* 295; *C&S (CC)* 20. C's view of the constitutional function of the King is surveyed by Colmer pp 162–3.

[28] This sentence is omitted from *TT* (1835). Perhaps the preceding sentence seemed daring enough, or possibly HNC associated it with the conception of SC. C considers love and desire repeatedly in his notebooks; see e.g. *CN* IV 4729–30, 4848, 5097, 5462–3.

[1] See 13 May 1833 n 21, above.

[2] In the scene Vor dem Thor (Before the Gate) Goethe's Faust encounters grateful *Bauern* (peasants, boors; in Hayward's tr, "Rustics"). *Faust* I 749–1008. The remarks here on *Faust* were not published. The intimation that C had not seen *Faust* II was repeated and published in 36:546. On *Faust* see also 16 Feb 1833, above, and nn.

[3] *TT* (1835) made no attempt to name the example, which has defied identification.

C's general views of Goethe's work are sketched in the fragment quoted in *CL* IV 665n. For his attempts in 1812–16 to acquire a set of Goethe's works see *CRB* I 114; *CL* III 523, 525, IV 648, 698–9. In an annotation it is not clear whether he is describing Goethe's *Dichtung und Wahrheit* (4 vols 1811–33) or merely using it as a reference to describe Luke 2.46–51 as "Wahrheit und Dichtung (tho' after the poetic machinery, the fictions, are detached, it is not easy to discover what the *facts* are)". Note on Friedrich Schleiermacher (1768–1834) *A Critical Essay on the Gospel of St. Luke* tr Connop Thirlwall (1825) 45: *CM (CC)* IV. C's tr of "Kennst du das Land" from *Wilhelm Meisters Lehrjahre* (1795–6, bk III ch 1) was published in *PW* (1834) II 95, dated "? 1799" in *PW* (EHC) I 311. For a second stanza, see *CL* VI 837n.

[4] In declining to translate *Faust* in

A close reasoner and a good writer in general may be known by the pertinent use of his connectives.*ᶜ* Read that page of Samuel Johnson—you can't alter one*ᵈ* conjunction without spoiling the sense. It is a linked strain throughout. In your modern books, for the most part, the sentences in a page have*ᵉ* the same connexion with each other as*ᶠ* marbles in a bag. They touch, without adhering.[5]   [36:511]

Hazlitt drew old women very well from his inherent love of ugliness and deformity.[6]

Man does not move in cycles, though Nature does. Man's course is like an arrow, for the*ᵍ* portion of the great cometary ellipse which he occupies is no more than a needle's length to a mile.[7]   [36:516]

ᶜ connectives in ~~discourse~~   ᵈ ~~only~~ one   ᵉ have ~~about~~   ᶠ ~~that~~ as   ᵍ ~~his~~ the

---

1814, but assuring John Murray that he regarded it as a work of "genuine and original Genius", C defended "the Scenes of Witchery and that astonishing Witch-Gallop up the Brocken" against those who would fail to "enter into the philosophy of that imaginative Superstition, which justifies it". *CL* III 528. The witches that Goethe did not imitate from *Macbeth* appear in *Faust* I 2337–604, 3835–4222. A. W. Schlegel charged a German poet (Goethe) with falsely elevating Shakespeare's vulgar instruments of hell into "Parcen, Furien und Zauberinnen" ("fates, furies, and enchantresses" tr John Black). *Ueber dramatische Kunst* II ii 153. If C borrowed from Schlegel either the tripartite division or the elevation of witches into tragic dignity, he reversed Schlegel's interpretation of the two works without rejecting the devaluation of Goethe. The *Bristol Gazette* reported that C in Lect 2 of 2 Nov 1813 "began by commenting on the vulgar stage errour which transformed the *Weird Sisters* into witches with broomsticks. They were awful beings; and blended in themselves the Fates and Furies of the ancients with the sorceresses of Gothic and popular superstition". *Lects 1808–19 (CC)* I 531.

[5] With an improvement in both clarity and continuity, *TT* (1835) inserted this paragraph into the discussion of Johnson the Whig of 13 May 1833, above; in MS B its emphasis falls upon the deterioration of style, what C usually condemns as a borrowing from the shallowness of France.

[6] This sentence was not published. In "On the Pleasures of Painting" published in *London Magazine* (1821) and as the first essay in *Table Talk* (2 vols 1822, 2nd ed 1824), Hazlitt had described in detail his first painting, after the manner of Rembrandt, of a shrivelled old woman. Hazlitt said it was nearly invisible in 1821; a century later, in the Maidstone Museum, P. P. Howe found it opaque. *The Life of William Hazlitt* (1947) 53n. The scant records tell us more about Hazlitt's portraits in oil of men known to C than about drawings C could have seen of women. Hazlitt himself used the words "drew" and "pencil" more often than "painted" or "brushes" in describing the process of painting portraits.

[7] "ELLIPSIS, a figure formed by cutting a cone obliquely to its axis: It is in a curve of this kind that the planets move around the sun, and the satellites round their primaries." John Bonnycastle *An Introduction to Astronomy* (4th ed 1803). "COMET, an opaque, spherical and solid body, like a planet, performing revolutions about the sun in elliptical orbits, having the sun in one of their foci."

[h]In Natural History God's freedom is shown in the law of necessity. In the Moral History God's necessity or providence is shown in man's freedom.[8]   [36:517]

German is inferior to English in modifications of expression of the affections; but superior to it in modifications of expression of all objects of the senses.[9]   [36:514]

Your political economists say that it is a principle of their Science—that all things *find* their level. Which I deny, and say on the contrary that the true principle is that all things are *finding* their level—as water does in a storm.[10]   [36:513]

There is now no reverence for any thing; and the reason is that men possess Conceptions only, and all their knowledge is Conceptional only.[11] Now as to conceive is a work of the mere Understanding, and as all that can be conceived may be comprehended, it is impossible that man should

[h] f 90[v]

C. T. Watkins *A Portable Encyclopaedia* (1810). So also Erasmus Darwin *Botanic Garden* I i 105–36. Darwin I ii 537–74 and nn traced from Pythagoras to Haller and Lavoisier the scientific study of the natural cycles of matter. C's comment seems additionally to reflect an interest awakened by Vico in cycles of human history.

[8] From a further perspective C contrasts the cycles of nature with the moral freedom of the individual from geometric pattern. These comments combine C's early interest in necessity as presented by Hartley and Priestley with his increased interest in the historical unfolding of prophecy. In *Logic* C rejected the solution of Moses Mendelssohn to the controversy over freedom and necessity but drew upon him for an understanding of the problem. *Logic (CC)* 123 and n.

[9] Most of C's remarks in TT on the German language concern phonetics, grammar, or etymology, seldom as here the treatment of vocabulary as a reflection of national temperament.

[10] Adam Smith (1723–90) *Wealth of Nations* bk I ch 10 (3 vols 1811) I 134:

"If, in the same neighborhood, there was any employment evidently either more or less advantageous than the rest, so many people would crowd into it in the one case, and so many would desert it in the other, that its advantages would soon return to the level of other employments." Cf I 151, 153, and passim. Ricardian economists most easily explained *laissez-faire* by the analogy of water finding its own level. C had long objected to the application of this static model to the dynamics of an actual economy: *M Post* 14 Oct 1800; *EOT (CC)* I 255; *Friend (CC)* II 131 (I 198); *LS (CC)* 205. In 1833 he is restating metaphorically his retort in the *Courier* 30 May 1811: "*Things* may find their level; but the *minds* and bodies of men do not." *EOT (CC)* II 176.

[11] C said in *Logic* that his distinction of conceptions from ideas and intuitions is assumed throughout that work. *Logic (CC)* 233n. In *SM* App C he argued that the true sense of ideal truths can be had only in "the union of the Universal and the Individual". *SM (CC)* 62; cf *BL* ch 23 *(CC)* II 214–15. On conceptions vs ideas see also *C&S (CC)* 12–13.

reverence that to which he must always feel something in himself superior. If it were possible to conceive God in a strict sense, that is as[i] we
conceive a horse or a tree—even God himself *could* not excite any reverence, though he might fear or terror or perhaps love as a tiger does, or
a lovely woman. But Reverence, which is the synthesis of Love and
Fear, is only due from man, and indeed only excitable in man, towards
Ideal Truths, which are always Mysteries to the Understanding, for the
same reason that the motion of my finger behind my back is a mystery to
you now—your eyes are not made for seeing through my body.[j12] It is
the Reason only that has a sense by which Ideas can be recognized, and
from the [k]fontal light of Ideas only can a man draw Intellectual
Power.[l13]   [36:510]

---

8. June 1833.[1]

There can be no doubt of the gross violations of strict neutrality by this
Government in the Portuguese affair; but I wish the Tories had left the
matter alone, and not given room to the people to associate them with

[i] ~~that~~ as   [j] body—~~So the Understanding has no sense or power by wch it can see~~   [k] f 91
[l] This entry was followed by HNC's transcription of three of C's marginalia on Rabelais; see n 13, below

[12] That the ideas of reason and the truths of religion are "subjects of ridicule to those who will believe nothing but . . . from premises cognisable by the
understanding"—*Logic (CC)* 207—and that even to the reason God and the nou-
menal must always remain mysteries are assumptions underlying all C's teachings
from 1809 on. The proper attitude to-
wards such mysteries is reverence; in
Voltaire, Diderot, and their royal disciples "the Human Understanding . . .
was tempted to throw off all show of reverence to the spiritual and even to the
moral powers and impulses of the soul".
SM (CC) 75.
[13] Here on f 91, torn from MS B probably in the preparation of *LR* I 139–40,
follow four paragraphs on Rabelais, according to *LR* I 138n transcribed by HNC
from "some remarks written by Mr. C.
in Mr. Gillman's copy of Rabelais, about
the year 1825". The three annotations,
in Rabelais *Works* (4 vols 1784)—see 15
Jun 1830 n 1, above—transcribed varia-

tim, are those on II back flyleaf ("All Rabelais Personages are phantasmagoric
Allegories . . ."), II 254–5 ("It is impossible to read Rabelais without an admiration mixed with wonder . . ."), II
258–61 ("In Ch. 9. Pantagruel stands for
the *Reason* . . .").
[1] As HNC wrote to SC on 7 Jun (Fri)
that he would be spending the night with
his sister Fanny and her husband, Justice
John Patteson, 33 Bedford Sq (UT ms),
we can assume that his visit to C on Saturday was not early in the day. About
this time Thomas Pringle, secretary of
the Anti-Slavery Society and a supporter
of C's, made a visit, which C followed
with a conciliatory letter on the state of
slaves in the West Indies and their "present animal impulses". *CL* VI 940. It
seems probable that Pringle is the person
of liberal views persistently challenged
on the 8th. The reported remarks are
harsher than C's marginalia on a pamphlet presented to him by Pringle, *Analysis of the Report of a Committee of the*

that scoundrel Don Miguel.[2] You can never interest the common herd in[a] the abstract question—with them it is a mere quarrel[b] between the men, and though Pedro is a very doubtful character, he is not so bad as his brother, and besides we are interested for the girl.[3]   [36:518]

---

[c]It is very strange that men who make light of the direct doctrines of the Scriptures, and turn up their noses at the recommendation of a line of conduct suggested by Religious Truths, will nevertheless stake the tran quillity of an empire—the lives and properties of millions of men and women—on the faith of a maxim of modern political Economy. And this, too, a maxim true only, if at all, of England or a part of England, or of some other country;—namely,[d] that the desire of bettering the condition will induce men to labor even more abundantly and profitably than servile compulsion—to which maxim the past history and present state of all Asia and Africa give the lie.[4] Nay, even in England at this day every man at Manchester, Birmingham and[e] in other great manufacturing towns knows that the most skilful artizans, who may earn high wages, are constantly in the habit of working but a few days in the week, and of being[f] drunk the rest.[5] The love of Indolence is universal, or next to it.

[36:519]

_{[a] ~~with~~ in   [b] quarrell   [c] f 91^v   [d] viz.   [e] &c.   [f] ~~ever~~ being}

House of Commons on the Extinction of Slavery (1833): *CM (CC)* I 31–6.

[2] After coming to England in Jun 1831, Dom Pedro had set out in 1832 on an expedition against the usurper Dom Miguel, from whom he took Oporto on 8 Jul 1832. More recently a fleet fitted out by Pedro with Capt Charles Napier in command had been followed throughout May in *The Times*; in July Napier would defeat Miguel's navy off St Vincent; Dona Maria would be proclaimed Queen; Pedro would enter Lisbon as victor; and civil war would be more intense until Miguel's defeat in 1834. On 3 Jun 1833 Sir Henry Hardinge (1785–1856), 1st Viscount Hardinge of Lahore (1846), Tory M.P. for Newport, Cornwall, in speaking against the ministerial policy towards Portugal said he would not ask members to judge between Miguel and Pedro, but asked if Pedro were beyond reproach; if it were neutrality to send recruits from British ports, "Captain Napier being the avowed agent in this business"; and if the Portuguese would have

delayed their choice had they favoured Pedro along with his daughter. Hansard 3rd s XVIII 400–7.

[3] Maria da Gloria, Maria II (1826–53) of Portugal, Pedro's daughter, Miguel's niece. For C's interest in the Pedro–Miguel conflict from its inception see 2 Jul 1830 and nn 10–12, above. HNC was also deeply concerned. His "Last Composition", a dream of events in 1870 that he began to dictate to SC on 27 Dec 1848, includes the rhetorical question, "Who does not see God's hand for Portugal in substituting Pedro's daughter for his mean-souled murderous brother". UT ms.

[4] "A journeyman who works by the piece is likely to be industrious, because he derives a benefit from every exertion of his industry." Adam Smith *Wealth of Nations* bk I ch 10 (3 vols 1811) I 167–8. The men who made light of the Scriptures were likely to write on economics for the *Ed Rev* or *Westminster Review*.

[5] *TT* (1835) substituted "idling" for "being drunk", but inserted the ironic

The Ministerial Plan for the West Indies is really insane.[6] How can it lead to any thing but a forcible change of property?   [36:520]
You are always talking of the *rights* of the Negros;—as a rhetorical mode of stimulating the people of England *here*, I don't object, but I utterly condemn your frantic practice of declaiming about their Rights to the Blacks.[7] They ought to be forcibly reminded of the state in which their brethren in Africa still are, and taught to be thankful for the Providence which has placed them within means of grace.[8] I know no right except such as flows from righteousness, and as every Christian believes his righteousness to be imputed, so his right must be an imputed right. It must flow out of a Duty, and it is under that name that the process of Humanization ought to begin and be conducted throughout.   [36:521]

---

[g]Thirty years ago and more Pitt availed himself with great political dexterity of the apprehension,[h] which Burke and the conduct of some of the

[g] f 92   [h] ~~panic~~ apprehension,

---

sentence: "I believe St. Monday is very well kept by the workmen in London."

[6] The ministerial proposal of 14 May for the abolition of slavery would free every child under six at the time of the Act; all other slaves would enter an apprenticeship with a guarantee of freedom in twelve years, the owners to be indemnified by the Government in an amount to be doubled on 10 Jun. Hansard 3rd s XVII 1193–262, XVIII 547. Protests by slave-owners that the apprentices would have no motive to work probably accounts for the sequence from C's observation that "love of Indolence is universal" to condemnation of this plan. To Pringle—to whom, as indicated in n 1, above, these remarks were probably addressed—C wrote in mid-Aug of "the improbability that any wages that can be offered by the Planters should stimulate any *body* of men . . . to labor throughout the year in such a climate . . . when the Labor of some twenty days would enable the man to . . . feed & cloath his family according to all *their* wants & wishes". *CL* VI 952. C's corrections on the page proofs of Pringle's *African Sketches* (1834) are described in "Coleridge Advises Thomas Pringle" *Quarterly Bulletin of the South African Library* XXIII

(1969) 68–73. *TT* (1835) toned down the charge of insanity.

[7] On C's "lifelong discrimination between speaking *for* the people and speaking *to* them" see *EOT (CC)* I clxx, II 376; *Lects 1795 (CC)* 43; *Friend (CC)* II 137; Woodring 79–80, 168, 210–11.

[8] HNC had called in 1825 for "some moral stimulus which shall insure habitual industry and correct the profligate propensities of savage nature". *Six Months in the West Indies in 1825* (1826) 318–19. Passages of warning to the planters that "a wise government" asked only "substantial education and substantial protection of the slaves, and a smooth road towards ultimate emancipation" were footnoted as belonging to 1825 in the edition of 1832, pp 303n, 307n. In the conciliatory letter, most likely to Pringle, C from his bed of pain, calmed by "Calomel and a Black Dose", reiterated as "an ardent & almost life-long Denouncer of Slavery" that "Man is made a Beast" and that a slave (through Christ) "may be free with a freedom, compared with which his oppressor is a pitiable Slave". *CL* VI 940–1. In a larger context see "The Vices of Slaves No Excuse for Slavery" in *LR* I 300 and an annotation on Vindex *The*

Clubs in London had excited, and endeavored to inspire into the nation a[i] panic of property.[9] Fox, instead of exposing the absurdity of this by showing the real numbers and contemptible weakness of the disaffected, fell into Pitt's trap, and was mad enough to exaggerate even Pitt's surmises.[10] The consequence was a very general apprehension throughout the country of an impending revolution—when I will venture to say the people were more heart whole than at any time for one hundred years previously. I who had been travelling in Sicily and Italy, countries where there were real grounds for the fear, was deeply impressed with the difference.[11] Now after a long period of high national glory and influence, when a revolution of a most searching and general character[j] is actually at work and[k] the old institutions of the country are all awaiting their certain destruction—the people at large are perfectly secure, sleeping or[l] gambolling at the brink of a volcano.[12]

[36:522]

---

15. June 1833.

The necessity for external government to man is in an inverse proportion to the vigor of his self-government. Where the last is most complete, the first is least wanted.[a] Hence the more virtue, the more liberty.[1]

[36:523]

I think St Paul's Epistle to the Romans the most profound work in existence, and I hardly believe that the writings of the *old* Stoics, now[b] lost,

| [i] ~~an~~ a | [j] ~~sweep~~ character | [k] ~~in~~ and | [l] ~~&~~ or |
| [a] ~~necessary~~ wanted. | [b] ~~as~~ now | | |

Conduct of the British Government Towards the Church of England in the West India Colonies . . . (1831): *CM (CC)* v.

[9] See 5 Apr 1833 n 22, above.

[10] See 28 Apr 1832 n 12, above.

[11] *TT* (1835) corrected the tenses. After seeing Sicily in 1805 C was the more convinced that the English in 1793–6 were not near revolution.

[12] Mention of his visits to Naples and Syracuse made the image of the volcano for England's parlous state come more readily, but C like most others had written of the "volcanic force" of the French Revolution and Napoleon and had hoped often that they were "burnt out". *EOT (CC)* I 53, 139, 282, 422, III 237 (C to T. G. Street 2 Oct 1813); *Friend (CC)* II 147 (with a comparison of the French Republic to Vesuvius).

[1] In the letter of about this date on the manumission of slaves, probably to Pringle, C stated "the true notion of human Freedom—viz. that Control from without must ever be *inversely* as the Self-government or Control from within"— unless men are to become wild fiends. *CL* VI 940.

could have been deeper.[2] ͨUndoubtedly it is, and must be, very obscure to ordinary readers, but some of the difficulty is accidental, arising from the form in which the Epistle appears. If we could now arrange this work in the way in which we may be sure St Paul would himself do, were he now alive and preparing it for the press, his reasoning would stand out clearer. His accumulated parentheses would be thrown into notes, or extruded to the margin.[3] You will smile after this, if I say, that I think I understand St Paul, and I think so, because really and truly I recognize a cogent consecutiveness in the argument—the only evidence I know ͩ that you understand a book.[4] How different the style of this intensely passionate argument ͤ is from that of the catholic circular charge called the Epistle to the Ephesians[5]—and how different both from that of the Epistles to Timothy and Titus, which I venture to call ἐπιστολαι παυλοειδεις not παυλου.[6] Indeed I cannot think them the composition of St Paul.   [36:524]

ͨ f 92ᵛ   ͩ know ~~of~~   ͤ ~~Epistle~~ argument

[2] Depending largely upon Tennemann, C had condemned the Stoics in Lects 6–7 of the lectures on the history of philosophy—*P Lects* (1949) 218–21, 236–7—as worldly, proud, and confusing nature with God. Here he accepts the ancient tradition that the first Stoics, Zeno, Cleanthes, and Chrysippus of the third century B.C., whose philosophic works have not survived, were profound as Seneca and other later Stoics were not. See, however, for Seneca's affinity with Paul, *CN* IV 5072. There would seem to be continuity from the previous entry (36:523) to this sentence in the Stoic belief that living in harmony with nature requires self-government.

[3] C made the same points, including the devaluation of the Epistles to Timothy and Titus, in a note on Romans in Anne Gillman's Bible. *CM (CC)* I 459. In Green's copy of Schleiermacher *Über den sogenannten ersten Brief des Paulos an den Timotheos* (Berlin 1807) 193, C noted that he was convinced by Schleiermacher of the spuriousness of this book, but already held with Eichhorn that "the 3 Pastoral Epistles" were less than all Pauline. *CM (CC)* IV. Repeating this position in a marginal note on the anony-

mous *Eternal Punishment Proved to Be Not Suffering, But Privation* (1817), he added that the three epistles appear "mere *Centos* of Pauline Phrases by some Bishop of the Age succeeding the Apostolic". *CM (CC)* II 568.

[4] The converse of C's description of method in writing. *Friend (CC)* I 448–524. If an author lacks clear progression, if "incompatible assertions are harmonized by the *sensation*, without the *sense*, of connection"—*LS (CC)* 153—a comprehending reader of Paul will discover, rather than supply, the consecutiveness.

[5] See 19 May 1830 n 10, above.

[6] "Epistles Paul-like, not Paul's". On C's slow acceptance of the rejection of Paul's authorship of the Epistles to Timothy and Titus in Eichhorn *NT* III 315–410 see *CM (CC)* I 459n. His rejection is clear enough in marginalia on Jeremy Taylor *Polemicall Discourses* I 966 and Daniel Waterland *The Importance of the Holy Trinity Asserted* 114. *CM (CC)* V. In late 1824 the two epistles seem to be accepted by C as Paul's; on 12 Jan 1826 he accepted Eichhorn and Schleiermacher on the epistles' "unpaulinity". *CN* IV 5169, 5312.

Erasmus' paraphrase on the New Testament is very explanatory and clear; but you cannot expect any thing very deep from Erasmus.[7] The only fit commentator on Paul was Luther, not by any means such a gentleman as the Apostle, but almost as great a Genius.[8]   [36:525]

Have you been able to discover any principle in this Emancipation Bill for the Slaves, except a principle of fear of the Abolition Faction,*f* struggling with a fear of causing*g* some monstrous calamity to the Empire at large! Well! I will not prophesy*h*, and God grant that this tremendous and unprecedented act of positive enactment may not do the harm to the con-

f Faction, & a   *g* ~~doing~~ causing   *h* prophecy

---

[7] Desiderius Erasmus (originally Geert Geerts, 1469–1536). His *Novum testamentum* (Basel 1516) was the first edition of the Greek NT with notes appended; the notes were expanded in 1519 as *Annotationes in Novum Testamentum*. His paraphrases of Matthew and John (Basel 1522–3), incorporating his interpretations, were extended to other books of the NT and translated into English in 1548. C's esteem for the drunken manner of Rabelais is withheld from Erasmus' tantalising avoidance of sobriety. In *SM (CC)* 66 he called him "the prince of sound common sense". Nor had he any difficulty in declaring Erasmus' superiority to Voltaire. *Friend (CC)* II 112–14 (I 131–4); *P Lects* Lect 10 (1949) 306–7. He spoke favourably of Erasmus in Lect 1 of 28 Oct 1813 in Bristol and wrote favourably in N 28 f 63 and in a note on Fleury *Ecclesiastical History*. *Lects 1808–19 (CC)* I 516; *CM (CC)* II 703. Defending Erasmus for taking a Latin name and complaining against underpraise, he called *Moriae encomium*, *The Praise of Folly*, "the (perhaps) most exquisite Work of wit & wisdom extant! In its kind certainly the most exquisite." Annotation on *Encyclopaedia Londinensis*: *CM (CC)* II 529. Erasmus is contrasted with Luther in a work C admired, Michael Ignaz Schmidt *Geschichte der Deutschen* (5 vols Ulm 1778–83) I 287–8, 293, 301.

[8] "Both in Paul and in Luther (names which I can never separate) . . .", C had

written in Luther *Colloquia Mensalia* (1652) 190: *CM (CC)* III. In a letter of 3 Mar 1818 to William Hart Coleridge, breathlessly praising Luther for thundering against "mock-rationality", C paused, "And O what a genuine Son of Paul is he not!" *CL* IV 845. To judge by *Friend (CC)* I 426 he had been set thinking of St Paul as a gentleman by an anecdote concerning the deistic Anthony Collins in *Biographia Britannica* (2nd ed 5 vols 1778–93) I 628n *sub* John Shute Barrington, Viscount Barrington, who "staggered the infidelity" of the deist: ". . . Mr. Collins observed that he had a very great respect for the memory of St. Paul; and added, 'I think so well of him, who was both a man of sense and a gentleman, that if he had asserted he had worked miracles himself, I would have believed him.' Lord Barrington immediately produced a passage in which that apostle asserts his having wrought miracles: Mr. Collins seemed somewhat disconcerted, and soon after took his hat, and quitted the company." Post-Freudian biographers have seen in Luther's antagonisms an inclination to re-enact the rôle of St Paul; e.g. Mark U. Edwards Jr *Luther and the False Brethren* (Stanford, California 1976)—the title refers to Gal 2.4.

Henry Langley Porter, an assistant to Gillman, recorded C's definition of a gentleman: "One who in all the detail of ordinary life, and with all the consciousness of Habit, shews respect to others in

cept of humanity and freedom which I cannot but fear! But yet what *can* I hope, when all human wisdom and counsel is set at *'*naught, and Religious Faith—the only miraculous Agent amongst men—is not invoked or regarded! And that *unblessed* phrase—the Dissenting Interest—enters into the question!!⁹   [36:526]

---

22. June. 1833.¹

What an incomparably delightful and instructive book Bishop Hacket's life of Archbishop Williams is!² You learn more from it of that which is valuable towards an insight into the times preceding the Civil Wars than from all the ponderous histories and memoirs now composed about that period.   [36:527]

Charles seems a very disagreeable personage during James's life. There is nothing dutiful in his demeanor.³   [36:528]

ᶦ f 93

---

a way that implies anticipation of reciprocal respect to himself." VCL MS LT 50 c.

⁹ It was called to the attention of the Commons on 31 May that the Government's proposal for emancipation was the position of "the large, respectable, and powerful party, called the Anti-Slavery Society, composed principally of persons dissenting from the Church of England". Hansard 3rd s XVIII 205. C's brief notes on Sir Henry George Grey *Corrected Report of the Speech of Viscount Howick, in the House of Commons, May 14, 1833, on Colonial Slavery—CM (CC)* II 907–9—are harsh, but not up to HNC's blast of Oct 1832 in the Preface to his *Six Months* (3rd ed 1832) against those hacking at England's colonial power "with a pertinacious hatred, of which there is no example in the history of domestic treason or foreign hostility".

¹ HNC wrote from the Athenaeum on 19 Jun (Wed) that DC had arrived, would stay with them on Sunday, and would leave for Cambridge on Monday. UT ms. DC may have been present for the talk on the 22nd (Sat).

² John Hacket (1592–1670) *Scrinia Reserata: A Memorial Offer'd to the Great Deservings of John Williams, D.D.* (2 pts 1693). C's copy contains mostly favourable marginalia: *CM (CC)* II 926–51. There are also notes of 1823 on the work in BM MS Egerton 2800 ff 169–70. Praise of the work is stated or implied in *CL* v 294, 300; *CIS* (1840) 49–50 and n. In an introductory note to the book C commended to HC this story of a man "thridding his way thro' a crowd of powerful Rogues" to his own aggrandisement as archbishop and unpitied death. *CM (CC)* II 926–7. C's marginal notes on Hacket *A Century of Sermons upon Several Remarkable Subjects* (1675) express surprise that the author of the book on Williams could be so prostrate before the Latin Fathers. *CM (CC)* II 925. He noted similarly in *CN* IV 5073 that Hacket's sermons show "injurious influences of patristic reading".

³ Hacket tells how James was brought to tears when "the Prince did deviate from him . . . in Affection to the Spanish Alliance" and how Charles listened to

I think the spirit of the Court and nobility of Edward III. and Richard II. was less gross than in the following times of Henry VIII. &c; for in these the chivalry was gone, and the whole coarseness left by itself.[4] Chaucer represents a very high and romantic style of society amongst the gentry.[5]   [36:529]

---

29. June 1833.[1]

The bed on which I slept at Cambridge was as near as I can describe it a couple of sacks full of potatoes tied together. I understand the young men

---

indiscreet revelations about his father. *Scrinia* i 181–200. Hacket, in his richly metaphorical way, declared his preference for James. Ibid i 223–4. C cared for neither: James I was a "loathsome Lackwit" (*CN* IV 5058); Charles, "that demure Jesuit", "*deserved* Death" for attacking the fundamentals of society, and in fact brought about his own death as "infatuated Beginner of that abomination" of freeing "Army-agitators" from law. Note on a flyleaf of Jeremy Taylor *Worthy Communicant: CM (CC)* v, note on Beaumont and Fletcher *Dramatic Works: CM (CC)* I 395, and reaction upon reading Clarendon in Mar 1810: *CN* III 3741. HC was too lenient towards Charles, C thought, in *Worthies of Yorkshire: CM (CC)* II 60–1, 62–3. Reading in 1823 Lucy Aikin *Memoirs of James First*, C declared the Stuart kings "all cruel, all liars, all morally cowards, and two loathsome". *CN* IV 5055. Cf *CN* IV 5160 on each Stuart "a wretched Man with a bit of metal imagined on his head". On Charles's threats not to marry see Aikin II 318–50. Cf "The Martyr?— Yea, verily; but it was to the vice of Lying." Annotation on Peter Heylyn *Cyprianus Anglicus* (1671): *CM (CC)* II 1103.

[4] Edward III (1327–77), Richard II (1377–99), Henry VIII (1509–47). Robert Henry, after describing in the period C praises an "ostentatious kind of gallantry, expressive of the most profound respect and highest admiration of the beauty and virtue of the ladies", ex-

plained that the "revival of chivalry by Edward I. and Edward III. contributed not a little to promote valour, munificence, and this splendid kind of gallantry, among persons of condition", but he had noted also that the "general profligacy of the clergy could not fail to have an ill effect on the manners of the laity", giving rise to the universal opinion that "the times of Antichrist were drawing near"; subsequently he contrasted the enduring chivalry and refinement in France with the passivity of the English in a "more barbarous state of society" under the sanguinary governments of Henry VII and Henry VIII. *History of Great Britain* x 369–79, XII 348–54. C's sentence is phrased more elegantly in *TT* (1835).

[5] C returns to Chaucer more seriously on 15 Mar 1834 (first two paragraphs) (36:628), below.

[1] Charles Valentine Le Grice, seeing C on 18 Jun for the first time in thirty years, judged him a broken man. See Editor's Introduction, above, I lvii. But C went with Gillman and Green to Cambridge for the Third Meeting of the British Association for the Advancement of Science, which opened on the 24th. HNC expected to remain in London to be with DC on Sunday, but expected to go to Cambridge on the 24th. UT ms. In Connop Thirlwall's rooms in Trinity College, at some of the meetings, and at a formal dinner in the Hall of Trinity, scientists and students gathered around the poet with deference, reported ironi-

think it hardens them. Truly I lay down at night a man, and arose in the morning a Bruise.[2]   [36:533n]

I am glad you came in to punctuate my discourse, which I fear has gone on for an hour without any stops at all.[3]   [36:536]

My emotions at revisiting Cambridge were at first overwhelming. I could not speak for an hour; yet my feelings were upon the whole very pleasurable, and I have never, of late years at least, passed three days of such great enjoyment, and healthful excitement of mind and body. The men were amused at my saying[a] that that fine old Quaker philosopher Dalton's face was like All Souls' College.[4]

[b]I was exceedingly pleased with Faraday;[5] he seemed to me to have the

[a] ~~calling~~ saying   [b] f 93[v]

cally in October by Catherine Clarkson: "Miss Hutchinson tells me that Coleridge was at Cambridge at the late assemblage of *wise men* & though not able to rise till the afternoon he had a crowded levee at his bedside." *CRC* I 247–8. C's remarks on the 29th pursue the topics of the meeting, but they begin more personally than in the published version.

[2] By delaying the personal remarks in *TT* (1835) as a footnote to the remark on King's College Chapel (36:533) HNC obscured the origin in C's visit to Cambridge of all topics on 29 Jun, except the last.

[3] This remark comes more dramatically at the end of the day's talk in *TT* (1835), but the punctuation may have been HNC's entry when C was talking to persons more scientifically inclined than HNC.

[4] John Dalton (1766–1844), chemist, physicist, Quaker, author of *A New System of Chemical Philosophy* (3 vols 1808–27), noted for providing the first table of atomic weights. Adam Sedgwick, in a long tribute, announced at the Cambridge meeting that the King was conferring funds from the Civil List upon Dalton, a philosopher "whose hair is blanched by time, but possessing an intellect still in its healthiest vigour". *Report of the Third Meeting of the British Association for the Advancement of Science* (1834) x. Robert Owen tells us that

C visited Dalton in Manchester on "several occasions", but he was too full of himself to tell us more: "Mr. Coleridge had a great fluency of words, and he could well put them together in high-sounding sentences, but my few words . . . generally told well; and although the eloquence and learning were with him, the strength of the argument was generally admitted to be on my side." *The Life of Robert Owen Written by Himself* (2 vols 1857–8) I 49. John Unsworth pointed out that these visits could have occurred only in 1793: "Coleridge and the Manchester Academy" *Charles Lamb Bulletin* NS No 32 (1980) 149–58. On 28 Jul 1817 C had tried to explain to an uncomprehending Lord Liverpool the importance of Davy's dynamic theory of chemistry: "The recent relapse therefore of the Chemists to the atomistic scheme, and the almost unanimous acceptance of Dalton's Theory in England, & Le Sage's in France, determine the intellectual character of the age with the force of an experimentum crucis." *CL* IV 760. All Souls' College, Oxford, like Dalton's face, had venerable amplitude, but there were no students inside.

[5] Michael Faraday (1791–1867), chemist and physicist, long Davy's assistant; he reported in 1821 the first of his great experiments with electricity. C's probable influence on Faraday by way of Davy is proposed in Leslie Pearce Wil-

true temperament of Genius—that carrying on of the spring*c* and freshness of youthful nay boyish, feelings, into the mature strength of manhood.[6] I was also very much struck with Thirlwall, who was very attentive to me.[7] [36:533n]

It seems to me a great delusion to call or suppose the imagination of a
subtle fluid, or molecules penetrable with the same, a*d* legitimate hypothesis.[8] I think it a suffiction.[9] Newton took*e* it*f* as *fact* that bodies fall to the

c ~~buoyancy~~ spring   *d* an   *e* ~~knowing~~ took   *f* the

liams *Michael Faraday* (1965) 62–71;
Owen Barfield *What Coleridge Thought*
(1972) 244.
  [6] HNC in a footnote in *TT* (1835)
quoted *BL* ch 4 (1817) 85 (var)—*CC* I
80–1—which quoted in turn *Friend* No 5
(CC) II 73–4 (I 109–10).
  [7] C was a guest in the Trinity College
rooms of Connop Thirlwall (1797–
1875), historian, writer on Schleiermacher (see 15 May 1833 n 3, above),
translator of Niebuhr (1828), and later
(1840) bp of St David's. Thirlwall forced
C into different language on 16 Apr 1834
(at n 16) and 31 May 1834 (at nn 3–4).
  [8] In *Opticks, or a Treatise of the Reflections, Refractions, Inflections, and
Colours of Light*, of which C owned the
3rd ed (1721), Newton asked: "And is
not this Medium exceedingly more rare
and subtile than the Air, and exceedingly
more elastic and active? And doth it not
pervade all Bodies? And is it not (by its
elastic force) expanded through all the
Heavens?" In *Principia mathematica*
(1687) he had declared it inconceivable
that inanimate matter should affect other
matter without the mediation of something else. He had questioned Descartes'
"aetherial medium extremely rare and
subtile, which freely pervades the pores
of all bodies", but had found by experiment certain resistances explicable
"only from the action of some subtle
fluid". *The Mathematical Principles of
Natural Philosophy* tr Andrew Motte (2
vols 1729) II 107–9. At the close, after a
lofty tribute to eternal God, he added a
paragraph "concerning a certain most
subtle Spirit, which pervades and lies hid
in all gross bodies" (II 393).
  C had objected very early to the hy-

pothesis of a "subtile and elastic fluid".
Note on RS *Joan of Arc* II 34 (1796) 41–
2: *CM (CC)* IV. He attacked the materialism of Newton's hypothesis in Lect 12
of the lectures on the history of philosophy: *P Lects* (1949) 357. He is closest to
the observation of 1833 in *AR* (1825)
394n. The materialism of the "subtile
fluid" was near the centre of his part in
the debate between Abernethy and Lawrence: *CN* IV 4518; *TL* (1848) 66.
  Of the speakers at Cambridge who discussed fluids, the one most likely to set C
off was William Charles Henry, physician to the Manchester Royal Infirmary,
who described living bodies as essentially solids so organised "as to leave
spaces occupied by fluids of various natures". *Report* 59. W. R. Hamilton, who
had drafted on 3 Oct 1832 an account for
C of an atomistic theory based on the theory of the point introduced by Ruggiero
Giuseppe Boscovich (1711–87)—of
whom C had been aware since 1793:
Friend (CC) II 11—and had described
for C on 3 Feb 1833 his own theory of
conical refraction, talked with C in Thirlwall's rooms on 27 Jun, very probably
on some of the topics of 29 Jun. Graves
Life of Hamilton I 593, II 38, 49. Hamilton wrote to his sister on 30 Jun 1834 of
Faraday that "having long given up the
fancy of *two fluids*, he now sees no use
for even one, and now seems to regard
the electrical current as only a transfer-
ence of *power*" (II 96). Davy had retained the doctrine of imponderable
fluids for many years, but had rejected it
by 1807 and attacked it vigorously in
Annals of Philosophy (1815): Davy
Works V 432, VIII 348.
  [9] "Hypothesis: the placing of one

centre and upon that built up a legitimate hypothesis.[10] It was a subposition of something certain—but Descartes' vortices were not an hypothesis; they rested on no fact at all; and yet they did in a clumsy way explain, the motions of the heavenly bodies.[11] But your subtle fluid &c is pure gratuitous assumption—and for what use—it explains nothing.

Besides you are endeavoring[g] to deduce Power from Mass, in which you expressly say there is no power but the vis inertiæ.[12] Whereas the whole analogy of Chemistry proves that Power produces Mass.

[36:530]

The use of a Theory in the real sciences is to help the investigator to a complete view of all the hitherto discovered parts relating to it; it is a collected View, θεωρια, of all he yet knows in *one*.[13] Of course, whilst any

---

[g] ~~guilty~~ endeavoring

---

known fact under others as their *ground* or foundation. Not the fact itself but only its position in a certain relation is imagined. Where both the position and the fact are imagined, it is Hypopœēsis not Hypothesis, subfiction not supposition." *CN* III 3587 (of 1809); cf *Friend (CC)* I 477 and n; *BL* ch 5 *(CC)* I 101–2; *CL* V 467–8 ("a Suf*fiction* not a Supposition").

[10] C maintained respect for the laws of gravity, although with a wry irony towards Newton's "sublime discoveries" that "gave almost a religious sanction to the corpuscular system and mechanical theory". *P Lects* Lect 12 (1949) 342. Cf *CL* IV 760.

[11] Cf "Vortices of Descartes are now fully exploded". *Encyclopaedia Britannica* supplement (1801). C apparently referred to this article in *Omniana* (1812) § 122 and in *CN* I 928 if there "Vort. Supplement" may be read for "Verb Supplement". Descartes' vortices were used to explain the formation of the heavenly bodies in, e.g., *Principia philosophiae* pt III § 46. In this context, as in *AR* (1825) 394n, C frequently rejects Leibniz more firmly than Descartes. His discussion of Descartes in *BL* ch 8 *(CC)* I 129–36 evolved from his observation in Descartes *Opera philosophica* (3 pts in 1 vol Amsterdam 1677–85) that the origi-

nal sin of Cartesianism is the "utter disanimation of Body", put into contrariety instead of into opposition with soul. *CM (CC)* II 170–1. He defended Descartes in terms more appropriate to Leibniz in *B Poets: CM (CC)* I 82 and n. In the lectures on the history of philosophy he treated Descartes as "a truly great man", an enemy of scepticism, whose absolute separation of the soul as intelligence from body as matter, like his sterilisation of nature, was deplorably used by materialists and by Spinoza. *P Lects* Lects 12, 13 (1949) 344, 349, 365, 377. In a note of 1824 he recommended Descartes as an introduction to theology. *CN* IV 5121. SC thought C too indulgent towards Descartes. *BL* (1847) I 92n–4. Cf *BL (CC)* I 93–4 and nn.

[12] "Force of inertia", the resistance offered by matter to any force tending to alter its state of rest or motion. Its proportionality was declared in Newton's second law of motion.

[13] An important contribution to C's sequence of distinctions among idea, law, theory, hypothesis, supposition, suffiction. His influence can be seen in Abernethy, who first explained that the term theory, "like hypothesis, denotes the most plausible and rational mode of accounting for certain phaenomena, the causes of which have not been fully de-

facts remain unknown, no theory can be exactly true, because every new part must necessarily displace the relation of all the others. A theory therefore only helps investigation: it cannot invent or discover.[14] The only true theories are geometrical; because in geometry[h] premises are true and unalterable. But [i]to suppose that in our present exceedingly imperfect acquaintance with the facts[j] any theory is[k] altogether accurate, is absurd; it can't be true.[15]   [36:531]

Lyell's system of geology is half the truth—but not more.[l16] Much of what he affirms is true, most of what he denies is false—which is the general characteristic of all systems not embracing the whole truth. So it is with the recti-linearity or undulatory motion of Light: I believe both, though Philosophy has not as yet ascertained the conditions of their alternate existence, or the laws by which they are regulated.[17]   [36:531]

---

[h] geometry all the facts are   [i] f 94   [j] facts of the ease   [k] ean be is   [l] more. A gr

---

veloped'', and then went on to distinguish: "By the word theory I mean a rational explanation of the cause or connexion of an apparently full or sufficient series of facts: by hypothesis, a rational conjecture concerning subjects in which the series of facts is obviously incomplete." *An Inquiry into the Probability and Rationality of Mr. Hunter's Theory of Life* (1814 [1815]) 7–9.

[14] On "invent" vs "discover" see e.g. *CN* III 4181.

[15] In the essays on method C had distinguished between the theories of "the tranquil geometrician" and hypotheses in physics, in a passage said to derive, via Jacobi, from Vico *De antiquissima italorum sapientia* (1710) bk I ch 3. *Friend (CC)* I 476 and n. The same point is made in different language—"Every Physical Theory is in some measure imperfect, because it is of necessity progressive . . ."—in *Method* 58.

[16] Charles Lyell (1797–1875), professor of geology at King's College, London 1831–3. His uniformitarian *Principles of Geology* (3 vols 1830–3) ended such hypotheses as Cuvier's that fossil remains could be accounted for by a series of catastrophes. Vol III was reviewed in the *Athenaeum* 29 Jun 1833 pp 409–11. On 18 Jan 1831 C had written to J. H.

Green: "I have been more than usually interested with the article in the last Quarterly on Lyell's 'Principles of Geology'. Lyell's motto seems to be—As it was in the beginning, is now, and ever shall be, World without end. As far as I can judge by the Review, he has a *half*-truth by the tail—tho' not half *the* truth. He sees (dimly indeed) the Eternity in the Time; but not—which is of no less necessity—the *Time* in the Eternity." *CL* VI 854. C had been drawn in 1795–6 to the uniformitarian views of the deistic James Hutton (1726–97) *Theory of the Earth* (1785). *Lects 1795 (CC)* 101, 353–4 and nn; *CL* I 177, 222; *CN* I 243 and n. Lyell rejected theories like Hutton's as involving periodicity in the building and eroding of continents. "A great deal", cancelled in MS B (see textual n *l*), returned in *TT* (1835) with a different syntactical antithesis.

[17] There were several papers on light—a subject as popular as electricity—at the Cambridge meeting. William Whewell summarised Sir David Brewster's paper on "the two rival theories of light": 1. "material particles emitted by a luminous body"; 2. "undulations propagated through a stationary ether". *Report* xv.

Those who deny Light to be matter do not therefore deny its corporeity.[18]   [36:532]

The principle of the Gothic Architecture is Infinity, made imaginable. It is no doubt a sublimer effort of Genius than the Greek style, but then it more depends on execution for its effect. I was more deeply impressed with the marvellous sublimity and transcendant beauty of the King's College Chapel than ever. It is unparalleled.[19]   [36:533]

I think[m] Gerard Douw's schoolmaster in the Fitzwilliam Museum the finest thing of that sort I ever saw—whether you look at it at the common distance, or examine it with a glass, the wonder is equal.[20] And that glo-

[m] think the

[18] A larger context is needed than HNC gives. Trying most of his life to reconcile the limited but undeniable evidence of the senses with certainty in human knowledge of God, C was ambivalent and wavering towards philosophers who advanced dynamic or vitalistic theories of natural phenomena. Here he may be simply reporting a fact.

[19] The general as well as the particular remarks arose from C's revisit to the Chapel of King's College, Cambridge (built 1446–1515), usually spoken of as the "crowning glory" of the perpendicular style. In giving an imaginative student's view of the Chapel as an example of perceived beauty along with "the exterior and interior of York Cathedral" in his second essay of 1814 on genial criticism, C would seem to be specifying the interior of the Chapel. *BL* (1907) II 239. Allston reported C as saying: " 'Grecian architecture is a thing, but the Gothic is an idea.' And then C added: "I can make a Grecian temple of two brick-bats and a cocked hat.' " Flagg *Life of Allston* 65–6. Informed praise of the Chapel had begun in an essay by James Bentham (1706–94) printed in several editions of several works between *The History and Antiquities of the Conventual and Cathedral Church of Ely* (Cambridge 1771) and a popular edition of that work in 1817. In 1804, with C sitting next to him at dinner, the architect George Dance had attacked the ideal of Greek proportions: "Dance said that the *Temple at*

Pestum was only one remove, as Architecture, above Stone-Henge.—He derided the prejudice of limiting Designs in Architecture within certain rules . . .". Farington *Diary* VI 2276. In Lect 1 of 27 Jan 1818, as reported by Green, C called attention to the peculiarity of the art of the Northern nations, "how it entirely depended on a symbolical expression of the infinite"; as reported by H. H. Carwardine, C "Spoke of the inferior excitement of his own feelings produced by view of a fine specimen of ancient architecture, compared to the intensity of the emotions which had been produced by a view of the cathedral at York and the interior of King's Coll Chapel". *Lects 1808–19 (CC)* II 59, 62.

[20] Gerard Dou or Dow or Douw (1613–75), Dutch painter. *Schoolmaster and Boys*, oil on panel 25.5 cm × 18 cm, in the collection bequeathed to the University by Richard, 7th Viscount Fitzwilliam (1745–1816), which in 1833 was crowded into "two moderate-sized apartments" in Perse School. Gustav Waagen saw it in 1835: "An old schoolmaster and four scholars; the master holds a rod in his left hand, teaching a boy to read; another with a book is opposite him. To the knees; by candlelight. . . . The expression of the old man is incomparably true; the whole a scene of admirable humour, and, with all the finish, not laboured." *Treasures of Art in Great Britain* III 448.

rious picture of the Venus—so perfectly beautiful and perfectly innocent—as if Beauty and Innocence could not be dissociated.[21] The French
thing below is a curious instance of the inseparable grossness of the
French taste. Titian's picture is made perfectly bestial.[22]   [36:534]

---

[n]I think Sir James Scarlett's speech for the Defendant in the late action of
Cobbett [o]versus the[p] Times Newspaper, for a libel, worthy the best ages
of Greece or Rome—though to be sure some[q] of his remarks could not
have been very palatable to his Client.[23]   [36:535]

---

1. July. 1833.[1]

If I could believe that Mandeville really *meant* any thing more by his Fable of the Bees than a bonne bouche of solemn raillery,[2] I should like to

[n] f 94[v]   [o–p] v.   [q] ~~Deft~~ [= Defendant] some

---

[21] Titian (Tiziano Vecelli or Vecellio,
1477–1576) *Venus and Cupid with a
Lute-Player*, oil on canvas 151.7 cm ×
187.7 cm. "The female figure unites
with great clearness that warm, full,
golden tone which is so characteristic of
Titian . . . Unfortunately, the heads of
the female and of the Cupid in the Fitzwilliam picture are much disfigured by
re-paintings". Waagen III 446–7. The
overpainting is now thought to have been
done by Titian himself; Waagen was
misled in part by the copy in Dresden,
known as "Philip II and His Mistress".
There is another version in the Metropolitan Museum, New York, in C's part of
the collection of the Earl of Leicester at
Holkham. Unlike the small Dou, the
sumptuous Titian had had a notable career of ownership when Fitzwilliam
bought it from the Orléans collection in
1798.
[22] C's "French thing" is an enamel
20.5 cm × 15.5 cm made for Lord Fitzwilliam as a copy of record in 1815 by
Horace Hone (1756–1825), miniaturist.
TT (1835) in a footnote added HNC's
opinion: "I wish this criticism were
enough to banish that vile miniature into
a drawer or cupboard. At any rate, it
might be detached from the glorious
masterpiece to which it is now a libellous
pendant." HNC's note was not repeated

in *TT* (1836), but no correction was made
in the epithet "French". Malcolm Cor-
mack, as Keeper of Paintings and Drawings, provided in 1973 the information
about it given in this note, but did not
know when Hone's work was removed
to the reserve.
[23] Sir James Scarlett (1769–1844),
Tory M.P., created 1st Baron Abinger in
1835. His speech was reported in *The
Times* 29 Jun 1833. He said that *The
Times* had merely said that the Leeds *Intelligencer* said that Cobbett was a bank-
rupt; that Cobbett's sales had gone up
after the libel; that Cobbett was a genius
who could afford to laugh. Let him, said
Scarlett, call them "the b——y old
Times" and let them respond with disapproval. Cobbett was awarded damages
of £160, a verdict, said *The Times*,
which "appeared to us to be received
with evident surprise by all who heard
the case".
[1] 1 Jul was a Monday. From 3 to 27
Jul C was at Ramsgate with the Gillman
family. *CL* VI 941, 948.
[2] "It is, perhaps, a piece of simplicity
to treat of Mandeville's work, as other
than an exquisite *bon bouche* of Satire &
Irony! But as there have been, and are,
Mortals and man-shaped Mortals too,
very plausible Anthropöeids, and who
have adopted his positions in downright

ask those man-shaped apes who have taken up his suggestions in earnest
and seriously maintained them as bases for a rational account of Man and
the World—how they explain the very existence of those dexterous
cheats, those superior charlatans, the Legislators and Philosophers, who
have known how to play so well upon the peacock-like*a* pride and follies
of their fellow fools.³   [36:537]

a h̶a̶b̶i̶t̶s̶ peacock-like

---

opake Earnest, it may be worth while to
ask—how? by what strange chance there
happened to start up among this premier
species of Ouran Outangs, yclept Man,
these *Wise Men* . . . who so cleverly
took advantage of this *Peacock* Instinct
of Pride and Vanity?'' C's annotation on
Bernard de Mandeville (1670–1733) *The
Fable of the Bees; or, Private Vices,
Publick Benefits* (2 vols 1724) I 35: *CM
(CC)* III. A transcript of C's note reportedly in RS's copy of Mandeville (now in
Yale) reads: "Can anyone read Mandeville's fable of the Bees, & not see that it
is a keen satire on the inconsistency of
Christianity & so intended? S.T.C." C
wrote those words, with "Christians"
for "Christianity" (RS traced over in ink
the original pencilled notes), in a work
he disliked intensely, *Hints to the Public
and the Legislature on the Nature and
Effect of Evangelical Preaching* by a
Barrister, i.e. James Sedgwick (4th ed
1808) 68: *CM (CC)* IV. A third copy of
Mandeville, 2 vols Edinburgh 1772,
owned by W. G. Boswell-Stone (*N&Q*
20 Sept 1902), sold at Sotheby's 29 Oct
1903, and described by Warren E. Gibbs
in *MLN* XLVIII (1933) 23, probably derives from *TT*—in which the entry in MS
B ends "fellow fools"; *TT* (1835) and
Gibbs read "Fellow mortals", a post-
mortal change that C is not likely to have
made. The annotation quoted above
shows that the French of *bonne bouche*,
"delicious morsel", is C's, corrected for
gender (cf C's letter of 31 May 1830: *CL*
VI 840). Mandeville, born in Dortrecht,
Holland, practised medicine in London,
where he wrote and published a poem
The Grumbling Hive (1705), included in
The Fable of the Bees (1714). A paragraph in *TT* (1835) quoted *The Grum-*

bling Hive lines 59–70 on lawyers, praising the lines, and another paragraph
praising the lines on doctors (lines 71–
84). Whether from C, this is a joke on
HNC, who was a Registrar of Voters for
the Northern Division and received 100
guineas from the Ipswich Election
Board. Bernard. Lord Coleridge *Story of
a Devonshire House* 303–4.
  ³ The direct philosophical descendants of Mandeville were the utilitarian
economists, whom C thought bestial
enough, but the paragraph that follows
(36:538) shows that he refers to the doctrine of evolution as it had descended
from Edward Tyson (1650–1708) *Or-
ang-Outang, sive Homo Sylvestris; or,
The Anatomie of a Pygmie* (1699), particularly by way of Lord Monboddo *Of
the Origin and Progress of Language*
"Of the Orang Outang" (6 vols 1774–
92) I 270–361. Again and again C attacked Monboddo's hominoid without
speech as a substitute for Adam. *CL* IV
574–5, VI 599, 723 and n; *P Lects* Lect 7
(1949) 239; *C&S (CC)* 66 and n, 218.
Usually, as in the remarks of 1 Jul, C associated the believers in simian ancestry
with peacocks, sometimes italicised, but
he made no mention of Sir Oran Haut-
Ton in Thomas Love Peacock's *Melin-
court* (1817), which not only quotes
Monboddo throughout but has transparent references to C, *The Friend*, and RS.
On C's rejection of temporal evolution
see 29 Apr 1830 n 1, above; *AR* (1825)
111–12; *P Lects* (1949) 423 n 14; George
R. Potter "Coleridge and the Idea of Evolution" *PMLA* L (1925) 389–91. Debating with M. F. X. Bichat at second hand
in 1821 C noted sportively that after a
higher power made man Nature was allowed to try "*her* hand—& she produced

Look at that head of Cline by Chantrey.[4] Is that forehead and nose, those temples and that chin, akin to the monkey-tribe? No, no. To a man of sensibility, no argument could[b] disprove the bestial theory so convincingly as a quiet contemplation of that fine bust.   [36:538]

It is odd that as yet no one has treated distinctly of that higher Logic which Passion authenticates, and which is very often at variance with the Logic of mere Syllogism and Grammar. No great Poet, such as Dante, Shakspeare or Milton, can be entirely appreciated without adverting to this reasonableness—as it were—of Passion.[5] What mountains of trashy criticism have been accumulated upon a supposed blunder of Shakspeare's—which so far from being any blunder at all, was itself admirable on account of the very incongruity of grammar—and dislocation of figure, which the profound men of the Johnsonian school condemned as false metaphor &c.[6]

---

b ca̶n̶ould

---

the Apes". *CN* IV 4829; cf the sober assertion, in *CN* IV 4984, of apes as degenerate from man.

[4] A marble bust of the surgeon Henry Cline (1750–1827) was left by the sculptor Sir Francis Chantrey (1781–1841)—knighted 1835—to the University of Oxford. There is a copy or version carved in 1813 at St Thomas's Hospital. C is pointing to a bust in the possession of Gillman at The Grove. In the lecture or essay known as "On Poesy or Art" of 1818 (the first part of the essay is based on lecture notes for Lect 13 of 10 Mar 1818: *CN* III 4397), C said that "a new field seems opened for modern sculpture in the symbolical expression of the ends of life, as in . . . Chantrey's children in Worcester Cathedral, &c"—*LR* I 227–8: *BL* (1907) II 260 (the passage is not in the lecture notes)—by which C refers to Chantrey's most celebrated work, a group of sleeping children in Lichfield Cathedral.

In several senses, Chantrey is the sculptor of medical men. C wrote to J. H. Green on 16 Jan 1819, "I am more and more delighted with Chantrey". On 5 May 1828 Green's friend Chantrey might be the one true Pygmalion. *CL* IV 911, VI 738. In the album verses *Love, Hope, and Patience in Education*

(1829), which describes the three graces of the title arranged as a statuesque group, a stanza later struck included the line, "On marble Lips, a CHANTRY has made breathe". *CL* VI 799n (C's note, for Sotheby); *PW* (EHC) I 482n. In "On Poesy or Art" C wrote: "The charm, the indispensable requisite, of sculpture is unity of effect." *LR* I 226: *BL* (1907) II 260. That C thought Chantrey possessed of the power of profound unity is clear from his remarks in *CN* IV 4630 and 5280 (on the bust of WW). For C on painting vs sculpture, in a conversation with Sir George Beaumont in 1804, see App F 27, below.

[5] This paragraph was not cancelled by a vertical line in MS B, has not survived in MS F, and was not published. C's own *Logic* does not engage the higher reasonableness of passion. He comes near in the contrast of the mental processes of Hamlet and Dame Quickley in *The Friend (CC)* I 450–6. He declared King Lear's despair in the storm "more terrific than any Michael Angelo inspired by a Dante could have conceived". Annotation on Shakespeare *Dramatic Works* ed Ayscough (1807) II 948: *CM (CC)* IV, used in Lect 6 of 28 Jan 1819: *Lects 1808–19 (CC)* II 333.

[6] "Johnson = the Frog-Critic—How

I cannot agree with all the solemn abuse poured out upon Bertram in All's Well that Ends Well.[7] He was a young nobleman in feudal times just bursting into *c*youth with all the feelings of pride of birth and appetite for pleasure and liberty natural to such a character. He had of course never regarded Helena otherwise than as a dependant in the family—and with all that which she possessed of goodness and fidelity and courage, which might atone for her inferiority in other respects, Bertram must necessarily have been ignorant.[8] And after all, her prima facie merit was having inherited a recipe from her old father the Doctor, by which she cures the King—a merit, which supposes an extravagance of personal loyalty in Bertram to make conclusive*d* to him in such a matter as that of taking a wife. Bertram had surely good reason to look upon the King's forcing him to marry Helena as*e* a very tyrannical act. Indeed it must be confessed that Helena's character is not very delicate, and it required all Shakspeare's consummate skill to interest us for her; and he does this chiefly by the operation of the other characters—the mother, Lafeu &c. We get to like Helena from their praising and commending her.[9]

[36:539]

c f 95   *d* ~~very winning~~ conclusive   *e* Word supplied by the editor, from *TT* (1835)

nimbly it leaps—how excellently it swims—only the fore-legs (it must be admitted) are too long & the hind ones too short—''. BM MS Egerton 2800 f 37, which may have been used in the 1808 lectures: *Lects 1808–19 (CC)* I 138.

[7] Particularly Johnson's last note on *All's Well That Ends Well* in *The Plays of William Shakespeare* (8 vols 1765) III 399: "I cannot reconcile my heart to Bertram; a man noble without generosity, and young without truth; who marries Helen as a coward, and leaves her as a profligate: when she is dead by his unkindness, sneaks home to a second marriage, is accused by a woman whom he has wronged, defends himself by falsehood, and is dismissed to happiness." A. W. Schlegel had answered that Bertram was a military portrait exposing the injustice of men towards women in the name of family honour, in a story that proves the power of women to overcome at last the violence of men. *Ueber dramatische Kunst und Litteratur* (1809–11) II ii 105.

[8] *TT* (1835) read: "in a great measure ignorant". C's brief surviving notes elsewhere—annotations on Shakespeare *Works* ed Theobald (1773) III 7, 25–9, 33, 57–8 and *Dramatic Works* ed Ayscough (1807) I 283, facing 286: *CM (CC)* IV—leave this paragraph as his most important statement on *All's Well*.

[9] In Act I Helena declares openly to others her love for Bertram, while confessing the distance of rank between them. She converses pertly of her virginity to Parolles; she will in time substitute herself when Bertram chooses to lie with Diana. On the prescription from her father, see I i 19–40, iii 225–62. The Countess, Bertram's mother, praises Helena at I iii 105–9, and Lefeu at II i 82–90. In II iii the King forces Bertram's consent. In his notes on the general characteristics of Shakespeare (BM MS Egerton 2800 f 40, probably used for Lect 5 of 10 Feb 1818), C cited this play as evidence of "Signal adherence to the great Law of nature, that opposites tend to attract and temper each other": "thus the Countess's beautiful Precepts to Bertram by elevating her character elevates

In Beaumont and Fletcher's tragedies, the comic[f] scenes are[g] never so interfused amidst the tragic as to produce a unity of the tragic on the whole, without which the intermixture is a fault. In Shakspeare, this is always managed with transcendant skill. The fool in Lear contributes in a very sensible manner to the tragic wildness of the whole drama.[10] Beaumont and Fletcher's serious plays or tragedies are complete hybrids—neither fish nor flesh upon any rules Greek, Roman or Gothic—and yet they are very delightful, notwithstanding.[11] No doubt they imitate the ease of gentlemanly conversation better than Shakspeare, who was not able *not* to be too *associated* to succeed completely in this.[12]   [36:540]

When I was a boy[h] I was fondest of Æschylus; in youth and middle age I preferred Euripides; now in my [i]declining years I admire Sophocles.[13] I

[f] comedyic   [g] is are   [h] boy &   [i] f 95[v]

---

that of Helena . . . & softens down the parent in her which Shakespear does not mean us not to see but to see & forgive and at length to justify''. *Lects 1808–19 (CC)* II 129. One of C's warmest memories of Dorothea Jordan was her recitation of *All's Well* III ii 102–32. VCL S MS 5 (3).

[10] The "never" at the beginning of this entry becomes "rarely" in *TT* (1835). With reference to *The Laws of Candy*, which he thoroughly disliked, C noted that Fletcher's comic scenes "not only do not re-act upon & finally *fuse* with, the tragic Interest, an excellence peculiar to Shakespere & Hogarth (see Lamb's Essay . . .) but they are dull & filthy in themselves—''. Annotation on Beaumont and Fletcher *Fifty Comedies and Tragedies: CM (CC)* I 366. A. W. Schlegel defended the Fool on the two grounds of comic relief and historical accuracy; he referred also to the Fool's wisdom. *Ueber dramatische Kunst und Litteratur* II ii 75–8.

[11] SC wrote to HNC 16 Nov 1836: "When I think of King and no King, Philaster, and the Beggars Bush, it does seem . . . that my father has so wound up his conception to an ideal of which Shakespeare was the type that he could tolerate nothing in the shape of a drama that was less than perfect, however beautiful in its own inferior line.'' UT Grantz

644. Beaumont and Fletcher are discussed often in the correspondence of SC and HNC. The TT of 1833, more obviously than in earlier years, reflects HNC's own interests in a way to suggest that he first steered C to certain topics. Entry 36:540 is the point of departure in Joseph W. Donohue Jr *Dramatic Character in the English Romantic Age* (1970).

[12] I.e. Beaumont and Fletcher would study and reproduce gentlemanly conversation *ab extra*, whereas it was too much a part of Shakespeare for his usual wise detachment?

[13] In a note on Milton's discussion of tragedy, which may be as early as 1807–8, C distinguished between the picturesque of Shakespeare and "the Statuesque—as Sophocles''; Sophocles produces "a Whole by the separation of Differents" rather than by harmonising them. Annotation on *B Poets: CM (CC)* I 72. When C generalised into "Ancients, statuesque—Moderns, picturesque" his debt to Schlegel is clear, and this way of contrasting ancients and moderns derives from Schiller for both Schlegel and C. BM MS 34225 f 167[v], which the editor of *Lects 1808–19 (CC)* I 492 connects with Lect 7 of 15 Dec 1812. See Schlegel *Ueber dramatische Kunst und Litteratur* I 15 (Lect I). At Cambridge, in 1792, C had borrowed *Aeschyli tragoediae* ed

can now at length see that Sophocles is the most perfect. Yet he never rises to the sublime simplicity of Æschylus—simplicity of design, I mean—nor diffuses himself inʲ the passionate outpourings of Euripides. I understand why the ancients called Euripides the most tragic of their dramatists; he evidently embraces within the scope of the tragic poet many passions—love, conjugal affection, jealousy and so on—which Sophocles seems to have considered incongruous with the ideal statuesqueness of the tragic drama. Certainly Euripides was a greater poet than Sophocles; his chorusses may be faulty as chorusses, but how beautiful and affecting they are as odes and songs. I think the famous—Ευιπ-που, ξενε &c of Sophocles[14] cold in comparison with many of the odes of Euripides—Εϱως, Εϱως in Hippolytus.[15]   [36:541]

There is nothing very surprising in Milton's preference of Euripides, though so unlike himself.[16] It is very common—indeed very natural—for

ʲ ~~into~~

Thomas Stanley (1663), then still the major edition, and his prize poem was especially influenced by Aeschylus. His Cambridge friend and rival, Samuel Butler, produced a new edition of Stanley's text and Latin translation with additional notes (4 vols Cambridge 1809–16). Minor notes on Aeschylus survive, *Agamemnon* ed (with English and German translations) by James Kennedy (Dublin 1829) and *Prometheus Vinctus* ed Charles James Blomfield (Cambridge 1810), H. F. Cary's copy, lent and returned. *CM (CC)* I 24–7. C had the text of all these poets in *Poetae graeci veteres* (Geneva 1614). For Hazlitt's tribute to C's conversation on the Greek tragedians see App F 28, below.

[14] *Oedipus at Colonus* 668–719. Tr R. C. Jebb 1886: "Stranger, [in this land] of goodly steeds". In a footnote *TT* (1835) quoted in Greek the first three lines of the chorus.

[15] *Hippolytus* 525–64. "Love, Love". In a footnote *TT* (1835) quoted in Greek the first five lines of the chorus. The entry as published then continued with praise of Euripides *Hecuba* 905–52 and in a footnote gave in Greek the first five lines of the chorus, with a translation of the entire chorus undersigned "J.T.C."

in *TT* (1835), changed in *TT* (1836) to a longer acknowledgement. Unfriendly reviewers would have been pleased to know that HNC's ms contained no mention of *Hecuba*. In 1824 C was reading *Orestes* in *Euripidis quae extant omnia* ed and tr Joshua Barnes (3 vols Leipzig 1778–88). *CN* IV 5136. *Gillman SC* No 471.

[16] "The books in which his daughter, who used to read to him, represented him as most delighting, after Homer . . . were Ovid's *Metamorphoses* and Euripides." Samuel Johnson "Milton" *The Works of the English Poets* (4 vols 1790) I 204. The original source was Deborah Milton Clark, who told Dr Thomas Ward, who told Birch in 1737: "Isaiah, Homer, and Ovid's metamorphoses were books, which they were often called on to read to their father . . .". *The Works of John Milton* ed Thomas Birch (2nd ed 2 vols 1753) I lxxvi. Thomas Newton added from Ward that Deborah, from reading aloud to her father, could recite passages from Homer and Ovid, "and another Gentleman has informed me, that he has heard her repeat several verses likewise out of Euripides". Milton *Poetical Works* (3 vols 1761) I lxxvi. William Hayley *The Life of Milton* (2nd

men to *like* and even admire an exhibition of power, very different in kind from any thing of their own. No jealousy arises. Milton preferred[k] Ovid too, and I dare say he admired both as a man admires a lovely woman, with a feeling into which jealousy or envy cannot enter. With Æschylus or Sophocles he might have *matched* himself.[17]   [36:541]

In Euripides you have oftentimes a very near approach to Comedy, and I hardly know any poet in whom you can find such models of serious and dignified conversation.   [36:541]

Newton was a great man, but you must excuse me if I think that it would take many Newtons to make one Milton.[18]   [36:545]

The collocation of the words is so artificial in Shakspeare and Milton that you may as well think [l]of pushing[m] a brick out of that wall with your finger as of displacing a word without injury from one[n] of their sentences.[o] Perhaps you may make the passage better—but it will be by changing it for something else.[19]   [36:542]

A good lecture upon style might be composed by taking on the[p] one hand the slang of L'Estrange and even of Roger North,[20] which became so

---

[k] ~~admired~~ preferred   [l] f 96   [m] pushing ~~the corner~~   [n] ~~the~~ a one
[o] sentences ~~of S~~   [p] the ~~extremes of~~

---

ed 1796), an edition C annotated, named (p 206) Euripides, Homer, Plato, and Sallust (above Tacitus) as Milton's favourites. Milton's own prose seems to treat Euripides, Sophocles, and Aeschylus more or less equally.

[17] Allusions to Ovid, especially to the *Metamorphoses* and *Fasti*, run throughout Milton's poetry and prose. "That Ovid among the Latin poets was Milton's favourite, appears not only from his elegiac but his hexametric poetry." Thomas Warton, quoted in Milton *Poetical Works* ed E. Hawkins (4 vols 1824) I 45–6.

[18] When Adam Sedgwick told SC in 1823 that Newton was a far greater man than Milton, shortly after she had been with C for the first time since childhood, she dissented, and retained the belief that Newton could be "far better estimated by one unlearned in mathematics and astronomy" than Milton "by one who

does not *understand* poetry". *Sara Coleridge and Henry Reed* ed Leslie Nathan Broughton (Ithaca, N.Y. 1937) 84. For C on Newton vs Milton see also 8 Oct 1830 n 4.

[19] The second sentence of this paragraph is omitted from *TT* (1835), and the first is qualified. C's emphasis is on the artfulness. *TT* (1835) quoted in a footnote the version HNC had published in his review of Aug 1834 in *QR*. *CH* 626.

[20] Sir Roger L'Estrange (1616–1704), Royalist pamphleteer and journalist; Roger North (1653–1734), lawyer, historian, politician until 1688. *TT* (1835) in a footnote called attention to C's near-exemption of North in *Friend (CC)* I 359–62. C wrote a note on the "full fragrance" of this "Black-guard Slang" or "Thames-Waterman's Language" in *The Emperor Marcus Antoninus His Conversation with Himself* and *The Mythological Picture of Cebes* tr Jeremy

fashionable after the Restoration as a mark of loyalty—and on^q the other the Johnsonian magniloquence^r or the^s balanced metre of Junius, and then showing how each extreme is faulty upon different grounds.[21]

It is quite curious to remark the prevalence of the cavalier slang-style in the Divines of Charles II. Barrow could not, of course, adopt such a mode of writing throughout, because he could not in it have communicated his elaborate thinking and lofty rhetoric; but even he not^t unfrequently lets slip a phrase here and there in the regular Roger North way— much to the delight, no doubt, of the largest part of his audience.[22] See particularly, for instances of this, his sermon on the Supremacy. South is full of it.[23]   [36:542]

^{q} ~~of~~ on ^{r} ~~pomposity~~ magniloquence ^{s} the ~~Gibbonian magniloquence~~ ^{t} ~~could~~ not

---

Collier: *CM (CC)* I 182–3. Yet on a flyleaf of the volume C defended Collier's style for "a Life, a Spirit, a Zest" absent from "the pompous enigmatic Jargon of modern Prose" introduced in Johnson's *Rambler*—C had been set off by Johnson's rejection of "colloquial barbarisms"—*CM (CC)* I 156 and n—as he seems to have been earlier in starting a list of "the true colloquial Barbarisms". *CN* I 666. SC provided a long note on L'Estrange in *BL* (1847) II 58–9 n 18. C called the phrase "what you would be at" the "only L'Estrange vulgarism" in Leighton at a period "when to write in loose slang had become a mark of loyalty". Annotation on *The Genuine Works of Archbishop Leighton* ed Erasmus Middleton (4 vols 1819) IV 245: *CM (CC)* III. Cf "A free and easy style was considered as a test of loyalty . . . as a badge of the cavalier party". Lect 14 of 13 Mar 1818: *Lects 1808–19 (CC)* II 235.

[21] HNC first wrote "Johnsonian pomposity or Gibbonian magniloquence", and then substituted Junius for Gibbon, either to create or to recapture from C a greater contrast among writers at the opposite pole from Restoration slang. On Junius see n 28, below.

[22] Isaac Barrow (1630–77), classical and mathematical scholar, noted for his sermons and his *Treatise of the Pope's Supremacy* (1680), and for resigning first a professorship of Greek at Cambridge and then one in mathematics in favour of his pupil Isaac Newton. C's set of "Barrow's Works: 2 Vol." went from Rydal Mount to DC; these may have been from *Works* ed John Tillotson (4 vols 1683–9). *WW LC* 316. C attended closely to Barrow's language, not for the first time, in 1802–3. *CN* I 1274–5, 1660. Noting in Nov 1803 Barrow's inferiority to Hooker and Taylor "in dignity of Style", he wondered why Barrow and Thomas Burnet wrote elegantly in Latin but in English were as "pert as their subjects & ideas would permit their words to be"; his explanation here also is loyalist aversion to the Puritans. *CN* I 1655. *SM* closes with a quotation from "the excellent Barrow" Sermon 20 from *Forty-five Sermons, upon Several Occasions: Works* III 229. *SM (CC)* 51–2.

[23] It was notably Barrow's *Pope's Supremacy* that C found "pert, frisky, & vulgar" in Nov 1803: "He seems to me below *South* in dignity—at least South never sinks so low as B. sometimes." *CN* I 1660. On Barrow see also 5 Jul 1834 second entry (36:659), below. Robert South (1634–1716) was court preacher from 1667. We hear of C's great interest in this subject in 1798–9: "Upon one occasion, he expatiated with suitable quotations, and no small display of note and comment, on the style and matter of our old English divines, from the dawn of the Reformation to the times of South and Barrow." Carlyon I 93. A note on South's sermon "Christianity

Johnson's fame now rests principally upon Boswell.[24] It is impossible not to be amused with such a book. But his bow-wow manner must have had a good deal to do with the effect produced;[25] for no one, I suppose, will set Johnson before Burke—and Burke was a great and universal talker—yet now we hear nothing of this except by some chance remarks in Boswell. The fact was, Burke, like all men of Genius who love to talk at all, was very discursive and continuous—hence he is not reported; for he seldom said the sharp short things that Johnson *almost always* *did,*[w] which produced a more decided effect at the moment and which are so much more easy to carry off.[26] Besides as to Burke's testimony to John-

u-w almost did   *v* f 96[v]

mysterious" f 51[v] (after 11 Sept 1831) was not used for *TT*; see 26 Oct 1831 n 1, above. Boswell reported Johnson's discussion of "the best English sermon for style" on 7 Apr 1778: "*South* is one of the best, if you except his peculiarities, and his violence, and sometimes coarseness of language." Boswell *Life of Johnson* ed G. B. Hill, rev L. F. Powell (6 vols Oxford 1934–51) III 248.

[24] James Boswell (1740–95) *The Life of Samuel Johnson, LL.D.* (2 vols 1791). Johnson's *Works* had been reprinted as frequently as the *Life* from 1791 until 1825, when there were three separate editions; more recently, *The Beauties of Johnson* ed Alfred Howard (1833) had sufficed. *TT* (1835) carried an advertisement for Murray's latest edition of the *Life*, "having for its ground work Mr. Croker's Edition of Boswell's Johnson", illustrated by Clarkson Stanfield (8 vols). On Macaulay's savage review of Croker's edition see 27 Dec 1831 n 6, above.

[25] *OED* cites for "bow-wow", among other examples, Scott's contrast of his own work with Jane Austen's, in his journal for 14 Mar 1826, published in 1832: "The Big Bow-wow strain I can do myself like any now going", and George Gilfillan's Introduction to the poems of James Beattie in 1854: "The deep bow-wows of Johnson's talk".

[26] C is saying here what he said more bluntly in a note of May 1808, that Johnson was "a man of *no genius*"; in fact, a man of "silly opinion"; of "pernicious

Opinion"; and an "inadequate Critic" and "bad Poet" (*Irene*). *CN* I 661, II 3214, III 3321; other instances of disparagement are listed in 3321n. In public references C achieved a similar effect less directly, as in praising "the beauty and independent worth of the citations" in Johnson's *Dictionary. Friend (CC)* I 52–3. In a note on *Gotthold Ephraim Lessings Leben* ed K. G. Lessing (3 pts in 2 vols Berlin 1793–5) II iii 281–2, C called Johnson's objection to imitative harmony, like nine tenths of his critical comments, "a mere sophism". *CM (CC)* III. By speaking of Johnson's "verbiage", C led Lady Beaumont in 1808–9 to share his disrespect for an author she had previously admired; Farington, who was told at second and third hand, obviously thought it an intriguing blasphemy. *Diary* IX 3278, 3289, 3425–6. In Lect 15 of 16 Jan 1812 C "excited a hiss once by calling *Johnson* a fellow'", for which he apologised, "observing that it was in the nature of evil to beget evil, and that he had . . . in censuring Johnson fallen into the same fault". *CRB* I 58: *Lects 1808–19 (CC)* I 398.

De Q, beginning in 1828, often contrasted Burke's organic style, in writing and conversation, with Johnson's mechanical style. *De Q Works* V 134, X 269–70. *TT* (1835) in a footnote came closer to the point in declaring C more continuous than Burke. In N 54 C contrasted as conversationalists himself as Aeolian harp and Johnson as single drum. *IS* 185. Much of the vigour of C's

son's powers, you must remember that Burke was a great courtier, and after all, Burke said and wrote more than once that he thought Johnson greater in talking than in writing—and even greater in Boswell than in real life.[27]   [36:544]

The style of Junius is a sort of Metre, the law of which is a balancing of thesis and antithesis.[28] When he gets out of this metre into a sentence of five or six lines long, nothing can exceed the slovenliness of the English.[29] But still the antithesis of Junius is a real antithesis of images or thought; but the antithesis of Johnson is very rarely more than verbal.[30]

[36:542]

---

attacks on Johnson must come from this self-aware contrast. HNC's note in *TT* (1835) also reports the comment on C as monologist by Mme de Staël.

[27] "As Johnson always allowed the extraordinary talents of Mr. Burke, so Mr. Burke was fully sensible of the wonderful powers of Johnson." When told he should have talked more, "O no (said Mr. Burke) it is enough for me to have rung the bell to him." Boswell *Life* ed Hill rev Powell IV 26–7. On Burke as dinner bell see 5 Apr 1833 (at n 22), above (36:478). Croker's edition of 1831 (v 212n) provided C with testimony: "Sir James Mackintosh remembers that, while spending the Christmas of 1797 at Beaconsfield, Mr. Burke said to him, 'Johnson showed more powers of mind in company than in his writings; but he argued only for victory; and when he had neither a paradox to defend, nor an antagonist to crush, he would preface his *assent* with *Why, no, Sir.*' " HNC's note in *TT* (1835), "said, I believe, to . . . Mackintosh", implies that he was unaware of Croker's note.

[28] Letters signed Junius, scandalously attacking George III and his ministers, appeared in the *Public Advertiser* 1769–72; as a book in *Junius* (1772, enlarged ed 3 vols 1812). There were many piracies. Speculation concerning the identity of the author was not ended by Byron's suggestion in *The Vision of Judgment* st 80 that he was "*really—truly*—nobody at all". De Q had written in *Bl Mag* XXIV (Dec 1828) 901–2 that Junius constructed sentences with "an elegance, which, after all, excluded eloquence and

every other *positive* quality of excellence", for "general terseness, short sentences, and a careful avoiding of all awkwardness of construction—these were his advantages". Cf *De Q Works* X 118–19. C annotated *The Letters of Junius* (1797), noting (pp 38–40): "Perhaps, the fair way of considering these Letters would be as a Kind of satirical Poems— the short, and for ever balanced sentences constitute a true metre; & the connection is that of satiric poetry, a witty logic, an association of ideas by amusing semblances of cause and effect . . . ". *CM (CC)* III.

[29] *TT* (1835) inserted here: "Horne Tooke and a long sentence seem the only two antagonists that were too much for him." Hazlitt wrote in "The Late Mr. Horne Tooke" *The Spirit of the Age* (2nd ed 1825) 112: "He no where makes so poor a figure as in his controversy with Junius. He has evidently the best of the argument, yet he makes nothing out of it." The controversy between Junius and Horne Tooke in the *Public Advertiser* 9 Jul–17 Aug 1771 included a plaintive Junius on 15 Aug: "I see the pitiful advantage he has taken of a single unguarded expression in a letter not intended for the public." *Junius* (2 vols 1805) II 142. Horne Tooke's victory is declared in Alexander Stephens *Memoirs of John Horne Tooke* (1813) 406–7.

[30] Cf Johnson never says "any thing in a common way. The best specimen of this manner is in Junius, because his antithesis is less merely verbal than Johnson's". Lect 14 of 13 Mar 1818: *Lects 1808–19 (CC)* II 237.

The definition of good prose is—Proper words in their proper places;—of good Verse[x]—the properest words in their proper places.[31] The propriety is of course relative. The words in prose ought to express the meaning and no more; if they attract attention to themselves, it is a fault. In the very best styles, as Southey,[32] you read page after page, understanding the author perfectly without once noticing the medium of communication; it is as if he had been speaking to you all the while. But in Verse you must do more; there the words, the media, must be beautiful and ought to attract your notice—yet not so much and so perpetually as to destroy the[y] unity which ought to result from the whole poem. This is the general rule, but of course subject to some modifications according to the different species of prose or verse. Some prose may approach towards Poetry, as Oratory, and therefore a more studied exhibition of the media may be proper; and some Verse may border more on mere narrative, and there the style should be simpler. [z]But the great thing in Poetry is to effect a unity of impression upon the whole; and a too great fulness and profusion of point in the parts will prevent this.[33] Who can read with pleasure more than a hundred lines or so of Butler at one time?[a] Each couplet or quatrain is[b] so whole in itself[c] that you can't connect them. There is no fusion; just as it is in Seneca.[34]   [36:542]

> [x] "Verse" is written over "Prose"   [y] the ~~total~~   [z] f 97
> [a] time ~~& yet how good & polished~~   [b] are   [c] themselves

[31] C had written to James Gillman Jr on 9 Nov 1832: "I was once asked for a definition of Good Prose and replied—'Proper words in their proper places.' And what then is good Verse, rejoined the Querist: and my answer was—'The *most* proper words in the *most* proper places.' " *CL* VI 928. Swift's words were widely known: "Proper words in proper places, make the true definition of style." *Letter to a Young Gentleman, Lately Enter'd into Holy Orders* (1721), in *Prose Works* IX (1948) 65. This is an example of one device of C's often counted as plagiarism. By way of Swift he hit upon a way to dramatise a definition of poetry, and the whole was too effective to sacrifice a part.

[32] Later precisionists would say "like" or "such as" Southey's, or three sentences further down, "as Oratory does". HNC recorded and retained throughout "as" plus noun.

[33] C is much less rigidly formulaic here than in the discussions of unity of impression in *BL* ch 14 *(CC)* II 14–15 and in Lect 2 of 21 Nov 1811: *Lects 1808–19 (CC)* I 206–7. *TT* (1835) introduced a Latin tag, *quocunque modo*, after the word "Poetry" in this sentence.

[34] In Lect 14 of 13 Mar 1818 C said that Seneca's thoughts, "striking as they are, are merely strung together like beads, without any causation or progression". *Lects 1808–19 (CC)* II 234. On Seneca, see also 25 Jun 1830 n 9, above. Samuel Butler (1612–80), author of the verse satire *Hudibras* (3 vols 1663–8). In the passage added to 1 Jul 1833 (at n 2) (36:527), above, lines from Mandeville are said to have "great Hudibrastic vigour". C cited *Hudibras* for wit and humour, and for modulations of metre, more often than for limitations and defects. *C 17th C* 145, 489, 526, 614–17, 661. C had lamented in one of his earliest poems, *Monody on the Death of Chatterton* (1790) lines 16–18: *PW* (EHC) I 13:

Imitation is the mesothesis of Likeness and Difference; the Difference is as essential to it as the Likeness, for without the Difference, it would be Copy or Fac-simile.[35] But, to borrow a term from astronomy, it is a librating mesothesis;[36] for it may verge more to Likeness as in Painting, or more to Difference, as in Sculpture.   [36:543]

It is a poor compliment to pay to a painter to tell him that his figure stands out of the canvas,[d] or that you start at the likeness of the portrait. Take almost any daub, and cut it out of the canvas[d] and place the figure looking in or out of a window, and any one may take it for life—or take one of Mrs Salmon's wax queens or generals, and you will feel the difference between a Copy, as they are, and an Imitation of the Human Form, as a good portrait ought to be.[37] Look at that flower vause of Van

---

[d] canvass

Ah me! yet Butler 'gainst the bigot foe
Well-skill'd to aim keen Humour's dart,
Yet Butler felt Want's poignant sting
. . .

[35] C distinguished imitation from copy with the same examples in a letter of 30 May 1814 to Charles Mathews on two approaches to acting and in a note on *The Tempest*. *CL* III 501 (cf VI 1038 to Byron, 1815); annotation on Shakespeare *Dramatic Works* ed Ayscough I sig b5, used for Lect 1 of 17 Dec 1818: *Lects 1808–19 (CC)* II 264. He was almost ceaseless in applying the distinction: e.g. *CN* II 2211, 2274; *BL* ch 18 *(CC)* II 72; BM MS Egerton 2800 f 21ᵛ, probably used in Lect 4 of 1 Apr 1808: *Lects 1808–19 (CC)* I 83. Versions of the distinction had been common since Aristotle. John Ruskin's rejection of the distinction made by Aristotle and C—*Modern Painters* pt I § 1 ch 4 (vol I 1843)—was rebutted by SC in a letter of 3 Jul 1850. *SC Memoir* II 329–30; *Sara Coleridge and Henry Reed* ed Broughton 50.

HNC's rearrangement of the talk of this date awkwardly divided the comments on imitation and copy; if for a good reason, then to make his point that C "had an eye, almost exclusively, for the ideal or universal" (36:456n).

[36] "LIBRATION, an apparent irregularity of the moon's motion, which makes

her appear to librate about her axis, in such a manner that the parts of her eastern and western limbs become visible and invisible alternately." Bonnycastle *Introduction to Astronomy* 431. On mesothesis see 18 Mar 1827 n 2, above.

[37] Mrs Salmon (1670–1760), one of the forerunners of Mme Tussaud. When Mrs Salmon and her husband moved from St Martin's-le-Grand to Fleet St near Chancery Lane, Addison celebrated the appropriateness of her shingle, a salmon, in *Spectator* No 28 (2 Apr 1711). Contemporary books with topographical plates of London include "Mrs Salmon's Waxworks" at this address or across the street, where she moved in 1795. The references usually cited are those by Boswell and Hogarth. Richard D. Altick *The Shows of London* (Cambridge, Mass 1978) 52–3. To make the same point Adam Smith cited the waxworks "of Mrs. Wright". "Of the Nature of That Imitation Which Takes Place in What Are Called the Imitative Arts" *Essays on Philosophical Subjects* ed Dugald Stewart (1795) 168. Waxworks illustrate the principle of similitude with difference more casually than C's example in his notes for Lect 13 of 10 Mar 1818: "The impression on the wax is not an imitation but a *Copy* of the Seal—the Seal itself is an Imitation". *CN* III 4397 f 50.

Huysum—and at these wax peaches and apricots. The last are likest to the original, but what pleasure do they give? None.[38]   [36:546]

I could write as good verses now as ever I did, if I were perfectly free from vexations and were in the ad libitum hearing of fine music, which has a sensible effect in harmonizing my thoughts, and *in animating and, as it were, facilitating my inventive faculty.[39] The reason of my not finishing Christabel is not that I don't know how to do it; for I have, as I always had, the whole plan entire from beginning to end in my mind;[40]

*f 97v

[38] Jan van Huysum (1682–1749), the most popular of a family of still-life painters. An authority of C's day noted of a Huysum sold in 1795, "Vase with Flowers. The merits of this artist are so well known, it is needless to say more than that it is a capital and beautiful picture." William Buchanan *Memoirs of Painting* (2 vols 1824) I 242. And another: "This illustrious painter has surpassed all who ever painted in that style, and his works excite admiration by their strict imitation of nature." John Gould *Biographical Dictionary of Painters, Sculptors, Engravers, and Architects* (new ed 2 vols 1838) I 239. In 1819 C counted Huysum among the great masters. *CN* IV 4630. The spelling "vause", obsolescent in 1833, may have recorded C's pronunciation; Byron rhymes the word with "grace" and "place" in *Don Juan* VI st 97. Do the wax peaches tell us something of Mrs Gillman? *TT* (1835) enlarged "None" to "None, except to children". In his discussion of copy vs imitation in Lect 1 of 17 Dec 1818, C asked "why we prefer a Fruit Piece of Vanhuysen's to a marble Peach on a mantle piece—or why we prefer an historical picture of West's to Mrs Salmon's Wax-figure Gallery". Annotation on *The Tempest* in Shakespeare *Dramatic Works* ed Ayscough I sig b5: *Lects 1808–19 (CC)* II 265. C thanked Eliza Nixon on 14 Jun 1834 for her gift of "sweet flowers so Van Huysum-like arranged". *CL* VI 984. In *TT* (1835) HNC attached a valuable note to 36:546 on C's knowledge of painting and music.

[39] He had not previously suggested that proximity to fine music would revive his song. On the survival of capacity, he oscillated. To Mrs Aders on 25 Mar 1823 he wrote what he had been saying off and on since 1802, "unused as for so many many years I have been to versifying of any kind, and dried up as, I fear, my poetic Spring will be found by the *severities* of austere Metaphysics"—he will nevertheless attempt to translate a single poem of Schiller's for a friend of hers. *CL* V 271. When Lady Beaumont urged him in 1828 "to resume Poetry", he scrawled on the margins of her request, as if in torment, that "scarce a week of my Life shuffles by, that does not at some moment feel the spur of the old genial impulse", but the same moment "awakes the Sense of . . . Life *unendeared*"; his mind now had a "*continuity*" that would have to be broken if he were to "begin anew". *CL* VI 731n. HNC received a more favourable response by not asking C to do something.

[40] C had noted on his birthday in 1823: "Were I free to do so, I feel as if I could compose the third part of Christabel, or the song of her desolation." *CN* IV 5032. Gillman gave us the events proposed by C for Cantos III and IV. Lamb, he said, urged C not to proceed. *C Life* (G) 301–3. In 1870, replacing SC's Preface to their edition of C's *Poems* (1852) with his own "Introductory Essay", DC gave in a footnote (p xliii) a version of C's intentions differing from Gillman's. The two are reprinted in *Christabel* ed EHC (1907) 32–3, 52n. For WW's comments on C's completing the poem see App F 29, below.

but I fear I could not carry on with equal success the execution of the Idea—the most difficult, I think, that can be attempted to Romantic Poetry—I mean witchery by daylight.[41] I venture to think that Geraldine, so far as she goes, is successful—but I doubt any one being able to go much farther without recourse to some of the common shifts. Besides after this continuation of the Faust, who can have courage to attempt a reversal of the judgment of all criticism against Continuations?[42] Let us except Don Quixote,*f* however—although the continuation is not uno flatu[43] with the original conception.

Some music is above me; most music is beneath me. I like Beethoven, Mozart, or some of the aerial compositions of the elder Italians, Palestrina &c. And I love Purcell.[44]   [36:546]

f ~~Cervantes~~ Don Quixote

[41] *TT* (1835) omitted the final clause, but HNC in a footnote called attention to the review (by himself) in *QR*. C noted during an electrical storm in Oct 1804: "Vivid flashes in mid day, the terror without the beauty.—A ghost by day time/ Geraldine." *CN* II 2207. WW's remarks to JTC (see App F 29, below) are among several indications that C often called the attention of friends to the daring of "witchery by daylight". An unpublished review, clearly by an intimate and thought to be by John J. Morgan, divides the summarising of the two extant parts with a comment: "We have hitherto seen the mysterious Geraldine shrouded in night; shown either by the uncertain light of a clouded moon, or by the glimmer of a dim and oscillating lamp;—at a time too when all nature around her was still, and at rest. The poet has now to introduce this supernatural being in the light, and joyousness of day. This difficulty has been overcome with great judgement, if we may not rather say, that, what was a difficulty, has been changed into a beauty." *W&C* 180. The first purported continuation, *Christobell*, in the *European Magazine and London Review* LXVII (Apr 1815) 345–6 was accepted as genuine by John Heraud in his "Reminiscences" of C, *Fraser's* X (Oct 1834) 394. *TT* (1835) carried a rebuttal by HNC (for which see also App F 29, below), dropped in 1836.

[42] Hayward's translation is probably referred to in the words "this continuation"; *TT* (1835) inserted (of *Faust* pt II) "which they tell me is very poor".

[43] "Of the same inspiration". Pt I of *Don Quixote* was published 1605, pt II 1615.

[44] Cf 5 Oct 1830 n 3, above. C wrote in N 52: "Yet I wish I did know something more of the wondrous mystery of this mighty *Art Magic*, were it but to understand why it is that ignorant as I am I should feel so utter, so extreme a difference between the Musical Compositions of Beethoven, Mozart, and our own Purcell for instance, and those of the equally celebrated Rossini and others which are just like nonsense verses to me, which I know to be meant for a Poem because I distinguish the rhymes." *IS* 214. Another time his list is "Haydn, Mozart, Cimarosa, and Beethoven". BM MS Egerton 2800 ff 66, 54–5: *IS* 156. *OED* defines "air", "aerial music", C's "aerial composition", as "song-like music" (1590) or "a piece to be sung as a solo with or without accompaniment"; the Elizabethan "ayre" was a simpler form of the madrigal. C mentioned Henry Purcell (1659–95), in C's day easily the most significant of English-born composers, in a comment on music in 1817. *CN* III 4337, echoed in *CL* IV 762. *TT* (1835) replaced the "&c" with Giacomo Carissimi (c 1604–74). HNC am-

God has taken for his share the best sort of music—sacred: the next best^g has fallen to the lot of the Devil—the military.⁴⁵ [36:546]

Good music never tires me, nor sends me to sleep. I feel refreshed by it and strengthened, as Milton seems to have been.⁴⁶ [36:546]

I am clear for public schools as the general rule, but for particular children private education may be proper. For moving in the best English society—I don't call the London exclusive clique the best society—*the defect of a* public education, upon the plan of our great schools and Oxford and Cambridge, is hardly to be supplied.⁴⁷ But the defect is visible positively in some men, and only negatively in others. The first offend you by habits and modes of thinking and acting attributable to their private education; in the others you only regret that the ease and freedom of the established and national mode of tuition is not added to their good qualities. [36:547]

I doubt the expediency of making even elementary mathematics a part of the routine in the system of the great schools.⁴⁸ Encouragement and fa-

---

^g best, ~~the military,~~   ^h f 98   ⁱ ~~the~~ ["a" supplied from *TT* (1835)]

---

plified in a note C's remarks on Palestrina and Carissimi. The preceding note by HNC in *TT* (1835) referred to C's "reverence" for Ludwig van Beethoven (1770–1827) and the prodigy known for short as Wolfgang Amadeus Mozart, in contrast with his "utter distaste" for Gioacchino Rossini (1792–1868), whom C would know for independent arias and probably chamber or piano music as well as his reputation in opera. C paid an involved compliment to Mozart in a letter of 24 Jan 1818 to the musical director William Ayrton and one to Beethoven in a letter of 9 Oct 1825. *CL* v 496, vi 1044. C quoted his own passage on the developmental strains of Cimarosa from *The Friend* in Lect 10 of his lectures on the history of philosophy. *Friend (CC)* i 129–30 (ii 111); *P Lects* (1949) 305–6. For an anecdote of 1818 of C and a musician, told by Gillman, see App F 30, below.

⁴⁵ Striking a more secular note in the margin of HC *Worthies*, C wrote: "Music is the Twilight between Sense and

Sensuality." *CM (CC)* ii 65.

⁴⁶ Most of the biographers had said that Milton, in Thomas Newton's words, "after dinner played on the organ, and either sung himself or made his wife sing". "Life" *Works* ed Hawkins (1824) i lxxxix. In another note on the same page of HC *Worthies* (see n 45, above), C called attention to Milton's Sonnet 20; he might have included No 13 to Henry Lawes. In *L'Allegro* lines 135–44 "soft Lydian Airs" are preferred; in *Comus* lines 84–8 a swain (like Lawes) with "soft Pipe and smooth-dittied Song" can "hush the waving Woods".

⁴⁷ "Defect": want, the lack of education from one of the "great schools". C's extended list of 1806, when he planned an essay on the pronunciation of Greek and Latin, included "Eton, Winchester, Westminster, St Paul's, Charterhouse, Christ's Hospital, Harrow, &c &c". *CN* ii 2859.

⁴⁸ The educational methods of Brougham and other utilitarians had begun to be considered by the masters of

cilities should be given, but not more, and I think more would *j*be thus effected*k* than by compelling all. Much less would I incorporate German or French or any modern tongue into the school labors.   [36:548]

S. T. C. 4. Aug. 1833.[1]

Dear Sir Walter Scott and myself were exact, but harmonious, opposites in this—that every*a* old ruin or hill or river called up in his mind a host of historical or biographical associations—just as a bright plate of brass, when beaten, attracts the swarming bees;[2] whilst, notwithstanding Dr

j-k be effected   *a* ~~he~~ every

---

the "great schools". On C's neglect of mathematics in his youth see JTC's report of C's TT 20 Apr 1811 and n 17, above. In a note to this entry in *TT* (1835) HNC quoted a marginal note of C's on Sir Francis Head (anon) *Bubbles from the Brunnens of Nassau* (1834). The identification was removed in 1836. See also 16 Apr 1834 n 8, below.

[1] From early July HNC and SC had been away from Hampstead. UT mss, DCL mss. After returning from Ramsgate, C was invited on 3 Aug to "a social evening" for the purpose of meeting Ralph Waldo Emerson, but declined on the plea of "pre-engagements". *CL* VI 949. Emerson's consequent visit to Highgate occurred on the 5th (or 4th). Emerson's letters concerning the visit are lost. Charles Emerson wrote on 6 Sept 1833: "I have a letter from Waldo dated Aug. 4. He has seen Coleridge." *The Letters of Ralph Waldo Emerson* ed Ralph L. Rusk (6 vols New York 1939) I 393. The discrepancy of dates is variously explicable. That C had seen a good deal of Mr and Mrs J. G. Lockhart at Ramsgate accounts for the subject of HNC's brief record of 4 Aug (Sun).

[2] The simile is more pointed for bees, as well as for Scott, than most of C's apian metaphors. C had written of himself in 1804: "Of all men, I ever knew, Wordsworth himself not excepted, I have the faintest pleasure in things contingent & transitory. I never, except as a

forced Courtesy of Conversation, ask in a Stage, whose House is that—nor receive the least additional pleasure when I receive the answer." *CN* II 2026 f 5ᵛ. In *LS* (1817) C had praised Scott's work for its "innocent, refined, and heart-bettering amusement" and its rivalry of RS in "the mass of interesting and highly instructive information scattered throughout". *LS* (*CC*) 210n. At first C thought too little of *The Lay of the Last Minstrel* (1805) to see any resemblance to *Christabel*. *CL* III 42. But C's friends began to tell him that Scott's thefts from *Christabel* in the *Lay* would ruin the sale of his own work when it came out. *CL* II 1191 and n. When the *Ed Rev* attacked C's poem in 1817 and the *QR* ignored it, C felt that Scott should repeat publicly his private praise. *CL* V 437. In 1820 Scott compounded his errors by misquoting unpublished verses of C's in *Ivanhoe*. In *Quentin Durward* ch 29 (1823) C found another mangled theft. *CL* IV 716, V 379–81; annotation on the novel in *Novels and Romances of the Author of Waverley* (7 vols Edinburgh 1825) VII 236: *CM* (*CC*) IV. When C thought it too late, Scott paid tribute to *Christabel* in the 1830 edition of the *Lay*, though censuring him for "caprice and indolence" in depriving "charming fragments" of completion that his "extraordinary talents" made desirable. Nevertheless, the "but harmonious", inserted above the line in MS B, is part of C's view of their

Johnson, I really believe I should walk over the plain of Marathon without taking[b] more interest in it than any other plain of similar features.[3]
Yet I receive as much pleasure in reading the account of the battle in Herodotus, as any one can.[4] Charles Lamb[c] wrote an essay on a man who
lived in past time;[5] I thought of adding another to it of one, who lives not
in *time* at all, past, present or future.   [36:549]
    Walter Scott was such an excellent and noble creature, and his genius
and acquirements were so great and peculiar, that in common society I
should always give him unqualified praise. Amongst friends I would
venture to say that I think his poetry not worth much.[6]

Mrs Lockhart's[d] vivacity of expression hides her prettiness of feature.
You must catch a glimpse at her when she is calm.[7]

> [b] ~~receiving the least pleasure~~ taking   [c] C. Lambe   [d] L's

---

symbiosis. On Scott's private praise see
C Life (G) 278–9. By the time of Scott's
bankruptcy in 1826, C's sympathy for
the person had run out. *CL* vi 562–3,
602–3. When Scott found SC at Keswick
"really a lovely vision of a creature",
she responded by finding him "like an
old, lame, fat, honest, good-natured admiral". *C Fille* 39.

[3] "The man is little to be envied,
whose patriotism would not gain force
upon the plain of Marathon, or whose
piety would not grow warmer among the
ruins of *Iona*." Samuel Johnson *A Journey to the Western Islands of Scotland*
(4th ed 1785) 347.

[4] Herodotus 6.102–20. WW, visiting
at Ambleside on 11 Jul 1844, was asked
if this entry gave a true picture of C's
mind. "At first Mr. Wordsworth said,
'Oh! that was a mere bravado, for the
sake of astonishing his hearers!' but
then, correcting himself, he added, 'And
yet it might in some sense be true, for
Coleridge was not under the influence of
external objects. He had extraordinary
powers of summoning up an image or a
series of images in his own mind, and he
might mean that his idea of Marathon
was so vivid, that no visible observation
could make it more so.' " *W Prose*
(1876) iii 442.

[5] One must repeat HNC's note in *TT*

(1835): "I know not when or where". In
the spirit noted by HNC, Lamb wrote to
Bryan Waller Procter 22 Jan 1829: "I am
born out of time. . . . When my sonnet
was rejected, I exclaimed, 'Damn the
age; I will write for Antiquity!' " *LL* iii
203.

[6] Pleasure from the novels, pleasant
encounters with the Lockharts, and the
personal manner of "Dear Sir Walter"
kept C mollified. All the major poets of
the time held a similar opinion of Scott's
poetry. It was, said WW, "altogether superficial", with "very little productive
power" and crowded with inversions. *W
Prose* (1876) iii 445, 457, 462. C found
Scott's novels lacking in "that sort of
Prose which is in fact only another kind
of Poetry", of which Laurence Sterne
provided examples. *CL* vi 778.

[7] Scott's daughter, Charlotte Sophia
(1799–1837), who married John Gibson
Lockhart in 1820. The Lockharts, who
usually went to Brighton, went to Ramsgate for their holiday in 1833; C was with
her on the 12th, 24th, and probably other
days in July; on the 26th he gave her a
lesson in metrics and wrote to Green that
"Scott's favorite Daughter" was "truly
an interesting and love-compelling
Woman". *CL* vi 942–7. Lockhart's
biographer describes her as subdued but
"clever, in an intuitive, feminine way

*a*10. Aug. 1833. S. T. C.

A person nervously weak has a sensation of weakness, which is as bad to him as muscular weakness; the only difference is the chance of removal.[1]   [36:550]

Some of the richest land in England for grain is in the isle of Thanet; the rents are very high and the farms much sought after; but the farmer's*b* life is a very anxious one, his stake is so high.[2]

Hooker and Bull being read in the Jesuit colleges is a curious instance of the power of mind over the most profound of all prejudices.[3]   [36:551]

There are permitted moments of exultation through Faith when we cease to feel our own emptiness, save as a capacity of our Redeemer's fullness.*c*[4]   [36:551]

a f 98ᵛ   *b* ~~stake is~~ farmers's
c Following this entry HNC copied verses of C's, on ff 98ᵛ–9; see n 4, below

---

that reproduced her father's deep wisdom". Marion Lochhead *John Gibson Lockhart* (1954) 149. The entries on Scott and on his daughter were cancelled with a vertical line in MS B, but they were not published and have not survived in MS F.
[1] Upon his return from Ramsgate, where he had benefited from "Dyasson's Warm Salt Shower-Baths", C recommended that HNC provide SC with six or eight weeks of such a place. *CL* vi 948.
[2] A vertical line through f 98ᵛ includes this sentence, but it was not published. The Isle of Thanet, in the northeast corner of Kent, includes Ramsgate, Broadstairs, and Margate.
[3] MS F for 8 Oct 1830 on the Athanasian creed says: "Pray look at the preface to my Jesuits' edition of Bull in Latin, & you will see what they think of him." See 8 Jul 1827 n 2, above, and *CN* i 800.
[4] Although exaltation through faith may have come up in a discussion of Hooker or Bull, there is a division mark of 3 mm in MS B; in *TT* (1835) the division fell between pp 226–7 and was lost for later editions by the compositor of *TT* (1836).

Following this entry in MS B, ff 98ᵛ–99, HNC transcribed *My Baptismal Birthday* and lines 28–34 of the hexameters "William, my teacher, my friend!" beginning "O what a life is the Eye". *PW* (EHC) i 490–1 (var), 305 (var). C recited the birthday verses to Emerson 5 Aug: *English Traits* (1856) 7. On the 10th the statement ending in "our Redeemer's fullness" could have led to the birthday verses in reference or recital of the whole. This recent metrical experiment would lead by association to the earlier. In *My Baptismal Birthday* line 10 here reads:

Make war against me! On my front I show

i.e. "front" as in *Friendship's Offering* (1834); *PW* (1834) ii 152 reads "heart". In *Hexameters*, differing from text and variants given by EHC and as written by C in Böhme *Works—CM (CC)* i 672—line 31 reads: "(Yea! and he smiled on the breast as the babe that smiles in his slumber)". *TT* (1836) inserted at this point 36:552, on a poet's need for "a species of applause".

*a*14. Aug. 1833. S. T. C.[1]

I always made a point of associating images of cheerfulness and light-someness with death and the grave, when instructing my children.[2] To be sure, I believe little Hartley did astonish a party of very grave persons, *b*his aunt's*c* connections, who asked him if he had learnt any hymns, by saying*d* that Papa had taught him a pretty Resurrection Hymn, which he repeated with great glee as follows:*e*

> "Splother! splother! splother!
> Father and mother!
> Wings on our shoulders—
> And Up we go!"[3]

---

*f*The Quakers educate upon a principle of suppressing all appearance of passion, where the exhibition of it can be injurious to their worldly interests; but they neither teach nor practise any inward subduing of the appetites; and accordingly they are the most sensual of any race of men I ever knew, within the sanction of certain public ordinances.[4] A*g* Quaker

a f 99   *b-e* For the variant in MS F see App C, below   *c* ~~mother's~~ aunt's
d ~~replying affirmatively~~ saying   *f-j* For the variant in MS F see App C, below   *g* ~~The~~ A

[1] This Wednesday's conversation provided so much copy that in the published version the entries spread over five days. Self-consciousness induced by Lockhart made C apologise almost two weeks later to Anne R. Scott, Sir Walter's niece, for releasing on her "the supposed excess of my intellectual powers". *CL* VI 959. With HNC he could open all the stops.

[2] In *BL* ch 22 C had objected to WW's lines in the *Intimations* Ode on the child's view of the grave as "but a lonely bed without the sense of light" and the implication therefore that the child in *We Are Seven* thought the dead to be "lying in a dark, cold place". C protested that a child of six "would have been better instructed in most christian families". *BL (CC)* II 140–1. WW removed from the Ode the four lines C objected to, but *We Are Seven* was irreparable on this point. Their difference was psychological as well as religious. DW made a journal entry after she and WW lay side by side in a trench on 29 Apr 1802—a critical time for that circle—as "both lay still, and unseen by one another; he thought that it would be as sweet thus to lie so in the grave, to hear the *peaceful* sounds of the

earth, and just to know that our dear friends were near". *DWJ* (1958) 152.
[3] "Qu +", in pencil on this entry in MS F, is a query probably by DC. The entry was not published.
[4] C's attack of 3 Jan 1834, below (36:614), on the Quaker system of faith was published with no mitigation. This assault on their commercial character, slightly moderated in MS F, was reduced to three brisk sentences in *TT* (1835). HNC added a sentence to MS F on the violence of Quakers during the recent election; if C made the remark, the source of his understanding was almost certainly HNC. C had felt *The Friend* hedged by his dependence upon Quakers for subscribers and readers—*(CC)* I 102 (II 69), 244 (II 169), II 18 n 3; *CL* III 15–19—and had paid them the double-edged compliment in 1817 that among Quakers, "if anywhere", we "may expect to find Christianity tempering commercial avidity". *LS (CC)* 185. He was more favourable in a marginal note on Marcus Aurelius—*CM (CC)* I 176—and earlier in the *M Post* 18 Dec 1801: *EOT (CC)* III 71–2.

is made up of Ice and Flame—he has no composition, no kindly mean temperature, no Christian gentleness and cheerful charity. Hence he is never interested about any public measure, but he becomes a downright fanatic, and oversteps in his furious irrespective zeal every decency and every right opposed to his course. Of course there are some exceptions, especially amongst the women, but I believe what I say is true of Quakers in general—and I have seen a good deal of them.[5]   [36:553]

*h*Their affecting not to pay tithes is actual dishonesty; they buy for a price calculated on its*i* payment. *Their* duty is to pay their own debts: they have nothing to do with the dedication of the money, the tenth part, which is not theirs, nor formed any part of their purchase. In truth the Quakers, who, though they pretend to be persecuted, are and have been the most petted of the Protestant sects, cultivate with intense correctness a little worldliness of their own: and I once ventured to tell a party of them that I thought they were like a string of double hunched camels trying to get through a needle's eye.[6]

I have never known a trader in philanthropy, who was not wrong somewhere or other: individuals so distinguished are usually unhappy in their family relations—men *not* benevolent to individuals, but almost hostile to them, yet lavishing money and labour and time on the race, the abstract notion.*j*[7]   [36:554]

When I read the eleventh chapter of Romans to that fine old man Mr Montefiore at Ramsgate, he shed tears.[8]   [36:555]

h f 99*v*   *i* ~~the~~ its   *j* See *f-j*, above

[5] C's earliest known problem was with Charles Lloyd (1775–1839). The "exceptions" must at least have included William Allen (1770–1843), lecturer at Guy's Hospital 1802–26 (*CL* iii 144, 170, 493–5). On 21 Apr 1811, above (JTC's records), he claimed that attendance at one Quaker meeting in Cambridge had cured his enthusiasm. For a possible linkage with Thomas Clarkson see HCR's report of C's remarks of 11 Jun 1811, App F 31, below.

[6] C represents himself as assigning Quakers twice the difficulty of getting into heaven that Christ ascribed to the merely rich man in Matt 19.24.

[7] Although a separate entry in *TT* (1835), this sentence continues the discussion of Quakers. *TT* (1835) added a harsh Coleridgian sentence on patriotism

vs cosmopolitism, along the lines of *The Friend* No 24 *(CC)* ii 323–4 (i 292–4); *SM (CC)* 63; and *CN* iii 3654 f 8. In 1809 an "ingenious and eloquent Philanthropist" meant a Burdettite. *CL* iii 210–11. Cf *Watchman (CC)* 139 and n. The funeral sermon for John Owen by a friendly acquaintance of C's, Joseph Hughes *Attachment to Life* (1822), had associated the highest philanthropy with the British and Foreign Bible Society.

[8] *TT* (1835) expanded the reading to Rom 9, 10, 11. All three chapters concern Paul's hope for conversion of the Jews to Christianity. We must assume a transition in the talk from false Quaker philanthropists to the father of a true Jewish philanthropist, Sir Moses Haim Montefiore (1784–1885). With the name a blank, *TT* (1835) inserted "Jew of sen-

The two images farthest removed from each other which can be comprehended under one term, are, I think, Isaiah—"Give ear O Earth" &c[9]
and Levi of Holywell Street—"Old Clothes!"—both of them *Jews*! Im-
mane quantum discrepant![10]   [36:556]

I consider Sallust's two works—especially the Catilinarian conspiracy—
romances founded on facts; no adequate causes are stated, and there is no
rcal continuity of action.[11] In Thucydides, you are aware from the beginning that you are reading the reflections of a man of great genius and experience upon the characters and operation of the two great political principles in conflict in the civilized world in his time; his narrative of events
is of minor importance to you and it is evident that he selects for the purpose of illustration. It is Thucydides himself, whom you read throughout, under the names of Pericles and Nicias &c.[12] [k]But in Herodotus it is
just reverse. He has as little subjectivity as Homer—and delighting in the
great fancied epic of events, he narrates them without impressing anything of his own mind upon the narrative. It is the charm of Herodotus
that he gives you the spirit of his age—of Thucydides that he reveals to
you his own, which was above the age.[13]

[k] f 100

---

sibility". C's visits to Ramsgate in 1819,
1822, 1824, 1825, and 1828 (*C at H* 90,
138) were renewed in July of this year
1833. Daniel Stuart wrote to HNC 7 Oct
1835 that he had given C "30£ per summer to go to the seaside, to the amount in
all of about 200£". VCL S MS F 6 f 7.

[9] Isa 1.2. A footnote in *TT* (1835) told
of C's memorisation of much of Isaiah,
although he was "remarkably deficient
in the technical memory of words".

[10] Horace *Odes* 1.27.6 (var). "Their
discrepancy is monstrous".

[11] Gaius Sallustius Crispus (86–c 34
B.C.), Roman historian and political par-
tisan of Julius Caesar. Two monographs,
History of the Jugurthine War and *Conspiracy of Catiline*, have come down in-
tact; only fragments remain of his *History of the Roman Republic*. Sallust
followed Thucydides closely as a model.
Some assessments grant to his work unusual fidelity to documentary sources,
others find inaccuracy. Gibbon ch 31
mentioned the palace of Sallust in order
to say in a footnote that he "usefully

practised the vices which he has so eloquently censured".

[12] Thucydides 1.22 said of the great
set speeches, which are dramatically
placed, that in default of exact memory
he made the speakers say what was
called for in each situation.

[13] This, not only an unusual contrast
of the two foremost Greek historians,
might seem also to reverse C's conclusions, as reported by HNC as C's Lect 10
of the 1818 series, wherein Thucydides
describes particular evils and "Herodo-
tean history . . . attempts to describe human nature itself on a great scale as a
portion of the drama of providence". *LR*
I 152–3. Most of the lecture is actually
taken from C's notes on Dante and his
age, for Lect 5 of 11 Mar 1819, in N 29,
with interpolations, possibly from other
sources, such as this on Thucydides and
Herodotus. See *CN* III 4498 and n; *Lects
1808–19 (CC)* II 394. In brief, "all history must be providential". *CIS* (1840)
7. The purpose of history, C wrote to
J. H. Frere 6 Jun 1826, "is to exhibit the

The difference between the composition of a history in modern and ancient times is very great; still there are certain principles upon which a history of a modern period may be written, neither sacrificing all truth and reality like Gibbon nor*l* descending into the mere anecdotal.*m*14

[36:557]

———

Gibbon's style is detestable; but his style is not the worst thing about him.15 His history has proved an effectual bar to all real familiarity with the temper and habits of imperial Rome; few or none read the original authorities, even those which are classical—and certainly no distinct knowledge of the actual state of the empire can be obtained from Gibbon's rhetorical sketches. He takes notice of nothing but what may produce*n* an effect; he skips on from eminence to eminence without ever taking you through the valleys*o* between; in fact his work is a collection of all the splendid anecdotes which he could find in any book concerning any persons or nations from the Antonines to the capture of Constantinople. When I read a chapter in Gibbon I seem to be looking through a

l or   *m* anecdotieal   *n* be produce   *o* vallies

___

moral Necessity of the Whole in the freedom of the component parts: the resulting Chain necessary, each particular link remaining free''; Hume, Gibbon, and William Robertson show the necessity as the old annalists show the freedom of the links; in "Herodotus, and the Hebrew Records, alone both are found united". *CL* vi 583.

14 C's polarities nearly always point to reconciliation in the middle way. Gibbon becomes the type of modern historian with a thesis to expound. C opposed anecdotes without significant illustration for history or biography; cf *Friend* No 7 *(CC)* ii 107 (i 181), ii 286 (i 357); *SM* and *LS (CC)* 14, 153. There is a valuable note on C's views of history in *CM (CC)* i 795 n 1.

15 C had objected for at least three decades to Edward Gibbon (1737–94) *The History of the Decline and Fall of the Roman Empire* (6 vols 1776–88). He drew upon Gibbon for one of his earliest lectures: *Lects 1795 (CC)* 169–71 and nn. In May 1810 he noted some of the defects in Gibbon that a tutor should point out to a pupil, from "the monotonous and ef-

feminate structure of his Periods'' and his periphrastic artifice, through his "truly gallican'' references to sexual appetite, and on to the most execrable, Gibbon's sneers at Christianity: "Yet with all these faults he is still our greatest Historian . . . & compared with Hume in any light but that of a natural style, he is to be canonized''. *CN* iii 3823; entries 3814–22 are further reactions to Gibbon. C also owned John Whitaker *Gibbon's History of the Decline and Fall of the Roman Empire . . .* (1791), in which Gibbon's organisation is complained of more than his style, which is often "stiff, affected, and latinised'' (p 15). Whitaker 1–5 may have contributed to the classification of historians in Lect 10 of 1818, as reported by HNC. *LR* i 152–3. Richard Porson's defence of Gibbon in *Letters to Mr. Archdeacon Travis* (1790), which C read (see 29 Dec 1822 nn 7–8, above), worried in the Preface (xxix–xxxii) over Gibbon's verbosity, waste of elegance and splendour on trifles, occasional obscurity, and refusal to acknowledge error, as in his controversy with Henry Edwards Davis in 1779.

luminous haze or fog, figures come*ᵖ* and go, I know not how or why, all
larger than life or distorted or discoloured; nothing is real, vivid, true; all
*�q*is scenical and by candle light as it were. And then he calls it a history
of the Decline and Fall of the Roman Empire. Was there ever such a
gross misnomer? I protest I do not remember a single attempt made
throughout the work to investigate the causes of the decline or fall of that
Empire.*ʳ* How miserably deficient is the narrative of the important reign
of Justinian!¹⁶ And that poor piddling*ˢ* scepticism— which Gibbon mis-
took for Socratic philosophy—has led him to misstate*ᵗ* and mistake the
character and influence of Christianity in a way which even an avowed
Infidel or Atheist could not have done. Gibbon was a man of immense
reading, but he had no philosophy, and he never fully understood the
principle upon which the best of the old historians wrote. He attempted
to imitate their artificial construction of the whole work—their dramatic
ordonnance of the parts—without understanding that their histories were
intended more as documents illustrative of the truths of political philosophy than as mere chronicles of events.

The key to the declension of the Roman Empire is*ᵘ* the Imperial Character overlaying and finally destroying the National Character. Rome under Trajan was an Empire without a Nation.*ᵛ*¹⁷   [36:557]

———

I like Johnson's political pamphlets better than any other part of his
works; particularly his Taxation no Tyranny is very clever and spirited,
though he only sees half of his subject, and that not in a very philosophical manner.¹⁸ Plunder—Tribute—Taxation are the three gradations of

ᵖ ~~pass~~ come   *q* f 100ᵛ   *ʳ* Empire. ~~You are told of barbarians & tyrants & transgresses of~~
ˢ pidling   *ᵗ* mistate   *ᵘ* ~~was~~ is   *ᵛ* Nation. ~~As a mfe of course, it fell before the attacks~~

¹⁶ Chs 40–4. Gibbon stigmatised Justinian as "not the most conspicuous object of his own times" (ɪᴠ 320). C wrote
a note on a later edition for James Gillman Jr on Gibbon's "absurd misappli-
cation of the understanding". *CM (CC)*
ɪɪ 844.

¹⁷ Jeremy Taylor's *Polemicall Discourses* i 1030–5, for reasons not clear,
set C to supplying some of the deficiencies in Gibbon's enumeration of the reasons for the spread of Christianity. Part
of this marginal note is congruent with
36:557: "The zealous Despotism of the
Cæsars with the consequent exclusion of
men of all ranks from the great interests
of the Public Weal . . . This extinction

of Patriotism aided by the melting down
of States and Nations in the one vast yet
heterogeneous Empire . . . sufficient to
preclude all living interest in the peculiar
institutions and religious forms of Rome
. . .". *CM (CC)* v.

¹⁸ *Taxation No Tyranny; an Answer to
the Resolutions and Address of the American Congress* (1775) in Samuel Johnson
Works (11 vols 1787) x 93–143. Cf x
100: "A tax is a payment exacted by authority from part of the community for
the benefit of the whole. From whom,
and in what proportion such payment
shall be required, and to what uses it
shall be applied, those only are to judge
to whom government is entrusted."

action by the sovereign on the property of the subject; the first is mere violence, bounded by no law or custom, and is properly an act only between conqueror and conquered, and that too in the moment of victory: the second supposes law, but a law proceeding only ʷfrom, and dictated by one party, the conqueror; by it he consents to forego his right of plunder upon the conquered giving up to him a fixed commutation: the third implies compact, and negatives any right to plunder—taxation being professedly for the direct benefit of the party taxed, that by paying a part, it may through the labors and superintendence of the sovereignˣ be able to enjoy the rest in peace. As to the right to tax being only commensurate with direct representation, it is a fable, falsely and treacherously brought forward by the Whigs, who knew its hollowness well enough.[19] You may show its weakness in a moment by observing that not even the universal suffrage of the French or Benthamites avoids the difficulty; for although it may be allowed to be contrary to decorum that women should legislate, yet there can be no reason why women should not choose their representatives to legislate; and if it be said that they are merged in their husbands, let it be allowed, where the wife has no separate property; but where she has a distinct taxable estate, in which her husband has no interest, what right can her husband have to choose for her the person whose vote may affect her separate interests? Besides, at all events, a single unmarried adult woman of age, possessing a £1000 a year, has surely as good a right to vote, if Taxation without representation is tyranny, as any man in the kingdom.[20] The truth of course is that direct representation is a chimera, impracticable in fact, and useless or noxious if practicable.   [36:558]

In Paradise Lost—in every one of his poems—it is Milton himself whom you see; his Satan, his Adam, his Raphael—they are all John Milton, and it is a sense of this intense egotism that gives me the greatest pleasure in reading Milton's works.[21]   [36:562]

ʷ f 101   ˣ sovran

[19] Johnson (x 121) made an appeal to "virtual representation"; specifically against the colonists he had been sarcastic (x 118): "The necessary connexion of representatives with taxes, seems to have sunk deep into many of those minds, that admit sounds without their meaning." In *TT* (1835) "Whigs" became "those". In a letter to HNC of 23 Feb 1832 C had bemoaned Joseph Hume's tie of taxation to direct representation. *CL* vi 884–5.

[20] For "man" *TT* (1835) substituted

"ten-pounder", meaning a voter under the Reform Act. On votes for women, see 21 Nov 1830 n 6, above. The fuller argument here indicates that C's earlier suggestions were meant seriously. In a note on RS *The Doctor* (vols i, ii 1834) ii 61, C objected to the "Nothingizing of the Female" when the name is absorbed "into the name and family of the Husband". *CM (CC)* iv.

[21] This is similar to what C had said of Thucydides, just above. It is Keats's

Horne Tooke was once holding forth on language, and turning to me asked me[y] if I knew what the meaning of the final *ive* was in English words.[22] I said I thought I could tell what he, Horne Tooke, thought himself. "Why, what?" said he.[z] "Vis"[23] I replied, and he acknowledged I had guessed right. I told him however that I could not agree with him and believed the final *ive* came from *ick*, vicus, οἶκος—the root [a]denoting collectivity and community, and was opposed to the final *ing*, which signifies separation, particularity and individual property, from ingle, a hearth or one man's place of rest: οἶκος, vicus, denoted an aggregate of ingles. The alteration of the *c* or *k* of the root into the *v* was evidently the digamma,[24] and hence we have the *icus* and ivus indifferently as finals in Latin.[25] The precise difference of the etymologies is apparent in the phrases:—The Lamb is sportive—i.e. has a nature or habit of sporting. The Lamb is sporting—i.e. the animal is now performing a sport. Horne Tooke upon this said nothing to my etymology, but I believe he found he could not make a fool of me as he did of Godwin and some others of his butts.[26]   [36:559]

---

[y] me ~~what my opinion was~~   [z] H.T.   [a] f 101[v]

"egotistical sublime", but not the spectator *ab extra* that C declared WW and Goethe to be. On 26 Mar 1804 the painter James Northcote reported that when he had called Milton ambitious, arrogant, and tyrannical in C's presence, C answered that Milton "was next *to our Saviour in Humility*". Farington *Diary* VI 2277. HCR heard C 23 Dec 1810: "We spoke of Milton. He was, said Coleridge, a most determined aristocrat, an enemy to popular elections, and he would have been most decidedly hostile to the Jacobins of the present day. He would have thought our popular freedom excessive. He was of opinion that the government belonged to the wise, and he thought the people fools. In all his works there is but *one* exceptionable passage,—that in which he vindicates the expulsion of the members from the House of Commons by Cromwell. Coleridge on this took occasion to express his approbation of the death of Charles. "Of Milton's 'Paradise Regained,' he observed that however inferior its kind is to 'Paradise Lost,' its execution is superior. That was all Milton meant in the preference he is said to have given to his

later poem. It is a didactic poem, and formed on the model of Job.
    "Coleridge remarked on the lesson of tolerance taught us by the opposite opinions entertained concerning the death of Charles by such great men as Milton and Jeremy Taylor." *CRD* I 162–3; cf the draft version in *CR (BCW)* 35–6.
    Stimulated by James Gillman in Sept 1820, C made a subtler distinction with regard to Milton's ego in the poetry: "the *Poet* appearing & wishing to appear *as* the *Poet*—a man likewise". *CN* IV 4714.
    [22] English -*ive* is an adoption from French *if*, feminine -*ive*, from Latin -*ivus*. *OED*. This entry connects with two lists in the notebooks 1820–6. *CN* IV 4754, 5307.
    [23] "Power".
    [24] In *TT* (1835) "the work of the digammate power".
    [25] With this entry as a prominent example, Joshua H. Neumann protested: "Coleridge's etymologies frequently run far afield, the worst of them recalling the famous etymological blunders of Carlyle and Ruskin." "Coleridge on the English Language" *PMLA* LXIII (1948) 651.
    [26] See 7 May 1830 n 15, above. God-

How very absurd the conduct of the Scotch Kirk has been with regard to poor Irving! They might with ample reason have visited him for the monstrous indecencies of those exhibitions of the Spirit—perhaps they would not have been justified in overlooking such disgraceful breaches of decorum—but to excommunicate him for his language about Christ's body is very foolish.[b][27] Irving's expressions are highly inconvenient and in

---

[b] foolish. ~~In the first place~~

---

win accepted the taunts philosophically. C. Kegan Paul *William Godwin: His Friends and Contemporaries* (2 vols 1876) I 147, II 105–6, 144. HNC seems never to have heard C say anything interesting about another member of that circle, Thomas Holcroft, playwright, translator, friend of Godwin and Lamb. For Cottle's report of C's remarks on Holcroft in 1807 see App F 32, below.

[27] On Irving, his language, and his troubles see 9 May 1830 nn 11–12, above. When the Scottish Presbytery of London, acting for the Kirk of Scotland, decided against Irving, *The Times* of 3 May 1832 had said more harshly what C said here: Irving's own utterances were harmless until "he entered into partnership with knaves"; the Caledonian Chapel in Regent Square would now be closed to "unknown tongues". More recently Irving's views of the corporal essence of Jesus had been condemned by the Presbytery of Annan. Thomas Moore had listened at Lockhart's on 9 Nov 1833 to C's account of the problems: "Was too far from Coleridge, during dinner, to hear more than the continuous drawl of his preachment; moved up to him, however, when the ladies had retired. His subjects chiefly Irving and religion; is employed himself, it seems, in writing on Daniel and the Revelations, and his notions on the subject, as far as they were at all intelligible, appeared to be a strange mixture of rationalism and mysticism. Thus, with the rationalists, he pronounced the gift of tongues to have been nothing more than scholarship or a knowledge of different languages; said that this was the opinion of Erasmus, as may be deduced from his referring to Plato's Timaeus on the subject. (Must

see to this.) Gave an account of his efforts to bring Irving to some sort of rationality on these subjects, to 'steady him,' as he expressed it; but his efforts all unsuccessful, and, after many conversations between them, Irving confessed that the only effect of all that Coleridge had said was 'to *stun*' him,— an effect I can well conceive, from my own short experiment of the operation." *Memoirs, Journal, and Correspondence* ed Lord John Russell (8 vols 1853–6) VII 7–8.

C reported to Green at the end of May 1830 that he had talked during the recent, second visit of Thomas Chalmers about Irving's "unlucky phantasms"; the presence of Scottish ladies kept him from going beyond his squib on Mackintosh to say that "while other Scotchmen were content with Brimstone for the Itch, Irving had a rank itch for Brimstone". *CL* VI 840. Like Trench on 10 Oct 1832 (above), McLellan had heard only sympathetic words on 27 Apr 1832 of "our once dear brother laborer in Christ, Rev. Mr. Irving": "Never can I describe how much it has wrung my bosom. I had watched with astonishment and admiration the wonderful and rapid development of his powers. Never was such unexampled advance in intellect as between his first and second volume of sermons, the first full of Gallicisms and Scoticisms, and all other cisms. The second discovering all the elegance and power of the best writers of the Elizabethan age. And then so sudden a fall, when his mighty energies made him so terrible to sinners." *Journal* 231. Only the reference to style here sounds like C's own language.

bad taste, but his meaning such as it is, is orthodox—as is plain enough to common reason.[c] The body of Christ—as body only[28]—was not capable of sin or righteousness,[d] any more than my body or yours; that his humanity had[e] a capacity of sin follows from its own essence. He was of like passions as we—and was tempted. How *could* he be tempted, if there was no formal capacity of falling?[29]   [36:561]

Johnson had neither eye nor ear—for Nature, therefore, he cared, as he knew, nothing. His knowledge of town life was minute, but still imperfect as not contrasted with the better life of the country.[30]   [36:558]

It is very extraordinary that in our translation of the Psalms, which professes to be from the Hebrew, the name Jehovah—ὁ ὤν—the Being or God—should be omitted, and instead of it, the Κύριος or Lord of the Septuagint adopted. The Alexandrian Jews had a superstitious dread of writing the name of God—and put Κύριος—not as a translation, but a mere mark or sign—everyone understanding for [f]what name it really stood. We who have no such feeling ought surely to restore the Jehovah, and thereby bring out in the true force the testimony of the Psalms to the divinity of Christ, the Jehovah[g] or manifested God.[31]   [36:560]

---

[c] reason. ~~I never understood Irving to say that Xst.~~

[d] ~~virtue~~ righteousness   [e] ~~was~~ had   [f] f 102   [g] ~~manifested~~ Jehovah

[28] *TT* (1835) inserted "or rather carcass (for body is an associated word)". John Ranicar Park (1778–1847), stimulated by *LR*, elicited from SC a correspondence on this subject in 1839–40. C rejected, SC wrote, a division between material body and immortal spirit: "My father on the contrary believed that man is ⟨essentially⟩ a spiritual being, whose invisible substance contains the principles both of spirituality (that is of intelligent personality—reason) and of animality, which last power is the efficient cause of the phænomenal body." UT Grantz 1179.

[29] *TT* (1835) added here a paragraph on Irving's rhetoric, with a simile from Thomas Fuller. See 36:561 n 1.

[30] This Wordsworthian analysis of Johnson's limitations is consolidated in print with the earlier remarks on Johnson. Why is it exactly where it is in MS B?

[31] God is named as Jehovah 5321 times in the Hebrew text of the OT, but only four times in AV. The name is made of the tetragrammaton JHVH, with the vowels of Adonai, which means "Lord," added as a reminder that it should be read aloud as Adonai. Both names are translated as Κύριος in the Septuagint and as "LORD" in AV. AV, however, follows Luther in distinguishing the two typographically, using LORD (sometimes GOD) for Jehovah. The restoration of Jehovah, "which expresses the divine existence", was recommended by William Newcome *An Historical View of the English Bible Translations* (Dublin 1792) 316–17 (see 17 Aug n 22, below). This interpretation of the name was traditional, being implied by Exod 3.14: Ἐγώ εἰμι ὁ ὤν (Septuagint)—"I Am that I Am" (AV). (The form Jehova is rejected and the etymology doubted by more recent scholars.) C's interpretation of ὁ ὤν in John 1.18, Rom 9.5, and elsewhere as confirming a

Claudian deserves more attention than is generally paid to him.[32] He is the link between the old classic and the modern way of thinking in verse. You will observe in him an oscillation between the objective poetry of the ancients and the subjective mood of the moderns. His power of pleasingly reproducing the same thought in different language is remarkable—as in Pope.[33] Read particularly the Phœnix, and see how the single image of renascence is varied.[34]   [36:563]

---

traditional identification of Christ with the Jehovah of the OT appears to be his own. See *CM (CC)* I 460–1, *CN* IV 5256, and nn. An entry in N Q ff 13ᵛ–14ᵛ on the subject, referring to Ps 37, was probably written about the time of this entry in TT. *TT* (1835) included a long footnote to forestall possible charges of plagiarism from *Remains of . . . Daniel Sandford* (1830) I 207 (see 5 Jul 1834 n 13, below). HNC dealt similarly with C's handling of Col 1.13–20 in *SM—(CC)* 44 and n—and in another passage of C's from "long before he knew that the late Bishop Middleton was of the same opinion". Sandford I 165 cited Middleton on "begotten before all creatures" in a diary entry dated 22 Dec 1825. C may have taken his explanation of Κύριος from William Newcome *An Historical View of the English Biblical Translations* (Dublin 1792) 316–17—see 17 Aug n 22, below. Newcome said that יְהֹוָה "the word Jehovah, which expresses the divine selfexistence", was not known until the sixteenth century, but " אַרְיָ Jah" was there in the Bible to be properly translated. Newcome quoted William Green (c 1714–94) *Poetical Parts of the Old Testament* (Cambridge 1781), which C may also have known: "It seems better to retain the original word Jehovah, than to translate it LORD. First, because it is the peculiar and incommunicable name of God. Secondly, because being his titular name too, the propriety of it is more observable when opposed to the Gods of the heathen, as it frequently is." Newcome 317. For C's similar approach to the interpretation of John 1.18 see *CM (CC)* I 460–1 and nn.

[32] Claudius Claudianus (c 370–c 408), the last classical poet of eminence. C's copy, *Cl. Claudiani quae exstant* ed Nikolaas Heinsius (Amsterdam 1650), was given to him by RS in Jun 1810, went next to WW and then to HC. *WW LC* 323. Thomas Arnold transcribed C's note from the book in 1884: *CM (CC)* II 44–5. Late in 1805 C was reminded of Claudian by modern poets anxious "to be always *striking*": Claudian, "who had powers to have been any thing—observe in him the anxious craving Vanity! every Line, nay, every word *stops*, looks full in your face, & asks & *begs* for Praise". *CN* II 2728. When C received the Elzevir edition in 1810, he was struck at once with the *Vita* (*CN* III 3876) and then for several years quoted in the *Courier* from the poems: *EOT (CC)* II 184, 187, 389, 393, 403. C translated much of Claudian's elegiac verse (ed unidentified) into very literal English for retranslation into Latin by Henry (and possibly James) Gillman c 1824–5. Berg Collection NYPL "Notes on Latin Elegiac Verse Making". One couplet reappears in *PW* (EHC)'I 1009 in Latin and in English, adapted and addressed to Eliza [Nixon], a young Highgate friend and neighbour. On Claudian see also 2 Sept 1833 (at n 17), below.

[33] C is not known to have praised this ability in marginalia on Pope (Copy A of *B Poets* VIII, which included Pope, was lost early on: see *CM—CC*—I 39).

[34] *The Phoenix*, Idyll 1 (Amsterdam 1650) 233–6. C quoted lines 34 as the motto on the title-page of *The Friend* (1818) and lines 49–54 (var) on 9 Dec 1814. *Friend (CC)* I 1; *EOT (CC)* II 410. In *Omniana* No 177 (1812) II 30 he published the wish "to see Claudian's splendid Poem on the Phoenix translated into English verse in the elaborate rhyme and gorgeous diction of Darwin". In a footnote in *TT* (1835) HNC gave several passages from the poem; see 36:563.

17. Aug. 1833.

I think highly of Sterne—that is, of the first part of the Tristram Shandy; for as to the latter part about the widow Wadman it is stupid and disgusting—and the Sentimental Journey is poor sickly stuff.[1] There is a great deal of affectation in Sterne to be sure; but still the characters of Trim and the two Shandies are most original and delightful. Sterne's morals are bad—but I don't think they can do much harm to any one whom they would not find bad enough before. Besides the oddity and erudite grimaces under which much of his dirt is hidden take away the effect for the most part; although to be sure the book is scarcely readable by women.[2]

[36:564]

Men of Humor are always men of Genius;[3] Wits rarely are so, although a man of Genius may amongst other gifts possess Wit, as Shakspeare.

[36:565]

[1] Laurence Sterne (1713–68) *The Life and Opinions of Tristram Shandy, Gentleman* (9 vols 1760–7); *A Sentimental Journey Through France and Italy, by Mr. Yorick* (2 vols 1768). Uncle Toby's "affair with widow Wadman" is mentioned in *Tristram Shandy* bk III ch 24; Corporal Trim (see next sentence) has an important rôle in the courtship of Toby and the widow, bks VIII–IX.

[2] In a footnote in *TT* (1835) HNC added a further comment on the superiority of Walter Shandy and the inferiority of the *Sentimental Journey*. In notes for Lect 9 of 24 Feb 1818 on Rabelais, Swift, and Sterne, on humour as a "disproportionate *generality*" given "universality", as in Mr Shandy, for in humour "the Little is made great and the great Little in order to destroy both", C praised the "moral *good* of Sterne", but censured him for making "the best dispositions of our nature the pandars & Condiments for the basest". *Lects 1808–19 (CC)* II 172–3, 174. In Lect 7 of 25 Mar 1819, on Cervantes, he again defined humour, and its congeniality with pathos, "so exquisite in Sterne & Smollett", as "a certain reference to the General, and the Universal, by which the finite great is brought into identity with the Little, or the Little with the Finite Great, so as to make both *nothing* by comparison with the Infinite". *CN* III 4503: *Lects 1808–19 (CC)* II 417. Much of this came from Jean Paul Richter (*CN* III 4503n), but not C's particular responses to Sterne. He found Sterne's sexual knowingness, his "dallying with the Devil", to be severely censurable, but to arise in part from every humourist's inclination to pardon or palliate "All follies *not selfish*". BM Add MS 34225 ff 68, 79, notes for Lect 9 of 1818: *Lects 1808–19 (CC)* II 174, 173. He was less tolerant in a contrast of 1809 between brutalising the affections with Pope or dissolving "all bonds of morality by the inevitable Shocks of an irresistible Sensibility with Sterne". *CN* III 3562. He borrowed a copy of Sterne for the lecture of 1818 (*CL* IV 1045), and his other references are usually from memory. In most of the allusions after 1819 Sterne leads the list of the great English novelists of the eighteenth century in a plan of C's to show how they differed from Scott—*CL* V 25, 33–4, VI 602, 778—notably in "that sort of Prose which is in fact only another kind of Poetry, nay, of metrical Composition, tho' metre *incognito*, such as Sterne's Le Fevre, Maria, Monk &c". In *Logic (CC)* 110 C cited *Tristram Shandy* bk V ch 43 for its parody of James Harris *Hermes*.

[3] ". . . Cleverness is a sort of Genius

Genius must have Talent as its complement and implement, as Imagination must have Fancy; in short, the higher intellectual powers can only act through a corresponding energy of the lower.[4]   [36:566]

I quite agree with Strabo, quoted by Ben Jonson in his splendid dedication of the Fox[5]—that there can be no great poet who is not a good man, though not perhaps a *goody*[a] man.[6] His heart must be pure: he must have learned to look into his own heart, and sometimes to look *at* it; for how can [b]he who is ignorant of his own heart, know any thing of, or be able to move, the heart of any one else?[7]   [36:568]

Rossetti's[c] view of Dante is in great part just; but he has pushed it beyond all bounds of common sense.[8] How could a poet—and such a poet as

a goodly   *b* f 102[v]   *c* Rosetti's

---

for instrumentality. It is the brain in the hand. In literature Cleverness is more frequently accompanied by wit, Genius and Sense by humour." *Friend (CC)* I 420; cf *CL* IV 667. In keeping with the qualification in *The Friend*, *TT* (1835) said "always in some degree". Julian Young, though he gave an exception, complained: "I have heard Coleridge say, more than once, that no mind was thoroughly well organized that was deficient in the sense of humour: yet I hardly ever saw any great exhibition of it in himself". *Memoir of Charles Mayne Young* 116.

[4] Cf C's objection to WW's Preface of 1815: ". . . he has mistaken the co-presence of fancy with imagination for the operation of the latter singly. A man may work with two very different tools at the same moment; each has its share in the work, but the work effected by each is distinct and different." *BL* ch 12 *(CC)* I 294.

[5] *The Works of Ben Jonson* ed William Gifford (9 vols 1805) III 162 and n, dedication of *Volpone; or, The Fox* to "The Two Famous Universities". In a footnote *TT* (1835) gave the Greek of Strabo (c 63 B.C.–A.D. c 24) *Geography* 1.2.5. C had copied the passage into a notebook in 1801 *(CN* I 1057) and used it in *Omniana* No 126 and in Lect 14 of 13 Mar 1818: *Lects 1808–19 (CC)* II 241 J. H.

Green cited *TT* for the passage in his Hunterian Oration (1847).

[6] HNC received a note in what appears to be HCR's hand: "Another time he replied to some commonplace sentimental morality 'Oh Sir you mistake it altogether—That is not goodness, that is goody-ness'—The Goody is in your T: T:". VCL S MS S F 11.3. I.e. he is reminded of the anecdote by entry 36:568, but the wording may be a comment also on *TT* (1835) as a whole. C used the word "goodiness" in the *Courier* 20 Jan 1810 (earliest appearance in *OED*) and later. *EOT (CC)* II 91, 364, 390; *CL* III 531; *CN* IV 5131.

[7] A characteristic shift of self-knowledge from the head to the heart. In a ms addition to *The Friend* for Thomas Allsop C wrote for the "Youthful Reader": "O learn early, that if the Head be the Light of the Heart, the Heart is the Life of the Head; yea, that Consciousness itself . . . is but the Reflex of the Conscience, when most luminous . . .". *Friend (CC)* I 523n.

[8] Gabriele Rossetti (1783–1854), Italian poet and political exile from Naples; professor of Italian in King's College, London, since 1831; father of four Victorian writers of note. At the instigation of J. H. Frere, who had known Rossetti in Naples and Malta, C recommended him to H. F. Cary on 13 Dec 1824, the

Dante—have written the details of the allegory as conjectured by Rossetti?[d] The boundaries between his allegory and his pure picturesque are plain enough, I think at first reading.[9]   [36:576]

---

[e]Lord Grey has contrived to unite the two worst modes[f] of governments—or at least to exercise them by alternation—an unprincipled[g] cabinet despotism in quiet seasons as now with regard to the Bank,[10] and[h] the base spirit of democracy in[i] times of popular violence.[j]

---

[d] Rosetti?   [e-j] For the variant in MS F see App C, below   [f] ~~forms~~ modes

[g] ~~an imperious~~ unprincipled   [h] & ~~a wild~~   [i] ~~of &~~ in   [j] See [e-j], above

---

first year of Rossetti's residence in London. *CL* v 403–4. In the same letter C recommended with some irony the ms, in which Rossetti "believes himself to have the filum Ariadneum in his hand", which soon became the work referred to in 1833, *La Divina Commedia . . . con comento analitico di Gabriele Rossetti* (2 vols 1826–7). Rossetti found in the *Inferno* an allegory expounding the doctrines of a secret, secular freemasonry. HCR observed on 27 Mar 1832, "Cary is by no means a convert to the opinions of Rossetti". *CRB* I 405. Some of the friendlier reactions to his interpretations are reported in E. R. Vincent *Gabriele Rossetti in England* (Oxford 1936) 36–66. Rossetti followed the "comento analitico" with *Sullo spirito antipapale, che produsse la riforma: disquisizione* (1832), which discovered a similar message in Petrarch and Boccaccio. Herman Merivale reviewed both works indulgently in *Ed Rev* LV (Oct 1832) 531–51. Rossetti gave C a copy of *Sullo spirito* and some poems in ms later to be published in *Versi* (Lausanne 1847). It is not clear that C took an opportunity in 1825 at the George Freres' "to hear the more of Signor Rossetti's poem". *CL* v 431.

[9] In 1796–7 C held the then conventional view of Dante Alighieri (1265–1321) as epitomising "the gloomy Imagination". *Watchman* 25 Mar 1796 *(CC)* 133; review of M. G. Lewis *Ambrosio; or the Monk* (1796) in *C Rev* Feb 1797. *MC* 372. In Feb 1804 WW provided a Dante at C's request, *Dante* ed Pompeo Venturi (3 pts Lucca 1732)—*CM (CC)* II

132—which remained with WW c 1810–c 1830. *WW LC* 324. In 1817, after listening on the beach at Littlehampton to C's views of Homer, H. F. Cary gave him a copy of his translation, *The Vision; or Hell, Purgatory, and Paradise* (3 vols 1814), in which C had been quoted in the Preface. C praised the translation in his lectures on Dante in 1818 and 1819. *Lects 1808–19 (CC)* II 185–6, 395. Adding to his Preface in the 2nd ed of 1819, Cary wrote that C's promotion of the work had made the new edition possible. On 11 May 1818 C had brought Cary together with the publishers Taylor and Hessey to sign an agreement for a new edition. Robert Wylie King *The Translator of Dante . . . Henry Francis Cary (1772–1844)* (1925) 118–19. C made deferential corrections in the 1819 edition: *CM (CC)* II 133–8. WW said: "Ariosto and Tasso are very absurdly depressed in order to elevate Dante." *W Prose* (1876) III 465. SC was afraid rather that the elevation of Dante would cloud the proper sense of Milton's superiority. *BL* (1847) II 24–9 n 13. HCR noted on 22 Nov 1831: "I read Cary's *Life of Dante*—insignificant—and looked into his translation. I fear it will rather retard than promote my study of the great poem." *CRB* I 394.

[10] Earlier in the year Viscount Althorp, Chancellor of the Exchequer, had dissolved a secret committee of inquiry and undertaken personal negotiations with officials of the Bank of England; on 31 May he brought before the Commons an agreement by which the monopoly of

To resolve Laughter into an expression of Contempt is contrary to fact, and laughable enough.[11] Laughter is a convulsion of the nerves; and it seems as if Nature cut short the rapid thrill of pleasure on the nerves by a sudden convulsion of them, to prevent the sensation becoming painful.[12] Aristotle's definition is as good as can be: Surprise at perceiving[k] any thing out of its usual place, when the unusualness is not accompanied by a sense of serious danger.[13] *Such* surprise is always pleasurable; and it is observable that surprise accompanied with circumstances of danger becomes tragic. Hence Farce may often border on Tragedy; indeed Farce is nearer Tragedy than Comedy is.[14]   [36:577]

---

[k] ~~seeing~~ perceiving

---

the Bank was to end in return for the provision that notes of the Bank for amounts £5 and above were to be legal tender except at the Bank. The parliamentary debate of June–July had resumed in August. This entry was moderated in MS F, but not published.

[11] "*Sudden Glory*, is the passion which maketh those *Grimaces* called LAUGHTER; and is caused either by some sudden act of their own, that pleaseth them; or by the apprehension of some deformed thing in another, by comparison whereof they suddenly applaud themselves." Thomas Hobbes *Leviathan* pt 1 ch 6 (1651) 27. Hobbes's earlier statement of the point in *Human Nature; or the Fundamental Elements of Policie* (1650) was taken up by Addison in *Spectator* No 47 (24 Apr 1711).

[12] When De Wette in *Theodor* wrote that laughter comes merely from contradiction or absurdity, C responded in the margin: "Laughter is a physical phænomenon: and must be physically explained. . . . It is the Law of Pleasure to pass into Pain, and this is especially the case where . . . the nerves are unprepared & withdrawn from the control of the Will: and Laughter is the nascent Convulsion by which Nature breaks off the train of sensations before they reach a painful state." *CM (CC)* II 191. David Hartley, although he did not use the word convulsion specifically in this connexion, described laughter as "a nascent Cry", a "Surprize, which brings on a momentary Fear first, and then a mo-

mentary Joy in consequence of the removal of that Fear". *Observations on Man* (1749) I 252, 437. Hazlitt, drawing either from C or from C's sources, defined laughter as "convulsive and involuntary movement, occasioned by mere surprise or contrast". Lect 1 on wit and humour in *Lectures on the Comic Writers* (1819): *H Works* VI 6.

[13] Francis Hutcheson quoted *Poetics* 5.1 on comedy in his refutation of Hobbes, Addison, and Mandeville in *Reflections upon Laughter, and Remarks upon the Fable of the Bees* (Glasgow 1750) 5: "some mistake, or some turpitude, without grievous pain, and not very pernicious or destructive". Most works on laughter quoted instead Aristotle *Nicomachean Ethics* 4.8–9 on unseemly ridicule as a sort of vilification, but Aristotle does not there "resolve" all laughter into this kind to be avoided. A theory of surprise entered with Cicero *De oratore* 2.71, in which laughter, though having as its province baseness and deformity, arises when expectation is deceived.

[14] With reference to *The Comedy of Errors*, C gave a neutral definition: "A proper farce is mainly distinguished from comedy by the license allowed, and even required, in the fable, in order to produce strange and laughable situations. The story need not be probable, it is enough that it is possible. . . . In a word, farces commence in a postulate, which must be granted." *LR* II 114–15; *Sh C* (1960) I 89.

Hebrew is so simple, its words are so few and near the roots, that it is impossible to keep up any adequate knowledge of it without constant application. The meanings of words are chiefly traditional.[15] The loss of Origen's Heptaglott Bible, in which he had written out the Hebrew words in Greek characters, is the heaviest Biblical literature has ever experienced. It would have fixed the sounds as known at that time.[16]

[36:570]

Animals have the vowel sounds; Man only can utter consonants. It is natural therefore that the consonants *[l]*should be marked first—the framework of the word—and no doubt a very sensible living language might be written quite intelligibly to the natives without any vowel sounds marked. The words would be recognized as in short hand, thus—Gd crtd th Hvn nd the rth. I wish I understood Arabic; and yet I doubt whether to the European philosopher or scholar it is worth while to undergo the immense labors of acquiring that or any other Oriental tongue.[17] [36:571]

Men of genius are rarely much annoyed by the company of vulgar people; because they have a power of looking at such persons as objects of amusement,*[m]* of another race altogether.[18] [36:567]

[l] f 103   *[m]* amusement— ~~keeping~~

[15] Luther based his rules for translating the Bible on the realisation that the "majestical and glorious" Hebrew of the early books was not only free of the compound words that mark Greek, Latin, and German, but with Moses and David was plain and simple, with few of the "colored and figured words" introduced by Solomon. *Colloquia Mensalia* 501–2. On C's attention to Hurwitz *The Elements of the Hebrew Language* (1829) see *CM (CC)* II 1188–90 and nn.

[16] See n 17, below, also 3 Jan 1834 (at n 26), below.

[17] Origen's *Hexapla* consisted of the OT in Hebrew with a transliteration into Greek characters and up to seven Greek translations in columns side by side, with the Septuagint in the centre. It is possible that no complete copy was ever made from the massive original ms. Eichhorn *AT* ch 2 § 68 I 146–8 argued that the earliest texts of the OT could have been written and understood without vowels, as were the early texts of the Koran, while modern Persian was still

easily read without them, and that this must to some extent have been the case with the *Hexapla*, for he adduced words in which the vowels in Origen's transliteration differed from the correct ones. Later, *AT* ch 2 § 113 I 331–5 and ch 3 §§ 168–9 I 331–5, he frequently called the work a "Polyglotte", cited Jerome (who used the original ms), listed variant readings, and described how Origen collected the Greek versions, giving alternative names ranging from *Tetrapla* to *Enneapla*, but no *Hexapla*, nor, of course, *Heptaglott*.

[18] C (as reported) seems momentarily to have forgotten what awareness of the impermanency of his own powers led him to retort against Friedrich Schlegel's assertion that genius, unlike talent, is what one is, not what one has: "I assert the contrary viz. that the Man of Genius *has*, not is, a Genius. . . . We *are* it only while we have it, as our pitying Angel, whom yet we may alienate." Annotation in *Athenaeum: CM (CC)* I 149.

I should never be very forward in offering*n* to pour spiritual consolation into*o* any one in distress or disease;[19] I believe, to be of any service, such resources must be self-evolved in the first instance. I am something of the Quaker's mind in this, and am inclined to *wait* for the Spirit.   [36:573]

The most common effect of this mock evangelical spirit, especially with young women, is Self Inflation and Busy Bodyism.[20]   [36:574]

How strange and awful is the synthesis of life and death in the gusty winds and falling leaves of an autumnal day![21]   [36:575]

I think there is a perceptible difference in the elegance and correctness of the English in the versions of the Old and New Testament. I cannot yield to the authority of many examples of usages which may be alleged from the New Testament Version. St Paul is very often most inadequately rendered, and there are slovenly and vulgar phrases which would never have come from Ben Jonson or any good writer of the times.[22]   [36:569]

The distinction between Accent and Quantity is clear, and was no doubt observed by the ancients in the recitation of verse. But I believe such recitation to have been always an artificial thing, *p*and that the common conversation was entirely regulated by accent. I do not think it possible to *talk* any language without confounding the quantity of syllables with their high or low tones; you may sing or recitative the difference well enough. Why should the marks of accent have been considered exclusively necessary for teaching the pronunciation to the Asiatic Hellenist, if the knowledge of the accented syllable did not carry the stress of time

n ~~attempting~~ offering   *o* ~~into~~   *p* f 103ᵛ

[19] The change of wording incompletely carried out in MS B was accomplished in *TT* (1835).

[20] This entry and the preceding must have emerged from a particular episode. C wrote the next day, 18 Aug, to Charles Aders: "I heard with unspeakable anguish and indignation of a scene that had lately taken place, by an incursion of the *little* Doctor's wife—and almost involuntarily, tho' to myself only, expectorated my spleen in three or four stanzas, which I have not yet made outward in Ink or Pencil, but which I will sometime or other put you in possession of." *CL* vi 956–7.

[21] With this feeling reference in mid-August to falling leaves, HNC preserves

the depth of C's self-perception amid adroit turns in the long conversation.

[22] In Anne Gillman's Bible C made objections to the King James version of Luke 5.32, 8.46 "vulgarly mistranslated"; Rom 9.3–5 "poorly and hungrily translated"; 2 Cor 7.11, 10.8; Gal 1.6; Eph 4.9; Col 1.14–15; 2 Thess 1.12; Heb 3.14; Rev 17.3. *CM (CC)* I 455, 460–71. William Newcome, on his way to becoming abp of Armagh, cited thirty-four authorities who agreed with him that revision was overdue. *An Historical View of the English Biblical Translations* (Dublin 1792) 113–86. For an aspect of the controversy over revision involving Thomas Middleton and Granville Sharp, see *CN* II 3275 and n.

with it? If ἄνθρωπος[23] was to be pronounced in common conversation with a clear distinction of the length of the penultima as well as of the elevation of the antipenultima, why was not that long quantity also marked?[24] It was surely as important an ingredient in the pronunciation as the accent. Besides can we altogether disregard the practice of the modern Greeks? Their confusion of the accent and quantity in verse is of course a barbarism, though a very old one, as the versus politici of Tzetzes and the Anacreontics prefixed to Proclus will show:[25] but these

[23] Ancient Greek metre was primarily quantitative; that is, it consisted in the alternation of long and short syllables in regular patterns, variable in accordance with discoverable rules. C's comparative mastery of this scheme is demonstrated by early specimens of his Greek and Latin verse and his winning of the Browne prize for a Greek Sapphic ode in 1792. See e.g. *CL* I 6, 34, 35, 56. After HC's dismissal from Oriel C helped him with an essay on metre, including "a new scheme of Prosody as applied to the choral and lyrical Stanzas of the Greek Drama". *CL* v 93. In a fragment possibly associated with this abortive project he mentioned the seminative work of Voss, Apel, Boekh, and Hermann (BM MS Egerton 2800 ff 56–57ᵛ), and, elsewhere, of Bentley and Porson (BM MS Egerton 2800 f 54ᵛ, *CM—CC—*1376).

Accent (προσῳδία, prosody) was in classical Greek essentially a matter of pitch, as C implies here, and was not directly related to the rhythm of prose or verse, whereas when applied to English verse accent is now synonymous with stress. Here C seems to feel quantity as the main element in stress, but on 26 Jul 1833 (*CL* VI 944) he distinguished force, pitch, and length unambiguously. See also *CM (CC)* I 377.

Two rival pronunciations were still common in C's time, one stressing the syllables marked by the written accents, the other placing the stress according to the Latin accentual rules. The apparent incompatibility between verse rhythm and accents that resulted was thought to be decisive against accents and led to the dropping of accents by the Oxford University Press in several publications and in the teaching of many schools. The correct view, and the evidence for it, had

been given by John Foster in *An Essay on the Different Nature of Accent and Quantity, with Their Use and Application in the English, Latin, and Greek Languages* (1762; 3rd ed 1820). C borrowed the 2nd ed (Eton 1763) from the Bristol Library 25 Oct 1796 and 13 Dec–9 Mar 1797, and used it for his review in *C Rev* (Feb 1797) of Samuel Horsley *On the Prosodies of the Greek and Latin Languages* (1796), identified as C's and reprinted by George Whalley in *RES* NS II (1951) 238–47 and discussed by Charles I. Patterson in *PMLA* LXVII (1952) 973–88. The compromise that C puts forward here in TT is to be understood as the basis of his comments on choral lyric in 1806. *CN* II 2835. It was expounded by William Primatt in *Accentus Redivivi* (1764) and reported by Horsley *On the Prosodies* 123–62 with disapproval, as a rule "sanctioned by some of the scholars of our two universities".

C had in the 1797 review, as here, not distinguished clearly between stress and quantity. In a footnote in *TT* (1835) HNC opposed C's opinion, using evidence of varying cogency, taken from Foster.

[24] Written accents were first introduced by Aristophanes of Byzantium, head of the library at Alexandria, hence *TT* (1835) added "or African". ῎Ανθρωπος (man) is a bad example, as the ω rather than ο shows that the syllable is long. The Greek alphabet has two long vowels, two short, and only three are "doubtful". An extra sentence in *TT* (1835) allows for this.

[25] C had a text of Joannes Tzetzes, Byzantine poet and grammarian of the twelfth century, Βιβλίον ἱστορικόν, τὸ διὰ στίχων πολιτικῶν ἄλφα καλούμενον, known also as *Chiliades*, in *Poetae graeci veteres carminis heroici scrip-*

very examples prove what the common pronunciation in prose then
was. [36:572]

---

28. Aug. 1833.

Baron von Humboldt,[1] brother of the traveller,[2] paid me the following
compliment at Rome: "I confess, Mr. Coleridge, I had my suspicions
that you were here in a political capacity*a* of some sort or other, but upon
reflection I acquit you. For in Germany and, I believe, elsewhere on the
continent, it is generally understood that the English government, in order to divert the envy and jealousy of the world at the power, wealth and
ingenuity of your nation, makes a point as a ruse de guerre of sending out
none but fools of gentlemanly birth and connections as diplomatists to
the courts abroad. An exception is sometimes made for a clever fellow,
if a libertine and thoroughly unprincipled."[3] [36:578]

---

a ~~character~~ capacity

---

tores ed J. Lectius (Geneva 1606) II 274–
86, and his *versus politici* are discussed
and quoted by Foster (1820) 112–14. In
a footnote *TT* (1835) gave illustrations
from Aristophanes and Tzetzes, taken
from Foster, and also from the Latin
poet Aurelius Prudentius Clemens (on
whom see also 2 Sept 1833 and n 18, below). The Anacreontics were, apparently, the two poems prefixed to Proclus
Εἰς τὴν Πλάτωνος θεολογίαν . . . *In
Platonis theologiam* ed and tr (Latin) Ae-
milius Portus (Hamburg 1618). They are
eight-syllable lines scanned by stress of
the accented syllable, such as were
called Anacreontics in Byzantine times.
The author is Andreas Wisius, a German
of the early seventeenth century, known
only for his Greek verses in modern
metres.

There must certainly have been a time
in the course of the change from ancient
pitch to modern stress accent when the
divergence C suggests between common
speech and verse did exist. It can be assumed that this happened some time before the end of the fourth century A.D.,
when Gregory Nazianzen wrote hymns
with stress on the accented syllables and
Nonnus perhaps was already writing his
quantitative hexameters with quantity
and accent coinciding at the ends of

lines.

[1] Karl Wilhelm, Freiherr von Humboldt (1767–1835), philologist and diplomat, Prussian ambassador in Rome
1801–8. In *BL* C said that Humboldt
warned him "*directly*" to leave Rome in
order to avoid retaliation by Napoleon
for his essays in the *M Post*. *BL* ch 10
(CC) I 216. Taking an opportunity in *The
Friend* of 1818 to say that he had read
WW's "sublime ode" (*Ode: Intimations
of Immortality from Recollections of
Early Childhood*) to Humboldt in Rome,
he paid a compliment to his "extensive
knowledge and just appreciation of English literature and its various epochs"
that may have owed something to Humboldt's presence in London as minister to
Britain (1817). *Friend (CC)* I 510n.
Humboldt lent C a volume of A. W.
Schlegel's *Spanisches Theater*. *CL* III
359.

[2] Alexander von Humboldt (1769–
1859), naturalist and author of travel
books, whom C met with his brother in
Rome. *IS* 417 n 30 connects him by way
of BM Add MS 36532 to the torpedo of
31 Mar 1830 (at n 9) (36:140).

[3] *TT* (1835) added a question, plausi-
bly Coleridgian, which is transitional to
the next entry.

What dull coxcombs your diplomatists at home generally are![4] I remember dining at Mr Frere's once in company with Canning and a few other interesting men.[5] Just before dinner *Lord Walpole* called on Frere, and asked himself to dinner.[6] From the moment of his entry he began to talk to the whole party, and in French—all of us being genuine English (I was told his French was *b*execrable). He had followed the Russian army into France and seen a good deal of the great men concerned in the war: of none of these things did he say a word, but went on gabbling about cookery, and dress and*c* the like. At last he paused for a little—and*d* I had remarked how a great image may be reduced to the ridiculous by bringing the constituent parts into prominent detail, and mentioned the grandeur of the deluge*e* and the preservation of life in the Genesis and also in Milton,[7] and the ludicrous*f* effect produced by Drayton's description in his *g*"Noah's Flood".*h*[8] Lord Walpole here resumed and spoke in raptures

b f 104   *c* & ~~such things~~   *d* & ~~in the~~   *e* deluge ~~in~~ t   *f* ~~contemptible &~~ ludicrous   *g–h* Qu.

4 C had referred to "hacknied diplomatists and the mere men of office" in the *Courier* 20 Dec 1809: *EOT (CC)* II 65. To James Gillman Jr he wrote on 10 Aug 1829 of "diplomatico-statistic Knowingness". *CL* VI 810. These have been the normal attitudes of self-respecting men of letters not themselves diplomats.

5 We can identify some of the number of opportunities C had to dine with "men so judicious, and so nobly principled, no less than highly gifted, as Mr Canning, and that model of a *fine* yet manly Intellect, Mr J. Frere". *CL* IV 671. The occasion was more likely to have been in 1816–18 or 1820 than in 1825–6, when Frere returned from Malta for a year. *CL* IV 538, 646, 654, 660, 881, 917, V 15, 37–8, 55–6, 91, VI 538. Frere had tried to get Lord Liverpool to provide an annuity for C in 1826, and C believed that Canning was about to achieve a pension for him when he died 8 Aug 1827. *CN* IV 5362; *CL* VI 539, 670–4, 680, 701–2, 705, 714. All this is a long way from C's private memory in 1803 that when "Frere with false heart" assured him at Cambridge that he would win a prize, he answered, "Why, Sir! the Boot fits you, Sir! I cannot get my Leg in." *CN* I 1656. In 1808–9 C had championed Frere vs Sir John Moore in Spain. *CL* III 200–1, 200n.

6 Horatio Walpole (1783 1858), from 1822 4th Baron Walpole and 3rd Earl of Orford (2nd creation), attaché at St Petersburg 1806, at Madrid 1808, secretary to the embassy at St Petersburg 1812–15, minister *ad interim* 1813–15, a commissioner for Indian affairs 1818–22. He was described by Capt Rees Howell Gronow as a small man "addicted to wearing hats with large brims and low crowns". *Reminiscences and Recollections* (2nd ed 2 vols 1889) II 298. He is "Lord ——" in *TT* (1835). The *M Chron* of 9 Jun 1835, citing this entry and the preceding as evidence that the views HNC attributed to C on the Reform Bill were wrong views, filled in the blank with Lord Londonderry. SC passed on from HNC to Mrs Henry Moutray Jones word that "the Ambassador alluded to was a 'far less able man' ". UT Grantz 1149 (var).

7 HNC's note in *TT* (1835) identified Gen 6–7 and *Paradise Lost* XI 728–869.

8 Drayton *Noah's Floud* lines 265–70, from *The Muses Elizium* (1630), quoted in the text of *TT* (1835) by HNC from *B Poets* III, as C might in fact have done. Some thirty-two years earlier C had linked Drayton's lines 457–8 on salamanders with William Alexander's *Doomes-day* st 29 as "a fine elucidation of an idea *spectrally* & at once given . . . Most exquisitely ludicrous". *CN* I 1026

of a picture which he had lately seen of Noah's Ark, and said the animals were all marching two and two, the little ones first, and that the elephants[i] came last in great majesty and filled up the foreground. "Ah! no doubt, my lord," said Canning, "your elephants, wise fellows! staid behind to pack up their trunks!" This floored the ambassador for half an hour.   [36:579]

In the sixteenth and seventeenth centuries almost all our ambassadors were distinguished men.[9] Read Lloyd's State Worthies.[10] The third rate men of those days possessed an infinity of knowledge and were intimately versed not only in the history, but even in the[j] heraldry[k] of the countries in[l] which they were resident.[m] Men were almost always, except for mere compliments, chosen for their dexterity and experience—not as now, by Parliamentary interest.   [36:579]

The sure way to make a foolish ambassador is to bring him up to it. What the deuce can an English minister abroad really want but an honest heart, a love for his country, veracity and the ten commandments? Your art diplomatic is stuff—no great man now would negotiate upon any such shallow principles.[11]   [36:580]

---

[i] elephants ~~were particu~~   [j] the ~~family her~~   [k] heraldry ~~as it were~~   [l] ~~to~~ in
[m] ~~sent to~~ resident.

---

and n. In an annotation on *B Poets* C rescued Drayton from Robert Anderson's "miserable Imitation of the slanderous aphorisming Detraction of Dr Johnson". *CM (CC)* I 55.

[9] A footnote in *TT* (1835) countered with HNC's opinion, buttressed by a quotation from Diego Hurtado de Mendoza (c 1503–75).

[10] David Lloyd (1635–92) *State-Worthies, or the Statesmen and Favourites of England Since the Reformation* . . . (2nd ed 1670). C quoted the work in *The Friend (CC)* I 212, "strongly" recommended it "as the Manual of every man who would rise in the world", and said that it "should be the Manual of every public man". *CN* III 3625, *CL* III 241 (letter to Sharp 10 Oct 1809). Whatever the validity of C's generalisation in this entry, Lloyd is not without such remarks as one on Sir William Compton, Gentleman of the Bedchamber to Henry VIII,

that "he was too narrow for his Fortune, and more attentive to his private advantage, than to the publick affairs" (p 145).

[11] The standard work on diplomacy was François de Callières (1645–1717) *De la manière de négocier avec les souverains* (Paris 1716) tr as *The Art of Negotiating with Sovereign Princes* (1716, 3rd ed 1838). It appeared in English under other titles also. Besides loyalty, courage, dignity, knowledge of languages, laws, customs, and geographical situation, Callières recommended presence of mind, caution in love, craft at the card-table, and flair in penetrating the secrets of others. A much later authority said that many diplomats "are beginning to wonder whether his unexceptionable tenets have any bearing on their working conditions in this day and age". Charles Roetter *The Diplomatic Art* (Philadelphia 1963) 113.

If a man is not tending upwards to be an Angel, depend upon it, he is tending downwards to be a Devil. He can not stop at the Beast. The most savage of men are not Beasts—they are worse.[12] [36:581]

---

[n]The conduct of the Mahometan[o] and Western Nations on the subject of Contagious Plague illustrates the two extremes of error on the nature of God's government of the world. The Turk changes Providence into Fatalism; the Christian relies upon it—when he has nothing else to rely on.[13] He does not practically rely upon it at all.[p][14] [36:582]

---

[a]2. Sept.[1]

The English affect stimulant nourishment = Beef and Beer.[2]

[n] f 104[v]   [o] ~~Eastern~~ Mahometan

[p] Following this entry HNC copied on f 104[v] C's verses on Cologne; see n 14, below   [a] f 105

[12] *TT* (1835) added "a great deal worse".

[13] The European Christian could always explain events or customs in the Levant with reference to "the fatalism of the Turk", but C's remark is directed against the hollow faith around him. C recognised that it was easier to see Providence after the events in "the stupifying influence of terror or actual calamity", as he had in the *Courier* 25 Jul 1816—*EOT (CC)* II 433; cf *LS (CC)* 165n—than to subordinate empirical and prudential considerations to a faith that Providence would guide the reason. His reservations about quarantine, on 7 Apr 1832 (at n 7) (36:364), presupposed that Providence would be consonant with moral conduct by individual and society.

[14] *TT* (1836) inserted at this point two entries, reversed and combined from MS B f 73[v], where they were transcribed from EC's "book MS", i.e. his transcriptions from C's notebooks (36:583). HNC copied at this point in MS B f 104[v] the two sets of verses by C on Cologne: *PW* (EHC) I 477 (var).

[1] Monday, following the visit of 28 Aug (Wed). The first entry appears in tabular form, with bars serving as ditto marks to repeat "The" and "affect" for each nation after the English. For the Prussians a third bar seems to indicate the omission of a parallel to "excitants"

and "sedatives" that HNC failed to catch. *TT* (1835) omitted the Prussians altogether. It also omitted, for the Russians, an illegible word or abbreviation preceding "to Narcotic" (printed as "narcotics"). This table is anticipated, if not in C's soberer comparisons of national characteristics, then in the *Courier* 30 May 1811: "Nor can it be denied, whatever may be its causes, that there exists a certain nationality of constitution, which occasions the poison of spirituous drinks to act with greater malignity in some countries than in others." *EOT (CC)* II 175. He had declared: "It is the Race that determines in part the choice of Soil & Climate—not these that give the character of the Race." Annotation on Steffens *Die gegenwärtige Zeit* (2 vols Berlin 1817) I 101: *CM (CC)* IV.

The latter half of this conversation is assigned in *TT* (1835) to 4 Sept, but C wrote on the 2nd (Mon) to Green: "Henry Coleridge goes off Devon-ward for his part Vacation and part Registering Barristership to morrow. I wonder, the Whigs employ such an inveterate Tory!" *CL* VI 960. Letters exchanged between HNC and SC, and SC's journal headed "in married time", show that HNC reached Devon on 5 Sept and returned home 11 Oct (Fri). UT mss.

[2] C's classification of drugs according to their effects seems to be a composite

The[b] French,[b] excitants, irritants = Nitrous oxide, Alcohol, Champagne.[3]
The[b] Austrians,[b] sedatives = *Hop bonum.* Hyoscyamus.[4]
The[b] Prussians,[b]———— = *Tongue-Bark*, Iron + Morphine.[5]

[b] Dash as ditto for "The" and after each race for "affect"

---

from Beddoes, Blumenbach, John Brown, other intensive study of physiology and pharmacy, and much personal experience. Most contemporary pharmacologies—e.g. John Murray *A System of Materia Medica and Pharmacy* (Edinburgh 1810), with a number of later editions—divided "general stimulants", as distinguished from local stimulants, into narcotics, tonics, antispasmodics, and astringents. C distinguishes here between narcotics, agreed to act in part to "diminish the actions and powers of the system", and sedatives, which could not be suspected of the stimulative effect at certain stages from certain amounts of narcotics. In 1803 he had counted as opposite temptations "narcotics" and "exhilarants". *CL* ii 919. On tonics see 19 May 1830 n 7, above. For the English, C's emphasis is on indulgent nourishment. Annotating Sir Thomas Browne, C noted the anti-aphrodisial effects of opium and bhang as "narcotic Stimulants". *CM (CC)* i 777.

[3] On nitrous oxide see 29 Apr 1830 n 5, above. C. T. Watkins *A Portable Cyclopaedia* (1810) summarised under "Gas" Davy's findings: "When breathed alone for a minute or two, it generally produces a pleasant thrilling, particularly in the chest and extremities . . . The mind meanwhile is often totally abstracted from all surrounding objects." If "stimulant" and "irritant" are taken as approximately equal in C's formula, the contrast is between the nourished English and the exhilarated French.

[4] Hop, *Humulus lupulus*, used to flavour beer, was recommended by most pharmacologists of C's day as a stimulant, but Beddoes had found that the effect of hop and tea on frogs resembled the second stage of narcotics in diminishing the powers of the system. *Hygëia* i

35–6. *Hyascamus niger*, hog bean, black henbane, one of the nightshades, is indigenous to Britain. Murray described its dried leaves as similar to opium in first quickening the pulse and then inducing diminished sensibility, stupor, or in large doses a profound sleep. On 17 Feb 1803 C wrote to Thomas Wedgwood: "Do bring down some of the Hyoscyamine Pills"; in Sept 1825 he wrote to EC that he had discontinued "the Calomel, which I took in very small doses with Jalap & extract of Hyoscyamus". *CL* ii 934, v 490.

[5] Peruvian bark, from three varieties of cinchona, was widely prescribed as a tonic. There is a full account in *The Edinburgh New Dispensatory* (Edinburgh 1797) 139–42. Beddoes prescribed it "against fevrous conditions". It was recommended by Thomas Bateman (1816) for erysipelas and various other ills from which C was thought to suffer; see 19 May 1830 n 8, above. For C it could be as innocent as an ingredient in a dentifrice. *CN* iv 4790. Central to one of his prescriptions of 1796 was "hard extract of Peruvian Bark, a Dram". *CN* i 235. On 3 Feb 1801 he wrote to Davy that he took "large quantities of Bark" with no salubrious effect. *CL* ii 672. The qualifier printed here as *"Tongue"* is doubtful at best. If the hyphen be taken as a comma, however, with "tongue, bark" intended, then the suggestion of Hermione de Almeida has cogency: adder's tongue, used medicinally to soothe (as in Keats's *Lamia* ii 224), was retained by C in his early poem *Melancholy* even after he learned that this was not an acceptable name for the fern he meant, hart's tongue. *PW* (EHC) i 74 and n. In opposing the Brunonian advocacy of such exciters as opium, cinchona, musk, and spiritous liquors, Richard Saumarez recom-

The[b] Russians,[b] Stim[t] Narcotic = Opium, Tobacco, Beng.[6] [36:584]

It is worth particular notice how the style[c] of the Greek[d] orators in the time of political independence, so full of connective particles, some of passion, some of sensation only—escaping the classification of mere grammatical logic—became in the hands of the declaimers and philosophers of the Alexandrian æra and still later entirely deprived of this peculiarity![j] So it was with Homer as compared with Achilles Tatius, Non-

---

[c] ~~Greek~~ style   [d] ~~time~~ Greek

---

mended cinchona only for tanning animal skins. *A New System of Physiology* (2nd ed 1799) I 86–7. Morphine extracted from opium, of which it is the principal alkaloid, has a powerfully hypnotic effect: the Prussians are presented here as sluggish. During the Napoleonic wars C viewed the Prussian leaders as infected with French philosophy, but he attributed to the average Prussian, despite a "want of true Patriotism", quicker feelings than "the phlegmatic Hollander". *CN* I 177, III 3367.

[6] Opium, the dried juice from the capsules of the poppy plant, *Papaver somniferum*, was taken by C and other Westerners of his time as laudanum, a tincture. By international convention, opium and laudanum were much later declared synonymous. John Brown, who recommended opium as the highest stimulant, "a truly blessed remedy" of "divine virtue", denied that it was a sedative: it is a stimulant that acts on the Turks as wine does on the British, he said. *Elements of Medicine* tr Beddoes § 230. There are full details of availability and current practice in *Edinburgh New Dispensatory* 143–5, 207–9. Beng, spelled also, C tells us, "Bhang, or Bang, or Banghee", is the dried flowering top of Indian hemp, *Cannabis sativa*, of which hashish and marijuana are derivatives. C's letters of 1–17 Feb 1803 (*CL* II 919–21, 927, 933–4) on the acquisition of bhang are classic sources, as for Molly Lefebure *Samuel Coleridge Taylor: A Bondage of Opium* (1974). "The Bang is the powder from the dried leaves of the Cannabis Indica, or Indian Hemp/ It is commonly blended with opium, & in Turkey and Barbary with Saffron & Spices. It is either chewed in large Pills, or soaked in the Powder. I have both smoked & taken the powder/ so did my ever-honoured ever-lamented Benefactor, T. Wedgewood: the effects on both were the same, merely narcotic, with a painful weight from the flatulence or stifled gas, occasioned by the morbid action on the coats of the Stomach. On others however it had produced, as we were informed by Sir J. Banks, almost frantic exhilaration. We took it in the powder, and as much as would lie on a Shilling. Probably, if we had combined it with opium and some of the most powerful essential oils, to stimulate & heat the stomach, it might have acted more pleasantly. . . ." C's annotation on Robert Percival *An Account of the Island of Ceylon* (1803) 152: *CM (CC)* IV. The illegible letters may be "stim" for stimulant, to make a contrast with the British of narcotic vs nourishment. For Grattan's account of C's remarks on opium-eating, in 1828, see App F 33, below.

[7] C's first group would include Lysias (c 459–c 380 B.C.), Isocrates (436–338 B.C.), Demosthenes (383–322 B.C.), and Aeschines (c 390–314 B.C.). The Alexandrian declaimers' works have survived only in fragments. The staccato style of Hegesias of Miletus was condemned and parodied by Cicero, but connective particles do appear in passages quoted from him in Greek by other writers, as they do also in the quotations from philosophers of the period in the footnotes to Tennemann *Geschichte der Philosophie* and in the writings of Plotinus and the later Neoplatonists approximately contempo-

nus, Tryphiodorus and the like.[8] In the latter, I suppose there are fewer single words by one half in the same number of lines as in Homer. All those notes of sound, those modifying marks of feeling, those appoggiaturas of time in the Iliad and Odyssey—especially the former—are utterly lost, and[e] Nonnus seems to fancy no verse ran well except in words making a dipodia by themselves.[9] How completely the true sense of harmony must have been lost![10]

The old Latin poets attempted to compound as largely as the Greeks— hence in Ennius such words as *belligerentes*[f] &c.[11] In nothing did Virgil show his judgment more than in rejecting these, except just where common usage had sanctioned them, as omnipotens. He saw that the Latin was too far advanced in its formation, and of too rigid a character to admit such composition or[g] agglutination. In this respect Virgil's Latin is very admirable and deserving preference. Compare it with Lucan or Statius and count the number of words used in an equal number of lines, and observe how many more short words Virgil has.[12]　　　　[36:585]

---

e & ~~the~~　　　*f* Dash in ms　　　*g* & or

---

rary with the later writers C mentions below. As reported here, he seems to be exaggerating what was certainly a tendency and eventually in the modern language became a fact. Cf, on Aristotle and connectives, *P Lects* Lect 5 (1949) 190.

[8] Achilles Tatius (3rd or 4th century A.D.), Greek rhetorician of Alexandria, author of a discursive erotic romance. When C saw an edition in Greek and Latin listed in a catalogue in 1808, he made a note to order it, "if I have it not already". *CN* III 3276 and n. Nonnus (3rd or 4th century A.D., till recently thought to be 5th century), Greek epic poet of Egypt; his long *Dionysiaca* and verse paraphrase of the gospel of St John are noted for their metrical and linguistic innovations. Tryphiodorus (5th century A.D.), Greek poet and grammarian, author of a poem on the sack of Troy, the only work of his to have come down to us.

[9] In compressing this passage *TT* (1835) removed the *Odyssey*, the second reference to Nonnus, and some of C's flowers of rhetoric.

[10] *TT* (1836) inserted here a paragraph slightly modified from N L (*CN* III 3497). Polybius (c 204–125 B.C.), histo-

rian of the Roman world, thus entered *TT*.

[11] Quintus Ennius (c 239–169 B.C.), "the father of Roman poetry". Of his *Annales*, which established the dactylic hexameter as the metre for Latin epic, some 500 lines remain. See line 193, "Non cauponantes bellum sed belligerantes" ("Not chaffering war but waging war"); and cf line 176, "Bellipotentes sunt magis quam sapientipotentes". ("They are war-strong more than wisdom-strong"). E. A. Warmington *Remains of Old Latin* (4 vols LCL 1935–40) III 70, 66. In *Omniana* (1812) C asked "youthful bards" to take warning from compound epithets in Greek that translate into such as "tail-horn-hoofed Satan". *TT* (1884) 353. In 1805 he noted that the names Thrasybulus and Demosthenes, as parallels to "Praise-God-Barebones &c", must explain "the conversational nature of the compound Epithets among the Greeks". *CN* II 2732. At the beginning of *BL* he both condemned double epithets and apologised for his own early practice of them. *BL* ch 1 *(CC)* I 6–7, 6n–7.

[12] Marcus Annaeus Lucanus (A.D. 39–65), Latin poet and prose writer born in

*h*I cannot quite understand the grounds of the high admiration which the ancients expressed for Propertius—and I own Tibullus is rather insipid to me.[13] Lucan was a man of great powers—but what was to be made of such a shapeless fragment of party warfare*i* and so recent too! He had fancy rather than imagination, and passion rather than fancy. His taste was wretched to be sure—still the Pharsalia is in my judgment a very wonderful work for such a youth as Lucan was.[14]

I think Statius a truer poet than Lucan, though he is very extravagant sometimes. Valerius Flaccus is very pretty in particular passages.[15] I am ashamed to say, I have never read Silius Italicus.[16] Claudian I recommend to your careful perusal, in respect of his being the first of the Moderns—or at least the transitional link between the Classic and the Gothic mode of thought.[17]

h f 105*v*   *i* "as" inserted above "warfare"

Spain. Publius Papinius Statius (A.D. c 45–c 96), Latin poet born in Naples. In judging Daniel's *Civil Wars* superior in "spite of a few dazzling Passages" in Lucan's *Pharsalia*, epic on the war between Caesar and Pompey, C wrote: "The Pharsalia is really a Hibbitihoy poem—neither man nor boy. It is to me just what I should have expected from a youth well educated & of strong natural Talents at 19: and great works might have followed if he had lived". Daniel *Poetical Works: CM (CC)* II 126. HNC's notes in *TT* (1835) identified the poets selectively. Of Statius, C quoted from the *Thebaid*, epic poem in twelve books admired by Dante, Chaucer, Pope, and Gray, and from the occasional poems of *Sylvae*. *CN* I 1179; *Lects 1795 (CC)* 51, 388; *PW* (EHC) II 1113 (also *CL* I 289); *EOT (CC)* I 66. A suspicion of preference for the unpreferred will hang over C's advocacy of the *Achilleis* (Achilliad), usually regarded as ended at bk II by the poet's death: "This is the general belief; but I think, erroneous. It seems to me an entire poem—Achilles Puer." Annotation on Dante tr Cary: *CM (CC)* II 134. Recommending it to Sotheby in Jul 1829 as a work to translate, C again insisted: "The interest of the Tale, the Novelty, the interesting criticisms, you might prefix, on the genius & characteristic traits of Statius—conspire to rec-

ommend it—& then it is a finished *Whole* of only two Books". *CL* VI 798. C always granted Virgil's mastery of language; see 8 May 1824 n 12, above.

[13] Sextus Propertius (c 50–c 15 B.C.), Roman elegiac poet, too amatory for C's full approval. Albius Tibullus (c 54–c 18 B.C.), elegiac poet just right for Eton (see 11 Apr 1833, at n 11, above) (36:493). C left with WW an edition of Catullus, Tibullus, and Propertius: *WW LC* 322; and see *BL (CC)* II 242, *Logic (CC)* 10.

[14] See n 12, above. Two sentences above, HNC modified MS B to "party as warfare", but ignored the change in *TT* (1835).

[15] Gaius Valerius Flaccus, Roman poet (1st century A.D.); his *Argonautica* is one in a series of adaptations from Apollonius Rhodius. C twice borrowed the *Argonautica* (Leyden 1724) at Cambridge. *Jesus Library Borrowings* 571, 574. He copied a passage, presumably not for prettiness, into a notebook in 1805 and used it in *BL* ch 10. *CN* II 2653, *BL (CC)* I 217.

[16] Tiberius Catius Silius Italicus (c 25–101), Latin epic poet and proconsul; *Punica*, in seventeen books, c 14,000 lines.

[17] Claudian, in the words of J. W. Mackail, who shared C's admiration, was a "singular and isolated figure", the "posthumous child of the classical

Prudentius is curious for this, that you see how Christianity forced allegory into the place of Mythology.[18] Vincentius, too, has much to be admired:[19] Mr Frere used to esteem these Latin Christian poets very highly, and no man in our times was a more competent judge.[20]

[36:586]

I call Persius *hard*—not obscure. He had a bad style; but I dare say, if he had lived, he would have learned to express himself in easier language. There are many passages in him of exquisite felicity, and his vein of thought is manly and pathetic.[21]

[36:586]

world'' who, with Prudentius, marks "the separation of the dying from the dawning light"; the "last eminent man of letters who was a professed pagan". *Latin Literature* (1895) 267–8. See also 14 Aug 1833 and n 31, above.

[18] Aurelius Prudentius Clemens (348–c 410), Christian Latin writer born in Spain, author of hymns, poems of dogma, and verse tales of martyrs. C explained more fully in Lect 3 of 3 Feb 1818: ". . . the first Allegory compleatly modern in its form is the Psychomachia or Battle of the Soul, by Prudentius, a Christian Poet of the 5th Century—facts that fully explain both the origin and nature of narrative Allegory, as a substitute for the mythological imagery of Polytheism, and differing from it only in the more obvious and intentional disjunction of the sense from the symbol, and the known unreality of the latter—so as to be a kind of intermediate step between Actual Person, and mere Personification". BM MS Egerton 2800 f 49v: *Lects 1808–19 (CC)* II 102.

[19] Omitted from *TT* (1835). C may have said or meant Venantius, for Venantius Honorius Clementianus Fortunatus (c 540–c 600).

[20] John Hookham Frere, who had been a student at Cambridge in C's day and later one of the satirists of C's circle in the *Anti-Jacobin*, paid for the shorthand record of C's lectures on the history of philosophy. *CL* IV 917. C admired his then-unpublished translations from Aristophanes. *CL* V 93 and n, VI 559; *CN* III 4331–2; *Friend (CC)* I 18; *P Lects* (1949) 414 n 16. And see 28 Aug 1833 n 5,

above. *TT* (1835) inserted the Greek from C's will on Frere as "lover of beauty, noble and good". *CL* VI 999. As early as 8 May 1816 C wrote to John Murray: "I assure you, I regard the day, when I first saw Mr Frere, among the most memorable Red Letter Days of my Literary Life". *CL* IV 637. Frere thanked HNC for *LR* III on 22 May 1838 as one, he said, that C, "with all his partiality towards me, would have regarded I fear as little better than a mere conceptualist". The letter, at UT, is accompanied with the transcript of the one from Frere to Mrs Gillman on 31 May concerning *C Life* (G), with a reservation about the remark on Canning but with "entire coincidence of opinion in everything which is said of Mr Coleridge, of his stupendous powers of mind and the angelical purity and simplicity of his nature". He is also quoted as calling C "one of the best and kindest of men and by far the greatest genius it was ever my lot to meet with". *C at H* 9.

[21] Aulus Persius Flaccus (34–62), Roman hexameter satirist born in Etruria. C wrote: "The style of Persius is half sophistic, i.e. abrupt, jagged, thorny; & half declamatory—; and the metre corresponds". Annotation on Flögel *Geschichte der komischen Litteratur: CM (CC)* II 760–1. C had quoted from *Satires* 3.67 to his brother George 10 Mar 1798 (*CL* I 397) and (var) in the Prospectus of *The Friend (CC)* II 17. In his copy of *Satirarum liber* ed Isaac and Méric Casaubon (1647) he expressed gratitude to his time for giving him an education "to understand and taste" such books and for

How very pretty those lines of Hermesianax in Athenaeus are about the poets![22]   [36:587]

I have already told you that in my opinion the Destruction of Jerusalem is the only subject for an Epic *j*poem now left[23]—yet with all its great capabilities it has this one insurmountable defect—that whereas a poem, to be epic, must have a personal interest, in this subject no skill or genius could possibly preserve the interest for a hero from being merged in the interest for the Event. The fact is the Event is too sublime and overwhelming.   [36:588]

An Epic poem must either be National or Mundane.[24] As to Arthur, you could not by any means make a poem on him national to Englishmen. What have *We* to do with him? Milton saw this,[25] and with a judgment at least equal to his genius,[26] he took a Mundane theme—one common to all mankind. His Adam and Eve are all men and women inclusively. Pope satirizes Milton for making God the Father talk like a school divine[27]—Pope was hardly a man to criticize Milton. The truth is

j f 106

---

making available such inexpensive copies. *CM (CC)* IV. C wrote pedagogically to James Gillman Jr 24 Oct 1826 of "the surly, soldierly, lordly, patrician, magistratual and legislatorial character of the Romans", which co-operated with the original poverty of Latin to give "a sort of *memorandum* character . . . eminently suited to Satires, moral sentences, Points, aphorisms & the like"; hence "Juvenal, Persius, Martial, Lucan, Sallust, Seneca, and Tacitus". *CL* VI 639.

[22] Athenaeus (2nd–3rd century A.D.), Greek scholar. *TT* (1835) gave the first lines of the Greek, *The Deipnosophists* 13.597. Athenaeus says that the elegiacs are from the *Leontion* of Hermesianax of Colophon (b c 300 B.C.). A. W. Schlegel translated the lines, the longest surviving fragment of Hermesianax, into German in *Athenaeum* (3 vols Berlin 1798–1800) I 118–19. See, for Schlegel and for Greek elegiacs, below (at n 32) and 23 Oct 1833 (at nn 1–5).

[23] See 24 Apr 1832 (at n 5), above.

[24] "Belonging to the world" (Johnson's *Dictionary*); "universal".

[25] Arthur was a British chieftain against the Saxons; not, like Alfred, an

Englishman that C could call his own. Milton, in his Latin poem *Mansus* lines 78–88, contemplated the summoning of Arthur into a major poem, but renounced such "Fable or *Romance*" in *Paradise Lost* I 576–81 (cf x 27–31 on "long and tedious havoc" feigned for "fabl'd Knights" and the similar *Paradise Regained* II 358–61).

[26] C had begun to complain by 1802 of the tendency of philosophers and critics to regard as incompatible "Judgment with Imagination, & Taste". *CN* I 1255. HNC's record here should be recognised as preceding the title, "Shakspeare's Judgment Equal to His Genius", which he assigned in *LR* II 60 to his version of C's lecture note of Mar 1808 on the subject. *CN* II 3288; cf Lect 4 of 1 Apr 1808: *Lects 1808–19 (CC)* I 72.

[27] *Epistles and Satires of Horace Imitated* Epistle II i 101–2:

In quibbles, Angel and Archangel join,
And God the Father turns a School-Divine.

Cf C's lecture note of 1819: ". . . as far as Pope's censure of our Poet . . . is just, we must attribute it to the character of his

the[k] judgment of Milton in the conduct of the celestial part of his story is very exquisite. Wherever God is directly acting as the Creator without any exhibition of his own essence, Milton adopts the sternest and simplest language of the Scriptures.[28] He ventures upon no poetic diction, no amplification, no pathos or affection. It is truly the Voice[l] or the Word of the Lord coming to and acting on the subject Chaos. But, as some personal interest was demanded for the purposes of poetry, Milton takes advantage of the dramatic representation of God's address to the Son, the filial Alterity,[29] and in *those addresses* slips in, as it were, by stealth, language of affection or thought or sentiment. Indeed, though Milton was in fact a high Arian in his mature life, he does for the necessity of poetry give a greater objectivity to the Father and the Son than he would have justified in argument. He was very wise [m]in adopting the strong anthropomorphism of the Hebrew[n] Scriptures at once. Compare Paradise Lost with Klopstock's Messiah and you will learn to appreciate Milton's judgment as much as his genius.[30]   [36:589]

---

[k] the ~~exquisite~~　　[l] Voice ~~of th~~　　[m] f 106[v]　　[n] ~~Bible~~ Hebrew

---

Age . . .''. *CN* III 4494 f 143[v]; Lect 4 of 4 Mar 1819: *Lects 1808–19 (CC)* II 387. And cf his defences and mutterings against Johnson's view of ''the Paradise Lost as a Task''. *CN* II 2026 f 8, 2075; *BL* Satyrane's Letters II *(CC)* II 188.

[28] In Lect 10 of 1818, as reported by HNC, C wrote: ''. . . Milton confines the poetic passion in God's speeches to the language of scripture; and once only allows the *passio vera*, or *quasi-humana* to appear, in the passage, where the Father contemplates his own likeness in the Son before the battle'' (*Paradise Lost* VI 710–18). *LR* I 174. On HNC's conflations of two lectures on Milton, see *CN* III 4498n and *Lects 1808–19 (CC)* II 184, 382, 425.

[29] See 8 Jul 1827 above (second sentence) (36:93).

[30] Klopstock *Der Messias* (1748–73). Cf C's Lect 10 of 1818, as given by HNC: ''The inferiority of Klopstock's Messiah is inexpressible. . . . In Milton you have a religious faith combined with the moral nature . . . In Klopstock there is a wilfulness . . .''. ''The feigned speeches and events in the Messiah shock us like falsehoods'', but in *Para-*

dise Lost ''no particulars, at least very few indeed, are touched which can come into collision or juxta-position with recorded matter''. *LR* I 173. Of C on 4 Apr 1823 Tom Moore reported: ''In talking of Klopstock, he mentioned his description of the Deity's 'head spreading through space,' which, he said, gave one the idea of a hydrocephalous affection.'' *Journal* II 624. After he had talked with Klopstock in 1798 and begun to read *The Messiah*, he reacted to the phrase ''the German Milton''—''a very German Milton indeed!'' *CL* I 445; *BL* Satyrane's Letters III *(CC)* II 206. Klopstock had shocked C and WW by declaring ''Glover's blank Verse superior to Milton's''. *CL* I 442; *W Prose* I 91; *BL* ch 22 *(CC)* II 133–4 (Milton's characters suggested by Scripture, Klopstock's ''*derived* from'' it). In Germany ''Milton was called the Homer, and Klopstock the Virgil, of Christianity'', according to William Taylor of Norwich *Historic Survey of German Poetry* (3 vols 1828) I 234. C's copy of Klopstock *Der Messias. Ein Heldengedicht* (Halle 1749) remained with WW c 1810 to c 1830. *WW LC* 338.

It is not that the German can express external imagery more fully than English, but it can flash more images at once on the mind than the English can.[31] As to mere power of expression, I doubt whether the Greek surpasses the English. Read a very pleasant and acute dialogue in Schlegel's Athenaeum (vol. [I]*°*) between a German, Greek, Roman, Italian, Frenchman on the merits of their languages.[32]   [36:591]

The Conquest of India by Bacchus might afford scope for a very brilliant poem of the fancy and understanding.[33]   [36:590]

I wish the naval and military officers, who write accounts of their travels,

---

° Blank left in ms

[31] Presumably by agglutination and compounding and by the effect of these on word order. On 24 Oct 1826 C wrote to James Gillman Jr that Latin had an occasional disadvantage in comparison with English that "in most instances you must have heard the whole sentence before you can ascertain the sense of any part". *CL* VI 639. *TT* (1835) italicised "fully" and "at once", but the immediate comprehension of the part before completion of the sentence, stressed in the letter, would suggest that English could *express* external imagery more quickly than the German.

[32] "Die Sprachen. Ein Gespräch über Klopstocks grammatische Gespräche" *Athenaeum* ed A. W. and F. Schlegel (3 vols Berlin 1798–1800) I 3–69. The speakers are Poesie, Grammatik, Deutscher, Deutschheit, Französe, Grieche, Engländer, Römer, Italiäner, and Grille (a cricket), who closes the discussion. Engländer has much the least to say for his language. In C's annotated copy his marginalia begin immediately after this colloquy. See *CM (CC)* I 132. As indicated by "W" in the table of contents, it was written by A. W. Schlegel. In 1823 C made a comparison of languages in a reaction against Schlegel and Steffens's *Caricaturen*. *CN* IV 4943.

HNC had written: "Greek—the shrine of the genius of the old world; as universal as our race, as individual as ourselves; of infinite inflexibility, of indefatigable strength, with the complication and the distinctness of nature herself . . .

speaking to the ear like Italian, speaking to the mind like English . . ."; in comparison with Scandinavian and other early Teutonic literature, he found "fewer mere pictures for the mind's eye" than in Greek and Latin. *Introductions to the Greek Classic Poets* General Introduction (1834) 22, 28–9.

[33] "Conquest of India by Bacchus in Hexameters" was among C's projects in Nov 1803. *CN* I 1646. He here declares it a subject of no profundity. In Lect 2 of 5 Feb 1808 at the Royal Institution, discussing the origin of drama, he noted: ". . . with the ancients Bacchus, or Dionysus, was among the most aweful & mysterious Deities—in his earthly character the conqueror and civilizer of India, and allegorically the Symbol—in the narrower and popular notion—of festivity, but worshipped in the mysteries as representative of the ⟨organic⟩ energies of the Universe, that work by passion and Joy without apparent distinct consciousness—and rather as the cause or condition of skill and contrivance, than the result . . . Bacchus was honored as the presiding Genius of the heroic Temperament and character . . .". *Lects 1808–19 (CC)* I 44–5. In a marginal note c 1828 C wrote of the re-conductor "from the Disorder or second Hades", the Redeemer, "to be born on earth & worshipped . . . as the Infant Bacchus". Faber *Dissertation on the Mysteries of the Cabiri: CM (CC)* II 584. Parenthetically C referred any reader of his note to Nonnus *Dionysiaca* (bks XIII–XL).

would spare their sentiment. The Magazines introduce this cant. Let them read the old Captains, Dampier &c &c.[34]   [36:592]

---

15. Oct. 1833.

The Trinity is the Idea. The Incarnation, which implies the Fall, is the Fact. The Redemption is the mesothesis of the two—the Religion.[1]

[36:593]

If[a] you bring up your children in a way which puts them out of sympathy with the religious feelings of the Nation in which they live, the chances are that they will ultimately turn out Ruffians or Fanatics.[2]   [36:594]

---

*a*23. Oct. 1833

Elegy is the natural poetry of the reflective mind; it *may* treat of *any* subject but it must treat no subject for itself, but always and exclusively with

a ~~I would rather~~ If   *a* f 107

[34] Three recent books of travel in India were reviewed in the *Ed Rev* LVII (Jul 1833) 358–70: Capt Thomas Skinner (c 1800–43) *Excursions in India, Including a Walk Over the Himalaya Mountains to the Sources of the Jumna and the Ganges* (2 vols 1832); Capt George Rodney Mundy (1805–84) *Pen and Pencil Sketches, from the Journal of a Tour in India* (2 vols 1832); Maj Edward Caulfield Archer *Tours in Upper India, and in Parts of the Himalaya Mountains, with Accounts . . . of the Native Princes* (2 vols 1833). On Dampier *A New Voyage Round the World* (1697) see 17 Mar 1832 n 3, above.

[1] On 2 Sept C had asked J. H. Green to review with him "the Tetractys" of the "Tri-unity"; in late October he would request Green to bring over Waterland's *Vindication* with C's marginalia on the Trinity. *CL* VI 961–2. In Jan 1825 he had written to Samuel Mence that in all books on redemption "Metaphors have been obtruded as the Reality", in part because writers failed to see or feared to say that "the Will is the obscure *Radical* of the Vital Power".

CL V 406. In a marginal note on Richard Field *Of the Church* C defined the redemption as the reconciliation of human impotence with divine omnipotence, the removal of the antithesis between creature and God. *CM (CC)* II 676. For William Page Wood's report of C on redemption 18 Dec 1828 see App F 34, below.

[2] C's letters of Oct 1826 to James Gillman Jr on liberal education (*CL* VI 628–33, 635) take for granted a conformity with the national religion that his vigorous defences of Andrew Bell against Joseph Lancaster in 1808 and after (*CL* III 86ff) show that he could not take for granted publicly. HNC had written in *A Letter to Winchelsea* (1829) 15–16: "You may live, my Lord, to know that a deeper mine is digging under the Church than the Roman Catholics could ever dig, or would ever fire. You may live to know that the Divorce of Scientific from Religious Education is as mysterious, as iniquitous, and seven times as dangerous as Babylon and the Lady of the Seven Hills."

reference to the poet himself.[b] As he will feel regret for the Past or Desire for the Future, so Sorrow and Love become the principal themes of Elegy. It presents every thing as lost and gone or absent and future.[c] The Elegy is the exact opposite to the Homeric Epic, in which all is purely external and objective, and the[d] poet is a mere voice.[1]

The true Lyric Ode is subjective too; but then it delights to present things as actually existing and visible, although associated with the poet[2] or colored highly by the subject of the Ode itself. [36:595]

I think the Lavacrum Pallados of Callimachus very beautiful—especially the episode of the mother of Tiresias and Minerva.[3] I have a mind to try how it would bear translation; but what metre have we to answer the Elegiac couplet of the Greeks?[4]

I greatly prefer the Greek rhythm of the short verse to Ovid's—though I do not dispute his taste with reference to the genius of his own language. Schlegel gave me a copy of Latin Elegiacs on the King of Prussia's going down the Rhein, in which he had almost exclusively adopted the manner of Propertius. I thought them very elegant.[5] [36:596]

[b] (himself). ~~Whatever his It's themes, however, generally will be The~~
[c] future. ~~But in the true Lyric, wēh is~~ [d] ~~no~~ the

[1] The context shows that Greek poetry is the subject. HNC had discussed elegies and lyric odes in the section of his proposed continuation of his *Introductions* published as a review of John Herman Merivale's (mostly Robert Bland's) *Collections from the Greek Anthology* (3rd ed 1833) and *Bibliotheca Graeca* vol XIX ed Christian Friedrich Wilhelm Jacobs and Valentin Christian Friedrich Rost (Gotha and Erfurt) in *QR* (Jul 1833) XLIX 349–81.

[2] For "poet" all published versions have followed *TT* (1835) in reading "past", a misprint. C describes the lyric ode as a middle thing, balancing the subjective with the actually present, in distinction from the subjectively reflective elegy and the objective Homeric epic.

[3] Callimachus, Greek poet born c 310 B.C. in Cyrene; associated with the Alexandrian Library, perhaps as head. Hymn 5 (of six extant) *On the Bath of Pallas* lines 57–130, in elegiac couplets. *TT* (1835) in a footnote gave the opening lines in Greek. C had the works of Callimachus in *Poetae graeci veteres* (1614) I 535–56. This hymn was one of three

specimens of Greek elegiacs translated into German elegiacs by A. W. Schlegel in *Athenaeum* I 130–9. C made two disapproving annotations on the definition of elegy in F. Schlegel's introduction to "Elegien aus dem Griechischen" in *Athenaeum* I 107–40. *CM (CC)* I 145–7.

[4] One line of dactylic hexameter and a second with "two and a half dactyls followed by another two and a half", originally accompanied by the flute. C. M. Bowra *Early Greek Elegists* (Cambridge, Mass 1938) 3–7.

[5] A. W. Schlegel's Latin elegiacs with German elegiac translation are entitled *Rhenus principem adorans hospitem. Faustam navigationem regis augustissimi et potentissimi Friderici Guilelmi III, quum . . . navi vaporibus acta Bonnam praeterveheretur d. XIV Sept. MDCCCXXV, publice pieque celebrat carmine A. G. a Schlegel.* An edition of the Latin only is entitled *Faustam navigationem . . .* Both were published at Bonn in 1825.

At the Aders's chateau in Jul 1828—perhaps when C was given the elegiacs—J. C. Young was suspicious of

You may find a few faults in Milton's Latin verses—but you will not persuade me, if these poems had come down to us as written in the age of Tiberius, that we should not have considered them as very beautiful.[6]   [36:597]

I once thought of making a collection to be called "The Poetical Filter" upon the principle of simply omitting from the old pieces of lyrical poetry which we have, those parts in which [e]the whim or bad taste of the author[f] or the fashion of the age prevailed over his genius.[7] You would be surprized at the number of[g] exquisite *wholes* which might be made by this simple operation [h]and perhaps by the insertion of a single line or half line out of poems which are now utterly disregarded on account of some odd or incongruous passages in them, just as whole volumes of Wordsworth's poems were formerly neglected or laughed at solely because of some few *wilfulnesses* of his[8]—whilst five sixths of his poems at that very time would have been admired and indeed popular, if they had ap-

[e-f] the whim or bad taste ⟨of the⟩ author's   [g] of the   [h] f 107[v]

the cordiality of C and Schlegel: "Coleridge told him that there never had been such a translation of any work in any language as his of Shakespeare. Schlegel returned the compliment, scratched *his* back in turn, and declared that Coleridge's translation of Schiller's *Wallenstein* was unrivalled for its fidelity to the original, and the beauty of its diction." *Memoir of Charles Mayne Young* 112. Schlegel was in London in 1814 and 1823. *CL* v 303; *CRB* I 149, 298; *CRC* I 190. C was haunted from 1811 by charges of plagiarism from Schlegel. *CL* III 343, 359–60, 446, IV 831, 839 and nn, 899–900nn, 924.

[6] Johnson, in his life of Milton, had granted "classic elegance" to these works: "The Latin pieces are lusciously elegant; but the delight which they afford is rather by the exquisite imitation of the ancient writers, by the purity of the diction, and the harmony of the numbers, than by any power of invention or vigour of sentiment." C had Johnson's lives frequently at hand in *E Poets*. A record of respectful attention to the *Poemata* was available in Milton *Poetical Works* ed Hawkins IV 249–394 and I 46–9 (a defence by Thomas Warton in 1785 against Johnson's preference for the Latin poems of Thomas May and Abraham

Cowley). C annotated Milton *Poems upon Several Occasions* ed Warton (2nd ed 1791), which included the defence (pp xvi–xxi).

If the age of Tiberius is confined to his reign, A.D. 14–37, then C may give Milton no greater competition than Manilius, whom A. E. Housman is thought to have studied out of masochism; but probably C's stress, like Warton's, was on Milton's mind as "deeply tinctured with the excellencies of ancient literature".

[7] The "filter" is C's own taste. He practised this filtering on individual passages frequently in his notebooks, as in a number of the fragments and metrical experiments collected in *PW* (EHC) II 988–1019, and in quotations throughout his published works. *BL* chs 17 and 22 in effect recommend that the reader use C's filter on the poems of WW. His procedure belongs to the tradition of identifying beauties and defects, as he indicated in a letter of 14 Dec 1807 to RS. *CL* III 42.

[8] *OED* cites this entry as the earliest use of "wilfulness" to mean a "wilful act". *TT* (1835) modified the rest of this paragraph with qualifications and additions favourable to WW, not in conflict with C's recorded opinions.

peared without those drawbacks under the name of Byron or Moore or Campbell or any of the favorites of the day.[9]   [36:598]

I think there is something very majestic in Gray's Installation Ode— but as to the Bard &c.[10] I must say I think them frigid[i] and artificial— there is more real lyric feeling in Cotton's Ode on the approach of winter.[11]   [36:599]

Compare Nestor, Ajax, Achilles &c. in the Troilus and Cressida of Shakspeare's with their namesakes in Homer. The old heroes seem[j] to have been all at school ever since. I scarcely know a more striking instance of the strength and pregnancy of the Gothic mind.[12]   [36:600]

---

[i] ~~rather~~ frigid   [j] ~~all~~ seem

[9] Thomas Moore (1779–1852), "national lyrist of Ireland" (*DNB*), friend and biographer (1830) of Byron. To C, Moore was an ingratiating social lion— which was bad enough—and the author of titillating lyrics in *The Poetical Works of the Late Thomas Little, Esq.* (1801; 15th ed 1822). In 1817, when C seems to have thought Moore the hateful reviewer of *Christabel* in the *Ed Rev*, he wrote to HCR: "I have read two pages of Lalla Rook or whatever it is called. Merciful Heaven! . . . Why, there are not 3 lines together without some adulteration of common English . . .". *CL* IV 740. Thomas Campbell (1777–1844), named among the Scottish luminaries, probably ironically, in *Friend (CC)* I 423. C wrote to Francis Wrangham on 10 Jan 1818 that "the best thing I ever heard of Campbell, the Pleasures of Hope man, was a toast he gave lately at Longman's Saturday public dinner . . . BUONA-PARTE—for having shot a bookseller!"; C begged Wrangham not to mention any particulars "to any of your London correspondents". *CL* IV 802. C attracted wide attention from his Lect 5 of 2 Dec 1811 when, as Byron reported, he "attacked the *Pleasures of Hope*, and all other pleasures whatsoever". *Byron's Letters and Journals* ed Leslie A. Marchand (12 vols 1973–82) II 140–2, 147; cf *Lects 1808–19 (CC)* I 262–3, 272.

[10] *TT* (1835) supplied "and the rest of his lyrics". Thomas Gray (1716–71) anon *Ode Performed in the Senate-House at Cambridge, July 1, 1769, at* the Installation of His Grace, Augustus-Henry Fitzroy, Duke of Grafton, Chancellor of the University (Cambridge 1769); collected as "Ode VII. For Music" in *The Poems of Mr. Gray* ed William Mason (York 1775) II 37–43 and in *The Works of Thomas Gray* ed Thomas James Mathias (2 vols 1814), which C annotated by noting exceptions to his general approval. In a tolerant reference to Gray's grapplings with Plato, C referred to him in Lect 4 of the lectures on the history of philosophy as "our amiable countryman—our sweet poet and scholar". *P Lects* (1949) 165. He had quoted a line from *The Bard*, probably from memory, in *Watchman* 1 Mar 1796 (*CC*) 40. C's singularity in 1833 is not in judging *The Bard* as Johnson judged it, but in selecting for praise the Installation Ode, to which Gray never put his name.

[11] Charles Cotton (1630–87) *Winter*, beginning "Hark, hark, I hear the north wind roar", from *Poems on Several Occasions* (1689), *E Poets* VI 768 (there is another *Winter* by Cotton at VI 709). In a footnote *TT* (1835) quoted WW's praise, with his long extract, at the end of his Preface of 1815. *W Prose* III 37–9. Lamb called WW's attention to the poem in 1803. *LL* (M) II 98–103, 106n. C praised "not a few poems" by Cotton, as both conversational and beyond improvement in language, in *BL* ch 19 *(CC)* II 91–2. SC provided a long note on Cotton in *BL* (1847) II 97–100 n 3.

[12] Modifying Schiller's naïve and self-consciously sentimental, a contrast of the

Well of Lord Byron I will only say—
    Si non *alium* late spargebat odorem,
    Laureus erat.[13]

Let a young man separate I from Me as far as he possibly can, and remove the Me till it is almost lost in the remote distance.[k] *I am Me* is as bad a fault in intellectuals and morals as in grammar—whilst none but One—God—can say "I Am I" or "that I Am".[14]   [36:605]

Dr Johnson seems to have really been more powerful in reasoning viva voce in conversation than with his pen in hand. It seems as if the excitement of Company called [l]something like reality and consecutiveness into his reasoning which in his writings I cannot see. His antitheses are almost always verbal only—and sentence after sentence in the Rambler may be pointed out, to which you cannot attach any definite meaning whatever. In his political pamphlets there is more truth of expression than in his other works for the same reason that his conversation is better than his

---

[k] distance. ~~The worst~~   [l] f 108

---

natural and the sophisticated, C had made a similar point in a marginal note on the Stockdale Shakespeare *Dramatic Works* ed Ayscough on the interleaves II 857–8: "But I am half inclined to believe, that Shakspeare's main object, or shall I rather say that his ruling impulse was to translate the ⟨poetic⟩ Heroes [of] Paganism into the not less rude but more intellectually vigorous, more *featurely* Warriors of Christian Chivalry, to substantiate the distinct and graceful Profiles or Outlines of the Homeric Epic into the flesh and blood of the Romantic Drama . . .". *CM (CC)* IV. Used in Lect 3 of 25 Feb 1819: *Lects 1808–19 (CC)* II 378. "Gothic", describing the romances of chivalry, had been extended from Richard Hurd's attention to *The Faerie Queene* in *Letters on Chivalry and Romance* (1762) to most European narratives before Locke. *TT* (1835) on Claudian (36:586) substituted "Classic" and "Gothic" for the "ancient" and "modern" of MS B.

[13] "If he had not spread about *another*

scent he would be a laurel." Cf Virgil *Georgics* 2.131–2, "et, si non alium late iactaret odorem, laurus erat". Either C or HNC substituted in memory *spargebat* for *iactaret*, "fling out". The entry was used in the Preface of *TT* (1835), dropped from *TT* (1836).

[14] Exod 3.14. C accepted from Schelling the identity of subject and object in consciousness, "I am because I affirm myself to be". *BL* ch 12 *(CC)* I 275; *CL* IV 768; *Logic (CC)* 85. If self-consciousness is an act, as Fichte had pointed out, then for C the contemplation of "Me" would be a triplication of inwardness, appropriate only for an infinite being. "Me" is properly an object observed by some other consciousness. Moral action therefore begins in the separation of "I" from "Me". "I am I" refers by underlying pun to the Greek verb εἰμί, Latin *sum*, "the verb that represents existence". William Vincent *The Origination of the Greek Verb. An Hypothesis* (1794) 9–10, quoted in *Logic (CC)* lxv–lxvi.

writing in general.[15]   [36:602]

Unless Christianity be viewed and felt in a high and comprehensive way, how large a portion of our intellectual and moral nature does it leave without object or action![16]   [36:604]

When I am very ill indeed I can *read* Scott's novels and them almost only. I cannot then *read* the Bible—my mind *reflects* on such matters at such times.[17]   [36:603]

Dryden's genius was of that sort which catches fire by its own motion;[*m*] his chariot wheels *get* hot[*n*] by driving fast.[18]   [36:601]

---

m motion; ~~he *gets* warm by~~   *n* ~~warm~~ hot

[15] *TT* (1836)—not (1835)—added for clarification: "He was more excited and in earnest." In a note to *Don Juan* XXI 19 Byron had declared the wrath and partiality of Mitford's *Greece* "virtues in a writer, because they make him write in earnest". HNC had heard C express during July and August similar views of Johnson's prose, what he referred to in 1826 as "pomp or Johnsonian mouthing". *CL* VI 637. In speaking of Johnson as a conversationalist C is not describing himself. He was stimulated by either a small audience or a large to teach and "to leave a *sting* behind" (*CL* IV 924), but he was excited into stronger reasoning so much more obviously by reading than by "Company" that he cannot have missed the distinction, although the observers of his borrowing in his lectures and books have not always seen it.

[16] In *TT* (1835) this entry is entitled "Scope of Christianity". Against sectarianism, C offers such expansions as that from "clergymen" to "clerisy" in *C&S*.

[17] C had written on 29 Oct 1829 that "Blackwood and Sir Walter's novels have been my comforters in many a sleepless night". *CL* VI 821. Without giving a reason, E. L. Griggs dates as "22 October 1833?" C's request to borrow *The Black Dwarf* and *Old Mortality*

"till tomorrow night". The entry is reworked for clarity in *TT* (1835), in which it is dated 1 Nov. SC had heard C "speak with admiration of the Rubens-like power of painting motion displayed by Sir Walter Scott in some of the latter chapters of *Rob Roy*"; she proposed "chapter xvi. of the second volume", specifically "pages 260–3", which she compared with *Inferno* XXII 118–51 as exemplifying C's praise of both Scott and Dante. *BL* (1847) II 447. C probably influenced her judgements of "the *Scotch* novels" in 1850. *SC Memoir* II 374–5. For Grattan's report of WW's and C's reactions to Scott's novels in 1828 see App F 35, below.

[18] In *BL* ch 18 C explained more fully that the vividness of Donne and Dryden derives as much "from the force and fervour of the describer, as from the reflections, forms or incidents which constitute their subject and materials. The wheels take fire from the mere rapidity of their motion." *BL (CC)* II 72. Did C not remember, or was only HNC unaware, that Pope had written in the Preface to his translation of *The Iliad* (1715) that Homer's imagination "becomes on Fire like a Chariot-Wheel, by its own Rapidity"? The chariot-wheels enter MS B as a revision.

Epitaph on S. T. C.
9. Nov. 1833.[1]
S. T. C.

Stop Christian Passer by!—Stop, child of God,
And read with gentle breast.—Beneath this sod
A poet lies, or that which once seemed He.—
O lift one thought in prayer for S. T. C.
That he who many a year with toil of breath
Found death in life, may here find life in death.
Mercy for praise—to be forgiven for fame
He asked, and hoped through Christ. Do thou the same!

*a*How many books are still published about Charles I. and his times! such is the fresh and enduring interest of that grand crisis of morals, religion and government. But these books are none of them works of any genius or imagination; not one of these authors seems to be able to throw himself back into that age; there would be less praise and less blame on both sides, if they did that.[2]   [36:606]

---

21. Dec. 1833.

*a*I hardly know what to think of the application of Malachi's prophecy of the Messenger.[1] What did John the Baptist in fact do—and how can he be said to have prepared the way of Christ on earth?[2] Besides, I cannot

---

o f 108ᵛ   *a–b* For the variant in MS F see App C, below

[1] On 29 Oct C wrote to Prati that "a friend & relation" to whom he had lent the 2 vols of Vico "is now in Devonshire & will not return till the end of November". *CL* VI 965–6. He had lent the Vico to HNC. Although there is no correspondence between HNC and SC at UT for this period, the schedule for registration would have returned him to the circuit in November. SC, who had addressed her letters of 12 Sept through 6 Oct from "Mama's room", had intensified her "nervous illness" in advanced pregnancy.

C's epitaph, sent to Green in a letter postmarked 29 Oct and to Lockhart in a letter postmarked 6 Nov (*CL* VI 963, 973), and given here as HNC transcribed it on MS B f 108. (In the ms the title precedes the date.) For the epitaph see also

C's annotations in Nehemiah Grew *Cosmologia Sacra: CM (CC)* II 903–6.

[2] C may have had particularly in mind the controversy over John Hampden's speech (see 4 May 1833 at n 13) (36:502) and such works as the Earl of Ashburnham's two volumes in 1830 to defend his ancestor John Ashburnham from "the misrepresentations of Lord Clarendon", reviewed in the *Ed Rev* LII (Oct 1830) 26–43. He would not have forgotten his distaste for Lucy Aikin *Memoirs of James First*.

[1] Mal 4.5.

[2] It was traditional to refer both Mal 4.5 and the words of Jesus concerning John the Baptist in Matt 11.10 back to Isa 40.3 (AV), "The voice of him that crieth in the wilderness, Prepare ye the way of the Lord . . .". Matt 3.1–3 and Luke 3.4

reconcile John's direct declaration to the Jews that he was not Elias—the Elias whom they meant.[3] The voice in the wilderness he was—but that does not answer the description of Malachi.[4] Our Lord's language is peculiar—if ye will receive it, this is that[b] Elias &c.[5] When I reflect upon this subject, and observe the distinction taken in the Prophets between the suffering and teaching [c]Christ—the Priest who[d] was to precede and the triumphant Messiah, the Judge—and how Jesus always seems to speak of the son of Man in a *future* sense and yet always as identical with himself, I sometimes think that Our Lord himself in his earthly career was the Messenger and that the way is *now still preparing* for the great and visible advent of the Messiah of Glory. I mention this doubtingly.[6]

——————— [36:607]

What a beautiful sermon or essay might be written on the growth of Prophecy![7]—from the germ, no bigger than a man's hand in Genesis till the column of cloud gathers size and height and substance, and assumes the shape of a man—girt like the smoke in the Arabian Nights' story, which comes up and at last takes a genii's shape.[8]   [36:608]

---

b See *a–b*, above   *c–d* Xt, ⟨Priest⟩ who P

---

identify John as the forerunner prophesied by Isaiah; the language of Luke 3.15–16 makes the parallel passages in Matt 3.11 and Mark 1.7 witness to the fulfilment.

[3] John 1.21. Paul, C's favourite, calls attention to John's denial in Acts 13.25. For Elias, the Greek form of Elijah, see e.g. Matt 17.3, 27.47.

[4] Those arguing opposite to C pointed to Luke 1.17, which does "answer the description" of both Mal 4.5 and Isa 40.3 (AV).

[5] Matt 11.13–14. The first half of this entry was omitted from *TT* (1835). The scrap in MS F lacks only "Elias &c", which would have begun the first line of that part of the entry retained for publication.

[6] C is drawing also upon such passages as James 2.1, "the Lord of glory", and Luke 24.26, "Ought not Christ to have suffered these things, and to enter into his glory?"

[7] Cf 13 Apr 1830 nn 1–4, above (36:123). C wrote important letters on prophecy to EC on 11 Nov 1825 (despite John Davison's fine *Discourses on*

Prophecy, the "subject appears to be a Mine, the richest Veins of which still remain to be opened"); to EC on 8 Feb 1826 (the relation of the NT to the prophecies of the OT); and to H. F. Cary in May 1827 (on the connexion of prophecy as "Organization Successive" and the logic of ideas). *CL* v 510, vi 556–8, 684–5. In 1795 he had shared the widespread interest of that time in Biblical prophecies that "even now are fulfilling and unfulfilled". *Lects 1795 (CC)* 152. The growth of prophecy had coincided with degeneration in God's chosen people "from the Captivity to the Birth of Christ". Annotation on Eichhorn *Apokryphischen Schriften: CM (CC)* ii 421. Where Davison found waves and troughs, C sought progressive revelation. Robert Lowth, who dealt much more narrowly with style than C, proclaimed what C practised: "The genius of the prophetic poetry is to be explored by a due attention to the nature and design of prophecy itself." *Lectures on the Sacred Poetry of the Hebrews* ii 65.

[8] *TT* (1835) in a footnote quoted from "The Story of the Fisherman. The Ninth

*ᵉ*The Logic of the Ideas⁹ is to that of Syllogisms as the infinitesimal calculus to common arithmetic—it proves but at the same time supersedes.¹⁰   [36:609]

---

1. Janȳ 1834.¹ S. T. C

What is it that W. S. Landor wants to make him a poet?² His powers are certainly very considerable; but he seems to be totally deficient in that modifying faculty, which compresses several units into one whole. He does not possess Imagination in its highest form;—that of stamping il più nell'*ᵃ* uno.³ Hence his*ᵇ* poems,*ᶜ* taken as wholes, are unintelligible; you have eminences excessively bright and all the ground around and between them in darkness. Besides which he never learned how to write

---

ᵉ f 109   *ᵃ* nel   *ᵇ* ~~in~~ his   *ᶜ* poe~~try~~ms

Night" *Arabian Nights Entertainments* (1778) I 41–3. There is a similar transformation from cloud to disclosed jinn in "The Merchant and the Geni. The First Night", not in HNC's edition but in 1811 I 37.

⁹ The Platonic assertiveness of "the Ideas", as if they could be numbered, was dropped from the "ideas" of *TT* (1835). Giving the examples of prescience and freewill, C had defined ideas in a note on Davison as "intuitions not sensuous, which can be expressed only by contradictory conceptions, or, to speak more accurately, are in themselves necessarily both inexpressible and inconceivable, but are suggested by two contradictory positions". *CM (CC)* II 152.

¹⁰ Derived from Kant *Vermischte Schriften* (4 vols Halle and Königsberg 1799–1807) II 1–54. *Logic (CC)* 214–15, 215 n 1, 224. For further definitions of ideas see 63–4, 236–7, 298.

¹ HNC returned to Heath's Court on 24 Dec. His letter to SC on the 28th, postmarked 30 Dec in London, predicted his arrival in Hampstead twenty-four hours after the letter. UT ms. He visited C on 1 Jan 1834 (Wed).

² Landor's works as edited by Charles G. Crump (1891–3) comprise six vols of *Imaginary Conversations*, two further vols of prose, and two of verse. In Oct 1799 C described what he found revealed in Landor's then anonymous *Gebir* (1798) as "a *powerful* or *ebullient* Faculty". *CL* I 540. When Landor wrote on 14 Dec 1808 that he would like to subscribe to *The Friend*, C was glad to have "a specimen of the Handwriting of so remarkable a man, and of a Genius so brilliant and original". *Friend (CC)* II 440–1. In Oct 1810 a notebook entry by C combined close observation with an echo from *Gebir*. *CN* III 3990. On 6 Nov 1831 Landor answered a report from HCR: "I grieve at the illness of Coleridge tho I never knew him.—I hope he may recover; for Death will do less mischief with the Cholera than with the blow that deprives the world of Coleridge." Ms in Dr Williams's Library. When HCR took Landor to Highgate 29 Sept 1832, they "seemed to like each other": "Landor spoke in his dashing way, which Coleridge could understand and he concurred with him." *CRB* I 414. SC thought this still important news for DC to be told nine months later. SC to Mrs DC 15 Apr, 11 May 1833. UT mss. The justice of C's evaluation does not remove the surprise that HNC and his advisers should think the remarks appropriate for publication in 1835.

³ See 27 Dec 1831 nn 2–3, above.

simple and lucid English; he might have profited much by Southey in this respect.[4]   [36:610]

After all you can say, I think the chronological order is the best for arranging a poet's works. All your divisions are in particular instances inadequate, and they destroy the interest which arises from watching the progress, maturity and even decay of Genius.[5]   [36:612]

The Useful, the Agreeable,[6] the Beautiful,[7] and the Good are distinguishable.[8] You are wrong in resolving Beauty into Expression or Interest; it is quite distinct; indeed it is opposite—not contrary. Beauty is an immediate presence between (*inter*) which and the beholder nihil *est*.[9] It is always one and tranquil—whereas the Interesting always disturbs and is disturbed. I exceedingly regret the loss of those Essays on Beauty which I wrote in the Bristol Mercury—Gutch or Gudge's paper, I think.[10] I would give much to recover them.   [36:611]

---

[4] The final clause, not published, points to the private correspondence and public friendship of Landor and RS. They had both entered Oxford in 1792, but the friendship began with RS's "very kind" review of *Gebir* in *C Rev* Sept 1799. *CL* I 573; *S Life* (Simmons) 33, 85.

[5] "Your divisions" is presumably generic for "anybody's divisions" in any edition of the works of any true poet. WW's classification of his own poems, from 1802 on, with his defence of this procedure in 1815, might come first to mind. HNC was preparing a new edition of C's poems, to be published by William Pickering, in which the divisions of 1828 were retained—Juvenile Poems, Sibylline Leaves, Miscellaneous Poems, dramas, etc. In a recent letter to HNC (probably of Dec 1833) explaining how he had been diverted from aid towards the collection of early poems, C handed the reins to HNC: "do not let my doings or no doings interfere with the Progress of Pickering". *CL* VI 975.

[6] In 1814 C distinguished between two senses of the Agreeable: first, "whatever agrees with our nature" because "congruous with the primary constitution of our senses"; second, that which has been made agreeable "by force of habit" or by association either with what was "dear and pleasing" or with "pleasure or advantage" that followed. "On the Principles of Genial Criticism" *BL* (1907) II 231.

[7] In a letter of 20 Feb 1828 to HNC, C identified in himself "the tranquil Complacency in Beauty, as distinguished from the Interesting, the Agreeable, the Delicious". *CL* VI 729. He distinguished the beautiful from the agreeable at greater length for J. H. Green 12 Aug 1829. *CL* VI 811.

[8] The agreeable and the good, C noted in 1814, act on the will, as beauty does not. "On the Principles of Genial Criticism" *BL* (1907) II 239–43.

[9] "There is nothing": C allows no intermediary purpose, thought, or emotion between the beauty in a beautiful object and its beholder. Beauty is not "interesting", because its appeal is to disinterest. In 1809 C had noted "the *disinterestedness* of all Taste". *CN* III 3584. The disinterest of aesthetic judgement is central to Kant's argument in *Kritik der Urtheilskraft* pt 1 (1790).

[10] Three essays "On the Principles of Genial Criticism in the Fine Arts" in *Felix Farley's Bristol Journal* ed John Mathew Gutch (1776–1861) in Aug–Sept 1814, reprinted in *BL* (1907) II 219–46.

*a*3. Jan. 1834.

Mr Kenyon has sent me a poem entitled "Rhymes on Tolerance".[1] The proper title would be "Intolerant*b* (I will not say intolerable) Rhymes on Tolerance". Ought not a man, who writes a book expressly to inculcate tolerance, learn to treat with respect or at least with indulgence articles of faith which tens of thousands ten times told of his fellow subjects or fellow creatures believe with all their souls, and upon the truth of which they rest their tranquillity in this world and their hopes of salvation in the next—those articles being at least maintainable against his arguments, and most certainly innocent in themselves?—Is it fitting to run Jesus Christ in a silly parallel with Socrates?—the being whom thousand millions of intellectual creatures—of whom I am one humbler unit, take to

a f 109ᵛ   *b* "Intolerant ~~Rhymes on~~

SW&F (CC). Although the uncertainty over the name is conceivably C's, Gutch had been at Christ's Hospital with C and with Lamb, who was in touch with him in 1819. LL II 236–9. TT (1835) carried a note omitted in 1836: "I preserve the conclusion of this passage, in the hope of its attracting the attention of some person who may have local or personal advantages in making a search for these essays, upon which Mr. C. set a high value. He had an indistinct recollection of the subject, but told me that, to the best of his belief, the essays were published in the Bristol Mercury, a paper belonging to Mr. Gutch. The years in which the inquiry should be made, would be, I presume, 1807 and 1808.—ED." The editor was identified by Josiah Wade, through whom HNC sent Gutch, then at Worcester, LR I and II. Wade to HNC 26 Sept 1836. UT ms. Cottle published an inaccurate version of the essays in *E Rec*.
[1] John Kenyon (1784–1856) anon *Rhymed Plea for Tolerance. In Two Dialogues. With a Prefatory Dialogue* (1833). C's copy, now in the BM, bears an inscription "To S. T. Coleridge Esqꞓ With the Author's respects and regards"; autograph corrections (but fewer than in the copy Kenyon presented to Harvard College 7 Mar 1834); and C's marginal objections to the Preface and the first ten pages. CM (CCᶜ) III. This copy, of the 2nd issue, contains notes on C, WW,

RS, Lamb and "Omissions and Additions" later inserted into the text (1839). C's *France: An Ode* is cited in a passage on supporters of Revolution who later recanted (p 141 n 10), and *Fears in Solitude* is cited pp 142–3 n 14. Scott, said Kenyon (p 144 n 2), had "that practical tolerance—that *humanness* (to use a word of Mr. Coleridge's) . . .". The "Prefatory Dialogue" includes eighteen lines of tribute (pp 19–20) to a "comprehensive soul" recognisable as C. SC, who gave the lines in *BL* (1847) II 411, said that the passage "concluded, when first written, with a reference to the unhappy thraldom of his powers", which Kenyon had witnessed at Bath in 1815, when C "was not so well regulated in his habits and labours" as he afterwards was (410n). WW liked the verse, but predicted reactions like C's: "Christians, however, will justly think that Tolerance is carried too far, by a philosophy that places all creeds so much upon the same footing." *CRC* I 252, *WL* (*L* rev) II 658. Kenyon and RS had been friends since c 1804; he had lived near, and visited, Poole. Initiated through Poole, C's relations with Kenyon, "a man of fortune, highly educated", had been cordial in 1814–15 and 1819. *CL* III 540, IV 557, 916. In *TT* (1835) the first two sentences of the entry were rewritten to omit Kenyon's name and the title of his poem.

be their Redeemer with an Athenian philosopher, of whom we should know nothing except through his glorification in Plato and Xenophon? And then to hitch Latimer and Servetus together![2] To be sure there was a stake and a fire in either case, but where the rest of the resemblance is, I cannot see. What ground is there for throwing the odium of Servetus' death upon Calvin alone? Why, the mild Melancthon wrote to Calvin in the name of all the Reformed churches in Germany to thank him for the act[3]—Zwingli did the same in the name of the Swiss churches, and the Archbishop of Canterbury did the like in the name of the Church of England.[4] Before a man deals out the popular slang of the day about the great leaders of the Reformation, he should learn to throw himself back to the age of the Reformation—when the two great parties in the Church were eagerly on the watch to charge heresy on the other. Besides if ever a poor fanatic thrust himself into the fire—it was Servetus. He was a rabid enthusiast, and did every thing he could in the way of insult and ribaldry to

[2] When Kenyon suggested that with a spirit of tolerance "Christ and Socrates had not died by hemlock and the cross, nor Servetus and Latimer by fire" (p vi), C made in the margin, more briefly, the objections he makes here. *CM (CC)* III. For C on Socrates as portrayed in the works of Plato and Xenophon see 7 Jan–13 Feb 1823 and n 1 and 1 May 1823 and n 15, above.

[3] In an annotation on *A Harmonie upon the Three Evangelists*, C denounced Calvin as worse than Servetus. *CM (CC)* I 477. Hugh Latimer, bp of Worcester, accused and silenced periodically for his Lutheran teaching and for encouraging Puritans, was burnt at Oxford in 1555. C had an anti-Sabellian distaste for Michael Servetus (Miguel Serveto y Revés, 1511–53), Spanish theologian and physician who opposed trinitarianism in *De trinitatis erroribus* (1531) and was tried before the Inquisition for his *Christianismi restitutio* (1553). After escape, he was imprisoned at the behest of John Calvin (Jean Chauvin or Caulvin, 1509–64), tried at Geneva, and burnt at the stake. Letters from Luther's collaborator Melanchthon (Philipp Schwarzert, 1497–1560) condemning the expressed opinions of Servetus were read at the trial. In a footnote *TT* (1835) gave the key words in the

Melanchthon letter C refers to. The letter appears in Calvin *Opera quae supersunt omnia* ed Wilhelm Baum, Eduard Cunitz, and Eduard Reuss (59 vols Brunswick 1863–1900) VIII 267, a work that includes all known documents pertinent to the trial. Rees XXXII under "Servetus" (an account hostile to Calvin) said: "The mild and otherwise moderate and benevolent Melanchthon sanctioned the deed by a congratulatory letter addressed to the magistrates of Geneva."

[4] Huldreich or Ulrich Zwingli (1484–1531), Swiss Protestant reformer, rector of the Great Minster in Zurich, and the abp of Canterbury, Thomas Cranmer (1489–1556), both disappeared from *TT* (1835), which generalised to conform with discoverable facts. Cranmer was himself committed to the Tower on 8 Sept 1553. In the trial of Servetus letters were solicited and received from the magistrates of all the Protestant cantons of Switzerland: "The magistrates of Zurich answered, that they had consulted their ministers, and intreated the council of Geneva to oppose strenuously SERVETUS's heresy." *Bibliotheque angloise* II pt 1 § 7, tr Sir Benjamin Hodges in *An Impartial History of Michael Servetus, Burnt Alive at Geneva for Heresie* (1724) 165.

provoke the feelings of the Christian Church. He called the Trinity—the Cerberus of Christianity &c[5]—*c*Indeed how should the principle of religious toleration have been acknowledged at first? It would require stronger arguments than any which have been brought forward yet, to prove that men in authority have not a right involved in an imperative duty to deter those under their control from teaching or countenancing doctrines which they believe to be damnable—and even to punish with death those who violate such prohibition. I am sure Bellarmine would have had no trouble in turning Locke round his fingers upon this ground alone.[6] But the only true argument—apart from Christianity—for toleration is that *it is of no use* to attempt to stop heresy or schism by persecution. You *cannot* preserve men in*d* the faith by such means—though you may stifle for a while any open appearance of dissent. The experiment has now been tried—and it has failed—and *that* is a great deal the best argument against a repetition of it for the magistrate.[7]   [36:613]

c f 110   *d* ~~from~~ in

[5] *TT* (1835) gave one phrase in Servetus' Latin rather than the ms "Cerberus of Christianity". Cf a letter to the Syndics and Senate of Geneva from the Pastors and Readers, Ministers of the Church at Zurich 21 Oct 1553: Servetus "often calls the coeternal trinity of God a three-headed monster, and a certain tripartite *Cerberus* . . . (trinitatem coeternam Dei triceps monstrum, ac cerberum quendam tripartitum) . . .". *Impartial History* 171. At the trial, Servetus said that he was not describing the Trinity but misrepresentations of it by Tritheists.

[6] Roberto Francesco Romolo Bellarmino (1542–1621), Italian Jesuit who defended the temporal power of the Pope in disputations against James I and William Barclay. In *Disputationes de controversiis Christianae fidei adversus hujus temporis haereticos* Bellarmine argued explicitly that persons in authority have a responsibility to deter others from damnable teaching. HNC included in "Omniana" C's explanation of his preference for William Penn over Locke's *Epistola de tolerantia* (1667) in answer to "the sublime and oft-times plausible arguments of Bellarmin, and other Romanists". *LR* I 312–15. Locke published three further letters on toleration in 1689–92.

TT (1835) here inserted three sentences, the first against "a *right* to toleration", the others concluding that the state has a right to exclude "hideous doctrine and practice" because Paul IV (1476–1559, Pope 1555–9), if granted the authority to command Catholics to separate from the national church of England, had then also the authority to command rebellion against Elizabeth (whom the Pope did not acknowledge as Queen).

[7] After first requesting a visit from HNC, apparently to discuss *TT* and materials for *LR*, HCR "objected to him the passage in *Table Talk* on toleration, which he thought not in favour of persecution". *CRB* II 506. On 17 Nov 1835 HCR wrote a letter to HNC about the remarks on toleration. For the letter and HNC's reply, see App F 36, below.

Among several notes on toleration in Baxter *Reliquiae Baxterianae*, C said that arguments "such as those adduced by Locke, had been fairly and fully and repeatedly confuted by both Romish and Protestant Divines; and the *true* grounds it would not perhaps *even now* be quite safe for a writer to bring forwards. We owe the blessing wholly to God, with no intervention or instrumentality of Human Wisdom." *CM (CC)* I 256. In *The*

I know this—that if a parcel of fanatic missionaries were to go to Norway and were to attempt to disturb the fervent and undoubting Lutheranism of the fine independent inhabitants of the interior of that country,[8] I should be right glad to hear that the busy fools had been quietly shipped off—any where. I don't include the people of the seaports in my praise of the Norweigians—I speak of the agricultural population. If that country could be brought to maintain a million more of inhabitants, Norway might defy the world: it would be αὐταρκής[9] and impregnable. But it is much under-handed[10] now. [36:613]

I have drawn up four or perhaps five Articles of Faith, by subscription or rather assent to which I think a large comprehension might take place.[11] My articles would exclude Unitarians and, I am sorry to say, the Roman Catholics, but with this difference—that the exclusion of the Unitarians would be necessary and perpetual, that of Roman Catholics depending on the individual's own conscience and intellectual light. I mean that the Roman Catholics hold the faith in Christ, but unhappily they also hold certain opinions, partly ceremonial, partly devotional ordinances, partly speculative, which have so fatal a facility of being degraded into base, corrupting and even idolatrous practices, that if the Roman Catholic will make *them* of the essence of his religion, he must of ᵉcourse be excluded. As to the Quakers, I hardly know what to say.[12] An article on the Sacra-

ᵉ f 110ᵛ

Friend of 1818 C agreed with Jacobi that "The only true spirit of Tolerance consists in our conscientious toleration of each other's intolerance". *Friend (CC)* I 96.

[8] Always an admirer of Sweden, C recorded a wish in Apr 1812 to see Norway part of a Scandinavian "Gothland". *CN* III 4147 f 6ᵛ. In 1814 Norway was joined in union with Sweden under the Swedish king. In Feb 1819 C denied that Britain was morally superior to "Sweden, Norway, Germany, The Tyrol". *CN* III 4482.

[9] "Sufficient to itself".

[10] *OED* cites this entry for the first observed use of "underhanded" to mean "undermanned".

[11] The divisiveness of sects is deplored in a note added to the 1812 edition of *The Friend*: see *(CC)* II 72n. In variance from the entry in TT, C wrote with scorn of the British and Foreign Bible Society as a symptom of "that Coalition-system in Christianity, for the expression of which Theologians have invented or appropriated the term, *Syncretism*". *LS (CC)* 200. In *SM* he denounced the Lancastrian system for "teaching those points only of religious faith, in which all denominations agree". *SM (CC)* 40. HCR noticed a contradiction between C's objection to bibliolatry and his approval of the Bible Society in 1812. *CRB* I 59.

[12] Followers of George Fox in the Religious Society of Friends called themselves Children of Light, rejecting the sacraments as inessential to Christian life. C goes on to equate Christian Light with baptism and Christian life with celebration of the Eucharist, and thus questions whether the Quakers on their own terms are Christians.

ments would exclude them. My doubt is whether Baptism and the Eucharist are properly any *parts* of Christianity, or not rather Christianity itself;—the one the initial conversion or Light, the other the sustaining and invigorating Life—both together the φῶς καὶ ζωή[13] which are Christianity. A line can only *begin* once; hence there can be no repetition of Baptism; but a line may be endlessly prolonged by fresh additions; hence the sacrament of love and life lasts for ever. But there is no knowing what the modern Quakers are or believe, excepting this, that they are altogether degenerated from their ancestors of the seventeenth century.*f* I should call modern Quakerism a Socinian Calvinism. Penn was a Sabellian, and seems to have disbelieved even the historic fact of the life and death of Jesus—most certainly Jesus of Nazareth was not Penn's Christ, if he had any.[14] It is amusing to see the modern Quakers appealing now to history for a confirmation of their tenets and discipline—by so doing in effect abandoning the strong hold of their founders. As an imperium in imperio I think Quakerism a conception of Lycurgus.[15] Modern Quakerism is like one of those gigantic trees which are seen in the forests of North America—apparently flourishing and preserving*g* all its greatest stretch and spread of branches; but when you have cut through an enormously thick and gnarled bark, you find the whole inside hollow and rot-

---

f century. ~~Judging by Penn & Barclay~~   *g* ~~throwin~~ preserving

[13] "Light and life"; cf John 1.4: "and the life was the light of men".

[14] William Penn (1644–1718), English Quaker who founded Pennsylvania and its city Philadelphia (1681–2). In Ireland he was imprisoned for writing *The Sandy Foundation Shaken* (1668), a tract against the doctrine of the Trinity. C had noted in 1810: "Of all the *Heresies* respecting the Person of Christ Sabellianism (to which, by the bye, the famous W. Penn professed himself an adherent) is the only one, quite & certainly clear from Polytheism, but yet it was Idolatry—for it made God himself an *Idol*." *CN* III 3968. The Roman Christian theologian Sabellius was excommunicated c 220 for the doctrine of "one *hypostasis*, or singular individual essence, of the Father, Son, and Holy Ghost". Ralph Cudworth *The True Intellectual System of the Universe* bk I ch 4 (2nd ed 1743) I 605. Penn had written that "*Mankind was* (and consequently is) *antecedently to Christ's Coming in the Flesh*, enlight-ened with such a Measure of Light, as was Saving in itself". Penn and George Whitehead *The Christian-Quaker and His Divine Testimony Vindicated* (1673–4) I 32. C's friend Thomas Clarkson had only slightly mitigated this offence to C by quoting Penn's words to Fox: "in my confession at the close I said, that we believed in Christ, both as *he was the man Jesus, and God over all blessed for ever*". *Memoirs of the Private and Public Life of William Penn* (2 vols 1813) I 127.

[15] *TT* (1835) modified to "the original Quakerism a conception worthy of Lycurgus". In its revised form the originally cryptic notation could mean merely "worthy of a great lawgiver". Lycurgus, the possibly legendary founder of the Spartan constitution, was often mentioned by C in such general terms. On the Society of Friends as *imperium in imperio* cf 8 Apr 1833 (at n 12), above (36:485).

ten.[16] Quakerism, like such a tree, stands by its inveterate bark alone. *Bark* a Quaker, and he is a poor creature.   [36:614]

How[h] much the devotional spirit of the Church has suffered by that necessary evil the Reformation, and the sects which have sprung up subsequently to it! All our prayers seem tongue-tied. We seem to be [i]thinking more[j] of avoiding an heretical expression or thought than of opening ourselves to God. We do not pray with that entire, unsuspecting, unfearing, childlike profusion of feeling, which so beautifully appears in the writings of some of the older Saints of the Romish Church,[17] particularly that remarkable woman Sta Theresa.[18] And certainly Protestants in their anx-

---

[h] ~~The S~~ How   [i-j] more thinking
                              2   1

---

[16] Untraced. There are many such descriptions as William Bartram's of *Cupressus disticha*: "The large ones are hollow, and serve very well for beehives; a small space of the tree itself is hollow . . .". *Travels Through North & South Carolina* pt 2 ch 3 (Philadelphia 1791) 91. Gillman heard C employ a similar simile for the Unitarians: "During the first week of his residence at Highgate, he conversed frequently on the Trinity and on Unitarianism, and in one of these conversations, his eye being attracted by a large cowry, very handsomely spotted: 'Observe,' said he, 'this shell, and the beauty of its exterior here pourtrayed. Reverse it and place it to your ear, you will find it empty, and a hollow murmuring sound issuing from the cavity in which the animal once resided. This shell, with all its beautiful spots, was secreted by the creature when living within it, but being plucked out, nothing remains save the hollow sound for the ear. Such is Unitarianism; it owes any beauty it may have left to the Christianity from which it separated itself. The teachers of Unitarianism have severed from *their* Christianity its *Life*, by removing the doctrine of St. John; and thus mutilated, *they* call the residue the religion of Christ, implying the whole of the system, but omitting in their teaching the doctrine of redemption.' " *C Life* (G) 314.

[17] *TT* (1835) inserted two Anglican prelates, Jeremy Taylor and Lancelot

Andrewes (1555–1626), before "older and better saints of the Romish Church". C was not greatly interested in Andrewes, who had "a strong *patristic* leaven". Annotation on Donne *LXXX Sermons: CM (CC)* II 260. Finding Andrewes praised as "stupendiously profound" in Peter Heylyn's life of Archbishop Laud, *Cyprianus Anglicus*, C answered in the margin: "A wise, pious & right learned Man he was; but who could *now* from the perusal of his works have guessed at these stupendous Attributions?" *CM (CC)* II 1101. He often linked Taylor with Leighton, as in a conversation of 1807 reported by Cottle *Rem* 334: "He thought favourably of Lord Rochester's conversion as narrated by Burnet; spoke of Jeremy Taylor in exalted terms, and thought the compass of his mind discovered itself in none of his works more than in his 'Life of Christ,' extremely miscellaneous as it was. He also expressed the strongest commendation of Archbishop Leighton, whose talents were of the loftiest description, and which were, at the same time, eminently combined with humility. He thought Bishop Burnet's high character of Leighton justly deserved, and that his whole conduct and spirit were more conformed to his Divine Master, than almost any man on record."

[18] In *TT* (1835) HNC provided a note on the Spanish saint Theresa or Teresa (1515–82). C was moved to fervent committed notes when he read her life in

iety to have the historical argument on their side have brought down the Romish errors too late. Many of them began, no doubt, in the Apostolic age itself; I say errors—not heresies as Epiphanius, blockhead! calls them.[19] The Ebionites heretics! Ebion is Hebrew for Beggar—and the name was adopted by some poor mistaken men who sold all their goods and lands and were then obliged to beg. Barnabas was one of their chief mendicants.[20] St Paul made a collection for them.[21]

*k*You should read Rhenferd's*l* account of the early heresies.[22] I think he enumerates about eight of Epiphanius' heretics to be mere nicknames given the Christians by the Jews.[23] Read the Hermas*m* or the Shepherd, of the genuineness of which and of the epistle of Barnabas I have no doubt. It is perfectly orthodox—but full of the most ludicrous tricks of Gnostic fancy; the wish to find the New Testament in the Old Testament. Gnosis is perceptible in the Epistle to the Hebrews—but kept*n* exquisitely within the limit of propriety.*o* In the others it is rampant; and most truly "puffeth up," as Paul said of it.[24]   [36:615]

---

k f 111   *l* Renfurt's   *m* Hermes   *n* kept ~~so~~   *o* propriety ~~that~~

1810 in RS's copy of *The Works of the Holy Mother St. Teresa of Jesus, Foundress of the Reformation of the Discalced Carmelites* (2 vols 1669–75). *CN* III 3907, 3909, 3911, 3917 and nn. His notes in the 2 vols were published by HNC in *LR* IV 65–71. *CM (CC)* V. Allsop's report on the relation of Theresa to *Christabel* is discussed in Arthur H. Nethercot *The Road to Tryermaine* (Chicago 1929) 26, 42, 207–11, and by later critics.

[19] Epiphanius (c 315–403), a Father of the Eastern Church. His *Panarion* included the Ebionites among the many kinds of heretic. Rhenferd set C right about these "heresies". See below, nn 22, 23.

[20] Barnabas, meaning "son of encouragement", was the name given to one Joseph, a Levite of Cyprus, who sold his land to benefit the apostles. Acts 4.36–7. He later served with Paul in Antioch.

[21] *TT* (1835) hedged the statements at the end of this paragraph. 1 Cor 16.1, 2 Cor 9.1, Acts 11.29–30, and Rom 15.25 concern Paul's collection for the saints.

[22] Rhenferd "Dissertatio de fictis Judaeorum haeresibus" and "Dissertatio

de fictis Judaeorum et Judaizantium haeresibus" *Opera philologica* (Utrecht 1722) 76–164. Cf 8 Jul 1827 n 14, above.

[23] C had written marginalia concerning Rhenferd's corrections to Epiphanius' "slanderous Blunders" in Eichhorn *AT*, Fleury *Ecclesiastical History*, and Oxlee *The Christian Doctrine of the Trinity* . . . I 4–5: *CM (CC)* II 437, 700, 709–10, III. C's view of the Ebionites as one among the variant groups of "orthodox apostolic Christians, who received Christ as the *Lord*", gained relief solicited by Paul, and derived from no person called Ebion "unless indeed it was Sᵗ Barnabas, who in his humility might have so named himself" is most fully explained in a marginal note on Waterland *Importance of the Doctrine of the Holy Trinity* 286–96: *CM (CC)* V.

[24] 1 Cor 8.1. A similar packaging of these subjects is apparent on 8 Jul 1827, 6 Jun 1830, and 31 Mar 1832, above. See also C's annotation on Fleury *Ecclesiastical History* in *CM (CC)* II 707, 714. Reading Joseph Nightingale *A Portraiture of Methodism* (1807) in Jun 1810, C meditated on the influential "vileness"

What between the Sectarians and the Political Economists, the English are denationalized. England I see as a country—but the English nation seems obliterated.[25] What can *integrate* us again? Must it be another threat of foreign invasion?   [36:616]

I never can digest the loss of most of Origen's works.[26] He seems to have been almost the only very great scholar and genius combined amongst the early Fathers. Jerome was very inferior to him.[27]   [36:617]

The invocation of the Saints is founded on an amiable and affectionate feeling. It certainly has a tendency in it to supersede the faith in the one Redeemer and to confound the distinction between the omnipresence of God, and mere creaturely presence. Yet with a change to the third person—oret Mater pro nobis &c.[28]—much mischief might have been avoided.[29]

---

of Epiphanius' account of the Gnostics. *CN* III 3901. In May 1827 C wrote to H. F. Cary that he was more at ease with *Hermas*, Barnabas, and Clement than with Daniel, Timothy, and Titus. *CL* VI 683.

[25] C's essay "On the Law of Nations", with its sequel, makes the nation a moral bond of people and state, "where the powers and interests of men spread without confusion through a common sphere . . . distinct yet coherent, and all uniting to express one thought and the same feeling". *Friend (CC)* I 292.

[26] C had read a full and admiring account of the scope of Origen's lost works in Fleury *Ecclesiastical History* I 338, 351–2, 357–8. He outlined in the margin of I 341 Origen's "noble scheme of Education". *CM (CC)* II 722. He defended Origen in marginalia on Luther *Colloquia Mensalia* 54 and Taylor *Polemicall Discourses* i 414: *CM (CC)* III, V. C would be fascinated by the theory of Gilles Quispel that writings by Origen recovered in the twentieth century at Toura, along with discoveries at Nag Hammadi, show an indebtedness to the Gnostic Valentinus.

[27] St Jerome, one of the four chief Doctors of the Church, author of histori-

cal and exegetical works, and author of the standard Latin version of the Bible, the Vulgate. C cited Jerome without respect in *The Friend* (CC) I 38. Fleury I 358 said of Origen: "There are a great many of his commentaries and homilies remaining; but most of them are only very loose translations by *Rufinus*, St *Jerome*, and other authors who are unknown." In C's Protestant world Jerome was a subject for Catholic painters.

[28] In the Litanies of the Saints, "Sancta Maria, ora pro nobis" ("Holy Mother Mary, pray for us"). C proposed a change to "Let the Mother pray for us", as he had in *C&S* ch 12 *(CC)* 105: ". . . it is not allowable in directing our thoughts to a departed Saint, the Virgin Mary for instance, to say Ora pro nobis, Beata Virgo, though there would be no harm in saying, Oret pro nobis, precor, beata Virgo". In a marginal note on Johnson *Works* quoted in *C&S (CC)* 105 n 2, C declared the difference of little significance in comparison with "that diluted Pope, an anti-national Clergy". C's language in *C&S* refers to the Order of the (High and Low) Mass in the Missale Romanum.

[29] HNC carried this entry to MS F, but it was not published. C could not be allowed to tolerate the invocation of saints.

4. Jan. S. T. C.

I was once remarking to Joseph Cottle[1] the fact of women having been good poets, historians, mathematicians, romancers, novelists &c, but that I had never heard of a woman being a philosopher or metaphysician. Upon which he said gravely—"that there was one named Mol-Branch;—that he had himself not read her works, but he had heard that the French esteemed them very highly."[a2]

---

[a]22. Feb. 1834[1]

Assume the existence of God—and then the harmony and fitness of the physical creation may be shown to correspond with and support such an assumption; but to set about *proving* the existence[b] of a God by[c] such

[a] On the following five leaves (ff 111v–113v) HNC copied passages from C's N 18; see n 2, below
[a] f 113v [b] existence ~~itself~~ [c] by ~~the works~~

[1] Joseph Cottle (1770–1853), Bristol bookseller who had known C since 1794 and published muddled recollections of him. This entry was not published. When C wrote to continue the colloquy after HNC left he was still in a jocular mood. See his letter of "Saturday Night" (4 Jan): *CL* VI 975–6.

[2] C's copy of Nicolas Malebranche (1638–1715) *De la recherche de la verité* (2 vols Amsterdam 1688) appears in *WW LC* 341; it is now in VCL. C wrote to Josiah Wedgwood 18 Feb 1801: "I had . . ." (before studying Locke) "groped my way thro' the French of Malbranche". *CL* II 679. Yet he also wrote, in Oct 1810: "I have not read his Book". *CN* III 3974. He appealed in Thesis X *BL* ch 12 to "the position of Malbranche, that we see all things in God". *BL (CC)* I 285. He could have found the statement in Kant *De mundi sensibilis atque intelligibilis forma et principiis* IV scholion: *Vermischte Schriften* II 474.

The next date in *TT* (1835) is 12 Jan, assigned to part of the talk of 3 Jan (36:614–17). The next four leaves of MS B, on leaves torn from it probably by HNC himself (but preserved at VCL), contain fifteen items copied by him, with variations, from C's N 18. On f 111v: from *CN* III 4073 (on "*Crathmocraulo*"), 3920, 4043, 3834. On f 112; from *CN* III 4073 (end of entry) (*TT* 36:619), 4084 (*TT* 36:618), 4086, 3826, 4087 (*TT* 36:620), 4082, 3752 (*TT* 36:413). On f 112v: 3890 (*TT* 36:213n), 3880. On f 113: 3749, 3740. Three of these, copied on f 112, were printed in *TT* (1835) under the date 20 Jan 1834 (36:618–20); they were cancelled in the usual way with a vertical line to indicate publication. The last entry on that leaf was not so cancelled; it was inserted in *TT* (1836), with modifications, under the date 25 Jul 1832 (36:413). Inserted as a footnote under the date 30 May 1830 in *TT* (1836) was the entry from N 18 of the hypothesis that Christ was quoting Ps 22 in Matt 27.46 (36:213n).

[1] There are no dated entries in MS B between 4 Jan (Sat) and 22 Feb (Sat). On 14 Jan SC gave birth to the twins Florence and Berkeley; they were baptised on the 15th, died on the 16th, and were buried on the 18th. On 19 Jan SC wrote to Elizabeth Crump Wardell that she was in "nervous misery". DCL ms. Hilary term had begun for HNC at Lincoln's Inn.

means is a mere circle—a delusion. It can be no proof to a good reasoner, unless he presumes his conclusion.[2]   [36:621]

Kant once set about proving the existence of God, and a masterly effort it was.[3] But in his later great work the Critique of the Pure Reason, he saw its fallacy—and said of it that *if* the existence *could* be *proved* at all—it must be in the manner indicated by him.[4]   [36:621]

I never could feel any force in the arguments for a plurality of worlds.[5] A lady asked me—"What then could be the intention in creating so many great bodies so apparently useless to us!" I said, I did not know, except perhaps to make dirt cheap.[6] What in the eye of an intellectual and om-

---

[2] *TT* (1835) inserted the stronger language that the philosopher who thus argues "violates all syllogistic logic".

[3] Kant "Der einzig mögliche Beweisgrund zu einer Demonstration des Daseyns Gottes" (1763) *Vermischte Schriften* II 57–246. In HCR's copy (II 78–9) C agreed with Kant in rejecting those who "deduce" God, "as those, who derive a God from the order of the material World not only confounding Certainty with Evidence, but mistaking for Evidence mere sensuous Vividness". *CM (CC)* III. After ruminations on the knowledge of God in N 29 (*CN* IV 4786) C returned to Kant's demonstration of "the *One*" God on 27 Jan 1824 (*CN* IV 5110).

[4] *Kritik der reinen Vernunft* (1781) bk II ch 3 §§ 3–6 disposes of the ontological, cosmological, and physico-theological arguments for God's existence. Annotating De Wette *Theodor*, C took from Kant an answer satisfactory at least in the moment of C's note: "The idea of God is *altogether* transcendent: what therefore we are able to believe concerning him must be determined by the Conscience & the Moral Interest, under the *negative* condition only of not contradicting Reason." *CM (CC)* II 183. According to Carlyon (I 185) C heard in 1799 of Kant's proof of God, by demonstrating that no proof was possible, without showing any sign of assent. That Kant did indeed take possession of C in 1801

"as with a giant's hand"—*BL* ch 9 *(CC)* I 153—needs no demonstration. On 8 Apr 1825 C wrote to JTC that he valued Kant not as a metaphysician but as a logician (*CL* v 421), meaning that he could not accept Kant's rejection of the transcendent, of ideas as constitutive.

[5] C here rejects out of hand a favourite speculation of his beloved Bruno. If there is a direct transition from the previous comment on Kant, it may be by way of Kant's "Gedanken von der wahren Schätzung der lebendigen Kräfte" (1747)—*Vermischte Schriften* I 1–282—which C praised with regard to "a *plurality* of self-subsisting Souls" proposed by Berkeley, in *AR* (1825) 392n–3 and mentioned admiringly with Kant's *Allgemeine Naturgeschichte und Theorie des Himmels* (1755) in *Logic (CC)* 194–5. Almost any questioning of Newton was welcome to C. In *C&S (CC)* 174–5 he derided the proposal of Edmund Halley in 1692 that there might be a habitable inner globe within the earth.

[6] *TT* (1835) inserted: "The vulgar inference is *in alio genere*", in another kind. The sentence implies a failure of logic by passing from one kind of inference to another that cannot be derived from the first; *LS (CC)* 99 n 4 explains the derivation from Aristotle *Posterior Analytics* 1.7.75a. C rejected propositions evolved from false transitions of this sort. *Logic (CC)* 90, 190.

nipotent Being*d* is the*e* whole sidereal system to the soul of one man, for whom Christ died? [36:622]

---

1. March. 1834.

I am by nature a reasoner. A person who should suppose I meant by that word an arguer, would not only not understand me, but would understand the contrary of my meaning. I can take no interest whatever in hearing or saying any thing merely as a fact—merely as having happened. It must refer to something within me before I can regard it with any curiosity or care. My mind is always energic[1]—I will not say energetic; I require in every thing what for lack of another word, I may call *propriety*— that is, a reason why the thing *is* at all, and why it is *there*.[2] [36:623]

---

*a*Shakspeare's intellectual action was *b*unlike that of*c* Ben Jonson or Beaumont and Fletcher. The latter see the totality of a sentence or a passage and then project it entire. Shakspeare goes on creating—evolving B. out of A. and C. out of D. &c., just as a serpent moves, which makes a fulcrum of its own body, and seems for ever twisting and untwisting its strength.[3] [36:624]

---

*d*A common source of error in printing is repeating a word—the compositor's eye being caught with it a little below or above. There are scores of such errors in the first edition of Shakspeare, all of which are faithfully preserved in the very latest of our impressions. When I first read the description of Cleopatra's sailing on the Cydus, Anthony and Cleopatra, Act II, scene 2, and came to the lines

> Her gentlewomen, like the Nereids
> So many mermaids, tended her i' the eyes,
> And made their bends adornings; at the helm
> A seeming Mermaid steers.[4]

d Being ~~as a~~ *e* ~~all~~ the *a* f 114 *b-c* ⟨un⟩like the~~at~~ ~~motion~~ of ~~of a serpent~~
d-g For the variant in MS F see App C, below *e-f* the⟨se⟩ ~~second~~ first

[1] Possessing, though not necessarily expressing, energy; "powerfully operative", as in *Lines on a Friend Who Died of a Frenzy Fever* lines 39–40: *PW* (EHC) I 77:

To me hath Heaven with bounteous
   hand assign'd
Energic Reason and a shaping mind . . .

[2] *TT* (1835) added for clarity: "or *then* rather than elsewhere or at another time".
[3] The distinction is that of C and De Q between a simple style, in which the difficulties have not begun, and a complex, organic style with life and growth.
[4] *Antony and Cleopatra* II ii 206–9. Some of the typographical errors in *An-*

I said *^ethese first^f* mermaids must be a mistake—Shakspeare could never have described one class of attendants as mermaids and then particularized a distinct attendant as a seeming mermaid. It must be sea maids or sea nymphs.[5] And so I afterwards saw it was in North's translation of Plutarch, whence Shakspeare took the description.[*g*6]

I believe the true reading in Macbeth is *"blank height* of the dark" instead of "blanket": height after hēt.[*h*7]   [35:625]

Crabbe and Southey are something alike; but Crabbe's poems are founded on observation and real life, Southey's on fancy and books.[8] In

---

g See *d-g*, above   *h* Insertion of this entry left no space in the ms for a divisional bar

---

tony and Cleopatra in the first folio (1623) were corrected in the second (1632).

[5] This entry was cut from MS F; *TT* 35:625 on *Macbeth* was crowded in instead. C's suggestion appears more briefly in *LR* II 145 and (var) *Sh C* (1960) I 78–9, from C's note in Shakespeare *Works* ed Theobald (8 vols 1773) VII 120–1: *CM (CC)* IV. The general and specific points in this paragraph are made in a variant sequence in notes attached to *Cymbeline* in the Stockdale Shakespeare ed Ayscough (1807) 893, 899. *Sh C* I 104–5; *CM (CC)* IV. In *The Dramatic Works of Shakespeare* with notes by Joseph Rann (6 vols Oxford 1786–94) V 276 C found it less clear what to substitute for the "mermaids" he regarded as an "evident [cor]ruption". *CM (CC)* IV. The modern chain of high regard for *Antony and Cleopatra* begins with C, *LR* II 142–5, more widely known through *NLS* I 145–8.

[6] "Her Ladies and gentlewomen also, the fairest of them were apparelled like the nymphes *Nereides* (which are the myrmaides of the waters) . . .". Plutarch "Antony" (Marcus Antonius) *The Lives of the Noble Grecians and Romanes* tr Sir Thomas North in 1579 from the French of Jacques Amyot, with later editions.

[7] Published in *TT* (1835) with an expansion for clarity (35:625): " 'Height' was most commonly written, and even printed, *hēt*." C made the proposal to amend *Macbeth* I v 53 in J. J. Morgan's copy of the Theobald edition of Shake-

speare (8 vols 1773) VI 300–1. *Sh C* I 65; *CM (CC)* IV. Of this emendation Alexander Dyce wrote to HNC: "What can I say of this, except that it is quite as bad a conjecture as Gilbert Wakefield's 'Bea te Sexti'!" UT ms. As Dyce reported in a note to the line in his Shakespeare of 1857, the entry, "on my urging its absurdity to the editor, was omitted in the second edition of that valuable miscellany". The omission carried away HNC's own objection in a footnote to the passage: "But, after all, may not the ultimate allusion be so humble an image as that of an actor peeping through the curtain on the stage?" The line, ridiculed by Johnson, has continued to trouble explicators.

Dyce's strictures would not have driven C from the position HCR heard him take at Collier's 23 Dec 1810: "On my noticing Hume's obvious preference of the French tragedians to Shakespeare, Coleridge exclaimed: 'Hume comprehended as much of Shakespeare as an apothecary's phial would of the falls of Niagara if placed under them.' " *CRD* I 162.

[8] According to C in 1814, he and William Lisle Bowles then counted George Crabbe (1754–1851) among "the cleverest literary characters of our knowledge" qualified to write essays that would expose the limitations of the *Ed Rev. CL* III 539. The R. H. Brabants had invited C to meet Crabbe in 1815. *CL* IV 557. C was polite in public towards "the Kehama of our laurel-honouring laureat"—*EOT (CC)* II 384—and other po-

Crabbe there is an absolute defect of the imaginative power. What facility he seems to have had—just like Southey in this.[9]   [36:626]

---

*ª*15. March 1834*ᵇ*

I take unceasing delight in Chaucer.[1] His manly cheerfulness is especially delicious to me in my old age. How exquisitely tender he is, and yet how perfectly free from the least touch of sickly melancholy or morbid drooping! The sympathy of the poet with the subjects of his poetry is equally remarkable in Shakspeare and Chaucer; but what the first effects by a strong act of imagination, of mental metamorphosis, the last does

ª f 114ᵛ   *ᵇ* 1815.

---

etry of RS. His defences of RS when *Wat Tyler* was published and attacked in 1817 extended to specific praise of the longer poems. *EOT (CC)* ɪɪ 449–60, ɪɪɪ 147–8; *BL* ch 3 *(CC)* ɪ 63–7. SC, in a letter to Mrs DC, emphasising her own dislike of Mrs WW most of all the set but agreeing with HC's expressed opinions on SH's "moral inconsistency" and "overweening Wordsworthianism", confirms that C agreed with HC in disliking "the Laureate Poetry". UT Grantz 359. The modification of this entry in print, presumably meant to appease RS, endangered that purpose by having C add that he could read almost anything "with some pleasure".

[9] *TT* (1835) added a paragraph on current fiction, probably as a separate entry. It comes at the top of the page in both 1835 and 1836. The transition can be made by way of *The Doctor*, about which HNC wrote to RS, its anonymous author, on 5 Mar. UT ms. In the addition C praised Capt Marryat's *Peter Simple* (1834) and "Tom Cringle's Log", which had appeared in *Bl Mag* 1829–33. Later in Mar C wrote to HNC: "I send back the Lewis—I have been exceedingly amused likewise with Peter Simple". *CL* vɪ 980. (On the Lewis see 15 Mar and n 18, below.) C had received *Bl Mag* without charge since c 1819. *CL* vɪ 884. *TT* (1835) carried a note dropped in 1836 perhaps because it made C a "*goody* man": "Mr. Coleridge said, he

thought this novel [*Peter Simple*] would have lost nothing in energy if the author had been more frugal in his *swearing*.—Eᴅ."

[1] Geoffrey Chaucer (c 1340–1400). Thomas Speght had provided notes and a glossary for *The Workes of our Antient and Learned Poet, Geffrey Chaucer* (1598). Dryden, Pope, and WW were among those who had modernised poems from *The Canterbury Tales* and passages from *Troilus and Criseyde*. RS *Select Works of the British Poets, from Chaucer to Jonson* (1831) had not modernised Chaucer (1–60) or Skelton *The Boke of Philip Sparow* (68–75). To Godwin, who had just completed a life of Chaucer, C wrote on 10 Jun 1803 of "my reverential Love of Chaucer" and promised a series of review-essays; on 1 Feb 1804 he outlined the plan for Sir George Beaumont; by Sept 1807 the essays were to be lectures. *CL* ɪɪ 951, 1054, ɪɪɪ 30. In Lect 3 of 3 Feb 1818, praising Chaucer's "great powers of invention" and "love of nature", C compared his power of characterisation with Shakespeare's. In Lect 14 of 13 Mar 1818 he expressed admiration of Chaucer's prose. *Lects 1808–19 (CC)* ɪɪ 104–5, 236, 238, 241. *TT* (1835) in a footnote quoted C on Chaucer's cheerfulness, from *BL* ch 2; in ch 19 he had cited and quoted Chaucer as a master of natural, unstudied style. *BL (CC)* ɪ 33, ɪɪ 92–3.

without any effort merely by^c the inborn kindly^d joyousness of his nature. How well we seem to know Chaucer! how absolutely nothing do we know of Shakspeare!

I cannot in the least allow any necessity for Chaucer's poetry, particularly the Canterbury Tales, being considered as obsolete.[2] Let a few plain rules be given for sounding the final *è* of ^{e}syllables and expressing the^f termination of^g such words as na*tion*, oc*ean* &c. as dissyllables—or let the syllables to be sounded in such cases be marked by a competent metrist. That of itself will, with a very few trifling exceptions, where the errors are inveterate, enable any reader to feel the perfect smoothness and harmony of his verse. As to understanding his language, if you read twenty^h pages with a good glossary, you surely can find no further difficulty even^i as it is;—but I should have no objection to see this done: Strike out those words which are now obsolete, and I will venture to say that I will replace every one of them by words in^j modern use out of Chaucer himself or Gower his disciple.[3] I do not want this myself—I rather like to see the significant terms which Chaucer unsuccessfully offered as candidates for admission into our language; but surely so very slight a change of the text may well be pardoned even by black-letterati for the purpose of restoring^k so great a poet^l to his ancient and most deserved popularity. [36:628]

Shakspeare is of no age. It is idle to endeavor to support his phrases by quotations from Ben Jonson and Beaumont and Fletcher, &c. His ^{m}language is entirely his own, and the younger dramatists imitated him. The^n construction of Shakspeare's sentences, whether in verse or prose, is the necessary and homogeneous vehicle of his peculiar manner of thinking. His is not the style of the age. His blank verse is more particularly an absolutely new creation. Read Daniel—the Civil Wars, or the Triumphs of Hymen.[4] The style and language are just such as a very pure and

^{c} by ~~his~~ ^{d} kindl~~inessy~~ &
$^{e-f}$ ~~& separating the syllables *tion* such~~ ⟨of syllables & ~~of~~ expression ⟨ing⟩⟩
^{g} ~~of as~~ of ^{h} 4~~0~~ 20 ^{i} ~~as~~ even
^{j} ~~of~~ in ^{k} ~~introducing~~ restoring ^{l} poet ~~once more into~~ ^{m} f 115 ^{n} ~~S's~~ The

[2] See Willmott's note, App S, vol II, below.

[3] John Gower (c 1325–1408), author of poems in Latin, French, and English, called by Chaucer "moral Gower". Upon the suggestion that Milton *L'Allegro* lines 23–4 derived from Gower, C answered: "In the name of common sense, if Gower could write the lines without having seen Milton, why not Milton have done so tho' Gower had never existed?" Annotation on Milton *Poems upon Several Occasions* ed Thomas Warton (1791) 44. *CM (CC)* III. In 1804 C declared Daniel as much above Gower and John Lydgate as below Chaucer. *CN* I 1835. Possibly on 15 Mar 1834 C was making a similar point with emphasis on plain style, with the remarks concerning Shakespeare a detour on the way to Daniel.

[4] In Lamb's copy of Samuel Daniel

manly writer of the present day would use;[5] it seems[o] quite modern in comparison with Shakspeare. Ben Jonson's blank verse is very masterly and individual, and perhaps Massinger's is even still nobler.[6] In Beaumont and Fletcher it is constantly slipping into lyric poetry.[p] [36:629]

As for editing Beaumont and Fletcher, the task would be immensi laboris.[7] The confusion is now so great, the errors so enormous, that the editor must use a boldness quite unallowable in any other case. All I can say as to Beaumont and Fletcher is, that I can point out well enough where[q] something has been lost, and [r]that something[s] so and so was probably in the original;[t] but the law of Shakspeare's thought[u] and verse is such that I feel convinced that not only could I detect the spurious, but supply the true word.[8] [36:630]

I believe Shakspeare was not a whit more intelligible in his own day than he is now to an educated man, except for a few local allusions of no consequence. As I said, he is of no age—nor of any religion, or party, or profession. The[v] body and substance of his works came out of[w] the unfathomable depths of his own oceanic mind—his observation and reading supplied him with the drapery of his figures.[9] [36:629]

Herrick has many very pretty verses.[10]

Lord Byron, as quoted by Lord Dover, in Walpole's Letters to

[o] ~~is~~ seems [p] poetry ~~or~~ [q] ~~that~~ where [r-s] theat ~~something~~ something
[t] original; ~~& that in~~ [u] ~~mind~~ thought [v] ~~His~~ The [w] of ~~his own (the depths)~~

Poetical Works (2 vols 1718), C wrote two letters to improve Lamb's opinion of the *Civil Wars* (1st ed 1609). *CM (CC)* II 118, 119–20. In annotations on the volume he praised *Civil Wars* v 113 for accent and scansion that assist the sense and vi 14 for "the strain of political morality"; he admitted vexation at the incongruous speech of Nemesis to Pandora at vi 32–47. *CM (CC)* II 123, 124–6. In *B Poets* IV he noted his mixed reactions to shorter poems by Daniel. *CM (CC)* I 44–7. In *E Poets* III 451 he wrote in praise of *Hymen's Triumph* (1615), "of which Chalmers says not one word", and in denigration of Daniel's sonnets. *CM (CC)* II 15. In a footnote *TT* (1835) quoted *BL* ch 18: *(CC)* II 78.

[5] *TT* (1835) inserted "Wordsworth, for example"—supported by *BL* ch 22, explained perhaps by Daniel's direct influence on WW. See *BL (CC)* II 146–7.

[6] In 1814 or later C analysed the "distinct unemphasized spondaism" of three lines in Massinger *The Bashful Lover*. *CN* III 4212.

[7] "Of enormous labour". Cf Ovid *Metamorphoses* 1.728: "ultimus immenso restabas, Nile, labori"; 5.490: "et frugum genetrix, immensos siste labores". On the task cf 16 Feb 1833 nn 30–1, above.

[8] Cf the boast that begins 5 Apr 1833 (at n 11), above (36:473).

[9] In a footnote *TT* (1835) quoted *BL* ch 15 on "myriad-minded". *BL (CC)* II 19 and n. A final sentence by HNC in 1835 was dropped in 1836: "I have sometimes thought that Mr. C. himself had no inconsiderable claim to the same appellation."

[10] This is the first remark by C on the Cavalier poet Robert Herrick (1591–1674) to surface. Thomas Maitland had

Mann,[11] says that the Mysterious Mother raises Horace Walpole far above every author living in his, Byron's, time.[12] Upon which I venture to remark: 1. that I [x]do not believe Lord Byron spoke sincerely;[y] for I suspect he made a tacit exception in favor of himself at least.

2. That it is a miserable mode of comparison which does not rest on difference[z] of kind, but consists in measuring heights between things of the same degree. It proceeds of envy and malice and detraction to say that A. is higher than B. unless you show that they are in pari materia.[13]

3. The Mysterious Mother is the most disgusting, detestable, vile composition that ever came from the hand of man.[14] No one with one spark of true *manliness*, of which Horace Walpole had none, could have

[x] f 115[v]   [y] ~~truly~~ sincerely;   [z] difference ~~or identity~~

published the complete poems as *The Works of Robert Herrick* (2 vols Edinburgh 1823), reprinted as *The Poetical Works* (1825). Herrick was not included in *B Poets* (13 vols), *E Poets* (21 vols), or RS *British Poets* (n 1, above). He later became a favourite for anthologists and illustrators. This entry, not followed by a divisional bar in MS B, was not published.

[11] George James Welbore Agar-Ellis, 1st Baron Dover of the 2nd creation (1797–1833) "Sketch of the Life of Horace Walpole" *Letters of Horace Walpole, Earl of Orford, to Sir Horace Mann* (3 vols 1833) I xxi–lxiii.

[12] Arriving at Walpole's "still more remarkable production" *The Mysterious Mother* (1768), a drama of incest, Lord Dover continued (xli–xlii): "In speaking of the latter effort of his genius, (for it undoubtedly deserves that appellation,) an admirable judge of literary excellence has made the following remarks:—'It is the fashion to underrate Horace Walpole . . . He is the *Ultimus Romanorum*, the author of the "Mysterious Mother," a tragedy of the highest order, and not a puling love-play . . . He is the father of the first romance and of the last tragedy in our language, and surely worthy of a higher place than any living writer, be he who he may.' " That the quotation comes from Byron's Preface to *Marino Faliero* (1821) was pointed out by the reviewer of the *Letters of Walpole* in *G Mag* NS I (Jan 1834) 24, which HNC had

brought promptly to C. *CL* VI 975–6.
[13] "Of the same kind". EHC responded that Byron, besides favouring Walpole's audacity, would have "the reasonable hope and expectation that this provocative eulogy of Walpole's play would annoy the 'Cockneys' and the 'Lakers' ". *The Works of Lord Byron: Poetry* (7 vols 1898–1905) IV 339. After numbering this paragraph of the entry "2." and the next "3.", HNC went back to f 115 to insert "1.".
[14] Walpole's titular character, the Countess of Narbonne, tells her son Count Edmund and his wife Adeliza that she is the mother of both; Adeliza stabs herself. C would not be appeased by Walpole's own Preface of 1791: "The Author . . . is sensible that the subject is disgusting, and by no means compensated by the execution. He cannot be blamed more than he blames himself for having undertaken so disagreeable a story . . ."; nor would C have liked the Postscript, in which Walpole said that the "subject is so horrid" that he "thought it would shock" too much to be staged. *The Mysterious Mother: A Tragedy* (2nd ed 1791) iii, 84. The reviewer in *G Mag* praised in it "a vigorous conception of character, and a powerful delineation of passion", but thought that to select such a subject was to "forego all claims to judgment and good taste". As early as 1796 C planned a satire "in the manner of Donne" against Walpole. *CN* I 171.

written it. As to the blank verse, it is indeed better than Rowe's or Thomson's,[a] which was so execrably bad;[15] any approach therefore to the manner of the old dramatists was of course an improvement—but the loosest lines in Shirley[16] are superior to Walpole's best.[17]   [36:631]

M. Lewis's Jamaica journal is delightful; it is almost the only unaffected book of travels or tours I have read of late years.[18] You have the man himself, and not an inconsiderable man—certainly a much finer

[a] Thompson's

[15] Nicholas Rowe (1673–1718), dramatist and poet laureate, was coupled by C with Johnson, in an annotation on Donne *Poems*, as inferior to Elizabethan and Jacobean poets to the same degree that modern Latin poets were inferior to the major Roman poets. *CM (CC)* II 240. A fair judgement of Rowe's blank verse would be based on *The Tragedy of Jane Shore* (1714).

Of James Thomson (1700–48), Scottish poet resident in and near London from 1725, C had written on 7 Nov 1817 to H. F. Cary, probably with *The Seasons* (1726–30) in mind, that "since Milton without any exception our Blank-verse Poets (and I exclude those who, like Mallet & too often my honored Thomson, give us rhyme-less or rather rhyme-craving Pentameter Iambics for Blank *Verse*) have sought for variety solely in their pauses or cadences, except where a rough Line is introduced for a particular effect". *CL* IV 782. In linking Thomson with Rowe in "execrably bad" verse, C probably meant the tragedies, e.g. *Sophonisba* (1730), *Tancred and Sigismunda* (1745). In 1795 C wrote to George Dyer of "that most lovely Poem, the Castle of Indolence". *CL* I 154. In *B Poets* C defended Thomson as "the Honor, yea, the Redeemer of Scotland". *CM (CC)* I 74. He rendered mixed judgement on the blank verse of "Thompson" as "immeasurably below" Cowper's, in a note in *BL* ch 1 *(CC)* I 25n. Thomson's poetry was sufficiently excellent to make C suspect he had an English father. *CM (CC)* I 75.

C had had a chance to review Hazlitt's recollections of 1798: "It was in this room that we found a little worn-out copy of the *Seasons*, lying in a window-seat, on which Coleridge exclaimed, '*That* is true fame!' He said Thomson was a great poet, rather than a good one; his style was as meretricious as his thoughts were natural." "My First Acquaintance with Poets" *Liberal* No 3 (1823) II 43–4. Hazlitt quoted C's remark several times, once as from "a friend of his and ours". *H Works* V 88, VII 125, XVII 120, XX 216.

[16] James Shirley (1596–1666) *Dramatic Works and Poems* ed William Gifford and Alexander Dyce (6 vols 1833). To judge from surviving evidence, C had previously maintained silence concerning Shirley, an associate of Massinger and Ford and (in printed editions) of Beaumont and Fletcher. Not later than 1800 Lamb had known two plays by Shirley from Robert Dodsley *A Select Collection of Old Plays* (12 vols 1744) IX 97–252. *LL* (M) I 229. He had extracted scenes from seven or eight plays in *Specimens of English Dramatic Poets* (1808).

[17] Instead of a divisional bar at the end of the entry on f 115[v], HNC wrote "Ld D⟨over⟩ Cobalt & Zinc", circled those words, and continued, "1st Vol. initio".

[18] Matthew Gregory Lewis (1775–1818) *Journal of a West India Proprietor, Kept During a Residence in the Island of Jamaica* (1834). The "Advertisement" explained: "The following Journals of two residences in Jamaica, in 1815–16, and in 1817, are now printed from the MS. of Mr. Lewis; who died at sea, on the voyage homewards . . .". HNC had lent the volume to C. *CL* VI 980.

mind than I ever supposed before from his[19] romances &c.[20] It is by far his best work, and will live and be popular.[21] Those verses on the Hours are very pretty;[22] but the Isle of Devils is like his romances, a fever dream, horrible without point.[23]   [36:632]

---

16. April 1834.[1]

I found that every thing in Sicily had been exaggerated by travellers, except two things—the wretchedness of the people, and the folly of the Government—and they did not admit of exaggeration.[2]   [36:633]

[19] Prior to "romances" on f 115[v], HNC wrote "nov", i.e. novels. Lewis had published *The Bravo of Venice* (1805) and *Feudal Tyrants* (1806), each with the subtitle "*A Romance . . . from the German*"; and *Romantic Tales* (4 vols 1808).

[20] C had reviewed Lewis's most widely known work, *The Monk: A Romance* (3 vols 1796) in *C Rev* XIX (Feb 1797) 194–200, as a work "truly terrific" in its "*physical* wonders", but uneven in style, unconvincing in "*moral miracle*", and shamelessly immoral in "libidinous minuteness" and in turning "the grace of God into wantonness". *MC* 370–8. (On C's authorship see *CL* I 318 and n, VI 733 and n.) C owned a copy of *The Castle Spectre* (1798), which he denounced for horrors and "agonizing pangs" without human feelings, though effective in its situations, in a letter to WW 23 Jan 1798 (*CL* I 378–9); he was assessing this most famous of Lewis's melodramas, produced at Drury Lane in 1797, as a model for himself and WW. In 1814 C associated it with "froth, Noise, & impermanence". *CL* III 522. To Mary Elizabeth Robinson in 1802 C declined to serve as "an infamous Pander to the Devil" by letting his name be associated with those of "Monk" Lewis and "Thomas Little" Moore. *CL* II 905.

[21] Lockhart, reviewing the volume in *QR* L (Jan 1834) 374–99, had declared the journal the best in all Lewis's works and predicted a longer life for his prose

than for even the best of his poems, *The Isle of Devils*. C and his contemporaries judged more accurately the superiority of travel books then recent than they judged the taste of later generations for such writing. Lewis's journal was reprinted in 1845 and again in 1929, when Mona Wilson began her Introduction to it: "I first read this book because Coleridge had praised it . . . Coleridge was right that in it we get the best of Lewis."

[22] *The Hours: Journal* p 7. Where twenty-four maids, or Hours, kept charge of Virtue's flock, False Love crept in at eve, seduced one, and thereby let the wolf break in: "An Hour once fled, has fled for ever . . .".

[23] *The Isle of Devils. A Metrical Tale: Journal* pp 261–89 ("This strange story was found by me in an old Italian book, called 'Il Palagio degli Incanti' . . ."— p 260). Irza, aged fourteen, washed ashore on an isle of imps, is taken to a cave by the master fiend; when she bears a child, he clubs it to death. They tend the grave together and she bears a second child. When a friar comes to return her to Cintra, the fiend dives into the sea, clutching the child.

[1] HNC went to Heath's Court for Easter (30 Mar) and wrote to SC from there through 4 Apr, when he reported progress on his review of C's *Poetical Works* for *QR*: "I cannot finish the paper on S.T.C. as I hoped". UT ms. Spring vacation made a Wednesday (16 Apr) available to him for the next talk.

[2] C had apparently expected his read-

*It is interesting to pass from Malta to Sicily—from the highest specimen of an inferior race, the Saracenic, to the most degraded class of a superior race, the European.[3] [36:634]

You may learn the fundamental principles of political economy in a very compendious way by taking a short tour through Sicily, and simply reversing in your own mind every law, custom and ordinance you meet with. I never was in a country where every thing proceeding from Man was so exactly wrong. You have peremptory ordinances *against* making roads, taxes on the passage of vegetables from one miserable town to another, and so on.[4] [36:633]

a f 116

---

ers to supply "Sicilian" when he told of "most bitter complaints" against the "—— Government" in a piece on Ireland in the *Courier* 13 Sept 1811: "Government! (exclaimed a testy old Captain of a Mediterranean trading vessel) call it *Blunderment*, or *Plunderment*, or what you like—only not a *Government*." Better government could with sense and good will ameliorate the peasantry of Sicily and Poland, "as rude and averse from industry, as ill-instructed, ill-cloathed, ill-housed, and ill-satisfied as the lower Irish". *EOT (CC)* II 281n. In *The Friend* No 27 he gave the specific example of "interference with the corn Trade". *Friend (CC)* II 362 (I 570). He had noted an excess of churches in Syracuse, with priests as "numerous as an Egyptian plague". *CN* II 2261.

HNC made notes in MS A p 102 from his own reading in John James Blunt (1794–1855) *Vestiges of Ancient Manners and Customs Discoverable in Modern Italy and Sicily* (1823).

[3] In *The Friend* No 27 C contrasted at religious processions "the apparent apathy, or at least the perfect sobriety, of the Maltese, and the fanatical agitations of the Sicilian Populace". *Friend (CC)* II 359 (I 566). In *The Prelude* (1805) X 947–52, WW addressed C

> who now,
> Among the basest and the lowest fallen
> Of all the race of men, dost make abode
> Where Etna looketh down on Syracuse,

The city of Timoleon! Living God! How are the Mighty prostrated!

Emerson paraphrased C as saying in 1833 that "in Malta, the force of law and mind was seen, in making that barren rock of semi-Saracen inhabitants the seat of population and plenty". *English Traits* (1856) 7.

Malta had a mixed population from successive colonisation by Phoenicians, Greeks, Carthaginians, Romans, Arabs in 870, and Normans from Sicily in 1090, after which Malta was ruled by various European monarchs until the Holy Roman Emperor Charles V assigned it in 1530 to the Order of the Hospitallers of St John of Jerusalem, who had been driven from Rhodes by the Turks. More recent French and British rule had little effect on the population, but C's racial contrast, as reported, is sharper than history warrants. Although the Arabs who conquered Sicily in the ninth century were displaced by the Normans in 1060–91, the Normans absorbed and promulgated Arabic learning.

[4] Emerson (pp 6–7) confirms C's account: ". . . on learning that I had been in Malta and Sicily, he compared one island with the other, 'repeating what he had said to the Bishop of London when he returned from that country, that Sicily was an excellent school of political economy; for, in any town there, it only needed to ask what the government enacted, and reverse that to know what

Do you know any parallel in modern history to the absurdity of our giving a legislative assembly to the Sicilians? It exceeds any thing I know. These precious legislators passed two bills before they were knocked in the head—the first was to render lands[b] inalienable and the second to cancel all debts due before the date of the bill.[5]

And then consider the gross ignorance and folly of our laying a tax upon the Sicilians. Taxation in its proper sense can only exist where there is a free circulation of capital, labor and commodities throughout the community.[6] But to tax people in countries[c] like Sicily and Corsica, where there is no internal communication, is mere robbery and confiscation. A crown taken from a Corsican living in the sierras or valleys[d] would not get back to him again in twenty years.[7]   [36:633]

_____

What can Sir Francis Head mean by talking of the musical turn of the Maltese?[8] Why all animated Nature is discordant there! The very cats

_____

[b] ~~the~~ lands   [c] ~~a~~ countr~~y~~ies   [d] vallies

_____

ought to be done; it was the most felicitously opposite legislation to any thing good and wise. There were only three things which the government had brought into that garden of delights,—namely, itch, pox and famine.' "

[5] C apparently refers with exaggeration to actions by the Parliament (modelled after the British) convened in Palermo 20 Jul 1812 and dissolved by Ferdinand III in Jul 1814. *A Reg* (1812) History 191, (1813) 174, (1814) 88–90. The barons had announced similar acts in Feb 1811. Guido Libertini and Giuseppe Paladino *Storia della Sicilia dai tempi più antichi ai nostri giorni* (Catania 1933) 608–9.

[6] C made various notes in 1804 on taxation, corruption of the judiciary, and administrative confusion as causes of Sicilian poverty. *CN* II 2193, 2213, 2231, 2261.

[7] Corsica with a similar history of colonisation and conquest to that of Malta, had remained French after achieving freedom from the British in 1796. To C during Napoleon's ascendancy Corsica was notorious for "assassins and banditti" in the population rather than in the government. *EOT (CC)* II 58.

[8] Francis Bond Head (1793–1875),

knighted 1835, 1st Bt 1836, lieutenant governor of Upper Canada 1835–7; author (anon) of *Bubbles from the Brunnens of Nassau. By an Old Man* (1834). In "The Renegade" (p 184) he contrasted a loud blast on a cow's horn to announce that the condemned man is proceeding to the gallows with "the lovely and love-making notes of the guitar" where "the ear has been constantly accustomed to good Italian music". Although Head was of complicated lineage, it is not clear why he was "Sir" in 1834. He had been an occasional contributor to the *QR* since 1827.

The copy of *Bubbles* presented by John Murray to SC (now VCL no 96) was lent in March to C, who wrote in it a letter to HNC wondering who the author was, noting the difference between his own recollections of the Maltese and Head's, and protesting what C thought a dishonesty in the author's attack on the public schools and universities of England (as having "too long" remained "almost the only pools stagnant in the country"). *CL* VI 977–8 and nn; *CM (CC)* II 978–80. HNC lent the book to JTC 21 Sept 1834, when it included C's letter and marginalia—and when JTC was alerted to make suggestions for

caterwaul more horribly and pertinaciously there than elsewhere.[9] The children—which stand and scream at each other [e]for an hour together out of pure love to dissonance. The dogs are deafening &c.[10]   [35:635]

No tongue can describe the moral corruption of the Maltese when the Island surrendered to us. There was not a family in which a wife or a daughter or both was or were not kept as[f] mistresses. A marquess of good family applied to Sir Alexander Ball to be appointed his valet. "My valet," said Ball, "what can you mean, Sir?" The marquess said he hoped he should then have the honor of presenting petitions to his Excellency. "O that is it, is it," said Ball; "my valet, Sir, brushes my clothes and brings them to me.—If he dared to meddle with matters of public business, I should kick him downstairs!"[11]

Malta was an Augean stable, and Ball had all the inclination[g] to be a Hercules. His task was most difficult, although his qualifications were remarkable. General Oakes[h] solicited him for the renewal of a pension to an abandoned woman, who had been notoriously treacherous to us.[12] Oakes[h] had promised the woman—the fact was, she had sacrificed her

---

[e] f 116ᵛ   [f] ~~by~~ as   [g] inclinaōn ~~& ability~~   [h] Okes

---

omissions from *TT*. BM Add MS 47447 f 114. For HNC's footnote, which printed most of the letter (var) with an addition of his own, see 35:635, below. The entry and the footnote were both dropped from *TT* (1836), and the portion of C's letter attached to 36:548 as a footnote, concerning the "New-Broomers", ceased to be identified with *Bubbles from the Brunnens*.

[9] C's longest of several notations in 1804–5 on Maltese noise included vivid details on cats, children, and dogs. "But it goes thro' every thing—their Street-Cries, their Priests, their Advocates/ their very Pigs yell rather than squeek . . .". *CN* ii 2614. His two entries on the "deep Quiet of Malta" apparently refer to political and military security.

[10] In *TT* (1835) "&c" becomes "and so throughout"—i.e. in reversal of all that Head says—before a conclusion to the paragraph: "Musical indeed! I have hardly gotten rid of the noise yet."

[11] Alexander John Ball (1757–1809), Bt 1801, rear-admiral 1805, had blockaded Malta almost from its capture by the French on 12 Jun 1798 until the surrender 5 Sept 1800 (he had been captain of the *Alexander* in the victory at Aboukir Bay 2–3 Aug 1798). He was appointed chief commissioner and in 1801 Governor of Malta. C gave a fuller version of the "Valet de Chambre" anecdote in the *Courier* 19 Apr 1811, in which the "marquess" of *TT* is "a Maltese, well drest, with all the air and manners of a gentleman, and (as it afterwards came out) of a good family". *EOT (CC)* ii 120–1. C was private secretary to Ball Jul 1804–Jan 1805 and public secretary 18 Jan–6 Sept 1805. C's admiration is attested in *Friend (CC)* ii 99–100, 252–6, 287–308, 347–69 (i 169–71, 532–80); *CL* ii 1141, 1171, iii 265; *CN* ii 2438. For a questioning of Sir John Stoddart's reports and John Rickman's gossip that C and Ball fell out at the end, see *CN* ii App B.

[12] Sir Hildebrand Oakes (1754–1822), 1st Bt 1813, brigadier-general 1802, major-general 1805, lieutenant-general 1811; Civil Commissioner of Malta 1810–13. William Hardman *A History of Malta . . . 1798–1815* ed J. Holland Rose (1909) 508–12, 517, 526. Oakes is not identified by name in *TT* (1835).

daughter to him. Ball was determined as far as he could to prevent Malta being made a nest of patronage; he considered, as was the fact, that there was a contract between England and the Maltese.[13] Hence the Government at home—Dundas[14]—disliked him, and never allowed him any other title than that of Civil Commissioner. We have, I believe, nearly succeeded in alienating the hearts of the inhabitants from us. Every officer in the island ought to be a Maltese except the immediate executive—£100 a year to a judge to keep a gilt carriage would satisfy, where an Englishman must have £2000.   [36:636]

---

*i*There are to my grief the names of some men to the Cambridge petition for admission of the Dissenters to the University, whose cheeks I think must have burnt with shame at the degrading patronage and befouling eulogies of the Times—and at seeing themselves used as the tools of*j* the open and rancorous enemies of the Church.[15] How could Thirlwall*k* bear to see himself held up for the purpose of inflicting insult upon men, whose worth and ability and sincerity he well knew—and this by a faction banded together like dogs and cats and serpents against a Church which he reveres. The *time* and the occasion and the motive ought to have satisfied him that, even if the thing were right or harmless in itself—not now nor with these was*l* it to be done.[16]   [36:637]

i f 117   *j* & of   *k* Therwall   *l* was ~~the~~

[13] When Baron Hobart as Secretary for War and the Colonies was using Malta as a place of patronage in 1803, Ball asked Granville Penn to impress upon him "the impolicy of appointing more Englishmen to the civil government of this island". BM Add MS 37268 f 82, quoted in Sultana 103.

[14] Henry Dundas, 1st Viscount Melville (1742–1811), Secretary of War 1794–1801, 1st Lord of the Admiralty 1804–5. Sultana 196, citing in refutation of C Ball's reference to Dundas in 1804 as "the boldest of the present ministers", possessing "the most comprehensive mind", took the sequence in *TT* to imply without evidence that Ball protested against a policy of patronage under Dundas before 1801.

[15] Religious qualifications for degrees from Cambridge and Oxford had been imposed since 1616. In Feb 1834 Dr Cornwallis Hewett's request for selective exemptions from the tests for his medical students had been tabled by the Senate of Cambridge University. He called a meeting in his rooms and secured signatures from sixty-three members of the Senate for a petition to admit persons for certain degrees without regard to religious opinion. The petition was presented by Earl Grey to the Lords on 21 Mar and by Spring Rice to the Commons on 24 Mar. Hansard 3rd s XXII 497–522, 569–98. As the favourable account in *The Times*, "Admission of Dissenters to the University of Cambridge", appeared on 17 Apr, the remarks recorded by HNC probably occurred later than 16 Apr; they are assigned to 1 May in *TT* (1835). A bill in support of the petition was introduced and passed by the Commons on 17 Apr; it would pass the third reading on 28 Jul but be rejected by the Lords on 1 Aug.

[16] Connop Thirlwall, Fellow and Tutor of Trinity College, Cambridge, lecturer there 1832–4. (See 29 Jun 1833 at n 7, above.) Previous to the petition, he was admired by C. *TT* 36:533n. *TT*

3. May. 1834.

Those who argue that England may safely depend upon a supply of foreign corn, if it grew none of its own or an insufficient quantity, forget that they are subjugating the necessaries of life itself to the mere luxuries or comforts of society.[1] Is it not certain, that the price of corn abroad will be raised upon us immediately as it is known that we must buy—and when that is once known, in what sort of situation shall we be? Besides the argument supposes that agriculture is not a positive good to the nation taken as a mode of existence for the people[2]—which is false and pernicious—and if we are to become a great horde*a* of manufacturers, shall we not even more than at present excite the ill will of all the manufacturers of other nations?[3] It has been already shown in evidence, that our man-

a ~~pile~~ horde

(1835) suppressed Thirlwall's name (along with that of *The Times*) and again when the subject recurred on 31 May.

[1] Burke's act of 1773 (13 Geo III cap 42) had made the importation of corn easier. The price above which imported corn was free of duty was raised, and related measures gave economic protection to the large landowners, in 1791, 1804, and 1815. Canning had tried to lower this cost to the poor in 1827 and Wellington had succeeded in 1828; bad harvests of 1828–31 had led to large importations at the sliding scale fixed in 1828; good harvests of 1832–3 had lowered the price. Joseph Hume had renewed the debate on 6 Mar 1834 by proposing "a fixed and moderate duty on the import at all times of foreign corn" with an equivalent bounty for export. Hansard 3rd s XXI 1197–1216.

C was unusual in opposing simultaneously the Corn Laws and the classical economists. According to Cottle, C had opposed the Corn Law of 1791 at Bristol and Bath in 1795 as "cruelty to the poor, and the alone cause of the prevailing sufferings, and popular discontent". *E Rec* I 182–3; *Lects 1795 (CC)* xxxiii. C objected in the marketplace at Calne to the law of 1815—"the poorest pay the most, not only *virtually*, as being so much less able to pay it, but actually, as making Bread so very much larger a proportion of his whole sustenance". *CL* IV 549–

50.

[2] J. R. McCulloch (anon) "Changes Required in the Corn-Laws" *Ed Rev* LVIII (Jan 1834) 271–307 had acknowledged the possibility of an argument like C's against dependence upon foreign corn, on grounds that "the power and prosperity of a great nation cannot be otherwise than precarious, if she depend upon others for any considerable portion of her subsistence" (p 274); he had answered first that since most English were in manufacturing and dependent upon foreign markets, other countries needed to send England food in exchange for manufactured products (276–8, 297–8); repeating the possible argument that "any serious deficiency could not be made up by importation", he asked in conclusion (306): "But who says that we are to neglect our agriculture?"

[3] An article in the *QR* LI (Mar 1834) 228–83, written by RS and revised by J. W. Croker (according to *The Wellesley Index to Victorian Periodicals* I 714–15), replied to McCulloch along the line less important to C than the positive good of agriculture (p 256): "The more perseveringly it may be attempted to force our manufactures upon foreigners, to the ruin of their own, and the more decidedly such a design may be favoured by the English government, the less will that design be likely to succeed."

ufacturers act upon the cursed principle of deliberately injuring foreign manufacturers, if they can, even to the[b] ultimate disgrace of the country and loss of themselves. [36:638]

---

[a]19. May 1834.[1]

How grossly misunderstood the character of the Christian Sabbath or Lord's Day is even by the Church! To confound it with the Jewish Sabbath, or rest its observance upon the fourth commandment[2] is, in my judgment, heretical, and would so have been considered in the primitive church. That cessation from labor on the Lord's day could not have been incumbent on Christians for two centuries after Christ, is apparent; because during that period, the greater part of the Christians were either slaves or in official situations under Pagan masters or superiors, and had duties to perform for those who did not recognize the day. And we know St Paul sent back Onesimus to his master—telling him that being a Christian, he was free in his mind indeed, but still must serve his earthly master, although he might laudably seek for personal freedom also.[3] [b]If the early Christians had refused to work on the Lord's Day, rebellion and civil war must have been the immediate consequence. But there is no intimation of any such cessation.[c] The Jewish sabbath was commemorative of the termination of the great act of creation; it was to record[d] that the world had not been from eternity, nor had arisen as a dream of itself, but that God had created it[e] by distinct acts of power, and that he had hallowed the day or season in which he rested or desisted from his work.[4]

---

[b] to   [a] f 117[v]

[b-c] In the ms the sentences follow "solemnized", below, but were marked with an x for insertion after "also"

[d] p̶u̶t̶ record   [e] itself̶

---

[1] When SH saw C on 8 May she was "shocked by the changed appearance of my dear old Friend. . . . He will never rise from his bed more. . . ." Before she left for Rydal in early June "he was not quite so well as the week before". *SHL* 414, 421. Although there is a gap in C's letters from early April until 27 May, he must have been in full voice for the talk dated 19 May (Mon). If the talk occurred on the 18th, the day encouraged the subject—the sabbath.

[2] Exod 20.8, Deut 5.12.

[3] Paul's epistle to Philemon accompanies Onesimus and commends him to the master "no longer as a slave but more than a slave, as a beloved brother". RSV 16. C's interpretation is supported by Col 4.1–9 and, among others, Eichhorn *NT* III 298, 300.

[4] Exod 20.8–11, 17, 31.13–17; Deut 5.12–15. SH copied for C about 1801 a passage on the distinction of sabbath and Lord's day in a book C owned before 1810. *CN* I 1000B, from Peter Heylyn *The History of the Sabbath* (2nd ed 1636) 236–7. *WW LC* 335. Heylyn, who mentioned Lutherans but not Luther, re-

When our Lord rose[f] from the dead, the old creation was as it were superseded, and the new creation began,[5] and therefore the first day and not the last day—the commencement and not the end of the work of God was solemnized.

Luther in speaking of the good by itself, and the good for its expediency, instances the observance of the Christian day of rest,—a day of repose from manual labor and of activity in spiritual labor—a day of joy and cooperation in the work of Christ's creation.[6] "Keep it holy," says he, "for its use' sake—both to body and soul—but if any where the day is made holy for the mere day's sake—if any where any one sets up its observance upon a Jewish foundation, then I order you to work on it, to ride, to dance, to feast on it—any thing that shall reprove this encroachment on[g] the Christian spirit and liberty.'"[7]

[h]The English reformers evidently had the same view. But the Church in the Stuarts' time was unhappily so identified with the undue advancement of the royal prerogative, that the puritanical Judaising of the Pres-

<hr>

[f] ~~came~~ rose   [g] of   [h] f 118

<hr>

mained otherwise an adequate source for most of C's remarks on the keeping of Sunday; e.g. *Omniana* I 161–4; *LR* I 282–4 (var); *TT* (1884) 349–50.

[5] 1 John 2.8. The texts for the Lord's day as the first meeting day of the week kept to commemorate the resurrection are Acts 20.7, 1 Cor 16.2, Rev 1.10. Jesus defends the plucking of corn on the Jewish sabbath in Mark 2.23–8. C distinguished between the Jewish sabbath as "a day of Inaction" and the Lord's day as "a Day of Restoration" in a note on Richard Byfield *The Doctrine of the Sabbath Vindicated. CM (CC)* I 873.

[6] Luther asserted on Christ's authority that God's work can be done on Sunday; it is proper on that day to hear, learn, do, and live God's word. Sermon "Vom Sabbath und Gottesdienst" (17th Sunday after Trinity) and sermon at the dedication of the Castle Church in Torgau, 5 Oct 1544. *Martin Luthers Werke* ed H. L. A. Vent (10 vols Hamburg 1827–8) I 175–7 (cf II 8–10—he counted playing, dancing, and going for a walk as transgressions against the Third Commandment, II 210); *D Martin Luthers sowohl in Deutscher also Lateinischer Sprache verfertigte und aus der letztern*

in die erstere übersetzte sämtliche *Schriften* ed J. G. Walch (24 vols Halle 1740–53) XII 2488-2503, XXII 1505. Cf also his commentary of 1535 on Gal 4.10. *Schriften* ed Walch VIII 2469–72.

To George Fricker C wrote on 4 Oct 1806 that the Bible did not lead him "to attach any criminality to cheerful and innocent social intercourse on the Lord's day . . . and though I have been taught by Luther, and the great founders of the Church of England, that the Sabbath was a part of the ceremonial and transitory parts of the law given by heaven to Moses; and that our Sunday is binding on our consciences, chiefly from its manifest and most awful usefulness, and indeed moral necessity", he honoured George's firmness in declining his invitation for a Sunday evening. *CL* II 1189. In one copy of Baxter *Reliquiae* C wrote a note similar to his comments in TT; in George Frere's copy he wrote to the same general purpose but granted a command "by implication" in the NT (Luke 23.56). *CM (CC)* I 268–9, 334. C probably knew of Richard Baxter *The Divine Appointment of the Lords Day Proved* (1671).

[7] Not found as given.

byterians coincided with the patriots of the nation in resisting the efforts of the church to prevent the alteration of the character of the day of rest. After the Restoration the*i* church adopted the view taken by its enemies.[8] It is curious to observe, in this infidel and politico-economy Parliament,[9] how this Sabbatarian spirit*j* unites itself with a rancorous hostility to that one institution, which according to reason and all experience can alone insure the continuance of any general religion in the nation at large.[10] Some of these gentlemen—who are for not letting a poor man have a dish of baked potatoes on a Sunday, religionis gratia[11]—are foremost among those who will vilify, weaken and impoverish the National Church. I own my indignation is very strong against such contemptible fellows.*k*

The early church distinguished the day of Christian rest so strongly from a fast, that it was unlawful for a man to bewail even his own sins— as such only—on that day. He was to bewail the sins of *all*—and to pray as one of the whole of Christ's body.[12]

I sincerely wish to preserve a decent quiet on Sunday. I would prohibit compulsory labor, and put down operas, theatres &c., for this plain reason, that if the rich be allowed to *play*, the poor will be forced, or be induced, to work. I am not for a Paris Sunday. But to stop coaches and to let the gentleman's carriage run—is monstrous.[13]   [36:639]

---

i & R the   *j* spirit ~~of hostility to~~   *k* ~~quacks & sabit~~ fellows.

[8] C made a note in 1804 on the usefulness of Sunday: "Sabbath promotes *public Spirit*/ Men lay aside their peculiar Professions/ One bond of feeling—hence the Sabbath breaking of Industry & its pernicious Consequences." *CN* II 1968. He noted that a proper line of argument in the 1630s would have been "the exposure of the Sabbatical Superstition, as a Judaic incroachment on the privileges & liberty of the Christian Festival". Annotation on Byfield: *CM (CC)* I 874. Carlyon (I 100–2) found amusement in C as a sabbatarian; he might have found it equally amusing that C's views coincided with those of Sermons 21–3 on Mark 2.27 in Samuel Horsley *Sermons* (4th ed 3 vols 1816) II 180–250.

[9] After writing "this Parliament" and "this spirit", HNC inserted "infidel & politico economy" and "Sabbatarian"; *TT* (1835) expanded to "this semi-infidel and Malthusian Parliament".

[10] Sir Andrew Agnew, Bt (1793–

1849), introduced in 1832, 1833, and 11 Mar 1834 a bill "to promote the better observance of the Lord's Day", defeated in the Commons on 30 Apr 1834, yea 125, nay 161; debated in the Lords 5 May, defeated and dropped 15 May. Hansard 3rd s XXII 54–5, XXIII 314, 356, 473–5, 1006–26. *M Chron* had opposed the bill from 29 Mar 1833 on; *The Times* of 17 May 1833 had called it "that monstrous piece of absurdity".

[11] "For religion's sake". *TT* (1835) inserted "(God forgive that audacious blasphemy!)". The bill called for bakers' shops to be closed on Sunday—the poor had their potatoes and roast cooked at the baker's fire.

[12] C's source untraced. In *TT* (1835) this paragraph followed that on Luther.

[13] The bill called for no work on Sunday except that of "menial servants acting in the necessary service of their employers". There were to be penalties for letting out to hire any carriage, gig, or

Your argument against the high prizes in the Church might be put strongly thus: "Admit that in the beginning it might *l*have been fairly said that some eminent rewards ought to be assigned to stimulate and record transcendant merit, what have you to say now after centuries of experience to the contrary? Have these high prizes been given to the highest genius, virtue or learning? Is it not rather the truth, as Jortin said, that twelve votes in a contested election will do more to make a man a bishop than an admired commentary on the twelve minor prophets?[14] To all which, I say again that you ought not to reason from the abuse which may be rectified against the inherent uses of the thing! Appoint the most deserving—and the prize will answer its purpose. As to the Bishops' incomes, in the first place the net receipts—that which the Bishop may spend—have been confessedly exaggerated beyond measure;[15] but waiving*m* that, and allowing the highest estimate to be correct, I should like to have the disposition of the episcopal revenue in any one year by the late or present Bishop of Durham or the present Bishop of Exeter compared with that of the most benevolent nobleman in England.[16] I firmly believe the former give away in charity of one kind or another—public, private,

l f 118ᵛ   *m* waving

horse, etc for travelling, but if a man kept his own horses and carriage he was free to travel as he wished on Sunday. Lamb, in paragraphs addressed to RS in the *London Magazine* Oct 1823, recast as "The Tombs in the Abbey" in *The Last Essays of Elia* (1833), had joined others in protesting that the poor were no longer permitted to inspect Westminster Abbey on the only day they were free to do so. Aside from its failures to set aside Sunday as a day of rest, Paris was for C the essence of depravity, as in *Friend (CC)* I 61 (II 52); *LS (CC)* 208. The revolution of 1830 in Paris had been fiercely anti-clerical.

[14] John Jortin (1698–1770) *The Life of Erasmus* (2 vols 1758–60) I 483; (3 vols 1808) I 436, quoting "a certain author": "Art thou dissatisfied, and desirous of other things? Go, and make twelve votes at an election. It shall do thee more service than to make a commentary on the twelve minor prophets." The passage is quoted, with a second acknowledgement of "anonymous authority", in John Disney *Memoirs of the Life and Writings of John Jortin* (1792) 276–7. It is not specified in those places that the result of dis-

satisfaction with unrewarded authorship will be a bishopric. Borrowing the passage in a letter to Mrs Elizabeth Evans 5 Feb 1793, C had inserted the phrase "and procure thee greater preferment", and had provided a similar specification in Lect 6 of LRR in 1795. *CL* I 48; *Lects 1795 (CC)* 221. As often, his memory seems to combine accuracy with regard to the actual words with an interpretation he provided for those words upon initial encounter.

[15] In *Conciones ad Populum* C had berated "the Religion of Mitres and Mysteries . . . the Eighteen-Thousand-Pound-a Year Religion of Episcopacy". *Lects 1795 (CC)* 66–7.

[16] *TT* (1835) substituted for Exeter "London or Winchester". Shute Barrington (1734–1826), bp of Durham 1791–1826, succeeded by William Van Mildert (1765–1836), dean of St Paul's 1820–6, one of the founders of Durham University (1832). Henry Phillpotts (1778–1869), bp of Exeter 1830–69, known as a vehement conservative on all issues, including most recently the Tithes Bill. HNC's friend Charles James Blomfield (1786–1857), bp of London

or official—three times as much in proportion as the latter. You may have a hunks[17] or two now and then—so you would more certainly, if you were to reduce the incomes to £2000 per annum; but as a body, in my opinion, the clergy of England do in truth act as if their property were impressed with a trust to the utmost extent that could be demanded by those who affect, ignorantly or not, to set up that lying legend of a tripartite or quadripartite division of the tithes by law.[18]   [36:640]

---

31. May 1834.[1]

I think Sir Charles Wetherell's Speech very effective. I doubt if any other lawyer in Westminster Hall could have done the thing so well.[2]

[36:641]

1828–56, editor of Aeschylus and of works begun by his brother Edward, a classical scholar who died in 1816. Charles Richard Sumner (1790–1874), bp of Winchester 1827–69. He had succeeded Van Mildert as bp of Llandaff and dean of St Paul's in 1826. Active like Blomfield in seeking endowments for new churches, he had urged also new schools for the poor. He had published a translation of Milton's *De doctrina Christiana* (1825) and voted for Catholic Relief (1829). It is inconceivable that the anti-hierarchical "you" of this entry was HNC.

[17] Miser or curmudgeon.

[18] The growth of opposition to pluralities, episcopal prizes, tithes, and religious monopoly, led first by Joseph Hume and other Benthamite Radicals, with helpful noise from Cobbett, but by 1834 spreading through Nonconformists, Catholics, and Churchmen in Scotland, Ireland, and England, is summarised by Halévy III 130–73. The decline of this coalition from internal dissension may perhaps be dated from an event C would take as an escalation of the threats, a meeting for disestablishment at the London Tavern on 12 May with Hume in the chair. Perhaps C mistakenly feared that something would come of two bills introduced by Brougham on 16 May to eliminate pluralism and non-residence. Hansard 3rd s XXIII 1104–7.

Brougham had written in the *Ed Rev* LVIII (Jan 1834) 498–507 of the "great unpopularity" of the Church and its tithes. The Commons had been debating since 20 Feb a modification of the Tithes Bill for Ireland passed in 1833. On 16 Apr George Faithfull (1790–1863), Radical M.P. for Brighton, proposing a tripartite division by which the greater part would go "to the relief of the nation", argued that tithes in earlier times had been divided among church, clergy, and the poor. Hansard 3rd s XVII 188–90. On 6 May Lord John Russell had declared in the Commons that the revenues of the Church of Ireland were excessive. Hansard 3rd s XXIII 666.

[1] On 27 May C, "who at an advanced age writes from a Bed of Sickness'', described his own education at Christ's Hospital and Cambridge in a testimonial for the Rev James Gillman. *CL* VI 983–4. The next day, noting that Charles and Eliza Aders had gone to dine with C, HCR observed: "Poor Coleridge is, I fear, beyond all hope of recovery or of any future exertion of his very great talents." And on 30 May: "A very sad account of Coleridge, he can scarcely be seen by any one, and his constitution is very fast breaking up". *CRB* I 442. Yet clearly there was an upturn at about this date, Saturday 31 May.

[2] As counsel for the University of Oxford at the Privy Council hearing on the

I cannot say how I grieve at Thirlwall's[a] conduct—but I do not see how Wordsworth[b] could have acted otherwise as Master [c]of the College.[3] I am afraid Thirlwall[d] is not aware how much some feelings upon a former occasion have influenced him.[4]

Young Christopher Wordworth's[e] pamphlet is very clever and well reasoned—I only regret that in some parts he has not taken a higher tone, and shown the injustice of this attack upon the Universities.[5]

A National Church requires and is required by the Christian Church for the perfection of each.[6] For if there were no National Church, the mere spiritual Church would either become like the Papacy a dreadful tyranny over mind and body—or else fall abroad into a multitude of enthusiastic sects as in England in the seventeenth century. I do not believe that in a country of any religion, liberty of conscience can be preserved except by means and under the shadow of a National Church—a political

a Thirlwall's   *b* W.   *c* f 119   *d* Thirwall   *e* C. W.'s

---

question of a charter for London University, Sir Charles Wetherell (1770–1846) spoke against the petition on 24 and 26 Apr. Charles C. F. Greville, clerk to the Council, noted on the 25th that "Wetherell made an amusing speech, and did not conclude", and later that "Wetherell made a very able speech, which he afterwards published". *The Greville Memoirs 1814–1860* ed Lytton Strachey and Roger Fulford (8 vols 1938) III 32, 34. The first portion of the speech was reported in *The Times* 25 Apr, but C is referring to the whole speech as published by Wetherell; see n 14, below. Wetherell was known for "the indiscretion and violence of his speeches as an ultra tory and protestant champion from 1826 to 1832". *DNB*. He provoked riots in Bristol in 1831.

[3] On 21 May Thirlwall published *A Letter to the Revd Thomas Thurton on the Admission of Dissenters to Academical Degrees*, which he followed up with *A Second Letter to the Revd Thomas Thurton*. He recommended the admission of Dissenters and the abolition of required attendance at chapel, in part on the grounds that chapel and all other teaching and show of religion at Cambridge was "the least impressive and edifying that can well be imagined".

Christopher Wordsworth (1774–1846) as Master of Trinity College requested Thirlwall's resignation. John Sterling reported to Trench on a dinner of the Apostles: "They give melancholy accounts of the coldness produced among the people at Trinity by the late controversy. I think Thirlwall quite right as to the compulsory chapel-going; but as long as the system lasts, he was bound, I think, either to conform to it or to resign his lectureship, and certainly the writing such a pamphlet as his was a queer kind of conformity." R. C. Trench *Letters and Memorials* I 159. Shortly before his death C expressed to Whewell "the deepest sorrow at Thirlwall's letters". Isaac Todhunter *William Whewell* (1876) II 196.

[4] Among endless possibilities C may have in mind the reactions to Thirlwall's translation of Schleiermacher's essay on Luke in 1825. See *CL* VI 543.

[5] Before Thirlwall's first pamphlet Christopher Wordsworth Jr presented the conservative position in one *On the Admission of Dissenters to Reside and Graduate* (Cambridge 1834).

[6] "In relation to the National Church, Christianity, or the Church of Christ, is a blessed accident, a providential boon . . . the envoy indeed and liege subject of another state . . . ". *C&S (CC)* 55.

establishment connected with, but *distinct* from, the spiritual Church.[7]

[36:642]

Sometimes I hope that the rabid insolence of the Dissenters may at last awake a jealousy in the laity of the Church of England. But the apathy and inertness are profound.[8]   [36:643]

Whatever the Papacy may have been on the Continent, it was always an unqualified evil in this Country. It destroyed what was rising of good, and introduced*f* a thousand evils of its own. The Papacy was and still is essentially extra-national; it affects, *temporally*, to do that which the Spiritual Church of Christ can alone do—to*g* break down the distinctions of nations. Now as the Papacy is itself local and peculiar, of course this attempt is nothing but a direct attack on the political independence of other nations.[9]

The institution of Universities was*h* the single check on*i* the Papacy.[10] The Popes always hated the Universities. The cœnobitic establishments of England it converted into monasteries and other monking receptacles. You see it was at Oxford that Wicliffe alone found protection and encouragement.[11]   [36:644]

---

f ~~prevented~~ introduced   *g* to ~~make all men~~   *h* ~~has~~ was   *i* of

[7] In a note on Baxter *Reliquiae* C despaired of a proper medium between "a Church Comprehensive" and "a Co-existence of independent Churches". *CM (CC)* I 307. It followed therefore, he thought, that the Anglican clergy should lay claim to tithes only "as Officers & Functionaires of the Nationalty". Note on Donne *LXXX Sermons: CM (CC)* II 294. Beginning as a rejection of arguments by Dissenters that the Church should relinquish various claims to exclusion, C's remarks turn to reject the claims on the other flank of a greater catholicity than the National Church afforded.

[8] *TT* (1835) added to "rabid insolence" an "undisguised despotism of temper". *TT* (1836) omitted "rabid insolence". Both editions ended with an ironic phrase, "too providential".

[9] In *C&S* C said that he made a note on 2 Jul 1828: "When I say the Pope, I understand the papal hierarchy, which is, in truth, the dilated Pope . . ."; a few pages later he declared that the "erection of a temporal monarch under the pretence of a spiritual authority", possible to

Mahomet, was imperfectly realised by the papacy because it would require "the extinction or entrancement of the spirit of Christianity". *C&S (CC)* 136, 138.

[10] In 1825, when Thomas Campbell made public his proposal for the secular metropolitan foundation that became in 1828 the University of London, C outlined for Joseph Hughes, a Baptist, his proposed lectures "On the History of Universities generally". *CL* VI 1054; cf V 446, 448. On the papacy vs the universities see also 6 May 1833 (sentence after n 6), above.

[11] Vaughan and Le Bas (see 13 May 1833 n 24, above) had shown that Wycliffe was encouraged and more nearly protected at Oxford than anywhere else; the papal bull ordering his imprisonment in 1377 was "at last received, though with manfiest coldness and reluctance" (Le Bas 175); he was sheltered as a lecturer at Oxford in 1379–82. Rees, under "Oxford" (vol XXV), said that Wycliffe "loosened the shackles of papal thraldom", but acknowledged that Boniface had freed Oxford from ecclesiastical authority in 1301.

Schiller's blank verse is bad. He moves in it as a fly in a glue bottle. His thoughts have their connection and variety—but there is no corresponding movement in the verse.[12] How different from Shakspeare's endless rhythms! ʲThere is a nimiety—a too-muchness—in all Germans. It is the national fault. Lessing had the best notion of blank verse. The trochaic termination of German words renders blank verse almost impossible. We have it[k] in our dramatic hendecasyllable—but then we have a power of inter-weaving the iambic ad libitum.[13]   [36:645]

Brougham's interruption of Wetherell's[l] speech, put me in mind of a young Scotch advocate—willing to show forth his raw cleverness at the open expence of good feeling and decorum! To talk in that strain, when he was there on oath to advise his Sovereign.[14]

14. June 1834.[1]

The Roman Catholic Emancipation Act—carried in the unprincipled manner it was—was in effect a Surinam toad,[2] and the Reform Bill and

ʲ f 119ᵛ   ᵏ it ~~a lot in the~~   ˡ W's

[12] As the contrast with Shakespeare indicates, C has in mind Schiller's dramas, particularly *Wallenstein*, in lines of five stresses without rhyme. C wrote to Godwin 28 Feb 1823 that Ludwig Tieck assured C "he could never read my Wallenstein but as an Original—nor did he hesitate to declare that in *diction* and *metre* it was decidedly superior to Schiller's". *CL* v 269.

[13] *TT* (1835) read "iambic close *ad libitum*", clarifying the contrast of flexibility in line-endings with the trochaic termination of words in German. The antecedent of "it" has C referring to lines of eleven syllables that end in a trochaic. In the classical hendecasyllabic line from Catullus, as imitated by Tennyson, trochaics would come in the third and fourth feet.

[14] *Substance of the Speech of Sir Charles Wetherell, Before the Lords of the Privy Council, on the Subject of Incorporating the London University* (1834) indicates interruptions by the Lord Chancellor (Brougham) at pp 2,

19–21 (on the name of "university" without the power of granting degrees), 34–6 (on the King's not being the head of the Church of Scotland), 41, 45, 47, 49–51, 58, 61–2, and 82–3. Wetherell had alluded unfavourably to Brougham on pp 10, 25–6. The entry was cancelled with a vertical line, but was not printed and has not been found in MS F.

[1] SC had begun a letter to HNC nervously on the 12th and posted it to Lincoln's Inn on Friday. UT ms. 14 Jun was the following day, Saturday. On both 5 and 9 Jul C mentioned a recovery "within the last eight days". In a letter of 9 Jul to Eliza Nixon, with whom he was exchanging current novels, he mentioned Henry Taylor as a young man "you may have seen on one of our latest Thursday evening Conversaziones". *CL* vi 988. Green was making his usual Sunday visit when HCR went to Highgate on 8 Jun: "No talk beyond a jocular compliment to me for my health". *CRB* i 443.

[2] C had added a passage to Satyrane's Letters in *The Friend* No 16 on "Mr.

the Dissenters' admission,[3] and attacks on the Church are so many toadlets one after another detaching themselves from their parent.   [36:646]

I cannot understand Sir Robert Peel's declaration that if the circumstances recurred, he would act precisely in the same way, except by supposing in him a very strange insensibility to principle.[4]

[a]Sir Robert Peel says that there is nothing in the Roman Catholic religion inconsistent with the duties of citizenship and allegiance to a territorial sovereign. If that is admitted by any one, there can be no answer to the argument from numbers. Certainly if the religion of the majority is innocuous to the interests of the *nation*—the majority have a natural [b]right to be trustees of the nationalty—the property set apart for the nation's use—and rescued from the gripe of private hands.[c]   [36:647]

[d]The movement of the Times newspaper is a spiral line. I have watched that paper for seven or eight years past, and I am persuaded that there is one fundamental object the[e] prosecution of which has never been omitted by it for a moment. On every subject the Times is inconsistent with itself, and sets a sail to every wind, except on one—and that is the reestablishment and final domination of the Roman Catholic church in Ireland. It is not leagued with O'Connell's party—but with the quieter and higher part of the Roman Catholic proprietors and clergy, who hate

---

[a-c] Written at the foot of the leaf and continued at the top of f 120 and marked with an x for insertion after "principle"
       [b] f 120   [c] See [a-c], above   [d] f 119ᵛ   [e] the ~~callous~~

Pitt's window Tax, with its' pretty little *additionals* sprouting out from it like young toadlets on the back of a Surinam toad". *Friend (CC)* II 212. C referred to this passage in talking to Lord Adare on 30 Jun 1834: "He laughed a good deal when he alluded to some comparison, I believe he said in the *Friend*, about little toads, and the Emancipation Bill, and the Reform Bill, &c." Graves *Life of W. R. Hamilton* II 95. It has been supposed that C found the toads in J. G. Stedman *Narrative of a Five Years' Expedition Against the Revolted Negroes of Surinam* (2 vols 1796) I 260 (*CN* I 124n), but they were a prolific species; e.g. Lazzaro Spallanzani saw at Bologna, then at Geneva, "the famous toad of Surinam . . . so remarkable for its property of bringing forth the young at the back". *Dissertations Relative to the Natural History of Animals and Vegetables* tr Thomas Beddoes (2 vols 1789) II 100–2.

To Sotheby in Apr 1808 C wrote that "my Thoughts are like Surinam Toads—as they crawl on, little Toads vegetate out from back & side, grow quickly, & draw off the attention from the mother Toad". *CL* III 94–5. For William Page Wood's report of C on Catholic emancipation (preceded by a discourse on St Paul) see App F 34, below.

[3] See 16 Apr 1834 n 15 and 31 May 1834 nn 3–5, above.

[4] Peel said on 11 Mar that he did not wish to modify Catholic emancipation, on which Grattan, Canning, and Castlereagh had agreed; on 25 Apr he repeated that with regard to Catholic emancipation he had only done his duty. Hansard 3rd s XXII, XXIII 72. He had concurred on 11 Mar that the Catholic oath was on the same footing as the King's oath; the Catholics had no reason to complain of the oath. Ibid XXII 27–8, 30.

O'Connell. You never see the smallest hesitation on this point—and as the crisis approaches, you will see how much more boldly it will speak.⁵ /How lamentable it is to hear the Duke of Wellington express himself doubtingly on the abominable sophism that the Coronation oath only binds the King as executive—making a Highgate oath of it.⁶ But the Duke is conscious of the ready retort which his language and conduct on the Roman Catholic Bill affords. He is hampered by that affair.

[36:648]

20. June 1834.¹

In the argument on the Corn laws there is a μετάβασις εἰς ἄλλο γένος.² It may be admitted that the great principles of Commerce require the interchange of commodities to be free; but commerce which is barter has no proper range beyond luxuries or conveniences*—it is the complement to the full existence of a State. But how can it be shown that the principles applicable to an interchange of conveniences* or luxuries apply to an interchange of Necessaries? No State can be such properly that is not self-subsistent at least; for no state that is not so is independent.³ The nation that cannot exist without the commodity of another nation is in effect the slave of that nation. In common times interest will prevail and prevent a ruinous exercise of the power; but interest will yield in individuals and nations to stronger passions. Is Holland an authority to the contrary? If so, Tyre and Sidon and Carthage are so! Would you put England on the footing of Holland, which can be overrun in a campaign and starved in a year!

[36:649]

*f 120   *a* conveniencies*

⁵ In leading articles of 3–4 Jun *The Times* spoke boldly enough against Peel and his more liberal followers as like the "costly, jobbing, pompous, and unproductive humbugs" practising their "common trickery" in recent years; they would have Church property genuinely "amenable to the will and wisdom of Parliament" (4 Jun).

⁶ "But he must say, that those who contended that this oath did not apply to him in his legislative capacity, did not act quite fairly in advising his Majesty to commit himself to this measure in his executive capacity." Wellington in the Lords 6 Jun 1834: Hansard 3rd s xxiv 298. C returns here to the subject and language of 9 Mar 1833 (at nn 4–6), above (36:464), again charging a perversion of the doctrine of the King's "two bodies".

¹ Two days earlier, 18 Jun, SC wrote to HNC at Lincoln's Inn that she was low and tearful. UT ms. 20 Jun was a Friday.

² "Transition to another kind". Debate had flared on 12 Jun. Hansard 3rd s xxiii 1392–4.

³ RS and Croker had written similarly in the *QR* li (Mar 1834) 256: "A commonwealth must be ill-constituted and insecure, unless it be self-sufficient in all things needful for the subsistence and well-being of the community; and this cannot be, unless it produces for itself all such things as nature or habit have rendered so far indispensable, that the use of them cannot be forgone without great and general distress."

D'Israeli Junior makes trees coeval with Chaos,[4] which is next to Hans Sachs,[b] who describing Chaos, said it was so pitchy dark that even the very *cats* ran against each other.[5]   [36:651]

The entire tendency of modern political economy is to denationalize. It would dig up the charcoal foundations of the temple of Ephesus to burn as fuel for a steam engine![c6]   [36:650]

[b] Saxe,   [c] For the addition "Friend 56", which follows, see n 6, below

[4] Benjamin Disraeli (1804–81), 1st Earl of Beaconsfield (1876) *The Revolutionary Epick. The Work of Disraeli the Younger, Author of "The Psychological Romance"* (1834) refers early to a forest with shuddering branches, but in a simile and before the throne of Demogorgon in a world that is already old (bk I st 2 line 7, p 2), and on p 9 "To the dark world that man had not defiled, | Where the eternal Forest spread its form . . ." (bk I st 9 lines 6–7). But C refers specifically to bk I st 10 lines 25–7:

Yea! mid their struggling life
The Forest sinks, nor roots conate with
Chaos
Withstand their energy . . ."

Contemporaries besides C who ridiculed the poem are mentioned in Robert Blake *Disraeli* (1966) 111. A chorus of mortals in Byron's *Heaven and Earth* (1823) pt 1 sc 3 lines 866–7 sings of

The forest's trees (coeval with the hour
When Paradise upsprung . . .)

[5] C transcribed in HEHL MS HM 8195 pp 750–652, with the date 17 Jun 1799, a *Fastnachtspiel* by the Meistersinger Hans Sachs (1494–1576), probably from the version by Anton F. X. Sebastian Sailer (1714–77): *Adams und Eves Erschaffung, und ihr Sündenfall. Ein geistlich Fastnachtspiel mit Sang und Klang. Aus dem Swäbischen in's Oesterreichische versetzt* (Vienna 1783). C's favourite was clearly *Die ungleichen Kinder Eve, wie sie Got der Herr anredt*, from which he recounted episodes in 1799, in Lect 2 of 5 Feb 1808

(though this is disputed), and in Lect 2 of 30 Jan 1818. See Carlyon I 93–4, *Lects 1808–19 (CC)* I 50 and n 19, II 82–3 and nn 37–40. Cf Carlyon from notes of 1799: "What would be thought, for instance, in the present day, of a play of Hans Sachs, which Coleridge had met with, in which Eve is represented as telling Cain and Abel to take care to have their hair combed, and their faces and hands well washed, for that the Almighty was about to pay them a visit." C told how Cain did the Lord's Prayer poorly, how his descendants were to be tinkers and shoemakers. But, he said, the play was "far superior to the vicious sentimentality of nine-tenths of the plays of Kotzebue and others of his school". Carlyon I 94. Describing some of C's books and papers in 1800, Lamb called it "that drama in which Got-fader performs". *LL* (M) I 217. The play bears various titles in different editions of Sachs. Coming upon a reference to it in Flögel *Geschichte der komischen Litteratur*, C wrote: "I have read this Comedy" and "can truly say, that Flögel has given a most lame and pitiful account of it". *CM (CC)* II 780. A leaf of passages copied by C is bound into *Hans Sachsens sehr herzliche Schöne und wahrhafte Gedicht, Fabeln und gute Schwenk* (Nuremberg 1781), now in the BM. *CM (CC)* IV.
The remarks on Disraeli and Sachs are cast in anecdotal form, but C became serious about "the original fluidity of the planet" in *TL* (1848) 67–8, in which he rejected a "chaos of heterogenous substances, such as our Milton has described", for the "only serviceable fiction" of "one vast homogenous drop".
[6] *TT* (1835) read "the modern or Malthusian political economy". This entry is

23. June 1834.

Socinus worshipped Jesus Christ, and said that God had given him the power of being omnipresent.[1] David, with a little more acuteness, *^a*suggested that mere audition or presence in a creature could not justify worship from men;—that a man, however glorified, was no nearer God in essence than a common scoundrel.[2] Prayer, therefore, was inapplicable. And how could a man be mediator between God and man? How could a man with sins himself offer*^b* any compensation for or expiation of sin? unless the most arbitrary caprice were admitted into the counsels of God? Then at last it was discovered that there was no such thing as sin.[3]

Priestley was*^c* the author of the modern Unitarianism.[4] I owe, under

^a f 120ᵛ   *^b* ~~be~~ offer   *^c* ~~is~~ was

written in a different script from the rest of 20 Jun, and HNC has added in still another script "Friend 56", in reference to the first essay on truth in *The Friend— (CC)* I 38–9—in which C applies to moral prudence, or "expediency", the analogy first recorded from Theopompus of Chios (4th century B.C.), reaching C by way of Lessing *Anti-Goeze (Sämmtliche Schriften* VI 297–8), as Emerson noted in his copy of *The Friend—CC* I 39n. HNC recognised that C was trying to sound original only on the subject of political economy.

[1] "Socinus pleaded for the *adoratio Christi* as obligatory on all Christians, and urged that the *invocato Christi* should not be forbidden." He argued that "after his baptism Christ had been conveyed to heaven, where he had beheld his Father, and heard from him the things which he was afterwards sent back to earth to teach. Raised again to heaven after his resurrection, he was made the head of all creation, with divine authority over the world, and in that sense God. He was thus no 'mere man,' and deserved divine honour." Hastings *Encyclopaedia of Religion* XII (1922) 521. On Socinus see also 1 May 1823 n 11, above.

[2] Francis Dávid or Davidis (1509–79), born in Kolozsvár (Klausenburg), became a Lutheran in Wittenberg (1552) and in 1564 a Calvinist bishop of the Hungarian churches of Transylvania. He

questioned the propriety of prayer to Christ, along the lines summarised by C. Rees XI under "David, Francis". Socinus was called upon to oppose his views. *Lexikon für Theologie und Kirche* ed Michael Buchberger (11 vols Freiburg 1957–67) II 182. For C it is Priestley who learned from French philosophers that sin is an outmoded illusion.

[3] *TT* (1835) inserted at this point the paragraph on "absolute Will" that closed the day's talk in MS B (below, last paragraph). *TT* (1836) inserted first a paragraph on Philo Judaeus, which is annotated at 7 Jan–13 Feb 1823 n 23, above (36:32), then the paragraph on "absolute Will".

[4] Joseph Priestley (1733–1804), nonconformist minister and theologian; man of science, particularly chemistry; defender of the French Revolution. On C's early admiration see the impressive columns on Priestley in the index to *Lects 1795 (CC)*; Woodring 67, 86–100, 169. The bad eminence of Priestley had been noted by John Whitaker *The Origin of Arianism Disclosed* (1791) 498–500. C's copy had remained with WW. *WW LC* 360. Modern English Unitarianism is sometimes traced from John Biddle (1616–62). Hastings XII 522.

HNC wrote to Thomas Tracy of Newburyport, Mass 10 Sept 1837: "With us the Unitarians, as a class, are distinguished by deadness to the imaginative, scorn of the mysteries, & a proud addic-

God, my return to the faith to my having gone much further than the Unitarians, and so came round to the other extreme. I never falsified the Scripture. I always told them that their interpretations of the Scripture were intolerable; and that if they were to affect[d5] to construe the will of their neighbour as they did that of their Maker, they would be scouted out of society. I said then plainly and openly, that it was clear enough that John and Paul were not Unitarians: But at that time I had a strong sense of the repugnancy of the doctrine of vicarious atonement to the moral being, and I thought nothing could counterbalance that. "What care I," I said, "for the Platonisms of John or the Rabbinisms of Paul? My conscience revolts."[6]

Always believing in the government of God, I was an optimist; but as I could not but see that the *present* state of things was not the *best*, I was necessarily led to look to a future state.[7]   [36:652]

You may conceive the difference in kind between Fancy and Imagination in this way—that if the check of the senses and the reason were withdrawn, the first would become delirium, and the second mania.[8] The fancy brings together images which have no connection natural or moral,

---

[d] ~~venture to~~ affect

---

tion to things of sense & the conclusions of the mere understanding. They are almost exclusively a wealthy, middle-ranked class, immersed in the world, & characterized by coldness & indifference to religion, except just upon the controverted points upon wch they dissent from the Church." HUL MS Am 661 (5).

[5] I.e. to attempt. In MS B "to venture" became "to affect"; *TT* (1835) read "to offer".

[6] Drawing upon Priestley, C had argued in Lect 5 of LRR in Bristol that atonement, wherever mentioned by the Prophets or by Paul, was "a necessary means relative to man not a motive influencing the Almighty", a voluntary submission by Christ in order to "confirm the Faith or awaken the Gratitude of Men". *Lects 1795 (CC)* 203–4. By Jul 1802 C was declaring redemption through Christ a mystery to be believed by faith, in letters not only to his brother George but even as "negative Unitarianism" to his former colleague John Prior Estlin. *CL* ii 807, 821.

[7] On C's "pious confidence of Optimism" in 1795–6 see *CL* i 168, 205; *Lects 1795 (CC)* lxi–lxvi. In Mar 1796 he found Mrs C's labour pains "inexplicable in the system of optimism". *CL* i 192.

[8] The distinction of *BL* chs 4, 13 between imagination that "dissolves, diffuses, dissipates, in order to re-create" and fancy that "has no other counters to play with, but fixities and definites" has been often scrutinised as central to C's doctrines in art. *BL (CC)* i 82–8, 304–5. Pertinent ms evidence is brought to bear in the analysis of J. R. de J. Jackson *Method and Imagination in Coleridge's Criticism* (1969). C offers here in analogy, as in *BL* ch 4, a distinction between delirium, a temporary disorder or alienation of the surface of the mind from its permanent core, and mania, a raging madness (so Johnson's *Dictionary*) from the depths of the mind, likely to be permanent (*TT* 36:142). In *Logic* C associated delirium with the understanding and the senses. *Logic (CC)* 127.

but are yoked together by the poet by some accidental coincidence: Hudibras—Lobster.[e9] The imagination modifies images and gives unity to variety; it sees all things in one—il più nell'uno.[10] There is the epic imagination, the perfection of which is in Milton; and the dramatic, of which Shakspeare is the absolute master. [f]The first[g] gives unity by throwing back into the distance, as after[h] the magnificent approach of the Messiah to battle, the poet by one touch—"far off their coming shone!"[11]— makes the whole one image: and so at the conclusion of Satan's address to the entranced angels in which every sort of image from all the regions of earth and[i] air is introduced[j] to diversify and illustrate, the reader is brought back to the single image by

> He called so loud [k]that all the hollow deep
> Of Hell resounded.[12]

The dramatic imagination[l] does not throw back, but brings close; all nature is stamped with one meaning, as in Lear, &c.[13]   [36:653]

---

[m]At the very outset, what are we to think of the soundness of this modern system of Political Economy, the tendency of every rule of which is to denationalize mankind, and to make love of country a[n] foolish superstition?[14]   [36:654]

---

[e] HNC left a two-line space after this, perhaps intending to quote the verses
[f-g] 1ˢᵗ   [h] ~~in~~ after   [i] ~~or~~ &
[j] ~~called~~ introduced   [k-l] &c. 2ᵈ [missing words supplied from *TT* (1835)]   [m] f 121   [n] ~~an~~

9 *TT* (1835) quoted Butler *Hudibras* II ii 29–32. C had quoted the lobster couplet in 1804 to illustrate "the conjunction disjunctive of Wit" (*CN* II 2112) and in 1833 as an example of enjoyable "sharp contrast" (*CL* VI 960). In *BL* ch 4 a line misquoted from Otway serves for the artificial collocation of fancy as here Butler's dawn "like a lobster boyl'd". See *BL (CC)* I 84.

10 "The many in one". Lowes *RX* 603 n 7 found a merging in this passage of the utilisation of St Francis of Sales in TT of 27 Dec 1831 (36:343) and Jeremy Taylor *Via Pacis* Decad 1 for Sunday § 8, preserved in *CN* I 876: "He to whom all things are one, who draweth all things to one, and seeth all things in one, may enjoy true peace of mind and rest of spirit."

11 *Paradise Lost* VI 768 (var). *TT* (1835) as well as MS B misread "their

coming" for "his coming"; was it C or HNC who failed to see that the Messiah shines out from among the thousands?

12 *Paradise Lost* I 314–15. In a footnote *TT* (1835) quoted I 300–15.

13 *TT* (1835) read "Lear throughout". Whether C cited other examples from Shakespeare or specified a passage in *King Lear*, HNC was unable in 1835 to recover the detail.

14 This is a supplement to 20 Jun 1834 (at n 6), above (36:650), on the denationalising tendency of political economy from Adam Smith to David Ricardo. RS and Croker had written in the *QR* LI (Mar 1834) 234: "the pseudo-science of political economy, which in this country might be esteemed the great folly of the age, if it were not felt in its consequences to be one of the great evils, and if there were not reason to apprehend that eventually it may prove the greatest curse".

God is the absolute Will. It is his name and the meaning of it. It is the Hypostasis. As begetting his*[o]* own Alterity—the Jehovah, the Manifested—he is the Father; but the Love and Life—the Spirit—proceeds from both.[15]   [36:652]

———————— *p*

*a*28. June 1834.[1]

You may not understand my system, or any given part of it, or you may be disgusted with it and reject it—well and good; but this I say, if you

> *[o]* ~~the~~ his
> *[p]* The last entry of table talk in MS B, which follows the bar, HNC cancelled: ~~St Paul's classic distinction of the human being into Will & Spirit & soul—~~
> Ff 121ᵛ, 122, and 123 are blank; ff 122ᵛ and 123ᵛ contain notes by HNC
> *[a]* MS C p 40

[15] The antithesis to the Priestleyans, represented in HNC's transfer of this paragraph in 1835 to an earlier position, is clear in a note of C's on Andrew Fuller *The Calvinistic and Socinian Systems Examined and Compared* (Market Harborough 1793): whereas the Calvinist "not only believes [in] a will, but that it is equivalent to the *ego ipse*", whereas the Priestleyan uses the word *will* "for the mere result and aggregate of fibres, motions, and sensations". *CM (CC)* II

801. On the absolute will in the Trinity cf 8 Jul 1827 (at n 3), above (36:93); two letters to EC in 1826 (*CL* VI 600, 641); *CN* I 1710 and n; J. A. Heraud *An Oration* (*C Talker* 259–60); and a note written for DC in *The Friend—(CC)* I 515n. Based on conversations with C, W. R. Hamilton diagrammed the relations of will, mind, and life for Lord Adare in 1842. After "A. Will" come B and C, Mind and Life:

B. MIND.
a. *Faith.*
α Interaction. β Causation.
γ. Identity.

b. *Thought.*
α. Induction. β. Deduction.
γ. Analogy.

c. *Sense.*
α. Co-apparition.

β. Succession.

γ. Similarity.
. . . .
C. *Life.*
a. Self-preservation.

b. Imagination.

c. Emotion.

Graves *Life of W. R. Hamilton* II 370, 373.

Except for the cancelled words on St Paul's distinction of will, spirit, and soul, this entry is the last of TT in MS B. The remaining leaves, ff 122ᵛ and 123ᵛ, contain miscellaneous notes by HNC.

[1] MS B contained inadequate space for further talk—of the few remaining leaves, only ff 121ᵛ, 122, and 123 were

blank, whereas f 122ᵛ contained HNC's notes on "Accents" and du Bellay and f 123ᵛ his notes on Hesiod and other classical poets. The next entry of TT begins on p 40 of the notebook later labelled "Sara's Poetry" (and here called MS C). The first of the two final days of recorded talk, 28 Jun, was a Thursday, one of the very few occasions when HNC's record may have coincided with C's weekly

once master it or any part of it, you cannot hesitate to embrace it as the truth; all doubt is over.[2] You cannot be sceptical about it.

All that metaphysical disquisition at the end of the first volume of the Biographia Literaria is unformed and immature; it contains the fragments of the truth, but it is not full, nor thought out.[3] It is wonderful to myself to think, how infinitely more profound my views now are, and yet how much clearer they are. The circle is completing; the idea is coming round to, and to be, the common sense. [36:655]

The regular generation of the modern, worldly Dissenter was[b] thus: Presbyterian, Arian, Socinian, Unitarian.[4] [36:656]

Is it not extraordinary to see these Dissenters calling themselves the descendants of the old Dissenters and yet clamoring for a divorce of Church and State? Why, Baxter, Bates and all the rest of them would have thought a man an atheist, who had proposed such a thing.[5] They

---

[b] i̶s̶ was

---

conversazióne. If so, the company must have been unusually small. On 30 Jun a young visitor was shown into C's "small room, half full of books in great confusion, and in one corner was a small bed, looking more like a couch, upon which lay certainly the most remarkable looking man I ever saw; he quite surpassed my expectations; he was pale and worn when I first entered, but very soon the colour came into his cheeks and his eye brightened, and such an eye as it is! such animation, and acuteness! so piercing! He began by . . . telling me how ill he had been for three months, but he is now getting a little better. . . .". Edwin Wyndham, then Viscount Adare, reporting to W. R. Hamilton. Graves II 94. Alexander Grosart identified as William Whewell (much interested in the Thirlwall affair) a visitor to C quoted by R. P. Graves, but it was probably Wyndham's testimony relayed by Hamilton: "He said that he had visited Coleridge about a month before his death, and had perceived at once his countenance pervaded by a most remarkable serenity. On being congratulated on his appearance, Coleridge replied that he did now, for the first time, begin to hope, from the mitigation of his pains, that his health was undergoing a permanent improvement . . . but that what he felt most thankful

for was the deep, calm, peace of mind which he then enjoyed; a peace such as he had never before experienced, or scarcely hoped for. This, he said, seemed now settled upon him; and all things were thus looked at by him through an atmosphere by which all were *reconciled and harmonised.*" W Mem II 290; W Prose (1876) III 470 and n.

[2] With other adjustments to the tone, *TT* (1835) replaced "embrace" with "acknowledge".

[3] Vol I of *BL* (1817) ends with ch 13 "on the imagination, or esemplastic power", preceded by a philosophical chapter on the relation of object to subject, with ten theses knitted together from Schelling, Fichte, and other transcendental idealists, *BL (CC)* I 232–306.

[4] First, in descent from Calvin, no episcopate. Next, adoption of the doctrine of Arius (c 256–336) that God created before any other creature a Son, neither eternal nor equal with the Father. Then the two stages of descent—under Socinus and finally Priestley—towards anti-trinitarian denial both of Christ's divinity and of the need for vicarious atonement. Socinianism, according to C inevitable in young men, is "not a religion, but a theory". *CN* III 3743; *LR* I 375.

[5] Richard Baxter is the favourite often

were rather for merging the state in the church. But these our modern gentlemen, who are blinded by political passions, give the kiss of alliance to the harlot of Rome and walk arm in arm with those who deny the God who redeemed them, if so they may wreak their insane antipathies on the Church. Well! I suppose they have counted the cost, and know what they would have.[6]   [36:657]

5. July 1834.[1]

I do not remember a more beautiful piece of prose in English than the consolation addressed by Lord Brooke (Fulke Greville)[a] to a lady of quality on certain conjugal infelicities.[2] The diction is such that it might have been written now, if we could find any one who combined so thoughtful a head and tender heart and exquisite taste.   [36:658]

Barrow frequently debased his language to prove his loyalty. It was indeed no easy task for a man of so much genius, and such precise mathematical mode of thinking to adopt even for a moment the slang of L'E-

[a] Ld Brooke (F. G.)

---

cited in TT. William Bates, who became "the other great leaders" in TT (1835), Baxter's contemporary and friend (1625–99), called "the silver-tongued", delivered Baxter's funeral sermon; the mildest of the nonconformists, he was the author of, among other works, *The Harmony of the Divine Attributes* (1674) and *The Four Last Things* (1691). In a marginal note dated 12 Sept 1830 C said that Baxter was called a Dissenter "with about as much right, as I might charge a man with desertion whom I had thrown out of a window in the hope of breaking his neck!" Part of a long note on John Miller *Sermons Intended to Show a Sober Application of Scriptural Principles to the Realities of Life* (Oxford 1830) 25–35: *CM (CC)* III.

[6] "Thinking that the very fact of the existence of an established Church, supported as a national institution, and represented by its dignitaries in the highest branch of the legislature, stamped them, as religionists, with a mark of inferiority, it was not wonderful that they employed the power, with which they were now invested, to bring down the established Church to the same level on which they

themselves stood; annihilate all the rights, powers, and privileges which belonged to its members; and, by depriving it of all support from the funds of the state, convert it into a self-constituted religious community. . . . Methodists and Presbyterians differed widely from Catholics; but Catholics, Presbyterians, and Methodists all differed widely from the episcopal Church of England." *A Reg* for 1834 History 164.

[1] In a longish letter of this date (a Saturday) C spoke of "progressive improvements" in his health for the last eight days. *CL* VI 986.

[2] Fulke Greville, Baron Brooke "A Letter to an Honorable Lady" in *Certaine Learned and Elegant Workes* (1633) ii 257–94. In six chapters of an unfinished work, Greville recommended respect, reverence, sense, understanding, and reason; in a passage in ch 5 that C called "almost divine" Greville wrote of "a well-beloved Wife": ". . . shee neither made the World her Judge, nor the Market her Theater, but contented her sweet minde with the triumphs of Patience, and made solitarinesse the tombe of her Fame . . .". *CM (CC)* II 878.

strange and Tom Brown;[3] but he *[b]*succeeds in doing so sometimes. I remember in his discourse on the Pope's supremacy—and the conduct of Peter at the time of our Lord's apprehension in the garden, he says—"Then up went Peter's anger, and out popped his sword".[4] With such exceptions, Barrow must be considered as closing the first great period *[c]*of the English*[d]* language. Dryden begins the second.[5] Of course there are numerous subdivisions.   [36:659]

Peter Wilkins is, to my mind, a work of uncommon beauty;[6] and yet Stothard's*[e]* illustrations have added beauties to it.[7] I think the latter part of Peter Wilkins, like*[f]* the chapter in Joseph Andrews between Mr B. my

[b] p 41   *[c–d]* of English   *[e]* Stodart's   *[f]* &

[3] This topic returns from 1 Jul 1833 (at n 33), above (36:542). C had said in Lect 14 of 13 Mar 1818: "A free and easy style was considered as a test of loyalty, or at all events, as a badge of the cavalier party; you may detect it occasionally even in Barrow, who is, however, in general remarkable for dignity and logical sequency of expression; but in L'Estrange, Collyer, and the writers of that class, this easy manner was carried out to the utmost extreme of slang and ribaldry." *Lects 1808–19 (CC)* II 235. When Lessing said that L'Estrange is known for one of the purest and most distinguished styles, C responded: "Lestrange's *Slang* is indeed the master *Slang* of his age—unless Ned Ward & Tom Brown be thought his Corrivals—and as to the 'Rheinheit', it puts me in mind of the Hibernian, who spit *clean* in a man's mouth, as he was gaping." Annotation on *Sämmtliche Schriften* VIII 94–5: *CM (CC)* III.

[4] *TT* (1835) omitted the instance, perhaps to avoid repetition from the more general reference in *TT* 36:542 (1 Jul 1833, at nn 22–3, above), perhaps because C had strained the evidence. In the *Tatler* report of Lect 14 of 13 Mar 1818 C made a similar statement: ". . . the action of S[t] Peter, in cutting off the ear of the High Priest's servant, is thus stated,—'Up rose his blood, and out popped his sword.'" *Lects 1808–19 (CC)* II 240. Barrow had written of Peter's actions when Christ was seized by the soldiers: ". . . presently up was his

spirit, and out went his Sword in defence of him". *A Treatise of the Pope's Supremacy* (1680) 43. In 1802 C noted examples of Barrow's slang: *CN* I 1274.

[5] To Klopstock, as reported in "Satyrane's Letters", WW (presumably) recommended "the prose works of Dryden as models of pure and native English". *Friend (CC)* II 246. With a delayed reference to C, Herbert Read amplified the point made in TT: For "Bunyan, Milton, Taylor, Browne, Donne, Bacon, Hooker" there was no "corporate sense", but by Dryden's time the corporate sense made literature a profession; "Dryden himself was the first writer to be wholly conscious of this sense, and it is a tribute to his real greatness that he himself became its first exemplar." *English Prose Style* (1928) 204.

[6] Robert Paltock (1697–1767) *The Life and Adventures of Peter Wilkins, a Cornish Man, Relating Particularly, His Shipwreck Near the South Pole . . .* by R.S. a Passenger in the *Hector* (2 vols 1751).

[7] Thomas Stothard (1755–1834), R.A. 1794, "one of the most popular and prolific artists of the turn of the century". His illustrations to *Peter Wilkins* first appeared in vol XII of "The Novelist's Magazine" series (2 vols 1783). For the *Bijou* (1829) he made a drawing of Christabel aghast at the look Geraldine gives Sir Leoline and made another to accompany *The Garden of Boccaccio* in *Keepsake* II (1829) facing 282. An engraving by C. Mottram (1815, copy in

lord's steward and Parson Adams,[8] if extracted, would form a very fair satire on the Malthusians. They clip the Glumms' wings in order to make them shoemakers and carpenters, &c![9] Richard Hart Davis' story is an imitation of Peter Wilkins; but there

V&A) shows Stothard and C at breakfast with WW, Sheridan, and several painters at Samuel Rogers's. An unsigned letter to Stothard (1828?) assured him, "Mr Coleridge knew you perfectly well—& recollected his meeting you at Mr Greens". Ms in Boston Public Library (U.S.A.), printed in G. E. Bentley Jr "Coleridge, Stothard, and the First Illustration of 'Christabel' " *Studies in Romanticism* xx (1981) 114–15. "He admired the Elegance of Geraldine & indeed the Beauty of the whole Draught—When I ventured to ask him whether Leoline ever was to marry the lady—he made answer That his affection to Geraldine was merely *parental*—He said that Leoline was an aged man,— hurried by his chivalrous feelings back to the days of his youth, so much so, that if you remember he declared that he would himself encounter in a tilt the wretches who had ran away with Geraldine—For he sees in her, the traces of her father— or thinks he sees—& she recalls to his mind his former friendship & ancient quarrel with Roland de Vaux—". At the words "or thinks he sees", or earlier, we can suspect that the reporter has taken over from C in order to instruct Stothard.

[8] Henry Fielding (1707–54) *The History of the Adventures of Joseph Andrews and His Friend Mr Abraham Adams* (2 vols 1742) bk iii ch 13 "A curious dialogue which passed between Mr. Abraham Adams and Mr. Peter Pounce, better worth reading than all the works of Colley Cibber and many others". Peter, the steward, who opposes the poor rates and charity, asks: "How can any man complain of hunger . . . in a country where such excellent salads are to be gathered in almost every field?" C owned and annotated a copy of *Joseph Andrews*, which has since disappeared. *CM (CC)* ii 689–90. The reference to Fielding was omitted from *TT* (1835).

[9] The Stothard illustrations were available in "A New Edition" (2 vols London and Edinburgh 1816). C's remarks are metaphorical for events in the text, chs 46–7, in which Peter seeks to save the throne by introducing diversity of crafts and thus freedom—what good to make watches if everybody made them and everybody had one?—and then to insert the people of Alkoe into international commerce. HNC, to achieve clarity of transition from the praise of Stothard, substituted a different remark in *TT* (1835): "What an exquisite image that of Peter's Glum fluttering over the ship, and trying her strength in lifting the stores!" RS, in the last of his complaints to HNC concerning C's errors, charged C with faulty memory, for "Peter's *Glum* should be Peter's *Gawrie*" and the print "represents Youwarkee *towing a chest*", with no trial of strength. HNC responded on 27 Jun 1835: "I was aware of the injury I had done dear Youwarkee in Glumming her; it was a slip. I never saw Stothard's designs; but if I remember rightly, there is a passage in P.W. descriptive of Youwarkee's trying her strength in lifting the first batch of stores, & Sara fancies she has seen that scene drawn & by Stothard; but perhaps it is what you mention." UT mss. The engraving at issue is the frontispiece to vol i, first engraved for the 1783 edition, reworked for the 1816. HNC wrote to RS 24 Apr 1836: "Did you hear that the author of Peter Wilkins has been discovered? One Robert Paltock of Clement's Inn. Pickering bought the agreement with Dodsley, I think, at a sale the other day." UT ms. When HNC acquired a copy of the work in *Gilbert's Clergyman's Almanack* (1842) he wrote on a front endleaf: "Robert Paltock author of Peter Wilkins—Agreement with Dodsley."

are[g] many beautiful things in it, especially his finding his wife crouching by the fire—she having in his absence plucked out all her feathers, to be like him![10]   [36:660]

There was a book published by Eagle at Bristol—part of which was true—which gave me much pleasure.[11]

How charming, how wholesome Fielding always is! To take him up after Richardson is like emerging from a sick room heated by stoves into an open lawn on a breezy day in May.[12]   [36:661]

I have been very much interested in the account of Bishop Sandford[h] published by his son.[13] He seems to have been a thorough gentleman

[g] Word supplied by the editor from *TT* (1835)   [h] Sanford

[10] *The Life and Surprizing Adventures of Crusoe Richard Davis* (2 vols 1756, 2nd ed 1801), identified in *M Rev* xv (1756) 656 as by Adolphus Bannac. The episode C refers to, when the narrator's feathered wife Mary tells of the "excess of pain and misery" as she tried different ways of reducing herself to something like human skin, appears in *The Voyages and Discoveries of Crusoe Richard Davis* (1801) 43–5.

After inserting a remark that "Robinson Crusoe and Peter Wilkins could only have been written by islanders", *TT* (1835) added a paragraph on C's project of a narrative on this "pre-occupied ground". On a flyleaf of *The Life and Adventures of Robinson Crusoe* (2 vols 1812), vol II of a copy belonging to Henry Gillman, C wrote in Jul 1830: "The Rob. Crusoe is like the Vision of a happy Night-mair", in which the excited imagination does not draw the reader away from "common Flesh and Blood". *CM (CC)* II 167.

[11] Probably William Williams (1727–91) anon *The Journal of Llewellin Penrose, a Seaman*. In an available edition (4 vols London: John Murray; Edinburgh: William Blackwood 1815), the "Advertisement" is signed John Eagles; the dedication is to Benjamin West as one who had known Williams and John Eagles's father. John Eagles (1783–1855) *Bristol Riots: Their Causes, Prog-*

ress, and Consequences (Bristol 1832) was published by Gutch and Martin. The *Journal*, in places highly reminiscent of *Robinson Crusoe*, tells of piracy, other adventure, and the flora and fauna of Caribbean islands.

[12] *TT* (1835) preceded this remark with two praising Fielding on more intellectualised grounds: "What a master of composition Fielding was! Upon my word, I think the Oedipus Tyrannus, the Alchemist, and Tom Jones the three most perfect plots ever planned." In Fielding *The History of Tom Jones, a Foundling* (4 vols 1773) C wrote that no young man could read Fielding "without feeling himself a better man—at least, without an intense conviction that he *could* not be guilty of a *base* Act". *CM (CC)* II 693. He took the opportunity there to comment unfavourably on Samuel Richardson, evidence that he had not purged his animus of 1804, when he was unable "not to be vexed that I must admire—aye, greatly, very greatly, admire *Richardson/* his mind is so very vile a mind—so oozy, hypocritical, praise-mad, canting, envious, concupiscent". Fielding's talent was for observation, not meditation, but Richardson was not philosopher enough to understand the difference. *CN* II 2471.

[13] *Remains of the Late Right Reverend Daniel Sandford, D.D. Oxon. Bishop of Edinburgh in the Scottish Episcopal*

upon the model of St Paul, whose manners were the finest of any man upon record.[14]   [36:662]

Is it judicious in the admirers of Walter Scott to call him the Shakspeare of Scotland?[15] Walter Scott[i] stands alone and will not be surpassed or equalled in his line; but so far from being like Shakspeare, he is[j] the reverse. Would it not be doing David Teniers injustice to compare him with Michael Angelo?[16]

I think the late conversation and disclosure between Mr Littleton and O'Connell the lowest step of degradation to which the Whig Government has yet descended![17] It is absolutely incredible—not so much for its

---

[i] W. S. ~~is at the head of~~   [j] ~~was~~ is

Church, with a memoir, by the Rev John Sandford, vicar of Chillingham (2 vols Edinburgh and London 1830). C's praise of the book is quoted in 36:560n (14 Aug 1833 n 31, above). Thomas Poole's niece, Elizabeth Poole (b 1799), married one of the bishop's sons, Archdeacon Sandford, curate at Wells. *Poole* II 262, 273. HNC wrote to JTC 7 Aug 1834: "If you meet with Bp Sandford's Life by his son, read it by all means. It is a good book." BM Add MS 47447 f 105. To Poole he wrote on 3 Sept: ". . . the last book wc̄h my Uncle read through was Bp Sandford's Life. He was remarkably pleased with the execution of the Memoir, & deeply impressed with the Bp's character. He wrote several notes—one exquisite one upon a very exquisite passage in the Memoir in wc̄h the Bp's courteous demeanor to his daughters is mentioned . . . honourable use shall be made of it." BM Add MS 35344 ff 110–11. SC wrote similarly to Poole on 5 Sept. Ibid f 105. C's annotated copy of *Sandford*, only one note of which has been preserved (*NTP* 298–9), has since disappeared. *CM (CC)* IV. HNC was exchanging visits with some of the Sandfords by Nov 1834. *Minnow* 183; Elizabeth Sandford to HNC 14 Nov 1834: UT ms.

[14] See 15 Jun 1833 (at n 8), above.

[15] In *The Spirit of the Age* (1825) Hazlitt had contrasted Scott as "a learned, literal, a *matter-of-fact* expounder of

truth or fable", a "*prophesier* of things past", with a "*maker*", a creative poet, who soars above his subject. *H Works* XI 59–60. C's three sentences were not published by HNC. *Scott: The Critical Heritage* ed John O. Hayden (1970) indexes twenty-five comparisons of Scott with Shakespeare before 1834. The reviewer of *Quentin Durward* in the *New Monthly Magazine* VIII (1823) 82–7 had found "such touches of nature and feeling as often remind us—what more *can* we say?—of Shakespeare himself". Hayden 275.

[16] C's admiration for Teniers, one of the masters of Dutch realism, is clear from 24 Jul 1831, above (36:302). Reynolds's *Discourses* had increasingly offered Michelangelo Buonarroti (1475–1564) as the greatest model for emulation. If C's applause in 1799 was conventional, after he had been to Rome he could count Michelangelo among those at "the culmination of the 'divine Philosophy' ", could welcome Samuel Rogers home fraternally as another who had seen the Sistine Chapel, which "no poet or philosopher can have seen in vain", and could contrast Michelangelo's unifying imagination with the fanciful "petrifactions" of Bernini. *CL* IV 569, 759, V 15, VI 1012.

[17] Edward John Littleton, 1st Baron Hatherton (1791–1863), in 1834 chief secretary to the Lord Lieutenant of Ire-

wickedness, as its folly! Surely these ministers must go soon! They cannot hold.[18]

---

[k]I think I could have conformed to the Roman Catholic Church before the Reformation. The errors existed, but they had not been made articles of faith before the Council of Trent. If a Roman Catholic asked[l] me the question put to Sir Henry Wotton, I should content myself by answering that I could not exactly say when my religion began, but that it was some sixty or seventy years before his, which began at the Council of Trent.[19]   [36:663]

[k] p 42   [l] h̶a̶d̶ asked

land, already charged with "thimble-shifting" because he modified the Tithes Bill to appease Daniel O'Connell—Hansard 3rd s XXIV (1834) 1154, 1206—told O'Connell in an interview on 23 Jun that the new Coercion Bill for Ireland would be moderate. When Lord Grey said at a cabinet meeting on 29 Jun that the bill would include provision against public meetings, Littleton told O'Connell of his disappointment. On 3 Jul O'Connell spoke in the Commons of his conversation of 23 Jun; on the 4th Grey said the issue was settled when Littleton told O'Connell it was not; on 5 Jul Littleton resigned. *The Times* 4–5 Jul 1834. Half of the *DNB* article on Littleton is concerned with the events of 23 Jun–5 Jul 1834.

[18] On 9 Jul the Grey ministry resigned, to be replaced by a ministry formed by Melbourne, dismissed on 17 Nov by William IV.

[19] On the Council of Trent see 10 Mar 1827 n 13, above (36:73). The anecdote concerning Sir Henry Wotton (1568–1639) is told by Izaak Walton in his "Life of Wotton" prefixed to *Reliquiae Wottonianae* (1651). A priest Sir Henry had met in Rome "sent to him by a boy of the Choir this question, writ on a small piece of paper; *Where was your Religion to be found before* Luther? To which question *Sir Henry* presently underwrit, *My religion was to be found* then, *where yours is not to be found* now, *in the written Word of God.*" In 1810 C noted Wotton's reply, in a discussion of the Church

of England vs the Roman Catholic Church. *CN* III 3872 f 37. Cf a squib in the *Courier* of 2 Aug 1817: *EOT (CC)* II 478. More tolerantly, to the question, Where was Protestantism before the fork in the river, C had proposed the answer, "Why, w[h]ere yours was, to be sure". *CN* IV 4802. But in 1826 he had been much irritated to find in *The Times* "the old *lie* that ours was the innovation". *CN* IV 5221.

TT (1835) concluded C's talk, under the heading "July 10. 1834. Euthanasia", with a passage from a letter from C to DC. *CL* VI 705. A portion of the original letter that includes this passage has survived among HNC's papers at VCL: S MS F 3.16. As the fragment contains an uncomplimentary reference to HNC, DC may have made it available only after C's final illness. C actually wrote to J. H. Green on the subject of euthanasia 29 Mar 1832 (*CL* VI 895), with a greater interest in his prospective autopsy. Next in fact on MS C p 42 comes the passage from *Sandford* published in *TT* (1835) II 238n (36:560n), then "Inscription for a Timepiece", published in *TT* (1835) II 360 and again in *LR* I 60; third, "Time fleets;—but Conscience gives immortality to the fleeting acts of Time. S.T.C."; fourth, the beginning of the letter to Adam Kennard (concluded on p 44).

According to *SC Memoir* I 110, HNC last saw C on Sunday, 20 Jul, but the day when he was last admitted to C's room is less clear in an autograph of SC to Miss

Lawrence (29 Sept), which says that SC and Mrs C "were first informed of his danger on the 20th", that when C "knew that his time was come" he told Mrs Gillman he "desired to see no more of those he loved upon earth"—"He did however take leave of my husband & saw some of his other friends after this— but my mother and I were content with his blessing brought to us by Henry & my brothers were not sent for because the medical men were of opinion that the agitation of seeing us & them would be more than he ought to encounter." VCL ms. C died on the 25th. HNC wrote in the letter to his brother James on 8 Aug concerning "Aunt S": "She is the widow of a great man—the greatest, in my judgment, since Milton. The impression he has made is profound, tho' at present in this country not very extensive. In America his influence is more general, &, if I mistake not, there will be a burst of power & glory around his memory very shortly in England." BM Add MS 47558 f 119.

EDITOR'S APPENDIXES

ABBREVIATIONS IN THE MANUSCRIPTS OF H. N. COLERIDGE EXPANDED IN THE PRESENT EDITION

ABBREVIATIONS IN THE MANUSCRIPTS OF H. N. COLERIDGE EXPANDED IN THE PRESENT EDITION

Initials for proper names otherwise identified in a particular entry are excluded from this list.

Apb. of C.	Archbishop of Canterbury
acc̄t.	account
accumulōn	accumulation
admon	administration
amplificōn	amplification
an̄r, anōr	another
applicon	application
apptēd	appointed
authy, authȳ	authority
Bart	Baronet
Bp, Bps	Bishop, bishops
bror, brōrs	brother, brothers
circēs	circumstances
C	S. T. Coleridge
C. J.	Christ Jesus
C. L.	Charles Lamb
C. of E.	Church of England
Commissōr	Commissioner
communicōn	communication
examon	examination
F. R.	French Revolution
Gov.	Government
i.e.	that is (id est)
illustrōn	illustration
J. C.	Jesus Christ
mar̄, mre	matter
modificōn	modification
mor, mōr	mother

m͞trs	matters
N. A.	North America
N. T.	New Testament
N. W.	Northwest
objōn	objection
obligo͞ns	obligations
operōn	operation
opōn	opinion
ōr, ōrs	other, others
O. T.	Old Testament
P.	Parliament (*as in* Act of P.)
parlār	particular
possōn	possession
Pr	Professor
Prot.	Protestant
Publicōns	Publications
Q. R., Qu. R.	*Quarterly Review*
R. C.	Roman Catholic
R. Catholic	Roman Catholic
Reformōn	Reformation
repre͞sives	representatives
STC, S.T.C.	S. T. Coleridge
S. W.	Southwest
tho'	though
thro'	through
w͞ch	which
w͞d	would
whēr	whether
W. H.	Westminster Hall
Xst, Xtian	Christ, Christian
Xtianity	Christianity

MANUSCRIPT E

MANUSCRIPT E

MS E is a transcription by HNC of the entries from C's conversation in MS A of 1822–4, with numbers assigned by him to each entry. MS E begins where the entries in MS A physically begin; HNC made slight changes in the order of subsequent entries. As the occasional verbal changes between MS A and MS E are not reflected in *TT* (1835) or *TT* (1836), it can be assumed that MS E, completed on 2 Jan 1827, was not utilised by HNC in the preparation of TT for publication. MS E occupies seventeen leaves of a workbook labelled on the first leaf in indication of the contents preceding the memorabilia of C's conversation:

Letters written during a tour in France
from August 6ᵗʰ to September 29ᵗʰ 1822.

Given to Sara Coleridge by her admiring and
affectionate friend and cousin
Henry Nelson Coleridge.
2. Jan. 1827.

The leaves of table-talk bear no page or folio numbers. The entries appear on rectos only, but the three notes by HNC appear on the verso preceding the page to which each refers. HNC assigned numbers 3 and 43 each to two successive entries. Entry 34 and one other entry have been cut from the ms.

Table Talk of S. T. C.

---

1. Negatively there might be more of the sayings of Socrates in the Memorabilia of Xenophon than in Plato; that is to say, there is less of what is *not* Socrates';—but the general spirit and impression left by Plato is more Socratic.

---

2. There was a want of harmony in Lord Byron. It was unnatural to connect very great intellectual powers with utter depravity. Such combination did not exist in rerum natura.

---

3. Old Mortality is the best of the Scotch Novels. Guy Mannering also good.

---

3. He ridiculed the ghost story in Wesley's Life. Define a ghost—visibility without tangibility—that is also the definition of a shadow; therefore they must be the same, because no two different things can have the same definition.

4. If a ghost is a soul, a soul is substance, and though we might not see it, yet we must feel it, as the wind. A visible substance without susceptibility of impact is an absurdity. Ghosts are always said to perform trifling and foolish tricks; but the soul w͞ch is reason could not spin spoons &c.

---

5. This is not a logical age. A friend had lately given him some political pamphlets of the 17ᵗʰ century in the time of Charles and the Cromwellate. *There* the premises were frequently wrong, but the deductions were always legitimate; whereas in these days the premises are commonly sound, but the conclusions false. He had paid a merited tribute to Oxford in his work on Logic for preserving that study in the schools. Geometry is not a substitute for Logic.

---

6. Xtianity proves itself, as the Sun is seen by his own light. It is; its evidence is involved in its existence.

7. Either we have an immortal soul or we have not; if we have not, we are beasts,—the first and wisest beasts perhaps, but still beasts; we only differ in degree, not in kind;—but we are not beasts by the concession of materialists and by our own consciousness; therefore it must be the possession of a soul within us that makes the difference.

---

8. Read the 1ˢᵗ chapter of Genesis without prejudice and you will be convinced at once. After the creation of the animals, Moses pauses;—"Let us make Man ~~after~~ in our image, after our likeness."—and the passage, "Man became a living soul."

---

9. He had finished a work on Logic, but had still the preface to write. He had also completed one half of his work on St John's Gospel. He expounded its aims and purposes. It is to demonstrate a priori the ⟨possibility and⟩ probability of a Revelation; the latter half will be on the historical evidence for w͞ch he has many materials. St John had a twofold object in his Gospel and Epistles; to prove the divinity and the actual human nature and bodily suffering of Jesus Christ, that he was God and Man. The notion that the effusion of blood and water from the Saviour's side was intended to prove the real death of the sufferer originated with some modern Germans, and is ridiculous. There is a very small quantity of water *occasionally* in the præcordia, but in the pleura, where wounds are not mortal, there is a great deal. St John meant to show he was a real man, and says, "I saw it with my own eyes! It was real blood, composed of lymph and crassamentum and not a mere celestial ichor!"

10. The verse of the Three Witnesses is spurious; it spoils the reasoning. St John's logic is Oriental consisting chiefly in *position*, whilst St Paul displays all the intricacies of the Greek system. Porson had shown that the balance of external authority is against the verse.

11. Xtianity might be believed without the six first chapters of Daniel; it was within us; it was associated with our mothers' chair.

---

12. Pindar was the sacerdotal poet. Religion appeared in his writings mild and benignant; in Æschylus terrible, malignant and persecuting. Sophocles was the mildest of the three tragedians, but the persecuting aspect was still maintained. Euripides was like a modern Frenchman, never so happy as when giving a slap at the Gods altogether. It was a mistake to suppose Pindar a wild and extravagant poet. He was a Tory. Ἀφίσταμαι. Something sacred about him.

---

13. Kotzebue represents the petty kings in the islands of the Pacific exactly as Homer's kings. All supposed descended from the Gods. Riches commanding influence.

---

14. S. T. C. was reciting his tragedy at some house, and was in the midst of Alhadra's description of the death of her husband, when a scrubby boy with a shining face set in dirt burst open the door with—"Please, ma'am! Master says, Will you ha' or will you not ha' the pin round?"—

---

15. The servant maid at Mr G's. came once into the room and said there was some one below, who asked if there was any poet there, and she knew, she said, that Mr C. was a Poet. Down goes S. T. C. gravely to the door and opens it, when a louting boy screamed in his face, "Any ~~poets~~ *pots* for the Angel?"

15. Credat Judæus—

---

16. John Kemble would correct any body. He was discoursing in his measured manner after dinner, when the servant announced his carriage; he took no notice of this and went on; after this had been repeated twice at intervals, the servant said upon entering the fourth time, "Mrs Kemble says, Sir, she has the *rheumatise* and cannot stay."—"Add *ism*" said Kemble, and proceeded in his discourse.

---

17. Mathews was performing before the King. The King was pleased with the imitation of Kemble, and told this anecdote. "I liked Kemble very much; he was one of my earliest friends. Once he was talking and

out of snuff; I offered him my box; he declined taking any—"He a poor actor could not put his fingers into a royal box." I said—"Take some, you will ob*lee*ge me. Kemble remarked "It would become your royal jaws better to say 'oblige me'."

---

18. St John used Λόγος technically; Philo-Judæus had so used it before, and it was commonly understood of the *Schechinah*. "With God" is an unfortunate translation of "Πρὸς τὸν Θεὸν"; that would be σὺν τῷ Θεῷ. Πρὸς meant the utmost possible proximity without confusion, likeness without sameness. The Jewish Church understood the Messiah to be a divine person. Philo-Judæus expressly cautions against supposing it a mere personification, a mere symbol; it was a substantial self-existent Being. Those who were afterwards called Gnostics, were a kind of Arians, and thought the Λόγος was an after-birth. They placed Ἄβυσσος and Σιγη before him. Therefore St John said, Ἐν ἀρχῇ ἦν ὁ Λόγος. He was begotten in the first simultaneous burst of Godhead, if such expression can be used, when speaking of Eternal Existence.

---

19. Snuff is the final cause of the human nose.

---

20. Great writers wrote best when calm and exerting themselves upon subjects unconnected with party or passion. Burke never shows his powers except he is in a passion. The French Revolution was alone a subject fit for him. We are not yet aware of the important consequences of that event. We are too near it.

---

21. Goldsmith did every thing happily.

---

22. "Δακρύοεν γελάσασα" looked like an expression of Moschus or Bion. Pindar called it *[a]*

---

23. A rogue is a roundabout fool; a fool in circumbendibus.

---

24. He did not believe St Paul to be the author of the Epistle to the Hebrews; he thought Luther's conjecture very probable, that it was Apollos an Alexandrine Jew. The plan was too studiously regular for St Paul. It was evidently written during the yet existing glories of the Temple. For 300 years the Church had not affixed St Paul's name to it; but its inspiration, independently of its genuineness as to St Paul, was never doubted.

[a] Blank left in ms

25. The three first Gospels showed the history, that is, the fulfillment of the prophecies in the facts; St John declared explicitly the doctrine *oracularly* and without argument, because, being pure reason, it could only be proved by itself. St Paul wrote for the Understanding and proved the doctrine by human logic.

---

26. The Understanding suggests the materials of reasoning; Reason decides on them. The first can only say;—This *is*, or *ought* to be, so;—the last says;—It *must* be so!

---

27. The Persians came from *Elam who was a son of Japheth*;† hence their European superiority. Kant had declared the existence of three races of mankind. If two races cross, a third is produced different from either, e.g. a white and negro produce a mulatto;—but *different species** produce by chance; sometimes the offspring are like the father, sometimes the mother, e.g. Englishman and Spanish woman.

---

28. Othello was not a negro, but a high and chivalrous Moorish Chief. Shakspeare learned the character from the Spanish poetry, wch was prevalent in England in his time. Jealousy is not the point of his passion; it was agony that the creature whom he had believed angelic, with whom "he had garnered up his heart," and whom he could not help still loving, should be proved impure and worthless. It was the struggle *not* to love her. It was a moral indignation and regret that virtue should so fall,— "'Tis pity on it, Iago." In addition, his honor was concerned. Iago would not have succeeded but by hinting that his honor was compromised. There was no ferocity; his mind was majestic and composed. He deliberately determined to die, and spoke his last speech with a view of showing his attachment to the State, though it had superseded him. Schiller has the material sublime; to produce an effect he sets a whole town on fire, and throws infants with their mothers into the flames, or locks up a father in an old tower. Shakspear drops a handkerchief and the same or greater effects follow. Lear is the most tremendous effort of Shakspeare, as a Poet; Hamlet, as a Philosopher or Meditator, and Othello is the union of the two. There is something gigantic and unformed in the two former; whilst in the last every thing assumes its due place and proportion, and the whole mature powers of his mind are displayed in admirable equilibrium.

†This is a mistake. Elam was son of Shem. X.Gen.22.v.
*rather "*varieties of the same species*"

29. Privilege was a substitution for law, where from the nature of the circumstances a law could not act without clashing with greater and more general principles. The House of Commons must of course have the power of taking cognizance of offences against its own rights. Sir F. Burdett might have been sent to the Tower for the speech he made; but when afterwards he published it in a pamphlet, and they took cognizance of it, they forgot the right distinction of privilege and law. As a speech they alone could notice it consistently with their necessary prerogative of freedom of debate; but when it became a book, then the law was to look to it, and there being a law of libel, Privilege wch acts only as a substitute for other laws, could have nothing to do with it. C. Wynn said "he would not shrink from affirming that if the H. of C. chose to burn one of its own members in Palace Yard, it had the inherent power to do it." This is for want of a due distinction between Privilege and Law.

_____

30. There are two principles in every European and Xtian state, permanency and progression. In the civil wars of England, wch were as new and fresh now as they were 150 years ago, and will be so for ever to us, these two principles came to a struggle. It was natural that the great and the good of the nation should be found in the ranks of either side. In Mahometan states there is no permanency and therefore they sink directly. They existed and *could* only exist in their efforts of progression; when they ceased to conquer, they fell to pieces. Turkey would long since have fallen, if it had not been supported by the rival interests of Europe. They had no Church; religion and state were one; there was no counterpoise, no mutual support. This is the very essence of Unitarianism. They had no past; they were not an historical people; they existed only in the present. China was an instance of permanency without any progression. The Persians were a superior people; they had a history and a literature; they had always been considered even by the Greeks as quite distinct from the other barbarians. The Afghans were a brave republican people. Europeans and Orientalists may be well represented by two figures standing back to back; the latter looking towards the East, that is, backwards; the former westward, that is, forwards.

_____

31. Kean was original, but copied from himself. His rapid descents from the hyper-tragical to the infra-colloquial, though sometimes productive of great effect, were often unreasonable. He was not thorough gentleman enough to play Othello.

_____

32. Sir J. Mackintosh was the King of the Men of Talent. He was an elegant converser. He once gave breakfast to S. T. C. and Sir H. Davy,

then an unknown young man. There was much conversation about Locke &c. Afterwards Mackintosh said to S. T. C. "That's a very extraordinary young man; but he is gone wrong upon some points." There was a freshness about the mind of the Davy wc̄h was strongly contrasted with that of Mackintosh. Davy's thoughts were like the flower plucked wet with the dew; nay more, you could see them growing in the rich garden of his mind. The mind of Mackintosh was a hortus siccus, full of specimens of every kind of plant, but dwarfed, ready cut and dried. He was like a liquor shop, where if you ask for gin, out they pour it from this phial; if for brandy, from that; so whatever was the subject, Mackintosh had a pre-arranged discourse upon it. In short he was, as the chief of men of Talent, of course very powerful; but he possessed not a ray of Genius. After leaving Davy you would remember many sayings and things wc̄h would stick by you for days, and set you thinking for yourself; but, although you would admire Mackintosh and be much taken with his fluency and brilliancy, you would carry off nothing. S. T. C. proposed to write on his forehead, "Warehouse to let." He dealt too much in generalities for a lawyer. He was deficient in power of applying his principles to the particulars in question. Robert Smith had more logical ability, but he always aimed at conquest by any means. Mackintosh was candid.

---

33. Canning was so very irritable, surprisingly so for a wit who was always giving hard knocks. He should have put on an ass's skin before he went into Parliament. The Cabinet could hardly stand; it was composed of such jarring materials. Canning and Plunkett must both feel mortified and wounded. Lord Liverpool was the stay of the Ministry, but he was not a man of a directing mind. He could not ride on the whirlwind. He served as the isthmus to connect one part of the Ministry with the other. He always gave the common sense of the matter.

[Item 34 has been cut from MS E. It was almost certainly the paragraph on the national debt that follows at this point in MS A p 104 (36:37).]

35. The poor laws were the necessary accompaniments of increasing commerce and manufacturing systems. In Scotland they did without them till Glasgow and Paisley became great manufacturing places, and then people said, "We must subscribe for the poor, or we shall have poor laws!" So they made themselves poor laws in order to avoid having poor laws. It was to absurd to talk of Queen Elizabeth's Acts creating the Poor Laws. The inequality and mischief consisted in the agricultural interest having to pay them all; for though perhaps in the end the land became more valuable, yet at the first the farmers bore all the brunt. The poor rates were the consideration given for having labor at demand. It was the

price. There ought to be a fixed revolving period for the equalization of rates.

---

36. The conduct of the Whigs was inconsistent. It originated in the fatal error wch Fox committed in persisting, after the three first years of the French Revolution, when every shadow of Freedom was vanished, in eulogizing the men and measures of France. So he went on gradually departing from all the principles of English policy and wisdom, till at length he became the panegyrist through thick and thin of a military frenzy under the influence of wch even the very name of Liberty was detested. Thus his party became the absolute abettors of the invasion of Spain, and did all in their power to thwart the efforts of this country to resist it. At present, when the invasion is by a Bourbon, and the cause of the Spaniards neither united nor sound in many respects, they would precipitate this country into a crusade. S. T. C. in 1808–9 met Lord Darnley accidentally when Lord D. said to him, "Are you mad, Mr C.?" "Why my Lord? What have I done that argues derangement of mind?" "Why, I mean those essays of yours on the 'Hopes and Fears of a People invaded by foreign armies'; the Spaniards are absolutely conquered; it is absurd to talk about their chance of resisting!" "Very well, my Lord! We shall see! But will your Lordship permit me in a year or two's time to retort your question upon you, if I should have grounds for so doing?" "Certainly, that's fair."

Two years afterwards, when affairs were altered in Spain, S. T. C. met Lord D. again about the same place, and after some little conversation, he said, "Does your Lordship remember giving me leave to retort a certain question upon you about the Spaniards? Who is mad now?" "Very true! it is very extraordinary. It was an ingenious conjecture!" "I think that is hardly a fair term. Has any thing happened wch I had not foretold, or from other causes, or under other conditions?"

---

37. Many votes were given for Reform in the H. of C. wch were not sincere. While it was well known that the measure never could be carried in Parliament, it was as well to purchase some popularity by voting for it. When Hunt and his associates, before the Six Acts, created a panic, the Ministers lay on their oars for three or four months, until the general cry even from the Opposition was, "Why do not the Ministers come forward with some measure?"

---

38. The present Ministry existed on the weakness of the Opposition. The latter had pledged themselves to such desperate measures that they never would have the support of the country.

39. The present adherents of the Romish Church were not Catholics; we are the Catholics. We can prove that we hold the doctrines of the primitive Church for the first 300 years. The Council of Trent made the Papists what they are. A foreign Romish Bishop had declared that the Protestants were more like the Catholics before the Council of Trent, than their present descendants. The course of Xtianity and the Xtian Church may be likened to a great river wch covered a large channel, and bore along with its waters mud and gravel and weeds, till it met a great rock in the middle of the stream; by some means or other the water flows purely and separated from the filth in a deeper and narrower course on one side of the rock; and the refuse of the dirt and troubled waters went off on the other, and then cried out, "We are the River." A person said, "But you will call them civilly Catholics?" "No! I will not! I will not tell a lie upon so solemn an occasion!" They are not Catholics. If they were, then we should be heretics, and Roman Catholics makes not difference. Catholicism is not capable of degrees. Properly speaking there can only be one body of Catholics ex vi termini; if Roman Catholics be allowed, then there may be English, Irish &c., wch with regard to a difference in religious tenets is absurd.

40. The Romish Religion is so flattering to the passions of men, that it is impossible to say how far it would spread amongst the highest orders, if the disabilities attending its profession were removed.

41. Milton's Latin style is perhaps better than his English. His style is as characteristic of him as a stern Republican, as Cowley's is of him as a Gentleman.

42. Literal interpretation of the Bible was the best after all. The Zenda-vesta must have been copied from the writings of Moses; for in the description of the Creation, the first chapter of Genesis is taken literally except that the Sun is created *before* the light, and the herbs and plants before after the Sun; wch are the two points they did not understand, and therefore altered as errors. There are only two accts of Creation properly so called; the world and Man; the intermediate Acts seem more as the results of secondary causes, or at any ⟨rate⟩ a modification of materials.

43. Pantheism and Idolatry naturally end in each other; for all extremes meet. The Judaic religion was the exact medium, the true compromise.

43. There is a difference in the credibility to be attached to Ghosts and Dreams. Dreams had nothing in them wch was absurd and nonsensical,

and though most of the coincidences may be readily explained by the diseased system of the dreamer and by the great and surprizing power of Association; yet it was impossible to say whether or not an inner sense existed in the mind, wch was but seldom developed, and wch might have a power of presentiment. All the external senses have their correspondents in the mind; the eye can foresee before the object is distinctly apprehended;—why should there not be a corresponding power in the soul? The power of prophecy might have been merely a spiritual excitation of this dormant quality; hence the Seers often required music &c. Every thing in nature had a tendency to move in cycles, and it would be a miracle if out of such myriads of cycles moving concurrently, some coincidences did not take place. No doubt many such happen in the day time, but then our senses drive out the remembrance of them, and render the impression hardly felt; when we sleep, the mind works without interruption. Terror produces them, and the Imagination, wch creates such a picture out of a small particle. In St Paul, ''speaking with tongues,'' means the speaking with the tongue without consciousness. 1. Cor.

Ghosts are absurd. When a real ghost, that is, some man dressed up has appeared, the effects have always been, when believed, most terrible, convulsion, idiocy, madness, death. But after all *these* stories of ghosts, the next day the Seer is quite well, has perhaps a slight headache or so, and that is all. Alston told of a youth in the University of Cambridge near Boston, that he determined to frighten a Tom Painish companion. He appeared in costume; the other said ''This is a good joke.''—I know who you are—come have done! I shall be offended—I will give you five minutes—and then by Heaven I will fire my pistol.''—He fired without effect, and instantly dropped lifeless.

The eye by a slight convulsion often saw a portion of the body, wch it of course projected forward, wch explained many stories of persons seeing themselves lying dead.

If a ghost be a spirit, it must be a substance; like the wind and therefore capable of impact, but it is not. If it be a shadow, it must have a substance of wch it is the shadow. Unless there is an external substance, the bodily eye *cannot* see it; therefore that wch is supposed to be seen, is in fact not seen, but produced from the mind. External objects naturally produce sensation; but here sensation, as it were, produces the object.

---

44. He had no doubt the Jews believed in a future state. The story of the witch of Endor proved it.

---

45. The pet texts of a Socinian were enough to confute him. If Christ were a mere man, it would have been ridiculous to call himself the Son

of Man; but being God and Man, it became a peculiar and mysterious title. If he were a mere man, Christ's saying—"My father is greater than I," would have been as unmeaning. It would be laughable enough to hear S. T. C. say—"My Remorse succeeded indeed, but Shakspeare is a greater dramatist than I;"—but how immeasureably more foolish would it be for a man, however good and wise, to say—"but Jehovah is greater than I."

---

46. Plato's works are logical exercises for the mind; nothing positive is advanced. Socrates may be fairly represented in the moral parts, but in the metaphysical disquisitions it is Pythagoras. Xenophon is quite different.

---

47. He approved of Milton's definition or ~~Law~~ rule of poetry; that it was "simple, sensuous, impassioned"; easy to be apprehended, abounding in sensible images, and informing them with the spirit of the Mind.

---

48. Wordsworth never had any of those losses of personality wch Hartley had so often. In composing the Wanderings of Cain, Wordsworth would not put down any thing he thought good, lest it should be thrown away. The latter poetry of W., though it had its merits, was different and inferior to his former. The three books of the Æneid were bad. Landor's orthography seemed absurd. There was nothing to be expected from Egypt. Every thing really fine in that country, was Grecian.

---

49. Remarkable contrast between the religion of the tragic and the popular poets of Greece. The former are always opposed to the Gods. The ancients had no idea of a *Fall* of Man, though they had of a gradual degeneracy. Prometheus was Jesus Christ and the Devil together. There were the popular, the sacerdotal and the mysterious religions.

---

50. If you take from Virgil his language and rhythm, what do you leave him?

---

51. He thought Granville Penn's book against Buckland a miserable performance. Science would be put an end to, if every phenomenon was to be referred to an actual miracle. It was absurd to refer every thing to the deluge. The deluge, wch left an olive branch standing, and bore up the Ark peaceably on its bosom, could not have caused the tremendous rents and fissures observable on the Earth. The tropical animals discovered in England and Russia could not have been transported in the perfectly natural state in wch they are found by such a flood; they must evidently have

been the natives of the places in wch they are found. The climates must have been altered; and supposing an inconceivably sudden evaporation to have produced an intense cold, the Solar heat would not be sufficient afterwards to overcome it. The Polar cold was not to be accounted for merely by the comparative distance of the Sun. No rain is mentioned previously to the deluge. The rainbow did not exist before.

52. The Earth is Memory; the Air and Heaven are Futurity.

53. The fondness for dancing was the reaction of the reserved manners of English women; it was the only way in wch they could throw themselves forth in natural liberty.

54. We had no idea of the perfection of the ancient tragic dance. The pleasure received had for its basis Difference, and the more unfit the vehicle was, the more lively was the curiosity and intense the delight at seeing the incongruity overcome.

55. The ancients understood some principles in acoustics wch we have lost. They conveyed the voice distinctly in their theatres by means of a pipe, and created no echo or confusion. Our theatres were fit for nothing; they were too large, or too small.

56. Nothing of Lord Byron's would live, nor much of the poetry of the day. The *art* was so neglected; the verses would not scan.

[Entry 57 was written here, cut out, and later returned to be kept with MS E.]

57. Up to 21. a father has power; after that age, authority or influence only. Show me one couple unhappy on account of limited circumstances, and I will show you ten wretched from other causes. S. T. C. would of himself disapprove marriage between first cousins, but the Church had decided otherwise on the authority of Augustine, and that was enough. A slight contrast of character was very material to happiness in marriage.

H. N. Coleridge—from m.s. of Table Talk of STC.

S.C. 1849

[On page facing entries 56 and 57:]
~~This is~~ These are all the Memorabilia, my love, I have. It would be well worth your while to be very attentive to your father's conversation, when

you are with him, and endeavour afterwards to preserve some of it, as I have ~~done~~ done. Especially as he talks to you on plainer subjects. Thine devotedly *HNC*.

2. Jan. 1827.

APPENDIX C
MANUSCRIPT F

MANUSCRIPT F

MS F comprises scraps and full leaves excised from a revision of Henry Nelson Coleridge's original record of his uncle's conversation. The revision, made in the autumn of 1834, was submitted to his brothers John and Edward and to his cousin Derwent for approval or disapproval of individual entries or of specific language in entries not condemned to excision. The 38 retained and recovered fragments, 37 of them in the Victoria College Library, account for nearly all of those entries in MS B cancelled with a vertical line but not published in *TT* (1835). The few exceptions, such as the comments of 12 May 1830 on Brougham and Queen Caroline, may somewhere exist as fragments, but there are various other ways of accounting individually for their absence. One would not expect the seven words of 25–6 Aug 1827 on C's dislike of Christopher Wordsworth to survive as a fragment. A few items in MS F lack final words or phrases; appearing on the leaf following the excision, these words were presumably crossed out and not transferred to the surviving fragment. For entries published in revised form, no paragraphs or sentences dropped after MS B remain among the fragments of MS F.

The numbers appearing on the upper right are page numbers in MS F, written and underlined in ink. The + and × marks at the beginning of entries were written in pencil by HNC's chosen censors to indicate degrees of disapproval. The numbers following the + or × of disapproval were added in pencil, probably before the entries were excised, certainly before the fragment with two anecdotes of 24 Jul 1830 was attached to MS E by some later member of the family. A few of these numbers, along with the mark preceding them, have been erased; numbers 22 and 23, with their respective +s, have been inked over.

The anomalous number 319 that precedes the remarks of 24 Jul 1832 on the slave-trade has no equivalent elsewhere in the fragments of MS F; more than 400 entries would have preceded it in a full transcription.

The dates centred above entries without brackets are given as they appear in MS F. Bracketed dates are those of the corresponding entry in MS B.

[24 Feb 1827]

+ 1　I have a difficulty in believing, according to the common interpretation, that any miraculous gift of tongues is intended to be recorded in the 2ᵈ chapter of the Acts of the Apostles. The only language previously used in divine service was Hebrew; & the text says that after the descent of the Holy Ghost, the Xtians came forth & spoke Ἑτέραις γλωσσαις— with other tongues—that is, as I cannot help thinking, with secular or profane tongues; & this it was that seems to have caused such astonishment in the foreign Jews, that the Apostles should speak of the things of God in any other language but Hebrew;—just, for example, as if an Italian or Spanish priest should in the midst of the solemnization of the Mass break all at once into his vernacular dialect instead of the Latin.

[24 Jun 1827]

+　The whole frame of a woman is mysterious. The indrawing of the source of life denotes modesty, the robe of a woman's soul; the prominence of her bosom shows the large action of tenderness & maternal [care.]

[8 Jul 1827]

Mr Frere said of that incident in the*[a]*　　　　of the Bible's being*[a]*
　　　that spirits could do a great many things, but he doubted their carrying parcels.

――――――

25. August. 1827.[1]

The doctrine of the polarization of Light is superseding the Newtonian theory. It is the green ray which is the most magnetic, & not the blue. Conceive it in this formula.

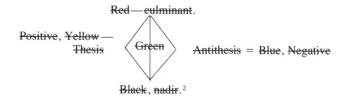

[25–6 Aug 1827]

St John's Gospel I hold to be genuine & self-sufficing authority for every thing it contains. St Luke's I take as fair ground for belief as to Facts. St Matthew's I suppose was one of the several Gospels to the Hebrews.

[29–30 Aug 1827]　　　　　　　　　　　　　　　　　　　　　　*31*

he had written "the Liberty of Prophesying" as a ruse de guerre, because the Church at that time needed toleration.

[a] Blank left in ms

[1] The entire entry was first cancelled by horizontal lines, and then cut from the leaf for preservation.
[2] On the verso, in pencil, probably by EC, with reference to a statement about Luther on the next leaf: "What was meant by biblical here—a note now & then will be necessary."

4. Four scraps from MS F, H. N. Coleridge's
revision between Coleridge's death and the publication of *Table
Talk* (1835). Victoria College Library, reproduced
by kind permission

[13 Apr 1830]

× × +4   It sometimes strikes me that from the second to the thirteenth chapter of Exodus is an insertion by another hand. There have been doubts as to the genuineness of the book of Joshua, but the internal evidence in its favor seems to me irresistible.

+ 5   Observe the different coloring given by the poetic spirit of David to the battles & other events recorded in prose in the books of Chronicles.

[25 Apr 1830]

+ 6   Mead ⟨& Lardner⟩ in my judgment, is are right in denying the reality of the supposed demoniac possessions in the New Testament, but ⟨Mead is⟩ wrong in saying that they were only bodily diseases. They were most evidently madmen;—δαιμόνιον ἔχει καὶ μαίμνεται—he hath a devil, & is mad; in English idiom he hath a devil, that is; he is mad. At all events the effect, the phænomenon, was that the man was mad. We very aptly render the form of the expression by our vulgar— 'The Devil is in him'. The spirit becomes devilish in madness. The belief that little individual devils got inside the man is surely absurd.

+ 7   The narrative of the ejection of devils in the 8th chapter of St Luke is, I believe, considered the great instance for reality ⟨of⟩ diabolic possession. Now let me entreat you to reflect calmly upon this scene. St Luke wrote his history from the accounts & documents of other persons, some of whom were eyewitnesses, & some were not. He tells you what was told to him with the strictest veracity, & draws no conclusions from the nar-rative. During or just after our Lord's miraculous cure of a madman, a neighbouring herd of swine is frightened, & run into the sea. Those are the facts. Like most madmen, the man in this case assumed the name of some other person or thing. ''I am Legion'' (or a Legion,

39

or the Legion) says he,—the Roman name running in his fevered imagination. He then asks, as a madman, to rush into the swine, that hated & galling mark & sign of the Jewish subjugation to Roman dominion. The swine are frightened, and the Jewish mob, who firmly believe every ⟨mental or nervous⟩ disease to be caused by diabolic influence—just as the Greeks imputed all unaccountable deaths to Apollo or Diana—cried out ''the Devils have entered the swine.''

+ 8   Are you apprehensive that this is dealing too freely with the text of the Evangelist? I can imagine it; but let us be cool, & consider the truth thoroughly, & be sure of this, that truth will do the Truth no harm at all. Now I ask you carefully to compare the awfully solemn manner in wᶜʰ the Prophets in the Old Testament relate the communications of God to them, as Moses in Deuteronomy—"The Lord God spake unto me, saying—Thou &c." & ~~look at the language~~ Isaiah & others with the preface to St Luke's gospel. You know the terms he uses. Now, ~~permit~~ with reference to the common theory of Scripture inspiration, permit me to state the following analogy:—

+9 The Duke of Wellington made me his secretary & said:—"You shall write a history of the War, & I will give you from my own mouth a detailed account of all that took place. I will dictate the language or at least the matter to you." Then, having received a perfect account of the whole war from the Duke's own mouth, suppose me to begin ~~th~~ my book thus:—'Whereas several corporals, some in service & some not, & a serjeant's wife have written accounts & pamphlets concerning the war—I also have availed myself of their assistance, & have attempted to set forth the following history—& never hint one word about the Duke's authority. What should you think of it?—[3]

40.

+10 Is it possible that the vulgar notion of inspiration can be true? Will it not lead to blasphemy—& to absurdity? Try the Psalms by this test. The Spirit of God doubting what He knew infallibly!—fearing what he could not fear!—hating what he could not strictly hate! The Spirit of Grace is indeed in the Scriptures, ~~but~~ & that is surely enough for us.

+11 The Apostles were teaching & preaching Xtianity. They had something else to do besides simply recording anecdotes of our Saviour's life & actions. St John in his gospels mentions nothing but what was the occasion & foundation of a doctrine. St Luke clubs nearly eight chapters together of our Lord's parables without any reference to time or place.

[27 May 1830]   *59.*

The first six ~~words~~ chapters of the book of Daniel cannot have been written by the author of the rest. They are full of Greek words. Now there could have been no Greek words in any thing written by Daniel, & there *are* no Greek words in the rest of the book.

The fourth monarchy in Daniel is clearly the Greek. There is no sort of intimation of the Romans. The monarchies are designated by their known heraldic signs.

6. June 1830.   *63.*

++14 Such is the narrow & unwise temper of the day, that if I or any other writer were to maintain & satisfactorily prove the truth of all the

[3] Pp 39 and 40 are watermarked "C.
WILMOT 1833."

great articles of faith holden by the Church of England, & to demonstrate their harmony with the laws of Morals & Mind,—if I were to silence the opposition, or even convince the incredulity, of the sceptic by taking away his most ready weapon of attack;—yet if I were to doubt the authenticity of the book of Daniel, or suggest that Inspiration did not mean Dictation—I fear, indeed I am sure, I should be almost universally condemned, & sneered at as being unorthodox & an enemy to the Church! Yet what is the fact? Is not this supposed inspiration of the Bible the handle wch every infidel & railer at religion invariably lays hold of? Well may they do so! & yet how unjustly if understood in the only way compatible with fact or common sense! What a mass of gratuitous difficulties—shall I not say, horrible blasphemies—does the Church create &, as it were, appropriate by this strange doctrine!

+ I well remember, when only nine years old, listening with intense eagerness to the story of Jael killing Sisera as read in church, & to the war song of Deborah—the most sublime composition in the world—& when the words, "Blessed shall Jael be &c." were read, putting down my head between my hands & knees, & murmuring from my soul as even now I do—"Cursed shall Jael be above women!" She murdered the innocent sleep.

+ Deborah's song—when we think for a moment what light she had, ⟨& consider⟩ her intention, her nation & the circumstances in wch she was placed—is, as I have said, the sublimest of human compositions: but the Holy Ghost to have inspired that Song! It is awful to utter the supposition.

+ Many of the most high-minded men I ever knew[4]

64.

were kept a long time from admitting the truths of Revelation solely & exclusively because of the verbal-inspiration doctrine, which they had been taught to believe to be part of the Xtian Religion.

[7 Jun 1830]

In the accounts we have of the Savoy Conference ⚏[5] it is clear that the Churchmen never from the beginning intended to yield a single letter, good, bad or indifferent.

---

[4] P 63 is watermarked "J. WHAT-MAN TURKISH MILL 1833."
[5] HNC presumably prepared or intended a note on the Savoy Conference, but it has not survived among the fragments of MS F.

[24 Jul 1830]   *73.*

My father, after explaining & insisting on a text in the pulpit, used always to say in his sermons:—"But that I may give you this injunction in the most solemn manner, hear the very words uttered by the Spirit of God";—& then he thundered out the Hebrew or Greek original. It did more good than all the rest of his sermon. The clowns in the gallery put out their necks, & opened their mouths, & were evidently impressed with a sense of something grand & holy.

+ 15   My dear brother George preached once morning & evening at Ottery on Scandal & Smuggling. In the afternoon people congratulated my mother. She, however, looked rather blank upon the occasion, & said,—"George was, no doubt, very clever & fine; but for her part, she must say, she did not like any new doctrines!"

[8 Oct 1830]

Hence, amongst other things, the Athanasian Creed was preserved; a composition, the original of wch was in Latin & cannot be traced within fifty years of the man whose name it bears—wch emanated from no general council—wch in the beginning & end is ⟨highly inconvenient, if not⟩ intolerant & persecuting, & in the middle is heretical in a high degree. I mean in particular the flagrant omission, or rather implicit denial, of the essential article of the Filial subordination in the Godhead, an article of faith wch Bull & Waterland have so labored to enforce in their writings wch have made the Church of England the classical authority on the subject of the Trinity even in the eyes of the Church of Rome itself,—& by not holding to wch Sherlock staggered to & fro between Tritheism & Sabellianism.

Pray look at the preface to my Jesuits' edition of Bull in Latin, & you will see what they think of him.

———

+ 16   In considering the question, how far a man is bound in point of conscience & honor to assent to every thing contained in the Prayer Book, before he takes Orders, I recommend you to put a clergyman in these four different points of view—1. in the desk. 2. in the pulpit. 3. as a pastor & 4. as a man of letters. Now if the points upon wch you have a difficulty are such, that they are quite collatoral to the liturgy, & such that it would be most impertinent to introduce any discussion of them in the pulpit, & worse than impertinent to broach them in your pastoral communications with your flock—& wch therefore have no proper place but in your book room & with your learned friends—I cannot understand how any doubts or difficulties of such a kind should deter you from taking Orders. I put all subscriptions for the

83

present out of the question; for, undoubtedly, if you can not do the duty of a clergyman of the Church of England without violating your conscience, you must not take Orders, if the Articles were abolished tomorrow.

+   You will remember that the Church of England binds you by one of her own articles to believe that she is fallible,—that all Churches have erred, & that the Scriptures are alone infallible. You have the strictest obligation, therefore, upon you to carry in mind that the doctrines of the Church of England may be erroneous, in so far as you are unable to reconcile them with the word of God. Accordingly it is beyond a doubt that you may conscientiously reject in your own mind the Athanasian Creed, whether as heretical or uncharitable or both, & still remain a faithful Church minister.[6] Besides in the desk, you are not using your own words or staking your own authority or warranting any thing;—it is well understood that you are only a voice, an officer of the Church. If you are amongst peaceful people, don't read the Athanasian Creed; if you suspect an informer, read it, because the Rubric,[7] wch is by Act of Parliament, orders it.

× × +   In the Pulpit you appear for yourself;—& I would there explain the true doctrine of the Trinity, & either leave the contrast to be observed by the ~~audience~~ congregation, or I would point out with decency the imperfections of the Creed wch I had been obliged by law to read in the morning. You are no more under an obligation to leave the Church, or not enter it, because of the Athanasian Creed, than a judge is obliged to leave the bench because he disapproves the actual law. The fact is, I believe, nine-tenths of the enlightened & reflecting clergy of the Church of England condemn this Creed.[8]

+   As Pastor, I am sure your doubts need not trouble you;—they do not enter into the performance of any pastoral duty.

---

[6] On the verso of the fragment from p 82, opposite this passage, is written in pencil, probably by EC: "× Does he mean that a clergyman as a voice of the church, may read a service which he deems *unscriptural*? ~~by~~ which I understand by heretical."

[7] *Rubric* is underlined in pencil; the annotator begins by matching the × × attached to the next paragraph: "× × But you *swear* to comply with the Rubric."

[8] A vertical line in pencil along the left margin, accompanied by a "Qu", queries the two final sentences of this paragraph.

+   I am supposing, of course, that you are not a Socinian or Unitarian, but that you believe in the redemption of man by the blood of Jesus, & that our salvation is by grace alone. Unless you believe[9]

84.

this, you cannot, indeed, without the grossest want of faith & honesty enter the Church; for these are points on wc̄h you must insist in the pulpit & in the cottage.

+   As to articles of discipline, the only way to assent to them is to obey them. Beyond obedience there can be no obligation.

[14 Aug 1831]

We have in my judgment behaved very unfairly to Ireland. We have not civilized the natives, & yet we have interfered so far as to prevent them from cutting each other's throats to any useful extent. We were bound to let the Irish run an equal race with other savages:—either civilize them forcibly, or else leave them to keep down their verminous population in the way common to all other savage tribes—by mutual homicide. 25 years ago I said in sport that the time might come when the English themselves would cry out against the Union. That time seems approaching, & if things go on in Ireland much longer as they now do, the cry will be a loud one. The true[10]

100.

English character has very sensibly suffered since the peace from the deluge of Paddyism in England, wc̄h the Union originated, & will, if preserved, augment. The connection of Ireland with England has been from first to last a source of unqualified evil & weakness to England; the soldiers & sailors obtained from Ireland might have been obtained, & better, in England & Scotland, & their whole number has been required to keep Ireland itself in that sort of murderous armistice, in wc̄h for the most part it has ever been.

[27 Dec 1831]

You see how Macaulay was worsted on the score of his facts by Croker, who seems to have made an excellent speech indeed.

---

[9] On the verso, in pencil, probably by EC, with reference to 21 Nov 1830 on Brougham: "I should omit the *guts*."
[10] The passage on Ireland to this point was written hurriedly by HNC on the verso of the remaining portion (p 100), probably because he left the earlier portion on p 99 crossed out.

[31 Mar 1832]

+ 19[11] My deep conviction is that the true course is, to recognize Xtianity in the Scriptures, not to piece it up by a selection of texts. So long as I thought it absolutely necessary to make every part & parcel of the writings contained in the collection called the Bible agree with, & tend to, the proof of Xtianity, I read in terror, & according as the mood was, I either outraged my common sense & reason, or else violated the plainest dictates of the moral conscience. But all would not do. Thank God! the verbal inspiration doctrine did not make an infidel of me, as it has to my knowledge done with many. I rejected it altogether. I saw the absurdity, the blasphemy attending it. I became sensible that such a mode of interpreting the Scriptures has no more warrant in the example & practice of the ancient Church & the greatest lights amongst the fathers, than it can have in reason. That wch is most beautiful, most natural, yea, most justifiable when regarded under the actual conditions of time, place & action, becomes a millstone round the neck of a sincere believer, a stumbling-block in the path of every devout reasoner, if considered with reference to the requisitions of this strange doctrine.

+   What! because Deborah, a mother in Israel, flushed with conquest, in the expression of her triumph, in the last working up of her sublime war ode, called Jael blessed for ridding Israel of its great enemy—am I, a disciple of Christ Jesus in England in the nineteenth century, to think that Jael was really blessed, was really not cursed, for the most cruel, most brutal, most dastardly act of assassination, that ever yet combined murder with treachery & a violation of the sacred rights of proffered hospitality!

[4 Apr 1832]

+   If I could contemn any men for their religious tenets, it would be the Unitarians; for they themselves universally call all believers in the orthodox doctrine either fools or knaves. To be sure, they were forced to make an exception of me, & it annoyed them that they were so forced; but they had flattered me so much as the champion of their cause, that they could not pretend that I was not master of all they could say for themselves; & they could not for the life of them make out that I had any sinister or interested motive; so they set me down for a visionary, & fond of a paradox as a theme for display in conversation.

[11] In the margin, in pencil: "Move this."

24. July 1832.[12]

319   The struggle about the Slave Trade & the Middle Passage excited my most violent emotions. Yet I then stated in the Watchman ⚜ —& I lost some friends by doing so—that no good would be done by applying to Parliament—that it was unjust—& that in twenty years after a parliamentary abolition, the horrors of the Slave Trade would be increased twenty fold. Now all acknowledge that to be true.

⚜ *More* Africans are now transported to America for slavery, the Middle Passage is more horrible, & the Servitude is worse.

[9 Aug 1832]

+ 2 1   The 1ˢᵗ Epistle of Peter is no doubt genuine; that is, I suppose it was in substance supplied by Peter. Of course, the Apostle could ⟨not⟩ have written the Greek text, wc̄h in all probability was composed by Mark, a disciple of Paul's. In truth, you see the Pauline phrases stuck in every where. But it is a most valuable work.

+   The 2ᵈ Epistle cannot possibly be genuine. The mention of St Paul's Epistles collectively, unless all that passage is interpolated, is decisive. The Epistolion was not collected for a long time after this age, & the term γράφαι—Scriptures—was never applied in the early apostolic age to any thing but the Old Testament.

+   I have no doubt myself that this 2ᵈ Epistle, & those to Titus & Timothy, were composed long after the apostles' time. It is evident that Church-government had assumed a certain degree of complexity at the date of those two works.

+   Suppose these three Epistles removed, would the evidence for a single fundamental article of our Faith be weakened? Can you not find in other parts of the New Testament canon all that you ~~can~~ could wish to find in these Epistles, & much better expressed?

August 15. 1832.

+ 2 2   I was complaining yesterday that a paper of mine was lost;— "No, Sir!" said Harriet,—"nothing is lost in your room, but every thing mislaid." If you knew the poor creature who said this, you would think it inspiration.

---

[12] HNC crowded the date against the entry after the initial transcription, perhaps after the scrap was cut from the leaf, and either after or simultaneously with the "319"; the deep indention would have allowed room for the date had the "319" not blocked the space.

[20 Jan 1833] *188.*

+ 23   The Quarterly Review gravely setting to work to prove Seward's Narrative not authentic is rather amusing.

[31 Mar 1833]

+ 25 [13]   I certainly did mean Sir James Mackintosh in "The Two Round Spaces"; but as to meaning to lampoon him, as Fraser's Magazine says, from resentment, I never had other than kind feelings towards him all my life. ~~He~~ Mackintosh was taken slightly ill in passing through Grasmere; the snow was deep, & I remember being tickled, as I looked on the humble church-yard, with the thought that if he, a great lawyer & Scotchman, should die ~~there,~~ his burial ~~& sepulchre~~ there ⟨with a great tombstone in the middle of the ground⟩ would be an odd circumstance. I never in my life wrote the verses down; but I repeated them, & copies were made, & ultimately printed without my knowledge.

[8 Apr 1833]

Can any humiliation be more complete, more pointed & unequivocal, than the House of Lords passing without a division the amendments of the Commons in this Irish coercion Bill! It is really quite extraordinary.

[14 Aug 1833]

Qu +   I always made a point of associating images of cheerfulness & lightsomeness with death & the grave, when instructing my children. To be sure, I believe little Hartley did astonish a party of very grave persons, who asked him if he had learned any hymns, by saying that Papa had taught him a pretty Resurrection Hymn, wch he repeated with great glee & jubilation of look as ~~he~~ follows,—

> Splother! splother! splother!
> Father & mother!
> Wings on our shoulders—
> And Up we go!—

———

The Quakers educate upon a principle ~~upon~~ of suppressing all appearance of passion, where the exhibition of it can be injurious to their worldly interests; but so far as I could ever see, they neither teach, nor practise any inward subduing of the appetites, & are a sensual race of

[13] Watermark: "EEN & 1834." It is not clear from MS B what an excised item 24 could have been. Hypothetically, something not in MS B could have been added to MS F, then excised, and later published in *LR*, destroyed, or lost; a simple alternative is a misnumbering of excised entries at this point.

men within the sanction of certain public relations.[14] A Quaker is made up of ice & flame; he has no composition, no mean temperature, ~~no gentleness~~. Hence he is ~~never~~ rarely interested about any public measure, but he becomes a fanatic, & oversteps in his irrespective zeal every decency & every right opposed to his course. ~~I understand their violence during the canvass & registration for the last election exceeded any thing witnessed by the oldest barristers~~. Of course there are many exceptions, especially amongst the women; but I believe what I say is true of the Quakers

174

in general, & I have seen a good deal of them first & last.

Their affecting not to pay tithes is ⟨little short of actual⟩ dishonesty. They buy for a price calculated on its payment. *Their* duty is to pay their own debts; they have nothing to do with the dedication of the money, the tenth part, which is not theirs, nor formed any part of their purchase. In fact, the Quakers, who, though they pretend to be persecuted, are & have ~~always~~ been ⟨for a century past⟩ the most petted of the Protestant sects, cultivate with intense earnestness a little worldly Goshen of their own; & I once ventured to tell a party of them that I thought they were like a string of double hunched camels trying to get through the eye of a needle.

[17 Aug 1833]

Lord Grey has contrived to unite the two worst styles of governing, or at least to exercise them by alternative,—an unprincipled cabinet despotism in quiet seasons as now with regard to the Bank, & the base spirit of democracy in times of popular violence.

[21 Dec 1833]

I hardly know what to think of Malachi's prophecy of the Messenger. What did John the Baptist in fact do; & how can he be said to have prepared the way for Christ on earth? Besides, I cannot reconcile John's direct declaration to the Jews that he was not Elias, the Elias whom they meant. The voice in the wilderness he was, but that does not answer the description of Malachi. Our Lord's own language is very peculiar:—"If ye will receive it, this is that[15]

---

[14] Separate fragments were created by a cut at this point, as if the rest were excised before the opening portion, which has itself subsequently broken in half from folding.

[15] The rest is missing. The fragment is watermarked: "REE 18."

[3 Jan 1834]

The invocation of Saints is founded on an amiable & affectionate feel-ing. It certainly has a tendency in it to supersede the faith in the one Re-deemer, & to confound the distinction between the omnipresence of God, & mere creaturely presence. Yet with a change to the third per-son—oret Mater pro nobis &c. much of the mischief might have been avoided.

[1 Mar 1834]

A common source of error in printing is the repetition of a word—the compositor's eye being caught with it a little below or above. There are scores of such errors in the first editions of Shakspeare, most of them faithfully preserved in the very latest of our impressions. When I first read the description

197.

of Cleopatra's sailing on the Cydnus in the Antony & Cleopatra, & came to the lines, still thus printed—

> Her gentlewomen, like the Nereids,
> So many mermaids, tended her i' th' eyes,
> And made their bends adornings; at the helm
> A seeming mermaid steers:— ⚓ A. II.1.2.

I said "Those *first* mermaids must be a mistake.⁺⁺ Shakspeare would never have described one class of attendants as[b] mermaids, & then par-ticularized a distinct attendant as a *seeming* mermaid. It must be sea maids or sea nymphs." And so I afterwards saw it was in North's trans-lation of Plutarch, whence the description is taken. ⚓

[b] Underlining of word cancelled

APPENDIX D
THE CONFESSIONAL

THE CONFESSIONAL

The early pages of MS A are H. N. Coleridge's personal diary, including but not confined to reports of S. T. Coleridge's conversation. A few brief entries are given in the annotations to the Table Talk, above. The sequence below, from 1823, appears in MS A pp 102–3.

13th February

———

Kept Hilary Term. Suffering for that angel Sara.

21st March

———

Sara and myself are solemnly engaged to each other. She has promised never to marry any one but me. She wrote me, while in London, two notes, wch I keep under lock and key, and gave me two ringlets of her hair, wch I had made into two rings; one of them with my own hair intertwined with hers and set round with pearls I gave to her the last morning, when we parted, and the other her own hair entirely I keep myself. She took from her own neck a coral necklace, wch I now wear round mine. I wrote her four letters. She has since communicated the whole affair to Fanny,[1] and Fanny's letter I keep. It is feeling and prudent. She advises us to keep the matter a secret, till I can claim Sara without a chance of refusal.

Now as I value my honour and happiness I ought to study with all my might to preserve the love I feel in its utmost force and purity. It should ever be before me, and deter me from every base and improper action. I never can meet any woman so exquisitely sweet again; and who loves me more devotedly.

———

My Xmas Hymn appeared in the Xtian Remembrancer of March.[2] Read

---

[1] Frances Duke Coleridge (1796–1842), daughter of Col James Coleridge and SC's cousin, who married John Patteson in 1824.

[2] HNC *Lines Written on Christmas Morning, Before Light* in the *Christian*

Walton's Lives again.[3] Sanderson's valuable for the history of the times.

Ugo Foscolo on Petrarch.[4] Entertaining.

Blunt's 'vestiges of ancient manners in Italy and Sicily' elucidates many parts of Virgil and Ovid.[5]

Southey's account of the Madras System exposes the rogueries and quackery of Lancaster.[6]

1ˢᵗ April.

Curran's speeches.[7] full of Irish faults and beauties. He seems to have been an honest and undaunted patriot.

Aminta, perhaps more praised than it deserves.[8]

Remembrancer v (March 1823) 157–9. It begins:

The Winds are sleeping,
The Earth is steeping
Her mighty bosom in nectareous dew;
The yellow moon
Sails in her noon
Of winter beauty thro' a sea of blue.

[3] Izaak Walton (1593–1683) *The Lives of Dʳ John Donne; Sir Henry Wotton; Mr. Richard Hooker; Mr. George Herbert; and Dʳ R. R. Sanderson* ed T[homas] Zouch (York 1796); further eds 1807, 1817.

[4] Ugo Foscolo *Essays on Petrarch* (1823).

[5] John James Blunt *Vestiges of Ancient Manners and Customs Discoverable in Modern Italy and Sicily* (1823).

[6] Robert Southey *The Origin, Nature, and Object, of the New System of Education* (1812).

[7] J. P. Curran (1750–1817, Irish orator and judge) *Speeches of the Right Honourable John Philpot Curran* (new ed, addns 1817).

[8] Torquato Tasso *Aminta* (1573), pastoral drama.

TABLE-TALK BY WILLIAM WORDSWORTH

TABLE-TALK BY WILLIAM
WORDSWORTH

Twice in MS B (Victoria College Library S MS 20) H. N. Coleridge reported
remarks by Wordsworth:

*a*15. Oct. 1829. Mr Wordsworth.

―――――――

The Decline & Fall of the Roman Empire is the grandest subject for history in the world. Gibbon was preeminently happy in the selection of it.
But he did not sufficiently keep it before his eyes. A third or more of his
work is quite foreign to the subject of his history. His matter is always
valuable, but *other* matter *b*ought to have been there. His style is abominable; he knew little of English Literature, & lost his English in France.
He is not Saxon enough in his construction. Five out of ten of his sentences end in a genitive case with the preposition *of*. His range of construction is very narrow. His answer to Warburton is more full of vernacular graces.

―――――――

The ancient historians considered the perfection of composition as of
more importance than the mere preservation of facts. Hence a multitude
of interesting links are omitted. Southey's mode of writing history is
more useful to mankind. Sallust's preface to the Catilinarian conspiracy
looks hypocritical, & the motives wch he assigns to the conspirators are
inadequate & absurd. We have not the greatest works of Sallust now.

Crispus Romana primus in historia[1]—could never have been said of
the two little works we now have. Some of the fragments of his other
works are exceedingly valuable, & contain facts & observations wch
were marvellously applicable to the events of the earlier years of the
French Revolution. Thucydides is in all respects the greatest of historians. He is artificial, but yet he really grapples with the facts. Herodotus

a f 8^v   *b* f 9

[1] Martial 14.191, of Sallust (Gaius   "The first Roman historian".
Sallustius Crispus, 86–c 34 B.C.); tr

545

is not to be considered simply as an historian, but as a man of general inquisitiveness after Knowledge, as a traveller & an antiquarian. Livy has always satisfied me, & Machiavel, one of the greatest of men, must have thought Livy's selection of facts judicious when he sat down to comment on them.

The character of the Solitary is compounded of what I knew of two men.

I shall, favente Phœbo,[2] write a sonnet on Dora's dancing a quadrille on the summit of Langdale Great Pike.

S. T. C. never did *converse* in the common sense of the word; he would lay hold of another person's suggestion, & then refine upon it, divide & subtilize it till he had made it entirely his own. He borrowed largely, ᶜbut he had a right to do so, for he gave away as largely. He is now too often dreamy; he rarely comes into contact with popular feelings & modes of thought.—You cannot incarnate him for a minute. The activity of his imagination, wc̄h I must call morbid, disturbs his sense & recollection of facts. Many men have done wonderful things—Newton, Davy &c, but S. T. C. is the only wonderful man I ever knew. He has been much in-debted to the German writers. He, however, thought the modern Ger-mans degenerate, their philosophy sickly & their theology latitudinarian.

Killarney possesses more individual parts of beauty than the Cumberland Lakes, & one point of view finer than any; but many separate parts in the English lakes are finer than the corresponding ones at Killarney. In shape it is like Derwent-water. The Mountains are too far off. The limestone banks are very favorable.

The authorized translation of the Bible was made at the most favorable time for the quality of our language. The higher classes speak ill from retaining the language of the nursery to a great degree, but upon the whole they speak in general very vernacularly. The middle classes are usually too bookish. Men of business often speak more naturally now than women, because women speak so much from novels.

ᶜ f 9ᵛ

[2] "If favoured by Phoebus".

16. Oct. 1829.

Water-slope is a word wanted; also a word for the waves in the running stream wċh are so different from the waves of the sea. *Cloudage* is also wanted for a ~~differen~~used mass of clouds.

Parterres & flowering bushes are quite fitting in a sequestered place for a lady with her novel or work-box; but they must not be brought into contact with the grand forms of Nature.

---

*d*Milton's "The cypress with *innumerable* boughs
      Hides me"—[3]
is admirably correct. The interweaving of the boughs of cypress are a sort of vegetable timber-yard.

    Milton, when he said "the twisted eglantine",[4] mistook *honeysuckle* for eglantine.

No man ever attained to such eminence with so little merit as Campbell. The Pleasures of Hope would have been a work of promise from its declamatory flow & its harmony, if it had also contained *anything* sterling. He is a thorough Anti-Xtian, & thereby places himself out of sympathy with the best & largest part of society.

Sotheby never had any real poetry in him—no imagination, but a flux of poetic diction.

I never could get through Cadenus & Vanessa.[5] So far as poetry is involved in imagination & in the calling forth of our sympathies with the beautiful forms of Nature, Swift had perhaps none of it; but he had the most rare felicity of language; every word is in its right place; his thoughts are weighty & his wit penetrating. My three favorite pieces

d f 10

---

[3] *Paradise Lost* IX 1089–90 (var: "Ye cedars" for WW's "The cypress").
[4] *L'Allegro* line 48.

[5] Jonathan Swift *Cadenus and Vanessa* (1726).

are—Rochefoucault[6]—Monkies[7]—Barrack House.[8] His epitaph is detestable & unchristian. Qu. the meaning of sæva indignatio.[9] Swift sometimes purchased his correct rhyming at the expence of grammar—*"never did exist"*.[10]—He probably loved Pope, & thought Pope loved him. *"Pope will mourn a month."*[11]

---

[e]11. March. 1831.

W.W. You may rely on this as a principle, that unless ~~the~~ a man can be made to take *pride* in serving or yielding to the influence of another, he will hate that other, though his services may be due on the score of interest, gratitude or any other affection. Interest will never be a match for the stronger Passions. Rich & Poor there must ever be; formerly under the system of a mitigated feudality the power & the subjection were merged in the affections; the dependant was proud of the relation, & felt that he was necessary to his lord or patron. Now that charm is almost entirely & for ever broken; the edges of riches & indigence bear sheer on each other; now it is all almsgiving-charity. Rawson, the most beneficent of human beings, got no other earthly reward for a life of incessant charities to the poor but the nickname of Soup Rawson.[12]

Three leaves of further remarks by Wordsworth, in H. N. Coleridge's hand, have been loosely inserted at the University of Texas into the MS A workbook. The leaves are 20 cm × 16.1, watermarked "J Glover 1824". HNC's crowding of "(Wordsworth—Oct. 1829)" into an open space after the second paragraph suggests that an earlier identification appeared on a previous leaf. The last paragraph breaks off in mid-sentence. The text of the three leaves follows.

Chantry could make nothing of W Scott's face for a long time, and was quite distressed about it. At length he caught him in the act of beginning

[e] f 36

---

[6] *The Life and Character of Dean Swift, upon a Maxim in Rochefoucault;* expanded as *Verses on the Death of Dr. Swift, D.S.P.D. Occasioned by Reading a Maxim in Rochefoucault* (line 207 quoted, var, at end of paragraph).

[7] *The Beasts' Confession to the Priest?*

[8] *The Grand Question Debated Whether Hamilton's Bawn Should Be Turned into a Barrack or a Malt House,* or perhaps *Vanbrug's House, Built from the Ruins of White-Hall That Was Burnt.*

[9] "Fierce indignation."

[10] *Verses on the Death of Dr. Swift* line 248.

[11] See n 6, above.

[12] Probably WW's friend, William Rawson (1748/9–1828), a Halifax merchant.

a grotesque story, and has most happily, yet at great hazard, ventured to fix a transitory expression in marble.

Chantry said he considered W's bust the finest thing he had done.   (Wordsworth—Oct. 1829)

Chantry has not attained to the ideal of his art; he owns it himself and says there is no taste for it in England, and Nymphs and Gods will not sell. He is a portrait painter in marble, but an admirable one. He must not be made responsible for every bust he executes in the way of trade. Flaxman attempted the ideal more.

Southey's is a picturesque face.

Lawrence's picture of young Lambton is a wretched histrionic thing;[13] the public taste must be vitiated indeed, if that is admired.

It may be questioned whether the future development of science will not render the poetical feeling for the objects of nature rare or impossible—as in water, if its constituents were perpetually familiar to the mind. Imagination enters into every act of the mind. There is a wonderful analogy between the various emotions of waters and the temper and thoughts of man. In the "Fons Bandusiæ", nothing but the supposition of devout reverence for the nymph of the spring can reconcile us to Horace's apparent pleasure in speaking of slaying a kid and [?staining] the stream with its blood.[14] Perhaps it is as poetical or more so to consider the water as a Power of Nature. In a poem on a Well W. has conceived the Influence in a novel way, wch he did not mention.

W. noticed the perfect beauty of form of the tufted fern or Prince's feather.

ꞌWhy are we so interested about ⟨contemporary⟩ facts, wch do not concern us, whilst we are perfectly ~~con~~ indifferent to ~~the same~~ similar events that have happened a few years back? Perhaps in order to fasten our minds on the present selves and induce us to carry on the cconomy of the world. Newspapers and magazines are read to a most pernicious extent; they cannot improve the mind in any way; they injure it, weaken it and debase it grievously.

———————

There were to be two other parts in the "Recluse", not so long as the "Excursion"; one of them severer and entering into the metaphysics of the mind, the other easier and more diffuse on the influences of nature.

ꞌp 2

[13] Sir Thomas Lawrence's portrait of Charles William Lambton (1818–31), eldest son of John George Lambton, 1st Earl of Durham; it was painted in 1825.

[14] Horace *Carmina* 3.13.

But it is impossible to reconcile the exact truth with poetry. Lucretius did all that was possible; yet his illustrations are the only valuable parts of his poem. If we abandon the old mythical conception of Gods and Nymphs &c. what can we substitute? We may call the phænomena of the visible world Powers if we please, but in fact they are not so. These are not Powers in any proper or usual sense. To call them *Laws* is no better, and yet how can we deal with the face of Nature and Nature's goings on ~~if~~ under this notion of their being only Rules or Laws? W. said he could not do it, and he regretted he had ever attempted such a subject. So long as he was called upon to operate with the imagination on the visible world, and to evoke the spirit that seems to lie hidden in its varied forms in sympathy with man, he felt he was able to do it; but to deal with ~~the world~~ nature as it really in a ᵍreligious view is, was what he could not manage. He thought himself entitled to avail himself as a verseman of many notions wc̄h he was not prepared to defend literally as a proseman, and he complained of the way in wc̄h he had been made answerable for mere plays of the Imagination.

He had often turned his thoughts to the composition of a heroic Poem, but his difficulty was as to what *Manners* could be properly adopted. He thought Milton's delay must be accounted for on this ground, and not for a want of a subject. There are many fine subjects. There is no difficulty as to Passion or Sentiment, because the human nature in its depths is always the same; but the costume and manners are varying, and it is hard to say what style is to be taken.

Nothing great or ennobling could be learnt from without or a posteriori; the seeds of all grandeur of thought and feeling are in the man himself, tho' called forth and developed by occasions and circ̄es [= circumstances]. Imagination enters into every thing. The ancient philosophers, tho' so often wrong in particulars, were far superior to many moderns in proposing the improvement of the mind as the grand object of their labors. They were ~~in~~ more spiritually in ~~their~~

ᵍ p 3

REPORTS OF CONVERSATIONS
WITH COLERIDGE ON SUBJECTS IN
TABLE TALK

REPORTS OF CONVERSATIONS
WITH COLERIDGE ON SUBJECTS IN
TABLE TALK

1. See 27 Apr 1823 n 8, above, on Mackintosh.

James Fenimore Cooper (1789–1851) shaped his own comparison of C and Mackintosh when sitting next to C at William Sotheby's on 22 Apr 1828: "The dissertations of Mr. Coleridge cannot properly be brought in comparison with the conversation of Sir James Mackintosh. One lectures, and the other converses. There is a vein of unpretending philosophy, and a habit of familiar analysis in the conversation of the latter, that causes you to remember the substance of what he has said, while the former, though synthetic and philosophical as a verbal critic, rather enlists the imagination than any other property of the mind. Mackintosh is willing enough to listen, while Coleridge reminded me of a barrel to which every other man's tongue acted as a spigot, for no sooner did the latter move, than it set his own contents in a flow." *Gleanings in Europe: England* ed Donald A. Ringe et al (Albany, NY 1982) 261. Samuel Rogers also preferred Sir James: "Coleridge spoke and wrote very disparagingly of Mackintosh: but Mackintosh, who had not a particle of envy or jealousy in his nature, did full justice, on all occasions, to the great powers of Coleridge." Alexander Dyce *Recollections of the Table-Talk of Samuel Rogers* ed Morchard Bishop (1952) 147. Recalling that C "had a mortal antipathy to Scotchmen, produced perhaps, or at any rate strengthened, by the remarks of the Edinburgh reviewers on the Lake poets", Dyce himself queried whether Mackintosh were not the "certain North-Briton" of whom C said "Sir, he is a Scotchman, and a rascal, and I do not lay the emphasis on *rascal*." *The Reminiscences of Alexander Dyce* ed Richard J. Schrader (Columbus, Ohio 1972) 178.

SC added to *TT* (1851) 15n confirmation from Mackintosh's "intimate friend", the Rev Robert Hall (1764–1831), that the images in his "spacious repository" were imported. " 'I know no man,' he said repeatedly and emphatically, 'equal to Sir James in talents. The powers of his mind are admirably balanced. He is defective only in imagination.' At this last statement I [Olinthus Gregory] expressed surprise, remarking that I never could have suspected that the author of the eloquent oration for

Peltier was deficient in fancy. 'Well, Sir,' said Mr. H. 'I don't wonder at your remark. The truth is, he has imagination, too; but, with him, imagination is an acquisition, rather than a faculty. He has, however, plenty of embellishment at command; for his memory retains every thing. His mind is a spacious repository, hung round with beautiful images, and when he wants one he has nothing to do but reach up his hand to a peg, and take it down. But his images were not manufactured in his mind; they were imported.' *B*. 'If he be so defective in imagination, he must be incompetent to describe scenes and delineate characters vividly and graphically; I should apprehend, therefore, he will not succeed in writing history.' *H*. 'Sir, I do not expect him to produce an eloquent or interesting history. He has, I fear, mistaken his province. His genius is best adapted for metaphysical speculation; but, had he chosen moral philosophy, he would probably have surpassed every living writer.' *B*. 'I admired exceedingly some of his philosophical papers in the Edinburgh Review, his articles for instance, on Madame de Staël's Germany, and on Dugald Stewart's Preliminary Dissertation; but there seemed to me a heaviness about them, and I do not think that Mr. Jeffrey could expound a metaphysical theory with more vivacity and effect.' *H*. 'With more vivacity, perhaps, but not with equal judgement or acuteness. He would not go so deep, Sir; I am persuaded that if Sir James Mackintosh had enjoyed leisure, and had exerted himself, he would have completely outdone Jeffrey and Stewart, and all the metaphysical writers of our times.' '' Olinthus Gregory ''A Brief Memoir of the Rev. Robert Hall'' *The Works of the Rev. Robert Hall* ed Gregory (2nd ed 6 vols 1832–3) VI 122–3.

2. See 1 May 1823 n 11, above, on Socinians and Unitarians.

The Rev Thomas A. Methuen reported C's conversation of 1815: ''The severity of his remarks relative to the Socinian body, from which he had happily seceded, was generally great. Once, for instance, he said to my father, taking up a large conch and applying it to his own ear, 'This shell may fitly represent the whole body of the Unitarians; for though it is dead and hollow, it still makes a great appearance, and no inconsiderable noise.' So, when writing, at my request, some notes on *Waterland's* well-known queries with the Deists (a work which I fear I have lost, enriched as it was with the numerous annotations of my guest), he remarked, at the conclusion of the Preface, 'On the whole, Socinianism may fitly be considered as a dance, in which self-complacent blank-headedness and blank-heartedness are the two blind fiddlers.' The edge of his animadversions on the Socinian party was, no doubt, considerably increased by the recollection of his former association with them, and by his consequent familiarity with their favourite opinions and delusive arguments. This I collected from the tone of his occasional references to the subject. Nor did it strike me that the severity of his strictures extended beyond the *system*, to its admirers and abettors." "Retrospect of Friendly Communication with the Poet Coleridge" *Christian Observer* XLV (1845) 259.

Emerson felt no restraint in C's attack on Unitarians in 1833: ". . . he burst into a declamation on the folly and ignorance of Unitarianism—its high unreasonableness; and taking up Bishop Waterland's book, which lay on the table, he read with vehemence two or three pages written by himself on the fly-leaves—passages, too, which, I believe, are printed in the 'Aids to Reflection'." *English Traits* (1856) 5. Alexander Dyce rejected from the record of Samuel Rogers's talk a notation concerning C at an earlier date: "At a dinner-party, among other abuse which he poured out on the Unitarians, he declared that 'they were fools.' Lord Holland, who was present, observed, 'Then the Trinitarians must be three fools.' " *Recollections of the Table-Talk of Samuel Rogers* ed Bishop 239.

3. See 18 Mar 1827 n 10, above, on electricity, magnetism, and galvanism.

C's ideas of the dynamic philosophy were partly grasped but oversimplified by such a hearer as Philarète Chasles (1798–1873): "He repudiated none of the dogmas of Christianity, for he believed they were conformable with reason, experience, and history. The material mystery of life, or the physical union which produced the phenomena, he thought was electricity, magnetism, and galvanism, which seemed to him to accord with the spiritual mystery of the soul associated to an intelligence served by organs. He thought all philosophical doctrines were explained through Christianity, which contained them all. He believed in progress developing itself through the phases of humanity; and in traditions of the past, vegetation becoming animal life in its progress, and the lower animal ascending to the higher." *Notabilities in France and England* (New York 1853) 121–2, tr from *Études sur les hommes et les moeurs aux XIX*ᵉ *siècle* (Paris 1850).

4. See 18 Mar 1827 n 13, above, on Spinozism.

C was reported to have three definitions of Spinozism in 1799: "His concentrated definition of Spinozism was, 'Each thing has a life of its own, and we are all one life'; but the expanded doctrine amounts to this,

'That there is but one substance in nature; that this one substance is endued with an infinite number of attributes, among which are extension and cogitation . . . that God is a self-existent and infinitely perfect Being, the cause of all things which exist, but yet not a different Being from them, since there is but one Being and one Nature, which Nature produces within itself. . . .' " Or second, "The great principle of Spinozism is, that there is nothing properly and absolutely existing but matter, and the modifications of matter; among which are even comprehended thought, abstract and general ideas, comparisons, relations, combinations of relations, &c. . . . Or [third] it has been defined to be 'a species of Naturalism, or Pantheism, or Hylotheism,' as it is sometimes called, that is, the dogma which allows of no other God but Nature or the Universe, and therefore makes matter to be God." Carlyon I 193–4.

Twenty-odd years later C held forth on a Thursday at Highgate: "He cited the strong eloquence of Tillotson and Clark[e], and reaching Leibnitz, he followed that great philosopher over the bridge of communication which he extended from earth to heaven. Leibnitz led to Spinoza. We heard him with the ardent glow of genius refute the impalpable pantheism of Spinoza, who gave a soul to the universe without individuality, and motion to matter without a mover. In the mazes of these metaphysical speculations, the poetical genius of Coleridge would flow on, or disport in circles like the harmonious and luminous ocean. From the refutation of Spinoza, 'who,' says he, 'withdraws God from the universe,' he proceeded in beautiful and sublime strains to illustrate the tenets and principles of religion, till, reached to the summit, where he could advance no farther or higher, he bowed himself in humility and reverence to the earth, and murmuring some sweet and mysterious verses from Dante's Paradise, he closed.

"I withdrew, filled with the highest and deepest admiration. Never had I seen in human being the union of such glowing eloquence and subtle acumen." Chasles *Notabilities in France and England* 120–1.

John Frere (1807–51), nephew of C's friend the statesman and satirist, recorded C's remarks on Spinoza in 1830: "C. Almost all thinking Jews are Deists. I wonder Mr. —— should ever have talked with you on those subjects; the persecution which a Jew would undergo from his brethren if it was known that he did so, is not to be calculated. The life, you know, of Spinoza was twice attempted, but he professed Christianity, at least in his way in a letter to a friend; for he said that if the Logos could be manifested in the flesh, it must converse and act as Jesus did. At the same time his notions of a God were very Pantheistic, a ☉ⁱᵉ whose center is everywhere and circumference nowhere. He had no notion of a Conscious Being of a God—but with these ideas to talk of God becoming flesh appears to me very much like talking of a square circle.

"Spinoza is a man whom I most deeply reverence, I was going to say whom I reverence as much as it is possible for me to reverence any creature. He was on the borders of the truth, and would no doubt had he lived have attained it.

"But bless me! to talk of converting the Jews, people are not aware of what they undertake.

"Mr. —— said to me, and I thought very beautifully, 'Convert the Jews! Alas, Sir, Mammon and Ignorance are the two giant porters who stand at the gates of Jerusalem and forbid the entrance of Truth.'" E. M. Green "A Talk with Coleridge: Abstract of a discourse on the state of the country in December 1830, written at the time by John Frere" *Cornhill Magazine* 3rd s XLII (1917) 406.

5. See 8 Jul 1827 n 7, above, on Mrs Jordan's voice.

Sarah Flower Adams (1805–48), at the Lambs' about 1825, heard C bend the subject of conversation towards Mrs Jordan's voice: "He spoke of the effect of different sounds upon his sensations; said, of all the pains the sense of hearing ever brought to him, that of the effect made by a dog belonging to some German conjuror was the greatest. The man pretended that the dog could answer, 'Ich bedanke mein herr' when anything was given to it; and the effort and contortion made by the dog to produce the required sound, proved that the scourge, or some similar punishment, had been applied to effect it. In contrast to this was the homage he rendered to the speaking voice of Mrs. Jordan, on which he expatiated in such rapturous terms, as if he had been indebted to it for a sixth sense. He said that it was the exquisite witchery of her tone that suggested an idea in his 'Remorse,' that if Lucifer had had permission to retain his angel voice, hell would have been hell no longer." "An Evening with Charles Lamb and Coleridge" *Monthly Repository* NS IX (1835) 167; Bertram Dobell *Sidelights on Charles Lamb* (1903) 309.

6. See 8 Jul 1827 n 28, above, on Scott.

Scott recorded details of an evening with C on 22 Apr 1828: "Lockhart and I dined with Sotheby, where we met a large dining party, the orator of which was that extraordinary man Coleridge. After eating a hearty [dinner,] during which he spoke not a word, he began a most learned harangue on the Samo-thracian Misteries—which he considered as affording the germ of all tales about fairies past, present, and to come. He then diverged to Homer, whose Iliad he considerd as a collection of poems by different authors at different times during a century. There was, he said, the individuality of an age, but not of a country. Morritt a zealous worshipper of the old bard was incensed at a system which would turn him into a polytheist, gave battle with keenness, and was joined by Sotheby, our host. Mr. Coleridge behaved with the utmost complaisance and temper, but relaxd not from his exertions. 'Zounds! I was never so bethumped with words.' Morritt's impatience must have cost him an extra sixpence worth of snuff.'' *The Journal of Sir Walter Scott* ed J. G. Tait (1950) 526. John Bacon Sawrey Morritt (c 1772–1843), a classical scholar, had maintained against Jacob Bryant the historical existence and known site of Troy.

7. See 7 May 1830 n 15, above, on Godwin.

HCR listened to C on 30 Mar 1811: "On returning to Lamb's, found Coleridge and W. Hazlitt there. A half-hour's chat. Coleridge spoke feelingly of Godwin and the unjust treatment he has met with. Godwin, it seems, is severely wounded by Southey's review of his *Life of Chaucer* in the *Annual Review*. Coleridge did not justify the review, but in apology ingeniously observed that persons who are themselves very pure are on that very account *blunt* in their moral feelings. . . .

"Coleridge spoke with severity of those who were once the extravagant admirers of Godwin, and afterwards, when his fame declined, became his most angry opponents. . . . I noticed the infinite superiority of Godwin over the French writers in moral tendency and feeling. I had learned to hate Helvétius and Mirabeau and retained my love for Godwin. This was agreed to as a just sentiment by Coleridge, etc. Coleridge said there was more in Godwin after all than he was once willing to admit, though not so much as his enthusiasts fancied. He had declaimed against Godwin openly, but visited him notwithstanding he could not approve even of Wordsworth's feelings and language respecting Godwin. Southey's severity he ascribed to the habit of reviewing. Southey had said of Coleridge's poetry that he was a Dutch imitator of the Germans. Coleridge quoted this, not to express any displeasure, but to show in what way Southey could speak even of him." *CRB* I 28–9; cf *CR (BCW)* 39.

8. See 9 May 1830 n 12, above, on Irving.

On 31 May 1830 at Mr Hoare's of Hampstead Heath Thomas Chalmers heard C speak of his health and other matters: "He began—in answer to the common inquiries as to his health—by telling of a fit of insensibility in which, three weeks before, he had lain for thirty-five minutes. As sensibility returned, and before he had opened his eyes, he uttered a sentence about the fugacious sense of consciousness, from which he passed to a discussion of the singular relations between the soul and the body. Asking for Mr. Irving, but waiting for no reply, he poured out an eloquent tribute of his regard—mourning pathetically that such a man should be so throwing himself away. Mr. Irving's book on the 'Human Nature of Christ' in its analysis was minute to absurdity; one would imagine that the pickling and preserving were to follow, it was so like a cookery book. Unfolding then his own scheme of the Apocalypse—talking of the mighty contrast between its Christ and the Christ of the Gospel narrative, Mr. Coleridge said that Jesus did not come now as before— meek and gentle, healing the sick and feeding the hungry, and dispensing blessings all around, but he came on a white horse; and who were his attendants?—famine, and war, and pestilence.'' William Hanna *Memoirs of the Life of Thomas Chalmers* (4 vols 1851) III 262.

9. See 9 May 1830 n 14, above, on Homer.

Fenimore Cooper heard C's impromptu eloquence at Sotheby's on 22 Apr 1828, along with Scott (quoted above, App F 6), J. G. Lockhart, and others: "When the ladies had retired, the conversation turned on Homer, whom, it is understood, Mr. Sotheby is now engaged in translating. Some one remarked that Mr. Coleridge did not believe in his unity, or rather that there was any such man. This called him out, and certainly I never witnessed an exhibition as extraordinary as that which followed. It was not a discourse, but a dissertation. Scarcely any one spoke besides Mr. Coleridge, with the exception of a brief occasional remark from Mr. Sotheby, who held the contrary opinion; and I might say no one *could* speak. At moments he was surprisingly eloquent, though a little discursive, and the whole time he appeared to be perfectly the master of his subject and of his language. As near as I could judge, he was rather more than an hour *in possession of the floor*, almost without interruption. . . . There seemed to be a constant struggling between an affluence of words and an affluence of ideas, without either hesitation or repetition. . . . In fact, the exhibition was much more wonderful than convincing.'' *Gleanings* (1982) 127.

HC wrote to DC in Aug 1830: "There must be better arguments for the position [of the multiple authorship of the Homeric epics] than ever I have heard, or Henry has advanced, or our Father would never have advocated it, as we both have heard him do, tho' *entre nous* a German fancy goes a great way with him, and had he been, like me, an almost daily reader of Homer, he would have been as thorough a believer in him as I am." *HCL* 109–10. HC and DC visited Highgate together in 1821, and HC never heard C talk after 1822. WW concurred with HNC that "the Books of the Iliad were never intended to make one Poem" and that the *Odyssey* came from a different age. *WL* (*L* rev) II 318.

10. See 27 May 1830 n 14, above, on Job.

John Frere recorded C's remarks of Dec 1830: "Now in the Book of Job (which is undoubtedly very ancient, before the law for there is no mention of the law in it, undoubtedly the most ancient book in the world) the word Satan meant only this officer, the prime vizier of the Sultan (you remember in the 'Arabian Nights' the Caliph and his vizier are very fond of going their rounds for the same purpose). God Almighty is shown to us under the semblance of a mortal king holding his court, and his officer comes, as the book tells us, 'from going his rounds on the earth and walking up and down in it,' but mind there is nothing like malignity attached to him.

"The King asks him concerning Job—the officer answers that he is a perfect man—but (adds he) 'He has yet had no temptation; he is prosperous, and he might alter if his circumstances were altered.'

"The King then commands him to try and to destroy his possessions. (N.B.—This is a mistake, *He gives him leave*.)

"Again on another day the same things happen and when the officer is asked about Job he says 'He is yet integer but many men will do this. I can say nothing for his integrity as long as his possessions only are touched; but stretch out your hand against his person and see if he will curse Thee then?' It is evident that there is no suggestion, no evil in the officer at all—indeed the belief in Angels and that sort of poultry is nowhere countenanced in the Old Testament and in the New, nowhere else." Green "A Talk with Coleridge" *Cornhill* XLII 408. The allusion to the *Arabian Nights* is a representative touch.

11. See 4 Jun 1830 n 4, above, on Donne.

Methuen gave an example of C's power in 1815 to quote from vital Christian theology: "He once asked me if I recollected what Dr. Donne had said respecting the conversion of St. Paul. On my replying in the negative, my friend delighted me with the following invaluable extract from his writings: 'Christ was the lightning flash that melted him, Christ was the mould that formed him.' " *Christian Observer* XLIV 261. William Page Wood (later Baron Hatherley) reported of 29 Jan 1829: "In the evening with B. Montagu to Coleridge's. He had been seized with a fit of enthusiasm for Donne's poetry, which I think somewhat unaccountable. There was great strength, however, in some passages which he read. One stanza or rather division of his poem, on the 'Progress of the Soul,' struck me very much; it was, I think, the fourth, in which he addresses Destiny as the 'Knot of Causes.' The rest of the poem seemed the effusion of a man very drunk or very mad.'' *Memoir of Hatherley* I 175.

12. See 2 Jul 1830 n 14, above, on C's aggressive behaviour.

Methuen gave two examples from 1814–15 of the aggressiveness C attributed to himself. The first came when Methuen asked C why he had so suddenly left Box (where he was staying with his old friend John Morgan): ''His reply, accompanied with no slight playfulness of manner, was, 'My dear Sir, I was actually driven from my lodgings.' I naturally enquired as to the cause of his expulsion: 'Oh,' said he, 'I was informed, to my surprise and horror, that a barrel of gunpowder was regularly kept in the cellar over which I then lodged; and on begging that it might be immediately removed, the servant maid significantly observed to me, 'Why, Sir, I thought it was the *shot* that killed, and not the *powder*.' I rejoined, 'Yes, and if I was a little bird, I should think so too.'

''On another occasion, when he was residing in a certain town, being asked by an acquaintance, 'What society do you find there, either of an intellectual or interesting kind?' he replied, 'Alas, I find little of either sort; and, as to the *brains* of the inhabitants, a —— (naming an insect not unacquainted with the superficies of human craniology) might easily walk through them without being up to his ancles.' '' *Christian Observer* XLIV 259. In a more typical form of such anecdotes, C would suggest that he directly insulted one of the inhabitants.

13. See 24 Jul 1830 n 11, above, on C's father.

John Coleridge's irritability comes to the fore in an anecdote from C, retold by William Jerdan in 1853 and amplified later in his *Men I Have Known* (1866), of C ''I think, when a junior pupil'' acting in a play prepared by his father for performance before parents who had come to collect their sons: ''I remember one of his pleasant stories, told *con gusto*, like that of his reading 'Remorse' with Mr. Kinnaird, of a school performance of a drama on the breaking-up day, in which he played a part. Unluckily the character demanded a laugh, which the juvenile actor delivered thus, 'ha! ha! ha! ha!' with due pause and emphasis of indiscretion between every ha! His father called out 'laugh—laugh,' upon which he repeated the ha's more emphatically than before, when the incensed pedagogue rushed upon the stage, and, cuffing the unfortunate performer, cried, 'Laugh, Sir, laugh; why don't you laugh?' to which the only response was the 'hah, hah, hah's,' with bursts of crying between, and certainly, at last, amid the uncontrollable laughter of the audience. It was a treat to hear the old man eloquent, with his sonorous voice and glittering eye, tell and act this juvenile tale, and compare himself to the boy in the Lupercalian sacrifice who was obliged to laugh when the priest pricked his forehead with the knife reeking with the blood of the victim goat.'' Jerdan *Autobiography* (4 vols 1852–3) III 313. For the revised version see *C Talker* 275.

14. See 19 Sept 1830 n 30, above, on modern poetry.

John Frere recorded in Dec 1830 a dialogue with C:

''*C*. Is there anything stirring now in the world of letters, anything in the shape of poetry lately produced, for I see nothing of the sort, nor even a Review that is not a year old?

''*F*. No, Sir, at least I have heard no talk of any such thing; these continual burnings occupy all men's thoughts and conversation.

''*C*. And what remedies are proposed? They talk I suppose of retrenchments, but what good can retrenchment do? Alas! revolutionary times are times of general demoralization; what great men do they ever produce? What was produced by the late Revolutionary Spirit in France? There must be something uppermost to be sure in such disturbances; some military superiority, but what great—I mean truly great—man was produced?

''In England the same spirit was curbed in and worsted by the moral sense, afterwards there followed times of repose, and the Muses began to show themselves. But now what is going forward? The depravity of the spirit of the times is marked by the absence of poetry. For it is a great mistake to suppose that thought is not necessary for poetry; true, at the time of composition there is that starlight, a dim and holy twilight; but is not light necessary before?

''Poetry is the highest effort of the mind; all the powers are in a state of equilibrium and equally energetic, the knowledge of individual existence is forgotten, the man is out of himself and exists in all things, his eye is in *a* fine &c.

''There is no one perhaps who composes with more facility than your Uncle [John Hookham Frere]; but does it cost him nothing before? It is the result of long thought; and poetry as I have before observed must be the result of thought, and the want of thought in what is now called poetry is a bad sign of the times.'' Green ''A Talk with Coleridge'' *Cornhill* XLII 402–3.

15. See 14 Aug 1831 n 26, above, on Locke.

HCR reported C's remarks on 23 Dec 1810: "Of Locke he spoke, as usual, with great contempt, that is, in reference to his metaphysical work. He considered him as having led to the destruction of metaphysical science, by encouraging the unlearned public to think that with mere common sense they might dispense with disciplined study. He praised Stillingfleet as Locke's opponent; and he ascribed Locke's popularity to his political character; being the advocate of the new against the old dynasty, to his religious character as a Christian, though but an Arian—for both parties, the Christians against the sceptics, and the liberally-minded against the orthodox, were glad to raise his reputation; and to the nationality of the people, who considered him and Newton as the adversaries of the German Leibnitz. Voltaire, to depress Leibnitz, raised Locke." *CRD* I 163; cf *CR (BCW)* 36.

16. See 27 Dec 1831 n 5, above, on Macaulay.

After describing De Q's way of talking in "beautifully rounded and balanced paragraphs", the publisher James Hogg paraphrased one conversation: "We talked, among many other things, about Macaulay, and about his prodigious power and love of talk. De Quincey remarked that such passion for speaking was usually the sign of a weak and shallow mind, but that Macaulay was a remarkable exception to this rule—that he was the only man of real power and substantial acquirements of whom he had ever heard, who was possessed by 'an actual incontinence of talk.' Even Coleridge, regarded as the greatest talker of the day, would not always talk, whilst Macaulay seemed ready to pour forth a flood of disquisition and information at any given time. With Coleridge there was always one difficulty, and sometimes two. It was sometimes a great difficulty to get him to begin to talk; it was always so to get him to stop." *De Quincey and His Friends* (1895) 128.

Sir Robert Inglis gave SC an opportunity to study Macaulay at close range on 13 Nov 1849: "He was in great force, and I saw the likeness (amid great unlikeness) to my father, as I never had seen it before. It is not in the features . . . but resides very much in the look and expression of the material of the face, the mobility, softness, and sensitiveness of all the flesh. . . . The eyes are quite unlike—even opposite in expression,— my father's in-looking and visionary, Macaulay's out-looking and objective. His talk, too, though different as to sentiment and matter, was like a little, in manner, in its labyrinthine multiplicity and multitudinousness, and the tones so flexile and *sinuous*, as it were, reminded me of the departed eloquence." Edith Coleridge *Memoir and Letters of Sara Coleridge* (2 vols 1873) II 276–7.

17. See 31 Mar 1832 n 5, above, on versification.

HNC's remarks, in *QR* LII (1834) 7–8 (*CH* 626–31), on C's attention to versification can probably be taken as only slightly modified from what C himself had said. After noting C's attention to rhythm, metrical arrangement, the tone and quantity of words, and "even minuter points of accentual scansion", he continued: "We do not, of course, mean that rules of this kind were always in his mind while composing . . . but we certainly believe that Mr. Coleridge has almost from the commencement of his poetic life looked upon versification as constituting in and by itself a much more important branch of the art poetic than most of his eminent contemporaries appear to have done. And this more careful study shows itself in him in no technical peculiarities or fantastic whims, against which the genius of our language revolts; but in a more exact adaptation of the movement to the feeling, and in a finer selection of particular words with reference to their local fitness for sense and sound. Some of his poems are complete models of versification, exquisitely easy to all appearance, and subservient to the meaning, and yet so subtle in the links and transitions of the parts as to make it impossible to produce the same effect merely by imitating the syllabic metre as it stands on the surface. . . . In some of the smaller pieces, as the conclusion of the 'Kubla Khan,' for example, not only the lines by themselves are musical, but the whole passage sounds all at once as an outburst or crash of harps in the still air of autumn. The verses seem as if *played* to the ear upon some unseen instrument. And the poet's manner of reciting verse is similar. It is not rhetorical, but musical: so very near recitative, that for any one else to attempt it would be ridiculous; and yet it is perfectly miraculous with what exquisite searching he elicits and makes sensible every particle of the meaning, not leaving a shadow of a shade of the feeling, the mood, the degree, untouched." C repeated as a rhapsode, HNC says, *Iliad* 1.348ff. "A chapter of Isaiah from his mouth involves the listener in an act of exalted devotion. We have mentioned this, to show how the whole man is made up of music; and yet Mr. Coleridge has no *ear* for music, as it is technically called."

18. See 31 Mar 1832 n 6, above, on Mrs Barbauld.

HCR, a friend of Mrs Barbauld and the Aikins who recorded much concerning them, including the attitudes of WW, Lamb, and C, repeated from Elton Hamond C's quip that "Barbauld must have had a very warm constitution, for he had clasped an icicle in his arms for forty years before he found it was cold''. *CRB* I 56. Several persons, perhaps many, heard C make the comparison that Hood in 1836 said C "used to" make between the "void Aikin", meaning Arthur as editor of *A Rev*, and "an aching void". *C Talker* 89, 307; *The Letters of Thomas Hood* ed Peter F. Morgan (Toronto 1973) 260. HCR called C's ridicule of Mrs Barbauld in his last lecture of the 1811–12 series (Lect 17 of 27 Jan 1812) "ungenerous & unmanly". *Lects 1808–19 (CC)* I 407.

Gillman gave an anecdote concerning Mrs Barbauld: "Mr. Coleridge once met Mrs. Barbauld at an evening party. He had not long been present, and the recognition of mere acquaintanceship over, than, walking across the room, she addressed him in these words:—'So, Mr. Coleridge, I understand you do not consider Unitarians Christians.' 'I hope, Madam,' said he, 'that all persons born in a Christian country are Christians, and trust they are under the condition of being saved; but I *do* contend that Unitaria*nism* is not *Christianity*;' to which she replied, 'I do not understand the distinction.' " Gillman continued: "Coleridge frequently observed, 'I do not so much care for men's religious opinions,— they vary, and are dependant on that which usually surrounds them—but I regard with more attention what men *are*.' " *C Life* (G) 164–5.

19. See 23 Apr 1832 n 5, above, on Vico.

HCR took tea at the Gillmans', with Basil Montagu and Edward Irving, on 16 Jun 1825: "I think I never heard Coleridge so very eloquent, and yet it was painful to find myself unable to recall anything of what had so delighted me, that is, anything that seemed worthy to be noted, so that I could not but suspect some illusion arising out of the impressive tone and the mystical language of the orator. He talked on for several hours without intermission, his subject the ever recurring one, religion, but so blended with mythology, metaphysics and psychology that it required great attention to find really the religious element. I observed that when Coleridge quoted Scripture or used well-known religious phrases Irving was constant in his exclamations of delight, but that he was silent at other times. Dr. Prati came in, and Coleridge treated him with marked attention. Indeed Prati talked better than I ever heard him. One sentence (Coleridge having appealed to him) deserves repetition: 'I think the old Pantheism of Spinoza far better than modern Deism, which is but the hypocrisy of Materialism'—in which there is an actual sense and I believe truth. Coleridge referred to an Italian Vico who is said to have anticipated Wolf's theory concerning Homer (which Coleridge says was his at college). Vico wrote *Sur une nouvelle Science*, viz. Comparative History. Goethe notices him in his Life as an original thinker and great man. Vico wrote on the origin of Rome. Coleridge drew a parallel between the West India planters and the negroes, the subjection between them and the condition of the plebs of Rome towards the patricians; but when I inquired concerning the origin of the inequality Coleridge evaded giving me an answer. Coleridge very eloquently expatiated on history and the influence of Christianity on society. His doctrines assume an orthodox air, but to me they are unintelligible. . . ." *CRB* ı 320–1.

20. See 24 Apr 1832 n 1, above, on the theory of colours.

Grattan heard C wind into the subject of the theory of colours at Brussels in Jun 1828: "There were several gentlemen of the party. Coleridge talked much and indiscriminately with those next him or about him. He did not appear to talk for effect, but purely for talking's sake. He seemed to breathe in words. Wordsworth was at times fluent but always commonplace; full of remark but not of observation. He spoke of scenery as far as its aspect was concerned; but he did not enter into its associations with moral beauty. He certainly did not talk well. But in fact he had no encouragement. He had few listeners; and what seemed rather repulsive in him was perhaps chiefly from its grating contrast to the wonderful attraction of Coleridge. His was a mild enthusiastic flow of language; a broad, deep stream, carrying gently along all that it met with on its course, not a whirlpool that drags into its vortex, and engulfs what it seizes on. Almost everything he talked about became the subject of a lecture of great eloquence and precision. For instance his remarks on grammar and its philosophy. His illustrations from chemistry and colours came here into play quite naturally, and led him on, but by no means abruptly into a complete, and it must be added a rather complex, essay on the nature of colour, prismatic effects and the theory of light. He was no doubt familiarly acquainted with Goethe's doctrine or theory of colours, and probably with an Italian translation of Aristotle's treatise, which neither I nor any of his listeners had more than passingly heard of. For in alluding to Newton's theory, which Goethe had written in refutation of, (comparing light to a closed fan, saying that a mixture of all colours made white, etc.) he called it 'an incubus on natural philosophy;' and he branched off from his main subject, to trace the analogy between natural grammar and colour, the whole of which he made very interesting if not very lucid, and as to its originality I am not competent to judge.* It was difficult to believe that all this was uttered extempore, or indeed without much elaborate arrangement. The thoughts and words appeared stereotyped; and in the fanciful system, as in all his discourse, there was a strong flavour of Kantean transcendentalism and mysticism." *Beaten Paths* II 110–12. Grattan's note, 111n: "* The following which I noted down at the time is a specimen of the theory. 'The first part of grammar, *identity*, is analogous to red. This second part, *position*, to blue. The third, the *thesis*, to yellow. The fourth, the *antithesis*, to green. The fifth, the *synthesis*, to another green totally. Black with its lustre as in ebony gave the best notion of solidity; and without it, as in the mouth of a cavern, of vagueness. It is at once the zenith and nadir of colour. Red and black always combine together in painting; and black is always used in giving notions of firmness.' "

21. See 28 Apr 1832 n 1, above, on McLellan.

Henry Blake McLellan (1810–33), after receiving his BA from Harvard in 1829, attended the Andover Theological Seminary for two years and spent the first of two winters at Edinburgh University. He stopped in London on his way to the Continent. In his journal he recorded his visit to Highgate to see C:

"*Saturday, April* 27. Walked to Highgate to call on Mr Coleridge. I was ushered into the parlor while the girl carried up my letter to his room. She presently returned and observed that her master was very poorly, but would be happy to see me, if I would walk up to his room, which I gladly did. He is short in stature and appeared to be careless in his dress. I was impressed with the strength of his expression, his venerable locks of white, and his trembling frame. He remarked that he had for some time past suffered much bodily anguish. For many months (thirteen) seventeen hours each day had he walked up and down his chamber. I inquired whether his mental powers were affected by such intense suffering; 'Not at all,' said he, 'my body and head appear to hold no connexion; the pain of my body, blessed be God, never reaches my mind.' After some further conversation and some inquiries respecting Dr Chalmers,[1] he remarked 'The Doctor must have suffered exceedingly at the strange conduct of our once dear brother laborer in Christ, Rev. Mr Irving.[2] Never can I describe how much it has wrung my bosom. I had watched with astonish-

---

[1] Thomas Chalmers (1780–1847), theologian, professor of divinity at Edinburgh from 1828 to 1843, when he founded the Free Church of Scotland. He had accompanied Edward Irving to Highgate in May 1827, when he found C's conversation "most astonishing, but, I must confess, to me still unintelligible". *C Talker* 127. He and his family had cordially befriended McLellan. *Journal* 138–220 passim.

[2] Irving had been assistant to Dr Chalmers at St John's, Glasgow, 1819–22. Because of Irving's approval of "speaking with tongues", the trustees of his Regent Square Church had taken action on 26 Apr to force him from the pulpit. On his return from Highgate, McLellan

ment and admiration the wonderful and rapid development of his powers. Never was such unexampled advance in intellect as between his first and second volume of sermons. The first full of Gallicisms and Scoticisms, and all other cisms. The second discovering all the elegance and power of the best writers of the Elizabethean age. And then so sudden a fall, when his mighty energies made him so terrible to sinners.' Of the mind of the celebrated Puffendorf[3] he said, 'his mind is like some mighty volcano, red with flame, and dark with tossing clouds of smoke through which the lightnings play and glare most awfully.' Speaking of the state of the different classes of England, he remarked 'we are in a dreadful state; care like a foul hag sits on us all; one class presses with iron foot upon the wounded heads beneath, and all struggle for a worthless supremacy, and all to rise to it move shackled by their expenses; happy, happy are you to hold your birth-right in a country where things are different; you, at least at present, are in a transition state; God grant it may ever be so![4] Sir, things have come to a dreadful pass with us, we need most deeply a reform, but I fear not the horrid reform which we shall have; things must alter, the upper classes of England have made the lower persons, *things*; the people in breaking from this unnatural state will break from duties also.'

"He spoke of Mr Alston[5] with great affection and high encomium; he thought him in imagination and color almost unrivalled." *Journal of a Residence in Scotland, and Tour Through England, France, Germany, Switzerland and Italy, with a Memoir of the Author, and Extracts from His Religious Papers* ed Isaac McLellan, Jr (Boston, Mass 1834) 230–2.

McLellan may have visited C again before he wrote in a letter of May: "Of all the men whom I have ever met, the most wonderful in conver-

---

dropped into a meeting, listened to Irving, and heard a woman speak with a "voice"; after hearing a second sermon the next Sunday evening, he concluded that Irving's principal error was to believe that one might achieve perfection in this life. *Journal* 231–5. Irving's "unlucky phantasms" were the main topic when Chalmers visited C again on 31 May 1830: "Dr Chalmers with his Daughter & his very pleasing Wife honored me with a Call this morning and spent an hour with me—which the good Doctor declared on parting to have been 'a *Refreshment*' such as he had not en-

joyed for a long season." Letter to J. H. Green: *CL* VI 839–40.

[3] Freiherr Samuel von Pufendorf (1632–94), German jurist and historian, author of *De jure naturae et gentium* (Lund 1672, tr 1710 *Of the Law of Nature and Nations*). C cited him by name in *The Friend: CC* II 322n (I 291n).

[4] C's praise contrasted with the remarks of other prominent Englishmen before and after this visit. RS and WW, with whom McLellan talked on 9 Apr 1833, thought the U.S. so wide that it surely must dismember. *Journal* 356–8.

[5] Washington Allston.

sational powers is Mr. S. T. Coleridge, in whose company I spent much time. With all his talent and poetry, he is a humble and devout follower of the blessed Jesus, even as 'Christ crucified.' I wish I had room for some of his conversation. When I bade him a last farewell, he was in bed, in great bodily suffering, but with great mental vigor, and feeling a humble resignation to the will of his heavenly Father. As I sat by his side I thought he looked very much like my dear grandfather, and I almost felt as if one spoke to me from the dead. Before I left him he said, 'I wish before you go, to give you some little memento to call up the hours we have passed together.' He requested me to hand him a book from his book-case, with pen and ink, then sitting up in bed he wrote a few lines and his name, kindly and most undeservedly expressing the pleasure he had had in my company. He will not live long I fear; but his name and memory will be dearer to the ages to come than to the present.'' *Journal* 70.

22. See 6 Aug 1832 n 1, above, on ''Scotch''.

HCR smiled on 29 Mar 1811 when the presence of the Sydney Smith family proved no damper to C's fulminations on the Scots: ''We talked of politics. It was amusing to observe how Coleridge blundered against Scotchmen and Frenchmen. He represented the *Edinburgh Review* as being a concentration of all the smartness of all Scotland. Edinburgh is a talking town, and whenever in their conversaziones a single spark is elicited, it is instantly caught, preserved, and brought to the *Review*. He denied humour to the nation. Smith appealed in behalf of Smollett. Coleridge endeavoured to make a distinction: that is, maintain his point and yet allow the acknowledged merits of Smollett. He abused Condillac just as Mrs. Smith had whispered to me: '*Ah, que c'est un grand homme ce Condillac!*'

''Before Lamb came, Coleridge had spoken with warmth of his excellent and serious conversation. Hazlitt imputed his puns to humility.

''Coleridge declaimed about Rogers, whom he represented as most feelingly alive to criticism and public opinion. At first, he warmly eulogized Bloomfield, whom he neglected the moment he saw the world neglect him. . . .

''We spoke of national characters, national dislikes, etc. Coleridge playfully said: 'I always say ''a *Scotch* rascal,'' as if the infamy lay in the being *Scotch*.' Coleridge's antipathy to the Irish I cannot share in. But then, he has no aversion to Turks or Jews, so I am the best Christian after all.'' *CRB* I 28–9; cf the draft in *CR (BCW)* 38–40. On ''Scotch rascal'' cf Dyce's report in App F 1, above.

23. See 2 Jan 1833 n 1, above, on Landor's visit to Highgate 29 Sept 1832 and on R. C. Trench's in October.

HCR took Landor to Highgate to see C: "We sat not much more than an hour with him; he was horribly bent and looked seventy years of age— nor did he talk with his usual fire but quite in his usual style. A great part of his conversation was a repetition of what I had heard him say before— an abuse of the Ministry for taking away his pension, he speaking of himself as having devoted himself not to the writing for the people, whom the public could reward, but for the nation, of which the King is the representative. The stay was too short to allow of our entering upon literary matters. He spoke only of Oriental poetry with contempt, and he showed his memory by alluding to Landor's juvenile poems in which were some said to be by: [?] but which were in fact original. Landor and he seemed to like each other. Landor spoke in his dashing way, which Coleridge could understand and he concurred with him. Indeed, I found Landor both with Coleridge and Lady Blessington more of an assentor than I should have expected." *CRB* I 413–14. In 1800 Landor had published *Poems from the Arabic and Persian* "with Notes, by the Author of Gebir". The poems were a hoax, perpetrated to deride translations published by Sir William Jones 1772–87. HCR seemed to have understood the conversation less well than C and Landor understood each other.

After C's death Landor remembered the visit to C with HCR: "He had recovered his health when I saw him, and told me that he had not been better for many years. Poor man! He put on a bran-new suit of black to come down and see me, and made me as many fine speeches as he ever could have done to a pretty girl. My heart aches at the thought that almost the greatest genius in the world, and one so friendly to me, is gone from it." Letter to his sisters 27 Aug 1834: John Forster *Walter Savage Landor: A Biography* (2 vols 1869) II 55. To Mrs Septimus Hodson, Landor wrote at about the same time: "He was very infirm in his limbs when I saw him, but he retained all his energy of mind, and all his sweetness, variety, and flexibility of language." ASL, Berg Collection, NYPL, quoted in Robert Henry Super *Walter Savage Landor: A Biography* (New York 1954) 232. Foster misdated the visit May 1832, and mistakenly declared Landor disappointed with C (II 242)—unless he drew on unspecified knowledge. In the spring of 1833, when Landor had returned to Florence, SC wrote to Mrs DC (Mary Pridham): "Crabbe Robinson (tell Derwent) has taken W. S. Landor to Highgate to see my father. They never used to be over kind I thought—for my father was neither a worshipper of Landor, like my Uncle Southey, nor even as great an admirer as Mr Wordsworth, & certainly Landor never quoted (I believe, a line from my father) nor mentioned even once his name with honour though he is always lauding the other two.'' UT Grantz 146.

R. C. Trench wrote to his wife 10 Oct 1832: ''I have had a long interview with Coleridge, who speaks of 'poor dear Mr. Irving,' and says it makes his heart break every time he thinks of him. 'The old man eloquent' has been suffering very much, and is very infirm—waiting for the redemption of the body, longing, as he told me, to be redeemed from the body of this death; 'for in this we groan,' he added, with mournful earnestness. He seems full of hope and faith, and uttered lively oracles in our hearing for more than an hour. He altogether dissents from the scheme of prophetic interpretation which I have adopted.'' *Letters and Memorials* ed M. Trench (2 vols 1888) I 123–4.

24. See 16 Feb 1833 n 13, above, on *Faust*.

HCR reported on 13 Aug 1812: ''I went by appointment to Coleridge, with whom I spent several hours most agreeably alone. I read to him a number of scenes out of the new *Faust*. He had read before the earlier edition, and he now acknowledged the genius of Goethe in a manner he never did before. At the same time, the want of religion and enthusiasm in Goethe is in Coleridge's mind an irreparable defect. The beginning of *Faust* does not please Coleridge, nor does he think Mephistopheles a character. I urged that Mephistopheles ought to be a mere abstraction, and no character, and Coleridge had nothing satisfactory to oppose to this remark. I read to Coleridge the *Zueignung*, and he seemed to admire it greatly. He had been reading Stolberg lately, of whom he seems to have a sufficiently high opinion. He considers Goethe's *Mahomets Gesang* as but an imitation of Stolberg's *Felsenstrom*, [not] considering that the *Felsenstrom* is but a piece of animated description, without any higher import, while Goethe's poem is a profound and significant allegory, exhibiting the nature of religious enthusiasm. The Prologue in Heaven to *Faust* did not offend Coleridge as I thought it would, notwithstanding it is a parody on Job. Coleridge said of Job: 'This incomparable poem has been most absurdly interpreted. Job, far from being the most patient of men, was the most impatient of men, and he was rewarded for his impatience: his integrity and sincerity had their recompense, because he was superior to the hypocrisy of his friends.'

''Coleridge praised *Wallenstein* but censured Schiller for a sort of ventriloquism in poetry,—by the bye, a happy term to express that common fault of throwing the feelings of the writer into the body, as it were, of other personages, the characters of the poem. In *Ruth*, as it stands at present, there is the same fault; Wordsworth had not originally put into the mouth of the lover many of the sentiments he now entertains, and which would better have become the poet himself.'' *CRB* I 107.

On 20 Aug at James Burney's HCR was relieved when C came in: ''With him I had a very interesting conversation about *Faust*. The additions in the last edition he thinks the finest parts. He thinks the character of Faust himself not *motiviert*. He would have it explained how he was thrown into a state of mind which led to the catastrophe. This does not seem to me a powerful objection. The last stage of the process is given. We see Faust wretched—he has acquired the utmost that finite powers can obtain, and he languishes for infinity. Rather than be finitely good he would be infinitely miserable. This is, indeed, reducing the wisdom and genius of Goethe's incomparable poem to a dull, commonplace moral idea; but I do not give it as the thing, only the abstract form. All final results and most general abstractions are when thus reduced seemingly trite. Coleridge talks of writing a new *Faust*! He would never get out of a few barren, vague conceptions; he would lose himself in dreaming— his whole intellectual apparatus, employed by himself to no other purpose than to keep the different implements in exercise—I cannot say order. Coleridge gave a very spirited sketch of *Faust* to Captain Burney, and I admired his power of giving interest to a prose statement.'' *CRB* I 108.

On 8 Dec at John Morgan's C wished ''Goethe's works for the sake of availing himself of his songs in his operas''. *CRB* I 114. On 2 Mar 1813 C was more ranging: ''In the evening accompanied Aders to see Coleridge. Coleridge was very eloquent, and on music, of which he seemed to speak with more feeling than knowledge. Purcell was his hero. He spoke with more than usual candour of Goethe, and said if he spoke in seeming depreciation of him, it was only because he compared him with the very greatest poets. He said that Goethe appeared to him from a sort of caprice to have underrated the kind of talent he had in his youth so eminently displayed, viz. the power of exhibiting man in a state of exalted sensibility as in *Werther*. Afterwards he delighted to exhibit objects in which a pure sense of the beautiful was chiefly called into exercise. These purely *beautiful* objects—not objects of desire or passion—he coldly delighted to exhibit as a statue does his succession of marble figures, and therefore he called Goethe picturesque. He spoke of Lessing's *Laocoön* as very unequal and in its parts contradictory; his examples destroying his theory. He spoke of *Reinecke Fuchs*, and said the moral of the piece is that if there be a conflict between dull blundering knaves, such as Isegrim the Wolf and Bruin the Bear, and such complete clever scoundrel[s] as Reynard, Reynard ought to be victorious. It is the prize due to his talents, and though poor and defenceless creatures like the hare, the hens, etc., must perish, for such is the constitution of nature, such creatures do not excite our sympathy. I never before heard him argue in favour of Buonaparte. He accused Schlegel of *Einseitigkeit* [narrowness] in his exclusive admiration of Shakespeare, and in his former work about the Greek poetry.'' *CRB* I 122–3.

25. See 16 Feb 1833 n 24, above, on *Wallenstein* and *Faust*.

In 1830 John Frere listened carefully to C on several of the subjects of TT of 16 Feb 1833:

''*C*. I have been asked why I did not translate the camp scenes in 'Wallenstein.'

''The truth is that the labour would have been immense, and besides it would not have been borne in English, to say nothing of the fact that Mrs. Barbauld reviewed my translation of the rest of the play and abused it through thick and thin, so that it sold for wastepaper. I remember your uncle telling me that he had picked it up—he approved it, so did Canning to whom he showed it—and so might one or two more, but the edition sold for wastepaper.

''*F*. Had you ever any thought of translating the 'Faust'?

''*C*. Yes, Sir, I had, but I was prevented by the consideration that though there are some exquisite passages, the opening chorus, the chapel and the prison scenes for instance, to say nothing of the Brocken scene where he has shown peculiar strength in keeping clear of Shakspear, he has not taken that wonderful admixture of Witch Fate and Fairy but has kept to the real original witch, and this suits his purpose much better. I say that a great deal of it I do not admire, and some I reprobate. The conception of Wagner is bad: whoever heard of a man who had gained such wonderful proficiency in learning as to call up spirits &c. being discontented?

''No, it is not having the power of knowledge that would make a man discontented—neither would such a man have suddenly become a sensualist. The discourses too with the pupil are dull. The Mephistapholes (*sic*), or whatever the name is, is well executed, but the conception is not original. It was —— who had before said, 'The Devil is the great humourist of the world.' There are other parts too which I could not have translated without entering my protest against them in a manner which would hardly have been fair upon the author, for those things are understood in Germany in a spirit very different from what they would infuse here in England. To give you an example, the scene where Mephistopheles is introduced as coming before the Almighty and talking with Him would never be borne in English and this whole scene is founded on a mistranslation of a passage in Scripture, the opening of Job. You remember how Satan means properly one who goes his rounds, and hence it came to mean one of those officers whom the King in Eastern countries used to send round to see how his subjects were going on. This power was soon abused and the Satans used to accuse people falsely, and hence the word came to have the meaning now attached to it of a calumniator, a διάβολος, an accuser.''

After continuing on Job (see App F 10, above), C remembered the subject:

"I return however to 'Faust.'

"*F*. Did you ever see Shelley's translation of the Chorus in 'Faust' you were just mentioning?

"*C*. I have, and admire it very much. Shelley was a man of great power as a poet, and could he only have had some notion of order, could you only have given him some plane whereon to stand, and look down upon his own mind, he would have succeeded. There are flashes of the true spirit to be met with in his works. Poor Shelley, it is a pity I often think that I never met with him. I could have done him good. He went to Keswick on purpose to see me and unfortunately fell in with Southey instead. There could have been nothing so unfortunate. Southey had no understanding for a toleration of such principles as Shelley's.

"I should have laughed at his Atheism. I could have sympathised with him and shown him that I did so, and he would have felt that I did so. I could have shown him that I had once been in the same state myself, and I could have guided him through it. I have often bitterly regretted in my heart of hearts that I did never meet with Shelley.'' Green "A Talk with Coleridge" *Cornhill* XLII 406–9.

26. See 4 May 1833 n 2, above, on colonies and colonisation.

John Frere reported a colloquy of Dec 1830 (see App F 14, above, of which the following is a direct continuation): "There is a want of the proper spirit; if a nation would flourish (politically speaking) there must be a desire in the breast of each man of something more than merely to live—he must desire to live well; and if men cannot live well at home they will go and live well elsewhere. The condition upon which a country circumstanced as ours is exists, is that it should become the Mother of Empires, and this Mr. W. Horton feels, but his plans are not extensive or universal enough. I had a conversation with him, but could not make him enter into my views. We ought to send out colonies, but not privately or by parishes; it should be a grand National concern; there should be in every family one or more brought up for this and this alone.

"A Father should say, 'There, John now is a fine strong fellow and an enterprising lad, he shall be a colonist.'

"But then some fool like Lord —— gets up and tells us 'Oh no! America should be a warning.'

"Good Heavens, Sir! a warning, and of what? Are we to beware of having 2 [sets ?] of men bound to us by the ties of allegiance and of affinity; 2 [sets] of men in a distant part of the world speaking the language of Shakspear and Milton, and living under the laws of Alfred. But a warning they should be to us, to give freely and in good time that liberty which is their due, and which they will properly extort from us if we withhold.

F. Is it not moreover true, Sir, that we should show ourselves really a Mother and not a Stepmother to those Empires which we found? We should with a nursing hand lead them through the dangers of infancy; but why keep them in leading strings when they are able to act for themselves? We should relax our hold by slow degrees as they are able to bear it, and nurture them to be free and manly states, and not the slaves of any, still less of their own Mother. What Mother ever complains of the ingratitude of her Son because he does not follow at her apron-strings all the days of his life? Why then do we complain of America, who with greater justice might complain of us that we have been far from remembering one great duty, namely that a Mother if need be should even sacrifice herself for her child?

"*C.* What you say is very true; but with regard to the execution of a plan of Colonisation, why should we not make the absurd system of Poor Laws subservient to the measure?

"Why not, since as Sir N. T. [Nathaniel Tooke] told Bartle the other day, An offer and refusal is as good as an acceptance, propose to any person requiring assistance of the overseer the following terms:—We have it is true bound ourselves by a most foolish promise to find you work; we have none here, but if you choose to go out to the Swan River, you shall have as much as you want, and we will carry you out there, your wife and your children too, if you have them, and you shall get your livelihood in an honorable independent way—and mind you are now to consider us discharged of our promise to find you work." Green "A Talk with Coleridge" *Cornhill* XLII 403–4.

27. See 1 Jul 1833 n 4, above, on painting vs sculpture.

George Dance and Farington heard C discuss painting and sculpture with Sir George Beaumont 25 Mar 1804: "The Conversation after dinner and throughout the evening was very metaphysical in which Coleridge had the leading & by far the greatest part of it.—His habit seems to be to analyze every subject. A Comparison was made between the powers required, or rather what was requisite for painting and Sculpture. Sir George was decidedly of opinion that it required much more to make a complete work in Painting than to arrive at perfection in Sculpture. He instanced *Colouring* which alone had occupied the greatest talents to arrive at excellence yet it was but a part of what was necessary to make a picture.—Coleridge concurred with him.—Upon it being observed that in Sculpture to make a *perfect form* it was necessary not to Copy any individual figure for nothing human is perfect, but to make a selection of perfect parts from various figures & assemble them together & thereby constitute a perfect whole, Coleridge observed that it was the same in good poetry,—Nature was the basis or original from which all should proceed. He said that perhaps there was not in any poem a line which separately might not have been expressed by somebody, it was the assembling so many expressions of the feelings of the mind and uniting them consistently together that delighted the imagination.'' Farington *Diary* VI 2275–6.

28. See 1 Jul 1833 n 13, above, on the Greek tragic poets.

Hazlitt paid a tribute to C in *The Spirit of the Age* (2nd ed 1825) 63: ''One of the finest and rarest parts of Mr. Coleridge's conversation, is when he expatiates on the Greek tragedians (not that he is not well acquainted, when he pleases, with the epic poets, or the philosophers, or orators, or historians of antiquity)—on the subtle reasonings and melting pathos of Euripides, on the harmonious gracefulness of Sophocles, turning his love-laboured song, like sweetest warblings from a sacred grove; on the high-wrought trumpet-tongued eloquence of Æschylus, whose Prometheus, above all, is like an Ode to Fate, and a pleading with Providence, his thoughts being let loose as his body is chained on his solitary rock, and his afflicted will (the emblem of mortality)
'Struggling in vain with ruthless destiny.'
As the impassioned critic speaks and rises in his theme, you would think you heard the voice of the Man hated by the Gods, contending with the wild winds as they roar, and his eye glitters with the spirit of Antiquity.''

29. See 1 Jul 1833 n 40, above, on *Christabel*.

WW commented to JTC on 28 Sept 1825 on C's plan for *Christabel*: ''Wordsworth said he had no idea how 'Christabel' was to have been finished, and he did not think my Uncle had ever conceived in his own mind any definite plans for it; that the poem had been composed while they were in the habit of daily intercourse and almost in his presence, and when there was the most unreserved intercourse between them as to all their literary projects and productions, and he had never heard from him any plan for finishing it. Not that he doubted my Uncle's *sincerity* in his subsequent assertions to the contrary, because, he said, schemes of this sort passed rapidly and vividly through his mind, and so impressed him that he often fancied he had arranged things which really and upon trial proved to be mere embryos. I omitted to ask him what seems obvious now, whether in conversing about it he had never asked my Uncle how it was to end; the answer would have settled the question. He regretted that the story had not been made to end the same night in which it begun. There was a difficulty and danger in bringing such a personage as the witch to the daylight and the breakfast table. And unless the poem was to have been long enough to give time for creating a second interest, there was a great probability of the conclusion being flat after such a commencement.'' Bernard, Lord Coleridge *This for Remembrance* (1925) 589; *W Prose* (1876) III 427 (var).

The first ''continuation'' of *Christabel*, in the *European Magazine* in 1815, was taken as genuine by Heraud (''Reminiscences'' in *Fraser's* Oct 1834), but rejected by HNC in a footnote in *TT* (1835) to the passage on C's finishing the poem, a note dropped from *TT* (1836): ''I should not have thought it necessary, but for the opinion expressed in Fraser's Magazine for October, 1834, p. 394., to remark here, that the verses published in the European Magazine, No. LXVII., and dated April, 1815, purporting to be a conclusion of Christabel, are not by Mr. Coleridge. With deference to the critic, I must take the liberty to say that they have not a particle of the spirit of the genuine poem; and that the metre and rhythm are copied by one whose eye was better than his ear. Besides, Coleridge's Bracy was not Merlin, neither was his Geraldine the Lady of the Lake. In fact, the genuine poem was well known, by recitation and transcription, nearly twenty years before its publication; and the writer of the conclusion had, of course, seen it. I believe I could name the Avellaneda of Christabel—but he is now gone, and it would reflect no credit upon his memory.''

30. See 1 Jul 1833 n 44, above, on C on music.

Gillman related an anecdote of 1818: ''At this time an intimate and highly accomplished friend of my wife's, who was also a very sensible woman, a fine musician, and considered one of the best private performers in the country, came on a visit. The conversation turned on music, and Coleridge, speaking of himself, observed, 'I believe I have no ear for music, but have a taste for it.' He then explained the delight he received from Mozart, and how greatly he enjoyed the dithyrambic movement of Beethoven; but could never find pleasure in the fashionable modern composers. It seemed to him 'playing tricks with music—like nonsense verses—music to please me,' added he, 'must have a subject.' Our friend appeared struck with this observation, 'I understand you, sir,' she replied, and immediately seated herself at the piano. 'Have the kindness to listen to the three following airs, which I played on a certain occasion extempore, as substitutes for words. Will you try to guess the meaning I wished to convey, and I shall then ascertain the extent of my success.' She instantly gave us the first air,—his reply was immediate. 'That is clear, it is solicitation.'—'When I played this air,' observed the lady, 'to a dear friend whom you know, she turned to me, saying, "what do you want?"'—I told her the purport of my air was to draw her attention to her dress, as she was going out with me to take a drive by the seashore without her cloak.' Our visitor then called Coleridge's attention to her second air; it was short and expressive. To this he answered, 'that is easily told—it is remonstrance.' 'Yes,' replied she, 'for my friend again shewing the same inattention, I played this second extemporaneous air, in order to remonstrate with her.' We now listened to the third and last air. He requested her to repeat it, which she did.—'That,' said he, 'I cannot understand.' To this she replied,—'it is I believe a failure,' naming at the same time the subject she had wished to convey. Coleridge's answer was—'That is a sentiment, and cannot be well expressed in music.' " *C Life* (G) 357–8.

31. See 14 Aug 1833 n 5, above, on the Quakers.

The linkage of Quakers with philanthropy suggests that C may have been thinking also of his old acquaintance and correspondent, Thomas Clarkson (1760–1846), who, though not a member of the Society of Friends, was closely associated with Quakers. HCR was disturbed by C's remarks on 11 Jun 1811: "C. made some strong remarks on a most excellent man whom he professed to admire, even in making strictures that might be thought to depreciate him—Mr. Clarkson. 'I have long,' said C., 'looked on him rather as an abstraction than as an individual who is to be loved because he returns the love men bear to their equals. Clarkson is incapable of loving any except those to whom he has been a benefactor. He is so accustomed to *serve* that he cannot love those whose happiness he can no longer promote. As others are benevolent from vanity, he is made vain by beneficence.' 'Many years ago I called him the moral steam engine, the giant with one idea. I am sorry that the reverence I feel for him as an abstract is in danger of being weakened. The abstract is deteriorating.' This par[ticu]lar remark was occasioned by Cl. having joined the Jacobins in signing a requisition for a reform meeting. This C. cd. not forgive." *CR (BCW)* 41.

32. See 14 Aug 1833 n 26, above, on Holcroft.

Joseph Cottle heard C on the subject of Holcroft in 1807: "Mr. C. now changed the subject, and spoke of Holcroft; who he said was a man of but small powers, with superficial, rather than solid talents, and possessing principles of the most horrible description; a man who at the very moment he denied the existence of a Deity, in his heart believed and trembled. He said that Holcroft, and other Atheists, reasoned with so much fierceness and vehemence against a God, that it plainly showed they were inwardly conscious there *was* a GOD to reason against; for, a nonentity would never excite passion.

"He said that in one of his visits to London, he accidentally met Holcroft in a public office without knowing his name, when he began, stranger as he was, the enforcement of some of his diabolical sentiments! which, it appears, he was in the habit of doing, at all seasons, and in all companies; by which he often corrupted the principles of those simple persons who listened to his shallow, and worn-out impieties. Mr. C. declared himself to have felt indignant at conduct so infamous, and at once closed with the 'prating atheist,' when they had a sharp encounter. Holcroft then abruptly addressed him, "I perceive you have *mind*, and know what you are talking about. It will be worth while to make a convert of *you*. I am engaged at present, but if you will call on me to-morrow morning, giving him his card, I will engage, in half an hour, to convince you there is no God!'

"Mr. Coleridge called on him the next morning, when the discussion was renewed, but none being present except the disputants, no account is preserved of this important conversation; but Mr. C. affirmed that he beat all his arguments to atoms; a result that none who knew him could doubt. He also stated that instead of *his* being converted to atheism, the atheist himself, after his manner, was converted; for the same day he sent Mr. C. a letter, saying his reasoning was so clear and satisfactory, that he had changed his views and was now '*a theist*.' The next sun probably beheld him an atheist again; but whether he *called* himself this or that, his character was the same.

"Soon after the foregoing incident, Mr. Coleridge said, he found himself in a large party, at the house of a man of letters, amongst whom to his surprise, he saw Mr. and Mrs. Holcroft, when, to incite to a renewal of their late dispute, and before witnesses, (in the full consciousness of strength) Mr. C. enforced the propriety of teaching children, as soon as they could articulate, to lisp the praises of their Maker; 'for,' said he, 'though they can form no correct idea of God, yet they entertain a high opinion of their *father*, and it is an easy introduction to the truth, to tell them that their Heavenly Father is stronger, and wiser, and better, than their *earthly* father.'

"The whole company looked at Mr. Holcroft, implying that *now* was the time for him to meet a competent opponent, and justify sentiments which he had so often triumphantly advanced. They looked in vain. He maintained, to their surprise, a total silence, well remembering the severe castigation he had so recently received. But a very different effect was produced on Mrs. Holcroft. She indignantly heard, and giving vent to her passion and her *tears*, said, she was quite surprised at Mr. Coleridge talking in that way before her, when he knew that both herself and Mr. Holcroft were atheists!

"Mr. C. spoke of the unutterable horror he felt, when Holcroft's son, a boy eight years of age, came up to him and said, 'There is no God!' So that these wretched parents, alike father and mother, were as earnest in inculcating atheism on their children, as christian parents are in inspiring their offspring with respect for religious truth.

"Actions are often the best illustration of principles. Mr. Coleridge also stated the following circumstance, notorious at the time, as an evidence of the disastrous effects of atheism. Holcroft's tyrannical conduct toward his children was proverbial. An elder son, with a mind embued with his father's sentiments, from extreme severity of treatment, had run away from his paternal roof, and entered on board a ship. Holcroft pursued his son, and when the fugitive youth saw his father in a boat, rowing toward the vessel, rather than endure his frown and his chastisement, he seized a pistol, and blew his brains out!*" *Rem* 329–32.

33. See 2 Sept 1833 n 6, above, on opium.

When Grattan spoke to C in 1828 as to "a regular glutton" in opium-eating, he got a quick response: "I talked to him of his indulgence in this enjoyment as a matter of course. On this he displayed infinitely more vivacity and energy than I had yet thought him susceptible of. He quite took the thing to heart. And, with an earnest anxiety to be rightly understood, and an evident hope that I would in some measure forward his views to that effect, he laboured to assure me that the most false notions existed on the subject. He admitted that he had at times taken opium, as the only means of relieving dreadful visitations of nightmare, which had

---

"* The father's remark on the occasion was, 'There's an end of him! A fine high-spirited fellow!' "

frequently so afflicted him as to make him leap from his bed in agonies of undefinable terror. He might have quoted Milton (leaving out one word)—

—'Sleep hath forsook and given me o'er
To (death's) benumbing opium as my only cure.'

"In speaking thus he seemed suddenly to recollect, and then recited, some lines which he said were never published, powerfully expressive of his sufferings, more so than his 'Pains of Sleep.' He shuddered and panted as he repeated them in a deep murmur, and gave me a vivid notion of the horrors to which he must have been habituated. But he solemnly protested against ever having taken opium in anything like excess, or for the purpose of mere excitement.

" 'It would have been a deep and wanton crime in me,' said he, raising his hands and eyes towards heaven, by no means a common movement with him, for he used but little gesticulation even when speaking with strong emphasis.

"He spoke with absolute abhorrence of the 'Confessions of an English Opium-eater,' called it 'a wicked book, a monstrous exaggeration,' and dwelt with great reprobation on the author for 'laying open his nakedness to the world.' He considered him to have behaved grossly in bringing him (Coleridge) into the book, as an authority for the excesses he avowed; and declared that 'when he suspected Mr. de Quincy of taking opium, he had on several occasions spent hours in endeavouring to dissuade him from it, and that gentleman invariably assured him in the most solemn manner that he did not take it at all, while by his after confessions it appeared that he was drinking laudanum as other men drink wine.' "
Grattan II 130–1.

34. See 15 Oct 1833 n 1, above, on redemption.

William Page Wood was more pleased with C on the subject of redemption, 18 Dec 1828, than on most subjects: "Coleridge's sentiments are formed on the Lutheran exposition of the Gospel scheme, which he considers to be derived from the exposition given by St. Paul and St. John, the two most gifted apostles. He conceives a genuine faith is the gradual substitution of Christ's reviving influence which causes the natural man to throw off as it were, by successive sloughs, the mortal vices. He conceives that an internal Church which 'cometh not by observation' is preparing in the minds of men; whilst an external Church must at the same time, by its salutary influence on the mind, keep up the internal action which would otherwise gradually wear out; that this was the scheme ordained from the beginning of our earth and the very object of its existence, at least after the fall; that the Jewish prophets looked forward to an eternal life by redemption, as the expressions of Ezekiel, for instance, 'that the wicked man turning away from his wickedness shall save his soul alive,' have otherwise no meaning, being certainly physically incorrect; that evil is merely subjective, not objective; that it is falsehood, the devil, who is a liar from the beginning, wishing to reconcile the impossibilities of being at the same time a creature, and yet equal to the Creator. He finely illustrated the subjectiveness of evil producing objective good by supposing the parts of a machine in a manufactory to be animated, and anxious to tear and bruise each other, and the manufactured article, which, at last, however, arrives at perfection by this very means. This, it is true, leaves untouched the origin of evil, and perhaps favours too much the doctrine of necessity.'' *Memoir of Hatherley* I 160–1.

35. See 23 Oct 1833 n 17, above, on Scott.

Grattan reported of 1828 along the Meuse: ''On some occasion . . . the novels of Walter Scott became the subject of conversation. I made the common, but I thought unanswerable, remark that their great popularity with various nations, even in translation, when the attractions of Scotch idiom and national colouring were almost wholly lost, was incontestable proof of their great merit. To this Wordsworth replied that 'it proved, if anything, the direct contrary—*because* ''The Sorrows of Werter,'' ''Ossian's Poems,'' and several other such worthless works, were universally translated and read.' Coleridge nodded his head at this, but whether assentingly or in sleep I cannot positively say, but I fear it was the former. I did not think it worth replying to; and I fancied it savoured of jealousy as well as want of critical acumen, and of *candour*, a less pardonable deficiency. . . .

''I think it was on the day previous to this conversation, as we were driving along, that Coleridge was holding forth, in his oracular but not dogmatical tone and style on the decay of literature and the degradation of taste. It must be remarked that he avowedly never read any of the light literature of the day, being wholly engaged for years previously on his 'great work.' He however heard the names of successful novels and popular authors, and confounded them altogether in his brain, which was certainly no respecter of persons. He had heard of *me* as one of the herd, what he no doubt considered the 'small deer' of literature; but of what I had written he had not the slightest notion. As he was talking away, a quarter to us and three parts to himself, both Wordsworth and I caught the words, 'Yes, this may be truly called the penultimate stage of English literature—there may be one station lower. We have Waverley novels and their school, Highway and Byway tales and their imitators.—We have'—but a coarse laugh of full two-horse power bursting from Wordsworth, and an irresistible faint echo from me (while our charming female fellow-traveller blushed deeply) put a stop to his remarks. I turned off the interruption much to his satisfaction by joining his strictures, and leaning on the arm of his criticism, as it were, to crush with weightier pressure the victims of whom I myself made one. Wordsworth was highly amused.'' *Beaten Paths* II 128–32. We get a better sense of Grattan, the author of *Highways and Byways* (7 vols 1823–7), than of C.

36. See 3 Jan 1834 n 7, above, on toleration.

Objecting to the passage on toleration in *TT* (1835), HCR on 17 Nov 1835 wrote a letter to HNC of which he carefully preserved a copy: ''I return you the second volume of the 'Table-talk,' which I have looked over again with renewed pleasure and sorrow. Born among the Dissenters, and reckoning among them many highly esteemed friends, I regret that you should have given permanence to so many splenetic effusions against them. As to the single passage which you send underlined, as if it did not justify my construction, you will pardon my saying, which I do most conscientiously, that I found it worse than I had imagined. Mr. Coleridge says: 'The only true argument, apart from Christianity, for a discriminating toleration, is that it is of no use to attempt to stop heresy or schism by persecution, unless, perhaps, by massacre!' Now, 'apart from Christianity' by no means implies that Mr. Coleridge meant that Christianity is opposed to this discrimination, but rather, 'independently of the arguments for it from Christianity.' You must be aware that he who recommends 'a *discriminating* toleration' rather recommends the discrimination than the toleration; and, of necessity, must approve of that being persecuted which is not tolerated. Now, what is that? In the preceding page, he insinuates that it is the *imperative duty* of the magistrate to punish with death the teachers of damnable doctrines. If so, the Romanists did no more than their duty in putting the Protestants to death; for they conscientiously think that damnation follows schism. As to the only true argument against persecution, that it is of no use,—'Of no use!' a Spaniard would truly say; 'for three hundred years the Kings of Spain have found it effectual in saving the souls of millions under their care.'

''There are, in this same article, equally palpable errors. Mr. Coleridge says, 'A right to toleration is a contradiction in terms.' If so, a right to liberty is a contradiction; for the famous formulary, 'Civil and Religious Liberty,' merely means that in certain personal matters of civil concern and conscience, the State must let the individual alone. But the most marvellous sentence is that in which Mr. Coleridge affirms that the Pope had a right to command the Romanists of England to separate from the National Church and to rebel against Queen Elizabeth. I thought that the liberal and intelligent in all Christian Churches were agreed in disclaiming this latter right, and conceding the former.

" 'The Romanist who acknowledges the Pope as the Head of his Church, cannot possibly consider the Church of England as any Church at all.' Mr. Coleridge, when he uttered this, forgot his own admirable and subtle distinction, that we ought not to say the Church *of*, but the Church *in*, England. Mr. Coleridge refers to the necessary criterion, but does not go on to state what it is. Yet, surely, he would not have denied, what Warburton so ably maintains, that Church Establishments are framed for their utility to the State, not for their truth." *CRD* II 180.

On 18 Nov HNC answered in fuller explanation: "He meant what I think he has said, that apart from Xtianity, not arguing as a Xtian, who has no sword but that of the spirit—he could find no satisfactory argument for toleration but the tried inutility of persecution. You say that persecution is not ineffective, if systematic, as in Spain—to which C agrees partially—'you may stifle any open appearance of dissent'—but he says 'you cannot keep people in the faith of it.' Whether the people of Spain have been kept in the faith in the sense of C by fear of persecution is perhaps not so clear a matter of fact as you would assume. But this is immaterial.

"You appear to object to the expression discriminating toleration. C certainly meant this. Does not every one? Would any man admit whatever hideous doctrine or practice any man or number of men may assert to be his or their religion? For instance a Suttee in Smithfield? or the mysteries of Kali or the Bona Dea or Corybas in the aisles of St Paul's. Must not some criterion in any case be adopted by the state? as C says.

"As to the Pope's Bull against Queen E.—did you ever by chance read it?—C repeats Hooker's argument—and in his day no Romanist dreamed of doubting the power and the right Aevo.

"I repent many passages in the T.T.—several have been omitted by me in the reprint which Murray has not yet published. But I see no fault at all in this on which you comment—nor fear any one who considers it calmly, ever citing it as an authority for persecution.

"The passage in the Remains was in print long ago—it is in substance Bellarmin's argument, and C gives it you as the most that can be said for persecution—see it answered elsewhere in the Remains." VCL ms.

COLLATION TABLE

COLLATION TABLE

This table follows the order of entries in Volume I of the present edition. Under "Topic", entry numbers are given, within brackets, for those paragraphs published in *TT* (1835) or *TT* (1836). The second column gives the folio number in MS B or the page number in MS A or B except for the initial material, mostly of 1811, provided to HNC by JTC. The dates "1835" and "1925" in this column designate as sources *TT* (1835) and Bernard, Lord Coleridge, *This for Remembrance* (1925). The entry numbers for MS E are those assigned by HNC in 1827. In the column for MS F, "MS F" marks those entries which have been found among the ms fragments of HNC's revision for publication. Volume and page are given for the two-volume *TT* (1835); page for the one-volume *TT* (1836).

TOPIC	ORIGIN (MSS A, B, C)	MS E	MS F	*TT* (1835)	*TT* (1836)
JTC 20 Apr 1811 [665]	1835			I 343–52	312–16
JTC 21 Apr 1811 [666]	1835			I 352–7	316–19
JTC Superstition [310n]	MS, Penn			I 243n–4	126n–7
JTC 9 Jan 1823 [47]	1925			I 39–46	21–4
	MS A				
St. John, etc. [25–28]	97	9–11		I 19–20	10–11
Pindar	97				
Greek tragedians [16]	97	12		I 17	9
Kotzebue [17]	97	13		I 17	9
DC	99				
Othello, etc. [1, 2]	99	28		I 1–3	1–2
Privilege	99–101	29		I 7–9	4–5
Progression [9]	101	30		I 9–12	5–6
Socrates [15]	96	1		I 16–17	9
Byron [4]	96	2		I 3	2
Scott [3]	96	3		I 3	2
Ghosts [13]	96	3, 4		I 14	7
Unlogical age [14]	96	5		I 16	8–9
Christianity [cf 28]	96	6		cf I 20	cf 11
Soul [11]	96	7		I 12–13	7
Genesis 1 [12]	96	8		I 13–14	7

587

TOPIC	ORIGIN (MSS A, B, C)	MS E	MS F	*TT* (1835)	*TT* (1836)
Ghosts [13]	96, 98	4		I 14–16	7–8
Reading *Osorio* [7]	98	14		I 5–7	3–4
Pots/poets	98	15			
Kemble [5, 6]	98	16		I 3–4	2
Mathews [6]	98	17		I 4–5	2–3
Logos [31, 32]	98, 100	18		I 22–3	12
Snuff [21]	100	19		I 18	10
Burke [19]	100	20		I 18	9–10
Goldsmith [20]	100	21		I 18	10
Iliad 6.484 [18]	100	22		I 17–18	9
Rogue [22]	100	23		I 18	10
Hebrews [29, 30]	100	24		I 21	11
Race [10, 65]	100	27		I 12, 55–6	6, 30
Reason [33]	102	26		I 23	12
Kean [34]	102	31		I 24	13
Mackintosh [35]	102, 104	32		I 24–5	13
Canning [36]	104	33		I 25–6	13–14
National debt [37]	104	[34]		I 26	14
Poor Laws [38]	104	35		I 27	14
Whigs [39]	104–5	36		I 28–30	15–16
Votes on Reform [40]	105	37		I 30	16
The Opposition [40]	105	38		I 31	16
Catholicism [41, 42]	105–6	39		I 31–3	16–17
Romish religion [43]	106	40		I 33	17–18
Milton's Latin [54]	106	41		I 50	26
Zendavesta [44]	106	42		I 34–5	18
Pantheism [45]	106	43		I 35	18
Ghosts [46]	107	2nd 43		I 35–9	19–21
Seeing ghosts [13]	107–8	2nd 43		I 15–16	8
Witch of Endor [48]	108	44		I 46	24
Socinians [49]	108	45		I 47–48	25
Plato [50]	108	46		I 48–9	26
Milton on poetry [53]	108	47		I 50	26
WW and HC	108–9	48			
Landor	109	48			
Ancient Egypt [52]	109	48		I 49	26
Greek religion [51]	109	49		I 48	26
Virgil [55]	109	50		I 50	27

TOPIC	ORIGIN (MSS A, B, C)	MS E	MS F	*TT* (1835)	*TT* (1836)
G. Penn [56, 57]	109–10	51		I 50–2	27
Earth, heavens [58]	110	52		I 52	27
Dancing [59]	110	53, 54		I 52	28
Acoustics [60]	110	55		I 53	28
Byron [61]	110	56		I 53	28
Intermarriage [62, 63, 64]	110	57		I 54–5	29
	MS B				
Gift of tongues			MS F		
Daniel [66]	1			I 56	30
Ecclesiastes [66]	1			I 56	30
Races [65]	1			I 55–6	30
Jewish history [67]	1ᵛ			I 57	31
Future state [48]	1ᵛ			I 46–7	24–5
Irish Catholics [70]	1ᵛ			I 58–9	31–2
Understanding [75]	1ᵛ			I 61–2	33
King John [72]	1ᵛ			I 59–60	32
Skelton [72]	1ᵛ			I 60	32
Proverbs [68]	1ᵛ			I 57	31
Energy [71]	1ᵛ–2			I 59	32
Sarpi [73]	2			I 60	33
Bartram [74]	2			I 61	33
Grammar [76]	2–2ᵛ			I 62–5	33–5
Magnetism, etc [77]	2ᵛ			I 65	35
Colours [371]	2ᵛ			II 44	162
Spinoza [69]	2ᵛ			I 57–8	31
Spenser [78]	3			I 66–7	35–6
Volpone [86]	3			I 72	39
Measure for Measure [85]	3			I 71–2	39
Beaumont, Fletcher [87]	3			I 72–3	39
Othello [79]	3			I 67–8	36–7
Love [84]	3			I 70	38
Woman's frame	3ᵛ		MS F		
English Bible [88]	3ᵛ			I 74	39
French Bible [88]	3ᵛ			I 74	40
Sotheby [88]	3ᵛ			I 74	
Perception [89]	3ᵛ			I 74	40
Craniology [90]	3ᵛ			I 75–6	40
''Jockies'' anecdote [91]	3ᵛ			I 76	40

TOPIC	ORIGIN (MSS A, B, C)	MS E	MS F	*TT* (1835)	*TT* (1836)
Hamlet [80]	4			I 68–9	37
The Trinity [93]	4			I 77	41
Athanasian Creed [94]	4			I 77–8	41–2
Don Quixote [425]	4ᵛ			II 87	184
Hamlet [84]	4ᵛ			I 70	37
Mrs. Jordan	4ᵛ				
The Pope [97]	4ᵛ			I 80–2	43–4
Barnabas, Hebrews [225]	4ᵛ			I 170	89
Church Fathers [107]	4ᵛ			I 84–5	45
Rhenferd [108]	4ᵛ			I 85	45
Frere on Scott	4ᵛ		MS F		
Cycles of language [99]	4ᵛ			I 82	44
Cant [95]	4ᵛ–5			I 78	42
Scale of being [96]	5			I 79	42
Reason [cf 33]	5				
Maxims, Polonius [81]	5			I 69	37
Man of maxims [82]	5			I 69	37
History of Popedom [97]	5			I 80	43
Scanderbeg, Scott [98]	5			I 82	44
Becket, Scott [98]	5			I 82	44
Light [371]	5		MS F	II 44–5	162
Colours [111]	5ᵛ			I 86	46
Colour-blindness [110]	5ᵛ			I 85–6	45–6
William III [114]	5ᵛ			I 87	46–7
Burke on taste [104]	5ᵛ			I 84	45
Bolingbroke [103]	5ᵛ			I 84	45
Ariosto, Tasso [105]	5ᵛ			I 84	45
Berkeley, Spinoza [115]	5ᵛ			I 88	47
Reformation [113]	5ᵛ			I 87	46
Athanasian Creed [94]	5ᵛ			I 77–8	41–2
Gospels	5ᵛ		MS F		
Algernon Sidney [103]	5ᵛ			I 84	45
Luther [100]	5ᵛ			I 82	44
Royal Society	5ᵛ				
Böhme [109]	5ᵛ			I 85	45
Baxter [101]	6			I 83	44
Restoration [112]	6			I 86–7	46
Prose and poetry [106]	6			I 84	45

TOPIC	ORIGIN (MSS A, B, C)	MS E	MS F	*TT* (1835)	*TT* (1836)
Christopher Wordsworth	6				
Genius [116]	6			I 88	47
Desire [117]	6			I 88	47
Taylor [118]	6			I 89	47
Hooker [119]	6			I 89	47
Ideas [120]	6			I 89–90	48
Taylor's *Prophesying*	6ᵛ		MS F		
Painting [122]	6ᵛ			I 91	49
Messiah [123]	6ᵛ			I 91–2	49
Unity of God [124]	6ᵛ			I 92–3	49–50
Hurwitz	6ᵛ				
The Trinity [125]	6ᵛ–7			I 93–4	50
Christianity [126]	7			I 94	50
Jews [127]	7–7ᵛ			I 95–8	51–2
Miracles of Moses [128]	7ᵛ			I 99–100	52–3
Exodus 2–13	7ᵛ		MS F		
Joshua	7ᵛ		MS F		
David	7ᵛ		MS F		
Pantheism [129]	7ᵛ			I 100	53
Poetic promise [130]	7ᵛ–8			I 100–1	54
Death [132]	8			I 101	54
Patients [131]	8			I 101	54
George IV	8				
Good and bad men [133]	8			I 101	54
My system [134]	8			I 102	54
Nominalists [135]	8			I 102	54–5
Schoolmen [136]	8ᵛ			I 103	55
Animal magnetism [140]	8ᵛ			I 106	56–7
Spinoza [138]	8ᵛ			I 104–5	56
Plato [139]	8ᵛ			I 105	56
Fall of man [141]	10			I 107–8	58
Madness [142]	10ᵛ			I 109–10	58
Mead, Luke	10ᵛ–11		MS F		
Gospels	11ᵛ		MS F		
Nature	11ᵛ				
Plants, etc [145]	11ᵛ			I 111	59
Insects [146]	11ᵛ			I 111	59
Brown, Darwin [143]	11ᵛ			I 110	58

TOPIC	ORIGIN (MSS A, B, C)	MS E	MS F	TT (1835)	TT (1836)
Nitrous oxide [144]	11ᵛ			I 110	58–9
Lover of Church [150]	11ᵛ			I 112	60
Black Colonel [149]	11ᵛ			I 112	59
Dogs [147]	12			I 111	59
Ant and bee [148]	12			I 111	59
Netherlands [151]	12			I 113–14	60
Holland [152]	12			I 115	60–1
Strasbourg	12				
Religion [153]	12			I 115–16	61
Walkerites [156]	12			I 116–17	62
Cocceius [155]	12			I 116	61
Women [154]	12ᵛ			I 116	61
Horne Tooke [157]	12ᵛ–13			I 117–20	62–3
That from *das* [158]	13			I 120	63
Plat-Deutsch [159]	13			I 121	64
Horne Tooke [160]	13–13ᵛ			I 121–2	64
Jacobins [161]	13ᵛ			I 122	64
Matronage [162]	13ᵛ			I 122	64
Tooke, Godwin [163]	13ᵛ			I 122–3	64–5
Persian poetry [164]	13ᵛ			I 123–4	65
Munro and Raffles [166]	13ᵛ			I 125	66
Ezekiel 37.3 [165]	13ᵛ–14			I 125	66
Brougham [167]	14			I 125–6	66
Horner [167]	14			I 126	66
Canning [168]	14			I 126	66
Shakspeare [169]	14–14ᵛ			I 127–8	67
Cymbeline I vi 36 [170]	14ᵛ			I 128	
Hamlet III i 58	14ᵛ				
Henry V II iv 57 [170]	14ᵛ			I 128	
Trinity, Irving [174]	14ᵛ–15			I 131–2	69
Reason, Understanding [172]	15			I 130	68
Homer [171]	15			I 128–30	67–8
Odyssey	15				
Languages [173]	15ᵛ			I 130–1	68
Patriarchs [175]	15ᵛ			I 132–3	69–70
Isaac [176]	15ᵛ			I 133	70
Jacob [177]	15ᵛ			I 133–4	70

TOPIC	ORIGIN (MSS A, B, C)	MS E	MS F	*TT* (1835)	*TT* (1836)
Passion [178]	15ᵛ–16			I 134–5	70–1
Grammar schools [181]	16			I 135–6	71
Arrogant men [182]	16			I 136	71
Love [179]	16			I 135	71
Democracy [184]	16			I 136	72
Queen Caroline	16				
Eucharist [185]	16ᵛ			I 137	72
Sacramentaries [186]	16ᵛ			I 137–8	72
Arnauld [187]	⸜16ᵛ			I 139	73
Sacraments [188]	16ᵛ			I 139	73
John 19.11 [189]	16ᵛ–17			I 139–41	73–4
Christ [190]	17			I 141–2	74–5
Mosaic books [191]	17			I 142–3	75
Prophecies by Moses [192]	17			I 143	75
Talent and genius [193]	17			I 144	75
Jonson on grammar [181]	17			I 136	71
Motives [194]	17ᵛ			I 144	75
Principle of life [195]	17ᵛ			I 144–5	76
Functional life [196]	17ᵛ			I 145–6	76
Hysteria [197]	17ᵛ			I 146	76
Hydro-carbonic gas [198]	17ᵛ			I 146	76
Bitters and tonics [199]	17ᵛ–18			I 146–7	77
Specific medicines [200]	18			I 147	77
Ephesians, Colossians [201]	18			I 147–8	77
Oaths [202]	18			I 148–9	77–8
Flogging [203]	18–18ᵛ			I 149–50	78
Americans [205]	18ᵛ			I 150	79
War of 1812 [206]	18ᵛ			I 150	79
Lines for Miss Barbour	18ᵛ				
One's country [207]	18ᵛ			I 151	79
Conversation of C, WW	18ᵛ				
Mosaic and Homeric	18ᵛ				
Job [208]	19			I 151	79–80
Imagery of Job [210]	19			I 152	80
Satan in Job [211]	19			I 152	80
Warburton's dating [212]	19			I 153	80
Job 19.25 [209]	19			I 151–2	80

TOPIC	ORIGIN (MSS A, B, C)	MS E	MS F	TT (1835)	TT (1836)
Daniel	19ᵛ		MS F		
Psalms [213]	19ᵛ			I 153	81
Ancient Mariner [214]	19ᵛ			I 155	82
"Grinning for joy" [215]	19ᵛ			I 157–8	83
Undine [216]	19ᵛ			I 158	83
Undine and Scott	20				
Congregational singing [220]	20			I 163–4	86
Hooker on the Bible [221]	20			I 164–5	86
Dreams [222]	20			I 165	86
Pilgrim's Progress [218]	20–20ᵛ			I 160–1	84
John Martin [217]	20ᵛ			I 159	83
Martin's Slay-good [218]	20ᵛ			I 159–60	84
Prayer [219]	20ᵛ			I 161–2	85
Church and George III	20ᵛ				
Plain style, Bunyan [218]	21			I 160	84
Taylor [223]	21			I 165–8	87–8
English Reformation [224]	21–21ᵛ			I 168–9	88–9
Bishops' errors	21ᵛ–2		MS F		
Deborah's song	22		MS F		
John and Paul [227]	22			I 171–2	89–90
Catholicity, gnosis [225]	22–22ᵛ			I 170–1	89
Tertullian [226]	22ᵛ			I 171	89
Party spirit [229]	22ᵛ			I 174	91
WW's religion	22ᵛ		MS F		
Reviews [228]	22ᵛ–23			I 172–4	90–1
Blanco White's review	23				
RS's *Bunyan* [231]	23–23ᵛ			I 174–5	91
Laud [232]	23ᵛ			I 175–6	91–2
Puritans [233]	23ᵛ			I 176	92
Presbyterians [234]	23ᵛ			I 176	92
Bishops at Breda [235]	23ᵛ			I 176	92
Savoy Conference	23ᵛ		MS F		
Study of Bible [236]	23ᵛ			I 177	92
Bunyan and Bible [231]	23ᵛ–24			I 175	91
Rabelais [237]	24			I 177–8	92–3
Swift on William III [237]	24			I 178–9	93
Bentley [238]	24			I 179	93

TOPIC	ORIGIN (MSS A, B, C)	MS E	MS F	TT (1835)	TT (1836)
Pisan frescoes [239]	24–24ᵛ			I 179–80	94
Improvement in arts [240]	24ᵛ			I 180	94
History of painting [241]	24ᵛ			I 181	94–5
Seneca [242]	24ᵛ			I 181	95
B—— M—— empty	24ᵛ				
He is insane	24ᵛ				
Aristotle and Plato [243]	25			I 182–4	95–6
Wellington [244]	25–25ᵛ			I 184–5	96–7
Foreign policy [245]	25ᵛ			I 185	97
Miguel and Pedro	25ᵛ–26				
Hollywell Jew [248]	26			I 187	98
Bourrienne [246]	26			I 186	97
Papacy, Reformation [249]	26ᵛ			I 188–90	99
Leo x [250]	26ᵛ–27			I 190	99
Thelwall [251]	27			I 190–1	100
Thelwall and C [252]	27			I 191	100
Stella [253]	27			I 191–2	100
Smuggling [254]	27			I 192	100–1
C's father	27ᵛ		MS F		
C's brother George	27ᵛ		MS F		
Spurzheim [255]	27ᵛ–28			I 193–4	101–2
France in 1830 [256]	28			I 195–6	102
Charles x	28				
Royalty of Spain	28				
State and Church [260]	28			I 200–1	104–5
U. S. not a state	28				
Basil Hall [257]	28ᵛ			I 196–8	102–3
Chapman	28ᵛ				
English Reformation [258]	28ᵛ–29			I 199–200	104
Democracy [259]	29			I 200	105
State and Church [260]	29			I 200–1	104–5
Government [261]	29			I 201	105
Brussels riot [285]	29ᵛ			I 215	112
Belgium	29ᵛ				
Gendarmerie [262]	29ᵛ			I 201–2	105
Young men today [263]	29ᵛ–30			I 202–4	105–6
RS's history	30				
Thucydides, Tacitus [264]	30–30ᵛ			I 205	107

TOPIC	ORIGIN (MSS A, B, C)	MS E	MS F	*TT* (1835)	*TT* (1836)
RS	30ᵛ–31				
Nature in poetry [RS] [265]	30ᵛ			I 205	107
Modern metre [RS] [266]	31			I 205–5	107
Hazlitt	31				
Lamb, Hazlitt, Hood	31ᵛ				
Gentle [Lamb] [267]	31ᵛ			I 206	107
Huskisson's death	32				
Logic [Whately] [268]	31ᵛ			I 206–7	107–8
Rhetoric [269]	31ᵛ			I 207	108
Hurwitz on *bineh* [75]	32			I 61–2	33
Varro, Zeno [270]	32			I 208	108
Socrates [271]	32			I 208	108
Greek philosophy [272]	32			I 209	108–9
Plotinus [273]	32ᵛ			I 209	109
Tertullian [274]	32ᵛ			I 209	109
Scottish, English Lakes [275]	32ᵛ			I 210–11	109–10
Devon [276]	32ᵛ			I 211	110
Where C wrote poems	32ᵛ–33				
Love [WW] [277]	33			I 211–12	110
Sympathy and love [277]	33			I 212	110
Luther on wedded life [278]	33			I 212	110
Hell [280]	33			I 213–14	111
Women [279]	33			I 212–13	110–11
Fear in politics [281]	33ᵛ			I 214	111
Ear for music [282]	33ᵛ			I 214–15	111
Belgians [285]	33ᵛ			I 215	112
English liturgy [283]	33ᵛ			I 215	111
School uniforms [284]	33ᵛ			I 215	112
Kepler, Newton etc [286]	33ᵛ–34			I 216–17	112–13
Experiment [287]	34			I 217–18	113
Bacon [288]	34			I 218	113
Reformation [289]	34–34ᵛ			I 218–19	113–14
Bull and Waterland [94]	34ᵛ			I 78	42
Athanasian Creed	34ᵛ		MS F		
Clergy and creeds	34ᵛ–35ᵛ		MS F		
[Brougham] [290]	35ᵛ			I 219	114
House of Commons [291]	35ᵛ–36			I 219–20	114

TOPIC	ORIGIN (MSS A, B, C)	MS E	MS F	TT (1835)	TT (1836)
Government [292]	36–36ᵛ			I 221–3	115–16
Grey [293]	36ᵛ			I 223–4	116
Statesmen [294]	37ᵛ			I 225–6	117
Nation [295]	37ᵛ			I 226	117
Ministers, Brougham	37ᵛ				
Representation [296]	37ᵛ–38ᵛ			I 226–8	118–19
Whigs [297]	38ᵛ			I 228–9	119
Napier [298]	38ᵛ			I 229–30	119
RS's history [299]	38ᵛ–39			I 231	120
Buonaparte [298]	39			I 230	119–20
Patronage of arts [300]	39ᵛ			I 232	120–1
Muskets from Tower	39ᵛ				
Old women [301]	39ᵛ			I 233	121
British Gallery [302]	39ᵛ–40ᵛ			I 233–7	121–3
Modern paintings [306]	40ᵛ			I 238–9	124
Italian and Dutch painters [303]	40ᵛ			I 238	123–4
Rubens [302]	40ᵛ–41			I 237	123
Carlo Dolce [304]	41			I 238	124
Reynolds' *Connoisseurs* [305]	41			I 238	124
Chillingworth [307]	41ᵛ			I 240–1	125
Hooker [308]	41ᵛ			I 241	126
Catholic peasantry [309]	42			I 242	126
Boy in Valetta [310]	42			I 242–3	126
Asgill [311]	42–42ᵛ			I 244–5	127
French peers [312]	42ᵛ			I 245–6	128
Creation of peers	42ᵛ				
Arousal on Reform	43				
Mixed evil in man [313]	43			I 247	128
St. Simonists [314]	43			I 247	128
Good and true [315]	43ᵛ			I 247–8	129
Iron [318]	44			I 249	130
Galvanism [319]	44			I 250	130
Heat [320]	44			I 250	130
Aeriforms	44				
Roman Catholicism [316]	44			I 248	129
Policy toward Holland [317]	44–44ᵛ			I 248–9	129

TOPIC	ORIGIN (MSS A, B, C)	MS E	MS F	*TT* (1835)	*TT* (1836)
Colonial character [321]	48			I 250–3	130–2
Five powers and Holland [322]	48ᵛ–49			I 254–7	132–4
Leopold as conjurer [293]	49			I 223–4	116
Leopold's asses [323]	49			I 257–8	134
Sir George Murray	49				
O.P.Q. on happiness [324–5]	49–49ᵛ			I 258–60	134–5
Political action [326]	49ᵛ–50			I 261–3	135–7
Reason, understanding [327]	50			I 263–5	137
Ireland	50ᵛ		MS F		
Locke's sums [328]	50ᵛ			I 265	137–8
Drayton, Daniel [329]	50ᵛ			I 265–6	138
C's system [330]	50ᵛ–51			II 1–2	139–40
Death [331]	51			II 2–3	140
Illness [332]	51			II 3	140
Genius [333]	51ᵛ			II 3–4	140
Advocate and client [334]	51ᵛ–52			II 4–7	141–2
French peers [335]	52ᵛ–53			II 7–9	142–3
Ministers, Reform [336]	53–53ᵛ			II 9–12	143–5
Religion [337]	53ᵛ–54			II 13	145
Union with Ireland [338]	54			II 13–14	145–6
Irish Church [339]	54			II 14–15	146
Organic, inorganic [340]	54–54ᵛ			II 15–16	146–7
History [342]	54ᵛ			II 17	147
Persons and things [341]	54ᵛ			II 16	147
Beauty [343]	54ᵛ–55			II 18–19	148
Macaulay, Croker	55		MS F		
Children [346]	55			II 20	149
Dogs and children [347]	55			II 21	149
Infamous Reform	55				
Church and State [344]	55–55ᵛ			II 19–20	148–9
Dissenters [345]	55ᵛ			II 20	149
Tory and Whig [348]	55ᵛ			II 21	149–50
Spinoza's premise [115]	55ᵛ			I 88	47
Church and nationalty [349]	56			II 23	150
Ministers, Reform Bill [350]	56–56ᵛ			II 23–5	151

TOPIC	ORIGIN (MSS A, B, C)	MS E	MS F	*TT* (1835)	*TT* (1836)
Disfranchisement [351]	56ᵛ			II 25–6	152
Genius feminine [WW] [352]	56ᵛ			II 26	152
Pirates [353]	56ᵛ			II 26–7	152
Astrology, alchemy [354]	57			II 27–8	153
Reform Bill [355]	57			II 28	153
Crisis [356]	57			II 29	153–4
Poets musical or picturesque	57ᵛ				
Milton not picturesque [418]	57ᵛ			II 83–4	182
Mrs Barbauld on *AM* [214]	57ᵛ			I 154–6	82
David Scott's *AM*	57ᵛ–58				
John 3.4 [357]	58			II 29–30	154
Bible as dictated	58–58ᵛ		MS F		
Inspiration vs dictation [358]	58ᵛ–59			II 30–1	154–5
Gnosis and canon [359]	59			II 32–3	155–6
Formation of canon [360]	59			II 33–4	156
Unitarianism [361]	59–59ᵛ			II 34–6	156–7
Unitarians the worst sect	59ᵛ		Ms F		
Moral law of polarity [363]	59ᵛ–60			II 36–7	158
Epidemic disease [364]	60–60ᵛ			II 38–40	158–60
Harmony [365]	60ᵛ			II 41	160
Intellectual revolutions [366]	61			II 42	160
Modern style [367]	61			II 42	160–1
Asgill [311]	61			I 245	127
Spanish and Italians [368]	61			II 43	161
Defoe, Asgill, Swift [376]	61			II 48	164
Vico [369]	61			II 43	161
Vico, Spinoza [370]	61			II 44	161
Colours [371]	61ᵛ			II 44–5	162
Destruction of Jerusalem [372]	61ᵛ			II 46–7	162–3
Vox populi, vox dei [373]	61ᵛ–62			II 47	163
Black [374]	62			II 48	163
Identity [375]	62			II 48	163
Asgill's style [376]	62			II 48	164
M—— ("Adiaphori") [380]	62			II 51	165

TOPIC	ORIGIN (MSS A, B, C)	MS E	MS F	*TT* (1835)	*TT* (1836)
Horner [and Brougham] [379]	62			II 50	165
Horne Tooke [377]	62ᵛ			II 49	164
Fox and Pitt [378]	62ᵛ			II 49–50	164
Aristocratic government [383]	62ᵛ			II 54	166–7
Citizens and Christians [381]	62ᵛ			II 51–2	165
Park on the Constitution [382]	62ᵛ–63			II 52–4	166
De vi minimorum [384]	63			II 54–5	167
Luther's works [385]	63			II 55	167
Hugh of St. Victor [385]	63			II 55	167
Greek, English, Latin [386]	63–63ᵛ			II 56–7	168
Roman picturesque [387]	63ᵛ			II 57	168
Roman mind [388]	63ᵛ			II 57–8	168–9
Metre, rhythm	63ᵛ				
Roman wars [389]	63ᵛ			II 58–9	169
Charm for cramp [*CM*] [390]	64			II 59–60	169
Greek [391]	66			II 60–1	170
Theta and German [393]	66			II 62	171
Christian names [395]	66			II 63–4	171
Greek duals etc [392]	66			II 61–2	170
Valckenaer [396]	66			II 65	172
Remembering facts [397]	66ᵛ			II 65–7	172–3
Schmidt [398]	66ᵛ			II 67–8	173
Homer [396]	66ᵛ			II 64	171–2
Jacobins [*CM*] [399]	[stub]			II 68	173
Head clear [*CM*] [400]	[stub]			II 68	173–4
WW a spectator [404]	67			II 71–2	175
The Excursion [401]	67			II 69	174
WW's dialogues [402]	67–67ᵛ			II 69–70	174
The Prelude [403]	67ᵛ			II 70–1	174–5
WW contemplative [404]	67ᵛ–68			II 71–2	175
C and French Revolution [405]	68			II 72–4	175–6
Slave trade	68–68ᵛ		MS F		
Infant schools [406]	68ᵛ			II 74–5	177

TOPIC	ORIGIN (MSS A, B, C)	MS E	MS F	TT (1835)	TT (1836)
C's system [407]	68ᵛ			II 76	177
Sublimity [408]	68ᵛ			II 76	177–8
Proverbs, Ecclesiastes [409]	69			II 76	178
Solomon [410]	69			II 77	178
Madness [411]	69			II 77	178
Faith [414]	69			II 77–8	178–9
Lamb on *sermoni propriora* [412]	69			II 77	178
Dobrizhoffer [415]	69			II 79–81	179–80
Scotch and English [416]	70			II 81–2	181
Genius [417]	70			II 82	181
Milton ignored painting [418]	70ᵛ			II 83–4	181–2
Baptismal service [419]	70ᵛ			II 85	183
Epistles: Peter, Titus, Timothy	70ᵛ–71		MS F		
Jews on Scripture [420]	71			II 85	183
Sanskrit [421]	71			II 86	183
Hesiod [422]	71			II 86	183
Virgil's *Georgics* [423]	71			II 86–7	183–4
Genius metaphysical [424]	71			II 87	184
Don Quixote [425]	71			II 87	184
Rabelais [237]	71			I 177–8	92–3
Swift [237	71			I 178	93
Malthus [426]	71–71ᵛ			II 88	
Steinmetz [427]	71ᵛ			II 89	184
Keats [428]	71ᵛ			II 89–90	184–5
Christ's Hospital [429]	72			II 90	185
Mrs Boyer [430]	72			II 90–1	185
Malta and Melita [431]	72			II 91–4	185–7
Maltese architecture [432]	72			II 94	187
English and German [433]	72–72ᵛ			II 94–5	187
Best state of society [434]	72ᵛ			II 95	187
Confusion in C's room	72ᵛ		MS F		
Pantheism begets polytheism	72ᵛ				
Blumenbach's five races [65]	72ᵛ			I 56	30

TOPIC	ORIGIN (MSS A, B, C)	MS E	MS F	*TT* (1835)	*TT* (1836)
Chemistry, nosology [435]	73			II 96	188
Abipones, immortality [*CM*] [415]	73				180
Androgynous minds [*CM*] [436]	73			II 96	188
Woman as flower [*CM*] [583]	73ᵛ				270
Compassion [*CM*] [583]					270
Woman's friendship [*CM*] [117n]	73ᵛ			I 88n	47n
Envy [*CM*] [116]	73ᵛ			I 88	47
Philosopher's language [*CM*] [437]	74ᵛ			II 96–7	188
Juries [438]	75ᵛ			II 97	188
Mason's poetry [444]	75ᵛ			II 99	189
Caesarean operations [441]	75ᵛ			II 98	189
Quacks [440]	75ᵛ			II 98	189
Professional fees [439]	75ᵛ			II 97–8	189
Inherited disease [442]	75ᵛ–76			II 98	189
Nervous cases [443]	76			II 99	189
American Union [445]	76			II 99–100	190
All and whole [446]	76			II 100–1	190
Ninth Article [447]	76			II 101	191
Preaching the holy life [449]	76ᵛ			II 102	191
Old divines [450]	76ᵛ			II 102–3	191
Sin and sins [448]	76ᵛ			II 101–2	191
Emotive sermons [451]	76ᵛ			II 103	191–2
Preaching extempore [452]	76ᵛ–77			II 103	192
Church at Reformation [453]	77			II 104	192
Church at present [454]	77			II 104	192
Seaward's narrative and *QR*	77		MS F		
Union with Ireland [455]	77			II 104–7	192–3
Dissenters and Church [456]	77–77ᵛ			II 108	194
England and Ireland [455]	77ᵛ			II 107–8	194
Faust and Michael Scott [457]	77ᵛ–79ᵛ			II 108–18	194–9
Beaumont and Fletcher [458]	79ᵛ			II 118–20	199–200

TOPIC	ORIGIN (MSS A, B, C)	MS E	MS F	TT (1835)	TT (1836)
Ben Jonson [459]	79ᵛ			II 120–1	200
Massinger, *Samson Agonistes* [460]	79ᵛ			II 121	201
Military appointments [461]	80			II 122–3	201–2
Penal code in Ireland [462]	80			II 124	202
Coronation oaths [464]	80			II 127–8	204
Divinity as profession [465]	80ᵛ			II 128	204
Professions and trades [466]	80ᵛ			II 128–9	204
Political economy [467]	80ᵛ			II 129	205
[Discussion expanded]				II 129–30	205
All and whole [468]	80ᵛ			II 131	206
Reducing prices [467]	80ᵛ			II 131	205–6
Churchmen [463]	80ᵛ–81			II 124–6	202–4
National debt [469]	81			II 131–2	206–7
Property tax [469]	81–81ᵛ			II 133–5	207–8
Mackintosh not lampooned	81ᵛ		MS F		
A poem either music or sense [470]	81ᵛ			II 135	208
Massinger, Shakspeare [471]	81ᵛ–82			II 135–9	208–10
Hieronomo [472]	82			II 139–40	210
Love's Labour's Lost [473]	82–82ᵛ			II 141–4	211–12
Gifford as editor [474]	82ᵛ			II 144	212–13
Shakspeare [475]	82ᵛ			II 145	213
Old dramatists [476]	82ᵛ			II 145–6	213
WW's *Cintra*	82ᵛ				
C and statesmen [477]	83			II 146–7	213–14
Burke [478]	83			II 147	214
Scientific lectures [479]					214
Monarchy vs democracy [480]	83			II 148–9	214–15
Reformed House of Commons [481]	83ᵛ			II 149	215
Irish Coercion Bill	83ᵛ		MS F		
United States of America [482]	83ᵛ			II 150–1	215–16
Basil Hall [483]	83ᵛ–84			II 151	216
Modes of unity in a state [485]	84			II 153–4	217

TOPIC	ORIGIN (MSS A, B, C)	MS E	MS F	*TT* (1835)	*TT* (1836)
Cavaliers and Malthusians [488]	84			II 155	218
Democracy and slavery [486]	84			II 154	217
The Times on North and South [484]	84–84ᵛ			II 151–3	216–17
Land and money [487]	84ᵛ			II 154–5	218
Methods of investigation [489]	84ᵛ–86			II 155–60	218–20
Wedded love in old drama [492]	86			II 163–4	222
Tennyson's poems [493]	86			II 164–5	222–3
Church of Rome [490]	86–86ᵛ			II 161–2	221
Romans and Italian tribes [491]	86ᵛ			II 163	222
Baxter and Luther [*CM*] [494]	86ᵛ			II 165	223
Wit and madness [495] [cf *CL* VI 719]				II 165–6	223
Colonisation [496]	87			II 166–7	223–4
Machinery [497]	87			II 167	224
Papacy and schoolmen [501]	87–87ᵛ			II 169–70	225–6
Roman conquest [499]	87ᵛ			II 168–9	224–5
Constantine [500]	87ᵛ			II 169	225
Capital [498]	87ᵛ			II 168	224
Charles I, Civil War [502]	87ᵛ–88			II 171–3	226–7
Reformed House of Commons [503]	88–88ᵛ			II 173–4	227–8
Food, medicine, poison [504]	88ᵛ			II 175–6	228
John Wilson [506]	88ᵛ? [cut]			II 177–8	229
Wilson on Lamb [505]	88ᵛ			II 176–7	228–9
Shakspeare's sonnets [507]	89			II 178–81	229–31
Johnson the Whig [511]	89ᵛ			II 184–5	232–3
Sidney and D'Alva [512]	89ᵛ			II 186–7	234
Wycliffe [509]	89ᵛ			II 182	231–2
James I [511]	89ᵛ–90			II 186	233
Love [508]	90			II 181–2	231
Love after enjoyment	90				

TOPIC	ORIGIN (MSS A, B, C)	MS E	MS F	TT (1835)	TT (1836)
Asgill and Johnson the Whig [511]	90			II 185	233
Goethe [515]	90			II 187–8	234
Connectives in writing [511]	90			II 185	233
Hazlitt admired ugliness	90				
Cycles [516]	90			II 188	234
Man's Freedom [517]	90ᵛ			II 188	235
German and English [514]	90ᵛ			II 187	234
Things finding their level [513]	90ᵛ			II 187	234
Reverence for ideal truths [510]	90ᵛ–91			II 183–4	232
Miguel and Pedro [518]	91			II 188–9	235
Bettering one's condition [519]	91ᵛ			II 189–90	235–6
Ministers and West Indies [520]	91ᵛ			II 190	236
Negro emancipation [521]	91ᵛ			II 190–1	236
Fox and Pitt [522]	92			II 191–2	236–7
Virtue and liberty [523]	92			II 193	237
Epistle to the Romans [524]	92–92ᵛ			II 193–4	237
Erasmus—Luther [525]	92ᵛ			II 194	238
Emancipation of slaves [526]	92ᵛ–93			II 195	238
Hacket's life of Williams [527]	93			II 196	238
Charles I [528]	93			II 196	239
Manners and chivalry [529]	93			II 196–7	239
Bed at Cambridge	93			II 200n	241n–2
Entrance to punctuate [536]	93			II 202	242
Cambridge—Dalton	93			II 200n	241n
Faraday, Thirlwall	93ᵛ			II 200n	241n
Hypothesis and Suffiction [530]	93ᵛ–94			II 197–8	239
Theory [531]	94			II 198–9	239–40
Lyell's geology [531]	94			II 199	240
Light [532]	94			II 199	240
Gothic architecture [533]	94			II 199–200	240
Paintings, Douw and Titian [534]	94			II 201–2	241

TOPIC	ORIGIN (MSS A, B, C)	MS E	MS F	*TT* (1835)	*TT* (1836)
Scarlett's speech [535]	94ᵛ			II 202	241–2
Mandeville [537]	94ᵛ			II 203	242
Bestial theory, Chantrey's Cline [538]	94ᵛ			II 204	243
Bertram in *All's Well* [539]	94ᵛ–95			II 205–6	243
Beaumont and Fletcher [540]	95			II 206	243–4
Greek tragedians [541]	95–95ᵛ			II 207–8	244–5
Milton on Euripides, Ovid [521]	95ᵛ			II 209–10	246
Euripides [541]	95ᵛ			II 211	246
Newton [545]	95ᵛ			II 218	250
Style: Shakspeare, Milton [542]	95ᵛ–96			II 211	246–7
Cavalier slang—Junius [542]	96, 96ᵛ			II 212–13	247–8
Johnson, Boswell, Burke [544]	96–96ᵛ			II 216–18	249–50
Prose and verse [542]	96ᵛ–97			II 214–15	248
Imitation and copy [543]	97			II 215	248–9
Painting (imitation, copy) [546]	97			II 218–19	250
Christabel and music [546]	97–97ᵛ			II 221–2	251–2
Music [546]	97ᵛ			II 220	251
Public schools [547]	97ᵛ–98			II 222–3	252
Mathematics in school [548]	98			II 223–4	252
Scott and C [549]	98			II 225–6	253
Scott's poetry	98				
Charlotte Lockhart	98				
Nervous weakness [550]	98ᵛ			II 226	253
Thanet	98ᵛ				
Hooker, Bull and Jesuits [551]	98ᵛ			II 226	254
Faith [551]	98ᵛ			II 227	254
Children and death	99		MS F		
Applause [552]					254
Quaker ice and flame [553]	99			II 227	254
Quakers	99–99ᵛ		MS F		
Philanthropists [554]	99ᵛ			II 227–8	254

TOPIC	ORIGIN (MSS A, B, C)	MS E	MS F	*TT* (1835)	*TT* (1836)
Montefiore [555]	99ᵛ			II 228	255
Jews [556]	99ᵛ			II 228–9	255
Sallust, Herodotus, Thucydides [557]	99ᵛ–100			II 229–30	255–6
Modern historians— Gibbon [557]	100–100ᵛ			II 230–3	256–7
Johnson—Taxation [558]	100ᵛ–101			II 233–5	257–8
Milton's egotism [562]	101			II 240–1	261
Horne Tooke [559]	101–101ᵛ			II 236–7	259
Scotch kirk and Irving [561]	101ᵛ			II 239–40	260–1
Johnson's limitations [558]	101ᵛ			II 236	258–9
"The Lord" in Psalms, etc [560]	101ᵛ–102			II 237–8	259–60
Claudian [563]	102			II 241	261
Sterne [564]	102			II 242–3	262
Humour and genius [565]	102			II 244	263
Genius [566]	102			II 244	263
Great poets, good men [568]	102–102ᵛ			II 245	263
Rossetti's Dante [576]	102ᵛ			II 253	267
Lord Grey	102ᵛ		MS F		
Laughter [577]	102ᵛ			II 253–4	267
Hebrew—Origen [570]	102ᵛ			II 246	264
Vowels and consonants [571]	102ᵛ–103			II 246–7	264
Men of genius [567]	103			II 244–5	263
Consolation in distress [573]	103			II 252	266–7
Mock evangelicals [573]	103			II 252	267
Autumn day [575]	103			II 252	267
Old and New Testaments [569]	103			II 245–6	263–4
Greek accent and quantity [572]	103–103ᵛ			II 247–51	264–6
Humboldt [578]	103ᵛ			II 254–5	268
Modern diplomatists [579]	103ᵛ–104			II 255–7	268–9
Diplomatists in Lloyd's *Worthies* [579]	104			II 257–8	269
Principles of diplomacy [580]	104			II 258	270

TOPIC	ORIGIN (MSS A, B, C)	MS E	MS F	*TT* (1835)	*TT* (1836)
Man not stationary [581]	104			II 258–9	270
Fatalism and providence [582]	104ᵛ			II 259	270
National temperament, drugs [584]	105			II 259–60	271
Greek and Latin writers [585]	105			II 260–1	271–2
Latin poets [586]	105ᵛ			II 261–3	272
Persius [586]	105ᵛ			II 262	272
Athenaeus [587]	105ᵛ			II 263	273
Destruction of Jerusalem [588]	105ᵛ–106			II 263–4	273
Epic poem [589]	106–106ᵛ			II 264–6	273–4
German and English [591]	106ᵛ			II 266	274
Bacchus' conquest of India [590]	106ᵛ			II 266	274
Military travellers [592]	106ᵛ			II 266	274–5
Incarnation and Redemption [593]	106ᵛ			II 267	275
Religious education [594]	106ᵛ			II 267	275
Elegy and ode [595]	107			II 268–9	275–6
Callimachus, Ovid, A. W. Schlegel [596]	107			II 269	276
Milton's Latin verses [597]	107			II 269–70	276
"The Poetical Filter" [598]	107–107ᵛ			II 270–1	276–7
Gray and Cotton [599]	107ᵛ			II 271	277
Troilus and Cressida [600]	107ᵛ			II 272–4	278–9
Byron's laurels	107ᵛ				
"I" and "me" [605]	107ᵛ			II 275–6	279
Johnson [602]	107ᵛ–108			II 274–5	279
Scope of Christianity [604]	108			II 275	279
Scott's novels [603]	108			II 275	279
Dryden [601]	108			II 274	279
C's epitaph	108				
Times of Charles I [606]	108ᵛ			II 276	280
Malachi's prophecy	108ᵛ		MS F		
Messenger of the Covenant [607]	108ᵛ			II 277	280
Prophecy [608]	108ᵛ			II 277–8	280–1
Ideas and syllogisms [609]	109			II 278	281

TOPIC	ORIGIN (MSS A, B, C)	MS E	MS F	*TT* (1835)	*TT* (1836)
Landor [610]	109			II 279	281
Poems in chronological order [612]	109			II 280–1	282
Useful, agreeable, beautiful, good [611]	109			II 279–80	281–2
Kenyon on tolerance [613]	109ᵛ–110			II 281 5	282–4
Norwegians [613]	110			II 285	284
Articles of faith—Quakers [614]	110–110ᵛ			II 286–8	284–6
Devotional spirit [615]	110ᵛ–111			II 288–90	286–7
England, country and nation [616]	111			II 291	287
Origen [617]	111			II 291	287
Invocation of the saints	111		MS F		
Cottle on "Mol-Branch"	111				
Sublimity [619]	112			II 291–2	287
Men like musical glasses [618]	112			II 291	287
Atheist's idea of God [620]	112			II 292	287
Sforza's decision [413]	112				
Proof of God's existence [621]	113ᵛ			II 292	288
Kant's attempt [621]	113ᵛ			II 292–3	288
Plurality of worlds [622]	113ᵛ			II 293	288
C as reasoner [623]	113ᵛ			II 294	288–9
Shakspeare's plots [624]	114			II 295	289
Antony and Cleopatra II ii 206–9	114		MS F		
Macbeth I v 53 [625]	114			II 295–6	
Crabbe and RS [626]	114			II 296	289
Chaucer [628]	114ᵛ			II 297–9	290–1
Shakspeare and his age [629]	114ᵛ–115			II 299–300	291–2
Editing Beaumont and Fletcher [630]	115			II 301–2	292
Shakspeare [629]	115			II 301	292
Herrick	115				
Byron and Horace Walpole [631]	115–115ᵛ			II 302–4	292–3
"Monk" Lewis [632]	115ᵛ			II 304	293

TOPIC	ORIGIN (MSS A, B, C)	MS E	MS F	*TT* (1835)	*TT* (1836)
Sicily [633]	115ᵛ, 116			II 304–6	294
Malta and Sicily [634]	116			II 306	294
Sir F. Head on Malta [635]	116–116ᵛ			II 306–8	
Sir Alexander Ball in Malta [636]	116ᵛ			II 308–10	295–6
Cambridge and Dissenters [637]	117			II 310–11	296
Corn Laws [638]	117			II 312–13	296–7
Christian Sabbath [639]	117ᵛ–118			II 313–18	297–9
Church prizes and revenues [640]	118–118ᵛ			II 318–20	299–300
Wetherell's speech [641]	118ᵛ			II 320	300
Thelwall	118ᵛ–119				
C. Wordsworth Jr.'s pamphlet	119				
National Church [642]	119			II 320–1	300–1
Dissenters [643]	119			II 321	301
Papacy in England [644]	119			II 321–2	301
Schiller's versification [645]	119–119ᵛ			II 323	301–2
Brougham and Wetherell	119ᵛ				
Roman Catholic emancipation [646]	119ᵛ			II 324	302
Peel on emancipation [647]	119ᵛ–120			II 324–5	302
The Times on emancipation	120				
Wellington on Coronation Oath [648]	120			II 325	303
Corn Laws [649]	120			II 326–7	303
Disraeli's poem [651]	120			II 328	304
Political economy [650]	120			II 327	304
Socinianism [652]	120–120ᵛ			II 328–30	304–5
Fancy and imagination [653]	120ᵛ			II 330–4	305–7
Modern political economy [654]	121			II 334	307
C's faith [652]	121			II 329	305
	MS C				
C's system, *Biographia* [655]	40			II 334–5	307
Presbyterian to Unitarian [656]	40			II 335	308

TOPIC	ORIGIN (MSS A, B, C)	MS E	MS F	*TT* (1835)	*TT* (1836)
Dissenters [657]	40			II 335–6	308
Lord Brooke [658]	40			II 336–7	309
Barrow and Dryden [659]	40–41			II 337	309
Fanciful tales of travel [660]	41			II 337–9	309–10
Fielding and Richardson [661]	41			II 339	310
Scott's admirers	41				
Littleton and O'Connell	41				
Roman Catholic religion [663]	42			II 339–40	310–11
Passage from Sandford [560n]	42			II 238n	260n
Inscription for a Timepiece	42			II 360	
"Time fleets"	42				
"To Adam Steinmetz Kennard"	42–44				319–20